W9-DFS-287

NAME-WORD FINDER

METAPHOR FINDER

SOPHISTICATED SYNONYMS

the

PHRASE FINDER

the PHRASE FINDER

THREE VOLUMES IN ONE
COMPRISING

NAME-WORD FINDER
METAPHOR FINDER
SOPHISTICATED SYNONYMS

Compiled by

J. I. RODALE

Author of The Word Finder, The Saia Book, etc.

With the Collaboration of

EDWARD J. FLUCK, Ph.D.

Formerly Instructor in Classical Languages at Muhlenberg College

RODALE PRESS
EMMAUS, PENNSYLVANIA

Note:

This volume is composed of three different books bound together, separated by title cards.
THE METAPHOR FINDER begins on page 897, SOPHISTICATED SYNONYMS on page 1125.

FIRST PRINTING, NOVEMBER, 1953
SECOND PRINTING, JUNE, 1954
THIRD PRINTING, APRIL, 1955

MANUFACTURED IN THE UNITED STATES OF AMERICA

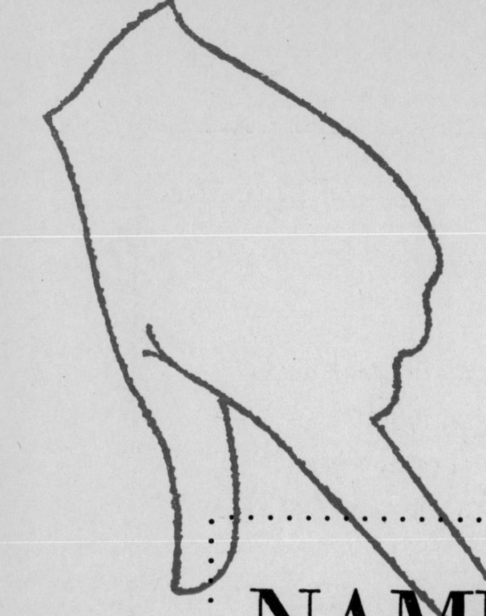

NAME-WORD FINDER

WITH DICTIONARY OF BIOGRAPHY, MYTHOLOGY, AND LITERATURE

EMMAUS, PENNSYLVANIA

RODALE PRESS, INC.

NAME-WORD FINDER

WITH DICTIONARY OF BIOGRAPHY, MYTHOLOGY, AND LITERATURE

EMMAUS, PENNSYLVANIA

RODALE PRESS

Contents

Introduction

NAME-CALLING is such a universal and ancient habit that one is tempted either to inquire into its original purpose and intrinsic value, or else to repeat critically, "What's in a name?" To be sure, "a rose by any other name would smell as sweet." Yet—when we wish to draw an instantaneous mental picture of a lovely young girl, especially one caught in the toils of a tragic love, we generally resort to the time-saving expedient of identifying her (in name only) with some similar person already existing in the full flesh of fiction or history. In the character of *Juliet,* Shakespeare has taught us all that her name now implies, and she enjoys a pre-existence well established by tradition within our knowledge. Similarly, a young and amorous gallant has been a *Romeo* ever since the Bard's first presentation of his impetuous hero.

Faithful friends are still, from the days of Greece and Rome, *Orestes and Pylades,* or *Damon and Pythias,* or *Aeneas and his fidus Achates.* From Biblical times the classical prototype for longevity comes to us as *Methuselah,* and for just as many centuries *Jezebel* has connoted a bepainted and nefarious lady. To call a man a *Shylock,* or a *Scrooge,* or a *Harpagon,* or to say that he is *apprenticed to Mammon,* is to establish his reputation for "avarice." Habiliments imparting the idea of "intrigue" are worn by such masculine names as *Volpone, Machiavelli, Rasputin,* and the class-word *Jesuit.* The same notion of machination on the distaff side is conveyed by the mere mention of *Lucrezia Borgia, Messalina, Becky Sharp,* or *Catherine the Great.* In the fictional place-name *Graustark,* or the personal one of a popular author of plots of intrigue, *E. Phillips Oppenheim,* is contained the same idea of scheming and espionage in background and type.

This heritage of eponyms, or "calling-names," brought into our everyday vocabularies from all eras and civilizations is enormously rich. English literature itself has deposited a hoard of *Fagins* and *Micawbers* and *Lochinvars* in our memories for use whenever we wish to give someone else with similar characteristics a descriptive label which will be understood by all who hear or read our words. The attempt has now been made to include in this volume all these personal "tags" that were displayed so prominently by their original bearers as to have left a new and convenient addition to our dictionaries of description. All these "name-words" are either proper nouns or derived from proper nouns. They are not restricted to those designating people, however, but include the names of famous places, buildings, eras, battles and the like (such as *Marathon, Waterloo, Attica, Parthenon, Augustan*).

Though the prime desideratum of the research that went into this volume was to present a collection of all those name-words which would be as universally understood as the ones already cited, the list as it now stands is far too extensive to justify any claim that each and every one of its members will be equally familiar to all readers. Furthermore, since the potential usefulness of a name was always measured in terms of how it might best fill the need of a writer or speaker wishing to employ it for anecdotal illustration, many of the too common ones were excluded on the ground that in passing into our vocabularies they have shed their initial capitals and are now written entirely in lower-case. An example is that of the overly famous fourth Earl of Sandwich, catapulted to unwarranted linguistic eminence as the result of a single historical achievement which is recalled almost daily at the luncheon tables and snack-bars of millions of Americans.

Consequently, many of the choicer name-words filling the ranks depleted by such omissions will require exposition and explanation in their introduction. For surely there will be critics to take issue with the admission of *Erysichthon* under the key-word HUNGRY, asking angrily, "Who but a pedantic graybeard would ever speak of *Erysichthonian hunger?*" This complaint is apparently in order, until knowledge of the name's content teaches us that appetite can be so inordinate as to drive its victim to gnaw away at and consume his own body!

Such uncommon and, it may be objected, recherché entries were made with the express intention of rendering this volume useful to the public speaker, writer, or layman in search of material for building stories or illustrative parables out of the idea he has in mind. To say that *Philyra,* for example, is even respectably well known as the designation of a "linden tree" is of course not true, but to a reader whose mind may conceivably be in pursuit of either a descriptive word or a story concerning such a tree, the inclusion should fill some need somewhere, even though it merely tells of a beautiful Hellenic maiden who was transformed into the original specimen of that tree.

All these eponyms, names formed from those of some prototypic exponent of a quality or characteristic and given to other people exhibiting the same traits, have been drawn from the pages of world literature, mythology, religion, art, science and history, from the remote past down to our own times. Such names as are still fresh on our lips, as coming from current literature or events, were for the most part omitted on the assumption that no one needs a book of reference to remind him of *Anthony Adverse,* or *Scarlett O'Hara,* or *Amber.* This is not to say that all candidates for admission have had to achieve the literal immortality of being no longer among us. In general, however, the compiler can plead only personal predilection for the election of such celebrities as *Marie Laurencin* and *Fritz Kreisler* to the hierarchy of a majority that now lives only, or principally, in our memories.

There are innumerable occasions on which allusion to a single well-chosen name can, with one incisive stroke, convey a more lasting impression than an array of sentences attempting dissective description of a person. Like the essence of a rare perfume, however, name-calling should be applied sparingly by the writer, if he would make its effect most provocative. It is obvious that the appearance of words from mythology on a newspaper's sporting page would not be likely to find an appreciative audience there, though poets, essayists and editorialists might borrow these same names to wonderful advantage. Again, it should be emphasized that this material will derive its greatest effect from being used with both discrimination and moderation, never to excess. Nor is it recommended that these name-words be marshaled to make a parade of ostentatious and superficial pseudo-knowledge. Instead, casual reference to a hitherto unfamiliar name should instil into a reader the desire to learn more about the bearer of that name than is conveyed in the necessarily abbreviated account found in the relevant biography in this volume. Further reading into the original source material is always to be encouraged, since one of the prime purposes of this compilation is to whet its user's appetite to delve more deeply into the stories behind these names. An interesting bed-side volume, it may profitably be read name-by-name, from cover to cover, in small doses meted out to synchronize with the brief periods of relaxation sought in a book before sleep.

HOW TO USE *THE NAME-WORD FINDER*

All name-words entered were first considered for their usefulness and then evaluated with care by reference to authoritative sources. In the alphabetized pages of the Index, printed in the forepart of this compilation in order to bring each name to the immediate attention of the reader, they are collected under "key-words" that define the pertinent implications of the name-words found under each heading. Those "key-words" consist of illustrative phrases, nouns, adjectives, verbs, and in a few cases adverbs, selected as the author felt them to be properly suggestive and in the effort to anticipate the needs of a user consulting a book of reference.

The name-words contained in this Index of Key-Words are presented, when compounds, in the normal order of given name and surname. That is, under the key-word CREDULITY the reader will find *Ichabod Crane,* printed in that order, though if he should wish to consult the account of that fictional character in the text of the book proper, he would naturally follow ordinary dictionary procedure and turn to the "C's," where he would find it listed as *Crane, Ichabod.*

Since this key-word CREDULITY, like its indexed companions, was selected so as to present not only the names of credulous people, but also anything that might describe or incite to credulity, the user will find among its name-words that of the *Stockwell Ghost,* a fraud that imposed itself convincingly upon many gullible persons in its day. At the end of the list of name-words following that key-word, as in all the other lists, there are included parenthetical cross-references to other key-words that function as synonyms wherever possible. These cross-references are not always presented in the same part of speech, for in the arduous task of compiling the name-words themselves, the filing of the key-words under which they are listed and the construction of the Index to them had to be left till last. Thus, under key-word CREDULITY, itself a noun, will be found a cross-reference to a list that includes two adjectives (*see GULLIBLE, DUPE, UNSUSPECTING*).

In the case of key-words which, being basic English or unique in meaning, afford no substitute, the cross-references cannot consist of synonymous ideas. In these cases, the function of the reference is to:

(1) explain the use of the key-word (*e.g.,* the WHEEL of *St. Catherine* and *Ixion,* since it was one of torture, gives a cross-reference to TORTURED, under which other name-words appropriate to this idea will be found);

(2) supply ideas related by connotation to one or more of the name-words in the group (*e.g.,* WIDOW may suggest HUSBAND-HUNTER as well as BEREAVED, and therefore supplies references to both those key-words for information on additional "widowed" name-words);

(3) refer the reader to opposite ideas or antonyms, where words of similar meaning are unavailable (*e.g.,* WIFE-BEATER suggests the vengeance exacted by one who is HENPECKED, WIFE-HUNTER

contains a cross-reference to HUSBAND-HUNTER, and the irreplaceable key-word FIREMAN also puts one of that profession out of work with a reference to NON-INFLAMMABLE);

(4) explain the allusions contained in the linking of a particular name-word to the key-word under which it is classified (*e.g.,* AFRICA, with its name-words *David Livingstone* and *Ethiopian,* shows cross-references to EXPLORER and UNCIVILIZED, where additional related material may be found);

(5) point to an idea that may be in the mind of the user of the Index when he looks up the key-word, though not the one intended by the author in so classifying the name-word involved (*e.g.,* HORSESHOE is given the cross-reference LUCKY, an idea not conveyed by the name-word listed under the former).

The key-words were chosen for the *emphasis* which they place *on the principal qualities of the name-words* they define. If, therefore, it is the name of a "*romantic* heroine" that is desired, the reader should refer to the key-word ROMANTIC rather than to HEROINE. Similarly, "*rustic* heroines" and "*tragic* heroines" should be looked for under the primary word under consideration, since the general word HEROINE will merely direct attention to the specific words, which contain larger and less generalized groups of name-words.

The cross-referenced key-words should aid the user of this volume in finding the exact name-word he desires. In the event that a suitable name is not found in the list contained under the first key-word consulted, reference should then be made to each of these other key-words for the name-words they suggest. For example, should the need arise to make use of a name and a story illustrative of ILLUSION, that key-word proposes names of the following persons and places: *Barmecidal* (a rich Arabian Nights banquet existing only in the imagination of a famished beggar); *Barataria* (an imaginary island-city in "Don Quixote"); *Lollius* (a non-existent but supposedly authoritative writer cited as source-material by medieval penmen); *Parmenides* (a Greek philosopher who investigated the differences between reality and illusion); *Zeuxis* and *Parhassius* (two ancient Greek painters, the one of whom deceived the birds of the air into pecking at grapes he had painted, while the other actually prevailed upon his rival to believe a pictured curtain was an actual fabric) ; *El Dorado* (the fabled "Golden Land" sought by the Spanish conquistadores); *Mme. Benoîton* (a character who never appears but is frequently mentioned in a comedy by Sardou); *Ivory Gate* (the gate of sleep and insubstantial dreams in Vergil's underworld); *Velasquez* (an artist whose portrait of a Spanish admiral was so true-to-life that an Emperor ordered it to return to the fleet); the *Island of St. Brandan* (an illusory flying isle that was the subject of a medieval legend and search); *Fear Fortress* (an imaginary castle that vanishes into thin air when approached by a courageous person); *Henri Matisse* (French post-impressionist painter whose canvases suggest the illusion of space); and *Matsys* (a Flemish artist who painted a house-fly with such *trompe l'œil* perfection that viewers endeavored to brush it from a portrait).

But this list of names pertinent to "illusions" is further supplemented by cross-references to HALLUCINATION, APPARITION, DELUDED, PECULIARITY and ECCENTRIC, which afford such additional names as those of *Bélise* (a literary character of Molière's who imagines all men to be enamored of herself); *Jabberwock* (Lewis Carroll's mythical monster); *White Ladies* (spectral fairies in French and German folklore); *Mrs. Veal* (Defoe's fictitious walking apparition); *Jacob Marley* (Dickens character whose ghost appears to Ebenezer Scrooge); *Phooka* (a malicious leprechaun in Irish folk tale); and a total of nineteen other equally arresting names.

From such a storehouse it should be a pleasant task, indeed, to find means with which to enliven almost any particular reference made to the word "illusion." In it, mirages are not limited to the oases seen by thirsting travelers in the desert, nor to the phosphorescent lights of the *ignis fatuus,* the will o' the wisp playing over marsh lands at night. In the iridescent eye of his imagination, the truly enchanted writer catches fleeting glimpses of "St. Brandan's Isle," and of "White Ladies" and "Ivory Gates" as well. "Barmecidal feasts" and "Zeuxian grapes" are the tantalizing visions that come to him in the lean and hungry hours before dawn. "Fear Fortress," like the storied walls of Jericho, tumbles down in defeat before his bold approach, and "El Dorado" becomes his attained goal.

The main body of the book, the Dictionary of Names, consists of biographies and facts concerning the name-words themselves. Necessarily brief, they supply sufficient source or bibliographic matter to enable the reader to search out the original documentary appearance of any particular name, if he desires to acquire more detailed information about it than it was possible to give in a work of this plan. In the case of all persons and events other than fictitious ones, dates have also been supplied to aid the reader in placing an otherwise strange name in its chronological background.

First is explained the application of the name-word to the key-word under which it is classified in the Index. The name itself is then employed in one or more phrases illustrating it in apt usage. Often in the form of famous quoted passages, these phrases sometimes render the name in adjectival speech, such as *Medusan hair, Jeffersonian statesmanship, Egerian counsel,* or *Edwardian pageantry.* Since name-words lend themselves readily to the completion of similes, many are treated as such in phrases like *profligate as Messalina, illusory as St. Brandan's isle,* and *lifelike as Myron's cow.* Elsewhere, the name is illustrated in metaphoric or in plain, unfigurative phrases, for the stimulation of the reader's own creative mind, not necessarily as a criterion for imitation or paraphrase by him.

In conclusion, the author would deprecate the critical cries of many readers sure to deplore the absence of many (to them) familiar and equally noteworthy names from these lists. In a project of the scope of any compilation similar to this, such oversight or editorial exclusion is as unintentional as it is inevitable. Despite these sins of omission, may the shades of those not entered in these rolls refrain in their umbrage from destroying whatever value this volume may have!

EDWARD J. FLUCK, PH.D.

Index of Key Words

A

ABANDON (n.)
Hathor; Paphian; Sardanapalus.
(see *unconventional, profligacy, dissolute, reprobate, self-indulgence*)

ABANDON (v.)
Rahu; Odur.
(see *deserter, forswear, renunciation, traitorous, faithless*)

ABANDONED
Lear; Children in the Wood; Effie Deans; Ion; Limbo; Oenone; Tarzan; Ariadne; Freya; Père Goriot.
(see *deserted, forsaken, neglected*)

ABASED
Ichabod.
(see *humiliation, degradation, shamed*)

ABBREVIATIONS
Tironian.
(see *abridge, shortcut*)

ABDUCTION
Jack-in-the-Green; Talassius; Helen of Troy; Europa; Hylas; Proserpina; Sabine; Hippodamia; Meg Merrilies; Ion Perdicaris.
(see *kidnaper, elopement*)

ABERRATION
Masochism; Havelock Ellis; Freudian; Richard von Krafft-Ebing; Marquis de Sade.
(see *perversion, abnormality, peculiarity, hallucination*)

ABETTOR
Rahab; Elspeth; Elbridge Gerry.
(see *ally, assistance, helpfulness, aid*)

ABJECT
Ichabod; Gibeonite; Uriah Heep.
(see *contempt, beggar, degradation, servility*)

ABLE
Acacetus; Cincinnatus.
(see *clever, accomplished, talent, adroit, ingenuity, skill, efficiency, capable*)

ABRIDGE
John Audley.
(see *shortcut, contract*)

ABRUPT
Philoxenus; Betsy Trotwood.
(see *blunt, unceremonious, brusque, rude, inconsiderate, discourteous*)

ABSENT
Mme. Benoîton; Lara.
(see *unseen, invisible*)

ABSENT-MINDED
Jean de La Fontaine; Laputa; Stultorum Feriae; Sganarelle; Sacripant.
(see *forgetful, inattentive, heedless, dreamer*)

ABSOLUTE
Hegelian.
(see *complete, perfection, idealistic, supreme, philosophy*)

ACCOMMODATING
Teirtu; Phormio.
(see *obliging, kindness, polite, courtesy, generosity*)

ACCOMPANY
Laodamia.
(see *attendant, escort*)

ACCOMPLICE
Barnaby Rudge; Maximilian of Mexico.
(see *ally, abettor*)

ACCOMPLISHED
Lorenzo the Magnificent, Johannes Factotum.
(see *education, experience, consummation, proficient, able, versatile, talent*)

ACCORD
James Monroe
(see *concord, harmony, unity, amity, agreement*)

ACCOUCHEMENT
Upis; Eilithyia; Virbius; Suben; Genetyllis; Doctor Slop.
(see *delivery, childbirth, lying-in*)

ACCURACY
Euclidean; Jean Hardouin; Rosa Bonheur; Parthian; Pierre Larousse; Edward Cocker; Alexander Agassiz; Jane Austen; Karl Baedeker; Bernouilli; Bulwer-Lytton; Polybius.
(see *exactitude, correctness, precision, truth, carefulness*)

ACCUSED
Silas Marner; Johannes Eckhart.
(see *impeachment, convicted, acquittal, blame, defendant*)

ACERBITY
Zoilus
(see *harsh, stern, asperity, morose, sullenness, ill-tempered, hypercritical*)

ACHIEVEMENT
Cecil Rhodes; Will Ladislaw.
(see *accomplished, exploits, feat*)

ACKNOWLEDGMENT
Levana.
(see *recognition*)

ACQUIESCENCE
Jephthah; Job.
(see *submission, resignation*)

ACQUITTAL
Clarence Darrow.
(see *release, deliverance, blameless, faultless, innocence*)

ACRES
Samuel Maverick
(see *landowner, plantations*)

ACTING
Thespian; Thalia (see Muse); Melpomene; Rialto.
(see *pantomime, histrionic, theatrical*)

ACTION
Campus Martius.
(see *motion, force, drill*)

ACTIVE
Wat Tyler; Ulysses; Gyes.
(see *vigorous, busy, diligent, industrious, energetic*)

ACTOR
Sir Henry Irving; David Garrick; Joseph Jefferson; Chaplinesque; Rosci-

ADVANTAGE
Elbridge Gerry.
(see *superiority, profit, privileged*)

ADVENTITIOUS
Novensides.
(see *accidental, casual, chance, unintentional*)

ADVENTURE (authors)
Victor Hugo; Alexandre Dumas; James Fenimore Cooper; E. Phillips Oppenheim; Ouida; Jules Verne; Daniel Defoe; Jack London; Ossian; Sir Thomas Malory; Walter Scott; Herman Melville.
(see *chance, danger, eventful, perilous, explorer, discoverer*)

ADVENTURESS
Lola Montez; Moll Flanders; Comtesse de LaMotte.
(see *social climber*)

ADVENTUROUS
Leatherstocking; John Smith; Mr. Midshipman Easy; Jolly Roger; John Gilpin; Richard Hakluyt; Jean Valjean; Aeneas; Argonauts; Roderick Random; Jason; Ulysses; Aramis; Athos; Porthos; Robinson Crusoe; Paridel; Marco Polo; Ruggiero; Long Tom Coffin; Captain Lismahago; Roland; Montesinos; Red Cross Knight; Gilgamesh; Elizabethan; Odyssey; Louis Joliet; Robert La Salle; Captain Kidd; Balboa; Jacques Marquette; Prester John; Richard Haliburton; "Kit" Carson; Gabriele d'Annunzio; Gloriana; Sindbad the Sailor; Tarzan.
(see *bold, daring, courageous, venturesome, chivalrous, enterprising, fortune-hunter, gold-seeker, reckless, foolhardy, rash*)

ADVERSITY
Naomi; Jane Eyre.
(see *misfortune, calamity, afflicted, misery, ill-luck, distressed*)

ADVICE
Moneta; Hesiodic; Gilgamesh; Fasti; Monsieur Josse; Dangle; Phaedrus; Mrs. Glasse.
(see *exhortation, persuasion, admonitory*)

ADVISER
Mentor; Calchas; Egeria; Munin; Ahithophel; Deborah; Faithful Eckhardt; Gonzalo; Nathan; Friar Laurence.
(see *counselor, guide, monitor*)

AESTHETIC
Oscar Wilde; Aurora Leigh; André Gide; Harold Skimpole.
(see *artistic, beauty*)

AFFABLE
Rasiel; Madame Eglantine; Washington Irving; Oriana.
(see *courtesy, polite, urbanity*)

AFFECTED
Little Pedlington; Pharisee; Lord Plausible; Mrs. Partington; Gorgibus; Sir Fopling Flutter; Lord Foppington; Bavius and Maevius; Holophernes; Cheshire Cat; Della Cruscans; Osric; Dundreary; Goody Two-Shoes; Lord Ogleby; Tilburina; Madelon; Euphuistic; Amorphus; Madame Eglantine; Lady Wishfort; Miss Carolina Skeggs; Sir Piercie Shafton; Joseph Surface.
(see *vanity, assumed, feigned, artificial, insincere, foppish, pretentious, conceited, coxcomical*)

AFFECTIONATE
Corporal Trim; Amoret; Leilah; Eugene Field; Susan Nipper; Bob Cratchit; Schumann-Heinck; Calpurnia; Bucephalus; Amelia; Platonic; Naomi; Amy Dorrit.
(see *tenderness, kindness, sympathetic, warm-hearted, love, lovers*)

AFFIANCED
Vor.
(see *betrothal*)

AFFIRMATIVE
Urim and Thummim.
(see *approval*)

AFFLATUS
Hippocrene; Heliconian.
(see *inspiration, ecstasy*)

AFFLICTED
Job; Old Man of the Sea; Isenbras.
(see *distressed, harass, persecution*)

AFIRE
Phaëthon; Tophet.
(see *burning, blaze, bonfire, fire*)

AFRAID
Fear Fortress.
(see *fearful, frighten, terrified, timidity, apprehensive*)

AFRICA
David Livingstone; Ethiopian.
(see *explorer, uncivilized*)

AFTERLIFE
Jordan; Phaedo, Padalon; Dis; Margaret Fox; Nastrond; Fortunatae Insulae.
(see *hereafter, eternity, lower world, underworld*)

AFTERTHOUGHT
Epimetheus.
(see *hindsight*)

AGE
Olympiad.
(see *dates, time*)

AGED
Lord Ogleby; Nestor; Enoch Wray; Graiae; Elli.
(see *old, senility, anile, old age, old man*)

AGELESS
Peter Pan; Dorian Gray; Khartaphilos.
(see *youth, rejuvenation*)

AGGRESSION
Rubicon; Philip of Macedon; Jehu; Julian the Apostate; Ignatius Loyola; Penthesilea.
(see *attack, assault, hostility, invader, marauder, raider, loot, spoils*)

AGITATOR
Giuseppe Mazzini; Jack-Amend-All; Cadean; Coxey's Army; Vicente Blasco-Ibañez.
(see *reformer, demagogue, radical, Communist, uprising*)

AGNOSTIC
Robert Green Ingersoll; Protagoras.
(see *doubting, unbeliever, skepticism*)

AGONY
St. Vitus; Laocoön; Calvary; Tartarus; Gethsemane; Golgotha; Deianira; Via Dolorosa; Black Hole of Calcutta.
(see *anguish, tortured, tormented, distressed, pain, suffering*)

AGREEABLE
Will Wimble; Euphrosyne.
(see *appropriate, affable, sociability*)

AGREEMENT
James Monroe; Rahab; Freischuetz; La Tosca; Hernani.
(see *pact, promise, compact, accord, harmony*)

AGRICULTURE
Piso; Triptolemus; Vacuna; Rhea; Ceres; Tammuz; Nebo; Vergilian; Odin; Hesiodic; Osiris; Ops; Jean Millet; Iasion; Dagon; Aristaeus; Isis; Terra; Quirinus; Picumnus and Pilumnus; Centoatl; Gula; Saturn; Pallas; Eleusinian; Tellus; Damoetas.
(see *grain, seed, corn, wheat, rye, maize, vegetables, fruit, vineyard, plant life, plow, harvest*)

AGRICULTURIST
Triptolemus Yellowley; St. Walston; Vaissya; Telchines.
(see *farmer, husbandry*)

AID
Thaddeus Kosciusko; Logistilla; Aegis; Matsya; Eumaeus; Elbridge Gerry; Eilithyia; Sister Anne; Aladdin; Nadejda von Meck; Launfal.
(see *assistance, succor, relief, alms, subsidize, bounty, helpfulness*)

AIM (v.)
William of Cloudeslie; Cephalus; Annie Oakley; Sagittary; William Tell.
(see *marksmanship*)

AIMLESS
Land of Nod; Meander; Simple Simon.
(see *meandering, desultory, roundabout*)

AIR
Jumala; Apsaras; Anaximenes; Indra.
(see *breeze, zephyr, wind*)

AIRPLANE
Abaris; Jules Verne; Peter Wilkins; Zetes.
(see *flying, winged*)

AIRY
Ariel; Nell Gwyn.
(see *ethereal, buoyant, vivacious*)

ALARM
Pan; Pavor; Phlegyas; Manlius Capitolinus.
(see *fearful, apprehensive, terrified, frighten, panic, startle*)

ALARMING
Stheno; Medusa.
(see *terrifying, fearful, dreadful, dire*)

ALCHEMIST
Zanoni; Subtle; Trismegistus; Paracelsus; Christian Rosenkreuz; Archdeacon Frollo.
(see *magic, thaumaturgy*)

ALCOHOLISM
Stephen Foster; Zombi; Mr. Krook.
(see *drunkenness, inebriation*)

ALERT
Vigiles; Heimdall; Vigilantes; Clara Barton; Mercutio; Sister Anne.
(see *watchful, vigilance, circumspect, wary*)

ALIAS
Outis; Smectymnuus.
(see *pseudonym*)

ALIEN
Novensides.
(see *foreign, exotic, strange*)

ALIKE
Twelve Peers; Donatello; Dromios; Menaechmus; Antipholus.
(see *similarity, likeness, identical, resemblance, twins, duplicate, equality*)

ALLEGIANCE
Ruth; Zedekiah.
(see *fidelity, loyalty, homage, duty, obedience*)

ALLEGORY
John Bunyan; Golden Ass; Phaedrus; Tarquinius Superbus; Jean de La Fon-

taine; Elsa; Lohengrin; Charles Perrault.
(see *fable, symbolism*)

ALLIANCE
Semo Sancus.
(see *treaty-making, compact, oath, unity*)

ALL-INCLUSIVENESS
Boswellian.
(see *comprehensive, encyclopedist*)

ALLITERATION
John Lyly.
(see *rhetoric*)

ALL-KNOWING
Marcus Terentius Varro; Onca; Mithras; Hagen; Helios; Merlin; Odin.
(see *omniscient*)

ALL-POWERFUL
Zeus; Rheingold; Woglinda, Wellgunda, and Flosshilda; Jove; Kama.
(see *omnipotent*)

ALL-RULING
Jove.
(see *power*)

ALL-SEEING
Helios; Mithras; Indra; Argus-eyed.
(see *sight, far-sighted*)

ALLURING
Mata Hari; Lola Montez; Queen Labe; Pierre Louys; Lilith; Marie Laurencin; Leda; Cleopatra; Calypso; Carmen; Cestus; Nefertiti; Lais; Thais; Aphrodisian; Pied Piper; Phryne; Siren; Parthenope; Peitho; Lamia; Lorelei; Leucothea; Ligeia; Mother Bunch; Ogygia; Stheneboea.
(see *tempter, temptress, enticement, beguilement, lure, seduction, attractiveness, engaging, persuasion, ensnare, coaxing*)

ALLUSION
Miss Tox.
(see *reference, hinting, suggestion, insinuation, innuendo*)

ALLY (n.)
Rhesus; Sarpedon.
(see *helpfulness, friendly, abettor, accomplice*)

ALMANAC
Gotha; Fasti; Nostradamus; Hesiodic.
(see *calendar, register*)

ALMOND
Phyllis.
(see *nuts*)

ALMS
Islam; Guy of Warwick; Philip.
(see *aid, succor, assistance, relief, subsidize, bounty, helpfulness*)

ALOOF
Anaxarete; Essenes.
(see *unfriendly, unsympathetic, disinterested, unfeeling, cold-hearted*)

ALPHABET
Abecedarians; Thoth; Cadmean; Palamedes.
(see *spelling, misspelling*)

ALTER
Ikhnaton; Elbridge Gerry; Peter Klaus; Spoonerism.
(see *change, modification, metamorphosis*)

ALTERCATION
Marlovian.
(see *strife, quarrelsome, wrangling*)

ALTERNATING
Meliboeus; Stultorum Feriae; Seven Against Thebes; Box and Cox; Barabbas; Dioscuri.
(see *reciprocation*)

ALTERNATIVE
Kilmansegg; Oenomaus.
(see *choice*)

ALTRUISTIC
Romola; Damon and Pythias; Sikh; Benthamite; Alcestis; Dioscuri; Castor and Pollux.
(see *philanthropic, unselfish*)

AMANUENSIS
Tironian; Baruch.
(see *scribe, secretary*)

AMATEUR
Dangle; Raffles; Harold Skimpole.
(see *dilettante*)

AMATORY
Petrarchan; Venus (see Aphrodisian); Anacreontic.
(see *amorous, erotic, ardent, enamoured, passionate, love, longing, tenderness, lovers, impassioned*)

AMAZING
Perseus; Balboa.
(see *prodigious, miraculous*)

AMAZON
Penthesilea; Hippolyte; Parthenia; Radegund.
(see *virago, termagant, shrew, scold, masculinity*)

AMBASSADOR
Marco Polo; Washington Irving.
(see *delegation, representative, emissary*)

AMBER
Heliades.
(see *precious stone*)

AMBIGUOUS
Tyndareus.
(see *equivocation, enigmatic, vague*)

AMBITION-CRAZED
Mecca; Abimelech.
(see *over-ambitious*)

AMBITIOUS
Alfred Lammle; Icarian; Jugurtha; Bellerophon; Khufu; Napoleon Bonaparte; Aimwell; Alexander the Great; Macbeth; Bifrost; Ephialtes; Herostratus; Livia; Lady Macbeth; Mithradates; Agathocles; Mark Antony; Fulvia; Mr. and Mrs. Leo Hunter; Genghis Khan; Themistoclean; Querno; Fenton; Pirithous; Uriah Heep; Theseus; Vathek; Louis XIV; Peregrinus Proteus; Tullia; Bob Acres; Henry Esmond.
(see *aspiring, emulate, eager, desire*)

AMBROSIA
Shri.
(see *nectar*)

AMBUSH
Jack-in-the-Green; Zacocia; Quintilius Varus; Trasimene Lake; Frontinus.
(see *snare, ensnare, man-trap*)

AMELIORATE
Theodorus.
(see *improvement*)

AMERICAN
Yankee; Uncle Sam; Brother Jonathan.
(see *Yankee, nationalism*)

AMIABLE
Queen of Hearts; Gibsonesque; Amelia Sedley; Honeywood.
(see *loveliness, sweetness, engaging, charm, attractiveness. kindness, tenderness, benignant, alluring*)

AMITY
James Monroe; Pax; Concordia.
(see *concord, harmony, friendly*)

AMOROUS
Paphian; Phaedra; Oreads; Nymphs; Menander; Oceanids; Napaeae; Peregrinus Pickle; Nereids; Naiads; Tannhaeuser; Amaryllis; Alpheus; Philander; Arthur Pendennis; Casanovian; Tracy Tupman; Jack-in-the-Green; Leda; Damoetas; Lesbia; Horatian (Horace); Byblis; Selene; Anchises; Don Juan; Catullan; Calypso; Erato; Indra; Mrs. Frail; Huncamunca; Rudolph of Mayerling; Mejnoun and Leilah.
(see *erotic, ardent, enamoured, passionate, love, longing, tenderness, lovers, amatory, impassioned*)

AMORPHOUS
Tiamat.
(see *irregular, shapeless, misshapen, vague*)

AMPHIBIOUS
Oannes.
(see *frog, reptile, fish*)

AMPLITUDE
Rubensian.
(see *fertility, abundance, wealth, plenty, opulence, fat*)

AMUSEMENTS
Edwardian.
(see *entertainment, divert, merriment, pleasure, games*)

AMUSING
Launce; Autocrat of the Breakfast Table; Gilbert and Sullivan; Mark Twain; Pickwickian.
(see *lively, ludicrous, droll, comical, funny, farce, riaiculous*)

ANALYTICAL
Havelock Ellis; Sidney Carton; James Joyce; Freudian; Lucian; Lord Bryce; Euripidean; Pinkerton; Proustian; Carl G. Jung; William James.
(see *dissection, solution, thoughtful*)

ANARCHIST
Pierre J. Proudhon; Sansculotte.
(see *demagogue, lawless, radical*)

ANATOMY
Michelangelo; Herophilus; Leonardo da Vinci.
(see *dissection, vivisection*)

ANCESTOR
Manes; Adam; Pyrrha; Shem; Ask and Embla; Ascanius; Lares; Tiki; Manu; Phut; Deucalion; Latinus.
(see *forebear, progenitor*)

ANCIENT
Pelasgians; Phorcus; Ogyges; Cecrops; Iapetus; Leleges; Methuselah; Stonehenge; Sabine.
(see *old, antiquity, archaic, obsolete, old-fashioned, primeval*)

ANECDOTAL
Athenaean; Caius Tranquillus Suetonius.
(see *raconteur*)

ANGEL
Zophiel; Zephon; Zadkiel; Uriel; Rasiel; Botticelli; Arioch; Ithuriel; Nama; Israfel; Jacob's Ladder; Michael.
(see *seraph, cherub*)

ANGER
Aeshina; Cambyses; Ivan the Terrible.
(see *wrathful, rage, fury, frenzy, resentful, indignation, choleric, ill-tempered*)

ANGLER
St. Ulric; Izaak Walton.
(see *fisherman*)

ANGLOPHILE
Charles Montesquieu.
(see *British*)

ANGUISH
Faustian; Gustave Doré; Calvary; Via Dolorosa; Golgotha; Cyparissus; Scopas.
(see *agony, tormented, tortured, suffering, distressed*)

ANILE
Witch of Edmonton; Mme. Pernelle; Lady Wishfort; Elli.
(see *aged, senility, old age*)

ANIMALS
Jean de La Fontaine; Aesop; Phaedrus.
(see *heifer, cow, cattle, oxen, bull, horse, mare, lion, elephant, cat, dog, hound, jackal, ape, monkey, bear, boar, buffalo, crocodile, pig, snake, dragon, griffin, frog, weasel, ram, sheep, rats, tortoise, whale, worm, faun, deer, fox, wolf, goat*)

ANIMATE (v.)
Stator.
(see *encouragement, inspiration*)

ANNALS
Eusebius; Tacitus.
(see *chronicle, register*)

ANNIHILATION
Ragnarok; Gorboduc; Siva.
(see *extermination, destruction*)

ANNOUNCER
Talleyrand; Flamininus; Gabriel; Fung-hwang; Stentorian.
(see *reporter, raconteur, journalist, rumor, gossip, tattler, harbinger, herald*)

ANNOY
Dangle.
(see *molested, bother, harass, nuisance, tormentor*)

ANNUAL
Fasti.
(see *year*)

ANNULMENT
Tess of the d'Urbervilles.
(see *divorce*)

ANOINT
Mithras; Gilead; Sarpedon.
(see *bathe, balm, ointment*)

ANONYMOUS
Bona Dea.
(see *unknown, unidentified, incognito*)

ANSWER (n.)
Abdemon; Urim and Thummim; Ferracute.
(see *response, rejoinder*)

ANTAGONISTIC
Turnus; Cato the Censor; Cato of Utica; Zoroaster; Ormuzd; Sir Mador.
(see *hostility, contradictions, conflict, opposition, inconsistent, incongruous*)

ANTEDILUVIAN
Pelasgians; Og; Iapetus; Deucalion; Pantibiblia.
(see *primeval, antiquity*)

ANTHEM
Francis Scott Key.
(see *hymn*)

ANTHROPOMORPHIC
Tiki.
(see *god, demigod, superhuman*)

ANTI-CHRISTIAN
Ganelon; Julian the Apostate.
(see *pagan, heathen, irreligious*)

ANTICIPATION
Spes.
(see *expectation, contemplative, hopeful, trusting*)

APOSTLE
Francisco Xavier; Manichaeus; St. Denis; St. Matthew; St. Mark; Luke; St. John; Philip; Peter.
(see *evangelistic, missionary*)

APOTHECARY
Galen.
(see *druggist*)

APOTHEOSIZED
Machaon; Arsinoë; Devarshis.
(see *acclaimed, homage, demi-god, divine, exaltation*)

APOTROPAIC
Ver Sacrum.
(see *scarecrow, avert*)

APPAREL
Zouave; Herr Teufelsdroeckh; Miss Flora McFlimsey; Longchamps; Silk-Stocking.
(see *clothing, dress, raiment, attire, costume, habiliments, garments, robe, equipment, wardrobe*)

APPARITION
Jabberwock; White Ladies; Mrs. Veal; Phooka; Jacob Marley.
(see *ghost, specter, phantom, spirit, bogy, hobgoblin, sprite, supernatural, chimerical, illusion, preternatural, visions*)

APPEALING
Childe Rolande; David Copperfield.
(see *attractiveness, amiable, engaging, charm*)

APPEARANCES
Major Bath; Caleb Balderstone.
(see *pretense, simulated, sham*)

APPEASEMENT
Aeschines; Austin Chamberlain; Edouard Daladier.
(see *peace-maker, propitiatory, reconciliation*)

APPETITE
Gargantuan; Erysichthon; Milo; Grangousier.
(see *hungry*)

APPLE
Hippomenes; Iduna; Hesperides; Milanion; Dorothea.
(see *fruit*)

APPREHEND
Yacumama.
(see *suspicion*)

APPREHENSIVE
Lady Dedlock; Dionysius; Harpagon; Eurylochus.
(see *fearful, afraid, distrustful, suspicion, anxiety, uneasy*)

APPRENTICE
Tappertitian.
(see *greenhorn, pupil*)

APPRISE
Munin.
(see *informer, notify, adviser, admonitory, warning*)

APPROPRIATE (adj.)
Miss Tox; Pindaric.
(see *adaptable, agreeable, conform, felicity*)

APPROVAL
Kriss Kringle; Libro d'Oro; Gotha.
(see *praise, consent*)

AQUEDUCT
Appius Claudius Caecus; Frontinus.
(see *water*)

ARABIAN
Lawrence of Arabia; Kedar.
(see *nomad*)

ARBITER
Phormio; Petronius; Philaeni; Hoyle; Perrin Dendin; Zeus; Jean Hardouin; Amorphus; Diogenes; Forsete.
(see *umpire, referee, lord, governor*)

ARBITRARY
Judge Lynch; Elbridge Gerry.
(see *domineering, overbearing, dictator, irresponsible, despotic, autocratic, unrestrained, tyrant, uncontrolled, absolute, imperious*)

ARCHAEOLOGICAL
Lawrence of Arabia; Prosper Mérimée; Jonathan Oldbuck; Stonehenge; Pompeii.
(see *antiques, antediluvian, primeval*)

ARCHAIC
Pelasgians.
(see *ancient, obsolete, bygone*)

ARCHANGEL
Rasiel; Michael; Uriel.
(see *angel, seraph, cherub*)

ARCHER
William of Cloudeslie; William Tell; Phut; Teucer; Ullur; Philoctetes; Sagittary; Adam Bell; Scythian; Kedar.
(see *bowman*)

ARCHFIEND
Belphegor.
(see *devil, demon, Satan, fiendish, diabolical*)

ARCHITECT
Trophonius; Ictinus; Imhotep; Solness; Vitruvius; Leonardo da Vinci; Christopher Wren.
(see *builder*)

ARCHITECTURE
Incan; Parthenon.
(see *construction, masonry*)

ARCTIC
Boreal.
(see *northernmost, cold*)

ARDENT
Tracy Tupman; Peter the Hermit; Islam; John Huss; Jane Eyre; Cestus; Leilah; Philander.
(see *amorous, erotic, enamoured, passionate, love, longing, tenderness, lovers, amatory, impassioned*)

ARDUOUS
Boethius; Salt River.
(see *difficulty, laborious, onerous, troublesome*)

ARGUMENTATIVE
John Willet; Captain Lismahago; Widow Blackacre; Tweedledum and Tweedledee; Socrates; Square and Thwackum.
(see *controversy, disputatious*)

ARIA
Giuseppe Verdi; Giacomo Puccini.
(see *opera, tuneful, melodious*)

ARID
Vritra; Sahara; Paran; Proserpina.
(see *dry, parched, barren*)

ARISTOCRATIC
Lady Clara Vere de Vere; Miss Lucretia MacTab; Almack's; Gotha; Jenkins; Isagoras; Gainsborough; Libro d'Oro; Belgravian; Jeames; Silk-Stocking; Robert E. Lee; Eupatridae; Alcaeus; Sadducees; Miss Carolina Skeggs.
(see *nobility, patrician, gentility, courtly, privileged*)

ARK
Manu; Deucalion; Noah; Pyrrha.
(see *boat, ship*)

ARMOR-PLATE
Völund; Vulcan; Mulciber; Orc.
(see *shield, iron, bronze, steel*)

ARMS
Lua.
(see *weapons*)

ARMY
Sam Browne; Campus Martius; Marius; Frontinus; Iphicrates.
(see *militaristic*)

ARMY CHAPLAIN
Ulrich Zwingli.
(see *minister*)

ARMY DOCTOR
Dioscurides.
(see *doctor, physician, surgeon*)

AROMATIC
Rosemary; Gilead.
(see *fragrant, sweet-smelling*)

AROUSE
Candaules; Maenad.
(see *incitement, excitement, animate*)

ARRAIGNMENT
Pasquinade.
(see *accused, impeachment, denunciatory*)

ARROGANT
Rajput; Xerxes; John Osborne; Tarquinius Superbus; Misenus; King Ryance; Antinous; Orgoglio; Junker; Marsyas; Sir Matthew Mite; Laenas; Coriolanus; Salmoneus; Lucius Mummius.
(see *haughtiness, supercilious, disdainful, blustering, insolent, overbearing, dogmatic, egotistic, pompous, lofty, self-important, self-assurance*)

ARROW
Adam Bell; Abaris; Philoctetes; Sagittary; Scythian; St. Sebastian.
(see *missiles, marksmanship*)

ARSENAL
Tvashtri.
(see *weapons*)

ARSON
Phaëthon; Herostratus; Phlegyas; Armida; Whiteboyism; Mr. Rochester; Surtur.
(see *fire-bug*)

ART-CRITIC
Pliny the Elder; Longinus; Giorgio Vasari.
(see *critic, connoisseur*)

ARTERIES
Herophilus.
(see *vein, blood*)

ARTFUL
Volpone; Widow Wadman; Patelin; Sinon.
(see *cunning, crafty, wily, subtlety, insidious, designing, intrigue, deceitful, sly*)

ARTICULATE
Vaticanus; Vach.
(see *utterance, pronunciation*)

ARTIFICE
Rhampsinitus; Wooden Horse; Galinthias.
(see *cunning, deceitful, imposture trickery, duplicity, guile, stratagem. ruse, wily, machinator*)

ARTIFICIAL
John Lyly; Alexandrianism; Dalcrozean; Célimène; Euphuistic; Miss Carolina Skeggs.
(see *affected, vanity, assumed, insincere, feigned, foppish, pretentious, conceited, coxcomical*)

ARTISAN
Mentor; Tvashtri; Bezaleel; Telchines.
(see *mechanical, craftsmanship, laborer*)

ARTIST
Polygnotus; Raphael; Titian; Nero; Will Ladislaw; Gustave Doré; Rembrandt; Burne-Jonesian; Botticelli; Attic; Andrea del Sarto; Arion; Dante Gabriel Rossetti; Leonardo da Vinci; Pre-Raphaelite; Muse; Praxiteles; Benvenuto Cellini; Christopher Wren.
(see *painter, colorist, pastels, singer, sculpture, architect, ballet*)

ARTISTIC
O. Henry; Heliconian; Edgar Allan Poe; Aurora Leigh; Mimi; Hadrian; Hippocrene; Godey; Oscar Wilde; Parthenon; Delmonico; Harold Skimpole.
(see *aesthetic*)

ARTLESS
Imogen.
(see *unaffected, candid, naive, guileless, unsophisticated, ingenuousness, sincerity, unsuspecting*)

ART PATRON
Pisistratus; Medici; Lorenzo the Magnificent; Maecenas; Nadejda von Meck.
(see *patron, patroness*)

ARTS AND CRAFTS
Quetzalcoatl; Telchines; Isis; Oannes; Ea; Siva.
(see *civilization, craftsmanship*)

ASCETIC
Francisco Xavier; Yogi; Lara; Ignatius Loyola; Francis of Assisi; Gymnosophist; St. Jerome; St. Theresa; Thaumaturgus; Jansenists; Jonathan Edwards; Rose of Lima; Labadists; Tertullian; Essenes; Simeon Stylites; John the Baptist.
(see *austerity, rigid, severity, stern, puritanic, renunciation, self-denial, abstinence*)

ASEXUAL
Abelites; Viraj.
(see *chastity, eunuch, virgin*)

ASHAMED
Valentine; Merope.
(see *shamed, humiliation, remorse*)

ASHEN
El Greco; Mr. Toodle.
(see *colorless, pallor*)

ASH-TREE
Yggdrasil.
(see *trees*)

ASIATIC
Rimski-Korsakov; Genghis Khan.
(see *exotic, bizarre, foreign, strange*)

ASLEEP
Somnus.
(see *sleep, repose*)

ASPERITY
Zoilus.
(see *virulent, crabbed, bitterness, sullenness, ill-tempered*)

ASPERSION
Lara.
(see *calumnious, detractor, slander, defame*)

ASPIRING
Fenton; Herostratus; Livia.
(see *emulate, eager, ambitious, desire*)

ASSASSIN
Junius Brutus Booth; Cassius; Brutus. Zelotes; Modo.
(see *murderer, killer, tyrannicide*)

ASSAULT
Adrastus; Enceladus; Ephialtes; George Edward Pickett; Gigantes.
(see *attack, onslaught, aggression, charge*)

ASSEMBLING
Osiris.
(see *unifier, piecemeal*)

ASSEMBLY-LINE
Henry Ford.
(see *industrialist, manufacturer*)

ASSEMBLY-PLACE
Yggdrasil; Almack's; Sanhedrin; Tabard.
(see *meeting-place, rendezvous*)

ASSISTANCE
Logistilla; Eumaeus; Eilithyia; Nadejda von Meck; Pirithous; Iolaus; Achates; Patroclus; Gunther; Sister Anne; Kederli; Maecenas.
(see *helpfulness, succor, aid, alms, patron, ally*)

ASSOCIATION
Siamese.
(see *indissoluble*)

ASTROLOGY
Trismegistus; Nostradamus; Ahithophel; Chaldean.
(see *fortune-telling, star-worshiper*)

ASTRONOMY
Urania (see Muse); Galileo; Johannes Kepler; Eratosthenes; Rasselas; Omar Khayyam; Hesperus; Hipparchus; Saturn.
(see *star, constellation, star-gazer*)

ASTUTE
Becky Sharp; Volpone.
(see *shrewd, sagacity, intelligent, ingenuity, sharper, perspicacity*)

ASYLUM
Alsatia.
(see *sanctuary, shelter*)

ATELIER
Della Robbia.
(see *artist*)

ATHEIST
Marlovian; Lorenzo; Euhemeristic; Protagoras; Goddess of Reason.
(see *godless, free-thinker, irreligious, agnostic, un-godfearing*)

ATHLETICS
Atalanta; Lysippus; Polycleitus; Olympian Games; Gymnopaedia: Milo; Polydamas.
(see *gymnastics*)

ATLANTIC
Oceanids.
(see *ocean-god, sea-deities*)

ATLAS
Heinrich Kiepert.
(see *map-maker, cartographer, geographer*)

ATOMIC
Lucretian; Epicurean; Democritus.
(see *universe, creation, minute, small*)

ATONEMENT
Dostoievskian; Atys; Cassiopeia; Owain; Hesione; Azazel.
(see *expiation, purgatory*)

ATROCITY
Mezentius; Myrmidons; Absyrtus; Theodosius; Tamerlane.
(see *heinous, cruelty, villainy, depravity, wickedness, savage, ferocious, criminal, horror*)

ATROPHY
Lamarckian.
(see *emaciated, consumptive*)

ATTACK (n.)
George Edward Pickett; Adrastus; Seven Against Thebes.
(see *aggression, assault, hostility, onslaught, charge*)

ATTENDANT
Favonius; Moth; Corporal Trim; Cristoph Wagner; Xury; Abishag.
(see *companion, association, escort*)

ATTIC
Mimi.
(see *roof*)

ATTIRE
Herr Teufelsdroeckh; Miss Flora McFlimsey.
(see *apparel, dress, clothing, raiment, costume, habiliments, wardrobe*)

ATTORNEY
Eugene Wrayburn; John Wemmick; Mr. Tulkinghorn; Papinian; Clarence Darrow; Dodson and Fogg; Seneca the Elder; Sargeant Buzfuz.
(see *lawyer, counselor, solicitor*)

ATTRACTIVENESS
Dolly Varden; Tom Jones; Hebe; Mother Bunch.
(see *amiable, loveliness, sweetness, engaging, charm, kindness, tenderness, benignant, alluring*)

AUCTION
Peter Funk; Tattersall's.
(see *barter, bid*)

AUDACITY
Marsyas; Misenus; Jean de La Fontaine; Robert Macaire; Phaëthon.
(see *bold, hardy, daring, fearless, intrepid, courageous, venturesome*)

AUGURY
Tarquinius Priscus; Tages; Vala; Veleda.
(see *prognostication, soothsayer, prediction, prophecy, harbinger, ominous*)

AUNT
Miss Lucretia MacTab.
(see *spinster, family tree*)

AUSTERITY
Thélème; Torquemada; Rose of Lima; Livia; Laconian; Ignatius Loyola; Jansenists; Xenocrates; Emersonian; St. Jerome; Curius Dentatus; Cato the Censor; Stoic; Fabricius; Labadists; Malvolio; Essenes.
(see *severity, stern, harsh, ascetic, formality, stiff, inflexible, strict, rigid, rigorous*)

AUTHENTIC
Simon Pure; Jean Hardouin.
(see *purity, trustworthy, unpolluted*)

AUTHORITATIVE
Areopagitical; Downing Street; King Log; Mrs. Harris; Capitoline; Hafen Slawkenbergius; Hoyle.
(see *standardized, dictator, imperious, dogmatic*)

AUTOCRATIC
Judge Lynch; Caesarean (2); Ivan the Terrible; Pisistratus.
(see *absolute, tyrant, oppression, overbearing, disdainful*)

AUTOGRAPH
John Hancock.
(see *signature*)

AUTOMATIC
Amphion; Teirtu; Bradley Headstone; Robotian; Mrs. Jarley.
(see *mechanical*)

AUTUMN
Thallo; Quadrifrons; Brisingamen; Lucius Opimius; Linus; Kabibonokka.
(see *seasons, harvest*)

AVARICIOUS
Alfred Lammle; Baba Abdalla; Ahab; Squeers; Shylock; Arthur Gride; Harpagon; Frothi; Gobseck; Père Grandet; Laban; John Osborne.
(see *greed, covetous*)

AVENGE
Theodosius; Kriemhilde; Thyestes; Melusina; Rigoletto; Polydorus; Robin and Makyne; Macduff; Latona; Laertes; Anteros; Ulysses; Ibycus; Ate; Alastor; Hippolyte; Dirae; Amphion; Orestes; Antiope; Ultor; Mary Ambree; Weird Sisters; Nemesis; Michael; Dinah; Eumenides; Edmond Dantès; Parthenia.
(see *revenge, punishment, vengeance, retaliation, retribution*)

AVERT
Fescennine; Laius; Ver Sacrum.
(see *prevent, deterrent*)

AVIATOR
Abaris.
(see *flying, airplane*)

AWAKENING
Sleeping Beauty; Kiak-Kiak.
(see *arouse, revive*)

AWARD
Cecil Rhodes; Alfred Nobel.
(see *gifts, present, reward, kudos, prize*)

AWE
Demogorgon.
(see *dreadful, fearful, terrifying*)

AWE-INSPIRING
Olympian.
(see *grandeur, magnificence*)

AWKWARD
Diggary; Miss Betsy Thoughtless; Abraham Slender; Dominie Sampson.
(see *uncouth, gauche, rude, clumsy, boorish*)

AXIOMS
Goethe; Tupperian.
(see *maxims, proverb, sententious*)

AZTEC
Quetzalcoatl; Tezcatlipoca.
(see *Indian*)

B

BABBLER
Poll Parrot; Lalage
(see *prattle, chatterbox, gossip, loquacious*)

BABIES
Mary Cassatt; Levana.
(see *infant, bambino*)

BACHELOR
Watkins Tottle; John Wemmick; Mirabel; Benedick; Coelebs.
(see *wife-hunter, misogyny*)

BACKBITE
Zedekiah; Mrs. Candour.
(see *defame, malign, slander, calumnious, libel, aspersion, abusive*)

BACKSLIDER
Pliable.
(see *deserter, apostasy*)

BACK-TO-NATURE
Walden Pond; Henry Thoreau; John Burroughs; Rousseauian; Tarzan; Mowgli; Rima.
(see *naturalism*)

BACKWARD
Postverta and Prorsa.
(see *return*)

BACKWOODS
Tarheel.
(see *uncivilized, woods*)

BAD LUCK
Sejus; Harmonia's Necklace.
(see *ill-luck, misfortune, unlucky*)

BAFFLING
Arrowsmith; Man with the Iron Mask.
(see *thwarted, bewilderment, perplexity*)

BAKER
Pistor; Fornax; Picumnus and Pilumnus; St. Wilfrid.
(see *cookery*)

BALANCE
Canephoroe; Caryatids; Dalcrozean.
(see *poise*)

BALEFUL
Hagen; Set; Skadhi.
(see *injurious, pernicious, deadly, evil, sinister, mischief-maker*)

BALL
Fortuna.
(see *round*)

BALLAD
Ginevra.
(see *song, poetry*)

BALLET
Vaslav Nijinsky; Bathyllus; Terpsichore; Giselle; Anna Pavlova; Edgard Degas; Sergei Diaghilev; Marius Petipa; Isadora Duncan; Taglioni; Michel Fokine.
(see *dancing*)

BALLOON
Jules Verne.
(see *flying*)

BALM
Gilead; Fierabras.
(see *ointment, unguent, panacea, curative, healing, soothe*)

BAMBINO
Della Robbia.
(see *babies, worship*)

BAMBOOZLE
Patelin.
(see *beguilement, cheat, dupe, mislead, hoax*)

BAN
Lysistrata; Charles C. Boycott.
(see *curse, excommunicated, denunciatory, execrate, penalty*)

BANDIT
Jonathan Wild; Gamaliel Ratsey; Rob Roy; Mohock; Gilderoy; Jack Sixteen-String; Fra Diavolo; Adam Bell; Sciron; Spartacus; Sinis; Hernani.
(see *outlaw, robber, brigand, freebooter, footpad, highwayman, marauder, gangster*)

BANEFUL
Grigori E. Rasputin; Auster.
(see *baleful*)

BANISHMENT
Isagoras; Idomeneus; Man in the Moon; Ishmael; Julia; Protagoras; St. John.
(see *exile, expatriate, ostracism, proscription*)

BANKER
Lombard; Fondlewife; Joseph Bounderby.
(see *financier, money-lender*)

BANQUET
Lucullan; Amphitryon; Saehrimnir; Deipnosophistae.
(see *feast, entertainment, eating*)

BANTER
Joe Miller; Fescennine.
(see *raillery, ridicule, mockery, derisive, joke, jester*)

BAPTISM
Constantine; Mithras; Cornelius; John the Baptist; Kistnerappan.
(see *bathe, immersion, convert*)

BARBARITY
Carthaginian; Tezcatlipoca; Tauri; Ethiopian; Jack Ketch; Tatar; Gothic; Huns; Lemnian; Mezentius; Scythian; Myrmidons; Zamore; Phalaris..
(see *cruelty, savage, brutal, ferocious, inhumanity*)

BARBECUE
St. Lawrence.
(see *roasted, burned*)

BARBER
Figaro.
(see *razor, bearded*)

BARBS
Laberius.
(see *censorious, critic, abusive*)

BARD
Ossian; Demodocus; Walther von der Vogelweide; Phemius; Orpheus; Arion; Minnesinger; Meistersinger; Taliesin.
(see *minstrelsy, poetry*)

BAREBACK
Europa; Ivan Mazeppa.
(see *ride, horseback*)

BAREFOOT
Kunigunde; St. Theresa; Tarheel; Kneippism; Ignatius Loyola; Isadora Duncan.
(see *ascetic, poverty, dancing*)

BARGAIN (v.)
Rahab; Glaucus; La Tosca; Tom Walker; Tarpeian Rock; Esau; Peter Fabel; Peter Schlemihl; Hernani.
(see *contract, covenant, compact, barter*)

BARMAID
Maritornes; Young Marlow; Mistress Quickly; Kate Hardcastle.
(see *tavern, waitress*)

BARREN
Baca; Ishtar; Sahara; Marah; Paran.
(see *arid, desert, dry*)

BARTER
Glaucus; Mimir.
(see *exchange, trader, bargain, swap*)

BASE
Caliban; Catiline; Fagin; Ganelon; Jonas Chuzzlewit.
(see *shameless, disrepute, disgrace, discredit, infamous, villainy, dishonor*)

BASHFUL
Daphne; Watkins Tottle; Miles Standish; Harley.
(see *shy, timidity, coy, diffident, modesty*)

BASIN
Mambrino.
(see *kettle*)

BASKET
Canephoroe.
(see *utensils*)

BAS RELIEF
Della Robbia; Scopas.
(see *sculpture*)

BASSO
Feodor Chaliapin.
(see *singer, deep*)

BASTARDY
William the Conqueror; Effie Deans; Lady Dedlock; Esther Summerson; Sabrina.
(see *unmarried mother, love-child, illicit*)

BATHE
Kneippism; Ashtavakra; Baptes; Susanna; Salmacis; Naaman.
(see *immersion*)

BATTERED
Irus; St. Stephen.
(see *beating, pelted, bruised*)

BATTLE (n.)
Valkyries; Plataea; Enyo; Odin; Saxnot; Armageddon; Arimaspians; Gettysburg; Tyr; Horatii and Curiatii; Walter Scott; Aceldama; Berserker.
(see *conflict, contest, fighting*)

BAWDY
Long Meg of Westminster; Mother Douglas; Paphian: Plautus; Fescennine.
(see *obscenity, indecency, lascivious, lewdness, unchaste*)

BAZAAR
Rialto.
(see *exchange, barter*)

BEACHCOMBER
Jack London.
(see *vagrancy*)

BEACON
Pharos.
(see *lighthouse, lantern, light*)

BEAK
Stymphalian.
(see *claw*)

BEAKERS
Antoine Lavoisier.
(see *laboratory, chemist, cup*)

BEANS
Jack and the Bean Stalk.
(see *vegetables*)

BEAR (n.)
Callisto; Valentine and Orson.
(see *animals*)

BEARDED
Ahenobarbus; King Ryance; Nazarite; Don Ferolo Whiskerandos; Anthony VanDyke.
(see *bewhiskered, whiskers*)

BEAST
Behemoth; Dabbat.
(see *brutish, animals, savage*)

BEATING
Orbilian; Judy; Oliver Twist; St. Stephen; Mr. Creakle.
(see *flogging, thrashing*)

BEAU
Macaroni; Tattle; Squire of Dames.
(see *coxcomical, foppish, lady-killer, dude*)

BEAUTIFUL (female)
Venus; Freyja; Iduna; Mme. de Montespan; Lakshmi; Una; Trilby; Nymphs; Anasuya; Oreads; Valkyries; Delilah; Oriana; Guinevere; Lola Montez; Deirdre; Cassiopeia; Shri; Charis; Andromeda; Ophelia; Cleopatra; Amoret; Juno; Helen of Troy; Mme. de Maintenon; Oceanids; Miranda; Cinderella-like; Maia; Messalina; Ginevra; Hebe; Tyndaris; Nereids; Penthesilea; Phryne; Poppaea; Nefertiti; Napaeae; Neaera; Sol; Moll Flanders; Naiads; Isolde; Portia; Hesperides; Nana; Leda; Zémire; Mrs. Siddons; Chloris; Callirrhoë; Callipolis; Statira; Queen of Sheba; Lais; Brunhilde; Lucrezia Borgia; Calypso; Hypatia; Cytherea; Beatrice; Aspasia; Armida; Rebekah; Haidee; Clodia; Aphrodisian; Marie Antoinette; Leilah; Mme. Recamier; Rhodope; Theodora; Thais; Marie Laurencin; Gerda; Alcina; Jessica; Circean; Abishag; Bathsheba; Chryseis; Campaspe; Esther; Esmeralda; Catherine Glover; Flora MacIvor; Dinah Morris.
(see *comely, fair, pretty, charm, elegance, exquisite, loveliness, grace*)

BEAUTIFUL (male)
Candaules; Endymion; Hoenir; Ganymede; Narcissus; Bathyllus; Antinous; Anchises, Hyperion; Adonis; Abdallah; Kama; Agathocles; Karoon; Acis; St. Sebastian.
(see *handsome*)

BEAUTY
William Butler Yeats; Phidian; Edgar Allan Poe; Pre-Raphaelite; Christopher Wren; Georgian; Minnesinger; Eden; John Keats; Botticelli.
(see *elegance, grace, comely, loveliness, attractiveness, charm*)

BEDIZENED
Lady Wishfort; Jezebel.
(see *showy, flashy, gaudy*)

BEDLAMITE
Tom O' Bedlam.
(see *lunatic, crazy, insanity, deranged*)

BEDSTEAD
Og; Procrustean.
(see *cradle*)

BEEF
Zagreus.
(see *cattle, bull*)

BEER
Gambrinus; Sabazius; Hymir.
(see *drink*)

BEES
Hymettan; Lama; Rhoecus; Aristaeus; Vergilian; Hyblaean; Melissa.
(see *honey, insects*)

BEFRIEND
St. Lawrence; Manlius Capitolinus; Mrs. Jarley; Samaritan; Mr. Brownlow.
(see *helpfulness, patron, aid, assistance, benefactor, friendly*)

BEGGAR
Belisarius; Bezonian; King Petaud's Court; Irus; Abram-man; Edie Ochiltree; Lazarus; Tom O'Bedlam; Guy of Warwick.
(see *mendicant, pauper, indigent*)

BEGIN
Janus; Johnny Newcome.
(see *greenhorn, self-starting*)

BEGUILEMENT
Delilah.
(see *alluring, tempter, ensnare, temptress, enticement, lure, seduction, attractiveness, engaging, persuasion, coaxing*)

BEHEAD
Louis XVI; St. Winifred; Xerxes; Henry VIII; St. Catherine; Crispin; St. Denis; John the Baptist; Radegund; St. James.
(see *decapitation*)

BEHIND-THE-TIMES
Rip Van Winkle.
(see *old-fashioned*)

BEING
Hegelian.
(see *realistic, actual, life-giving, substance*)

BELEAGUER
Lars Porsena; Tydeus.
(see *besieger, blockade, siege*)

BELIEF
Joseph of Arimathea; Simeon; Mary Baker Eddy.
(see *persuasion, trusting, reliance, convert, faith, religious*)

BELLE
Lady Wishfort.
(see *beautiful, coquettish*)

BELLES-LETTRES
Edmund Burke.
(see *litterateur*)

BELLIGERENT
Marsi; Mars; Wild Boar of Ardennes; Sikh; Tullus Hostilius; Genseric; Hippolyte; Riffian; Thalestris; Saxnot; Picti; Kumara; Quirinus; Amazonian; Berserker; Shatriya.
(see *war, hostility, pugnacious, quarrelsome, antagonistic, opponent, rivalry*)

BELLOW (v.)
Achelous; Stentorian.
(see *roar*)

BELL-RINGER
Quasimodo.
(see *tinkle, curfew*)

BELOVED
Queen of Hearts; Neaera; Chloë; Robin Hood; Zuleika; Doctor Charles Primrose; Endymion; Calidore; Benjamin; Fiametta; Nathanael; Stella.
(see *sweetheart, lovers, darling*)

BELT
Sam Browne.
(see *girdle*)

BEMOAN
Queen of Tears; Miss Flora McFlimsey.
(see *lamentation, moan, mourning, sorrow*)

BENEFACTOR
Mme. de Montespan; Nadejda von Meck; Larunda; Major Bath; Jack the Giant-Killer; Florence Nightingale; Promethean; Hadrian; Mme. Marie Curie; Ptolemy; Louis Pasteur; Maecenas; Parsifal; Count Zinzendorf; Atticus; Joseph Pulitzer; Saturn; Androclean; Ahuramazda; Shamash; Ephialtes; Flavius Vespasian; Hiawatha; Jacob's Ladder; Periander; Mithras; Titus Vespasianus; Yama; Barzillai; Fung-hwang.
(see *succor, savior, patron, supporter, friendly*)

BENEVOLENT
Uncle Toby; Zeno; Jean Valjean; Parson Abraham Adams; Pisistratus; Xenocrates; Tabitha-Dorcas; Lord Ogleby; Mr. Brownlow; Thomas Allworthy; Joseph of Arimathea; Harley.
(see *benignant, obliging, humaneness, tenderness, charitable, generosity, philanthropic, altruistic, unselfish, kindness*)

BENIGHTED
Pinchwife.
(see *ignorance, unintelligent*)

BENIGNANT
Zephyrus.
(see *amiable, loveliness, sweetness, engaging, charm, attractiveness, kindness, tenderness*)

BEPAINTED
Lady Wishfort; Jezebel.
(see *rouged, cosmetics, painted*)

BEREAVED
Laodamia; John Wemmick.
(see *sorrowful, grief, broken-hearted, sadness, doleful*)

BESIEGER
Tydeus; Lars Porsena.
(see *siege*)

BESMEARED
Mr. Toodle.
(see *grimy, dirty*)

BESOTTED
Baba Abdalla; Thyia.
(see *intoxicated, drunkenness, sot, intemperate, inebriation*)

BESTIAL.
Comus.
(see *degradation, brutal, brutish, sensuality, low-born, depravity, villainy*)

BETRAYAL
Aceldama; Gethsemane.
(see *treachery, perfidy, infidelity*)

BETRAYED
St. Lucia; Philomela; Merlin; Margaret; Madama Butterfly; Uriah; Norma; Rigoletto; King Mark; Fulvia; Maximilian of Mexico; Polydorus; Samson; Deiphobus; Florimel; Jaffier; Sisera.
(see *mislead, ensnare, delude, seduced, dupe*)

BETRAYER
Ephialtes; Kriemhilde; Ganelon; Tarpeian Rock; Prusias; Delilah; Judas; Sinon; Agravaine.
(see *seducer, untrustworthy, faithless, double-dealing, disloyal, deceitful, turncoat*)

BETROTHAL
Vor.
(see *affianced*)

BEWAIL
Jeremiad; Queen of Tears.
(see *lamentation, mourning, moan, sorrow, grief*)

BEWARE
Greeks Bearing Gifts.
(see *cautious, wary*)

BEWHISKERED
Dundreary; Don Ferolo Whiskerandos.
(see *whiskers, bearded*)

BEWILDERMENT
Ophelia.
(see *perplexity, maze, muddle-headed, mystery*)

BEWITCH
Master Leonard; Cleopatra; Sylvia.
(see *fascinating, spellbinder, enchantment, captivating, magic*)

BIAS
Monsieur Josse; Tacitean; Livian; Alfred Dreyfus; Leicester; Dedlock.
(see *partiality, prejudice, bigotry*)

BIBLIOPHILE
Antonio Magliabecchi; Grolieresque.
(see *bookish*)

BIBULOUS
Sir Toby Belch; King Cole.
(see *besotted, tippler*)

BICKERING
Big-Endians; Tweedledum and Tweedledee; Billingsgate.
(see *wrangling, quarrelsome, squabble, altercation, disputatious*)

BID
Balaam; Peter Funk.
(see *proposal*)

BIGAMY
Brigham Young.
(see *much-married, adulterous*)

BIG-NOSED
Hafen Slawkenbergus; Cyrano de Bergerac.
(see *nose*)

BIGOTRY
Isabella I; Zelotes; Abecedarians; St. Bartholomew's Day; Basile; Bloody Mary; Parson Trulliber; Doctor Slop.
(see *prejudice, intolerance, obstinate, opinionated, dogmatic, fanatical*)

BIND
Yggdrasil; Yue-Laou.
(see *confinement, chained*)

BIOGRAPHY
Plutarch; Agricola; Cornelius Nepos; Caius Tranquillus Suetonius; Boswellian; Giorgio Vasari.
(see *historian*)

BIOLOGIST
Empedocles.
(see *animals, plant life, scientific*)

BIRD LANGUAGE
Fafner; Francis of Assisi; Rima.
(see *birds*)

BIRDS
Mother Carey; Phineus; Walther von der Vogelweide; Etruscan; Oppian; Garuda; Stymphalian; John James Audubon.
(see *sparrow, nightingale, hawk, owl, crow, pigeon, parrot, eagle, woodpecker, swallow, guinea hens, geese, crane, swan, doves, herons, peacock, raven, magpies, vulture, partridge*)

BIRTH
Badebec; Clothos; Eupatridae; Latona; Matuta; Vala; Libitina; Partula;

Ferona; Upis; Eilithyia; Virbius; Genetyllis; Hera.
(see *childbirth, lineage, offspring, creation, progeny*)

BISEXUAL
Hermaphroditus.
(see *self-renewing, parthenogenesis*)

BITE
Nicander.
(see *chew, eating*)

BITS
Lapithae.
(see *horsemanship*)

BITTERNESS
Dostoievskian; Ishmael; Henrik Ibsen; Julian the Apostate; Emily Brontë; Democritus; Zakkum; Catullan; Naomi; Byronic; Juvenalian; Zoilus; Hipponax; Swiftian; Marah.
(see *gall, rancorous, hatred, malice, malign, spiteful, enmity, asperity, acerbity, severity, harsh, ill-tempered*)

BIZARRE
Gothic; Rider Haggard.
(see *fantastic, strange, whimsical, outlandish*)

BLACK
Rahu; Nox; Quashee; Hela; Erebus; Sambo; Ethiopian; Stygian; Cimmerian; Kali; Kaaba; Mnevis.
(see *darkness*)

BLACK-AND-BLUE
Irus.
(see *livid, crushed, battered*)

BLACK-FACE
Master Leonard.
(see *negro*)

BLACKMAIL
Silas Wegg; Sir Francis Clavering; Maffia.
(see *bribery, extortion, protection-money*)

BLACKSMITH
Völund; Brontes; Vulcan; Wayland the Smith; Joe Gargery; Tubal-Cain; Tvashtri; Mulciber; Mime; Dactyli.
(see *smithy, forge*)

BLADE
Morglay.
(see *sword, broadsword, razor*)

BLAME
Momus.
(see *censorious, condemned, disapproval, reproachful, accused*)

BLAMELESS
Kunigunde; Epictetus.
(see *faultless, innocence, impeccable*)

BLAND
Hymettan; Hyblaean.
(see *mildness, affable, suave, amiable, complacent*)

BLASÉ
Vathek; Dorian Gray.
(see *boredom, ennui, sophisticated, cynic*)

BLASPHEMOUS
Capaneus; Belshazzar; Front de Boeuf.
(see *impiety, sacrilegious, profanation*)

BLATANT
Guppy; Donnybrook Fair.
(see *bellow, vociferous, noisy*)

BLAZE
Herostratus; Flamen; Yezd.
(see *flame, burning, glowing*)

BLEAK
Egdon Heath.
(see *cold, drear, cheerless*)

BLEND
Chiron; Centaur; Salmacis.
(see *unite, mixture, fusion*)

BLESSED
Job; Avalon; Fortunatus; Jabez.
(see *happiness, blissful, holiness, hallowed, sacred*)

BLESSING
Cleobis and Biton; Tiny Tim; Jacob's Ladder; Fung-hwang.
(see *advantage, glory, honor, thanksgiving, gratitude*)

BLIGHT
Robigus.
(see *pestilence, rust*)

BLINDNESS
Orion; Rhoecus; Belisarius; Wandering Willie; Bernouilli; St. Cecilia; Appius Claudius Caecus; Phineus; Ruggiero; Daphnis; Zedekiah; Miltonic; Tobit; Melesigenes; Helen Keller; Edgard Degas; Hodur; St. Lucia; Nydia; Oedipus; Nyctymene.
(see *sightless, unseeing*)

BLINKING
Nyctymene.
(see *sight, glance*)

BLISSFUL
Vaikuntha; Mejnoun and Leilah; Olympian; Lalla Rookh; Elysian; Eden.
(see *joy, rapt, ecstasy*)

BLOCKADE
Lars Porsena; Tydeus.
(see *siege*)

BLOCKHEAD
Boeotian; Trissotin; Shallow.
(see *simpleton, foolish, dunce*)

BLOND
Neoptolemus; Pyrrhus; Titian.
(see *yellow, hair*)

BLOOD
St. Januarius; Nessus; Ymir; Ve; Hyacinthus; Acis; Doctor Sangrado; Hoenir.
(see *vein*)

BLOODCURDLING
Apache.
(see *terrifying, fearful*)

BLOODSHED
Modo; Enyo; Gorboduc.
(see *slaughter, carnage, butchery, murder, massacre, homicidal*)

BLOODTHIRSTY
Myrmidons; Mme. Thérèse Defarge; Laestrygonian; Les Tricoteuses; Tullia; Tezcatlipoca; Robespierre; Aceldama; Hela; Kali.
(see *cruelty, savage, ferocious, inhumanity, barbarity, ruthlessness, murder*)

BLOSSOM
Charis; Juventas; Nanna; Flora; Pincian; Chloris.
(see *flowers*)

BLUE
Edie Ochiltree; Sakhrat.
(see *emerald*)

BLUE-STOCKING
Cornelia Blimber; Armande.
(see *learned, scholarly, pedantic*)

BLUFF
John Bull; Nathaniel Winkle; Squire Western; Philoxenus; Sganarelle.
(see *good-natured, hearty, blunt, frank*)

BLUNDERING
Lord Balmerino; Verges; Moses Primrose; George Primrose; Abraham Slender; Teague; Sir Martin Mar-All; Mrs. Slipslop; Spoonerism.
(see *mistaken, bungle, awkward, stupid*)

BLUNT
Tommy Atkins; Laberius; Theodore Dreiser.
(see *abrupt, outspoken, unceremonious, brusque*)

BLUSH
Pierre Loti.
(see *embarrassment, red, rosy*)

BLUSTERING
Drawcansir; Bobadil; Aquilo; Mussolini.
(see *roar, loud, bully, domineering. boastful, boisterous*)

BOAR
Varaha; Oeneus; Wild Boar of Ardennes; Meleager; Sindre; Saehrimnir.
(see *swine, pig*)

BOARDING-HOUSE MISTRESS
Mrs. M. Todgers.
(see *proprietress*)

BOASTFUL
Ralph Roister Doister; Xerxes; Niobe; Misenus; Marsyas; Aganice; Irus; Goliath; Thrasonic; Thamyris; Huggins and Muggins; Rodomontade; Sir Kay; Don Adriano de Armado; Tartarin; Parolles; Falstaffian; Astolfo; Anchises; Basilisco; Marquis of Carabas; Amorphus; Jack Brag; Cassiopeia; Drawcansir; Gasconnade; Crispin; Scaramouch; Gnatho; Miss Carolina Skeggs; Sacripant; Almanzor; Lreux.
(see *braggart, blustering, vainglorious*)

BOAT
Hringham.
(see *ship, fleet, man-of-war*)

BOATMAN
Phaon; Charon.
(see *ferryman*)

BOAT-RACE
Portunus.
(see *pilot, helmsman*)

BODY
Lais; Jerry Cruncher; Candaules.
(see *corpse, cadaver*)

BODYGUARD
Pisistratus; Varangians.
(see *escort, protector, defender, custodian*)

BOG
Serbonian Bog; Slough of Despond.
(see *marsh, swamp, mire*)

BOGY
La Befana; Prinz Ruprecht; Berchta: Empusa.
(see *apparition, hobgoblin*)

BOIL (v.)
Pelias; Morgiana.
(see *hot*)

BOISTEROUS
Squire Western: Termagant; Tityre-Tu; Giovanni Boccaccio.
(see *noisy, tumultuous, turbulence, vociferous. loud*)

BOLD
Captain Macheath; Lazarillo de Tormes; Ferdinand Magellan; Laenas; Paulina; Robert Macaire; Jolly Roger; Richard Haliburton; Deiphobus; Actaeon; Europa; Judith; Jack London; Lochinvar; Jezebel; Phaëthon; Selim; Iachimo; Priscilla, the Puritan Maid; Spartacus.
(see *fearless, intrepid, valor, courageous, bravery, adventurous, audacity, daring, heroism*)

BOLT
Capaneus; Indra.
(see *arrow, dart, missiles, thunderbolts, lightning*)

BOMBARDMENT
Francis Scott Key; St. Stephen.
(see *assault, pelted*)

BOMBASTIC
Della Cruscans; Pistol; Osric; Mrs. Malaprop; Mrs. Partington; John Lyly; Geronimo; Bombastes Furioso; Aldiborontiphoscophornio; Sir Piercie Shafton.
(see *inflated, turgid, stilted, grandiloquent, magniloquence, pompous*)

BONES
Ve; Junner.
(see *body*)

BONFIRE
Ucalegon.
(see *fire*)

BONUS
Marius.
(see *reward, gifts, subsidize*)

BOOKBINDING
Grolieresque.
(see *bibliophile*)

BOOKISH
Antonio Magliabecchi; Cristoph Wagner; Astolfo; Pantibiblia; Callimachus.
(see *pedantic, studious, scholarly*)

BOOMERANG
Thrym; Mjöllnir.
(see *scythe*)

BOORISH
Laconian; Damoetas; Miss Betsy Thoughtless.
(see *rustic, clown, loutish, awkward. clumsy, coarse*)

BOOTY
Genseric; Chryseis.
(see *loot, spoils, pillage*)

BORDERS
Mason and Dixon; Terminus.
(see *limit, frontier*)

BOREDOM
Peronella; Querno; Paridel; Old Man of the Sea; Xenophon; Emma Bovary; Gratiano.
(see *ennui, tedious*)

BORROWER
Panurge; Jeremy; Echo.
(see *loan*)

BOSSED
George Dandin.
(see *henpecked*)

BOTANIST
Theophrastus; Dioscurides; Lamarckian.
(see *naturalism*)

BOTHER (n.)
Old Man of the Sea.
(see *annoy, plague, troublesome, nuisance*)

BOUNDARY
Mason and Dixon; Terminus.
(see *limit, frontier*)

BOUNTY
Icarius; Dolly Madison; Ceres; Nadejda von Meck; Saehrimnir; Santa Claus.
(see *aid, assistance, succor, relief, alms, subsidize, helpfulness, generosity*)

BOURGEOIS
Monsieur Jourdain; Mme. Sans-Gêne; Babbitt.
(see *Philistine, smug*)

BOVINE
Hathor.
(see *cow*)

BOW (v.)
Ramman.
(see *obeisance*)

BOWER
Flora.
(see *grottoes*)

BOW-LEGGED
Sambo.
(see *splayfoot*)

BOWMAN
Parthian; William of Cloudeslie; Ullur; Adam Bell; Philoctetes; Teucer; William Tell; Scythian; Sagittary; Kedar; Phut.
(see *archer*)

BOXING
Amycus; Dioscuri; Phorbas; Osiris; Marquis of Queensbury.
(see *fisticuffs*)

BOYISH
Penrod; Pancras; Moth; Saint Nicholas; Wagon Boy; Fidelio.
(see *childlike*)

BOY-SERVANT
Xury; Teague.
(see *page*)

BRACE (v.)
Stator.
(see *strength, supporter*)

BRACELET
Tarpeian Rock.
(see *jewelry*)

BRAGGART
Tartarin; Mussolini; Gasconnade; Irus; Bessus; Basilisco; Bobadil; Jack Brag; Ralph Roister Doister; Rodomontade; Thamyris; Drawcansir; Anchises; Aganice; Amorphus; Adriano de Armado; Scaramouch; Sacripant; Shallow; Almanzor.
(see *boastful, blustering, vainglorious*)

BRAIN
Ve.
(see *mind*)

BRAIN-CHILD
Rishi.
(see *thoughtful*)

BRANDED
Sir Edward Hugh Redgauntlet; Jim Crow; Hester Prynne; Meleager; Samuel Maverick; Althaea.
(see *stain, shamed*)

BRASS
Tubal-Cain.
(see *copper, bronze, metallurgy*)

BRAVERY
Zouave; Laconian; Idomeneus; Glaucus; Joan of Arc; Joseph Andrews; Melantius; Leonidas; Cloelia; Arria; Argantes; Doctor Charles Primrose; Deiphobus; Horatius Cocles; Mercutio; Priam; Pocahontas; Rajput; John Ridd; Rebecca the Jewess; Valley Forge; Jacques Marquette; Philaeni; Marsi; Manlius; Ajax; Penthesilea; Lord Nelson; Marmion; Mayeux; Naomi; Uncle Toby; Nisus; Euryalus; Mettius Curtius; Euphorbus; Gurth; Scaevola; Gyas; Sarpedon.
(see *bold, courageous, daring, chivalrous, fearless, intrepid, audacity, valor, gallantry, heroism*)

BRAWLING
Marlovian; Termagant; Bobadil; Clodius; Tityre-Tu; Katharine; Thyia.
(see *quarrelsome, disputatious, wrangling, squabble, bickering, altercation, melee*)

BRAWN
Milo; Polydamas; Little John; Samson.
(see *muscular, power, vigor, robust, strength*)

BRAZEN
Falstaffian; Talus.
(see *bold, impudent*)

BREACH-OF-PROMISE
Mrs. Bardell; Dodson and Fogg.
(see *proposal, forswear*)

BREAD
Fornax; Mithras; Pistor; St. Wilfrid.
(see *baker*)

BREAST-FEED
Rumina.
(see *suckle*)

BREATH
Auster.
(see *breeze*)

BREECHES
Gammer Gurton; Sansculotte.
(see *pantaloons*)

BREEDING
Mendelian; Glaucus; Jukes Family.
(see *heredity*)

BREEZE
Zephyrus; Vaya; Apsaras.
(see *wind, west wind, zephyr*)

BREEZY
Hippoclides.
(see *flippant, nonchalant*)

BRIBERY
Philip of Macedon; Jemmy Twitcher; Curius Dentatus; Lucius Opimius; Aceldama; Amphiaraus; Harmonia's Necklace; Jugurtha.
(see *corrupt, graft, suborn*)

BRIDE
Lucy Ashton; Ginevra.
(see *matrimony, wedlock*)

BRIDEGROOM
Talassius; St. Keyne.
(see *wife-hunter*)

BRIDESMAID
Pronuba.
(see *marriage*)

BRIDGE
Bilfrost; Horatius Cocles; Rialto.
(see *aqueduct*)

BRIDLES
Lapithae.
(see *horsemanship*)

BRIEF
Callimachus; Pharnaces.
(see *succinct, laconic, pithy, terse, epigrammatic, sententious, short-cut*)

BRIGAND
Paul Clifford; Robert Macaire; Jemmy Twitcher; William of Cloudeslie; Cacus; Jonathan Wild; Fra Diavolo; Captain Macheath; Sciron; Sinis.
(see *robber, footpad, highwayman, freebooter, marauder, outlaw, bandit, gangster*)

BRIGHT
Phoebe and Phoebus; Thia; Apollo; Harpocrates; Helios; Delia; Sol; Hyperion; Aglaia.
(see *shining, glowing, lustrous, glittering, dazzling*)

BRILLIANT
Kubla Khan; Aspasia; Franz Liszt; Acestus; Chesterfieldian; Thais; Paganini; David Garrick; Johnsonian; Clodia; Fanny Kemble; the name Barrymore; Paul Gauguin; Oscar Wilde; François Voltaire; Byronic; Mme. Pompadour; Balzacian; Phryne; Aglaia; Gloriana; Mme. de Sévigné.
(see *illustrious, eminent, glory, celebrity, clever, keen, intellectual, unusual, impressive*)

BRIMSTONE
Cotton Mather.
(see *Hell, denunciatory*)

BRINE
Oceanus; Salacia.
(see *sea, ocean-god*)

BRITISH
Jeames; Tommy Atkins; John Bull.
(see *anglophile, nationalism*)

BROAD-MINDED
Chaucerian; Appius Claudius Caecus; Wife of Bath.
(see *foresight, tolerance, good-natured*)

BROAD-SHOULDERED
Fierabras.
(see *shoulder*)

BROADSWORD
Morglay.
(see *sword, rapier, sabre*)

"BROKE"
Duke Humphrey; Beau Brummel.
(see *impecunious, poverty, impoverished*)

BROKEN-HEARTED
Parthenope; Paul and Virginie; John Chivery; Selim; Smike; Haidee.
(see *disconsolate, inconsolable, dispirited, sadness, melancholy, sorrowful, heart-broken*)

BRONZE
Dodonean; Cabiric; Tubal-Cain; Benvenuto Cellini; Etruscan; Rhoecus.
(see *metallurgy, brass, copper*)

BROODING
Hamlet; Tschaikovsky; Alcyone; Melpomene.
(see *melancholy, hypochondriac, doleful*)

BROTHEL
Mother Douglas.
(see *prostitute, pimp*)

BROTHER-COMPLEX
Canace; Electra; Byblis.
(see *aberration*)

C

CACOPHONOUS
Arthur Honegger; Ismenias.
(see *harsh, discord*)

CADAVER
Jerry Cruncher; William Burke.
(see *corpse, body*)

CAKE
Fornax; Pistor.
(see *bread, baker*)

CALAMITY
Frothi; Sejus; Lerna.
(see *disaster, misfortune, catastrophe, ruination, adversity, afflicted, evil, ill-luck*)

CALCULATING
Fenton; Dorine; Mrs. Martha Bardell; Becky Sharp.
(see *scheming, crafty, designing, selfish, wary, cautious, circumspect*)

CALCULATIONS
Eratosthenes; Bernouilli.
(see *mathematics*)

CALCULUS
Leibnitzian; Isaac Newton; Bernouilli.
(see *mathematics*)

CALENDAR
Fasti; Eusebius; Julian.
(see *year, time, almanac*)

CALIPH
Vathek.
(see *Arabian, king*)

CALLIGRAPHIC
Spencerian.
(see *handwriting*)

CALLOUS
Regan.
(see *unfeeling, apathy, indifferent, hard-hearted*)

CALLOW
Johnny Newcome.
(see *inexperience, unsophisticated, immature*)

CALM (n.)
Pax; Platonic; Arria; Bertolde; Alcyone; Polyxena; Polycleitus; Sir Guyon; King Log; Irene; Les Tricoteuses; Spinoza.
(see *peaceful, tranquillity, placid, repose, quiet*)

CALUMNIOUS
Basile; Lady Sneerwell.
(see *abusive, reproachful, opprobrious, scurrilous, ribald, invective, denunciatory, injurious, offensive, insulting, insolent*)

CAMEO
Pyrgoteles; Gibsonesque.
(see *jewelry*)

CAMP
Bret Harte.
(see *tent, out-of-doors*)

CAMP-MEETING
Beulah.
(see *religious*)

BROTHERLY
Fourierist; Dioscuri; Sikh; Zeno; Castor and Pollux; Labadists; Valentine; Orson.
(see *fraternal, friendly*)

BROWBEAT
Uncle Pumblechook; Mr. Fang; Mr. Creakle.
(see *bully, overbearing, insolent*)

BRUISED
Irus.
(see *battered, contuse*)

BRUSHWOOD
Man in the Moon.
(see *shrub, bush*)

BRUSQUE
Philoxenus; George Warrington.
(see *rude, blunt, abrupt, bluff, gruff, discourteous, impolite*)

BRUTAL
Marquis de Sade; Vandalism; Morgante; Jonas Chuzzlewit; Parson Trulliber; Simon Legree; Peregrine Pickle; Myrmidons; Robert the Devil; Attila; Argantes; Ferdinand Fathom; Gymnopaedia; Robotian; Troglodytae; Busirus; Centaur; Lemnian; Yahoo; Mr. Fang; Mr. Creakle; Front de Boeuf; Bill Sikes; Squeers.
(see *savage, ferocious, cruelty, inhumanity, unfeeling, barbarity, ruthlessness*)

BRUTISH
Gadarene.
(see *beast*)

BUBBLING
Pierre Pérignon.
(see *effervescent, foam*)

BUCCANEER
Vitalians; Vikings; Varangians; Sir Henry Morgan; Jean Lafitte; Dick Deadeye; John Silver.
(see *piracy, corsair, freebooter*)

BUCKTEETH
Wild Boar of Ardennes.
(see *malformed, ugliness*)

BUDS
Chloris.
(see *blossom, flowers*)

BUFFALO
Yama.
(see *animals*)

BUFFOON
Touchstone; Jack Pudding; Wamba; Pantaloon; Patelin; Querno; Harlequin; Merry-Andrew; Scaramouch; Hanswurst.
(see *mountebank, jester, clown, zany, foolish*)

BUGBEAR
Lamia.
(see *hobgoblin, specter, ogre, bogey*)

BUILDER
Romulus and Remus; Vitruvius; Amphion; Cadmean; Imhotep; Ictinus; Solness.
(see *architect*)

BULK
Gigantes; Henri Matisse.
(see *magnitude, dimensions, large, massiveness, amplitude*)

BULL
Zagreus; Phalaris; Apis; Mithras; Minos; Pasiphaë; Dirce; Bacis; Europa; Achelous; Siva; Serapis; Mnevis.
(see *animals*)

BULLET
Freischuetz.
(see *marksmanship, rifle, pistol*)

BULL-HEADED
John Bull
(see *obstinate, pig-headed, self-willed, stubborn, opinionated*)

BULLY
Pistol; Uncle Pumblechook; Drawcansir; Thrasonic; Tityre-Tu; Hectorean; Mr. Fang; Mr. Creakle; Gradasso; Joseph Bounderby.
(see *browbeat, domineering*)

BULWARK
Aegis; Stonewall Jackson.
(see *fortress, security, safeguard, protection*)

BUMPTIOUS
Tappertitian.
(see *conceited, vainglorious, egotistic, opinionated, vanity*)

BUNGLE
Lord Balmerino.
(see *blundering, clumsy*)

BUOYANT
Ino; Thomas Traddles.
(see *resilient, cheerful, hopeful, vivacious, animate, spirited*)

BURDEN
Caryatids; Canephoroe; Old Man of the Sea; Ossa on Pelion; Og.
(see *encumbrance, impediment, troublesome*)

BURGLAR
Raffles; Bill Sikes; Jack Sheppard.
(see *robber, cracksman, thievery*)

BURGUNDY
Pierre Pérignon.
(see *wine*)

BURIAL
Mausolus; Pompeii; Père La Chaise; Stoke Poges; Libitina.
(see *entombed, sepulcher*)

BURIED ALIVE
Philaeni; Antonius Polemon.
(see *suffocation*)

BURLESQUE
Hudibrastic; Batrachomyomachia; Aldiborontiphoscophornio; Cockaigne; Candide; Plautus.
(see *caricature, travesty, parody, farce*)

BURLY
John Willet; McFingal.
(see *brawn, strength*)

BURNED
Capaneus; John Huss; Ulrich Zwingli; St. Lawrence; Creusa; Scaevola; Semele; St. John.
(see *cremated, roasted*)

BURNING
Tophet; Phlegethon; Gehenna.
(see *flame, hot, fire, scorch, afire, glowing*)

BUSH
Jack-in-the-Green.
(see *shrub, brushwood*)

BUSY
Martha; Rialto.
(see *diligent, industrious, officious*)

BUSYBODY
Sir Launcelot Greaves; Quidnunc; Paul Pry; Sir Benjamin Backbite; Widow Blackacre; Basile; Marplot.
(see *meddlesome, prying, officious*)

BUTCHERY
Absyrtus; Zagreus; Jack Ketch; Macduff; Tezcatlipoca; Fordicidia; Pelias.
(see *murder, slaughter, massacre, carnage, bloodshed*)

BUTLER
Diggary.
(see *servant*)

BUTTER
Widenostrils.
(see *milk*)

BUTTRESS
Stator.
(see *supporter, prop*)

BUXOMNESS
Rubensian.
(see *plump*)

BUY OFF
Jugurtha.
(see *bribery, suborn*)

BYGONE
Urth.
(see *past*)

C

CACOPHONOUS
Arthur Honegger; Ismenias.
(see *harsh, discord*)

CADAVER
Jerry Cruncher; William Burke.
(see *corpse, body*)

CAKE
Fornax; Pistor.
(see *bread, baker*)

CALAMITY
Frothi; Sejus; Lerna.
(see *disaster, misfortune, catastrophe, ruination, adversity, afflicted, evil, ill-luck*)

CALCULATING
Fenton; Dorine; Mrs. Martha Bardell; Becky Sharp.
(see *scheming, crafty, designing, selfish, wary, cautious, circumspect*)

CALCULATIONS
Eratosthenes; Bernouilli.
(see *mathematics*)

CALCULUS
Leibnitzian; Isaac Newton; Bernouilli.
(see *mathematics*)

CALENDAR
Fasti; Eusebius; Julian.
(see *year, time, almanac*)

CALIPH
Vathek.
(see *Arabian, king*)

CALLIGRAPHIC
Spencerian.
(see *handwriting*)

CALLOUS
Regan.
(see *unfeeling, apathy, indifferent, hard-hearted*)

CALLOW
Johnny Newcome.
(see *inexperience, unsophisticated, immature*)

CALM (n.)
Pax; Platonic; Arria; Bertolde; Alcyone; Polyxena; Polycleitus; Sir Guyon; King Log; Irene; Les Tricoteuses; Spinoza.
(see *peaceful, tranquillity, placid, repose, quiet*)

CALUMNIOUS
Basile; Lady Sneerwell.
(see *abusive, reproachful, opprobrious, scurrilous, ribald, invective, denunciatory, injurious, offensive, insulting, insolent*)

CAMEO
Pyrgoteles; Gibsonesque.
(see *jewelry*)

CAMP
Bret Harte.
(see *tent, out-of-doors*)

CAMP-MEETING
Beulah.
(see *religious*)

CARD-PLAYER
Sara Battle; Hoyle; Sir John Suckling.
(see *gambling, games*)

CAREER
Odyssey.
(see *vicissitudes, fortune*)

CAREFREE
Faunus; Vedius Pollio; Lyaeus; Hippoclides; Mercutio; Pan; Puck.
(see *insouciance, nonchalant, lighthearted*)

CAREFULNESS
Protogenes; Dame Durden.
(see *cautious, circumspect, vigilance, discreet, wary, prudence*)

CARELESSNESS
Cassim Baba; Palinurus; Halgaver.
(see *thoughtless, heedless, inattentive, inadvertent, neglectful*)

CARETAKER
Mentor; Silvanus.
(see *custodian, warden, guardian, curator, keeper*)

CARICATURE
William Hogarth; Sir Fretful Plagiary; Thackerayan; Claude Monet; Plautus; Molière; Ryparographer; Dickensian; Aristophanic.
(see *travesty, parody, farce, burlesque*)

CARNAGE
St. Bartholomew's Day; Jack Ketch; Berserker; Ragnarok; Seven Against Thebes; Huitzilopochtli; Kali.
(see *slaughter, butchery, massacre, bloodshed*)

CARNAL
Belphegor; Alcina; Paphian; Pierre Louys; Potiphar's Wife; Gomorrah; Baubo; Obidicut; Babylonian; Sodoma.
(see *sensuality, lustful, lechery, lascivious, concupiscent*)

CARNIVAL
'Arry and 'Arriet; Halgaver.
(see *festival, merry-making*)

CARNIVEROUS
Laestrygonian; Empusa; Freki; Stymphalian.
(see *flesh-eating, cannibalism*)

CAROUSAL
Bacchic; Saturnalian.
(see *feast, entertainment, banquet, merry-making, revelry, orgiastic*)

CARPENTER
Peter Quince; St. Joseph.
(see *builder*)

CARPING
Momus; Susan Nipper; Zoilus; Sneer; Smelfungus.
(see *censorious, hypercritical, critic, faultfinder*)

CARRIER
Saint Fiacre; Skirnir.
(see *vehicle*)

CARTOGRAPHER
Anaximander; Heinrich Kiepert.
(see *map-maker, geographer*)

CARVE
Schamir.
(see *sculpture, chisel, cut, engraver*)

CASCADE
Minnehaha.
(see *water, falls*)

CAVE-DWELLERS
Tauri; Troglodytae.
(see *primeval, antiquity*)

CAVERN
Montesinos; Egeria.
(see *grottoes*)

CEILING-PRICE
Diocletian.
(see *economics, low-cost*)

CELEBRITY
Laura; Zabian; Mr. and Mrs. Leo Hunter.
(see *fame, glory, hono., reputation, eminent, distinctive*)

CELESTIAL
Vaikuntha.
(see *heaven, angel, seraph, God, divine, cherub*)

CELIBACY
Essenes.
(see *bachelor, virginity, abstinence, spinster, chastity, purity*)

CELTIC
William Butler Yeats.
(see *nationalism*)

CEMETERY
Mausolus; Aceldama; Père La Chaise; Stoke Poges.
(see *burial, sepulcher*)

CENOBITE
Pachomius.
(see *convent*)

CENSORIOUS
William Ralph Inge; Jonathan Edwards; Sir Benjamin Backbite; Cato the Censor; Walther von der Vogelweide; Mrs. Grundy; Puritanic; Basile; Appius Claudius Caecus; Parian; Philippic; St. Jerome; Momus; Hipponax; Smelfungus.
(see *captious, hypercritical, faultfinder*)

CENSUS
Libertas.
(see *population*)

CENTENARIAN
Enoch Wray; Khartaphilos; M. Valerius Corvinus.
(see *old man, patriarch, senility*)

CEREMONIOUS
Barataria; Scone; H. M. Stanley.
(see *courtly, formality, punctilious*)

CHAGRIN
Rumplestilzchen.
(see *annoy, humiliation, crestfallen*)

CHAINED
Zedekiah; Hesione.
(see *confinement, restraint, enslavement*)

CHAIN-STORE
Robert Hawley Ingersoll.
(see *assembly-line*)

CHALLENGE
Marsyas; Amycus; Barbara Frietchie; Pierides; Misenus; Gordius; Phorbas; Goliath; Sadducees.
(see *defiance, contest*)

CHAMBERLAIN
Fadladeen.
(see *steward*)

CHAMELEON
Lysias.
(see *reptile*)

CHAMPAGNE
Pierre Pérignon.
(see *wine*)

CHARM

Aspasia; Fritz Kreisler; Dolly Varden; Addisonian; Juventas; Queen of Hearts; Apelles; Mozartean; Agnes Wickfield; Ogygia; Anatole France; Perdita; Célimène; Titania; Handel and Haydn; Callipolis; Aglaia; Mme. de Sévigné.

(see *amiable, loveliness, sweetness, engaging, attractiveness, kindness, tenderness, benignant, spell-binder, enchantment, witchcraft, fascinating, alluring*)

CHASE

Tam O'Shanter; Dictynna.

(see *follow, hunter, pursuit*)

CHASM

Mettius Curtius.

(see *cavern*)

CHASTISE

Prinz Ruprecht.

(see *whipping, flogging, lashing, discipline*)

CHASTITY

Poor Richard; Rhea Silvia; Minerva; Glaucus; Joseph; Atys; Artemis; Lysistrata; Paphnutius; Pudicitia; Penelope; Phaon; Kunigunde; Georgian; Diana; Pitys; Rinaldo; Mejnoun and Leilah; Galahad; Daphnis; Callisto; Abelites; St. Anthony; Arethusa; Belphoebe; Britomartis; Dorigen; Virginia; Parsifal; Imogen; Sir Guyon; Hippolytus; Leucothea; Pelléas and Mélisande; Tenes; St. Winifred; Vestal; St. Filumena; Syrinx; Sangreal; Breidablik; St. Kevin.

(see *purity, virtue, modesty, continence, innocence, decency*)

CHATTERBOX

Poll Parrot; Alfred Jingle; Lalage; Mrs. Nickleby.

(see *prattle, tattler, gossip, babbler, loquacious*)

CHEAP

Pinchbeck; Brummagem; Etienne de Silhouette; Bermudas; Marcus Licinius Crassus; Barataria.

(see *low-cost, inferiority, meretricious*)

CHEAT

Patelin; William M. Tweed; Sir Giles Overreach; Ferdinand Fathom; Brennus; Alfred Lammle; Laomedon; Dousterswivel; Peter Fabel; Scapino; Subtle.

(see *trickery, imposture, rogue, knave, swindler, charlatan, mountebank*)

CHEEKS

Physignathus.

(see *face, features*)

CHEERFUL

Bob Cratchit; Clara Peggoty; Pippa; Weller; Pollyanna; Baubo; Euphrosyne.

(see *lively, animate, joy, happiness, joviality, gaiety*)

CHEERLESS

Tullianum.

(see *dreary, gloom, somber, dismal*)

CHEMIST

Louis Pasteur; Antoine Lavoisier.

(see *alchemist, science*)

CHERUB

Zadkiel; Zophiel; Zephon.

(see *angel*)

CHESS-BOARD

Rinaldo.

(see *games*)

CHEST

Osiris.

(see *cask, kettle*)

CHEW

Fletcherize.

(see *masticate, bite*)

CHRISTIAN
Galilean; St. Paul; John Bunyan; Charlemagne; Christian; Nazarite; Samaritan.
(see *religious, saintliness, patron saint, martyrdom, protestant, Presbyterian*)

CHRISTIAN SCIENCE
Phineas P. Quimby; Mary Baker Eddy.

CHRISTMAS
Kriss Kringle; Prinz Ruprecht.
(see *gifts, present*)

CHRONICLE
Parian.
(see *diary, record, history, annals*)

CHRONOLOGY
Eusebius; Fasti.
(see *time*)

CHURCH-MUSIC
J. S. Bach; Handel and Haydn; Giovanni Palestrina.
(see *requiem*)

CHURCHYARD
Thomas Gray; Old Mortality.
(see *cemetery*)

CICADA
Tithonus.
(see *insects*)

CIGARETTE
Carmen.
(see *tobacco*)

CINDERS
Mr. Toodle.
(see *grimy, dirty, smoke, coals*)

CIRCUITOUS
Meander.
(see *indirect, roundabout, meandering*)

CIRCUMFERENCE
Eratosthenes.
(see *dimensions, geographer*)

CIRCUMNAVIGATION
Ferdinand Magellan; Xerxes.
(see *mariner, voyager*)

CIRCUMSPECT
Mr. Tulkinghorn; Sister Anne.
(see *alert, cautious, wary, carefulness, watchful, vigilance, discreet, prudence*)

CIRCUMSTANCE
Giacomuzzo Sforza.
(see *eventful, factual, chance*)

CIRCUMVENT
Thermopylae.
(see *thwarted, trickery, outwit, beguilement, mislead*)

CIRCUS
P. T. Barnum.
(see *animals, showman*)

CITIZENRY
Quirites.
(see *franchise, voting*)

CITY-BRED
Gothamite.
(see *urbanity*)

CIVILIZATION
Lucretian; Oannes; Isis; Cecrops; Saturn; Quetzalcoatl; Evander; Saraswati.
(see *culture-bringer, refinement*)

CLAIM (n.)
Joe Dun.
(see *request, demand*)

CLAIRVOYANT
Bacis; Xanthos; Zal; Weird Sisters; Witch of Endor; Tiresias; Calchas; Mopsus; Swedenborgian; Spurinna Vestritius; Sibylla; Huldah.
(see *visions, insight, divination, trance*)

CLAN
Jukes Family.
(see *family, clique, racialism*)

CLANDESTINE
Laverna; Amy Robsart; Naaman.
(see *secrecy, hidden*)

CLARION
Gjallarhorn.
(see *trumpet, loud*)

CLARITY
Gymnosophist.
(see *brilliant, intellectual*)

CLASHING
Curetes; Symplegades.
(see *strike, pound*)

CLASP (v.)
Nemean Lion.
(see *embrace, hug*)

CLASS-CONSCIOUS
Karl Marx; Lady Clara Vere de Vere.
(see *labor movement, proletariat, caste*)

CLASS-HARMONY
Publilius Philo; Ciceronian.
(see *concord, accord, unity*)

CLASSICIST
Cornelia Blimber; Mozartean; Jean Auguste Ingres; Chloë; Handel and Haydn.
(see *linguist, cultured*)

CLAW
Stymphalian; Stheno.
(see *lacerate*)

CLEANLINESS
Nazarite; Poor Richard; Breidablik.
(see *faultless, purity, chastity*)

CLEAR
Bandusia; Delia; Hymettan; Hyblaean.
(see *bright, limpid*)

CLEAVE
Balisardo; Balmung; Schamir.
(see *split, sunder*)

CLEMENCY
Seneca the Younger.
(see *merciful, gentle, forgiving, compassionate, kindness*)

CLERGY
Obadiah Slope; Smectymnuus; Doctor Charles Primrose; Charles Honeyman; Cotton Mather; Parson Trulliber; Flamen; Robert Elsmere; Doctor Syntax; Maister Gowk-Thrapple.
(see *minister, preacher, priest, ecclesiastical*)

CLERK
St. Nicholas.
(see *scribe, secretary*)

CLEVER
Autolycus; Acontius; Ali Baba; Cacus; Acacetus; Hippomenes; Jack Horner; Jane Austen; Will Ladislaw; Mercury; Ben Jonson; Nerissa; George Warrington; Galinthias; Puss-in-Boots; Morgiana; Petruchio; Bellerophon.
(see *skill, ingenuity*)

CLING
Peleus.
(see *adherence, embrace, clasp*)

CLINIC
Mayo.
(see *doctor, physician*)

CLIQUE
Junker.
(see *clan, partisanship*)

CLOAK (n.)
Asmodeus.
(see *coat*)

CLOCK
Anaximander; Robert Hawley Ingersoll; Galileo; Sam Slick.
(see *sun-dial, time*)

CLOSE (v.)
John Audley; Symplegades.
(see *end*)

CLOSE-MOUTHED
Porcia.
(see *reticent, secrecy*)

CLOTHING
Miss Flora McFlimsey; Herr Teufelsdroeckh; Gymnosophist; Jack of Newbury; Longchamps; Silk-Stocking.
(see *apparel, handkerchief, hosiery, coat, jacket, pantaloons, hat, robe, shoemaker, shirt*)

CLOUD
Moses; Nephelococcygia; Eurus; Ve; Indra.
(see *mist, foggy*)

CLOUDBURST
Pluvius; Parjanya.
(see *rain, shower, storm*)

CLOWN
Merry-Andrew; Damoetas; Harlequin; Gobbo; Till Eulenspiegel; Touchstone; Teague; Wamba; Pantaloon; Jack Pudding; Launce; Scaramouch; Speed; Hanswurst.
(see *buffoon, foolish, jester, droll, zany*)

CLUMSY
Diggary; Hanswurst.
(see *awkward, bungle, blundering, ineptitude*)

COACHMAN
Tony Weller; St. Fiacre.
(see *driver*)

COAL-DUST
Mr. Toodle.
(see *dirty, filth, black*)

COALS
Kunigunde.
(see *fire, hot, cinders*)

COARSE
Billingsgate; Emile Zola; Wife of Bath; Juvenalian; Rabelaisian; Aristophanic; Troglodytae; Capulet; Parson Trulliber; Turcaret; Martial; Hipponax; Baubo; Joseph Bounderby; the Crawleys.
(see *crude, gross, ribald, indecency, vulgarity, rude, boorish, loutish, uncivilized*)

COAT
Joseph; Tabard; Taglioni.
(see *jacket*)

COAXING
Lalage.
(see *alluring, tempter, lure, temptress, enticement, beguilement, seduction, attractiveness, engaging, persuasion, ensnare*)

COBBLER
Crispin; Hans Sachs.
(see *tanner*)

COLORLESS
John Doe.
(see *characterless, unexpressive*)

COLOSSAL
Badebec; Thrym; Rameses; Titanic; Phidian.
(see *gigantic, huge, monstrous, enormous, vast, prodigious*)

COMBUSTION
Antoine Lavoisier; Mr. Krook.
(see *burning*)

COMEDY
Thalia (see Muse); Terence; Roscius; Nell Gwyn; Menander; Shakespearean; Vincent Crummles.
(see *farce, parody, burlesque, travesty, stage*)

COMELY
Zémire.
(see *grace, pretty, handsome, beautiful, fair*)

COMET
Jules Verne; Berenice; Belinda.
(see *constellation, star, planet*)

COMFORT
Pierrette; Goshen; Bethesda; Phaedo; Abishag.
(see *consolation, strengthener, encouragement*)

COMICAL
Aristophanic; Pooh-Bah; Quixotic; Artemus Ward; Barber of Seville; Peter Quince; Dickensian; Zeuxis; Bottom; Bob Acres; Pierrot; Figaro; Plautus; James Barrie; Cercopes; Chaplinesque; Dooley; Punch; Judy; Sancho Panza; William Hogarth; Molière.
(see *amusing, lively, ludicrous, droll, funny, farce, ridiculous, burlesque, humor, laughter*)

COMMANDER
Abraham Lincoln; Michael; Epaminondas; Ferdinand Foch; George Washington; Woodrow Wilson; Laenas; Manlius; Emperor Jones; Agamemnon; Zeus; Poseidon.
(see *chieftain, leader*)

COMMEMORATIVE
Pindaric; Taj Mahal.
(see *remembrance*)

COMMERCIAL
Mercury; Hamilcar; John Jacob Astor; Liburnians; Carthaginians; Rialto; Lloyd's.
(see *trader, merchant*)

COMMODIOUS
Skidbladnir.
(see *accommodate*)

COMMODORE
Commodore Trunnion.
(see *nautical, mariner*)

COMMONPLACE
Tupperian.
(see *trite*)

COMMOTION
Skimmington.
(see *turbulence, tumultuous, disorderly, violence, disturbance*)

COMMUNICATION
Vach; Caducean; Samuel Morse; Margaret Fox.
(see *conversation, messenger, despatch*)

COMMUNIST
Friedrich Engels; Leon Trotsky; Incan; Karl Marx; Labadists; Fourierist; Lenin; Mazdakite; Pierre J. Proudhon; Essenes; Sansculotte.
(see *radical, socialism*)

COMPACT (n.)
Manfred; Tarpeian Rock; La Tosca; Freischuetz; Peter Fabel.
(see *agreement, covenant, bargain, treaty-making, pact*)

COMPANION
Hylas; Wife of Bath; Nisus; Autocrat of the Breakfast Table; Ascanius; Zerbino; Corporal Trim; Aramis; Pirithous; Horatio; Hyacinthus; Cristoph Wagner; Panurge; Gyas; Lieutenant Hatchway; Abiathar; Patroclus; Iolaus; Jonathan; Luke.
(see *friendly*)

COMPASS
Perdix; Galileo.
(see *helmsman, mariner*)

COMPASSIONATE
Dickensian; Veronica; Clara Barton; Abraham Lincoln; Orlando; Richard Babley; Ferdinand Foch; Samaritan.
(see *tenderness, pity, sympathetic, benignant, merciful, clemency, kindness*)

COMPENSATION
Robin and Makyne; Alfred Adler; Spolia Opima; Hugh Strap.
(see *recompense, reward, equalizer*)

COMPETITION
Peter Funk; Canace; Turnus; Spolia Opima; Oenomaüs; Palamon and Arcite.
(see *rivalry, emulate, contest*)

COMPLACENT
Goody Two-Shoes.
(see *self-satisfied, contentment, smug*)

COMPLAINING
Adullamite; Miss Flora McFlimsey.
(see *querulous, faultfinder*)

COMPLETE (adj.)
Dan to Beersheba; Buddha; Thomas Cook; Petrarchan; Hermaphroditus; Dame Durden.
(see *perfection, consummation, entire, whole*)

COMPLIANCE
Ramman.
(see *submission, obedience, acquiescence, consent*)

COMPLICATION
Charybdis; Hydra; Henry James; Minos; Laocoön; Scylla; Serbonian Bog.
(see *intricate, entangled, confusion*)

COMPOSER
Wagnerian; J. S. Bach; Chopinesque; Franz Liszt; Mendelssohn-Bartholdy; Gustave Mahler; Rimski-Korsakov; Strauss.
(see *music*)

COMPOSITE
Hermaphroditus; Gryps; Chimaera; Centaur; Smectymnuus.
(see *hybrid*)

COMPOST
Picumnus and Pilumnus.
(see *agriculture*)

COMPOSURE
Pyrrhonian; Spinoza.
(see *tranquillity, calm, placid, self-control*)

COMPREHENSIVE
Tennysonian; Lord Burleigh; Pierre Larousse; Galsworthian.
(see *all-inclusiveness*)

COMPULSION
Ephebeia; Sganarelle; Cadean; Gibeonite.
(see *coercion, constraint, forced labor*)

COMPUTE
Olympiad.
(see *calculations, numbers*)

CONCEALED
Lycomedes; Man with the Iron Mask; Sisera; Rahab; Bermudas; Admetus; Delia; Curetes; Duessa; Amy Robsart; Lake Trasimene; Mokanna.
(see *secrecy, hidden, disguise, ambush, hide-out*)

CONCEITED
Sir Jerry Witwold; Lord Nelson; Narcissus; Junker; Misenus; Marsyas; Panglossian; Malvolio; Thamyris; Almanzor; Ralph Roister Doister; Sir Willoughby Patterne; Goody Two-Shoes; Arachne; Proetides; Pharisee; Arthur Pendennis; Richard Moniplies; Captain Lismahago; Dogberry; Mr. Tittlebat Titmouse; Tappertitian; Orgoglio; Dugald Dalgetty; Baillie Nicol Jarvie; Rev. Mr. Collins; Fadladeen.
(see *affected, vanity, insincere, foppish, pretentious, coxcomical, egotistic, opinionated*)

CONCENTRATION
Proustian; Isaac Newton.
(see *thoughtful, pensive, absorption*)

CONCERN
Bo-Peep.
(see *anxiety, solicitude, carefulness*)

CONCERTIZE
Mozartean.
(see *music, prodigy*)

CONCISE
Pharnaces; Giottesque; Martial; Tacitean; Thucydides.
(see *brief, laconic, succinct, terse, sententious, pithy*)

CONCORD
Constantine; Pax; Peleus; James Monroe; Concordia.
(see *agreement, amity, friendly, peaceful, unity*)

CONCUBINE
Leilah; Briseis; Lindabrides; Campaspe; Chryseis; Gomer (see Hosea); Bilhah (see Rachel); Hagar.
(see *mistress, paramour*)

CONCUPISCENT
Potiphar's Wife.
(see *lustful, lechery, lascivious, carnal, passionate*)

CONDEMNED
Tarpeian Rock; Gibeonite; Barathron.
(see *doomed, punishment, judgment, convicted, penalty*)

CONDUCT (n.)
St. Nicholas; Carneades.
(see *deportment, manners*)

CONFESSION
Tess of the D'Urbervilles; Robert Macaire; Raskolnikov; St. Catherine; Arthur Dimmesdale; St. Cecilia.
(see *acknowledgment*)

CONFIDANT
Dr. Watson; Viola; Friar Laurence.
(see *friendly*)

CONFIDENCE
Spes.
(see *trusting, faith, belief, reliance. dependable, cocksure*)

CONFIDENTIAL
Robert Browning; Porcia.
(see *privacy, trustworthy, faithful*)

CONFINEMENT
Man in the Moon; Sleeping Beauty; Limbo; Nora Helmer.
(see *imprisonment, captivity*)

CONSERVATIVE
Lucius Opimius; Bourbonistic; Hooverize; Lucius Cornelius Sulla; Silk-Stocking; Hunker; Sadducees.
(see *reactionary*)

CONSOLATION
Silas Marner; Isaian; Bethesda; Doctor Syntax; Boethius; Servius Sulpicius Rufus.
(see *comfort*)

CONSORT
Statira; Aspasia.
(see *companion, association, mistress*)

CONSPICUOUS
Pharos; Catherinette.
(see *eminent, distinctive*)

CONSPIRACY
Catiline; E. Phillips Oppenheim; Piso; Graustark; Darius; Jaffier; Lentulus Sura; Guy Fawkes; Lars Porsena; Porcia; Scaevola; Hernani.
(see *plot, collusion, intrigue, machinator*)

CONSTABULARY
Peeler; Vigilantes; Vigiles; Scotland Yard.
(see *policeman, detection*)

CONSTANCY
The Peachums; Paul and Virginie; Clytie; Patroclus; Achates; Zadok; Penelope; Pirithous; Theseus; Rosemary; Iolaus; Protesilaus; Pythias; Abiathar; Siguna; Selim.
(see *steadfast, fidelity, faithful, loyalty, devotion, trustworthy*)

CONSTELLATION
Astraea; Callisto; Orion; Cassiopeia; Pleiades; Hyades.
(see *star*)

CONSTITUTION
Lord Bryce; John Jay.
(see *law*)

CONSTRAINT
Cadean.
(see *compulsion, force, necessity, obligation, coercion, pressure*)

CONSTRUCTION
Ictinus; Vitruvius.
(see *builder, architect*)

CONSULTANT
Dr. Watson.
(see *adviser, counselor, deliberation*)

CONSUMMATION
Libitina.
(see *complete, achievement, death*)

CONSUMPTIVE
La Traviata; Mimi.
(see *atrophy, emaciated*)

CONTAGION
Bessy Bell.
(see *infection, disease, tainted, pestilence*)

CONTAIN
Kit-Cat Club.
(see *capacity*)

CONTEMPLATIVE
André Gide; Izaak Walton; Jaques; Martha; Essenes.
(see *thoughtful, studious, meditation*)

CONTEMPT
Jack-a-Lent; Don Adriano de Armado; Pentheus; Betsey Prig.
(see *disdainful, scornful, mockery, derisive*)

CONVEX
Sir John MacAdam.
(see *round*)

CONVEYANCE
Hippocampus.
(see *carrier, vehicle*)

CONVICTED
Tarpeian Rock; Barathron; Sacco-Vanzetti; Abel Magwitch.
(see *malefactor, criminal, condemned, guilt*)

CONVIVIAL
Bardolph; John Barleycorn; Horatian (Horace).
(see *feast, festival, sociability, jolly, joviality, symposium*)

COOKERY
Apician; St. Wilfrid; Meg Dods; Andhrimnir; Mrs. Glasse; Brillat-Savarin.
(see *kitchen, baker, cuisine*)

COOL
Bandusia.
(see *freezing, ice*)

COPPER
Dactyli.
(see *brass, bronze, metallurgy*)

COPY (n.)
Jean Auguste Ingres; Veturius Mamurius; Mme. Marie Tussaud; Florimel; Donatello; Dromios; Sosia; Sopherim; Antipholus; Menaechmus.
(see *reproduction, replica, facsimile, duplicate*)

COQUETTISH
Célimène; Nerissa; Widow Barnaby; Dolly Varden; Angelica.
(see *flirtatious, philanderer, courtship*)

CORD
Yue-Laou.
(see *unite*)

CORDIALITY
Dolly Madison.
(see *sincerity, hearty, ardent, affectionate*)

CORN
Dagon; Fornax; Proserpina.
(see *grain, maize*)

CORNET
Misenus.
(see *trumpet*)

CORNUCOPIA
Irene; Amalthaea.
(see *horns, plenty*)

CORONATION
Scone.
(see *king*)

CORPSE
William Burke; Jerry Cruncher; Zombi; Hraesvelger.
(see *lifeless, death*)

CORPULENCE
Rubensian; Henry VIII.
(see *fat, plump*)

CORRECTIVE
Cadean; Jack-Amend-All; Coxey's Army.
(see *reformable, improvement*)

CORRECTNESS
Euclidean; Crichton; Edward Cocker; Victorian; Belgravian.
(see *accuracy, precision; propriety, faultless*)

CORRESPONDENCE
Nadejda von Meck; Pliny the Younger.
(see *letter-writer, epistolographer*)

CORRUPT
Gomorrah; Tess of the D'Urbervilles; Richard Varney; Isaian; Augean; Alcina; Onias Menelaus; Abijah; Abigor; Fagin; Mirabel; Tammanyites; the Peachums; Piso; Friar Rush; Sextus Tarquinius.
(see *bribery, impure, depravity, wickedness, vicious, dissolute, debauchery, profligacy, reprobate, enticement, adulterous*)

CORSAIR
John Quelch; Lara; Sir Henry Morgan; Vikings; Varangians; Vitalians.
(see *piracy, buccaneer, picaresque*)

COSMETICS
Marie Laurencin; Lady Wishfort; Picti.
(see *painted, bepainted, rouged*)

COSMIC
Prajapati; Ptah.
(see *universe, world*)

COSMOGONY
Audhumla; Hesiodic.
(see *creation*)

COSMOPOLITE
Lola Montez; Henry James; City of Destruction.
(see *worldliness, international*)

COSSACK
Ivan Mazeppa.
(see *Russian, horsemanship*)

COSTLY
Pyrrhic Victory.
(see *high-priced, rich, sumptuousness, splendor, gorgeous*)

COSTUME
Zouave; Marie Laurencin; Herr Teufelsdroeckh; Max Reinhardt.
(see *apparel, dress, clothing*)

COUNCIL
Yggdrasil; Sanhedrin.
(see *adviser*)

COUNSELOR
Fasti; Mentor; Egeria; Ucalegon; Horatio; Nestor; Moses; St. Jerome; Nathan; Gamaliel; Naomi; George Washington; Moneta; Consus; Ahithophel; Gonzalo; Friar Laurence.
(see *adviser, lawyer, guide, monitor*)

COUNTERFEIT
Bayes's Troops; Florimel.
(see *forgery, spurious, imitation, copy, fraudulence, feigned, simulated, sham, faker, hypocrisy*)

COUNTERPART
Oliver (2); Sosia.
(see *duplicate, copy, twins*)

COUNTRY GENTLEMAN
Mr. Wardle; Squire Western; Sir Roger de Coverly; Bob Acres; the Crawleys.
(see *provincial, rustic*)

COUNTRY GIRL
Pamela.
(see *rustic, milkmaid*)

COUNTRYSIDE
Jean Millet; Damoetas; Tibullan; Theocritean.
(see *rusticity*)

COUPLE
Darby and Joan; 'Arry and 'Arriet; Jack and Jill.
(see *pair, lovers*)

COURAGE
Virtus.
(see *virtue*)

COURAGEOUS
Ajax; Barbara Frietchie; Phaedo; Thermopylae; Ivanhoe; Abraham Lincoln; Antigone; Zouave; Sophonisba; Mithradates; John Bunyan; John Brown; Ciceronian; Joan of Arc; Uncas; Spartacus; Horace Greely; Molly Pitcher; Naomi; Wellingtonian; Gunga Din; Mercutio; Judith; Oliver (2); Henry Thoreau; Sophoclean; Penthesilea; Arria; Ferdinand Magellan; Porcia; Agrippina the Younger; Martin Luther; Philaeni; Argantes; St. Ambrose; Horatius Cocles; Pocahontas; Stevensonian; Cromwellian; Cloelia; Bellerophon; Benthamite; Boadicea; Dugald Dalgetty; Godiva; Emersonian; Orlando; Jack the Giant-Killer; Vasco da Gama; Baillie Nicol Jarvie; Micawber; Mettius Curtius; Sir Daguenet; Dandie Dinmont; Esther.
(see *bold, fearless, bravery, intrepid, valor, heroism, daring, gallantry, chivalrous*)

COURIER
Skirnir; Hermes; Mercury.
(see *messenger, runner*)

COURTESAN
Menander; Manon (Lescaut); Theodora; Thais; La Traviata; Nana; Ninon de Lenclos; Lais; Lalage; Phryne; Aspasia; Moll Flanders; Lindabrides; Rhodope; Mme. Dubarry; Alexandre Dumas; Campaspe; Camille; Messalina; Delilah.
(see *prostitute, whore, harlot, strumpet, wanton, demi-mondaine, streetwalker*)

COURTESY
Quasimodo; Jack and Jill; Calidore; David Livingstone; Alcinous; Oriana; Terence; Nausicaa; Robert E. Lee; Handel and Haydn; Rebekah.
(see *polite, urbanity, affable, manners*)

COURTHOUSE
Clarence Darrow.
(see *tribunal, judgment*)

COURTIER
Raleigh; Rosencrantz and Guildenstern; Osric; Timias; Xerxes; Adriano de Armado; Fadladeen; Aelius Sejanus.
(see *knighthood*)

COURTLY
Calidore; Anacreontic; Lancelot; Robin Hood; Will Honeycomb; Beau Brummel; Sir Courtly Nice.
(see *elegance, polite*)

COURTSHIP
Priscilla, the Puritan Maid.
(see *husband-hunter, wife-hunter*)

COVENANT
Rahab; Freischuetz.
(see *agreement, treaty-making, pact*)

COVETED
Naboth; Rheingold.
(see *desire, greed*)

COVETOUS
Harpagon; Urvashi; Ahab; Laban.
(see *envy, avaricious, greed*)

COW
Isis; Hathor; Myron's Cow; Kamadhenu; Audhumla.
(see *heifer, bovine*)

COWARDICE
Fear Fortress.
(see *faint-hearted, timidity, fearful*)

CREDITOR
Joe Dun.
(see *loan*)

CREDULITY
Ichabod Crane; Othello; Orgon; Lentulus Sura; Sancho Panza; Roxane; Pyramus; Pollyanna; Minna; Malvolio; Calandrino; Camacho; Deianira; Captain Cuttle; Melantius; Parson Abraham Adams; Epimetheus; Géronte; Stockwell Ghost; Christopher Sly; Cousin Michel.
(see *gullible, dupe, unsuspecting*)

CREMATED
Agathocles; Ulrich Zwingli; Creusa; Kalanos; Evadne; Deianira; Hringham.
(see *burned, roasted*)

CREPUSCULAR
Ra.
(see *twilight, dusk*)

CRESCENDO
Gioacchino Rossini; Maurice Ravel.
(see *music, loud*)

CRESCENT
Tanit.
(see *moon*)

CRESTFALLEN
Fadladeen.
(see *discouraged, dispirited, dejected, despondent, melancholy, downcast, sadness*)

CRIMINAL
Tityus; Jukes Family; Tarpeian Rock; Alsatia; Nero; Raskolnikov; Robert the Devil; Robert Macaire; Barathron; Bill Sikes; Fagin; Scalae Gemoniae; Jack Sheppard; Maffia.
(see *wickedness, iniquity, delinquency, transgression, malefactor*)

CRIMINAL LAWYER
Clarence Darrow.
(see *attorney*)

CRIPPLED
Ashtavakra; St. Giles; Witch of Edmonton; Völund; Tiny Tim.
(see *lame*)

CRISIS
Ver Sacrum; Marcus Furius Camillus.
(see *emergency, straits, crucial*)

CRITERION
Diogenes.
(see *standardized, touchstone, rules*)

CRITIC
William Ralph Inge; Juvenalian; Jean de La Fontaine; Susan Nipper; Cato the Censor; Jonathan Edwards; Zoilus; Philoxenus; Sir Fretful Plagiary; H. G. Wells; Thersitean; Callimachus; John Ruskin; Thomas DeQuincey; Reverend Mister Chadband; Old Man of the Sea; Longinus; Laberius; Egeria; Walther von der Vogelweide; Nietzschean; André Gide; Quintilian; Elihu; Shavian; Sneer; Smelfungus; Stevensonian; Philippic; Mrs. Grundy.
(see *censorious, connoisseur, carping, captious, art critic*)

CROCODILE
Sebek.
(see *reptile*)

CRONE
Stheno; Sycorax.
(see *hag*)

CROOKED
Ashtavakra.
(see *misshapen, distorted, deformed*)

CROONER
Minnesinger.
(see *singer*)

CROPS
Iasion; Ops; Ge; Tellus.
(see *harvest, agriculture*)

CROSS (n.)
St. Ulrich; Constantine.
(see *crucifixion, worship*)

CROSS-DRESSING
Viola.
(see *transvestitism*)

CROSSROADS
Trivia.
(see *roads*)

CROTCHETY
Vainlove; Sir Mungo Malagrowther.
(see *whimsical, capricious, notion*)

CROW
M. Valerius Corvinus.
(see *birds*)

CRUCIAL
Pippa; Ides of March; Gettysburg.
(see *crisis, momentous*)

CRUCIFIXION
Manichaeus; Golgotha.
(see *cross*)

CRUDE
Bottom; Edward Bellamy; Innocents Abroad; Peter Quince; Moll Flanders; Fescennine.
(see *immature, harsh, coarse, rude, uncouth, awkward*)

CRUELTY
Robert the Devil; Enyo; Tiberian; Tom Walker; Xerxes; Mithradates; Neoptolemus; Witchfinder General; Draconian; Megaera; Lemnian; Etruscan; Punic; Machiavellian; Ahab; Cambyses; Caligula; Amarant; Calchas; Alberich; Alecto; Bluebeard; Genseric; Jean Paul Marat; Tisiphone; Genghis Khan; Jack Ketch; Jezebel; Huns; Hannibal; Hecate; Minos; Lycus; Laenas; Torquemada; Simon Legree; Pharaoh; Herodian; Vedius Pollio; Fra Diavolo; Tamerlane; Dirce; Polyphemus; Nero; Robespierre; Tullus Hostilius; Phalaris; Moloch; Procrustean; Tezcatlipoca; Tarquinius Superbus; Domitian; Danton; Pyrrhus (Neoptolemus); Medea; Mezentius; Abimelech; Creon; Salome; Bill Sikes; Marquis de Sade; Guy de Maupassant.
(see *unmerciful, inhumanity, merciless, unfeeling, pitiless, ruthlessness, dire, relentless, barbarity, inexorable, savage, ferocious, brutal, sanguine, truculent, bloodthirsty*)

CRUSADER
Thaumaturgus; Peter the Hermit; Rinaldo; Richard the Lion-Hearted; Ivanhoe.
(see *pilgrimage*)

CRUSHED
Tarpeian Rock; Laocoön; Acis; Symplegades.
(see *squeezed, bruised*)

CRYING
Job Trotter; Melusina; Heliades; Queen of Tears; Byblis.
(see *weeping, sobbing, tears, wail*)

CRYPT
Mithras.
(see *tomb*)

CUCKOLD (n.)
Diomedes; Claudius; Menelaus; Tyndareus; Malbecco; King Mark; Uriah; Amphitryon; Fondlewife; Marquis of Steyne.
(see *infidelity, adulterous*)

CUISINE
Apician; Delmonico.
(see *kitchen, cookery*)

CULTURE-BRINGER
Quetzalcoatl; Prometheus.
(see *arts and crafts, civilization*)

CULTURED
Leonardo da Vinci; Dolly Madison; Augustan; Hadrian; Ovidian; Phrygian; Lorenzo the Magnificent; Ptolemy; Quintilian; Periclean; Scipio Africanus; Sordello.
(see *refinement, civilization*)

CUNNING
Moth; "Kit" Carson; Daedalian; Fra Diavolo; Emilia; Volpone; Nessus; Milanion; Iachimo; Philip of Macedon; Reynard; Tarquinius Superbus; Galinthias; Hermes; Jugurtha; Machiavellian; Utgard-Loki; Melampus; Aelius Sejanus; Scapino; Arthur Gride; Sinon.
(see *wily, crafty, artful, sly, astute, designing, shrewd, intrigue, deceitful, trickery*)

CUP
Mentor; Sangreal.
(see *beakers, potions*)

CUP-BEARER
Ganymede; Hebe.
(see *waiter*)

CURATE
Parson Trulliber; Rev. Mr. Collins.
(see *preacher*)

CURATIVE
Paracelsus; Kneippism; Dioscurides; Gilead; Abaris; Telephus; Philoctetes; Tobit; Podalirius; St. Winifred; Theodorus; Carrol-Dakin; Bethesda; Melampus; Hygeia; St. Fiacre; Fierabras; Gula; St. Swithin; Serapis; Doctor Sangrado; Mary Baker Eddy; Naaman.
(see *remedy, healing, restore, therapeutics*)

CURATOR
Frontinus.
(see *guardian, custodian, keeper*)

CURFEW
William the Conqueror.
(see *bell-ringer, signal*)

CURIOSITIES
Mme. Marie Tussaud.
(see *phenomenon, wonder-worker, rare, spectacular*)

CURIOSITY
Elsa; Lohengrin; Lot's Wife; Morgiana; Quidnunc; Marplot; Paul Pry; Herophilus; Eve; Fatima; Peeping Tom; Pliny the Elder; Pentheus; Pandora; Socrates.
(see *inquisitive*)

CURL
Berenice; Belinda; Phrygian.
(see *ringlet*)

CURSE (n.)
Andvaranaut; Woglinda, Wellgunda, and Flosshilda; Thrinacian; Balaam; Kundry; Alcmaeon; Anu; Hippodamia; Tutankhamen; Hecate; Polycrates; Harmonia's Necklace; Rheingold; Dirae; Shimei; Ebal; Harry Gill; Lady of Shalott; Myrtilus.
(see *execrate, denunciatory*)

CUSTODIAN
Woglinda, Wellgunda, and Flosshilda; Gryps; Arioch; Hesperides; Dr. Bartholo; Mr. Jarndyce; Fafner.
(see *guardian, keeper, curator*)

CUSTOM
Rebeccaite.
(see *tax-complainer*)

D

DAGGER-MEN
Zelotes.
(see *assassin, murderer, ruffian*)

DAINTY
Galatea; Titania; Osric; Marie Laurencin; Gibsonesque; Trilby.
(see *elegance, exquisite, delicate, beautiful, fastidious*)

DALLIANCE
Amaryllis; Paphian; Casanovian.
(see *amorous, erotic, philanderer*)

DAMAGING
Luddites; Pyrrhic Victory.
(see *injurious, harmful, loss*)

DAMNATION
Vathek; Zakkum; Jonathan Edwards.
(see *condemned, doomed, perdition, punishment*)

DAMP
Hela.
(see *moisture, foggy*)

DANCING
Terpsichore; Bathyllus; Lola Montez; Giselle; Galli; Lydian; Hippoclides; Vaslav Nijinsky; Edgard Degas; Caryatids; Anna Pavlova; Muse; Esmeralda; Salii; Salome; Siva; Strauss; White Ladies; Isadora Duncan; Taglioni.
(see *ballet*)

DANGER
Mata Hari; Jack London; Leather-Stocking; James Fenimore Cooper; Andromeda; Yacumama; Joseph Conrad; Damoclean; Frankenstein; Cabiric; Circean; Alcina; Charybdis; Siren; Scylla; Simeon Stylites; Syrtes; Semele.
(see *perilous*)

DAPPER
Dundreary; Mr. Turveydrop; Beau Tibbs; Tattle; Mantalini; Macaroni; Jack Sixteen-String; Silk-Stocking.
(see *nimble, trimness, foppish, dude*)

DARING
Jael; Richard Haliburton; Jesse James; Jacksonian; Elizabethan; Leif Ericson; Aramis; D'Artagnan; Argonauts; Cleolia; Aloidae; Horatius Cocles; Christopher Columbus; Robinson Crusoe; Cornwallis; Roland; James Fenimore Cooper; Captain Kidd; Jack London; Barbara Frietchie; Jolly Roger; Hero and Leander; Athos; Robin Hood; Balboa; Capaneus; Judith; Europa; Fuzzy-Wuzzy; Icarian; Richard the Lion-Hearted; Lochinvar; Marco Polo; Porthos; Long Tom Coffin; Spartacus.
(see *bold, adventurous, fearless, bravery, intrepid, valor, courageous, heroism, undaunted*)

DARKNESS
Dis; Kuvera; Hela; Laverna; Nox; Niflheim; Ragnarok; Rahu; Stygian; Erebus; Hodur; Gustave Doré; Baldur; Cimmerian; Acheron; Set; Apepi; Ifurin.
(see *obscurity, gloom, despondent, cheerless*)

DARLING
Queen of Hearts; Fiametta.
(see *favored, pet, sweetheart, beloved*)

DART
Abaris.
(see *hurl, throw, flying*)

DEBONAIR
Philander; Sir Harry Wildair; the Crawleys.
(see *courtesy, affable, polite, refinement, urbanity, obliging, kindness, vivacious, buoyant, elegance*)

DEBT
Manlius Capitolinus; Alsatia; Joe Dun; Amy Dorrit; Nigel Olifaunt.
(see *obligation, loan*)

DECADENT
Pierre Louys; Dorian Gray; Vathek.
(see *degeneracy*)

DECAPITATION
Xerxes; Trophonius; St. Winifred; Kriemhilde; Hagen; Orillo; Crispin; Rhampsinitus; St. Denis; John the Baptist; St. James; Ciceronian.
(see *behead*)

DECEASE
Thanatos; Atropos; Padalon; Orcus; Mors.
(see *death*)

DECEITFUL
Wooden Horse; Cacus; Belise; Parthian; Reynard; Volpone; Zacocia; Galinthias; Job's Friends; Thessalian; Erlking; Laban; Outis; Nessus; Pecksniff; Parolles; Stockwell Ghost; Janus; Patelin; Tartuffian; Prusias; Buncombe; Modred; Ananias; Battus; Indra; Bagoas; Archimago; Ferdinand Fathom; Mr. Fudge; Goneril; Sinon; Sapphira; Scapino; Rebekah; Olivia.
(see *falsehood, fraudulence, insincere, trickery, wily, guile*)

DECEIVED
Epimetheus; Deiphobus; Arnolphe; Camacho; Alfred Lammle; La Tosca; Fondlewife; Lucia di Lammermoor.
(see *cheat, dupe, outwit, betrayed*)

DECENCY
Pudicitia.
(see *propriety, decorous, modesty, purity*)

DECEPTIVE (illusory)
Matsys' Fly; Myron's Cow; Parrhasius' Curtain; Miltiades; Simon Pure; Tatar; Pope Joan; Zeuxis; Velasquez; Lollius; Island of St. Brandan; Amphitryon.
(see *deceitful, delusive, illusion, mislead*)

DECISION
Areopagitical; Judge Bridlegoose; Rubicon; Thélème; Urim and Thummim; Seneca the Elder; Hoyle; Candida.
(see *judgment, decree*)

DECLAMATION
Asinius Pollio; Demosthenes.
(see *rhetoric, bombastic, pompous, oratory*)

DECLARATION OF WAR
Fetiales.
(see *war*)

DÉCOLLETÉ
Phryne.
(see *dress, robe*)

DECORATIVE
Paul Gauguin; Benvenuto Cellini; Byzantine; Joseph Marie Jacquard; Bezaleel; Grolieresque.
(see *enriched, embellishment*)

DECOROUS
Jean Martinet; Pudicitia; Crichton; Gibbet.
(see *decency, propriety, dignified*)

DECREE
Areopagitical; Norns.
(see *regulation, law*)

DEGRADATION
Gibeonite; Yahoo; Zeluco; Troglodytae; Paula Tanqueray; Hester Prynne; Scalae Gemoniae.
(see *dishonor, disgrace, ignominy, humiliation, degeneracy, decadent, corrupt*)

DEJECTED
Trophonius; Smike.
(see *dispirited, discouraged, downcast, despondent, doleful, crestfallen*)

DELAY
Lentulus Sura; Oenopion; Fabian.
(see *procrastination, postpone, dawdling*)

DELEGATION
Philaeni; Horatii and Curiatii.
(see *representative, emissary*)

DELIBERATION
Consus.
(see *meditation, thoughtful, reflective, circumspect, wary, cautious*)

DELICATE
Pre-Raphaelite; Mimi; Dante Gabriel Rossetti; Rosalind; Mozartean; Sir Roger de Coverly; John Keats; Jean Watteau; Florimel; Aucassin and Nicolette; Apsaras; Oberon; Attic; William Butler Yeats.
(see *dainty, soft, smoothness, elegance, slender, fragility*)

DELIGHT
Hathor; Faustian; Elysian; Charis; Alice in Wonderland; Queen of Hearts; Hephzibah.
(see *joy, charm, ecstasy, pleasure*)

DELINEATION
Cornelius Nepos; Plutarch; Lysias; Anton Chekhov; Andrea del Sarto.
(see *outline, drawing, description, characterization, character sketches*)

DELINQUENCY
Jukes Family.
(see *transgression, degeneracy*)

DELIQUESCE
St. Januarius.
(see *melt*)

DELIVERANCE
Libertas; Phorbas; Flamininus; Messianic; Zerubbabel; Gideon; Zechariah; Veturia and Volumnia; Vishnu; Moses; Azrael; St. George; Paean; Esther; Beowulf; Gibil; Shadrach; Sleeping Beauty; Sigura; Soter; Habakkuk; Mordecai; Sabra; Saul; Thecla.
(see *release, liberated, emancipator, redemption, escape, rescue*)

DELIVERY (birth)
Latona; Virbius; Upis; Badebec; Genetyllis.
(see *accouchement, childbirth, lying-in*)

DELL
Napaeae.
(see *grove, forests, woods*)

DELUDED
Belise; Camacho; Abu Hassan.
(see *aberration, irregular, eccentric, peculiarity, illusion, hallucination*)

DELUGE
Gilgamesh; Ut-Napishtim; Manu; Og; Noah; Deucalion; Ogyges; Ragnarok.
(see *flood, cataclysm, drowned*)

DELUSIVE
Lollius; Ivory Gate; Erlking.
(see *deceitful, deceptive, illusion*)

DEMAGOGUE
Pisistratus; Publicola; Publilius Philo; Dionysius.
(see *agitator*)

DEMAND (n.)
Joe Dun; King Ryance.
(see *claim, questioning, request*)

DEMARCATION
Terminus; Mason and Dixon.
(see *distinctive, limit, boundary*)

DEMENTED
Madge Wildfire; Bedlam; Proetides; Richard Babley; Meg Merrilies.
(see *insanity, lunatic, crazy, deranged, crack-brained*)

DEMIGOD
Theseus.
(see *pseudo-god, apotheosized*)

DEMIMONDAINE
Paula Tanqueray; La Traviata; Camille; Mrs. Frail; Mrs. Slipslop.
(see *mistress, courtesan*)

DEMISE
Mors; Thanatos.
(see *death*)

DEMOBILIZATION
Lysistrata.
(see *peace, pacifist*)

DEMOCRATIC
Periclean; Leo Tolstoi; John Ball; Tammanyites; Jeffersonian; Timoleon; Robert Burns; Lycurgus; Giuseppe Mazzini; Servius Tullius.
(see *republican*)

DEMON
Aeshina; Kuvera; Red Man; Lucifer; Master Leonard; Rahu; Berchta; Samael; Amaimon; Andhaba; Abaddon; Alastor; Garm; Abigor; Asmodeus; Nibelung; Gadarene; Uma; Ephialtes; Azazel; Daitya; Fenrir; Hymir.
(see *devil, fiendish, evil*)

DEMOTION
Stellenbosche.
(see *riddance, dismissal*)

DEMURE
Gibsonesque; Priscilla, the Puritan Maid.
(see *modesty, shy, coy*)

DENTIST
Kindhart.
(see *toothpick, toothless*)

DENUNCIATORY
Zephaniah; Demosthenes; Philippic; Nahum; John the Baptist; Juvenalian; Shimei; Ebal; Ezekiel; Malachi; Jeremiah; Doctor Slop; Habakkuk; Lawrence Boythorn; Amos.
(see *abusive, reproachful, opprobrious. scurrilous, invective, calumnious, injurious, offensive, insulting, insolent*)

DEPARTURE
Hegira.
(see *exodus, fleeing, escape*)

DEPENDABLE
Dugald Dalgetty; Pythias; Porcia.
(see *reliable, confidant, trustworthy*)

DEPENDENT
Mr. Turveydrop; Walther von der Vogelweide.
(see *parasite*)

DEPORTMENT
Mr. Turveydrop.
(see *conduct, manners*)

DEPOSED
Macduff; Cronus.
(see *degradation, dismissal*)

DEPRAVITY
Dorian Gray; Paul Clifford; Bill Sikes; Belial; Alcina; Nero; Jansenists; Acra-

sia; Richard Varney; Vathek; Dirk Hatteraick.
(see *corrupt, degeneracy, vicious, perversion, wickedness, profligacy, dissolute, reprobate, shameless*)

DEPRECATOR
Veturia and Volumnia.
(see *regretful*)

DEPUTATION
Philaeni; Horatii and Curiatii.
(see *representative, emissary*)

DERANGED
Proetides; Madge Wildfire.
(see *insanity, lunatic, madness, aberration*)

DERISIVE
Democritus; Democritus Junior; Betsey Prig; Etienne de Silhouette.
(see *scoffer, mockery, ridicule, scornful, contempt*)

DESCRIPTION
Alciphron.
(see *delineation*)

DESERT (n.)
Bedouin; Paran; Sinai; Baca.
(see *wilderness, solitude*)

DESERTED
Valentine and Orson; Philoctetes; Madge Wildfire; Oenone; Père Goriot.
(see *abandoned, forsaken*)

DESERTER
Helenus; Pliable; Odur; Amasa.
(see *forsaken, abandon, runaway, backslider, recreant, apostasy, turncoat*)

DESERVING
Fortunatae Insulae.
(see *merit, prize, reward*)

DESIGNER
Ictinus; Thomas Chippendale; Joseph Marie Jacquard; Thomas Sheraton.
(see *inventive, drawing, delineation*)

DESIGNING
Jesuit.
(see *crafty, insidious, artful, intrigue, sly, astute, subtlety, cunning, trickery, treachery*)

DESIRE (n.)
Candaules; Aphrodisian; Cestus; Kama; Cytherea; Urvashi; Astarte; Cupid; Deirdre; Gerda; Kalpa-Tarou; Kamadhenu.
(see *longing, eager, impulse, passion, yearning, love, lustful*)

DESPATCH (n.)
Samuel Morse.
(see *communication*)

DESPERADO
Catiline; Jesse James; Spartacus.
(see *gangster, marauder, reckless, ruffian, daring*)

DESPERATION
Deianira; Giselle; Soren Kierkegaard; Phlegethon; Acheron; Calvary; Melusina; Phyllis; Golgotha; Ophelia; Lady Macbeth; Childe Harold; Effie Deans; Lorenzo; Ver Sacrum; Macbeth; Gethsemane; Peter Schlemihl.
(see *hopeless, despondent, wretchedness, rash, reckless, precipitous, headlong, frantic*)

DESPICABLE
Pecksniff; Pistol; Jack-a-Lent.
(see *contempt, mean-spirited, abject, worthless*)

DESPISE
Reverend Mister Chadband.
(see *disdainful, contempt, scornful*)

DESPONDENT
Weeping Philosopher; Slough of Despond; Smike; Saul.
(see *dispirited, melancholy, discouraged, dejected*)

DESPOTIC
Tiberian; Tarquinius Superbus; Tamerlane; Louis XIV; Incan; Rameses; Khufu; Pisistratus; Periander; Mussolini; Torquemada; Cambyses; Henry VIII; Domitian; Isagoras; Ivan the Terrible; Minos; Eglon; Rehoboam.
(see *autocratic, dictator, absolutism, tyrant, oppression, arbitrary, wilful*)

DESTINATION
Manoa; Mecca; Thule; Melicertes.
(see *goal, haven*)

DESTINY (A)
Verthandi; Xanthos; Fortuna; Moerae; Norns; Weird Sisters; Zeus; Parcae; Excalibur; Skuld.
(see *lot, doom, fate*)

DESTINY (B)
Laius; Zadig; Jocasta; Manfred.

DESTINY (C)
Krupp Family; Thomas Hardy.

DESTITUTE
Effie Deans; Duke Humphrey; Beau Brummel.
(see *indigent, needy, distressed, impecunious*)

DESTRUCTION
Frankenstein; Juggernaut; Kilkenny Cats; Maelstrom; Philippic; Phooka; Vandalism; Huns; Deucalion; Boulangism; Asmodeus; Muspel; Siva; Ragnarok; Typhon-Typhoeus; Armageddon; Ogyges; Pentheus; Surtur; Sebek; Nebuchadnezzar; Moloah; Pompeii; Vala; Loki; Leucothea; Ligeia; Lorelei; Abaddon; Enyo; Ishtar; Hodur; Gomorrah; Andvaranaut; Kali; Woglinda, Wellgunda, and Flosshilda; Faithful Eckhardt; Scipio Africanus; Siren; Telchines.
(see *ruination, shipwreck, devastation, holocaust, ravaging, extinction, annihilation, death, slaughter, murder, massacre*)

DESULTORY
Mrs. Nickleby.
(see *rambling, disconnected, discursive, capricious*)

DETACHMENT
Prosper Mérimée.
(see *objectivity*)

DETAILED
Gothic; Lord Macaulay; Byzantine; Balzacian; Pre-Raphaelite; Protogenes.
(see *involved, intricate*)

DETECTION
Alphonse Bertillon; Ithuriel; Pinkerton; Dr. Watson; Sherlock Holmes; Monsieur Dupin; Justice Overdo; Scotland Yard.
(see *discovery, exposure, constabulary, policeman*)

DETENTION
Tolbooth.
(see *confinement*)

DETERMINATION
George-a-Green; Andrew Volstead; Christopher Columbus; Stonewall Jackson; Leicester Dedlock; Antonius Polemon; Charlemagne; Brom Bones; Trojan; Kate Hardcastle; Widow MacStinger.
(see *resolute, firm, constancy*)

DETERRENT
Thetis.
(see *hindrance, discouraged, obstacle*)

DETRACTOR

Zoilus; Lreux.

(see *aspersion, abusive, defame, disparage, censorious, slander, calumnious*)

DEVASTATION

Mithradates; Huns; Vandalism; Lucius Mummius; Muspel; Attila; General Sherman.

(see *ravaging, pillage, plunderer, sack, aestruction*)

DEVELOPMENT

Luther Burbank.

(see *evolution*)

DEVIL

Robert the Devil; Klingsor; Old Nick; Mephistophelian; Pandemonium; Sam Hill; Master Leonard; Eblis; Freischeutz; Vathek; Beelzebub; Abaddon; Belial; Abigor; Sir Urian; Alastor; Walpurgis; Friar Rush; Samael; Satanic.

(see *demon, evil, goblin*)

DEVOTION

Friar Tuck; Pirithous; Clytie; Euryalus; Amoret; Galatea; Enoch Arden; Amelia; Abdiel; Berenice; Boswellian; Brahmin; Laodamia; Hero and Leander; Jonathan; Achates; Damon and Pythias; Bucephalus; Desdemona; Dioscuri; Haemon; Iolaus; Galahad; Pylades; Lochinvar; Porcia; Ruth; Falstaffian; Man Friday; Horatio; Patroclus; Ophelia; Uncle Tom; Nisus; Nanna; Philaeni; Antigone; Sidney Carton; Pythias; Paul and Virginie; Rab; Theseus; Cordelia; Evadne; Selim; Siguna.

(see *affectionate, ardent, companion, love, friendly, religious*)

DEVOUR

Laestrygonian; Grangousier.

(see *ravenous, swallow, eating, greed*)

DEVOUT

Doctor Charles Primrose; Rose of Lima; Santa Rosalia; Parsifal; Jenkinson; Ephraim; Mahomet; Ashtavakra; Thomas à Kempis; St. Jerome; Cornelius; Aeneas; Spinoza; Simeon.

(see *religious, saintliness, holiness*)

DEW

Eos; Kneippism; Selene; Hrimfaxe.

(see *moisture, damp*)

DIABOLICAL

Iago; Phooka.

(see *fiendish, infernal, atrocity, wickedness, demon, devil, satan*)

DIAGNOSIS

St. Pantaleon; Wilhelm Roentgen; Hippocratic.

(see *curative, healing, therapeutics*)

DIALECT

Dooley; Kiplingese; Uncle Remus; Artemus Ward.

(see *jargon, linguist*)

DIALOGUE

Meliboeus; Lucian.

(see *conversation*)

DIAMOND

Golconda; Cagliostro; "Diamond Jim" Brady; St. Theresa; Cogia Hassan Alhabbal; Schamir; Kohinoor.

(see *precious stone, gem-engraving, jewelry*)

DIARY

Samuel Pepys; Jeames.

(see *register, chronicle*)

DICE

Phoecus; Palamedes; Judge Bridlegoose.

(see *gambling, chance, games*)

DIN
Bromius; Curetes; Flamininus.
(see *noisy, uproar, clashing*)

DINNER
Athenaean; Apician; Amphitryon; Deipnosophistae; Brillat-Savarin.
(see *banquet, feast*)

DIPLOMACY
Richelieu; Dolly Madison; Talleyrand; Franklinian; Washington Irving; Philip of Macedon; Thomas Paine; Lysander; Machiavellian; E. Phillips Oppenheim; Catherine the Great; Chesterfieldian; Mme. de Maintenon; Benjamin Disraeli; Fetiales.
(see *tact, management, political influence, politicians, politics*)

DIPSOMANIAC
Mr. Krook; Stephen Foster.
(see *drunkenness, tippler*)

DIRE
Dirae.
(see *dreadful, fearful, horror, disaster, calamity, destruction, cruelty, terrifying*)

DIRECT (adj.)
Theodore Dreiser; Ku-Klux; Ulysses Grant.
(see *sincerity, frank, outspoken*)

DIRECT (v.)
George Bradshaw; Karl Baedeker; Ciceronian; Itineraria; Pharos; Mrs. Glasse.
(see *management, control, regulation, rules, guide*)

DIRGE
Linus.
(see *elegy, funeral, mourning, requiem*)

DIRTY
Mr. Toodle; Halgaver.
(see *foul*)

DISADVANTAGEOUS
Sejus; Harmonia's Necklace.
(see *injurious, prejudice, harmful*)

DISAGREEMENT
Tweedledum and Tweedledee; Galen; Lavinia.
(see *discord, conflict, contention, dissension, strife, quarrelsome, disputatious*)

DISAPPEARANCE
Richard Haliburton; Tom Walker; Hamelin; Sangreal; Sir Patrick Spens; Launfal; Hendrick Hudson; Comte de LaMotte.
(see *vanish*)

DISAPPOINTMENT
Timon; Lear; Abdallah; Island of St. Brandan; Sister Anne; Marah.
(see *frustration, baffling, thwarted*)

DISAPPROVAL
Cotton Mather; Molly Maguire; Robert Green Ingersoll.
(see *denunciatory, censorious, objector*)

DISASTER
Charybdis; Pyrrhic Victory; Rheingold; Waterloo; Iliad; Frothi; Sejus; Scylla.
(see *mishap, misfortune, misadventure, adversity, calamity, catastrophe, ruination*)

DISBELIEF
Cassandra-like; Pyrrhonian.
(see *doubting, agnostic*)

DISC
Ikhnaton.
(see *round*)

DISCIPLE
Phaedo; Tabitha-Dorcas; Onesimus; Nathanael; Peter.
(see *adherence, supporter, pupil, evangelistic*)

DISCIPLINE
Ephebeia; Orbilian; Laconian; Jean Martinet; Iphicrates.
(see *training, drill, control, regulation, orderliness, punishment, chastise*)

DISCONNECTED
Alfred Jingle.
(see *desultory, meaningless, senseless*)

DISCONSOLATE
Laodamia.
(see *inconsolable, heart-broken, woe, broken-hearted, sorrowful, melancholy, sadness*)

DISCONTENTED
Sir Mungo Malagrowther; Mr. Redlaw; Louis XVI; Rasselas; Adullamite; Emma Bovary.
(see *dissatisfied, uneasy, restless*)

DISCORD
Ate; Babel; Tweedledum and Tweedledee; Modred; Montagues and Capulets; Empedocles; Thetis; Eris; Loki; Lavinia; Crabtree.
(see *disagreement, contention, opposition, strife, quarrelsome, dissension, wrangling, discord, harsh, cacophonous*)

DISCOURAGED
Smike.
(see *dispirited, dejected*)

DISCOURSE
Vach.
(see *conversation, communication, utterance*)

DISCOURTEOUS
Sir Kay; Philoxenus.
(see *impolite, brusque, abrupt, rude, ill-mannered*)

DISCOVERER
Robert LaSalle; Leif Ericson; Vasco da Gama; Jacques Marquette; David Livingstone; Christopher Columbus; Hendrick Hudson; Louis Joliet; Ferdinand Magellan; Richard Hakluyt; Richard Haliburton; Henry M. Stanley; John Smith; Madoc.
(see *explorer*)

DISCOVERY
Cacus; Morgiana; Pinkerton; Hilkiah.
(see *revelation, detection*)

DISCREDIT (v.)
Lucian.
(see *critic, disparage*)

DISCREDITED
Beau Brummel; Ichabod.
(see *disgrace, disfavor, dishonor*)

DISCREET
Mr. Tulkinghorn; Nicodemus.
(see *prudence, cautious, circumspect wary, wisdom, justice*)

DISCRIMINATING
Chesterfieldian; Dabbat.
(see *connoisseur, insight, penetrating, sagacity*)

DISCRIMINATION
St. Bartholomew's Day; Alfred Dreyfus; Jim Crow; Salic Law.
(see *bias, bigotry, prejudice*)

DISCURSIVE
Peripatetic.
(see *rambling, desultory*)

DISCUS
Palamedes.
(see *quoit*)

DISDAINFUL
Lady Clara Vere de Vere; Launfal.
(see *scornful, contempt, supercilious, haughtiness*)

DISEASE
Bessy Bell; Celsus; Niflheim; St. Roch; Romola; Rudra; Jukes Family.
(see *sickly, valetudinarian, epidemic, ill health*)

DISFAVOR
Coventry; Miltiades; Galba.
(see *unacceptable, discredit, disrepute, disapproval, disgrace*)

DISFIGURED
Amelia; Mayeux; Rosa Dartle.
(see *deformed, mar, ugliness, mutilation, misshapen*)

DISGRACE
Julia; Miltiades; Man in the Moon; Waterloo; Ichabod; Lentulus Sura; Hester Prynne; Salt River; Scalae Gemoniae.
(see *degradation, dishonor, disrepute, shame, ignominy, infamous, opprobrious, scandal*)

DISGUISE
Mata Hari; Duessa; Jack-in-the-Green; Luddites; Viola; Lalla Rookh; Lycomedes; Rosalind; Fidelio; Foigard; Friar Rush; Kate Hardcastle; Orsino; Tamar.
(see *concealed, masked, incognito, transvestitism*)

DISHONEST
Turcaret; Sampson Brass; Greeks Bearing Gifts; Samuel Maverick; Machiavellian; Squeers.
(see *falsehood, fraudulence, deceitful, perfidy, treachery*)

DISHONOR
Virginia; Leucothea; Hester Prynne; Barathron; Quintilius Varus; Hamelin; Scalae Gemoniae.
(see *disgrace, discredit, disrepute, infamous, shame, degradation, ignominy, opprobrious, scandal, abased*)

DISILLUSIONED
Wertherian; Robin and Makyne; Catullan; Troilus and Cressida; Lear; Obermann; Nora Helmer; Mokanna; Père Goriot.
(see *blasé, cynic*)

DISINHERIT
John Osborne.
(see *expatriate, excommunicated*)

DISINTERESTED
Henry James; Hugh Strap.
(see *impartial, unbiased, unselfish*)

DISINTERRED
John Wycliffe.
(see *excavated, unburied*)

DISLOYAL
Gobbo; Pecksniff; Modred; Anu; Judas; Benedict Arnold; Coriolanus.
(see *unfaithful, faithless, falsehood, perfidy, treachery*)

DISMAL
John Wemmick; Tullianum; Mrs. Gummidge.
(see *cheerless, gloom, darkness, drear, melancholy, sadness, doleful, lugubrious, mourning*)

DISMISSAL
John Drum; Stellenbosche.
(see *release, deposed*)

DISOBEDIENCE
Zanes; Jonah; Lot's Wife; Absalom; Fatima; Ebal; Lady of Shalott.
(see *infraction, mutiny, rebellious, obstinate*)

DISORDERLY
Bedlam; Tityre-Tu; Chaos; Tiamat; King Petaud's Court; Halgaver; Pandemonium.
(see *lawless, rebellious, turbulence, unmanageable, ungoverned, tumultuous, riot*)

DISPARAGE
Mrs. Candour.
(see *decry, aspersion, defame*)

DISPASSIONATE
Sir Guyon.
(see *temperance, self-control, imperturbable, composure, sobriety, impartial, unbiased, candid*)

DISPIRITED
Trophonius.
(see *dejected, discouraged, downcast, despondent, crestfallen*)

DISPLAY
Lantern Land; Alexandrianism; Sir Matthew Mite.
(see *pompous, ostentation, pedantic*)

DISPOSSESSED
Prospero; John Noakes; Perdita; Okie; Tom Styles.
(see *eviction, expropriation*)

DISPUTATIOUS
Tweedledum and Tweedledee; Canace; Captain Lismahago; John Noakes; Big-Endians; Mopsus; Dred Scott Case; Pico della Mirandola; Square and Thwackum; Smelfungus.
(see *captious, contention, bickering, dissension, quarrelsome*)

DISREPUTE
Bezonian; MacFlecknoe; Bardolph; Herostratus.
(see *discredit, dishonor, disgrace, degradation, abased*)

DISSATISFIED
Rasselas; Schopenhauerian.
(see *discontented, uneasy*)

DISSECTION
Celsus; Jerry Cruncher; Osiris; Herophilus.
(see *anatomy, mayhem, piecemeal*)

DISSENSION
Rheingold; Cephalus; Modred; Lavinia; Angelica; Tweedledum and Tweedledee; Montagues and Capulets.
(see *discord, contention, strife, disagreement*)

DISSOCIATE
Jim Crow; Charles C. Boycott.
(see *ostracism*)

DISSOLUTE
Casanovian; La Traviata; Toulouse-Lautrec; Sir Matthew Mite; Lentulus Sura; Mirabel; Lucio; Dionysus; Mark Antony; Tityre-Tu; Nancy; Paul Clifford; Catiline; Dick Swiveller; Barnadine.
(see *licentious, debauchee, lewdness, profligacy, depravity, reprobate*)

DISSUADER
Veturia and Volumnia.
(see *deterrent*)

DISTAFF
Frigga.
(see *spinner*)

DISTANCES
Itineraria.
(see *interval, remote*)

DISTANT
Rhipaei Montes; Jericho; Thule; Pytheas; Hyperboreans.
(see *remote, far-away*)

DISTENDED
Physignathus.
(see *distortion, misshapen, fat*)

DISTINCTIVE
Jim Crow; Eupatridae; John Hancock; Libro d'Oro; Peregrine White; Pelops; Gotha; Chandra.
(see *characteristic, eminent, original*)

DISTORTION
Henry Matisse; Mayeux; Elbridge Gerry.
(see *deformed, misrepresentation*)

DISTRACTED
Margaret; Armida.
(see *deranged, insanity, madness, frantic, crazy*)

DISTRESSED
Okie; Elsa; Adullamite; Gorgibus.
(see *anguish, agony, tormented, tortured, suffering*)

DISTRIBUTE
Icarius.
(see *generosity, share, hospitality*)

DISTRUSTFUL
Malbecco; Laocoön; Leontes; Kitely; Eurylochus.
(see *apprehensive, doubting, suspicion*)

DISTURBANCE
Molly Maguire; Thomas Hardy; Skimmington.
(see *agitator, commotion, disorderly, confusion*)

DISUSE
Lamarckian.
(see *modification, atrophy*)

DIVE (v.)
Helle.
(see *swimmer, fall*)

DIVERSE
Centaur; Chiron.
(see *variety, multiplicity*)

DIVERT
Merry-Andrew; Laius.
(see *amusing, entertainment, refreshment, pleasure*)

DIVIDE (v.)
Terminus; Elbridge Gerry; Diocletian; Mason and Dixon.
(see *split, share, cleave, demarcation*)

DIVIDEND
Androclean.
(see *reward*)

DIVINATION
Tages; Witch of Endor; Etruscan; Melampus; Urim and Thummim; Urganda; Agnes.
(see *foretell, soothsayer, augury, magic, prediction, prophecy*)

DIVINE (adj.)
Olympian; Swarga; Seven Sleepers of Ephesus.
(see *sacred, holiness, spirit, heaven, celestial, angel, seraph*)

DIVINITY
Jumala.
(see god, goddess)

DIVORCE (n.)
Antiope; Henry VIII; Diana Warwick.
(see *annulment*)

DORMANT
Hypnos.
(see *sleep, quiet, lethargy, restful*)

DOTAGE
Quintilius Varus; Géronte; Grangousier.
(see *senility, anile, old man*)

DOTE
Malbecco.
(see *uxorious, foolish, sentimentality*)

DOUBLE (n.)
Oliver (2); Sosia.
(see *twins, copy, reproduction, similarity, resemblance, alike*)

DOUBLE-DEALING
Janus; Cassius; Polonius; Jesuit; Prusias; Sir and Lady Pliant; La Tosca; Thessalian; Maskwell.
(see *deceitful, duplicity, artifice, fraudulence, dishonest, trickery*)

DOUBLE SENSE
Ralph Roister Doister.
(see *ambiguous, equivocation*)

DOUBTFUL
Buridan's Ass; Tyndareus; Pope Joan.
(see *wavering, undecided, uncertainty, hesitancy, dubious, ambiguous, enigmatic, equivocation*)

DOUBTING
Malbecco; Jean Hardouin; Anatole France; Doubting Thomas; Robert Elsmere; Slough of Despond.
(see *agnostic, unbeliever, skepticism*)

DOVES
Pleiades.
(see *pigeon, birds*)

DOWDY
Halgaver.
(see *slatternly*)

DOWNCAST
Smike; Trophonius.
(see *sadness, dejected, dispirited, despondent, crestfallen*)

DOWNFALL
Belvidera; Pharnaces; Waterloo.
(see *destruction, ruination*)

DOWNPOUR
Pluvius; Parjanya; Eurus.
(see *rain*)

DOWRY
Saint Nicholas.
(see *bride, bridegroom, wedding present*)

DOZE
Hypnos; Somnus.
(see *sleep, drowsy*)

DRAGGED
Dirce; Hector.
(see *punishment*)

DRAGON
Jabberwock; Cecrops; Zagreus; Tiamat;Triptolemus; Una; Saint George; Red Cross Kight; Cadmean; Beowulf; Fafner; Fortunio; Kederli; Andromeda; Orc; Rustam.
(see *serpent, monstrosity, griffin*)

DRAGOON
Richard Varney; The Crawleys.
(see *cavalryman, horsemanship*)

DRAMA
Thalia (see Muse); Jean Racine; Shakespearean; Dionysus; Menander; Melpomene; Pierre Corneille; Aga-

thon; Marlovian; Ben Jonson; Bulwer-Lytton; Molière; Shavian; Sophoclean.
(see *actor, pageantry, stage, histrionic*)

DRAMATIC
Giuseppe Verdi; Wagnerian; David Garrick; P. T. Barnum; Brontesque; Fanny Kemble; Thucydides; Livian; Feodor Chaliapin; Anna Pavlova; Mrs. Siddons; Byronic; Joseph Jefferson; Giacomo Puccini.
(see *theatrical, tragedy*)

DRASTIC
Andrew Volstead.
(see *momentous*)

DRAW-BACK
Rosamond Vincy.
(see *disadvantageous, imperfect, defective*)

DRAWING
Ictinus.
(see *artist, outline*)

DREADFUL
Dirae; Pavor; Vejovis; Ifurin.
(see *horror, dire, fearful, terrifying*)

DREAMER
Zechariah; Rip Van Winkle; Peter Klaus; Amphiaraus; Ephialtes; Daniel; John-a-Dreams; Joseph; Peter Pan; Pliny the Younger.
(see *visionary*)

DREAMLAND
Jacob's Ladder; Horn Gate; Land of Nod; Ivory Gate; Hypnos; Morpheus; Sin; Lotophagi; Somnus; Serapis.
(see *visions*)

DREAMY
Thomas DeQuincey; Pierre Loti; Praxiteles; Stephen Foster; Claude Debussy; Robert Schumann.
(see *impressionistic, vague, illusion*)

DREAR
Cimmerian; Stygian; Orcus.
(see *gloom, dismal, darkness, solitude, cheerless, loneliness, monotonous*)

DRESS (n.)
Mantalini; Taglioni; Herr Teufelsdroeckh; Miss Flora McFlimsey.
(see *apparel, attire, clothing, raiment, garments, habiliments, costume*)

DRILL (military)
Zouave; Campus Martius; Jean Martinet; Commodore Trunnion.
(see *discipline, militaristic*)

DRINK (n.)
Fabulinus; Bromius; Bacchic; Hippocrene; Dionysus; Bacchanal; Lenaea; Thyia; Maenad; Neptune.
(see *tippler, drunkenness, intemperate, wine, champagne, beer*)

DRIVER
Jehu.
(see *vehicle, fast*)

DROLL
Punch; Touchstone.
(see *amusing, lively, ludicrous, comical, funny, farce, ridiculous*)

DRONING
Calypso.
(see *singer*)

DROP (v.)
Helle.
(see *fall*)

DROUGHT
Pluvius; Vritra; Okie; Robigus; Haggai.
(see *arid, dry, parched*)

DROWNED
Misenus; Leilah; Physignathus; Ophelia; Nydia; Rhea Silvia; Sabrina; Tiberinus.
(see *overboard*)

DROWNING
Ran; Davy Jones.
(see *deluge*)

DROWSY
Peter Klaus; Morpheus; Hypnos; Sleeping Beauty; Somnus; Kiak-Kiak.
(see *sleep, lethargy*)

DRUDGE
Gibeonite.
(see *slave, menial, toil*)

DRUG (v.)
Lovelace.

DRUGGIST
Galen.
(see *pharmacist, medicine man*)

DRUNKENNESS
Trinculo; Mr. Krook; Martin of Tours; Saint Vincent; Faunus; Falstaffian; Tam O'Shanter; Borachio; Philip Wharton; Zombi; Naraka; Elpenor; Eccles; Hippodamia; Eurytion; Friar Rush; Satyr; Scythian; Teague; Christopher Sly.
(see *alcoholism, inebriation*)

DRY
Dry-as-Dust; Vritra; Auster; Baca; Cornelia Blimber.
(see *arid, parched, uninteresting, barren*)

DRY-EYED
Thaukt.
(see *unemotional, cold-hearted, stoical*)

DUALITY
Jekyll-Hyde; Gemini; Zoroaster.
(see *double, double sense, twins*)

DUBIOUS
Miss Kilmansegg.
(see *undecided, uncertainty, hesitancy, quandary, dilemma*)

DUDE
Mantalini; Macaroni; Beau Nash; Jack Sixteen-String; Joseph Sedley, Sir Courtly Nice; Silk-Stocking.
(see *dapper, foppish*)

DUEL
Edgar Ravenswood.
(see *swordsman, single-handed*)

DULL-WITTED
Claudius; Querno; Tupperian; Boeotian; Dry-as-Dust; MacFlecknoe; Shallow; Silence; Hoenir.
(see *stupid, blockhead, unintelligent*)

DUMBNESS
Helen Keller; Thaumaste.
(see *inarticulate, mute, silence, speechless, sign language*)

DUNCE
Sir Daguenet; Dr. Dodipoll.
(see *simpleton, foolish, blockhead*)

DUNCE-CAP
Flamen.
(see *cap, ignominy*)

DUNGEON
Tullianum; Tolbooth; Black Hole of Calcutta; John Howard; Margaret.
(see *imprisonment, penitentiary*)

DUPE
Camacho; Orgon; Ferdinand Fathom; Sampson Brass; Epimetheus; Maxi-

E

EAGER
Justice Overdo; Pandora; Bardolph; Herostratus.
(see *ambitious, emulate, desire, aspiring*)

EAGLE
Hraesvelger.
(see *hawk, vulture, birds*)

EARNEST
Mahomet; Cotton Mather; James Russel Lowell; Heraclitus; David Copperfield; Carlylean; Boanerges.
(see *zeal, eager, impassioned, importunate, warm-hearted, cordiality, sincerity, truthful, serious*)

EARTH
Demogorgon; Enceladus; Consus; Ve; Seb; Midgard; Rinde.
(see *universe*)

EARTH-GODDESS
Tellus; Demeter; Terra; Rhea; Ge; Lua; Hertha; Acca Larentia; Maia.
(see *nature, agriculture*)

EARTHQUAKE
Ymir; Poseidon; Alrinach; Amphiaraus; Trasimene Lake; Siguna; Hringham; Uzziah; Enrico Caruso.
(see *shake*)

EASE (n.)
Lotophagi; Nephelococcygia.
(see *leisure, contentment*)

EASE (v.)
Gilead; Lotophagi.
(see *soothe, painless*)

EASTWARD
Quetzalcoatl.
(see *forward*)

EAST WIND
Eurus.
(see *wind*)

EASY-GOING
Yankee; Phaeacian; Joseph Sedley; Charles Honeyman.
(see *naturalness, calm, unperturbed, unconcerned*)

EATING
Duke Humphrey; Apician; Fabulinus; Deipnosophistae; Joe; Brillat-Savarin.
(see *appetite, hungry, gastronome, gourmet, feast, banquet*)

ECCENTRIC
Herr Teufelsdroeckh; El Greco; Commodore Trunnion; Queer Card; David Crockett; Empedocles; Squire Western; Betsy Trotwood; Tom Pin~h; Horace Walpole; John Buncle; Gabriele D'Annunzio; Dandie Dinmont.
(see *aberration, irregular, peculiarity, idiosyncratic*)

ECCLESIASTICAL
Tertullian; Thomas Aquinas; Giovanni Palestrina.
(see *religious, priest, clergy, minister, preacher*)

ECHO
Selim; Echo.
(see *reiteration, repetition*)

ECLIPSE (n.)
Anaxagoras; Thales; Rahu; Fenrir.
(see *sunless, darkness, cloud*)

ELEGANCE

Edwardian; Attic; Agathon; Adonis; Jean Racine; John Lyly; Will Honeycomb; Gainsborough; Beau Nash; Trimalchio; Chesterfieldian; Belgravian; Terence; Osric; Nerissa; Petronius; Georgian; Silk-Stocking.

(see *grace, beauty, polite, gentility, courtly, dainty*)

ELEGY

Tibullan; Theocritean; Neniae; Propertian; Thomas Gray; Ovidian; Lycidas; John Chivery; Stoke Poges; Tyrtaeus.

(see *dirge, lamentation*)

ELEMENTARY

Abecedarians.

(see *rudimentary*)

ELEMENTS (weather)

Weird Sisters.

(see *rain, foggy, snow, mist, sun-god*)

ELEPHANT

Adrastus; Ganesa.

(see *thick-skinned, animals*)

ELEVATING

Hippocrene; Charis; Heliconian.

(see *exaltation*)

ELFIN

Oberon; Völund; Puck; Ymir; Robin Goodfellow; Erlking; Titania; Mozartean; Fenella.

(see *fairy, sprite, imp, diminutive, dwarf, pygmy, delicate, mischief-maker*)

ELIXIR

Ponce de Leon.

(see *philter, love-potion*)

ELLIPSES

Johannes Kepler.

(see *oval*)

ELOCUTION

Tutivillus; Demosthenes.

(see *speech, expression, utterance*)

ELONGATE

Bayard (1).

(see *protracted, lengthy*)

ELOPEMENT

Gretna Green; Selim; Jessica.

(see *runaway, fleeing, escape*)

ELOQUENCE

Atticus; Henry Ward Beecher; Ciceronian; Clarence Darrow; Nestor; Quintilian; Acacetus; Rienzi; Lord Burleigh; Gorgias; Thaumaturgus; Mercury; Hamiltonian; Mimir; Demosthenes; Saraswati; Hypatia.

(see *oratory, utterance, expression, rhetoric, grandiloquent*)

ELUSIVE

Jesuit; Proteus; Mme. Benoîton; Island of Saint Brandan; Artful Dodger; Lollius; Man with the Iron Mask; Mercury; Titania; Fra Diavolo; Anatole France; Henry James; Claude Debussy.

(see *evasive, equivocation, delusive, deceptive, fraudulence, deceitful*)

EMACIATED

Philetas.

(see *thin, gaunt, skinny*)

EMANCIPATOR

Timoleon; Libertas; Flamininus; Gideon; Messianic; Publicola; Zerubbabel; Thaddeus Kosciusko; Abraham Lincoln; Esther; Garibaldian; William Tell; Sinn Fein.

(see *liberator, freedom, freer, deliverance*)

EMBARRASSMENT

Queer Street; Merope.

(see *perplexity, entangled, harass, annoy, distressed, shame*)

ian; Acrasia; Armida; Mambrino; Aeaean; Loathly Lady; Lir; Malagigi.
(see *magic, sorcerer, witchcraft, charm*)

ENCIRCLE
Oceanus.
(see *girded, belt, embrace*)

ENCOMIUM
Agesilaus; Agricola; Della Cruscans.
(see *praise, eulogy, panegyric*)

ENCOURAGEMENT
Nadejda von Meck.
(see *favoring, promoter, aid, helpfulness, patroness*)

ENCROACHMENT
Naboth.
(see *usurper, intrusive*)

ENCUMBRANCE
Old Man of the Sea; Og; Rosamond Vincy.
(see *impediment, hindrance*)

ENCYCLOPEDIST
Pierre Larousse; Celsus; Marcus Terentius Varro; Athenaean; Suidas.
(see *all-inclusiveness, learned, comprehensive, lexicographer*)

END (n.)
Moerae; John Audley; Janus; Kiak-Kiak.
(see *finality, limit*)

ENDLESS
Danaides; Iliad; Luggnagg; Querno; Shesha.
(see *interminable, infinite, everlasting, never-ending, eternity, immortality*)

ENDURANCE
Epictetus; Gibraltar; Trojan; Marathon; Gymnopaedia; Stonewall Jackson; Valley Forge; Helena; Spartan.
(see *suffering, patience, fortitude, resignation, constancy, tolerance*)

ENEMY
Menalcas; Hannibal; Saracen.
(see *antagonistic, hostility, unfriendly*)

ENERGETIC
Hotspur; Lityerses; Ulysses; Richard the Lion-Hearted; Trojan; Marcus Furius Camillus; Catherine the Great; Agesilaus; Raleigh; Saint Paul; Justice Overdo; Martha; Penrod; Arthur Honegger; Edisonian.
(see *vigor, power, potent, enterprising, strength*)

ENGAGING
Queen of Hearts.
(see *amiable, loveliness, sweetness, charm, attractiveness, kindness, tenderness, benignant*)

ENGINEER
Sir John MacAdam; Vitruvius; Leonardo da Vinci; Robert Fulton.
(see *inventive, creative, ingenuity*)

ENGRAVER
Pyrgoteles.
(see *etcher, chisel, sculpture*)

ENGROSSED
Yogi.
(see *absorption*)

ENIGMATIC
Man with the Iron Mask; Mona Lisa; Tyndareus; Sphinx.
(see *occultism, ambiguous, unintelligible, incomprehensible, puzzle, perplexity*)

ENLIGHTENMENT
Attic; Atlantis; Goddess of Reason; Alumbrado; Munin; Periclean.
(see *instructive, cultured, education, learned, reason*)

ENMITY
Montagues and Capulets.
(see *hatred, hostility, malign, malice, malevolence, rancorous, feud*)

ENNUI
Rasselas; Emma Bovary; Paridel.
(see *languorous, boredom, tedious*)

ENORMOUS
Amarant; Og; Gigantes; Leviathanic; Gargantuan; Brobdingnagian.
(see *huge, vast, gigantic, tremendous, colossal, prodigious*)

ENRICHED
Cogia Hassan Alhabbal; Edmond Dantès.
(see *rich, wealth*)

ENSEMBLES
Max Reinhardt.
(see *group action*)

ENSLAVEMENT
Uncle Tom; Hypsipyle; Dionysius.
(see *slavery, subjugator, overlord*)

ENSNARE
Quintilius Varus; Lake Trasimene; Sinon.
(see *enticement, beguilement, lure, trap, man-trap, tempter*)

ENTANGLED
Og.
(see *ensnare*)

ENTERPRISING
Mrs. Partington; Rienzi; John Jacob Astor; Andrew Carnegie.
(see *bold, adventurous, daring, courageous, venturesome, chivalrous*)

ENTERTAINMENT
Phemius; Punch; Mother Goose; John Drum; Sir John Mandeville; Dolly Madison; Mark Twain; Oliver Wendell Holmes.
(see *feast, banquet, hospitality, amusements*)

ENTHUSIASTIC
Minna; Desdemona; Peter the Hermit; Merry-Andrew; Justice Overdo; Richard the Lion-Hearted; Triptolemus Yellowley; Penrod; Stevensonian.
(see *fanatical, bigotry, visionary, dreamer, eager, fervor*)

ENTICEMENT
Calypso; Lamia; Peitho; Ligeia; Leucothea; Lorelei; Leda; Friar Rush.
(see *alluring, temper, temptress, beguilement, lure, seduction, attractiveness, engaging, persuasion, ensnare, coaxing, corrupt*)

ENTIRE
Dan to Beersheba.
(see *whole, complete*)

ENTOMBED
Leucothea; Antonius Polemon.
(see *burial, sepulcher, tomb, buried alive*)

ENTRAILS
Etruscan; Tages.
(see *liver, augury*)

ENTRANCE (n.)
Annie Oakley.
(see *admittance*)

ENTRANCED
Yogi.
(see *charm, enchantment, ecstasy*)

ENVENOM
Locusta.
(see *poison, venomous*)

ENVIRONMENT
Hippocratic; Lamarckian.
(see *heredity*)

ENVY
Sir Kay; Joseph; Maud Muller; Ahab; Naboth; Polycrates; Wallenstein; Gorbodoc; Iago.
(see *hatred, jealousy, covetous, malice*)

EPHEMERAL
Omar Khayyam; Abu Hassan.
(see *short-lived, transience, fleet, brief*)

EPIC
Vergilian; Homeric; Miltonic; Dantean; Calliope (see Muse).
(see *heroism, poetry*)

EPICUREAN
Epicurus; Lucullan; Apician; Ninon de Lenclos; Aristippus; Aulus Vitellius; Atticus; Delmonico; Phaeacian; Farinata; Gilgamesh; Horatian; Henry VIII; Joseph Sedley; Deipnosophistae; Nellie Melba; Brillat-Savarin.
(see *gourmet, glutton, voluptuary, sensuality*)

EPIDEMIC
Saint Roch; Hippocratic.
(see *disease, plague, pestilence*)

EPIGRAMMATIC
Horatian (Horace); Oscar Wilde; Pharnaces; Callimachus; Omar Khayyam; François Voltaire; Martial; Giottesque; Juvenalian; Mrs. Mountstuart Jenkinson.
(see *concise, laconic, terse*)

EPISTOLOGRAPHER
Alciphron; Pliny the Younger; Mme. de Sévigné.
(see *letter-writer*)

EPITAPH
John Chivery; Franz Schubert.
(see *inscription*)

EQUALITY
Twelve Peers.
(see *alike*)

EQUALIZER
Publilius Philo;Thaddeus Kosciusko.
(see *unifier*)

EQUINE
Hippocampus.
(see *horse*)

EQUINOX
Hipparchus.
(see *storm*)

EQUIPMENT
Iphicrates.
(see *apparel, utensils*)

EQUITABLE
Minos; Rhadamanthus; Dike; Astraea; Aeacus; Themis; Forsete.
(see *justice, honesty, impartial, unbiased*)

EQUIVOCATION
Jesuit; Maskwell.
(see *prevarication, evasive, ambiguous, double-sense*)

ERECT (adj.)
Watkins Tottle.
(see *inflexible, stiff*)

EROSION
Okie; Santa Rosalia.
(see *atrophy*)

EROTIC
Cupid; Venus; Flora; Paphian; Bathyllus; Tracy Tupman; Richard von Krafft-Ebing; D. H. Lawrence; Mrs. Frail.
(see *amorous, ardent, enamoured, passionate, love, longing, tenderness, lovers, amatory, impassioned*)

ERRAND-BOY
Wagon Boy.
(see *messenger, boy-servant*)

ERROR
Queer Card; Ancaeus; Agave; Pyramus; Winifred Jenkins; Sir Martin Mar-All; Mrs. Slipslop.
(see *mistaken, blundering, wrong, incorrect*)

ERUDITE
Marcus Terentius Varro; Pico della Mirandola.
(see *learned, scholarly*)

ERUPTION
Titus Vespasianus; Pompeii.
(see *volcano*)

ESCAPE
Cloelia; Tam O'Shanter; Deucalion; Britomartis; Little Red Ridinghood; Jean Valjean; Erich W. Houdini; Edmond Dantès; Phrixus.
(see *fleeing*)

ESCAPISM
Manly; Graustark.
(see *unreal, delusive*)

ESCORT
Fabulinus; Lalla Rookh; Nausicaa.
(see *bodyguard, attendant, companion, protection, safeguard*)

ESOTERIC
Pythagoras; Christian Rosenkreuz; Eleusinian.
(see *secrecy, exclusive, initiated*)

ESPIONAGE
Mata Hari; Theodora; Solomon Pross; E. Phillips Oppenheim.
(see *spy, scout*)

ESPRIT
Mme. Recamier.
(see *wit, intelligent*)

ESSAYIST
André Gide; Lord Macaulay; Charles Lamb; Addisonian; Elia; Emersonian; Montaigne; Washington Irving; Stevensonian.
(see *writer*)

ESSENTIAL
Telephus; Hugo Grotius.
(see *necessity, rudimentary*)

ESTABLISHED
Procrustean; Platonic.
(see *fixed, substantial, rigid*)

ESTABLISHER
Stator.
(see *encouragement, assistance, protector*)

ESTATES
Samuel Maverick; Eupatridae; Licinius; Marquis of Carabas.
(see *property, landowner*)

ESTEEM
Joseph of Arimathea.
(see *admiration, honor, revered, reverence, veneration, worshipful, respectful*)

ESTRAY
Valentine and Orson.
(see *lost, wanderer, foundling*)

ETCHER
James A. Whistler.
(see *engraver*)

ETERNITY
Ormuzd; Khartaphilos; Phaedo; Luggnagg; Demogorgon; Anasuya; Nama; Vanderdecken; Soren Kierkegaard; Shesha.
(see *perpetual, endless, infinite, everlasting*)

ETHEREAL
Marie Laurencin; Apsaras; Florimel; Pierre Loti; Mignon; Mozartean.
(see *airy, celestial, heaven, refinement, delicate, fragility*)

ETHICAL
Lao-Tse; Adam Smith.
(see *moralizer, conduct, philosophy*)

ETHNOLOGY
Josephus; Strabo.
(see *nationalism*)

ETIQUETTE
David Livingstone; Mr. Podsnap; Jean Martinet; Rajput.
(see *ceremonious, manners, decorous*)

EULOGY
Neniae.
(see *praise, encomium, panegyric*)

EUNUCH
Bagoas; Atys; Galli; Xerxes.
(see *unmanned, castration, unmanly*)

EUPHONIOUS
Gorgias; Isocrates.
(see *mellifluous, sweet-sounding*)

EUPHUISTIC
Osric; John Lyly; Sir Piercie Shafton.
(see *diction, pompous, ornate, magniloquence, grandiloquent*)

EUTHANASIA
Antonius Polemon.
(see *incurable, unhealable*)

EVANGELISTIC
Wesleyan; Luke; Saint John; Saint Mark; Saint Matthew; Peter Poundtext; Philip.
(see *missionary*)

EVASIVE
Lollius; Ananias; Spenlow and Jorkins.
(see *deceitful, equivocation, prevarication, sophist*)

EVENING
Nox; Ra; Hesperus.
(see *night, dusk, twilight, sunset*)

EVENTFUL
Golden Ass; Hypsipyle; Fasti.
(see *momentous*)

EVERGREEN
Atys; Pitys.
(see *pine-tree, trees*)

EVERLASTING
Dantean; Tophet; Gehenna; Khartaphilos; Luggnagg; Vanderdecken.
(see *endless, unending, perpetual, interminable, eternity, imperishable, deathless, immortality*)

EVICTION
John Noakes; Tom Styles.
(see *dispossessed*)

EVIDENCE
Ion.
(see *proof*)

Petit André.
(see *hanged, decapitation, behead, guillotine*)

EXEMPLARY
Zeno; Leilah; Arria; Algeresque; Stella; King of Yvetot; Utopian; Aurora Leigh; Rev. Micah Balwhidder; Sir Willoughby Patterne.
(see *virtuous, paragon, perfection, model*)

EXEMPTION
Flamen.
(see *privileged, release, exclusive*)

EXHIBITIONIST
Peregrinus Proteus.
(see *extrovert*)

EXHORTATION
Zechariah; Haggai; Tyrtaeus.
(see *persuasion, encouragement*)

EXILE
Coventry; Man in the Moon.
(see *banishment, ostracism, proscription, expatriate*)

EXILED
Julia; Prospero; Calvinistic; Giuseppe Mazzini; Coriolanus; Karl Marx; Isagoras; Ishmael; Ovidian; Napoleon Bonaparte; Idomeneus.
(see *ostracism, banishment*)

EXODONTIST
Kindhart.
(see *toothless*)

EXODUS
Hegira; Moses.
(see *fleeing, escape*)

EXORCISM
Gibil.
(see *charm, enchantment, magic, witchcraft, sorcerer*)

EXOTIC
Xanadu; Zuleika; Mata Hari; Sir Matthew Mite; Rider Haggard; Pierre Loti; Novensides.
(see *foreign, strange, bizarre, outlandish*)

EXPAND
Paribanou; Hamilcar.
(see *increase, elongate*)

EXPATRIATE
Henry James; Gertrude Stein.
(see *banishment, exile, ostracism*)

EXPECTATION
Kilmansegg; Spes.
(see *anticipation, hopeful*)

EXPEDITION
Robert La Salle; David Livingstone; Jacques Marquette.
(see *explorer, adventurous, discoverer*)

EXPERIENCE
Odyssey; Lachesis; Periander; Nestor.
(see *vicissitudes, wisdom*)

EXPERIMENTATION
Galileo; Antoine Lavoisier.
(see *test, laboratory*)

EXPIATION
Azazel; Owain; Robert the Devil; Hesione.
(see *atonement*)

EXPLANATION
Bessus.
(see *excuse, solution*)

EXPLOITS
Rustam; Theseus; Hercules.
(see *feat, achievement*)

F

FABLE
Jean de La Fontaine; Phaedrus; Aesop; Uncle Remus.
(see *allegory*)

FABRICATED
Wardour Street.
(see *counterfeit, pseudo, spurious*)

FABULOUS
Prester John; Tintagel; El Dorado; Astolfo; Poictesme; Mme. Benoîton; Cockaigne; Hippocampus; Arion; Hyperboreans; Haroun al Raschid; Kamadhenu; Snark.
(see *fictitious, non-existent*)

FACE (n.)
Claudius Aesopus.
(see *features*)

FACETIOUS
Touchstone; Artemus Ward; Mrs. Partington.
(see *witty, humor, joke, droll, jester, funny, comical, gaiety, merriment*)

FACSIMILE
Mme. Marie Tussaud; Sosia.
(see *copy, reproduction, duplicate, alike, likeness, resemblance, similarity*)

FACTIONALISM
Montagues and Capulets.
(see *discord, dissension, rebellious, tumultuous, turbulence*)

FACTOTUM
Panurge; Acacetus; Barber of Seville; Bardolph; Till Eulenspiegel; Phormio; Handy Andy; Robotian; Weller; Pooh-Bah; Johannes Factotum; Gyes.
(see *versatile*)

FACTUAL
Theodore Dreiser; Euhemeristic.
(see *literal, realistic*)

FADDIST
Ikhnaton.
(see *whim*)

FAILURE
Bessy Bell; Stellenbosche.
(see *defective, ill-luck*)

FAINT-HEARTED
Pliable; Abraham Slender.
(see *timidity, afraid, fearful, bashful, shy*)

FAIR (adj.)
Callipolis; Oriana; Callirrhoë.
(see *beautiful, comely, pretty, handsome, attractiveness*)

FAIRY
Melusina; Demogorgon; Banshee; La Befana; Berchta; Oberon; Mab; Peter Pan; Urganda; Gloriana; White Ladies.
(see *supernatural, elfin, sprite*)

FAIRY TALES
Charles Perrault; Grimm Brothers.
(see *imaginary, fable, fabulous*)

FAITH
Ben Hur; John Bunyan; Epictetus; Land o' the Leal; Helena; Abraham

Lincoln; Spes; Shadrach.
(see *belief, trusting, reliance, confidence, fidelity*)

FAITHFUL
Little John; Nanna; Morgiana; Susan Nipper; Nutbrown Maid; Gunga Din; Jonathan Oldbuck; Oriana; Abiathar; Mentor; Imogen; Iolaus; Troilus and Cressida; Corporal Trim; Uncle Tom; Ruth; Pythias; Pylades; Porcia; Pirithous; Clara Peggoty; Partridge; Patroclus; Penelope; Zadok; David; Theseus; Zerbino; Euryclea; Euryalus; Eumaeus; Abdiel; Abraham; Evangeline; Dorigen; Caleb Balderstone; Achates; Bucephalus; Christian; Damon and Pythias; Faithful Eckhardt; Gelert; Hugh Strap; Brigid of Kildare.
(see *trustworthy, loyalty, reliable, dependable*)

FAITH-HEALER
Phineas P. Quimby; Mary Baker Eddy.
(see *miraculous, wonder-worker*)

FAITHLESS
Farinata; Punic; Job's Friends; Carthaginian; Feretrius; Laomedon; Oliver (1); Odur; Hosea.
(see *perfidy, treachery, dishonest, disloyal, untrustworthy*)

FAKER
Abram-man; Peter Funk; Dousterswivel.
(see *humbug, swindler, mountebank, charlatan, quackery*)

FALL (n.)
Helle; Elpenor; Arioch.
(see *downfall*)

FALLS (water) (n.)
Minnehaha.
(see *stream, water*)

FALSE ACCUSATION
Tenes; Genevieve; Susanna; Saint Stephen; Naboth; Sir Mador; Melissa.
(see *perjury, frame-up*)

FALSEHOOD
Archimago; Phaedra; Sapphira; Appius Claudius; Modred; Judas; Apocryphal; Job's Friends; Feretrius; Bayes's Troops; Belise; Ventidius; Sinon; Ivory Gate; Buncombe; Duessa; Ganelon.
(see *liar*)

FAME
Algeresque; Rhodope; John Hancock; Asaphic; Mr. and Mrs. Leo Hunter; Herostratus.
(see *celebrity, illustrious, glory, eminent*)

FAMILIAR
Witch of Endor.
(see *obliging, affable, courtesy, friendly*)

FAMILY
Manes; Forsyte; Lares; Sif; Penates.
(see *clan*)

FAMILY-TREE
Gotha; Libro D'Oro; Lady Clara Vere de Vere.
(see *lineage, ancestor, first, original*)

FAMINE
Minnehaha; Duke Humphrey; Sarah.
(see *starvation, hungry*)

FANATICAL
Peregrinus Proteus; Islam; Torquemada; Sir Edward Hugh Redgauntlet; Adolf Hilter; Isabella I; Zelotes; Old Mortality; Diogenes; Juggernaut; Hypatia; Habakkuk Mucklewrath; Riffian; Joanna Southcott.
(see *zeal, bigotry, enthusiastic, visionary*)

FANTASTIC

Erewhon; Judy; Poictesme; Alice in Wonderland; Grimm Brothers; Lucian; Rabelaisian; Cockaigne; Ikhnaton; Jules Verne; Pantagruel; Fata Morgana; Harlequin; Haroun al Raschid; Rider Haggard; Aristeas; H. G. Wells; Lagado; Sir John Mandeville; Brobdingnagian; Pierre Loti; Chimaera; Chiron; Horn Gate; Cervantean; Centaur; Gulliver; Don Adriano de Armado; Anubis; Alnaschar; Echidna; Peter Pan; Badebec; Bimini; Atlantis; Childe Rolande; Gryps; Xanadu; Swiftian.

(see *absurd, unreasonable, irrational, nonsense, ridiculous, incongruous, senseless, ludicrous, silly, stupid, ill-advised*)

FAR-AWAY

Thule; Utgard; Hyperboreans; Rhipaei Montes.

(see *remote, distant*)

FARCE

Vincent Crummles.

(see *amusing, lively, ludicrous, droll, comical, funny, ridiculous*)

FARMER

Vaissya; Saint Walston; John Greenleaf Whittier; Triptolemus Yellowley; Boeotian; Ops; Aristaeus; Centoatl; Triptolemus; Thestylis; Jean Millet; Cincinnatus; Hesiodic; Quirinus; Dandie Dinmont; John Ridd.

(see *agriculture, husbandry*)

FAR-REACHING

Maelstrom; Briarean.

(see *all-inclusiveness, comprehensive*)

FAR-SIGHTED

Heimdall.

(see *sight, sharp-sighted*)

FASCINATING

Queen of Hearts; Cleopatra; Punch; Witch of Endor; Sylvia.

(see *enchantment, spellbinder, charm, magic, captivating, witchcraft, sorceress*)

FASCIST

Mussolini; Adolf Hitler.

(see *autocratic, despotic*)

FASHIONABLE

Beau Nash; Beau Brummell; Jenkins; Godey; Miss Flora McFlimsey; Gothamite; Belgravian; Macaroni; Ninon de Lenclos; Sir Fopling Flutter; Lord Foppington; Silk-Stocking; Longchamps.

(see *modish, elegance, sartorial, finery*)

FAST (swift)

Jack and the Bean Stalk; Abaris; Liburnians; Milanion; Ladas; Jehu; Laelaps.

(see *swift, fleet, rapid, race, quick*)

FASTIDIOUS

Beau Nash; Anthony VanDyck; Epicurean.

(see *delicate, exquisite, finical*)

FASTING

Islam.

(see *abstinence, meatless, diet*)

FAT

Clara Peggoty; Rubensian; Tony Lumpkin; Dowsabel; Joseph Sedley; Hanswurst; Joe.

(see *corpulence, plump*)

FATAL

Andvaranaut; Lot's Wife; Ides of March; Lamia; Montagues and Capulets; Jocasta; Gorgons; Harmonia's Necklace; Rheingold; Morgante; Poly-

crates; Laius; Thomas Hardy; Krupp Family; Semele; Serbonian Bog.
(see *deadly, calamity, destruction, ruination, baneful, pernicious*)

FATE
Clotho; Moerae; Urganda; Atropos; Verthandi; Parcae; Norns; Lachesis; Skuld.
(see *destiny, doom, fortune*)

FATHER
Priam; Capulet; Sir Roger de Coverly; Anthony Absolute; Aegean; Tyndareus.
(see *progenitor, ancestor, forebear, parenthood, creator*)

FATHER-LOVE
Electra; Myrrha.
(see *incest, fixation*)

FATHER VS. SON
Sohrab; Rustam.
(see *unfilial, unpaternal*)

FATHOM (v.)
Wilhelm Roentgen.
(see *penetrating, diagnosis*)

FATUOUS
Mr. Turveydrop; Mrs. Partington.
(see *foolish, stupid, witless, absurd*)

FAULTFINDER
Momus; Smelfungus; Zoilus.
(see *critic, captious, carping, censorious, complaining*)

FAULTLESS
Bayard (2); Amy Dorrit; Grandisonianism.
(see *impeccable, perfection, innocence, blameless*)

FAUN
Donatello; Faunus.
(see *sylvan, nymph*)

FAVORED
Beau Brummell; Dick Whittington; Almack's; Lesbia; Benjamin; Israel; Antinous; Whiteheaded Boy; Joseph; Noah.
(see *indulgence, darling, beloved, choice, pampered*)

FAVORING
Favonius; Elbridge Gerry; Nike.
(see *advantage, benignant, helpfulness*)

FAWNING
Uncle Pumblechook; Jenkins.
(see *sycophant, obsequious, servility, flatterer*)

FEARFUL (afraid)
Menoetes; Emperor Jones; Harpagon; Cronus; Lady Macbeth; Lady Dedlock; Dionysius; Domitian; Slough of Despond.
(see *apprehensive, afraid, timidity, cowardly*)

FEARFUL (inspiring fear)
Tamerlane; Prinz Ruprecht; Vejovis; Berchta; Typhon-Typhoeus; Lemures; Erebus; Horace Walpole; Gigantes; Pavor; Timor; Medusa; La Befana; Fear Fortress; Banshee; Krupp Family; Demogorgon; Jormungandar; Rodilardus; Proserpina.
(see *dire, awe-inspiring, dreadful, horror, frightening*)

FEARLESS
Bayard (2); Leonidas; Jack the Giant-Killer; Laberius; Jolly Roger; Porthos; Boadicea; Charlotte Corday; Ferdinand Magellan; Molly Pitcher; Barnadine; Horace Greely; Jacksonian; Jean de La Fontaine; William Allen White.
(see *bold, courageous, daring, undaunted, bravery, intrepid, valor*)

FEAST
Lucullan; Neptune; Gloriana; Deipnosophistae.
(see *banquet, entertainment, reverly*)

FEAT
Rustam; Dorigen; Tom Hickathrift; Erich W. Houdini.
(see *exploits, achievement*)

FEATHER
Zal.
(see *plumes*)

FEATURES
Ve.
(see *face*)

FECUNDITY
Anaites; Fordicidia; Ishtar; Liber; Tellus; Isis.
(see *fertility, fruitfulness, prolific, productivity, reproductive*)

FEDERALIST
Jeffersonian; Hamiltonian.
(see *political groups*)

FEELING (n.)
Psyche.
(see *senses, sensitivity*)

FEIGNED
Simon Pure; Mrs. Candour; Miss Carolina Skeggs.
(see *affected, vanity, artificial, insincere, foppish, pretentious, conceited, coxcomical*)

FELICITY
Vaikuntha; Fung-hwang.
(see *appropriate, blissful, blessed, happiness*)

FEMININE
Bona Dea; Marie Laurencin; Rosalind; Florimel; Mut.
(see *soft, tenderness, delicate, womanly*)

FENCING
Laertes.
(see *duel, swordsman*)

FERMENT
Pierre Pérignon; Gambrinus.
(see *wine, beer*)

FEROCIOUS
Quilp; Morgante; Tezcatlipoca; Wild Boar of Ardennes; Lemnian; Manly; Myrmidons; Argantes; Berserker; Diocletian; Front de Boeuf; Garm.
(see *savage, wild, bloodthirsty, rapacious, barbarity, cruelty, inhumanity, ruthlessness*)

FERRYMAN
Charon; Phaon; Nessus.
(see *mariner*)

FERTILITY
Anaites; Pyrrha; Dagon; Feronia; Ge; Triptolemus; Cabiric; Ishtar; Hecuba; Flora; Fordicidia; Horae; Demeter (see Ceres); Pronuba; Thallo; Eleusinian; Priapus; Isis; Ops; Osiris; Freyja; Frey; Nefertem; Liber; Galli; Iasion; Lupercus; Selene; Silvanus; Hertha; Atargatis.
(see *abundance, amplitude, wealth, plenty, opulence, fecundity*)

FERVOR
Thaumaturgus.
(see *zeal, eager, vehemence, intensity, impassioned, ardent*)

FESTIVAL
Fescennine; Saturnalian.
(see *carnival, feast*)

FINALITY
Parthian; Areopagitical; Azrael; John Audley; Waterloo; Atropos.
(see *end*)

FINANCES
Moneta.
(see *money, investments, fortune-hunter*)

FINANCIER
J. P. Morgan; Rothschild; Lombard; Rockefeller; Marcus Licinius Crassus; Jay Gould; "Diamond Jim" Brady.
(see *money-lender, banker*)

FINE (n.)
Zanes.
(see *forfeit, penalty*)

FINERY
Freyja; Beau Tibbs; Gorgibus; Miss Flora McFlimsey; Manon (Lescaut); Silk-Stocking.
(see *dress, sartorial*)

FINGER-PRINTS
Alphonse Bertillon.
(see *identification*)

FINICAL
Protogenes.
(see *fastidious, dapper, foppish, coxcomical*)

FIRE
Muspel; Mulciber; Phlegethon; Yezd; Zoroaster; Yama; Promethean; Vulcan; Kunigunde; Abaddon; Padalon; Moloch; Agni; Uriel; Moses; Cacus; Cabiric; Utgard-Loki; Flamen;Tophet; Typhon-Typhoeus; Rudra; Ragnarok; Gibil; Sheol; Surtur; Sandalphon; Brigid of Kildare; Heraclitus; Democritus.
(see *conflagration, burning, blaze, kindle, ignite, pyre, flashes*)

FIRE-ALARM
Ucalegon.
(see *fireman*)

FIRE-BRAND
Althaea; Meleager.
(see *agitator, reformer, demagogue, torch*)

FIRE-BUG
Marcus Licinius Crassus; Herostratus.
(see *arson*)

FIREMAN
Vigiles.
(see *fire-alarm, non-inflammable*)

FIRM (adj.)
Barzillai; Saint Wulfstan.
(see *fixed, rigid, immovable, inflexible, steadfast, resolute*)

FIRST
Iapetus; Peregrine White.
(see *original, elementary, rudimentary, primeval, aboriginal*)

FIRST LADY
Dolly Madison.
(see *hospitality*)

FISH
Dagon; Oannes; Andvari; Matsya.
(see *ichthyologist*)

FISHERMAN
Rip Van Winkle; Oppian; Saint Ulric; Nimrod; Izaak Walton; Glaucus; Peter.
(see *angler*)

FISHFOOD
Vedius Pollio.
(see *worm*)

FLOGGING
Talus; Marsyas; Orbilian; Zobeide; Gymnopaedia.
(see *beating, lashing, whipping, thrashing, scourging*)

FLOOD
Ogyges; Og; Alrinach; Manu; Noah; Deucalion; Ut-Napishtim; Tiberinus.
(see *deluge, downpour*)

FLORID
John Lyly; Louis XIV.
(see *ornate, embellishment, decorative, luxurious, rococo*)

FLOWER GIRL
Nydia.
(see *gardens*)

FLOWERS
Nanna; Kama; Della Robbia; Chloris; Pincian; Flora; Hyacinthus.
(see *blossom, roses, heliotrope, lotus, sunflower*)

FLOWING
Hymettan; Hyblaean; Heidrum.
(see *smoothness, abundance*)

FLUENT
Thomas DeQuincey; Gorgias.
(see *glib, talkative, loquacious*)

FLUID
Saint Januarius.
(see *liquor*)

FLUNKEY
Jeames.
(see *lackey, manservant, servant, valet*)

FLUTE
Jubal; Krishna; Phrygian; Marsyas; Hamelin; Euterpe; Eumolpus; Syrinx.
(see *piper*)

FLYING
Abaris; Zetes; Asmodeus; Island of Saint Brandan; Peter Wilkins; Icarian; Loretto; Phrixus.
(see *winged, aviator*)

FOAM
Cytherea; Gambrinus; Dhanvantari; Hrimfaxe.
(see *beer, ocean-god*)

FOGGY
Niflheim; Trasimene Lake; Notus.
(see *mist*)

FOLIAGE
Sif.
(see *trees, plants*)

FOLK LORE
Uncle Remus; Grimm Brothers; Heinrich Heine.
(see *superstitious, fable*)

FOLLOW
Hamelin.
(see *pursuit, accompany, obedience*)

FOLLY
Asmodeus; Rasselas.
(see *foolish*)

FOOD
Apician; Delmonico; Deipnosophistae; Lucullan; Athenaean.
(see *sustenance, provisions, diet, epicurean, gastronome, hungry, eating*)

FOOLHARDY
Marsyas; Misenus; Phaëthon; Icarian.
(see *rash, venturesome, adventurous, reckless, hot-headed*)

FOOLISH
Jack Pudding; Sir Daguenet; Lot's Wife; Gothamite; Aeschines; Lentulus Sura; Basilisco; Janotism; Alice

Adams; Midas; Malvolio; Limbo; Alfred Lammle; Orgon; George Primrose; Epimetheus; Hanswurst; Damoetas; Launce; Baba Abdalla; Simple Simon; Quixotic; Trissotin; Calandrino; Dr. Dodipoll; Mrs. Partington; Scaramouch; Peter Schlemihl; Cousin Michel.
(see *dunce, senseless, silly, fatuous, inane, irrational, witless, clown, buffoon, nonsense, absurd, ridiculous, stupid*)

FOOLISH FEAR
Jabberwock.
(see *non-existent, unreal, unreasonable*)

FOOT-BATH
Sciron.
(see *bathe*)

FOOTMAN
Diggary; Jeames.
(see *lackey, manservant*)

FOOTPAD
Mohock; Gibbet.
(see *highwayman, brigand, bandit, robber, thievery, freebooter*)

FOOT-RACE
Phidippides; Hippomenes; Milanion; Atalanta.
(see *race, runner, marathon, sprinter*)

FOPPISH
Adonis; Lovelace; Lord Plausible; Jack Sixteen-String; Mr. Turveydrop; Mantalini; Macaroni; Beau Tibbs; Sir Fopling Flutter; Lord Foppington; Silk-Stocking; Sir Courtly Nice.
(see *affected, vanity, pretentious, conceited, coxcomical*)

FORBIDDEN
Lot's Wife; Bluebeard; Eve.
(see *taboo, ban, proscription*)

FORCE
Coxey's Army; Cadean; Ptah; Giacomuzzo Sforza.
(see *strength, power, might, energetic, vigor, coercion, compulsion*)

FORCED LABOR
Rameses; Gibeonite; Rehoboam.
(see *enslavement, slavery*)

FORCED MARRIAGE
Sganarelle; Onan.
(see *marriage, unloving*)

FOREBEAR (n.)
Manes; Manu; Tiki.
(see *ancestor*)

FORECLOSE
Tom Walker.
(see *prevent*)

FOREDOOMED
Banshee; White Ladies.
(see *predestination, doom*)

FOREIGN
Novensides.
(see *alien, exotic, outlandish, strange*)

FOREIGN MISSIONS
Mrs. Jellyby.
(see *missionary*)

FORERUNNER
John the Baptist.
(see *harbinger, herald*)

FORESIGHT
Johnny Appleseed; Alfred the Great; Rhoecus; Spurinna Vestritius.
(see *premonition, prudence, prognostication, anticipation*)

FORESTALL
Laius.
(see *foreclose, prevent*)

FORESTS
Artemis; Dryad; Dictynna; Silvanus; Tarzan; Diana.
(see *woods, grove*)

FORETELL
Jules Verne; Vala; Red Man; Zal; Postverta and Prorsa; Ocyroe; Xanthos; Nereus; Weird Sisters; Ibycus; Helenus; Dodonean; Witch of Endor; Veleda; Delphi; Sibylla; Huldah; Kalanos; Mother Shipton.
(see *prediction, prophecy, prophet, prophetess, prognostication, augury*)

FOREVER
Vanderdecken.
(see *perpetual, eternity, everlasting, endless*)

FOREWARN
Mother Carey.
(see *premonition*)

FORFEIT
Zanes.
(see *penalty, loss, confiscation*)

FORGE (n.)
Brontes; Tubal-Cain; Tvashtri; Mime; Wayland the Smith; Völund; Dactyli; Vulcan; Mulciber.
(see *smithy, furnace, blacksmith*)

FORGERY
Nora Helmer.
(see *counterfeit*)

FORGETFUL
Oeneus; Hippomenes; Mr. Redlaw; Epimetheus; Cassim Baba; Lethean; Lotophagi; Sigurd; Stultorum Feriae; Sheol.
(see *neglectful, inattentive, oblivion, carelessness, heedless, mindless, absent-minded*)

FORGIVING
Joseph; Gudrun; Azazel.
(see *pardon*)

FORMALITY
Petrarchan; Mozartean; Victorian; David Livingstone; Georgian; Mrs. Grundy; Henry M. Stanley.
(see *conventional, etiquette, punctilious, precision, methodical, ceremonious*)

FORMIDABLE
Barbarossa; Armada; Leviathanic.
(see *fearful, dreadful, awe-inspiring, terrifying, danger, tremendous*)

FORSAKEN
Laodamia; Effie Deans; Children in the Woods; Mariana.
(see *abandoned, deserted*)

FORSWEAR
Battus.
(see *renunciation, abandon*)

FORTHRIGHT
Philoxenus; Laberius.
(see *direct, outspoken, frank, unceremonious, brusque*)

FORTITUDE
Naomi; Gudrun; Phaedo; Stonewall Jackson; Hermione; Helena.
(see *endurance, bravery, resolute, patience*)

FORTRESS
Gibraltar.
(see *stronghold, castle, bulwark, safeguard, protection, security*)

FORTUNATE
Cinderella-like; Colonel Jack; Pandora; Fortunatus; Gyges; Cogia Hassan Alhabbal; Pip; Fortunio.
(see *lucky, success, prosperity, happiness, favored, advantage*)

(see *ingenuousness, sincerity, candid, outspoken, direct, artless, guileless, naive*)

FRANTIC
Thyia.
(see *frenzy, distracted, raving, madness*)

FRATERNAL
Dioscuri.
(see *brotherly*)

FRATRICIDE
Cambyses; Abimelech; Kriemhilde; Telamon; Timoleon; Cain; Seven against Thebes.
(see *unbrotherly*)

FRAUDULENCE
Pope Joan; Peter Funk; Thessalian; Laban; Ahab; Simon Pure; Cock Lane Ghost; Silas Wegg; William M. Tweed; Cagliostro; Subtle; Mrs. Veal; Alfred Lammle; Margaret Fox; Galinthias; Hippodamia; Dousterswivel; Friar Bungay; Stockwell Ghost.
(see *deceitful, dishonest, falsehood, sham, duplicity, imposture, guile, crafty, cheat, humbug*)

FRAYED
John Wemmick.
(see *dowdy*)

FREAK
Andhaba.
(see *monstrosity, dwarf, hunchback, hybrid, composite, malformed, misshapen*)

FREEBOOTER
Sir Henry Morgan; Jean Lafitte; Vikings; John Quelch; Rob Roy.
(see *robber, piracy, thievery, plunderer, buccaneer, pillage, highwayman, footpad, brigand, bandit, gangster, marauder*)

FREEDOM
Romany; Persius; Plataea; Timoleon; Thaddeus Kosciusko; Harmodius and Aristogiton; Bohemian; Garibaldian; Percy B. Shelley; Sinn Fein.
(see *independence, liberty-loving, deliverance, unrestrained*)

FREER
Flamininus; Messianic; Timoleon; Zerubbabel; Libertas; William Tell; Gideon; Abraham Lincoln; Moses; Esther; Gibil; Sigurd; Satyrane.
(see *emancipator, liberator*)

FREE-THINKER
Omar Khayyam; Robert Green Ingersoll; Desiderius Erasmus.
(see *skepticism, agnostic, atheist, unbeliever, un-godfearing, irreverent*)

FREE-WILL
Thélème.
(see *will, unrestrained, volition, spontaneous*)

FREEZING
Boreal.
(see *frost, frozen, cold, ice*)

FRENCH
Robert Macaire; Johnny Crapaud.
(see *nationalism*)

FRENZY
Thyia; Publius Decius Mus; Tzigane; Cybele; Rhea; Atys; Maenad; Zombi; Galli; Corybantic;Proetides; Pythian; Phrygian; Bassarid; Agave; Curetes.
(see *anger, wrathful, rage, fury, resentful, indignation, choleric, ill-tempered*)

FRESHEN
Cagliostro; Bimini.
(see *rejuvenation, refreshment, revive*)

FUNERAL
Neniae; Libitina; Old Mortality.
(see *burial, cemetery*)

FUNNY
Dickensian; Dooley.
(see *amusing, droll, facetious, comical, ludicrous*)

FURIES
Eumenides; Dirae.
(see *vengeance, avenge*)

FURNACE
Shadrach.
(see *smithy, blacksmith, forge*)

FURNITURE
Thomas Chippendale; Thomas Sheraton.
(see *bedstead, cradle*)

FURY
Cambyses; Berserker; Rumplestilzchen; Ivan the Terrible; Guido Franceschini.
(see *anger, wrathful, rage, frenzy, resentful, ill-tempered, choleric, indignation*)

FUSION
Hermaphroditus; Salmacis.
(see *blend, mixture, merging, hybrid*)

FUTILITY
Newcastle; Luggnagg; Danaides; Lantern Land; Mrs. Partington; Anna Karenina; Hamlet; Holophernes; Wertherian; Lollius; Thomas Hardy; Rebecca the Jewess; Sisyphean.
(see *useless, worthless, profitless, valueless, ineffectual*)

FUTURE
Janus; Postverta and Prorsa; Skuld.
(see *hereafter*)

G

GAIETY

Thelemite; La Traviata; Donnybrook Fair; Macaroni; D'Artagnan; Ninon de Lenclos; Pan; Mercutio; Lothario; Captain MacHeath; Nell Gwyn; Phaeacian; Pierrette; Tzigane; Sir Harry Wildair; Mohock; Robert Burns; Friar Tuck; Strauss; Romany; Goldsmithian; Charles Surface; Horatian (Horace); Saturnalian; James Steerforth.

(see *cheerful, lively, merriment, joy, joviality, mirth, hilarity, jolly, vivacious*)

GALL

Tobit.

(see *bitterness, rancorous, spiteful, malice, malign, acerbity, mordant*)

GALLANTRY

The Newcomes; Othello; Sir Roger de Coverly; Trissotin; Quixotic; Sir Harry Wildair; Mercutio; Cloelia; Excalibur; Jack and Jill; Uncle Toby; Timias; Cyrano de Bergerac; Rinaldo; Sir Thomas Malory; Pickwickian; Garibaldian; Will Honeycomb; Robert E. Lee; Leonidas; Lord Nelson; Glaucus; Squire of Dames; Lindor.

(see *courageous, chivalrous, bravery, valor, polite, courtesy, etiquette*)

GALLOWS

Gilderoy; Tess of the D'Urbervilles.

(see *hangman, hanged*)

GAMBLING

Judge Bridlegoose; Bret Harte; Asmodeus.

(see *dice, wager, card player*)

GAMES

Adrastus; Campus Martius; Pythian.

(see *sportsman, amusements, chess board, card player, dice, quoit*)

GAMIN

Gavroche.

(see *imp, boyish*)

GANGSTER

Laverna; Apache; Clodius.

(see *brigand, robber, highwayman*)

GARBLED

Mrs. Ramsbottom; Elbridge Gerry; Spoonerism.

(see *misrepresentation, misunderstood, miswriting*)

GARDENS

Diocletian; Alcinous; Ops; Vergilian; Libitina; Pincian; Flora; Vertumnus; Priapus; Andrew Fairservice; Saint Fiacre; Sallustian; Khem.

(see *flowers, fruit, orchard*)

GARLANDS

Della Robbia.

(see *flowers, fruit, foliage*)

GARMENTS

Jack of Newbury; Cestus; Herr Teufelsdroeckh; Miss Flora McFlimsey.

(see *apparel, clothing, dress*)

GARRET

Mimi.

(see *roof*)

GARRULOUS

Mrs. Nickleby; Sir Jerry Witwold; Corporal Trim; Lucio; Edie Ochiltree; Mrs. Sarah Gamp; Paulina; Lalage; Diggary; Alfred Jingle; Rev. Micah Balwhidder; Mrs.Caudle; Gratiano; Shallow; Mrs. Poyser.

(see *talkative, chatterbox, gossip, loquacious, long-winded*)

GASTRONOME
Deipnosophistae; Apician; Lucullan; Brillat-Savarin.
(see *epicurean, eating, dinner, appetite, gourmet*)

GATE
Portunus.
(see *entrance*)

GAUCHE
Diggary; Miss Betsy Thoughtless.
(see *awkward, clumsy, uncouth, ungraceful, tactless, blundering*)

GAUDY
Brummagem.
(see *tawdry, cheap, ostentatious, showy, meretricious, flashy*)

GAUNT
Miggs; El Greco.
(see *emaciated, lean, lanky, thin, skinny, slender, consumptive*)

GAZE
Vidar.
(see *stare*)

GEESE
Manlius Capitolinus; Mother Carey.
(see *goose*)

GEM-ENGRAVING
Pyrgoteles; Sabaean.
(see *precious stone, jewelry*)

GENEALOGY
Gotha; Lady Clara Vere de Vere.
(see *pedigreed, family-tree, ancestor, progenitor, lineage*)

GENERALSHIP
Wallenstein; Hamilcar; Lysander; Garibaldian; Marcus Furius Camillus; Robert E. Lee; Caesarean (2); Belisarius; Ulysses Grant; Scipio Africanus; Philip H. Sheridan; William T. Sherman.
(see *strategist, commander, chieftain*)

GENERATE
Nefertem; Khem.
(see *reproductive, procreation*)

GENEROSITY
Charlotte Corday; Bayard (2); La Befana; Baucis-Philemon; Johnny Appleseed; Alcestis; Sir Roger de Coverly; Captain Bountiful; Andrew Carnegie; Duncan; Portia; Dorcas; Martin of Tours; Betsy Trotwood; Timon; Johnsonian; Timias; Maggie Tulliver; Phaon; George Warrington; Tom Jones; Greatheart; Morgante; Maecenas; Godiva; Icarius; Isabella I; Baillie Nicol Jarvie; Nadejda von Meck; Boaz; Hugh Strap; Saturnalian; Santa Claus; Charles Surface; Honeywood; Rebekah.
(see *bounty, munificence, charitable, patron*)

GENIALITY
Mark Twain; Wife of Bath; Oliver Wendell Holmes; Chaucerian; Mr. Wardle; Anatole France; Thackerayan.
(see *cordiality, hearty, kindness, cheerful*)

GENIUS
Demogorgon; Periclean; Henry Ford; Homeric; Palamedes; Hippocrene; Fritz Kreisler; Paganini; Franz Liszt; Heliconian; Shakespearean.
(see *talent, ingenuity, inspiration, creative, inventive, proficient*)

GENRE
Jean Millet.
(see *painter*)

GENTILITY
Sara Battle; Mrs. Deborah Primrose;

GIFTS
Maecenas; Magi; Saint Nicholas; Prinz Ruprecht; Kriss Kringle; La Befana; Santa Claus; Saturnalian; White Ladies.
(see *present, donation, gratis, bonus, offering, prize, subsidize, bounty*)

GIGANTIC
Argante; Tityus; Briarean; Brobdingnagian; Nicneven; Titanic; Lapithae; Gargantuan; Enceladus; Fenrir; Front de Boeuf; Steropes; Hringham.
(see *tremendous, huge, massiveness, enormous, vast, prodigious*)

GILDED
Louis XV; Louis XIV.
(see *gold, ornate*)

GIRDLE
Hippolyte; Cestus.
(see *belt*)

GIRL-CRAZY
Tracy Tupman.
(see *passionate, philanderer, wife-hunter*)

GIRLISH
Juliet; Miranda; Agnes.
(see *virginity, maiden*)

GIRL-SHY
Watkins Tottle.
(see *misogyny*)

GLADIATOR
Spartacus.
(see *swordsman*)

GLANCE
Vidar.
(see *stare*)

GLARE (v.)
Euryale; Medusa.
(see *glower, menacing*)

GLEAN
Lityerses; Ruth.
(see *harvest*)

GLEE CLUB
Meistersinger.
(see *singer*)

GLENS
Napaeae.
(see *dell*)

GLIB
Jack-Amend-All.
(see *talkative, persuasion*)

GLITTERING
Watling Street.
(see *sparkling, flashes, bright*)

GLOOM
Emily Brontë; Cimmerian; Acheron; Avernian; Tullianum; Brontesque; Prisoner of Chillon; Thomas Gray; Weeping Philosopher; Hades; Stygian; Cocytean; Saturn.
(see *darkness, shade, cloud, sadness, dejected, despondent*)

GLORY
Periclean; Armada; Libertas; Gloriana; Spolia Opima; Solomon.
(see *fame, honor, illustrious, eminent, celebrity, exaltation, apotheosized, magnificence*)

GLOWER (v.)
Sir Edward Hugh Redgauntlet.
(see *stare, glare, lower*)

GLOWING
Iris.
(see *radiant, shining, bright*)

GLUTTON
Irus; Aulus Vitellius; Apician; Phaeacian; Rodilardus.
(see *gourmet, voracious, hungry, appetite*)

GOAL
Mecca; Manoa; Aurora Leigh; Thule; Fabulinus.
(see *destination*)

GOAT
Lupercus; Amalthaea; Master Leonard; Esmeralda; Heidrum.
(see *animals, herdsman*)

GOBLIN
Kuvera; Erlking; Phooka; Barguest.
(see *hobgoblin, bogy, specter, demon, apparition*)

GOD
Ka; Jumala; Olympian; Woden; Poseidon; Baal; Zeus; Baldur; Apollo; Endymion; Jacob's Ladder.
(see *demigod, divine, superhuman*)

GODDESS
Dryad; Cytherea; Egeria; Eilithyia; Napaeae; Oceanids; Oreads; Nymphs; Naiads; Maia.
(see *nymph, ocean-god, sea-deities*)

GOD-FEARING
Cornelius; Elihu; Obadiah; Gamaliel.
(see *reverence, piety, holiness, religious, devout, saintliness*)

GODLESS
Mezentius.
(see *irreligious, impiety, atheist, profanation, wickedness, un-godfearing*)

GOLD
Kilmansegg; Pactolus; Karoon; Incan; Woglinda, Wellgunda, and Flosshilda; Midas; Danaë; Benvenuto; El Dorado; Arimaspians; Nibelung; Hesperides; Phrygian; Mammon; Frothi; Sol; Shri; Sindre; Phrixus; Phidian.
(see *gilded, wealth, riches, hoard*)

GOLD-DIGGER
Fenton.
(see *venality, mercenary, money-mad*)

GOLD-SEEKER
Argonauts; Jason.
(see *fortune-hunter*)

GOLDSMITH
Della Robbia; Benvenuto Cellini.
(see *jewelry*)

GOOD (n.)
Ahuramazda; Zoroaster; Uriel; Ormuzd; Manichaeus.
(see *advantage, profit, welfare, prosperity, righteousness, virtue*)

GOOD FAIRY
Cinderella-like; Logistilla.
(see *fairy, benefactor, patroness*)

GOOD FAITH
Fides; Semo Sancus.
(see *honor, trustworthy*)

GOOD-NATURED
Will Wimble; Wife of Bath; Tom Jones; Susan Nipper; Madame Eglantine; John Bull; Ivan Ivanovitch.
(see *kindness, charitable, generosity, amiable, affable, benevolent, graciousness, obliging*)

GOOD OMEN
Fung-hwang.
(see *harbinger*)

GOOD SENSE
Sir Roger de Coverly; Joseph Andrews; Oliver Wendell Holmes.
(see *practical, intelligent*)

GOOSE
Seb.
(see *geese*)

GORGE (n.)
Thermopylae.
(see *mountainous*)

GORGEOUS
Duessa; P. T. Barnum.
(see *showy, glittering, shining, magnificence, splendor, resplendent*)

GOSSIP
Larunda; Sir Jerry Witwold; Mrs. Candour; Sir Benjamin Backbite; Anchises; Ascalaphus; Kriemhilde; Quidnunc; Lady Sneerwell; Caius Tranquillus Suetonius; Agravaine.
(see *tattler, talkative, chatterbox, busybody, rumor*)

GOURMET
Apician; Lucullan; Gioacchino Rossini; Hanswurst; Nellie Melba; Brillat-Savarin.
(see *banquet, epicurean, hungry, appetite, dinner, feast, gastronome*)

GOUT
Antonius Polemon.
(see *disease, sickly, ill health, valetudinarian*)

GOVERNESS
Jane Eyre.
(see *nurse*)

GOVERNOR
Agricola; Jumala.
(see *overseer, magistrate, supervisory*)

GRACE (physical)
Vaslav Nijinsky; Isadora Duncan; Taglioni; Anna Pavlova; Praxiteles; Dalcrozean; Rodinesque; Caryatids; Charis; Terpsichore; Graces; Thalia (see Muse); Belphoebe; Ariel; Juventas; Camilla; Burne-Jonesian; Apelles; Canephoroe; Lysippus; Gibsonesque; Edgard Degas; Gainsborough; Jean Watteau; Aglaia; Marius Petipa.
(see *comely, beautiful, dancing, rhythm*)

GRACELESS
Mrs. Jarley.
(see *puppet, awkward, gauche, clumsy*)

GRACIOUSNESS
Célimène; Lady Bountiful; Calidore; Mistress Quickly; Autocrat of the Breakfast Table; Addisonian; Dolly Madison; Elia; Robert E. Lee; Berchta; Mme. de Maintenon; Jenny Lind; Fritz Kreisler; Johnsonian; Florence Dombey; Anacreontic; Handel and Haydn; Gilbert and Sullivan.
(see *benevolent, good-natured, friendly, benignant, kindness*)

GRAFT (n.)
Jemmy Twitcher; Jugurtha.
(see *cheat, fraudulence, peculator, embezzlement*)

GRAIN
Dagon; Centoatl; Eleusinian; Proserpina; Ceres.
(see *seed, wheat, corn, rye, maize*)

GRAMMARIAN
Priscian; Pierre Larousse; Protagoras; Aristarchus.
(see *language, word-coiner*)

GRANDEUR
Michelangelo; Longinus; Homeric; Phidian.
(see *majesty, lofty, dignified, glory, eminent, magnificence, splendor, awe-inspiring*)

GROAN
Pan.
(see *moan, lamentation, mourning, bemoan, bewail*)

GROPE
Nydia.
(see *blindness*)

GROSS (adj.)
Caliban; Ryparographer; Baubo; Henry VIII; Emile Zola.
(see *sensuality, coarse, rude, vulgarity, obscenity, licentious*)

GROTESQUE
Punch; Gothic; Robotian; Toulouse-Lautrec.
(see *fantastic, bizarre, strange, hideous, whimsical, incongruous*)

GROTTOES
Oreads.
(see *cavern*)

GROUP ACTION
Cadean; Coxey's Army; Barabbas; Fourierist.
(see *mob-psychology*)

GROVE
Egeria.
(see *woods, forests*)

GRUESOME
Uma; Jack the Ripper; Gothic.
(see *frighten, ugliness, terrifying, grim*)

GRUFF
Betsy Trotwood.
(see *rude, impolite, bluff, brusque, discourteous*)

GRUMBLER
Miss Flora McFlimsey; Theophrastus.
(see *complaining, faultfinder*)

GUARANTEE (n.)
Palladium; Pythias.
(see *safeguard, protection, security*)

GUARDIAN
Oliver (1); Mimer; Penates; Graiae; Tanit; Pusan; Dr. Bartholo; Woglinda, Wellgunda, and Flosshilda; Manes; Talus; Nibelung; Mentor; Gryps; Michael; Argus-eyed; Arioch; Gibraltar; Heimdall; Fafner; Gelert.
(see *warder, protector, custodian, defender, tutelar*)

GUERRILLA
Lawrence of Arabia; Fra Diavolo; "Kit" Carson.
(see *frontiersman, woodsman*)

GUIDE
Karl Baedeker; Buffalo Bill; Pharos; Pausanias; Ciceronian; Nike; Ariadne; Sir Guyon; "Kit" Carson; Nestor; Moses; Aaron; Fortuna; Itineraria; George Bradshaw; Fabulinus.
(see *adviser, counselor, monitor, direct*)

GUILDS
Meistersinger; Asaphic; Tolbooth.
(see *labor movement*)

GUILE
Loki.
(see *crafty, cunning, artifice, deceitful, duplicity, subtlety, wily*)

GUILELESS
Nathanael.
(see *artless, unsophisticated, candid, frank, ingenuousness*)

GUILLOTINE
Louis XIV; Antoine Lavoisier; Marie Antoinette; Mme. Thérèse DeFarge.
(see *execution, behead, decapitation*)

H

HABILIMENTS
Herr Tuefelsdroeckh; Miss Flora McFlimsey.
(see *apparel, clothing, dress, raiment*)

HABITUAL
Commodore Trunnion.
(see *repetition, routine, inveterate*)

HADES
Amaimon; Avernian; Amenthes; Urugal; Sheol.
(see *lower world, infernal, underworld, Hell*)

HAG
Nicneven; Duessa; Hecate; Ulrica; Sycorax; Stheno; Loathly Lady.
(see *virago, termagant, anile, crone*)

HAIL
Nuriel; Alrinach; Telchines.
(see *rain, ice*)

HAIR
Berenice; Ahenobarbus; Ve; Cercopes; Don Ferolo Whiskerandos; Esau; Medusa; Arimaspians; Belinda; Orillo; Maritornes; Sif; Samson.
(see *curl, tresses, ringlet, lock, whiskers*)

HAIRBREADTH
James Fenimore Cooper; "Kit" Carson; Leatherstocking.
(see *adventurous, daring, reckless, foolhardy*)

HAIR SHIRT
Saint Theresa.
(see *penitential, penance, nun, ascetic*)

HAIR-SPLITTER
Osric.
(see *argumentative, controversy, disputatious*)

HALF-BREED
Ramona.
(see *hybrid*)

HALF-HEARTED
Laodicean.
(see *indifference, apathy, unconcerned*)

HALF-STARVED
Marchioness.
(see *hungry, ravenous, voracious*)

HALF-WITTED
Barnaby Rudge; Goose Gibbie.
(see *blockhead, moronic, simpleton*)

HALLOWED
Gettysburg; Semo Sancus.
(see *consecrated, dedication, sanctity, revered, veneration*)

HALLUCINATION
Belise.
(see *aberration, irregular, eccentric, peculiarity, illusion, deluded, mirage*)

HAMMER
Thrym; Mjöllnir; Sisera.
(see *forge, blacksmith, beating*)

HANDFUL
Gideon.
(see *little, small*)

Harry Gill; Scrooge; Père Grandet.
(see *cruelty, inexorable, implacable, relentless, unmerciful, merciless*)

HARDSHIP
Silas Marner; Okie.
(see *afflicted, burden, calamity, misfortune*)

HARDY
Cossack; Leif Ericson; Marsi; Vikings.
(see *strength, rigorous, robust, bold, bravery, daring*)

HAREM
Brigham Young; Xerxes; Fadladeen; Solomon; Rehoboam.
(see *polygamous, much-married*)

HARLOT
Camille; Dol Common; Paula Tanqueray; Tamar; Rahab; Doll Tearsheet; Nana; Theodora.
(see *whore, prostitute, courtesan, strumpet, demimondaine*)

HARMFUL
Auster; Njord; Amaimon; Sejus; Skadhi; Lerna.
(see *baneful, baleful, injurious, pernicious*)

HARMONY (accord)
Peleus; Pax; Graces; Irene; Concordia.
(see *accord, concord, unity, amity*)

HARMONY (musical)
Saint Cecilia; Giovanni Palestrina.
(see *music*)

HARP
Aeolian; Teirtu; Jubal.
(see *lyre*)

HARSH
Manlius; Zaleucus; Orbilian; Draconian; Carthaginian.
(see *stern, severity, cruelty, morose, hard-hearted*)

HARVEST
Linus; Jean Millet; Pentecost; Okie; Ops; Boaz; Consus; Terpsichore; Vacuna; Saint Roch; Lityerses; Saturn; Semo Sancus; Ceres.
(see *crops, productivity, agriculture, reap*)

HASTY
Tybalt; Peter the Hermit; Aegean; Pyramus.
(see *choleric, rash, reckless, swift, precipitous*)

HAT
Phrygian; Libertas; Gainsborough; Catherinette.
(see *cap, helmet*)

HATCHET
Giacomuzzo Sforza.
(see *split, cleave*)

HATEFUL
Lucifer; Domitian; Mussolini; Mezentius; Aelius Sejanus; Stygian.
(see *malevolence, malice, loathsome, villainy*)

HATRED
Zacocia; Emily Brontë; Roderigo; Alcaeus; Cain; Hamilcar; Gorboduc.
(see *hostility, enmity, malevolence*)

HAUGHTINESS
Laenas; Lady Clara Vere de Vere; Farinata; Edgar Ravenswood; Coriolanus; Junker; Vathek; Tarquinius Superbus; Mme. de Montespan; Sordello.
(see *arrogant, disdainful, supercilious, pride, snob*)

HEATHEN
Julian the Apostate; Saracen.
(see *pagan, idolatry, unconverted*)

HEAVEN
Uranus; Olympian; Usas; Tanit; Ymir; Urania (see Muse); Land o' the Leal; Jordan; Vaikuntha; Jumala; Watling Street; Elysian; Fortunatae Insulae; Swarga; Summanus; Breidablik; Padalon.
(see *sky, celestial, paradise*)

HEAVENLY MUSIC
Saint Cecilia.
(see *music of the spheres*)

HEAVY
Gunther.
(see *ponderous, massiveness, onerous, burden*)

HEDONIST
Zaluco; Xerxes; Volupia; Thelemite; Ninon de Lenclos; John Stuart Mill; Aristippus; Omar Khayyam; Gilgamesh.
(see *epicurean, voluptuary, selfish, pleasure*)

HEEDLESS
Hippoclides; Miss Betsy Thoughtless; Paulina; Ahaz.
(see *inattentive, unconcerned, carelessness, neglectful, thoughtless*)

HEEL
Krishna; Achilles.
(see *vulnerable*)

HEIFER
Io.
(see *cow*)

HEINOUS
Richard Varney.
(see *atrocity, hateful, villainy, infamous, wickedness*)

HEIR
Ascanius.
(see *inheritance, legacy*)

HEIRESS
Kilmansegg.
(see *rich, wealth*)

HEIRLOOM
Caius Verres.
(see *antiques*)

HELIOTROPE
Clytie.
(see *flowers*)

HELL
Avernian; Amaimon; Abigor; Yama, Zakkum; Tophet; Tartarus; Urugal; Acheron; Alastor; Naraka; Sam Hill; Cotton Mather; Koran; Eblis; Dantean; Barathron; Jonathan Edwards; Sheol; Stygian.
(see *punishment, tortured, infernal, lower world, underworld*)

HELMET
Mambrino.
(see *hat, cap*)

HELMSMAN
Palinurus; Menoetes; Sergestus.
(see *navigator, sailor, boatman*)

HELPFULNESS
Franklinian; David Harum; Hop o' My Thumb; Man Friday; Jack Robinson; Friar Tuck; Jack and Jill; Marcus Aurelius; Patroclus; Aladdin; Handy Andy; Thaddeus Kosciusko; Wagon Boy; Ariadne; Saint Christopher; Sabrina; Greatheart; Lohengrin; Eilithyia; Eumaeus; Matsya; Logistilla; Iolaus; Gunther; Candida.
(see *aid, assistance, succor, relief, alms, subsidize, bounty, ally*)

HELPLESSNESS
Naboth; Lazarus.
(see *powerless, defenseless, desperation*)

HEM AND HAW
Hottentotism.
(see *stammer, mumbling, inarticulate*)

HEMORRHAGE
Talus.
(see *blood*)

HENPECKED
George Dandin; Saint Keyne; Pinchwife; Skimmington; Jerry Sneak; Doctor Syntax; Mrs. Caudle; Don José.
(see *woman-hater, wife-beater*)

HERALD
Talthybius; Eos; Caducean; Paul Revere; Skirnir; Stentorian.
(see *announcer, messenger, harbinger, forerunner*)

HERBS
Dioscurides; Helios; Glaucus; Marsi; Melampus.
(see *vegetation, plants, botanist*)

HERDSMAN
Pales; Lycidas; Meliboeus; Tityrus; Damoetas; Thyrsis; Menalcas; Acis; Eurytion.
(see *shepherd, pastoral, rusticity*)

HEREAFTER
Skuld.
(see *future*)

HEREDITY
Aeschylean; Mendelian; Pelops; Jukes Family; Lamarckian; Lysander; Eupatridae.
(see *genealogy, family tree, lineage*)

HERETICAL
John Huss; Robert Green Ingersoll; Pico della Mirandola; John Wycliffe; Galileo; Savonarola.
(see *unbeliever, disagreement, sectarian, iconoclast*)

HERMIT
Gymnosophist; Saint Jerome; Montesinos; Pachomius; Walden Pond; Beltenebros; Santa Rosalia; Rousseauian; Troglodytae; Saint Giles; Guy of Warwick; John the Baptist; John Burroughs; Alexander Selkirk.
(see *ascetic, recluse, solitude, backwoods*)

HERO
Cid; Aeneas; Lars Porsena; Raleigh; Arnold von Winkelried; Ajax; Long Tom Coffin; Protesilaus; Miltiades; Rustam; Harmodius and Aristogiton; Telamon; Theseus; Achilles; Perseus; Peleus; Quetzalcoatl; Jesse James; Ivanhoe; Trojan; Saint George; Gideon; Odin; Jack the Giant-Killer; Ogier the Dane; Cornelius Nepos; Leonidas; Maccabees; Lord Nelson; Beowulf; Fierabras; Guy of Warwick; Siegfried; Tristan.
(see *romantic, tragic, rustic*)

HEROINE
Alcestis; Molly Pitcher; Helena; Mary Ambree; Electra; Antigone; Dido; Isolde; Brunhilde.
(see *romantic, tragic, rustic*)

HEROISM
Gettysburg; Thermopylae; Valhalla; Wagnerian; Euripidean; Calliope (see Muse); Marathon; Valley Forge.
(see *bold, courageous, daring, bravery, valor, prowess, intrepid, strength, power*)

HERONS
Ibycus.
(see *birds*)

HERO-WORSHIP
Boswellian; Livian.
(see *idolatry, apotheosized, demigod*)

HESITANCY
Lentulus Sura; Kilmansegg; Louis XVI; Buridan's Ass; Sganarelle; Athelstane.
(see *indecision, doubting, uncertainty, vacillation*)

HIDDEN
Trasimene Lake; Freudian; Delia; Admetus; Man with the Iron Mask; Amy Robsart; Rahab; Curetes; Havelock Ellis; Jack-in-the-Green; Sisera.
(see *concealed, secrecy, occultism, clandestine, abstruse, mystery, obscurity*)

HIDEOUS
Duessa; Kuvera; Ulrica; Typhon-Typhoeus; Yellow Dwarf; Quasimodo; Quilp; Melusina; Euryale; Medusa; Stheno; Loathly Lady.
(see *ugliness, dreadful, terrifying, horror*)

HIDE-OUT
Bermudas; Lycomedes.
(see *seclusion, isolation, outlaw*)

HIEROGLYPH
Trismegistus.
(see *writing, incomprehensible, code, undecipherable*)

HIGH
Gilderoy.
(see *lofty, tall*)

HIGH CASTE
Gainsborough; Brahmin.
(see *pedigreed, aristocratic, nobility*)

HIGH-PRICED
Pierre Renoir.
(see *costly*)

HIGH-SOULED
Rebecca the Jewess.
(see *magnanimous, generosity, unselfish*)

HIGH-SPIRITED
Diana Vernon; Hedda Gabler; Hezekiah.
(see *vivacious, spirited, nobleness*)

HIGHWAY
Watling Street; Sir John MacAdam; Appius Claudius Caecus.
(see *roads*)

HIGHWAYMAN
Captain MacHeath; Fra Diavolo; Bully Dawson; Jack Sixteen-String; Dick Turpin; Jemmy Twitcher; The Peachums; Paul Clifford; Jonathan Wild; Gamaliel Ratsey; Galloping Dick; Gibbet; Sinis; Sciron.
(see *brigand, robber, thievery, footpad, bandit, freebooter, marauder*)

HIKER
Walking Stewart.
(see *peripatetic, walk*)

HILARITY
Martin of Tours; Saturnalian.
(see *merriment, gaiety, mirth, jolly, joy, joviality, jubilation*)

HINDRANCE
Amy Robsart; Rosamond Vincy.
(see *impediment, encumbrance*)

HINDSIGHT
George Primrose; Epimetheus.
(see *impudent, unsuspecting*)

HINTING
Tacitean; Giottesque; Lara.
(see *suggestion, innuendo, insinuation, allusion*)

HIRE
Saint Fiacre.
(see *borrower, loan*)

HIRELING
Maximilian of Mexico.
(see *mercenary, puppet, cat's-paw*)

HISSING
Arthur Honegger.
(see *noisy, steam*)

HISTORIAN
Lord Macaulay; Thucydides; Livian; Josephus; Richard Hakluyt; Herodotean; Polybius; Asinius Pollio; Edward Gibbon.
(see *writer, past*)

HISTORY
Parian; Fasti; Clio (see Muse).
(see *annals, chronicle, record, biography*)

HISTRIONIC
Roscius.
(see *actor, theatrical, stage, drama*)

HIT (v.)
Jack-a-Lent.
(see *pelted, beating, strike, knockout, clashing*)

HOARD
Andvari; Gryps; Beowulf; Fafner.
(see *treasure, wealth, riches*)

HOAR-FROST
Andhrimner.
(see *frost, cold, ice, freezing, froze*)

HOAX
Bayes's Troops; Galinthias; Stockwell Ghost; Mrs. Veal; Jean Latude.
(see *sham, fraudulence, imposture, humbug, deceptive*)

HOBGOBLIN
Prinz Ruprecht; Robin Goodfellow; Empusa.
(see *apparition, bogy, specter, demon, goblin*)

HOBO
Jack London.
(see *vagrancy, wanderer, nomad, tramp*)

HOLD (v.)
Peleus.
(see *clasp, clutch, embrace, hug*)

HOLINESS
Santa Rosalia; Rishi; Paphnutius; Manichaeus; Mecca; Nama; Red Cross Knight; Saint Jerome; Rose of Lima; Pachomius; Grigori E. Rasputin; Simeon Stylites; Sakhrat; Sangreal.
(see *saintliness, sanctity, piety, purity, devout, divine*)

HOLLAND
Knickerbocker.
(see *Dutch*)

HOLLOW
Caleb Balderstone.
(see *insincere, treachery, pretense, faithless, unfeeling, hypocrisy*)

HOLOCAUST
Ragnarok; Surtur.
(see *destruction, slaughter, immolation, fire*)

HOMAGE
Magi.
(see *obeisance, reverence, respectful, deferential, worshipful, adoring*)

HOME
Penates.
(see *domestic, abode, residence, family, hearth*)

HOMELESS
Ishmael.
(see *outcast, exiled, expatriate*)

HOMELY
Dominie Sampson.
(see *plainness*)

HOMESICK
Demodocus.
(see *nostalgia, pining*)

HOMICIDAL
Cain; Modo.
(see *murder, filicide, tyrannicide, parricide, patricide, fratricide*)

HOMOSEXUALITY
Proustian; Lesbia; Laconian; Hyacinthus; Hylas; Pierre Louys; Agathon; Bathyllus; Sappho; Sergei Diaghilev.
(see *perversion, abnormality*)

HONESTY
Philoxenus; Diogenes; Theodore Dreiser; Brutus; Joseph Andrews; Tommy Atkins; Aristides; Orgon; Miramont; Clara Peggoty; Melantius; Cordelia; Fabricius; Manly; Galba; Oliver Twist; Montaigne; Gorgibus; Gonzalo; Richard Moniplies.
(see *integrity, justice, equitable, fidelity, sincerity, candid*)

HONEY
Mithras; Hyblaean; Hymettan; Glaucus; John the Baptist; Melissa.
(see *bees*)

HONOR
Cato the Censor; Canephoroe; Dike; Aepytus; Calidore; Pudicitia; Curius Dentatus; Olympian Games; Regulus; Jabez; Imogen; Timias; Attic; Nike; Lucretia; Madama Butterfly; Horatius Cocles; Gideon; Semo Sancus; Hernani.
(see *reputation, fame, virtue, esteem, chastity, purity*)

HOODWINK
Calandrino; Deianira; Aeschines.
(see *deceitful, cheat, trickery, dupe*)

HOOKS
Saint Catherine.
(see *tortured*)

HOPEFUL
Micawber; Spes; Helena; Leibnitzian.
(see *sanguine, optimistic, confidence, expectation*)

HOPELESS
Mignon; Cimmerian; Aladdin; The Newcomes; Sisyphean; Danaides; Serbonian Bog.
(see *desperation, abject, despondent, disconsolate, downcast*)

HORNS
Astolfo; Ammon; Amalthaea; Isis; Achelous; Gjallarhorn; Master Leonard; Hernani; Kneph.
(see *trumpet, cornucopia*)

HORROR
Mezentius; Echidna; Chimaera; Medusa; Harpies; Hela; Euryale; Graiae; Jocasta; Niflheim; Gothic; Horace Walpole; Edgar Allan Poe; Stheno.
(see *frighten, alarm, fearful, dire, dreadful*)

HORSE
Lapithae; Helios; Queen Labe; Arion; Dioscuri; Darius; Xanthos; Grani; Rhesus; Bayard (1); Rocinante; Tobias Hobson; Rosa Bonheur; Pacolet; Sleipnir; Houyhnm; Al Borak; Hrimfaxe.
(see *mare, mule, equine, war-horse*)

HUG

Nemean Lion; Peleus.

(see *embrace, clasp*)

HUGE

Gigantes; Tityus; Titanic; Polyphemus; Patagonian; Amarant; Leviathanic; Lapithae; Gargantuan; Enceladus; Aloidae; Cyclopean; Brobdingnagian; Behemoth; Ahiman; Og; Anak; Pantagruel; Orgoglio; Goliath; Hringham; Jormungandar; Junner; Jotunheim.

(see *vast, massiveness, bulk, gigantic*)

HUMANENESS

Hippocratic; Atalanta; Arion; Kubla Khan; Pierre Corneille; Jean Valjean; Parson Abraham Adams.

(see *kindness, benevolent, sympathetic, compassionate, clemency*)

HUMANIST

Quintilian.

(see *cultured*)

HUMANITARIAN

Friedrich Engels; Samaritan.

(see *philanthropic, altruistic*)

HUMANKIND

Prajapati; Midgard.

(see *man*)

HUMAN SACRIFICE

Tauri; Tlaloc; Ver Sacrum; Tezcatlipoca; Huitzilopochtli; Kali; Juggernaut.

(see *bloodshed, immolation, sacrifice*)

HUMBUG

Little Pedlington; Pecksniff; Silas Wegg.

(see *imposture, trickery, fraudulence*)

HUMILIATION

Brennus; Belisarius; Rigoletto; Masochism; Hezekiah; Miltiades; Isenbras; Job.

(see *abased, degradation, shamed*)

HUMILITY

Phaedrus; Nebuchadnezzar; Canute; Confucian; Cinderella-like; Uriah Heep; Abou Ben Adhem; William Allen White; Thomas Allworthy; Samaritan; Seneca the Younger.

(see *meekness, selflessness*)

HUMOR

Horatian (Horace); Democritus Junior; Aesop; Benedick; Lucian; Pantagruel; Elia; Joe Miller; Washington Irving; Anatole France; William Hogarth; Will Rogers; Thackerayan; Jane Austen; Mark Twain; Charles Lamb; Joseph Jefferson; Touchstone; Autocrat of the Breakfast Table; Oliver Wendell Holmes; Bret Harte; Jonathan Oldbuck; Mrs. Ramsbottom; David Harum; Marivaudage.

(see *facetious, witty, droll, funny, comical*)

HUNCHBACK

Quasimodo; Mayeux; Dick Deadeye; Rigoletto.

(see *deformed, misshapen, malformed*)

HUNDRED-EYED

Argus-eyed.

(see *vigilance*)

HUNDRED-HEADED

Typhon-Typhoeus.

(see *monstrosity*)

HUNGRY

Ugolino; Mithradates; Erysichthon; Milo; Freki; Barataria; Phineus; Duke Humphrey; Widenostrils; Joe.

(see *appetite, half-starved, voracious, ravenous*)

HUNTER
Tiglath-Pileser; Chiron; Oppian; Pan; Cephalus; Rahu; Mithradates; Ullur; Vacuna; Telamon; Orion; Gula; Esau; Freischuetz; Wild Boar of Ardennes; Wild Huntsman; Meleager; Nimrod; John Peel; David Crockett; Tartarin; Izdubar.
(see *outdoorsman, sportsman*)

HUNTRESS
Diana; Artemis; Belphoebe; Dictynna; Britomartis; Maid Marian; Camilla.
(see *sportswoman, Amazon*)

HURL
Gunther.
(see *throw, whirl*)

HURRICANE
Vaya; Typhon-Typhoeus.
(see *storm, wind*)

HUSBAND-HUNTER
Mother Bunch; Widow Barnaby; Agnes; Miss Tabitha Bramble; Rosa Dartle; Wife of Bath; Widow Wadman; Kate Hardcastle; Widow MacStinger; Mrs. Bardell; Candida.
(see *old maid, spinster*)

HUSBANDRY
Ops; Saint Walston; Sudra; Ceres.
(see *agriculture, agriculturist, farmer*)

HUSHED
Larunda.
(see *quiet, silence*)

HUSSAR
Richard Varney.
(see *cavalryman*)

HYBRID
Hippocampus; Harpy; Centaur; Pan; Chimaera; Echidna; Minotaur; Gryps; Luther Burbank; Sagittary; Narasinha; Snark.
(see *composite, half-breed, husbandry*)

HYDROGRAPHER
Louis Joliet.
(see *map-maker*)

HYDROTHERAPY
Kneippism.
(see *therapeutics*)

HYMN
Polyhymnia; Eumolpus; Paean; Giovanni Palestrina.
(see *song, psalmist*)

HYPERCRITICAL
Zoilus; Smelfungus.
(see *captious, carping, critic*)

HYPNOTISM
Phineas P. Quimby; Trilby; Franz Mesmer; Svengali.
(see *spellbinder, sleep*)

HYPOCHONDRIAC
Argan.
(see *morose, melancholy, despondent, dispirited*)

HYPOCRISY
Parolles; Ventidius; Regan; Job's Friends; Judas; Archimago; Balaam; Tartuffian; Pharisee; Foigard; Goneril; Archdeacon Frollo; Pecksniff; Uncle Pumblechook; Sir Jerry Witwold; Mrs. Jellyby; Ephraim Jenkinson; Reverend Mister Chadband; Uriah Heep; Jonathan Wild; Reynard; Sapphira; Joseph Surface; Rev. Mr. Stiggins; Mascarille; Maskwell; Olivia.
(see *insincere, deceitful, pretense*)

I

ICE
Nuriel; Ugolino; Hela; Kabibonokka.
(see *frozen, cold, frost, freezing, hail*)

ICHTHYOLOGIST
Alexander Agassiz.
(see *fish*)

ICONOCLAST
John Knox; Saint Eulalia; Ulrich Zwingli.
(see *heretic, reformer, protestant*)

IDEALISTIC
Poictesme; Plato; Periclean; Atlantis; Hyperboreans; Arcadian; Lalla Rookh; Coelebs; Aspasia; Utopian; Quixotic; Beatrice; Aucassin and Nicolette; Grandisonianism; Arrowsmith; Dostoievskian; Woodrow Wilson; Titian; Rousseauian; Hegelian; Sordello; Percy B. Shelley; Henriette; Hephzibah; Melchizedek.
(see *perfection, exemplary, imaginary, visionary, illusion*)

IDENTICAL
Oliver (2); Dromios; Twelve Peers; Menaechmus; Antipholus.
(see *alike, similarity, likeness, resemblance, twins, duplicate, equality*)

IDENTIFICATION
Euryclea; Ion; Perdita; Man with the Iron Mask; Alphonse Bertillon.
(see *recognition*)

IDEOLOGY
Karl Marx; Friedrich Engels.
(see *political science, labor movement*)

IDIOSYNCRATIC
Queer Card; Johnsonian; Marivaudage.
(see *peculiarity, eccentric, crotchety*)

IDLENESS
Tityre-Tu; Paridel; Nephelococcygia; Cockaigne; Marplot; Paul Pry; Will Wimble; Duke Humphrey; Rip Van Winkle; Lubberland; Les Rois Fainéants.
(see *indolence, lazy, unemployed, dawdling, lounger, ineffectual*)

IDOLATRY
Tiki; Tophet; Ahaz; Julian the Apostate; Baal; Ahab; Huldah; Habakkuk; Jeroboam; Athaliah; Terah.
(see *pagan, heathen*)

IDYLLIC
Hyperboreans; Theocritean; Lycidas; Tintagel; Arcadian; Atlantis; Mimi; Bessy Bell; Walden Pond; Paul and Virginie; Pierre Loti.
(see *pastoral, rusticity*)

IGNITE
Creusa; Muspel; Flamen; Mr. Krook.
(see *kindle, burning, fire, combustion*)

IGNOMINY
Ichabod; Scalae Gemoniae.
(see *dishonor, disgrace, disrepute, shame, opprobrious, scandal*)

IGNORANCE
Trimalchio; Winifred Jenkins; Miss Betsy Thoughtless; Miramont; Adriano de Armado; Squire Western; Mr. Tittlebat Titmouse; Perrin Dendin; Mrs. Malaprop; Topsy; Pinchwife;

ILLUSTRIOUS
Gotha; Chandra; John Hancock.
(see *brilliant, eminent, celebrity, glory, intellectual, unusual*)

IMAGE
Veronica; Laodamia.
(see *likeness, statue, resemblance*)

IMAGINARY
Alnaschar; Xanadu; Nephelococcygia; Belise; Centaur; Chimaera; Chiron; Poictesme; Cockaigne; Erewhon; Avalon; Weissnichtwo; Fata Morgana; Dick Whittington; Ivan Ivanovitch; El Dorado; Limbo; Fear Fortress; Jabberwock; Mrs. Harris; Lubberland; Snark.
(see *fictitious, fantastic, unreal, illusion, visions*)

IMAGINATION
Odyssey; Cervantean; Martial; Agathon; Mercutio; Quixotic; Alice in Wonderland; Rider Haggard; Edgar Allan Poe; William Butler Yeats; H. G. Wells; Jules Verne; Kubla Khan; E. Phillips Oppenheim; Giottesque; Spenserian; Kalpa-Tarou; Scheherezade.
(see *inventive, notion, hallucination, day-dream, dreamer*)

IMITATION
Veturius Mamurius; Caius Verres; Echo; Mme. Marie Tussaud; Brummagem; Bayes's Troops; Wardour Street; Poll Parrot; Pinchbeck; Sir John Millais; Salmoneus; Jannes and Jambres.
(see *copy, reproduction, resemblance, likeness, echo, duplicate*)

IMMATURE
Juventas; Tony Lumpkin; Nora Helmer.
(see *unfinished, unsophisticated, imperfect, youthful, juvenility*)

IMMERSION
Ran.
(see *baptism, overboard, drowning*)

IMMINENT
Ides of March; Phlegyas.
(see *threatening, danger, perilous*)

IMMODEST
Jezebel; Cotys.
(see *unchaste, indecorous, indelicate, shameless, gross, coarse, lewdness, obscenity*)

IMMOLATION
Nanna; Brunhilde; Evadne; Sardanapalus.
(see *sacrifice, self-destruction*)

IMMORALITY
Lentulus Sura; Marlovian; Theodora; Lysistrata; Ovidian; Julia; Lorenzo the Magnificent; Pierre Louys; Lady Bellaston; The Peachums; Catherine the Great; Dorian Gray; Marquis de Sade; Silk-Stocking.
(see *wickedness, vicious, sinful, corrupt, depravity, "loose," dissolute, profligacy, indecency, licentious*)

IMMORTALITY
Anasuya; Undine; Plato; Phaedo; Olympian; Ut-Napishtim; Phoenix; Valhalla; Orpheus; Osiris; Fortunatae Insulae; Asaphic; Dionysus Zagreus; Glaucus; Bifrost; Luggnagg; Beatrice; Struldbrugs; Proserpina.
(see *deathless, apotheosized, indestructible, perpetual, eternity, endless*)

IMMOVABLE
Rhadamanthine; Saint Wulfstan.
(see *fixed, stationary, unchangeable, inexorable*)

Abihu; Enceladus; Belshazzar; Aloidae; Phidian; Uzziah.
(see *irreverent, un-godfearing, irreligious, profanity, iniquity, blasphemous*)

IMPLACABLE
Hannibal; Lycus; Mme. Thérèse Defarge.
(see *vindictive, inexorable, unforgiving, relentless, rancorous, unmerciful, merciless, pitiless*)

IMPOLITE
Philoxenus.
(see *rude, discourteous, boorish, ill-mannered*)

IMPORTED
Novensides.
(see *alien, foreign, indigenous*)

IMPORTUNATE
Joe Dun; Guppy; Dangle.
(see *persistence, pressure, insistent*)

IMPOSSIBLE
Utopian; Gordius; Boethius; Navius; Eurystheus; Excalibur; Ossa on Pelion; Dorigen; Gulliver; Aladdin; Island of Saint Brandan; George Edward Pickett; Queen Dick.
(see *unattainable, absurd, impracticable*)

IMPOSTURE
Cagliostro; Laverna; Tartuffian; Rebeccaite; Abram-man; Subtle; Pope Joan; Foigard; Aimwell; Katerfelto; Margaret Fox; Alfred Lammle; Simon Pure; Cock Lane Ghost; Stockwell Ghost; Mokanna.
(see *cheat, deceitful, humbug, treachery, hoax, fraudulence, charlatan, mountebank*)

IMPOVERISHED
Catiline; Nigel Olifaunt.
(see *impecunious*)

IMPRACTICABLE
Alnaschar; Icarian; Nephelococcygia; Peter Schlemihl; Quixotic; Dora Spenlow.
(see *impossible*)

IMPREGNABLE
Ferracute; Gibraltar.
(see *invulnerable, invincible, unmovable*)

IMPREGNATE
Fordicidia.
(see *fecundity, fertility, pregnancy*)

IMPRESSIONISTIC
Claude Monet; Henry James; Max Reinhardt; Claude Debussy; Edouard Manet; Mary Cassatt; Proustian; James A. Whistler; Pierre Loti; Pierre Renoir; Maurice Ravel.
(see *sensuous*)

IMPRESSIVE
Wagnerian; Giovanni Palestrina.
(see *solemnity*)

IMPRINT
Veronica.
(see *image*)

IMPRISONMENT
Ephialtes; Danaë; Jean Latude; Edmond Dantès; Man in the Moon; Prisoner of Chillon; Bastille; Amy Dorrit; Jehoiachin; Abel Magwitch; Phidian.
(see *confinement, jail, captivity*)

IMPROBABLE
Lollius.
(see *impracticable*)

IMPROPRIETY
Priscian; Abihu; Hippoclides; Mrs. Mountstuart Jenkinson.
(see *indecorous, inappropriate*)

IMPROVEMENT
Theodorus; Luther Burbank.
(see *ameliorate, progressive, proficient*)

IMPRUDENT
Lady Teazle; Epimetheus.
(see *indiscretion, rash, injudicious, carelessness, ill-advised, heedless*)

IMPUDENT
Cagliostro; Thersitean; Weller; Pierrot; Falstaffian; Alfred Jingle; Crispin; Maid Marion; Puff.
(see *insolent, insulting, presumptuous, shameless, impertinent, rude, saucy, pert*)

IMPULSE
Pippa.
(see *influential, impetuous, incitement, sudden*)

IMPULSIVE
Zenobia; Gelert; Maggie Tulliver; Arthur Pendennis.
(see *rash, hasty, quick*)

IMPURE
Canace; Amfortas; Iachimo; Atys; Tess of the D'Urbervilles; Pierre Louys.
(see *adulterous, illicit, spurious, corrupt, unchaste, rakish, dissolute*)

INACCESSIBLE
Rhipaei Montes.
(see *unattainable*)

INACTIVE
Hypnos; Fabian; Jaques; Hamlet; Obermann.
(see *dormant, dilatory, quiet, drowsy, do-nothing, lethargy*)

INADEQUATE
Olibrius.
(see *defective, ineffectual, ineptitude, incompetence*)

INADVERTENT
Zaleucus; Cyparissus; Hypsipyle; Spoonerism.
(see *unintentional, heedless, neglectful, accidental*)

INANE
Simple Simon.
(see *silly, senseless, worthless, foolish, trifling*)

INAPPROPRIATE
Hippoclides; Olibrius; Mrs. Partington; Winifred Jenkins; Mrs. Malaprop; Saint Valentine; Mrs. Nickleby; Mrs. Mountstuart Jenkinson.
(see *malapropism, impropriety*)

INARTICULATE
Barkis; Tutivillus; Hottentotism.
(see *dumbness, mute, confusion, unintelligible*)

INARTISTIC
Philistines; Boeotian.
(see *philistine*)

INATTENTIVE
Cassim Baba.
(see *absent-minded, heedless, neglectful, carelessness*)

INAUSPICIOUS
Ides of March.
(see *unlucky, ill-luck, misfortune, ominous*)

INCARNATION
Krishna; Euphorbus; Vishnu.
(see *rebirth*)

INCENSE (n.)
Leucothea; Abihu.
(see *fragrant, perfume*)

INCEST
Thyestes; Arsinoë; Canace; Byblis; Ninon de Lenclos; Pasiphaë; Oedipus; Nyctymene; Jocasta; Myrrha; Sarah.
(see *father-love, brother-complex, impure, mother-complex*)

INCITEMENT
Peitho; Suada.
(see *exhortation, encouragement, persuasion*)

INCOGNITO
Trophonius; Vincentio; Guy of Warwick.
(see *unrecognized, disguise*)

INCOHERENT
Alfred Jingle.
(see *incongruous, inconsistent, meaningless, senseless*)

INCOMPETENCE
Martinus Scriblerus; Stellenbosche.
(see *unfit*)

INCOMPLETE
Lord Balmerino; Onan.
(see *unfinished, defective*)

INCOMPREHENSIBLE
Navius; Albert Einstein; Ka.
(see *unfathomable, unintelligible*)

INCONGRUOUS
Centaur; Chiron; Saint Valentine.
(see *absurd, unreasonable, irrational, fantastic, nonsense, ridiculous, senseless*)

INCONSEQUENTIAL
Batrachomyomachia; King of Yvetot; Mr. Toots.
(see *trivial, insignificant, petty*)

INCONSIDERATE
Harry Gill.
(see *uncharitable, thoughtless*)

INCONSISTENT
Trissotin; Jekyll-Hyde.
(see *incongruous, contradictions, alter, variable*)

INCONSOLABLE
Laodamia; Cyparissus; Weeping Philosopher.
(see *disconsolate, broken-hearted, heart-broken, cheerless*)

INCONSTANT
Rhoecus; Phebe.
(see *variable, fickle, mercurial, capricious, faithless, irresolute*)

INCONTINENCE
Argante; Eurytion.
(see *unchaste, lewdness, lascivious, lustful, licentious*)

INCORRECT
Priscian.
(see *ungrammatical, error, blundering, wrong*)

INCORRIGIBLE
Mirabel.
(see *remediless, hopeless, incurable, obdurate, shameless, recreant*)

INCORRUPTIBLE
Aristides; Fabricius.
(see *imperishable, indestructible, immortality, integrity*)

INDIRECT
Brom Bones.
(see *circuitous, roundabout*)

INDISCRETION
Anchises; Melusina; François Voltaire; Tattle; Emma Bovary.
(see *imprudent, rash, injudicious, unwise, heedless*)

INDISPENSABLE
Puss-in-Boots; Epaminondas; Monsieur Dupin.
(see *essential, necessity*)

INDISSOLUBLE
Hermaphroditus; Siamese.
(see *inseparable, indestructible, indivisible*)

INDISTINGUISHABLE
Saint Valentine; Dromios; Sosia; Antipholus.
(see *resemblance, alike, likeness*)

INDIVIDUALISTIC
Soren Kierkegaard; André Gide; Walt Whitman; Elbert Hubbard.
(see *personal, unique, characteristic, idiosyncratic*)

INDIVISIBLE
Parmenides.
(see *indissoluble, inseparable*)

INDOLENCE
Aulus Vitellius; Lotophagi; Phaeacian; Rosamond Vincy; Eugene Wrayburn; Gioacchino Rossini; Silk-Stocking; Cockaigne; Lubberland; Les Rois Fainéants.
(see *lazy, idleness, easy-going, inactive*)

INDOMITABLE
Fuzzy-Wuzzy.
(see *invincible, insurmountable*)

INDUCEMENT
Suada; Peitho.
(see *persuasion*)

INDULGENCE
Whiteheaded Boy; Mistress Quickly.
(see *graciousness, favored, pampered*)

INDUSTRIALIST
Andrew Carnegie; Robert Hawley Ingersoll; Henry Ford; Jack of Newbury.
(see *manufacturer*)

INEBRIATION
Lenaea; Eurytion; Trinculo; Thyia; Zombi; Martin of Tours; Eccles; Mr. Krook; Saint Vincent; Christopher Sly.
(see *alcoholism, drunkenness*)

INEDIBLE
Zakkum.
(see *bitterness, gall*)

INEFFECTUAL
Cassim Baba; Bumbledonian.
(see *inadequate, ineptitude, incompetence, useless, futility, powerless*)

INEPTITUDE
Lord Balmerino; Janotism; John-a-Dreams; Sir Martin Mar-All; Jeannot; Les Rois Fainéants.
(see *unfit, worthless, folly, foolish*)

INESCAPABLE
Daedalian; Javert; Serbonian Bog.
(see *inevitability, unavoidable*)

INEVITABILITY
Laius; Vala; Atropos; Vanderdecken; Ides of March; Old Man of the Sea.
(see *necessity, unavoidable*)

INEXHAUSTIBLE
Saehrimnir; Tityus; Launfal.
(see *indestructible, everlasting, self-renewing*)

INEXORABLE
Coriolanus; Hela; Thaukt; Pluto; Javert; Thomas Hardy.
(see *relentless, implacable, pitiless, merciless, hard-hearted, unmerciful*)

INEXPERIENCED
Moses Primrose; Johnny Newcome; Dangle; Miss Betsy Thoughtless.
(see *unpracticed, untrained, callow, greenhorn, immature*)

INEXPLICABLE
Erich W. Houdini; Ka.
(see *unintelligible, incomprehensible, inscrutable, mystery, enigmatic*)

INEXTRICABLE
Gordius.
(see *intricate, perplexity, entangled*)

INFALLIBLE
Odin; Fadladeen; Freischuetz.
(see *unerring, faultless, sure, oracular*)

INFAMOUS
Quisling; Gomorrah; Lentulus Sura.
(see *disrepute, disgrace, dishonor, base, heinous, shameless, scandal, ignominy, opprobrious*)

INFANT
Levana; Vaticanus.
(see *babies*)

INFANTICIDE
Aëdon; Medea; Cronus; Norma; Margaret; Effie Deans; Madge Wildfire; Procne.
(see *filicide*)

INFANTRY
Tommy Atkins.
(see *soldier, army*)

INFATUATION
Cupid; Ruy Blas.
(see *passionate, folly*)

INFECTION
Mr. Redlaw.
(see *contagion, disease, pollute, poison*)

INFERIORITY
Olibrius; Brummagem; Macflecknoe; Esau; King of Yvetot; Jukes Family; Alfred Adler; Samaritan; Jack-a-Lent.
(see *mediocrity, defective*)

INFERNAL
Anubis; Acheron; Hecate; Hela; Stygian; Hades; Tartarus; Pluto; Nastrond; Azazel; Lucifer; Belphegor; Abigor; Gustave Doré; Amaimon; Dantean.
(see *lower world, underworld, Hell, devil, diabolical, demon, fiendish, Satan*)

INFIDELITY
Hermione; Leonatus Posthumus; Pompeia; Tereus; Genevieve; Lady Dedlock; Hosea; Melissa.
(see *faithless, adulterous, unfaithful, disloyal*)

INFINITE
Shesha.
(see *endless, eternity, vast*)

INFLAMMABLE
Creusa; Muspel; Flamen; Mr. Krook.
(see *combustion, burning*)

INFLATED
Bombastes Furioso; Bottom.
(see *bombastic, turgid, magniloquence, grandiloquent, pompous, stilted, rhetoric*)

INFLEXIBLE
Medes and Persians.
(see *stiff, rigorous, immovable, firm, inexorable, obdurate*)

INFLUENTIAL
Cadean; Aegis; Pippa; Livia; Peitho; Abigor; Suada; Savonarola; Medici; Elbridge Gerry; Mme. Pompadour; Tammanyites; Godwinian; Calvinistic; Maelstrom; Wolseyan; Silk-Stocking.
(see *political influence, authoritative, momentous, potent, power*)

INFORMAL
Bertolde.
(see *unconventional, unceremonious, naturalness, easy-going, familiar, simplicity*)

INFORMATIONAL
George Bradshaw; Karl Baedeker; Pierre Larousse.
(see *enlightenment, instruction, advice*)

INFORMER
Aelius Sejanus; Munin; Mime; Ascalaphus; Larunda.
(see *tattler, divulge, gossip*)

INFRACTION
Zanes; Zaleucus.
(see *violation, non-observance, transgression, disobedience*)

INGENUITY
Acontius; Daedalian; Crichton; Galinthias; Perdix; Althaea; Palamedes; Fag; Bob Sawyer; Yankee; Puss-in-Boots; Franklinian; Scheherezade; Kate Hardcastle; Mascarille.
(see *inventive, skill, able, capable, clever*)

INGENUOUSNESS
Partridge; Mr. Toots; Henriette; Agnes.
(see *artless, candid, frank, guileless, honesty, sincerity, truthful, naive*)

INGLORIOUS
Ichabod.
(see *humiliation, dishonor, obscurity*)

INGRATITUDE
Hippomenes; Boethius; Goneril; Regan; Gunther; Mr. Redlaw; Roderick Random.
(see *ungrateful, thanklessness*)

INHERITANCE
Naboth; Esau; Nicodemus Boffin
(see *legacy, heir, heiress*)

INHOSPITABLE
Tauri; Hymir.
(see *unfriendly, ungenerous, intolerance, prejudice, bigotry*)

INHUMANITY
Vedius Pollio; Minotaur; Talus; Lemnian; Phalaris; Tauri; Tezcatlipoca; Jack Ketch.
(see *barbarity, cruelty, sadism, savage, brutal, ferocious*)

INIQUITY
Apollyon; Satanic; Habbakuk.
(see *injustice, wickedness, sin, sinful, evil, heinous*)

INITIALS
Major Bagstock.
(see *alphabet*)

INITIATED
Eleusinian.
(see *privacy, secrecy, esoteric, exclusive*)

INJUDICIOUS
Martinus Scriblerus.
(see *unwise, indiscretion, impudent, rash, ill-advised*)

INJURIOUS
Sejus.
(see *ill-luck, bad luck, harmful, baneful, disadvantageous, pernicious, ominous*)

INJUSTICE
Phaedrus; Boethius; Barabbas; Edmond Dantès; Alfred Dreyfus; Silas Marner; Jean Latude.
(see *unjust*)

IN-LAWS
George Dandin.
(see *mother-in-law, daughter-in-law, step-mother, son-in-law*)

INNKEEPER
Boniface; Martin of Tours; John Willet; Meg Dods; Tabard.
(see *landlord, landlady*)

INNOCENCE
Astraea; Arcadian; Hermione; Pelléas and Mélisande; Desdemona; Tenes; Hippolytus; Iphigenia; Miranda; Kunigunde; Pamela; Eden; Adam; Saint Ursula; Saint Wulfstan; Genevieve; Elaine; Pickwickian; Juliet; Virginia; Rev. Micah Balwhidder; Breidablik; Daisy Miller.
(see *innocuous, guileless, artless, purity, ingenuousness, simplicity, faultless, blameless*)

INNOCUOUS
Simple Simon.
(see *innocence*)

INNOVATOR
Philoxenus; Terpander; Ikhnaton; Iphicrates.
(see *unusual*)

INNUENDO
Tacitean; Lara; Phaedrus.
(see *suggestion, insinuation, allusion, indirect, hinting, sly*)

INOPPORTUNE
Sir Urian.
(see *disadvantageous*)

INORDINATE
Gargantuan.
(see *extravagance, intemperate, excessive*)

INQUISITION
Torquemada; Galileo.
(see *search, investigation, examining, zeal*)

INQUISITIVE
Socrates; Pandora; Argus-eyed; Lot's Wife; Quidnunc; Elsa; Marplot; Morgiana; Paul Pry; Pinkerton; Peeping Tom.
(see *curiosity, spy, investigation, prying, intrusive, meddlesome*)

INSANITY
Proetides; Caligula; Atys; Ophelia; Melampus; Gadarene; Orestes; Vaslav Nijinsky; Vincent van Gogh; Mignon; Lucy Ashton; Meg Merrilies; Guy de Maupassant; Richard Babley; Tom o'Bedlam; Robert Schumann; Madge Wildfire; Mr. Rochester; Haidee; Marquis de Sade; Lucia di Lammermoor; Maurice Ravel.
(see *deranged, lunatic, crazy, demented, aberration, madness*)

INSATIABLE
Barathron; Erysichthon.
(see *greed, voracious, rapacious*)

INSCRIPTION
Parian; John Chivery.
(see *writing*)

INSCRUTABLE
Ka; Sphinx; Mona Lisa; Man with the Iron Mask.
(see *incomprehensible, inexplicable, unfathomable, hidden, mystery*)

INSECTS
(see *ants, bees, cicada, grasshopper, worm, mosquito, spider*)

INSENSITIVE
Robotian.
(see *brutish, apathy, unfeeling, indifference, callous*)

INSEPARABLE
Charis; Lynceus; Zerbino; Nisus; Siamese; Saint Roch; Old Man of the Sea.
(see *indissoluble, indivisible*)

INSIDIOUS
Jesuit; Modred; Aelius Sejanus.
(see *artful, sly, guile, wily, crafty, cunning, intrigue, subtlety, designing, treachery*)

INSIGHT
Zal; Theophrastus.
(see *intuition, clairvoyant, penetrating, perspicacity*)

INSIGNIFICANT
Augustus Snodgrass; Pygmy; King of Yvetot; Sir Urian; Jack-a-Lent.
(see *unimportant, petty, trivial, picayune*)

INSINCERE
Parolles; Regan; Job's Friends; Sir Fretful Plagiary; Maskwell; Judas; Buncombe; Cheshire Cat; Major Bagstock; Lord Plausible.
(see *affected, feigned, faithless, dishonest, hollow, hypocrisy, double-dealing*)

INSINUATION
Tacitean; Lara; Phaedrus; Patelin; Lord Plausible.
(see *allusion, hinting, indirect, sly, suggestion, artful*)

INSISTENT
Joe Dun.
(see *persistence, importunate*)

INSOLENT
Antinous; Xerxes; Ephialtes; Steropes; Uncle Pumblechook; Sir Kay; Silas Wegg.
(see *abusive, rude, overbearing, domineering, contempt, insulting, supercilious*)

INSOLUBLE
Abdemon.
(see *inexplicable*)

INSOLVENT
Catiline; Alsatia; Queer Street; Robert Hawley Ingersoll.
(see "*broke,*" *indigent, needy, impecunious*)

INSOUCIANCE
Lyaeus; Hippoclides; Louis XV.
(see *nonchalant, indifference, apathy, unconcerned, carelessness*)

INSPIRATION
Bassarid; Abecedarians; Phryne; Parnassus; Rishi; Aganippe; Alumbrado; Euterpe; Phaedo; Pythian; Nymphs; Dulcinea; Urania (see Muse); Thalia (see Muse); Erato; Castalian; Tempe; Acestes; Polyhymnia; Pierian; Heliconian; Muse; Camenae; Hippocrene; Bandusia; Sleipnir; Calliope (see

Muse); Melpomene; Pegasus; Mahomet; Deborah; Joan of Arc; Tyrtaeus.
(see *exaltation, afflatus, elevating, impulse, insight, genius*)

INSTANT
Jack Robinson.
(see *quick, sudden, abrupt*)

INSTITUTIONS
John Howard.
(see *founder, establisher, organizer*)

INSTRUCTIVE
Seshat; Peripatetic; Giottesque.
(see *informational, enlightenment, scholarly, advice*)

INSTRUCTOR
Mentor; Panglossian; Eumolpus; Orbilian; Oannes; Rasiel; Gamaliel; Hoyle.
(see *schoolteacher, teacher, professor, counselor, adviser*)

INSTRUMENT (musical)
Jubal; Fritz Kreisler; Serge Rachmaninoff; Niccolo Paganini.
(see *music*)

INSUFFERABLE
Guppy.
(see *overbearing*)

INSULTING
Cambyses; Candaules; Latona; Peregrinus Proteus; Jim Crow; John Drum.
(see *abusive, reproachful, opprobrious, scurrilous, ribald, invective, calumnious, denunciatory, injurious, offensive, insolent*)

INSURANCE
Lloyd's.
(see *security*)

INSURMOUNTABLE
Ossa on Pelion.
(see *arduous*)

INSURRECTION
Cadean; Spartacus; Jacquerie; Rebeccaite; Roundheads; Wat Tyler; Waverly.
(see *rebellious, revolution, mutiny, uprising*)

INTAGLIO
Pyrgoteles.
(see *precious stone, jewelry*)

INTEGRITY
Benthamite; Xenocrates; Piso; Henry Ward Beecher; Thomas Allworthy.
(see *honesty, virtuous, good faith, ethical, upright*)

INTELLECTUAL
Aspasia; Laputa; Marcus Terentius Varro; Phrygian; Goddess of Reason; Kantian; Leibnitzian; Galileo; Leonardo da Vinci; Will Ladislaw; Lantern Land; Armande; Hypatia; Hugin; Periclean.
(see *learned, pedantic, scholarly*)

INTELLIGENT
Anaxagoras; Agesilaus; Phryne; Ahithophel; Mercutio; Attic; Cleopatra; Marco Polo; Portia; Riquet; Mayeux; Helen Keller; Christopher Columbus; Mme. Recamier; Mme. de Maintenon; Abraham Lincoln; Hoenir.
(see *thoughtful, astute, sagacity, shrewd*)

INTEMPERATE
Scythian; Bacchanal.
(see *inordinate, excessive, uncontrolled, unrestrained, self-indulgence, inebriation*)

INTENSITY
Alcaeus; Nama; Dantean; Romany; Bulwer-Lytton; Romeo; Proustian; Tschaikovsky; Dostoievskian.
(see *vehemence, ardent, earnest*)

INTERCESSOR
Sandalphon; Veturia and Volumnia.
(see *mediator*)

INTERFERENCE
Daitya; Paul Pry; Marplot.
(see *meddlesome, opposition, antagonistic*)

INTERMINABLE
Iliad; John Jarndyce.
(see *endless, long-winded, protracted, tedious*)

INTERNATIONAL
Fetiales; Lola Montez; Hugo Grotius; E. Phillips Oppenheim.
(see *cosmopolite*)

INTERNE
Bob Sawyer.
(see *doctor*)

INTERPRETER
Sopherim; Melampus; Tages; Euhemeristic; Zechariah; Joseph; Daniel.
(see *translator*)

INTERSECTION
Trivia.
(see *roads*)

INTERVAL
Hippomenes; Olympiad; Johannes Kepler.
(see *time, periodic, dates*)

INTERVENTION
Admetus.
(see *interference, mediator*)

INTIMIDATE
Laenas.
(see *browbeat, bully, frighten, coercion, terrifying, terrorist*)

INTOLERANCE
Torquemada; Alfred Dreyfus; Carlylean; Puritanic; Bloody Mary; Saint Bartholomew's Day.
(see *bigotry, prejudice, proscription, hatred, narrow-minded, persecution*)

INTOXICATED
Elpenor; Bassarid.
(see *inebriation, drunkenness, tippler, sot, besotted*)

INTRANSIGENCE
Tertullian; Giuseppe Mazzini; Perrin Dendin; Montagues and Capulets.
(see *uncompromising, obstinate, inflexible, strict*)

INTREPID
Argonauts; Boadicea; Barnadine; Ferdinand Magellan; Edgar Ravenswood; Christopher Columbus; Robert La Salle; Jack the Giant-Killer.
(see *bold, courageous, daring, undaunted, heroism, valor*)

INTRICATE
Alexandrianism; Minos; Daedalian; Serbonian Bog; Dred Scott Case.
(see *entangled, maze, complication*)

INTRIGUE
Xerxes; Terence; Volpone; Plautus; Ganelon; Dorine; Clodius; Athos; Scapino; Caiaphas; Aelius Sejanus; Lucrezia Borgia; Becky Sharp; Vanity Fair; Catherine the Great; Jesuit; E. Phillips Oppenheim; Machiavellian; Alexandre Dumas; Medici; Graustark; Grigori E. Rasputin; Jack-in-the-Green; Mascarille; Razor.
(see *plot, conspiracy, scheming, stratagem, machinator, ruse, wily*)

INTROSPECTION
Soren Kierkegaard; André Gide; Robert Schumann.
(see *pensive*)

INTROVERT
Carl G. Jung; Anna Karenina.
(see *brooding, self-absorption*)

INTRUSIVE
Marplot; Paul Pry.
(see *meddlesome, interference*)

INTUITION
Calpurnia; Zal.
(see *clairvoyant, insight, apprehensive*)

INVADER
Lars Porsena; Darius; Genseric; Genghis Khan; Attila; Huns; Hengist and Horsa; Sennacherib.
(see *marauder, attack*)

INVALID
Mary Baker Eddy.
(see *sickly, ill-health*)

INVECTIVE
Philippic; Pasquinade; Parian; Juvenalian; Shavian.
(see *abusive, reproachful, opprobrious, scurrilous, ribald, injurious, calumnious, denunciatory, offensive, insolent*)

INVENTIVE
Perdix; Palamedes; Lapithae; Mercury; Anaximander; Ea; Rhoecus; Jubal; Galileo; Giottesque; Alfred Nobel; Jules Verne; Samuel Morse; Edisonian; Robert Fulton; Quetzalcoatl; Bob Sawyer; Alexander Bell; Robinson Crusoe; Franklinian; Telchines.
(see *ingenuity, creative*)

INVESTIGATION
Ithuriel; Pliny the Elder; Copernican; Scotland Yard; Wilhelm Roentgen; John Howard; Pinkerton.
(see *examining, search, inquisition, research, explorer*)

INVESTMENTS
Get-Rich-Quick Wallingford.
(see *speculator*)

INVETERATE
Commodore Trunnion.
(see *obstinate, habitual, proficient*)

INVINCIBLE
Hector; Achilles; Agamemnon; Alexander the Great; Ron; Siegfried.
(see *indomitable*)

INVIOLABLE
Stygian; Plataea; Thrinacian.
(see *sacred, hallowed*)

INVISIBLE
Fortunatus; Mambrino; Perseus; Gyges; Autolycus; Abaris; Angelica; Jumala; Wayland the Smith; Jack the Giant-Killer; Gunther; Siegfried.
(see *unseen*)

INVITATION
Duke Humphrey.
(see *challenge*)

INVOLUNTARY
Deianira.
(see *automatic, spontaneous, mechanical, inadvertent, unintentional*)

INVOLVED
Laocoön.
(see *complication, maze, entangled, intricate*)

INVULNERABLE
Thetis; Utgard-Loki; Talus; Achilles; Siegfried; St. Sebastian.
(see *invincible*)

IRASCIBLE
Theodosius; Tatar; Capulet; Squire Western; Anthony Absolute.
(see *choleric, hot-headed, impatience, anger, wrathful*)

IRIDESCENT
Bifrost; Iris.
(see *light*)

IRISH
Teague; Sinn Fein.
(see *nationalism*)

IRON
Tubal-Cain; Etruscan; Dactyli; Krupp Family.
(see *cast-iron, steel*)

IRONY
Juvenalian; Lucian; Thomas Hardy; Thackerayan; Guy de Maupassant.
(see *sarcasm, mockery*)

IRRATIONAL
Leontes.
(see *absurd, unreasonable, fantastic, nonsense, ridiculous, incongruous, senseless, ludicrous, silly, stupid, ill-advised*)

IRREGULAR
Edgar Allan Poe; Francois Villon; Casanovian; Bohemian.
(see *aberration, eccentric, peculiarity, illusion, deluded, hallucination*)

IRRELEVANT
Mrs. Nickleby.
(see *inappropriate, illogical*)

IRRELIGIOUS
Protagoras; Pentheus; Lucretian; Nietzschean.
(see *irreverent, un-godfearing, godless, impiety, agnostic, atheist, blasphemous*)

IRREPLACEABLE
Epaminondas.
(see *necessity, essential, indispensable*)

IRRESISTIBLE
Lorelei; Leucothea; Siren; Cestus; Britomartis; Ligeia; Giselle; Jack the Giant-Killer; Maelstrom; Mata Hari.
(see *fascinating, enchantment, spellbinder*)

IRRESOLUTE
Palaemon; Buridan's Ass; Lentulus Sura; Louis XVI; Athelstane.
(see *undecided, indecision, inconstant, vacillation, hesitancy, fickle, mercurial*)

IRRESPONSIBLE
Manon (Lescaut): Pan; Spenlow and Jorkins; King Cole; Goldsmithian; Nell Gwyn.
(see *untrustworthy*)

IRREVERENT
Daitya; Ephialtes; Protagoras; Oeneus; Abihu; Mezentius; Capaneus; François Voltaire.
(see *irreligious, blasphemous, impiety, un-godfearing, profanation, godless*)

IRREVOCABLE
Rubicon; Norns.
(see *unchangeable, finality*)

IRRITABLE
Cambyses; Tatar; Lady Wishfort; Jonathan Oldbuck; Sir Fretful Plagiary.
(see *irascible, choleric, captious, fiery-tempered, petulance*)

J

JACKAL
Anubis.
(see *animals*)

JACKET
Zouave; Tabard.
(see *coat*)

JACK-OF-ALL-TRADES
Johannes Factotum; Till Eulenspiegel; Handy Andy.
(see *factotum, handyman*)

JAIL
Ephialtes; Tolbooth; Black Hole of Calcutta; John Howard; Amy Dorrit; Abel Magwitch; Tullianum; Bastille.
(see *penitentiary, imprisonment, lock-up, workhouse, dungeon, confinement, captivity*)

JAILER
Orgoglio; Solomon Pross; Aloidae.
(see *custodian, turnkey*)

JARGON
Babel; Widow Blackacre; Mumbo-Jumbo; Gertrude Stein.
(see *gibberish, nonsense, unintelligible, cant, senseless, meaningless*)

JAUNDICE
Walter Reed.
(see *disease*)

JAUNTY
Zouave.
(see *dapper, trimness, nimble, airy, dashing, showy, bedizened*)

JAVELIN
Meleager; Ron.
(see *spear, dart, missiles*)

JAW
Physignathus; Symplegades.
(see *face, features*)

JEALOUSY
Semele; Gorboduc; Aëdon; Cephalus; Agricola; Hylas; Juno; Hyacinthus; Medea; Leontes; Emilia; Nessus; Leonatus Posthumus; Eblis; Domitian; Desdemona; Malbecco; Roderigo; Doctor Bartholo; Kitely; Roxane; La Tosca; Othello; Wallenstein; Don José; Mariamne; Melissa; Sarah; Saul.
(see *suspicion, envy, watchful, vigilance, distrustful, apprehensive*)

JEER
Momus.
(see *derisive, scoffer, mockery, taunt, ridicule, sarcasm*)

JESTER
Moth; Pasquinade; Trinculo; Wamba; Rigoletto; Sir Daguenet; Yorick; Joe Miller.
(see *humor, buffoon, zany, droll, clown*)

JEWELRY
Monsieur Josse; Benvenuto Cellini; Brisingamen; Brummagem; Völund; Woglinda, Wellgunda, and Flosshilda; E. Phillips Oppenheim; "Diamond Jim" Brady.
(see *precious stone, gem-engraving, ruby, diamond, emerald, intaglio, necklace, ring, bracelet*)

JUMP
Salii; Hermod; Vaslav Nijinsky; Al Borak.
(see *leap*)

JUMPY
Saint Vitus.
(see *nervous, tension*)

JUSTICE
Forsete; Aeacus; Thor; Justinian; Varuna; Papinian; Artegal; Agesilaus; Servius Sulpicius Rufus; Aristides; Ibycus; Galba; Zeno; Nestor; Shamash; Domitius Ulpian; Rhadamanthine; Minos; Vigilantes; Ramman; Periander; Themis; Maat; Nemesis; Astraea; David; Benthamite; Samuel; Confucian; Dike; Arthurian; Poor Richard; John Jay; John Jarndyce; Pied Piper; Victor Hugo; George Washington; Gladstonian; Hugo Grotius.
(see *equitable, impartial, honesty, law, judgment*)

JUVENILITY
Juventas.
(see *youth, immature*)

K

KEEN (sharp)
Balmung; Heimdall; Vidar; Schamir.
(see *sharp, cleave, split*)

KEEN-SCENTED
Fanny Cleaver.
(see *nose, fragrant*)

KEEPER
Woglinda, Wellgunda, and Flosshilda; Gryps; Hesperides.
(see *custodian, caretaker, curator, watchman*)

KETTLE
Hymir.
(see *vat, basin*)

KEY
Sesame.
(see *entrance*)

KICK
Sciron.
(see *hit, strike*)

KIDNAPPER
Dirk Hatteraick.
(see *abduction*)

KILLER
Hodur; Modo; Lamia; Robert Macaire.
(see *murderer, assassin*)

KILL-JOY
Rev. Mr. Stiggins.
(see *doleful, mirthless, cheerless, morose, gloom*)

KINDLE
Flamen; Muspel.
(see *ignite, fire, inflammable*)

KINDNESS
Icarius; Azor; Baucis-Philemon; Manes; Mithras; Nausicaa; Nereus; Anatole France; Samaritan; Johnsonian; Mercutio; Lord Ogleby; Jonathan Oldbuck; Mrs. Jarley; Morgante; Abou Ben Adhem; Edie Ochiltree; Grimwig; Dick Swiveller; Uncle Toby; Betsy Trotwood; Captain Cuttle; King Log; Rev. Micah Balwhidder; Witch of Endor; Tom Pinch; John Jarndyce; Joe Gargery; Mr. Brownlow; Nicodemus Boffin.
(see *amiable, benignant, affectionate, benefactor, benevolent, generosity, charitable, philanthropic, sympathetic*)

KING
Oberon; Odin; Tarquinius Priscus; Sennacherib; Jehu; Menelaus; Croesus; Servius Tullius; Nebuchadnezzar; King Cole; Lear; Robert Bruce; King of Yvetot; Melchizedek; Saul; Numa; Romulus and Remus; Uzziah.
(see *emperor, prince, autocratic, tyrant, despotic*)

KISS
Rodinesque; Widow Wadman.
(see *embrace, hug*)

KITCHEN
Pistor.
(see *cookery, baker, recipes*)

KITE
Gilderoy; Franklinian.
(see *flying*)

KLEPTOMANIA
Mahu.
(see *steal, thievery*)

KNAVE
Scapino; Subtle; Nym; Machiavellian; Panurge; Richard Varney; Dousterswivel.
(see *villainy, scoundrel, rogue, rascal, swindler, mischief-maker, sharper, trickery*)

KNEEL
Santa Rosaiia.
(see *devout, prayer, piety*)

KNIGHTHOOD
Lancelot; Ivanhoe; Oliver (2); Orlando; Calidore; Lohengrin; Squire of Dames; Walter Scott; Parsifal; Sangreal; Scudamour; Gloriana; Amfortas; Tannhaeuser; Sir Thomas Malory; Galahad; Agravaine; Gawain; Almanzor; Launfal; Sir Mador.
(see *chivalrous, gallantry, paladin*)

KNITTING
Les Tricoteuses; Mme. Thérèse Defarge.
(see *weaver*)

KNOCKOUT
Amycus.
(see *slap, fisticuffs, boxing, beating, hit, strike*)

KNOWLEDGE
Onca; Minerva; Mimir; Imhotep; Delphi; Astolfo; Vach; Athena; Sesame; Jack the Giant-Killer; Thomas Aquinas; Pallas.
(see *learned, erudite, scholarly, studious, enlightenment, science, wit, judgment*)

KUDOS
Spolia Opima.
(see *glory, fame, praise*)

L

LABORATORY
Antoine Lavoisier; Lagado.
(see *chemist, physics, botanist, biologist, scientific*)

LABORER
Sudra; Gibeonite; Okie.
(see *worker, journeyman, artisan, toil*)

LABORIOUS
Eurystheus; Danaides; Sisyphean; Flaubertian; Salt River.
(see *industrious, painstaking, diligent, onerous, arduous*)

LABOR MOVEMENT
Karl Marx; Friedrich Engels.
(see *liberal, radical, guilds*)

LABOR-SAVING
Joseph Marie Jacquard.
(see *assembly line, efficiency*)

LACERATE
Naraka.
(see *mangle, claw, sunder, butchery, mayhem*)

LACHRYMOSE
Queen of Tears; Byblis; Job Trotter; Heliades; Weeping Philosopher.
(see *tears, weeping, crying, mourning, lamentation*)

LACKADAISICAL
Della Cruscans; Tilburina; John Chivery; Jeronimo.
(see *sentimentality, repining, pining, affected*)

LACKEY
Gibeonite.
(see *footman, flunkey, valet, manservant, servant*)

LACONIC
Pharnaces.
(see *terse, succinct, sententious, pithy, brief, close-mouthed, concise*)

LAD
Wagon Boy; Moth.
(see *youthful, juvenility, boyish*)

LADY-KILLER
Lord Nelson.
(see *philanderer, amorous, swain, lovers, paramour*)

LADY-LIKE
Marie Laurencin; Madame Eglantine.
(see *gentility, womanly, feminine, beautiful, graciousness*)

LADY-LOVE
Dulcinea; Fiametta; Callipolis; Callirrhoë; Delia.
(see *sweetheart, beloved, darling, mistress, paramour, lovers*)

LAGER
Gambrinus; Hymir.
(see *beer*)

LAGOON
Yacumama.
(see *pool*)

LAKE
Naiads; Juturna.
(see *nymph*)

LAME
Claudius; Hephaestus; Agesilaus; Völund; Saint Giles; Vulcan; Tyrtaeus.
(see *crippled*)

LAMENTATION
Aëdon; Daphnis; Cocytean; Jeremiad; Queen of Tears; Miss Flora McFlimsey; George Dandin; Byblis.
(see *wail, plaintive, lachrymose*)

LAMPOON
Hipponax; Archilochian; Alexander Pope; Juvenalian.
(see *satirism, ridicule, derisive, invective, censorious, sarcasm*)

LANCE
Ron.
(see *spear, javelin*)

LANDLADY
Mrs. Martha Bardell; Meg Dods.
(see *boarding-house mistress, proprietress, host*)

LANDLORD
Boniface; John Willet.
(see *innkeeper, host*)

LANDOWNER
Eupatridae; Rajput; William the Conqueror; Samuel Maverick.
(see *plantations, acres*)

LANDSCAPE
Ogygia; Jean Millet; Vincent van Gogh; Edouard Manet; Claude Monet.
(see *painter, scenic*)

LAND'S END
Thule.
(see *remote, distant*)

LANGUAGE
Euphuistic; Priscian; Aeschylean; Vach; Edmund Burke; Billingsgate; Jeronimo; Winifred Jenkins; Marivaudage.
(see *speech, diction, dialect, utterance, expression*)

LANGUOROUS
Lotophagi; Praxiteles; Della Cruscans; Tilburina; Lydia Languish; Silk-Stocking.
(see *ennui, lackadaisical, indolence, pining*)

LANKY
Philetas; Uncle Sam.
(see *tall, thin, skinny, lean, gaunt, emaciated*)

LANTERN
Pharos; Diogenes.
(see *light*)

LAP-DOG
Madame Eglantine.
(see *dog*)

LAPIDARY
Pyrgoteles.
(see *precious stone*)

LARGE
Brobdingnagian; Patagonian; Pantagruel.
(see *bulk, massiveness, huge, colossal, vast, gigantic, enormous, prodigious, amplitude*)

LARGE-EYED
Marie Laurencin; Hera.
(see *eye*)

LARGE-NOSED
Cyrano de Bergerac.
(see *big-nosed*)

LARGER
Benjamin.
(see *portion*)

LEAN
Rocinante; Philetas.
(see *skinny, thin, gaunt*)

LEAP
Salii; La Tosca; Vaslav Nijinsky; Hermod; Al Borak.
(see *jump*)

LEARNED
Laputa; Pierian; Eratosthenes; Onca; Suidas; Hippocratic; Thoth; Caius Laelius; Marcus Terentius Varro; Panglossian; Oannes; Atticus; Seshat; Aristotelian; Desiderius Erasmus; Cecil Rhodes; Ignatius Loyola; Confucian; Armande; Hafen Slawkenbergius; Cornelia Blimber; Lantern Land; Monsieur Jourdain; Ephraim Jenkinson; Sorbonist.
(see *erudite, studious, scholarly, bookish, bibliophile*)

LEATHER
Crispin.
(see *tanner, shoemaker*)

LECHERY
Tereus; Potiphar's Wife; Baptes; Silenus; Nessus; Obidicut; Mayeux; Grigori E. Rasputin; Archdeacon Frollo; La Tosca; Virginia; Argante; Marquis of Steyne; Iachimo; Silk-Stocking.
(see *lustful, lascivious, carnal, incontinence*)

LEECH
Struldbrugs; Mr. Turveydrop.
(see *parasite*)

LEER
Arthur Gride.
(see *scowl, contempt, derisive*)

LEFT-HANDED
Scaevola.
(see *hands, gauche*)

LEGACY
Persius.
(see *inheritance*)

LEGENDARY
Poictesme; Pantibiblia; Mme. Benoîton; Arthurian; Flying Dutchman; William Butler Yeats; Corinna.
(see *fictitious, fabulous, non-existent*)

LEGITIMACY
Levana; Tyndareus.
(see *birth, childbirth*)

LEISURE
Meander; Vacuna.
(see *ease*)

LENGTHY
John Jarndyce; Gustave Mahler.
(see *tedious, long-winded, protracted*)

LEPROSY
Uzziah.
(see *disease*)

LETHARGY
Hypnos; Lotophagi; Peter Klaus; Land of Nod.
(see *drowsy, sleep, hypnotism*)

LETTER-WRITER
Alciphron; Pliny the Younger; Ciceronian; Horace Walpole; Mme. de Sévigné.
(see *correspondence*)

LEVEL-HEADED
Agnes Wickfield; Sir Guyon.
(see *practical, unemotional, impartial, dispassionate*)

LEWDNESS
Paphian; Maritornes; Julia; Baptes; Acrasia; Belphegor.
(see *profligacy, lustful, lascivious*)

LEXICOGRAPHER
Suidas; Websterian; Pierre Larousse; Peter Mark Roget.
(see *encyclopedist*)

LIAR
Sinon; Sapphira; Galinthias; Laomedon; Ate; Naraka; Ananias; Nessus; Phaedra; Fag; Wooden Horse; Barber of Seville; Buncombe; Shallow; Mr. Fudge; Reynard; Peter Peebles; Baron Munchausen; Figaro; Mascarille.
(see *prevarication, equivocation, misrepresentation, falsehood*)

LIBEL
Mr. Fang.
(see *slander, defame, lampoon, malice, aspersion*)

LIBERAL (political)
Appius Claudius Caecus; Marius; Gracchi; Clarence Darrow; Giuseppe Mazzini; Charles Montesquieu; Lord Bryce; Gladstonian; Friedrich Engels; Lafayette.
(see *radical, labor movement*)

LIBERATED
Sleeping Beauty.
(see *deliverance, rescue*)

LIBERATOR
Harmodius and Aristogiton; Brutus; Messianic; Barbarossa; Gibil; Zerubbabel; Cassius; Libertas; Soter; Flamininus; Timoleon; Publicola; William Tell; Saint George; Garibaldian; Gideon; Thaddeus Kosciusko; Beowulf; Red Cross Knight; Kederli; Mordecai; Satyrane; Saul; Sinn Fein.
(see *emancipator, freer*)

LIBERTINE
Sallustian; Mirabel; Paridel; Thelemite; Iachimo; Lothario; Lovelace; James Steerforth; Don Juan; Roderick Random; Byronic; Charles Surface; Silk-Stocking.
(see *rakish, debauchee, profligacy, lechery*)

LIBERTY-LOVING
Sordello.
(see *patriotic, tyrannicide*)

LIBRARIAN
Aristarchus; Eratosthenes; Marcus Terentius Varro; Callimachus; Antonio Magliabecchi.
(see *bookish, bibliophile*)

LIBRARY
Pantibiblia; Pico della Mirandola.
(see *bookish, bibliophile, textbook*)

LICENTIOUS
Aulus Vitellius; Messalina; Ovidian; Poppaea; Petronius; Saturnalian; Belphegor; Faustina; Cotys; Julia; Emile Zola; Argante; Ninon de Lenclos; Mayeux; Mirabel; James Steerforth; Marquis of Steyne; Fescennine; Sir and Lady Pliant; Charles Surface; Philip Wharton; Marlovian; Marquis de Sade.
(see *unrestrained, dissolute, wanton*)

LIFE-GIVING
Sangreal; Ve; Lachesis; Ptah; Promethean.
(see *vitalize, revive, animate, reanimate*)

LIFE-GUARD
Ino.
(see *custodian, preserver*)

LIFELESS
Thanatos; Avernian; Mors.
(see *death*)

LIFE-LIKE
Apelles; Zeuxis; Myron's Cow; Mme. Marie Tussaud; Parrhasius' Curtain; Velasquez; Matsys' Fly.
(see *realistic, verisimilitude*)

LIFE-SIZE
Rubensian.
(see *large*)

LIGHT (n.)
Baldur; Eos; Phoebe and Phoebus; Sin; Semo Sancus; Shamash; Utu; Usas; Mithras; Harpocrates; Thia; Osiris; Surya; Helios; Hyperion; Saint Filumena; Zoroaster; Watling Street; Edisonian; Kohinoor; Phosphor.
(see *bright, dawn, sunlight, moon, moonlight, star, shining, glowing*)

LIGHT-FINGERED
Moll Cutpurse.
(see *shop-lift, thievery, pickpocket*)

LIGHT-HEADED
Lazarillo de Tormes; Master Froth.
(see *giddy, thoughtless, frivolous, indiscretion*)

LIGHT-HEARTED
Pippa; Ariel; Phebe; Elia; Gawain; Strauss.
(see *cheerful, gaiety, merriment, joy*)

LIGHTHOUSE
Palamedes; Pharos.
(see *guide*)

LIGHTNING
Capaneus; Agni; Salmoneus; Sagittary; Celadon; Dioscuri; Rudra; Zeus; Tages; Tlaloc; Typhon-Typhoeus; Vejovis; Semele; Indra.
(see *storm, thunder, thunderbolts, flashes*)

LIGHT-WEIGHT
Philetas.
(see *thin, lanky*)

LIKENESS
Dromios; Laodamia; Donatello; Menaechmus; Veronica; Antipholus; Sosia.
(see *alike, similarity, identical, resemblance, twins, duplicate, equality*)

LIMIT
Thule; Terminus.
(see *frontier, boundary, end*)

LIMPID
Hymettan; Hyblaean.
(see *clear, bright, purity*)

LINDEN TREE
Philyra.
(see *trees*)

LINEAGE
Rajput; Gotha; Libro d'Oro.
(see *genealogy, ancestor, progenitor, family tree*)

LINEN
Isis.
(see *spinner, weaver*)

LINGUIST
Pico della Mirandola; Zal; Mithradates; Prosper Mérimée; Lawrence of Arabia.
(see *language, translator*)

LION
Hippomenes; Milanion; St. Ignatius; St. Mark; Narasinha; Pakht.
(see *animals*)

LIQUEFY
Saint Januarius.
(see *melt*)

LIQUOR
John Barleycorn.
(see *alcoholism, ambrosia, mead*)

LISP
Lalage.
(see *speech*)

LIST (n.)
Libro d'Oro; Fasti.
(see *register*)

LITERAL
Martha; Cristoph Wagner.
(see *exactitude, strict, precision*)

LITIGIOUS
Lysias; Tom Styles; John Noakes; Peter Peebles; John Jarndyce.
(see *quarrelsome, bickering, disputatious, argumentative, contention*)

LITTERATEUR
Caius Laelius; Claudius; Nebo; Mme. Recamier; Quintilian; Longinus; Tabard; Maecenas; Dionysius; Aristarchus; Pantibiblia; Anatole France; Armande.
(see *bookish, bibliophile, writer*)

LITTLE
Vamana; Zaccheus.
(see *small, tiny, petite, dainty, diminutive, picayune, petty, trivial*)

LITURGICAL
Giovanni Palestrina.
(see *ecclesiastical, church-music*)

LIVELY
Nerissa; Dorine.
(see *amusing, active, nimble, vivacious, airy, spirited*)

LIVER
Tityus.
(see *entrails*)

LIVERYMAN
Tobias Hobson.
(see *horsemanship*)

LIVESTOCK
Apis.
(see *herdsman, cattle*)

LIVID
El Greco; Hela.
(see *black-and-blue, crushed, batterea*)

LOAFER
Sir Toby Belch; Eccles.
(see *lounger, idleness, indolence, vagrancy, lazy, dawdling*)

LOAN
Lombard.
(see *money-lender, usurer*)

LOATHSOME
Melusina.
(see *repellent, hateful*)

LOAVES
Fornax.
(see *baker, bread*)

LOBSTER
Palinurus.
(see *fish*)

LOCK (hair)
Sif; Belinda; Berenice.
(see *ringlet, curl*)

LOCKUP
Danaë; Tolbooth.
(see *jail, penitentiary, imprisonment, workhouse, dungeon*)

LOCOMOTIVE
Arthur Honegger.
(see *vehicle*)

LOFTY
Farinata; Ossian.
(see *sublimity, elevating, majesty, dignified, haughtiness, pride, arrogant*)

LOGARITHMS
Bernouilli.
(see *mathematics, geometry, trigonometry*)

LOGIC
Carneades; John Stuart Mill; Euhemeristic; Aristotelian; Adam Smith.
(see *reason, philosophy*)

LONELINESS
Peter Wilkins; Enoch Arden; Alexander Selkirk.
(see *solitude, isolation, segregation, deserted, separation, seclusion*)

LONGEVITY
Sarpedon; Methuselah; Tiresias; Theophrastus; Zanoni; Gorgias; Sarah; Terah; Seth; Shem.
(see *old age, old man*)

LONGING
Gerda; Daphnis; Urvashi; Stephen Foster; Auld Robin Gray.
(see *nostalgia, pining, repining, ennui, yearning*)

LONGITUDE
Eratosthenes.
(see *geographer, map-maker*)

LONG-LASTING
Mrs. Deborah Primrose; Iliad; Seven Sleepers of Ephesus; Epimenides.
(see *longevity, endurance, everlasting*)

LONG-LEGGED
Lysippus.
(see *lanky*)

LONG-NOSED
Hafen Slawkenbergius.
(see *big-nosed*)

LONG-SUFFERING
Job.
(see *patience, fortitude, submission, resignation*)

LONG-WINDED
Micawber.
(see *protracted, tedious, lengthy, loquacious*)

LOOK-OUT
Sister Anne.
(see *watch-tower, lighthouse, guide, vigilance*)

LOOM (n.)
Joseph Marie Jacquard.
(see *weaver*)

"LOOSE"
Lady Bellaston.
(see *immorality, dissolute, unchaste, wanton, licentious*)

LOOT
Vandalism; Vitalians; Varangians; Titus Vespasianus; Myrmidons; Telegonus; Lucius Mummius; Marcus Furius Camillus; Genseric; Achan; Caius Verres.
(see *plunderer, booty, spoils, freebooter, devastation, marauder, pillage*)

LOQUACIOUS
Lalage; Gratiano; Corporal Trim; Edie Ochiltree; Dogberry; Ciceronian.
(see *talkative, long-winded, garrulous, vociferous*)

LORD
Prajapati; Marquis of Carabas; Agamemnon.
(see *king, overlord, emperor, prince, autocratic, tyrant, despotic, dictator*)

cestis; Dido; Portia; Evangeline; Pierrette; Sigismunda; Rosemary; Haidee; Isolde; Perdita.

(see *mistress, concubine, demimondaine, courtesan, adulterous, passionate*)

LOVERS (male)

Abou Ben Adhem; Azor; Tannhaeuser; Romeo; Othello; Lancelot; Philander; Abdallah; Astrophel; Lord Nelson; Ivan Mazeppa; Acontius; Lord Ogleby; Ivanhoe; Pyramus; Sidney Carton; Selim; Hyacinthus; Haemon; Celadon; Hylas; Tattle; Strephon; John Chivery; Lindor; Scudamour.

(see *swain, philanderer, gallantry, passionate, adulterous*)

LOWBORN

Billingsgate.

(see *vulgarity, coarse, ill-mannered*)

LOW-COST

Wayland the Smith; Etienne de Silhouette.

(see *cheap, price-control*)

LOWER (scowl)

Sir Edward Hugh Redgauntlet.

(see *scowl, leer, glare, glower, menacing, stare*)

LOWER WORLD

Manes; Mercury; Amenthes; Sheol; Serapis; Mors; Larunda; Dantean; Anubis; Avernian; Dis; Echidna; Erebus; Nastrond; Padalon; Orcus; Hela; Proserpina; Utgard; Aeacus; Thanatos; Urugal; Vejovis; Hades; Isis; Amenti; Ifurin.

(see *underworld, infernal*)

LOYALTY

Achates; Aramis; Brunhilde; Dorigen; Damon and Pythias; Abdiel; the Peachums; Rev. Micah Balwhidder; Gunga Din; Athos; Blondel; Abiathar; Euryalus; Nutbrown Maid; Paul and Virginie; Land o' the Leal; Naomi; Nanna; Nisus; Thomas Paine; Ruth; Iolaus; Pythias; Jonathan; Uncas; Zadok; George Warrington; Horatio; Ben Hur; Ben Jonson; Imogen; Dirk Hatteraick; Patroclus; Pirithous; Jael; Theseus.

(see *allegiance, constancy, faithful, fidelity*)

LUCK (deities)

Lakshmi; Moerae; Tyche; Fortuna.

(see *destiny, chance, fortune, fate*)

LUCKY

Colonel Jack; Fortunio; Judge Bridlegoose; Gyges; Cogia Hassan Alhabbal; Pip.

(see *fortunate, prosperity, favored, success*)

LUDICROUS

Winifred Jenkins; Mrs. Partington; Lord Ogleby; Miss Lucretia MacTab; Mrs. Malaprop; Dickensian; Chaplinesque.

(see *absurd, unreasonable, irrational, fantastic, nonsense, ridiculous, incongruous, senseless, ill-advised, stupid, silly*)

LUGUBRIOUS

Gustave Mahler; Mrs. Gummidge.

(see *doleful, gloom, melancholy, sadness, mourning*)

LUKE-WARM

Laodicean.

(see *indifference, unconcerned*)

LUMINOUS

Sakhrat.

(see *bright, shining, glowing, radiant, resplendent*)

LUNAR

Tanit; Selene.

(see *moon, moonlight*)

LUNATIC
Luna; Abram-man; Tom o'Bedlam; Proetides.
(see *deranged, madness, insanity, demented, crazy*)

LURE (n.)
Marie Laurencin; Siren; Lorelei; Phryne; Lilith; Calypso; Aphrodisian; Pied Piper.
(see *alluring, tempter, enticement, persuasion*)

LURID
El Greco.
(see *gloom, pallor, dismal*)

LUSH
Gustave Mahler.
(see *ornate, embellishment, florid*)

LUSTFUL
Iachimo; Urvashi; Potiphar's Wife; Nessus; Virginia; Tess of the D'Urbervilles; Obidicut; Hippodamia; Sodoma; Sextus Tarquinius; Stheneboea; Appius Claudius; Pandemos.
(see *lascivious, lechery, lewdness, licentious, concupiscent*)

LUXURIOUS
Lydian; Etruscan; Capua; Phaeacian; Phrygian; Sybarite; Nephelococcygia; Cockaigne; Seric; Sabaean.
(see *epicurean, effeminate, sensuality, sensuous*)

LUXURY-LOVING
Sallustian; Lucullan; Alcinous; Sardanapalus; Poppaea; Manon (Lescaut); Mantalini; Silk-Stocking.
(see *voluptuary, self-indulgence, lavish, prodigal, extravagance, pleasure*)

LYING-IN
Suben.
(see *accouchement*)

LYRE
Jubal; Memnon; Thamyris; Terpander; Eumolpus.
(see *harp, music, instrument*)

LYRICAL (literature)
Catullan; Robert Burns; Goethe; John Keats; Heinrich Heine; Ben Jonson; Anton Chekhov; Byronic; Corinna; Anacreontic; Tennysonian; Blake-like; Algernon Swinburne.
(see *poetry*)

LYRICAL (music)
Stephen Foster; Jenny Lind; Chopinesque; Euterpe; Giacomo Puccini; Giuseppe Verdi; Franz Schubert; Terpander.
(see *melodious, tuneful, music*)

M

MACABRE
Uma; Horace Walpole; Jerry Cruncher; Lord Balmerino; Mme. Marie Tussaud.
(see *gruesome, ugliness, grim, terrifying, frighten*)

MACHINATOR
Aelius Sejanus; Machiavellian; Mascarille.
(see *conspiracy, plot, scheming, intrigue*)

MACHINE-MADE
Robotian.
(see *automatic, mechanical*)

MADNESS
Luna; Melampus; Agave; Caligula; Proetides; Pentheus; Orestes; Ophelia; Madge Wildfire; Gadarene; Adolf Hitler; Mr. Rochester; Lucy Ashton; Tom o'Bedlam; Vincent van Gogh; Lucia di Lammermoor.
(see *deranged, demented, insanity, crazy*)

MAGGOTS
Ymir.
(see *worm*)

MAGIC
Balisardo; Zanoni; Trismegistus; Apollonius; Britomartis; Dorigen; Astolfo; Golden Ass; Thoth; Alasnam; Alcinous; Aeaean; Aristeas; Marsi; Yogi; Anasuya; Abaris; Cestus; Perseus; Atlantes; Medea; Empedocles; Xanadu; Thessalian; Druids; Orillo; Prospero; Queen Labe; Vivian; Cagliostro; Archimago; Glaucus; Freischuetz; Pied Piper; Jack and the Bean Stalk; Ali Baba; Aladdin; Excalibur; Hiawatha; Avalon; Erich W. Houdini; Hamelin; Saehrimnir; Mambrino; Uther; Klingsor; Merlin; Jannes and Jambres; Telchines; Malagigi; Simon.
(see *sorcerer, sorceress, thaumaturgy, voodoo, enchantment, witchcraft, wizard*)

MAGISTRATE
Baillie Nicol Jarvie.
(see *officialdom*)

MAGNANIMOUS
Philaeni; Imogen.
(see *heroism, bravery, generosity, high-souled, nobleness, chivalrous, unselfish*)

MAGNETISM
Pippa; Grigori E. Rasputin; Franz Mesmer; Svengali.
(see *attractiveness, hypnotism*)

MAGNIFICENCE
Hadrian; Sallustian; Mausolus; Caesarean (2); Phidian; Capitoline; Grand Mogul; Solomon; Kubla Khan; Pharaoh; Genghis Khan; Nebuchadnezzar; Karoon; Babylonian; Wagnerian.
(see *grandeur, splendor, sublimity, riches, sumptuousness*)

MAGNILOQUENCE
John Lyly; Ossian.
(see *bombastic, grandiloquent, sesquipedalian, turgid, inflated, stilted*)

MAGNITUDE
Leviathanic; Hringham.
(see *gigantic, huge, colossal, vast, enormous, prodigious, large, bulk, massiveness*)

MAGPIES
Pierides.
(see *birds*)

MAIDEN
Parthenon; Minnehaha; Neaera; Sabine; Nausicaa; Chloë; Proserpina; Charis; Lady of Shalott; Priscilla, the Puritan Maid; Annie Laurie; Agnes; Sabrina.
(see *girl, youthful, virginity*)

MAIDSERVANT
Apsaras.
(see *servant*)

MAIL-ORDER
Robert Hawley Ingersoll.
(see *merchant*)

MAIZE
Centoatl.
(see *corn, grain, Aztec, agriculture*)

MAJESTY
Poseidon; Olympian; Pindaric; Jove; Parthenon; Capitoline; Agamemnon; Mrs. Siddons; Michelangelo; Brahmsian; Miltonic; Phidian; Hera.
(see *grandeur, lofty, high, dignified, imperial*)

MAKESHIFT
Stultorum Feriae.
(see *substitute, dilatory, alternative*)

MALAPROPISM
Priscian; Mrs. Slipslop; Mrs. Malaprop.
(see *inappropriate, impropriety, unfit, stupid, error*)

MALCONTENT
Shimei; Adullamite.
(see *discontent, dissatisfied, agitator, rebellious*)

MALEFACTOR
Abigor; Justice Overdo; Shimei; Lucifer; Ahriman.
(see *convicted, criminal, outlaw*)

MALEVOLENCE
Miggs; Yellow Dwarf; Phooka; Nicneven; Hagen.
(see *enmity, hostility, mischief-maker, bitterness, malice, resentful, envy*)

MALFORMED
Sindre; Dick Deadeye; Mayeux; Quasimodo; Rigoletto; Witch of Edmonton.
(see *misshapen, freak, deformed, monstrosity, hunchback, dwarf*)

MALICE
Graciosa; Tartuffian; Domitian; Abaddon; Quilp; Joseph Surface; Gorboduc; Sir Mungo Malagrowther; Erlking; Mrs. Candour; Miss Tabitha Bramble; Hagen; Nicneven; Old Nick; Luddites; Sir Benjamin Backbite; Basile.
(see *malevolence, rancorous, hatred, venomous, spiteful*)

MALIGN
Sejus; Phooka; Zoilus; Set; Caliban; Sebek; Nicneeven; Mumbo-Jumbo; Iago.
(see *injurious, baneful, baleful, pernicious, heinous*)

MALLEABLE
Nereus; Proteus; Telchines.
(see *flexible, change, metamorphosis, pliant*)

MALLET
Thrym.
(see *hammer*)

MALT BEER
Gambrinus; Sabazius; Hymir.
(see *ferment, drink*)

MALTREAT
Oliver (1).
(see *abusive, mistreatment*)

MAMA'S BOY
Little Lord Fauntleroy.
(see *sissified, effeminate*)

MAN (original)
Hoenir; Audhumla; Adam; Yama; Ask and Embla.
(see *original, ancestor, progenitor, lineage*)

MANAGEMENT
Telemachus; Frontinus; J. P. Morgan.
(see *control, direct, governor, surveillance*)

MAN-EATING
Stymphalian; Lycaon.
(see *cannibalism*)

MANEUVERS
Dalcrozean; Iphicrates.
(see *strategist, motion*)

MANGLE
Deiphobus; Naraka.
(see *lacerate, claw, sunder, butchery, mayhem*)

MANLINESS
Atlantes; Virtus; Dandie Dinmont; Adonis.
(see *heroism, bravery, courageous, daring, bold, intrepid*)

MANNERS
Petronius; Madame Eglantine; White Ladies.
(see *etiquette, deportment, courtesy, decorous, well-behaved*)

MAN-OF-WAR
Old Ironsides.
(see *ship*)

MANSERVANT
Lazarillo de Tormes; Xury.
(see *servant*)

MANSION
Breidablik.
(see *residence, abode, castle*)

MANSLAUGHTER
Modo.
(see *murder, homicidal, killer*)

MAN-TRAP
Rhampsinitus.
(see *ensnare, snare, stratagem, ambush*)

MANUFACTURER
Alfred Nobel; Jack of Newbury.
(see *assembly-line, industrialist*)

MANURE
Picumnus and Pilumnus.
(see *agriculture*)

MANY-HANDED
Yama; Uma; Kali.
(see *freak, composite*)

MANY-HEADED
Hydra; Shesha; Briarean; Typhon-Typhoeus.
(see *monstrosity, hybrid*)

MAP-MAKER
Anaximander; Eratosthenes; Heinrich Kiepert.
(see *geographer*)

MAR
Sir Martin Mar-All.
(see *harmful, disfigured, bungle, blundering, injurious*)

MARATHON
Ladas.
(see *runner, race, foot-race*)

MARAUDER
Telegonus; Vitalians; Vikings; Huns; Leleges; Varangians; Sir Henry Morgan.
(see *bandit, brigand, desperado, freebooter, plunderer, pillage, ravaging*)

MARBLE
Parian; Parthenon; Hymettan.
(see *rocks, stones*)

MARE
Queen Labe; Glaucus.
(see *horse*)

MARINE
Tiamat; Hippocampus.
(see *ocean-god, sea*)

MARINER
Peter Wilkins; Mother Carey; Carthaginian; Lloyd's; Vasco da Gama; Herman Melville.
(see *sailor, navigator, seafaring, privateer, corsair, buccaneer*)

MARKSMANSHIP
Freischuetz; Parthian; Adam Bell; Teucer; William Tell; David Crockett; Annie Oakley; William of Cloudeslie; Nimrod; Izdubar; Gungnir.
(see *aim, archer, bowman, targeteer*)

MAROONED
Prospero; Robinson Crusoe; Alexander Selkirk.
(see *shipwreck*)

MARRIAGE
Brigham Young; Vor; Talassius; Sif; Demeter (see Ceres); Cecrops; Hymeneal; Frigga; Semo Sancus; Mother Bunch; Pandemos; Pronuba; Yue-Laou; Hermaphroditus; Hera.
(see *wedlock, nuptial, matrimony, bride, bridegroom, bridesmaid*)

MARRIAGEABLE
Rosa Dartle; Benedick; Coelebs.
(see *old maid, husband-hunter, wife-hunter, bachelor*)

MARSH
Phooka; Serbonian Bog; Slough of Despond; Nastrond.
(see *bog, mire, swamp*)

MARTIAL
Junker; Kumara; Saxnot; Mars; Marsi; Gradasso; Tullus Hostilius; Tyrtaeus.
(see *militaristic, belligerent, war, soldier*)

MARTINET
Commodore Trunnion; Jean Martinet.
(see *drill, discipline, severity, strict*)

MARTYRDOM
Regulus; Dorothea; Pancras; Saint Lawrence; Saint Filumena; Saint Eulalia; Saint Pantaleon; Saint Denis; Saint Valentine; Saint Vitus; Saint Paul; Saint Catherine; Saint Ursula; Saint George; Saint Cecilia; Saint Vincent; Saint Lucia; Saint Januarius; Joan of Arc; Isaac; Saint Stephen; Hugh of Lincoln; Wat Tyler; John Brown; Agnes; St. Ignatius; St. James; Peter; Sergius; St. Sebastian.
(see *self-sacrificing, stoned, saintliness*)

MASCULINITY (female)
Enyo; Hippolyte; Maid Marian; Amazonian; Thalestris.
(see *unfeminine, amazon, virago, scold, shrew, termagant*)

MASCULINITY (male)
Rodinesque; Grandisonianism.
(see *manliness, brawn, muscular, robust, power*)

MASKED
Gamaliel Ratsey; Man with the Iron Mask.
(see *disguise, incognito, veil*)

MASONRY
Stonehenge; Pelasgians; Baruch.
(see *stones, stone-pile, builder*)

MASS (musical)
Giovanni Palestrina.
(see *church-music, requiem*)

MASSACRE
Ivan the Terrible; Mithradates; Ron; Marius; Lucius Mummius; Huitzilopochtli; Saint Bartholomew's Day; Esther.
(see *butchery, slaughter, carnage*)

MASSIVENESS
Leviathanic; Hringham; Rodinesque.
(see *bulk, gigantic, huge, colossal, vast, enormous, prodigious*)

MASTER-RACE
Nietzschean.
(see *superiority, superiority-complex*)

MASTICATE
Fletcherize.
(see *bite*)

MATERIALISTIC
Mammon; Philistines; Worldly Wiseman; Babbitt; Mrs. Martha Bardell.
(see *philistine, worldliness*)

MATERNITY
Suben.
(see *accouchement, lying-in, delivery, childbirth, birth*)

MATES
Mejnoun and Leilah; Jack and Jill.
(see *lovers, couple*)

MATHEMATICS
Isaac Newton; Eratosthenes; Bernouilli; Hipparchus; Leibnitzian; Euclidean.
(see *calculus, geometry, trigonometry, logarithms*)

MATRICIDE
Alcmaeon; Agrippina the Younger; Electra; Nero; Orestes.
(see *murder, homicidal*)

MATRIMONY
Picumnus and Pilumnus; Mother Bunch.
(see *marriage*)

MATRON OF HONOR
Pronuba.
(see *bride*)

MATTER-OF-FACT
Gradgrind.
(see *practical, prosaic, unimaginative, literal*)

MAUSOLEUM
Taj Mahal; Mausolus.
(see *tomb, burial, sepulcher*)

MAWKISH
Della Cruscans; Tilburina.
(see *lovelorn, sentimentality, vapid*)

MAXIMS
Hesiodic; Goethe.
(see *proverb, sententious, axioms*)

MAYHEM
Absyrtus; Deiphobus; Osiris; Pelias; Jack the Ripper.
(see *mutilation, piecemeal, lacerate, butchery*)

MAZE
Daedalian.
(see *intricate, bewilderment, perplexity, confusion*)

MEAD
Heidrum.
(see *liquor*)

MEAL-TICKET
Gnatho.
(see *parasite*)

MEANDERING
Salt River; Meander.
(see *wanderer, indirect, roundabout, slow*)

MEANINGLESS
Talassius; Barataria; Mrs. Ramsbottom; Mumbo-Jumbo; Winifred Jenkins.
(see *senseless, unintelligible, foolish, nonsense, absurd*)

MEAN-SPIRITED
Jonas Chuzzlewit; Joseph Surface; Old Nick; Malbecco; Wandering Willie.
(see *ungenerous, malice*)

MEATLESS
Mazdakite.
(see *fasting, vegetarianism, diet*)

MECHANICAL
Galileo; Mrs. Jarley; Teirtu; Robotian; Bradley Headstone; Sudra; Robert Fulton.
(see *automatic, repetition, involuntary, self-starting*)

MEDALLION
Benvenuto Cellini; Della Robbia.
(see *sculpture, bas-relief*)

MEDALS
Jonathan Oldbuck.
(see *prize, reward, archaeological, antiquary*)

MEDDLESOME
Amorphus; Ascalaphus; Lot's Wife; Witchfinder General; Andrew Fairservice; Marplot; Quidnunc; Capulet; Paul Pry; Grigori E. Rasputin.
(see *busybody, interference, prying, curiosity*)

MEDIATOR
Mithras; Sandalphon.
(see *arbiter, intercessor, umpire*)

MEDICINE
Vaidya; Dhanvantari; Podalirius; Gilead; Ocyroë; Paean; Imhotep; Saint Pantaleon; Caducean; Celsus; Hippocratic; Dioscurides; Aesculapian; Empedocles.
(see *herbs, curative, healing, doctor*)

MEDICINE MAN
Buffalo Bill.
(see *apothecary, druggist, pharmacist*)

MEDIOCRITY
Will Ladislaw; Grub-Streeter.
(see *inferiority, commonplace*)

MEDITATION
Siva; Polyhymnia; Rodinesque; Yogi; Martha.
(see *contemplative, pensive, thoughtful, reflective*)

MEDIUM (spiritualist)
Zanoni; Witch of Endor; Margaret Fox.
(see *fortune-telling, clairvoyant, prophet, spiritualist*)

MEEKNESS
Fierabras; Enoch Wray; Gethsemane; Lucy Ashton; Pamela; Mrs. Elizabeth Shandy; Raskolnikov.
(see *submission, humility, gentle, resignation*)

MEETING-PLACE
Philaeni; Tabard.
(see *assembly-place*)

MEGALITHIC
Stonehenge; Pelasgians.
(see *masonry*)

MELANCHOLY (authors)
Propertian; Thomas Gray; Thomas Hardy; Democritus Junior; Weeping Philosopher; Soren Kierkegaard; Emily Brontë; Byronic; Tibullan; Heraclitus.

MELANCHOLY (general)
Azor; Aëdon; Banshee; Trophonius; George Warrington; Egdon Heath; Edgar Ravenswood; Hamlet; Jaques; Saul.

MELANCHOLY (music)
Tzigane; Tschaikovsky; Gustave Mahler; Phrygian.
(see *despondent, hypochondriac, sadness, dejected, lugubrious, doleful*)

MELEE
Kriemhilde.
(see *fighting, brawling, conflict*)

MELLIFLUOUS
Hyblaean; Spenserian; Phemius; Isocrates; Hymettan.
(see *euphonious*)

MELODIOUS
Saint Cecilia; Ligeia; Lorelei; Leucothea; Philomela; Franz Schubert; Gilbert and Sullivan; Handel and Haydn; Giacomo Puccini; Giuseppe Verdi; Gioacchino Rossini; Strauss.
(see *tuneful, aria, music, song*)

MELT
Icarian.
(see *liquefy*)

MEMBERSHIP
Quirites.
(see *association, society*)

MEMORY
Proustian; Phaedo; Manfred; Ganesa; Euryclea; Cassim Baba; Mnemosyne; Odin; Rosemary; Pierre Loti; Munin; Antonio Magliabecchi.
(see *remembrance, recollection*)

MENACING
Minotaur.
(see *threatening, intimidate, alarm, frighten*)

MENDACIOUS
Fag; Mr. Fudge; Foigard; Sir John Mandeville; Mrs. Sarah Gamp.
(see *liar, deceitful, falsehood*)

MENDICANT
Francis of Assisi; Tom o'Bedlam; Edie Ochiltree.
(see *beggar, pauper, indigent, tramp*)

Riquet; Picus; Arethusa; Pierides; Philomela; Pitys; Perdix; Philyra; Aeaean; Dryope; Pleiades; Loathly Lady; Lir; Proteus; Telchines; Procne; Myrrha.
(see *transfiguration, chance, flexible*)

METAPHYSICS
Saint Augustine; Hegelian; Mary Baker Eddy.
(see *philosophy*)

METEOR
Saint Lawrence; Berenice; Belinda.
(see *planet, star, constellation*)

METHODICAL
Freudian; Ferdinand Fathom; Wesleyan; Eunomia; Bradley Headstone; Havelock Ellis.
(see *orderliness, systematic, exactitude, routine*)

METICULOUS
Jean Martinet; Protogenes; Flaubertian.
(see *precision, finical, carefulness, fastidious*)

METROPOLIS
City of Destruction.
(see *city-bred, urbanity, worldliness, cosmopolite*)

MICROSCOPE
Katerfelto.
(see *pseudo-scientific, scientific*)

MIDDAY
Ra.
(see *noon*)

MIDDLE-CLASS
Babbitt.
(see *bourgeois, philistine*)

MIDGET
Blefuscu; Vamana; Lilliputian; Tom Thumb; Sindre.
(see *dwarf, freak, stunted, pygmy*)

MIDNIGHT
Barguest.
(see *night*)

MID-OCEAN
Aegir.
(see *sea, ocean-god*)

MIDWIFERY
Virbius; Upis; Doctor Slop; Lucina.
(see *accouchement*)

MIGHT (n.)
Giacomuzzo Sforza; Milo; Samson; Armada; Leviathanic; Hercules; Guy of Warwick; Tarzan.
(see *power, strength, force, potent*)

MIGRATORY
Kabibonokka; Okie; Leleges; Terah.
(see *nomad, wanderer, roving, vagrancy*)

MILDEW
Robigus.
(see *pestilence, rust, damp*)

MILDNESS
Evander; Irene; Favonius; Saturn.
(see *clemency, compassionate, kindness, soft, suave, soothe*)

MILITANT
Richard the Lion-Hearted; Peter the Hermit; Ethan Allen; Boadicea; Bellona; Thalestris; Thor; Crusaders; Mahomet; Joan of Arc; Michael; Amazonian.
(see *fighting, contest, belligerent*)

MILITARISTIC
Wellingtonian; Frontinus; Spartan; Tullus Hostilius; Alfred the Great; Marcus Ulpius Trajan; Mars; Theodosius; Napoleon Bonaparte; Xenophon; Uncle Toby; Corporal Trim; Marius; Sir Lucius O'Trigger; Shatriya; Ephebeia; Mithradates; Sheridan; Laconian; Philip of Macedon; Rajput; Sergius.
(see *soldier, martial, war*)

MILK
Rumina.
(see *cow*)

MILKMAID
Phyllis; Thestylis.
(see *rusticity*)

MILKY WAY
Watling Street.
(see *sky, heaven, star*)

MILLINERY
Catherinette.
(see *hat, cap, helmet, headdress*)

MIMIC
Nerissa; David Garrick.
(see *imitation, mockery, counterfeit, pantomime*)

MIND
Odin; Hoenir; Hugin.
(see *intellectual, understanding, brain, senses, soul, spirit*)

MINDLESS
Bedlam; Poll Parrot.
(see *stupid, senseless, neglectful, carelessness, heedless*)

MINIATURE
Horatii and Curiatii.
(see *midget, little, diminutive, tiny*)

MINING
Bret Harte.
(see *metallurgy*)

MINISTER (n.)
Obadiah Slope; Charles Honeyman; Cotton Mather; Robert Elsmere; Rev. Mr. Collins; Maister Gowk-Thrapple; Parson Trulliber; Rev. Mr. Stiggins.
(see *preacher, clergy, chaplain, curate*)

MINORITY
Mason and Dixon; Alfred Dreyfus.
(see *prejudice, discrimination*)

MINSTRELSY
Phemius; Walther von der Vogelweide; Blondel; Demodocus; Minnesinger; Meistersinger; Taliesin.
(see *bard, singer, music*)

MINT (financial)
Moneta.
(see *finances, coins, capital, wealth, riches*)

MINUTE (adj.)
Protogenes.
(see *diminutive, tiny, little, miniature*)

MIRACULOUS
Empedocles; Elijah; Arion; Saint Filumena; Apollonius; Thaumaturgus; Pallas; Krishna; Shadrach; Hugh of Lincoln; Siva; Saint Januarius; Poictesme; Jonah; Tabitha-Dorcas; Saint Swithin; Sangreal; Servius Tullius; Loretto; Thecla; Sakhrat.
(see *supernatural, thaumaturgy, wonderworker*)

MIRAGE
Fata Morgana.
(see *illusion, deceptive, mislead, delusive*)

MIRE
Slough of Despond.
(see *marsh, swamp, mud, filth*)

MIRROR
Lady of Shalott; Alasnam; Perseus; Narcissus; Louis XV.
(see *reflection*)

MIRTH
Silence; Falstaffian; Panurge; Dickensian; Giovanni Boccaccio; Chaucerian; Cercopes; Rabelaisian; Euphrosyne.
(see *merriment, jolly, gaiety, joviality, hilarity, laughter, humor*)

MIRTHLESS
Marcus Crassus.
(see *lugubrious, soured*)

MISADVENTURE
Calandrino.
(see *misfortune, ill-luck, disaster, calamity*)

MISANTHROPY
Arnolphe; Scrooge; Manly; Sir Mungo Malagrowther; Timon.
(see *cynic, anti-social*)

MISCALCULATION
Busirus.
(see *error*)

MISCEGENATION
John Rolfe; Bug Jargal; Madama Butterfly; Malachi; Phinehas.
(see *mis-married*)

MISCHIEF-MAKER
Portia; Pandora; Ascalaphus; Mab; Ate; Phooka; Dickon Sludge; Loki; Erlking; Puck; Robin Goodfellow; Friar Rush; Crabtree; Sneer; Topsy; Penrod; Witchfinder General; Perrin Dendin.
(see *malevolence, meddlesome, interference, prying, troublesome, imp*)

MISEDUCATED
Richard Feverel; Martinus Scriblerus.
(see *pampered, pedantic*)

MISERLINESS
Argan; Harpagon; Arthur Gride; Père Grandet; Malbecco; Wandering Willie; the Crawleys; Tom Walker; Harry Gill; Gobseck; Squeers; Scrooge.
(see *greed, penny-pincher, avaricious, stingy*)

MISERY
Zeluco; Black Hole of Calcutta; Oliver Twist; Louis XVI; Struldbrugs; Pierre J. Proudhon; Valley Forge.
(see *distressed, wretchedness, woe, tribulation, grief, sorrow*)

MISFIT
Olibrius.
(see *inferiority*)

MISFORTUNE
Rheingold; Tristram Shandy; Iliad; Calandrino; Tutankhamen; Sir Mungo Malagrowther; Harmonia's Necklace; Sejus.
(see *disaster, calamity, adversity, ill-luck*)

MISGUIDED
Sir Francis Wronghead.
(see *wrong*)

MISINFORMED
Trimalchio.
(see *uninformed*)

MISJUDGMENT
Gelert; Sir Francis Wronghead.
(see *mistaken, miscalculate*)

MISLEAD
Sinon.
(see *deceitful, fraudulence, trickery, wily, guile*)

MIS-MARRIED
Francesca of Rimini.
(see *unhappy, divorce, annulment*)

MISOGYNY
Juvenalian; Jonathan Oldbuck; Saint Kevin.
(see *woman-hater*)

MISREPRESENTATION
Epicurean; Phaedra; Elbridge Gerry; Ralph Roister Doister.
(see *error, fraudulence, falsehood*)

MISSHAPEN
Quasimodo; Mayeux; Fanny Cleaver; Witch of Edmonton; Rigoletto; Toulouse-Lautrec.
(see *malformed, distorted*)

MISSILES
Saint Stephen.
(see *arrow, lance, pike, javelin, spear*)

MISSIONARY
Francisco Xavier; David Livingstone; Joseph of Arimathea; Manichaeus; Jacques Marquette; Crispin; Saint Denis; Saint Paul; Luke; Mrs. Jellyby; Saint James.
(see *evangelistic, apostle*)

MISSISSIPPI
Louis Joliet; Huck Finn.
(see *river, explorer*)

MISSPELLING
Artemus Ward; Mrs. Ramsbottom.
(see *alphabet, miswriting*)

MIST
Notus; Niflheim; Friar Bungay; Trasimene Lake; Jean Corot.
(see *foggy, cloud*)

MISTAKEN
Ancaeus; Cephalus; Agave; Pentheus; Lear; Sir Martin Mar-All; Queer Card; Mrs. Partington; Rustam.
(see *wrong, error*)

MISTREATMENT
Antiope; John Drum; Marchioness; Oliver (1).
(see *abused, maltreat*)

MISTRESS
Nana; Neaera; Manon (Lescaut); Chloë; Lindabrides; Tyndaris; Pompeia; Lady Bellaston; Emma Bovary; Lola Montez; Maid Marian; Mme. de Montespan; Delilah; Nell Gwyn; La Traviata; George Sand; Paula Tanqueray; Mme. Pompadour; Lalage; Mme. DuBarry; Ninon de Lenclos; Nancy.
(see *paramour, sweetheart, concubine, demimondaine*)

MISUNDERSTOOD
Justice Overdo; Socrates.
(see *error, wrong, misjudgment*)

MISWRITING
Mrs. Ramsbottom; Artemus Ward; Ralph Roister Doister.
(see *illiterate*)

MIXTURE
Chiron; Minotaur; Centaur; Hermaphroditus.
(see *jumble, variety, hybrid, composite*)

MOAN
Cocytean.
(see *sobbing, groan, lamentation, bemoan, mourning, bewail*)

MOB
Louis XVI; William Hogarth.
(see *rabble*)

MOBILE
Iphicrates.
(see *fickle, change, inconstant, active, nimble*)

MOB-LAW
Judge Lynch.
(see *group action*)

MOB-PSYCHOLOGY
Barabbas.
(see *demagogue, agitator*)

MOB SCENES
Max Reinhardt.
(see *tumultuous, turbulence, uprising*)

MOCKERY
Momus; Mephistophelian; Brennus; Tantalus; Alberich; Panurge; Thersitean; La Tosca; Faustian; Fanny Cleaver.
(see *derisive, ridicule, scornful, mimic, jeer*)

MOCK-HEROIC
Batrachomyomachia; Snark; Hudibrastic.
(see *farce, burlesque*)

MODEL (artist's)
Mme. Marie Tussaud; Phryne.
(see *figure*)

MODEL (exemplary)
Arria; Livia; Amelia; Cid; Utopian; Coelebs; Leilah; King of Yvetot; Giottesque; Grandisonianism; Sir Willoughby Patterne; Periclean; Ciceronian.
(see *paragon, exemplary, pattern*)

MODERATION
Charles Montesquieu; Sir Guyon; Corinna.
(see *temperance, sobriety, composure*)

MODESTY
Dike; Pudicitia; Parson Abraham Adams; Priscilla, the Puritan Maid; Hypatia; Pamela; Bob Cratchit; Rebecca the Jewess; Torquemada; Agricola; Tom Pinch; Thomas Allworthy; Mme. Marie Curie; Isaac Newton.
(see *chastity, purity, virtue, propriety*)

MODIFICATION
Lamarckian.
(see *alter, change*)

MODISH
Sir Courtly Nice; Silk-Stocking; Miss Flora McFlimsey; Gibsonesque; Longchamps.
(see *fashionable, ceremonious, conventional*)

MOISTURE
Thales.
(see *damp, water*)

MOLESTED
Phineus.
(see *annoy, disturbance, harass, tortured, plague, pestilence*)

MOMENTOUS
Pippa.
(see *significant, serious, grave*)

MONASTERY
Saint Fiacre; Pachomius; Bernard of Menthon; Saint Theresa; Brigid of Kildare.
(see *convent, monks, nun*)

MONEY
Moneta.
(see *coins, finances, capital, wealth, riches*)

MONEY-LENDER
Gobseck; Lombard; Arthur Gride; Shylock.
(see *usurer, loan*)

MONEY-MAD
Peronella; Polydorus; Guido Franceschini; Get-Rich-Quick-Wallingford.
(see *avaricious, greed, miserliness, speculator*)

MONITOR
Tertullian; Mentor; Talus.
(see *adviser, counselor, guide*)

MONKEY
Cercopes.
(see *ape*)

MONKS
Friar Rush; Savonarola; Pachomius; Jacques Marquette.
(see *monastery*)

MONOPOLY
Krupp Family.
(see *ownership, financier, privileged*)

MONOTHEISTIC
Islam; Marcus Terentius Varro; Xenophanes; Sikh.
(see *religious, pantheistic*)

MONOTONOUS
Calypso; Vanderdecken; Maurice Ravel.
(see *tedious, droning*)

MONSTROSITY
Pasiphaë; Enceladus; Lapithae; Busirus; Minotaur; Medusa; Typhon-Typhoeus; Echidna; Hydra; Phorcus; Gigantes; Geryon; Sagittary; Cerberean; Talus; Andhaba; Orc; Briarean; Argante; Frankenstein; Jabberwock; Genghis Khan; Dabbat; Horace Walpole.
(see *freak, hybrid, composite*)

MONTH
Fasti; Luna; Hipparchus; Julian.
(see *calendar, year*)

MONUMENTAL
Pierre Larousse; Khufu.
(see *encyclopedist, enormous, colossal*)

MOODINESS
Edgar Ravenswood; Umbriel; Edgar Allan Poe; Egdon Heath; Leontes; Ganelon; Jaques.
(see *morose, lugubrious, gloom, despondent, hypochondriac, saturnine*)

MOON (deities)
Bendis; Ishtar; Artemis; Isis; Thia; Luna; Rahu; Selene; Sin; Tanit; Phoebe and Phoebus; Chandra; Thoth; Yue-Laou; Junner; Mut.
(see *planet, star, constellation*)

MOONLIGHT
Endymion; Sir John Millais; Claude Debussy.
(see *milky way*)

MOOR (heath)
Egdon Heath; Thomas Hardy.
(see *heath, desert*)

MORALIZER
Livia; Tertullian; Sophoclean; Stoic; Panaetius; Zeno; Sallustian; Pamela; Cato the Censor; Aesop; Jaques; William James; Jansenists; Zoroaster; Lao-Tse; Giottesque; Poor Richard; Victorian; Henry Ward Beecher; Doctor Charles Primrose.
(see *sententious, didactic, proverb*)

MORAVIAN
Count Zinzendorf.
(see *Protestant*)

MORBID
Argan; Old Mortality; Dostoievskian; Soren Kierkegaard; Anton Chekhov; Peter Tschaikovsky.
(see *melancholy, moodiness, sadness*)

MORDANT
Archilochian; William Ralph Inge; Lucian; Hipponax.
(see *caustic, sarcasm, satirism, hypercritical*)

MORE
Benjamin.
(see *portion*)

MORNING
Matuta; Wabun; Ra; Phosphor.
(see *dawn, sunlight, noon*)

MORONIC
Barnaby Rudge; Goose Gibbie.
(see *defective, stupid, foolish, abnormality*)

MOROSE
Jaques; Silence; Edgar Ravenswood; Sir Mungo Malagrowther; Malbecco; Arnolphe; Tiberian; Weeping Philosopher; Schopenhauerian.
(see *crabbed, sullenness, perverse, surly, moodiness, gruff*)

MORTALITY
Yorick.
(see *death, destruction*)

MORTGAGE
Tom Walker; Nigel Olifaunt.
(see *pledge*)

MORTICIAN
Libitina.
(see *burial, tomb, entombed, funeral, sepulcher, cemetery*)

MOSQUITO
Walter Reed.
(see *insects*)

MOSS
Demogorgon.
(see *plant life, forests*)

MOTHER-COMPLEX
Coelebs; D. H. Lawrence; Oedipus.
(see *abnormality, fixation*)

MOTHERHOOD
Niobe; Cybele; Hecuba; Madonna; Eilithyia; Andromache; Cornelia; Effie Deans; Schumann-Heinck; Joanna Southcott; Mrs. Deborah Primrose; Mary Cassatt; Mut.
(see *birth, childbirth*)

MOTHER-IN-LAW
Naomi.
(see *in-laws*)

MOTION
Dalcrozean; Johannes Kepler; Arthur Honegger; Myron's Cow; Ve.
(see *gesticulation*)

MOTTOES
Martial.
(see *epigrammatic, pithy, didactic*)

MOUNTAINOUS
Arcadian; Og; Ve; Lapithae; Oreads; Montesinos; Heliconian; Junner; Sinai.
(see *forests*)

MOUNTEBANK
Merry-Andrew; Friar Bungay.
(see *charlatan, quackery, pretender, poseur*)

MOURNING
Cocytean; Via Dolorosa; Cassandra-like; Daphnis; Ishtar; Philomela; Memnon; Spurinna Vestritius; John Wemmick.

(see *lamentation, sorrow, grief, lachrymose*)

MOUSE-KILLER
Smintheus.
(see *rats*)

MOWER
Saint Walston.
(see *harvest, reap*)

MUCH-MARRIED
John Buncle; Henry VIII; Wife of Bath.
(see *fickle, inconstant, harem, capricious, girl-crazy, polygamous*)

MUD
Tiberinus.
(see *mire, swamp*)

MUDDLE-HEADED
Stultorum Feriae.
(see *stupid, absent-minded, forgetful*)

MULCT
Zanes.
(see *forfeit, penalty*)

MULE
Queen Labe.
(see *horse, hybrid*)

MULTIPLICITY
Quadrifrons; Gyes.
(see *composite*)

MUMBLING
Tutivillus.
(see *incoherent, inarticulate*)

MUMMY
Ptah.
(see *corpse*)

MUNIFICENCE
Maecenas; Nadejda von Meck; Ptolemy.
(see *bounty, generosity, reward, patron, patroness*)

MUNITIONS
Krupp Family.
(see *explosives, weapons, arms, arsenal*)

MURALS
Polygnotus; Etruscan.
(see *painter*)

MURDER
Modo; Areopagitical; Gracchi; Pliny the Younger; Herodian; Clarence Darrow; Horace Walpole.
(see *homicidal, manslaughter, massacre, slaughter, butchery, bloodshed*)

MURDERER
Aegisthus; Laestrygonian; Bluebeard; Tydeus; Pyrrhus (Neoptolemus); Jack the Ripper; William Burke; Robert Macaire; Guido Francischini; Macduff; Bill Sikes; Falkland.
(see *assassin, killer, cut-throat, tyrannicide, matricide, patricide, fratricide, parricide*)

MURDERESS
Medea; Locusta; Tullia; Clytemnestra; Tyndaris; Lamia; Althaea; Lady Macbeth.
(see *infanticide, filicide*)

MUSCULAR
Samson; Fierabras.
(see *brawn, broad-shouldered, might, power, strength, vigor*)

MUSIC (ancient deities and artists)
Jubal; Linus; Calypso; Pythian; Terpander; Chiron; Amphion; Eumolpus; Leucothea; Trismegistus; Ligeia; Dactyli; Israfel; Orpheus; Lydian; Lorelei;

Calliope (see Muse); Arion; Korah; Aeolian; Euterpe; Saraswati; Thamyris; Ismenias.
(see *melodious, harmony, symphonic, tuneful, aria, opera*)

MUSIC (composers)
Mendelssohn-Bartholdy; Brahmsian; Chopinesque; J. S. Bach; Franz Schubert; Serge Rachmaninoff; Giacomo Puccini; Gustave Mahler; Edvard Grieg; Ludwig van Beethoven; Tschaikovsky; Gilbert and Sullivan; Mozartean; Claude Debussy; Strauss; Maurice Ravel; Robert Schumann; Handel and Haydn; Rimski-Korsakov.
(see *composer*)

MUSIC OF THE SPHERES
Johannes Kepler.
(see *heavenly music*)

MUTE
Thaumaste; Fenella; Vaticanus.
(see *silence, dumbness, speechless, inarticulate*)

MUTILATION
Pelias; Jack the Ripper; Uranus; Tyr.
(see *mayhem, piecemeal, butchery, disfigured, crippled*)

MUTINY
Christopher Columbus; Hendrick Hudson.
(see *rebellious, revolution, riot, insurrection, uprising*)

MUTTER
Tutivillus.
(see *incoherent, inarticulate, grumbler*)

MUTUAL
Will Ladislaw; Damon and Pythias; Anteros.
(see *reciprocation*)

MYRTLE
Myrrha; Venus.
(see *trees*)

MYSTERY
Sphinx; Mignon; Comte de LaMotte; Mata Hari; Man with the Iron Mask; Demogorgon; Epimenides; Tom Walker; Viraj; Jumala; Monsieur Dupin; Jekyll-Hyde; Rudolph of Mayerling; Sir Patrick Spens; Lara; Childe Rolande; Amy Robsart; Lenore; Isis; Lollius; Ka; Lohengrin; Cock Lane Ghost; Rider Haggard; Lawrence of Arabia; Edgar Allan Poe; Horace Walpole; Samuel Taylor Coleridge.
(see *incomprehensible, abstruse, enigmatic, riddle, unknown, inscrutable, unintelligible*)

MYSTICISM
Zagreus; Dionysus Zagreus; Abecedarians; Johannes Eckhart; Empedocles; Pythagoras; Saint Theresa; Christian Rosenkreuz; Trismegistus; Francisco Xavier; Johannes Kepler; Gymnosophist; Swedenborgian; Omar Khayyam; Blake-like; William Butler Yeats; Eumolpus; Eleusinian.
(see *occultism, secrecy, allegory, symbolism*)

N

NAGGING
Xanthippe; Mrs. Caudle.
(see *harass, henpecked, scold, fault-finder*)

NAIL
Jael; Naglfar; Sisera.
(see *claw, stigmata*)

NAIVE
Doctor Charles Primrose; Partridge; Charles Perrault; Melantius; Bob Acres; Daisy Miller; Mme. Sans-Gêne.
(see *artless, ingenuousness, naturalness, simplicity, candid, plainness, unsophisticated*)

NAKEDNESS
Gymnosophist; Godiva; Candaules; Gymnopaedia.
(see *undress, nudism*)

NAP
Hypnos; Somnus.
(see *drowsy, lethargy, repose, sleep*)

NARROW-MINDED
Bowdlerize; Cato of Utica; Puritanic; Arnolphe; Philistines; Junker.
(see *bigotry, prejudice, partiality, mean-spirited*)

NATIONALISM
Arnold von Winkelried; Ivan Ivanovitch; Chauvinistic; Josephus; Maccabees; Thaddeus Kosciusko; Brother Jonathan; Rimski-Korsakov; John Bull; Francis Scott Key; Johnny Crapaud; Uncle Sam; Yankee; Cousin Michel; Nicholas Frog; Sinn Fein.
(see *racialism, patriotic, Celtic, Dutch, French, Irish, German-baiting, Russian, British, American, negro, Welshman*)

NATIVE FIGHTERS
Zouave; Fuzzy-Wuzzy; Sikh.
(see *India, Indian, guerrilla*)

NATIVES
Paul Gauguin.
(see *aboriginal, primeval, indigenous, uncivilized, backwoods*)

NATTY
Jack Sixteen-String.
(see *jaunty, foppish, dapper, dude*)

NATURALISM
Luther Burbank; William Wordsworth; Walden Pond; Rousseauian; Darwinian; Pliny the Elder; Alexander Agassiz; Lamarckian; John Burroughs.
(see *back-to-nature*)

NATURALNESS (character trait)
Penrod; Peter Pan; Cophetuan; Henriette; Bertolde; Satyrane; Mme. Sans-Gêne.
(see *naive, spontaneous, unaffected, unpretentious, unspoiled*)

NATURALNESS (writers)
Robert Burns; Pre-Raphaelite; Corneille; O. Henry; Henry Wadsworth Longfellow; Amy Lowell; Lysias; Jean Racine; Robert Browning; Paul Lawrence Dunbar; Emile Zola; Goldsmithian; Mark Twain.
(see *writer*)

NATURE
Rhea; Nymphs; Lucretian; Audhumla; Minnesinger; Thallo; Sabazius.
(see *world, universe, creation, landscape, countryside, rusticity*)

NATURE (painters of)
Jean Corot; Edouard Manet; Claude Monet; Rosa Bonheur; Sir John Millais.
(see *painter, genre*)

NAUTICAL
Long Tom Coffin; Lieutenant Hatchway; Commodore Trunnion; Sol Gills; Vasco da Gama; Herman Melville.
(see *sailor, marine, seafaring, privateer, corsair, buccaneer, sea-deities*)

NAVAL BATTLE
Salamis.
(see *fleet, man-of-war*)

NAVIGATOR
Ferdinand Magellan; Christopher Columbus; Richard Hakluyt; Vasco da Gama; Liburnians; Pytheas; Hendrick Hudson.
(see *mariner, discoverer, explorer, helmsman*)

NECESSITY
Telephus; Tobias Hobson.
(see *unavoidable, inevitability, compulsion, destiny, fate*)

NECKLACE
Manlius; Brisingamen; Harmonia's Necklace; Cagliostro; Comte de LaMotte.
(see *jewelry*)

NECTAR
Rahu.
(see *liquor, ambrosia*)

NEEDLE
Gammer Gurton.
(see *sharp*)

NEEDLECRAFT
Arachne.
(see *seamstress, sewing society, embroidery*)

NEEDY
Lazarus; Jeremy Diddler; Okie; Saint Lawrence.
(see *destitute, "broke," indigent, poverty*)

NE'ER-DO-WELL
Jeremy Diddler; Peter Peebles; Scaramouch.
(see *useless, idleness, knave, disrepute, do-nothing*)

NEGATIVE
Urim and Thummim.
(see *renunciation, forbidden*)

NEGLECTED
Children in the Wood; Lear; Topsy; Abel Magwitch; Père Goriot.
(see *abandoned, deserted, forsaken*)

NEGLECTFUL
Regan; Cassim Baba; Oeneus; Halgaver.
(see *carelessness, heedless, inattentive, inadvertent*)

NEGOTIATE
John Jay.
(see *bargain, compact, treaty-making*)

NEGRO
Bug Jargal; Sambo; Paul Lawrence Dunbar; Chloë; Quashee; Uncle Remus.
(see *black-face, Africa*)

NEIGH
Darius; Houyhnm; Sagittary.
(see *horse*)

NOBILITY (birth)
Eupatridae; Gotha; Chandra; Lady Clara Vere de Vere; Libro d'Oro; Silk-Stocking.
(see *pedigreed, aristocratic, patrician, gentility, courtier, majesty*)

NOBLENESS (character)
Zeno; Pythias; Publius Decius Mus; Aurora Leigh; Stoic; Long Tom Coffin; Miss Lucretia MacTab; Madama Butterfly; Cornelia; Lucretia; Imogen; Longinus; Calidore; Saint George; Parsifal; Lancelot; Alcestis; Andromache.
(see *magnanimous, dignified, high-souled*)

NOD
Lord Burleigh.
(see *bow, obeisance*)

NOISY
Rhea; Mohock; Pandemonium; Donnybrook Fair; Jefferson Brick; Joseph Bounderby; Termagant; Yahoo; Friar Rush; Stockwell Ghost; Curetes; Dionysus; Babel; Bacchanal; Brontes; Bacchic; Arthur Honegger; Bromius.
(see *boisterous, vociferous, blatant, brawling, uproar, tumultuous, loud*)

NOISELESS
Larunda.
(see *quiet, hushed, silence*)

NOMAD
Bedouin; Tzigane; Land of Nod; Leleges; Apache; Isaac; Khartaphilos; Saracen; Scythian; Okie; Jack London; Kedar.
(see *gypsy, wanderer, vagrancy, migratory*)

NO-MAN'S LAND
Tom Tiddler.
(see *contest, forbidden*)

NONCHALANT
Louis XV; Lyaeus; Hippoclides.
(see *easy-going, insouciance, unconcerned, indifference, apathy*)

NONCONFORMIST
Bohemian; Brand.
(see *intransigence, unconventional*)

NONENTITY
MacFlecknoe; John Doe; Lollius; King of Yvetot; Jack-a-Lent; Sir Urian; Augustus Snodgrass; Monsieur Sotenville; Mrs. Elizabeth Shandy.
(see *insignificant, futility, unimportant, figure-head*)

NON-EXISTENT
Weissnichtwo; Nephelococcygia; Utopian; Fear Fortress; Jabberwock; Mrs. Harris; Erewhon; Queen Dick; Lubberland; Snark.
(see *fabulous, fictitious, never*)

NON-INFLAMMABLE
Servius Tullius; Thecla.
(see *unharmed*)

NON-INTERVENTION
James Monroe; Gamaliel.
(see *isolation*)

NON-MILITARY
Quirites.
(see *pacifist*)

NON-MORAL
Mistress Quickly.
(see *immorality, "loose"*)

NON-OBSERVANCE
Zanes.
(see *heedless, carelessness, infraction, disobedience, transgression, violation*)

NONPLUS
Kilmansegg.
(see *perplexity, quandary*)

NONSENSE
Buncombe; Mrs. Ramsbottom; Lagado; MacFlecknoe; Gertrude Stein.
(see *absurd, unreasonable, irrational, fantastic, ridiculous, incongruous, ludicrous, senseless, silly, stupid, ill-advised*)

NOON
Bacis; Ra.
(see *sunlight*)

NORTHERNMOST
Hraesvelger; Kabibonokka; Rhipaei Montes; Thule; Hyperboreans.
(see *arctic, far away, aistant*)

NORTH WIND
Njord; Boreal; Aquilo.
(see *wind*)

NOSE
Cyrano de Bergerac; Hafen Slawkenbergius; Tristram Shandy.
(see *face, features*)

NOSELESS
Marie Laurencin.
(see *malformed, ugliness*)

NOSTALGIA
Demodocus; Hesperus; Fritz Kreisler; Stephen Foster.
(see *homesick, longing, pining*)

NOTES
Pliny the Elder; Captain Cuttle.
(see *record*)

NOTHINGNESS
Nirvana.
(see *oblivion, nonentity, non-existent*)

NOTIFY
Munin; Hermod.
(see *announcer, herald, harbinger, reporter, enlightenment, informer*)

NOTION
King Ryance.
(see *whimsical, capricious, crotchety*)

NOTORIETY
Herostratus; Henry VIII; Clodia; Mr. and Mrs. Leo Hunter; Oscar Wilde; Zabian; Pierre Louys; Jukes Family.
(see *publicity-seeker, disrepute, fame, celebrity*)

NOURISHER
Tellus; Hrimthursar.
(see *food, sustenance, provider*)

NOUVEAU RICHE
Nicodemus Boffin; Turcaret; Cogia Hassan Alhabbal; Trimalchio; Mr. Tittlebat Titmouse; Peronella.
(see *pretentious, showy, ostentation, pseudo-genteel, parvenu, rags to riches, upstart*)

NOVELIST
Emile Zola; Galsworthian; Victor Hugo; Nathaniel Hawthorne; Oliver Wendell Holmes; Dickensian; Alexandre Dumas; Joseph Conrad; Brontesque; Leo Tolstoi; Bulwer-Lytton; Daniel Defoe; Thackerayan; Balzacian; Walter Scott; Stevensonian.
(see *writer, fictitious*)

NOVELTY
Ikhnaton.
(see *unusual, innovator*)

NOW
Verthandi.
(see *time*)

NOWHERE
Erewhon.
(see *non-existent*)

NOZZLE
Hafen Slawkenbergius; Cyrano de Bergerac.
(see *nose*)

NUDISM
Candaules; Charis; Lady Godiva; Gymnosophist; Pierre Renoir; Edouard Manet.
(see *nakedness, undress*)

NUISANCE
Quidnunc; Paul Pry; Old Man of the Sea; Mohock; Marplot; Guppy.
(see *bother, impediment, annoy*)

NUMBERS
Bernouilli.
(see *mathematics*)

NUMISMATIST
Jonathan Oldbuck.
(see *coins*)

NUN
Pachomius; Saint Theresa; Flora MacIvor.
(see *convent, religious*)

NUPTIAL
Hymeneal; Pronuba.
(see *marriage, wedlock*)

NURSE
Siguna; Abishag; Baubo; Romola; Rebecca the Jewess; Elli; Euryclea; Ciara Barton; Clara Peggoty; Mrs. Sarah Gamp; Saint Filumena; Betsey Prig; Florence Nightingale; Acca Larentia; Meg Merrilies.
(see *rearing, succor, helpfulness, nourisher*)

NUTCRACKER
Symplegades; Tschaikovsky.
(see *crushed*)

NUTS
Iduna.
(see *almond*)

NYMPH
Upis; Hesperides; Leucothea; Dryope; Ligeia; Naiads; Napaeae; Nereids; Neaera; Maia; Oceanids; Oreads; Philyra; Lorelei; Salmacis; Hyades; Juturna; Undine; Swarga; Egeria; Woglinda, Wellgunda, and Flosshilda; Daphne; Melissa; Sabrina.
(see *goddess, spirit, maiden*)

O

OAK-TREE
Dodonean; Rhoecus; Milo.
(see *trees*)

OARSMAN
Elpenor.
(see *rower*)

OATH
Semo Sancus; Sigurd; Stygian; Feretrius; Regulus; Gungnir.
(see *vow, pledge, promise*)

OBDURATE
Pharaoh; Robin and Makyne; Thaukt.
(see *hard-hearted, obstinate, inflexible, inexorable, unfeeling, cantankerous*)

OBEDIENCE
Ramman; Leonidas; Latinus; Noah; Aaron; Samuel; Abraham; Katharine; Jerry Sneak.
(see *compliance, submission, subservient, duty, deferential, respectful*)

OBEISANCE
Gradasso.
(see *bow*)

OBITUARY
Mors; Neniae.
(see *death*)

OBJECTIVE (n.)
Manoa; Thule.
(see *destination, goal*)

OBJECTOR
Jean Hardouin.
(see *disapproval, protestation*)

OBLIGATION
Panaetius; Feretrius; Pythias; Telemachus; Regulus; Naomi.
(see *duty, agreement, compact, covenant, compulsion*)

OBLIGING
Phormio; Teirtu; Elbridge Gerry.
(see *accommodating, kindness, complacent*)

OBLIVION
Lethean; Lotophagi; Sheol; Salt River; Jaques; Mr. Redlaw.
(see *nothingness, forgetful, heedless, carelessness, neglectful*)

OBSCENITY
Baptes; Martial; Belphegor; Cotys; Fescennine; Ryparographer; Marquis de Sade; Baubo; Kali.
(see *indecency, indelicate, immodest, unchaste, shameless, gross, coarse, ribald, lewdness*)

OBSCURITY
Delphi; Moerae; Propertian; Heraclitus; Protogenes; Persius; Albert Einstein; Brontesque; Jericho; Stellenbosche; MacFlecknoe.
(see *unintelligible, vague, darkness, incomprehensible, doubtful, enigmatic, abstruse*)

OBSEQUIOUS
Phormio; Gnatho; Uncle Pumblechook; Rev. Mr. Collins; Arthur Gride; Laban.
(see *fawning, sycophant, deferential, servility*)

OBSERVANT
Vincentio; Chaucerian; Henry Thoreau; Robert Bruce; Emily Dickinson; Mme. de Sévigné; Mulvaney; Washington Irving; Balzacian; Alexander Agassiz.
(see *vigiliance, sharp-sighted, watchful*)

OBSESSED
Mr. Redlaw.
(see *fixation*)

OBSOLETE
Pelasgians.
(see *ancient, disuse, archaic, old*)

OBSTACLE
Amy Robsart.
(see *hindrance, impediment, difficulty*)

OBSTETRICIAN
Doctor Slop.
(see *midwifery, accouchement*)

OBSTINATE
Sir Francis Wronghead; John Willet; Pharaoh; Ganelon; Leicester Dedlock; Abraham Slender.
(see *self-willed, stubborn, wilful, perverse, inflexible, opinionated, obdurate*)

OCCULTISM
Trismegistus; Chaldean; Franz Mesmer; Christian Rosenkreuz.
(see *mysticism, secrecy, abstruse*)

OCEAN-GOD
Salacia; Amphitrite; Neptune; Ea; Phorcus; Poseidon; Varuna; Aegir; Ran; Tethys; Triton.
(see *sea-deities, water*)

OCTAGON
Padalon.
(see *square*)

ODES
Pindaric; Horatian.
(see *poetry*)

ODOROUS
Philoctetes; Gilead; Sabaean.
(see *fragrant, sweet-smelling, aromatic, perfume, stench*)

OFFENSIVE
Yahoo; Jack Ketch; Jim Crow; Betsey Prig.
(see *abusive, reproachful, opprobrious, scurrilous, ribald, invective, calumnious, denunciatory, injurious, insulting, insolent*)

OFFERING
Mettius Curtius; Hesione.
(see *present, gifts, sacrifice*)

OFFICIALDOM
Circumlocution Office; Downing Street.
(see *authoritative*)

OFFICIOUS
Polonius; Shallow; Pooh-Bah.
(see *self-important, dogmatic, imperious, meddlesome*)

OFFSPRING
Levana.
(see *babies, infant*)

OGRE
Kuvera.
(see *specter, ghoul, goblin, hobgoblin, bogy, bugbear*)

OIL
Morgiana; St. John.
(see *fat*)

OINTMENT
Anasuya; Gilead.
(see *balm, panacea, healing, curative, soothe*)

OLD
Pelasgians; Old Ironsides.
(see *ancient, antiquity, archaic, obsolete, old-fashioned, primeval, aged*)

OLD AGE
Elli; Graiae; Utgard-Loki; Terah.
(see *aged, longevity*)

OLD-FASHIONED
Cincinnatus; Godey.
(see *old, ancient, archaic, obsolete, primeval*)

OLD MAID
Miggs; Miss Tox; Miss Kilmansegg; Catherinette.
(see *spinster, husband-hunter, anile*)

OLD MAN
Tithonus; Methuselah; Géronte; Yue-Laou; Enoch Wray.
(see *senility, aged*)

OLIGARCH
Isagoras; Lucius Cornelius Sulla.
(see *aristocratic, dictator*)

OLIVES
Aristaeus; Pallas.
(see *fruit, trees*)

OMINOUS
Xanthos; Ides of March; Laelaps; Sejus; Tarquinius Priscus; Thrinacian; Jonah; Banshee; Phooka; Thomas Hardy; Egdon Heath; Harmonia's Necklace.
(see *ill-omen, inauspicious, ill-luck, premonition*)

OMISSION
Tutivillus.
(see *neglectful, defaulter*)

OMNIPOTENT
Jove; Zeus; Grand Mogul; Rheingold.
(see *all-powerful, power, potent*)

OMNIPRESENT
Aristeas; Old Man of the Sea.
(see *ubiquitous*)

OMNISCIENT
Helios; Mithras; Onca; Delphi; Atlantes; Hagen; Woglinda, Wellgunda, and Flosshilda; Odin; Merlin; Mimir; Jack the Giant-Killer; Marcus Terentius Varro.
(see *all-knowing, all-seeing*)

OMNIVOROUS
Grangousier; Widenostrils.
(see *ravenous, hungry, voracious*)

ONE-EYED
Polyphemus; Graiae; Steropes; Hagen; Arimaspians; Cyclopean; Osiris; Mimir.
(see *purblind, freak*)

ONE-HANDED
Tyr.
(see *hands*)

ONE-LEGGED
John Silver.
(see *peg-legged*)

ONEROUS
Augean.
(see *arduous, burden, difficulty, heavy, laborious*)

ONE-SIDED
Glaucus.
(see *unjust, partiality*)

ONSLAUGHT
George Edward Pickett.
(see *assault*)

OPEN AIR
Claude Monet; Edouard Manet.
(see *countryside, landscape, out-of-doors*)

OPEN-PICKINGS
Tom Tiddler.
(see *opportunist*)

OPERA
Wagnerian; Giuseppe Verdi; Gioacchino Rossini; Giacomo Puccini; Jean de Reszke; Schumann-Heinck; Nellie Melba; Adelina Patti; Enrico Caruso.
(see *aria, singer*)

OPINIONATED
Procrustean; Zelotes; Grimwig.
(see *dogmatic, conceited, cocksure, sure*)

OPIUM
Thomas DeQuincey.
(see *dope*)

OPPORTUNIST
Lara; Marmion; Fenton; Roderick Random.
(see *fortune-hunter, self-seeking, gold-digger, chance*)

OPPOSITION
Turnus; Pompey; Sadducees; Ormuzd; George-a-Green; Mrs. Partington; Molly Maguire.
(see *antagonistic, controversy, disputatious, altercation, hostility, resistance*)

OPPRESSION
Appius Claudius; Periander; Esther; Rameses; Old Man of the Sea; Eglon; Widow MacStinger; Sir Giles Overreach.
(see *tyrant, despotic, slavery, enslavement, injustice, persecution, taskmaster*)

OPPROBRIOUS
Scalae Gemoniae; Barathron; Bezonian.
(see *disrepute, dishonor, disgrace, reproachful, doom, penalty, condemned, abusive*)

OPTIMISTIC
Candide; Panglossian; Pollyanna; Micawber; Col. Mulberry Sellers; Mark Tapley; Leibnitzian.
(see *cheerful, hopeful, sanguine, confidence, expectation*)

OPULENCE
Dives; Queen of Sheba; Grand Mogul; Silk-Stocking; "Diamond Jim" Brady.
(see *abundance, amplitude, wealth, plenty, riches, rich*)

ORACULAR
Serapis; Sibylla; Dodonean; Sin; Trophonius; Fortuna; Delphi; Ammon; Pythian; Rishi; Urim and Thummim; Kneph.
(see *prophecy, prophet, ominous, foretell, clairvoyant*)

ORANGE
Yellow Dwarf.
(see *fruit*)

ORATORIOS
Handel and Haydn.
(see *church-music*)

ORATORY
Demosthenes; Ciceronian; Isocrates; Seneca the Elder; Quintilian; Websterian; Servius Sulpicius Rufus; Appius Claudius Caecus; Gorgias; Boanerges.
(see *rhetoric, elocution, eloquence*)

ORCHARD
Pomona; Vergilian.
(see *fruit*)

ORCHESTRATION
Rimski-Korsakov.
(see *instrument, music*)

ORDAIN
Seshat.
(see *instructive, enlightenment, establisher*)

ORDEAL
Kunigunde.
(see *tribulation, touchstone, proof, test*)

ORDERLINESS
Stator; Horae; Varuna; Eunomia; Manlius; Shamash; Poor Richard; Irene.
(see *systematic, methodical, regulation, tidy*)

ORGAN (musical)
Jubal; Saint Cecilia.
(see *music*)

ORGANIZER
Wallenstein; Alfred the Great; Ethan Allen; Thomas Cook; Florence Nightingale.
(see *establisher, instructor*)

ORGIASTIC
Bacchanal; Galli; Phrygian; Thyia; Sabazius; Cotys; Baptes; Dionysus; Rhea; Corybantic; Baal; Grigori E. Rasputin.
(see *revelry, merry-making, carousal, sensuality, self-indulgence debauchery*)

ORGULOUS
Mr. Darcy; Lady Clara Vere de Vere.
(see *pride, arrogant, haughtiness, supercilious, overbearing*)

ORIENTAL
Adrastus; Nefertiti; Baal; Babylonian.
(see *Asiatic, exotic*)

ORIGINAL
Euhemeristic; Iapetus; Adam; Peregrine White; John Hancock; Ask and Embla.
(see *first, primeval*)

ORNATE
Isocrates; Della Cruscans; Euphuistic; Propertian; Phrygian; Gorgias; Benvenuto Cellini; Edwardian; Byzantine; Sir Piercie Shafton; Edmund Burke; Alexander Pope.
(see *decorative, embellishment, florid*)

ORNITHOLOGY
John James Audubon.
(see *birds*)

ORPHAN
Silas Marner; Faustina; Dick Whittington.
(see *parentless*)

OSTENTATION
Alexandrianism; Martinus Scriblerus; Brummagem; Trimalchio; Peregrinus Proteus; Turcaret; Vanity Fair; Junker; Sir Piercie Shafton; Beau Tibbs; Joseph Bounderby; Major Bath; Sir Matthew Mite; "Diamond Jim" Brady.
(see *showy, display, pompous, pageantry, pretentious*)

OSTRACISM
Hagar; Ishmael; Danaë; Arioch; Themistoclean; Pariah; Oscar Wilde; Man in the Moon; Paula Tanqueray; Hester

Prynne; Coventry; Effie Deans; Charles C. Boycott.
(see *banishment, exile, expatriate, excommunicated*)

OUTDOORSMAN
Nimrod.
(see *out-of-doors, sportsman, hunter*)

OUTLANDISH
Novensides; Rumplestilzchen.
(see *foreign, strange, exotic, bizarre, unusual*)

OUTLAW
William of Cloudeslie; Hereward the Wake; Mohock; Jack Sixteen-String; Adam Bell; Maid Marian; Rob Roy; Friar Tuck; Robin Hood; Little John; Jesse James.
(see *bandit, brigand, freebooter, robber, highwayman, marauder*)

OUTLINE
Ictinus; Etienne de Silhouette.
(see *delineation, drawing*)

OUTNUMBERED
Leonidas; Thermopylae.
(see *hopeless, defeat*)

OUT-OF-DOORS
Napaeae; Naiads; Nereids; Nymphs; Oceanids; Oreads; Claude Monet; Edouard Manet.
(see *nature, countryside, scenic, outdoorsman*)

OUT-OF-THE-WAY
Bermudas; Stellenbosche; Jericho.
(see *remote, far-away, distant, seclusion*)

OUTSPOKEN
Laberius; Philoxenus; Tommy Atkins; Mme. Sans-Gêne; Marivaudage.
(see *frank, candid, bluff, blunt*)

OUTTALK
Vivian.
(see *persuasion, glib, cogent*)

OUTWIT
Hercules; Petruchio; Reynard.
(see *baffling, cheat, dupe, circumvent, swindler*)

OVAL
Nefertiti.
(see *ellipses*)

OVEN
Fornax.
(see *baker, furnace*)

OVER-AMBITIOUS
Thamyris; Aelius Sejanus; Pierides; Marsyas; Phaëton; Arachne; Justice Overdo.
(see *ambition-crazed, aspiring, ambitious*)

OVERAWING
Colossus.
(see *awe-inspiring, intimidate, browbeat, fearful*)

OVERBEARING
Junker; Lady Clara Vere de Vere; Peter Stuyvesant.
(see *imperious, domineering, supercilious, arrogant, haughtiness*)

OVERBOARD
Menoetes; Palinurus; Red Man; Sir Patrick Spens.
(see *drowned, shipwreck, float*)

OVERCAUTIOUS
Lentulus Sura.
(see *cautious, timidity, fearful, circumspect, vigilance*)

P

PACIFIST
Antenor.
(see *propitiatory, peace-maker*)

PACT
Hernani.
(see *agreement, compact, contract, bargain, treaty-making*)

PAGAN
Ossian; Argantes; Julian the Apostate; Saint Jerome; Morgante; Saracen.
(see *idolatry, unconverted*)

PAGE (court)
Moth.
(see *boy-servant*)

PAGEANTRY
Edwardian; Walter Scott; Max Reinhardt.
(see *display, ostentation, pompous, showy, splendor, magnificence*)

PAIN
Marquis de Sade; Philoctetes; Deianira; Masochism.
(see *sore, agony, anguish, suffering, tortured, woe*)

PAINLESS
Caesarean (1).
(see *panacea, soothe*)

PAINSTAKING
Flaubertian; Jeannot.
(see *laborious, carefulness, industrious, diligent*)

PAINTED
Picti; Jezebel; Tlaloc.
(see *bepainted, cosmetics*)

PAINTER
Parrhasius' Curtain; Protogenes; Apelles; Polygnotus; Zeuxis; Matsys' Fly; Rosa Bonheur; Botticelli; El Greco; Mary Cassatt; Andrea del Sarto; Pierre Renoir; Velasquez; Rembrandt; Jean Watteau; Rubensian; Michelangelo; Jean Corot; Jean Millet; Leonardo da Vinci; Gainsborough; James A. Whistler; Raphael; Edouard Manet; Claude Monet; St. Luke; John James Audubon; Toulouse-Lautrec; Giorgio Vasari; Tintoretto; Raphael of Cats; Henri Matisse; Sir John Millais.
(see *artist, colorist, pastels*)

PAIR
Mejnoun and Leilah; 'Arry and 'Arriet.
(see *couple, lovers*)

PALADIN
Orlando; Oliver (2); Ogier the Dane; Roland; Rinaldo; Malagigi.
(see *knighthood, chivalrous, gallantry, hero, champion*)

PALLOR
Tullus Hostilius; Sir John Suckling; Hagen; Trophonius.
(see *white, sickly*)

PAMPERED
Apis; Whiteheaded Boy; Nora Helmer.
(see *favored, coddled, indulgence, self-indulgence*)

PANACEA
Paracelsus; Gilead; Doctor Sangrado.
(see *remedy, medicine, curative, healing*)

PARRICIDE
Papinian; Front de Boeuf.
(see *patricide, matricide*)

PARROT
Kama; Poll Parrot.
(see *birds*)

PARTHENOGENESIS
Huitzilopochtli; Joanna Southcott.
(see *virginity, childbirth*)

PARTIALITY
Rebekah.
(see *prejudice, bias, bigotry, injustice, one-sided, favoring*)

PARTISANSHIP
Montagues and Capulets.
(see *factionalism, rivalry, antagonistic*)

PARTRIDGE
Perdix.
(see *birds*)

PARVENU
Trimalchio.
(see *nouveau-riche, pseudo-genteel, upstart, showy*)

PASS (ticket)
Annie Oakley.
(see *password*)

PASSION (deities)
Cestus; Cupid; Aphrodisian; Erato; Peitho; Obidicut; Paphian; Pandemos.
(see *fervor, ecstasy, blissful, love, sensuality, lewdness, lechery*)

PASSION (in art)
Scopas; Sophoclean; Euripidean; Catullan; Propertian; Brontesque; Tzigane; Walther von der Vogelweide; Tschaikovsky; Romany; Carlylean; Byronic; Sarah Bernhardt.
(see *pathos*)

PASSIONATE (men)
Romeo; Faustian; Mr. Rochester; Tracy Tupman; Peregrine Pickle; Arthur Pendennis; Grigori E. Rasputin; Marquis de Sade.
(see *philanderer, adulterous, lovers, girl-crazy, lady-killer, amorous, erotic, licentious, lascivious, debauchee, lustful, cuckold*)

PASSIONATE (women)
Phaedra; Zenobia; Dido; Nama; Cleopatra; Potiphar's Wife; Mimi; Kundry; Juliet; La Tosca; Isolde; Leilah; Manon (Lescaut); Guinevere.
(see *lovers, mistress, concubine, demimondaine, adulterous, courtesan, unmarried mother*)

PASSIONLESS
Belphoebe.
(see *apathy, stoical, cold-blooded, imperturbable, calm*)

PASSWORD
Sesame.
(see *pass*)

PAST
Limbo; Clio (see Muse); Urth; Postverta and Prorsa; Proustian.
(see *bygone, ancient, obsolete, yesterday, end*)

PASTELS
Mary Cassatt; Edgard Degas; Marie Laurencin.
(see *painter, artist, colorist*)

PASTORAL
Theocritean; Daphnis; Damoetas; Astrophel; Menalcas; Strephon; Corydon; Chloë; Montesinos; Lycidas; Tityrus; Meliboeus; Phyllis; Louis

PEDIGREED
Piso; Peregrine White; Silk-Stocking; Mr. Tittlebat Titmouse; Lady Clara Vere de Vere; Miss Carolina Skeggs.
(see *patrician, blue-stocking, lineage, genealogy, aristocratic, nobility*)

PEEPER
Lazarillo de Tormes; Susanna; Peeping Tom.
(see *glance, sly*)

PEG-LEGGED
John Silver; Silas Wegg.
(see *crippled*)

PELTED
Saint Stephen; Jack-a-Lent.
(see *stoned, battered, beating, hit, strike*)

PENALTY
Tisiphone; Alecto; Orbilian; Zanes; Zaleucus; Manlius; Megaera.
(see *punishment, retribution, chastise*)

PENANCE
Atys; Siva; Saint Christopher; Saint Ambrose; Saint Jerome; Owain; Mme. de Montespan; Robert the Devil; Nathaniel Hawthorne; Hester Prynne.
(see *humiliation, hair shirt, fasting*)

PENETRATING
Schamir; Vidar.
(see *sharp, keen*)

PENITENTIAL
Verticordia; Dismas; Hezekiah; Tannhaeuser; Giovanni Palestrina; Moll Flanders; Magdalene; Isenbras; Micah; Onesimus.
(see *repentance, remorse, contrite, regretful, sorrowful*)

PENITENTIARY
Tolbooth.
(see *jail, lockup, workhouse, dungeon, imprisonment, confinement*)

PENMANSHIP
Spencerian; John Hancock.
(see *handwriting*)

PENNY-PINCHER
Père Grandet; Arthur Gride; Gobseck; Harry Gill; Scrooge.
(see *miserliness, greed, avaricious, stingy*)

PENSIVE
Polyhymnia; Rodinesque; John-a-Dreams; Omar Khayyam.
(see *reverie, thoughtful, reflective, meditation*)

PERDITION
Tophet.
(see *hell, hades, ruination, destruction*)

PERENNIAL
Asaphic.
(see *permanent, imperishable, perpetual, deathless*)

PERFECTION
Hermaphroditus; Eden; Elysian; Atlantis; Hephzibah; Buddha; Utopian; Galahad; Devarshis; Henriette; Stella; Grandisonianism.
(see *faultless, impeccable, excellence, paragon, model, exemplary*)

PERFIDY
Sinon; Feretrius; Hannibal; Punic; Prusias; Carthaginian; Tarpeian Rock; Zacocia; Laomedon; Modred; Seven against Thebes.
(see *faithless, treachery, traitorous, dishonest, two-faced, venality, deceitful*)

PERFORMANCE
Franz Liszt; Paganini; Fritz Kreisler.
(see *virtuoso, concertize*)

PERFUME
Rosemary; Pierre Loti; Sabaean.
(see *fragrant, sweet-smelling, odorous, aromatic*)

PERFUNCTORY
Robotian.
(see *carelessness, indifference, heedless, neglectful*)

PERILOUS
Syrtes; Simeon Stylites; Damoclean; Jack London; Robinson Crusoe.
(see *danger, unsafe, precarious*)

PERIODIC
Olympiad.
(see *recurrence, interval, time, dates*)

PERIPATETIC
Aristotelian; Walking Stewart.
(see *itinerant, wanderer, roving*)

PERJURY
Naboth; Ahab; Laomedon.
(see *false accusation, forswear, perfidy, falsehood*)

PERMANENT
Medes and Persians.
(see *imperishable, perpetual, deathless, endless, unchangeable, perennial*)

PERNICIOUS
Sejus; Auster; Harmonia's Necklace; Rheingold.
(see *harmful, injurious, baneful, baleful, deadly, fatal, malign, malevolence*)

PERPETUAL
Luggnagg; Khartaphilos.
(see *unending, everlasting, eternity, interminable, perennial*)

PERPLEXITY
Gorgibus; Kilmansegg; Man with the Iron Mask; Queer Street.
(see *difficulty, doubtful, bewilderment, puzzle, straits, dilemma, quanaary, predicament*)

PERSECUTION
Io; Genseric; Elihu; Torquemada; Diocletian; Islam; Saint Bartholomew's Day; Bloody Mary; Falkland; Alfred Dreyfus.
(see *oppression, slavery, enslavement, afflicted, distressed, molested, murde.*)

PERSISTENCE
Demosthenes; Blondel; Robert Bruce; Hero and Leander; Javert; Evangeline; Petruchio; Jane Eyre; Fabian; Leicester Dedlock.
(see *steadfast, resolute, indefatigable, constancy*)

PERSONAL
Mme. de Sévigné; Soren Kierkegaard.
(see *individualistic, familiar, confidential, ego, self-absorption*)

PERSPICACITY
Sidney Carton; John Bull.
(see *sharp-sighted, shrewd, sagacity, astute, insight*)

PERSUASION
Peitho; Suada; Salome; Haggai; Pippa; Zechariah; Amphiaraus; Seneca the Elder; Sinon; Vertumnus; Veturia and Volumnia; Cassius; Amphion; Pocahontas; Worldly Wiseman; Clarence Darrow; Henry Ward Beecher.
(see *tempter, enticement, beguilement, ensnare, cogent, inducement, incitement, influential*)

PERT
Nerissa; Dorine; Susan Nipper.
(see *saucy, flippant, impudent, dapper*)

PERVERSE
Leicester Dedlock; Old Nick; Widow Blackacre; Sir Francis Wronghead.
(see *obstinate, stubborn, wilful, petulance, captious, ill-tempered*)

PERVERSION
Pasiphaë; Sodoma; Dorian Gray; Jack the Ripper; Richard von Krafft-Ebing; Masochism; Canace; Vathek; Marquis de Sade.
(see *aberration, abnormality, psychoneurotic, homosexuality*)

PESSIMISM
Schopenhauerian; Heraclitus; Soren Kierkegaard; George Warrington; William Ralph Inge; Weeping Philosopher; Henrik Ibsen.
(see *cheerless, dispirited*)

PESTILENCE
Stymphalian; Romola; Saint Roch; Sennacherib.
(see *plague, epidemic, contagion, deadly, malign, pernicious*)

PESTLE
Picumnus and Pilumnus.
(see *pound*)

PET (n.)
Little Eva.
(see *darling, favored, sweetheart*)

PETITE
Titania.
(see *dainty, tiny, little, diminutive*)

PETRIFYING
Gorgons; Furies; Medusa.
(see *fearful, frighten, terrifying, dreadful*)

PETTIFOGGER
Dodson and Fogg.
(see *lawyer, shyster*)

PETTY
Lilliputian; King of Yvetot; Tweedledum and Tweedledee; Jonas Chuzzlewit.
(see *picayune, trivial, unimportant, insignificant*)

PETULANCE
Mirabel; Lydia Languish; Baillie Nicol Jarvie; Sir Mungo Malagrowther.
(see *choleric, irascible, irritable, perverse, querulous, censorious*)

PHALANX
Epaminondas.
(see *generalship, strategist*)

PHALLIC
Priapus; Siva; Frey.
(see *orgiastic, reproductive, sensuality*)

PHANTOM
Saint Filumena; Mrs. Veal; Wild Huntsman.
(see *apparition, specter, ghost, visions, illusion, mirage*)

PHARAOH
Ikhnaton; Tutankhamen; Khufu.
(see *king, autocratic, despotic*)

PHARMACIST
Dioscurides; Galen.
(see *medicine, medicine man*)

PHENOMENON
Thrinacian; Vincent Crummles.
(see *miraculous, wonder-worker, prodigy*)

PHILANDERER
Jove; Widow Barnaby; Don Juan.
(see *girl-crazy, lady-killer, dalliance, amorous*)

PHILANTHROPIC

Samaritan; Boaz; Abou Ben Adhem; Publilius Philo; Daniel Deronda; Clara Barton; Florence Nightingale; Fourierist; John Howard; Elbert Hubbard; Rockefeller; Joseph Pulitzer; J. P. Morgan; Alfred Nobel; John Jacob Astor; Andrew Carnegie.

(see *altruistic, unselfish, humanitarian, benevolent, charitable*)

PHILISTINE

Philistines; Babbitt; Mr. Podsnap; Cristoph Wagner.

(see *materialistic, wordliness, narrow-minded*)

PHILOSOPHY (ancient)

Academia; Anaxagoras; Anaximenes; Anaximander; Parmenides; Pythagoras; Protagoras; Peripatetic; Plato; Stoic; Xenophanes; Epicurean; Lucian; Empedocles; Aristotelian; Thales; Pittacus; Heraclitus; Hypatia; Theophrastus; Polemon of Athens; Atticus; Horatian (Horace); Lucretian; Marcus Aurelius; Seneca the Younger; Manichaeus; Lao-Tse; Gilgamesh; Ciceronian; Democritus; Zeno; Epictetus.

(see *cynic, stoicism, idealistic*)

PHILOSOPHY (in literature)

Joseph Conrad; Edward Gibbon; William Wordsworth; François Voltaire; Thomas Hardy; Robert Browning; John Greenleaf Whittier; Panglossian; Square and Thwackum; Laputa; Mulvaney; Candide.

(see *moralizer, didactic*)

PHILOSOPHY (medieval and modern)

Baconian; Rousseauian; Henry Thoreau; Kantian; Schopenhauerian; Emersonian; Spinoza; Hegelian; Leibnitzian; Christian Rosenkreuz; William James; Leonardo da Vinci; Abelard and Héloise; Charles Montesquieu.

(see *materialistic, ethical*)

PHILTER

Sigurd; Isolde; Sophonisba; Mother Bunch; Quetzalcoatl; Friar Laurence.

(see *love potion, potions*)

PHOBIA

Pavor.

(see *neurosis, fearful*)

PHRASEOLOGY

Longinus; Horatian; Algernon Swinburne; Peter Mark Roget; Adriano de Armado; Alfred Jingle.

(see *diction, language*)

PHYSICIAN

Herophilus; Nicander; Ocyroë; Galen; Paean; Aesculapian; Melampus; Celsus; Hippocratic; Dioscurides; Machaon; Theodorus; Podalirius; Dhanvantari; Luke; Vaidya; Saint Pantaleon; Doctor Sangrado; Doctor Slop; Mayo; Walter Reed; Purgon.

(see *doctor, surgeon, healing, medicine*)

PHYSICS (science)

Albert Einstein; Galileo; Alexander Bell; Pliny the Elder.

(see *gravity, atomic, science*)

PHYSIQUE

Adonis; Rodinesque.

(see *body, muscular, athletics*)

PIANIST

Ignace Jan Paderewski; Chopinesque; Franz Liszt; Serge Rachmaninoff.

(see *music*)

PICARESQUE

Gil Blas.

(see *rogue, swashbuckling, adventurous*)

PINETREE
Pitys.
(see *trees*)

PINING
Tilburina; Lydia Languish; Narcissus; Daphnis; Byblis.
(see *repining, ennui, lackadaisical*)

PINION
Zetes; Icarian.
(see *winged, feather*)

PIONEER
Walt Whitman; "Kit" Carson; Samuel Maverick; Jacques Marquette; Bret Harte; Ramona.
(see *frontiersman, explorer, adventurous, innovator*)

PIPEDREAM
Alnaschar.
(see *visionary, impracticable*)

PIPER
Hamelin; Pan; Pied Piper; Syrinx.
(see *flute*)

PIRACY
John Quelch; Varangians; John Silver; Captain Kidd; Jolly Roger; Leleges; Lara; Jean Lafitte; Sir Henry Morgan; Vitalians; Barbarossa; Vikings; Dick Deadeye.
(see *freebooter, corsair, buccaneer, seafaring, marauder*)

PISTOL
Hedda Gabler.
(see *rifle*)

PITCHFORK
Man in the Moon.
(see *trident*)

PITHY
Philip of Macedon; Pharnaces.
(see *epigrammatic, sententious, terse, laconic*)

PITILESS
Vedius Pollio; Thaukt; Genseric; Jack Ketch; Pyrrhus (Neoptolemus); Hela; Bloody Mary; Lycus; Lemnian; Abimelech.
(see *merciless, unmerciful, relentless, hard-hearted, cold-hearted, ruthlessness*)

PITY
Via Dolorosa; Parsifal; Heliades.
(see *compassionate, sympathetic, merciful, clemency*)

PLACID
Darby and Joan; Alcyone; Bumbledonian; Irene.
(see *calm, composure, quiet, serenity, tranquillity, undisturbed*)

PLAGIARISM
Sir Fretful Plagiary.
(see *copy, imitation*)

PLAGUE
Chryseis; Saint Roch; Romola; Saint Sebastian; Phorbas.
(see *pestilence, epidemic, contagion, deadly*)

PLAIN (n.)
Campus Martius.
(see *smoothness*)

PLAINNESS
Epicurean; Curius Dentatus; Cincinnatus; John Knox; Jane Eyre; Gorgibus.
(see *ingenuousness, unaffected, sincerity, frank, candid, unsophisticated*)

PLAINTIFF
Lysias; John Doe; Mrs. Bardell.
(see *lawsuit, complaining*)

PLAINTIVE
Phrygian.
(see *sadness, sorrowful, elegy, dirge, melancholy, lugubrious*)

PLANET
Zadkiel; Johannes Kepler.
(see *star, constellation*)

PLANTATIONS
Aristaeus; Colonel Jack.
(see *orchard, acres, landowner*)

PLANT-BLIGHT
Robigus.
(see *rust, pestilence, damp*)

PLANT-LIFE
Shamash.
(see *nature, agriculture*)

PLANTS
Dioscurides; Demogorgon; Luther Burbank.
(see *herbs, vegetables, botanist, naturalism*)

PLATITUDINOUS
Sir Willful Witwould; Mrs. Mountstuart Jenkinson.
(see *sententious, commonplace, trite*)

PLATONIC
Tschaikovsky; Laura; Nadejda von Meck.
(see *passionless, apathy, chastity*)

PLAYWRIGHT
Aeschylean; Sophoclean; Euripidean; Plautus; Menander; Terence; Ibsen; Alexandre Dumas; Corneille; Racine; Molière; Shavian; Shakespearean; Sir Fretful Plagiary; Aristophanic; Marivaudage.
(see *drama, comedy, tragedy, farce*)

PLEASURE
Sybarite; Thelemite; Volupia; Hathor; Euphrosyne; Freyja; Lotophagi; Gilgamesh; Aristippus; Epicurean; John Stuart Mill; Omar Khayyam.
(see *voluptuousness, luxury-loving, entertainment, self-indulgence, sensuality, joy*)

PLEDGE
Regulus; Fides; Ver Sacrum; Tamar.
(see *guarantee, promise, hostage, security*)

PLENTY
Goshen; Irene; Lakshmi; Ops; Deae Matres; Amalthaea; Chicomecoatl; Fortuna; Saehrimnir; Heidrum; Lubberland.
(see *abundance, fertility, amplitude, wealth, opulence*)

PLIANT
Sir and Lady Pliant; Pliable.
(see *adaptable, obsequious, malleable, flexible*)

PLOT (v.)
Aelius Sejanus; Mata Hari; Rosencranz and Guildenstern; the Pages; Guy Fawkes; Jaffier; Harmodius and Aristogiton; Jean Latude.
(see *conspiracy, scheming, machinator, intrigue, stratagem*)

PLOW
Sita; Triptolemus; Boötes; Cincinnatus; Pallas.
(see *agriculturist, farmer*)

PLUCK
Trojan.
(see *spirited, courageous, resolute, valor, bravery, daring, manliness, heroism*)

PLUG
Talus.
(see *leak*)

PLUMES
Gainsborough; Hraesvelger; Kneph.
(see *feather*)

PLUMP
Dolly Madison; Clara Peggoty.
(see *amplitude, fat, buxomness*)

PLUNDERER
Caius Verres; Varangians; Sennacherib; Marcus Furius Camillus; Vitalians; Vandalism; Genseric; Achan; Lucius Mummius; Myrmidons; Telegonus; Naraka; Ferdinand Fathom.
(see *pillage, raider, ravaging, rapacious, loot, sack, spoils, predatory*)

POETASTER
MacFlecknoe; Mrs. Leo Hunter; Augustus Snodgrass; Querno; Della Cruscans; Bavius and Maevius.
(see *grandiloquent, magniloquence, turgid*)

POETRY (ancient)
Tempe; Euterpe; Erato; Calliope (see Muse); Anacreontic; Orpheus; Odin; Saraswati; Bragi; Pittacus; Pegasus; Sleipnir; Pindaric; Rishi; Pierian; Hippocrene; Heliconian; Aganippe; Parnassus; Bandusia; Castalian; Sappho; Homeric; Alcaeus; Phemius; Catullan; Propertian; Ovidian; Horatian; Vergilian; Tyrtaeus.

POETRY (modern)
Tennysonian; Sir John Suckling; Emily Dickinson; Lalla Rookh; Marlovian; Dante Gabriel Rossetti; François Voltaire; Samuel Taylor Coleridge; Robert Browning; Ben Jonson; John Keats; Walt Whitman; William Butler Yeats; William Wordsworth; Amy Lowell; Walther von der Vogelweide; Meistersinger; Miltonic; Oliver Wendell Holmes; Henry Wadsworth Longfellow; Minnesinger; John Greenleaf Whittier; James Russel Lowell; Kiplingese; Stevensonian; Spenserian; Walter Scott; Percy B. Shelley; Edgar Allan Poe; Shakespearean; Francois Villon; Algernon Swinburne.
(see *bard, minstrelsy*)

POISE
Canephoroe; Caryatids.
(see *balance, self-assurance, composure, dignified, unperturbed, undisturbed*)

POISON
Agathocles; Pico della Mirandola; Titus Vespasianus; Sophonisba; Sigismunda; Bagoas; Lucrezia Borgia; Nessus; Locusta; Agrippina the Younger; Skadhi; Nicander; Deianira; St. John; Ifurin; Sir John Suckling.
(see *venomous, toxicology*)

POLICEMAN
Peeler; Mr. Fang; Scotland Yard; Vigilantes; Javert; Vigiles.
(see *detection, discovery, vigilance, sleuth*)

POLICY-MAKING
Quintilius Varus.
(see *crisis, momentous*)

POLITE
Chesterfieldian; Miss Tox; Gibbet; Lawrence Boythorn.
(see *urbanity, courtesy, etiquette, well-behaved, manners, decorous, suave*)

POLITICAL GROUPS
Tammanyites; Silk-Stocking; Hunker; Salt River; Locofocos; Sinn Fein.
(see *democratic, republican, nationalism*)

POLITICAL INFLUENCE
Savonarola; Lorenzo the Magnificent; Mme. DuBarry; Richelieu; Cromwellian; Medici; Wolseyan; Dolly Madison; William M. Tweed; Grigori E. Rasputin; Maffia.
(see *influential, power*)

POLITICAL SCIENCE
Charles Montesquieu; Lord Bryce; Machiavellian; Adam Smith.
(see *law, international, economics*)

POLITICIANS (ancient)
Fulvia; Cato of Utica; Marius; Sulla; Ciceronian; Publilius Philo; Caesarean; Gracchi; Pompey; Asinius Pollio; Augustan; Periclean; Catiline.
(see *statesman*)

POLITICS (fictional)
Quidnunc; Jefferson Brick.
(see *roundabout*)

POLLUTE
Locusta.
(see *tainted, infection, poison, contagion*)

POLYGAMOUS
Brigham Young; Bluebeard; Mazdakite.
(see *much-married, bigamy, harem*)

POLYGLOT
Pico della Mirandola; Babel; Zal; Francisco Xavier.
(see *linguist*)

POLYSYLLABLES
Silas Wegg.
(see *sesquipedalian, magniloquence, grandiloquent*)

POMEGRANATE
Pronuba; Proserpina.
(see *fruit*)

POMPADOUR
Gibsonesque; Mme. de Pompadour.
(see *hair, headdress*)

POMPOUS
Scaramouch; Sir Piercie Shafton; Martinus Scriblerus; Monsieur Sotenville; Holophernes; Huggins and Muggins; Mr. Podsnap; Peregrinus Proteus; Pooh-Bah; Sir Matthew Mite; Mr. Turveydrop; Lantern Land; Laputa; Little Pedlington; Xerxes; John Lyly; Dogberry; Aldiborontiphoscophornio; Captain Lismahago; Major Bagstock; Major Bath; Don Adriano de Armado; Marquis of Carabas; Bombastes Furioso; Sargeant Buzfuz; Cambyses; Henry M. Stanley.
(see *showy, boastful, vainglorious, self-important, ostentation, display, bombastic*)

PONDEROUS
Leviathanic; Hringham.
(see *bulk, massiveness, might, heavy*)

POOL
Castalian; Bethesda; Juturna.
(see *lagoon, lake*)

POPLAR TREE
Heliades; Dryope.
(see *trees*)

POPULATION
Deucalion; Malthusian.
(see *creator, economics*)

PORCELAIN
Della Robbia; Josiah Wedgewood.
(see *pottery*)

PORNOGRAPHY
Ryparographer; Marquis de Sade.
(see *obscenity, indecency, shameless, indelicate, unchaste*)

PORT (harbor)
Palaemon; Portunus; Melicertes.
(see *shelter, asylum, destination*)

PORTER
Charon.
(see *ferryman*)

PORTION
Mazdakite; Benjamin.
(see *inheritance, legacy, divide*)

POSEUR
Monsieur Jourdain; Miss Carolina Skeggs; Lantern Land; Laputa; Alfred Lammle.
(see *affected, pretentious, imposture, charlatan, quackery*)

POSTHUMOUS
Ichabod.
(see *orphan*)

POSTPONE
Oenopion.
(see *defer, delay, procrastination*)

POSTURE
Dalcrozean; Isadora Duncan.
(see *tableau, dancing*)

POTAGE
Esau.
(see *food*)

POTENT
Milo; Balisardo.
(see *power, might, strength, force*)

POTIONS
Mother Bunch; Sigurd; Isolde; Quetzalcoatl; Friar Laurence.
(see *philter, love-potion*)

POTTERY
Perdix; Joseph Wedgewood.
(see *porcelain*)

POUND (v.)
Picumnus and Pilumnus; Mjöllnir.
(see *beating, strike, bruised, crushed*)

POVERTY (ancient)
Job; Naomi; Lucian; Protogenes; Lucius Opimius; Aglaos; Manlius Capitolinus; Fabricius; Martial.

POVERTY (economics)
Pierre J. Proudhon; Karl Marx; Sansculotte; Friedrich Engels.

POVERTY (fictional)
Oliver Twist; Marchioness; Algeresque; Dick Whittington; the Newcomes; Mimi; Major Bath; Parson Abraham Adams; Clara Peggoty; Panglossian; Peter Schlemihl; Duke Humphrey; Effie Deans; Pistol; Dominie Sampson.

POVERTY (group)
Okie; Jukes Family.

POVERTY (religious)
Saint Lawrence; Francis of Assisi.

POVERTY (residence)
Bermudas; Queer Street; Grub-Streeter.
(see *indigent, destitute, needy, straits, "broke," impecunious, pauper, beggar*)

POWER (military-political)
Nebuchadnezzar; King Log; Boadicea; Diocletian; Cleopatra; Alexander the Great; Pharaoh; Barbarossa; Krupp Family; Mark Antony; Agamemnon.
(see *might, strength, force, potent*)

PRECISION
Euclidean; Cornelia Blimber; Pierre Larousse; Bernouilli.
(see *exactitude, accuracy, correctness*)

PRECOCIOUS
Tages; Mozartean; Vincent Crummles; John Stuart Mill.
(see *prodigy, genius, proficient, talent*)

PREDATORY
Sir Henry Morgan; Stheno; Sampson Brass; Front de Boeuf; Sennacherib.
(see *plunderer, pillage, ravaging, sack, rapacious, greed, ravenous, loot, spoils*)

PREDESTINATION
Jansenists; Yue-Laou; John Knox.
(see *foredoomed, fate, necessity*)

PREDICAMENT
Kilmansegg; Queer Street.
(see *straits, quandary, dilemma, emergency*)

PREDICTION
Calchas; Delphi; Dodonean; Abaris; Apollonius; Postverta and Prorsa; Zal; Huldah; Tiresias; Veleda; Sibylla; Ammon; Mopsus; Tages; Camenae; Nereus; Ibycus; Amphiaraus; Ocyroë; Bacis; Xanthos; Vala; Spurinna Vestritius; Helenus; Nostradamus; Jeremiad; Isaian; Weird Sisters; Witch of Endor; Mrs. Nickleby; Red Man; Banshee; Jules Verne; Kalanos; Mother Shipton.
(see *foretell, prophet, seer, clairvoyant, prognostication, soothsayer, divination*)

PREGNANCY
Postverta and Prorsa; Metis; Lupercus; Lucina; Fordicidia; Feronia; Partula; Picumnus and Pilumnus.
(see *childbirth, delivery*)

PREHISTORIC
Stonehenge; Leleges; Iapetus; Ogyges; Pelasgians.
(see *ancient, archaic, primeval, antiquity*)

PREJUDICE
Mason and Dixon; Rev. Micah Balwhidder; Jim Crow; Leicester Dedlock; Doctor Slop; Squire Western; Isabella I; Edward Gibbon; Ku Klux; Monsieur Josse; Baillie Nicol Jarvie; Alfred Dreyfus.
(see *bias, bigotry, opinionated, dogmatic, partiality, intolerance, nationalism*)

PREMONITION
Calpurnia.
(see *warning, forewarn, ominous, ill-omen*)

PRESBYTERIAN
John Knox.
(see *Protestant*)

PRESCRIPTION
Mrs. Glasse; Doctor Sangrado.
(see *remedy, apothecary, medicine, recipes*)

PRESENT (gift)
Kriss Kringle; Prinz Ruprecht; Saint Nicholas.
(see *gifts, offering, prize, donation, wedding present*)

PRESENT (time)
Verthandi.
(see *time*)

PRESERVER
Vishnu; Ino; Stator; Soter.
(see *savior, protector, guardian, safeguard, defender*)

PRIEST
Zadok; Numa; Flamen; Druids; Atys; Nebo; Eumolpus; Foigard; Ezra; Magi; Jacques Marquette; Saint Ambrose; Melchizedek; Onias Menelaus; Phinehas; Père La Chaise.
(see *clergy, minister*)

PRIESTESS
Sibylla; Pythian; Norma.
(see *nun*)

PRIMEVAL
Iapetus; Pelasgians; Troglodytae; Tiki; Seb; Tiamat; Ogyges; Demogorgon; Viraj.
(see *ancient, old, antiquity, archaic, obsolete, old-fashioned*)

PRINCE
Beelzebub; Memnon; Maharajah; Adrastus.
(see *imperial, king, majesty, lord, overlord, chieftain*)

PRINCESS
Pocahontas; Graciosa; Lalla Rookh.
(see *queenly, nobility*)

PRINCIPAL
Ka.
(see *essential, first, original*)

PRISMATIC
Iris.
(see *light, iridescent, rainbow*)

PRISON
Tolbooth; Tullianum; Limbo; Black Hole of Calcutta; Bastille; John Howard; Amy Dorrit.
(see *dungeon, jail, lockup, workhouse, penitentiary*)

PRIVACY
Melusina; Soren Kierkegaard.
(see *seclusion, secrecy, concealed, solitude*)

PRIVATEER
Jean Lafitte; John Quelch; Alexander Selkirk.
(see *freebooter, corsair, buccaneer, pirate*)

PRIVILEGED
Incan; Molmutius; Eupatridae; Israel; Junker; Silk-Stocking.
(see *exemption, favored, franchise, advantage, reserved, exclusive*)

PRIZE
Alfred Nobel; Spolia Opima; Rachel.
(see *award, grant, gifts, present*)

PRIZE-FIGHTING
Marquis of Queensbury.
(see *boxing, fisticuffs, wrestling*)

PROBABILITY
Carneades.
(see *verisimilitude*)

PROBE
Wilhelm Roentgen.
(see *investigation, search, test, research*)

PROCRASTINATION
Fabian; John Jarndyce; Oenopion; Lentulus Sura.
(see *delay, defer, dilatory, postpone*)

PROCREATION
Lupercus; Prajapati; Pushan; Nefertem; Khem.
(see *creation, productivity*)

PROCURER
Pandarus; Khufu; Long Meg of Westminister; the Peachums; Squire of Dames; Mother Douglas.
(see *pimp, panderer*)

PRODIGAL
Zeluco; Sir John Suckling; Aulus Vitellius; Charles Surface; Abu Hassan; Heir of Linne.
(see *wasteful, lavish, extravagance, squanderer*)

PRODIGIOUS
John Buncle; Dominie Sampson; Badebec.
(see *huge, vast, enormous, extraordinary, miraculous*)

PRODIGY
Phoenix; Mendelssohn-Bartholdy; Mozartean; Paganini.
(see *phenomenon, genius, miraculous*)

PRODUCTIVITY
Ceres; Badebec; Nefertem; Tellus; Feronia; Priam; Iasion; Ge; Proserpina.
(see *fertility, prolific, abundance, fruitfulness*)

PROFANATION
Clodius; Abihu; Lucifer; Peregrinus Proteus; Milanion.
(see *impiety, irreligious, irreverent, violation, blasphemous*)

PROFESSOR
Holophernes; Teufelsdroeckh.
(see *teacher, schoolteacher, pedantic, learned*)

PROFICIENT
Johannes Factotum.
(see *versatile, skill, accomplished, able*)

PROFIT
Alnaschar.
(see *reward, advantage, useful*)

PROFITLESS
Lantern Land; Laputa.
(see *worthless, useless, valueless*)

PROFLIGACY
Piso; Polemon of Athens; Lentulus Sura; Zeluco; Clodius; Mark Antony; Marmion; Messalina; Clodia; La Tosca; Julia; Faustina; Lady Bellaston; Charles Surface; Captain MacHeath; Sir Harry Wildair; Peregrine Pickle; Philip Wharton; Marquis of Steyne; Silk-Stocking; "Diamond Jim" Brady.
(see *corrupt, immorality, depravity, roué, dissolute, shameless, debauchee*)

PROFOUND
Dostoievskian; Goethe; Socrates; Leonardo da Vinci.
(see *intellectual, learned, erudite, sagacity*)

PROGENITOR
Manes; Manu; Tiki; Prajapati; Pyrrha; Ptah.
(see *ancestor, forebear*)

PROGENY
Levana.
(see *offspring, lineage*)

PROGNOSTICATION
Sibylla; Cassandra; Ammon; Etruscan.
(see *foretell, prophet, clairvoyant, seer, soothsayer, prediction*)

PROGRESSIVE
Periclean; Sordello; Elizabethan; Victorian.
(see *liberal, improvement, reformer*)

PROHIBITIONIST
Andrew Volstead.
(see *teetotaler, temperance*)

PROLETARIAT
Pisistratus; Pierre J. Proudhon; Friedrich Engels; Karl Marx; Lenin.
(see *worker, laborer, labor-movement*)

PROLIFIC
Ishtar; Priam; Ge; Selene; Frey; Mozartean; Badebec; Feronia; Walking Stewart; Giuseppe Verdi; Rubensian.
(see *fertility, fruitfulness, fecundity, productivity*)

PROMENADE
Duke Humphrey.
(see *stroller*)

PROMISCUOUS
Clodia; Julia; Lady Bellaston; Lady Booby.
(see *immorality, dissolute, "loose," wanton, licentious*)

PROMISE
Fides; Feretrius; Regulus; Dorigen; Sigurd; Hernani; Jack-Amend-All; Jacob's Ladder.
(see *agreement, contract, pact*)

PROMONTORY
Palinurus.
(see *island*)

PROMOTER
Favonius; Lorenzo the Magnificent; Lars Porsena; Edwardian.
(see *progressive, enterprising, patron, encouragement*)

PRONUNCIATION
Desiderius Erasmus; Spoonerism.
(see *diction, language, speech, articulate*)

PROOF
Euphorbus; Ion.
(see *recognition, test*)

PROP
Telamon.
(see *supporter, brace*)

PROPAGANDISTIC
Uncle Tom; Ignatius Loyola.
(see *proselytizer, convert, doctrinaire*)

PROPERTY
William the Conqueror; Naboth.
(see *landowner*)

PROPHECY
Dodonean; Pythian; Delphi; Scipio Africanus.
(see *prediction, prognostication, foretell, clairvoyant, seer, soothsayer*)

PROPHET
Calchas; Phineus; Picus; Xanthos; Tiresias; Zal; Jeremiad; Helenus; Nathan; Spurinna Vestritius; Amphiaraus; Apollonius; Abaris; Silenus; Chiron; Balaam; Nahum; Bacis; Mopsus; Pan; Proteus; Manichaeus; Melampus; Lentulus Sura; Tages; Nereus; Tarquinius Priscus; Ibycus; Nostradamus; Ancaeus; Isaian; Haggai; Habakkuk; Hosea; Samuel; Daniel; Zephaniah; Elijah; Amos; Ezekiel; Zechariah; Piers Plowman; John the Baptist; Kalanos; Mokanna; Malachi; Micah; Obadiah.

PROPHETESS
Themis; Huldah; Ocyroë; Oenone; Ulrica; Vala; Nymphs; Postverta and Prorsa; Thetis; Cassandra-like; Sibylla; Veleda; Camenae; Witch of Endor; Deborah; Weird Sisters; Miriam; Joanna Southcott; Mother Shipton; Philip; White Ladies.

PROPITIATORY
Miss Tox.
(see *compliance, complacent, expiation*)

PROPOSAL
Malvolio; Mrs. Bardell.
(see *affianced, breach-of-promise, marriage*)

PROPRIETARY
Rajput.
(see *ownership, landowner, property*)

PROPRIETRESS
Mrs. Jarley; Mrs. M. Todgers.
(see *landlady, host*)

PROPRIETY
Pudicitia; Jean Martinet; Mrs. Grundy.
(see *decorous, etiquette, decency, manners, conventional*)

PROSAIC
Martha.
(see *unimaginative, literal, tedious, commonplace*)

PROSCRIPTION
Lucius Cornelius Sulla; Marius.
(see *expropriation, condemned, banishment, exile*)

PROSELYTIZER
Francisco Xavier; Ignatius Loyola; St. Sebastian.
(see *propagandistic, convert*)

PROSPERITY
Salus; Saturn; Shri; Lakshmi; Amalthaea; Frothi; Frey.
(see *wealth, riches, fortune, luck*)

PROSTITUTE
Dol Common; Manon (Lescaut); Nana; Magdalene; Rahab; Doll Tearsheet; Paphian; Mother Douglas; Theodora; La Traviata; Acca Larentia.
(see *street-walker, whore, strumpet, harlot*)

PROTECTION
Lloyd's; Aegis; Alsatia; Gibraltar; Palladium; Seven Sleepers of Ephesus.
(see *safeguard, shelter, bulwark*)

PROTECTION-MONEY
Rob Roy; Maffia.
(see *blackmail, extortion*)

PROTECTOR
Penates; Saint Patrick; Celadon; Cabiric; Aristaeus; Molmutius; Vigiles; Elijah; Vigilantes; Dïoscuri; Morgante; Imhotep; Leonidas; Licinius; Michael; Lares; Manes; Nancy.
(see *defender, champion, guardian, tutelar, warder, patron*)

PROTECTRESS
Laverna; Lucina; Rahab; Levana; Siguna; Althaea.
(see *patroness*)

PROTEGE
Smike; Richard Babley; Martial.
(see *favored*)

PROTESTANT
Ulrich Zwingli; Calvinistic; Martin Luther.
(see *religion, Presbyterian, Moravian, anti-clerical*)

PROTESTATION
Adullamite.
(see *disapproval, objector*)

PROTOGRAM
Smectymnuus.
(see *composite*)

PROTRACTED
Epimenides; Dred Scott Case; John Jarndyce; Iliad.
(see *lengthy, tedious*)

PROVERB
Poor Richard; Goethe; Apelles; Tupperian.
(see *maxims, aphorisms, epigrammatic, axioms*)

PROVIDER
Wagon Boy.
(see *provisions, nourisher, sustenance*)

PROVINCIAL
Abraham Slender; Monsieur Sotenville.
(see *rusticity, rude, country gentleman*)

PROVISIONS
Chicomecoatl.
(see *food, sustenance, provider*)

PROWESS
Horatii and Curiatii; Guy of Warwick; Gradasso.
(see *daring, bravery, valor, heroism, fearless, intrepid, courageous, gallantry*)

PRUDE
Puritanic; Bowdlerize; Mr. Podsnap; Jenkins; Victorian; Reverend Mister Chadband; Sir Jerry Witwold.
(see *coy, demure, modesty, straitlaced, affected, propriety*)

PRUDENCE
Metis; Minerva; Ganesa; Agricola; Epictetus.
(see *wisdom, discreet, carefulness, cautious, circumspect, good-sense, foresight, tact*)

PRYING
Marplot; Paul Pry; Lot's Wife; Morgiana; Quidnunc.
(see *meddlesome, busybody, curiosity*)

PSALMIST
Asaphic.
(see *poetry*)

PSEUDO
Wardour Street.
(see *imitation, counterfeit, spurious, forgery*)

PSEUDO-GENTEEL
Miss Carolina Skeggs; Madelon.
(see *social-climber, affected, pretentious*)

PSEUDO-GOD
Salmoneus; Empedocles.
(see *demigod, apotheosized*)

PSEUDO-MAGNIFICENCE
Emperor Jones.
(see *rococo*)

PSEUDONYM
Atticus; Outis; Delia; Democritus Junior; Madelon; Smectymnuus.
(see *incognito*)

PSEUDO-SCIENTIFIC
Lagado.
(see *charlatan, mountebank, quackery*)

PSYCHIATRIST
Alfred Adler; Havelock Ellis; Carl G. Jung; Freudian; Richard von Krafft-Ebing.
(see *aberration, abnormal, neurosis, fetishism, mother-complex, father-love, fixation*)

PSYCHOLOGICAL
Pierre Corneille; Anton Chekhov; D. H. Lawrence; Jean Racine; Robert Browning; Henry James; James Joyce; Dostoievskian; Joseph Conrad.
(see *delineation, characterization*)

PSYCHOLOGY
Psyche; William James; Fear Fortress; Phineas P. Quimby.
(see *mind, reason*)

PSYCHONEUROTIC
Elsie Venner; Hedda Gabler; Masochism; Marquis de Sade.
(see *neurotic*)

PUBLICAN
Zaccheus; St. Matthew.
(see *tax-complainer, toll-gate*)

PUBLIC GROUND
Tom Tiddler; Campus Martius.
(see *socialism*)

PUBLICITY-SEEKER
Salmoneus; Peregrinus Proteus; Empedocles.
(see *social-climber*)

PUBLIC WORKS
Asinius Pollio; Sesostris; Marcus Ulpius Trajan.
(see *philanthropic*)

PUFF (v.)
Physignathus.
(see *breath, gust*)

PUGILISM
Marquis of Queensbury.
(see *boxing, fisticuffs, wrestling*)

PUGNACIOUS
Tullus Hostilius; Amycus.
(see *belligerent, truculent, quarrelsome, fighting, contention*)

PUNCTILIOUS
Jean Martinet; Rajput; Commodore Trunnion.
(see *meticulous, precision, finical, fastidious, carefulness*)

PUNCTUATION
Ralph Roister Doister.
(see *miswriting*)

PUNISHMENT (inflictors of)
Brahma; Ibycus; Torquemada; Eumenides; Nemesis; Alastor; Dirae; Furies; Feretrius; Varuna; Yama; Vishnu; Anteros; Melantius.
(see *sadism, cruelty, lashing, whipping, scourging, horsewhip, flogging, beating*)

PUNISHMENT (places of)
Hades; Stygian; Naraka; Tartarus; Nastrond; Sheol; Niflheim.
(see *hades, hell, lower world, underworld, infernal*)

PUNISHMENT (victims of)
Arachne; Tantalus; Salmoneus; Marsyas; Francesca of Rimini; Tityus; Andhaba; Capua; Ixion; Ivan Mazeppa; Idomeneus; Raskolnikov; Cassiopeia; Niobe; Caryatids; Callisto; Farinata; Dirce; Man in the Moon; Amphion; Anchises; Miriam.
(see *victim, martyrdom, behead, decapitation*)

PUNSTER
Outis; Speed; Launce.
(see *quipster*)

PUPIL
Abecedarians.
(see *studious*)

PUPPET
Judy.
(see *pawn, dupe, cat's-paw*)

PUPPET-KING
Maximilian of Mexico; Zedekiah.
(see *king*)

PURBLIND
Nyctymene.
(see *short-sighted*)

PURCHASER
Peter Funk.
(see *payment*)

PURGATORY
Saint Patrick.
(see *expiation, lower world, atonement*)

PURIFICATION
Pales; Lupercus; Fordicidia; Eleusinian; Dostoievskian; Epimenides; Eumolpus; Kistnerappan.
(see *purity, sacrifice*)

PURITANIC
Roundheads; Priscilla, the Puritan Maid; Reverend Mr. Stiggins; Mr. Podsnap.
(see *ascetic, strict, strait-laced, prude*)

PURITY (emblems of)
Breidablik; Pudicitia; Parthenon; Vestal; Madonna; Diana; Artemis; Minerva; Gefjon; Sangreal.
(see *chastity, holiness, virginity, virtue, innocence, continence, impeccable, faultless*)

PURITY (female)
Kunigunde; Zémire; Nama; Miranda; Nutbrown Maid; Saint Winifred; Belphoebe; Imogen; Juliet; Pamela; Godiva; Britomartis; Oriana; Iphigenia; Sabra.

PURITY (male)
Selim; Abelites; Paphnutius; Lohengrin; Hippolytus; Joseph; Parsifal; Gymnosophist; Saint Anthony; Galahad; Sikh.

PURSUIT
Dirae; Orestes; Eumenides; Alpheus; Arethusa; Furies; Liburnians; Britomartis; Erlking; Banquo; Tam o'Shanter; Galloping Dick.
(see *chase, race, hunter*)

PUZZLE
Osiris; Kilmansegg; Queer Street; Abdemon; Man with the Iron Mask.
(see *riddle, dilemma, quandary, enigmatic*)

PYGMY
Lilliputian; Blefuscu; Vamana; Sindre; Yellow Dwarf; Tom Thumb.
(see *midget, dwarf, stunted, freak*)

PYRAMIDS
Khufu.
(see *slave labor, Pharaoh*)

PYRE
Sardanapalus; Peregrinus Proteus; Evadne; Deianira; Hringham; Kalanos; Thecla.
(see *cremated, self-destruction, immolation*)

PYTHON
Zombi.
(see *serpent, snake*)

Q

QUACKERY
Little Pedlington; Paracelsus; Laputa; Katerfelto; Lantern Land; Friar Bungay; Belphegor; Subtle; Puff.
(see *charlatan, humbug, mountebank, pretender, imposture*)

QUAIL (v.)
Ruggiero.
(see *fearful, downcast, dispirited*)

QUANDARY
Queer Street; Kilmansegg; Belvidera.
(see *dilemma, puzzle, riddle, perplexity, straits, difficulty*)

QUANTITY
Benjamin.
(see *bulk, massiveness*)

QUARRELSOME
John Noakes; Tybalt; Sir Lucius O'Trigger; Peter Peebles; Xanthippe; Widow Blackacre; Tweedledum and Tweedledee; Centaur; Hera.
(see *belligerent, pugnacious, bickering, wrangling, irascible, choleric, petulance, disputatious, dissension*)

QUEENLY
Juno; Mab; Statira; Semiramis; Clytemnestra; Penthesilea; Dido; Hecuba; Elizabethan; Marie Antoinette.
(see *princess, nobility, imperial, majesty*)

QUERULOUS
Jaques; Mrs. Gummidge.
(see *complaining, faultfinder, discontented, petulance, irascible*)

QUEST
Gilgamesh; Ithuriel; Mambrino; Manoa; Sleeping Beauty; Doctor Syntax; Sangreal; Parsifal; Galahad.
(see *search, crusader, pursuit, journey, investigation*)

QUESTIONING
Abdemon; Lucian; Socrates; Jean Hardouin; Pyrrhonian.
(see *inquisitive, investigation, research*)

QUICK
Gyes; Mercury; Ladas; Jack and the Bean Stalk; Jack Robinson.
(see *nimble, rapid, speed, swift, fast, fleet*)

QUICKSANDS
Syrtes; Edgar Ravenswood.
(see *bog, marsh, swamp*)

QUICKSTEP
Zouave.
(see *drill*)

QUICK-TEMPERED
Kilkenny Cats; Katharine.
(see *ill-tempered, irascible, choleric, anger*)

QUIET
Hypnos; King Log; Harpocrates; Pax; Larunda.
(see *serenity, tranquillity, peace, calm, silence*)

QUIPSTER
Trinculo; Joe Miller; Touchstone.
(see *punster, joke, witty, humor*)

QUITTER
Pliable.
(see *cowardly, faint-hearted, fearful, timidity*)

QUOIT
Palamedes; Hyacinthus; Myron's Cow.
(see *games, throw*)

QUOTER
Mrs. Harris; Dick Swiveller; Mrs. Mountstuart Jenkinson.
(see *repetition*)

R

RABBLE
Louis XVI; William Hogarth.
(see *group-action, mob-psychology, mob-law, vulgarity*)

RACE (running)
Hippomenes; Milanion; Bendis; Tam o'Shanter; Luna; Ladas.
(see *foot-race, runner, marathon, sprinter*)

RACEHORSE
Ladas; Pacolet; Tattersall's.
(see *horse-racing, horse*)

RACIALISM
Josephus; Maccabees; Madama Butterfly.
(see *nationalism, master-race*)

RACKET
Curetes.
(see *noisy, din, commotion, tumultuous, loud, boisterous, vociferous*)

RACONTEUR
Sindbad the Sailor; Scheherezade.
(see *anecdotal, tale-teller*)

RACY
Plautus; Giovanni Boccaccio; Chaucerian.
(see *spirited, lively, indelicate, obscenity*)

RADIANT
Phoebe and Phoebus; Usas; Utu; Thia; Delia; Aurora; Hyperion; Helios; Sol; Parian; Watling Street; Chloris; Célimène; Harpocrates.
(see *bright, shining, light, luminous, resplendent*)

RADICAL
Leon Trotsky; Pierre J. Proudhon; Friedrich Engels; Sacco-Vanzetti; Karl Marx; Lenin; John Stuart Mill; Godwinian; Locofocos; Sansculotte.
(see *liberal, communist, socialism*)

RAGE
Eris; Thyia; Cambyses; Rumplestilzchen; Mariamne.
(see *anger, wrathful, fury, frenzy, resentful, choleric, ill-tempered, indignation*)

RAGS TO RICHES
Pip; Roderick Random.
(see *self-made, fortune-hunter, luck, change, rich*)

RAIDER
Apache; Leleges; Vitalians; Varangians.
(see *marauder, bandit, desperado, freebooter, plunderer, pillage, ravaging*)

RAILLERY
Momus; Benedick.
(see *banter, irony, ridicule, derisive, mockery, satirism*)

RAIMENT
Herr Teufelsdroeckh; Silk-Stocking; Miss Flora McFlimsey; Longchamps.
(see *apparel, clothing, dress, costume*)

RAIN
Ullur; Tlaloc; Varuna; Alrinach; Frey; Eurus; Vritra; Anaites; Pluvius; Notus; Parjanya; Hyades; Indra; Japheth; Telchines.
(see *cloudburst, shower, storm, downpour, rainstorm*)

RAINBOW
Iris; Zeus; Bifrost; Midgard.
(see *colorful*)

RAIN PORTENT
Saint Swithin.
(see *weather man*)

RAINSTORM
Mother Carey.
(see *rain*)

RAKISH (libertine)
Lovelace; Silk-Stocking; Lothario; Casanovian; James Steerforth; Don Juan; Sir Harry Wildair; Iachimo; Tityre-Tu; Charles Surface; Mirabel.
(see *adulterous, impure, illicit, corrupt, unchaste. dissolute*)

RAM
Ammon; Kneph; Phrixus.
(see *sheep*)

RAMBLING
Peripatetic; Meander.
(see *desultory, disconnected, discursive, capricious*)

RANCH
Pales; Apis; Geryon; Glaucus; Samuel Maverick.
(see *herdsman, flocks, shepherd*)

RANCOROUS
Smelfungus; Zacocia; Doctor Slop.
(see *spiteful, vindictive, hateful, malevolence, malign*)

RANSOM
Chryseis; Ion Perdicaris.
(see *hostage, expiation, redemption, deliverance*)

RANT
John Lyly; Cambyses; Termagant; Jeronimo; Aldiborontiphoscophornio.
(see *bombastic, exaggeration, magniloquence*)

RAPACIOUS
Harpies; Freki; Caius Verres.
(see *ravaging, predatory, plundcrer, greed, avaricious*)

RAPE
Dinah; Menander; Lucretia.
(see *seduced, debauchery*)

RAPID
Ladas; Ullur; Grani; Galloping Dick; Liburnians; Sol; Phidippides; Milanion; Al Borak.
(see *fast, fleet, quick, speed, swift*)

RAPIER
Laertes; Morglay.
(see *sword, broadsword*)

RAPIST
Tityus; Eurytion; Sextus Tarquinius; Tereus; Lovelace.
(see *seducer, debauchee*)

RAPPING
Margaret Fox.
(see *spiritualist, medium*)

RAPT
Yogi; Vaikuntha.
(see *absorption, self-absorption, ecstasy*)

RARE
Thomas Chippendale; Phoenix; Rumplestilzchen.
(see *extraordinary, strange, unusual, exquisite, bizarre*)

REASON
Ve; Goddess of Reason; Houyhnm; Thomas Aquinas; Logistilla; Kantian; Aristippus; Anaxagoras; Ethan Allen.
(see *intelligent, rationalistic, mind, understanding, brain*)

REBELLIOUS
Arioch; Absalom; Sadducees; Tatar; Maccabees; Roundheads; Molly Maguire; John Ball; Zedekiah; Wat Tyler; Hezekiah; Modred; Spartacus; Ethan Allen; Thaddeus Kosciusko; Jack-Amend-All; Giuseppe Mazzini; Amasa; Rienzi; Jeroboam; Korah; Onan.
(see *disobedience, mutiny, defiance, insurrection, revolutionary*)

REBIRTH
Rhea; Zagreus; Sabazius; Empedocles; Tammuz; Aristeas; Dionysus Zagreus; Osiris; Eleusinian; Narasinha.
(see *reincarnation*)

REBUKE
Haggai.
(see *censorious, chastise, admonitory, reproachful, denunciatory*)

RECANTATION
Johannes Eckhart; Galileo.
(see *repudiation, renunciation*)

RECIPES
Mrs. Glasse; Apician; Mother Bunch.
(see *cookery*)

RECIPROCATION
Anteros; Daphnis.
(see *mutual*)

RECKLESS
Polyphemus; Front de Boeuf; Paris; Belial; Casanovian; Genseric; Alcibiades; Barnadine; Ate; Nell Gwyn; Mercutio; Don Juan; Peter the Hermit; Hotspur; Sir Harry Wildair; Jehu.
(see *rash, carelessness, thoughtless, inattentive, unconcerned, imprudent, indiscretion, hot-headed*)

RECLUSE
Abelard and Héloise; Troglodytae; Montesinos; Walden Pond; Manfred; Peter Wilkins.
(see *hermit, ascetic, retirement, seclusion, solitude*)

RECOGNITION
Perdita; Ion; Euryclea; Euphorbus.
(see *identification, acknowledgment, confession*)

RECOLLECTION
Proustian; Mnemosyne.
(see *memory, remembrance*)

RECOMPENSE
Spolia Opima; Hugh Strap.
(see *compensation, retribution*)

RECONCILIATION
La Traviata; Leontes; Ion; Concordia; Perdita; Cephalus; Hermione; Sir Mador.
(see *agreement, concord, harmony, appeasement, atonement, expiation*)

RECONNOITRE
Eurylochus.
(see *scout, spy*)

RECORD (v.)
Fasti; Thoth.
(see *register, annals, chronicle, diary, list*)

RECREANT
Hosea; Polydorus.
(see *apostasy, backslider, deserter, faint-hearted, mean-spirited, traitorous, cowardly*)

REGRETFUL
Oenone; Owain.
(see *repentance, penitential, remorse, contrite, sorrowful*)

REGULATION
Hoyle; Edward Cocker; Hooverize; Marquis of Queensbury; Eunomia.
(see *orderliness, law, management, control*)

REINCARNATION
Euphorbus; Vishnu; Dionysus Zagreus; Empedocles; Aristeas; Narasinha.
(see *rebirth, metamorphosis, transfiguration*)

REITERATION
Vanderdecken.
(see *repetition*)

REJOINDER
Parthian.
(see *response, answer*)

REJUVENATION
Cagliostro; Zombi; Pelias; Ponce de Leon; Phaon; Hygeia; Bimini; Iduna; Khartaphilos.
(see *renew, self-renewing*)

RELATIVITY
Albert Einstein.
(see *mathematics, physics*)

RELEASE
Barabbas.
(see *freedom, deliverance*)

RELEGATED
Man in the Moon.
(see *exile, banishment, ostracism*)

RELENTLESS
Mephistophelian; Draconian; Dirae; Melantius; Mme. Thérèse Defarge; Richelieu; Javert.
(see *ruthlessness, implacable, inexorable, obdurate, merciless, unforgiving*)

RELIABLE
Bucephalus; Abdiel; Mentor; Pythias; Porcia; Dugald Dalgetty.
(see *dependable, trustworthy, constancy*)

RELIANCE
Spes; Stonewall Jackson.
(see *self-assurance, confidence*)

RELICS
Jonathan Oldbuck.
(see *archaeological, antiques*)

RELIEF
Bethesda; Gilead.
(see *aid, assistance, succor, alms, subsidize, bounty, helpfulness*)

RELIGION
Mahomet; Euhemeristic; Numa; Egeria; Lao-Tse; Ikhnaton; Manichaeus; Zoroaster.
(see *holiness, saintliness, piety, reverence*)

RELIGIOUS
Parsifal; Handel and Haydn; Count Zinzendorf; Wesleyan; Abecedarians; Shadrach; Saint Augustine; Calvinistic; John Bunyan; Callimachus; Johannes Eckhart; Thomas á Kempis; John Huss; Pachomius; Giovanni Palestrina; Ulrich Zwingli; Red Cross Knight; Paphnutius; Santa Rosalia; Phineas P. Quimby; Martin Luther; Mary Baker Eddy; Dinah Morris.
(see *devout, god-fearing, nun, monks, preacher, clergy, patron saint*)

REMEDILESS
Telephus; Philoctetes.
(see *hopeless, unhealable*)

REPRESENTATIVE
Ivan Ivanovitch; Philaeni; Horatii and Curiatii.
(see *ambassador, delegation, emissary*)

REPRISAL
Robin and Makyne; Whiteboyism.
(see *retaliation, retribution, revenge, punishment*)

REPROACHFUL
Xanthos; Launce; Bezonian; Valentine; Philippic; Giottesque.
(see *abusive, opprobrious, scurrilous, ribald, invective, calumnious, denunciatory, injurious, offensive, insulting, insolent*)

REPROBATE
Silk-Stocking; Peregrine Pickle; Lorenzo.
(see *corrupt, dissolute, debauchee, profligacy, immorality, scoundrel*)

REPRODUCTION (copy)
Mme. Marie Tussaud; Jean Auguste Ingres; Veturius Mamurius; Menaechmus.
(see *replica, alike*)

REPRODUCTIVE
Ishtar; Isis; Siva; Dagon; Khem; Kneph; Venus.
(see *procreation, creation, fertility*)

REPTILE
Sebek; Yacumama.
(see *snake, serpent, rattlesnake, python, crocodile*)

REPUBLICAN
Polybius; Giuseppe Mazzini; Cato of Utica; Tacitean; Livian; Publicola; Sansculotte.
(see *democratic*)

REPUDIATION
Tess of the D'Urbervilles.
(see *renunciation, recantation, divorce, disinherit*)

REPULSE
Salt River; Manlius Capitolinus.
(see *downfall, rout, defeat*)

REPUTATION
Falkland.
(see *character, fame, esteem, honor, prestige, celebrity, disrepute*)

REQUEST (n.)
Semele; King Ryance.
(see *demand, claim, importunate*)

REQUIEM
Giuseppe Verdi.
(see *church-music, mass*)

RESCUE
Pocahontas; Ino; Zerubbabel; Sigurd; Saint George; Sister Anne; Hypsipyle; Fatima; Isaac; Zémire; David Livingstone; Azaziel; Azor; Blondel; Bernard of Menthon; Launfal; John Ridd; John Smith.
(see *deliverance, redemption, release, salvation, liberator*)

RESEARCH
Lagado; Callimachus; Clio (see Muse); Claudius; Herodotean.
(see *studious, learned, investigation, search, analytical, examining*)

RESEMBLANCE
Dromios; Sosia; Veronica; Menaechmus; Donatello; Antipholus.
(see *alike, likeness, similarity, identical, twins, duplicate, equality*)

RESENTFUL
Gorgibus; Latona.
(see *anger, rage, wrathful, fury, frenzy, indignation, choleric, ill-tempered*)

RESERVED
Talassius; Goshen.
(see *exclusive, privileged, favored, advantage*)

RESIDENCE
Dred Scott Case; Bermudas; Queer Street; Stellenbosche.
(see *address, abode, home*)

RESIGNATION (submission)
Stoic; Jephthah; Gethsemane; Phaedrus; Job; Marcus Aurelius; Auld Robin Gray; Griselda; Zadig; Gudrun; Enoch Wray.
(see *submission, acquiescence, compliance, patience, uncomplaining, stoical*)

RESILIENT
Thomas Traddles.
(see *buoyant, elastic, cheerful, vivacious*)

RESISTANCE
Pentheus; Leonidas; Pamela; Zelotes; Gideon; Adrastus; Stonewall Jackson; George-a-Green.
(see *intransigence, uncompromising, opposition, hostility*)

RESOLUTE
Hector; Leonidas; Arria; Appius Claudius Caecus; Brutus; Polyxena; Christian; Antonius Polemon; Charlemagne; Saint Ambrose; Joseph Andrews; Judith; John Bunyan; Leicester Dedlock; Christopher Columbus; George-a-Green; John Brown; Old Ironsides; Abraham Lincoln.
(see *steadfast, earnest, unflinching, determination, inflexible, undaunted, bold*)

RESONANT
Feodor Chaliapin; Stentorian; Sarah Bernhardt; Edmund Burke.
(see *sonority, sweet-sounding, voice*)

RESOURCEFUL
Penelope; Perseus; Blondel; James Fenimore Cooper; Friar Tuck; Sidney Carton; Daniel Boone; Scheherezade; Ali Baba; Petruchio; Hercules; Siegfried; Penrod; Crichton; Robinson Crusoe; Geronimo; D'Artagnan; John Jacob Astor.
(see *ingenuity, inventive, skill, able, capable, clever*)

RESPECTFUL
Joseph of Arimathea; Corporal Trim.
(see *deferential, courtesy, decorous, polite, ceremonious, worshipful*)

RESPLENDENT
Usas; Hyperion; Breidablik; Helios; Gloriana.
(see *bright, splendor, radiant, shining, light, gorgeous*)

RESPONSE
Echo; Ferracute.
(see *answer, rejoiner, echo*)

RESPONSIBILITY
Edward Cocker; Atlas.
(see *duty, obligation, trustworthy*)

RESTFUL
Beulah; Vedius Pollio; Hypnos.
(see *calm, quiet, repose, serenity, tranquillity*)

RESTLESS
Ulysses; Rasselas; Jack London; Childe Harold.
(see *roving, vagrancy, nomad, adventurous*)

RESTORE
Cagliostro; Lazarus; Saint Filumena; Orillo; Hygeia; Bimini.
(see *renew, revive, self-renewing, rejuvenation*)

RESTRAINT
Sir Guyon; Malthusian; Amaimon; Joe Gargery.
(see *self-control, discipline, control, coercion, suppression*)

RESTRICTION
Salic Law.
(see *restraint, constraint, limit, reserved*)

RESURRECTION
Dabbat; Gabriel; Phoenix; St. Mark.
(see *rebirth, reincarnation*)

RESUSCITATE
Protesilaus; Elijah; Haidee; Zombi; Tabitha-Dorcas.
(see *revive, reanimate*)

RETALIATION
Hipponax; Oliver (2); Robin and Makyne; Sir Mungo Malagrowther; Branchidae.
(see *retribution, revenge, punishment, avenge, vindictive*)

RETENTIVE
Antonio Magliabecchi.
(see *memory, remembrance, recollection*)

RETICENT
Nathaniel Hawthorne.
(see *close-mouthed, laconic, silence, secrecy*)

RETIREMENT
Jericho; Alsatia.
(see *seclusion, solitude, privacy, loneliness, isolation*)

RETRIBUTION
Ramman; Branchidae; Nemesis; Pied Piper; Tisiphone; Judas; Ultor; Robin and Makyne; Megaera; Ate; Alecto; Alcmaeon; Brahma; Nathaniel Hawthorne.
(see *retaliation, recompense, compensation, reward, revenge, vengeance, penalty*)

RETURN
Fabulinus; Tammuz; Hesperus.
(see *recurrence, restore*)

REVELATION
Manichaeus; Koran; Urim and Thummim; Eumaeus; Swedenborgian.
(see *inspiration, discovery, divulge, oracular*)

REVELRY
Donnybrook Fair; Dionysus; Bacchic; Bromius; Saturnalian; Bacchanal.
(see *carousal, merry-making, orgiastic, debauchery*)

REVENGE
Polydorus; Pied Piper; Kriemhilde; Melusina; Nemesis; Dinah; Macduff; Ultor; Orestes; Laertes; Theodosius; Latona; Ibycus; Völund; Robin and Makyne; Edgar Ravenswood; Hannibal; Thyestes; Rigoletto; Moby Dick; Edmond Dantès; Shylock; Eblis; Amphiaraus; Aepytus; Alcmaeon; Cassiopeia; Furies; Antiope; Whiteboyism; Alastor; Mary Ambree; Emily Brontë.
(see *vengeance, avenge, vindictive, retribution, rancorous, malevolence*)

REVERED
Buddha; Gideon.
(see *worship, venerable, adored, hallowed*)

REVERENCE
Abraham; Canute; Christian; Joseph of Arimathea; Madonna; Confucian; Aaron; Balboa.
(see *veneration, adoring, homage, esteem, obeisance*)

RIDE
Ivan Mazeppa; John Gilpin; Sheridan; Paul Revere; Mithradates.
(see *horseback, horsemanship, bareback*)

RIDICULE
Lucian; Hipponax; Cockaigne; Momus; Martinus Scriblerus; Parian; Shavian; Alexander Pope; Étienne de Silhouette.
(see *mockery, scornful, contempt, raillery, derisive, satirism, sarcasm*)

RIDICULOUS
Lagado; Abderian; Miss Tabitha Bramble; Winifred Jenkins; John Gilpin; John Lyly; Géronte; Pooh-Bah; Tartarin; King Ryance; Mrs. Ramsbottom; Aganice; Barataria; Batrachomyomachia; Jeannot.
(see *absurd, unreasonable, irrational, fantastic, nonsense, incongruous, senseless, ludicrous, silly, stupid, ill-advised*)

RIFLE
Krupp Family; Annie Oakley.
(see *pistol, weapons, marksmanship*)

RIGHTEOUSNESS
Joshua; Sir Launcelot Greaves; Lao-Tse; Noah; Shamash; Melchizedek.
(see *piety, holiness, god-fearing, saintliness, religious, devout*)

RIGHT HAND
Fides.
(see *honor, trustworthy*)

RIGHTS
Hugo Grotius; Dred Scott Case.
(see *justice, equitable, honesty, law*)

RIGID
Mrs. Jarley.
(see *inflexible, stiff, erect, strict, stern*)

RIGOROUS
Cato the Censor; Tertullian; Medes and Persians; Jean Martinet; George Dandin; Jansenists; Cato of Utica.
(see *ascetic, austerity, harsh, severity, strait-laced*)

RING (finger)
Andvaranaut; Rheingold; Pyrgoteles; Gyges; Polycrates.
(see *jewelry*)

RINGLET
Berenice; Sif; Belinda.
(see *lock, curl, hair*)

RIOT
Luddites; Pandemonium; Rebeccaite; Skimmington.
(see *confusion, chaos, uprising, commotion, tumultuous.*

RIVALRY
Canace; Montagues and Capulets; Statira; Twelve Peers; Eugene Wrayburn; Menalcas; Ormuzd; Roxane; Turnus; Palamon and Arcite.
(see *competition, strife, contest, antagonistic, controversy, opposition, altercation*)

RIVER (deities)
Stygian; Oceanus; Achelous; Tethys; Vritra; Woglinda, Wellgunda, and Flosshilda; Sabrina; Tiberinus.
(see *stream, water*)

ROADS
Pushan; Sir John MacAdam; Itineraria; Frontinus.
(see *highway, pathway, route, turnpike*)

ROAR
Stentorian; Ramman.
(see *uproar, bellow, shout*)

ROSES
Dorothea.
(see *flowers*)

ROSY
Lilith; Aurora.
(see *blush, red*)

ROUÉ
Lothario; Marquis of Steyne; Lovelace; Silk-Stocking.
(see *rakish, debauchee, profligacy, libertine, dissolute*)

ROUGED
Lady Wishfort; Picti; Jezebel.
(see *painted, cosmetics*)

ROUND
Giottesque.
(see *cycle*)

ROUNDABOUT
Circumlocution Office.
(see *circuitous, indirect, meandering*)

ROUT
Waterloo; George Edward Pickett; Pavor.
(see *defeat, repulse, downfall*)

ROUTE
Dan to Beersheba; Pausanias; Itineraria.
(see *itinerary, guide*)

ROUTINE
Circumlocution Office; Commodore Trunnion.
(see *repetition, inveterate, recurrence*)

ROVING
Aristeas; Romany.
(see *vagrancy, nomad, gypsy, wanderer, migratory, peripatetic*)

ROWER
Salt River.
(see *oarsman*)

RUBY
Kaaba.
(see *precious stone*)

RUDDER
Fortuna; Tiberinus.
(see *pilot*)

RUDE
Captain Lismahago; Philoxenus; Gothic; Sir Kay; Troglodytae; Gurth; Aquilo; Mme. Sans-Gêne.
(see *impolite, boorish, gruff, discourteous, uncouth, gauche*)

RUDIMENTARY
Abecedarians; William McGuffey.
(see *essential*)

RUFFIAN
Richard Varney; Captain MacHeath.
(see *villainy, rascal, knave, scoundrel, rogue, roisterer, bully*)

RUINATION
Pentheus; Fortunatus; Frothi; Jericho; Kriemhilde; Perrin Dendin; Catiline; Nana; Belvidera; Ragnarok.
(see *destruction, devastation, annihilation, calamity, catastrophe*)

RULES (method)
Hoyle; Marquis of Queensbury.
(see *regulation, methodical, orderliness*)

RUM
Reverend Mr. Stiggins.
(see *drink, inebriation, tippler, drunkenness*)

S

SABBATH
Sabazius
(see *sacred*)

SABOTEURS
Jacquerie; Luddites; Rebeccaite.
(see *pernicious, destruction, disadvantageous*)

SABRE
Morglay.
(see *sword, broadsword, rapier*)

SACHEM
William M. Tweed.
(see *chieftain, political influence*)

SACK (v.)
Varangians; Lucius Mummius; Attila; Huns; Vitalians.
(see *spoils, plunder, loot, marauder, predatory, ravaging*)

SACRED
Sakhrat; Hippocrene; Heliconian; Rishi; Pentecost; Mecca; Camenae; Apis; Aganippe; Egeria; Castalian; Eleusinian; Pierian; Polyhymnia; Kaaba; Sinai.
(see *worship, revered, consecrated, hallowed, divine, saintliness, venerable*)

SACRIFICE
Berenice; Jephthah; Hesione; Isaac; Idomeneus; Iphigenia; Antigone; Cecrops; Epimenides; Juggernaut; Moloch; Flamen; Polyxena; Crusaders; Calchas; Cassiopeia; Ver Sacrum; Saraswati.
(see *human sacrifice, self-sacrificing, immolation*)

SACRILEGIOUS
Ahaz; Abihu; Titus Vespasianus; Capaneus; Oeneus.
(see *impiety, blasphemous, irreverent, un-godfearing, profanation*)

SADDLER
Crispin.
(see *tanner*)

SADISM
Marquis de Sade; Domitian; Jack Ketch; Mr. Creakle; Gymnopaedia; Quilp; Phalaris; Jack the Ripper; Richard von Krafft-Ebing; Torquemada.
(see *cruelty, perversion, brutal, fiendish, barbarity, ferocious, savage*)

SADNESS
Linus; Omar Khayyam; Auld Robin Gray; Ossian; Heliades; Melpomene; Via Dolorosa; Philomela; Smike; Stephen Foster; Thomas Gray.
(see *melancholy, doleful, despondent, sorrow, mourning, grief*)

SAFEGUARD
Palladium; Aegis; Gibraltar; Rahab; Alsatia; Rhesus; Seven Sleepers of Ephesus; Polydorus; Rhampsinitus; Molmutius; Celadon.
(see *protection, security, defense, bulwark*)

SAGACITY
Tyr; Goddess of Reason; Wellingtonian; Marmion; Themistoclean; Periander; Ganesa.
(see *wisdom, ingenuity, perspicacity, prudence*)

SAGE
Devarshis; Atlantes; Pittacus; Merlin; Thales; Manichaeus; Rishi; Solon; Nathan.
(see *shrewd, astute, intelligent, learned*)

SAILOR
Long Tom Coffin; Flying Dutchman; Jolly Roger; Raleigh; Sergestus; Sindbad the Sailor; Glaucus; Vasco da Gama; Peter Wilkins; Captain Cuttle; Lieutenant Hatchway; Vanderdecken; Saint Eulalia; Dick Deadeye; Menoetes; Moby-Dick; Mother Carey; Trinculo; Saint Nicholas; Ferdinand Magellan; Dioscuri; Liburnians; Jack London; Mr. Midshipman Easy.
(see *seafaring, mariner, navigator, pilot*)

SAINTLINESS
Madonna; Paphnutius; Rose of Lima; Santa Rosalia; Saint Valentine; Saint Theresa; Saint Ulric; Saint Januarius; Saint Patrick; Santa Claus; Thomas à Kempis; Sabra; Thecla; Saint Sebastian.
(see *devout, religious, piety, holiness, patron saint*)

SALAAM
Gradasso.
(see *bow*)

SALON
Mme. Recamier; Aspasia.
(see *hospitality*)

SALTY
Oceanus; Salacia.
(see *sea, ocean-god*)

SALVATION
Jonathan Edwards; Shadrach; Raskolnikov; Simeon.
(see *deliverance, rescue, redemption*)

SAMPLE (n.)
Giottesque.
(see *exemplary, model, pattern*)

SANCTIMONIOUS
Obadiah Slope; Reverend Mister Chadband; Pharisee; Joseph Surface.
(see *cant, hypocrisy*)

SANCTITY
Saint Catherine; Paphnutius; Semo Sancus; Archdeacon Frollo.
(see *holiness, purity, saintliness, piety, religious*)

SANCTUARY
Alsatia; Molmutius; Loretto.
(see *shelter, temple*)

SAND
Pactolus; Syrtes.
(see *pebbles*)

SANGUINE
Gemini; Spes; Leibnitzian.
(see *hopeful, confidence, optimistic*)

SARCASM
William Ralph Inge; Susan Nipper; Hipponax; Archilochian; Jonathan Oldbuck; Catullan; Parian; Gungnir.
(see *irony, ridicule, derisive, mordant, satirism*)

SARCOPHAGUS
Tutankhamen.
(see *coffin*)

SARTORIAL
Herr Teufelsdroeckh; Zouave; Silk-Stocking; Longchamps.
(see *dress, apparel, costume, raiment, finery*)

SATAN
Beelzebub; Belial.
(see *devil, demon, infernal*)

SATIRISM (ancient)
Abderian; Phaedrus; Lucian; Martial; Hipponax; Juvenalian; Persius; Fescennine; Parian; Archilochian; Aristophanic; Gungnir.
(see *sarcasm, abusive, reproachful, invective, lampoon, censorious*)

SATIRISM (modern)
Charles Perrault; Piers Plowman; Desiderius Erasmus; Pasquinade; Bavius and Maevius; Jean de La Fontaine; Charles Montesquieu; Till Eulenspiegel; John Jarndyce; Pantagruel; Molière; Galsworthian; Alexander Pope; Henrik Ibsen; Anatole France; Hudibrastic; Little Pedlington; Herr Teufelsdroeckh; Erewhon; Shavian; Thackerayan; Swiftian; William Hogarth.

SATURATED
Mr. Krook.
(see *inebriation, drunkenness*)

SATURDAY
Melusina.
(see *sabbath*)

SATURNINE
Saturn; Silence; Leontes.
(see *morose, somber, sullenness, moodiness*)

SAUCY
Columbine; Dorine; Pierrot; Pierrette.
(see *pert, impudent, impertinent, insolent, flippant*)

SAVAGE
Tauri; Tatar; Pyrrhus (Neoptolemus); Mme. Thérèse Defarge; Myrmidons; Lemnian; Tezcatlipoca; Laestrygonian; Garm; Troglodytae; Barbarossa; Zamore; Macduff; Centaur; Peregrine Pickle.
(see *uncivilized, cruelty, barbarity, ferocious, bloodthirsty, wild*)

SAVIOR
Messianic; Azaziel; Alcestis; Ptolemy; Ino; Saint George; Rienzi; Soter; Stator; Veturia and Volumnia; Esther; Vishnu; Matsya.
(see *liberator, defender, preserver, protector, deliverance*)

SAW
Perdix.
(see *carpenter*)

SCALES (weight)
Palamedes.
(see *utensils, heavy*)

SCANDAL
Pompeia; Pope Joan; Lord Nelson; Rudolph of Mayerling; Caius Tranquillus Suetonius; Mrs. Candour; Lady Sneerwell; Daisy Miller.
(see *disgrace, dishonor, disrepute, defame, calumnious, backbite, slander*)

SCAPEGOAT
Admetus; Hesione; Azazel.
(see *victim, substitute*)

SCAR
Euryclea; Rosa Dartle.
(see *disfigured, mar*)

SCARECROW
Priapus.
(see *apotropaic*)

SCARLET WOMAN
Lilith; Delilah; Rahab.
(see *street-walker, prostitute, whore, harlot, strumpet*)

SCATHE
Skadhi.
(see *harmful, injurious, damaging, baneful*)

SCENIC
Arcadian; Tintagel; Tempe; Claude Monet; Edouard Manet.
(see *picturesque, landscape, countryside*)

SCEPTER
Ptah.
(see *imperial, majesty*)

SCHEMING
Cassius; Dorine; Plautus; Marmion; Patelin; the Pages; Menander; Quilp; Reynard; Terence; Philip of Macedon; Rosencrantz and Guildenstern; Emilia; Mata Hari; Machiavellian; Jesuit; Uriah Heep; Get-Rich-Quick Wallingford; Dousterswivel; Aimwell; Worldly Wiseman.
(see *crafty, wily, plot, stratagem, machinator*)

SCHOLARLY
Clio (see Muse); Academia; Abelard and Héloise; Pico della Mirandola; Saint Nicholas; Antonio Magliabecchi; Cecil Rhodes; Desiderius Erasmus; Alfred the Great; Emersonian; Albert Einstein; Aristarchus.
(see *learned, erudite, pedantic, studious*)

SCHOOL TEACHER
Holophernes; Orbilian; Bradley Headstone; Eugene Wrayburn; Squeers; Mr. Creakle; Dominie Sampson.
(see *teacher, instructor, professor*)

SCIENCE (deities)
Oannes; Ea; Nebo; Vidar; Imhotep.
(see *arts and crafts, knowledge*)

SCIENTIFIC
Herophilus; Eratosthenes; Anaxagoras; Empedocles; Anaximander; Aristarchus; Euclidean; Aristotelian; Lagado; Galileo; Copernican; Louis Pasteur; Antoine Lavoisier; Bernouilli; Mendelian; Franklinian; Mme. Marie Curie; Arrowsmith.
(see *physics, chemist, botanist, mathematics, astronomy, geologist, biologist*)

SCIMITAR
Morglay.
(see *sword*)

SCOFFER
Mephistophelian; Abderian; François Voltaire; Dorothea; Nietzschean.
(see *derisive, mockery, jeer, taunt, ridicule*)

SCOLD (n.)
Skimmington; Katharine; Xanthippe; Mrs. Caudle; Mme. Pernelle.
(see *shrew, termagant, virago, abusive*)

SCORCHED
Vritra; Phlegethon; Robigus.
(see *burn, cremated, roasted, parched*)

SCORNED
Phaedra; Pariah; Philip Wharton.
(see *jilt, despise*)

SCORNFUL
Democritus; Juvenalian; Rhoecus; Catullan.
(see *disdainful, insolent, contempt, defiance*)

SCOUNDREL
Ferdinand Fathom; Bezonian.
(see *knave, rogue, rascal, swindler, cheat, villainy*)

SCOURGING
Zobeide; St. Sebastian.
(see *whipping, flogging, lashing, horsewhip, beating*)

SCOUT (n.)
Caleb; Zophiel; Uncas; Eurylochus; Daniel Boone; Buffalo Bill; Deadwood Dick; "Kit" Carson.
(see *reconnoitre, spy*)

SCOWL
Sir Edward Hugh Redgauntlet.
(see *glare, leer, menacing, stare*)

SCRIBE
Tironian; Sopherim; Imhotep; Thoth; Ezra.
(see *clerk, secretary, amanuensis*)

SCRIPT
John Hancock; Spencerian.
(see *handwriting*)

SCULPTURE
Lysippus; Phidian; Dirce; Praxiteles; Pygmalion; Rhoecus; Scopas; Polycleitus; Saraswati; Myron's Cow; Della Robbia; Michelangelo; Leonardo da Vinci; Rodinesque; Père La Chaise.
(see *bas relief, statue*)

SCURRILOUS
Alexander Pope; Fescennine; Juvenalian.
(see *abusive, reproachful, opprobrious, ribald, invective, calumnious, denunciatory, injurious, offensive, insulting, insolent*)

SCYTHE
Saint Walston.
(see *blade, mower, reap*)

SEA-DEITIES
Varuna; Triton; Oceanus; Oceanids; Phorcus; Eurynome; Palaemon; Amphitrite; Nereids; Thetis; Glaucus; Poseidon; Melicertes; Njord; Ran; Neptune; Salacia; Ve; Aegir; Ymir; Red Man; Davy Jones; Mother Carey; Hymir.
(see *ocean-god, nymph, water*)

SEAFARING
Alexander Selkirk; Herman Melville; Alcinous; Vikings; Varangians; Vitalians; John Quelch; Moby Dick; Sindbad the Sailor; Sir Henry Morgan; Joseph Conrad; Jack London; Commodore Trunnion.
(see *sailor, freebooter, corsair, buccaneer, mariner*)

SEAL-RING
Pyrgoteles.
(see *ring, jewelry*)

SEAMSTRESS
Tabitha-Dorcas; Mimi; Dorcas.
(see *needlecraft*)

SEARCH
Diogenes; Sangreal; Mambrino; Manoa; Ithuriel; Hylas; Gilgamesh; Bo-Peep; Doctor Syntax; Javert; Sleeping Beauty.
(see *investigation, quest, research, examining, probe*)

SEASHELLS
Caius Laelius.
(see *pebbles*)

SEASONS
Proserpina; Linus; Horae; Rhea; Thallo; Quadrifrons; Ishtar.
(see *autumn, winter, springtime, summer*)

SECLUSION
Beltenebros; Walden Pond; Amy Robsart; Bessy Bell; Jack-in-the-Green; John Burroughs; Rousseauian.
(see *solitude, privacy, loneliness, isolation*)

SECOND-HAND
Fag.
(see *pawnbroker*)

SECRECY
Consus; Lycomedes; Ku Klux; Joseph of Arimathea; Lohengrin; Jaffier; Porcia; Christian Rosenkreuz; Vivian; Amy Robsart; Man with the Iron Mask; Falkland; Mr. Tulkinghorn; Molly Maguire; E. Phillips Oppenheim; Maffia.
(see *mystery, clandestine, concealed, hideout, privacy*)

SECRETARY
Tironian; Baruch.
(see *scribe, clerk, amanuensis*)

SECTARIAN
Mazdakite; Pharisee.
(see *partisanship, factionalism, intolerance*)

SECURITY
Alcyone; Rhesus; Molmutius.
(see *safeguard, protection, shelter, defense*)

SEDUCED
Leda; Callisto; Clarissa Harlowe; Norma; Madge Wildfire; Hetty Sorrel; Lucretia.
(see *unmarried mother, paramour, shamed*)

SEDUCER
Sextus Tarquinius; Paris; Iachimo; Tereus; Lovelace; Lothario; Arthur Donnithorne; Mirabel; Modred; James Steerforth.
(see *rapist, paramour, illicit, debauchee*)

SEDUCTION (deities)
Venus (see Aphrodisian); Loki; Mephistophelian; Comus; Eblis; Samael; Erlking.
(see *alluring, tempter, temptress, enticement, beguilement, lure, attractiveness, engaging, persuasion, ensnare, coaxing*)

SEDUCTRESS
Acrasia; Alcina; Circean; Tyndaris; Calypso; Queen Labe; Potiphar's Wife; Armida; Kundry; Vivian; Stheneboea; Mata Hari; Zuleika; Lucrezia Borgia; Carmen; Lilith; Lady Booby.
(see *sorceress, enchantment, siren*)

SEED
Tellus; Saturn; Semo Sancus; Proserpina.
(see *grain*)

SEER
Zal; Veleda; Urganda; Vala; Bacis; Sibylla; Melampus; Navius; Picus; Phineus; Abaris; Rishi; Amphiaraus; Nostradamus; Chaldean; Zephaniah; Zechariah; Witch of Endor.
(see *clairvoyant, prediction, prognostication, foretell, soothsayer*)

SEGREGATION
Man in the Moon; Mason and Dixon; Jim Crow.
(see *isolation, separation*)

SELF-ABSORPTION
Henry James; Rosamond Vincy; John-a-Dreams; Major Bagstock; Soren Kierkegaard.
(see *absorption, rapt, contemplative, egotistic*)

SELF-ASSURANCE
Laenas; Nerissa; Tappertitian; Fadladeen; Emperor Jones; Jonathan Edwards; Benvenuto Cellini; Huggins and Muggins; Leicester Dedlock; Widow Barnaby; Dugald Dalgetty.
(see *confidence, poise*)

SELF-CONTROL
Polemon of Athens; Persius; Abelites: Marcus Aurelius; Sir Guyon.
(see *temperance, level-headed, unemotional, restraint*)

SELF-DENIAL
Essenes; Saint Anthony; Honeywood.
(see *abstinence, temperance, sobriety, austerity, ascetic*)

SELF-DESTRUCTION
Laodamia; Antinous; Publius; Decius Mus; Amphiaraus; Mettius Curtius; Evadne; Sardanapalus; Peregrinus Proteus; Brunhilde.
(see *suicide*)

SELF-IMPORTANT
Leontes; Grand Mogul; Bottom; Sargeant Buzfuz; Pooh-Bah; Almanzor.
(see *pride, conceited, vanity, egotistic, pompous*)

SELF-INDULGENCE
Acrasia; Phaeacian; Aulus Vitellius; Zeluco; Borachio.
(see *hedonist, epicurean, voluptuary, luxury-loving*)

SELFISH
Anu; Rosamond Vincy; Parson Trulliber; Mr. Turveydrop; Becky Sharp; Junker; Mr. Redlaw; Arthur Pendennis; Monsieur Josse; Scrooge; Harold Skimpole; Arnolphe; Little Pedlington.
(see *ungenerous, narrow-minded, self-seeking*)

SELFLESSNESS
Spartan; Cornelia.
(see *altruistic*)

SELF-LOVE
Narcissus; Onan.
(see *egotistic, conceited*)

SELF-MADE
Joseph Bounderby; Colonel Jack; "Diamond Jim" Brady; Jacksonian; Silas Lapham.
(see *rags to riches*)

SELF-PITY
Propertian; Tibullan; Childe Harold; Stheneboea.
(see *introvert, brooding*)

SELF-RENEWING
Phoenix; Saint Filumena.
(see *renew, restore, automatic*)

SELF-SACRIFICING
Nydia; Nisus; Alcestis; Lycurgus; Sidney Carton; Godiva; Clara Barton; Enoch Arden; Daniel Deronda; Nanna; Arnold von Winkelried; Thomas à Kempis; Judith; Kalanos; Père Goriot.
(see *self-denial, altruistic, unselfish*)

SELF-SATISFIED
Laodicean; Pharisee; Diogenes; Babbitt; Goody Two-Shoes; Mr. Podsnap.
(see *smug, complacent*)

SELF-SEEKING
Baconian; Quisling; Martial; Roderick Random.
(see *ambitious, over-ambitious, selfish*)

SELF-STARTING
Teirtu.
(see *automatic*)

SELF-SUPPORTING
Walden Pond; Fourierist.
(see *independence*)

SELF-TORMENTOR
George Dandin; Malbecco.
(see *anxiety*)

SELF-WILLED
Creon; Mr. Rochester; Richard Moniplies.
(see *stubborn, determination*)

SENILITY
Quintilius Varus; Tithonus; Elli; Yue-Laou; Géronte; Enoch Wray; Lord Ogleby; Grangousier.
(see *aged, old, anile*)

SENSATIONALIST
Peregrinus Proteus.
(see *publicity-seeker*)

SENSELESS
Abderian; Lagado; Talassius; Mrs. Partington; Macflecknoe; Mrs. Ramsbottom; Alfred Jingle.
(see *absurd, unreasonable, irrational, fantastic, nonsense, ridiculous, incongruous, ludicrous, ill-advised, stupid, silly*)

SENSES
Hoenir; Kama; Ve.
(see *hearing, feeling, sight*)

SENSIBLE
Horatio; Franklinian; Alice Adams; Dooley; Agnes Wickfield; Will Rogers; David Harum; William Allen White; Autocrat of the Breakfast Table.
(see *good sense, practical, wisdom, discreet, sagacity*)

SENSITIVITY
Nydia; Florimel; Forsyte; Harley.
(see *gentle*)

SENSUALITY (deities and places)
Erato; Satyr; Paphian; Gomorrah; Freyja; Obidicut; Aphrodisian; Libitina; Baubo; Belphegor; Baal; Volupia; Cupid; Ishtar; Faunus; Nymphs; Maenad; Fescennine; Pandemos.
(see *carnal, lustful, lechery, lascivious, concupiscent*)

SENSUALITY (female)
Nana; Armida; Ninon de Lenclos; Lady Bellaston; Potiphar's Wife.
(see *scarlet woman, harlot*)

SENSUALITY (male)
Tiberian; Zeluco; Xerxes; Henry VIII; Lovelace; Marquis de Sade; Manly; Louis XV; Tannhaeuser; Silk-Stocking; Pierre Louys; Peregrine Pickle; Mayeux; Toulouse-Lautrec; Joseph Sedley.
(see *roué, rakish, libertine, philanderer, dissolute, seducer, rapist*)

SENSUOUS
Kama; Praxiteles; Lydian; Antinous; Rubensian; Burne-Jonesian; Algernon Swinburne; Maurice Ravel.
(see *impressionistic, languorous*)

SENTENTIOUS
Tupperian; Polonius; Fadladeen; Sancho Panza; Goethe; Poor Richard.
(see *terse, laconic, pithy, succinct, didactic*)

SENTIMENTALITY
Tilburina; Bavius and Maevius; Harley; Della Cruscans; Lalla Rookh; Paul and Virginie; Joseph Surface; Harold Skimpole; Don Ferolo Whiskerandos; John Chivery; John Wemmick; Wertherian.
(see *lackadaisical, repining, pining*)

SENTINEL
Heimdall.
(see *watchman, warder*)

SEPARATION
Terminus.
(see *isolation, segregation, solitude, borders, limit*)

SEPARATIONIST
Sinn Fein.
(see *nationalism, independence*)

SEPULCHER
Mausolus; Taj Mahal.
(see *coffin, sarcophagus, grave, tomb*)

SERAPH
Azaziel; Zadkiel; Zephon; Nama; Zophiel; Rasiel.
(see *angel, cherub*)

SERENITY
Irene; Alcyone; King Log.
(see *tranquillity, peace, calm, repose, quiet, composure*)

SERIOUS
Heraclitus; Marcus Crassus; Gammer Gurton.
(see *grave, solemnity, earnest, momentous*)

SERMON
The Crawleys.
(see *exhortation, preacher*)

SERPENT
Laocoön; Enceladus; Medusa; Phorbas; Pythian; Caducean; Hygeia; Melusina; Pallas; Echidna; Skadhi; Samael; Shesha; Yacumama; Apepi; St. John; Ifurin; Jormungandar.
(see *snake, reptile, rattlesnake, python, snakebite, snake-killer*)

SERVANT
Sudra; Moth; Fortunio; Eumaeus; Fag; Scapino; Gibeonite; Pamela; Maritornes; Clara Peggoty; Diggary; Cristoph Wagner; Young Marlow; Jack and Jill; Richard Moniplies.
(see *valet, manservant, footman, boy-servant, maidservant, waiter, waitress*)

SERVICEABLE
Johannes Factotum; Mrs. Deborah Primrose; Hop o' My Thumb; Man Friday.
(see *useful, helpfulness, practical*)

SERVILITY
Jenkins; Uncle Pumblechook.
(see *enslavement, slavery, obsequious, fawning, sycophant*)

SESQUIPEDALIAN
John Lyly; Aldiborontiphoscophornio.
(see *polysyllables, bombastic, grandiloquent, magniloquence*)

SETTLER
Ramona; Robert LaSalle; Knickerbocker; John Rolfe.
(see *frontiersman, colonist*)

SEVERITY
Rhadamanthine; Torquemada; Zaleucus; Medes and Persians; Orbilian; Galba; Draconian; Fabricius; Cato the Censor; Manlius; Judge Lynch.
(see *austerity, stern, inexorable, obdurate, rigorous, strict*)

SEWING SOCIETY
Tabitha-Dorcas.
(see *seamstress, needlecraft*)

SEXUALITY
Havelock Ellis; Freudian; Marquis de Sade; Masochism; Richard von Krafft-Ebing; Carl G. Jung.
(see *sensuality*)

SHABBY
Bermudas; Queer Street; Sansculotte.
(see *poverty, stingy, beggar*)

SHADE
Bandusia.
(see *darkness, dusk, shelter, protection*)

SHADOW
Rahu; Peter Schlemihl.
(see *imagine, phantom, reflection*)

SHAKE
Lord Burleigh.
(see *bow, obeisance*)

SHINING
Sol; Breidablik; Apollo.
(see *light, bright, glittering, glowing, luminous, radiant*)

SHIP
Hringham; Flying Dutchman; Liburnians; Naglfar.
(see *boat, man-of-war, fleet*)

SHIPWRECK
Scylla; Leucothea; Ligeia; Palaemon; Lorelei; Sergestus; Syrtes; Alrinach; Ino; Haidee; Paul and Virginie; Viola; Sir Patrick Spens; Peter Wilkins; Antipholus.
(see *ruination, perdition, destruction*)

SHIRT
Deianira; Garibaldian; Whiteboyism.
(see *hair shirt*)

SHOCK
Melusina.
(see *shake, surprise*)

SHOEMAKER
Hans Sachs; Crispin.
(see *tanner*)

SHOP-LIFT
Laverna.
(see *thievery, robber, steal*)

SHORT CUT
Puff.
(see *abridge*)

SHORTEN
John Audley.
(see *contract, brief, concise, succinct*)

SHORTHAND
Tironian.
(see *secretary*)

SHORT-LIVED
Aulus Vitellius; Galba; Omar Khayyam; Theophrastus; Abu Hassan; Little Eva.
(see *transience*)

SHORT-SIGHTED
George Primrose; Aeschines; Edouard Daladier.
(see *purblind, imprudent*)

SHORT-STATURED
Zaccheus.
(see *diminutive, little, small, tiny*)

SHOULDER (n.)
Pelops; Siegfried; Junner.
(see *broad-shouldered*)

SHOUT
Talassius; Jericho.
(see *shriek, roar, uproar, vociferous*)

SHOWER (rain)
Parjanya; Hyades; Pluvius; Eurus.
(see *rain, cloudburst, downpour, rainstorm, storm*)

SHOWMAN
Barnum; Buffalo Bill.
(see *theatrical, stage-director*)

SHOWY
Don Adriano de Armado; Trimalchio; "Diamond Jim" Brady; Buncombe; Peregrinus Proteus; Zouave.
(see *flashy, gaudy, bedizened, ostentation, exhibitionist*)

SHREW
Miggs; Mrs. Caudle; Xanthippe; Widow Blackacre; Katharine; Skimmington; Mrs. Poyser; Mme. Pernelle; Hera.
(see *scold, termagant, virago, sharp-tongued*)

SHREWD
Marcus Licinius Crassus; Periander; Volpone; Deucalion; Ganesa; Machiavellian; Richelieu; Yankee; David Crockett; David Harum; Andrew Fairservice; Fadladeen; Huck Finn; Becky Sharp; Brom Bones; Partridge; Nicodemus Boffin; John Jarndyce.
(see *astute, artful, cunning, sly, crafty, subtlety, sagacity, ingenuity*)

SHRIEK
Calliope (see Muse); Melusina; Barguest.
(see *shout, roar*)

SHRUB
Leucothea.
(see *bush, brushwood*)

SHY
Daphne; Barkis; Florimel; Miles Standish; Mr. Toots; Fear Fortress; Young Marlow; Watkins Tottle; Rima.
(see *timidity, coy, diffident, bashful*)

SHYSTER
Sampson Brass; Dodson and Fogg.
(see *lawyer, unjust, unprincipled, unscrupulous*)

SICKLY
Bessy Bell; Mimi; La Traviata.
(see *valetudinarian*)

SIEGE
Manlius Capitolinus; Lars Porsena; Titus Vespasianus; Fulvia; Wooden Horse; Marcellus; Seven against Thebes; Frontinus.
(see *blockade, assault, attack*)

SIEVE
Danaides.
(see *loss, plug*)

SIGH
Scalae Gemoniae; Tilburina; Umbriel; Lydia Languish.
(see *mourning, lamentation, lackadaisical*)

SIGHT
Lynceus; Heimdall.
(see *eyesight, far-sighted, purblind*)

SIGHTLESS
Nydia; Melesigenes; Grai: ·
(see *blindness, unseeing*)

SIGNAL
Hernani; Samuel Morse.
(see *token, sign-language*)

SIGNATURE
Miramont; John Hancock.
(see *script, handwriting*)

SIGNIFICANT
Lord Burleigh.
(see *momentous*)

SIGN-LANGUAGE
Francisco Xavier; Thaumaste.
(see *dumbness, mute, gesticulation*)

SILENCE
Larunda; Harpocrates; Sphinx; Lord Burleigh; Sleeping Beauty; Prisoner of Chillon.
(see *noiseless, hushed, quiet, calm, peace, mute, reticent*)

SILKEN
Yue-Laou; Silk-Stocking; Seric.
(see *soft*)

SILLY
Orgon; Marplot; Shallow; Janotism; Andrew Aguecheek; Peter Schlemihl; George Dandin.
(see *absurd, unreasonable, irrational,*

fantastic, nonsense, ridiculous, incongruous, senseless, ludicrous, stupid, ill-advised)

SILVERSMITH
Mentor; Benvenuto Cellini.
(see *goldsmith*)

SIMILARITY
Dromios; Sosia; Donatello; Antipholus.
(see *alike, likeness, identical, resemblance, twins, duplicate, equality*)

SIMPERING
Sir Fopling Flutter.
(see *affected, coxcomical*)

SIMPLETON
Calandrino; Sganarelle; Géronte; Verges; Damoetas; Janotism; Sol Gills; George Dandin; Jack-a-Lent; Moses Primrose; Andrew Aguecheek; Simple Simon; Jack Pudding; Colin Clout; Goose Gibbie; Barnaby Rudge.
(see *dunce, dull-witted, blockhead*)

SIMPLICITY (art)
Arcadian; Attic; Tibullan; Sir John Millais; Heinrich Heine; Giovanni Palestrina; Anatole France; Thomas Sheraton; Fritz Kreisler; Stephen Foster; Mother Goose; Paul Lawrence Dunbar; O. Henry; Emily Dickinson; Corinna; Walden Pond; Blake-like.

SIMPLICITY (of character)
Pamela; Fabricius; Cophetuan; Cato the Censor; Gorgibus; Perdita; Flavius Vespasian; Cincinnatus; Regulus; David; Francis of Assisi; John Knox; Jeffersonian; Labadists; Lao Tse; Mazdakite; Mme. Marie Curie; Partridge; Maud Muller; Juliet; Paul and Virginie; Uncle Toby; the Newcomes; Tiny Tim; Doctor Charles Primrose.
(see *naturalness, unpretentious, naive, unaffected, ingenuousness, artless, plainness, sincerity, frank*)

SIMULATED
Veturius Mamurius; Bayes's Troops.
(see *artificial, counterfeit, feigned, pretense*)

SIN
Abaddon; Aeschylean; Sodoma; Gomorrah; Isaian; Dostoievskian; Soren Kierkegaard; Kaaba.
(see *evil, iniquity, wickedness, transgression, immorality*)

SINCERITY
Cordelia; Alasnam; Dike; Baillie Nicol Jarvie.
(see *candid, frank, honesty, ingenuousness, guileless, truth*)

SINECURE
Stellenbosche.
(see *do-nothing, figure-head*)

SINFUL
Fierabras; Dorian Gray; Owain; Jonah; Grigori E. Rasputin; Adam; Friar Rush; Jeroboam.
(see *blasphemous, impiety, irreverent, un-godfearing, irreligious, profanation*)

SINGER
Ligeia; Leucothea; Phemius; Siren; Lorelei; Parthenope; Arion; Asaphic; Thamyris; Eumolpus; Orpheus; Pippa; Blondel; David; Minnesinger; Trilby; Meistersinger; Jenny Lind; Schumann-Heinck; Jean de Reszke; Nellie Melba; Adelina Patti; Enrico Caruso.
(see *minstrelsy, bard, song*)

SINGLE-HANDED (combat)
M. Valerius Corvus; Spolia Opima; Pittacus; Manlius; Ullur; Marcellus; Elhanan; Rustam; Horatii and Curiatii; Horatius Cocles; George a-Green; Sohrab.
(see *prowess, strength, power, conqueror*)

SLAVE
Caryatids; Gibeonite; Thestylis; Morgiana; Leilah; Uncle Tom.
(see *captivity, drudge, menial*)

SLAVE LABOR
Sesostris; Khufu; Colonel Jack; Simon Legree.
(see *forced labor, subjugator, overlord, enslavement*)

SLAVERY
Ichabod; Dred Scott Case; Abraham Lincoln; Mason and Dixon.
(see *captivity, enslavement*)

SLEEP (deities)
Hypnos; Somnus; Caducean; Morpheus; Selene; Endymion; Ivory Gate; Horn Gate; Kiak-Kiak.

SLEEP (fictional)
Sigurd; Epimenides; Peter Klaus; Cleobis and Biton; Palinurus; Seven Sleepers of Ephesus; Rip Van Winkle; Land of Nod; Mr. Wardle; Joe.
(see *lethargy, drowsy, doze, nap*)

SLEET
Nuriel.
(see *hail, ice, rain*)

SLENDER
Philetas; Lysippus.
(see *thin, skinny, lean*)

SLEUTH
Scotland Yard; Monsieur Dupin; Sherlock Holmes.
(see *detection, policeman*)

SLINGSHOT
Elhanan; Sinis; David.
(see *stones, weapons*)

SLIT (v.)
Schamir; Balmung.
(see *cut, cleave, split, sunder*)

SLOW
Meander.
(see *inactive, lazy, dilatory*)

SLOW-WITTED
John Willet; Athelstane; Cousin Michel.
(see *stupid, dull-witted, blockhead, unintelligent*)

SLUR (v.)
Tutivillus.
(see *inarticulate, unintelligible*)

SLY
Arthur Gride; Sinon; Volpone; Reynard.
(see *cunning, artful, crafty, wily, insidious, subtlety*)

SMALL
Vamana; Zaccheus; Pygmy; Lilliputian.
(see *little, tiny, diminutive, pygmy, dwarf*)

SMALLPOX
Nana.
(see *disease, epidemic, plague*)

SMART (alert)
Artemus Ward; David Harum.
(see *clever, ingenuity, intelligent, adroit*)

SMILE
Mona Lisa.
(see *laughter*)

SMITHY
Vulcan; Tubal-Cain; Mulciber; Völund; Mime; Tvashtri.
(see *blacksmith, forge*)

SMOKE
John Rolfe; Mr. Toodle.
(see *mist*)

SMOOTHNESS
Hymettan; Hyblaean.
(see *bland, mildness, soft, suave*)

SMOTHER
William Burke; Othello.
(see *choke, suffocation, strangle*)

SMUG
Mr. Podsnap; Pharisee; Jonathan Edwards; Reverend Mister Chadband; Babbitt; Goody Two-Shoes; Alumbrado.
(see *self-satisfied, complacent*)

SMUGGLER
Jean Lafitte; Don José; Dirk Hatteraick.
(see *illegal*)

SNAKE (divinity)
Sabazius; Hygeia; Zombi; Yacumama; Apepi.
(see *serpent, reptile, python, rattlesnake*)

SNAKEBITE
Elsie Venner; Nicander; Marsi; Laocoön.
(see *venomous*)

SNAKE-HAIRED
Stheno; Euryale; Medusa; Gorgons; Kali.
(see *slatternly*)

SNAKE-KILLER
Saint Patrick; Phorbas.
(see *deliverance, mouse-killer*)

SNARE
Wooden Horse; Trasimene Lake; Widow Barnaby; Quintilius Varus; Gethsemane; Kriemhilde.
(see *ensnare, ambush, trap, man-trap*)

SNARLING
Smelfungus; Kilkenny Cats.
(see *fighting, menacing, threatening, complaining, gruff*)

SNOB
Miss Lucretia MacTab; Jenkins.
(see *social-climber, pretentious, affected*)

SNOOPING
Quidnunc; Marplot; Paul Pry.
(see *inquisitive, curiosity, spy, prying, meddlesome*)

SNOUT
Hafen Slawkenbergius.
(see *nose, large-nosed*)

SNOW
Mother Carey; Kabibonokka; Hela; Heliconian; Bernard of Menthon; Telchines; Rinde.
(see *ice frost, frozen*)

SNOW-SHOES
Ullur.
(see *sure-footed*)

SNOW-WHITE
Rhesus.
(see *white*)

SOBBING
Queen of Tears; Cocytean.
(see *weeping, crying, lachrymose, sigh*)

SOBRIETY
Polemon of Athens; Marcus Crassus; Silence; Minna; Isabella I.
(see *abstinence, self-denial, temperance*)

SOCIABILITY
Rasiel; Evander; Edwardian.
(see *affable, friendly, geniality, neighborly*)

SOCIAL CLIMBER
Fenton; Becky Sharp; Jenkins; Peronella; Monsieur Jourdain; Libro d'Oro; Alfred Lammle; Mr. and Mrs. Leo Hunter; Sir Matthew Mite; John Osborne.
(see *snob, pretentious*)

SOCIALISM
Friedrich Engels; Mazdakite; John Ball; Dostoievskian; Pierre J. Proudhon; Leo Tolstoi; Rousseauian; Fabian; Lenin; Fourierist; Karl Marx.
(see *communist, radical*)

SOCIAL PROBLEM
Okie; Jukes Family; Raskolnikov.
(see *sociology*)

SOCIAL REGISTER
Silk-Stocking; Libro d'Oro; Gotha.
(see *aristocrat, nobility, Patrician, gentility, privileged, approval*)

SOCIETY
Dolly Madison; Gotha; Jenkins.
(see *fashionable, elegance, modish*)

SOCIOLOGY
Henrik Ibsen; Clarence Darrow; Malthusian.
(see *social problem*)

SOFT
Lydian; Zephyrus.
(see *malleable, mildness, gentle, bland, delicate, smoothness*)

SOFT-HEARTED
Mrs. M. Todgers.
(see *clemency, merciful, forgiving, compassionate*)

SOIL (n.)
Terra; Demogorgon; Ge; Picumnus and Pilumnus.
(see *earth*)

SOLAR
Hyperion; Utu; Sol.
(see *sun-god, sunlight*)

SOLDIER
Shatriya; Josephus; Dugald Dalgetty; Miles Standish; Sergius; Saint Sebastian.
(see *army, militaristic, warrior*)

SOLECISM
Priscian; Winifred Jenkins.
(see *ungrammatical*)

SOLEMNITY
Giovanni Palestrina; J. S. Bach; Semo Sancus; Stygian; Polyhymnia; Publius Decius Mus; Aldiborontiphoscophornio.
(see *grave, serious, awe-inspiring, majesty*)

SOLICITOR
Mr. Tulkinghorn.
(see *attorney, lawyer*)

SOLICITUDE
Mrs. Caudle; Calpurnia.
(see *anxiety, concern, carefulness*)

SOLIDITY
Bilfrost; Gibraltar.
(see *strength, power, massiveness*)

SOLITUDE
Nathaniel Hawthorne; Alexander Selkirk; Prisoner of Chillon; Manfred; Red Man; Henry Thoreau; Peter Wilkins; Walden Pond.
(see *loneliness, isolation, seclusion, privacy, wilderness*)

SOLOIST
Meistersinger.
(see *singer*)

SOT
Saint Vincent; Mr. Krook; Martin of Tours; Christopher Sly.
(see *drunkenness, inebriation, tippler, alcoholism*)

SOUBRETTE
Dorine.
(see *pert, saucy, flippant*)

SOUL
Psyche; Maat; Manu; Ve; Lemures; Pushan; Plato; Democritus.
(see *mind, spirit*)

SOULLESS
Peter Fabel; Robotian.
(see *unfeeling, lifeless*)

SOURED
Timon; Sir Mungo Malagrowther.
(see *crabbed, morose, cantankerous, surly, petulance, ill-tempered*)

SOUTH SEAS
Paul Gauguin; Alexander Selkirk.
(see *aboriginal, uncivilized*)

SOUTH WIND
Notus; Auster.
(see *wind*)

SPANGLED
Woglinda, Wellgunda, and Flosshilda.
(see *glittering, sparkling*)

SPANIEL
Chloë.
(see *dog*)

SPARKLING
Célimène; Pierre Pérignon.
(see *glittering, bright, shining, brilliant*)

SPARRING
Amycus.
(see *boxing, fisticuffs*)

SPARROW
Kama; Tobit.
(see *birds*)

SPEAR (n.)
Ithuriel; Quirinus; Odin; Gunther; Cephalus; Britomartis; Ron; Lua; Gungnir.
(see *lance, javelin, pike*)

SPECIMEN
Giottesque.
(see *exemplary, model, pattern*)

SPECTACULAR
P. T. Barnum; Watling Street.
(see *glittering, shining, showman*)

SPECTER
Phooka; Mr. Redlaw; Wild Huntsman; White Ladies; Mrs. Veal; Flying Dutchman.
(see *apparition, phantom, ghost, visions, illusion*)

SPECULATOR (stocks)
Col. Mulberry Sellers; Turcaret.
(see *fortune-hunter, chance, money-mad*)

SPEECH (deities)
Thoth; Vach; Fabulinus; Ve; Saraswati.
(see *language, conversation, communication*)

SPEECHLESS
Larunda; Vaticanus.
(see *mute, dumbness, silence*)

SPEED
Liburnians; Ladas; Bayard (1); Acestes; Alcinous; Milanion; Pacolet; Jehu; Grani; Garuda; Galloping Dick.
(see *fast, swift, rapid, quick, fleet*)

SPELL-BINDER
Hypnos; Svengali; Vivian.
(see *enchantment, charm, magic, sorcerer*)

SPELLING
Mrs. Ramsbottom.
(see *misspelling, alphabet*)

SPENDTHRIFT
Mantalini; Silk-Stocking; Panurge; Peregrine Pickle; Heir of Linne.
(see *wasteful, extravagance, prodigal*)

SPICES
Sabaean.
(see *fragrant, aromatic*)

SPIDER
Arachne.
(see *insects*)

SPINNER (thread)
Rumplestilzchen; Verthandi; Berchta; Moerae; Arachne; Lachesis.
(see *weaver, loom*)

SPINSTER
Miggs; Miss Lucretia MacTab; Miss Tabitha Bramble; Miss Kilmansegg; Miss Tox; Rosa Dartle; Catherinette.
(see *old maid, husband-hunter*)

SPIRIT (deities)
Hoenir; Psyche; Fabulinus; Maat; Lares; Lemures; Rasiel; Pushan.
(see *soul, mind*)

SPIRITED
Mary Ambree; Zouave.
(see *high-spirited, vivacious, lively*)

SPIRITUALIST
Margaret Fox; Witch of Endor; Zanoni; Phineas P. Quimby; Yogi.
(see *medium, clairvoyant*)

SPITEFUL
Erlking; Nicneven; Ganelon.
(see *envy, malevolence, malign, hateful, rancorous*)

SPLAYFOOT
Plancus.
(see *flatfoot*)

SPLENDOR
Capitoline; Phrygian; Breidablik; Tutankhamen; Incan; Kubla Khan; Rameses; Karoon; Ptolemy; Ethiopian; Elizabethan; Aglaia; Solomon; Sallustian; Gainsborough; Kohinoor.
(see *magnificence, grandeur, sublimity, riches*)

SPLIT (v.)
Balisardo; Milo.
(see *cleave, sunder*)

SPOILS
Lua; Spolia Opima.
(see *loot, sack, pillage*)

SPONGER
Harold Skimpole; Sir Toby Belch; Gnatho.
(see *parasite*)

SPONTANEOUS
Skirnir; Androclean.
(see *volition, impulse, self-starting*)

SPORTSMAN
Nathaniel Winkle; Izaak Walton; Esau; John Peel; Nimrod.
(see *hunter, fisherman, athletics*)

SPORTSWOMAN
Artemis; Dictynna; Annie Oakley; Diana; Atalanta.
(see *huntress*)

SPOUSE
Pronuba.
(see *consort, wifely, conjugal, marriage*)

SPRING (water)
Hippocrene; Ea; Bethesda; Callirrhoë; Bandusia; Arethusa; Camenae; Castalian; Egeria; Quadrifrons; Juturna; Naiads; St. Keyne; Pierian.
(see *fountain, well*)

SPRINGTIME
Flora; Favonius; Chloris; Rhea; Juventas; Saint Valentine; Ver Sacrum; Hyperboreans; Minnesinger; Frey; Tammuz; Thallo; Venus; Robert Schumann; Maia.
(see *seasons*)

SPRINTER
Hippomenes; Phidippides.
(see *runner, race, foot-race, marathon, sure-footed*)

SPRITE
Puck; Ariel; Umbriel; Robin Goodfellow.
(see *apparition, fairy, elfin, goblin, hobgoblin, imp*)

SPURIOUS
Miss Carolina Skeggs; Pinchbeck; Apocryphal; Wardour Street.
(see *sham, feigned, counterfeit, meretricious, humbug*)

SPY
Solomon Pross; Zophiel; Caleb; Mata Hari; Rosencrantz and Guildenstern.
(see *scout, reconnoitre*)

SQUABBLE
Skimmington.
(see *wrangling, quarrelsome, brawling, altercation*)

SQUALL
Red Man; Mother Carey.
(see *storm, rainstorm, tempest*)

SQUANDERER
Mantalini; Nana; Pistor.
(see *wasteful, spendthrift, prodigal*)

SQUARE
Kaaba.
(see *octagon*)

SQUEEZE
Nemean Lion.
(see *choke, smother, suffocation*)

STAGE (deities)
Melpomene; Thalia (see Muse).
(see *theatrical, acting, comedy, tragedy*)

STAGE-DIRECTOR
Max Reinhardt; Sergei Diaghilev.
(see *showman*)

STAIN
Dorian Gray; Picti.
(see *dye, painted, disgrace, dishonor, corrupt*)

STAIRWAY
Scalae Gemoniae.
(see *fall, hurl*)

STAMMER
Hottentotism; Spoonerism; Demosthenes.
(see *mumbling, inarticulate*)

STEEP
Scalae Gemoniae; Gibraltar; Tarpeian Rock.
(see *high*)

STEIN
Gambrinus.
(see *beer*)

STENCH
Philoctetes; Sol Gills.
(see *odorous*)

STENOGRAPHER
Tironian.
(see *secretary*)

STEPMOTHER
Graciosa; Tenes.
(see *in-laws*)

STERILIZE
Louis Pasteur.
(see *milk*)

STERN (adj.)
Woden; Mr. Fang; Manlius; Livia; Laenas; Tertullian; Periander; Charlemagne; Jonathan Edwards.
(see *austerity, severity, rigorous, strict, inexorable*)

STEWARD
Jack Horner; Lreux.
(see *chamberlain*)

STICKLER
Jean Martinet; Mrs. Grundy; Sara Battle.
(see *punctilious, meticulous*)

STIFF
Watkins Tottle; Mr. Padsnap; Mrs. Jarley.
(see *rigid, erect, inflexible, rigorous, strict, inexorable*)

STIGMATA
Saint Catherine.
(see *nail, miraculous*)

STILTED
Martinus Scriblerus; Sir Piercie Shafton.
(see *formality, pompous, bombastic, pretentious, magniloquence*)

STINGING
Aristophanic; Archilochian; Gungnir.
(see *abusive, censorious, sarcasm*)

STINGY
Wandering Willie; Scrooge; Mrs. Jellyby; Squeers; Harry Gill.
(see *miserliness, penny-pincher, avaricious*)

STOCKY
Polycleitus.
(see *plump, bulk, massiveness*)

STOICAL (character)
Nutbrown Maid; Zadig; Polyxena; Andromache.
(see *passionless, apathy, imperturbable, patience, nonchalant, indifference*)

STOICISM
Persius; Yogi; Seneca the Younger; Zeno; Panaetius; Boethius; Epictetus.
(see *philosophy*)

STOKER
Mr. Toodle.
(see *furnace*)

STONECRUSHER
Sir John MacAdam.
(see *crushed*)

STONED
Achan; Saint Stephen.
(see *pelted*)

Hygeia; Antaeus; Alberich; Briarean; Cyclopean; Ajax; Pallas; Atlas; Gunther; Gibraltar; Guy of Warwick; Garuda; Milo; Thalestris; Cleobis and Biton; Rodinesque; Mithradates; Giacomuzzo Sforza; Aloidae; Tarzan.

(see *power, might*)

STRENGTHENER
Stator.

(see *encouragement, promoter, aid*)

STRICT
Jonathan Edwards; Essenes; Livia; Manlius; Puritanic; Mr. Podsnap; Medes and Persians; Orbilian; Jean Martinet; Jansenists.

(see *stiff, stern, rigorous, puritanic, austerity, severity*)

STRIFE
Montagues and Capulets; Lavinia; Turnus; Eris.

(see *discord, contention, quarrelsome, fighting*)

STRIKE (v.)
Feretrius; Jack-a-Lent.

(see *hit, slap, pound, beating*)

STRIPPED
Candaules; Gymnopaedia.

(see *nakedness, nudism, undress*)

STROLLER
Peripatetic; Walking Stewart.

(see *wanderer, roving*)

STRONGHOLD
Front de Boeuf; Gibraltar.

(see *castle, bulwark, safeguard*)

STRUMPET
Doll Tearsheet; Maid Marian; Vivian.

(see *harlot, whore, prostitute, streetwalker*)

STUBBORN
Grimwig; Johnsonian; Cato of Utica; Leicester Dedlock.

(see *obstinate, pig-headed, obdurate, inflexible, perverse, wilful*)

STUDIOUS
Claudius; Pico della Mirandola; Sorbonist.

(see *learned, scholarly, pedantic, erudite*)

STUNTED
Vamana; Sindre.

(see *small, little, dwarf, deformed*)

STUPID
George Primrose; Cousin Michel; John-a-Dreams; Tony Lumpkin; Querno; MacFlecknoe; Dogberry; Huggins and Muggins; Phrygian; Hoenir; Bumbledonian; Damoetas; Abderian; Perrin Dendin; Boeotian; Doctor Dodipoll; Jack Pudding; Sacripant; Verges; Abraham Slender; Giottesque.

(see *absurd, unreasonable, irrational, fantastic, nonsense, ridiculous, incongruous, senseless, ludicrous, silly, ill-advised*)

SUAVE
Lovelace; Silk-Stocking; Hyblaean; Hymettan.

(see *bland, mildness, soft, debonair, urbanity*)

SUBCONSCIOUS
Carl G. Jung.

(see *unaware*)

SUBJUGATOR
Tamerlane.

(see *conqueror, victorious, overlord, slave-labor*)

SUFFRAGIST
John Stuart Mill.
(see *franchise, voting*)

SUGARCANE
Kama.
(see *sweetness, honey*)

SUGGESTION
Emily Dickinson; Miss Tox; Titian; Fescennine.
(see *innuendo, insinuation, hinting*)

SUICIDE
Rudolph of Mayerling; Sir John Suckling; Haemon; Nydia; Peregrinus Proteus; Dido; Parthenope; Lucretia; Pleiades; Gracchi; Deianira; Publius Decius Mus; Madama Butterfly; Amy Robsart; Phyllis; Seneca the Younger; Sigismunda; Cato of Utica; Jaffier; Schopenhauerian; La Tosca; Adolf Hitler; Zenobia; Althaea; Hedda Gabler.
(see *self-destruction*)

SUICIDE WARRIOR
Arnold von Winkelried; Publins Decius Mus.
(see *fighting*)

SUIT (v.)
Kit-Cat Club.
(see *appropriate, adjustable, adaptable*)

SUITOR
Brom Bones; Barkis; Antinous; the Pages; Mr. Toots; Abraham Slender; Miles Standish.
(see *wife-hunter, beau*)

SULLENNESS
Mr. Redlaw; Saturn; Tiberian.
(see *crabbed, morose, cantankerous, soured, ill-tempered*)

SUMMER
Maid Marian; Quadrifrons.
(see *seasons*)

SUMPTUOUSNESS
Phrygian; Benvenuto Cellini; Lucullan; Kubla Khan.
(see *costly, magnificence, splendor, riches, luxurious*)

SUNDER
Balmung.
(see *cleave, split*)

SUN-DIAL
Anaximander.
(see *clock*)

SUNFLOWER
Clytie.
(see *flowers*)

SUN-GOD
Eos; Surya; Frey; Thia; Mithras; Uriel; Pushan; Shamash; Gishzida; Phoebe and Phoebus; Gula; Agni; Utu; Nefertiti; Ra; Baldur; Harpocrates; Bacis; Phaëthon; Sol; Helios; Hyperion; Junner; Kneph; Pakht.
(see *heat, warmth*)

SUNLESS
Rahu; Erebus; Cimmerian.
(see *darkness, shade, dismal, black*)

SUNLIGHT
Hyperboreans; Beulah; Danaë; Clytie; Lagado; Osiris; Jack and the Bean Stalk.
(see *light, bright, dazzling*)

SUNSET
Ra; Amenti.
(see *dusk, twilight*)

SURE
Cephalus; Freischuetz.
(see *confidence, poise, self-assurance, infallible, security, trustworthy*)

SURE-FOOTED
Atalanta.
(see *runner, race, fast, rapid, fleet*)

SURF
Ran.
(see *sea-deities*)

SURFACE
Rinde.
(see *superficial*)

SURGEON
Podalirius; Machaon; Saint Pantaleon; Vaidya; Celsus; Mayo; Walter Reed.
(see *doctor, physician*)

SURLY
Manly; Gurth.
(see *gruff, morose, petulance, perverse, ill-tempered, soured, discourteous*)

SURMOUNT
Telamon.
(see *triumphant, conqueror*)

SURPRISE
Pan; Lalla Rookh; Olibrius; Galinthias; Marivaudage.
(see *shock, startle, amazing*)

SURRENDER
Gethsemane.
(see *abandon, renunciation*)

SURVEILLANCE
Falkland.
(see *overseer, warden, guardian, custodian, watchful, vigilance*)

SURVEYOR
Mason and Dixon; Sir John MacAdam.
(see *roads, builder*)

SURVIVAL
Darwinian.
(see *endurance, persistence*)

SURVIVOR
Ut-Napishtim; Vopiscus.
(see *escape, unharmed*)

SUSPENSE
Phlegyas; Scheherezade; Victor Hugo.
(see *uncertainty, hesitance, perplexity, indecision, vacillation*)

SUSPICION
Imogen; Robert Macaire; Desdemona; Melissa; Mariamne; Kunigunde; Wallenstein; Cephalus; Cronus; Hermione; La Tosca; Dionysius; Cato the Censor; Bradley Headstone; Eurylochus; Saul; Pompeia; Jean Hardouin; Domitian; Leonatus Posthumus; Leontes; Malbecco; Job's Friends; Kitely.
(see *apprehensive, distrustful, doubting, jealousy, fearful, conjecture*)

SUSTENANCE
Demogorgon.
(see *food, nourisher*)

SWAIN
Acis; Meliboeus; Menalcas; Tityrus; Corydon; Thyrsis; Lindor.
(see *rustic, gallantry, lovers, suitor, beau*)

SWALLOW (bird)
Philomela; Procne.
(see *birds*)

SWALLOW (v.)
Grangousier.
(see *eating, drink, devour*)

SWAMP
Phooka; Nastrond; Serbonian Bog; Slough of Despond.
(see *bog, fen, marsh*)

SWAN
Cycnus; Elsa; Lohengrin; Leda; Lir; Anna Pavlova.
(see *birds*)

SWAP
Glaucus.
(see *barter, exchange, bargain, trader*)

SWASHBUCKLING
Hectorean; Alexandre Dumas; Gabriele D'Annunzio.
(see *blustering, braggart, boastful, bully, roisterer*)

SWEAR
Feretrius.
(see *oath, vow, pledge, promise, perjury, forswear*)

SWEATER
Joseph Marie Jacquard.
(see *knitting, clothing*)

SWEETHEART
Queen of Hearts; Fiametta; Chloë; Jack and Jill; Dowsabel; Callipolis; Maid Marian; Delia; Dulcinea; Evangeline; Neaera; Zuleika; Stella.
(see *beloved, darling, lady-love, beau, suitor, swain*)

SWEETNESS
Hymettan; Nausicaa; Eumolpus; Melissa; Florimel; the Pages; Kama; Philomela; Hyblaean; Jessica.
(see *amiable, loveliness, engaging, charm, attractiveness, kindness, tenderness, benignant*)

SWEET-SMELLING
Gilead; Leucothea.
(see *fragrant, aromatic, perfume, odorous, incense*)

SWEET-SOUNDING
Aeolian; Adelina Patti.
(see *melodious, harmony, tuneful*)

SWEET-VOICED
Israfel.
(see *euphonious, mellifluous, resonant, singer*)

SWIFT
Jack Robinson; Pacolet; Grani· Tam O'Shanter; Zophiel; Cossack· Belphoebe; Odin; Ladas; Dictynna; Jehu; Laelaps; Garuda; Achilles; Liburnians; Phidippides; Skirnir; Milanion; Galloping Dick; Hermes; Jack the Giant-Killer; Ariel; Geronimo; Ganymede; Acestes; Abaris; Ullur; Camilla; Arion; Mercury; Al Borak.
(see *rapid, quick, fast, fleet, speed, velocity*)

SWIMMER
Eurynome; Nereids; Thetis; Tethys; Cloelia; Amphitrite; Horatius Cocles; Hero and Leander; Atargatis.
(see *mermaia, life-guard*)

SWINDLER
Camacho; Bully Dawson; Jeremy Diddler; Alfred Lammle; Dousterswivel; Tartuffian; Alfred Jingle; William M. Tweed.
(see *cheat, fraudulence, trickery, charlatan, imposture, quackery, embezzlement*)

SWINE
Gurth; Wild Boar of Ardennes; Varaha; Gadarene; Eumaeus.
(see *pig, boar*)

SWOLLEN
Physignathus.
(see *inflated, tumor*)

SWORD
Excalibur; Balmung; Morglay; Lua; Balisardo; Gram.
(see *broadsword, rapier*)

SWORDSMAN
Porthos; Hereward the Wake; Athos; D'Artagnan.
(see *duel*)

SYCOPHANT
Ephraim Jenkinson; Jenkins; Rev. Mr. Collins; Uncle Pumblechook; Prusias; Martial; Rosencrantz and Guildenstern; Gnatho; Irus.
(see *obsequious, fawning, flatterer, servility*)

SYLVAN
Faunus; Ogygia; Maid Marian; Pan; Dryads; Artemis; Pales.
(see *forests, woods*)

SYMBOLISM
Charles Perrault; Paul Gauguin; Dante Gabriel Rossetti; Blake-like.
(see *allegory*)

SYMPATHETIC
Atticus; Joe Gargery; Eugene Field; Galsworthian; Balzacian; Havelock Ellis.
(see *affectionate, tenderness, kindness, warm-hearted, compassionate, benignant, pity*)

SYMPHONIC
Brahmsian; Beethoven; Franz Liszt; Rimski-Korsakov; Tschaikovsky; Gustave Mahler; Franz Schubert; Robert Schumann.
(see *music*)

SYMPOSIUM
Agathon; Deipnosophistae.
(see *feast, revelry, banquet*)

SYNONYMS
Peter Mark Roget.
(see *words, dictionary*)

SYSTEMATIC
Richard Feverel; Eunomia; Hoyle.
(see *methodical, orderliness*)

T

TABLEAU
Mme. Tussaud; Mrs. Jarley.
(see *posture*)

TABLE TALK
Deipnosophistae; Autocrat of the Breakfast Table.
(see *conversation, symposium*)

TABOO
Richard von Krafft-Ebing.
(see *forbidden, ban, proscription*)

TACT
Dolly Madison; Esther; Talleyrand.
(see *diplomacy, management, insight, understanding*)

TACTLESS
Baillie Nicol Jarvie; Job's Friends.
(see *blunt, inappropriate, outspoken, brusque, unceremonious, gruff*)

TAIL
Gigantes.
(see *tassels*)

TAINTED
Zakkum.
(see *corrupt, pollute, infection, poison, mildew, stain*)

TALENT
Acacetus; Minna; Arsinoë; Hippocrene; Heliconian.
(see *able, genius, clever, skill*)

TALE-TELLER
Sindbad the Sailor; Charles Perrault; Scheherezade; Herodotean.
(see *anecdotal*)

TALKATIVE
Vach; Lucio; Alfred Jingle; Widow Blackacre; Sir Willful Witwould; Diggary; Lalage; Gratiano; Edie Ochiltree; Mrs. Nickleby; Sir Jerry Witwold.
(see *loquacious, long-winded, garrulous, chatterbox, gossip*)

TALL
Lysippus; Ferracute; Patagonian; Og; Front de Boeuf; Fierabras; Thalestris; Amazonian; Ichabod Crane; Burne-Jonesian; Aloidae.
(see *high, stature, lanky, long-legged*)

TANNER
Crispin; Simon.
(see *cobbler*)

TANTALIZING
Tantalus.
(see *tempter, enticement, beguilement, lure, disappointment, frustration*)

TANTAMOUNT
Twelve Peers.
(see *alike, likeness, similarity, identical*)

TARGETEER
Cephalus; Annie Oakley; William of Cloudeslie; Adam Bell; William Tell; Freischuetz; Nimrod; Izdubar.
(see *marksmanship, archer, bowman*)

TASKMASTER
Simon Legree; Khufu; Pelias; Eurystheus.
(see *slave-labor, hard-hearted, overseer, laborious*)

TASSELS
Zouave.
(see *tail*)

TASTELESS
Trimalchio.
(see *inedible, vapid, showy*)

TATTLER
Kriemhilde; Crabtree; Larunda; Ascalaphus; Agravaine.
(see *gossip, busybody, rumor, divulge, babbler, informer*)

TATTOOING
Picti.
(see *embellishment, bepainted*)

TAUNT
Brennus.
(see *derisive, ridicule, mockery, jeer, scornful, insulting, scoffer*)

TAVERN
Martin of Tours; Mistress Quickly.
(see *barmaid, innkeeper*)

TAWDRY
Brummagem.
(see *meretricious, flashy, showy, sham, gaudy, spurious*)

TAX-COLLECTOR
Zaccheus; St. Matthew.
(see *toll-gate*)

TAX-COMPLAINER
Rebeccaite; Rehoboam; Whiteboyism.
(see *complaining*)

TAXFREE
Flamen.
(see *privileged, favored, advantage, reserved, exclusive, franchise*)

TEACHER
Mentor; Orbilian; Plato; Socrates; Chiron; Eumolpus; Protagoras; Quintilian; Gamaliel; Oannes; Sopherim; Rasiel; Squeers; Holophernes; Panglossian; Mr. Creakle; Bradley Headstone; George Primrose; Abecedarians; Alexander Agassiz.
(see *professor, school-teacher, instructor*)

TEARS
Heliades; Eos; Byblis; Demodocus; Weeping Philosopher; Queen of Tears; Saint Lawrence; Memnon; Niobe; Belvidera; Job Trotter.
(see *lachrymose, weeping, crying, sobbing, mourning, lamentation*)

TEDIOUS
Gratiano; Querno; Job; Vanderdecken; Circumlocution Office; Goody Two-Shoes; Dry-as-Dust; Tupperian; Lindor.
(see *laborious, uninteresting, monotonous, boredom, ennui, slow*)

TEETOTALER
Nazarite; Martin of Tours; Rev. Mr. Stiggins; Essenes; Andrew Volstead.
(see *abstinence, temperance*)

TELEGRAPH
Samuel Morse; Mother Shipton.
(see *communication*)

TELEPHONE
Alexander Bell.
(see *communication*)

TEMERITY
Laenas.
(see *rash, reckless, impulsive, foolhardy, heedless, venturesome, presumptuous, hasty, audacity*)

TEMPER
Hotspur; Theodosius.
(see *ill-tempered, fiery-tempered, hotheaded, quick-tempered, anger, irascible*)

TEMPERANCE
Polemon of Athens; Jonathan Edwards; Poor Richard; Corinna; Sir Guyon.
(see *abstinence, sobriety, self-denial*)

TEMPEST
Mother Carey; Rudra; Njord; Red Man; Walpurgis.
(see *storm, rainstorm, squall, hurricane, whirlwind*)

TEMPLE
Parthenon.
(see *chapel*)

TEMPTED
Paphnutius; Amfortas; Vathek.
(see *seduced*)

TEMPTER
Apollyon; Comus; Samael; Eblis; Sam Hill.
(see *temptress, enticement, beguilement, lure, seduction, attractiveness, engaging, persuasion, ensnare, coaxing*)

TEMPTRESS
Thaïs; Tyndaris; Circean; Alcina; Potiphar's Wife; Kundry; Eve; Calypso.
(see *tempter, enticement, beguilement, lure, seduction, attractiveness, engaging, ensnare, persuasion, coaxing, alluring*)

TENDERNESS
Rosalind; Hermione; Quasimodo; Annie Laurie; Imogen; Florence Dombey; Amoret; Tristan; Tibullan; Cophetuan; Jonathan; Dantean; David Harum.
(see *amiable, loveliness, sweetness, engaging, charm, attractiveness, kindness, benignant, affectionate*)

TENEMENT
Martial.
(see *abode, residence, poverty*)

TENSION
Spoonerism.
(see *uneasy, timidity, fearful, excitement*)

TENT
Paribanou; Kedar.
(see *camp, out-of-doors, nomad*)

TERMAGANT
Katharine; Xanthippe; Widow MacStinger; Skimmington; Doll Tearsheet; Mrs. Caudle; Enyo; Mme. Pernelle.
(see *shrew, scold, virago*)

TERRA-COTTA
Della Robbia.
(see *porcelain, pottery, vases*)

TERRIER
Dandie Dinmont.
(see *dog*)

TERRIFIED
Little Red Ridinghood; Emperor Jones; Prisoner of Chillon.
(see *fearful, apprehensive, afraid, horror, alarm, startle, shock*)

TERRIFYING
Graiae; Yama; Typhon-Typhoeus; Mars; Avernian; Gorgons; Mumbo-Jumbo; Jehu; Jabberwock; Pavor; Furies; Barguest; Ephialtes; Juggernaut; Ivan Mazeppa.
(see *fearful, dire, awe-inspiring, dreadful, frighten*)

TERRORIST
Leon Trotsky; Jean Paul Marat; Danton; Tamerlane; Geronimo; Genseric; Vandalism; Ivan the Terrible; Whiteboyism.
(see *saboteurs, raider, intimidate, marauder, desperado, plunderer*)

TERSE
Giottesque; Callimachus; Laconian; Martial; Horatian; Pharnaces; Ion Perdicaris.
(see *laconic, brief, sententious, concise, pithy, shortcut*)

TEST (n.)
Job; Alasnam; Pelops; Diogenes; Boötes.
(see *experimentation, tribulation, proof, ordeal, criterion, judgment*)

TEST-TUBES
Antoine Lavoisier.
(see *laboratory, chemist*)

TEXTBOOK
Jean Auguste Ingres; Herodotean; Pierre Larousse; Xenophon; William McGuffey.
(see *didactic, schoolteacher, bookish*)

TEXTILES
Jack of Newbury.
(see *weaver*)

THANKLESSNESS
Newcastle; Gunther; Goneril.
(see *ingratitude, ungrateful*)

THANKSGIVING
Vacuna.
(see *gratitude*)

THAUMATURGY
Apollonius; Thessalian; Zanoni; Saint Filumena; Hugh of Lincoln; Simon.
(see *wonder-worker, miraculous, sorcerer, magic*)

THEATRICAL
Rialto.
(see *acting, stage*)

THEOCRAT
Zelotes.
(see *monotheistic, power*)

THEOLOGIAN
Abelard and Héloise; Hugo Grotius; Thomas Aquinas; Pico della Mirandola; Leibnitzian; John Wycliffe; Desiderius Erasmus; Johannes Eckhart; Christian Rosenkreutz; St. Augustine; Martin Luther; Calvinistic; John Huss; Wesleyan; Sorbonist.
(see *religious, preacher*)

THERAPEUTICS
Kneippism; Wilhelm Roentgen.
(see *healing, curative*)

THESAURUS
Peter Mark Roget.
(see *dictionary*)

THICK-SKINNED
Ferracute.
(see *dull-witted, insensitive, callous*)

THIEVERY
Laverna; Comte de LaMotte; Jean Valjean; Moll Flanders; Moll Cutpurse; Jack Horner; Sacripant; the Peachums; Solomon Pross; Raffles; Rhampsinitus; Silas Marner; Cacus; Cagliostro; Autolycus; Alcmaeon; Andhaba; Jessica; Dismas; Bill Sikes; Foigard; Geryon; Taffy; Thrym; Cogia Houssam; Trophonius; Abramman; Arimaspians; Bezonian; Artful Dodger; Fagin; Cercopes; Bully Dawson; Diomedes; Hermes; Mercury; Mahu; Mohock; Naraka; Nym; Colonel Jack; Saint Nicholas; E. Phillips Oppenheim; Jack Sheppard; Abel Magwitch; Micah; Onesimus; Pandareos.

TIDY
Martha.
(see *housewifery, domestic, orderliness*)

TILES
Della Robbia.
(see *porcelain*)

TIME
Olympiad; Anaximander; Partula; Quadrifrons; Amaimon; Proustian.
(see *dates, month, year, eternity, present, past, future, never, periodic, interval*)

TIMIDITY
David Copperfield; Menoetes; Fear Fortress; Florimel; Watkins Tottle; Pliable.
(see *fearful, shy, cowardice, bashful, diffident, faint-hearted, afraid*)

TINKLE
Dodonean.
(see *bell-ringer*)

TINTED
Josiah Wedgewood.
(see *dye, stain*)

TINY
Vamana; Tom Thumb; Lilliputian; Hop o' My Thumb; Oberon; Titania; Fenella.
(see *little, small, diminutive, pygmy, midget*)

TIPPLER
Saint Vincent; John Barleycorn; Mr. Krook; Friar Rush; Fortunio; Silence; Mrs. Sarah Gamp; Teague.
(see *dipsomaniac, alcoholism, drunkenness, inebriation*)

TITANIC
Promethean; Hringham; Leviathanic.
(see *vast, massiveness, gigantic, enormous*)

TOAD
Johnny Crapaud.
(see *frog*)

TOBACCO
John Rolfe.
(see *smoke, plants*)

TOIL
Sisyphean; Gibeonite; Rachel.
(see *laborious, arduous, onerous, difficulty*)

TOKEN
Ion; Tamar.
(see *signal, evidence*)

TOLERANCE
Chaucerian; Charles Montesquieu; Seneca the Younger; Constantine.
(see *endurance, impartial, unbiased, broad-minded, patience*)

TOLL-GATE
Rebeccaite.
(see *tax-collector, tax-complainer*)

TOMB
Etruscan; Old Mortality; Mausolus; Taj Mahal.
(see *coffin, sarcophagus, grave, cemetery*)

TOMB-ROBBERY
Tutankhamen.
(see *thievery, sacrilegious*)

TONGUE
Panglossian.
(see *language, polyglot, linguist, utterance, speech*)

TONGUELESS
Larunda; Philomela.
(see *mute*)

TOOTHLESS
Graiae; Elli.
(see *old age, anile, senile*)

TOOTHPICK
Agathocles.
(see *eating*)

TOOTH-PULLER
Kindhart.
(see *toothless*)

TORCH
Bendis; Pharos.
(see *firebrand, light*)

TORMENTED (conscience)
Arthur Dimmesdale; Vathek; Orestes.
(see *anguish, agony, suffering, distressed, conscience-stricken, self-tormentor*)

TORMENTOR
Mab; Marquis de Sade; Torquemada; Furies; Lemures; Old Nick.
(see *punishment, sadism, cruelty, inquisition, persecution*)

TORTOISE
Sciron; Hermes.
(see *animals*)

TORTURED (physical)
Tantalus; Tityus; Io; Masochism; Saint Catherine; Saint Eulalia; Ixion; Dirce; Saint Lucia; Regulus; Hugh of Lincoln.
(see *anguish, agony, suffering, distressed, punishment*)

TOUCHSTONE
Diogenes; Alasnam.
(see *test, criterion, proof*)

TOUGH
Nemean Lion.
(see *stiff, rigid, inflexible, stubborn*)

TOURISTS
George Bradshaw; Karl Baedeker; Thomas Cook; Itineraria; Strabo; Pausanias.
(see *traveler, voyager, pilgrimage*)

TOURNAMENT
Walter Scott; Palamon and Arcite.
(see *contest, knighthood*)

TOWER
Pharos; Danaë.
(see *fortress, castle, stronghold, lighthouse*)

TOWN HALL
Tolbooth.
(see *assembly-place*)

TOXICOLOGY
Locusta; Nicander.
(see *poison, venomous*)

TRADER
Sudra; Vaissya; Marco Polo; Robert LaSalle; Carthaginian; Glaucus; Rialto.
(see *peddler, huckster, barter, exchange, swap*)

TRAGEDY
Banshee; Melpomene; Thespian; Seneca the Younger; Sophoclean; Shakespearean; Giacomo Puccini; Euripidean; Thomas Hardy; Aldiborontiphoscophornio; Henrik Ibsen; Vincent Crummles; Aeschylean.
(see *dramatic, calamity, disaster, catastrophe*)

TRAGIC HEROES
Pyramus; Pelléas and Mélisande; Beau Brummel; Enoch Arden; Othello; Oedipus; Orpheus; Tristan; Aegis-

thus; Abelard and Héloise; Orestes; Achilles; Hamlet; Romeo; Promethean; Agamemnon.
(see *hero*)

TRAGIC HEROINES
Desdemona; Electra; Isolde; Anna Karenina; Zenobia; Tess of the D'Urbervilles; Lady of Shalott; Ophelia; Dido; Brunhilde; Hecuba; Ginevra; Marie Antoinette; Clytemnestra; Antigone; Medea; Alcestis; Iphigenia; Juliet; Mimi.
(see *heroine*)

TRAINING (military)
Campus Martius; Ephebeia.
(see *discipline, drill*)

TRAITOROUS
Branchidae; Tarpeian Rock; Capua; Thermopylae; Ephialtes; Coriolanus; Ventidius; Judas; Gracchi; Helenus; Modred; Prusias; Ganelon; Rosencrantz and Guildenstern; Philip Wharton; Benedict Arnold; Jonathan Wild; Quisling.
(see *treachery, betrayal, perfidy, recreant, turncoat, faithless*)

TRAMP (n.)
Irus; King Petaud's Court.
(see *itinerant, vagrancy, beggar*)

TRANCE
Saint Theresa; Khartaphilos.
(see *ecstasy, hypnotism, dreamland*)

TRANQUILLITY
Farinata; Pyrrhonian; King Log; Irene; Alcyone; Pax.
(see *serenity, peace, calm, repose, quiet, undisturbed*)

TRANSFIGURATION
Cyparissus; Pitys; Milanion; Cycnus; Syrinx; Aëdon; Aeaean; Azor; Io; Anaxarete; Dryope; Hyacinthus; Lycaon; Heliades; Latona; Tereus; Thetis; Nereus; Galatea; Alcyone; Phaon; Riquet; Atys; Ascalaphus; Clytie; Melusina; Golden Ass; Saint Januarius; Siva; Astolfo; Battus; Jekyll-Hyde; Loathly Lady; Telchines; Proteus; Myrrha; Procne.
(see *metamorphosis*)

TRANSGRESSION
Eve; Zanes.
(see *violation, disobedience, sin, iniquity*)

TRANSIENCE
Omar Khayyam; Damoclean.
(see *ephemeral, short-lived*)

TRANSLATOR
Melampus; Saint Jerome; John Wycliffe.
(see *linguist*)

TRANSMIGRATION (spiritual)
Buddha; Pythagoras.
(see *rebirth, reincarnation, metamorphosis, transfiguration*)

TRANSVESTITISM
Lycomedes; Viola; Rebeccaite; Pope Joan; Fidelio; Omphale; George Sand; Parthenia; Radegund.
(see *disguise, incognito*)

TRAP
Trasimene Lake; Trophonius; Wooden Horse; Rhampsinitus; Quintilius Varus; Milo.
(see *snare, ensnare, man-trap, ambush, stratagem*)

TRAVELER
Strabo; Ulysses; Apollonius; Louis Joliet; Prester John; Sir John Mandeville; Ponce de Leon; Marco Polo; Johnny Appleseed; Magi; Walking Stewart; Mirabel; Richard Haliburton; Innocents Abroad; Henry Wads-

worth Longfellow; Richard Hakluyt; Washington Irving.
(see *tourists, voyager, itinerary*)

TRAVELERS-AID
George Bradshaw; Heinrich Kiepert; Thomas Cook; Pausanias; Itineraria; Bernard of Menthon.
(see *direct, v.*)

TRAVESTY
Sir Launcelot Greaves; Marivaudage.
(see *burlesque, farce, parody, caricature*)

TREACHERY (female)
Jezebel; Delilah; Bathsheba; Regan; La Tosca; Olivia.

TREACHERY (groups and places)
Parthian; Greeks Bearing Gifts; Punic; Gethsemane; Thessalian; Carthaginian.

TREACHERY (male)
Xerxes; Branchidae; Sinon; John Silver; Prusias; Alcibiades; Zacocia; Paris; Modred; Mime; Menalcas; King Mark; Macbeth; Laomedon; Sir Kay; Lycomedes; Judas; Sanballat.
(see *traitorous, betrayal, perfidy, recreant, turncoat, double-dealing, faithless, infidelity, disloyal, deceitful*)

TREASURE
Gryps; Andvari; Saint Lawrence; Fata Morgana; Fafner; Rheingold; Sindre; Goshen; Golconda; Trophonius; Kriemhilde; Jack and the Bean Stalk.
(see *gold, riches, wealth, hoard*)

TREATY-MAKING
Semo Sancus; Fetiales; John Jay.
(see *peacemaker, truce*)

TREE-CLIMBER
Zaccheus.
(see *pedestal*)

TREES
Napaeae; Yggdrasil; Hrimthursar; Ve; Dodonean; Dryad; Pomona; Silvanus; Kalpa-Tarou.
(see *ash tree, linden tree, poplar tree, bush, pine tree, evergreen, laurel, cypress, myrtle, oak tree*)

TREMENDOUS
Colossus; Hringham; Leviathanic.
(see *bulk, massiveness, huge, titanic, vast, prodigious*)

TRESSES
Sif.
(see *hair, ringlet, lock, curl, snake-haired*)

TRIAD
Vishnu; Graces; Charis.
(see *divinity, triplets*)

TRIBULATION
Job; Iliad; Ulysses; Griselda.
(see *troublesome, suffering, distressed, afflicted, grief, adversity, misery, woe, sorrow*)

TRIBUNAL
Areopagitical; Forsete; Sanhedrin.
(see *judgment, courthouse*)

TRICKERY
Sir Kay; Robin Goodfellow; Volpone; Utgard-Loki; Hermes; Greeks Bearing Gifts; Scapino; Perseus; Squeers; Sinon; Wooden Horse; Zacocia; Cacus; Stockwell Ghost; Galinthias; Philip of Macedon; Hippomenes; Katerfelto; Outis; Dousterswivel; Milanion; Jack Horner; Sampson Brass.
(see *fraudulence, artifice, ruse, stratagem, wily, double-dealing, deceitful, cheat*)

TRIFLING
Vainlove; Philander; Janotism; Big-Endians; Lantern Land; Tweedledum and Tweedledee; Jeannot.
(see *picayune, insignificant, petty, dalliance, frivolous*)

TRIGONOMETRY
Hipparchus.
(see *mathematics*)

TRIMNESS
Jack Sixteen-String; Gibsonesque.
(see *tidy, chic, elegance*)

TRIPLETS
Sabra.
(see *triad*)

TRITE
Sir Willful Witwould; Tupperian.
(see *unimaginative, uninspired, uninteresting*)

TRIUMPHANT
Ludwig van Beethoven; Pompey; Saint George.
(see *exultant, joy, jubilation, conqueror*)

TRIVIAL
Smelfungus; King of Yvetot.
(see *unimportant, insignificant, petty, picayune*)

TROLLOP
Maritornes; Doll Tearsheet; Dol Common.
(see *strumpet, street-walker, harlot, prostitute, whore*)

TROPICS
Paul Gauguin.
(see *heat*)

TROUBADOUR
Minnesinger.
(see *minstrelsy, bard*)

TROUBLESOME
Queer Street; Old Man of the Sea; Friar Rush; Eris.
(see *annoy, harass, burden, nuisance, difficulty*)

TROUPER
Vincent Crummles.
(see *actor*)

TRUCE
Glaucus.
(see *treaty-making, peace-maker*)

TRUCULENT
Wild Boar of Ardennes.
(see *ferocious, belligerent, savage, brutish, deadly, ruthlessness*)

TRUE-LOVE
Neaera.
(see *lady-love, sweetheart, darling, beloved*)

TRUMPET
Hernani; Triton; Gjallarhorn; Gabriel; Jericho; Misenus; Jubal.
(see *horns*)

TRUSTING
Captain Cuttle; Jaffier; Clarissa Harlowe; Amelia Sedley; Tyr; Orgon; Noah; Duncan; Witch of Endor.
(see *faith, belief, credulity*)

TRUSTWORTHY
Mentor; Spes; Zadok; Abdiel; Dugald Dalgetty; Porcia; Regulus; Garcia; Faithful Eckhardt.
(see *reliable, dependable, constancy, faithful*)

TRUTH
Maat; Dike; Una; Horn Gate; Simon Pure; Red Cross Knight; Varuna; Alasnam; Satyrane.
(see *honesty, honor, integrity, sincerity, ingenuousness, virtue*)

TRUTHFUL
Philoxenus; Juliet; Dorigen; Selim; Fabricius; Andromache; Eumaeus; Calidore.
(see *candid, frank, artless, guileless, outspoken*)

TUBERCULAR
La Traviata; Mimi.
(see *emaciated, sickly*)

TUMOR
Saint Fiacre.
(see *disease, swollen*)

TUMULTUOUS
Pandemonium; Donnybrook Fair; Chaos; Saxnot; King Petaud's Court; Rhea; Flamininus; Curetes.
(see *riot, turbulence, lawless, violence, disorderly*)

TUNEFUL
Franz Schubert; Stephen Foster; Giacomo Puccini; Giuseppe Verdi; Gioacchino Rossini.
(see *melodious*)

TURBULENCE
Francesca of Rimini; Ran; Paulina; Enyo; Centaur; Aegir; Thyia; Termagant; Locofocos.
(see *tumultuous, commotion, confusion, mutiny, insurrection, rebellious*)

TURGID
John Lyly; Aldiborontiphoscophornio.
(see *polysyllables, bombastic, grandiloquent, magniloquence, inflated*)

TURNCOAT
Benedict Arnold; Pliable; Amasa; Coriolanus; Thessalian; Tarpeian Rock; Capua; Herodian.
(see *apostasy, backslider, deserter, traitorous, faithless, recreant*)

TURNKEY
Miggs; Solomon Pross.
(see *jailer, custodian*)

TURNPIKE
Rebeccaite.
(see *highway, roads, pathway, route*)

TURPENTINE
Tarheel.
(see *oil, pine-tree*)

TUTELAR
Tanit; Lares.
(see *guardian, protector, patron, patron saint, custodian, defender*)

TUTOR
Panglossian; Square and Thwackum; Rasiel; Atlantes; Gamaliel.
(see *teacher, instructor, school teacher, professor*)

TWADDLE
Mrs. Slipslop; Spoonerism.
(see *prattle, gossip, chatterbox, nonsense, gibberish, jargon, senseless*)

TWILIGHT
Ra; Hesperus.
(see *sunset, dusk, evening*)

TWINS
Vopiscus; Dromios; Latona; Esau; Menaechmus; Dioscuri; Romulus and Remus; Antipholus.
(see *alike, similarity, likeness, identical, resemblance, duplicate, equality*)

TWITCHING

Saint Vitus.
(see *nervous*)

TWO-FACED

Janus.
(see *double-dealing, unfaithful, hypocrisy, deceitful*)

TYRANNICIDE

Cassius; Brutus; Harmodius and Aristogiton.
(see *liberator*)

TYRANT

Cambyses; Lorenzo the Magnificent; Mussolini; Pharaoh; Pittacus; Pisistratus; Creon; Rameses; Khufu; Dionysius; Aelius Sejanus; Isagoras; Tiberian; Lityerses; Mezentius; Domitian; Jean Paul Marat; Danton; Robespierre; Tamerlane; Minos; Periander; Tarquinius Superbus; Eglon; Jonas Chuzzlewit; Judge Lynch; Sir Matthew Mite; Rehoboam.
(see *despotic, autocratic, dictator, absolutism, oppression, arbitrary, overlord, domineering*)

U

UBIQUITOUS
Javert; Pooh-Bah; Pacolet; Old Man of the Sea.
(see *omnipresent*)

UGLINESS (female)
Gorgons; Stheno; Hela; Ulrica; Miss Tabitha Bramble; Euryale; Medusa; Loathly Lady.
(see *hag*)

UGLINESS (male)
Yellow Dwarf; Hagen; Punch; Riquet; Azor; Kuvera; Quilp; Mayeux; Mr. Fang; Quasimodo; Hipponax; Andvari; Thersitean.
(see *hideous, homely, misshapen, deformed, monstrosity, loathsome, repellent, dwarf*)

ULCERS
Celsus; Philoctetes.
(see *sore, cancerous*)

UMPIRE
Palaemon.
(see *arbiter*)

UNACCEPTABLE
Pariah; Coventry.
(see *ostracism, offensive, unwelcome, unpopular, outlaw*)

UNACHIEVABLE
Navius.
(see *impossible, unattainable*)

UNAFFECTED
Bertolde; Amy Dorrit.
(see *naturalness, simplicity, ingenuousness, artless, guileless, naive*)

UNAFFECTIONATE
Joseph Bounderby; Anteros.
(see *cold-hearted, hard-hearted, heartless, unfeeling*)

UNAFRAID
Laberius.
(see *fearless, courageous, daring, undaunted, bravery, intrepid*)

UNAGING
Dorian Gray; Peter Pan; Hyperboreans; Hebe; Juventas; Iduna; Kumara.
(see *youthful, rejuvenation, immortality*)

UNAMBITIOUS
Theophrastus.
(see *lazy, inaolence*)

UNAMIABLE
Sir Mungo Malagrowther.
(see *ill-tempered, ill-mannered, sullenness, crabbed, morose, gruff*)

UNANSWERABLE
Abdemon.
(see *puzzle, riddle, dilemma, quandary*)

UNATTAINABLE
Tantalus; Sylvia; Thule.
(see *impossible, unachievable*)

UNAUTHORIZED
Apocryphal; Judge Lynch.
(see *lawless, illegal*)

UNAVOIDABLE
Laius; Old Man of the Sea; Vanderdecken.
(see *inevitability, inescapable, necessity*)

UNAWARE
Sacripant.
(see *subconscious, inattentive, heedless, ignorance*)

UNBELIEVER
Dabbat.
(see *agnostic, doubting, skepticism*)

UNBIASED
Melantius.
(see *impartial, equitable, disinterested*)

UNBROTHERLY
Oliver (1); Romulus and Remus; Onan.
(see *fratricide*)

UNBURIED
Palinurus.
(see *disinterred*)

UNCANNY
Anton Chekhov; Mme. Marie Tussaud.
(see *preternatural, supernatural, ghost, eerie*)

UNCEREMONIOUS
Gretna Green.
(see *bluff, blunt, brusque, gruff, informal, casual*)

UNCERTAINTY
Tyndareus; Kilmansegg; Moerae; Weissnichtwo; Jumala.
(see *doubting, doubtful, ambiguous, enigmatic, hesitancy, indecision, suspense*)

UNCHANGEABLE
Procrustean; Medes and Persians; Parmenides.
(see *immovable, irrevocable, inexorable*)

UNCHARITABLE
Mrs. Jellyby; John Wemmick; Parson Trulliber; Miss Tabitha Bramble.
(see *censorious, harsh, severity, misanthropy*)

UNCHASTE
Canace; Maid Marian; Tess of the D'Urbervilles.
(see *adulterous, impure, illicit, corrupt, rakish, dissolute*)

UNCIVILIZED
Troglodytae; Zamore; Tarzan; Mowgli; Rima.
(see *wild, wilderness, wild man, savage, barbarity*)

UNCOMPLAINING
Aglaos; Griselda.
(see *resignation, submission, stoical, long-suffering, patience*)

UNCOMPROMISING
Saint Wulfstan; Tertullian; Giuseppe Mazzini.
(see *intransigence, inflexible, obstinate, narrow-minded, strict, intolerance*)

UNCONCERNED
Hippoclides.
(see *nonchalant, insouciance, carelessness, indifference, apathy, easy-going*)

UNCONTRADICTABLE
Squire Western.
(see *absolute, cocksure*)

UNCONTROLLED
Frankenstein; Zenobia; Aegean; Phaëthon.
(see *unmanageable, unrestrained, headlong*)

UNCONVENTIONAL
Johnsonian; Algernon Swinburne; Sir Harry Wildair; Maggie Tulliver; Walt Whitman; Henry VIII; Brand; Mme. Sans-Gêne.
(see *informal, lawless, eccentric, idiosyncratic*)

UNCONVERTED
City of Destruction.
(see *pagan, idolatry*)

UNCOUTH
Manly; Gurth.
(see *awkward, boorish, clumsy, loutish, rude, gauche, outlandish*)

UNCTUOUS
Obadiah Slope; Pecksniff.
(see *obsequious, fawning, sycophant, sanctimonious*)

UNCULTURED
Cristoph Wagner; Trimalchio; Philistines; Boeotian.
(see *uncivilized, illiterate, untutored*)

UNDAUNTED
Barnadine; Mark Tapley; Laberius; Widow MacStinger.
(see *daring, bold, intrepid, bravery, fearless, courageous*)

UNDECIDED
Buridan's Ass.
(see *irresolute, hesitancy, vacillation, doubting, quandary, dilemma*)

UNDECIPHERABLE
Mrs. Ramsbottom.
(see *hieroglyph, unintelligible, senseless*)

UNDERGROUND
Arethusa; Demogorgon; Alpheus.
(see *lower world, underworld*)

UNDERPRIVILEGED
Licinius; Publilius Philo.
(see *proletariat, slavery*)

UNDERSTANDING
James Monroe; Mme. de Maintenon; Eugene Field; Pierrette; Theophrastus; Columbine; Melampus.
(see *reason, mind, intelligent, insight, sympathetic, compassionate*)

UNDERTAKER
Libitina.
(see *death*)

UNDERWORLD
Padalon; Avernian; Dis; Hades; Orcus; Amenti; Ifurin.
(see *lower world, infernal*)

UNDERWRITERS
Lloyd's.
(see *security, guarantee*)

UNDIGNIFIED
Lazarillo de Tormes; Diggary.
(see *indecorous, ill-mannered, vulgarity*)

UNDISTURBED
King Log.
(see *calm, placid, quiet, serenity, tranquillity, peaceful, composure, worriless*)

UNDRESS
Lazarillo de Tormes.
(see *nudism, nakedness, stripped*)

UNEASY
Eurylochus; Damocles.
(see *apprehensive, fearful, distrustful, ill-at-ease*)

UNEMOTIONAL
Stoic; Anaxarete.
(see *cold-hearted, rationalistic, unfeeling, hard-hearted*)

UNEMPLOYED
Coxey's Army; Luddites.
(see *idleness, loafer*)

UNENDING
Sisyphean; Luggnagg.
(see *endless, eternity, immortality, everlasting, perpetual, interminable*)

UNEQUAL
Olibrius.
(see *inferiority, mediocrity*)

UNERRING
Odin; Gungnir; Ron; Freischuetz; Sagittary.
(see *infallible, exactitude, accuracy, sure*)

UNEXPECTED
Sir Urian; Tatar; Cinderella-like.
(see *surprise, shock, startle, sudden*)

UNEXPRESSIVE
John Wemmick.
(see *characterless, unemotional*)

UNFAITHFUL
Hosea; Pompeia; Manon (Lescaut); Hermione; Troilus and Cressida; Daphnis; Hetty Sorrel.
(see *faithless, untrustworthy, infidelity, treachery, perfidy, deceitful, disloyal, recreant, turncoat*)

UNFATHOMABLE
Albert Einstein; Mona Lisa; Sphinx.
(see *deep, profound, inscrutable, mystery, unintelligible, inexplicable*)

UNFEELING
Squeers; Gradgrind; Regan; Anaxarete; Thaukt.
(see *unemotional, cold-hearted, hard-hearted, heartless, apathy, merciless, pitiless, inhumanity*)

UNFEMININE
Enyo; Amazonian.
(see *amazon, virago, masculinity*)

UNFILIAL
Goneril; Anu; Regan; Tullia; Micah; Père Goriot.
(see *matricide, patricide*)

UNFINISHED
Lord Balmerino; Giottesque; Onan; Franz Schubert.
(see *imperfect*)

UNFIT
Olibrius.
(see *inferiority, inappropriate, irrelevant, impropriety, ineptitude*)

UNFLINCHING
Scaevola; Spartan; Philaeni.
(see *resolute, courageous, undaunted, fearless, bold, bravery, intrepid*)

UNFORGIVING
Lycus; Guido Francischini.
(see *relentless, implacable, inexorable, stony-hearted, hard-hearted, rancorous*)

UNFRIENDLY
Sir Mungo Malagrowther; Tauri; Xerxes.
(see *impiety, irreverent, blasphemous, antagonistic, opposition*)

UNGAINLY
Tom Pinch.
(see *uncouth, ungraceful, awkward, clumsy, boorish, loutish*)

UNGENEROUS
Sir Matthew Mite; Mrs. Jellyby.
(see *uncharitable, mean-spirited, stingy, miserliness, selfish*)

UN-GODFEARING
Ephialtes.
(see *impiety, irreverent, blasphemous, profanation, sacrilegious*)

UNGOVERNED
King Petaud's Court; Lucio.
(see *unmanageable, uncontrolled, unrestrained*)

UNGRACEFUL
Mrs. Jarley.
(see *awkward, clumsy, gauche, uncouth, ungainly*)

UNGRAMMATICAL
Alfred Jingle; Priscian.
(see *solecism*)

UNGRATEFUL
Hippomenes; Goneril; Gunther.
(see *ingratitude, thanklessness*)

UNGUENT
Gilead.
(see *ointment, panacea*)

UNHAPPY
Clarissa Harlowe; Belvidera; Midas; Daphnis; Undine; Childe Harold; Hedda Gabler; Agathocles; Francesca of Rimini.
(see *sadness, sorrowful, afflicted, grief, distressed, heart-broken, disconsolate*)

UNHARMED
Shadrach.
(see *unmarked*)

UNHEALABLE
Amfortas; Philoctetes.
(see *incurable*)

UNHYGIENIC
Black Hole of Calcutta.
(see *filth, foul*)

UNIDENTIFIED
Richard Roe; Man with the Iron Mask; John Doe; Sohrab.
(see *unknown, unrecognized, incognito*)

UNIFIER
Isocrates; Wallenstein; Garibaldian.
(see *unite, unity*)

UNIMAGINATIVE
Sancho Panza; Martha.
(see *matter-of-fact, prosaic, literal*)

UNIMPORTANT
King of Yvetot; Jack-a-Lent; Pygmy; Holophernes.
(see *insignificant, petty, picayune, inconsequential, trivial*)

UNINFORMED
Miss Betsy Thoughtless.
(see *untutored, ignorance, illiterate*)

UNINSPIRED
Tupperian; Robotian.
(see *prosaic, uninteresting, tedious, commonplace*)

UNINTELLIGENT
Bumbledonian.
(see *stupid, unreasonable, irrational, senseless, ill-advised*)

UNINTELLIGIBLE
Ka; Mrs. Ramsbottom; Gertrude Stein; Albert Einstein.

(see *incomprehensible, abstruse, meaningless, mumbling, inarticulate, enigmatic, inexplicable, insoluble*)

UNINTENTIONAL
Spoonerism; Deianira; Callirrhoë; Telegonus; Hodur; Cyparissus.
(see *casual, accidental, chance, adventitious, involuntary, spontaneous*)

UNINTERESTING
Dry-as-Dust; Xenophon.
(see *tedious, monotonous, boredom, ennui*)

UNIQUE
Pelops; Peregrine White; Epaminondas.
(see *rare, extraordinary, unusual*)

UNITE
Yue-Laou; Yggdrasil.
(see *unifier, unity*)

UNITED STATES
Brother Jonathan; Uncle Sam.
(see *American*)

UNITY
Siamese; Raphael; Graces; James Monroe; Constantine.
(see *harmony, amity, concord, accord, agreement*)

UNIVERSE
Brahma; Galileo; Johannes Kepler; Anaximenes; Urania (see Muse); Parmenides; Democritus.
(see *creation, world, nature*)

UNJUST
Brennus; Ahab; Abijah; Zoilus; Creon; Elbridge Gerry.
(see *partiality, injustice, iniquity, prejudice, bias, wickedness*)

UNKNOWN
Man with the Iron Mask; Sir Urian; Ka.
(see *unidentified, unrecognized, incognito, mystery, enigmatic*)

UNLIKELY
Lollius.
(see *impracticable*)

UNLOVED
Florence Dombey.
(see *abandoned, neglected*)

UNLOVING
Anteros.
(see *cold-hearted, unemotional, unfeeling*)

UNLUCKY
Yezd; Peter Schlemihl; Tristram Shandy; Jonah; Menelaus; Andvaranaut; Rheingold; Harmonia's Necklace.
(see *bad luck, ill-luck, misfortune, baleful, disaster, inauspicious*)

UNMANAGEABLE
King Petaud's Court.
(see *uncontrolled, ungoverned, impracticable*)

UNMANLY
Vathek; Bagoas; Queen Dick; Silk-Stocking.
(see *effeminate, sissified, foppish*)

UNMANNED
Uranus; Atys.
(see *castration, eunuch*)

UNMARKED
Samuel Maverick.
(see *unharmed*)

UNMARRIED MOTHER
Margaret; Effie Deans; Lady Dedlock.
(see *seduced, betrayed, bastardy*)

UNMASK
Ithuriel.
(see *exposure, divulge*)

UNPOLLUTED
Nazarite.
(see *cleanliness, purity*)

UNPOPULAR
Galba; Mme. DuBarry.
(see *hateful, unacceptable, offensive, unwelcome*)

UNPRACTICED
Johnny Newcome.
(see *artless, inexperienced, callow, greenhorn, immature*)

UNPRETENTIOUS
Bob Cratchit; Amelia Sedley.
(see *naturalness, plainness, simplicity, modesty*)

UNPRINCIPLED
Harold Skimpole; Roderick Random, Becky Sharp.
(see *unscrupulous, immorality, wickedness, vicious, knave, rogue*)

UNPRONOUNCEABLE
Houyhnm; Aldiborontiphoscophornio.
(see *sesquipedalian, bombastic*)

UNREAL
Mme. Marie Tussaud; Weissnichtwo.
(see *non-existent, fictitious, never*)

UNREASONABLE
Draconian; Leicester Dedlock; Fear Fortress; Leontes.
(see *absurd, irrational, fantastic, silly, nonsense, ridiculous, incongruous, ill-advised, senseless, ludicrous, stupid*)

UNRECOGNIZED
Guy of Warwick; Callisto; Laius; Telegonus; Protogenes; Man with the Iron Mask; Sohrab.
(see *incognito, unknown, unidentified*)

UNRELIABLE
Pliable; Mrs. Candour; Capua.
(see *untrustworthy, inconstant, fickle, irresponsible, treachery*)

UNREQUITED
Robin and Makyne.
(see *retaliation, avenge*)

UNRESTRAINED
Cybele; Argante; Frankenstein; Lucio; Samuel Pepys; Mme. Sans-Gêne.
(see *licentious, "loose," dissolute, inordinate, lawless, wanton, abandon*)

UNSAFE
Ides of March.
(see *danger, perilous, precarious*)

UNSCRUPULOUS
Uriah Heep; Jugurtha; Lothario; the Crawleys; Marmion; Lovelace; Widow Barnaby; Themistoclean; Sir Giles Overreach; Machiavellian; Roderick Random.
(see *unprincipled, ruthlessness, dishonest, trickery, fraudulence, villainy*)

UNSEEING
Nydia; Melesigenes.
(see *blindness, sightless*)

UNSEEN
Wayland the Smith; Mambrino.
(see *invisible, latent*)

UNSELFISH
Cyrano de Bergerac; Publius Decius Mus; Zeno; Sidney Carton; Ruth; Zémire; Auld Robin Gray; Tolstoi; Honeywood; Philaeni; Mettius Curtius; Stoic; Amy Dorrit.

(see *altruistic, philanthropic, self-denial, self-sacrificing, generosity, magnanimous*)

UNSMILING
Marcus Crassus; John Wemmick.
(see *sobriety, serious*)

UNSOPHISTICATED
Peter Quince; Doctor Charles Primrose; Moses Primrose; Bob Acres; Rev. Micah Balwhidder; Elaine; Agnes; Innocents Abroad; Daisy Miller; Mme. Sans-Gêne.
(see *artless, guileless, ingenuousness, simplicity, naturalness, naive*)

UNSPOILED
The Peachums; Miranda.
(see *naturalness, simplicity, plainness*)

UNSUSPECTING
Epimetheus; Duncan; Melantius.
(see *credulity, trusting, surprise*)

UNSYMPATHETIC
Thaukt; Gradgrind.
(see *cold-hearted, hard-hearted, callous*)

UNTIDY
Mrs. Jellyby; Halgaver.
(see *slatternly, disorderliness, chaos*)

UNTRAINED
Johnny Newcome.
(see *greenhorn, inexperienced, immature, artless, callow*)

UNTRUSTWORTHY
Zacocia; Pliable; Battus; Mr. Fudge; Bagoas; Carthaginian; Mrs. Candour; Gawain; Alcibiades; Wooden Horse; Laomedon; Nym; Prusias; Modred.
(see *faithless, unreliable, deceitful, dishonest, treachery, disloyal, deceptive*)

UNTUTORED
Topsy; Miramont.
(see *untrained, uninformed, ignorance, ingenuousness, artless*)

UNUSUAL
Phoenix.
(see *rare, extraordinary, out-of-the-way, outlandish, bizarre, exotic, novelty, strange*)

UNWELCOME
Dangle; John Drum.
(see *unacceptable, offensive, unpopular*)

UNWISE
Semele; Lot's Wife.
(see *foolish, indiscretion, injudicious, ill-advised, imprudent, stupid*)

UNWITTING
Rustam; Zaleucus; Telegonus.
(see *inadvertent, unintentional, accidental, involuntary*)

UPRIGHT
Epaminondas; Daniel; Calidore.
(see *integrity, honesty, virtuous, good faith, erect*)

UPRISING
Coxey's Army; Cadean; John Ball; Rebeccaite.
(see *mutiny, insurrection, rebellious, riot*)

UPROAR
Abaddon; Bedlam; Skimmington.
(see *commotion, disturbance, tumultuous, turbulence*)

UPSIDE DOWN
Cercopes.
(see *disorderly, confusion*)

UPSTART
Lady Booby; Trimalchio.
(see *nouveau riche, parvenu, snob, pretentious*)

URBANITY
Ovidian; Addisonian; Gothamite; Terence.
(see *courtsey, polite, manners, suave, elegance*)

USEFUL
Karl Baedeker; Puss-in-Boots; Sam Browne; Mulciber; Handy Andy; Vulcan; Man Friday; Johannes Factotum; Hop o' My Thumb.
(see *advantage, helpfulness, serviceable*)

USELESS
Dogberry; Shallow; Khufu; George Primrose; Holophernes; Danaides; Les Rois Fainéants.
(see *futility, profitless, valueless, ineffectual, worthless*)

USURER
Arthur Gride; Sir Giles Overreach; Shylock; Gobseck; Tom Walker.
(see *money-lender, loan*)

USURPER
Tarquinius Priscus; Candaules; Tullia; Athaliah.
(see *expropriation, dispossessed*)

UTENSILS
Widenostrils.
(see *vat, kettle, basin*)

UTTERANCE
Vach.
(see *speech, language, conversation, communication*)

UXORIOUS
Candaules; John Buncle; Claudius; the Crawleys; Jerry Sneak; the Pages; Fondlewife; Watkins Tottle; Kitely; Pistol; Pinchwife; Sir and Lady Pliant.
(see *lady-killer*)

V

VACANT
Sleeping Beauty.

(see *loneliness, isolation, seclusion, leisure, idleness*)

VACILLATION
Buridan's Ass; Pilate; Sganarelle; Fortuna; Mussolini.

(see *hesitancy, indecision, irresolute*)

VACUOUS
Abderian; Monsieur Sotenville.

(see *empty-headed, inane*)

VAGARY
King Ryance.

(see *whim, crotchety, capricious, idiosyncratic*)

VAGRANCY
Friar Tuck; Wandering Willie; Edie Ochiltree; Abram-man; Bedouin; Land of Nod; Irus; Apollonius; Okie; Gil Blas; Jack London.

(see *gypsy, roving, nomad, itinerant, wanderer*)

VAGUE
Ka; Jumala; Island of Saint Brandan; Demogorgon.

(see *ambiguous, uncertainty, doubtful, mirage, illusion*)

VAINGLORIOUS
Basilisco; Gasconnade; Xerxes; Thrasonic; Ralph Roister Doister; Isenbras.

(see *boastful, braggart, blustering, conceited, vanity, self-important, pretentious*)

VALET
Crispin; Barber of Seville; Lazarillo de Tormes; Man Friday; Scapino; Figaro; Xury; Ruy Blas; Leporello; Mascarille; Razor.

(see *manservant, footman, flunkey, lackey, waiter, attendant*)

VALETUDINARIAN
Argan.

(see *sickly, ill health, invalid*)

VALOR
Zouave; Hector; Virtus; Othello; Saul; Achilles; Penthesilea; Elhanan; Nestor; Coriolanus; Euphorbus; Idomeneus; Sir Thomas Malory; Bayard (2); Sarpedon; Leonidas; Horatius Cocles; Marsi; Lord Nelson; Arthurian; Orlando; Oliver (2); Thermopylae; Excalibur; Marmion; Jack the Giant-Killer.

(see *bold, courageous, daring, chivalrous, bravery, prowess, intrepid, heroism*)

VALUABLE
Samuel Pepys; Godey.

(see *useful, serviceable, advantage, rare, costly*)

VALUELESS
Holophernes.

(see *worthless, useless*)

VAMPIRE
Lamia; Empusa.

(see *ghoul, temptress*)

VANISH
Sir Patrick Spens; Atlantis; Sangreal; Island of Saint Brandan.

(see *disappearance, invisible*)

VANITY (female)
Minna; Belise; Brisingamen; Vanity Fair; Cassiopeia; Lady Wishfort; Lady Clara Vere de Vere; Miss Lucretia MacTab; Proetides; Freyja.

VANITY (male)
Lucian; Beau Tibbs; Sacripant; Lord Nelson; Asmodeus; Rasselas; Caleb Balderstone; Aeschines; Domitian; Oscar Wilde; Major Bagstock; Dick Swiveller; Malvolio; Marquis of Carabas; Sir Matthew Mite; Narcissus; Peter Peebles; Mayeux; Gnatho; Artemus Ward; Holophernes; Parolles; Gawain; Thamyris; Arthur Pendennis; Joseph Sedley; Sir Fretful Plagiary.
(see *affected, feigned, artificial, foppish, pretentious, conceited, coxcomical*)

VAPID
Tupperian.
(see *inane, trite, prosaic*)

VARIABLE
Bayard (1); Proteus; Vertumnus.
(see *change, mercurial, alter, malleable, metamorphosis*)

VARIETY
Montaigne; Joseph Marie Jacquard; Thomas Gray; Quadrifrons.
(see *multiplicity, diverse*)

VASES
Mentor.
(see *pottery*)

VASSALAGE
Zedekiah.
(see *slave, enslavement, feudal*)

VAST
Enceladus; Tityus; Behemoth; Titanic; Leviathanic; Sahara; Hringham.
(see *huge, enormous, prodigious, gigantic, colossal*)

VAT
Lenaea.
(see *kettle*)

VEGETABLES
Vertumnus.
(see *vegetation*)

VEGETARIANISM
Mazdakite; Shavian; Essenes.
(see *fasting, diet*)

VEGETATION
Maia; Euphrosyne; Favonius; Tammuz; Anaites; Pincian; Shamash; Osiris.
(see *plants, plant life, vegetables*)

VEHEMENCE
Juvenalian.
(see *impetuous, violence, ardent, zeal, fervor, earnest*)

VEHICLE
Garuda; Hippocampus.
(see *carrier, conveyance*)

VEIL
Veronica; Mokanna; Isadora Duncan.
(see *masked, concealed, disguise*)

VEIN
Talus.
(see *blood, arteries*)

VELOCITY
Phidippides; Arthur Honegger; Galileo.
(see *speed, rapid, fast, quick, swift, fleet, race*)

VENALITY
Jugurtha.
(see *bribery, money-mad*)

VENDETTA
Montagues and Capulets.
(see *feud, strife, enmity, hostility, dissension, discord*)

VENERABLE
Faithful Eckhardt; Enoch Wray; Nestor; Abraham; Methuselah; Moses.
(see *revered, adored, patriarch*)

VENERATION
Capitoline; Sakhrat; Apis; Sangreal; Joseph of Arimathea.
(see *worship, reverence, esteem, homage, obeisance*)

VENGEANCE
Branchidae; Ibycus; Boulangism; Nahum; Polydorus; Shylock; Laertes; Macduff; Melusina; Lucretia; Hecuba; Patroclus; Nana; Rigoletto; Samson; Salome; Orestes; Dinah; Boadicea; Medea; Hamilcar; Robin and Makyne; Edmond Dantès; Theodosius; Thyestes; Rhoecus.
(see *revenge, avenge, vindictive, retaliation, retribution, vengeful, rancorous*)

VENGEFUL (deities)
Nemesis; Tisiphone; Jove; Ultor; Latona; Frothi; Kriemhilde; Völund; Megaera; Furies; Alecto.
(see *vengeance*)

VENISON
Esau.
(see *deer*)

VENOMOUS
Nicander; Lucrezia Borgia; Medusa; Medea; Locusta; Thessalian.
(see *poison, deadly, virulent*)

VENTURESOME
Jack London; Leif Ericson; Louis Joliet; D'Artagnan; Vikings; Icarian.
(see *adventurous, bold, daring, enterprising, courageous, chivalrous*)

VERBOSE
Euphuistic; Don Adriano de Armado; Aldiborontiphoscophornio; John Lyly.
(see *loquacious, long-winded, turgid, grandiloquent, bombastic, talkative*)

VERDICT
Sacco-Vanzetti; Areopagitical; Papinian.
(see *decision, judgment, acquittal, convicted*)

VERISIMILITUDE
Jules Verne; Mme. Marie Tussaud.
(see *life-like, realistic, probability*)

VERSATILE
Marcus Terentius Varro; Abaris; Vertumnus; Thomas Gray; Chiron; Clodia; Daedalian; Gyes; Themistoclean; Lorenzo the Magnificent; Leonardo da Vinci; Moth; Handy Andy; Pico della Mirandola; Raleigh; Goethe; Johannes Factotum; Palamedes.
(see *talent, variable, adaptable, factotum, genius*)

VETERAN
Commodore Trunnion.
(see *proficient, accomplished, skill*)

VICE
Petronius; Zeluco; Asmodeus; Paul Clifford.
(see *wickedness, sin, immorality, depravity*)

VICIOUS
Louis XV; Jack the Ripper; Jekyll-Hyde; Marquis de Sade; Jezebel; Fenrir; Tiberian; Yahoo; Lucio; Jonathan Wild; Dorian Gray; Pyrrhus (Neoptolemus); Vathek.
(see *corrupt, shameless, unprincipled, degeneracy, evil, iniquity, profligacy*)

VIRAGO
Thalestris; Omphale; Termagant; Maid Marian; Widow Blackacre; Radegund; Xanthippe; Hippolyte; Skimmington; Katharine; Mme. Pernelle.
(see *shrew, scold, termagant, amazon*)

VIRGINITY
Kunigunde; Britomartis; Polyxena; Nausicaa; Leucothea; Saint Winifred; Tenes; Vestal; Rhea Silvia; Minerva; Parthenon; Iphigenia; Saint Ursula; Saint Eulalia; Saint Lucia; Tanit; Saint Filumena; Pallas; Abishag; Gefjon; Cloelia; Dorothea; Parthenia; Agnes; Sabrina.
(see *purity, chastity*)

VIRTUE
Sangreal; Land o' the Leal; Gerda; Socrates; Victorian; Poor Richard; Zeno; Lucretia; Abelites; Atlantes; Plato.
(see *honor, honesty, integrity, good, innocence, continence*)

VIRTUOSO
Paganini; Fritz Kreisler; Franz Liszt; Ignace Jan Paderewski; Serge Rachmaninoff; Nellie Melba; Adelina Patti; Marius Petipa; Vaslav Nijinsky; Anna Pavlova.
(see *skill, connoisseur*)

VIRTUOUS
Dorigen; Curius Dentatus; Alasnam; Cincinnatus; Tenes; Piso; Persius; Pamela; Kunigunde; Susanna; Jack the Giant-Killer; Zamore; Bayard (2); Amelia; Thomas Allworthy; Virginia; Cato the Censor; Parson Abraham Adams; Thecla.
(see *upright, nobleness, purity, chastity, exemplary, blameless, modesty*)

VIRULENT
Billingsgate; Zoilus.
(see *venomous, malevolence, deadly, malign, caustic, abusive*)

VISIONARY
Bifrost; Col. Mulberry Sellers; Quixotic; Thule; Alnaschar; El Greco; Zelotes; Walking Stewart; Joanna Southcott.
(see *dreamer, imagination, unreal, fantastic, illusion, chimerical*)

VISIONS
Ivory Gate; Horn Gate; Jacob's Ladder; Lynceus; Vidar; Saint Theresa; Pachomius; Saint Filumena; Fanny Cleaver; Joan of Arc; Benvenuto Cellini; Eleusinian; Constantine; Zechariah; Ezekiel; Abou ben Adhem.
(see *apparition, supernatural, specter, phantom, hallucination, dreamland*)

VITALIZE
Bimini; Cagliostro; Galatea.
(see *animate, reanimate, renew*)

VIVACIOUS
Dorine; Rosalind; Nell Gwyn.
(see *lively, gaiety, light-hearted, high-spirited, cheerful*)

VIVISECTION
Herophilus.
(see *dissection, mayhem, piecemeal*)

VOCABULARY
James Joyce; Peter Mark Roget.
(see *diction, dictionary, language, lexicographer, phraseology*)

VOCIFEROUS
Boanerges.
(see *loud, noisy, blatant*)

VOICE
Sarah Bernhardt; Echo; Jenny Lind; Enrico Caruso; Adelina Patti; Stentorian; Thamyris; Eumolpus; Nellie Melba.
(see *utterance, speech, singer*)

W

WAGER
Sindre; Tattersall's.
(see *pledge, gambling*)

WAIF
Valentine and Orson; Huck Finn; Abel Magwitch.
(see *estray, foundling*)

WAIL
Cocytean; Fabulinus; Heliades; Queen of Tears.
(see *lamentation, moan, bemoan, bewail, crying, weeping, sobbing*)

WAITER
Diggary; Xury; Ganymede.
(see *steward, attendant, manservant, lackey, valet*)

WAITRESS
Mistress Quickly; Maritornes; Kate Hardcastle; Hebe.
(see *maidservant, barmaid*)

WALK (v.)
Peripatetic; Walking Stewart.
(see *promenade*)

WALTZ
Strauss; Giselle; Maurice Ravel.
(see *dancing, ballet*)

WANDERER
Edie Ochiltree; Peripatetic; Aeneas; Ulysses; Aristeas; Sindbad the Sailor; Walther von der Vogelweide; Khartaphilos; Ishmael.
(see *roving, nomad, traveler, vagrancy, itinerant, gypsy*)

WANTON
Flora; Sardanapalus; Silenus; Vivian; Baal; Poppaea; Sir and Lady Pliant; Nell Gwyn; Lorenzo; Paphian; Faustina.
(see *dissolute, licentious, "loose," lustful, lewdness, carnal, concupiscent, immorality*)

WAR (symbols)
Rubicon; Spolia Opima; Junker; Paean; Krupp Family; Pallas.
(see *war-god, enmity, hostility, strife, fighting, battle, assault, attack*)

WAR (writers on)
Herodotean; Frontinus; Count Leo Tolstoi; Alcaeus; Bragi; Thucydides; Tyrtaeus.
(see *poetry, historian, novelist*)

WARDER
Woglinda, Wellgunda, and Flosshilda.
(see *keeper, custodian, guardian, turnkey, curator*)

WARDROBE
Miss Flora McFlimsey; Herr Teufelsdroeckh.
(see *apparel, clothing, attire, raiment, garments*)

WAR-GOD
Hodur; Valkyries; Kumara; Eris; Abaddon; Skanda; Huitzilopochtli; Saxnot; Minerva; Gula; Mulciber; Vulcan; Janus; Quirinus; Set; Bellona; Tyr; Uma; Odin; Woden; Ullur; Enyo; Mars; Ares.
(see *war*)

WAR-HORSE
Bucephalus.
(see *horse*)

WARM-HEARTED
Schumann-Heinck; Sol Gills.
(see *affectionate, tenderness, kindness, sympathetic, love, compassionate*)

WARMTH (heat)
Flora; Helios; Agni; Muspel; Shamash; Hyperion; Surya; Harpocrates.
(see *heat, fire, glowing*)

WARNING
Koran; Giselle; Latinus; Isaian; Marsyas; Faithful Eckhardt; Jonathan; Cotton Mather; Zechariah; Zephaniah; Tom Walker; Moneta; Spurinna Vestritius; Mother Carey; Jacob Marley.
(see *admonitory, ominous, ill-omen, augury*)

WARRIOR
Hippolyte; Apache; Genseric; Ahab; Shatriya; Camilla; Tiglath-Pileser; Cid; Rhesus; Marsi; Tullus Hostilius; Picti; Diomedes; Elhanan; Zerbino; Turnus; Telamon; Leleges; Rinaldo; Pyrrhus (Neoptolemus); Pittacus; Ossian; Menelaus; Rajput.
(see *soldier, militaristic, single-handed, champion*)

WARY
Mr. Tulkinghorn.
(see *cautious, carefulness, watchful, prudence, discreet*)

WASTE
Pistor.
(see *superfluous, excessive, inordinate*)

WASTREL
Philip Wharton; Mark Antony; Silk-Stocking; Mantalini; Antinous; Tityre-Tu.
(see *squanderer, prodigal, spendthrift*)

WATCH (time)
Robert Hawley Ingersoll.
(see *clock*)

WATCHDOG
Garm; Bernard of Menthon; Cerberean; Gelert.
(see *dog, vigilance*)

WATCHFUL
Vigiles; Argus-eyed; Vincentio; Cotton Mather; Horae; Polyphemus; Kitely; Vigilantes; Sister Anne; Prinz Ruprecht; Zophiel; Arioch; Sol; Robert Bruce; La Befana; Simeon Stylites; Cerberean.
(see *alert, vigilance, circumspect, wary*)

WATCHMAN
Verges; Sister Anne.
(see *sentinel, warder, guardian*)

WATCH-TOWER
Pharos.
(see *tower*)

WATER (deities)
Oceanus; Poseidon; Njord; Amphitrite; Arethusa; Camenae; Neptune; Aegir; Ran; Achelous; Varuna; Egeria; Tlaloc; Ea; Anaites; Juturna; Naiads; Vritra; Hymir; Alpheus; Kistnerappan.
(see *sea-deities, ocean-god, nymph*)

WATER (springs)
Hagar; Castalian; Callirrhoë; Hippocrene; Mimir; Saint Winifred; Bandusia; Pierian; Rebekah.
(see *fountain, well, spring, stream, river, waterfall*)

WATER-CURE
Kneippism.
(see *curative, healing*)

WATERFALL
Minnehaha.
(see *water, stream*)

WATER SUPPLY
Frontinus.
(see *aqueduct*)

WAVERING
Buridan's Ass.
(see *hesitancy, irresolute, doubting, indecision, vacillation, uncertainty*)

WAX-WORK
Mrs. Jarley; Mme. Marie Tussaud.
(see *unreal, life-like*)

WAYFARER
Johnny Appleseed.
(see *tourists, traveler, itinerant, nomad*)

WEAK-WILLED
George Dandin; Amfortas; Aeschines; Austin Chamberlain; Cassim Baba; Edouard Daladier; Mrs. Frail; Claudius; Louis XVI; Sir Daguenet; Pilate.
(see *wavering, unwise, injudicious, imprudent, indiscretion*)

WEALTH (deities of)
Plutus; Mammon; Frey; Nibelung; Kuvera; Frothi.
(see *riches, treasure, gold, hoard*)

WEALTH (individual)
Silk-Stocking; Karoon; Agathocles; Zaccheus; Lucullan; Polycrates; Haroun al Raschid; Fortunatus; Barzillai; Mme. de Montespan; Nana; Amalthaea; Queen of Sheba; Ptolemy; Lorenzo the Magnificent; Launfal; Atticus; Croesus; Marcus Licinius Crassus; Prester John; Sallustian; Maharajah; Dives; Marquis of Carabas; Tutankhamen; Aladdin; Pip; Medici; Midas; Grand Mogul; Sir Matthew Mite; Gyges; Tarquinius Priscus; Jay Gould; Rothschild; Rockefeller; John Jacob Astor; J. P. Morgan; Andrew Carnegie.
(see *rich, gold-seeker, fortune-hunter*)

WEALTH (places of)
Golconda; Lydian; Incan; Manoa; El Dorado; Capua; Goshen; Pactolus; Phrygian; Sabaean; Seric.
(see *abundance, fertility, amplitude, plenty, opulence*)

WEAPONS
Tvashtri; Ron; Lua; Iphicrates.
(see *arms, arrow, spear, lance, javelin, pike, rapier, scimitar, sword, broadsword, sabre, slingshot, rifle, pistol, cannon, arsenal*)

WEASEL
Galinthias.
(see *animals*)

WEATHER-CONTROL
Thallo; Shamash; Horae.
(see *seasons*)

WEATHERMAN
Rasselas.
(see *prophet, rain portent*)

WEAVER
Arachne; Jack of Newbury; Joseph Marie Jacquard; Silas Marner.
(see *spinner, thread*)

WEDDING PRESENT
Creusa.
(see *gifts, present*)

WEDLOCK
Talassius; Sif; Hymeneal; Yue-Laou; Mother Bunch; Frigga; Vor; Brigham

WHISKERS
Don Ferolo Whiskerandos.
(see *bewhiskered, bearded*)

WHISPER
Mr. Creakle.
(see *rustle, sigh*)

WHITE
Parian; Rhesus.
(see *snow, frost, pallor*)

WHITE-HAIRED
Zal.
(see *aged, old age*)

WHOLE
Saehrimnir.
(see *complete, entire*)

WHOLESOME
Diana; Lady Teazle; Maud Muller.
(see *health, robust, vigor, hearty*)

WHORE
Dol Common; Doll Tearsheet; Rahab; Paphian; Nana; Jezebel; Tamar.
(see *strumpet, street-walker, harlot, prostitute*)

WICKEDNESS
City of Destruction; Beelzebub; Eblis; Set; Satanic; Gomorrah; Sodoma; Onan; Ahriman; Apollyon; Lucifer; Belial; Hagen; Friar Rush; Nastrond; Enceladus; Master Leonard; Klingsor; Nero.
(see *iniquity, evil, sin, vice, immorality, depravity, impiety*)

WIDOW
Wife of Bath; Widow MacStinger; Mrs. Martha Bardell; Naomi; Tamar.
(see *husband-hunter, bereaved*)

WIFE-BEATER
Bluebeard; Sganarelle; Punch.
(see *misogyny, cruelty, henpecked*)

WIFE-HUNTER
Mr. Toots; Doctor Syntax; Coelebs; Miles Standish.
(see *bachelor, girl-crazy*)

WIFELY
Dorigen; Andromache; Alcestis; Jack and Jill.
(see *spouse, conjugal*)

WILD
Dionysus; Tauri; Phrygian; Steropes; Rima.
(see *uncivilized, savage, barbarity, ferocious*)

WILDERNESS
Azazel; Kedar; Paran; Sinai; Baca.
(see *desert, soltitude*)

WILD MAN
Valentine and Orson; Romulus and Remus; Tarzan; Mowgli.
(see *unrestrained, lawless*)

WILFUL
Sganarelle; Lydia Languish; Antigone.
(see *obstinate, stubborn, perverse, cantankerous, pig-headed, self-willed, obdurate*)

WILL (n.)
Nietzschean; Skuld; Thélème.
(see *volition, free-will, determination, decision*)

WILLING
Sabine; Barkis; Joseph Andrews.
(see *spontaneous, adaptable, eager, ready*)

WILL-POWER
Helen Keller; Epictetus.
(see *self-control, continence, temperance*)

WILY
Zacocia; Scapino; Aelius Sejanus; Widow Wadman; Vivian; Machiavellian; Volpone.
(see *insidious, artful, cunning, sly, crafty, subtlety, deceitful, treachery, intrigue*)

WIND (n.)
Aeolian; Njord; Vaya; Boreal; Auster; Notus; Ramman; Hraesvelger; Sleipnir; Dodonean; Jack and the Bean Stalk; Aquilo; Eurus; Favonius.
(see *east wind, north wind, south wind, west wind, air, gust, hurricane*)

WINE
Pierre Pérignon; Ancaeus; Dionysus; Bromius; Liber; Lenaea; Lyaeus; Mithras; Odin; Lucius Opimius.
(see *vintage, grapes*)

WINE-BIBBER
Saint Vincent; Bassarid; Silenus.
(see *tippler, sot, drunkenness, inebriation*)

WINE, WOMEN, AND SONG
Alcaeus; Horatian (Horace); Satyr; Omar Khayyam; Minnesinger.
(see *merry-making, carousal, revelry, orgiastic*)

WINGED
Hraesvelger; Zetes; Caducean; Icarian; Azaziel; Peter Wilkins; Zophiel; Stymphalian; St. Mark; St. Matthew.
(see *pinion*)

WINGED HORSE
Pegasus; Ruggiero; Al Borak.
(see *flying*)

WINTER
Hymir; Baldur; Aegir; Proserpina, Kabibonokka; Quadrifrons.
(see *cold, ice, snow, seasons*)

WIRELESS
Samuel Morse.
(see *telegraph, communication*)

WISDOM (Biblical)
Elihu; Solomon; Esther; Deborah; Ahithophel; Magi.
(see *wisdom, religious*)

WISDOM (deities of)
Ea; Ganesa; Nereus; Nebo; Metis; Onca; Thoth; Mimir; Vach; Minerva; Odin; Vidar; Saraswati; Athena; Sin; Thor; Baldur; Devarshis; Goddess of Reason; Woden; Pallas.
(see *knowledge, reason, mind, insight, judgment, understanding, sagacity*)

WISDOM (philosophical)
Baconian; Kantian; Emersonian; Poor Richard; Caius Laelius; Anaxagoras; Anaximenes; Pythagoras; Epictetus; Stoic; Plato; Aristotelian.
(see *philosophy*)

WISDOM (political)
Pittacus; Augustan; Solon; Lycurgus; Talleyrand; Canute; Abraham Lincoln; Cromwellian; Periclean; George Washington; Alfred the Great; Aristides; Periander; Caesarean (2); Agesilaus; Ciceronian.
(see *political science*)

WISDOM (practical)
Aesop; Chiron; Mrs. Nickleby; Deucalion; Panglossian; William Allen White; Will Rogers; Enoch Wray; Prospero; Columbine; Jack the Giant-Killer; Antenor; Ulysses; Nestor; Candida.
(see *good sense*)

WISDOM (religious)
Delphi; Confucian; Numa; Buddha; Parsifal; Saint Ambrose; Christian Rosenkreuz; Nathan; Gamaliel.

(see *wisdom, biblical, religion*)

WISHFUL
Lady Wishfort; Midas; Leibnitzian.

(see *eager, desire, longing*)

WISTFUL
Pierrot; Giacomo Puccini; Stephen Foster; Chaplinesque; Fritz Kreisler.

(see *contemplative, meditation, pensive, reflective*)

WIT (general)
Ninon de Lenclos; David Crockett; Talleyrand; Attic; Sir John Suckling.

(see *intelligent, intellectual, understanding, esprit*)

WITCHCRAFT
Setebos; Walpurgis; Nicneven; Witch of Edmonton; Lilith; Hecate; Witch of Endor; Aganice; Duessa; Ulrica; Sycorax; Esmeralda; Tam O'Shanter; General Witchfinder; Joan of Arc; Mme. De Montespan; Cotton Mather.

(see *sorcerer, sorceress, magic, thaumaturgy, wonder-worker, exorcism, enchantment*)

WITLESS
Pantaloon.

(see *dull-witted, half-witted, foolish, stupid, silly, unintelligent*)

WITTY (authors)
Molierè; Plautus; Terence; Joe Miller; Mme Recamier; Oscar Wilde; Omar Khayyam; François Voltaire; Aesop; Goldsmithian; Archilochian; Marital; Autocrat of the Breakfast Table; Shavian; Cerventean; Johnsonian; Desiderius Erasmus; Rabelaisian; Aristophanic.

(see *humor, jester, joke, facetious, droll, funny, repartee*)

WITTY (fictional characters)
Benedick; Sam Slick; Weller; Diana Warwick; Nerissa; Lady Wishfort; Figaro; Touchstone; Mulvaney; Rosalind; Barber of Seville; Teague.

WIZARD
Navius; Zanoni; Malagigi.

(see *sorcerer, wonder-worker, thaumaturgy, soothsayer, seer*)

WOE
Via Dolorosa; Acheron; Jeremiad; Iliad.

(see *sorrow, grief, tribulation, misery, anguish, agony, melancholy, suffering, heart-broken, unhappy*)

WOLF
Little Red Ridinghood; Lycaon; Odin; Tyr; Freki; Fenrir; Mowgli.

(see *animals*)

WOMAN-HATER
Jonathan Oldbuck; Juvenalian; Saint Kevin.

(see *girl-shy*)

WOMANKIND
Alasnam; Marie Laurencin.

(see *lady-like, lady-love*)

WOMANLY
Florimel; Eve; Rosalind; Jenny Lind.

(see *feminine*)

WONDER-WORKER
Sakhrat; Thaumaturgus; Zanoni; Apollonius; Thessalian; Saint Filumena; Hugh of Lincoln; Loretto; James and Jambres.

(see *thaumaturgy, wizard, sorcerer, magic*)

WOODEN-LEGGED
John Silver; Silas Wegg.
(see *crippled*)

WOODPECKER
Picus.
(see *birds*)

WOODS
Little Red Ridinghood; Dryad; Artemis; Silvanus; Pan.
(see *forests, sylvan, grove*)

WOODSMAN
Leatherstocking; Uncas; Deadwood Dick; Daniel Boone.
(see *frontiersman, explorer*)

WORD-COINER
James Joyce; Adriano de Armado.
(see *vocabulary, creative*)

WORDS (deities of)
Thoth; Fabulinus; Vach.
(see *speech, language, utterance*)

WORKER
Luddites; Okie; Gibeonite; Johannes Factotum; Karl Marx.
(see *laborer, journeyman, artisan, toil, handyman, factotum*)

WORKHOUSE
Oliver Twist; Tolbooth.
(see *jail, penitentiary, imprisonment, lockup, dungeon, confinement, forced labor, slave labor*)

WORLD
Audhumla; Jotunheim; Kedar.
(see *universe, creation, earth, nature*)

WORLDLINESS
City of Destruction; Wordly Wiseman; Mirabel; Vanity Fair.
(see *sophisticated, carnal, sordid, selfish, ambitious, pride, irreligious*)

WORM
Schamir.
(see *fishfood, maggots, insects*)

WORRILESS
Lyaeus.
(see *insouciance, carefree, nonchalant, light-hearted*)

WORSHIP (objects of)
Quetzalcoatl; Beatrice; Apis; Ka; Druids; Madonna; Kaaba; Kiak-Kiak; Mnevis; Sinai.
(see *revered, adored, reverence, holiness*)

WORSHIPFUL
Chauvinistic; Magi; Cecrops.
(see *devout, solemnity, respectful, venerable*)

WORTHLESS
Clodia; Brummagem; MacFlecknoe, Limbo.
(see *useless, valueless, futility*)

WOUND (n.)
Philoctetes; Amoret; Amfortas; Telephus.
(see *sore, cancer, lacerate*)

WRANGLING
Tybalt; Tweedledum and Tweedledee.
(see *altercation, brawling, quarrelsome, squabble, bickering, disputatious.*)

WRATHFUL
Aeshina; Hector; Achilles; Ajax; Nahum; Agamemnon; Elihu.
(see *anger, rage, fury, frenzy, resentful, indignation, choleric, ill-tempered*)

WREATHS
Della Robbia.
(see *foliage, flowers*)

WRESTLING
Antaeus; Marquis of Queensbury; Milo; Gunther; Elli.
(see *boxing*)

WRETCHEDNESS
Okie; Struldbrugs.
(see *misery, poverty, woe, tribulation, suffering, agony*)

WRINKLES
Tithonus.
(see *old age, aged*)

WRITER
Grub-Streeter; Sudra.
(see *litterateur, scribe, clerk, secretary, playwright, poetry, historian, novelist, essayist, journalist, ghost-writer*)

WRITING
Seshat; Spencerian; Evander; Nebo; Trismegistus.
(see *handwriting, miswriting, spelling, misspelling*)

WRONG (adj.)
Queer Card; Belise.
(see *error, incorrect, mistaken*)

X

X-RAY
Wilhelm Roentgen; Vidar.
(see *penetrating, sight*)

Y

YANKEE
Sam Slick.
(see *American, United States*)

YAWN
Paridel.
(see *drowsy, sleep, ennui, boredom*)

YEAR
Quadrifrons; Hipparchus; Julian.
(see *annual*)

YEARNING
Samuel Maverick.
(see *cattle*)

YEARNING
Leilah; Lydia; Languish.
(see *longing, pining, desire, covetous*)

YELLOW
Yellow Dwarf; Vincent van Gogh; Tiberinus.
(see *gold, blond*)

YELLOW FEVER
Walter Reed.
(see *disease*)

YESTERDAY
Urth.
(see *past*)

YOUNGEST
Benjamin; Peregrine White.
(see *immature, inexperienced, callow, greenhorn*)

YOUTH (spirit of)
Kumara; Aurora; Apollo; Iduna; Hebe; Juventas; Ponce de Leon; Hygeia; Bimini; Hyperboreans; Peter Pan; Cagliostro.
(see *juvenility, adolescence, childhood*)

YOUTHFUL (female)
Nymphs; Oceanids; Oreads; Napaeae; Nereids; Naiads; Juliet; Agnes.
(see *girlish, maiden*)

YOUTHFUL (male)
Johnny Newcome; Romeo; Moth; Wagon Boy; Zephon.
(see *boyish, lad*)

YOUTH MOVEMENT
Ephebeia.
(see *discipline, drill*)

NAME-WORD FINDER

PART II

BIOGRAPHICAL EXPLANATIONS

Dictionary of Names

A

AARON

Aaron was the first high priest of the Jews, acme of priestly pomp, dignity, and reverence, the man who with Moses led the Children of Israel out of Egypt, and observed with reverence, devotion and implicit obedience the many laws and rites and ceremonies laid down for the guidance of the Israelites.

with Aaronic reverence for every ceremony

ABADDON

Abaddon is the Hebrew name of the evil spirit or destroying angel whom the Greeks called Apollyon. Medieval demonographers believed him to be the chief of the demons of the seventh hierarchy. To them he was the causer of wars, combustions, and uproars. In Klopstock's *Messiah* he is pictured as a fallen angel, still showing traces of his pristine beauty under the ravages of sin.

a malicious Abaddon of a fellow

ABARIS

Abaris was a Hyperborean or Scythian priest of Apollo whose history is entirely mythical. He was given a golden arrow with magical powers by the god. It could carry him riding through the air and rendered him invisible at the same time. The same golden dart also cured diseases and invested its owner with the prophetic abilities of Apollo, its donor. Before his death Abaris was said to have given his magic dart to Pythagoras, the philosopher.

swift as Abaris on his dart
invisible as Abaris streaking by

ABDALLA, BABA

Baba Abdalla, in the *Arabian Nights' Entertainments,* is a man who, not satisfied with being made rich by a dervish, demands a box of magic ointment as well. By misusing the latter he ultimately loses both his wealth and his sight.

with the purblind greed of Baba Abdalla

ABDALLAH

Abdallah, the father of Mahomet, was so beautiful that when he married Amina, two hundred virgins broke their hearts from disappointment in love.

a heart-breaking Abdallah

ABDEMON

Abdemon was the Tyrian said to have answered all the riddles Solomon propounded to Hiram, king of Tyre, at the famous contest of puzzling questions that was held by the two monarchs. He also proposed insoluble ones to Solomon, thus winning for Hiram a large sum of money.

expert as Abdemon at answering riddles

ABDERIAN

Abderian, the name given to the inhabitants of Abdera, refers to a Thracian town, the inhabitants of which were proverbially stupid and given to senseless and incessant laughter; hence, stupid, senseless, ridiculous. For Democritus (460 B. C.) the "laughing philosopher," who lived at Abdera, see under *Democritus.*

an unfortunately Abderian expression

ABDIEL

Abdiel is the seraph mentioned in Milton's *Paradise Lost* as refusing to join Satan in his revolt. He is also mentioned in the Jewish cabalists, and his name is synonymous with faithful and loyal devotion.

an Abdiel loyal to his master

ABECEDARIANS

The Abecedarians were a sect of German Anabaptists who in the 16th century rejected all learning as a hindrance to religious inspiration. Mystics of a sort, they believed that even "A—B—C" was an obstacle to direct contact with God. In another sense, Abecedarian refers to people who either teach or learn the alphabet, thus working with something in its elementary or rudimentary state.

grammatical as an Abecedarian

ABELARD AND HELOISE

Peter Abelard (1079-1142) was the famous French teacher of philosophy and rational theology. The tutor of Héloise, he developed for her an unparalleled devotion, matched only by hers for him, that has become one of the world's great stories of frustrated love. When Héloise found herself about to bear him a son, he proposed marriage under the condition that it be kept secret, in order that his churchly career might remain unassailable. However, Fulbert, the uncle of Héloise, did not keep the secret, and Héloise sought refuge in the convent of Argenteuil. Abelard embraced the life of a monk, and the two lovers never saw each other again. His correspondence with her has become, however, one of the great documents of pure and almost holy love.

Abelardian correspondence with his Héloise

ABELITES

The Abelites were an African sect, mentioned by St. Augustine as marrying but not procreating their kind. Their purpose in sexual abstinence was to prevent the handing down of inherited sin.

frigid and chaste as an Abelite

ABIATHAR

Abiathar, "father of abundance," was a high priest of Israel who remained faithful to David as a companion during the latter's exile (*1 Samuel, xxii,* 20).

like Abiathar, faithful in his superior's disgrace

ABIGOR

Abigor was a demon of high degree and rank in medieval demonology. A grand-duke in the infernal regions, he suggests evil power and wrongdoing.

an Abigor exalted in corruption

ABIHU

Abihu was the second son of Aaron. For joining his brother Nadab in employing common fire to burn incense, he was slain with him to expiate the sacrilege (*Lev.*, x).

the blundering Abihu of the congregation

ABIJAH

Abijah is the name of several persons in the Old Testament, the most important of whom is the Abijah who was one of the unjust judges preceding the Kingdom. His name, therefore, is used of a corrupt or perverted legal decision.

an unjust judgment worthy of Abijah

ABIMELECH

Abimelech was the pitilessly ambitious son of Gideon who killed 69 of his brothers in order to make himself king of Shechem. He spared only one, Jotham (*Judges,* ix, 1-57).

fratricidal as Abimelech

ABISHAG

Abishag, "author of error," was the beautiful young Shunammite woman whom David took to nurse and comfort him in his old age (*1 Kings,* i, 1-4).

seeking some winsome Abishag to pamper his dotage

ABRAHAM

Abraham, the first and most eminent of the Jewish patriarchs, was called the "Father of the Faithful," because of his wise and fatherly leadership and his own complete faith in God and obedience to His mandates; hence, patriarchal, devout, blessed.

the world has need of an Abraham with Abraham-like patience

ABRAM-MAN

An Abram-man was originally a mendicant lunatic from the Abraham Ward in London's infamous Bedlam. Later the name came to be used of any beggar who feigned lunacy and who for all his seeming madness had enough wit to steal and thieve as he went along.

an Abram-man cloaking his thefts under the excuse of irresponsibility

---

ABSALOM

Absalom was the disobedient, undutiful, rebellious son of King David, found slain in the forest of Ephraim. His death brought inconsolable grief to King David, whose lament, "Absalom, Absalom, my son Absalom," has become a classic cry of grief.

the rebellious spirit of an Absalom

ABSOLUTE, ANTHONY

Anthony Absolute was the crotchety, gouty, comically irascible and domineering father of young Captain Jack Absolute in Sheridan's comedy of manners, *The Rivals,* a play so universally and continuously popular that Sir Anthony has become the nickname for any father of that type.

well does he know he faces a Sir Anthony Absolute.

ABSYRTUS

Absyrtus in Greek legend was the son of Aeëtes, the king of Colchis, and the brother of Medea who took him with her when she fled with Jason. As her father pursued her, she resorted to an atrocity in order to effect her safe elopement. She cut the body of Absyrtus into pieces and cast the fragments into the Black Sea at Tomi, the name of which is derived from a Greek root meaning "to cut." In his grief over gathering up the dissected limbs of his son, Aeëtes gave up the pursuit of Medea.

mayhem as atrocious as that done to Absyrtus

ABU HASSAN

Abu Hassan, the prodigal hero of *The Sleeper Awakened* in the *Arabian Nights' Entertainments,* is a young man of Bagdad who, by a stratagem of Haroun-al-Raschid, was twice made to believe himself caliph for a day, and who afterward became in reality the caliph's chief favorite and companion.

deluded as Abu Hassan

ACACETUS

Acacetus was a name given to Mercury because of his eloquence. Meaning in Greek literally "not bad," the name connotes anyone who does everything well.

a clever modern-day Acacetus

ACADEMIA

The Academia was originally a piece of land near Athens and belonging to the Attic hero Academus, who revealed to Castor and Pollux the whereabouts of Helen, their sister, who had been abducted by Theseus. Subsequently a gymnasium was built on the ground and adorned with plane and olive plantations, statues and other works of art. Plato made it his school and his followers taught there after him, whence Platonism and its practitioners are referred to as Academics.

a philosophy suggestive of the Academia.

ACCA LARENTIA

Acca Larentia was the wife of the shepherd Faustulus and the nurse of Romulus and Remus after they had been taken from the she-wolf. Livy says that the story of the wolf (*lupus*) arose from her being called *Lupa* ("prostitute") because of her amorous ways with other men. She was also conceived of as an earth-goddess and the mother of the Lares.

amorous as Acca Larentia

ACELDAMA

Aceldama was the "field of blood" near Jerusalem. It was purchased by the priests with the bribe Judas took for betraying Jesus after Judas, repentant, had thrown the money down. Though it was then used as a cemetery for strangers, the name of Aceldama still connotes any slaughter house, such as a battlefield, or a place of betrayal and death.

a battlefield gory as Aceldama

ACESTES

Acestes is a Sicilian mentioned in the *Aeneid's* account of the competitive games held in honor of the anniversary of the funeral of Anchises, Aeneas's father, as having discharged an arrow from his bow with such speed and force that it took fire in the air as it flew. The phrase *Acestes' arrow* thus connotes action that is lightning-swift, or inspired thought.

brilliant as Acestes' arrow

ACHAN

Achan is the name of the Israelite of the tribe of Judah, who was stoned to death for plundering and looting in the sack of Jericho (*Josh.*, vii).

a selfish despoiler like Achan

ACHATES

Achates was the friend of Roman Aeneas who was so faithful and so loyal that his name gave the Latin phrase *fidus Achates* to the language, and Achates still stands for exceptional loyalty and devoted constancy in friendship.

he and his Achates waited

ACHELOUS

Achelous, Greek god of the river of that name, son of Oceanus and Tethys, and the eldest of his 3000 brothers, was involved with Hercules in a fight over Deianira, the hero's wife. Taking the form of a roaring bull, he was overcome by Hercules, who deprived him of one of his horns. He regained it however, by offering the horn of Amalthaea (*q. v.*) to his victor. He was regarded as the representative of fresh water, as opposed to the brine of seas. Hence, the phrase *Acheloan cups* refers to water in general.

a bellowing as of Achelous in flood

ACHERON

Acheron was the river of woe and despair in the lower world. Charon ferried the souls of the dead over its streams, and the Phlegethon, river of fire, and Cocytus, river of lamentation, flowed into it. Though the name signifies joylessness and bitter sorrow, it is sometimes used to designate hell itself.

dark Acherontian despair
hopeless Acherontic sorrow

ACHILLES

Achilles was a legendary Greek hero famous for valor, invincibility, unappeasable wrath, and invulnerability, except in his heel, by which his mother, Thetis, had held him when she dipped him into the river Styx to render him invulnerable. His "wrath" is the subject of Homer's *Iliad.*

sulking like an Achilles
with Achillean wrath resounds

ACIS

Acis, the son of Faunus, was a beautiful Sicilian shepherd beloved by the nymph Galatea. Polyphemus the Cyclops, his jealous rival, crushed him under a huge rock, and the bereaved nymph forthwith changed his gushing blood into the river Acis at the foot of Mt. Aetna. Handel composed a pastoral opera on this theme.

a rustic swain as handsome as Acis

ACONTIUS

Acontius was a beautiful youth from Ceos. He came to Delos to celebrate the festival of Diana and became enamored of Cydippe, a noble Athenian girl betrothed to marry another man. In order to gain her for himself, Acontius resorted to a clever stratagem. He tossed her, while she was sitting before the temple of Diana, an apple inscribed with the words, "I swear by the sanctuary of Diana to marry Acontius." Diana heard her reading the message aloud and caused her to become incurably ill when she was on the point of marrying Acontius' rival. She was made well only when her father allowed her to wed Acontius.

clever at love as Acontius

ACRASIA

Acrasia was the Circe-like enchantress who lived in the "Bower of Bliss," according to Spenser's *Faerie Queene.* She transformed her lovers into monsters and held them captive until she herself was finally cast into chains and her bower destroyed by Sir Guyon. Her name means literally "self-indulgence," and she represents intemperate sexual appetite and its depraving effects.

self-indulgent in sexuality as Acrasia

ACRES, BOB

Bob Acres, the lovable but comically ambitious country squire in Sheridan's play, *The Rivals,* comes to town to be polished into a gay young blade and to sue for the hand of a rich wife. Eager to be a town gentleman, but laughably naive and marked with the self-consciousness of his country breeding, he furnishes the delightful note of comedy throughout the play.

just one more Bob Acres come to town

ACTAEON

Actaeon was the hunter who surprised Diana bathing. This so enraged her that she changed Actaeon into a stag, and he was destroyed by his own hounds. The name is still used of one who profanes beauty or purity or privacy by untoward glances.

limited to an Actaeon-glimpse

ADAM

Adam, the first human being created, according to the Bible, was placed in the Garden of Eden. The name is also used to specify the first person to sin, and his sin is made the excuse for every sin that man is heir to. A kind of scapegoat for the human race, Adam is sometimes made the equivalent of original sin.

it's the old Adam in us
the fault goes back to Adam

ADAMS, ALICE

Alice Adams is the title character of Booth Tarkington's Pulitzer Prize-winning novel (1922). It is the story of a girl who faced reality sensibly after overcoming a character that was prone to make foolish attempts at pretense.

the pretentious Alice Adams of her town

ADAMS, PARSON ABRAHAM

Parson Abraham Adams is the learned but unworldly 18th century curate in Fielding's *Joseph Andrews.* Memorable for his simple modesty and credulity, he was anxious to read a man of the world his sermon on "vanity," preached patience under affliction, and had every virtue under heaven except that of superiority to the common failings of humanity or of knocking down a rascal insulting the innocent. Very poor himself, he was treated by the rich as if he were a servant and even their servants deemed it a condescension to treat him on equal terms.

humane and benevolent as Parson Adams

ADDISONIAN

Addisonian refers to Joseph Addison, eighteenth century essayist, whose style and personality are equally marked by grace, charm, urbanity, and smoothness. His writing has been the pattern for all English prose writers who seek those qualities, as his manners have been the pattern for pleasant courtesy.

with an Addisonian ease and grace
unsullied Addisonian rectitude

ADHEM, ABOU BEN

Abou Ben Adhem, a Persian in the poem by Leigh Hunt, dreamed that when an angel came to him, writing the names of those who loved the Lord, he said, "Write me as one who loves his fellowman," and again dreamed that the angel came to show his name leading all the rest. Abou Ben Adhem is now used to imply a person whose love of God shows in his love of his kind.

not churchy, perhaps, but an Abou Ben Adhem nevertheless

ADLER, ALFRED

Alfred Adler (1870-1937), originally a follower of Freud, established his own school of psychology in 1912 in Vienna. He opposed Freudian emphasis on sexuality as the all-determining factor in psychoanalytics. Stressing the "ego," he probed the inferiority-complex and the "compensation" mechanisms it creates in the abnormal psyche.

needs Adlerian help for his inferiority complex

ADMETUS

Admetus, king of Pherae in Thessaly, treated Apollo so kindly when Zeus had bound the younger god to him as serf for having slain the Cyclopes that Apollo intervened in Admetus' fate. Destined to early death unless he could find a volunteer to substitute for him, Admetus was unable to find anyone except Alcestis, his wife, noble enough to die in his stead. Heartbroken at her death, he was yet obliged to entertain the drunken Hercules and to conceal his sadness from his guest until the latter, having discovered his woe, intercepted Thanatos, the messenger from Hades, and restored Alcestis to life and to her husband.

an Admetus in need of a scapegoat

ADONIS

Adonis was the beautiful youth loved by Venus and was passionately fond of hunting, in which sport he was finally killed by a boar. From his blood sprang a flower, the anemone. In Greek poetry he is often called "beautiful as day," and the name indicates perfect manly beauty. Ironically used, the name connotes a beau or coxcomb.

one must admit that he is an Adonis

ADRASTUS

Adrastus was a king of Argos. The founder of the Nemean games, he collected and led the famous attack on Thebes (see *Seven against Thebes*). When the expedition was defeated, Adrastus escaped on the fabulous swift horse, Arion. In his old age he led the second assault on Thebes, that of the *Epigoni,* on his successful return from which he died of grief because his only son, Aigialeus, had fallen in the attack.

Adrastus was also the name of the Indian prince from the banks of the Ganges who aided the King of Egypt against the crusaders. Clad in a serpent's skin and riding an elephant, he was slain by Rinaldo, according to Tasso in *Jerusalem Delivered.*

launched the attack of an Adrastus

ADRIANO DE ARMADO

Don Adriano de Armado, in Shakespeare's *Love's Labor's Lost,* is a pompous and boastful Spanish courtier "with a mint of phrases in his brain." A coiner of words, though awkward and ignorant, he is the military braggart in the state of peace as Parolles (*q. v.*) is in that of war.

a braggart like Don Adriano de Armado

ADULLAMITE

Adullamite comes from Adullam, the cave to which discontents followed David, and is consequently applied to malcontents congregating in any obscure place to air their grievances and "nurse their discontent."

no patriot frequents Adullam's cave
an Adullamite gloom

AEACUS

Aeacus was the son of Jupiter and Aegina, after whom the island on which he was born was named. At that time the island was unpopulated except for ants which Jupiter transformed into men (the Myrmidons) so that Aeacus might have someone to rule over. So renowned for his piety and justice was he that after his death he was made a judge in the lower world.

an equitable Aeacus of a judge

AEAEAN

Aeaean refers to the sorcery and enchantment practiced by Circe on her magic isle of Aeaea, in the *Odyssey.* By her cruel arts men were transformed into docile lions, tigers, wolves and swine.

a lethal Aeaean enchantment

AEDON

Aëdon was the wife of Zethus and jealous of the six sons and six daughters of Niobe, her sister-in-law. Mistaking him for the eldest son of Niobe, Aëdon killed her own only son, Itylus. Jupiter relieved her of her grief by changing her into a nightingale, whose plaintive tunes thus represent the melancholy lamentations she poured forth for her child.

infanticide as unintentional as that of Aëdon

AEGEAN

Aegean refers to Aegeus, the father of Theseus, who threw himself into the sea—thereafter called the Aegean Sea—in a passion of grief when he heard the false rumor that his son had been killed. Aegean has since implied passionate, grief-stricken, hasty action.

in unrestrained Aegean grief

AEGIR

Aegir, in Scandinavian mythology, was the wild and turbulent god of the stormy winter sea. *Aegir's Daughters* are the rolling waves of mid-ocean.

down to Aegir's briny depths

AEGIS

The Aegis was originally the storm cloud around the thunderbolt which Jupiter gave to Apollo and Athena. Later it was the shield of Jupiter, forged by Vulcan and described as striking terror into those who beheld it. It is most commonly thought of as the defensive short cloak worn by Athena, covered with scales and adorned with the head of Medusa. Today the word *aegis* means any protecting power or influence.

under the aegis of his patron saint

AEGISTHUS

Aegisthus was the adulterous paramour of Clytemnestra, the queen of Mycenae and wife of Agamemnon. When the latter returned from his ten year siege of Troy, Aegisthus aided Clytemnestra in murdering him in his bath. He himself was consequently slain, along with Clytemnestra, by Agamemnon's children, Orestes and Electra. (See under names of the other principle characters as well.)

an Aegisthus at cuckoldry

AENEAS

Aeneas, the son of Anchises and Venus, was the Trojan prince destined to found the Roman race of historical times. After Troy fell to the Greek siege (1184 B. C.) and his wife, Creusa, disappeared in the confusion, he fled with his father and his son, Ascanius (also called Iulus, from which name the Julian family of the classical Caesars claimed descent). With a handful of Trojan survivors he undertook a long voyage in search of a new home. His adventures, as told in the *Aeneid,* are modeled on those of Ulysses (Odysseus) in Homer's *Odyssey*.

Ultimately, after an abortive love-affair with Dido, queen of Carthage, who committed suicide when he abandoned her, he came to Italy, his destined home. He asked King Latinus for the hand of Lavinia, his daughter. As she was betrothed to Turnus, another aboriginal Italian king, he won her only after a long war. Founding Lavinium, he inherited Latinus' kingdom on the latter's death. He was noted for his filial piety and his high devotion to the will of the gods. Achates was the constant and faithful companion of all of his labors.

the vicissitudes of an Aeneas

AEOLIAN

Aeolian, from Aeolus, the Greek god of the winds, is now commonly applied to the music of wind instruments. There is a story that Aeolus had all the winds in a bag, and would keep them or release them as he chose on request. *Aeolian harp* means music produced as the wind blows through harpstrings.

with aeolian sweetness
delicate aeolian murmuring
impressionable as an Aeolian harp

AEPYTUS

Aepytus was the youngest son of Cresphontes, king of Messenia, and Merope. When his father and brothers were murdered during an insurrection, he alone escaped, but Merope, his mother, was forced to marry Polyphontes, the usurper of the throne. After he had grown to manhood, he returned to his native land and put Polyphontes to death to avenge his father's murder. The eponymous kings of Messenia after him were named Aepytids in his honor.

an Aepytus avenging his father's death

AESCHINES

Aeschines was the great Athenian orator of the fourth century B. C. who opposed his rival, Demosthenes, in favoring appeasement of Philip, the ambitious king of Macedon. He actually supplied the latter with a pretext for his invasion and subjugation of Greece. Excessively vain and devoid of political sagacity, since he allowed himself to be hoodwinked by Philip's obvious machinations to rule over all the Hellenes, he was nevertheless acquitted of Demosthenes' charges that he was a fifth columnist working in Philip's interests and against those of his own country.

hoodwinked as Aeschines

AESCHYLEAN

Aeschylean refers to Aeschylus (525-456 B.C.), generally regarded as the founder of Greek tragedy into which he was responsible for the introduction of a second actor (for dialogue), scenery and stage-dress. It also typifies a literary diction and themes similar to his. His language is sonorous, ornate and figurative, replete with bold metaphors and rolling polysyllabic words. The themes of his seven extant plays (he wrote some ninety) exhibit an intensely religious and moral spirit that probes into such doctrines as the heredity of crime, the inevitability of destiny and fatality, and the belief that men learn only through suffering and atonement (*mathema pathema*).

His tragedies were originally composed in trilogies of three plays, each dealing with a different stage in the crisis of the principal characters. The *Oresteia* (or "Story of Orestes") is the only one to survive complete, and includes the *Agamemnon, Choephoroe* ("Libation-Bearers") and the *Eumenides* ("The Furies"). This vast theme of towering crime and atonement was imitated in recent times by O'Neill in his lengthy *Mourning Becomes Electra.* The other plays of Aeschylus dealt likewise with stories from Greek mythology, of which the *Prometheus Bound* creates the mightest dramatic effect. *The Persians,* however, was based on the historical event of the Persian Wars, in which he himself took part.

Aeschylean language, sonorous and rolling
Aeschylean crime and punishment

AESCULAPIAN

Aesculapian comes from Aesculapius, the Greek god of medicine and healing, mentioned in Homer's *Iliad* as having the "greatest skill in the healing art." It is recorded that he not only healed the sick but restored the dead to life, and that Jupiter, in punishment, killed him with a thunderbolt. The knowledge of medicine was transmitted in secret from father to son in his family.

with Aesculapian skill
born with the Aesculapian touch

AESHINA

Aeshina is the demon of anger in Avestan mythology and corresponds to the Asmodeus of the apocryphal Old Testament Book of Tobit.

wrathful as Aeshina

AESOP

Aesop (619-564 B. C.), celebrated Greek fabulist, was a slave who was set free because of his humor and pleasantry. His fables, endowing animals with the sense, the wit, and the reasoning of human beings, are the earliest, the shortest, the most sensible, and at the same time the most amusing of all the literature of fable. The Greeks erected a statue in his honor, and his work has been translated into every language, thereby becoming a part of the universal background of literature.

Aesop, greatest wit and moralist that ever lived

a psychology as elementary as Aesop's

an Aesop-like perception of cause and effect

AESOPUS, CLAUDIUS

Claudius Aesopus was the famous Roman tragic actor of the first century B. C. Horace thought him as fine as Roscius, the great comic actor of the day. A friend of Cicero, he kept alive the memory of the great statesman while he was in exile by constant allusions to him on the stage. Cicero spoke of his great power of facial expression and gesture.

a face as expressive as Aesopus's

AGAMEMNON

Agamemnon, the son of Atreus and leader of the Greeks against Troy, is immortalized both in Homer's *Iliad* and in Aeschylus' tragedy *Agamemnon.* Wrathful—the Iliad opens with his quarrel with Achilles—invincible, valorous, loyal, the greatest and best of the heroes of the Trojan War, he nevertheless comes to a tragic end when, on his return home, he is murdered by his wife Clytemnestra and her paramour, Aegisthus. In vengeance, they are killed by Orestes and Electra, Agamemnon's children. (See Clytemnestra, Orestes, Electra, Iphigenia.)

has the Agamemnon-quality that marks the great leader

AGANICE

Aganice was a Thessalian woman of ancient times who was able to calculate eclipses and pretended to have the moon under her command and to be able to draw it from heaven whenever she elected. Her boastfulness eventually made of her a laughing-stock and a butt for ridicule.

boasts Aganicean supernatural powers

AGANIPPE

Aganippe is the spring at the foot of Mount Helicon in Boeotia, Greece. It was regarded as sacred to the Muses, who could thus be called Aganippides. It had the virtue of imparting poetic inspiration.

drink of the waters of Aganippe

AGASSIZ, ALEXANDER

Alexander Agassiz (1839-1910) was a famous Swiss geologist and icthyologist, invited to Harvard College as resident, to Cornell as non-resident. His method of teaching is suggested in the story that he would place a student before a fish to "see what he could see," and would receive every report with the phrase, "There's more," over and over again, until the student had actually seen all, and had learned to observe keenly and completely. The words *observant, keen, thorough, complete,* attach themselves to any mention of Agassiz.

has adopted Agassiz methods

AGATHOCLES

Agathocles was a Sicilian whose strength and physical beauty provoked the interest of Damas, a noble Syracusan, who drew him from his humble origins. On the latter's death he married his rich widow and became one of the wealthiest citizens of Syracuse. Overly ambitious, he was soon exiled but collected an army and soon made himself sovereign of the city in 317 B. C. In a few years he had mastered all of Sicily that was not subject to Carthage. Though he succeeded in conquering and coming to terms with that rival power, his last days were embittered through domestic unhappiness. His grandson, ambitious of succeeding to the throne, murdered his son, and Agathocles, fearful of the safety of the rest of his family, had to send his wife and her two children to Egypt for sanctuary. He himself died shortly thereafter, artfully poisoned with the quill with which he cleaned his teeth. He was placed on the funeral pyre and cremated while still alive, being unable to give any signs that he was not dead.

Agathoclean vicissitudes

AGATHON

Agathon was an effeminate Athenian tragic poet of the fifth century B. C. He celebrated his victory in a playwrights' contest with a banquet that furnishes the scene for Plato's dialogue on love, the *Symposium.* An innovator, he was the first to use imaginary characters and imaginary subjects in his tragedies. A lover of luxury and of beautiful words, he was a well known homosexual of his day.

with Agathonian elegance and effeminacy

AGAVE

Agave was the daughter of Cadmus and the mother of Pentheus, both kings of Thebes. While celebrating the orgiastic rites of Bacchus (Dionysus) on Mount Cithaeron, she met her son Pentheus who was opposed to the worship of the new god. Inspired by Bacchus to believe him a wild beast, she tore him to pieces and carried his head triumphantly to Thebes. When returned to her senses, she went into exile. Pentheus stands for conservatism, Agave for credulous acceptance of novelty. The story is told in Euripides' play, the *Bacchae.*

an Agave raving with excitement

AGESILAUS

Agesilaus (441-361 B. C.) was the king of Sparta who ousted his nephew, the rightful heir, from the throne. His political opponents made capital of his lameness by quoting an ancient oracle that warned against a "lame reign" at Sparta, but his energy and intelligence enabled him to win victories over the Persians and Thebans for his country. In order to earn a financial subsidy when Sparta was in need he conducted a mercenary expedition in aid of an Egyptian prince against Persia and met his death in so doing. His friend, Xenophon, wrote an encomium of him in the *Agesilaus,* which describes his piety, justice, wisdom and patriotism.

an encomium befitting Agesilaus

AGLAIA

Aglaia is one of the Three Graces (v. *Charis*) of classical mythology. Her name signifies "brilliance," "brightness," and "splendor."

a brilliant Aglaian charm

AGLAOS

Aglaos was the proverbial poorest man in Arcadia in ancient times. Apollo declared him to be happier than Gyges because he found him "contented with his lot."

contented and uncomplaining as Aglaos.

AGNES

Agnes, in Molière's *L'Ecole des Femmes,* is the ingenuous and unsophisticated young girl whose name has passed into popular use to designate any young woman untutored in affairs of the heart.

Agnes is also the name of the virgin martyr under Diocletian (304 A. D.) who became the patron saint of young girls. The festival of St. Agnes' Eve (January 20-21) was celebrated with quaint rites intended to reveal to maidens their future husbands by a process of divination.

a husband-hunting Agnes

AGNI

Agni, in Hindu mythology, is the god of lightning and the sun's fire of the ancient Aryans. One of the three chief divinities of the Vedas, he is represented as having two faces, seven arms and three legs.

a day warmed by Agni

AGRAVAINE

Agravaine, surnamed *l'Orgueilleux* or "the proud" in medieval romance, is brother to Sir Gawain and a knight of the Round Table. Ever open-mouthed, he gossiped of Lancelot's improper relationship with Guinevere and betrayed the guilty couple to King Arthur.

a tattler like Sir Agravaine

AGRICOLA

Cnaeus Julius Agricola was the distinguished Roman governor of Britain from 77 to 83 A. D., whose life was immortalized in the laudatory biography written by his son-in-law, Tacitus. He secured the island as far north as the firths of Forth and the Clyde and invaded Caledonia (ancient Scotland) to rout the last of the native rebels who had taken refuge there. On his return to Rome he found the emperor Domitian jealous of his fame and exploits, and his death was rumored to have been received with pleasure, if not actually motivated by the emperor.

the modest achievements of an Agricola

AGRIPPINA THE YOUNGER

Agrippina the Younger was the granddaughter of Agrippa and Julia, daughter of Augustus, and the wife of the emperor Claudius (41-54 A. D.) whom she was said to have poisoned in order to vacate the throne of Rome for Nero, her son by a previous marriage. A strong-willed and imperious woman, she opposed Nero's love affairs with Acte and Poppaea Sabina, and for her efforts was murdered at the order of her own son and by some of his henchmen. A previous attempt to drown her by capsizing a ship having failed, the assassins burst into her bed chamber the same evening. Courageously she is said to have bared her body for them and to have bidden, "Strike the womb that bore the monster!"

an imperious Agrippina-like hold on her son

AGUECHEEK, ANDREW

Andrew Aguecheek, a fool and coward in Shakespeare's *Twelfth Night*, was a silly, simple, timid country squire, painfully aware of his own shortcomings. The name is used now to indicate any self-conscious rustic simpleton.

a neighbor he has, an amusing but pathetic Sir Andrew Aguecheek

AHAB

Ahab was the seventh king of Israel (897 B. C.), idolater, warrior and the husband of Jezebel. Because he coveted the vineyard of Naboth adjacent to the palace and could not secure it by purchase or exchange, he had Naboth falsely accused of breaking a fast and stoned to death. When confronted by the conscience of Elijah, he said, "Hast thou found me, O mine enemy?" The prophet predicted that the dogs would lick his blood in punishment of his injustice, but by humbling himself he deferred extermination for himself and passed it on to his son. He also introduced the worship of Baal.

cruel and unjust as Ahab

AHAZ

Ahaz was the king of Judah (735-720 B. C.) who had to pay tribute to Tiglath—Pileser of Assyria, because he did not heed the advice of the prophet Isaiah. The latter, together with Hosea and Micah, denounced him as idolatrous and sacrilegious.

sacrilegious as Ahaz

AHENOBARBUS

Ahenobarbus ("red beard") was the name of an illustrious Roman family of the Domitian *gens.* According to legend, Castor and Pollux had announced to an early member of the family the Roman victory over the Etruscans (496 B. C.), and to demonstrate their supernatural origin had stroked his beard, originally black, and turned it to red.

an expert Ahenobarbus at changing the color of her hair

AHIMAN

Ahiman was one of the three sons of Anak at Hebron. He and his brothers, Sheshai and Talmai, were so gigantic in stature that they terrified the spies (*Numbers,* xiii, 22), though they were later conquered by Caleb.

as huge as Ahiman

AHITHOPHEL

Ahithophel was a counselor and adviser of David, and was accounted the wisest man in Israel (*2 Samuel,* xvi, 23): "And the counsel of Ahithophel, which he counselled in those days, was as if a man had enquired at the oracle of God." A student of the stars and of astrology, this man of superhuman wisdom was a co-conspirator with Absalom, joining him in his revolt but committing suicide later when his advice was rejected. He was probably the grandfather of Bathsheba (*q. v.*)

the unusual intelligence of an Ahithophel

AHRIMAN

Ahriman is the spirit or principle of evil in the Zoroastrian religion. To him the ancient Persians attributed all the woes existing in the world. Unlike Ahuramazda, the eternal principle of good, Ahriman is created and will one day perish.

a wicked man who does honor to Ahriman

AHURAMAZDA

Ahuramazda is the eternal principle of good in the Zoroastrian religion of the ancient Persians. The creator of all things, the earth, sun, moon and stars, he assigns to everything its proper place and regulates its movements. During the 12,000 years that the world will endure he will be in perpetual conflict with Ahriman, the spirit of evil, until the world will at length be consumed, evil exterminated, and a new world created over which Ahuramazda will be supreme and sole monarch.

perpetual Ahuramazdan beneficence

AIMWELL

Aimwell is a gentleman of broken fortunes and the young hero of Farquahar's *Beaux' Stratagem.* He impersonates a wealthy nobleman in order to put himself in the way of a rich marriage as a means of recouping his fortunes.

a scheming and ambitious Aimwell

AJAX

Ajax, a Homeric hero of great size and strength and terrible in wrath, was second only to Achilles in fame, strength, and manly beauty among the Trojan warriors. His wrath was so passionate that when Ulysses worsted him in the contest for the possession of Achilles' armor, Ajax, in a frenzy of rage, took his own life. His name stands for strength, bravery, courage, and invincible wrath.

with the mighty wrath of an Ajax
strong as Ajax' red right hand

ALADDIN

Aladdin, according to the *Arabian Nights' Entertainments,* was the son of a poor widow in China. He found a magic lamp, the genius of which then came into his service, built him a beautiful palace and made him wealthy. After marrying the daughter of the sultan of China, he hung up his lamp, allowed it to become rusty, and eventually lost it. His palace was magically transported to Africa, where an African magician gave him a wonder-working ring which was a "preservative against every evil." The genius of the ring then gratified his every wish. The expression *to finish Aladdin's window* means to attempt to do the impossible, *i.e.,* to set the 24th window in Aladdin's palace with the same frame of precious stones with which the genius of the lamp had set the other 23 windows. It was a hopeless task.

no Aladdin's lamp or ring to help him

ALASNAM

Alasnam, in the *Arabian Night's Entertainments,* was given a magical mirror by one of the genii. A "touchstone of virtue," it told him whether a maiden would remain faithful to him or not by clouding if a sincere woman looked into it and clearing if she were true. He became the possessor of eight golden statues but had to seek a still more precious one to put on the ninth pedestal. He found it in the person of the most beautiful and virtuous woman of her race. This woman he married.

Alasnam's talent for finding good women

ALASTOR

Alastor, according to Greek mythology, is a surname of Zeus the Avenger, and his Roman counterpart was, Jupiter Vindex. In medieval demonology he was the devil who executed the sentences of the prince of Hell. The name Alastor also signifies the evil genius, or Nemesis, of a house, and was used by Shelley in his poem *Alastor, or The Spirit of Solitude.*

the unrelenting revenge of Alastor

ALBERICH

Alberich, the uncouth and malignant dwarf in the famous Nibelung stories, learns from the Rhine-maidens of the Rhine-gold they guard, steals it, and makes for himself a ring that confers upon its possessor power over the world. Alberich, strong, crafty, full of guile, with the possession of the ring, becomes the king of the Nibelungs. He is portrayed in Wagner's *Ring-cycle* music dramas, or operas.

has the guile of an Alberich

ALCAEUS

Alcaeus was the great Greek lyric poet of the seventh to the sixth century B. C. A contemporary of Sappho, he was like her an aristocrat and left his native island of Lesbos when it became a dictatorship. His poems run the gamut of political and personal themes and sing of wine, love, war and hatred. His name is associated with the Alcaic stanza which he invented and which was much used by his later Roman admirer, Horace.

with Alcaic hatred of dictators

ALCESTIS

Alcestis is the noble wife of Admetus, king of Pherae in Thessaly, in Euripides' tragedy of that name. Since Apollo had entreated the Fates to grant deliverance from death to Admetus if his father, mother, or wife would die in his stead, Alcestis generously offered herself when Admetus' aged parents refused to shorten their own days in order to save their son. Because of her goodness she was excused and brought back from the lower world by Hercules.

an Alcestis of a wife
Alcestean anguish

ALCIBIADES

Alcibiades (450-404 B. C.) was a brilliant, versatile, shrewd Greek leader and a pupil of Socrates, but also reckless and untrustworthy. He was popular largely because of his good looks and astonishing escapades. He had a popularity that enabled him to carry any measure he advocated, although thoughtful Athenians were apprehensive for the future of the state in consequence. Eventually, inflated with success, he proposed taking Sicily as a base of operations against Sparta in the Peloponnesian War. In this final adventure, the moment he felt fear he betrayed his own cause and fled the country; hence, reckless, popular, unsafe, treacherous.

may prove a modern Alcibiades

ALCINA

Alcina, in Ariosto's *Orlando Furioso,* is the counterpart of Homer's Circe. A seductive nymph, she embodied all voluptuous delights. The sister of Logistilla (reason) and Morgana (lasciviousness), after enjoying her lovers she transformed them into trees, stones, fountains or beasts, according to her whim.

a corrupting and depraving Alcina

ALCINOUS

Alcinous, in Homeric legend, was the grandson of Neptune (Poseidon) and the father of Nausicaa. The happy ruler of the Phaeacians on the island of Scheria (Corfu), he was famed for his beautiful gardens, the luxurious habits of his court, his courteous hospitality, and the sea-faring prowess of his people. Ulysses, shipwrecked on his shores, wept when the minstrel Demodocus sang of the fall of Troy and proceeded to relate to his host of his wanderings since that time. Alcinous then provided the hero with rowers and a ship with magic speed of oar to escort him back to the island of Ithaca, his home.

courteous hospitality worthy of Alcinous

ALCIPHRON

Alciphron (c. 200 A. D.) was a Greek sophist and epistolographer. He wrote fictitious letters purporting to have been written by Athenians of various classes of society and depicting Athenian life in the fourth century B. C.

as ardent a letter-writer as Alciphron

ALCMAEON

Alcmaeon was a Greek warrior who killed his mother, Eriphyle, to avenge Amphiaraus, his father, whom she had betrayed to his death for the sake of getting Harmonia's necklace (*q. v.*). He was pursued by the Furies for his matricide, and was himself eventually slain for having stolen Harmonia's necklace from his first wife, Alphesiboea, in order to give it to her successor, Callirrhoë.

an Alcmaeon who will find his retribution

ALCMENA

(see *Amphitryon*)

ALCYONE

Alcyone was the wife of Ceyx, the son of the morning star. When he was drowned at sea, her grief was so intense that in pity the gods changed her into the halcyon bird (kingfisher) and him into a tern and reunited them.

The phrase *halcyon days* was used by the ancients to refer to the fourteen days of calm weather that occurred immediately before and after the shortest day of winter, when the halcyon was brooding. Since her nest was supposed to float on the sea, she was regarded as a harbinger of peace and security.

brooding as Alcyone

ALDIBORONTIPHOSCOPHORNIO

Aldiborontiphoscophornio is the sesquipedalian name of a solemn and pompous character in Carey's *Chrononhotonthologos* (1734), "the most Tragical Tragedy that was ever tragedized by any Company of Tragedians" and a burlesquing parody on the bombast of the contemporary stage.

a name as unpronounceable as Aldiborontiphoscophornio

ALECTO

Alecto, a daughter of Nox (Night) and Acheron, the river of woe in the lower world, was one of the three Furies who visited punishment on the wicked Tartarus. Like her sisters, Tisiphone and Megaera, she brandished a flaming torch as, with snakes writhing in her hair, she meted out retribution with her whip.

the cruel vengeance of an Alecto
vindictive as Alecto

ALEXANDER the GREAT

Alexander the Great (356-323 B. C.), King of Macedonia, was so inexhaustible a world conqueror that he mourned only that there were no more worlds to conquer. His name is synonymous with utter conquest, acknowledgement of power, and lust for power. He founded Alexandria in Egypt.

a very Alexander among men

ALEXANDRIANISM

Alexandrianism is derived from the city of Alexandria, the cultural capital of the Hellenistic Age following the death of Alexander the Great. It was used by the Romans as a term of literary criticism, and its chief characteristics were artificiality, beauty and intricacy of form, and an elaborate, far-fetched display of mythological learning. The word today connotes much the same meaning, namely intricacy, artificiality and elaboration of form in writing.

writings full of Alexandrianisms

ALFRED THE GREAT

Alfred the Great (849-901), King of the West Saxons in the ninth century, was, in turn, military leader, law-giver, organizer and scholar. He first drove out the Danes, but when later he realized that he would be overwhelmed he made a wise treaty. He yielded them the north of England and held the south, where he set up a code of laws and founded many institutions (among them trial by jury) that are still the basis of English civilization. He encouraged learning by becoming himself a learner, importing teachers, and establishing schools in monasteries, in general laying the foundation of English culture, civilization, and law. His own nobility and wisdom are broadly reflected in the *Proverbs of Alfred.*

with the foresight of an Alfred the Great

ALGERESQUE

Algeresque comes from Horatio Alger whose books for boys pictured the ordinary poor boy rising to great fame and success through his own virtue, resourcefulness, wit, and exemplary behavior, in a series of incredible coincidences and situations. It means sudden, spectacular, and heroic.

dreamed himself an Algeresque hero

ALICE in WONDERLAND

Alice in Wonderland is the eight-year-old who in Lewis Carroll's book by that name goes down a rabbit-hole and enters a world of fantasy and delight and wonder, where animals live their own carefree, irresponsible, and inimitable happy existence in a series of adventures and whimsical situations. All are designed to fill children from seven to seventy with delight. The whole fantastic whimsy is shot through with a wisdom and philosophy and art that make the story a classic for all time.

looking about America with an Alice-in-Wonderland delight

ALLEN, ETHAN

Ethan Allen (1737-1789) organized the men of Vermont as the "Green Mountain Boys," celebrated for their exploits during the American Revolution. He is less known but equally significant as the earliest American deist. His book on *Reason, the Only Oracle of Man* opposes Calvinism and its doctrine of original sin.

a militant rebel like Ethan Allen

ALLWORTHY, THOMAS

Thomas Allworthy is the foster-father of Tom in Fielding's *Tom Jones.* A man of modest integrity, distinguished for his worth and benevolence, he is said to have been drawn from the author's friend, Ralph Allen, of Bristol, mentioned by Pope in the lines:

"Let humble Allen, with an awkward shame,
Do good by stealth, and blush to find it Fame."

as modestly virtuous as Allworthy

ALMACK'S

Almack's (now called Willis') was the old Assembly Room in King's Street, St. James, London, where exclusive society held its balls, the invitations to which were supervised by a select circle of titled persons and were a distinction almost as eagerly sought as the privilege of being introduced at Court. The owner was a Scotchman, MacAll, who inverted his name to disguise his nationality.

an Almack perennial

ALMANZOR

Almanzor is the extravagantly egotistical knight-errant in Dryden's *Conquest of Granada.* Drawcansir (*q. v.*) is a burlesque caricature of him.

self-conceited as Almanzor

ALNASCHAR

Alnaschar is the fifth brother of the barber in the *Arabian Nights' Entertainments.* He invested all his money in a basket of glass-ware and calculated to make a handsome profit on it, dreaming that by investing that profit he would eventually become rich enough to marry the vizier's daughter. During a quarrel with his imaginary wife he kicked the basket, breaking all his glass-ware. The phrase *Alnaschar's dream* means counting your chickens before they are hatched.

a pipe-dream worthy of Alnaschar

ALOIDAE

Aloidae is the patronymic of Otus and Ephialtes, reputed sons of Aloeus but actually sired by Poseidon. When only nine-years-old, each of these giants measured nine cubits in breadth and twenty-seven in height. Renowned for their strength and daring, they put the god Ares in chains and kept him prisoner for thirteen months. Before their beards began to appear, they conceived the impious project of threatening the Olympian gods with war. Piling mount Pelion on Olympus and Ossa on Pelion (*q. v.*) in their enterprise, they were slain by Apollo for their presumption.

monstrous as the Aloidae

ALPHEUS

Alpheus is a river god in Greek mythology and the son of Oceanus and Tethys. Originally a hunter, he fell in love with the nymph Arethusa. When she fled from him, he pursued her under the sea, but she was changed into a spring which came up in the harbor of Syracuse.

the amorous pursuit of an Alpheus

ALRINACH

Alrinach is the demon of Eastern mythology who presides over floods, earthquakes, rain and hail. Also causing shipwrecks, she is said when visible to assume female form.

weather stirred up by Alrinach

ALSATIA

Alsatia is a cant name for Whitefriar, a district of London that formerly had privileges of sanctuary for insolvent debtors and criminals of all types. Hence, its name betokens an asylum or place of safety for lawless persons.

disappeared in a protecting Alsatia

ALTHAEA

Althaea, in Greek mythology, was the wife of Oeneus and the mother of the hero Meleager. It was prophesied that the infant Meleager would die at the same time as a brand of wood then burning in the hearth, so Althaea quenched the brand. Meleager survived to become, among other things, the murderer of Althaea's brothers, whereupon she thrust the brand back into the flames. Meleager died as soon as it was consumed, and Althaea killed herself.

the ingenuity of an Althaea

ALUMBRADO

Alumbrado is the Spanish word meaning "enlightened." The name was first applied to a Spanish sect that arose in 1575 and claimed special illumination. It has since been applied to any person who considers himself a perfectionist.

a smug, punctilious Alumbrado

AMAIMON

Amaimon, or Amaymon, is one of the four kings of Hell in medieval demonology. He ruled over the northern (or eastern) part, and could be restrained from doing ill from the third hour until noon and from the ninth hour until evening. Asmodeus was his lieutenant.

an Amaimon restrained from harmdoing

AMALTHAEA

Amalthaea is the name of the goat with whose milk the infant Jupiter was fed. He broke off one of her horns and endowed it with magic powers whereby it would instantly fill with whatever the possessor wished. Thus, Amalthaea's horn became the cornucopia. According to more rationalizing accounts, Amalthaea was the name of the nymph by whom Jupiter was nursed in his infancy.

prosperity flowing from Amalthaea's horn

AMARANT

Amarant is a cruel giant in medieval romance. He was killed in Palestine by Guy of Warwick.

enormous and cruel as Amarant

AMARYLLIS

Amaryllis, the name given to a country girl in the poetry of Theocritus and of Vergil, was thereafter used in practically all lyric poetry for any mistress or sweetheart. Dalliance with the maidens instead of attention to the tasks of the moment has come to be called "sporting in the shade with Amaryllis."

to forget his Amaryllis and get on with his work

AMASA

Amasa was the son of David's half-sister, Abigail, who deserted his uncle and king in order to command the rebel forces of Absalom. After his victory David gave him the place held by his cousin Joab, but this attempt to allay disaffection in Judah failed, for shortly after, Joab assassinated Amasa.

a turncoat like Amasa

AMAZONIAN

Amazonian is from the Amazons, a fabled race of strong female warriors, terrible in battle. The story runs that they mated with neighboring tribes, to whom they sent all sons to be reared, but that they kept their daughters. The Queen of the Amazons was unconquered until Hercules, to whom all things were possible, killed her.

an overwhelming Amazonian woman

Amazonian dames that in their deeds affected to be men

AMBREE, MARY

Mary Ambree is the heroine of an old English ballad. To avenge her lover's death she fought against the Spaniards at the siege of Ghent in 1584. Her name has since become proverbial for a woman of heroic spirit.

the avenging spirit of Mary Ambree

AMBROSE, ST.

St. Ambrose (340-397 A. D.) was the patriotic, wise and resolute governor of Milan who later was baptized Arian bishop of that city. His advocacy of the Christian cause was one of the final blows against paganism. He even dared to reprove the emperor Theodosius for his punitive massacre at Thessalonica by imposing penance on him. Among his writings are a treatise on the duties of priests and many commentaries on parts of the scriptures.

Ambrosian courage to reprove wrongdoing

AMELIA

Amelia is the title-character of a novel by Fielding (1751). The virtuous and devoted wife of Captain Booth, a profligate and weakling, she is a model of conjugal affection. Her character is said to have been drawn from Fielding's own wife, even down to an accident which disfigured her beauty.

with the devotion of an Amelia

AMEND-ALL, JACK

Jack Amend-All was a nickname for John Cade (1410-1450). In English history he was a rebel and a reformer who promised to correct existing evils and abuses. The name may now be used to characterize any zealous champion of the underprivileged or anyone insistently calling for reforms.

a corrective Amend-All

AMENTHES

Amenthes is the lower world in Egyptian mythology. The abode of the dead, it is the equivalent of Hades, and its name means "hiding-place."

gone to Amenthes

AMENTI

Amenti is the name of the Egyptian goddess of the dead and also that of the lower world itself, into which the sun was supposed to descend at night. To Amenti and the tribunal of Osiris, there the souls of the departed were conducted by Anubis for dispatch to heaven or hell by decision of the 42 judges.

passed to Amenti

AMFORTAS

Amfortas, son of Titurel, was the chief of the knights of the Holy Grail in their castle at Montsalvat, but through yielding to the wiles of Kundry he was wounded sorely by the sacred spear which the knights revered as the one to have pierced the side of Christ. When the spear was redeemed by Parsifal, the wound of Amfortas was healed.

with the frailty of Amfortas
yielding, like Amfortas, to temptation
tempted, as was Amfortas

AMMON

Ammon was an Egyptian god represented either as a ram or as a man with ram's head and curved horns. His famous oracle at the Siwah oasis in the Libyan desert was visited by Alexander the Great, who thereafter was pictured on his coins as wearing the ram's horns in his hair. The Greeks identified Ammon with Zeus.

a prognosticating Ammon

AMORET

Amoret is the twin sister of Belphoebe in Spenser's *Faerie Queene*. A personification of beauty, she expresses the affectionate devotion of a loving and tender wife to Sir Scudamore, her husband. Timias finds her in the arms of Corfiambo (sensual passion), combats the monster, but in so doing wounds the lady.

a loving and devoted Amoret

AMORPHUS

Amorphus is a character in Jonson's *Cynthia's Revels*. An affected braggart, he arbitrates other people's quarrels, but is himself no fighter. The meaning of his name probably reflects the etymology of the adjective "amorphous," which is defined as "without determinate shape, structureless."

a pretentious Amorphus, meddling in others' affairs

AMOS

Amos, a tender of sycamores and a shepherd, was one of the minor Hebrew prophets of the eighth century B. C. With exhortations and visions he denounced the luxury, extravagance, and crime of his people.

a condemnatory Amos

AMPHIARAUS

Amphiaraus was the Argive seer and hero who married Eriphyle. Polynices bribed her with Harmonia's necklace to persuade her husband to be one of the Seven against Thebes, even though Amphiaraus knew that none of the Seven attackers of Thebes would return alive, except for Adrastus. When he reluctantly yielded to the persuasions of his wife, he enjoined on his children the duty of avenging his death by killing Eriphyle. He was swallowed up by a chasm in the earth, and his son, Alcmaeon, avenged him as ordered. His shrine near Oropus delivered oracles through dreams.

an Amphiaraus predicting his own death

AMPHION

Amphion and his brother, Zethus, were the sons of Antiope and Jupiter. When they were grown to manhood, they avenged the cruel treatment of their mother by Dirce by tying the latter to a mad bull which dragged her to her death. This scene is portrayed in the group of classical sculpture known as the Farnese Bull. Later Amphion and Zethus became the rulers of Thebes. The former was such an excellent musician that when it came time to build the walls of the city he merely took up his lyre and played, whereupon the stones placed themselves into position under the spell of his music.

the persuasive music of Amphion

AMPHITRITE

Amphitrite, in Greek mythology, is the goddess of the sea. The daughter of Nereus, she became the wife of Neptune (Poseidon). With reference to the sea, her name means literally the "wearing away of the shore on all sides."

an Amphitrite of the waves

AMPHITRYON

Amphitryon was the king of Thebes and husband of Alcmena. Jupiter, enamored of Alcmena, took on the appearance of Amphitryon whose wife, as a result, underwent a double pregnancy. She bore twins, Iphicles, the son of Amphitryon, and Hercules, the son of Jupiter. The marital deception is the subject of a play by Roman Plautus, by Dryden, by Moliére, and by a modern playwright, J. Giraudoux. From the comedy by Molière (1668) the name has come to mean a host at a dinner party, inasmuch as Jupiter in the guise of Amphitryon gave a banquet. The latter came home in time to attend and claimed the honor of being host.

cuckolded like Amphitryon

AMYCUS

Amycus was a son of Neptune (Poseidon) and king of Bithynia. A mighty boxer, he used to challenge strangers to spar with him and then slay them. When the Argonauts came to this country, Pollux accepted his challenge and knocked him out. His people broke into the ring to avenge their king but were routed by the Argonauts.

a burly Amycus with his fists

ANACREONTIC

Anacreontic is from Anacreon, a Greek poet (563-478 B. C.) who wrote gay, convivial, erotic lyric poetry so generally admired that the name is now applied to any especially graceful verse in praise of love and wine.

praised her in Anacreontic verse
the Anacreontic mood of the courtier's easy and voluptuous life

---

ANAITES

Anaites was the ancient Persian goddess of water, vegetation, and all fertility. She was identified by the Greeks with Cybele, Artemis, and Aphrodite.

invoke Anaites to give the gardens some rain

ANAK

Anak was the eponymous ancestor of the Anakim ("long-necked men"), a race of giants of southern Canaan who were annihilated by the ancient Israelites (*Joshua*, xi, 21; *Numbers*, xiii, 33).

monstrous as the Anakim

ANANIAS

Ananias, a follower of Christ, was reputed to have been stricken dead, along with his wife Sapphira, when Peter accused him of lying. The name is now used to imply deliberate lying, and at one time there was in America an Ananias Club, a jocular term used half seriously, to which public men were publicly and jocosely assigned.

is cursed with an Ananias tongue

ANASUYA

Anasuya is the wonder-working wife of the Rishi Atri in Hindu mythology. She gave Sita an ointment with which to keep herself forever beautiful.

a face-cream invented by Anasuya

ANAXAGORAS

Anaxagoras (c. 500-430 B. C.) of Ionia was a friend of Pericles and one of the most eminent of the early Greek philosophers. His book *On Nature* maintains that the universe is directed by Spirit or Intelligence. Also a scientist, he was the first to explain the solar eclipses. Later he was accused of impiety and compelled to leave Athens where he had taken up residence.

the wisdom of Anaxagoras

ANAXARETE

Anaxarete was a maiden of Cyprus whose desperate lover, Iphis, hanged himself at his door. For her coldness she was changed by Venus into a statue.

a cold-hearted Anaxarete, spurning love

ANAXIMANDER

Anaximander of Miletus was a practical scientist and philosopher of the early sixth century B. C. A friend and contemporary of Thales, he is said to have constructed a sun-dial and a map of the world.

practical as Anaximander

ANAXIMENES

Anaximenes of Miletus was a Greek philosopher of the sixth century B. C. He believed in a single cosmic material element as the substance from which the universe is made. Claiming this to be *air*, he believed that by condensation and rarefication it gave rise to all the other forms of matter.

abstruse as Anaximenes

ANCAEUS

Ancaeus was a son of Neptune (Poseidon). A seer predicted that if ever he planted a vineyard he would not live to enjoy the wine from it. Laying aside a cup of wine made from his own grapes to pursue a wild boar, he was killed in his own vineyard by the animal. This gave rise to the proverb, "There's many a slip 'twixt the cup and the lip."

an Ancaeus to avoid the vineyard.

ANCHISES

Anchises was a member of the royal house of Troy. His youthful beauty equaled that of the immortal gods, and Venus (Aphrodite) fell in love with him, bearing him a son, the hero Aeneas. Anchises, however, boasted of his intercourse with and amorous conquest of the goddess and for his indiscretion was struck blind or paralyzed by the thunderbolt of Zeus, who was angered that a mortal should dare to sully the reputation of a goddess. When Troy fell to the Greeks, Aeneas carried his aged father out of the burning city on his shoulders and took him along on his fated trip to Italy to found a new national home for the remnants of the Trojan people. Anchises died en route and was buried at Mount Eryx on Sicily.

an Anchises boasting of his amours

ANDHABA

Andhaba is a Hindu demon with a thousand arms and heads and two thousand eyes and feet. When he tried to carry off the tree of paradise, he was slain by Siva.

as much a monstrosity as Andhaba

ANDHRIMNER

Andhrimner, in Scandinavian mythology, is the creator of hoar-frost and the cook for the gods in Valhalla.

panes thickly frosted by Andhrimner

ANDREWS, JOSEPH

Joseph Andrews, the title character of a novel by Fielding, was created to ridicule Richardson's *Pamela*. He is a footman who marries a maid-servant. Thackeray describes him as "brave, but his voice too musical to halloo to the dogs; his bravery in riding races for the gentlemen of the countryside, his constancy in refusing temptations, make an altogether refreshing bit of goodness." Hence, the name means excessively good, selectively brave, eagerly willing; honest, and resolute.

the Joseph Andrews type

ANDROCLEAN

Androclean is from Androcles, a Greek slave who was thrown to the lions in the arena, but, according to the legend, was recognized by one of the lions as the person who had many years before in Africa extracted a thorn from its foot. The name has been brought into new prominence by Shaw in his satire *Androcles and the Lion.* It is now applied to any person who is spared disaster in consequence of an earlier spontaneous act of kindness on his part.

rather an Androclean story. His accuser remembered the man who had given him lodging the night of the blizzard.

ANDROMACHE

Andromache was the loving wife of Hector, "the bulwark of Troy," and the mother of his son Astyanax. One of the noblest and loveliest of the female characters in the *Iliad,* she saw her dead husband dragged around the walls of the city and her child hurled from its walls when the city fell. She herself became the slave-concubine of Pyrrhus (Neoptolemus), the son of Achilles, who took her to Epirus. Later she married Helenus, Hector's brother. The classical type of the true wife and mother, she is the subject of a tragedy by Euripides.

the nobleness of an Andromache
as stoical as Andromache in grief
Andromachean smiles through tears

ANDROMEDA

Andromeda was a princess of Ethiopia whose mother had boasted that her daughter was more beautiful than the Nereids. Whereupon, Poseidon sent a monster to lay waste their land, but was dissuaded from that destruction by her father's promise to chain Andromeda to a rock, where she would be at the mercy of the sea monster. Here it was that Perseus found her, slew the monster, and married the maiden. She had been promised to Phineus, who appeared at the wedding, fought Perseus, and was slain. Andromeda at her death was placed among the stars.

rescued from danger as dire as Andromeda's

ANDVARANAUT

Andvaranaut was the last ring of Andvari's treasure and bore the curse of destruction to each of its owners. Ultimately it became the famous Ring of the Nibelungs, popularized in the music-dramas of Richard Wagner.

the Hope diamond, a modern Andvaranaut

ANDVARI

Andvari is the fish-shaped dwarf in old Norse mythology. He possesses a fabulous treasure, which is wrested from him by Loki and becomes the hoard of the Nibelungs.

ugly and rich as Andvari

ANGELICA

Angelica is an infidel princess of great beauty and coquetry in the epics of of Boiardo and Ariosto. Sent from farthest Asia to sow dissension among the Christians in Paris, she is desperately loved by Orlando but is indifferent to him, loving Rinaldo herself as a result of drinking from a magic fountain. Rinaldo, however, cannot abide her until both drink again of the magic waters, which now have the opposite effect. Orlando is driven mad with jealousy when she marries Medoro, a young Moor, and returns with him to India. She possesses a magic ring which defends her from all spells when on her finger and makes her invisible when in her mouth.

as coquettish as Angelica

ANNUNZIO, GABRIELE D'

Gabriele d'Annunzio (1863-1938) was the famous Italian romantic novelist, poet and dramatist. Likewise an aviator, soldier and patriot of World War I, he occupied Fiume for Italy in 1919 but had to surrender it in 1921. In 1924 he was honored by his country by being created Prince of Montenevoso. He is most renowned for his swashbuckling, egotistical adventures and for his ungallant discarding of his erstwhile mistress, the great tragic actress Eleanore Duse, whose love for him he publicized in his novel *Il Fuoco*, "The Flame."

swashbuckling in the d'Annunzio tradition

ANTAEUS

Antaeus was a giant whose enormous strength depended on his being in contact with Mother Earth. No matter how exhausting the exertion, his strength was renewed every time he touched the ground. Hercules killed him completely off the ground, holding him there and crushing him. *Antaean strength* now is apt to be used of the natural, healthy, physical strength completely renewed in sleep, when a man figuratively throws himself on the ground to rest.

healthy players with Antæan strength

ANTENOR

Antenor was the wisest of the Trojan elders in Greek legend. He advised the return of Helen to Menelaus, her husband, but when Troy fell because she was not given back to the Greeks he escaped and founded Padua in Italy.

as wise as Antenor

ANTEROS

Anteros ("anti-love") was the Graeco-Roman deity opposed to Eros, or Love, and struggling against him. According to another interpretation, his name meant "return-love," either as the symbol of reciprocal affection or, more probably, as the avenging Eros who punishes those who do not respond to love with love.

summon Anteros to avenge a cold heart

ANTHONY, SAINT

Saint Anthony of Padua was the patron saint of the poor, and, according to one legend, patron saint of swineherds. It was, therefore, customary to dedicate to him a pig of each litter, which is perhaps the reason an undersized pig was called an Anthony. His name has also become associated with the idea of complete purity and chastity.

a porker for St. Anthony

ANTIGONE

Antigone is the heroine of Sophocles' tragedy *Antigone*. When Creon, a conquering tyrant, had declared that the slain enemies should not be buried, Antigone sought out and buried the body of her brother, and was herself ordered to be buried alive in punishment. To appreciate the devotion in her act, one must remember that burial in those days took on a special significance, when only the souls of the *buried* dead might be admitted to the abode of the blessed. Antigone therefore represents the devotion, courage and will to risk her own life for the eternal salvation of those she loved.

Antigonean courage

ANTINOUS

Antinous was a Bithynian youth of uncommon beauty who became the favorite of the Roman emperor Hadrian and accompanied him on all his journeys. In 122 A.D. he drowned himself in the Nile in order to avert an ill omen that concerned Hadrian, who, in grief, enrolled him among the gods, founded the city of Antinoopolis in his honor, and filled the Roman Europe with statues of the handsome lad that still abound in continental museums.

a youth of Antinoan beauty

The name is also that of the most insolent of the suitors for Penelope's hand in the *Odyssey*. He was the first of the suitors to be slain by Odysseus (Ulysses).

with Antinoan arrogance

ANTIOPE

Antiope was the first wife of Lycus, a king of Thebes in Boeotia. He divorced her because she was made pregnant by Jupiter, to whom she bore two sons, Zethus and Amphion. Antiope was subsequently treated with great cruelty by Dirce, the second wife of Lycus, but her sons avenged her by tying Dirce to a mad bull, which dragged her to her death. They then threw her body into a fountain near Thebes, which was henceforth known as the fountain of Dirce.

an Antiope seeking revenge through her sons

ANTIPHOLUS

Antipholus of Ephesus and Antipholus of Syracuse, in Shakespeare's *Comedy of Errors*, are twin brothers who were lost to each other by a shipwreck in infancy. Though identical in appearance, they are as different in temperament as are their twin slaves, the Dromios (*q. v.*)

can't tell Antipholus from Antipholus

ANTOINETTE, MARIE

Marie Antoinette (1755-1793) was Queen of France, wife of Louis XVI, archduchess of Austria, delightful and intelligent, was marvelously trained by an uncle, Franz Josef, in the ways of rule, but given no chance to use her political wisdom in France. Helpless before the growing discontent of the French people and the ineptitude of the king, she was a victim of the destruction of royalty. She was imprisoned for nine months after the execution of the king, and was finally executed after a series of most infamous indignities. She is remembered and most often referred to in her happier and gayer early years as the beautiful young Queen. With her lovely dresses and beautiful surroundings she lived in the Little Trianon, where the courtiers mimicked the simple fashion of shepherds and shepherdesses, surrounded by the graceful appurtenances of royal country life. Her story is marvelously told in Louisa Muhlbach's novel, *Marie Antoinette and Her Son.*

the esprit of Marie Antoinette

ANTONY, MARK

Mark Antony (82-30 B.C.) was a supporter of Caesar, with whom he crossed the Rubicon. Politically popular at the time of Caesar's assassination, he made himself master of Rome. He was attacked for his overweening ambitions by Cicero in a series of speeches modeled on those of Demosthenes against Philip of Macedon and so known as "Philippics." In revenge he formed the Second Triumvirate with Octavian and Lepidus and caused the proscription and murder of the great orator. After Philippi (42 B.C.), he and Octavian divided the Roman world between them, Antony taking the East as his sphere of influence. At Alexandria he lived the life of an Oriental ruler, engaging in riotous, profligate and debauched activities with Cleopatra, who bore him three children. Estranged from Octavian, he even donated large slices of the Roman East to the "harlot queen of the Nile," as Cleopatra was then known in Rome. Defeated at Actium and in Egypt by Octavian, he committed suicide. Shakespeare's play *Antony and Cleopatra* gives a romantically distorted version of the historical facts.

a profligate Mark Antony, drunk with power

ANU

Anu, in Hindu mythology, is the son who refused to bear a curse pronounced on his father. In consequence of his unfilial attitude he was himself put under a curse, to the effect that his posterity should not possess dominion. Anu is also the supreme god of the Assyro-Babylonian pantheon.

with the unfilial disloyalty of Anu

ANUBIS

Anubis, the son of Osiris, corresponds in Egyptian mythology to Hermes (Mercury). It was his duty to conduct the souls of the dead before the judgment seat in the lower world. In art he was represented as having a human body and the head of a jackal or dog.

resisting the summons of Anubis

APACHE

Apache is the name of a tribe of Indians noted for their warlike disposition and their disastrous raids as well as for the wild yells that heralded their approach and their activities; hence it connotes nomadic, warlike, formidable, bloodcurdling.

In French, the name designates a group of lawless people inhabiting the demimonde of Paris, and resembling our American gangsters with their gun molls.

lively brood, usually yelling like Apaches

emitting bloodcurdling Apache yells

APELLES

Apelles, the greatest painter of antiquity, was born at Colophon in Ionia in the first half of the 4th century B.C. The favorite painter of Alexander the Great, he executed several portraits of him. He also painted Bucephalus, Alexander's horse, so realistically that a living horse mistook it and began to neigh. Grace and charm characterized his paintings of *Aphrodite Anadyomene,* which depicted the goddess of love wringing the sea water,from which she was born, out of her hair. When a cobbler criticized the drawing of a sandal in one of his pictures he altered it, but as the cobbler then proceeded to criticize the drawing of the leg, Apelles uttered the proverb, "A cobbler should stick to his last."

beauteous as Apelles' Aphrodite

APEPI

Apepi, in Egyptian mythology, is the giant serpent that fed the forces of darkness and evil against the sun-god Ra, by whom they were consumed daily. The struggle at morning symbolized the conflict of dark against light, evil against good.

a snake as monstrous as Apepi

APHRODISIAN

Aphrodisian is from Aphrodite (Venus), goddess of love and beauty, and commonly represents unrestrained love and inordinate desire. In art and poetry she is pictured as sprung from the foam of the sea on the Greek island of Cythera, in which connection she is usually called Cytherea. The wife of the lame blacksmith, Vulcan, she was not remarkable for conjugal fidelity, but was caught in a net during an amour with Ares (Mars) for all the gods to see. She also dallied with Adonis, and by the Trojan Anchises became the mother of Aeneas. Hence, she was regarded by the Romans as the progenitor of their race.

fresh and rosy, an Aphrodite rising from the sea

APICIAN

Apician refers to a gourmet's fondness for the well-stocked dinner-table. The word is derived from the name of a Roman glutton, Apicius, who was so fond of eating that when his income was reduced by extravagances to a sum he considered inadequate to the maintenance of his epicureanism he committed suicide rather than submit to living on a plain diet. This ancient gastronome lived during the reign of Tiberius (A.D. 14-37). A work on cookery and recipes from ancient days is falsely attributed to him, since his name had become synonymous with expensive dinner tastes.

an Apician fondness to linger over dinner

APIS

Apis was the sacred bull of Memphis and symbolical of the Egyptian god Apis, sometimes identified with Osiris and Serapis. He lived in a splendid palace with walks and courts for his entertainment. His birthday was a holiday for all Egypt, his death marked by national mourning. He was not allowed to live more than twenty-five years, at the end of which he was sacrificed and buried in great pomp.

a rancher's zealous concern for each bull as though it were Apis

---

APOCRYPHAL

Apocryphal, from the Apocrypha, refers to books or writings commonly hidden from the public. The word now is applied to certain books of the Bible, marking them as uncanonized or not to be included. The general use of the word indicates not authenticated, therefore false, unreal, or of doubtful origin.

spurious as the Apocrypha

APOLLO

Apollo is known variously as the god of music and poetry, god of the sun and of light, god of health and healing, but always as the perfect representation of youthful, manly beauty. His favorite residence was on Mount Parnassus, and he had oracles at Delphi and Delos. Artemis (Diana) is his twin sister.

bright and glowing as a young Apollo
bright as Apollo's lute

APOLLONIUS

Apollonius of Tyana in Cappadocia (c. 4 B. C.) was a vagrant Pythagorean philosopher and mystic who traveled through all the lands of the then known world, acquiring so much fame as a thaumaturge and wonder-worker that divine honors were lavished on him. Eventually settling down at Ephesus, he is said to have proclaimed the death of the emperor Domitian the very moment that it occurred. He also wrote a life of Pythagoras.

Apollonian miracles and wonders

APOLLYON

Apollyon is the destroying angel of Hell, also one of the many names applied to Satan, the principle of evil. Bunyan personifies him in his *Pilgrim's Progress* as opposing Christian; hence, evil, wickedness, temptation.

an Apollyon-like onslaught
Apollyon—smoke issuing from his belly and fire from his mouth, Doré's picture will stay with me till I die

---

APPIUS CLAUDIUS

Appius Claudius, one of the Roman consuls in the year 451 B. C., was also one of the decemvirs, a board of ten men appointed to draw up the earliest codification of Roman law. In his second term of appointment he became oppressive. Enamored of a beautiful young girl, Virginia, he attempted to gain possession of her by having one of his dependents claim her as a slave. When he pronounced judgment in favor of his henchman, Virginia's father plunged a knife into her breast and led the uprising that overthrew him from power.

legalistic as Appius Claudius

APPIUS CLAUDIUS CAECUS

Appius Claudius Caecus, "the blind," was a Roman censor in 312-308 B. C. He built the first highway, the Appian Way, from Rome to Brindisi on the Adriatic coast, and also constructed the first aqueduct to bring water into Rome. In his old age he resolutely and stubbornly opposed the overtures of Pyrrhus for peace. A man of broad views and originality, he gave new life to the Senate by admitting rich plebeians and freed-men to that august body. He also composed many aphorisms and was a notable orator.

versatile as Appius Claudius Caecus

APPLESEED, JOHNNY

Johnny Appleseed, an American pioneer, a gentle, amiable, and rather aimless wanderer, friendly and pleasant, traveled the Ohio Valley in early days, scattering appleseeds from a bag he habitually carried, a custom which explains, the Ohio natives say, the many apple trees growing where no farmer has planted them. The name is now used of any friendly traveler who leaves growing plants or trees as a token of his one-time presence.

the doctor is a regular Johnny Appleseed; he is always bringing plants from his garden for a patient's yard

---

APSARAS

Apsaras, according to Hindu mythology, was one of a class of female spirits residing in the breezes. All of the Apsarases were wives of the Gandharvas, the heavenly singers at the banquets of the gods, and handmaidens of Indra, the Vedic deity presiding over the spirits of the middle realm (the air).

a maidservant as ethereal as Apsaras

AQUILO

Aquilo is the Roman god of the north wind, identified by the Greeks with Boreas. He is a type of blustering and rudeness.

blasts of Aquilo chilling the earth

AQUINAS, THOMAS

Thomas Aquinas (1225-1274) was the oblate of the Benedictine Monastery at Monte Cassino, Italy, who rose to become the greatest teacher of theology in the University of Paris. A defender of Aristotle, he wrote a critique of Platonism, and his *Summa Theologica* is the basis of almost all modern Roman Catholic theology. Called the "Angelical Doctor," he insisted on the capacity of the reason to act as a sufficient and genuine cause of true knowledge.

a new Aquinas to expound theology

ARACHNE

Arachne, in Greek mythology, was the Lydian maiden who challenged Athena (Minerva) to compete with her in weaving. Insulted by the goddess for her overweening conceit, she hanged herself in despair but was turned into a spider by Athena so that she might ever ply her craft. The phrase *Arachne's labors* connotes the arts of spinning and weaving.

busy as Arachne at her weaving
needlecraft worthy of Arachne

ARAMIS

Aramis is one of the immortal three of Dumas' *Three Musketeers,* who cavort from one adventure to another all over Europe, a part of the one-for-all and all-for-one code of boon companions ever since. (See *Athos* and *Porthos*).

he needs no brother; he has his Aramis and Porthos

ARATUS

Aratus (born c. 315 B. C.) was a Greek of Asia Minor who spent part of his life at the court of Antigonus Gonatas in Macedonia where he composed hymns for the marriage of that monarch. He also wrote the *Phaenomena,* an astronomical poem that describes the stellar regions and the relative positions of the principal stars and constellations, their risings and settings, and various predictive weather signs. His work was translated into Latin by Cicero and had great influence on the ancients' knowledge and theories of astronomy.

another Aratus looking at the stars

ARCADIAN

Arcadian is from Arcadia, a mountainous region in southern Greece with lonely and impressive scenery Its inhabitants claimed to be the oldest people in Greece and resisted the Dorian invasion (twelfth century B.C.) and later Spartan aggressions. Its mythological associations are numerous. According to one account, Jupiter (Zeus) was born there, on Mount Lycaeus. Hermes and Pan were originally Arcadian deities. The natives derived their name from Arcas, the son of Zeus and Callisto, and were proverbial for the contented, pastoral simplicity of their life and for their rustic and idyllic innocence. The phrase *et in Arcadia ego* connotes supreme content and happiness.

full of Arcadian delights

ARCHILOCHIAN

Archilochian refers to the stinging satire of Archilochus (B. C. 714-676), one of the earliest of the Greek poets, who was born on the island of Paros of a noble father and a slave mother. Driven by poverty to migrate to Thasos, he became engaged to Neobule. When her father, Lycambes, broke off the betrothal, Archilochus lampooned the whole family with such mordant satire that father and daughter are said to have hanged themselves in shame.

with trenchant Archilochian wit

ARCHIMAGO

Archimago is the magician who typifies hypocrisy and deceit in Spenser's *Faerie Queene.* Assuming the guise of the Red Cross Knight, he deceives Una (Truth) into believing him the true Knight (Piety), but is finally exposed by Sansloy. Archimago is cast into a dungeon for his falsehood. Later the arch-hypocrite is at liberty again and employs Braggadocchio to attack the Red Cross Knight.

a deceitful hypocrite of an Archimago

ARCHIMEDES

Archimedes (287-212 B. C.) of Syracuse was one of the greatest mathematicians of antiquity, and an astronomer and inventor in physics and mechanics as well. He invented the compound pulley and the "screw of Archimedes," a contrivance for raising the level of irrigation water that is still used in the canals of Egypt. "Give me a place to stand and I will move the earth" was one of his boasts. In the thrill of discovery he shouted *"Eureka"* ("I have found it"), when in his bath he discovered specific gravity as a means of testing whether base metal had been put into Hiero's crown. He was killed by Marcellus at the capture of Syracuse, the siege of which had been delayed by many of his own devices.

another Archimedes in inventiveness

ARDEN, ENOCH

Enoch Arden, the hero of Tennyson's sentimental narrative poem *Enoch Arden,* marries his childhood sweetheart, goes to sea, is marooned and reported lost for many years. He finally returns to his house and through the window sees his wife, his boyhood friend Philip, and their family of children, all happily engaged in the usual evening household tasks. Sensing perfect domestic peace and realizing the ensuing complicated unhappiness were he to reveal himself, he turns away and soon dies in a far-off town, alone. His name suggests self-sacrifice, renunciation, and loneliness.

war is sure to bring about an occasional Enoch-Arden-case

AREOPAGITICAL

Areopagitical refers to a final legal judgment and comes from the Areopagus (Mars Hill or the Hill of Ares) in Athens. Here it was that in ancient times Ares was tried for the murder of Hallirrhothius, who had attempted to ravish his daughter Alcippe. Here also Orestes was tried for the murder of his mother Clytemnestra, Athena putting the case before a tribunal of Athenian citizens. The name *Areopagus* was later applied to the body which met there to judge cases of murder, mayhem, arson and poisoning. The name today applies to any tribunal whose judgment is authoritative. Milton's essay, *Areopagitica,* is a plea for unlimited liberty in printing.

awaiting the Areopagitical verdict

ARES

(see *Mars*)

ARETHUSA

Arethusa was one of the Nereids and an attendant on Diana. According to Ovid, the river-god Alpheus fell in love with her while bathing in his stream in Arcadia. When the chaste nymph shunned him, Diana took pity an her and metamorphosed her into a well, which flowed under the Adriatic to Ortygia, an island in the harbor of Syracuse. But Alpheus still pursued her and passing by the same underground channel from Greece and Sicily, he reappeared in her fountain, mingling his waters with hers.

coy and chaste as Arethusa

ARGAN

Argan, the title character of Molière's *Le Malade Imaginaire,* is a miserly hypochondriac who finds himself in this predicament: he cannot afford to be sick unless his apothecary will charge less; but if he buys fewer of his drugs, he will suffer in health. The name Argan thus connotes a congenital valetudinarian who is always nursing his health.

enjoys the morbid health of an Argan

ARGANTE

Argante is the name of a giantess who personifies unbridled licentiousness in Spenser's *Faerie Queene.* Called "a daughter of the Titans," she is made to seem hideous in her lecherous incontinence.

Argantean licentiousness

ARGANTES

Argantes is the bravest of the infidel knights in Tasso's *Jerusalem Delivered.* A courageous Circassian, brutally fierce, and a despiser of the Nazarenes, he was slain by Rinaldo.

courageous and pagan as Argantes

ARGONAUTS

The Argonauts are in Greek legend a group of sailors and adventurers who sailed with Jason in search of the Golden Fleece. The word is now used of gold-seekers, or of any one who ventures forth openly in search of wealth.

organizing another of his Argonautic ventures
gleams like the galleon rare of Argonautic dreams

ARGUS-EYED

Argus-eyed refers to Argus, the legendary Greek with a hundred eyes, who guarded the heifer Io. Legend has it that upon his death the hundred eyes were transferred by Juno to the tail of the peacock. The name is now used of a person so watchful that he sees all, knows all and is, in other words, incurably curious and inescapably watchful.

my Argus-eyed neighbor will broadcast this
a purblind Argus, all eyes and no sight

ARIADNE

Ariadne, the daughter of Minos of Crete, fell in love with Theseus when he came to convey the tribute to the Minotaur in the labyrinth, and gave him a thread to guide himself out, on condition that he would marry her. He took her with him, but soon deserted her on the island of Naxos. She later married Dionysus, who placed among the stars the crown he gave her as a wedding gift. Hence, Ariadne suggests both a guide in difficulty and a group of stars.

need an Ariadne's thread to guide one through the daedalian mazes of the book

---

ARIEL

Ariel is an airy spirit of light and speed, graceful, tricksy, beneficent, literally out of this world. The chief literary use is in Shakespeare's *The Tempest,* in which Ariel does the bidding of Prospero by land, by air, by sea. The name has been used as the title of a biography of Shelley, whose spirit was, like Ariel's, quick, light, joyous.

Ariel, engirdling the earth.
swift as Ariel in his flight

ARIMASPIANS

The Arimaspians of classical mythology were a one-eyed people of Scythia. They were constantly at war with the griffins who guarded the gold mines, and are frequently represented in Greek art as figures in oriental attire locked in combat with griffins. They used the gold they purloined from the monsters to adorn their hair. Milton in *Paradise Lost* speaks of them as stealthy thieves.

greedy and thieving as the Arimaspians

ARIOCH

Arioch, in *Daniel,* ii, 14, is the captain of Nebuchadnezzar's guard into whose custody Daniel was given. In Milton's *Paradise Lost* he is one of the rebellious angels overthrown by Abdiel and cast out of heaven. The name means "a fierce lion."

rebellious as Arioch
watchful as Arioch

ARION

Arion was a legendary Greek poet from the island of Lesbos. He became so famous as a minstrel and lyre player that he went on a concert tour of the Greek cities in Italy. Returning to Greece a rich man, he was thrown overboard by the greedy sailors who wanted to rob him of his wealth. But dolphins which had heard his sweet music while he was still aboard ship carried him on their backs unharmed to Taenaros.

Arion is also the name of the fabulous horse, offspring of Ceres and Demeter, that had the power of speech and on its right side the feet of a man. It was owned by Hercules who gave it to king Adrastus.

music as sweet as Arion's

ARISTAEUS

Aristaeus was the son of Apollo and the water nymph Cyrene in Greek mythology. The protector of vine and olive plantations, he was also the patron deity of husbandmen and shepherds and instructed men in the management of bees.

an apiarist taught by Aristaeus

ARISTARCHUS

Aristarchus of Samothrace was the head of the great library at Alexandria from 180 to 145 B. C. The "founder of scientific scholarship," he edited the works of Homer, Hesiod, Alcaeus, Anacreon and Pindar. He also wrote on literary and grammatical subjects.

needs an Aristarchus to edit his work

ARISTEAS

Aristeas is the "Wandering Jew" of popular Greek tradition. He was a poet who alternately appeared and disappeared over a period of some 400 years. He appeared first as a teacher of Homer, and thereafter in different ages and places in utterly different character. He visited all the mythical nations of the earth and was considered by Herodotus as a magician, whose soul could leave and re-enter its body at will.

roving and ubiquitous as Aristeas

ARISTIDES

Aristides, an Athenian statesman and general of the 5th century B. C. and called "Aristides the Just," is recorded by all historians as "eminently good." The name is now applied to any public man who is notably just and honest.

the new judge is a true Aristidian

ARISTIPPUS

Aristippus of Cyrene (435-366 B. C.) was the founder of the Cyrenaic school of philosophy. A predecessor of Epicurus, he taught that pleasure, which should be a sensation of mild character, is the true end of life. All pleasures differ in degree and duration but are equal in value. Some, however, are conducive to pain, and so man must distinguish between those he wants, inasmuch as all pleasures need the reason to control and temper them.

pursuing Aristippan pleasures

ARISTOGITON

(see *Harmodius and Aristogiton*)

ARISTOPHANIC

Aristophanic refers to the coarse and ribald nature of the comedies of Aristophanes (448-380 B. C.), master of satire and chief exponent of Attic Old Comedy. His plays contain deft caricatures of the leading personalities of his day, men like Socrates, Cleon the demagogue, and the tragedians Aeschylus, Sophocles and Euripides. In the *Lysistrata* he inveighs against war, in the *Knights* against political demagogism, in the *Clouds* against the educational doctrines of the Sophists, and in the *Wasps* against lawyers and litigation. Eleven of his comedies are extant. The principal characteristics of his humor are a rather broad and racy, though healthy, indecency and a sharp, stinging satire.

his books have an Aristophanic flavor

ARISTOTELIAN

Aristotelian comes from Aristotle (384-322 B. C.), the Greek philosopher admitted to be "the most remarkable man of all history," according to Plutarch, and the founder of the Peripatetic School of Philosophy, where he introduced formal reasoning and logic;

hence, learned, logical, scientific. He was the pupil of Plato and the teacher of Alexander the Great.

with an Aristotelian air quite overwhelming

ARMADA

Armada refers loosely to any fleet of warships, but is specifically the Spanish fleet sent against England in 1588. The name is commonly used in literature of a fleet that has been notable in some crisis.

a whole Armada of glorious sail

ARMADO, DON ADRIANO DE

Don Adriano de Armado is the verbose and fantastic Spanish braggart in Shakespeare's *Love's Labour's Lost.* Represented as a pompous lover and court retainer, he was designed to ridicule John Florio, "the Resolute," a pedantic philologist and lexicographer. He is contemptuous of everything common, is boastful yet poor, and has at the same time a majestic gait and the lowest propensities. He is also a coiner of words.

another wordy Armado

ARMAGEDDON

Armageddon is commonly taken to refer to the great final battle between the forces of Good and Evil. In the Bible it is used as the name of the place of the great final battle of the world.

the first whisper of the great Armageddon

ARMANDE

Armande is one of the learned ladies of Molière's *Les Femmes Savantes.* Her love for Clitandre does not meet with reciprocity, for he prefers her sister Henriette who is not a *femme savante.* Armande is, thus, one of the prototypes of the literary and intellectual blue-stocking.

a learned Armande at her librarian's desk

ARMIDA

Armida is the beautiful sorceress in Tasso's *Jerusalem Delivered.* Instigated by Satan to disturb the plans of the Crusaders, she is employed by Satan to seduce Rinaldo and other Christian warriors. In an enchanted palace on a remote island she holds Rinaldo in voluptuous bondage until two messengers from the Christian army bring a talisman to liberate him. Pursuing Rinaldo she attacks him in battle until he confesses his love and persuades her to become a Christian. According to another version, unable to allure Rinaldo back, she set fire to her palace in distraction, rushed into combat and was slain. Her story is the subject of operas by Gluck and Rossini.

amorous delights learned in Armida's enchanted palace

ARNOLD, BENEDICT

Benedict Arnold was an American general who turned traitor so flagrantly that his name has ever since been synonymous with any arrant treachery to one's country.

Arnoldean betrayal

ARNOLPHE

Arnolphe is the selfish and morose cynic of Molière's comedy, *L'Ecole des Femmes.* His pretended misanthropy and hatred of the world springs from his absorbing self-interest. He tries to bring up a young girl, Agnes, in virtuous innocence, and only succeeds in teaching her to deceive him.

a narrow-minded Arnolphe

ARRIA

Arria was the wife of Caecina Paetus, who, when the latter was ordered to commit suicide because he was under the disfavor of the emperor Claudius, "taught her husband how to die." She courageously stabbed herself first, then handed him the dagger and said *Paete, non dolet* ("Paetus, it does not hurt"). Her name has been since then a byword for calm and resolute stoicism in the face of disaster.

the example of an Arria to nerve one

ARROWSMITH

Arrowsmith is the principal character in Sinclair Lewis' novel of that name. It shows the struggles and experiences of a young idealist in science who meets every sort of difficulty, prejudice, and obstacle that a matter-of-fact, selfish, and practical social and professional set-up can offer to his kind.

he is having an Arrowsmith experience that is trying his mettle

---

'ARRY and 'ARRIET

'Arry and 'Arriet are the names jocularly given to the young British cockney and his girl when they are out skylarking at county fairs and holidays in London.

a big, confused, noisy 'Arry-an-'Arriet occasion

ARSINOE

Arsinoë was the name of several Macedonian princesses who were rulers of Egypt. The most important of them was Arsinoë II, the wife in turn of Lysimachus, Ptolemy Ceraunus and of her own brother, Ptolemy II. A woman of rare vigor and talent, she was an unusual ruler both in war and in peace, and the years of her reign until her death in 270 B. C. were "Egypt's golden age." Even before her death she was deified.

a born leader like Arsinoë

ARTEGAL

Artegal is the hero of the fifth book of Spenser's *Faerie Queene* and the impersonator of Justice. He is also the poet's friend and patron, Lord Grey. His main object is to rescue Irena (Ireland), whose heritage has been withheld by the tyrant Grantorto. A chivalrous knight-errant, he subdues the spirit of mischief and violence wherever he encounters it. He finally marries Britomart.

a chivalrous and just Artegal

ARTEMIS

Artemis is the Greek name for the Roman Diana, a huntress, goddess of the chase and of the moon. Known also as Delia and Cynthia, she was protector of forest life, the guardian of the wild life of forest and stream, and the symbol of chastity. Apollo was her twin brother.

every hunter is out with an occasional Artemis, on a hunting holiday

---

ARTHURIAN

Arthurian is from King Arthur, the semi-fabulous king of Britain who assembled the Knights of the Round Table and pledged them to carry into the then-savage kingdom his principles of truth, law, and justice instead of violence and brutality. He and his court were a pattern of valor, breeding and grace.

too late for Arthurian idealism
a case of Arthurian justice

ASAPHIC

Asaphic means of or pertaining to Asaph, one of the chief singers in the Temple in the time of David and Solomon. He was also the eponymous head of one of the guilds of singers, who were known as "sons of Asaph." The Asaphic psalms (50 and 73-83) have the name of Asaph superinscribed. Mr. Tate, who wrote the second part of *Absalom and Achitophel,* praised Dryden under this name.

a song of the lasting fame of Asaph

ASCALAPHUS

Ascalaphus was the son of Acheron and was turned into an owl for his mischief-making. When Pluto gave Proserpina permission to return to earth provided that she had not eaten anything while in the lower world, Ascalaphus volunteered the information that she had tasted of a pomegranate. For his thankless task of "squealing," Proserpina's mother, Ceres, had him metamorphosed into the "wise bird."

an informer and gossip like Ascalaphus

ASCANIUS

Ascanius was the young son of Creusa and Aeneas, whom the hero led to safety out of burning Troy to accompany him on his journeys to find another country in which to settle the remnants of the Trojan race. Ultimately becoming heir to his father's new kingdom in Italy, he founded the city of Alba Longa. Also known as Iulus, he was claimed with mistaken etymology to be the ancestor of the famous Julian family of classical times.

heir to a fortune as great as that of Ascanius

ASHTAVAKRA

Ashtavakra is the hero of a story in the *Mahabharata,* one of the two great epics of ancient India. He was born crippled and crooked, but became straight by bathing in the Samanga river.

crooked as Ashtavakra

ASHTON, LUCY

Lucy Ashton is the heroine of Scott's *Bride of Lammermoor* and of Donizetti's opera. Betrothed to Edgar Ravenswood, the "gentle Lucy" is forced by her mother to marry the Laird of Bucklaw instead and goes mad on her bridal night.

mad as Lucy Ashton

ASK AND EMBLA

Ask and Embla, in Scandinavian mythology, were the first man and woman. They were created by Odin, Vili, and Ve (*qq. v.*) out of an ash and an elder tree respectively.

original as Ask and Embla

ASMODEUS

Asmodeus is the destructive spirit of whom many stories are told in Jewish demonology. The demon of vanity and dress, he is called "king of the devils" in the Talmud. In modern times he is jocularly spoken of as the destroyer of marital happiness. He heads the fourth of the nine ranks of malicious, revenging devils. Wierus makes him superintendent of gambling houses. LeSage makes him the companion of Don Cleofas in *Le Diable Boiteux,* or "The Devil on Two Sticks," and he bears the Don through the air like an arrow simply by having him hold on to his cloak. Presiding over the follies of mankind rather than their crimes, he is malicious rather than malignant, and he delights in scoffing, gibing and teasing.

versatile as Asmodeus to annoy

ASPASIA

Aspasia of Miletus was the famous mistress of Pericles. Belonging to a class of women known as *hetaerae,* or female companions, she so charmed the leader of the Athenians by her beauty and high intelligence that he left his wife and lived in illegitimate union with her for the rest of his life. Aspasia's home was a salon for the best literary and philosophical society of Athens and was visited even by

Socrates. Her son by Pericles was granted Athenian citizenship in deference to the greatness of the father. W. S. Landor's *Pericles and Aspasia* is a collection of imaginary letters between the lovers.

a modern Aspasia of intellectual society

ASS, GOLDEN

The *Golden Ass* or *Metamorphoses* is a Latin romance by Lucius Apuleius that tells of the transformation of a young Greek, Lucius, into an ass by means of a magic ointment. He suffers many picturesque vicissitudes, falling into the hands of robbers who make him their unwilling and much abused accomplice in their exploits. Later he serves a strange wandering priest of Cybele and becomes a popular performing ass. By favor of the goddess Isis, he is eventually restored to human shape and intiated into the mystic rites of Isis and Osiris. The whole lively tale may be an allegory of human life, depicting the sensual degradation of the soul and its recovery.

a life as full of changes as the Golden Ass's

ASTARTE

Astarte, the female counterpart of Baal, and the Phoenician goddess of fertility and reproduction, was worshiped in orgies marked by voluptuousness and frenzy. She is in some mythologies identified with Aphrodite and Venus, always with some representation of love and desire.

Astartean lust

ASTOLFO

Astolfo, or Astolpho, is a famous character in the romantic tales concerning the supposed adventures of Charlemagne and his paladins. Generous, brave, courteous and handsome, he is the English cousin of Ariosto's *Orlando Furioso.* A boaster, he undertakes great feats, including a visit to Alcina's isle on the back of a whale. When Alcina wearied of him and turned him into a myrtle, he was disenchanted by Melissa and took a flight to the moon, from which he returned with Orlando's wits in a phial to cure the latter's madness. The magic horn given him by Logistilla enabled him to drive whole armies into panic, and the book that the same fairy gave him permitted him to know everything.

like a blast from Astolfo's horn

an Astolfo's book to tell you everything

ASTOR, JOHN JACOB

John Jacob Astor (1763-1848), one of the wealthy men of early America, made his money first in musical instruments, then in fur trading, in connection with which he set up the first line of fur-trading stations; then in shipping, until he became a person to reckon with in transportation. A fortunate and extensive purchase of land in New York City and the erection of commodious public buildings eventually enriched him immensely for those days—"he made $250,000 in sixteen years." His continued success enabled him to give $400,000 to found the Astor Library, and to amass twenty million dollars, a fortune due largely to his sagacity and to his "close and constant application to business."

many an ambitious Astor went out west

ASTRAEA

Astraea was the goddess of justice and daughter of Jupiter and Themis. During the Golden Age she lived on earth, but with the spread of sin she was the last of the immortals to leave it and was metamorphosed into the constellation *Virgo.*

reluctant as Astraea to believe his guilt

ASTROPHEL

Astrophel is the name used by Sir Philip Sidney to depict himself as the lover of Stella (*q.v.*), in real life Penelope Devereux, to whom he was at one time betrothed. He celebrated her praises in the famous sonnet-sequence, "Astrophel and Stella," published in 1591. The name Astrophel is a metagrammatic translation of the abbreviation of his name to Phil. Sid., Sid. being understood as the contraction of Latin *sidus*, "star," which in Greek is *astron*, and Phil. standing for Greek *philos*, a "friend" or "lover." Hence, Astrophel means "star-friend."

Spenser commemorated his friendship with Sidney in the pastoral ode called "Astrophel."

thoughts lost like Astrophel's in the stars

ATALANTA

Atalanta was the fleet-footed Greek maiden who would yield only to a suitor who could outstrip her in a race. She was finally won by Hippomenes who outran her by a trick suggested to him by Aphrodite. The goddess gave him three golden apples to drop in Atalanta's path as they ran. Atalanta stooped each time to pick up the apple, and lost the race.

with the winged speed of an Atalanta
fleet and slim as Atalanta

ATARGATIS

Atargatis was a Syrian goddess of fertility whose chief cult was at Hieropolis. Worshiped at Askelon under the name of Derceto and the form of a mermaid, she was also venerated in Rome as Dea Syria.

breasting the waves like Atargatis

ATE

Ate, the daughter of Jupiter, was the goddess of blind recklessness, discord and mischief. Driven out of heaven, she took refuge with mankind and was later regarded as an avenging deity bent on exacting retribution. In Spenser's *Faerie Queene* she is a lying and slanderous hag, a friend of Duessa.

with the blind mischief of Ate.

ATHALIAH

Athaliah, the daughter of Ahab and Jezebel, was the wife of Jehoram and and the usurper of the throne of Judah (2 *Kings*, xi, 1). She introduced the worship of the Phoenician god Baal into Israel.

idolatrous as Athaliah

ATHELSTANE

Athelstane, surnamed the Unready, in Scott's *Ivanhoe*, is the slow-witted Thane of Coningsburgh. A Saxon of royal descent, he is suitor to Rowena.

hesitant as Athelstane

ATHENA

Athena, the Greek goddess of wisdom, arts, industry, agriculture, science and laws, is fabled to have sprung full-grown from the brow of Jove. For her, Athens was named. She is the equivalent of the Roman Minerva, and represents wisdom and knowledge.

She's a terrible woman, a very Athena of a woman, not a woman to marry. Why man, she would always know as much as you do!

ATHENAEAN

Athenaean is from Athenaeus (c. 200 A. D.), the author of the *Deipnosophistae*, or, "Connoisseurs in Dining." The book deals with the dinner conversations held in Rome by a group of 23 learned men who talk of food in all its aspects and on a wide range of other subjects. The author was a collector of excerpts and anecdotes which he edited in the form of conversation. His knowledge was encyclopedic.

Athenaean dinner conversations

ATHOS

Athos is one of the *Three Musketeers* of Dumas' famous novel, men whose adventures take them careening in and out of great royal intrigues in kings' palaces, into back streets and cellars, highways and byways all over Europe and out on the high seas, always with utter daring, utter resourcefulness, and, above all, utter loyalty to each other. They originated the famous "one-for-all and all-for-one" brand of loyalty.

don't molest him; he has a Porthos and an Aramis
inseparable as Athos and his comrades

ATKINS, TOMMY

Tommy Atkins is the name given to any private in the British army, as Johnny Reb and Yankee were given to American soldiers. Collectively it means the British infantry, made more famous in Kipling's *Barrack Room Ballads*. It suggests blunt and honest feeling and opinion among soldiers.

the Tommy Atkins honesty

ATLANTES

Atlantes is a sage and magician in Ariosto's *Orlando Furioso*. Living on Mount Carena in a castle with a wall of glass, he tutored the young Rogero in all the manly virtues. Possessing powers of enchantment, he rode about on a hippogriff.

all-powerful as Atlantes

ATLANTIS

Atlantis is a mythical island said to have sunk into the ocean in the early ages, but Plato, for purposes of idealizing, located it in the far west, and described it as an ideal state. Bacon's *The New Atlantis* outlines an ideal community known for the scientific enlightenment of its inhabitants; hence ideal, enlightened, scientific.

the new land is a very Atlantis

ATLAS

Atlas, giant leader of the Titans, and of superhuman strength, was given the responsibility of bearing the universe on his shoulders. One version of the story says that he was punished by being charged to hold up the heavens. At any rate, his name suggests superhuman strength.

an Atlantean vigor of arm
stood, with Atlantean shoulders fit to bear the weight of mightiest monarchies

---

ATROPOS

Atropos is the one of the three Fates that cuts the thread of life. Hence, she typifies Death, the end of human experience. For the other two, see *Clothos* and *Lachesis*.

the finality of Atropos

ATTIC

Attic is from Attica, the region of Greece environing Athens, its capital. It thus connotes all the qualities of superiority that distinguished Athens and the Athenians of the great age from their less enlightened and cultured neighbors. The ones most commonly suggested by the name are the *simple elegance* of Athenian art, the *trenchant intelligence* of men like Pericles, Sophocles and Plato, the *delicate wit* popularized in the expression "Attic salt," and the *inviolable honor* signified by the phrase "Attic faith."

with Attic wit and intelligence

ATTICUS

Titus Pomponius Atticus (109-32 B.C.) was a Roman writer, epicurean and philosopher. The intimate friend and publisher of Cicero, he spent many years in Athens in retreat from the Civil Wars raging in Italy, and there it was that he acquired the cognomen *Atticus* ("the Athenian"). Cicero turned to him constantly for sympathy and help in the trials of his stormy political life. A very wealthy man, Atticus was a lavish patron of the arts and literature. Because of his reputation for learning and eloquence, his name was applied as a pseudonym to Addison by Pope in the latter's *Epistle to Dr. Arbuthnot*

has his Atticus to befriend him

ATTILA

Attila (406-453), king of the Huns, was an aggressive leader in a succession of marches over Asia, invasions so devastating that he became known as "the Scourge of God."

From the fury of the Huns, O Lord, deliver us"

OLD LITANY

with Attila-like destruction

ATYS

Atys was a beautiful Phrygian youth who was loved by the goddess Cybele. She made him her priest on condition of perpetual chastity. When he broke his vow she caused him to become insane. In his frenzy he castrated himself and was changed into a fir tree. Catullus has depicted the orgiastic tumult of his emotions in a Latin poem, translated into English by Leigh Hunt.

a frenzied Atys driven to penance

AUCASSIN AND NICOLETTE

Aucassin and Nicolette, a famous pair of lovers in an old French romance, a dialogue of exquisite verse and prose, appear in English in a modern version by Andrew Lang. First and last they represent idealistic love, so purely romantic that their names have taken their place among the great lovers of universal fame.

an Aucassin-and-Nicolette romance that ignores domesic cares and pay-checks

---

AUDHUMLA

Audhumla, in old Norse cosmogony, is the cow from whose udders flowed the four rivers of milk which nourished the giant Ymir, out of whom the world was shaped. Bōrr, the first man, was made by her licking salt from the snow. Odin was Bōrr's son. Audhumla thus represents the power of creative nature acting upon chaos.

has the creative powers of Audhumla

AUDLEY, JOHN

John Audley is an 18th century theatrical term for making an abridgment. In the year 1749 a man named Shuter had a troupe of actors which toured English fairs. It was his habit to lengthen the exhibition for the audience until a sufficient number of people had gathered outside to make a new audience, a practice not unknown in modern American carnival shows. The existence of a new audience was made known by an employee's calling out "John Audley," as if paging someone seated in the audience. Then the first show was brought to a sudden end in order to make room for the new audience. The phrase *We will John Audley it* thus came to mean "shorten" or "cut" in modern theatrical parlance.

needs to be John Audleyed

AUDUBON, JOHN JAMES

John James Audubon (1785-1851), American ornithologist and artist who specialized in painting the birds of North America from life, was born in Haiti, the natural son of a French merchant and a Creole woman. Later legally adopted by his father, he emigrated to America where he became a general storekeeper, tutor, and drawing teacher in turn.

He was forced to take his work to England in order to find a publisher, after which his *Birds of America* and *Ornithological Biography* established his reputation as a bird authority. Chapters of the Audubon Society throughout America are devoted to studying the habits and appearance of native birds.

Audubonian knowledge of the fowls of the air

AUGEAN

The Augean stables are named from Augeas, King of Elis, whose stables were cleaned of thirty years' filth by Hercules, as one of the many supposedly impossible tasks imposed on him. He cleaned them by turning the course of the river Alpheus to run through them.

the new administration may find Augean stables

AUGUSTAN

Augustan refers to the age of Augustus Caesar (B.C. 63-A.D. 14), first of the Roman Emperors, and supreme head of the State after his defeat of Antony and Cleopatra. Born Caius Octavius, he assumed the name of his great-uncle, Julius Caesar, when adopted by him in his will, following the assassination of 44 B.C. From that year he was thus known as Caius Julius Caesar Octavianus (Octavian), until in 27 B.C. the Senate conferred on him the honorific cognomen *Augustus*, to express their veneration of him as head of the Roman priesthood. (Both this name and that of Caesar were latter conferred on subsequent emperors as a matter of course.)

He had the political sagacity to veil actual sovereignty under republican forms, and achieved the most splendid annals of Roman history. He saw Rome transformed "from a city of bricks to a city of marble," and developed its prestige and culture to the point of a Golden Age. In support of his program for regeneration following the period of the bloody civil wars, he made use of the genius of men like Maecenas, Agrippa, Vergil, Horace, and Livy. The achievements of his time were so admirable that any similarly remarkable period in any country is characterized as Augustan.

the longed-for Augustan age
wisdom worthy of an Augustus

AUGUSTINE, ST.

St. Augustine (A.D. 354-430) was the famous African teacher of rhetoric in Rome and Milan who was converted to Christianity in his thirty-fourth year and became the bishop of Hippo and leader of the early Christian Church. He taught that the soul is superior to the body and so can suffer nothing from it. The subtler points of Christian metaphysics are expounded in his *Confessions* and *City of God.*

reasoning with Augustinian subtlety

AURELIUS, MARCUS

Marcus Aurelius (121-180), a Roman Emperor and philosopher, believed that an individual is living best when he understands the law of nature, resigns himself to the will of the gods and acts in a way that will react to the good of all men. He adopted as his guiding principles duty, resignation, frugality, and self-control. His *Meditations*, translated and published in almost every language of the world, are based upon those maxims, and the book finds appreciative readers today because it is common to all time, all humanity.

with a Marcus Aurelius universality

AURORA

Aurora, the young and beautiful goddess of the dawn, is often represented as driving the chariot of the sun across the night skies to meet the eastern sky at dawn. Her name is used to suggest youth, radiance, and color.

blushing like Aurora
the rosy fingers of Aurora
Aurora throws her fair
fresh-quilted colors in the air

AUSTEN, JANE

Jane Austen (1775-1817), the daughter of a clergyman, drew her characters from the fairly properous middleclass people she knew, and is unrivaled in her accurate portraits and characterization, her freedom from the usual sentimentality, and her introduction of a note of pure comedy. Her novels are really companion pieces to the comedies of manners by Goldsmith and Sheridan. The film version of her *Pride and Prejudice* was hailed with delight in the twentieth century. She represents keen character portrayal and comic personality in what Scott called her "supreme portraits of society."

with a Jane Austen insight into the family motives and intrigues

---

AUSTER

Auster is the Latin name for the personification of the south wind. The modern Sirocco which blows over Mediterranean countries, it is harmful and pernicious to plants and human health. Hot and dry in Italy, it is a damp wind in England and generally brings wet weather. The root of the name Auster is also found in the appellative for the continent of Australia.

the baneful breath of Auster

AUTOCRAT OF THE BREAKFAST TABLE

The Autocrat of the Breakfast Table is a sobriquet used by Oliver Wendell Holmes in a series of dissertations purporting to be the conversation of a group of people who lived in a boarding-house in the Boston of the middle 1880's. The arrangement enabled Holmes to make the book the vehicle for his own wise and witty, sensible and derisive comments concerning a miscellaneous lot of subjects of current interest. Holmes himself is the Autocrat, the self-appointed and warmly accepted master of ceremonies at the breakfast table.

the welcome Autocrat of club dinners

AUTOLYCUS

Autolycus, the son of Mercury and Chione, was the craftiest robber and thief of antiquity. He could change the appearance of both himself and his stolen goods so as to make them unrecognizable, or could make himself and the pilfered merchandise invisible. He stole the flocks of his neighbors and changed their markings. Sisyphus alone outwitted him by branding his sheep under their feet. In Shakespeare's *Winter Tale* he is a peddler and called the son of Mercury because he was born under that "thieving planet."

as crafty a thief as Autolycus

AVALON

Avalon is the name of an ocean island and of a castle of loadstone built on it in medieval romance. "Not far on this side of the terrestrial paradise," it was the abode and burial place of King Arthur and the residence likewise of Oberon and Morgaine la Fée. The island of the blest in Celtic mythology, its name means "apple island."

an Avalon for his dreams

AVERNIAN

Avernian refers to Lake Avernus in Campania (near Naples), a small, deep volcanic crater filled with water and shut in by steep, wooded heights. It was so gloomy and terrifying in aspect that the Romans believed it to be the entrance to the lower world. Because of noxious fumes rising from it, no bird could fly over it without plummeting, suffocated, into its depths. The name was also often used to designate the lower world itself, as in Vergil's famous phrase *facilis descensus Averno,* "easy is the descent to Hell."

Avernian gloom and horror

AZAZEL

Azazel is the name of the act of dismissing the goat, or scapegoat, in the Mosaic ritual of atonement (*Lev.*, xvi, 8). It may actually be the appellation of the person to whom the goat was sent, probably some demon of the wilderness.

In Milton's *Paradise Lost,* Azazel is the standard-bearer of the infernal hosts.

despatched to Azazel for expiation

AZAZIEL

Azaziel is a seraph in Byron's "Heaven and Earth." He falls in love with a mortal, Anah, the granddaughter of Cain. When the flood came, he carried her under his wing to some other planet.

a rescuing Azaziel

AZOR

Azor is the frightful but kind-hearted monster in Mme. Villeneuve's fairy tale, *Beauty and the Beast.* Once a handsome and graceful young prince, he had by enchantment been transformed into a hideous shape from which he could be rescued only by the love of a devoted young woman. To have the life of her father, Zémire finally consents to marry Azor, won by his respectful affection and deep melancholy. He is immediately restored to his former self. The allegory suggests that innate beauty can be preserved and immortalized only by the touch of pure love.

like Azor, made handsome by the touch of love

AZRAEL

Azrael, according to Mohammedan mythology, and also mentioned in the Bible, is the angel of death. The Mohammedan story is that he had been visible to the person stricken until Mohammed prayed that he become invisible. The Bible declares: "the last to die will be Azrael, angel of Death."

to every man comes Azrael
waiting for the wings of Azrael

also caused her death, inasmuch as along with the giant she also produced 68 sellers of salt, each leading a mule by the halter, 7 camels with stores of eels, 9 dromedaries carrying hams and smoked tongues, and 25 wagons laden with leeks, garlic, onions and shallots.

prodigiously fruitful as Badebec

BAEDEKER, KARL

Karl Baedeker (1801-1859) printed the first good guide books to be used by travelers. His name has come to be used not only of these guide books, but of any travelers' guide, and is sometimes applied to persons whose knowledge of places is unusually extensive, accurate and freely informative.

his presence makes a Baedeker unnecessary

with Baedekerized comprehensiveness

BAGOAS

Bagoas was the eunuch, trusted and favored by Artaxerxes III whom he poisoned in 338 B. C. Put to death by Darius III because of a similar deceitful attempt on his life, he left a memory so dishonorable that his name became a synonym for eunuch for many of the Latin writers.

deceitfully crafty as Bagoas

BAGSTOCK, MAJOR

Major Bagstock is a "blue-faced," apoplectic officer in Dickens' *Dombey and Son*. Wooden-featured and self-absorbed, he always speaks of himself in initials, as "J. B.," "old J. B.," or "Joey B." He turns out to be only a fair-weather friend of Dombey.

self-engrossed as Major Bagstock

BALAAM

Balaam was an Oriental prophet who, urged by the king and induced by love of gain, cursed Israel and was astonished and confused to hear the ass he was riding break into speech and rebuke him for his selfish curse. Terrified, Balaam repented and God's power turned the curse into a blessing to the people. His name has also been used of persons who make profession of religion for the sake of gain.

Balaam-like, changes the burden of his song at will

BALBOA

Balboa was the Spanish navigator who in 1513 discovered the Pacific Ocean, on which occasion he first thanked God and set up the cross, then stepped into the water and took possession in the name of the sovereign of Castille. He is recorded as a "wonderful manager of the Indians" and "the best head that ever protected a camp."

with the emotions of a Balboa

stared with the glad wonder and surprise of a Balboa

BALDERSTONE, CALEB

Caleb Balderstone is servant and butler to Ravenswood in Scott's *Bride of Lammermoor*. Old, but proud and faithful, he resorts to fantastic expedients to conceal his master's poverty, struggling without food, furniture or essential comforts to maintain an appearance of affluence.

proud and vain as Balderstone

BALDUR

Baldur was the Norse god of the summer sun, the noblest, gentlest and wisest of all the gods and so fair that a brilliant white light streamed from his person. As a result of the machinations of Loki he was slain by his twin brother, Hodur, the blind god of war. His death typifies the disappearance of the sun from the horizon during the winter months in the North.

as dark as when Baldur died

BARTHOLO, DR.
Dr. Bartholo, in Beaumarchais' *Barbier de Seville,* is an old doctor and the jealous guardian of Rosine. He tries to keep her and her lover separated so that he may marry her himself.

a guardian as vigilant as Dr. Bartholo

BARTHOLOMEW'S DAY, ST.
St. Bartholomew's Day, August 24, 1572, was the infamous occasion of a frightful massacre of French Protestants that was begun in Paris on the eve of the festival. Secretly ordered by Charles IX, at the instigation of his mother, Catharine de' Medici, it was remarkable for its incredibly fiendish cruelty. Authorities estimate that from 30,000 to 70,000 persons were atrociously slaughtered in this pitiless persecution.

a purge to make Bartholomew's Day look pale by comparison

BARTON, CLARA
Clara Barton (1821-1912) was an American nurse noted for her general philanthropy, but especially for having founded the Red Cross organization. Her own observations and experiences in military hospitals during the Civil War and in the Franco-German war, her work among the poor and her experience in the distribution of food to the destitute in Paris made her see the need for such an organization, and gave her the practical knowledge of methods of administering mass relief. She is revered throughout the world for making available practical, effective, and instant help in any emergency in any land.

many a man remembers a Clara Barton who helped him through his need

---

BARUCH
Baruch was the amanuensis, secretary, and friend of the prophet Jeremiah (*Jer.,* xxxvi), and the supposed author of the Apocryphal book of the Old Testament that bears his name. Another Baruch was a pious Jew of Jerusalem who undertook, as mason, to repair part of the city's wall (*Neh.,* iii, 20).

a secretary as amicable as Baruch

BARZILLAI
Barzillai ("iron of the Lord," "strong and firm") was the rich man of Gilead who helped David to escape from Absalom (*2 Samuel,* xvii, 27).

no Barzillai to help him

BASILE
Basile is a slanderer in Beaumarchais' *Barber of Seville* and *Marriage of Figaro.* His name has become proverbial in the French language for a calumniator, a bigot and a niggard.

a malicious Basile, making a profession of slander

BASILISCO
Basilisco is the foolish and braggart knight in an old play, *Soliman and Perseda,* so popular that his name has become proverbial for boastfulness. Shakespeare makes the Bastard in *King John* say, when asked by his mother why he boasted of his ill-birth, "Knight, knight, good mother, Basilisco-like." That is, his boasting had made him a knight.

a foolish and boastful Basilisco

BASSARID
The Bassarids, or "wearers of fox skins," were devotees and votaries of Bacchus (Dionysus). As such they were partners for the Maenads and worshiped their god with orgies of wine. Swinburne in *Atalanta in Calydon,* speaks of them as follows:

"And Pan by noon and Bacchus by night . . .
Follows with dancing and fills with delight

The Maenad and the Bassarid . . ."

The Bassarids were conceived of as dancing about the god in a state of intoxicated possession and as tearing animals to pieces in their frenzy.

frenzied by drink as a Bassarid

BASTILLE

A Bastille was originally any tower or fortress for protection, but now is best known as the name of the great French prison for political prisoners, famous in Paris for four centuries, and especially notorious when its destruction in 1789 became one of the significant events in the French Revolution. The name is synonymous with captivity, imprisonment, and government disfavor.

ahead of such intrigue looms the Bastille
even a Bastille can fall

BATH, MAJOR

Major Bath is a poor and pompous but noble-minded gentleman in Fielding's *Amelia.* The punctilious benefactor of the heroine, he tries to conceal his poverty by bold speech and ostentatious bearing. Though his oaths are sworn "by the honor and dignity of a man," he is yet caught cooking some gruel in a saucepan for his ailing sister.

a down-at-the-heels but proud Major Bath

BATH, WIFE OF

The Wife of Bath is one of the prominent figures in Chaucer's *Canterbury Tales,* a seasoned traveler, good-humored, coarse, jovial, companionable. Broad in beam, in speech, and in action, she is typical of the fairly prosperous common townswoman of the fourteenth century. She "had had five husbandes at the chirche doore" and was apparently on a search for a sixth among the twenty-nine pilgrims on their way to Canterbury.

there was a jolly Wife of Bath on the bus

BATHSHEBA

Bathsheba was the beautiful wife of Uriah the Hittite. After committing adultery with David before the treacherous murder of her first husband, she married her lover and became by him the mother of Solomon (2 *Samuel,* xi).

a paramour beauteous as Bathsheba

BATHYLLUS

Bathyllus of Samos was a beautiful youth loved by Polycrates, the tyrant of the island. He was also the subject of homosexual love poems by the Greek master of erotic lyric verse, Anacreon, and received the aesthetic admiration of Roman Horace at a later date.

Bathyllus of Alexandria was the freedman and favorite of the wealthy Roman Maecenas. He brought to perfection the imitative dance or ballet, the pantomine of which the Romans were so fond. Excelling in his personification of Leda and in comic characterizations, he was so popular in this genre of drama that his name became synonymous with pantomimic acting.

with the graceful charm of Bathyllus

BATRACHOMYOMACHIA

The *Batrachomyomachia,* or "Battle of the Frogs and Mice," is a parody of Homeric epic and is of the exaggerated consequence of a storm in a puddle. This delightful bit of "much ado about nothing" tells of a mouse who, invited to ride on a frog's back to survey the watery kingdoms, is drowned when the frog dives in fright over a water-snake. A great war buds from this pitiable incident and is quelled only by the personal intervention of Zeus, who, his thunderbolts failing to daunt the doughty warriors, sends an army of crabs which forthwith sends the original combatants squealing back to their natural habitats.

an inconsequential Batrachomyomachia

BATTLE, SARA

Sara Battle, an old gentlewoman, mistress of whist, a martinet of a player, the arbiter of rules, was always a winner at any game she played. Her name still suggests any genteel old lady, stern stickler for rules, who takes her cards seriously and entertains and voices the highest scorn for the trifling player. The character derives from Lamb's *Essays of Elia.*

as usual, Sara-Battled her way to first prize

BATTUS

Battus was a shepherd whom Hermes turned into a stone because he had broken a promise that he had made to the god.

untrustworthy as Battus

BAUBO

Baubo, in Greek mythology, was the nurse of Demeter (*q. v.*) or a minor goddess associated with her worship at Eleusis. It was said that she tried to cheer the bereaved deity, while giving her hospitality during her search for her lost daughter Proserpina, with ribald conversation. In Goethe's *Faust,* Baubo personifies gross sensuality.

conversation as inappropriate as Baubo's

BAUCIS AND PHILEMON

Baucis and Philemon, a peasant and his wife who offered simple friendly hospitality to Jupiter and Mercury when they were traveling in disguise, were thereafter immortalized for their kindness by being turned, at their death, into trees. Meantime their cottage had been turned into a temple, and the two peasants into its priests. The names have become synonymous with generosity, friendliness, and simple hospitality.

with a sweet Baucis-and-Philemon spirit, set me down to supper

---

BAVIUS AND MAEVIUS

Bavius and Maevius were Roman poetasters sarcastically referred to in Vergil's third *Eclogue*:

"He may with foxes plough and milk he-goats,
Who praises Bavius or on Maevius dotes."

Since that time both names have been used in allusion to any bad or indifferent versifier. In English literature the words *Baviad* and *Maeviad* refer to Gifford's satires on the Della Cruscan school of poets. This group was founded by some young Englishmen at Florence, Italy, in the latter part of the eighteenth century. Their work consisted entirely of silly and sentimental affectations.

poems of Bavian or Maevian quality

BAYARD (1)

Bayard was a famous horse of incredible speed, and belonged to the four sons of Aymon, a semi-mythical character in Carolian romance. This steed could adapt his size to carry either one or all four sons at a time, merely by elongating his body to conform to the number of riders he was carrying. Many wonderful feats were ascribed to him, and the phrase *keep Bayard in the stable* signifies keeping what is valuable under lock and key.

accommodating as Bayard

BAYARD (2)

Bayard, known as the knight *sans peur et sans reproche,* saved the French from utter rout by the English in 1513. For that and for many other achievements he was almost worshiped by the French, and was, in fact, the pattern of chivalry to youth the world over.

a Bayard-like chivalry

BAYES'S TROOPS

Bayes's Troops is a frequent allusion to the sham perpetrated in Buckingham's farce, *The Rehearsal*, in which a mock battle is fought between foot-soldiers and large hobby-horses. At last, Drawcansir fells all the participants on both sides. When Smith asks how they are to go off stage, Bayes replies, "As they came on—upon their legs." Whereupon they all jump up alive again.

as sham as Bayes's Troops

BEATRICE

Beatrice Portinari was an Italian lady of rare beauty of person and character, whom Dante had seen when she was eight years old and had worshiped remotely through many years. She is the lady he immortalized in his *Divina Commedia,* the *Vita Nuova* and his sonnets with such impassioned description that many great artists have painted pictures of her, using Dante's idealized conception of Beatrice as their model.

the star of Beatrice-devotion
no Beatrice lighted his days

BEAU BRUMMEL

(see *Brummel, Beau*)

BEAU NASH

(see *Nash, Beau*)

BEDLAM

Bedlam was an early London asylum for the insane, and in time a name applied to any crazed person. The name now is used both of persons and of a confused, uproarious, mad place.

a harmless Bedlam passed this way
the bedlam brainsick duchess

BEDOUIN

The Bedouins were nomadic Arabs in the desert, actually shepherds and herdsmen, but the vagabonds and robbers among them were so famous that Bedouin has come to signify only vagabonds, vagrants, and robbers.

drifted light-hearted, free, and proud like the Bedouin

BEECHER, HENRY WARD

Henry Ward Beecher (1813-1887), preacher, orator, and lecturer, was noted both for his zeal and for his eloquent flow of racy and original thought. His quaint humor was shot through with high moral earnestness. He was an active force in the anti-slavery agitation in America, and was respected everywhere for his integrity and high character, as well as admired for his unsurpassed eloquence and persuasiveness.

bids fair to be a second Beecher

BEELZEBUB

Beelzebub, originally from Baal, god of the Philistines, became Beel-zebub, and is used to indicate Satan, Prince of Evil. Beelzebub is looked upon as second only to Satan as an evil force.

domineering as a Beelzebub

BEETHOVEN, LUDWIG VAN

Ludwig van Beethoven (1770-1827), a pianist and composer, wrote music that is strong and powerful, sometimes tempestuous and towering, sometimes tender, usually robust in its melody, but always grand and always moving. It has a depth and a breadth that covers the whole range of human emotion, and most of his compositions end on a note of triumph.

His opera, *Fidelio,* and nine powerful symphonies, along with violin and piano concerti, constitute his major works.

a Beethoven-like range

BEFANA, LA

La Befana is the good fairy of Italian children, filling their stockings with toys when they go to bed on Twelfth Night. According to legend, she was too busy with house affairs to look after the Magi when they went to offer their gifts, and said that she would see them on their return. But they took another route and every Twelfth Night Befana watches to see them. She is otherwise used as a bogie to frighten children. Her name is a corruption of the word *Epiphania.*

gifts from the generosity of Befana

BEHEMOTH

Behemoth, an animal mentioned in Job ("Behold now behemoth; he eateth grass with thee"), apparently meant some great, strong, huge and powerful animal. The word is frequently found in old stories, and is beginning to be loosely used of anything huge beyond belief.

a very behemoth of a building

BELCH, SIR TOBY

Sir Toby Belch, the bibulous, jolly, comic uncle in Shakespeare's *Twelfth Night,* was a tippling loafer and jovial sponge. He was a coarse realist, rough, independent, awkward, and impudent, but so comic that his name has lived to be applied to all such persons.

unctuous as Sir Toby Belch

BELGRAVIAN

Belgravian, from Belgrave, an ultra-fashionable section of London, consequently suggests elegance, aristocracy, and fashion, the opposite of Bohemianism.

from the Belgravian fortresses of the city

BELIAL

Belial, from the expression "sons of Belial" in the Bible and in many other allusions, has come to be another name for Satan, or for persons given over wholly to evil ways.

the usual Belial racket in the early dawn

BELINDA

Belinda is the heroine of Pope's *Rape of the Lock.* In a frolic of gallantry Lord Petre cut off a lock of her hair, but this liberty occasioned a bitter feud between the two noble families, hitherto very friendly. Pope says that Belinda wore on her neck two curls, and when Belinda, bereft of the one ringlet, demanded it back, it was found to have flown to the skies, like Berenice's, and to have become a meteor. The poem was written with the design of effecting a reconciliation.

controversial as Belinda's lock

BELISARIUS

Belisarius (c. 505-565) was the most famous of Justinian's Byzantine generals and repelled the enemies of the Empire many times. His courage, however, was for the most part unrewarded, for Justinian suspected him of conspiracy against his life, deprived him of all his property, put out his eyes, and forced him to live as a beggar in Constantinople. His story is dramatically recreated in Robert Graves' novel, *Count Belisarius.*

a fallen Belisarius of a beggar

BELISE

Bélise is a self-appreciative young lady in Molière's *Les Femmes Savantes.* Vain and imaginative, she thinks that all men are in love with her.

deluded as Bélise

BELL, ADAM

Adam Bell is the hero of a famous old ballad that has his name for a title. A legendary English outlaw and wild, north-country bandit of the generation before Robin Hood, he was celebrated for his skill in archery.

Adam Bell's talent with the bow and arrow

BELL, ALEXANDER

Alexander Graham Bell (1847-1922), Scotch physicist and inventor, was brought to Boston University to teach vocal physiology, there developed his father's system of visible speech, and went on to invent the telephone, which he exhibited in 1876. He was celebrated for his accuracy, his patience, his determined concentration.

the Bell-telephone patent

BELL, BESSY

Bessy Bell is a character in Allan Ramsay's ballad, founded on fact and called "Bessy Bell and Mary Gray." Daughters of two country gentlemen in the neighborhood of Perth, England, they tried to escape the plague of 1666 by building themselves a secluded bower in a romantic spot called Burnbraes. Here they were supplied with food and other essentials by a young gentleman who was in love with both of them. After a time he fell sick of the disease and unwittingly communicated it to them. All three sickened and died in their idyllic isolation.

lives in a greenwood bower, like Bessy Bell of ballad-fame

BELLAMY, EDWARD

Edward Bellamy, author of *Looking Backward,* a book that at the time, 1888, was held to be an utterly fantastic pipe-dream, foretold many things then scarcely projected, now highly developed and known to every child in America. The book has recently been republished and is looked upon as a comic strip, so crude and behind the times are the things at that time considered miracles.

the Man from Mars may well be another Bellamy dream

BELLASTON, LADY

Lady Bellaston is a profligate and fashionable sensualist in Fielding's *Tom Jones.* One of Tom's mistresses, she conducts herself and converses as flippantly as the court beauties of the reign of Louis XV.

as "loose" as Lady Bellaston

BELLEROPHON

Bellerophon, son of Glaucus, king of Corinth, mounted on Pegasus, was sent to the King of Lycia bearing a sealed message that he was to be put to death. To that end the King of Lycia sent him to kill the Chimera, an impossible task, but with the help of Pegasus he accomplished it. Legend has it that Bellerophon attempted to mount to heaven on Pegasus. Jupiter, however, sent a gad-fly to sting the horse. Bellerophon was thrown, became lame and blind in consequence, and henceforth wandered lonely through the Aleian field, consumed by grief and avoiding the paths of men.

Bellerophontic achievement

BELLONA

Bellona, goddess of war in Roman mythology, is related as companion, sister or wife to Mars, the god of war; hence, is always associated with the activities of war. She prepared the chariot of Mars when he was going to war, and herself appeared on the battlefield with disheveled hair, a torch in her hand, and a whip to animate the combatants.

formed to a Bellona fury

BELPHEGOR

Belphegor was a Canaanitish divinity, worshiped particularly by the Moabites on Mount Phegor. The rites of this licentious, lewd fellow were spectacular for their obscenity. Wierus called him the ambassador in France from the infernal court of Beelzebub, but according to Machiavelli he was an archfiend who had formerly been an archangel. His name is sometimes used in quite another sense, to signify a "quack."

a Belphegor dallying in the fleshpots of Babylon

BELPHOEBE

Belphoebe is the virgin huntress whom Spenser used in the *Faerie Queene* to represent Elizabeth the woman as distinguished from the queen. She is a moonbeam, light without warmth; a white flower wihout perfume. The sister of Amoret, she is equally chaste, but of the Diana and Minerva type. Cold as an icicle, passionless and immovable, her beauty is that of a marble statue as she moves with fleet grace through the forests. Her only love is that of chivalry.

chaste and cold as Belphoebe

BELSHAZZAR

Belshazzar, the last king of Babylon (538 B.C.), in a marvelous feast drank wine in praise of the gods in the vessels of gold and silver that his father, Nabonidus, had taken from the temple at Jerusalem. Whereupon a handwriting appeared on the wall, which Daniel interpreted to mean that Belshazzar should lose his kingdom to the Medes and Persians, a prophecy that was fulfilled that night. Belshazzar, hence, means blasphemous, impious, doomed.

The morrow proved it true;
Belshazzar's grave is made,
His kingdom passed away;
The Mede is at his gate,
The Persian on his throne.
Byron

BELTENEBROS

Beltenebros is a name for a jilted lover who retires into obscurity after receiving the cruel rebuff of the object of his affection. Meaning "darkly beautiful" or "fair forlorn," it was originally taken by Amadis of Gaul after he retired to his hermitage, Poor Rock, upon severance from Oriana, his lady-love.

another Beltenebros, sulking in lovelorn isolation

BELVIDERA

Belvidera is the heroine of Otway's tragedy, *Venice Preserved.* The wife of Jaffier, who joined in a conspiracy with his friend Pierre against the Venetian senate, she prevailed on her husband to disclose the plot in order to save the life of her father, himself a senator. Therein she caused the death of her husband, who stabbed himself and his friend rather than die under the torture inflicted by the perfidious senate. A model of beauty, conjugal tenderness, purity and agonized suffering, she was described by Sir Walter Scott as causing more tears to fall in pity for her than fell for Juliet or Desdemona.

unhappy Belvidera, the cause of her husband's downfall

BENDIS

Bendis was the Thracian goddess of the moon, and was identified at Athens with Artemis (Diana). Her temple was in the city's port, the Piraeus, and her festival was celebrated with a torch-race.

worshiping Bendis with an eye on the moon

BENEDICT

Benedict, from Benedick, a bachelor of long standing in Shakespeare's play *Much Ado About Nothing,* is a name now used of a newly married man, usually one who has been a bachelor for many years.

Benedict trembling at the altar

BENJAMIN

Benjamin was the favorite son of Jacob and Rachel, whose father reluctantly allowed him to accompany his brothers to Egypt, where he was favored by his brother, Joseph, who had insisted that he be brought. *Benjamin's mess* means a larger than ordinary portion of anything, because Joseph sent from his own table meat for his brothers' table, and made Benjamin's portion five times as much as he gave the other brothers.

a serving for Benjamin

BENOITON, MME.

Mme. Benoîton is a character who never appears, though constantly mentioned, in Sardou's comedy "La Famille Benoîton" (1865). She is proverbial for the type of person many of us have heard about over a long period of time, and yet one whom we never have actually seen or met.

elusive as Mme. Benoîton

BENTHAMITE

Benthamite is from Jeremy Bentham (1748-1832), an eminent English lawyer who abandoned the practice of law in order to attack its iniquities, to "reform jurisprudence," and to bring about a re-examination of the laws on the basis of the happiness of the greatest number. He was at first ridiculed, but finally feared, and eventually universally respected and admired for his courage, his sagacity, and his independence. Macaulay says, "He found jurisprudence a gibberish and left it a science." At any rate, he introduced the reform of jurisprudence and stands today for fairness, justice, and integrity in behalf of all men alike.

a Bentham-passion for fair dealing

BEOWULF

Beowulf is the semi-mythical Swedish hero of the eighth century Anglo-Saxon epic poem. King of the Geatas, he liberates Hrothgar, king of Denmark, from Grendel, a bloodthirsty man-eating monster who slays nightly all those sleeping in the king's palace. After destroying a water-demon, he reigns in peace for fifty years until he receives a mortal wound while slaying a dragon that guards a fabulous hoard.

heroism worthy of Beowulf

BERCHTA

Berchta, or Frau Bertha, is a fairy in the folk-lore of south Germany who corresponds to the north German Hulda ("gracious lady"). The impersonation of the Epiphany, like the Italian *Befana,* she is represented as a gentle white lady who tends neglected cradles and is the patroness of spinners. After Christianity had converted pagan deities into demons, she became a bogie with a large foot and a long iron nose. In this guise she was used as a bugbear to frighten and intimidate naughty children.

fears of Berchta in the children's minds

BERENICE

Berenice was the devoted wife of Ptolemy III who vowed to sacrifice her hair to Aphrodite if her husband were to return home the conqueror of Asia.

She suspended a lock in the temple of the goddess, but it was stolen the first night. Conon of Samos told the king that it had been wafted to heaven by the winds, where it was regarded as forming the constellation of seven stars that is still known as *Coma Berenices*, or Berenice's lock. This charming tale of devotion and sacrifice was the subject of a poem in Greek by Callimachus, the Latin translation by Catullus, and Pope's English paraphrase, *The Rape of the Lock.*

with the conjugal devotion of Berenice

BERGERAC, CYRANO DE

Cyrano de Bergerac (1619-1655), actually a dramatist and duelist, became known to the world as a romantic figure in Rostand's play, in which de Bergerac is immortalized for his extraordinarily large nose and for his equally extraordinary, unselfish chivalry in courting and winning his cousin Roxane, whom he himself loved, for a handsome, less brilliant, but physically more prepossessing young Frenchman; hence, selfless, chivalrous, noble-hearted.

the de Bergerac brand of chivalry more than matches the Quixotic

---

BERMUDAS

The Bermudas were an out-of-the-way place in London, chosen for residence by those who had occasion to live cheaply or in concealment. This nineteenth century hide-away was comprised of the obscure and intricate alleys and narrow passageways north of the Strand, near Covent Garden. The shabby genteel would hire a knocker in some West-End square, where mail could be left for them, but actually lived in the Bermudas.

slinks in and out of the Bermudas
lives in some Bermudan hall-apartment

BERNARD OF MENTHON

St. Bernard of Menthon (923-1008) was a Roman Catholic monk who founded hospices on the Great and Little St. Bernard passes. Later becoming arch-deacon of Aosta and the patron of Alpinists, he had named after him the species of dog of unknown origin which has been bred for over 1000 years at the monastery founded by him. This powerful and large breed has gained immortal fame from its ability to rescue travelers lost in Alpine snowstorms.

as helpful to travelers as Bernard of Menthon

BERNHARDT, SARAH

Sarah Bernhardt (1844-1923), known as the "divine Sarah" and famous for her resonant *voix d'or* ("*golden* voice") was the most brilliant and universally acclaimed actress of her century. From the time of her early appearances in Racine's *Phèdre* and Hugo's *Hernani* she was renowned for her amazing power of emotional acting and for the realism and pathos of her death scenes. Active and amazingly energetic to the last of her eighty years, she made triumphant tours of North and South America, Australia and all the capitals of Europe.

Bernhardtian genius and passion

BERNOUILLI

Bernouilli is the name of a Swiss family famous in the annals of science. In the period of a century, eight of its members cultivated various branches of mathematics. The properties of numbers were first discovered by Jacques B. (1654-1705), a professor of mathematics at Basle, who wrote *A Method of Teaching Mathematics to the Blind* from his own experience at teaching a blind girl several branches of the science. He and his brother Jean quarreled over the solution to Jacques' famous problem of isoperimetrical figures, which engaged the attention of all continental mathematicians. Like Archimedes, he requested that the logarithmic spiral be engraved on his tombstone. His brother Jean (1667-1748) discovered exponental calculus.

another Bernouilli, expert in numbers

BERSERKER

Berserker was a redoubtable Scandinavian warrior who went into battle unharnessed, his strength and fury taking the place of armor which he despised as unmanly. He could take on the form and ferociousness of wild beasts, and fire and iron could not harm him. His twelve sons inherited his name as well as his bellicose ferocity. Our English word *berserk* is derived from his name.

wading in carnage, like Berserker

BERTILLON, ALPHONSE

Alphonse Bertillon (1853-1914), a Frenchman, devised a method, thus far infallible, of identification by means of physical imprints, best known in America as the current system of finger-printing.

either your conscience or Bertillon will bring you to your knees

---

BERTOLDE

Bertolde is the hero of a witty play by J. Cesare Croce, Italian prose-writer. A comedian by profession, he is astonished at nothing and is as much at ease with kings and queens as with persons of his own rank and vocation. The phrase *imperturbable as Bertolde* suggests not being disconcerted by anything, or surprised and thrown off guard.

as sure of himself as Bertolde

BESSUS

Bessus is a cowardly and bragging captain in Beaumont and Fletcher's *A King and No King.* He explains away all of his cudgelings and defeats with an unfailing supply of excuses.

as full of explanations as Bessus

BETHESDA

Bethesda was the pool of miraculous healing powers at Jerusalem, mentioned in *John,* v, 2. Hence, it can be used of any spring of curative waters or of a source of spiritual relief or comfort, as, for example, a chapel.

makes frequent pilgrimages to Bethesda

Bethesdan comfort and consolation

BEULAH

The Land of Beulah is a place of rest and perpetual light in Bunyan's *Pilgrim's Progress.* Symbolizing a Christian's peace of mind, it lies on the hither side of Death. The pilgrims tarry in it until their summons comes to cross the stream and enter the Celestial City. "Here, because they were weary, they betook themselves awhile to rest. But a little while soon refreshed them here; for the bells did so ring, and the trumpets continually sounded so melodiously, that they could not sleep, and yet they received as much refreshing as if they had slept their sleep ever so soundly." Here they met nothing that was offensive to their senses or minds. Whence Beulah Land is a common name for religious camp-meeting sites.

refreshed as by a sojourn in Beulah

BEZALEEL

Bezaleel was the artificer who executed the art works on the Hebrew tabernacle (*Exodus,* xxxvi, 2-6) and beautified it with furnishings.

a craftsman as skilled as Bezaleel

BEZONIAN

Bezonian is the name given by Pistol to Shallow in Shakespeare's *King*

Henry IV. The name is derived from the Italian word *bisogno,* meaning "need" or "want." It was frequently used by the old dramatists as an opprobrious term for "beggar," "low fellow," or "scoundrel." Strictly speaking, it is not a proper name, but it has been so widely thought to be one that its usage as such is firmly established.

a beggarly Bezonian scoundrel

BIFROST

Bifrost, or "the trembling way," is the bridge between heaven and earth in Scandinavian mythology. Like the bridge to Valhalla, it was regarded as a rainbow and supposed to be constructed of precious stones of various colors. Of extreme solidity in spite of its seemingly delicate iridescence, it was built with great art.

climbing over Bifrost to get at his pot of gold

BIG-ENDIANS

Big-endians were the people of a land in Swift's *Gulliver's Travels* in which the two parties based their political and religious doctrines on whether an egg should be opened on the big end or the little end; hence the names Big-endian and Little-endian have come to be applied to any persons disputatious about trifles. Under the former Swift satirized the Roman Catholics of England; under the latter he ridiculed the English Protestants.

two or three Big-endians spoiled the party

BILLINGSGATE

Billingsgate refers to the fishwives at the London market at Billingsgate, whose inveterate use of vulgar and abusive language was so common and so notorious that all loud female bickering and abusive vituperation has come to be called Billingsgate.

the lovely lady suddenly lapsed into her very best Billingsgate

an Edwardian manner and a Billingsgate tongue

BIMINI

Bimini is the name of the two fabulous islands supposed by the natives of Puerto Rico to belong to the Bahama group, but lying far out in the Atlantic. Superstitious belief placed on them a marvelous fountain that had the power of restoring youth. It was an object of eager quest for Ponce de Leon, who in his search for Bimini found Florida.

as rejuvenated as if she had discovered Bimini

BITON

(see *Cleobis and Biton*)

BLACKACRE, WIDOW

The Widow Blackacre is a perverse virago, a quarrelsome and argumentative busybody in Wycherley's *The Plain Dealer.* Macaulay considered her the author's best comic characterization, and likened her to the Countess in Racine's *Plaideurs,* "talking the jargon of English instead of French chicane."

an argumentative busybody like the Widow Blackacre

BLACK HOLE OF CALCUTTA

The Black Hole of Calcutta was a name given to a small and close dungeon in Fort William, Calcutta. It was a room only 20 feet square, poorly ventilated, and not intended to hold more than two or three prisoners at a time. On the capture of Calcutta by Surajah Dowlah, June 18, 1756, the entire British garrison of 146 men was locked up at night in this room. In the morning only 23 were found to have survived the excruciating agonies of heat, thirst and want of air. The sufferings of those imprisoned were recorded by one of the men, and the Black Hole is now synonymous with barbaric cruelty, unhygienic confinement and dungeoned miseries.

a jail as overcrowded as the Black Hole of Calcutta

BLACKSTONE, SIR WILLIAM

William Blackstone (1723-1780) was the eminent English jurist whose *Commentaries on the Laws of England* was so clear and so well arranged that it became an essential book for all students of law, and in America became the authority that settled practically all questions of law. It stood with the Bible, the medical book, and the dictionary, on every bookshelf in America, and many a lawsuit was settled authoritatively and inexpensively by a trip to that shelf; hence, authoritative, final, accepted.

Lincoln was the Blackstone of his community

BLAKE-LIKE

Blake-like is from William Blake (1757-1827), an English poet whose childlike rapture in natural phenomena and simple beauty, along with a certain lyric simplicity and clearness of expression, set him apart even from the lyric poets of his own time. A symbolic quality in his drawing makes his engraving a collector's item. A mystic, he had visions—fields of angels, trees of wings—which filled his soul with intense ideas of beauty; hence, mystic, visionary, symbolic, rapturous.

a certain Blake-like rapture and glad amazement

BLEFUSCU

Blefuscu is the name of an island inhabited by pygmies in Swift's *Gulliver's Travels.* "Situated to the north-east side of Lilliput, from whence it is parted only by a channel of 800 yards wide," it was ruled over by an Emperor. Swift, of course, meant this pygmy nation to signifiy France to his readers.

an aristocratic midget from Blefuscu

BLIMBER, CORNELIA

Miss Cornelia Blimber is the daughter of Dr. Blimber, the head of a first-class educational institution conducted on the forcing and cramming principle, in Dickens' *Dombey and Son.* She is a very learned blue-stocking, bespectacled, grave and precise, with "no light nonsense about her." The pedantic spinster had become "dry and sandy with working in the graves of deceased languages."

with a Ph.D. in Latin and Greek, she is a modern-day Cornelia Blimber

---

BLONDEL

Blondel was the minstrel and boon companion who accompanied King Richard I of England on all his journeys and crusades, the two singing together their hearty songs. When King Richard was imprisoned in some unknown place by Leopold of Austria without privilege of ransom, Blondel roamed Europe, singing under every prison window the first stanza of a song the two had composed, until, at the Castle of Durrenstein, a great voice answered with the second stanza. Knowing the whereabouts of the king, Blondel effected his rescue; hence, loyal, persistent, resourceful, determined.

would that every great heart had a faithful Blondel

BLOODY MARY

Bloody Mary is the name given to Mary Tudor, Queen of England (1553-1558), whose reign was distinguished for its sanguinary persecutions of the adherents of the Church of England. Two hundred persons are said to have been burnt at the stake within a period of four years for their attachment to the Reformed doctrines.

pitiless and intolerant as Bloody Mary

BLUEBEARD

Bluebeard, in an early French story, forbade his beautiful young wife, Fatima, to open a certain door in their castle, but she mischievously and curiously managed to get the key and open the door, only to discover the bones of her husband's six earlier wives. When Bluebeard saw a telltale stain on the key, and was about to kill her for her disobedience, her brothers arrived and killed Bluebeard. His name is now used of any man whose several wives have died mysteriously.

has a Bluebeard chamber in his mind into which none but he may look

---

BOADICEA

Boadicea was the wife of Prasutagus, king of a British tribe in the first century. After her husband's death, Boadicea, incensed by the brutal greed of the Roman procurator Catus, took up arms against the Roman colonists, and 70,000 Romans fell before her armies. Later she was defeated and took poison to avoid falling into the conqueror's hands; hence, intrepid, vengeful, energetic, courageous, fearless.

history records few Boadiceas

BOANERGES

Boanerges, a name meaning "Sons of Thunder," is said to have been applied to the disciples James and John, and to have meant loud and earnest oratory; hence, loud, vociferous, thunderous, zealous.

there they thunder away, Boanergic and futile

BOAZ

Boaz was the wealthy Bethlehemite who generously allowed Ruth (*q. v.*), a relative's widow, to glean in his fields at harvest time, later marrying her and thus becoming an ancestor of David (*Ruth,* ii-iv).

like Boaz, inclined to marry his brother's widow

BOBADIL

Captain Bobadil was a blustering, brawling, braggart soldier in Jonson's *Every Man in His Humor,* and the name has ever since been applied to that sort of person, wherever found.

a very Bobadil, he nevertheless had swaggered his way among his betters

surprised to find a Bobadil in that gracious company

BOCCACCIO, GIOVANNI

Boccaccian is from Giovanni Boccaccio (1313-1375), celebrated Italian novelist and storyteller noted specially for his romantic and witty tales in the *Decamerone,* which he wrote in 1353 at the request of his mistress, Princess Mary, the natural daughter of Robert, King of Naples. Boccaccio probably recorded the sort of rough-and-ready, rather coarse but always comic stories then extant in Italy. The name Boccaccian is now applied to any broad, robustious, usually ribald and racy stories.

robustious belly-shaking Boccaccian mirth

BOEOTIAN

Boeotian refers to the inhabitants of Boeotia, the district of Greece to the immediate north of Attica and with Thebes as its principal city. Surrounded by mountains, its people were largely given to the rustic pursuits of agriculture and herd-grazing. The sophisticated Athenians called them "Boeotian pigs" and said that they were as dull and thick as their atmosphere. Though Hesiod, Pindar, Plutarch and Corinna were Boeotians, the people as a whole were proverbial for their stupidity, and the expression "Boeotian ears" is still used today to refer to people who are unable to appreciate music or rhetoric.

a Boeotian blockhead, rude and uncultured

BOETHIUS

Boethius (480-524 A. D.) was a Roman Christian in the service of Theodoric. Having studied Greek at Athens, he undertook and failed in the impossibly arduous task of translating all of Plato and Aristotle into Latin, with a commentary thereon. His most famous work is the *Consolatio Philosophiae,* which he wrote when, accused of secret correspondence with the Emperor of the East, he was languishing in prison prior to being tortured to death. A medley of poetry and prose in five books, it professed to be "dictated by the afflicted Muses" in order to console the prisoner for the triumph of injustice. Vastly admired since then, it has been translated by King Alfred, by Chaucer, and by Queen Elizabeth.

Boethian in its stoical consolation

BOFFIN, NICODEMUS

Nicodeums Boffin, in Dickens' *Our Mutual Friend,* is a kind-hearted and illiterate old man who inherits an estate, "Boffin's Bower," from his late employer. Shrewd and devoted to his wife the *nouveau riche* Boffin is known as "the golden dustman."

sudden wealth, like that of Boffin

BOHEMIAN

Bohemian was originally a name applied to a wandering group from Bohemia, Austria, who entered France as gypsies, but later the name was applied to groups of people who live a free and easy life in open protest against convention and formality.

has Bohemian tastes and happy-go-lucky habits

the bookshop with its air of Bohemianism

BONA DEA

The Bona Dea was an anonymous Roman goddess and earth-spirit, patroness of women and known only as "the good goddess." Identified variously with Fauna, Maia, and Ops, she confined her worship so exclusively to women that men were not even permitted to know her name. Her annual rites, held in December, were profaned in 62 B. C. when the profligate rake Clodius Pulcher, an irreverent member of the café society of the day, attended them in female disguise in order to prosecute an amorous intrigue with Caesar's wife. This scandal occasioned the Dictator's resounding exclamation, "Caesar's wife must be above suspicion."

a Bona Dea ritual "for ladies only"

BONAPARTE, NAPOLEON

Napoleon Bonaparte, Emperor of France (1804-1814 and 1815), rose from an entirely private station to the highest pinnacle of greatness through military power and intellectual endowment. Admired by the world, worshiped by his soldiers, trusted by the people, conqueror of almost all of Europe through a surpassingly brilliant series of personal and military events, he was nevertheless defeated by Wellington's English army at Waterloo, was finally distrusted by his own people, abdicated his throne, and was exiled to St. Helena where he died in 1821. Napoleonic and Bonapartian have come to mean many things to the world—brilliant military genius, ambition, power, selfishness, defeat, devotion.

Bonapartean glory
Napoleonic ambition

BONES, BROM

Brom Bones, the Yankee suitor for the hand of Katrina Van Tassel in Irving's *Legend of Sleepy Hollow,* disposes of Ichabod Crane, his learned and lanky rival, by stuffing him with grisly tales of a headless horseman, then impersonating the ghostly apparition and scaring Ichabod out of his wits and out of the neighborhood. Hence, the name applies to any persistent suitor who routs a rival by Yankee ingenuity.

a Brom-Bones invention

BONHEUR, ROSA

Rosa Bonheur (1822-1899) was a French painter of animals, whose father instructed her in painting, and insisted upon her working directly from living models, until her work attained remarkable fidelity and accuracy. *The Nivernaise Ploughboy* and *The Horse Fair* are her best known pictures. Her name still stands for unsurpassed skill in the painting of animal pictures.

there is a Rosa Bonheur quality in the child's drawing, crude as it is

---

BONIFACE

Saint Boniface is the jolly, genial, shrewd and hearty innkeeper in Farquhar's *Beaux' Stratagem,* whose name is now used of genial innkeepers the world over, wherever the friendliness of the host is a recognized part of the attraction of the service rendered.

a rosy Boniface made us welcome and furnished us good cheer

BOOBY, LADY

Lady Booby is a female of frail virtue in Fielding's *Joseph Andrews.* She attempts to seduce its hero, her footman, whose virtue she is, however, unable to conquer. Designed as a caricature of Richardson's *Pamela,* she is represented as a vulgar *nouvelle riche,* whom the parson is compelled to reprove for laughing in the church.

vulgar as Lady Booby

BOONE, DANIEL

Daniel Boone (1738-1820), famous American hunter, trapper, scout, and explorer, was born in Bucks County, Pennsylvania, and went on into Kentucky, North Carolina, and finally Missouri. In turn he fought the Indians, befriended them, was adopted by them, and finally attacked by them. He set up the town of Boonesboro in Kentucky, but lost his own land there by means of a defective title. Later he acquired a great tract in Missouri and lost it too because the title was not valid when Spain ceded that territory to the United States. He is remembered as an intrepid, fearless, indomitable scout whose adventures figure in many a story.

the true Daniel-Boone courage

BOOTES

Boōtes was the son of Ceres and the inventor of the plow. He was later translated to heaven and made a constellation. According to another account, he was a son of Lycaon and Callisto and was slain by his father who served his body at Jupiter's table, wishing to test the omniscience of the god. Jupiter restored him to life and placed him among the stars.

devoted to the plow like Boötes
no Boötes to test your knowledge

BOOTH, JUNIUS BRUTUS

Junius Brutus Booth, a great English actor, was the father of two equally famous actor sons, Edwin and John Wilkes, the latter the assassin of President Lincoln.

histrionic as the Booths

BO-PEEP

Bo-Peep is the chief character in a Mother Goose ditty, said to have originated as a popular song at a time when Elizabeth was fearful lest she lose the loyalty of a section of her people. The populace, knowing their own kind and that their good fortune depended on the protection of the queen, evolved the verse:

Leave them alone, they will come home
Bringing their tails behind them

like a distracted Bo-Peep

BORACHIO

Borachio is a villainous follower of King John in Shakespeare's *Much Ado About Nothing*. His name is derived from the Spanish *borracho,* a leathern wine bottle dressed with resin and pitch to keep the wine sweet, and he plays on its origin thus: "I will, like a true drunkard (*borachio*), utter all to thee." Hence, the name has become a stock literary epithet for inebriated and excessive self-indulgence.

looking villainous and swilling his wine like the original Borachio

---

BORAK, AL

Al Borak is the name of the legendary winged horse that carried Mohammed to the seventh heaven. Of incredible swiftness, at each step she took a leap as far as the longest sight could reach.

a jump as long as Al Borak's

BOREAL

Boreal, from Boreas, ruler of the north winds, consequently suggests freezing and bitter cold.

seek shelter from the Boreal blasts
gladly greet the Boreal snows

BORGIA, LUCREZIA

Lucrezia Borgia (1480-1519), Duchess of Ferrara, was the daughter of Cardinal Rodrigo Borgia (Pope Alexander VI), born in Rome of an aristocratic Spanish family. Famed for her beauty and charm, she was corrupted by the court of Rome with its intrigues and machinations and acquired the reputation of being an unusually adroit poisoner. There is no serious evidence, however, of incestuous relations between her and her father and brother, Cesare, as scandalmongers of the time charged. She established a sort of cultural salon and was patroness to such geniuses as Ariosto, Titian, Dosso Dossi and Cardinal Bembo.

dark Borgian rumors

BOSWELLIAN

Boswellian is from James Boswell (1740-1795), devoted admirer of Dr. Samuel Johnson, the greatest literary figure of the eighteenth century in England. Boswell's *Biography of Johnson,* while conspicuous for its minuteness of detail and its indiscriminate recordings of both significant and insignificant sayings and incidents, nevertheless set a pattern for biography that has never been surpassed.

recorded with Boswellian detail
every man has his Boswell

BOTTICELLI

Botticelli, an eminent Florentine painter (1447-1515), did many of the Vatican frescoes, and is specially known for the famous Botticelli angels. He emphasized beauty of form, and put into each countenance beauty of soul and character, all against a background of natural landscape. He declared himself to be a "painter of ideas."

with a Botticelli-angel grace and beauty

BOTTOM

Bottom, a crude and ordinary peasant weaver in Shakespeare's *Midsummer Night's Dream,* is so elated to find himself in a play the rustics are performing as their gesture of loyalty at their Duke's wedding festivities that he misses no chance to bring himself to the fore. In the play he wears an ass' head, in which guise, by Puck's mischievous enchantment, he is beloved of Titania, queen of the fairies, which makes him so self-important and pompous that his name now indicates persons of low birth absurdly inflated by any chance publicity.

has the glad presumption of a Bottom

BOULANGISM

Boulangism is from George S. Boulanger, who in 1886-89 advocated a French policy of militarism inspired by a desire for revenge upon Germany, a desire so strong as to name that spirit wherever it appeared thereafter.

take care not to go Boulangering about

BOUNDERBY, JOSEPH

Joseph Bounderby, a banker, merchant, and big, loud man in Dickens' *Hard Times,* is a coarse and ostentatious bully, a self-made man "perfectly devoid of sentiment."

the Joseph Bounderby of the town

BOUNTIFUL, LADY

Lady Bountiful was a generous country woman prominent in Farquahar's play, *The Beaux' Stratagem.* The name is now applied to any mistress of the manor who goes about bestowing gracious gifts and generous help wherever they are needed.

the Lady Bountiful of the village

BOURBONISTIC

Bourbonistic means United States conservatism, based upon an obstinate opposition to progress. The word is, of course, derived from the notorious French Bourbons and Bourbonism, devoting their means to established Bourbon policies, and now indicates a disposition to stand by old standards regardless of their utility.

easy to adopt a rocking-chair Bourbonism

BOVARY, EMMA

Emma Bovary is the title character of Flaubert's famous novel, *Madame Bovary.* She is the passionately romantic wife of a prosaic provincial physician. Weary of her dull life, she seeks distraction with lovers. As her indiscretions accumulate, she falls heavily into debt and discontent, from which she can free herself only by taking poison and killing herself.

bored and discontented as Emma Bovary

BOWDLERIZE

Bowdlerize is from Thomas Bowdler (1754-1825), who edited the first expurgated edition of Shakespeare. Bowdlerized is now applied to any unnecessary or ridiculous censorship or expurgation.

pedagogical Bowdlerizing, ridiculously prevailing over artistry

---

BOX and COX

Box and Cox are two characters in John Morton's farce in which Box and Cox, one a night- and one a day-worker, rent the same room, though they never see each other, and a series of comic situations arises therefrom. The term is now used of any two persons who handle the same job, surreptitiously and laughingly calling it a Box-and-Cox arrangement.

a neat, convenient, and deceptive Box-and-Cox game

BOYCOTT, CHARLES C.

Charles Cunningham Boycott (1832-1897) was a retired British army captain who became agent for the estates of absentee landlords in County Mayo, Ireland. For refusing to receive rents at figures estimated by the tenants, his life was threatened, his mail and food supply intercepted, and he became the victim of economic and social ostracism by Irish Land League agitators, a practice of "persuasion" by pressure which came to be known by his name.

ostracized like Charles Boycott

BOYTHORN, LAWRENCE

Lawrence Boythorn, in Dickens's *Bleak House,* is a handsome old man whose bark is more effective than his bite. "The very fury of his superlatives . . . seemed to go off like blank cannons and hurt nothing." A true gentleman and chivalrously polite, he has a sterling quality in his laughter. Walter Savage Landor is said to have been the author's model for this character.

fulminating expletives like Lawrence Boythorn

BRADSHAW, GEORGE

George Bradshaw (1801-1853) was an eminent English publisher of the first railway guides, which were so complete and so famous that Bradshaw is synonymous with any comprehensive and infallible travel information.

must first absorb a bit of Bradshaw
an impressive Bradshaw

BRADY, "DIAMOND JIM"

"Diamond Jim" was the sobriquet of James Buchanan Brady (1856-1917), self-made American who rose from bellboy to financier, and who made famous collections of diamonds and other jewels. His name is as familiar an appurtenance of the era of the Gay Nineties as is that of Lillian Russell, and, despite the fact that he endowed the Urological Institute named after him at Johns Hopkins, in popular memory it connotes ostentatious display and profligacy.

a gem to catch the eye of "Diamond Jim"

BRAG, JACK

Jack Brag, the hero of a novel of the same name by Theodore Hook, is a vulgar, pretentious braggart who employs art to insinuate himself into aristocratic society, where his innate vulgarity stood out in bold relief. He was accepted for a brief while because of his knowledge of the technicalities and slang of the kennel and the turf, which he thought would lead gentry to suppose him to be "to the manor born."

ostentatious as Jack Brag

BRAGI

Bragi, in Norse mythology, is the god of poetry whose songs record the deeds of warriors. The son of Odin and one of his principle skalds in Valhalla, he is married to Iduna who keeps in a box the immortalizing apples that protect the gods from growing old.

a strain of Bragian grandeur

BRAHMA

Brahma, the supreme, self-existent god of the Hindus, usually pictured as having four heads and four arms, is the creator of the universe. With Vishnu, the preserver, and Siva, the destroyer, he forms the divine trinity. Said to have visited the earth nine times and in various forms, he will again appear a tenth time in the guise of a warrior on a white steed, in order to bring retribution upon all incorrigible offenders.

the creative instinct of Brahma
Brahman retribution

BRAHMIN

Brahmin, a Hindu word, originally meant a group of persons and families of distinction who eventually became a hereditary caste. The name still has that meaning, but is sometimes loosely used of persons who seem to wish to imply themselves superior for inherent reasons.

snobbish Brahmins

BRAHMSIAN

Johannes Brahms (1833-1897) composed much choral, chamber, and symphonic music that is marked by rich, grand, solid tones, full of intensely human feeling. His work grew out of his own experiences and emotions and his particular surroundings at the time of composition.

Brahmsian majesty of tonal color

BRAMBLE, MISS TABITHA

Miss Tabitha Bramble is the prototype of the man-hunting spinster of comic Valentine cards. The sister of Matthew Bramble in Smollett's *Expedition of Humphry Clinker,* she is described as being excessively starched, vain and ridiculous, and soured by her unsuccessful labors to get herself a husband. Malicious, greedy and uncharitable, she finally inveigles Captain Lismahago into marriage because she dangles her snug fortune before him.

crabbed and dour as Miss Bramble

BRANCHIDAE

The Branchidae were a family in charge of the temple of Apollo near Miletus in Asia Minor. Accused of revealing its treasure to Xerxes, they were escorted by the Persian king to Sogdiana, where their treachery to their native town would be safe from vengeance. Generations later, however, Alexander the Great reached their sanctuary in his career of conquest of the East. He savagely destroyed their new town and massacred all its inhabitants in retaliation for their ancestors' crime.

the guilt of the Branchidae will ultimately find them out

BRAND

Brand, the hero of Ibsen's play of the same name, is an uncompromising nonconformist, a rebel against social conventions.

like Brand, at variance with society

BRASS, SAMPSON

Sampson Brass is the knavish attorney in Dickens' *Old Curiosity Shop.* Servile, dishonest and affectedly sentimental, he makes his legal clients his lawful prey. The prototype of the shyster lawyer, he conducts his business in a thoroughly tricky and crafty manner, making dupes of all who trust him.

as much a shyster as Sampson Brass

BREIDABLIK

Breidablik, in Scandinavian mythology, is the heavenly mansion of Baldur, into which nothing unclean can enter. A "wide-shining splendor," it is the land of fewest crimes.

chaste as Breidablik

BRENNUS

Brennus was the leader of the Gauls who defeated the Roman army and occupied most of the city in 390 B. C., failing however to starve out the resisters besieged on the Capitol. When the ransom gold was being weighed out by the Romans in order to liberate their city from occupation, a complaint was made to Brennus that he was using false weights. Thereupon, the Gallic chieftain threw the additional weight of his sword into the scales, tauntingly exclaiming *Vae Victis,* "Woe to the vanquished," a phrase that became ever after a reminder of Roman humiliation.

an unjustly taunting Brennus

BRIAREAN

Briarean is from Briareus, a son of Coelus (Heaven) and Terra (Earth) and a giant with a hundred arms and fifty heads. According to Hesiod, he defended Jupiter against the Titans; but other poets say that he assisted giants in their attempt to storm Mount Olympus, and was buried alive under Mount Aetna as a punishment. Briarean suggests a person superhuman in physical strength and faculties, capable of reaching or grasping in many directions at once.

a Briarean reach
of monstrous, Briarean size

BRICK, JEFFERSON

Jefferson Brick, in Dickens' *Martin Chuzzlewit,* is a fiery and noisy American journalist and politician.

blatant as Jefferson Brick

BRIDLEGOOSE, JUDGE

Judge Bridlegoose (*Bridoie*) is the ignorant arbiter in Rabelais' *Gargantua and Pantagruel.* He makes his legal decisions and decides all cases at law by means of resorting to a throw of a dice-cup.

making his decisions by chance, like judge Bridlegoose

BRIGID OF KILDARE

Brigid of Kildare (453-523), as St. Bridget, the patroness of Ireland, was of such extraordinary piety in her youth that the king of Ulster freed her from the control of her father, a prince of Ulster. Of the four monasteries founded by her, that of Kildare is famous for the "Fire of St. Bridget," which was inextinguishable, for the nuns never allowed it to go out. Every twentieth night St. Bridget returned to tend this fire personally. She is commemorated by a feast-day on the 1st of February.

faithful as Brigid of Kildare

BRILLAT-SAVARIN, ANTHELME

Anthelme Brillat-Savarin (1755-1826) was a French politician and writer who is better known for his gastronomic talents. A member of the National Assembly, he fled to Switzerland to escape proscription during the Terror. In 1793 he sought securer safety in the United States, where he supported himself by playing in the orchestra of a New York City theatre. After the fall of Robespierre he returned to France (1796) and became a judge on the Court of Cassation during the Consulate. Though he was the author of several books on political economy and law, his fame today rests on his *Physiologie du Gout* ("Physiology of the Sense of Taste"), a treatise on the art of dining. A literary guide-book for gourmets, it has appeared in numerous editions. The name of Brillat-Savarin is also immortalized in the existence of a chain of Savarin Restaurants, such as the one located in

New York's Pennsylvania Station, and by various food products named after him, *e.g.*, Savarin Coffee.

a bill-of-fare approved by Brillat-Savarin

BRISEIS

Briseis, the daughter of Briseus, a priest at Lyrnessus, is the war-prize and concubine of Achilles in the *Iliad*. Against her will, she is forced from him by Agamemnon, when he is compelled to give up his own concubine, Chryseis. This so enrages Achilles that he refuses to go into battle, but remains sulking in his tent until his friend Patroclus is slain by Hector.

controversial as Briseis

BRISINGAMEN

Brisingamen was the name of the famous necklace of the goddess Freya, who left her husband Odin to obtain it from the fairies. Odin consequently deserted her because her love was changed into vanity. Symbolically interpreted, Freya typifies the beauty of the year, and the necklace signifies the rich flowers and tints of autumn, which Freya puts on. Odin's leaving her represents the passing of the fertility of the genial year, when winter is at hand. The necklace was later stolen by Loki, the personification of sin.

as fond of her jewelry as Freya was of Brisingamen

BRITOMARTIS

Britomartis ("sweet maid") was a Cretan fertility goddess identified with the Greek Artemis, because she was fond of the chase, and also named Dictynna. The latter name, from a Greek word for a "fish net," may allude to the legend of her falling over a cliff and landing safely in some fishermen's nets, when she was eluding the amorous pursuit of Minos. Another version has it that she escaped the king's pursuit only by fleeing to Aegina. In Spenser's *Faerie Queene*, Britomart is a "lady knight," represented as being armed with a magic spear which nothing could resist. She is the personification of virginal purity of heart and mind.

chaste as Britomartis

BROBDINGNAGIAN

Brobdingnagians were a people in a region described in Swift's *Gulliver's Travels* as a land inhabited by persons of enormous size. There everything else was on the same proportionate scale, and the whole was a satire on the follies of man. The inhabitants of Brobdingnag were represented as giants, about "as tall as an ordinary spire-steeple."

our faults enlarged as in a Brobdingnagian mirror

BROMIUS

Bromius, signifying "noisy, boisterous," is one of the many names of Bacchus (Dionysus), this one alluding to the din attendant on wine-bibbing activities. Hence, a *Bromian drink* is wine, and *Bromian* (from the Greek verb to "roar") as an adjective connotes riotous merrymaking.

Bromian confusion in the tavern

BRONTE, EMILY

Emily Brontë (1818-1848) was the sister of Charlotte Brontë, and wrote *Wuthering Heights*, which holds its place among the powerful novels of the world. It is marked by emotional intensity, a certain gloom of spirit and background, and a struggle of the human soul torn by hatred and revenge. Bitterness, struggle, and melancholy are the chief elements she represents.

with Brontesque revenge

BRONTES

Brontēs ("thunder") was the name of one of the three Cyclopes, his brothers being Steropes and Arges. These one-eyed giants were the blacksmiths of antiquity, forging Zeus's thunderbolts in the crater of volcanic Mount Aetna in Sicily. They were said to have been the monstrous offspring of Uranus (Heaven) and Ge (Earth).

noisy as Brontēs at his forge

BRONTESQUE

Brontesque is from Charlotte Brontë, (1816-1855), whose novels were marked by keen perception and delineation of character, passionate knowledge of life, powerful and vigorous expression, and a singular felicity with words. Both Hugh Walpole and Mrs. Gaskell pay high tribute to her unusual power, and her *Jane Eyre* is one of the great novels of English literature, powerful even in its gloomy and tragic atmosphere. Her sisters, Anne and Emily, were likewise novelists, the latter being the author of *Wuthering Heights*. All three wrote under the pseudonym of Bell.

the inevitable Brontesque gloom

BROWN, JOHN

John Brown, originally from Connecticut, migrated to Ohio, then to Kansas. There espousing the anti-slavery cause, with other believers he drove out of Kansas a pro-slavery party ten times their own number. From Canada, later, he secretly organized a party to invade Virginia and personally free the slaves, intending to incite a servile rebellion. In 1859, with twenty men, he surprised Harper's Ferry, captured forty men, and seized the arsenal and the army. The Virginia Militia attacked, wounded and killed Brown, but reported themselves "amazed at his courage and his sayings." His spirit is immortalized in the song "John Brown's body lies a-moldering in the grave," and in Stephen Vincent Benet's book, *John Brown's Body*.

BROWNE, SAM

A Sam Browne is from Samuel J. Browne (1850-?), an intrepid and gallant colonel with the British army in India, but ironically remembered chiefly for his invention of a military belt, originally worn by officers only, and marked by a supporting piece worn over the shoulder.

correct Sam-Browne attire

BROWNING, ROBERT

Robert Browning (1812-1889), one of the six great English poets (Chaucer, Spenser, Shakespeare, Milton, Browning, Tennyson), struck out and away from the usual conventional and regular form and subject of verse, rhyme, and stanza to establish a natural expression of his own. Vigorous, independent, dramatic in style, his verse can best be read as if it were talk, talk that is energetic, interesting, varied, sometimes dramatic, sometimes confidential, sometimes tender. Friendly, approachable, alertly curious about "whate'er he looks upon, and his looks go everywhere," occasionally humorous, he is the companion walking beside his reader, thinking aloud.

the Browning vitality

BROWNLOW, MR.

Mr. Brownlow, in Dickens' *Oliver Twist*, is the benevolent old gentleman who befriends the title-character.

kindly as Mr. Brownlow

BRUCE, ROBERT

Robert Bruce (1274-1329), king of Scotland, is particularly remembered by the story of his moment of discouragement, when he saw a spider try and try again, over and over, to fasten a thread of its web, until at last it succeeded, whereupon Bruce sprang up and went to the attack once more, and that time was successful. Since that time it is said that no one named Bruce ever injures a spider.

a Robert-Bruce perseverance

BRUMMAGEM

Brummagem is a corruption of the name of the English city of Birmingham, a great mart and manufacturing center of gilt toys, cheap jewelry, imitation gems, mosaic-gold and such tawdry fineries. The word thus connotes, through derivation from the Latin name for the city, "Bremenium," any worthless or inferior imitation.

collects gaudy brummagem from Woolworth's

BRUMMEL, BEAU

George Byan Brummel (1778-1840) was the "glass of fashion and the mold of form" in London, when he was a favorite and a companion of the Prince of Wales. He had, consequently, unlimited credit and influence, and free passage anywhere in the *beau monde.* When, however, he was no longer in favor, his creditors descended, his world frowned upon him, and he died practically of starvation, attended only by a faithful old servitor, but still proud, pathetically gallant, and in his last delirium happy in the illusion that the Prince had come to see him. It is this story that was perfectly and effectively presented by Richard Mansfield in the play *Beau Brummel.*

his is a kind of Beau-Brummel history

BRUNHILDE

Brunhilde, one of the young and stalwart Valkyries, beautiful and the favorite of her father Wotan, is one of the most dramatic figures in the story of the Nibelungen Ring, as Wagner interprets it in his operas. Devoted to her father, Brunhilde only once disobeyed him, acting in what she thought was his interest, a disobedience Wotan never forgave. She later immolated herself on Siegfried's funeral pyre. Strong, young, steadfast, she is one of the most heroic and dramatic of the women in Wagner's operas.

with Brunhildean magnificence
with Brunhildean wrath

BRUTUS

Junius Brutus is known in history as a liberator, and in Shakespeare's *Julius Caesar* as an honest patriot who placed his love of country, and a resolve to maintain it as a republic, before his personal affection for Julius Caesar. To that end he lent himself to the assassination of Caesar that was plotted by less noble and envious conspirators.

many a Brutus gave his life

BRYCE, LORD

James Bryce (1832-1922) was a British jurist, historian, diplomat and statesman, created Viscount of Dechmont in 1914. His reputation as an historian was already established by his *Holy Roman Empire* when he came to the United States as British ambassador from 1907 to 1913. An ardent Liberal, he wrote his great work, *The American Commonwealth,* in examination of the political institutions of this country from the point of view of an historian and a constitutional lawyer. This definitive study has since been considered a classic in its field.

with shrewd Brycean analysis

BUCHEPHALUS

Bucephalus ("bull-head") was the name of the celebrated war-horse of Alexander the Great. When it was offered for sale to Philip, his father, it was so wild and unmanageable that he refused to buy it for himself. Alexander, noting that it shied at its own shadow, turned its head to the sun, caressed it and mounted it successfully. Plutarch says that Philip then predicted, "O son, thou must needs have a realm that is meet for thee, for Macedon will not hold thee." A strong mutual affection bound Alexander and Bucephalus, which carried its master in his eastern campaigns. When the horse died in India at the age of thirty, Alexander founded the city of Bucephala in its honor.

he and his Bucephalus may be seen any stormy day, when there is no work to keep them at home.

BUDDHA

Buddha is a being who, according to the Ceylonese Buddhists, through many transmigrations came to have unlimited knowledge and unlimited wisdom. The many legends concerning the first Buddha surpass all other legends in utter extravagance. One tells that an Evil Power that came to test Buddha rode on an elephant one hundred fifty miles high, and threw at him immeasurable mountains that turned to wreaths of flowers as they struck him. The true Buddha points his followers the way to Nirvana, the ultimate end of existence. Buddhists believe in a continued existence of being under different forms, in the accumulation of merit, and in Nirvana, the cessation of a distinct and separate existence. More than one-third of the human race, according to an authority, are followers of Buddha.

passive as a bronze Buddha

BUFFALO BILL

Buffalo Bill (William F. Cody, 1846-1917) was an American scout, Indian fighter, and showman known as a "medicine man" in the early days of America.

the stage of Buffalo Bill tactics

BULL, JOHN

John Bull is the personification of England, as Uncle Sam is of the United States. John Bull is bluff, portly, kindhearted, good-natured. But perspicacious and not too readily credulous, he expects credentials. Washington Irving, an ambassador to England, characterizes John Bull in an essay by that name in his English *Sketch Book,* though this collective name for the English nation was first used in Arbuthnot's satire, *The History of John Bull,* in which the French are also satirized as *Lewis Baboon* and the Dutch as *Nicholas Frog.*

John Bull pertinacity

BULWER-LYTTON

Bulwer-Lytton (1831-1891), novelist and dramatist, wrote many novels and plays, always with historical accuracy and dramatic intensity. His play *Richelieu,* perfectly interpreted by Sir Henry Irving, is universally known and frequently revived, always with great acclaim. *Rienzi* and *The Last Days of Pompeii* are novels with the same powerful interest. Brilliant, gifted, scholarly, his work holds its own today among the great works of the world.

with the permanency of a Bulwer-Lytton novel

BUMBLEDONIAN

Bumbledonian is from Mr. Bumble, an inefficient, pompous, blundering beadle in Dickens' *Oliver Twist,* satirizing the unintelligent, self-serving, self-satisfied officialdom of English welfare institutions in Dickens' century. The word hence means stupid, inefficient, placid, indifferent, the lowest type of bureaucracy.

a Bumbledonian scandal.
waited on by an unctuous Mr. Bumble
threatens to become a first-class Bumbledom

BUNCLE, JOHN

John Buncle, "a prodigious hand at matrimony, divinity, a song, and a peck" is the title character in *The Life and Opinions of John Buncle, Esq.* by Thomas Amory. He marries seven wives, loses all in the flower of their age, is inconsolably bereft for two or three days, then resigns himself to the decrees of Providence, and marries again. A kind of innocent Henry VIII, he is said to be the representative of his author, an eccentric person of whose history little is known.

a much-married John Buncle

BUNCOMBE

Buncombe is the county in North Carolina mentioned in a Congressional representative's phrase "talking for Buncombe." In current usage the word has come to mean insincerity of speech, palaver to please political constituents or anybody else. It is indulged in with the aim of gaining applause or even deceiving, and so connotes specious show and nonsense.

he must be talking for Buncombe

BUNYAN, JOHN

John Bunyan (1628-1688), a thinker converted to Christianity by an itinerant preacher, began preaching himself, but fell afoul of the law that forbade any preaching except that of the established church and was thrown into prison for twelve years. In prison he wrote *Pilgrim's Progress,* in which Christian sets out on the road to the Celestial City. His effort, often discouraging, always difficult, but eventually rewarding, is actually the story of Bunyan's own life "woven in tapestry." Told in simple language with simple Biblical dignity, it is a classic for all the ages so long as souls struggle each toward its own salvation.

in a Bunyan cloud of golden dream
a John Bunyan simplicity

BURBANK, LUTHER

Luther Burbank (1849-1926), famous American naturalist, is known for his brilliant achievement in combining and improving plants and animals by selective breeding. His purpose was to perpetuate the good features and eliminate all undesirable features by combining, crossing, grafting—a purpose in which he was so successful that his name has become a verb expressing that kind of endeavor.

engaged in burbanking his corn
a Burbank triumph

BURIDAN'S ASS

Buridan's Ass is a name used to describe a man of indecision, like one "on double business bound, who stands in pause where he should first begin, and both neglects." The origin of the phrase is to be found in an expression of John Buridan, thirteenth century French philosopher, who phrased this paradox: "If a hungry ass were placed exactly between two measures of oats in every respect equal, it would starve to death, because it would be unable to decide to which to go in order to satisfy its hunger."

indecisive as Buridan's ass

BURKE, EDMUND

Edmund Burke (1729-1797), Irish statesman, orator and writer, championed the cause of the American colonies in the tense times prior to their severance from England. A member of The Club, a literary circle presided over by Dr. Samuel Johnson, he was a master of English prose in the grand manner. His speeches are rich in imagery and poetic cadences and make full use of rhetorical ornamentation. In the protracted case against Warren Hastings for maladministration of India (1786-1794), he managed the prosecution. Though liberal in his attitude toward America, he disapproved of the French Revolution, seeing in it an attack on the settled institutions of society (*Reflections on the French Revolution*).

Burkean sonority of language

BURKE, WILLIAM

William Burke (1792-1829) was an Irish laborer who suffocated and murdered fifteen victims in order to sell their cadavers to surgeons. With William Hare as his accomplice, he centered his activities in Edinburgh until, apprehended and convicted by Hare's having turned King's evidence, he was hanged on January 29, 1829. His infamous name has supplied the English language with the verb *burke*, meaning to "smother by suffocation" and to "suppress," as a question or a publication. A *burker* is a body-snatcher.

ghoulish as William Burke

BURNE-JONESIAN

Burne-Jonesian is from Sir Edward Burne-Jones (1833-1898), an English artist of the Pre-Raphaelite school, whose painting of figures is marked by tall, graceful, lyric movement, deep wide-set eyes, a delicately molded rather long face with a full chin—a spiritual, yet sensuous kind of beauty.

the perfect Burne-Jonesian
a Burne-Jonesian grace

BURNS, ROBERT

Robert Burns (1759-1796), the handsome, gifted, brilliant Scotch plowboy, is among the most lyrical of all English poets. With a natural gift for song, Burns recorded in a melody never surpassed the natural scenery of Scotland, her rivers, streams, and bird-song. He loved her people, their fun and frolic and their feelings and their tenderness and goodness, and poured it all forth in a stream of song. To the youthful freshness of his songs he added a fiercely passionate protest against hypocrisy and caste, and eventually a plea for and a prophecy of democracy, when

"... man to man, the warl' o'er
Shall brothers be for a' that ..."

with the spontaneity of a Burns

BURROUGHS, JOHN

John Burroughs (1837-1921) was a distinguished American naturalist and writer of popular essays on nature, among them *Ways of Nature, Bird and Bough, Locusts and Wild Honey*, and *Field and Study*. A friend of Walt Whitman, to whom he dedicated a volume of analytical notes on the character and work of the great poet, he lived in Thorelian Walden-Pond (*q.v.*) seclusion in a cabin named "Slabsides" in the New York hills.

like John Burroughs, retiring in nature

BUSIRUS

Busirus was an Egyptian king who habitually sacrificed any stranger to feed his horses, and finally seized Hercules, who broke his chains and killed the monstrous king.

made a Busirian mistake when he tackled Jimmy
a Busirus trick

BUZFUZ, SARGEANT

Sargeant Buzfuz, in Dickens' *Pickwick Papers*, a pompous, hectoring self-important, and fussy lawyer, is Mrs. Bardell's counsel in her suit for breach-of-promise against Mr. Pickwick.

under the cross-fire of a Sargeant Buzfuz

BYBLIS

Byblis, the daughter of Miletus and Idothea, conceived a frantic passion for her brother Caunus, whom she pursued hopelessly through several lands. Frustrated in her amorous intentions and exhausted with sorrow, she wept herself into a fountain because denied her incestuous desire.

lachrymose as Byblis

BYRONIC

Byronic is from Lord Byron (1788-1824), the English poet noted for his tempestuous, bold, alternately gay and reckless spirit and style, and his morbid and melancholy passions, as well as for brilliant and powerful poetry. *Byronic* has a multitude of meanings because of Byron's multifarious moods; the word practically takes its meaning from its context, as emotional, dramatic, melancholy, bitter, tempestuous, reckless, brilliant.

like Byron's tempest-anger, tempest-mirth
trying to pump up Byronic emotion
peculiarly Byronic air

BYZANTINE

Byzantine generally indicates the elaborately decorated style of Byzantium, the capital city of the Eastern Empire, notable for its art, literature, and especially for its architecture, marked by the round arch, cross, circle, and dome, ingeniously combined.

with Byzantian regulation of architecture
Byzantine magnificence

C

CABIRIC

Cabiric is from the Cabiri, gods ot fertility worshiped in Asia Minor, at Samothrace, and in Boeotia. Also protectors from dangers, especially those of the sea, they were of Oriental origin and their mysteries were solemnized with great magnificence. They were connected with fire as well as with the forces of creative life, and were called "sons of Vulcan" because of their mastership of metal-work.

splendid Cabiric metal-work

CACUS

Cacus was a monster and brigand who lived in a cave on Rome's Aventine hill. He stole some of the cattle of the Spanish giant Geryon from Hercules, as that hero was resting by his hill on his way back to Greece. Cleverly driving them into his cave tail-foremost, he escaped immediate discovery for his theft, but the lowing of the rest of the cattle was answered by those in the cave. His deceit detected, he was attacked and slain by Hercules. Cacus was probably an ancient Roman fire-god.

a clever ruse, worthy of Cacus

CADEAN

Cadean refers to the insurrection of Jack Cade, an Irish peasant who headed 20,000 armed men in 1450, in order to "procure redress of grievances," and was killed while resisting arrest. Introduced into Shakespeare's *King Henry VI,* his name has since been used in the phrase *Jack Cade legislation,* as meaning pressure from without.

Cadean tactics to right wrongs

CADMEAN

Cadmean is from Cadmus, the Phoenician who founded Thebes on a spot to which he was guided by Athena, goddess of wisdom. There he killed a dragon and sowed the dragon's teeth that sprang out of the ground as fully armed men who fell to fighting each other until there were only five left. These, with Cadmus, founded the city of Thebes. The term *Cadmean victory* springs from the story of the men's destruction of each other, and means a victory in which the victor suffers as much as the vanquished. Cadmus is also credited with having brought the first alphabet to Greece.

costly as a Cadmean victory

blessed be Cadmus, or whoever first invented books

Misfortunes are like the creations of Cadmus, they destroy one another.—Bulwer-Lytton

the Cadmuses who sowed the teeth of letters

with Cadmean malice sow the dragon's teeth

CADUCEAN

Caducean, as in Keats' phrase *caducean charm,* is from caduceus, the wand carried by Hermes (Mercury) as messenger and herald of the gods. Surmounted by wings and with two serpents entwined about it, it became the symbol of eloquence and of office, and was also used by Hermes to give sleep to whomever he chose and to conduct, as psychopomp, the souls of the dead to the lower world. Since Asclepius, the god of healing, is represented in classical art as also holding a staff entwined with a serpent, the caduceus was adopted by the United

States Army Medical Corps and by medicos in general as the emblem of their profession.

caducean powers of communication

CAESAREAN (1)

Caesarean is the name of the operation of delivering a child by surgery, rather than by the natural process of birth, and it is so called because of the legend that Julius Caesar was delivered in this fashion.

CAESAREAN (2)

Caesarean, from Julius Caesar (100-44 B. C.), called "the greatest general and the greatest man that ever lived," suggests that he was at once aggressive, powerful, and discreet in domestic as well as in foreign affairs. Bold but not reckless, crafty but not dishonest, he thought things through to the end before undertaking them, in a career that made him master of the world on a most magnificent scale.

Caesarean grandeur
Caesarean magnificence

CAGLIOSTRO

Cagliostro was the assumed name of Giuseppe Balsamo (1743-1795), one of the most impudent and successful impostors of all time. The subject of Dumas' *Joseph Balsamo* and of works by Schiller and Goethe, he was a supposed magician who promised everlasting youth to all who would pay for his secret. A fraudulent professor of medicine, he was imprisoned in the Bastille for complicity in the notorious Affair of the Diamond Necklace, which was purchased by Cardinal Rohan for Marie Antoinette at the instigation of the Countess de la Motte, to whom it was delivered but from whose hands it also vanished (1785-1786). Subsequently condemned to death by the Inquisition at Rome, his sentence was commuted, though he died in prison at the Chateau of St. Leo for a later adventure.

a Cagliostro adept at charlatanism

CAIAPHAS

Caiaphas was the high-priest who sought the death of Jesus and presided at the session of the Sanhedrin at which His arrest was planned (*Matthew*, xxvi, 3). As head of the nation, he had to deliver Him to Pilate with the execution request. He was well known for his capacity for intrigue.

intriguing as Caiaphas, seeking a conviction

CAIN

Cain, the first son of Adam, killed his brother Abel; hence his name stands for hate and murder, a meaning preserved in the phrase "the brand of Cain."

a fratricidal Cain

CALANDRINO

Calandrino is a name typifying a simpleton and is first found in a story in Boccaccio's *Decameron* (Day 8, Tale 9). His mishaps and misfortunes were described by Macaulay as having "made all Europe merry for more than four centuries." Literally born to be fooled and hoodwinked, his name has become synonymous with any type of gullible credulity which prods its victim into ridiculous misadventures.

unhappily gullible as Calandrino

CALCHAS

Calchas was the famous Greek soothsayer who recommended that Agamemnon sacrifice his daughter Iphigenia to Artemis, when the Greek fleet bound for Troy was becalmed at Aulis. Later at Troy he advised the Greeks in all their difficulties. He died of grief when he met Mopsus, a soothsayer superior to himself, who predicted things he himself did not know.

a Calchas bent on sacrifice
a Calchan prediction

CALEB

Caleb was the Israelite leader who was one of a party of twelve sent out to spy in the Land of Canaan (*Numbers,* xiii, 6). He later took part in its conquest and became one of the commissioners authorized by Moses to distribute its land.

as viligant as Caleb

CALIBAN

Caliban is a character in Shakespeare's *The Tempest,* servant to Prospero, a savage, low and deformed slave, unreasoning, unmoral, malignant and envious, brooding and baleful; hence, the name suggests malignant, unreasoning, base, gross.

that most dangerous thing, a Caliban with a mind

CALIDORE

Calidore is the knight who is a prototype of courtesy in Book Six of Spenser's *Faerie Queene.* Intended as a portrait of Sir Philip Sidney and the most courteous of all knights, he is called the "all-beloved." It is he who muzzles and chains the Blatant Beast, a portrayal of Scandal or Rumor having 100 tongues and a poisonous sting, and drags it off to Faerie Land.

with Calidorean courtesy

CALIGULA

Caligula is a nickname of Caius Caesar, a Roman Emperor (37-41 A. D.), who went insane a few months after he assumed the throne and subjected Rome to four years of insane decrees. He was literally crazy about sports, and ordered spectators to be seized indiscriminately and thrown to the beasts; he proposed to make his horse consul. Finally he so insulted the praetorian guards that they killed him. The term "a Caligula" implies the crazy use of an absolute power, the ultimate in insane cruelty.

one Caligula is all the history of the world could support

CALLIMACHUS

Callimachus (born c. 310 B. C.) was a learned critic and poet who was connected with the great library at Alexandria as a bibliographer. He also wrote hymns to the gods and was a famous epigrammatist, composing expressions of personal emotion and sketches of lovers' troubles. His most famous works were *The Lock of Berenice* and the *Aitia,* a poetic explanation of the origins of local religious traditions. His is the proverbial saying "A big book is a big nuisance," which he uttered in defense of his own preference for short writings.

critical as Callimachus

CALLIOPE

(see *Muse*)

Calliope was the Muse of epic and heroic poetry, and was represented in ancient works of art as carrying waxen tablets and a stylus for writing. She was also the mother of the minstrels Orpheus and Linus. Her name has been given to the steam-whistle musical instrument that is a feature of American circuses.

a pompous Calliopean outburst

CALLIPOLIS

Callipolis is the wife of Muly Mahamet in *The Battle of the Alcazar* (1594) by George Peele. She is also referred to in Shakespeare's 2 *Henry IV.* Sir Walter Scott uses the name repeatedly as a synonym for lady-love, sweetheart, and charmer. In *Kenil-*

worth he calls her "most fair Callipolis . . . divine duchess of dark corners." In *The Abbott* a modest character, Roland Graeme, calls the beautiful Catherine his "most fair Callipolis," and elsewhere the author says, "Hark ye, most fair Callipolis . . . if thou takest all that trouble of skewering thyself together, like a trussed fowl, that there may be more pleasure in the carving, even save thyself the labor."

a new Callipolis to charm him

CALLIRRHOE

Callirrhoë, the daughter of the river-god Achelous and wife of Alcmaeon, inadvertently caused the death of her husband by requesting that he retrieve Harmonia's necklace from his first wife and give it to her. For this he was killed by his first wife's brothers. Another Callirrhoë is the lady-love of Chaereas in Chariton's pastoral Greek romance, *The Loves of Chaereas and Callirrhoë.* The name is also applied to the most celebrated well in Athens because of its meaning "fair-flowing," and it has always carried a romantic connotation.

fair as Callirrhoë

CALLISTO

Callisto was a nymph in the retinue of Artemis (Diana), goddess of the chase and of chastity. Ravished by Jupiter, she bore him a son, Arcas, the legendary ancestor of the Arcadians. In punishment she was changed into a she-bear by Artemis or the jealous Hera (Juno), and in that guise roamed about the forests until, unrecognized, she met her now matured son out hunting. He would have killed her had not Jupiter changed them both into constellations, Callisto into Ursa Major (the Great Bear) and her son into Arctophylax.

punished by heaven, like Callisto

CALPURNIA

Calpurnia, the wife of Caesar, pleaded with Caesar not to go to the Senate House on the morning of the Ides of March, the day against which Caesar had been warned by the soothsayers as marked with doom for him. The story of her affectionate pleading and her solicitude is retold in Shakespeare's *Julius Caesar,* which adds to the soothsayers' warning a dream Calpurnia had, suggesting that evil would befall her husband if he ventured forth on that day.

touching Calpurnian plea

CALVARY

Calvary is the hill where Christ suffered the agony of despair and of crucifixion; hence *Calvary* is now sometimes used to indicate the supreme anguish of any human spirit in the hour of suffering what seems to be a final crisis.

every soul has had its Calvary

CALVINISTIC

Calvinistic refers to John Calvin (1509-1564), the great Protestant reformer who departed from the teachings of the Roman Church and preached the new doctrines of predestination, irresistible grace, total depravity, particular redemption and final perseverance of the saints. He faced persecution, danger, and exile, but in Geneva established a large group of believers. He was finally, after a period of exile, recalled to Geneva, where it is said that today, after hundreds of years, the influence of his sound morality, learning, and religion is still felt.

with Calvinistic fervor

CALYPSO

Calypso was the sea-nymph who detained Odysseus (Ulysses) for seven years on the island of Ogygia. She loved the hero and promised him immortality if he would remain with her, but, as he longed more for his wife Penelope and his home at Ithaca, he refused to stay with her. The gods forced her to consent to his going. Her name suggests a beautiful seductress. It has also lent itself to a style of musical composition, a *Calypso-song,* a lyrical style of West Indian Negro origin, influenced by jazz. Often improvised and monotonously droning, its words are frequently based on some topical news event.

Calypsonian seductions
amorous and beautiful as Calypso

CAMACHO

Camacho, the "richest of men" in Cervantes' *Don Quixote,* gets cheated out of his bride Quiteria, "fairest of women," after having made elaborate wedding preparations. Basilius pretends to kill himself and Quiteria is given to him in marriage as a matter of form, since he is supposed to be dying. Basilius then jumps up and shows that his wounds were a mere pretense, but Camacho has already been irretrievably duped.

an easy Camacho to dupe

CAMBYSES

Cambyses, king of Persia (529-522 B. C.), conquered Egypt and treated the people with great cruelty, insulting their religion and killing their god Apis with his own hands. Tyrannical toward his own people and family, he even killed his own brother, Smerdis, for suspected designs on the throne.

Another Cambyses is a pompous, ranting character in Thomas Preston's *A Lamentable Tragedy.* He is known to modern readers by Falstaff's allusions to him in Shakespeare's 1 *Henry VI*: "I must speak in passion, and I will do it in King Cambyses' vein."

tyrannical as Cambyses

CAMENAE

The Camenae ("foretellers") were originally water-nymphs in old Italian religion. Their sacred spring was outside the Porta Capena at Rome and was dedicated by King Numa. From it the Vestals drew the water for their rites. Because of their gift of prophecy and inspiration they were later identified with the Greek Muses.

inspired at the Camenae's spring

CAMILLA

Camilla was a virgin princess of the Volscians in ancient Italy, famous for her fleetness of foot, her grace, and her ability in war. A huntress, she was also a devotee of Diana. She assisted Turnus in his war against Aeneas, exhibiting undaunted bravery. After slaying many Trojan followers of Aeneas, she was herself killed by Arruns. Dr. Samuel Johnson called her "the first female warrior."

when swift Camilla scours the plain
with Camillan belligerence
the fleetness of a Camilla

CAMILLE

Camille, the heroine of the younger Dumas' *La Dame aux Camélias,* is a well-known courtesan, Marguérite Valéry by name, who is redeemed from a life of sin by her love for Armand Duval. Dumas' novel and subsequent play about her was made the basis of the libretto of Verdi's *La Traviata* (*q. v.*)

another wayward Camille, reclaimed by love

CAMILLUS, MARCUS FURIUS

Marcus Furius Camillus was a great Roman general of the fourth century B. C. The conqueror of Veii, one of Rome's early rivals, he was subsequently exiled on a charge of misappropriating booty from the plunder of that city. Recalled in the crisis of the

Gallic invasion of Rome by Brennus and his hordes, he drove out the enemy. Five times he was created Dictator in moments of national emergency. Plutarch has left an absorbing biography of this energetic patriot.

unconquerable as Camillus

CAMPASPE

Campaspe was the Greek courtesan who became the favorite concubine of Alexander the Great. She is also said to have been the model for the famous painting of Venus Anadyomene (rising from the sea) by Apelles (*q. v.*). *Alexander and Campaspe* is the subject of a play by John Lyly.

beauteous as Campaspe

CAMPUS MARTIUS

The Campus Martius was an open space to the northwest of ancient Rome and was used as a training and exercise ground for early Roman armies. Dedicated to Mars (whence its name, "Mars Field"), it was also the place of assemblage of citizens for the purpose of voting. In 220 B. C. the censor C. Flaminius erected in it the Circus that bore his name. Inasmuch as its spacious plain was available for all types of games and sports, including equestrian drills, the name Campus Martius connoted any field of action.

as proud of their local green as if it were the Campus Martius

---

CANACE

Canace, the daughter of Aeolus, is the Greek mythological maiden who was passionately enamored of her brother Macareus. She committed incest with him and bore him a daughter Isse. When her father discovered the illicit affair, he forced Canace to kill herself.

Another Canace in Chaucer's *Squire's Tale* and Spenser's *Faerie Queene* is courted by a number of suitors, but her brothers Cambalo and Algarsife would not yield her in marriage to anyone who could not overthrow them in combat. Whence the phrase *Algarsife and Canace strife* (as suggested by Milton's *Penseroso*) connotes controversial rivalry in competition.

a brother-complex like Canace's
as disputed over as Canace

CANDAULES

Candaules was the last Heraclid king of Lydia (7th century B. C.) who exposed his wife unclad to Gyges, his officer, in order to show her matchless beauty of form. Insulted and shamed, the queen induced Gyges, who had been inflamed by her charms, to murder Candaules, marry her and usurp the throne.

uxorious as Candaules bragging of the beauty of his wife

CANDIDA

Candida, the title-character of a play by Shaw (1897), is a rationalistic woman who chooses as husband a man who needs her rather than a poet who loves her.

the resolute decision of a Candida

CANDIDE

Candide, the hero of Voltaire's *Candide,* bears all sorts of misfortunes, discouragements, untoward events, and insults with a cynical and philosophical indifference in a satirical burlesque of optimism. The book represents the height of Voltaire's satirizing powers.

has endurance, but is no Candide

CANDOUR, MRS.

Mrs. Candour is a noted slanderer and backbiter who poses at being a trustworthy friend in Sheridan's *School for Scandal.* Thomas Moore said of her, "The name of 'Mrs. Candour' has become one of those formidable by-words which have more power in putting folly and ill-nature out of countenance than whole volumes of the wisest remonstrance and reasoning."

as reliable as Mrs. Candour

CANEPHOROE

The Canephoroe ("Basket-bearers") were maidens of noble Athenian families selected to carry on their heads at the festival of the Panathenaea the baskets that contained sacred implements. Their graceful attitude and superb poise and sense of balance, as depicted on the Parthenon frieze, have made them a favorite subject to sculptors and other artists. Figures representing them were sometimes used as Caryatids (*q.v.*) for architectural support of the entablature of a temple and other roofing structure.

beautifully poised as a Canephora

CANUTE

Canute was king of the Danes when they overran Britain in the eleventh century, and king of Denmark and Norway, the most powerful monarch of his time. His reign was marked by prudence, diplomacy (he married the widow of the Saxon Ethelred), and by an almost monastic piety and reverence. It was to rebuke the flatterers who called him "all-powerful" that he ordered his chair set on the seashore and commanded the incoming tide to retire. The waves continued to rush in, giving point to his sermon that one Being and one alone is really all-powerful.

the sermon of a Canute
the force of a Canute preachment

CAPANEUS

Capaneus was a Greek chieftain who was one of the famous Seven against Thebes (*q. v.*). Because he had dared to defy Zeus, he was struck by lightning for his blasphemous impiety as he was scaling the walls of the beleagured city. His wife, Evadne, threw herself on his flaming body, as though on his funeral pyre, to die with him.

blasphemous as Capaneus

CAPITOLINE

Capitoline refers to the venerable hill overlooking the Roman Forum. On its summit was the great temple of Jupiter Optimus Maximus, the tutelary guardian of the city, and his wife and daughter, Juno and Minerva. Magistrates sacrificed there when taking office, as did generals celebrating a triumph. On the northeast summit was the *arx* or citadel, the stronghold of the ancient city. The name of the hill, Capitolium, was said to have been due to the fact that a human head (*caput*) was found there while builders were digging the foundations for the temple. Today the name connotes imperial majesty, power and splendor, as associated with the mature period of Rome's primacy.

with Capitoline splendor and magnificence

CAPITOLINUS, MANLIUS

Marcus Manlius Capitolinus was the heroic Roman who successfully repulsed a night attack by the Gauls on the *arx,* or citadel of the Capitoline hill, in 390 B. C. Brennus and his Gallic hordes had occupied all of the city except for the citadel, which they would have captured had not Capitolinus been awakened by the agitated cries of some geese enclosed in it with the besieged. Thereafter the feeding of the sacred geese became a devoir of the Roman State, and a goose was ostentatiously arrayed and carried in annual procession. Later Manlius Capitolinus intervened on behalf of the debt-burdened poorer citizens of

Rome, was accused of aiming to make himself tyrant and hurled from the Tarpeian Rock (*q. v.*).

a Manlius to befriend the poor

CAPUA

Capua was the chief city of Campania in antiquity, famous for its wealth and luxury. After the battle of Cannae (216 B. C.) it defected from its allegiance to Rome and went over to Hannibal. Captured after a lengthy siege, it was severely punished by Rome as an object lesson to the capital's other allies. Its senators and leading citizens were beheaded, the others exiled, and its territory became the property of the Roman State.

Capuan luxury and fickleness

CAPULET

Capulet, the father of Juliet in Shakespeare's *Romeo and Juliet,* is represented as the head of one of the two families at feud in the play. He was so coarse, irascible, and, withal, jovial, that the name is now used to suggest those qualities.

the Capulets of the world are always making trouble

CARABAS, MARQUIS OF

The Marquis of Carabas, a character in Perrault's *Puss in Boots,* is a stuffy nobleman of boundless pretensions and vanity, wanting to restore the slavish foolery of the reign of Louis XIV. The name is now used as a title to designate a man who possesses or boasts of possessing large estates like a feudal lord, or of any pompous person proud of a fat purse.

as boastful of his wealth as the Marquis of Carabas

CARLYLEAN

Carlylean is from Thomas Carlyle (1795-1881), philosopher, essayist, and historian of the French Revolution, who in vigorous, irregular language, sometimes so abrupt as to be almost incomprehensible, arraigned existing social order. Worshiping right-minded action in any guise, he cherished certain oft-repeated convictions: that happiness consists in finding one's work and doing it; that all history is the story of the one man that dominated his particular period; that biography answers two questions—What effect had society upon the man, and what effect had the man on society? Carlyle's word painting in his *History of the French Revolution* is unforgettable: he flung portraits of men and events in their own lurid colors against a background of history so that the two are inseparable thereafter.

Carlylean sneer
Carlylean philosophy
the tremendous vigor of a Carlyle

CARMEN

Carmen is a vital, passionate, seductive and beautiful Spanish gypsy girl, non-moral, filled with the joy of living, and fickle. She first appears in Mérimée's story, and later in Bizet's opera *Carmen,* where she is a cigarette maker, alluring and seductive and fickle, finally stabbed by her lover José.

with a Carmen-like provocativeness

CARNEADES

Carneades of Cyrene (214-129 B. C.) was a Greek philosopher of the New Academy. In opposition to the Stoics and the Epicureans he believed that certain knowledge was unattainable, but that, though surety was impossible, probabilities could be formed and that these only could serve as guides to conduct. Cicero accepted his views, and the doctrine of logical probabilism has become the basis of skepticism.

Carneadean insistence on skepticism

CARNEGIE, ANDREW

Andrew Carnegie (1837-1919), the great Scotch-American industrialist, made a fortune in steel, primarily, and generously shared his first great acquisition of wealth with some of the men who had helped acquire it. He was one of the world's great philanthropists, spending millions of dollars to endow libraries, schools, and research foundations for the advancement of teaching, medicine and peace.

with the foresight of a Carnegie

CARROL-DAKIN

Carrol-Dakin are the names of the two scientists who in World War I discovered and used with marvelous success an antiseptic, ever since called the Dakin solution, and the most effective treatment for wounds known up to that time.

obviously a Dakin-solution case

CARSON, "KIT"

Christopher ("Kit") Carson (1809-1868) was an American hunter and scout whose position in the latter period of American pioneer history was analogous to that of Daniel Boone and David Crockett at an earlier period. Receiving his early training in the rigors and hardships of life in frontier settlements, he became after 1826 a professional guide to conduct emigrants and drovers across the plains and mountains separating them from the Pacific Coast. While Indian agent at Taos, New Mexico, he exerted a strong coercive influence on the warlike Apaches and gained a thorough knowledge of their traits and language. After serving as chief scout on the Federal side in charge of border warfare in the Civil War, he became Indian agent at Fort Lyon, Colorado, until his death. His hairbreadth exploits and deeds of cunning against the Indians have made him familiar to every American schoolboy and are immortalized in many stories and tales.

an adventurous "Kit" Carson to guide them

CARTHAGINIAN

Carthaginian refers to the country and people of Carthage, a maritime power on the north coast of Africa that came into grim and unrelenting conflict with Rome in the third and second centuries B. C. This contest catapulted the rivals into the famous Punic Wars, ending with the cruel extirpation of the Phoenician power in 146 B. C. Preeminently a ruling class of overlords, the Carthaginians have passed into historical record, under the obloquy of Roman opinion of them, as having a character that was both perfidious and barbarous. Plutarch described them as sour and morose, harsh to subjects, quick to anger, obstinate and treacherous.

with Carthaginian treachery

CARTON, SIDNEY

Sidney Carton is the principal character in Dickens' *Tale of Two Cities,* the key person and resolving element in the several crises of the French and English characters caught in the French Revolution. In spite of his dissolute career and his indifference with regard to his own concerns, Carton's unfailing care for the woman he loved, which extended to her husband and to all those whose lives were her concern, and his resourcefulness in every situation have made him a synonym both for unselfishness and for an amazing keenness of mind.

a Sidney-Carton selflessness

CARUSO, ENRICO

Enrico Caruso (1873-1921), sensational Italian operatic tenor, studied singing while holding jobs as a mechanic and factory accountant in Naples. Achieving world-wide fame for his rich and magnificent voice, he made his debut at the Metropolitan Opera House in *Rigoletto* (1903) with such tremendous success that he became the leading tenor of that house for 18 years. His extensive repertoire included more than 40 French and Italian operas. The possessor of a dynamic temperament, he was so impressed with panic by the catastrophic San Francisco earthquake and fire in 1906 that he is said to have rushed about shouting, "Give me Vesuvius, give me Vesuvius."

the golden tones of a Caruso

CARYATIDS

Caryatids were draped female statues used by the Greeks in place of columns for the architectural support of roofing structure. Derived from "maidens of Caryae," a town in Laconia, the name and the burdened position of the figures may reflect the slavery to which the women of Caryae were reduced by the Greeks as a punishment for joining the Persians in their invasion of Greece. However, groups of girls also executed ritual dances at the town's annual festival of Artemis, sometimes striking the attitude depicted in the statues. The best known sculptural examples are the six Caryatids supporting the entablature of the Porch of the Maidens on the southern side of the Erechtheum on the Athenian Acropolis.

with Caryatidal poise and grace

CASANOVIAN

Casanovian is from Giovanni Casanova, an eighteenth century Italian adventurer, famous for his gay, reckless, wandering, but always aristocratic life. Associating always with high society, he dabbled sometimes with letters, and wrote entertaining memoirs of his time. His name is synonymous with reckless, gay, dissolute, usually irregular but always charming, adventures and experiences.

the Casanovian dissoluteness of the times

CASSANDRA-LIKE

Cassandra-like refers to Cassandra, the daughter of Priam, who had received from Apollo the gift of prophecy. Later Apollo, angry, ordained that her prophecies, which usually predicted dire events, should never be believed. When she predicted the fall of Troy, she was declared crazed. Her name now is applied to any discredited prophet of calamity, and *Cassandra-like* indicates generally doleful predictions.

a prophet that, Cassandra-like, tells truth without belief

CASSATT, MARY

Mary Cassatt (1855-1926) went from her native Pittsburgh to Europe to study painting in Spain and France, coming under the influence of Manet, Renoir, Degas, and the Impressionists. A pastelist of note, she became world-famous for her paintings of babies, children, and mothers, which were the chief subjects of her inspiration. Her work shows unusual firmness of drawing and bold tonal color.

looks like one of Mary Cassatt's mothers with her baby

CASSIOPEIA

Cassiopeia was the wife of Cepheus, king of the Ethiopians, and the mother of Andromeda. She was so vain and proud of her beauty that she boasted she was more beautiful than the Nereids. In order to ravage the country in revenge Poseidon sent a sea-monster which could be appeased only by the sacrifice of Cassiopeia's daughter. After Andromeda was rescued by Perseus, the vain mother was placed among the stars, becoming known as "The Lady in the Chair."

Cassiopeian vanity

CASSIUS

Cassius was a Roman citizen known in history as a liberator who loved the republic and feared that Caesar might establish an empire. In Shakespeare's *Julius Caesar* he is featured as so envious that he plotted the assassination of Caesar for his own ends, under the guise of patriotism, cleverly enlisting others, Brutus among them, who honestly feared that Caesar might become a king. A Cassius means a crafty, persuasive, selfish, dangerous person.

for every great man there is one Cassius
with the dissembling craftiness of a Cassius

CASTALIAN

Castalian is from Castalia, a nymph who, pursued by Apollo, cast herself into a spring on Mount Parnassus in order to escape the god's unwelcome attentions. Sacred to Apollo and the Muses who are hence called Castalides, it was "a pool of clear, cold water, lying deep in its rock-cut basin at the foot of the sheer cliff." The Pythia, or priestess of Pythian Apollo, used to bathe in its limpid waters, and the spring has always been regarded as a source of poetic inspiration.

inspiring as the Castalian spring

CASTOR AND POLLUX

(see *Dioscuri*)

CATHERINE, ST.

St. Catherine was a martyr of the early church, who confessed Christianity at a feast of Maximinus in 307 at Alexandria. For this she was tortured to death and beheaded. Whence, in heraldry a catherine-wheel is a figure of a wheel with its tires armed with hooks, representing the fiendish means of her death.

Another St. Catherine was a Dominican nun of Siena (1347-1380). Of great fame for her sanctity, she was said to have received the stigmata, or the semblance of Christ's wounds, at the crucifixion.

as tortured as St. Catherine

CATHERINE THE GREAT

Catherine II, or the Great, married Peter III of Russia in order to strengthen friendship between Russia and Prussia. In her determination to become a Russian in order to rule her people better, she acquired a complete understanding of their nature and character. Her worldly-wise actions were dictated by the conditions in which she lived, particularly by the misery of her married life. Completely immoral in her sexual relations with men, she took an active part in all political intrigues. Of forceful character, she effected great reforms in her adopted country and aimed her foreign policy at securing the greatness and safety of Russia. Her sole misfortune seems to have been that she lived too long (1729-1796), as the Russian people became quite disgusted with her sexual activities with young men even when she was of advanced years.

with a zeal for reform like Catherine's

CATHERINETTE

A Catherinette is a Parisian young woman who, having attained her twenty-fifth birthday still unmarried, pays homage as a spinster to her patron St. Catherine on that saint's feast day. Wearing millinery that is imaginative to the point of being bizarre, the Catherinettes acknowledge their single state publicly by promenading the streets of the French metropolis in fantastically conspicuous bonnets.

a hat to distinguish a Catherinette

CATILINE

Lucius Sergius Catiline (108-62 B. C.) was an impoverished Roman patrician, dissolute but energetic. When he had ruined both his reputation and his fortune, he tried to re-establish himself by revolution, his only supporters being desperadoes like himself. His early attempts at a general subversion of Roman authority having been frustrated, he renewed his ambitions during Cicero's consulship (63 B. C.). An outcast from solvent society, he and his impoverished army of fugitive slaves and economic derelicts were defeated in the following year. His name suggests any base political conspirator.

a new Catiline to conspire against the state

CATO OF UTICA

Marcus Porcius Cato "of Utica" (95-46 B. C.) was the great grandson of Cato the Censor, and like him was a man of rigid character, narrow and somewhat short-sighted. The chief political opponent of Caesar and the Triumvirate, he was an ardent Republican and known as the "conscience of Rome." When he finally realized that the old Republic had collapsed and that an age of dictatorship had arrived, he committed suicide at Utica in Africa rather than yield to the new Caesarean political views.

Catonian stubbornness

CATO THE CENSOR

Marcus Porcius Cato "the Censor" (234-149 B. C.) was famous for his austerity, frugality and strictness in reforming the lax morals of the Roman nobility and checking their luxury and extravagance. Advocating a return to the simplicity of rural life, he was fearlessly honest in attacking powerful offenders (including the Scipios) and bluntly opposed to the sophisticated refinements of Greek culture. A bitter hatred and suspicion of Carthage caused him to end all his speeches in the Senate with the famous words *Carthago delenda est* ("Carthage must be destroyed").

Catonian morality

CATULLAN

Catullan refers to the passionate emotions of Valerius Catullus (B. C. 87-47), Roman prodigal and poet who wrote both intensely amorous and bitterly sarcastic poems to his capricious mistress Clodia (whom he calls Lesbia in his verses), a rich, beautiful and infamously licentious Roman lady. His poetry speaks of his vehement love for her, their frequent rifts and reconciliations, and of his final scorn for her unfaithfulness and broken honor. His poems are mostly short, but extremely varied in mood and felicitous in expression. They also include venomous attacks on Julius Caesar and his political henchmen.

Catullan outbursts of passion

CAUDLE, MRS.

Mrs. Caudle is a character in a series of sketches called *Mrs. Caudle's Lectures,* by Douglas Jerrold. Printed in *Punch,* they were popular in the nineteenth century and pictured the garrulous and admonishing wife, not abusive and not nagging, but endlessly talkative.

a Mrs. Caudle lecture

CECILIA, SAINT

Saint Cecilia (?-176) was a Roman virgin. After her martyrdom in Sicily, she was sainted as the patron of music, especially of organ music. She has been the subject of paintings by many famous masters, who have usually pictured her as blind and seated at an organ, with angels hovering about listening, and flowers dropped from heaven upon the keys. Cecilian is synonymous with harmony, melody, and sweetness.

Cecilian harmony

CECROPS

Cecrops was the legendary first king of Athens and the founder of its civilization. A hero of the Pelasgic race, he was reigning when Poseidon (Neptune) and Athena contended for the possession of Attica, the former offering a horse and the latter an olive tree. Cecrops decided in favor of the goddess and, according to the wisdom she bestowed on him, he instituted marriage, abolished bloody sacrifices, and taught his subjects how to worship the gods. In art he was represented as half-dragon, and the word *Cecropian* signifies an ancient and mythical founder.

of Cecropian antiquity

CELADON

Celadon is the lover of Amelia, a "matchless beauty" in Thomson's *The Seasons.* When Amelia became frightened by a storm that had overtaken them, Celadon clasped her in his arms and said, " 'Tis safety to be near thee, sure, and thus to clasp perfection." Immediately a flash of lightning struck her dead. The name is also poetically applied to any swain or rustic lover.

the Celadon and Chloë of the village

CELIMENE

Célimène is the name of a fine lady in Molière's *Misanthrope.* It has become proverbial for an artificial, coquettish, but sparkling and charming woman.

coquettish as Célimène

CELLINI, BENVENUTO

Benvenuto ("Welcome") Cellini was the great Italian sculptor, goldsmith, metal artist, and autobiographer (1500-1571). His most celebrated works include a gold medallion of "Leda and the Swan," a magnificent bronze statue of "Perseus with the head of Medusa" that is one of the most typical monuments of the Renaissance, a sumptuous salt cellar for Francis I and a medal of that monarch. His works of decorative art are rather florid for modern taste. Cellini's *Memoirs,* not published until 1728, are full of spicy animation, his amours and hatreds, and his love of the ornate in art. They also reveal his aplomb and self-applause, and disclose the supernatural visions he had while imprisoned in the Castel Sant' Angelo for embezzling jewels from the pontifical tiara.

exquisite Celliniesque jewelry

CELSUS

Aulus Cornelius Celsus was a Latin encyclopedist who wrote on agriculture, medicine, philosophy, and a variety of other subjects during the reign of Tiberius (14-37 A. D.). Only his books on medicine are extant today, and they are based largely on Hippocrates. They show humanity and a balance between theory and experience. The author recommended dissection of criminals and propounded sound rules for good health, including discussions on diet. The section on surgery shows that difficult and dangerous operations were already undertaken in that day. Other parts of the work deal with fevers, internal diseases, wounds, ulcers, and general principles of the medical profession.

abides by the health rules of his Celsus

CENTAUR

The Centaurs, whose name means "bull-killers," were represented in classical art as having bodies the lower half of which was horse, the upper that of a man. Said to have been the offspring of Ixion and a cloud, they led a turbulent, quarrelsome, pugnacious and savage life. Chiron was the most famous of the Centaurs. The name has come to suggest figuratively any person or thing regarded as an incongruous blend of diverse elements.

a Centaurian mixture
with Centaurian incongruity
Centaurian brutishness

CENTOATL

Centoatl is the Mexican goddess (or god) of maize and of agriculture.

Centoatl guaranteeing a bountiful harvest

CEPHALUS

Cephalus, the husband of Procris, was tempted by the goddess Aurora, whose amorous overtures he resisted, to try the fidelity of his wife. Changed by Aurora into a wealthy stranger, he successfully tempted his wife to purchase his gifts with her favors. When he revealed his true self, Procris in shame fled to Crete where Artemis (Diana) presented her with a dog and an unerring spear, and sent her back to her husband in the guise of a handsome youth. In order to get the dog and the spear Cephalus promised to yield to the amorous desires of the youth, who then was revealed to him as his wife. In spite of a reconciliation, Procris continued to fear the love of Aurora and jealously watched Cephalus every time he went hunting. Thinking that he had heard an animal stirring in a bush one day, Cephalus hurled his spear only to kill his suspicious wife.

unhappy Cephalus, object of his wife's suspicions

CERBEREAN

Cerberean is from Cereberus, the three-headed monster that guards the gates of the lower world; hence the symbol for baleful, inescapable, malignant vigilance.

ever on guard, with wide Cerberean mouths

CERCOPES

The Cercopes were a monkey-like race of men who tried to steal Hercules' weapons. In revenge the hero strung them upside down on a pole which he carried across his shoulders. While in this position they made so many jests about his hairiness that Hercules was amused and disposed to let them go. They are a common comic subject in both classical literature and art.

upside down like the Cercopes

CERES

Ceres is the goddess of agriculture, the beneficent spirit of growth in grain and other vegetation, whence the word *cereal.* There is a story that Ceres left Olympus once in anger to live on earth among men, conferring blessings where she was kindly received and not allowing the earth to produce where she was repulsed. The mother of Proserpina, whose rape by Pluto made her queen of the lower world, Ceres grieves for her daughter half of each year, as symbolized by the death of vegetation in the wintertime.

fruitful as Ceres
through verdant vales, and Ceres' golden reign

Ceres, most bounteous lady,
Thy rich leas of wheat, rye,
Barley, oats, and peas.
HERRICK

CERVANTEAN

Cervantean refers to Cervantes, the late sixteenth century Spanish novelist and dramatist, author of *Don Quixote,* and famous for a delicate, romantic, absurd, and extravagant kind of adventure, tinged with a sensitive wit, and a deep appreciation of gallantry, chivalry, and honor. His name suggests imagination, wit, extravagance, romance, fantasy.

a Cervantean perfection of comic character

Cervantean invention and whimsicality

CESTUS

Cestus, in Homer, is the girdle of Venus, the decorations of which are so magically exciting that they necessarily provoke ardent love. Whoever wore it immediately became an irresistible objection of passion and desire. In Tasso's *Jerusalem Delivered* Armida wore a similar alluring garment.

needs Cestus to make her alluring

CHADBAND, REVEREND MR.

The Reverend Mr. Chadband is a character in Dickens' *Bleak House* and a type of hypocritical piety. Affecting to condemn the carnal world, he nonetheless enjoys life's luxuries with great relish.

hypocritical as the Rev. Mr. Chadband

CHALDEAN

The Chaldeans were an Oriental people noted for their fortune-telling, originally based on Chaldean astrology, magic, and occult learning. They were the soothsayers of their time and seers of note.

sought a Chaldean answer

CHALIAPIN, FEODOR

Feodor Chaliapin (1873-1938) underwent numerous professional vicissitudes, being in turn a porter, shoemaker, hunter and streetsweeper, before hitting on art as a career. First a dancer, he soon found that his magnificently dramatic bass voice was the finest operatic vehicle for the transmission of Russian nationalistic music-drama that could be discovered in many a generation. From his 1913 London appearance as *Boris Godunov* in Moussorgsky's opera of the same name he was a world sensation. Later appearances under Sir Thomas Beecham in *Ivan the Terrible, Prince Igor,* and in *La Khovantchina* brought him so much fame that he came to New York's Metropolitan, where he achieved brilliant and unforgettable success. His vigorous theatrical ability and superb voice made his performance of *Boris* unique and inimitable.

the dynamically vibrant voice of a Chaliapin

CHAMBERLAIN, NEVILLE

Neville Chamberlain, the English Prime Minister in 1939, was one of the representatives called to the Munich Conference, who with the French Daladier consented to Hitler's demand that Germany be allowed to take the Sudetenland from Czechoslovakia, with the understanding that that, and that alone, was all that Germany wanted. The possession of the Sudeten was the first step in the march of Germany into Austria, Poland, etc., resulting in World War II. Regardless of what virtues Chamberlain may have had, he will always be remembered for the fatal policy of appeasement, pusillanimous, timid, infamous, pathetic.

Chamberlainian transigence

CHANDRA

Chandra, in Hindu mythology, is the name of the moon as both planet and deity. It is often applied as a suffix to the name of a distinguished person, as in Ramachandra, and hence connotes any eminent or illustrious character.

Chandra bathing the heavens with light

CHAOS

Chaotic comes from Chaos, the god of disorganization, disorder, confusion, mad intermingling of the four elements—fire, earth, air, water. Ruler of space before creation, and in the old stories still ruler of the space outside the realm of an ordered universe, his name connotes confusion, disorder, tumult, unrest.

anarchic as Chaos

CHAPLINESQUE

Chaplinesque is from Charlie Chaplin, a comic actor of the screen, whose appeal lay in a ludicrous and rather wistful helplessness as he shuffled around on his inert and flapping feet, doggedly, obediently, half-bewildered, and irresistibly funny.

a wistful Chaplinesque humor

CHARIS

Charis is the personification of grace and beauty in Greek mythology. In the *Iliad* she is described as the wife of Hephaestus (Vulcan), though in the *Odyssey* Aphrodite is that god's wife. The idea of personified grace was at an early age divided into a plurality of beings, and so elsewhere in mythology the concept is described as a triad, the Charites or the Latin Graces. The daughters of Zeus, their names were Euphrosyne, Aglaia, and Thalia. In early times they were depicted as clad, but later were represented nude. Appearing as unsuspicious maidens in the full bloom of life, they usually embrace each other. As friends of the Muses they lend their beauty to everything that delights and elevates gods and men, and by their refined gentleness they enhance the enjoyment of life.

inseparable as the Charites

CHARLEMAGNE

Charlemagne (742-814) was the imposing central figure in the songs of the French troubadours, and in old French romance a hero of war and adventure. He was actually a statesman and reformer, who, in the opinion of Bryce, "laid the foundation of all that is noble and beautiful and useful in the Middle Ages." In the hour of his death he caused his body to be placed on the throne, his royal robes around him, his sword by his side, a Bible open on his lap, that he might lay at the feet of his God his royalty, his power, and his soul. He it was who commanded all the conquered peoples to be baptized and to obey the laws of Christianity — a mass conversion and compulsory Christianity that nevertheless became habitual as the years rolled on.

kingly as Charlemagne on his throne in the West
like Charlemagne, at a word transform a heathen world

CHARON

Charon, son of Erebus, ferries the souls of the departed across the river Styx to their destined abode. The name is now jocosely applied to any ferryman. John Kendrick Bangs makes Charon a constant character in his witty *Houseboat on the Styx.*

man stands on the bank of Time, awaiting Charon, common carrier for all humanity
thick as Charon's ferry with phantoms

CHARYBDIS

Charybdis suggests Scylla and Charybdis, the former a dangerous rock on the Italian side of the Strait of Messina, the latter a whirlpool on the Sicilian side. In the *Odyssey* Homer pictures the Sicilian side of the Strait as a low rock containing an immense fig-tree, under which dwelt Charybdis, who thrice every day swallowed down and sucked in the waters of the sea and three times threw them up again. The phrase "between Scylla and Charybdis" consequently means to be beset by danger whichever way one turns.

a Scylla and Charybdis situation

CHAUCERIAN

Chaucerian is from Geoffrey Chaucer (1340-1400), the first English poet famous the world over for his broad human stories of the people of his time. Written as it is of people he knew and talked with, his work is inevitably a perfect picture of the people, their trades, their religion, their lives, their laughter, their broad mirth; it is broad, racy, uproarious, a reflection of what amused and entertained fourteenth century England. Happy, tolerant, wise, mirthful, Chaucerian suggests these qualities. What Boccaccio is to Italy, Chaucer is to England.

Chaucerian gayety
with the Chaucerian joy of life

CHAUVINISTIC

Chauvinistic comes from Nicholas Chauvin, whose enthusiasm for and admiration of Napoleon was so exaggerated and so constantly forced down the throats of his comrades that they came to speak of an expression of boundless enthusiasm for a cause or for a leader as chauvinism. The word is still used for an uncalled-for or extravagant expression of patriotism.

ridiculously chauvinistic

CHEKHOV, ANTON

Anton Chekhov (1860-1904) is almost universally regarded as the master of the Russian short story. His art, which is psychological, records a given state of mind and the morbid experiences it suffers under the buffetings of opposition. The construction of his stories, most of which relate the undoing of a life, is extremely musical and lyrical, and the stories themselves reveal the author's uncanny ability to evoke moods. A playwright as well, he wrote many fine plays, such as *Uncle Vanya, The Three Sisters,* and *The Cherry Orchard.* The word *Chekhovian* suggests lyrical enchantment and clearly delineated evocation of a mood.

Chekhovian moodiness

CHESHIRE CAT

The Cheshire Cat is the cat appearing in Carroll's *Alice in Wonderland* to give Alice advice. An apparition, the grin appears first as the cat materializes, and when the cat disappears the grin is the last to fade. The constant, unmeaning smile assumed by persons who wish to be ingratiating is often referred to as a Cheshire-cat grin, hence affected, insincere, calculating.

grin like a Cheshire cat, from ear to ear

CHESTERFIELDIAN

Chesterfieldian is from Lord Chesterfield (1694-1773), in his day not only "the glass of fashion and the mold of form" in England, but also a wise, politic, and diplomatic statesman. Himself genteel, elegant, suave, ingratiating, and highly successful, it was his dearest wish that his son be equally acceptable, to which end he wrote *Lord Chesterfield's Letters to his Son,* in which he recorded the principles and the policies that would, in his opinion, foster those qualities and lead to success.

with Chesterfield's sauve grace
adopted a Chesterfieldian gloved manner
elegant as a Chesterfield

CHICOMECOATL

Chicomecoatl is the name of the Aztec goddess of abundance and provisions.

blessed from the cornucopia of Chicomecoatl

CHILDREN IN THE WOOD

The Children in the Wood, afterward called *The Babes in the Wood,* were actually the children left to an uncle, with a substantial legacy that was to be theirs at maturity, or the uncle's in case they did not live to legal maturity. The covetous uncle hired two ruffians to murder the children, but the task was not to their liking. They left the babes in the woods, where they died, and the robins covered them over with leaves. Years later one of the ruffians, jailed for some offense, told of the deed, and the story was woven into a ballad titled *The Babes in the Wood,* a name that now means cruelly neglected, abandoned, forsaken.

children curiously love a babes-in-the-wood sadness in their stories

---

CHILLON, PRISONER OF

The Prisoner of Chillon was actually François de Bonnivard (1496-1570), whom Charles III imprisoned for six years in the dungeon of Chillon on Lake Geneva for some political crime. Byron combined this fact with some details from a story of Dante's and pictures Bonnivard's sorrow during his imprisonment, but shows him finally so accustomed to the gloom and the silence and safety, so divorced from all memory of or desire for active living, that when liberation comes, the space and the freedom terrify him.

the Prisoner-of-Chillon dread of the world never left him

CHIMAERA

The Chimaera was the strange fire-breathing monster, the forepart of whose body was that of a lion while its hind quarters were those of a dragon and its mid-section that of a goat. It lived in Lycia, which it devastated along with other countries of Asia Minor until it was destroyed by Bellerophon. The explanation of the origin of this fanciful creature is to be sought in a volcano of the same name in Lycia. The word has come to mean any absurd, impracticable or horrible fantasy, as in the English word *chimerical.*

of Chimaera-like absurdity
Chimaeran horror

CHIPPENDALE, THOMAS

Thomas Chippendale was an early English furniture designer. Chippendale chairs are marked by seats wide at the front, with sharp corners, the tops wide, often with "ears" at the corners. The whole is graceful in outline, sometimes ornate, but rather sturdier in design and less tasteful than others. The name is now loosely and derisively applied to furniture, delicate and fragile and wholly inadequate for casual use.

the incongruous Chippendale screamed at its stalwart owner

CHIRON

Chiron was the wisest and most famous of the Centaurs and noted for his skill in music, medicine, prophecy and hunting. Taught by Apollo and Artemis, he was himself the teacher of Achilles, Peleus, Diomedes and many other Greek heroes. Hercules was also his friend, but one of that hero's poisoned arrows struck Chiron as they were fighting with the other Centaurs. Chiron, though immortal, gave that precious gift to Prometheus because he did not care to continue living in pain. Jupiter placed him among the stars as the constellation *Sagittarius,* "the archer."

a teacher with the skill of Chiron
has Chironian wisdom

CHIVERY, JOHN

John Chivery, in Dickens' *Little Dorrit,* is the sentimental son of a turnkey, hopelessly in love with Miss Amy Dorrit. He spends his time composing epitaphs declaring his death from heartbreak. The following is a specimen: "Here lie the mortal remains of JOHN CHIVERY, Never anything worth mentioning, Who died about the end of the year one thousand eight hundred and twenty-six, Of a broken heart, Requesting with his last breath that the word AMY might be inscribed over his ashes, Which was accordingly directed to be done, By his afflicted parents."

with the elegiac sorrow of John Chivery

CHLOE

Chloë is the shepherdess-heroine of Longus' celebrated Greek pastoral romance *Daphnis and Chloë.* It has been common ever since in pastoral poetry to denote a mistress, sweetheart, or a maiden. Negresses and spaniels in recent times are frequently dubbed with the name. Ravel's exquisitely sensuous and impressionistic symphonic suite, of the same name as Longus' novel, is a musical depiction of bucolic simplicity.

a classical Chloë in a pastoral setting

CHLORIS

Chloris in Greek mythology is the goddess of buds, flowers, and the spring, like the Latin Flora. She was the wife of Zephyrus, the personification of the West wind, who carried her off by force, desirous of her beauty. To him she bore a son, Carpus.

presiding like Chloris over her bowl of flowers

CHOPINESQUE

Frederic Chopin (1809-1849), held to be the greatest of all composers of piano music, was born in Poland of French-Polish ancestry. His music is permeated with romantic intimacy, is emotional, sensitive, full of lyric melody, and is sometimes heroic, sometimes nostalgic. He has been called a miniaturist because of his many short, perfect, single-mood compositions.

exquisitely complete as a nocturne by Chopin

CHRISTIAN

Christian is the pilgrim in John Bunyan's *Pilgrim's Progress,* who went on a journey from the City of Destruction to the Celestial City, over a path symbolic of the experiences of a lifetime. He is beset by all the troubles and the temptations and succored by the help and the blessing that any real Christian experiences in his effort toward real Christian living, and carries on his back a great burden that falls from him as he stands before the Cross in the Holy City.

like Christian, beset about by temptations

CHRISTOPHER, SAINT

Saint Christopher is the 3rd century saint who, as a penance for having once served the devil, was required to carry pilgrims across a certain river. It is said that unwitting, he carried Christ in the form of a little child, and the child grew heavier and heavier on his shoulders. When St. Christopher set him down, Christ in His own form stood before him and said, "Blessed art thou; thou hast carried the sins of the world." Chaucer makes one of his pilgrims to Canterbury wear an image of Saint Christopher. The name means "Christ-bearer."

burdened as was Saint Christopher

CHRYSEIS

Chryseis was the beautiful daughter of Chryses, the priest of Apollo, in the *Iliad.* Taken prisoner by Achilles, she fell by lot in the distribution of booty to Agamemnon, who refused to accept her father's ransom money and rebuffed him with harsh words. She was forced to act as Agamemnon's concubine, until Apollo sent a plague on the Greek camp and she was forthwith released.

a war-prize as lovely as Chryseis

CHUZZLEWIT, JONAS

Jonas Chuzzlewit, the cousin of Martin, hero of Dickens' novel *Martin Chuzzlewit,* is noteworthy for his mean brutality, small tyranny, and voracious greed. Goaded by base instincts, he ultimately becomes a murderer and a suicide.

a brutal Jonas Chuzzlewit
Chuzzlewitian tyranny

CICERONIAN

Ciceronian refers to the consummate oratory and statesmanship of Marcus Tullius Cicero (106-43 B.C.), Roman patriot and political leader who strove for class-harmony between the capitalistic Equites ("knights") and the aristocratic Senators, impeached Verres (*q.v.*) for his extortionate governorship of Sicily (70 B.C.), and quashed the abortive revolution of Catiline (*q.v.*) in the year of his consulship (63). For executing several of the conspirators without a trial he was forced to go into exile, later returning to Rome to a life of literary retirement in which he composed his masterly philosophic and rhetorical essays. On the murder of Julius Caesar he put himself at the head of the republican party, attacking Mark Anthony (*q.v.*) in a series of denunciatory Philippics (see *Demosthenes*). But with the formation of the second triumvirate among Anthony, Lepidus, and Octavius (Augustus) his name was put on the proscription list of state enemies and he was murdered while attempting to flee the country. His head and hands were cut off and nailed to the Rostra in Rome by order of his arch-enemy Anthony.

His literary style was regarded as so faultless and pure in its rolling sonority, balanced clauses, and intricate, periodic sentence-structure that it became the model for imitation in oratorical schools of many subsequent ages. The word *cicerone,* derived from his name and of Italian origin, came to mean a glib and loquacious guide who explains antiquities to a traveler.

pure as Ciceronian Latin
sonorously Ciceronian eloquence

CID

The Cid was the title given to Don Rodrigo Laynez, a famous Spanish hidalgo of the eleventh century, by the five Moorish generals whom he had conquered. Also known by the abbreviated name of Ruy Diaz and Count of Bivar, he was placed in charge of all the armies of King Sancho in 1065, whence came his appellation of *Campeador,* or warrior and champion. He died at Valencia in 1100 at the age of seventy-four. The details of his history are lost in a cloud of romantic fiction, but he is regarded as a model of the heroic virtues of his age and as the flower of Spanish chivalry. He is the subject and hero of Corneille's *Le Cid* and of Herder's *Cid.*

chivalrous as the Cid

CIMMERIAN

The Cimmerians were a people who dwelt in utter darkness, in a remote region; hence, the word means gloom, darkness, dreariness. The word is also used to indicate the desert abode of the souls of the unblest, the opposite of the Elysian fields, abode of the blest.

in dark Cimmerian desert ever dwell
the Cimmerian depth
Cimmerian gloom

CINCINNATUS

Lucius Quinctius Cincinnatus (519-439 B. C.) was the plain-living Roman called from his plough in order to save the Roman army when it was blockaded by the Aequi on Mount Algidus. Made Dictator for the emergency, he defeated the enemy and then returned to his farm. He is a type of old-fashioned simplicity and frugality.

simple and frugal as Cincinnatus

CINDERELLA-LIKE

Cinderella-like is from *Cinderella,* an old folk-story of the neglected but beautiful household drudge serving her more favored relatives. Finally befriended by a fairy godmother who sent her in marvelous beauty and gorgeous array, she wore glass slippers to a ball where a prince fell in love with her, but at the stroke of twelve she was magically whisked back to reality. In her haste she dropped one of the slippers, by means of which the prince found her, the only maiden in the kingdom whose foot fit the slipper, and married her. The word is now used of any humble and beautiful maiden to whom good fortune comes unexpectedly.

the whole Cinderella-like story came to light

CIRCEAN

Circean is from Circe, an evil enchantress whose magic drink turned human beings into swine, according to Homer's *Odyssey;* others say she transformed men into beings with human form, but the heads of beasts. The word is now used of any beautiful woman who exercises an evil influence deliberately.

a wild Circean life
Circean mockery
lulled by sweet Circean song

CIRCUMLOCUTION OFFICE

The Circumlocution Office, in Dickens' *Little Dorrit,* is the name, now become proverbial, for the official red tape of the English public-office system, where each employee tries to shuffle off every act to some one else, and before anything is done it has to pass through so many departments that every fly is crushed on the wheel.

typical buck-passing of the Circumlocution Office

CITY OF DESTRUCTION

The City of Destruction, in Bunyan's *Pilgrim's Progress,* is the imaginary Babylon from which Christian flees to find the Celestial City. It symbolizes the worldliness of the unconverted.

a cosmopolis as evil as the City of Destruction

CLAUDIUS

Claudius was the antiquarian emperor of Rome (41-54-A. D.) who was taken from his literary studies and placed on the throne by the praetorian guard after the murder of Caligula. Lame and popularly regarded as a bit dull-witted, he had a fundamental weakness of character and lack of interest in his imperial duties that made him the slave of his wives and freedmen. In his reign the southern part of Britain was, however, made a Roman province. Devoted to Etruscan researches, he was cuckolded by one wife, Messalina, and poisoned by another, Agrippina, who could not await his death in order to place her son Nero on the throne.

studious as Claudius

CLAVERING, SIR FRANCIS

Sir Francis Clavering, in Thackeray's *Pendennis,* is a fortune-hunting baronet who marries the plebeian Mrs. Amory to recoup his financial losses. He is subsequently blackmailed by Altamont, Mrs. Amory's first husband.

as calculating about marriage as Sir Francis Clavering

CLEAVER, FANNY

Fanny Cleaver, in Dickens' *Our Mutual Friend,* is the deformed little dolls' dressmaker who smells "miles of flowers and bushels of roses" as she works. "The person of the house," she is also often referred to as "Jenny Wren," and sees visions of happy people coming to comfort her for the pain and mockery in which she lives.

pathetic as Fanny Cleaver

CLEOBIS AND BITON

Cleobis and Biton were two Argive youths who drew their mother's chariot a distance of 25 stades so that she might attend a festival to Hera at Argos. On their arrival the youths were praised by the townsmen for their strength and their mother was blessed by the women. Then the mother prayed to Hera that her sons might receive the greatest blessing bestowed upon men. The youths, who were resting from their toil in the goddess's temple, fell into a sound sleep from which they never awoke. After the deity had thus showed that it is better for a man to die than to live, statues were erected at Delphi to commemorate the youths and their noble, filial service to their mother.

dutiful as Cleobis and Biton

CLEOPATRA

Cleopatra, the last Ptolemaic queen of Egypt (69-30 B. C.), was endowed, Plutarch says, with "captivating graces and high mental qualities," sufficient at least to captivate Julius Caesar, who warred with her brother Ptolemy on her account. After Caesar's death she captivated Mark Antony, who in his infatuation almost forgot his duties as general. After his retreat and suicide, Cleopatra, rather than become the captive of Octavius, committed suicide by means of the bite of an asp conveyed to her secretly in a basket of fruit. Her name is synonymous with great magnificence, power, and intelligence, as well as with grace, charm, beauty, and passionate devotion.

a starry-eyed Cleopatra
glorious sorcery of Cleopatra

CLIFFORD, PAUL

Paul Clifford, the hero of Bulwer-Lytton's novel of the same name, was a romantic highwayman. Familiar with the dens of depravity and vice and steeped in dissipation, he afterwards became reformed by the redemptive power of love.

redeemed like Paul Clifford from his errant ways

CLIO

(see *Muse*)

Clio was the Muse of history. A symbol for scholarly research and the study and analysis of events of the past, she was represented in ancient works of art as carrying an open scroll of manuscript or a chest of books.

an authoritative history guided by Clio

CLODIA

Clodia was the sister of Clodius Pulcher and the wife of the Roman consul Quintus Metellus Celer. Beautiful, promiscuous and profligate, she took the poet Catullus to be one of her lovers, and as Lesbia, was alternately praised and damned in his ardent verses. The enemy of Cicero, she was attacked in his speech in defense of Caelius, Catullus' successor in her fickle affections, whom she charged with attempting to poison her. Altogether unprincipled, though wealthy, brilliant and versatile, she seems to have had everything except character.

worthless as Clodia, yet praised in art

CLODIUS

Publius Clodius Pulcher, brother of Clodia, was a Roman patrician notorious for his violence and profligacy. In 62 B. C. he attended the female rites of the Bona Dea clad as a woman, in order to consummate an amour with Caesar's wife. For this profanation he was prosecuted, though acquitted, by Cicero. In revenge he forced the great statesman into exile. His subsequent quarrel with Milo resulted in each leader's organizing of gangs of thugs, and frequent street fights and brawls followed. In one of these riots in 52 B. C. he was murdered, and such was his popularity with the masses of Roman citizens that Pompey had to take extreme measures as sole consul in order to keep order in the city.

a play-boy popular as Clodius

CLOELIA

Cloelia was a Roman virgin given to the Etruscan king Porsena as a hostage during his war with the young republic. She escaped her confinement and swam the Tiber back to Rome. Returned to Porsena, she was released with some of the other hostages by him in admiration of her gallant and courageous deed. He also rewarded her with a splendidly caparisoned horse and sent to the Romans a statue of a woman on horseback.

as daring a swimmer as Cloelia

CLOTHOS

Clothos is the one of the three Fates who holds the distaff on which is wound the thread of life, hence endows a life with its general texture. The other two were Lachesis and Atropos.

with a prayer to Clothos

CLOUT, COLIN

Colin Clout, a name used by Spenser to indicate any ordinary rustic, was later used in many odes and amorous verses. Even now in England the name indicates the honest, pleasant, and amiable rustic.

all the Colin Clouts were at the fair

CLYTEMNESTRA

Clytemnestra was the daughter of Tyndareus and Leda, and the sister of Castor, Pollux and Helen of Troy. Wife of Agamemnon and queen of Mycenae, she contracted a paramour, Aegisthus, during her husband's ten year siege of Troy. Under pretext of justice for Agamemnon's sacrifice of their daughter, Iphigenia (*q.v.*),and his bringing Cassandra into their home as his concubine Trojan prize, she murdered her husband in his bath on his return from Troy. She herself was killed by her children, Electra and Orestes, in revenge for her act. The story of her murder of Agamemnon is told in Aeschylus' play, *Agamemnon*, that of her own death in Sophocles' *Electra*. She is the classical prototype of the adulterous wife and husband-killer. (*See Agamemnon, Electra, Crestes,* etc.)

with the hatred of a Clytemnestra
Clytemnestran hatred of her husband

CLYTIE

Clytie was a water-nymph and the daughter of Oceanus. She fell in love with Apollo the Sun-god but met with no reciprocation. In grief she turned into a sunflower or heliotrope, even then constantly keeping her face turned toward the object of her devotion as he rode through the skies on his daily course.

as fond of the sun as Clytie

COCKAIGNE

Cockaigne is a fabulous land of luxury and idleness, in part intended to ridicule the fanciful stories of Avalon (*q. v.*). Called Lubberland by English sixteenth poets, it referred in burlesque to London and its suburbs. Boileau applied the name to Paris, and the Neapolitans also have a festival called Cocagna. In Germany Hans Sachs made it the subject of his humorous poem *Schlaraffenland*. The lotus-land of poetry, it is applied in British humor to cockneydom and a poor man's notion of paradise.

lives in an imaginary Cockaigne

COCKER, EDWARD

Edward Cocker (1632-1675) was the author of an arithmetic so completely accurate that it became the authority for all calculations. The expression "according to Cocker" came to mean completely regular or acceptable, just as "according to Hoyle" means meeting every conventional requirement, not only in cards, but in any particular field of discussion.

all according to Cocker

COCK LANE GHOST

The Cock Lane Ghost was an imposture perpetrated by a young girl and her family living in Cock Lane in London. Several noted men eventually undertook to solve the mystery that had baffled other investigators. Dr. Samuel Johnson was among them, and he later wrote an account of the Cock Lane Ghost, telling that the mysterious "knockings" had been produced by means of a board concealed on the girl's person. Since that any supposedly alarming event has been referred to as a Cock Lane Ghost.

timid politicians, always listening for a Cock Lane Ghost

COCLES, HORATIUS

Horatius Cocles (the "one-eyed") was the hero of old Roman legend who with two companions defended the Sublician bridge against the whole Etruscan army under Porsena, while his countrymen broke down the bridge behind them. When the task had been nearly finished, he sent his companions to join the rest of the Roman army. As soon as the bridge was destroyed he plunged into the Tiber and swam across to Rome amid a hail of enemy arrows. A statue was erected in his honor, and he was granted as much land as he could plow around in one day. His valiant exploit is the subject of one of Macaulay's *Lays of Ancient Rome*.

a Cocles at single-handed combat

COCYTEAN

Cocytean is from Cocytus, one of the principal rivers of Hades in classical mythology (see *Acheron, Stygian*). Since its very name signifies "wailing," and "lamentation," the epithet *cocytean* is descriptive of gloom and grief.

sobs of Cocytean intensity

COELEBS

Coelebs is a name for a bachelor in search of a model wife. Originally a synonym for a bachelor's ideal, it was the appellation of a character in Hannah More's novel *Coelebs in Search of a Wife* (1809). He ultimately marries a woman who meets the exact requirements in qualities that were described by his dead mother.

Coelebs in search of a perfect woman

COGIA HASSAN ALHABBAL

Cogia Hassan Alhabbal, in the *Arabian Nights' Entertainments*, is the name of a poor rope-maker who becomes rich from finding a diamond in a fish.

as nouveau riche as Cogia Hassan Alhabbal

COGIA HOUSSAM

Cogia Houssam is the captain of the Forty Thieves in the *Arabian Nights' Entertainments.*

a light-fingered Cogia Houssam

COLE, KING

King Cole, a traditional 3rd century British king of great wealth, now a figure for a nursery rhyme, devoted himself to a life jolly and merry, utterly ignoring any of the responsibilities of royalty. The name is hence applied to persons in great position who seem wholly unaware of their obligations, and intent only upon the pleasures their position affords.

a pleasant King-Cole sort of ruler
King Cole's monarchy of mirth

COLERIDGE, SAMUEL TAYLOR

Samuel Taylor Coleridge (1772-1834), a critic and poet of high rank, friend of Wordsworth and Lamb, was also a charming conversationalist, as is apparent in his *Table Talk.* His poetry has an atmosphere, that Lamb called a "wizard twilight" that has nevertheless a semblance of truth that induces a suspension of disbelief. He can make an enduring picture out of an airy nothing, as he does in *Christabel* and *Kubla Khan,* and can give an air of mystery and beauty to the simplest event, as he does in the *Ancient Mariner.*

full of the Coleridge atmosphere

COLLINS, REV. MR.

The Reverend Mr. Collins, in Jane Austen's *Pride and Prejudice,* is a conceited toady and sycophant.

obsequiously fawning like the Rev. Mr. Collins

COLOSSUS

Colossal from Colossus, a statue of Apollo set up in 280 B.C. at Rhodes, about 120 feet high, has come to be used of any person of amazing strength or greatness, especially one who uses his power to awe the world or to control great areas of action. It is also used to indicate the amazing size or extent of any thing or any scheme.

he doth bestride the world like a Colossus
the whole project is unbelievably colossal

COLUMBINE

Columbine is the sweetheart of Harlequin, the clown, with whom she makes the love-pair of early Italian comedy. She is always pretty, wise, and bright, with a heart of understanding, pity, love, and optimism. Because of her merry tongue, happy quips, delightful sauciness and instant resourcefulness she is beloved and popular in audiences all over the world, and a stock character for graceful and fanciful comedy in any language.

with the womanly heart of a Columbine under all her merry quips

---

COLUMBUS, CHRISTOPHER

Christopher Columbus (1446-1506), the discoverer of America, Italian courtier and explorer, was easily obsessed by the study of the sea, geography, navigation, and unknown horizons. Himself a maker of maps and charts, he asked the Portuguese for ships to make an exploring expedition. They dallied and Spain referred him to a council that disapproved, but finally Isabella gave him two ships and his friends a third. Despite a crew that was afraid, discontented, and talked of drowning him, Columbus sailed on and found land, returning triumphant to Spain. He made a second, a third, and a fourth voyage. From one of these an envious and malicious rival maneuvered that Columbus should be returned to Spain in chains, but the indignant Spanish public had him released. On his final journey he faced famine and mutiny, and returned to Spain, where he died in 1506, never knowing the importance and extent of his discovery.

Columbian adventures

COMMON, DOL

Dol Common, in Jonson's *Alchemist,* is a prostitute who is in league with Subtle.

the Dol Common of the town

COMUS

Comus is the creature of Milton's imagination and the child of Bacchus, god of wine and revelry, and Circe, with her evil power of transforming men into beasts. He is the moving evil force in Milton's masque *Comus,* representing the dangers besetting three young persons making their way through a forest. They are saved from the temptations and the evil wiles by their faith in the powers of good and in the guardian angels of heaven who watched over them. Comus is synonymous with the temptations of the flesh and the devil.

managed to elude the Comus of city streets

callous as Comus to moral babble

innocently disguised as ever Comus was

CONCORDIA

Concordia was the Roman goddess who personified harmony and amity. She had several temples, the earliest of which was built by Camillus (*q. v.*) to commemorate the reconciliation between the patricians and the plebeians in 367 B. C. The Senate frequently met in the temple of this goddess, who is represented in art as a matronly figure holding the cornucopia in her left hand.

Concordia ruling the household

CONFUCIAN

Confucian is from Confucius (551-478 B.C.), the great Chinese sage, philosopher, and teacher who established and taught what must now be considered the basic principles of Chinese thought and education, teachings that are looked upon with veneration in his own country, and with respect by the civilized world. His name has become the symbol of his principles, his learning, and his philosophy, much as Christianity is the symbol of Christian principles throughout the world.

famed as the sayings of a Confucius

CONRAD, JOSEPH

Joseph Conrad (1857-1924), a Pole who ran away at sixteen to be a British sailor, at sixty began to write novels in English of the sea, storms, and of men against that background. He particularly pictured character under the strain of unusual circumstances or in great danger, emphasizing man's reaction to such crises, and the personal crises they precipitate. He wrote, in what one critic calls "golden prose," the most vivid and splendid sea stories in literature, stories unusual, mysterious, adventurous, involving man in struggle with nature. A profound thinker, Conrad declares "the ultimate test of character is loyalty to the persons or the principles that have been the best influences in a person's life."

the realism of a Conrad

CONSTANTINE

Constantine the Great (274-337 A.D.) was created Emperor of Rome on the death of his father and predecessor Constantius. At this time the government was divided among two senior rulers, called Augusti, and two juniors, called Caesars. Constantine defeated his rival Augustus, Maxentius, near Rome in 312. On his way to the struggle he claimed to have seen a vision of the cross and beneath it the words "In hoc signo vinces," so he placed Christian monograms on the shields of his troops before doing battle. In 324 Licinius, Emperor of the East, surrendered to him, making him sole monarch of the empire. Always tolerant of Christians, he presided over the Council of Nicaea (325) in an effort to establish unity within the church and state. In 330 he transferred the seat of government to Byzantium, renaming it Constantinople and dying there in 337, baptized a Christian.

the unifying genius of a Constantine

CONSUS

Consus was a somewhat vague and elusive Roman god associated in part with the earth and its harvests. Also considered as presiding over secret deliberations and counsels, he was identified in later times with Neptune. At his festival horse and chariot races were held in the Circus Maximus on August 18th, and the occasion was known as the Consualia.

like Consus at a horse race

COOK, THOMAS

Thomas Cook (1808-1892), an English wood-turner by profession, was the English travel agent famous as the organizer of the "grand circular tour" of Europe. His first venture in the travel field was the hiring of a special Midland Counties Railway Company train to conduct 570 passengers from Leicester to Loughborough to attend a meeting of a temperance society of which he was a member. The first publicly advertised excursion ever run in England, it was followed by a more ambitious pleasure trip from Leicester to Liverpool with visits to the Isle of Man, Dublin and the Welsh coast. In 1855 he conducted an excursion to the Paris exhibition, and in the following year organized the first "grand tour" of Europe. His son and three grandsons were all engaged in the same firm as Thomas Cook and Son, and the name became synonymous for a courteous host who takes care of all the needs of the most timid of tourists in a strange land.

complete as a Cook's tour

COOPER, JAMES FENIMORE

James Fenimore Cooper (1789-1851) wrote stories of American pioneers, Indian scouts, hardy frontiersmen, intrepid sailors, with all the dangers, hair breadth escapes, and reckless adventuring that marked the lives of those men. The looseness of structure and the hand-made coincidences do not at all obscure the raciness of his stories of the romance of the early days as he saw it in his own neighborhood. A pioneer himself in the field of pioneer life in American literature, Cooper stands for excitement, daring, and superhuman prescience, all of which are evident in his novel, *The Last of the Mohicans.*

a racy Cooper-narrative

COPERNICAN

Copernican is from Copernicus, the noted and brilliant astronomer of the sixteenth century and the first to advance the theory that the earth rotates on its axis. He was laughed at for his pains, although his theory is the basis of the entire conception of the universe today.

the result of Copernican reasoning

COPHETUAN

Cophetuan is from Cophetua, an African king who saw, was fascinated by, and married a beautiful and artless beggar maid. The whole is so simple and natural a story that it has been made the subject of a painting by Lord Leighton and a poem by Lord Tennyson. Cophetuan, therefore, means a natural, simple, and wholesome love of a great person for a person of humble origin.

a Cophetuan romance

COPPERFIELD, DAVID

David Copperfield, the appealing but timid young hero of Dickens' novel by that name, came up through a difficult childhood situation into and through boys' schools that well-nigh reduced him to stupidity, while a cruel step-father drove him to such desperation that he ran away to an eccentric but kindly old aunt, Betsy Trotwood. Through it all he was so lovable that wherever he went he attracted some one bit of unaffected devotion, usually among lowly, simple, artless, people.

an artless David-Copperfield sort of youth

CORDAY, CHARLOTTE

Charlotte Corday (1768-1793) was a French girl who believed that the excesses and the terrorism of the French Revolution could be ended if Marat, the most cruel of the triumvirate of Danton, Robespierre and Marat, was killed. She sacrificed herself to denunciation and certain death by gaining admission through a ruse to Marat's quarters and stabbed him. Her name indicates patriotic, daring, sacrificial patriotism.

there's many a Charlotte Corday in the underground

CORDELIA

Cordelia, in Shakespeare's *King Lear*, is the aged monarch's youngest and favorite daughter, who, though sincere in her filial devotion, is disinherited in favor of her deceitful and hypocritical sisters Goneril and Regan. When they have cast their father aside in shameful neglect, Cordelia comes to rescue him but is captured and put to death. Lear, realizing the noble depths of Cordelia's love for him, dies of a broken heart.

a Cordelia in her father's heart

CORINNA

Corinna was a Greek lyric poetess of the sixth century B.C. In a simple style she wrote of the legends of her native land. She criticized Pindar for having too few myths woven into the fabric of his odes, but when he went to the opposite extreme and included too many, she uttered the proverbial expression attributed to her: "One should sow by handfuls, not with the whole sack." Thus her own work was always tempered with moderation and simplicity.

Corinnan insistence on moderation

CORIOLANUS

Coriolanus is the hero of one of the most stirring of the early Roman legends. Born Caius (or Cnaeus) Marcius, he received his surname for valor displayed at the capture of the Volscian town of Corioli. In 491 B.C., however, he was impeached and exiled because of his haughtiness toward the Roman plebeians who feared and disliked him. Taking refuge with the Volscians, he offered them his aid in a war against his native city and was appointed general of the Volscian army for the enterprise. He was victorious on his march all the way to the Cluilian dike near Rome. The Romans, alarmed, sent envoy after envoy to him encamped there in order to dissuade him from his traitorous project, but he remained obdurate to their pleas. At length his mother Veturia and his wife Volumnia came with his two children to intercede with him. They successfully prevailed on him to lead back the hostile army and to remain in exile for the rest of his life.

Another account says that the Volscians put him to death on his return for his disloyalty to them.

another Coriolanus bitter at his country

CORNEILLE, PIERRE

Pierre Corneille (1606-1684) was the great French dramatist whose first work gained applause, the critics said, "because it catered to the vicious taste of the public." Be that as it may, his work ranged all the way from simple comedy to sublime tragedy, always with a good plot and a profound understanding of inner personal conflicts and of the clash of wills. He was the first to free the drama from its slavery to the Greek and Roman classic style and make his characters talk like human beings.

startled his public with his Corneille frankness

CORNELIA

Cornelia was the virtuous and accomplished mother of the Gracchi, whose education she supervised. She was adored by the people, who erected a statue to her with the simple inscription, "To the Mother of the Gracchi." She is famed the world over for her answer when asked about her jewels, "These are my jewels," as she pointed to her sons. She stands for nobility, dignity, and wise motherhood.

rivals Cornelia's pride

CORNELIUS

Cornelius was the Roman centurion stationed at Caesarea who became the first Christian convert (*Acts,* x). "A devout man and one that feared God," he had visions of the Holy Spirit and caused both himself and his household to be baptized in the Christian brotherhood.

a proselyte like Cornelius

CORNWALLIS

Cornwallis (1738-1805), daring and dashing, and by common consent called the most able British general during the Revolution in America, was a wonderful leader in the expected military situation and the regulation military tactics, but disturbed by the unexpected and wholly original ingenuity of the Americans. The name is now used of any gallant and admirable military leader who is forced to surrender because he has failed to appraise all the facts.

the bewilderment of a Cornwallis

COROT, JEAN

Jean Corot (1796-1875) was the French landscape painter whose pictures are marked by the atmospheric quality of early morning mistiness or of twilight, the foliage delicately diffused yet suggesting mass, and the whole remarkably true to nature. He is famous, too, for his catching and getting into his scenes his own emotion upon beholding them, a quality made evident both in his canvases and in his diary concerning the occasion of the painting.

endowed with the enchanting Corot-like quality
almost a Corot atmosphere
the stage was set in Corot tones

CORVUS, M. VALERIUS

Marcus Valerius Corvus gained his surname of "raven" from a brave event in his illustrious career in the annals of early Rome. In B. C. 349 he accepted the challenge of a gigantic Gaul to meet him in single-handed combat. In the conflict that ensued he was assisted to victory by a raven, which settled on his helmet and flew in the face of the barbarian. Reaching the age of 100 years, he was often referred to by later writers as a memorable example of the favors of fortune.

as friendly as Corvus's raven

CORYBANTIC

Corybantic refers to the fantastic frenzy of the Corybantes, priests of Cybele, the goddess of reproduction who haunted forests and mountains. Their festivals in celebration of the goddess were marked by loud orgies, noisy music, and self-inflicted wounds, in the most extravagant of demonstrations.

degenerated into a Corybantic orgy

CORYDON

Corydon, a simple shepherd swain in Vergil's *Eclogues,* has since been used as a type name in English pastoral poetry. It suggests any enamoured rustic in actual life.

to meet her Corydon in leafy lanes

COSSACK

The Cossacks were a pastoral Russian people, with skilled horsemen, who were from ancient times the basis of the Russian cavalry. Swift in attack, hardy, fearless, they were a formidable part of Russian military strength. The word has come to mean hard, fearless horsemanship anywhere.

swift as a Cossack

COTYS

Cotys, or Cotytto, was the Thracian goddess of immodesty and obscenity. In *Comus* Milton speaks of her as "goddess of nocturnal sport, dark-veiled Cotytto." She was worshiped at Corinth and Athens with rites that were known as *Cotyttia.* Associated with the Phrygian deity Cybele, she had her orgiastic and licentious liturgies presided over by special priests known as *Baptes* (*q.v.*).

indecent enough to shock even Cotys

COVENTRY

"To send to Coventry" means to ignore a person. The meaning grows out of an old story that Coventry so disliked soldiers that no woman there was permitted to speak to a soldier. Consequently, for a soldier to be sent to Coventry meant social exile, a fact so generally accepted that social exile of any kind came to be called being "sent to Coventry."

apparently being sent to Coventry

COVERLY, SIR ROGER DE

Sir Roger de Coverly is the lovable, elderly, beneficent, but positive country squire in Addison's Roger de Coverly Papers from the *Spectator.* He was beloved for his kindly grace, respected for his management of his great estate, and his native wisdom, and esteemed for his faultless dignity, integrity, and high character. He also delighted his friends by his amusing methods of securing church attendance in his parish, his superstitions, his fear of the rowdyism of a town, his shy devotion to the widow, and his simple gratitude for gracious attentions.

with a Roger-de-Coverly aimiability

COXEY'S ARMY

Coxey's Army refers to the group of 122 unemployed men whom Jacob S. Coxey assembled during the second presidency of Grover Cleveland. Setting out from Massillon, Ohio, on March 25, 1894, they reached Washington, D. C., on May 1st. Coxey was apprehended and imprisoned for twenty days on charges of trespassing and carrying a banner in the Capitol grounds.

a group of unemployed as restless as Coxey's Army

CRABTREE

Crabtree is the name of a mischief-maker in Sheridan's *School for Scandal.*

a Crabtree at stirring up discord

CRANE, ICHABOD

Ichabod Crane, the fantastically tall, long-necked and superstitious schoolmaster in Irving's *Legend of Sleepy Hollow,* is remembered for his timidity and his terror-stricken flight when pursued by what he believed to be a headless horseman.

the voice of a Webster and the look of an Ichabod Crane

CRAPAUD, JOHNNY

Johnny, or Jean, Crapaud is a sportive designation of a Frenchman or of the French nation collectively. The origin of the name may be found in a prediction of Nostradamus that adumbrated the taking of Arras from the Spaniards under Louis XIV after a long and desperate siege. The prophecy had declared that the city would fall to *anciens crapauds* ("ancient toads"), for the armorial bearings of the French nation had formerly been three of those amphibians.

the accent of a Johnny Crapaud

CRASSUS, MARCUS

Marcus Crassus, a Roman praetor in 105 B.C., was so sober-faced and serious that he never laughed. On one occasion at sight of an ass eating thistles he heard someone say, "Like lips, like lettuce," and was forced to smile.

couldn't smile any more than Crassus

CRASSUS, MARCUS LICINIUS

Marcus Licinius Crassus, grandson of Marcus Crassus the praetor, became one of the richest men in Rome because of his shrewd financial dealings. He owned silver mines and succeeded in buying up a large slice of Rome by bidding for houses when they were burning and consequently priced cheaply. A triumvir with Caesar and Pompey in 60 B.C., he was defeated and murdered at Carrhae, in 53, in his war with the Parthians in the East.

shrewd financial dealings worthy of Crassus.

CRATCHIT, BOB

Bob Cratchit is the poor clerk and the father of the family in Dickens' *Christmas Carol.* He is the man whose simple Christmas Day with his family, from the hour he starts out carrying Tiny Tim to church, through the Christmas dinner, on to the late visit of Scrooge, has made its way into the heart of the world. Bob Cratchit is an example of the modest, tender, pleasant, unassuming father of a family he loves.

as kindly and cheerful as a Bob Cratchit

CRAWLEYS, THE

The Crawleys are one of the important families in Thackeray's *Vanity Fair.* Sir Pitt is a rich, miserly, and coarse baronet and country squire. The Reverend Bute, his brother, is a fox-hunting, horse-playing parson who lets his wife compose his sermons. Rawdon, Pitt's younger son, is a handsome, debonair, and unscrupulous dragoon who is very much in love with Becky Sharp, whom he has married secretly.

unoriginal as Bute Crawley's sermons

CREAKLE, MR.

Mr. Creakle is a bullying schoolteacher in Dicken's *David Copperfield.* Fiery-faced and speaking in an angry whisper, he delights in punishing the boys over whom this incapable brute has no right to authority.

a teacher as sadistic as Mr. Creakle

CREON

Creon was the tyrannical king of Thebes and contemporary of Oedipus who ruled the city after the siege of The Seven (*q.v.*). By cruel edict he forbade burial to the corpse of one of the besiegers, Polynices, but the latter's heroic sister, Antigone, honored divine justice above human and gave it symbolic interment. By sentencing her to death for disobeying his orders, Creon inadvertently caused the death of his own son Haemon, her betrothed, and of his grief-crazed wife.

orders as arbitrary as Creon's

CRESSIDA

(see *Troilus*)

CREUSA

Creusa, in Greek mythology, was a princess of Corinth who became the second wife of Jason. Medea, whom she had supplanted in his favors, sent her a wedding present of a crown and robe steeped in inflammable chemicals, and when she donned it, consuming fires destroyed her by a horrible death.

Another Creusa was the first wife of Aeneas. When the hero fled Troy after its destruction, she was separated from him and detained in the homeland by will of the Great Goddess.

burned to a crisp like Creusa

CRICHTON

The Admirable Crichton was actually James Crichton, 1567, a Scotch gentleman, scholar, and adventurer noted for his resourcefulness. Barrie made him the chief character in a play of that name, in which he is a paragon of tact, ingenuity, and resourcefulness in directing and saving his so-called superiors when they are cast upon an island, but steps back into his old role of service when they all revert to their conventional life.

a very Crichton in any emergency

CRISPIN

Crispin is the name of an impudent and boastful valet, a stock character in Italian and French comedy. It is also the name of a Christian saint who with his brother Crispinian went to Soissons in Gaul to do missionary work. Supporting themselves by their skill in the shoemaker's trade, they were beheaded by order of the emperor Maximian in 287. Saint Crispin is regarded as the patron of cobblers, saddlers, and tanners.

as skillful as St. Crispin at working with leather

CROCKETT, DAVID

David Crockett (1786-1836) received his early training as a frontiersman in the Tennessee backwoods, where his feats as a hunter, trapper, and marksman made him nationally famous. After serving in the Creek War under Andrew Jackson, he became a colonel in the Tennessee militia and entered the State Legislature, gaining election more by his story-telling ability than by political speeches. A Jackson Democrat, he served three terms as Representative to Washington, where his shrewd wit and eccentric manners became proverbial. Because he split with Jackson over the latter's Indian policy, he lost out on a fourth term in the national capital and in disgust emigrated to Texas, where he fell fighting in defense of the Alamo on the 6th of March.

has Davy Crockett's flair for the woods

CROESUS

Croesus was a Greek king so renowned for his wealth that "rich as Croesus" has become one of the most familiar of phrases descriptive of fabulous riches.

all the riches of Croesus could not buy content

CROMWELLIAN

Cromwellian refers to Oliver Cromwell, English statesman and reformer, Lord Protector (dictator) of England from 1653 to 1658, the period of the Commonwealth. Cromwell was noted for his power, statesmanship, wisdom, and courage, and for his organizing ability. The name is used today in compliment to the courage and statecraft of a person. His army, made up exclusively of men who read the Bible, prayed and believed in God and was never defeated.

the Cromwellian soldier never met defeat
a Cromwellian band
the righteous fervor of a Cromwell

CRONUS

Cronus, called Saturn by the Romans, was the son of Uranus and Ge (Heaven and Earth). He castrated his father and deprived him of the government of the earth for having confined his children to the lower world. Married to Rhea, Cronus became the father of Hestia, Demeter, Hera, Hades, Poseidon, and Zeus. Because he had been warned that one of his own children would one day depose him, he swallowed all of Rhea's babies as soon as they were born, but Zeus was saved by a wile of his mother's in substituting a stone wrapped in swaddling clothes for the infant himself. When he had matured, Zeus was successful in dethroning Cronus.

another Cronus, deposed from power

CROW, JIM

Jim Crow has become a typical name for a negro in the southern States ever since it was first used in a refrain in T. D. Rice's minstrel song "Jim Crow," produced in 1835. To less prejudiced Northerners the name has offensive connotations of unfair segregation and insulting discrimination of negroes from whites in public vehicles, restaurants, theaters, and other public places.

herded into a Jim Crow segregation

CRUMMLES, VINCENT

Vincent Crummles, in Dickens' *Nicholas Nickleby,* is the eccentric star and manager of a cheap theatrical troupe playing in the Portsmouth Theater. The father of Ninetta Crummles, billed as the "Infant Phenomenon," he has his entire family on the stage, including a dog that lived and died on it. Always seeking for novelties to present, he approaches Nicholas with an offer, saying, "There's genteel comedy in your walk and manner, juvenile tragedy in your eye, and touch-and-go farce in your laugh. You'll do as well as if you had thought of nothing else but the lamps from your birth downwards."

as devoted to the stage as Vincent Crummles

CRUNCHER, JERRY

Jerry Cruncher is a character in Dickens' *Tale of Two Cities,* who is an employee of Tellson's Bank by day and a body-snatcher and self-styled "resurrection man" by night. The cold-blooded ghoul sells his cadavers to physicians for anatomical dissection and study.

ghoulish as Jerry Cruncher

CRUSADERS

The Crusaders were persons who went on a series of military expeditions (1096-1271) supported by Christian monarchs to rescue sacred places of Palestine from the Mohammedans when the Pope called upon the world for a holy crusade in a personal appeal that accomplished the greatest triumph of human oratory, concluding with "Jesus Christ summons you!" The response was immediate and frenzied, under the slogan "It is the will of God." The cross was sewed to every Crusader's garment; a moratorium of debts, imprisonments, and of war during the Crusades was declared, and for two centuries there was religious frenzy, tumult, disorder, license, and crime, bringing about greater power of the church, an end of feudal aristocracy, a spread of chivalry, a stimulation of intellectual development, trade, commerce, and exploration. The name Crusader has come to mean any person who at personal sacrifice of time and energy devotes himself to any idea he believes will help the good of the world, or even of his own small section of the world.

has assumed the proportions of a crusade

CRUSOE, ROBINSON

Robinson Crusoe was the hero of a story by Daniel Defoe, based on the adventures of Alexander Selkirk, a Scottish sailor who was left for four years on the island of Juan Fernandez in 1704 with only his gun, his axe, and a little ammunition. Crusoe's adventures, his life on the island day by day, his man Friday, record all the possible and quite probable ways in which he maintained a not unhappy and altogether exciting existence, all told with an accuracy and a vividness that has held boys of all ages spellbound since the day of its publication.

Robinson Crusoe ingenuity

CUPID

Cupid is the son of Venus and god of love and intense longing, amorous dalliance, and desire. He is usually pictured with bow and arrow, in accordance with the story that he goes about shooting love into the hearts of people at random or mischievously. "Succumbed to Cupid's dart" is the poet's way of saying that one fell in love. His Greek name, Eros, gives us the English word *erotic.*

Cupid, he that shot so trim when King Cophetua loved the beggar maid

---

CURETES

The Curetes were mythical Cretan earth-spirits. Rhea entrusted the care of her infant son Zeus to them, after she had saved the child from being swallowed by his fother Cronus (*q.v.*). By clashing their weapons in a frenzied warlike dance they drowned out the cries of the infant, thus preventing his father from finding where he was concealed. They later remained as priests of Rhea in her temples in Crete.

a tumultuous din, created by the Curetes

CURIE, MME. MARIE

Madame Marie Curie (1867-1934) was the Polish physicist and chemist who discovered radio-active substances, an achievement that advanced the world immeasurably in the treatment of theretofore irremediable ailments. She was remarkable not only for her skill, endurance and perseverance in the face of repeated disappointments, but for her utter simplicity, modesty, and dignity in the face of the world-fame and acclamation showered upon her success.

the modesty of a Madame Curie

CURIUS DENTATUS

Manius Curius Dentatus is famous as a type of old Roman honor, virtue, austerity and frugality. As consul in the years 290, 275 and 274 B.C. he defeated the Samnites, refusing a bribe of gold they offered him and bringing the war to a close. After defeating

Pyrrhus, an invader of Italy from Epirus, he retired to his farm, rejecting any share of war booty for his reward.

honorable as Curius

CURTIUS, METTIUS

Mettius Curtius was the distinguished Roman after whom the Lacus Curtius, a marshy spot in the Forum, was named. According to legend, a great chasm appeared in the earth on this spot in B. C. 362, and the soothsayers stated that it could be filled only by casting into it Rome's greatest treasure. Thereupon Curtius, a noble youth, mounted his horse in full armor and declared that Rome held no greater treasure than a brave and gallant citizen. He leaped into the abyss and the earth closed over him.

as patriotic as Mettius Curtius

CUTPURSE, MOLL

Moll Cutpurse was a notorious London pickpocket, whose name was finally used for any woman thief in the old puppet shows, and is still used in England of any light-fingered woman. Hence, the name suggests thievery, shoplifting, "snapping up of trifles" in any degree. Moll is the heroine of Middleton's comedy, *The Roaring Girl.*

the Moll Cutpurses have turned into shoplifters

CUTTLE, CAPTAIN

Captain Cuttle is a character in Dickens' *Dombey and Son.* A kindly and good-natured sailor, he is as simple as a child, credulous, trustful, and generous. One of his favorite expressions is "When found, make a note of."

neglecting Captain Cuttle's advice, he never found it again

CYBELE

Cybele, the mother of the gods, was worshiped in Asia Minor in such wild and enthusiastic orgies that her worship has become associated with that of Bacchus. The Corybantes, who performed their orgiastic dances in the forests, were her priests.

Cybelean rites

CYCLOPEAN

Cyclopean is from Cyclopes, a family of giants, each having one eye in the middle of his forehead. Mythology says they made thunderbolts for Vulcan; Homer refers to them as giant shepherds. The word is now commonly used to indicate tremendous strength.

glaring as the Cyclopean eye

CYCNUS

Cycnus is the name of several characters who were metamorphosed into swans in Greek mythology. One, the son of Poseidon, was slain by Achilles in the Trojan war and subsequently transformed into the graceful bird. Another, a Ligurian prince and a friend of Phaëthon, was likewise transfigured and placed among the stars. From the form Cygnus comes the English word *cygnet.*

Cycnus gliding in majesty over the lake

CYPARISSUS

Cyparissus, in Greek mythology, was a son of Telephus (*q. v.*). Having unintentionally killed his favorite stag, he was seized with such inconsolable transports of grief that he was metamorphosed into a cypress tree.

grief as unassuageable as Cyparissus'

CYTHEREA

Cytherea, another name for Aphrodite, is the personification of love, the goddess born, fresh and beautiful, of the sea-foam. She is called Cytherea because the worship of Aphrodite was introduced into the island of Cythera, off the southern coast of Greece, where some authorities say she first rose from the sea.

sweeter than Cytherea's breath
fresh as sea-born Cytherea
warm as Cytherea

D

DABBAT

Dabbat, in Mohammedan religion, is the beast or monster regarded as the third sign of the coming resurrection. This symbol of the Apocalypse will appear with the Antichrist, called Daggial, and will separate the believers from the unbelievers.

discriminatory as Dabbat

DACTYLI

The Dactyli ("fingers") were supernatural beings who resided on Mount Ida in Phrygia and who were credited with the discovery of the metallurgic art of working iron and copper by means of fire. Connected with the worship of Rhea, or Cybele, they were sometimes confused with the Curetes, Corybantes, and Cabiri (*qq.v.*). They were also said to have introduced rhythm and music into Greece.

as flushed as the Dactyli at their forge

DAEDALIAN

Daedalian is from Daedalus, the Athenian who built the labyrinth in which the Minotaur was confined. He had been an artificer and a skillful worker, but had committed murder and fled to Crete. Daedalian means cunningly wrought, intricate, confusing, ingenious.

cannot escape the Daedalian political intrigue

DAGON

Dagon was the Philistine national god who, according to the Bible, had richly adorned temples in Gaza and other Phoenician cities. Represented as having the face and hands of a man but the tail of a fish, he was generally regarded as a symbol of fertility and reproductive power. Since his name resembles both the word for fish (*dag*) and that for grain (*dagan*), others take him to be a god of agriculture, corn, and grain.

needs Dagon to restore his strength

DAGUENET, SIR

Sir Daguenet, in Arthurian romance, was King Arthur's court jester and fool. Though deformed and weak in body, he was not lacking in courage on the occasion when, wearing the armor of a sick knight and impersonating Sir Lancelot, he succeeded in frightening off the Cornish knight Mark. He was himself accoladed by King Arthur.

gallant as Sir Daguenet

DAITYA

The Daitya were a Hindu race of demons, evil spirits, and giants who battled with the gods and interrupted sacrifices.

Daityan interference

DALADIER, EDOUARD

Daladier was the French minister representing France at the fatal Munich Conference in 1939, when France and England, called to conference by Hitler, then Dictator of Germany, agreed to let Hitler take the German-populated fringe of Czechoslovakia, called the Sudeten. This was the first step in the German march into World War II. His name has since been used for a weak, appeasing, gullible foreign policy.

as pathetic as Daladier

DALCROZEAN

Dalcrozean is from Emile Jaques-Dalcroze (1865- - -), a Swiss composer and teacher of musical eurhythmics, whose great work has been the development of the eurhythmic instinct in close conjunction with the sense of hearing and the instinct for tone. Based on defined relations between bodily movements and the movements of sound, it was applied particularly to the development in children of graceful, kinesthetic balance and gestures. In our time many of the posturings and stances have come to seem rather artificial and absurd, according to the standards of modern theatrical usage.

motions as studied as Dalcrozean maneuverings

DALGETTY, DUGALD

Dugald Dalgetty is a mercenary soldier of fortune in Scott's *Legend of Montrose*. Characterized by his pedantry, conceit, self-assurance and greediness, he is at the same time a man of real courage, completely trustworthy to those who pay him for his services, and his sword is at the beck and call of all the highest bidders.

as dependable as Dugald Dalgetty

DAMOCLEAN

Damoclean is from Damocles, a Syracusan whose extravagant admiration of royal luxury, magnificence, and wealth was tempered by Dionysius. The latter, to demonstrate the transience of royal good fortune, invited him to a banquet over which a sword was suspended by a single hair. The term *Damocles' sword* has since been used to suggest how precarious a thing is luxury, fame, and glory.

public acclaim is a precarious thing —a Damocles sword

DAMOETAS

Damoetas is the name of a herdsman and a rustic in the pastoral poetry of Theocritus and Vergil. In Sidney's *Arcadia* he is a foolish country clown. The name ranges, consequently, in application from use for a gentle, amorous, and simple swain to overtones of boorishness and bucolic stupidity.

watching his herds like Damoetas

DAMON AND PYTHIAS

Damon and Pythias, ancient and ideal friends from Syracuse, Sicily, were so ready to do or die for each other that Damon, when Pythias was once condemned to death, offered himself as hostage while Pythias was allowed to go and transact some final business. On Pythias' return, the Tyrant of Sicily, Dionysius, touched by such patent devotion and loyalty, pardoned him and begged to be a sharer in their friendship. In some versions Pythias is known as Phintias.

a Damon and Pythias loyalty

DAN TO BEERSHEBA

Dan to Beersheba means all the way from Dan, at the uppermost tip of Palestine, to Beersheba, the lowermost point; hence it signifies all the way, throughout, and is equivalent to the English expression, from *A* to Z.

they howled like dervishes all the way from Dan to Beersheba—madly happy

---

DANAE

Danaë was the daughter of Acrisius, the king of Argos, who confined her in a brazen tower to forestall an oracle that predicted his death at the hands of her son. Zeus loved her and succeeded in visiting her in the form of a shower of gold. A favorite subject in Renaissance painting, this metamorphosis is interpreted as a shower of sunbeams pouring over her nude body. Less romantically, it may be considered as bribe money proffered a greedy chaperon. In any case, she bore a son, Perseus, and she and her child were placed in a chest by Acrisius and set adrift at sea. Landing on the island of Seriphos, Danaë and Perseus received the hospitality of Dictys and Polydectes, the latter of whom wooed her in vain.

luxuriating in the sunshine like Danaë

DANAIDES

The Danaides were the fifty daughters of Danaus. They had fled with their father from his brother Aegyptus, pursued by Aegyptus's fifty sons. Danaus compelled his daughters to marry and then to murder the fifty sons, but for punishment in Hades the fifty Danaides are compelled to draw water in a sieve perpetually to fill a bottomless cask; hence, the significance futile, laborious, useless, endless.

obedient and unhappy Danaides

DANDIN, GEORGE

George Dandin, the hero of Molière's comedy of the same name, is a wealthy French citizen who marries the daughter of a noble and lives with his wife's parents, who always take her side in a disagreement and place him in the wrong. Forever lamenting his disagreeable fate with the words, "'Tis your own fault, George Dandin," he has become proverbial for any silly and simple-minded fellow who is henpecked by his wife and mother-in-law and subject to their rigorous rule.

henpecked as George Dandin

DANGLE

Dangle is a theatrical amateur in Sheridan's *The Critic*. Said to have been a characterization of a Mr. Thomas Vaughan, the author of an indifferently successful play, he besieges a theater manager with impertinent flattery and unasked for advice of a gratuitous and unwelcome nature.

the inexpert advice of a Dangle

DANIEL

Daniel was a Hebrew prophet and judge who as a child was brought with his three brothers to the King to be trained to speak Chaldean and to do the bidding of the King. He grew to be an interpreter of dreams, interpreted the dream of Nebuchadnezzar and prophesied his fall from his high estate and the loss of his reason, declaring that he would live as a beast of the field. It was Daniel, too, who interpreted the handwriting on the wall for Belshazzar, and foretold his doom. His name also lives as one of the most upright of the judges.

would try the skill of a Daniel

D'ANNUNZIO, GABRIELE

(see *Annunzio, Gabriele d'*)

DANTEAN

Dantean (also Dantesque) means in the style of Dante's *Inferno,* graphic, intense, epic in its scope. It is impressive, elevated, and solemn in style, hence giving the name Dantean to any attempt at or imitation of his inimitable expression. Dantean is also sometimes used of a love like that of Dante for the noble Beatrice, whom he cherished in his heart for years after he saw her passing by on a street in Italy; hence, a tender, passionate, life-long love.

a Dantesque picture, grim and terrible

a remote, reverent, Dantean worship

DANTES, EDMOND

Edmond Dantès, the hero of Dumas' novel *The Count of Monte Cristo,* is a young sailor who has been unjustly imprisoned for 14 years in the gloomy Chateau d'If in Marseilles harbor, as the victim of a plot. After making a bold and daring escape by simulating death and being cast into the sea in a sack, he takes possession of a treasure on the Isle of Monte Cristo and ultimately brings vengeance to bear on each of his persecutors.

a courageous break for freedom like that of Edmond Dantès

DANTON

Danton (1759-1794) was one of the three great leaders of the French Revolution in the height of its extreme terrorism, along with Robespierre and Marat. He was tyrannous, cruel, and incredibly callous to human anguish. He was finally, after the peak of the Revolution, himself destroyed by Robespierre.

capable of becoming a Danton

DAPHNE

Daphne was a nymph who, according to Greek mythology, when pursued by Apollo prayed to the gods for deliverance and was turned into a laurel tree, which became thereafter Apollo's favorite tree and is held sacred to him.

swifter than fleeting Daphne's twinkling feet
more swift than Daphne in her race
as shy as Daphne 'fore Apollo's love

DAPHNIS

Daphnis was the son of Hermes and a nymph. A Sicilian shepherd beloved by a nymph, he was blinded by her either because he did not reciprocate her love or because he was unfaithful to her. He spent the rest of his life composing mournful songs and lamentations on his unhappy fate, works which are supposed to be the origin of pastoral poetry. According to Theocritus, he was a chaste shepherd who refused to love and was punished by Aphrodite with a longing for some one unattainable, in consequence of which he pined away and died.

pines like Daphnis

DARBY AND JOAN

Darby and Joan, in an old story of a happy and elderly married couple, lived a peaceful and contented domestic life, pleased with each other, thoughtful and considerate and satisfied; hence, typical of conjugal happiness and placid content.

a happy Darby and Joan existence

DARCY, MR.

Mr. Darcy is the proud lover and suitor of Elizabeth Bennet in Jane Austen's *Pride and Prejudice.*

orgulous as Mr. Thomas Darcy

DARIUS

Darius was an Achaemenid prince who in 512 B.C. formed a conspiracy with six other men to overthrow the usurper of the throne of Persia. The seven chiefs had agreed that the one whose horse neighed first at a given time and place subsequent to their victory over the usurper should become king. Darius succeeded to the throne. The most important event in his reign was the commencement of the great war against Greece, provoked by a revolt of the Ionian Greeks. Except for the first invasion of Greece, however, marked by his victory at Marathon and defeat at Salamis, the prosecution of his further plans was left to his son Xerxes.

proud of his horse as Darius

DARROW, CLARENCE

Clarence Darrow was so successful a defense lawyer in the large number of important cases drawing national attention which he undertook that it was felt that he never lost a case, however conclusive the evidence against his client. Recognized as the leading criminal lawyer in the United States, he was also retained by the labor organizations of his time in nearly all their litigation. Some of his most celebrated cases were the Steinenburg murder case, the Leopold-Loeb defense, and the Debs strike case. In 1925 he defended J. T. Scopes at the Tennessee evolution trial involving the teaching of Darwinism in the public schools of that state. He was also the author of *Crime, Its Cause and Treatment* and many other books on social and economic questions, and placed on society the blame for delinquency.

a prolonged Darrow-like defense

D'ARTAGNAN

D'Artagnan, the chief of the four heroes in Dumas' *The Three Musketeers,* is ingenious, resourceful, daring, the leader in the many adventures engaging the three musketeers in their escapades all over the world, be it country road or city alley, king's palace or squalid cellar. In all alike it was the quick mind and the alert swordplay of D'Artagnan that saved the day; hence, daring, venturesome, resourceful, gay.

with D'Artagnan's own skill in swordplay

DARTLE, ROSA

Rosa Dartle is a disfigured woman in Dickens' *David Copperfield.* In spite of an old scar which had once cut through her mouth, downward toward the chin, she had some appearance of good looks. "A little dilapidated—like a house—with having been so long to let," she gave the impression of wanting to be married, and her excessive thinnness seemed to be the result of some consuming fire within her that prompted her to say frequently, "I want to know."

a husband-hunting Rosa Dartle

DARWINIAN

Darwinian is from Charles Darwin (1809-1882), eminent English naturalist of the nineteenth century, who won undying fame by his *Origin of the Species.* This proposed the evolution of new species originated from old, and perpetuated by natural selection. His theory became a matter of such widespread dissension, such violent disagreement, and such vehement discussion that the whole theory is known as Darwinism. Advocates of the theory are known as Darwinians. Even the little irregularity rather like the point of an animal's ear, but occasionally appearing on the human ear, is known as a Darwinian.

fanatical excitement about the Darwinian theory

DAVID

When David, son of Jesse, was a shepherd lad, he killed Goliath, the champion of the Philistines, with a sling, restored the moody King Saul with his shepherd songs, and after Saul's death became king of Israel. He transformed the people from a pastoral to a conquering nation. He also planned the magnificent temple that Solomon finished. To David are credited the Psalms, songs of devotion and trust, lyric and beautiful.

Davidian minstrelsy

DAWKINS, JOHN

John Dawkins is a nimble-fingered pickpocket in Dickens' *Oliver Twist.* He is otherwise known as the "Artful Dodger" (*q.v.*).

the light-fingered John Dawkins of the crowd

DAWSON, BULLY

Bully Dawson, a notorious bully and highwayman, a swaggering sharper, lived in the infamous part of London and terrorized the famous part. According to the Spectator, "half the town kicked him, and he kicked half the town." His name is still the word for a defiant, reckless highwayman and swindler.

rid the town of its Bully Dawson

DEADEYE, DICK

Dick Deadeye, in Gilbert and Sullivan's *H. M. S. Pinafore,* is a hunchbacked sailor and pirate, the foil for the hero Ralph Rackstraw.

buccaneering like Dick Deadeye

DEADWOOD DICK

Deadwood Dick is the celebrated scout, frontiersman, and Indian fighter who is the hero of dime-novel romances. This fictional character is said to have been modeled on Robert Dickey (1840-1912), an American trapper.

a woodsman as agile as Deadwood Dick

DEAE MATRES

Deae Matres ("mother-goddesses") was the Latin name for the three Teutonic divinities of plenty and abundance.

blessed by the Deae Matres

DEANS, EFFIE

Effie Deans is the tragic heroine of Scott's *Heart of Midlothian.* The daughter of a poor cowherd, she is ruined and abandoned by Geordie Robertson, her lover. Pilloried and outcast, she is driven to infanticide of her bastard child and condemned as a murderess.

another poor, unmarried Effie Deans

DEBORAH

Deborah was the famous prophetess and judge of Israel (*Judges,* iv, v). Her court was held in a spot named after her in the hills of Ephraim. In the dark days of the oppression she became the adviser and inspirer of Barak, and with him she planned the campaign that resulted in the overthrow of the Canaanites. Her victory is the subject of the vivid and fervent *Song of Deborah.*

astute and wise as Deborah

DEBUSSY, CLAUDE

Claude Debussy (1862-1918) was a French musician who broke away from all the conventional standards to write work at first startling, but later accepted as beautiful, and now considered a step forward in all musical composition. His music is sensitive, mysterious, dreamy, and elusive, full of tone-painting and impressionism, as in the sumptuous orchestral work "The Afternoon of a Faun," the pianistic "Clair de Lune," and the opera *Pelléas and Mélisande.*

Debussyan moonlight

DECIUS MUS, PUBLIUS

Publius Decius Mus was the Roman consul who at the time of the Latin War (340 B.C.) gained victory for his side by the solemn act of *devotio.* Vowing himself to death in battle if the gods would grant success to the Romans and take the enemy troops along to Hades with him, he charged into the thick of the foe in a kind of patriotic suicide. His son, of the same name, committed a similar act of self-sacrifice against the Samnites in 295 B.C.

a Decius Mus to lead the suicide-squad

DEDLOCK, LADY

Lady Dedlock, wife of Sir Leicester in Dickens' *Bleak House,* had an illegitimate child, Esther Summerson (*q.v.*), by Captain Hawdon before her marriage, and subsequently lives in constant fear of discovery. At the end of a life miserable with apprehensive remorse, she is found dead on the grave of her first lover.

another Lady Dedlock, fearing exposure and disgrace

DEDLOCK, LEICESTER

Sir Leicester Dedlock is an honorable and trustful gentleman in Dickens' *Bleak House.* No one can shake him of his prejudices and fossilized ideas. He is obstinate, high spirited and completely unreasonable, though he has been cuckolded by his wife, Lady Dedlock.

prejudiced as Dedlock

DEFARGE, MME. THERESE

Mme. Thérèse Defarge is the wife of a Parisian wine-seller in Dickens' *Tale of Two Cities.* One of the Jacquerie, she conveys messages in code in her knitting. Embodying the implacable blood-thirst of the Terror, the relentless hag counts the number of guillotine executions, knitting happily as she tolls them off.

knitting as savagely as Mme. Defarge

DEFOE, DANIEL

Daniel Defoe (1661-1731), a reporter and journalist in London who late in years chanced upon Alexander Selkirk, a sailor who had for years been marooned on a desert island, let his imagination play with the story until he had evolved *Robinson Crusoe,* a world classic in adventure. His narrative is so simple in style, so objective, and has so perfectly the trick of achieving an amazing verisimilitude that fools the reader into complete belief, the name Defoe has ever since meant the ability to make a person believe the unbelievable. Defoe also wrote *Moll Flanders* and *The History of the Plague in London,* both with the same quality of utter reality.

Defoe's air of truth

DEGAS, EDGARD

Edgard Degas (1834-1917) was the French painter in whose work can be seen the influence of the blindness that closed over his vision. His delicate pastels of groups of ballet dancers, performing before footlights and represented informally in poses depicting them engaged in such tasks as fastening their slippers, are remarkable for their plasticity. He also modeled silhouettes of women and horses, which were not cast in bronze until after his death, and executed drawings that are prized for their delicacy of line.

posturing like a Degas ballerina

DEIANIRA

Deianira was the wife of the hero Hercules. Hoodwinked by the Centaur Nessus, who was slain by Hercules for offering violence to his wife, Deianira believed Nessus' words when he told her before dying that if she sent Hercules a shirt steeped in his blood it would preserve her husband's love. The blood being poisoned, it caused the hero such agonies that he threw himself on a funeral pyre and perished. In remorse and despair the gullible Deianira then put an end to her own life.

credulous as Deianira

DEIPHOBUS

Deiphobus was the son of Priam and Hecuba who married Helen of Troy after the death of Paris. When the avenging Greeks captured the Trojan citadel, he was betrayed by the perfidious Helen and brutally killed and mangled by her first husband, Menelaus. Next to Hector he had been the bravest and boldest of all the Trojans.

another Deiphobus betrayed by his own wife

DEIPNOSOPHISTAE

The Deipnosophistae ("connoisseurs in dining") were a group of twenty-three learned men who, in the work of that name by Athenaeus, met for dinner in Rome on several occasions and conversed about food in all its aspects, as well as about a host of other things. The name Deipnosophist, hence, refers to an interesting conversationalist at a dinner party and to one adept at table talk.

as fluent at the table as the Deipnosophistae

DEIRDRE

Deirdre in old Celtic literature is the spirit and personification of all beauty, all sweetness, all womanliness, with a singleness of passion and a loyalty that might well be the pattern for a Juliet or a Desdemona. When her guardian, King Conchobar, was about to marry her she ran away with her lover, Usna, but returned on the king's promise to pardon her lover and his brothers. The king betrayed his promise, put the brothers to death, and Deirdre's sorrow was so great that she killed herself. The legend constantly appears in Celtic literature, most beautifully in Fiona Macleod's *Fall of the House of Usna,* where in the preface she is called "the essence of tragic loveliness."

even as Deirdre, soul of all love, all desire

DELIA

Delia is the pseudonym with which the Roman poet Tibullus (*q.v.*) calls his sweetheart and lady-love. Her real name is thought to have been Plania, the Latin root of which would correspond in meaning with the Greek Delia, meaning *bright, clear, radiant* and *manifest.* Delia is also a surname of Diana (Artemis), meaning one born on Delos, the bright and clear island.

hides his love under the name Delia

DELILAH

Delilah, the beautiful scarlet woman of the Philistines, and mistress of Samson, beguiled him into telling her the source of his strength so that she might betray it to the Philistines, who then robbed him of his strength and held him captive for many years. Delilah is now used of any alluring and treacherous woman.

many a strong man owes his downfall to a Delilah

no man leaps from Delilah's lap to Abraham's bosom

DELLA CRUSCANS

The Della Cruscans, so called from the Crusca or Academy in Florence, were a school of sentimental poetasters started by a group of young Englishmen in the latter part of the eighteenth century. Conspicuous for their lackadaisical and sentimental effusions, sentimentality and bad taste, they wrote high flown panegyrics about each other and created quite a furor at the time.

lackadaisical as a Della Cruscan

DELMONICO

Delmonico, chef and restaurateur in New York, was so famous for cooking and fine food that the name has come to imply the acme of the culinary art.

savors of Delmonico's

DELPHI

The Delphic Oracle is the shrine of Apollo at Delphi, where the oracle appears as a vapor, "the breath of Apollo," from a fissure in the ground. This oracle was sought as a matter of course by the authorities in Asia and in Rome, and always by the Greeks, before they set out on any significant undertaking. It was believed that no colonization would prosper unless it had been approved by the Delphic oracle.

Oh were there but some oracle,
some Delphic utterance wise
to guide

DEMETER

(see *Ceres*)

Demeter is another name for Ceres, the goddess of the fruitful earth and of marriage and the special protector of fertility. She was the mother of Proserpina, queen of the lower world.

Demeter's bounty

DEMIURGIC

Demiurgic is from Demiurge, Plato's name for the Creator of the world. In other philosophies it is a force building the world as directed by a Superior Being, and in still others it is regarded as the source of evil. Hence, *demiurgic* may be found in quite widely differing contexts, to indicate either good or evil creation.

Demiurgic energy

DEMOCRITUS

Democritus of Abdera (born c. 460 B.C.) was an ancient writer on natural philosophy, morals, mathematics, and music. He believed the universe to be composed of atoms moving about in space and grouping themselves into bodies, which, though constantly changing and disintegrating themselves, cannot harm the eternal nature of their atomic elements. He supposed the soul to consist of fire, itself the rarest and subtlest form of atomic structure. Because he was pictured by Juvenal as laughing at the follies of mankind, though maintaining that happiness (in moderation) is the *summum bonum* of life, he became known as the Laughing Philosopher and was thus contrasted with Heraclitus (*q.v.*), the Weeping Philosopher.

a gleeful Democritus, poking fun at
the foibles of his fellows

DEMOCRITUS JUNIOR

Democritus Junior is the pseudonym under which Robert Burton (1576-1640) published his celebrated *Anatomy of Melancholy*. In quaint language and with considerable humor he presented a view of all the modifications of that disease and the manner of curing it. The pseudonym alludes to Democritus of Abdera (*q.v.*), the famous "laughing philosopher" of antiquity, and is also found in the inscription of Burton's monument in Christ Church Cathedral. The name connotes one who derides and laughs at other people's folly.

whimsically derisive as Democritus
Junior

DEMODOCUS

Demodocus is the famous minstrel and bard at the Phaeacian court of king Alcinous in the *Odyssey*. As he sings of the fall of Troy he moves Ulysses (Odysseus) to tears and stimulates the hero to tell of his adventures since leaving Troy. His music also evokes nostalgia and a longing for his home in Ithaca in the heart of the wanderer.

nostalgic as the music of Demodocus

DEMOGORGON

Demogorgon is a vague and mysterious power whose very name is so tremendous that Statius only alludes to it, speaking of him as "the Most High of the triple universe, whom it is unlawful to know." Boccaccio speaks of him as the primeval god, and in Shelley he is an eternal power who ousts the gods of false theology. According to Ariosto, the fairies were all subject to him and he inhabited a palatial temple in the Himalayas, where he summoned them before him every fifth year to give an account of their deeds. Elsewhere, he is a genius of the soil or earth, reputed to be the life and sustenance of plants and pictured as an old man covered with moss as he lives underground.

as vague and mysterious as Demogorgon

DEMOSTHENES

Demosthenes (384-322 B.C.), the greatest of the ancient Greek orators, had to overcome a stammering speech defect and a weak voice to attain his eminence. Thus, he is said to have spoken with pebbles in his mouth to cure himself of the former, to have quoted poetic verses while running up hill and to have harangued by the sea shore in order to strengthen his voice and to accustom himself to the hurly-burly and turbulence of the popular assemblies. Foreseeing that Philip of Macedon (*q.v.*) was plotting to subjugate all of Greece, he devoted all his powers to warning his countrymen in a series of impassioned speeches leveled at that unscrupulous monarch. Hence, any speech of impassioned denunciation has come to be known as a Philippic.

the perseverance of a Demosthenes in voice control

DENDIN, PERRIN

Perrin Dendin is an ignorant peasant who is applied to as a judge in Rabelais' *Pantagruel.* His characterization is intended as a satire on lawyers who prefer the ruin of their clients to the slightest concession.

a stupid Perrin Dendin of an arbiter

DENIS, SAINT

Saint Denis, or Denys, was the apostle to the Gauls, the first bishop of Paris, and the patron saint of France. He underwent martyrdom by decapitation in the third century, and in art is represented as raising himself in order to carry his severed head, which he transported for six miles to lay it down on the spot where stands the cathedral bearing his name.

beheaded like Saint Denis

DE QUINCEY, THOMAS

Thomas DeQuincey (1785-1859), one of the best read and best informed men of London, read so voraciously that the story went round that he flung finished books on the floor until every room in the house was impassable, then turned the key and rented another house. A dreamer, too shy to "go up" for the examinations for a degree, he was nevertheless the most scholarly of critics, a master of English style, unsurpassed for his impassioned prose and sustained melody of sound. Some of the finest passages in the language are found in his *Dream Fugues.* His romantic style, his vigor and eloquence, his power to picture the terrible, the gorgeous, are exemplified in his incomparable *Flight of a Tartar Tribe.* His *Confessions of an Opium Eater* lay bare a period of his own life with the illuminating interpretation of a highly intelligent man.

like a DeQuincey confession

DERONDA, DANIEL

Daniel Deronda is the title-character and hero of George Eliot's novel about a philanthropic Jew who sacrificed his own life in the endeavor to restore their former political prestige to the Hebrew people.

a self-sacrificing Daniel Deronda

DESDEMONA

Desdemona, the beautiful and enthusiastic daughter of Brabantio in Shakespeare's *Othello,* was so enraptured by the tales of heroism and daring that Othello, a noble Moor, told, that despite his color and her family's objections she married him and was supremely happy, adored by her husband. Meantime, Othello's lieutenant, Iago, angered by Othello, determined to make him suffer in consequence, and in a roundabout way secured a handkerchief of Desdemona's which he swore had been given as a love token. Othello, in a frenzy of grief, smothered Desdemona, discovered Iago's trick, and killed himself in remorse.

a Desdemona-devotion

DEUCALION

Deucalion was the son of Prometheus, whom the latter warned that Zeus, irate over the sins of mankind, proposed to destroy the earth by a flood. He built an ark for himself and Pyrrha, his wife, and when the waters of the deluge receded they landed on Mount Parnassus. Advised by an oracle to throw over their shoulders "the bones of their mother" in order to repopulate the earth, they correctly interpreted this as referring to the stones of Mother Earth and did as they were told. From the stones cast by Deucalion men sprang up, from Pyrrha's, women. Their eldest son was Hellen, the legendary ancestor of the Hellenic race, who was himself the father of Dorus, Xuthus, and Aeolus, progenitors respectively of the Dorian, Ionian, and Aeolian Greeks.

antediluvian as Deucalion

DEVARSHIS

The Devarshis, in Hindu religion, are sages who, having attained perfection on earth, were subsequently exalted to heaven as demigods.

with the wisdom of the Devarshis

DHANVANTARI

Dhanvantari, in Hindu religion, is the physician of the gods, generated by the churning of the ocean with a cup of amrita (ambrosia) in his hands.

the medical skill of Dhanvantari

DIAGHILEV, SERGEI

Sergei Diaghilev (1872-1929) was the great impresario of the *Ballet Russe* who collaborated with dancer Michel Fokine and painter Leon Bakst to perfect Russian ballet by the artistic blending of choreography, costuming, stage sets, lighting, and music, commissioning the greatest composers and artists of his day to work toward this goal. Presenting dance versions of such popular orchestral pieces as Rimski-Korsakov's *Scheherezade* and Debussy's *L'Après-midi d'un Faune,* he also engaged Stravinsky to write musical scores for the ballets *L'Oiseau de Feu* and *Petrouchka.* Vaslav Nijinsky was his most sensational star and protégé, until a break occurred between the two, Nijinsky marrying to escape the homosexual bond between them. Though Diaghilev visited New York with his company, he exhibited the group principally in London, Paris, and Monte Carlo.

the Diaghilev of the dance studio

DIANA

Diana was the goddess of the moon, protector of maidenhood, and the goddess of the chase and of hunting. Hence, she stands for chastity, freedom, and wholesome outdoor sport with its attendant health. Her Greek name was Artemis as huntress, Selene as moon-goddess, Hecate as witch, and Delia or Cynthia as born at Cynthus on the island of Delos. Apollo was her twin-brother.

looks like a young Diana in the field

DIAVOLO, FRA

Fra Diavolo, or "Brother Devil," was the sobriquet of Michele Pezzo (1771-1806), the famous Italian brigand who in early life was a friar known as Fra Angelo ("Brother Angel"). His bandit activities were associated with the political turmoil in S. Italy in the time of the French invasion. His nickname arose from the audacious cunning with which he eluded arrest after his numerous robberies and murders had made him famous and a romantically popular figure. He carrier on guerrilla raids against the French troops with abominable cruelty and perpetrated many atrocious mass-slaughters. Finally captured, he was hanged at Naples in November of 1806, in spite of the intercession of the British who greatly admired his military prowess. Scribe wrote a libretto for an opera by Auber about this hero.

as elusive as Fra Diavolo

DICKENSIAN

Charles Dickens (1812-1870), master novelist, has peopled the language of the world with more significant names than has any other one author. Mr. Micawber, Uriah Heep, Mr. Pickwick —one could scarcely catalog them. His caricatures, his ludicrous situations, and his glorification of the ridiculous have never been approached, the depth of his tenderness, his compassion, his indignation, never surpassed. He won the ear of the public by breezy, exuberant, rollicking mirth, and having won it, he poured into it, through his merciless though comic exposure, knowledge of the abuses existing in poorhouses, schools, courts, laws. *Bleak House,* Mr. Bumble, Mr. Squeers, were revelations of evils at a time when England was inclined to correct evil conditions. Though Dickens contributed to the fun of the world, he also contributed to its betterment.

with Dickensian mirth

DICKINSON, EMILY

Emily Dickinson (1830-1886), a poet practically unrecognized in her own day, came into prominence on the late publication of her verses. They are always simple, usually short snatches from her own thought, and are notable for their perfect clarity and their unusual insight and penetration. Their brevity is deceptive; by a single stroke they open a world of suggestion, glimpse a world of thought and feeling.

an Emily Dickinson glimpse

DICTYNNA

Dictynna is a surname of Britomartis (*q.v.*) and Diana. Derived from the Greek word for "hunting net," the name was applied to these mythological deities as goddesses of the chase.

a Dictynna-like sportswoman

DIDDLER, JEREMY

Jeremy Diddler, a swindler in Kenney's farce, *Raising the Wind,* is always borrowing money and never paying. Nonchalantly asking for what he will, he is a needy, seedy, clever vagabond living by his wits and his consummate presumption; hence, swindler, borrower, ne'er-do-well, sponger.

Diddler's respect for a loan

DIDO

Dido was the daughter of Belus, king of Tyre, and the wife of Sychaeus, whom her brother Pygmalion murdered for his wealth. Fleeing from her treacherous brother, she went to Africa where she purchased as much land as could be covered with a bull's hide. After the bargain was completed, she craftily cut the hide into small shreds and strips, thereby securing a larger piece of territory. On it she built the city of Carthage, near which Aeneas was shipwrecked on his voyage from Troy to Italy. Dido (also called Elissa) fell in love with him and committed suicide when he rejected her and passed on to Italy.

The story of her tragic passion for the Trojan prince who was destined to become the founder of the Roman people of historical times was made by Vergil the original reason for the deadly hatred of Rome and Carthage that culminated in the Punic Wars, and Hannibal was regarded as her avenger. The great drama of Dido and Aeneas is told in the sixth book of Vergil's *Aeneid.* Henry Purcell, an English musician of the seventeenth century, used the story for the libretto of his opera, *Dido and Aeneas.*

the tragic despair of a Dido

DIGGARY

Diggary is a gauche and garrulous servant in Goldsmith's comedy, *She Stoops to Conquer.* A born laborer, he is used as butler and footman by Mr. and Mrs. Hardcastle on grand occasions. Laughing and talking with the guests while serving, he is as awkward as possible.

an awkward Diggary to wait table

DIKE

Dike, or Astraea, is a daughter of Zeus and Themis (*q.v.*) and, like her mother, the personification of justice in Greek mythology. An attendant of Nemesis, she also presides over good faith, modesty and truth. Her sisters are Eunomia ("wise legislation") and Eirene ("peace"). At the advent of the materialistic Iron Age she left earth for Olympia, informing Zeus of every injustice done on earth.

equitable as Dike

DIMMESDALE, ARTHUR

Arthur Dimmesdale is the Puritan clergyman in Hawthorne's *Scarlet Letter.* His conscience torments him for years by the burden of guilt which he is unable to confess. At length he makes a public confession of his adultery with Hester Prynne, who has been ignominiously branded with the scarlet "A."

conscience-vexed, like Arthur Dimmesdale

DINAH

Dinah, the daughter of Jacob by Leah (*Genesis xxx, xxxiv*), was violated by Shechem, the son of Hamor, after her father had moved from Aram to Canaan. The sons of Jacob, especially Simeon and Levi, subsequently avenged the rape of their sister by slaying all the inhabitants of Shechem and rescuing Dinah. The story may be a reflection of a tribal dispute rather than an account of a personal violation.

a Dinah rescued by her brothers

DIN, GUNGA

Gunga Din is the Hindu watercarrier in Kipling's poem of that name in *Barrack Room Ballads.* He is loyal, courageous, and highly lauded by his master, so unforgettably that his name is often applied to any loyal, fearless, and unselfishly faithful servitor. The tribute, "You're a better man than I am, Gunga Din" has become part of the language.

Gunga Din . . . white, clear white inside
When he went to tend the wounded under fire

The Gunga Dins are about to come into their own

DINMONT, DANDIE

Dandie Dinmont, in Scott's *Guy Mannering,* is the eccentric but courageous and manly Scotch farmer who owns two terriers that are claimed to have been the progenitor of a breed of very courageous dogs named "Dandie Dinmont terriers" after him.

the courage of a Dandie Dinmont

DIOCLETIAN

Diocletian, Roman emperor from 284 to 305 A.D., was born in Dalmatia of obscure parentage. After he gained the throne, he associated Maximianus with him to repel the barbarians' encroachments on the far-flung ramparts of the empire, making him a co-Augustus (or senior ruler) and selecting Constantius Chlorus and Galerius to be co-Caesars (or junior rulers). Having thus divided the government of the provinces among four men, he himself chose the East. His famous economic Edict of Prices (301 A.D.) was an interesting attempt in ancient times, though a failure, at setting ceiling prices on clothing, foodstuffs and other commodities. It also attempted to stabilize wages. He is equally famous for the fierce persecution of Christians which he instituted in 303. Two years later he abdicated, compelling his reluctant colleague and co-Augustus to do likewise. Retiring to his sumptuous palace at Spalato on the Dalmatian coast of the Adriatic, he spent the rest of his life in philosophic contemplation and in rural pleasures, such as that of cultivating his garden.

shares his power and divides his responsibilities like Diocletian

---

DIOGENES

Diogenes (412-323 B.C.), the noted Greek Cynic philosopher, declared that man needed few possessions, and to demonstrate he lived in a tub. He also believed that man had lost his sense of honor and his integrity, wherefore he went about in the daytime carrying a lantern in search, he said, of an honest man. Hence, Diogenes implies a self-satisfied but churlish and cynical person.

Diogenean skepticism

DIOMEDES

Diomedes (also called Tydides, or son of Tydeus) was one of the most renowned of the Greek chieftains at the siege of Troy. He performed many heroic deeds and with Ulysses stole the Palladium (*q.v.*) on which the safety of the city depended. An impetuous, fiery and chivalrous warrior, he vanquished many of the city's defenders and wounded Ares (Mars) and Aphrodite (Venus). The latter, enraged, caused his wife, Aigialeia, to be unfaithful to him during his absence. In grief over her deceit he wandered to Italy where he was said to have founded many cities in Apulia.

as valliant as Diomedes

DIONYSIUS

Dionysius I was a man of low birth who by demagoguery made himself master of Syracuse from 405 to 367 B.C. He conquered half of Sicily and extended his dominions to continental Italy. Possessing more power than any other Greek before Alexander, he became a tyrant in the worst sense of the word. Living in a fortified residence on the island of Ortygia, he was extremely suspicious and apprehensive of treachery, to guard against which he adopted excessive precautions. His flair for literature led him to write a prize-winning play, *The Ransom of Hector,* and he died from the effects of his drinking orgies in celebration of this victory. His brother-in-law, Dion, had introduced Plato to him, but the great philosopher's teachings neither convinced nor impressed the tyrant, who, legend says, sold him into slavery from which his Athenian friends later ransomed him. Dionysius I was succeeded by his son of the same name, equally unpopular for his misrule of the island.

Dionysian suspicions of treachery

DIONYSUS

Dionysus, youthful, beautiful, but effeminate god of wine, usually called Bacchus, was worshiped in rites noisy and riotous, wild and dissolute. There is a story that when the men of a ship he had hired headed toward Asia to sell him as a slave, he demonstrated that he was a god by turning the masts and oars into serpents, himself into a lion, causing ivy to grow around the vessel. The sailors who, stricken with madness, had leaped into the sea, he turned into dolphins.

a Dionysian celebration

DIONYSUS ZAGREUS

Dionysus Zagreus (the latter, a Thracian name signifying "torn to pieces") was the son of Zeus and Persephone, according to Orphic legend. Incited by the jealous Hera, the Titans killed and devoured him, but Athena rescued his heart from their cannibal feast and gave it to Zeus, who destroyed the Titans with a thunder bolt. From their ashes sprang the race of men, who have consequently some part of the divine nature in them. Zeus later swallowed Zagreus' heart, and out of it was born a new Dionysus, the son of Semele. Elements of ecstasy and mysticism were found in the ritualistic worship of Zagreus and his rebirth.

as mysterious as Zagreus

DIOSCURI

The Dioscuri, or "sons of Zeus," were Castor and Pollux (the latter was known as Polydeuces to the Greeks). Worshiped as deities, they were protectors of mariners to whom they appeared in storms as electrical flashes now known as St. Elmo's Fire. Castor was famous for his skill in taming and managing horses, Pollux for his skill in boxing. In the fight that ensued after they carried off the daughters of Leucippus, Castor was killed. Pollux, immortal and fondly devoted to his twin brother, asked to be allowed to die also. Zeus, accordingly, granted them to spend alternate days in Heaven and in Hades together or to take turns at dwelling in Hades. Later they were identified with the constellation Gemini (twins) and their name popularized in the oath *by jiminy*.

devoted as the Dioscuri

DIOSCURIDES

Dioscurides was a Greek physician serving in the Roman army in the reign of Nero (54-68 A.D.). The author of a professional work known as the *Materia Medica,* he described in its five books about 600 plants and their medical properties. At the time of the revival of learning he was regarded as the father of the science of pharmacy.

mixing his medicines like Dioscurides

DIRAE

Dirae is the Roman name of the Greek Eumenides, or Furies (*q.v.*), given to them because of their dire and dreadful appearance. In the poem of this name attributed to Vergil, the minstrel heaps curses and imprecations on the soldiers who have dispossessed him of his land.

horrendous as the Dirae

DIRCE

Dirce was the second wife of Lycus, a king of Boeotia, who had divorced his first wife, Antiope, because she became pregnant by Jupiter. Dirce subsequently treated Antiope with great cruelty, but was punished for this by the sons of Antiope who tied her to a mad bull which dragged her about until she was dead. They then threw her body into a fountain near Thebes, which was thereafter called the fountain of Dirce. The story of her death is portrayed in the famous sculptural group from antiquity, which is called the Farnese Bull.

a cruel Dirce deserving of a cruel punishment

DIS

Dis was in Roman religion the male god of the underworld and the equivalent of the Greek Pluto ("wealth"), of whose name his own may be a translation by contraction from the Latin word *dives* for "rich." The cult of Dis and Proserpina, his queen in the lower world, was founded during the first Punic war (249 B.C.) by order of the Sibylline Books. In later times both Dis and Orcus (his synonym) paled into mere symbols of death and the afterlife.

summoned by Dis

DISMAS

Dismas, Desmas, or Dysmas, is the legendary and traditional name of the repentant thief who was crucified at Christ's side.

penitent as Dismas

DISRAELI, BENJAMIN

Disraeli (1804-1881), statesman and prime minister who succeeded Gladstone, was a marvellous diplomat and dexterous empire builder. It was he who arranged the purchase of Egypt's 176,000 shares of the Suez Canal for twenty million dollars, thereby opening the gateway to India, and eventually adding Empress of India to Queen Victoria's many titles. His personality and diplomacy have been revived by George Arliss's acting of the name-part in Parker's marvellous play *Disraeli.*

with the suave diplomacy of a Disraeli

DIVES

Dives, the rich man in Christ's parable about Lazarus, is hence used of any rich man, particularly one who ignores the needs of others. There is a story, built later, that Dives ate only from plates of gold and wore only cloth of gold. Erroneously regarded as a proper name, it is actually the Latin adjective meaning "rich," and was taken from the Latin version of the Bible (Vulgate) as betokening a man's name.

a disappointed Dives

DODGER, ARTFUL

Artful Dodger is a clever young pickpocket in Dickens' *Oliver Twist.* His name is now used to indicate any person adept at petty crime and shrewd at dodging the consequences; hence, thieving, crafty, elusive.

yes, he's charming, insouciant, but an Artful Dodger nevertheless

---

DODIPOLL, DR.

Doctor Dodipoll is the name of a foolish and doddering character in a comedy (1600) by an unknown author. The phrase *as wise as Dr. Dodipoll* means, hence, to be a dunce and not wise at all.

the puny intellect of a Dr. Dodipoll

DODONEAN

Dodonean is from Dodona, the most ancient and venerable oracle in Greek Epirus. Dedicated to Zeus, it gave its responses from its lofty oak trees through which the wind rustled, thus revealing the will of the supreme god. Bronze vessels suspended from the branches of the trees were set in motion by the wind and came in contact with each other, thus rendering the sounds of the god's replies more distinct. The oracular responses were interpreted first by men, later by aged women, and the priests in charge of the temple were known as Selli. In later times the prestige of the oracles of the Dodonean oaks yielded to the more famous oracle of Apollo at Delphi.

listening for a prediction from the rustling of his Dodonean oaks

---

DODS, MEG

Meg Dods is the crabbed old innkeeper in Scott's *St. Ronan's Well.* She was so good a housewife that a cookery book of some repute was named after her, though it was written by Mrs. Johnstone, a Scottish authoress.

smells from Meg Dods's kitchen

DODSON AND FOGG

Dodson and Fogg are the pettifogging law partners who became legal advisers to Mrs. Bardell (*q. v.*) in her breach-of-promise suit against Pickwick, in Dickens' *Pickwick Papers.* They challenge Mr. Pickwick to call them "swindlers" and "thieves" or to assault them.

a case for the dossiers of Dodson and Fogg

DOE, JOHN

John Doe is the sham name used for the plaintiff in legal papers, in blanks, or where the actual name is to be inserted later. It is sometimes used of a person with no special claim to identity or no established character; *i.e.*, a nonentity, a disparaging term. The sham name for a legal defendant is Richard Roe.

a kind of negative John Doe citizen

DOGBERRY

Dogberry is a blundering and conceited constable, absurd and "solemn as an ass" in Shakespeare's *Much Ado about Nothing.* He is pompous, officious, and useless in his office, but garrulous and vainglorious; hence, his name is used of the loquacious but stupid incumbent of any office.

the whole system is full of Dogberrys

DOMBEY, FLORENCE

Florence Dombey, a pitiably loveless and motherless child in Dickens' *Dombey and Son,* was brought up by a father who cared nothing for girls and who was frigid, egotistical, selfish. Florence, despite the empty childhood, grew into unusual loveliness and grace of character.

a delightful Florence Dombey sort of child

DOMITIAN

Domitian was the younger son of Vespasian and the last of the Flavian emperors of Rome (81-96 A.D.). His lack of success in the wars which he planned wounded his vanity and aroused his suspicious fears of more successful leaders like Agricola (*q.v.*). Thus he came to delight in the misfortunes and sufferings of others. In the later years of his reign he relentlessly purged the Senate of all noble and distinguished men and plunged Italy into a ghastly blood-bath of cruelty and tyranny. Denounced as a jealous monster in the pages of Tacitus, and branded for his vices by the scalding satire of Juvenal, he was finally murdered by the connivance of his wife, Domitia, after many other attempts on his life had failed.

a hated Domitian to tyrannize over them

DONATELLO

Donatello, the hero of Hawthorne's *Marble Faun,* is a young Italian count who bears a remarkable resemblance to the marble statue of a faun with pointed ears by Praxiteles. He leads a simple but animal life until he is transformed by a sudden crime.

a likeness as striking as that of Donatello to Praxiteles's statue of the Faun

---

DONNITHORNE, ARTHUR

Arthur Donnithorne is the weak but good-natured young squire who seduces Hetty Sorrel in George Eliot's *Adam Bede.*

the Arthur Donnithorne of her guilt

DONNYBROOK FAIR

Donnybrook Fair, held annually in August in Donnybrook, Ireland, was the occasion of much gaiety and fun celebrated in Irish song and story. But so constantly was it also the occasion of debauchery and fighting, and of many broken heads, that the fair was finally suppressed in 1855. The name is now applied to any gay but riotous and tumultuous occasion. A "true Donnybrook man" means always a gay and reckless fighting Irishman.

jostling together like the heads and sticks at a Donnybrook fair

---

DOOLEY

Mr. Dooley is the pen name of Finley Peter Dunne (1867-1936), an American who, in irresistible Irish dialect, commented on current social, domestic, political, national and foreign affairs with a most keen, penetrating, and astute insight. Yet he was withal so comic that the whole country read him, quoted him, was influenced by him, and respected him. Winning the popular ear with his side-splitting comments, he thereby managed to convey to the listening public a great deal of good sense.

world needs another Mr. Dooley, another Will Rogers

DORADO, EL

El Dorado was supposed by Spaniards of the 16th century to be a land of fabulous wealth—*Dorado* is, in fact, Spanish for "golden" or "gilded." Expeditions were sent to discover this country, believed to be situated in the interior of South America, somewhere between the rivers Orinoco and Amazon. Though all such attempts proved abortive, rumors of its existence persevered until the beginning of the 18th century.

The name may have been applied at first to a man, *el rey dorado.* Sir Walter Raleigh describes the levee of this "golden king" whose chamberlains every morning, after having rubbed his naked body with aromatic oils, blew powdered gold over him through long canes. After the name came more popularly to be used as the designation of a country, however, the whole of Guiana was sometimes included in the term. Francis Orellana, a companion of Pizarro, first spread in Europe the account of this golden land. The word is now used for any land of great riches, for any new-found gold-field, or even for "a castle in Spain."

searching for the El Dorado of his dreams

DORCAS

Dorcas was a woman in the Bible recorded as "full of good works and almsdeeds which she did." When she died her friends sent for Peter and "weeping showed him the coats and garments which Dorcas made when she was with them." Peter prayed and raised her from the dead. Many charitable sewing societies bear her name, indicating their continuance of her good works.

a veritable Dorcas in her town

DORE, GUSTAVE

Gustave Doré, great French artist and illustrator (1833-1883), ranks with Dante in his power to paint the grim, the horrible, the infernal, and the Bible suggestion of eternal punishment. For that reason he was selected to illustrate Dante's *Inferno,* Milton's *Paradise Lost,* the *Bible,* and other epics carrying the imagination into unknown depths of suffering.

grim as a Doré illustration

DORIAN

(see *Laconian*)

DORIGEN

Dorigen is a lady of high family in Chaucer's "Franklin's Tale." Married to Arviragus out of pity for his love and meekness, she was wooed during her husband's absence by

Aurelius but remained faithful to her marital vows, answering that she would never listen to her importuning extra-marital suitor until the rocks on the coast of Britain were removed. With the aid of magic Aurelius accomplished this feat and claimed his reward, and Arviragus forced her to keep her word. Aurelius, however, seeing how sad she and her husband were, said that he would rather die than hurt so true a wife and noble a husband.

a wife as true as Dorigen

DORINE

Dorine is the stock-in-trade name of the intriguing soubrette in old French theatrical nomenclature, as in Molière's *Tartufe.* The name can consequently be applied to any lively and pert young woman with scheming designs.

a scheming Dorine, saucy and calculating

DOROTHEA

Dorothea was an Alexandrian virgin who suffered death by martyrdom under Diocletian in the third century. Theophilus, the judge's secretary who was present at her agony, scoffingly requested her to send him fruit from Paradise, and at a dinner party held immediately after her execution an angel appeared with a basketful of roses and apples. Saying, "From Dorothea in Paradise," the divine being vanished. The miracle sufficed to convert the skeptic.

Dorothea's saint-day is February 6th. In art she is represented with a rose branch in her hand, a wreath of roses on her head, fruit by her side, and an angel carrying a basket with three apples and three roses. She is the subject of *The Virgin Martyr,* a play by Massinger and Dekker.

a fragrance as sweet as that of Dorothea's roses

DORRIT, AMY

Amy Dorrit is the unselfish and unaffected daughter of an imprisoned debtor in Dickens' *Little Dorrit.* Born and reared in Marshalsea prison, in which her father was confined for twenty-five years, she is the epitome of feminine virtue, still retaining her sweet and affectionate nature when a change in family fortunes frees them from jail. The prison chaplain performs the ceremony of her marriage to Arthur Clennan.

as devoted a child as Amy Dorrit

DOSTOIEVSKIAN

Dostoievskian refers to the writings and doctrines of Feodor M. Dostoievsky (1821-1881), great Russian novelist and thinker, whose works show unusual power and intensity as well as a lack of finish and proportion. Embittered by poverty and physical suffering, he fell victim to dark thoughts and morbid fancies, but from his four years of exile in Siberia (for participation in a revolutionary group) he obtained an eloquent ability to translate the dark and seamy side of Russian life into profoundly moving literature. His psychological studies of the balance of good and evil in man are familiar from his great novel *Crime and Punishment,* which declares the doctrine of purification through suffering alone. It also shows his characteristic belief that in every life, however derelict, there are ecstatic moments of self-dedication. He believed in the ideal of a Russian people forming a kind of social state bound together only by mutual love and kindness.

Dostoievskian purification of sin

DOUSTERSWIVEL

Dousterswivel, in Scott's *Antiquary,* is a scheming German swindler and rogue who obtains money under promise of finding buried treasure by use of a divining rod.

a cheating knave of the Dousterswivel type

DOWNING STREET

Downing Street, famous in London as the street where the Prime Minister of England lives, is consequently often used instead of his name. Just as we say "The White House approves . . .," so "Downing Street announced . . .," It is also the home of the Foreign and of many other government offices, although its implication as the voice of the Prime Minister is dominant.

the Downing Street reaction is still a conjecture

Downing Street has ventured no comment

DOWSABEL

Dowsabel, in early English stories, is a name used of the sweetheart of a country swain, usually suggesting a fat, hearty, good natured, rather mature girl, amusingly rustic.

like the sailor, he has a Dowsabel at every inn

lingering at the stile, beguiling his Dowsabel

DRACONIAN

Draconian is from Draco, an Athenian thesmothete about 620 B. C., who framed a set of laws so harsh and severe that Draconian has come to mean harsh, cruel, and bloody. The penalty for violation of even a minor law was death.

after all, this is no Draconian system

Draconian methods went under the hammer two thousand years ago

DRAWCANSIR

Drawcansir is a blustering, bullying braggart in Villier's play *The Rehearsal.* He takes part in a battle, and after killing all the combatants on both sides, makes an extravagantly boastful speech. The name has become a synonym for gross exaggeration.

exaggerated as Drawcansir

DRED SCOTT CASE

The famous Dred Scott Case arose from a claim for emancipation by a negro slave, Dred Scott, who was taken from his native state, Missouri, to live in the free states of Illinois and Minnesota (1834-1838). On his return to Missouri in the latter year, he claimed the rights of a free man because of his residence in free territory. In 1852 the Supreme Court of Missouri denied his claim, holding that he had returned to his former status. The Federal Circuit Court in 1854 decreed that as a citizen of Missouri he could be a party to a suit before that body but denied his claim. The United States Supreme Court quashed his hopes by ruling (1857) that a negro had no legal rights with a white man and might justly be reduced to slavery. The case is one of the most celebrated instances of the exhaustive efforts of legal machinery to determine the rights and status of a slave.

as intricate as the Dred Scott case

DREISER, THEODORE

Theodore Dreiser (1871-1945) molded and influenced the American novel of the twentieth century, cleansing it of Victorian stuffiness and giving it realism of plot and motion. In a bald and journalistic style that was the result of years of editing of periodicals and magazines, he wrote without embellishment about people and circumstances that would have been considered shocking, immoral, and sordid in the previous century. With a rather plodding honesty of detail he reached a milestone in the development of the modern novel with such books as *An*

American Tragedy, Sister Carrie, Jennie Gerhardt, The Titan, The Genius, and *A Hoosier Holiday.*

with Dreiserian plainness of talk

DREYFUS, ALFRED

Alfred Dreyfus was the victim of a notorious case of anti-Semitic prejudice in France (1894-1906). A captain in the French army, he was falsely accused of treasonously selling state secrets to Germany and was sent to Devil's Island for life-imprisonment. The famous novelist Emile Zola became champion of his cause, and Dreyfus was rescued from his living hell, after four years of suffering in unjust incarceration, only when it was proven that the documentary evidence against him bore signatures that were forged. His name has ever since been used as one of the most famous examples of malicious discrimination and biased persecution of minority groups.

like Dreyfus, a victim of religious intolerance

DROMIOS

Dromio of Ephesus and Dromio of Syracuse are twin brothers exactly alike and indistinguishable in appearance, though the former is stupid and the latter alert by temperament. They are attendants on the two Antiphiluses, identical twins constantly mistaken for each other, though they too are of different nature.

the resemblance of the Dromios

DRUIDS

The Druids were ancient priests of early Britain, with great knowledge and some power in magic. They are said to have acted as judges in matters of importance, as teachers, and in some localities were considered soothsayers and conjurers. Their places of worship were usually in the open on a hill. The name means priestly, wise, judicial, and suggests magic, conjuring and soothsaying.

had the air of an ancient Druid

DRUM, JOHN

John Drum is a name derived from Shakespeare and used in the phrase, *John Drum's Entertainment,* a proverbial expression for ill treatment. Most of the allusions, of anecdotal origin, seem to point to the dismissing of some unwelcome guest with more or less of ignominy and insult. Stanihurst says that to John Drum a man is "to hale him in by the head and thrust him out by both the shoulders." Brewer adds that the allusion is to drumming a soldier out of a regiment.

give him John Drum's treatment

DRYADS

The Dryads, or Hamadryads, were nymphs who presided over woods and trees, the oak being their favorite. They were believed to come into and pass out of existence along with the tree that was their particular abode. Consequently, they were regarded as the incarnate spirit of forests and wooded places; hence, graceful, swift, joyous lovers of trees.

Glide swift and silent as a dryad
That disappears among the trees
Hovey

DRY-AS-DUST

The Rev. Dr. Dry-as-Dust, mentioned by Scott in the introduction to his novels, and fully characterized by his name, suggests dullness, inanity, tedium, and lack of interest. The name is sometimes given to a dull, plodding author, particularly an historian or antiquarian.

another Dry-as-Dust on the lecture platform

DRYOPE

Dryope, in Greek mythology, was a Thessalian princess beloved by Apollo. The ancestress of the Dryopes, a race of ancient Thessaly, she was metamorphosed into a poplar tree for having unintentionally plucked a lotus, which was really a manifestation of a Hamadryad. According to other versions, she was transformed into a nymph herself or into a lotus.

inadvertent as Dryope's deed

DUBARRY, MME.

Marie Jeanne Becu, Mme. DuBarry (1746-1793), was the famous French courtesan and adventuress who became the mistress of Louis XV, over whom she had absolute influence. The power behind the unpopular throne, she was subsequently condemned to death by the Revolutionary Tribunal and beheaded on December 7, 1793. Her name is associated with the power a woman can exert over a monarch.

a modern-day DuBarry of the political scene

DUESSA

Duessa is the foul witch in Spenser's *Faerie Queene,* who in the guise of the lovely Fidessa entices the Red Cross Knight into the House of Pride, seduces him and turns him over a prisoner to Orgoglio, the giant. Become the latter's mistress, she is bedecked in gorgeous robes and ornaments and set upon a monstrous beast with seven heads. Una sends Prince Arthur to rescue the Red Cross Knight, kill Orgoglio and strip Duessa of her gorgeous disguise. Then found to be a hideous hag, she runs into the wilderness for concealment.

meretricious as Duessa

DULCINEA

Dulcinea is the peasant sweetheart beloved by Don Quixote in Cervantes' novel *Don Quixote.* For her the hero rode forth on his many absurd and fantastic quests, and her name now signifies a sweetheart who inspires her lover to acts of devotion.

Of late she hath played Dulcinea
To a line of ardent swains

DUMAS, ALEXANDRE

Alexandre Dumas (1802-1870), known as *père* or "the Elder" to distinguish him from his son of the same name, and creator of *The Count of Monte Cristo* and *The Three Musketeers,* was a master of cloak-and-dagger romance. Inns, palaces, cellars and highways are the background for his tales, and Athos, Porthos, Aramis, and d' Artagnan are among the real people of the world because of his astonishing artistry.

Alexandre Dumas (1824-1895) *fils,* or "the Younger," wrote *La Dame aux Camélias,* known as "Camille" to English readers, the basis of Verdi's operatic masterpiece, *La Traviata,* a tale of a jilted courtesan who dies of tuberculosis, the most poetic disease of the time.

Dumas-like dramaturgy

DUNBAR, PAUL LAWRENCE

Paul Lawrence Dunbar (1872-1906) was one of the first of the Negro poets to get recognition in American literature. He not only recorded the Negro reaction to life, to summer, nature, to the far-off hills, but has contributed to folklore with *G'way, Miss Lucy, When Malindy Sings,* and many other verses. The happy, emotional, fun-loving, tender mind of the negro, the joy of living of the Negro race, is apparent in his delightful poetry.

Dunbarian versification

DUNCAN

Duncan is the trusting Scottish king whose throne was taken by Macbeth. In history, Duncan was killed by Macbeth on a field of battle, but in

Shakespeare's play he was murdered by Macbeth while a guest in the latter's castle where he had stopped the night in compliment to his host, on whom he had conferred special grateful honors. His name stands for a trustful, unsuspecting person.

be duly guarded; be not a trusting Duncan

the simple trust of a Duncan

DUNCAN, ISADORA

Isadora Duncan (1878-1927) was the American-born dancer who, sponsored by the English actress Mrs. Patrick Campbell, became the toast of European capitals. After founding a dancing school for children near Berlin, she accepted an invitation to open another school in Moscow. She initiated a new convention for stage dancing, in which the tutu and the toe-slippers of traditional Russian ballet gave way to the classic Greek tunic, bare feet, and flowing drapery, and in which stately Dalcrozean posturing replaced technical virtuosity *sur les pointes*. Feeling that all great music was fundamentally danceable in free and easy movements, she set her most famous dances to the *Marseillaise,* Tschaikovsky's *Marche Slave,* and Chopin's *Marche Funèbıe.* She suffered a tragic death when a long scarf she was wearing while motoring caught in one of the wheels of her automobile.

impressive Duncanesque posturing

DUNDREARY

Dundreary is an insignificant titled person in Taylor's play, *An American Cousin,* made popular by E. O. Sothern's acting—a fatuous, inconsequential, facetious character, laughing idiotically over nothing. His appearance was marked by long whiskers with a shaven chin; he is usually pictured wearing a Prince Albert coat.

the old football picture and a lot of derby-hatted Dundrearys.

DUN, JOE

Joe Dun was a famous bailiff of Lincoln who lived in the reign of Henry VII. He was so energetic in collecting bad debts that when anyone was dilatory over a payment his neighbors would tell the creditors to "Dun him" (i.e., send Dun after him). The name is now used of anyone who presses for payment of a bill.

get Joe Dun after him

DUPIN, MONSIEUR

Monsieur Dupin is the detective in Poe's *Purloined Letter, Murders in the Rue Morgue,* and *The Mystery of Marie Roget.* He is, thus, the prototype of detectives such as Ellery Queen, Nero Wolfe, Sherlock Holmes, Philo Vance, M. Poirot, Perry Mason, Lord Peter Wimsey and other sleuths who work their sinuous ways through many serialized whodunits of more recent writers.

the M. Dupin indispensable to the solution of the mystery

DURDEN, DAME

Dame Durden is the title-character of an old English ballad about a careful housewife. She kept five servant gorls who carried the milking pails, and five serving men who used the spade and flail and loved the girls. The names of the girls were Moll, Bet, Doll, Kate, and Dorothy Draggletail; those of the enamored swains were John, Dick, Joe, Jack and "Humphrey with his flail."

In Dickens' *Bleak House,* Dame Durden is the pet-name and sobriquet given by Mr. Jarndyce to Esther Summerson (*q. v*), his conscientious ward.

an establishment as perfect as Dame Durden's

DUSE, ELEANORA

Eleanora Duse was a versatile Italian actress of comedy and tragedy. For some years she was associated with the romanticist Gabriele d'Annunzio, scoring great fame in *The Dead City* (1898) and *Francesca da Rimini* (1901). She avoided all make-up, making her art depend rather on intense naturalness than on stage effect. She died in 1924, in Pittsburgh, while on a theatrical tour of this country to escape, it was said, the pangs of her love for d' Annunzio, who had jilted her and publicized their romance in his novel, "The Flame of Life."

histrionic as Duse

E

EA

Ea, in Assyro-Babylonian mythology, is the god of the waters of the ocean, subterranean springs, and wisdom. He is also the healer of the sick, the inventor of the arts and sciences, and the supposed creator of man.

healed by the touch of Ea

EBAL

Ebal was the mountain in Palestine from which the curse for disobedience to the law was delivered. It lay to the north of the valley in which Shechem was situated (*Deut.*, xxvii, 13).

a curse fulminated from Ebal

EBLIS

Eblis, or Iblis, is the chief of the wicked Mohammedan jinn. An evil spirit or devil, he is the prince of the apostate angels, who are represented as exiled to the infernal regions for refusing to worship Adam. To justify his refusal Eblis said that he himself was formed of ethereal fire, whereas Adam was a mere creation of clay. In revenge for his relegation he tempted Adam and Eve and seduced them to their fall from innocence. The Arabians say that at the very moment of their prophet's birth the throne of Eblis was hurled to the bottom of hell and the idols of the Gentiles were overturned.

an Eblis to tempt them from innocence

ECCLES

Eccles is the name of a sponging loafer, parasite, and drunkard in T. W. Robertson's play *Caste* (1867), one of a series of realistic "cup and saucer" comedies by that author.

a do-nothing like Eccles

ECHIDNA

Echidna was the monster, half woman and half serpent, who was the daughter of Tartarus, or Hell. The wife of Typhon, she became by him the mother of the fantastic and horrible hybrids of Greek mythology that indicate an oriental origin (cf. Assyrian and Hindu deities). Some of them were the Chimaera, the many-headed dog Orthus, the 100-headed dragon that guarded the apples of the Hesperides, the Theban Sphinx, Cerberus, Scylla, Gorgon, and others. She dwelt in the lower world until she was killed in her sleep by Argus, the "all-seeing."

productive of evil as Echidna

ECHO

Echo, in mythology, was a nymph who loved Narcissus, and in her grief for him dwindled away until only her voice remained. While actually echo means any repetition of a sound, figuratively it is applied to persons who imitate or emulate another person's ideas, opinions, expressions, or personality.

the only perfect lover is Echo

ECKHARDT, FAITHFUL

Faithful, or Trusty, Eckhardt is a venerable old man with a white staff, in German legend. Sometimes represented as a companion of Tannhaeuser (*q. v.*), he warns people away from the seducing fiends of the Venusberg, the mountain of fatal delights. He also appears every Maundy Thursday evening to announce the coming of Frau Holle at the head of the hosts of the departed. On this occasion he warns all persons, especially children, to go home in order to escape injury from the headless bodies and two-legged horses that traverse the streets that night.

no Eckhardt to warn him of his peril

ECKHART, JOHANNES

Johannes "Meister" Eckhart (1260-1327) was a German theologian who became the founder of religious mysticism. Preaching in the vernacular rather than in Latin, he occupied an administrative position in the Dominican Order. A practical reformist and speculative mystic, he was accused of Pantheism, brought to trial, and compelled to make a public recantation of all of his suspected religious errors. His sermons and tracts were hard to understand because of their abstruse expression and terminology.

a mystical Eckhart speculating on religious problems

EDDY, MARY BAKER

Mary Baker Eddy (1821-1910), after having experimented, as an invalid, with many kinds of physical healing, turned to an intensive study and analysis of the Bible to evolve the system of mental cure and health that is associated with the Christian Science Church, which she chartered in 1879. A renowned spiritual and religious leader, she embodied the principles of her metaphysics in the work *Science and Health.*

the faith of a Mary Baker Eddy

EDEN

Eden refers to the Garden of Eden, home of our first parents, but it has since broadened to mean any region of consummate beauty and freshness, utter innocence, and ineffable bliss.

every man finds an Eden of his own

EDISONIAN

Edisonian is from Thomas Edison (1847-1931), inventor, scientist, and electrician, who was called a wizard and noted for his discovery and development of hundreds of practical uses of electricity, first in connection with light, finally in all its fields. Marked by an amazingly inventive mind, a tenacity of purpose, and a concentration that has given rise to many laughable stories, his name is synonymous with progress and a high degree of genius.

almost an Edisonian concentration
living as we do in the Edisonian age

EDWARDIAN

Edwardian refers to the characteristics of the reign of Edward VII, the "Peacemaker," Victoria's son and king of England from 1901 to 1910. Representative of the aged Queen for many years prior to his assumption of the throne, he was popular for his preoccupation with the arts of living, his love of pageantry and brilliant court functions, and a strong predilection for contemporary social amusements. He frequently entered horses at the Derby and had a thoroughly British taste for sports. Ready to promote all worthy causes (*e.g.*, projects for housing of the poor and a hospital fund named after him) and public utilities of a non-political nature, including the trusteeship of the British Museum, he was conspicuous for his public appearances and as a promoter of international friendliness. The name *Edwardian* has come recently to connote ornate and overgenteel lavishness.

an Edwardian insistence on elegance

EDWARDS, JONATHAN

Jonathan Edwards (1703-1758) was the noted New England preacher of "hell fire and damnation" from whose very name has been coined the term

Edwardeanism to express his theological doctrines of the sovereignty of God, regeneration, pardon of sin, remission of the penalty, and justification through the righteousness of another. In his last year at college he was converted to the belief that the election of some to salvation and of others to eternal condemnation was an "exceedingly pleasant, bright and sweet doctrine." A man of stern resolutions and of an ascetic temperance in eating and drinking, he published lists of names of people suspected of reading improper books and was so censorious of others that he became unpopular for his strict principles and smug self-assurance.

smugly critical as Jonathan Edwards

EGDON HEATH

Egdon Heath is the ominous and forbidding moor that is the setting for Thomas Hardy's grimly melancholy novel, *The Return of the Native.* It dominates the fictitional characters just as it controls the somber mood of the story.

a bleak and Egdon Heath-like setting with a personality of its own

---

EGERIA

Egeria was one of the Camenae (*q.v.*) and the Roman goddess of fountains and childbirth. In her grove with its well gushing forth from a dark recess she used to meet Numa, an early king of Rome, to advise and counsel him on the forms of religious worship that he introduced. The Vestals drew their water from her sacred spring, which Numa subsequently dedicated to the nymphs who were known as the Camenae.

Egerian wisdom in counsel

EGLANTINE, MADAME

Madame Eglantine is the prioress characterized by her good-natured affability in Chaucer's *Canterbury Tales.* A mixture of manners and costume, of vanity and ignorance of the world, she has a lady-like delicacy of manners at table, is fond of lap-dogs, and is sprightly and gay. She affects with great difficulty, however, a pretense of courtly hauteur.

good-natured as Mme. Eglantine

EGLON

Eglon was a king of Moab and an ally of Ammon and Amalek against Israel. After he had held the Jewish people in intolerable and tyrannical suppression for eighteen years, he was murdered by Ehud, a left-handed Benjamite who secured an interview with him under pretense of bringing the annual tribute (*Judges*, iii, 15-25).

a despotic oppressor of the Eglon type

EILITHYIA

Eilithyia, the daughter of Zeus and Hera, was the Greek goddess of childbirth. Her sacred cave was shown on the island of Crete, and the Romans identified her with their Juno Lucina. In the *Iliad* her concept is pluralized, Homer there speaking of the Eilithyiae, but in the *Odyssey* she is an individual who assists mothers through the dangers and difficulties of parturition.

a young mother calling Eilithyia for aid

EINSTEIN, ALBERT

Albert Einstein is an eminent German-Swiss physicist, whose theories of uniform motion (1905) and gravitation (1915) stirred the scientific world and set in motion new realms of research. The theories are so incomprehensible to the ordinary mind that *Einstein* has come to mean anything so obscure, intangible, unfathomable and scholarly as to be generally incomprehensible.

some men are Einsteins—nobody at home understands them couched in Einsteinian language

ELAINE

Elaine, the lily maid of Astolat of the Arthurian legend, lived with only her father, her brothers, and an old dumb servitor in a tower quite remote from the court. She grew up utterly gay, innocent, unconventional, unsophisticated, and unbelievably fascinated and eager-eyed over the stories of chivalry her brothers told her. Her lack of sophistication explains her mistaking the casual courtesy of Sir Lancelot, when he chanced to come by Astolat, for love, and she saw no reason why she should not tell him, as a child would tell, of her love and her wish to be his wife. His gentleness and courtesy of refusal, bound as he was to Guinevere, is one of the finest things in Tennyson's *Lancelot and Elaine.* But that refusal left Elaine to die broken hearted.

with the childlike innocence of an Elaine

ELECTRA

Electra was the daughter of Agamemnon and Clytemnestra and the sister of Orestes and Iphigenia. During Agamemnon's ten year siege of Troy, Clytemnestra had taken unto herself a paramour, Aegisthus, with whose help she murdered her husband in his bath after his return from the siege. In reprisal, Electra goaded her brother into assisting her in the vengeance slaying of their adulterous mother. After they had perpetrated the matricide, Orestes gave Electra in marriage to his faithful friend, Pylades.

The story of Electra's murder of her mother is told in Sophocles' extant play, *Electra,* and is magnificently recast in modern form by Eugene O'Neill's lengthy *Mourning Becomes Electra.* Into it, however, the modern playwright introduces Freudian complexes and neuroses, and represents Electra as suffering first from an abnormal love for her father, then from an equally jealous passion for her brother, the seeds of both fanned, of course, by her unrelenting detestation of her mother.

the passionate possessiveness of an Electra

an Electra complex

ELEUSINIAN

Eleusinian refers to the mysteries celebrated in the worship of Demeter, her daughter Persephone, and Iacchus (Dionysus) at Eleusis, a town near Athens where stood a great sanctuary of the earth goddess. Arising from an agrarian festival, the rites developed to include a feast of purification and fertility having reference to the annual sowing of grain in autumn. Connected with this was the descent into Hades and a subsequent rebirth in future life. The rites were held in a darkened hall where flashes of light brought visions to the initiated. These visions probably depicted mythological scenes relating to the doctrine of life after death.

esoteric as the Eleusinian mysteries

ELHANAN

Elhanan, the son of Jair, a Bethlehemite, was the valiant Jewish fighter against the Philistines and the slayer of Goliath the Gittite (*2 Samuel,* xxi, 19), though according to *1 Samuel,* xvii, 4, the latter was killed by David. This contradiction is avoided in *1 Chronicles,* xx, 5, where the text reads that "Elhanan slew (not Goliath, but) Lachmi, the brother of Goliath." In either case, he was a brave warrior who achieved the destruction of a foe in single combat.

a giant-slaying Elhanan

ELIA

Elia is the pen name of Charles Lamb in a series of essays, the *Essays of Elia,* a graceful, pleasant, reflective rambling on many subjects, some natural, many whimsical, but all universal in their appeal. Hence, the name refers to any writing of that nature.

with Elia's pleasant chat

ELIHU

Elihu, the youngest of the four friends of *Job* (xxxii-xxxvii), speaks in wrath against the persecuted man and his other friends because the former justified himself and not God, and the latter convicted Job without being able to give him an answer. After saying, "Great men are not always wise, neither do the aged understand judgment," he reproves Job by reasoning that omnipotent God cannot be unjust and that His wisdom is unsearchable.

a youthful critic like Elihu

ELIJAH

Elijah is the prophet who, at God's command, went forth alone to a solitary place where he was fed by ravens. Then he proceeded to a town where a widow gave him of her unfailing cruse of oil and meal, the same widow whose child Elijah later raised from the dead. He listened for the voice of God in the whirlwind, in the earthquake, and in the fire, and heard it at last in a still small voice. It was Elijah who anointed Elisha, the day he smote the seas with his mantle, so that they walked over on dry land, just before he bestowed that mantle on Elisha, and was taken up to heaven in a chariot of fire drawn by horses of fire. References to all these events are common in all literature, varying according to the context.

Elijah's mantle will undoubtedly fall on X

ELIZABETHAN

Elizabethan is from Elizabeth, Queen of England (1558-1603), during whose reign the island made its most astonishing and splendid progress in power, exploration, internal affairs, colonization, invention, art, music, and letters. The name now suggests great prosperity, intellectual progress, accomplishment, luxury, and culture.

like the glories of the Elizabethan era

and great Elizabethan deeds still ring through all the world

ELLI

Elli, in Norse mythology, is the aged nurse of Utgard Loki (*q. v.*). A toothless crone, she alone can dominate Thor in a wrestling match, for she is in reality Old Age, who eventually triumphs over all men.

anile as Elli

ELLIS, HAVELOCK

(Henry) Havelock Ellis (1859-1939) was the famous English physican, psychologist, editor and author whose work in the field of sex has been a bit overshadowed by the greater popularity of the Freudian school. Though the subject matter of his studies of the causes of sexual aberrations is repugnant to all except the sympathetically minded and the scientist, his *Studies in the Psychology of Sex, The World of Dreams,* and *The Dance of Life* are written in a clear and beautiful style and have won him some fame as a literary artist. He always shows a broad intelligence and generous sympathy with all the psycho-neurotic aberrations of "the weak, erring children of men," as he probes at the causes of the fetishes, sadistic and masochistic neuroses, etc. of his clinical patients in an effort to make for understanding and liberation. His "case histories" have made absorbing reading for thousands of dilettantes in the realms of sex.

as methodical as Havelock Ellis in probing at the origins of desire

ELPENOR

Elpenor was one of the companions of Ulysses when the hero and his crew fell into the power of the enchantress Circe and were metamorphosed into swine on her magic isle of Aeaea. Intoxicated with wine, Elpenor fell asleep on the roof of the sorceress's dwelling one day, tumbled off, broke his neck, and was left unburied when Ulysses left the island unaware of his friend's fate. In the lower world he is the first spirit whom the adventurer meets, and he implores Ulysses that he may be buried and that his oar may be planted on his grave.

drunken as Elpenor and due for a fall

ELSA

Elsa was the young Duchess of Brabant in the German version of the legend of Lohengrin. Championed by the swan-knight who married her on condition that she not ask his origin, she yielded to her overwhelming curiosity and lost him forever. She is an allegorical type of Psyche of the Cupid and Psyche story.

as curious as Elsa

ELSMERE, ROBERT

Robert Elsmere is the title-character of a novel by Mrs. Humphry Ward about a young minister whose religious doubts prompted him to resign his calling.

a skeptical Robert Elsmere

ELSPETH

Elspeth, in Scott's *Antiquary,* is an apathetic old woman who is tortured by her conscience because of having participated in a crime perpetrated by her mistress.

a conscience-stricken Elspeth

ELYSIAN

Elysian is from Elysium, sometimes called the Elysian fields, the abiding place of the blessed. Hence, it indicates any ideally blissful state.

scarcely the Elysium we were led to expect
an Elysium of the mind

EMERSONIAN

Emersonian is from Ralph Waldo Emerson (1803-1882), American philosopher, essayist, lecturer, and poet, whose theories and preachments on the independence of the individual spirit and on self-reliance perhaps induced and certainly reflected much of the independence of the individual that has marked America. His best known works are his essays on the matters that concern the spirit of all mankind, the matters that make and shape the character and nature of man. His personal austerity and his scholarliness are proverbial, but his friendly and affectionate nature is clearly revealed in his poems and his letters.

Emersonian truths, stimulating, vital

EMILIA

Emilia, the wife of Iago in Shakepeare's *Othello,* is a vulgar and scheming woman of low cunning and loose principles. With a high degree of spirit and energy she becomes accessory to her husband's plot to steal Desdemona's handkerchief and to arouse the Moor's suspicious jealousy of his wife and Cassio. At Desdemona's death Emilia reveals the plot and is killed by Iago.

a scheming Emilia, crafty and cunning

EMPEDOCLES

Empedocles (455-395 B. C.) was the wealthy and versatile Sicilian philosopher and scientist who originated the theory of the four elements, air, earth, fire and water, which he believed formed the whole material universe, drawn together or dissociated by the opposing forces of Love and Discord. Also interested in medicine, he was reckoned as a magician on account of his success in curing disease. A biologist and inventor of the art of rhetoric as well, this mystic and eccentric genius contrived to make his death seem as miraculous as his life by hurling himself into the crater of Mt. Aetna with the hope that his sudden disappearance might lead people to suppose him a god or his belief in transmigration of souls a proven fact. But the volcano grudgingly threw up one or both of his golden sandals, thus betraying his ruse.

an Empedoclean belief in reincarnation

EMPUSA

Empusa, in Greek mythology, was a cannibalistic monster that was sent forth under divers shapes in order to frighten travelers. A hobgoblin, vampire, and bogy, it devoured human beings.

as carnivorous as Empusa

ENCELADUS

Enceladus was one of the Giants and a son of Ge (Earth), said to have been generated in her by impregnation from the blood of the mutilation of Cronus (*q. v.*). Enceladus and his brother Giants were represented as monsters, partly human, of vast size and with serpents for feet. For their assault on the gods, they were all defeated and imprisoned in the earth, Enceladus under Mt. Etna.

gigantic as Enceladus

ENDOR, WITCH OF

The Witch of Endor is the witch King Saul sought out in his extremity, even after he had had all the known witches destroyed, to beg her to bring up the spirit of Samuel to advise him. When Saul, upon Samuel's appearance and prediction of the loss of his kingdom, was faint and exhausted, the Witch of Endor brought him food and ministered to him. She thence became known for her honesty, skill, faith, and kindness, although the name *witch* has led many writers to use her name with the usual evil and ugly implications of that word.

a truthful and courageous Witch of Endor

ENDYMION

Endymion was the beautiful youth beloved by the moon-goddess, Diana, who lulled him to perpetual sleep that he might not repel her caresses. The name is synonymous with perpetual youth and with exceptional manly beauty.

in still Endymion's fragrant bower

ENGELS, FRIEDRICH

Friedrich Engels (1820-1895) was the life-long friend of Karl Marx and a German socialist writer. Interested in the condition of the proletariat and the working class from early in life, he went to England and became the co-founder of Marxian doctrines and ideology. He authored the famous *Manifesto of the Communist Party* and after Marx's death edited volumes II and III of *Das Kapital.* He has since been regarded by some as a humanitarian and liberating freethinker, by others as a radical and dangerous revolutionary.

a modern Engels, devoted to the cause of the proletariat

ENYO

Enyo was the Greek goddess of war, identified with the Roman Bellona. Accompanying Ares (Mars) to battle, she delighted in bloodshed and in the destruction of cities. Like the Amazons, she suggests an intrepid female warrior, a termagant, and a violent, turbulent woman.

as unfeminine as Enyo

EOS

Eos was the Greek goddess of the dawn who, like the Roman Aurora, at the close of night ascended to heaven in a chariot drawn by swift horses in order to announce the coming light of the sun. The lover of several beautiful youths, Orion, Cephalus (*q. v.*), and Tithonus, she requested Zeus to make the last-named immortal, but neglected to add that eternal youth also be given him. In consequence, he aged and shriveled down to the size of a grasshopper or cicada, but not before he had made her the mother of Memnon (*q. v.*), the leader of the Ethiopians in the Trojan war. When the latter was killed by Achilles, Eos was thought to have shed tears in the form of the natural phenomenon ever since known as dew.

rejoicing in the dawn like Eos

EPAMINONDAS

Epaminondas (c. 418-362 B. C.) was the great Theban statesman and commander who, with his friend Pelopidas, raised his city to be for a time the most powerful of the Greek states, invading and defeating Sparta four times. A fine tactician and strategist, he invented the phalanx formation, a heavy and solidly massed column of men, fifty deep, which could easily break through the usual thin lines of infantrymen prevailing at the time. When he was killed at the battle of Mantinea, his fellow countrymen, though crushingly victorious over their Spartan enemies, were forced to make peace because the unity and strength of Thebes depended on the genius of this one man alone. An indispensable and irreplaceable leader, he was also distinguished for his integrity and uprightness.

indispensable as Epaminondas

EPHEBEIA

The Ephebeia was the Athenian youth movement which compelled all young men of from 18 to 20 years of age (*ephebi,* or "youths") to register for military training. Like the Roman *Juventus* and the Fascist Italian *Giovinezza,* it imposed strict discipline on them and billeted them by tribes for guard and patrol duty. Begun in the 4th century B. C., it distinguished them by a standardized and uniform costume, which consisted of a broad-brimmed hat and a dark mantle, and gave them a daily remuneration of four obols. When compulsory military training was later abolished, the movement was remodeled into a school of philosophy and literature.

a youth movement as organized as the Ephebeia

EPHIALTES

Ephialtes and his brother Otus, the giant sons of Poseidon or Aloeus, attacked the gods of Greek mythology and tried to pile Mt. Pelion on Olympus and Ossa on Pelion in their attempt to climb to heaven. For their insolent impiety they were defeated by Zeus and the other gods. According to the *Iliad,* they imprisoned Ares, the war god, in a bronze jar for thirteen days; he would have perished, had he not been liberated by Hermes. A different tradition makes them beneficent heroes who founded cities and the worship of the Muses. Still another legend made an Ephialtes the demon of nightmare among the Greeks.

From the historical period of the Persian wars against Greece, Ephialtes is the name of the Malian traitor who, when Leonidas was defending the pass of Thermopylae (480 B. C.), guided a group of Persians over a mountain path in the rear of the embattled Greeks, thus enabling them to surprise and annihilate the heroic defenders.

another un-godfearing Ephialtes
a new Ephialtes to jail and imprison war
a nightmare inspired by Ephialtes

EPICTETUS

Epictetus (A. D. 60-140) was a famous Greek philosopher and teacher of Stoicism. A manumitted slave and lame from birth, he taught at Rome until expelled by Domitian. Gentle, amiable, and earnest, he believed in the government of the world by an all-wise Providence and wrote a *Manual* of instructions for wise living that is often compared with the *Meditations* of Marcus Aurelius. Convinced that practice of the words *endure* and *abstain* would free a man of wrong-doing and help him to live a peaceful life, he had a strong faith in the power of the will to overcome the cares and sorrows of life and in the necessity for mankind's independence of external circumstances.

as blameless as Epictetus

EPICUREAN

Epicurean is from Epicurus (341-270 B. C.), the Greek philosopher whose teachings have been misrepresented ever since the time of the wine-bibbing Horace (who called himself "a pig from the sty of Epicurus") as meaning a refined sensuous enjoyment, especially in matters of eating and drinking. In his school, known as the "Garden," he taught that to conduct oneself wisely one must trust in the evidence of the senses and not give way to superstitious belief in the supernatural. Believing that all things have a natural cause, he imitated Democritus in insisting that the universe and everything in it is made of atoms. Ethically he reasoned that since pleasure is the only good perceived by the senses, pleasure (in the sense of the absence of pain) must be a perfect harmony of body and mind that can be found only in plain living. An Epicurean, therefore, means one who seeks pleasure, but seeks it in a wise, refined and fastidious fashion.

given over to Epicurean living
as misunderstood as Epicurus
another misrepresented Epicurean

EPIMENIDES

Epimenides was a legendary Cretan poet and prophet. Sent out when a boy in search of a stray sheep, he sought shelter from the heat of the fierce mid-day sun in a cave, where he fell into a deep sleep which lasted 57 years. On waking and returning home, he found his younger brother grown an old man. He is said to have visited Athens and purified it from a plague by certain mysterious rites and sacrifices. The Apostle Paul has preserved (*Titus,* i, 12) his celebrated verse against his fellow-countrymen: "The Cretains are always liars, evil beasts, slow bellies."

slept as long as Epimenides

EPIMETHEUS

Epimetheus, or "Afterthought," was the brother of Prometheus, "Forethought," in Greek mythology. Forgetting the advice of his famous brother not to accept any gifts from the gods, he was easily duped by Zeus into marrying Pandora (*q. v.*), the beautiful guile by which the god intended to plunge mankind and Prometheus into prolonged suffering for the theft of fire. When Pandora's celebrated box was opened, out of it poured all the evils and distempers that plague the world, Hope alone remaining at the bottom to comfort the lot of Epimetheus and of all men after him. Epimetheus was the father of Pyrrha, who with her husband Deucalion (*q. v.*) were the only mortals to survive the great flood which Zeus sent as his final curse on sinful humankind.

another Epimetheus, easy to fool

ERASMUS, DESIDERIUS

Desiderius Erasmus (1466-1536) was the famous Dutch humanist, scholar, satirist and theologian whose attitude toward the ignorance and intolerant power of the Catholic clergy of his day is revealed in the famous motto, "Erasmus laid the egg and Luther hatched it." He edited numerous editions of both classical pagan and Church writers, and was the supreme arbiter of good taste for the aristocratic public seized with ardor for the restoration of the arts and learning. "The glory and the shame of the Catholic priesthood," he wrote witty satires that showed kings and princes, bishops and popes alike, as all in bondage to Folly. He also devised a modern pronunciation of ancient Greek, called Erasmian after him. His appearance is familiar from Holbein's numerous portraits of him.

as scholarly as Erasmus

ERATO

(see *Muse*)

Erato, whose name means literally "lovesome," was the Muse of erotic poetry. In ancient works of art she was pictured as carrying the lyre which was always used to accompany the reading of poems. The name is a symbol for passion and amorousness, and is, of course, related to that of the love-god himself, Eros (Cupid).

an Erato-inspired Valentine

ERATOSTHENES

Eratosthenes (3rd century B. C.) was a mathematician, geographer, literary critic, astronomer, grammarian, and poet in charge of the Alexandrian library. He calculated the circumference of the earth with amazing accuracy by measuring the angular distance of the sun at Alexandria from a vertical position at Assouan. He also drew the first rough system of latitudes and longitudes on the map of the world and made the first scientific attempt to fix the dates of legendary Greek history, establishing, for example, the date of the end of the ten year siege of Troy as 1184 B. C. (according to our Christian reckoning).

a mathematical Eratosthenes to solve the problem

EREBUS

Erebus is the region of utter darkness through which the souls of the departed must pass to their destined abode.

dark as Erebus

hopeless and as full of Fear
as are the blasted banks of Erebus

EREWHON

Erewhon, or "Nowhere" in anagram form, is an ideal and non-existent Utopian state in Samuel Butler's romance of that name, satirizing the Darwinian theory and conventional religion. In the sequel, *Erewhon Revisited,* the narrator finds himself the object of a topsy-turvy cult calling itself "Sunchildism."

a fictitious Erewhon of the imagination

ERICSON, LEIF

Leif Ericson, son of Eric the Red, was the Norseman sometimes credited with the first discovery of America. Eric the Red discovered and colonized Greenland in 983. It is by some people believed that in a later voyage, about 1000 A.D., Lief found the coast of either Labrador or Newfoundland, or possibly what is now known as New

England. Venturesome, hardy, daring, the Ericsons were, whatever they discovered, of the stuff Columbus was made of.

the blood of Leif Ericson is in the New England seaman

ERINYES

(see *Eumenides, Furies*)

ERIPHYLE

(see *Harmonia's Necklace*)

ERIS

Eris was the Greek goddess of discord and strife and the sister of Ares (Mars), whom she assisted in the tumult of war by provoking causes for hostility. Enraged because she was the only deity not invited to the marriage of Peleus and Thetis (the parents of Achilles), she threw into the midst of the guests a golden apple inscribed "to the fairest." Zeus ordered Hermes to take the rival claimants for the award, Hera, Athena, and Aphrodite, to Mt. Ida and to lay the decision before the Trojan Paris. Hera attempted to bribe him by offering the sovereignty of Asia, Athena proffered fame in war, and Aphrodite promised him the fairest woman in the world. When he decided in favor of Aphrodite's pledge of Helen, the Trojan war was motivated.

a contentious and trouble-making Eris

ERLKING

The Erlking, or king of the elves, is a malicious elementary spirit which is personified in Teutonic tradition as a goblin who prepares mischief and ruin for men and is especially spiteful to children. He spreads his delusive seductions to snare and destroy people who pass through his domains in Thuringia's Black Forest. Schubert's dramatic musical setting of Goethe's famous ballad recounting the death of a child from fright as the Erlking pursues the boy and his father through the forest is a well-known concert hall favorite.

ran as though pursued by the Erlking

EROS

(see *Cupid*)

ERYSICHTHON

Erysichthon was a Greek prince, son of the Thessalian king Triopas. He profanely cut down trees in a grove sacred to Demeter (Ceres) and was punished by the goddess with a terrible and insatiable appetite. So hungry did he become that, in a frantic endeavor to satisfy himself, he devoured his own flesh.

an appetite as insatiable as Erysichthon's

ESAU

Esau, "red all over like an hairy garment," was the son of Isaac and Rebecca, and the twin brother of Jacob (*Genesis*, xxv). A cunning hunter and a man of the field, he was destined to be subservient to his twin from the time when the Lord said to their pregnant mother, "Two nations are in thy womb . . . and the one people shall be stronger than the other people, and the elder shall serve the younger." Though Isaac loved Esau the huntsman "because he did eat of his venison," Jacob required his twin, returning tired and faint from the fields, to pay for a mess of potage with his birthright (inheritance) and thereby gained the ascendancy over him.

a bargain as necessary as Esau's

ESMERALDA

Esmeralda, in Victor Hugo's *Notre Dame de Paris,* is a beautiful gypsy dancing girl who keeps a pet goat. Beloved by Quasimodo (*q. v.*) and Claude Frollo, she is executed as a witch.

the Esmeralda of the dance

ESMOND, HENRY

Henry Esmond, the title-character of Thackeray's novel, is a brave and chivalrous youth in love with his wayward and capricious cousin, Beatrix, who involves him in the cause of James Stuart, the Old Pretender, with whom she is infatuated. She later marries her brother's tutor and secures him a bishopric. Lady Castlewood, Beatrix's mother, eventually marries Henry.

smitten by his cousin, like Henry Esmond

ESSENES

The Essenes, a Jewish sect in the time of Christ, were communists who forswore all types of fleshly indulgence. Vegetarians and teetotalers, they sacrificed only the fruits of the earth to God and kept the Sabbath so strictly that they would not even wash a plate or rinse a cup on that day. Always dressed in white and devoted to contemplation and study, they took no part in public affairs and interpreted the Jewish Scriptures allegorically. These ascetics preached voluntary poverty, community of wealth and goods, and celibacy.

as austere and self-denying as the Essenes

ESTHER

Esther (the Persian form of the Jewish name Hadassah), the heroine of the Old Testament book bearing her name, was the beautiful and courageous granddaughter of Kish, a captive Benjaminite during the Persian oppression under Ahasuerus (Xerxes, *q. v.*). Her loveliness, tact and wisdom attracted that monarch, who chose her as his queen in succession to Vashti, whom he had divorced for disobedience. With providential deliverance, Esther then averted a general massacre of her race that had been planned by the wicked Haman because Mordecai, Esther's cousin, would not do obeisance to him. Her salvation of her people gave rise to the feast of Purim.

lovely and courageous as Esther

ETEOCLES

(see *Seven Against Thebes*)

ETHIOPIAN

Ethiopian refers to Ethiopia, a rich African region, magnificent and powerful in its time, its people barbaric and splendid. The Bible and other world literature refer constantly to the splendor and the magnificence of Ethiopia; hence, the name suggests splendor, riches.

Jupiter went yesterday to feast amongst the blameless Ethiops

---

ETRUSCAN

Etruscan refers to the Etruscan or Tyrrhenian people who, though of Oriental origin, appeared in Italy in the 9th and 8th centuries B. C. and became powerful and industrious overlords of the indigenous Italian stock. Builders of fortified cities, they were skillful and artistic workers in bronze and iron. With extensive commercial activities, they supplied Rome with its Tarquin kings, the last of the early city's monarchs. Hheir elaborate, circular bee-hive tombs were embellished with mural paintings showing both their luxury and their cruel and somber practices. They instituted divination by studying the entrails of sacrificed animals and by interpreting the habits of birds and their flights, the latter taken over by the Romans for their *auspices*.

Etruscan architectural grandeur

EUCLIDEAN

Euclidean is from Euclid, the famous Greek geometrician of about 350-300 B. C., whose principles still govern the reasoning and the axioms of geometry. Hence, his name is synonymous with precision, mathematical accuracy, and regularity.

evident as Euclidean axioms

EUHEMERISTIC

Euhemeristic refers to the religious rationalism of Euhemerus (c. 300 B. C.), a Sicilian Greek writer whose *Sacred History* advanced the theory, known after him as *euhemerism,* that the mythological gods had their origin in kings and heroes who were deified after their death by those whom they had governed or benefited. This deriving of deity from a rationalistic study of history reduced all gods to the level of distinguished men who had once actualy lived, and subjected Euhemerus to frequent attacks for supposed atheism.

as rationalistic as Euhemerus

EULALIA, SAINT

St. Eulalia was a Spanish virgin martyred by torture under Diocletian, when she was only twelve years old, for having cast down the idols which a Roman judge had set up. Killed on February 12, 308, she became the patroness of the city of Barcelona and of sailors.

invoking St. Eulalia to keep their ship from foundering

EULENSPIEGEL, TILL

Till Eulenspiegel is the half-mythical prankster of German folklore. Though the portrayal of his character in literature was said to have been the work of Dr. Thomas Murner, a 16th century German satirist, Till himself was a wandering mechanic of 13th century Brunswick. A clown and an adventurer from birth (he was baptized in mud), he indulged in the famous series of "merry pranks" recorded in music by the popular tone-poem of Richard Strauss. A Jack-of-all-trades, he cheated the rich and helped the poor, hoodwinked smug and gullible Philistines into believing that he was a butcher, a baker, a wheelwright, a monk and even a learned philosopher, until he was finally hanged in the flesh. His spirit, however, remains as immortal as that of Puck.

a droll Eulenspiegel of a fellow

EUMAEUS

Eumaeus is the faithful swineherd of Odysseus (Ulysses) in the *Odyssey.* When his master returns to his home in Ithaca after an absence of twenty years spent at Troy and in devious wanderings on the way back, he reveals to him the insolence and riotous living of the suitors for the hand of Penelope, his wife. When the hero is ready to exact vengeance for their profligacy, Eumaeus aids him to slay the arrogant suitors.

a faithful Eumaeus to aid his master

EUMENIDES

Eumenides (see the *Furies*) is a euphemisitic name given the Furies, whose true name of Erinnyes the Greeks were afraid to speak. Eumenides means literally "well wishers" or "kind ones."

no escape from the Eumenides

EUMOLPUS

Eumolpus ("sweet singer") was the first priest of Demeter and the founder of the Eleusinian (*q. v.*) mysteries in that goddess's honor. He also purified Hercules from the murder of the Centaurs and instructed that hero, as well as Linus, in playing the lyre. He was said to have been the inventor of vocal accompaniments to the flute and to have written hymns of consecration. Also reputed to have been the first priest of Dionysus, he was believed to have introduced cultivation of the vine and of fruit trees.

sweet-voiced as Eumolpus

EUNOMIA

Eunomia, in Greek mythology, was one of the Horae (*q. v.*), daughters of Zeus and Themis and goddesses of the order of nature and the seasons. She represented "good order," and her sisters, according to Hesiod, were Dike ("justice") and Irene ("peace"), though their names are elsewhere given as Thallo ("spring") and Carpo ("autumn"). In art all are represented as blooming maidens. Eunomia had one of the minor planets named after her.

Eunomian orderliness

EUPATRIDAE

The Eupatridae were Athenian hereditary aristocrats and owners of vast landed estates of the time before Solon (*q. v.*). Local chiefs of the period before union of the communities later comprised in Attica, they were nobles and distinguished from the *Geomoroi* (yeomen) and *Demiourgai* (mechanics). The name *Eupatrid* is now used to connote any aristocrat, patrician, or person privileged by birth.

owns as much land as a Eupatrid

EUPHORBUS

Euphorbus was one of the bravest of the Trojan warriors and was slain by Menelaus, who dedicated his shield in the temple of Hera near Mycenae. Pythagoras (*q. v.*) claimed to be his reincarnation in a later age, recognizing and selecting his shield from an array of others in the temple in proof of his assertion.

another incarnation of Euphorbus

EUPHROSYNE

Euphrosyne ("mirth" or "cheer") was one of the Charites or Graces (see *Charis*), three daughters of Zeus. Presiding over the things that make life agreeable, joyful, and refined, Euphrosyne may have originally been a goddess of vegetation.

spreading Euphrosynean pleasantness

EUPHUISTIC

Euphuistic comes from Euphues, the principal character in Lyly's *The Anatomy of Wit,* a book marked by an affected, strained play on words and an elaborate, highflowen style. Hence, euphuistic means elaborate, artificial, ornate, figurative language.

a ridiculously Euphuistic style

EURIPIDEAN

Euripidean refers to Euripides (480-406 B.C.), the great Greek tragic poet who introduced romanticism and character analysis into drama and freed it of superstitious attitudes toward the gods of mythology. His themes concern characters locked in violent stress, especially women in the grip of passion—Medea meditating her dire vengeance on Jason, Phaedra burning with passion for the chaste Hippolytus her step-son. Though skeptical of the justice of heaven and bitter in his reflections on the unhappy aspects of suffering humanity, he also shows admiration for the heroism of women like Electra and Alcestis. His work was so universally popular that it was said that many Athenians taken captive during the disastrous Sicilian expedition of 415 B.C. purchased their liberty at Syracuse by reciting passages from his plays.

where is there a charm like that of Euripides?

knew no Euripides to loose his chains

EUROPA

Europa was the beautiful daughter of Agenor, the king of Tyre. Zeus fell in love with her and in order to prosecute an amour changed himself into a gentle white bull. He sported so tamely on the sea-shore, where she was playnig with her maidens, that she boldly climbed on his back. Whereupon the bull dashed off into the waves and swam away, carrying her to Crete. There she became the mother by the god of Minos, Rhadamanthus, and Sarpedon.

bold as Europa among her herds

EURUS

Eurus was the personification of the South-east or East Wind in classical mythology. In art he was represented as holding a vase inverted, as if pouring rain from it. The bringer of bad weather in general, Darwin in his *Economy of Vegetation* speaks of him as follows: "While southern gales or western oceans roll, And Eurus steals his ice-winds from the pole."

Eurus massing his dark clouds in warning.

EURYALE

Euryale, the "wide-wanderer," was the sister Gorgon (*q. v.*) of Medusa ("queen") and Sthenno ("mighty"). A daughter of Phorcys and Ceto, she had a hideous face, glaring eyes, and serpents in her hair and girdle, as did her sisters. Medusa was mortal and was consequently slain by Perseus, but Euryale and Sthenno were immortal.

ugly as Euryale

EURYALUS

Euryalus is a Trojan youth and the faithful and loving friend of Nisus in Vergil's *Aeneid*. The two companions joined with Aeneas on his celebrated flight to Italy after the fall of Troy and fought with great bravery against the native Rutulians there. Nisus perished in an attempt to rescue Euryalus from capture by the enemy during a night attack on their camp.

an ever faithful Euryalus to aid him

EURYCLEA

Euryclea is the old nurse of Odysseus (Ulysses) in Greek mythology. When her master returns home in disguise after his famous 20 year absence, it is she who recognizes and identifies him by a scar on his leg.

a memory for detail like Euryclea's

EURYDICE

(see *Orpheus*)

EURYLOCHUS

Eurylochus is the companion of Ulysses whom the hero of the *Odyssey* sends forth in charge of half of his crew in order to reconnoitre on Circe's Aeaean isle and determine what type of hospitality may await them there. When the sorceress invites them within her palace for entertainment, Eurylochus suspiciously refrains from entering and returns to the ship to report to Ulysses while the other men are being transformed into swine.

as impervious to magic as Eurylochus

EURYNOME

Eurynome, a Greek goddess of the sea, was a daughter of Oceanus and the mother by Zeus of the Graces (see *Charis*) and of Leucothea. Eurynome was also an epithet of Artemis in Arcadia, where she was worshiped as a mermaid.

breasting the waves like Eurynome

EURYSTHEUS

Eurystheus, the king of Tiryns, was the hard taskmaster of Hercules on whom he imposed the hero's famous twelve labors. The oracle at Delphi had enjoined on Hercules that he serve Eurystheus for a period of 12 years because in a fit of madness he had killed his own children. The labors were of such extraordinary difficulty that *to serve Eurystheus* has come to mean to accomplish the impossible. They included a descent into the lower world to bring back Cerberus for Eurystheus to see, the bringing back alive of the Arcadian stag with golden antlers and brazen feet, and the skinning of the ferocious Nemean lion. After all of Eurystheus' wildest whims had been gratified, Hercules was released from servitude to him.

a taskmaster as hard to please as Eurystheus

EURYTION

Eurytion, in Greek mythology, was the Centaur who became so inflamed with wine at the wedding feast of Pirithous and Hippodamia that he attempted to ravish the bride. As the result of his incontinent violation of hospitality, he and many of the other guests were slain in the celebrated battle of the Centaurs and the Lapiths that ensued.

Eurytion was also the name of the giant who guarded the cattle of Geryon (*q. v.*) and was slain by Hercules.

as uncontrollably drunk as Eurytion

EUSEBIUS

Eusebius (265-340), the bishop of Caesarea, was called the father of church history. His *Chronicle* contained an epitome of universal history and chronological tables of important events, and is the foundation of much of our knowledge of the dates of events in Greek and Roman history down to A.D. 325. He also wrote a biography of Constantine and a topography of Palestine.

the Eusebian flair for fixing dates

EUTERPE

(see *Muse*)

Euterpe was the Muse of lyric poetry and music. Her name means literally "well pleasing," and she was represented in ancient art as carrying the flute which was always an accompaniment to the reading of lyric poetry. Many poetic and singing societies were and still are named "Euterpean."

the presiding genius of the Euterpean Society
a Euterpean mood

EVADNE

Evadne, in Greek mythology, was the devoted wife of Capaneus (*q. v.*), one of the seven chieftains who marched against Thebes. When he was blasted by Zeus's lightning bolt for impiety as he was scaling the walls of the beleaguered city, Evadne cast herself in self-sacrifice into the flames of his burning body, as though it were a funeral pyre.

a husband-loving Evadne

EVANDER

Evander ("good man") was the son of Hermes and founded an Arcadian colony on Rome's Palatine hill before the Trojan war. He taught his neighbors the art of writing, milder laws, and the enjoyment of peace and social life. In the *Aeneid* he is represented as assisting Aeneas against Turnus (*q. v.*).

a civilizer like Evander

EVANGELINE

Evangeline was the Acadian maiden who, in the expulsion of the Acadians from Nova Scotia, was separated from her lover Gabriel and spent her life searching for him. The whole story is told in an appealing poem by Longfellow. Many times Evangeline came near to, or passed by, where Gabriel was, but not until she was an aging but still beautiful woman did she find him, dying in a hospital.

her search was as futile as that of Evangeline

EVE

Eve was the first woman, wife of Adam, living in the Garden of Eden. She is credited with having been tempted into eating of the fruit of a forbidden tree, and in turn tempting Adam to eat, whereupon both were banished from the garden.

like Eve persistent

a beauteous Eve lost him his Eden

EXCALIBUR

Excalibur was the name of King Arthur's famous sword, which he alone was able to draw from its stone sheath. On the sheath was an inscription proclaiming as heir to the throne of Britain the one who should be able to wrest the sword. When the latter was cast into a lake on the death of Arthur, a hand and arm rose from the water, snatched and flourished it three times, then disappeared. Tennyson related this incident in his *Morte d'Arthur.* The name Excalibur thus signifies high destiny, chivalry, valor and magic.

found an Excalibur to prove his superiority

EYRE, JANE

Jane Eyre, the heroine of Charlotte Brontë's novel of the same name, is a governess who stoutly copes with the most unpleasant adversities until by genuine force of character she wins the respect and love of her employer, Rochester, whom she then marries.

Jane Eyre's strength of character

EZEKIEL

Ezekiel was one of the 6th century B. C. prophets. The Old Testament book bearing his name contains his visions and pronouncements of judgment against his apostate people and their enemies, prophesying the former's eventual redemption. One of the major prophets of the captivity, he foretold the destruction of Jerusalem and prepared his nation for its restoration.

an Ezekiel calling down doom

EZRA

Ezra was the 5th century B. C. scribe and priest who originated public preaching. The historical Old Testament book named after him was edited and in part written by him.

preaching with the eloquence of Ezra

F

FABEL, PETER

Peter Fabel, whose legend is the subject of a play, *The Merry Devil of Edmonton,* is a person reputed to have sold his soul to the devil and then to have defaulted on his bargain by cheating him out of it. He died in the reign of Henry VII of England.

another Peter Fabel at abjuring an agreement

FABIAN

Fabian comes from Quintus Fabius Maximus "Cunctator," known as "the delayor" because he carried on military operations against Hannibal (217 B.C.) by a policy of wearing out the enemy by eluding him rather than by meeting him in open battle. The later Fabian societies are groups of socialists (England) who seek to win their ends without violence. In general, however, Fabian suggests delay.

Wellington pursued a Fabian policy in Spain

pursuing interminable Fabian tactics

FABRICIUS

Caius Fabricius Luscinus, one of the most popular heroes in the annals of the Roman Republic, was always considered as a type of old Roman honesty and frugality. One of the ambassadors sent to King Pyrrhus, who had invaded Italy in 280 B.C., he resisted all the attempts of the latter to corrupt him. In 278, when he was commanding the Roman army against this enemy, he actually disclosed to him that his doctor had made the Romans a treacherous proposal to poison the king. As censor in 275, he distinguished himself by the severity with which he curbed the growing taste for luxury. He lived in the starkest simplicity on his hereditary farm, and died as poor as he had lived, leaving no dowry for his daughters, for whom the Senate provided one in respect to the memory of their father.

Fabrician honesty and truthfulness

FABULINUS

Fabulinus was the deity who taught Roman children how to utter their first word, as Vagitanus taught them how to emit their first cry or wail. These *numina* ("powers," "wills") were legion in number and presided over every aspect of human action. Edusa taught children to eat; Potina instructed them in the talent of drinking; Abeona escorted one as he was departing on a journey, while Adeona guided him toward his goal, Iterduca escorted him on his way, and Domiduca saw to his return home. Aniconic and unanthropomorphized spirits, they pervaded the animistic religion of the early Romans prior to the acquisition of the major deities, who in later times were identified with the Greek pantheon.

Fabulinus prompted the child to utter his first syllable for his doting parents.

FACTOTUM, JOHANNES

Johannes Factotum is the name used to describe one who does all kinds of service for his employer, who is good at anything, and who can turn his hand to any kind of work. The Latin equivalent of Jack-of-all-trades, it is found in Greene's *Groatsworth of Wit* (1592), where there is mention of Shakespeare as "an absolute Johannes Factotum in his own conceit."

get your Johannes Factotum to do it for you

FADLADEEN

Fadladeen is the infallible, sententious, shrewd and conceited courtier in Moore's *Lalla Rookh.* The grand chamberlain of the harem, he pronounces weighty judgments on both trifling and serious affairs. His criticism of the several tales that make up the romance is racy and full of humor, and his crestfallen assurance when he finds out that the poet is the Prince in disguise is well conceived.

self-assured as Fadladeen

FAFNER

Fafner, in the old Norse version of the Siegfried story, is the dragon who guards the Nibelung's hoard. He is slain by Sigurd, who roasts and eats his heart, thereby gaining the power to understand the language of the birds. In the Wagnerian cycle he guards the Rheingold and is killed by Siegfried.

a Fafner-like dragon custodian

FAG

Fag, the lying and ingenious servant to Captain Absolute in Sheridan's *The Rivals,* "wears his master's wit as he does his lace, at second-hand." Though he never scruples to tell a lie at the Captain's command, yet it hurts his conscience to be found out.

a mendacious Fag

FAGIN

Fagin, the master of thieves in Dickens' *Oliver Twist,* abducts Oliver and tries to instruct him in the art of thievery. A villain and a professional tutor in crime, his name is now used of any low character who uses children to serve his own ends.

a roundup of the local Fagins
an end of Faginism in the town

FAIRSERVICE, ANDREW

Andrew Fairservice, in Scott's *Rob Roy,* is a pious and shrewd gardener at Osbaldistone Hall. He is of a meddlesome and cowardly character.

inquisitive as Andrew Fairservice among his plants

FALKLAND

Falkland, the hero of William Godwin's *Caleb Williams,* is in the beginning an impersonation of honor, intellect, benevolence, and a passionate desire for fame. Driven to commit a murder in a moment of ungovernable passion, he is urged to conceal the crime by his fanatical regard for his reputation, allowing an innocent man to be executed and his family ruined. His servant, Williams, an intelligent peasant-lad, obtains a clue to his master's guilt, though the latter extorts from him an oath that he will keep the secret. Finding it impossible thereafter to live under Falkland's restless surveillance, Williams escapes and is pursued by his master's unrelenting persecution. He is formally accused by Falkland of robbery and at last discloses before the tribunal his dreadful secret. Falkland then dies of shame and a broken heart.

as desirous of fame as Falkland

FALSTAFFIAN

Falstaffian is from Sir John Falstaff, comic and likable character in Shakespeare's series of *King Henry* plays and in *The Merry Wives of Windsor.* Falstaff is a corpulent, jovial, tippling old braggart, scorned and loved and tormented and indulged by his betters, including Prince Hal, later King Henry, despite his impertinent jibes, his unsought admonitions, his brazen assurances and exaggerations. In this character Falstaff organized a ragged regiment of his own kind, making some of the most uproarious scenes in the plays. Falstaffian means uproarious mirth, entertaining braggadocio, tipsy boasting, monstrous assurance, and lovable devotion.

a Falstaffian butt
rollicking peals of Falstaffian laughter
the unctuous roll of his Falstaffian voice

FANG, MR.

Mr. Fang is the brutal and bullying police magistrate in Dickens' *Oliver Twist*. If he had brought a suit for libel against his stern and whiskey-flushed face, he would have recovered heavy damages. His hard-hearted attempt to send Oliver to prison on suspicion of theft is thwarted by Mr. Brownlow.

another Mr. Fang at browbeating

FARINATA

Farinata degli Uberti was a Ghibelline noble of Florence whom Dante described in his *Inferno* as occupying a red-hot coffin, the lid of which was suspended over him till the coming of Doomsday. His mien, however, appeared as lofty, haughty, and tranquil as if he scorned hell itself. His horrible punishment was meted out because of his reputation for infidelity and epicurism.

as hot as Farinata's coffin

FASTI

The Fasti, or "days on which it is allowed to speak," were calendar-like lists, drawn up by Roman priests, of days on which legal business might auspiciously be transacted. Expanded into a kind of yearly almanac by the insertion of notes on historical happenings, sacrifices, festivals, and astronomical information, they gave a chronological schedule of each year's events, ultimately being used even in the sense of "history." Ovid wrote a poem by this name, intended to have a book for each of the twelve months of the year but actually composed for only the first six. It was designed to contain a list of all religious rites, customs, and beliefs for each month and an explanation of their origin.

consults his Fasti to see when it is best to do anything

FATA MORGANA

(see *Morgana, Fata*)

FATHOM, FERDINAND

Count Ferdinand Fathom is the title character in Smollett's picaresque novel of the same name. Proceeding with thoroughness and method to rob his benefactors, he plunders mankind and dupes all who trust him. In spite of being forgiven by all his victims, the repulsive scoundrel dies at last in misery and despair.

as methodical a cheat as Ferdinand Fathom

FATIMA

Fatima, the young and beautiful seventh wife of Bluebeard, having been told not to open a certain door in the castle, mischievously managed to get the key and open the door, only to find the bones of her husband's six other wives. Her disobedience discovered, she was about to be killed when her brothers, having learned of her discovery, rushed in, rescued her, and killed Bluebeard.

as curious as Fatima
with the fatal curiosity of a Fatima

FAUNTLEROY, LITTLE LORD

(see *Little Lord Fauntleroy*)

FAUNUS

Faunus was the Roman deity of woodlands, gifted with prophetic powers. He was also the protector of herds and crops, and identified with the Greek Pan. Originally there were a number of Fauni, or spirits of the countryside, and they were identified with the Greek Satyrs. All were equipped with horns and goat's feet, and their names suggest carousing, merriness, sensuality, and things wild and sylvan. They pursued the Nymphs with amorous intentions.

sensual as a Faun
a Faun pursuing his Nymph

FAUSTIAN

Faustian comes from Faustus, the principal character in many famous operas, plays, and stories, all based on an actual Dr. Faustus and all dealing with the student who sold his soul to the devil in return for a lifetime full of what he deemed the highest pleasure at the moment he summoned it. Those delights, along with their tragic consequences, and the supreme tragedy when the forfeit of his soul is required, have made a powerful story in many forms, especially in Goethe's *Faust*. Faustian suggests the height of human experience either in delight or in anguish. It is also used to refer to the story as a whole, as *Faustian mockery,* alluding to the mockery of Mephistopheles when he comes demanding Faust's soul.

Faustian dreams
transient Faustian delight
Faustian terror

FAUSTINA

Faustina the elder was the wife of the Roman emperor Antoninus Pius (A.D. 81-161) and was notorious for her licentious and wanton conduct, though she was deified after death and worshiped in the great temple of Antoninus and Faustina in Rome.

Her daughter, Annia Galeria Faustina, was the wife of Marcus Aurelius (A.D. 121-180), to whom she bore at least 13 children. Though she too was maligned by historians for her profligacy, the charges may have been false, for her husband lamented her death very bitterly and established charitable schools for orphaned girls in her honor, naming them *Faustinianae.*

a licentious Faustina cuckolding her husband

FAVONIUS

Favonius, from a Latin root meaning to *favor,* was the personification of the West Wind in classical mythology. The son of Aeolus and Aurora, and the lover of Flora, he was regarded as the harbinger and attendant of springtime and the promoter of vegetation. Identified by the Romans with the Greek Zephyrus, he was usually represented as the mildest of all the sylvan deities.

invokes Favonius to prosper his crops
a soft Favonian breeze

FAWKES, GUY

Guy Fawkes was the one of the conspirators who was found and executed as a leader in the famous Gunpowder Plot (1605), a scheme to blow up the House of Parliament and kill King James I and the members of Parliament, in protest against the Protestant control of the government. The name has come to mean any active participation in violent and secret revolutionary movements.

a Guy Fawkes . . . expecting every moment to be his last . . . for heroic devotion to a bad cause

---

FEAR FORTRESS

Fear Fortress was an imaginary, nonexistent, and hypothetical castle in a forest near Saragossa. The origin of all accidents, mishaps, and disasters was attributed to the owner of this invisible edifice, which represented the terrible obstacles that fear can conjure up, obstacles which vanish into thin air if they are approached with undaunted courage and bravery.

the lord of Fear Fortress has taken his courage

FENELLA

Fenella, in Scott's *Peveril of the Peak,* is an attendant on the Countess of Derby. A tiny, elf-like creature, she pretends to be a deaf-mute.

a diminutive Fenella

FENRIR

Fenrir, the terror of the gods in Norse mythology, is a giant wolf and water-demon, the son of Loki. He slays Odin and swallows up the sun at the Ragnarok (*q. v.*), after which he is himself slain by Vidar.

vicious as Fenrir

FENTON

Fenton, in Shakespeare's *Merry Wives of Windsor,* is an ambitious person who woos wealthy Anne Page for her money. After marriage, however, he soon discovers that she has wonderful inward treasures which quite transform him. The name is used for anyone who seeks to mend his fortunes by making an auspicious and fortunate marriage.

like Fenton, he must be after her money

FERETRIUS

Feretrius was the surname of Jupiter, the "striker," and was used by persons taking an oath at the sacrifice of an animal. The person swearing by this function of the deity thus invited the god to strike him just as he was striking the victim, if he should prove perfidious to his word.

every time he makes a promise he should swear by Feretrius

FERONIA

Feronia was an ancient Italian goddess associated with fertility. Vergil calls her the goddess of childbirth. At her famous shrine in Etruria a great fair was held once a year, at which a fire-walking rite was one of the features.

visited annually by Feronia

FERRACUTE

Ferracute, a giant who flourished in medieval fable, was of the race of Goliath, had the strength of forty men, and was twenty cubits tall. His skin was so thick that neither lance nor sword could pierce it. He possessed a bronze head which answered every question put to it.

as responsive as Ferracute's bronze head

FESCENNINE

Fescennine refers to the crude verses dramatized at Fescennium in ancient Etruscan Italy. Representing the somewhat ribald banter of country-folk celebrating the harvest and vintage festivals, they were sung in antiphonal, or responsive rivalry and were popularly believed able to avert misfortune. Performed also at marriages, they may have been of phallic inspiration. Highly satiric in character, the word *Fescennine* still betokens licentious and suggestive wit.

bawdy and suggestive as Fescennine doggerel

FETIALES

The Fetiales were Roman priests, probably of Jupiter Feretrius (*q. v.*), who were entrusted with the details and formalities of international relations and statesmanship. Playing an important part in the proprieties of making treaties and declaring war, they took on their missions a flint axe and a sceptre from the temple of the god. A soldier captured from the army of Pyrrhus was forced to buy a piece of real estate near the Circus Flaminius in 280 B.C. This was thereafter declared hostile ground, and into it a Fetial hurled a spear from the temple of Bellona in token of a declaration of war.

modern Fetials, intriguing in international diplomacy

FEVEREL, RICHARD

Richard Feverel, the hero of Meredith's *Ordeal of Richard Feverel,* is the victim of a false system of education foisted upon him by a dogmatic father.

miseducated as Richard Feverel

FIACRE, ST.

Saint Fiacre, famous for his miraculous cure of a tumor, was an Irish nobleman who founded a monastery near Paris. The patron saint of gardeners, he died about the year 670. His name was subsequently adopted by the Hotel de St. Fiacre, an inn in Paris where small coaches were first offered for hire in 1650, and from this name the word *fiacre* was coined as a synonym for a hackney.

a garden blessed by St. Fiacre

FIAMETTA

Fiametta ("little flame") was a name given by Boccaccio to a lady whom he loved, generally believed to have been Maria, a natural daughter of Robert, king of Naples. Used by him in many of his works, it typified a lady-love and sweetheart.

the Fiametta of his passions

FIDELIO

Fidelio is the name of an opera by Beethoven, in which Leonora, the wife of Fernando Florestan, a prisoner, assumes the guise of a boy (Fidelio) in order to save her husband's life.

In Shakespeare's *Cymbeline,* Imogen assumes the name Fidele when she apparels herself as a boy, and in Wycherley's *Plain Dealer* another young girl disguised as a boy bears the name Fidelia.

as faithful as Fidelio

FIDES

Fides was the Roman goddess of good faith and fidelity, whose cult was particularly directed toward honoring the solemn pledge of the right hand. Known also as Fides Publica, she was depicted as wearing a wreath of olive or laurel. Dius Fidius, another god of faithfulness, was one of the manifestations of Jupiter.

a promise sworn by Fides

FIELD, EUGENE

Eugene Field (1850-1895), a writer of poetry for and about children, has a tenderness and grace, a depth of love that has made his name the synonym for all that is dearest about children and deepest in the love for children.

with Fieldian grace

FIERABRAS

Sir Fierabras, the hero of a medieval romance relating to the time of Charlemagne, was the greatest giant ever to walk the earth, surpassing all other men in height, breadth of shoulder, and hardness of muscle. Possessor of Babylon, seigneur of Russia, lord of Cologne, master of Rome and Jerusalem, and even of the Holy Sepulchre, he carried away from the latter the crown of thorns and the balsam which embalmed the body of Christ, one drop of which would cure any sickness or heal any wound in a moment. After his pride had been laid low by Oliver, one of Charlemagne's paladins, he ended his days in the odor of sanctity, "meek as a lamb and humble as a chidden slave." He is an allegory of Sin overcome by the Cross.

humbled from his pride, like Sir Fierabras

FIGARO

Figaro, a comical and witty liar, originally a character in Beaumarchais' *Barber of Seville,* was so popular that he was used again and again in other stories until he has almost acquired a personality. He is sometimes a barber, sometimes a valet, always coolly outwitting all comers, always adroit and unscrupulous.

the world owes a debt to Figaro; Figaro has given it more laughs than all the rest of the comedies combined

---

FILUMENA, SAINT

Filumena is the name of a pseudo-saint whose worship commenced in the nineteenth century. Longfellow applied the name to Florence Nightingale, possibly from its resemblance to the Greek *philomela,* a nightingale, and also because, in a picture by Sabatelli, St. Filumena is represented as hovering over a group of sick and maimed, who were healed by her intercession.

In the cemetery of St. Priscilla, in 1802, a grave was found, containing the remains of a glass vase that had held blood, the indication of the burial place of a martyr. Three tiles, which served to close the grave, contained the words *Pax tecum, Filumena* ("Peace be with you, Filumena"). Shortly after, a devout artisan, a priest, and a nun were all visited by visions of a virgin martyr who told them the story of Diocletian's love for her, of her refusal, and subsequent martyrdom. On the way to Mugnano whither they were carried for presentation, her remains worked many miracles on her adorers, repaired her own skeleton, and made her hair grow. So many wonders were said to have been worked by this phantom saint that she was called *La Thaumaturge du XIXme Siècle* in a book printed in Paris in 1847.

as thaumaturgic as St. Filumena

FINN, HUCK

Huck Finn is the shrewd, untutored, impulsive, generous-hearted waif, in Mark Twain's *Huckleberry Finn,* who sails down the river on a raft with a runaway slave boy, Jim. Through his eyes one gets an almost epic view of the whole midwest in the days of early America.

the world would be a grim place without its Penrods, its Tom Sawyers and Huck Finns

---

FLAMEN

The Flamens, "those who blow," were the priestly kindlers of sacred fires in ancient Rome. The special priests of various deities, including Jupiter, Mars, and Quirinus (Romulus), they were fifteen in number, and their principal function was the performance of daily sacrifices. Exempted from military service and taxation, as the modern clergy, they were also prohibited from holding political office. As emblem of their position they wore a white-leather conical hat, and if this fell off during a sacrifice, the remiss Flamen had to abdicate his duties.

as good at kindling a fire as a Flamen

FLAMININUS

Titus Quinctius Flamininus, the conqueror of Philip V of Macedon in 197 B.C., was subsequently hailed as the "liberator of Greece" for proclaiming the freedom of all Hellenes at the Isthmian Games. The gift was purely illusory and of hollow reality, but the Greeks received the announcement of it with such an excess of jubilant outburst that crows circling above the open-air theater, scene of the official declaration, were said to have dropped dead into the arena.

as popular a liberator as a modern Flamininus

FLANDERS, MOLL

Moll Flanders, a crude woman of wonderful beauty but of a most checkered career, is the center of interest in DeFoe's *Moll Flanders*. An adventuress and thief through many years, she finally went to Virginia, where she lived honestly and died a penitent. As one critic put it, she was "rehabilitated" in Virginia. Her name connotes crude, dishonest, beautiful, penitent, courtesan.

a reformed Moll Flanders

FLAUBERTIAN

Flaubertian refers to the meticulous literary craftsmanship of Gustave Flaubert (1821-1880), the distinguished French novelist who sometimes spent as much as a week in searching for the best turn of phrase, the most definitive adjective, and in avoiding all general banalities of description. *Madame Bovary* (*q. v.*), his first novel, took him six years to write, and *Salammbo*, begun with some archaeological studies at Carthage in 1858, was not finished until 1862, even though he had worked on it in almost sullen silence during all of the intervening time. Similarly, his *Temptation of Saint Anthony* was begun in 1857 and not completed until 1874. A model of style and realism, his works contain scrupulously truthful portraiture of life.

writes with painstaking Flaubertian exactitude

FLETCHERIZE

Fletcherize comes from Dr. Horace Fletcher (1849-1919), who caught the public ear and attained some degree of fame and many followers at the turn of the century by declaring that normal health could be maintained by any one who would take the established amount of time to chew his food. The rush of people to obtain perfect information of this inexpensive way to maintain perfect health gave rise to the common expression, "Fletcherize your food."

the transient fads, like fletcherizing, exercising to music, and the like

---

FLORA

Flora was the Roman goddess of fertility, springtime, and flowers. Her annual festival, the Floralia, was celebrated from April 28th till May 1st, and was marked by extravagant merriment and lasciviousness, as indicative of the ardent, erotic stirrings caused by warmth and the rebirth of vegetation.

looking like Flora in her bower

FLORIMEL

Florimel is a character in Spenser's *Faerie Queene*, whose name is compounded of the Latin roots for "flower" and "honey," thus suggesting all the sweet and delicate elements of which her womanly nature is molded. She expresses the ethereal gentleness and shy sensitivity of her sex, as well as the perils to which those qualities are subjected in a world of force and violence. Fleeing alike from friend and foe in her timidity, she finds treachery in the very one whom she trusts. A maligant witch made a counterfeit of her "with fine mercury and virgin wax," so like the original that it was impossible to tell the difference until, placed side by side, the copy evanesced into nothingness.

ethereal and timid as Florimel

FLUTTER, SIR FOPLING

Sir Fopling Flutter, in Etherege's comedy *The Man of Mode*, is a simpering fop and a mincing man of fashion.

dandified as Sir Fopling Flutter

FLYING DUTCHMAN

The Flying Dutchman is a Dutch ghost ship in a superstition that a certain ship captain was condemned to sail

"drank up all the rivers which were between Fortunio and the dragon"; Strong Back, who "carried wine enough to fill them all"; Light Foot, Boisterer, and Gormand.

incredible as the adventures of a Fortunio

FOSTER, STEPHEN

Stephen Foster (1826-1864), a problem to his parents because of his "idle, dreaming ways" and (to them) "strange talent for music," grew up to achieve the most typically American mode of musical expression in his two hundred songs. "Oh, Susanna," one of the first, appeared in twenty different editions in less than three years, because of his habit of giving manuscript copies to minstrel performers. Throughout his life his expenses were always in excess of his income, and he was finally eclipsed by his habit of drink, dying in poverty in a cheap rooming house. Songs like "Old Folks at Home," "Beautiful Dreamer," and "My Old Kentucky Home" show his powerful ability to appeal to the fundamental human emotions of universal humanity. Wistful, delicate, and nostalgic, they were molded exclusively by American influences, and even Southerners accepted them as an authentic expression of plantation atmosphere.

dreamily nostalgic as a Foster song

FOURIERIST

A Fourierist is a person who practices or defends the communistic principles of François Fourier (1772-1837), French social reformer, who proposed to mass people into phalanges of approximately 1800 persons, subdivided into units of 24 to 32 persons responsive to any one of the four prevailing affections—friendship, love, ambition, and familism. Each of these units would occupy a beautiful and self-supporting tract, and the component members would derive their support from the labor of all, the surplus being divided into twelve shares (five for labor, four for capital, and three for talent). A number of attempts were made unsuccessfully to organize people in this way, the most famous being at Brook Farm.

as socially conscious as a Fourierist

FOX, MARGARET

Margaret Fox (1833-1893) was an acclaimed medium and spiritualist who declared that she could establish communication with the world after death by means of spirit rappings. With her sisters as assistants at her séances, she achieved some renown among the gullible in the United States and Europe, and her success led to extensive investigation of all types of spiritualistic phenomena. Though at one time she confessed to being an impostor, she later repudiated it.

with Margaret Fox pretensions to supernatural powers

FRAIL, MRS.

Mrs. Frail, in Congreve's *Love for Love,* is a woman of easy virtue whose amatory frailties are betokened by her name. The role was one of the favorite ones in the repertoire of Mrs. Anne Bracegirdle (1663-1748), eminent English actress of the day.

a demimondaine of the Mrs. Frail type

FRANCE, ANATOLE

Anatole France, the pen-name by which Jacques Anatole Thibault (1844-1924) is famous the world over as the author of such charmingly graceful stories as *The Crime of Sylvestre Bonnard, Thais,* and *Penguin Island,* grew up in the literary atmosphere of his father's book-stalls. He developed a beautifully simple style, opposed to the "rare" artistry of the Goncourts and their disciples, characterized by felicity of expression, translucent simplicity, and harmonious grouping of words. A skeptic in matters of philosophy and a genial and kind doubter in all other things, he shows in all his writings a delicately pungent satire and an elfin spirit that is both evanescent and elusive.

an Anatole France-like simplicity of style

FRANCESCA OF RIMINI

Francesca da Rimini was the daughter of Guido da Polenta, lord of Ravenna. Married to Lanciotto, the son of Malatesta da Rimini, a brave but deformed and hateful person, she fell hopelessly in love with his handsome brother Paolo. Caught in their adulterous passion by him, they were both slain in 1285. In the fifth Canto of his *Inferno,* Dante represents the hapless lovers as being blown about by a hellish whirlwind, locked in each other's arms, and able to pause in their incessant turmoil only long enough to tell their tale of sorrow to the passerby. The story has inspired countless poems, tragedies, and paintings, and is the subject of Tschaikovsky's breath-takingly dramatic symphonic poem.

an unhappy Francesca, forbidden to love

FRANCIS of ASSISI

Saint Francis of Assisi (1182-1226), the saint who established the Franciscan order of monks, consecrated to the practice of poverty, simplicity, and unworldliness, is also credited with so much sympathy with and understanding of birds that birds flew to him wherever he went. His statue has become almost routine for garden places.

a Franciscan simplicity

FRANCISCHINI, GUIDO

Guido Franciscini, in Browning's *Ring and the Book,* is the impoverished fortune-hunting Italian nobleman who seeks to repair his fortunes by marrying Pompilia, daughter of Pietro and Violante, but when he ill-treats the latter after the marriage, she confesses that Pompilia is not her child but the offspring of a Roman wanton. In a fury Guido so abuses his young wife that she runs away with a young canon. Guido, unrelenting, has the canon defrocked and Pompilia sent to a convent, but the frail girl is permitted to return to her home for the birth of her child. Still choking with frustration and rage, Guido then goes to their home, murders Pietro, Violante, and Pompilia, and is executed for his villainy.

unforgiving as Guido Franciscini

FRANKENSTEIN

Frankenstein is the scholar in Mrs. Shelley's novel of the same name. He creates in his laboratory a monster that has all the motive powers of a physical human being and gets out of Frankenstein's control. Maddened by unsatisfied human cravings, it commits atrocious crimes, and brings about the final ruin of its creator. The word now indicates any idea or movement that, out of control, does damage not foreseen and not intended by its sponsors, eventually bringing disaster to its authors. (The name has become so indelibly associated with the idea of the monster that it is frequently erroneously applied to the monster rather than to its student creator.)

in danger of becoming a Frankenstein creation

FRANKLINIAN

Franklinian is from Benjamin Franklin (1706-1790), practical American scientist, inventor, philosopher, diplomat, and active citizen. He originated an almost incredible number of American societies, institutions, and public services, among them colleges, debating societies, fire companies, a postal system, the *Saturday Evening Post,* every one of them still a going concern. It was Franklin who discovered electricity, invented the Franklin stove, and in general rose to every occasion with a practical solution for the matter in hand and with amazing resourcefulness. These same qualities made him an invaluable diplomat and ambassador on several important international matters. His recorded philosophy in *Poor Richard's Almanac* is part of the world's practical wisdom, and his name suggests resourcefulness in its every degree.

the ingenuity of a Franklin
the Briarean power of a Franklin

FREISCHUETZ

Freischuetz, or "Free-shooter," is the name of a legendary German hunter and marksman who was in league with the Devil. From him he secured seven balls, all of which were infallible. The first six, however, reached targets of the Freischuetz' choice, while the seventh belonged to the Devil and was directed at his pleasure. Legends of this character were popular among German troopers of the fourteenth and fifteenth centuries. The story first appeared in poetic version in Apel's *Ghostbook* (1810), and F. Kind made it into a libretto for Weber's famous opera.

unerring as the Freischuetz

FREKI

Freki ("voracious" or "hungry"), in Norse mythology, is the name of one of the two wolves that recline at Odin's feet when he is presiding on his throne. Freki and his fellow Geri eat all their master's meat, for he needs no food.

carnivorous as Freki

FREUDIAN

Freudian comes from Sigmund Freud (1856-1939), a physicist and physician, who disseminated widely his doctrine that much disease and many disorders could be diagnosed or explained through the interpretation of the patient's dreams, and that behavior generally could be explained through psychic analysis. The fact that much of the interpretation either originated in or led to sex-interest gave impetus to the popularity of the theory, until *Freudian complex,* loosely speaking, and to the unscientific mind, has come to suggest sex-interest.

a Freudian complex
Freudian interpretations

FREY

Frey, the son of Njord, is the god of the sun and the rain, and, hence, of fertility, prosperity and peace in Scandinavian mythology. All phallic emblems were sacred to him, and his union with Gerth, a giantess, symbolized the rebirth of plant life in springtime. He was one of the most popular of the Northern deities.

as prolific as Frey

FREYA

Freya, the Scandinavian equivalent of Venus, was the daughter of Njord and the sister of Frey. The goddess of love, beauty, sensual pleasure and fecundity, she was the wife of Odur, but was deserted by him because she loved finery even more than she did her husband. Half of the warriors who fell in battle belonged to her, the other half to Odin. Two cats drew her chariot.

as lovely as Freya

FRIAR BUNGAY

Friar Bungay, an historical personage whose history is inextricably overlaid with legend, is said to have "raised the mists and vapors which befriended Edward IV at the battle of Barnet." He was the personification of the charlatan of science in the fifteenth century, according to Bulwer-Lytton.

fraudulent as Friar Bungay

FRIAR LAURENCE

Friar Laurence, in Shakespeare's *Romeo and Juliet,* is the adviser, confessor, and friend of the young lovers. Undertaking to marry them, he then is forced to save Juliet from a second marriage by giving her the sleeping draught that leads to the drama's tragic consequences.

no Friar Laurence to consummate their union

FRIAR RUSH

Friar Rush, in medieval folklore, was a devil disguised as a monk and sent to corrupt his brethren. Originally a mischievous elf of the Robin Goodfellow type, he was despatched from the infernal regions to keep clerics in the same state of wickedness they were then in. His German name, Bruder Rausch, signifies either "noise" or "drunkenness," and his history was first printed in 1620.

troublesome as Friar Rush

FRIBBLE

Frible is an effeminate and feeble-minded coxcomb in Garrick's farce *Miss in Her Teens.* Much given to coddling himself, he is "sadly troubled with weak nerves." Though his countenance is superficially thoughtful, his head is actually blank.

a neurotic Fribble

FRIDAY, MAN

Cruscoe's Man Friday is the young savage he found on the supposedly uninhabited island in DeFoe's *Robinson Crusoe,* and kept as his servant and companion. The worshipful service rendered by the Man Friday has given that name to any one kindly and devotedly carrying out the wishes and purposes of another.

every president now must have his Man Friday

FRIETCHIE, BARBARA

Barbara Frietchie, an American woman who displayed the American flag boldly as the rebels marched through her town of Frederick, Maryland, won permanent acclaim by standing at the window beside the flag, challenging the passing enemy, and is immortalized in these lines by Whittier:

"Shoot, if you must, this old gray head,
But spare your country's flag. . . "

the Barbara Frietchies of today do not stand in windows; they fly planes

---

FRIGGA

Frigga, in Scandinavian mythology, is the goddess of marriage and domestic life. The wife of Odin, she is also the mother of Baldur and the other gods. Though she knows the fate of men, she does not prophesy. The constellation Orion is called her distaff, and Friday is named after her. Much confused with Freya (*q. v.*), she is known as Fricka in Wagner's *Ring* operas.

wedlock blessed by Frigga

FROG, NICHOLAS

Nicholas Frog is the humorous national designation given to the Dutch, in Arbuthnot's *History of John Bull.* Frogs are known as "Dutch nightingales."

croaking like Nicholas Frog

FROLLO, ARCHDEACON

Archdeacon Claude Frollo, in Victor Hugo's *Notre Dame de Paris,* is a noted alchemist absorbed in a bewildering search for the philosopher's stone. Though he has a great reputation for sanctity, he falls in love with a gypsy girl, Esmeralda (*q. v.*), whom he pursues with unrelenting fury because she will not yield to his passionate desires.

an Archdeacon Frollo of superficial holiness

FRONT DE BOEUF

Front de Boeuf, in Scott's *Ivanhoe,* is the brutal and parricidal Norman baron who is master of the stronghold of Torquilstone. A reckless and predatory overlord, he is gigantic in stature and a blasphemous and ferocious follower of Prince John.

ferocious as Front de Boeuf

FRONTINUS

Sextus Julius Frontinus (A.D. 40-103) was Roman governor of Britain, where he constructed the Roman road through Wales. Later curator of the aqueducts at Rome, he wrote a work on this subject, the *De Aquae Ductu,* in which he discusses the history, length, altitude, and capacity of the city's water lines. The author also of three books of military *Stratagems,* he illustrates in them his country's tactics before and during battles, describes the conduct of sieges and ambuscades, and discourses generally on the management of an army.

with the military knowledge of Frontinus

FROTH, MASTER

Master Froth is a foolish gentleman whose name explains his character, in Shakespeare's *Measure for Measure.* Without solidity enough for deep crime, he is yet far too light for virtue. A clown in the play argues as follows in favor of him: "Look upon his face. I'll be sworn upon a book that his face is the worst part about him; and if his face be the worst part about him, how could Master Froth do the constable's wife any harm?"

In Congreve's *Double Dealer,* Lord Froth is a solemn coxcomb married to a coquettish wife.

superficial as Master Froth

FROTHI

Frothi was the mythical Norse king associated with a golden age of unprecedented prosperity, known as *Frothi peace.* His avarice, however, eventually caused the giantesses who ground out his gold to mill for him vengeance, calamity, and disaster instead. According to some authorities, his gold was known as *Frothi's meal;* according to others, the term refers to his ruin.

prosperous as Frothi

FUDGE, MR.

Mr. Fudge was a contemptuous British designation bestowed upon any absurd or lying person. Its origin is explained in *Remarks upon the Navy* (London, 1700): "There was, sir, in our time, one Captain Fudge, commander of a merchantman, who, upon his return from a voyage, how ill fraught soever his ship was, always brought home to his owners a good cargo of lies."

the exaggerated mendacity of a Mr. Fudge

FULTON, ROBERT

Robert Fulton (1765-1815) was the famous American engineer and inventor who patented a machine for sawing marble, another for spinning flax, and a third for twisting hemp rope. Though he also invented a submarine, he was unable to interest any government of his day in it. While in France, he was commissioned by Robert R. Livingstone, U. S. ambassador to that country, to build a steamboat, with which he experimented on the Seine river. Back in the U. S., he built the *Clermont,* which steamed up the Hudson from New York to Albany and back. The first of a line of commercial steamboats, it operated with a profit for its owners.

the mechanical ingenuity of a Robert Fulton

FULVIA

Fulvia was the first wife of Mark Antony and an ambitious and masterful woman who played an important political role in the civil war that sprang up in Rome after the assassination of Julius Caesar. With Antony's brother Lucius she held Perugia firm against Octavian's siege, while her husband was disporting himself with Cleopatra in the East. Forced to surrender the town in 40 B.C., she died shortly thereafter. In Tennyson's *Dream of Fair Women* she is referred to as an injured wife.

as occupied as Fulvia while her husband was dallying with another woman

---

FUNG-HWANG

Fung-hwang is the richly colored, graceful, pheasant-like Chinese bird of good omen, displayed as a motif in both Chinese and Japanese decorative art. It is said to have appeared just before fortunate events of great public moment. Announcing the advent of an age of virtue, it put in its last appearance in the time of Confucius.

blessed by the appearance of Fung-hwang

FUNK, PETER

Peter Funk is the fictitious name of the person employed at auctions to bid on articles put up for sale, in order to raise their price. Though his purchases are always sham, since he never actually pays a cent of money, he is of great service in stimulating and encouraging timid potential customers to enter the contest and bid for objects competitively.

a Peter Funk who keeps raising the ante

FURIES

The Furies, avenging deities, fierce, violent, unresrained, inescapable, were so feared by the early Greeks that their name has been preserved to mean the personification of vengeance, violence and punishment. They were also known as Erinyes and Eumenides.

the Furies of an aroused conscience
pursued by the Furies of his memory
thither, by harpy-footed Furies, are the damned all brought

FURIOSO, BOMBASTES

Bombastes Furioso, the hero of Rhodes' opera of that name, was burlesque, bombastic, pompous, and swaggered about using ponderous inflated language. The whole was meant to be a satire on Ariosto's *Orlando Furioso*.

he is rather a Bombastes Furioso among the music critics, not too much credited

---

FUZZY-WUZZY

Fuzzy-Wuzzy is the name given to the Hottentots by the British Army in India in Kipling's *Barrack Room Ballads,* when he pays his respects to the fuzzy headed fighter in the native armies who had achieved the well-nigh impossible when they "broke the British square"; hence, surprising, indomitable, daring.

your Fuzzy-Wuzzy on the field of battle is inspired by all the Furies

G

GABLER, HEDDA

Hedda Gabler, the heroine and title-character of Ibsen's play of that name, is a neurotic and high-spirited young woman who is uncongenially married and is fond of playing with pistols. After tormenting an admirer and goading him to death, she finally commits suicide.

neurotic as Hedda Gabler

GABRIEL

Gabriel is the archangel appointed to carry tidings to heaven and to the world. His office is so well established that in song and in story it is assumed that Gabriel's trumpet will announce the resurrection on the last day.

fancies himself the appointed Gabriel of any great occasion

GADARENE

Gadarene is from Gadara, the place where Jesus cast the devils out of demoniac persons and into a herd of swine, which at once dashed madly into the sea. The word now, recalling the headlong rush, suggests demoniac, brutish.

run ravening as the Gadarean swine

GAINSBOROUGH

Gainsborough stems from the portrait painting by Thomas Gainsborough (1727-1788) in the days of plumes, large and beautiful hats, great beauty, and great elaboration of dress. The name has, therefore, come to be associated rather with elaborate and elegant dress and a certain delicacy and grace of feminine features than with the artist's skill. The Gainsborough hat has especially survived the years.

dressed in the best Gainsborough style

GALAHAD

Galahad, the son of Lancelot, is the pure and perfect Arthurian knight who finally achieved the quest of the Holy Grail. His name has always been the symbol of purity, devotion, and chastity.

a rare Galahad in a modern world

GALATEA

Galatea was one of the Nereids, or sea-nymphs, with whom the crude Cyclops, Polyphemus, fell desperately in love. His devotion, however, was unsatisfactory because unrequited, as Galatea showered her affections on the youth Acis. In a jealous rage Polyphemus crushed the latter under a rock. Galatea then transformed Acis into a river, which continued to bear his beloved name. In Handel's *Acis and Galatea* the contrast between the dainty Nereid and the uncouth, lumbering giant is delightfully represented by the music.

For Galatea, the beautiful sculptured maiden transformed into life because of the devotion of its creator, see *Pygmalion*.

pale as an unwakened Galatea

GALBA

Servius Sulpicius Galba became emperor of Rome for a brief six months following the suicide of Nero in 68 A.D. Elevated to the purple by his troops in Spain, he was honest and just. In his short reign, however, he was so severe that he became unpopular, was conspired against, murdered, and replaced by Otho. His name is, therefore, suggestive of ill-used power, unpopularity, and fickle and short-lived public favor.

another Galba, fallen from the fickle favor of Fortune

GALEN

Galen (129-199 A.D.), one of the most famous of ancient physicians, lived at Rome under the emperor Marcus Aurelius, who was his friend. He wrote over 100 treatises on his profession, and his name is today a generic name for an apothecary. The expression "Galen says 'Nay' and Hippocrates 'Yea'" means that when even doctors disagree, who is to decide?

a Galen in the local drug-store

GALILEAN

Galilean is a name given to Christ, probably because of his origin near the Sea of Galilee and his preachings there. The name was sometimes applied to his followers and to the early Christians.

Galilean wisdom

GALILEO

Galileo (1564-1642) was the renowned Italian astronomer, physicist, and experimental philosopher whose name is associated with the "new sciences" of his time that flung the bounds of the visible universe wide open. Remarkable for his intellectuality and mechanical inventiveness, he constructed an astronomical clock, the proportional compass or sector that is still used in geometrical drawing, probed into heretical theories of the solar sysem, and from Pisa'a leaning tower demonstrated the falsity of the current doctrine that heavy bodies fall with velocities proportional to their weight. His unlimited scientific curiosities provoked the enmity of the Church, which subjected him to inquisitions and recantations.

a new star-gazing Galileo

GALINTHIAS

Galinthias aided Alcmene of Thebes to give birth to the infant Hercules, when the Moerae (Fates) and Ilithyiae (*q. v.*) were endeavoring to delay the delivery at the request of jealous Hera. She surprised the opposing goddesses by startling them with the false news that Alcmene had already been delivered, whereupon they dropped their arms and broke the interfering spell. The deceived Moerae avenged this successful trick by transforming Galinthias into a weasel. In pity, Hecate made her her attendant in the lower world. Hercules afterward erected a shrine to her.

a trick of Galinthian ingenuity

GALLI

The Galli were eunuch priests of Cybele, the Asiatic goddess of fertility. Named from the Gallus river in Phrygia, they were said to have castrated themselves in imitation of Attis (*q. v.*). They worshiped the goddess with wild, orgiastic dancing and frenzied, clashing music.

orgies frenzied as those of the Galli

GALLOPING DICK

Galloping Dick was the sobriquet popularly bestowed upon Richard Ferguson, a notorious English highwayman who was executed at Aylesbury on April 4, 1800. The name was given him because of his bold riding when pursued.

flying down the bridlepath like Galloping Dick

GALSWORTHIAN

Galsworthian is from John Galsworthy (1867-1933), eminent English author of the twentieth century, dramatist and novelist. With an unusual combination of sympathy, penetration, and subtle satire, he lashed at the social situations and implications of English society, even while he drew with inherent sympathy the picture of fine English character. In general, his books and stories are among the truest and most comprehensive interpretations of English society today—a cross-section of English life.

Galsworthian penetration

GAMA, VASCO DA

Vasco da Gama (c. 1469-1525) was the Portuguese navigator who was the first to double the Cape of Good Hope and to reach India entirely by sea route. The hero of Camoen's *Lusiad,* he is pictured as wise, courageous, tender-hearted, pious, patriotic, and always in control of his emotions. He is also the hero of Meyerbeer's opera, *L' Africaine.*

a scout with the courage of Vasco da Gama

GAMALIEL

Gamaliel, a leader of the liberal school of Pharisees and the preceptor of St. Paul (*Acts,* xxii, 3), was the first of the seven great Rabbans, or outstanding Rabbis. It was by his advice (*Acts,* v, 34) that the Sanhedrin was persuaded not to molest the first preachers of Christianity: "For if this counsel or this work be of men, it will come to naught: But if it be of God, ye cannot overthrow it; lest haply ye be found even to fight against God."

The grandson of Hillel, a leading authority on interpretation of Biblical law, he was the grandfather of Gamaliel the younger, a leader of his people in the period of stress that followed the destruction of Jerusalem in 70 A. D., a scholar noted for his liberalism, and an innovator in Jewish ritual.

a teacher as wise as Gamaliel

GAMBRINUS

Gambrinus, mythical Flemish king and Duke of Brabant (1251-1294), was reputed to be the inventor of beer. He is always represented as a king holding a foaming glass of lager.

has Gambrinus's fondness for beer

GAMP, MRS. SARAH

Sairey Gamp, the old nurse in Dickens' *Martin Chuzzlewit,* was noted for her fondness for liquor and her constant references to her fictitious and useful friend, Mrs. Harris. The name Sairey Gamp is used to suggest any garrulous, perhaps tippling and not-too-scrupulous aged woman.

the glorious inconsequences of a Sairey Gamp

GANELON

Ganelon, Count of Mayence and one of Charlemagne's paladins, was known as the "Judas of knights." Though his master always trusted him, he consistently betrayed him and was perpetually engaged in machinations for the destruction of Christianity. Spite, obstinacy, dissimulation, false humility, and immeasurable powers of intrigue were the chief ingredients of his character. Jealous of Roland, he plotted with Marsillus, the Moorish king, to attack Roncevalles in order to destroy his rival. Six and a half feet tall, he had glaring eyes and flaming red hair. Friendless, moody, and solitary, he has become a byword for a traitor of the basest sort.

as full of treachery as Ganelon

GANESA

Ganesa is the name of the Hindu god of policy, prudence, and wisdom. He is represented in art as having four (or three) arms and the head of an elephant.

with Ganesan prudence and an elephantine memory

GANYMEDE

Ganymede, the cupbearer to the gods after Hebe, was, like Hebe, the most beautiful of mortals. Jove, having seen him among his playmates, took the form of an eagle and snatched him into heaven to be his cupbearer.

swift as Ganymede to serve

GARCIA

Garcia, from Elbert Hubbard's story, *A Message to Garcia,* is the Cuban patriot and general of the Spanish-American War to whom a message is sent. Its dramatic delivery emphasizes the faithfulness, resourcefulness, and initiative that should mark the perfect messenger fit to be trusted with any important message.

tenacious of his Garcia-message

GARGANTUAN

Gargantuan, from Gargantua, in Rabelais' satire, *Gargantua and Pantagruel,* refers to the friendly giant king, best remembered for his prodigious capacity for eating and drinking huge quantities. He could drink a river dry and is said to have swallowed five pilgrims in a salad, according to the story. Hence, his name signifies great size and a prodigious appetite.

a gargantuan fiction
with Gargantuan extravagance

GARGERY, JOE

Joe Gargery, the kindhearted, ignorant blacksmith who befriends Pip in Dickens' *Great Expectations,* expresses sympathy when his virago wife abuses Pip at the table, by giving him more gravy. Every time his wife breaks out into a fresh tirade, Joe reaches for little Pip's plate to put on even more gravy.

generous as Joe Gargery

GARIBALDIAN

Garibaldian refers to the patriotic efforts of Giuseppe Garibaldi (1807-1882) in securing the unification of Italy. After exiles in South America and New York for complicity in undertakings to effect the liberation of his native land from the piecemeal distribution made of it by the armies of France, Austria, Spain, and the independent Kingdom of Naples, he raised gallant volunteer armies which he commanded with such consummate generalship that he was able to defeat the Austrians and was proclaimed Dictator for the purpose of freeing Naples and marching on Rome. The type of red shirt worn by the patriot is still known as a garibaldi in honor of the most revered of all of Italy's patriots.

Garibaldian vigor in the cause of freedom

GARM

Garm, in Norse mythology, is the demon watchdog of Hel, goddess of the land of the dead. A bloody-breasted and ferocious monster, he broke loose from his chains at Ragnarok and killed the god Tyr, but was simultaneously killed by his victim.

beware of that dog—he's a Garm

GARRICK, DAVID

David Garrick was a brilliant English actor of the eighteenth century. His name is used to imply the acme of versatile and effective acting. The Garrick Club in London is the most exclusive of clubs for eminent actors. He was an irrepressible mimic—when suddenly missing at a dinner, his party saw in the courtyard outside a young negro boy rolling in delight to see Garrick mimicking a turkey cock, coat tail stuck out behind, in a seeming flutter of rage and pride.

the world has yet to produce a second Garrick

where wishful young Garricks strut the stage

GARUDA

Garuda is the emblem of strength and swiftness in Hindu mythology. He has the head and red wings of a bird but a golden body and the legs of a man, and serves as the vehicle on which Vishnu rides.

fleet as the wings of Garuda

GASCONADE

Gasconade refers to Gascony, a French province noted for its bragging, boasting, swaggering inhabitants. So vainglorious were the Gascons that any speech or writing in which one unduly praises his own achievements is apt to be called a gasconade.

issues his usual gasconade

GAUGUIN, PAUL

Paul Gauguin (1848-1903) was the famous French painter who was one of the principal founders of the symbolist school in art. Later he established a studio on the island of Tahiti, and his name is now associated with paintings of lush tropical climes, brilliant and decorative color schemes, natives, palm trees, and sarongs.

a Gauguinish riot of color

GAVROCHE

Gavroche is the gamin in Hugo's *Les Misérables,* so typical that his name has come to mean any street Arab or wandering urchin, shrewd and crafty and wise.

an impudent young Gavroche tagged along

GAWAIN

Gawain was a pleasant, handsome, courtly knight of the Round Table. A lover of pleasure and dalliance, he was always willing to turn aside from any quest or mission to follow his own desires, and willing to entrust the fulfilment of his mission to another, even though the responsibility was to have been his alone. Hence, his name connotes light, fickle, untrustworthy, frivolous.

an irresponsible Gawain-like fellow

GE

Ge, or Gaea, the personification of the earth, according to the Greeks and Romans (the latter of whom called her Tellus), was the first being to spring from Chaos. Having given birth to Uranus(Heaven) and Pontus (Sea), she became by the former the mother of the Titans, whom she hid from their jealous father. To one of these Titans, Cronus (*q. v.*), she gave a large iron sickle with which to mutilate Uranus and succeed to the hegemony of the early gods. Regarded as one of the gods of the nether world, she was also influential over marriage and death.

prays to fruitful Ge for a large crop

GEFJON

Gefjon was the Scandinavian goddess of virginity. All maidens who died chaste repaired to her after death to serve as her handmaids.

pure as Gefjon

GEHENNA

Gehenna was a place outside Jerusalem where refuse was dumped and burned, hence, later used to suggest hell. (See also *Tophet.*) "Hot as Tophet" and "hot as Gehenna" were polite ways of saying hot as hell. The fires were kept burning continuously for fear of pestilence.

ever-burning Tophet fires

GELERT

Gelert was the favorite greyhound of Llewellyn, son-in-law of King John of England. During the absence of his master he destroyed a ferocious wolf that attacked Llewellyn's infant son. On his return Llewellyn, seeing the dog's bloody mouth, rashly concluded that it had killed his son, who was fast asleep under a confused heap of bedclothes. When the dying yell of the faithful animal awakened the child, Llewellyn was smitten with remorse for his hasty and impulsive deed, and erected an elegant monument over the remains of the heroic dog. This legend has been versified by William Robert Spencer.

a loyal guardian like Gelert

GEMINI

The Gemini were twins, a zodiacal constellation containing the stars Castor and Pollux, but popularly known as the astrological sign indicating a dual nature, changeful and commanding and usually optimistic in disposition.

inseparable as the Gemini

GENETYLLIS

Genetyllis was the Graeco-Roman goddess who presided over and was the protectress of childbirth.

an accouchement made easy by Genetyllis

GENEVIEVE

Geneviève, sainted patroness of the city of Paris, which she saved from the Huns by her prayers (451) and from Clovis until his conversion to Christianity, was noted for her numerous deeds of mercy during plague, famine, and siege.

In medieval romance, another Geneviève was the wife of Count Palatine Siegfried of Mayenfeld in the age of Charles Martel. During his campaign against the Saracens he condemned her to death because he gave ear to a false accusation charging her with infidelity. Escaping to the forest of Ardennes, she lay in concealment there until her husband recgnized her innocence on finding her.

charitable as Ste. Geneviève

GENSERIC

Genseric (390-477) was the great marauding king of the Vandals who started his career of conquest by transporting some 80,000 of his people from Spain to Africa in search of a new home. Short of stature and lame, he had a tremendous capacity for war and was completely pitiless and reckless of human life. The terror of Constantinople and Rome, he captured Roman Africa, assaulted Rome and for fourteen days in a calm and businesslike way he emptied the city of its movable wealth. The latter years of his rapacious life were spent in a fiendish persecution of Catholic Christians everywhere.

a cruel and plundering Genseric

GEORGE, ST.

St. George was martyred by decapitation in Diocletian's persecution of Christians living in Cappadocia in 303. The legendary hero of the middle ages, he was pictured as slaying a dragon which held a princess captive. The allegory expressed the triumph of the Christian hero over evil, and is told in Percy's *Reliques* and Spenser's *Faerie Queene*, where George represents "Piety" and rescues Una, "Truth," from the dragon. The patron of soldiers, he has also been the patron saint of England since the establishment of the Order of the Garter by Edward III. St. George's cross is a red one on a white field.

triumphant as St. George over evil

GEORGIAN

Georgian, from the period of the Georges in England, connotes elegance, formality, and beauty of style in architecture, furnishings, and manners.

a Georgian elegance marked the mansion

GERDA

Gerda, the most beautiful of the goddesses in the Scandinavian pantheon, was noted for her piety and her virtue. At first sight of her, Frey was so seized by her loveliness that he could neither speak, sleep, nor drink. His messenger, Skirnir, thereupon promised to secure her for his wife, if Frey would give him in reward his magic sword that would strew a battlefield with carnage of its own accord. When Gerda promised to marry Frey in nine nights, the latter exclaimed:

"Long is one night,
Long are two nights,
But how shall I hold out three?
Shorter hath seemed
A month to me oft
Than of this longing time the half."

radiantly lovely as Gerda

GERONIMO

Geronimo (1834-1909), chief of the Apaches, a dreaded tribe of Indian wanderers, appeared on unexpected and devastating swift raids. The hero of many actual adventures, he was also in fiction a favorite hero in bloodcurdling stories.

boys in the yard playing Geronimo

GERONTE

Géronte is the name of a stock character in classical French comedy. A simple-minded, credulous, and ridiculous old man, he appears in Corneille's *Le Menteur* and in Molière's *Le Médecin malgré Lui.*

a dotard like Géronte

GERRY, ELBRIDGE

Elbridge Gerry (1744-1814) was an American statesman, a signer of the Declaration of Independence, and Vice-President of the United States in the last year of his life. While Governor of Massachusetts in 1812, he divided that State into representative districts in such a way as to give to one special political party preponderant and unfair advantage over the others. When Gilbert Stuart, the artist, saw the map of the new distribution, he converted the Essex County section of the new map into the figure of a salamander by adding a few strokes of the pen. "No, no," said Benjamin Russel, an ardent Federalist, when shown the altered drawing, "not a Sala-mander, Stuart, a Gerry-mander." The word gerrymander, established in our language since that time, means to distort, misrepresent, manipulate unfairly, and to garble with the intent of establishing an advantage.

another Gerry at jockeying for advantage

GERYON

Geryon was a triple-headed or triple-bodied Spanish giant and rancher. The owner of a magnificent herd of oxen guarded for him by his herdsman Eurytion and his formidable dog Orthrus, he was defeated and killed by Hercules, who had been sent by his taskmaster Eurystheus to steal the oxen and drive them back to Greece.

cattle as fine as Geryon's

GETHSEMANE

Gethsemane was the garden or orchard at the foot of the Mount of Olives, east of Jerusalem. The scene of Christ's agony and betrayal (*Matt.*, xxvi, 36), its name has been used since that time to connote any place or occasion of suffering, sorrow, and despair.

entered his Gethsmane with resignation

GET-RICH-QUICK-WALLINGFORD

Get-Rich-Quick-Wallingford is the genial and diverting rogue who is always meditating on schemes for making money in a series of amusing stories by George Randolph Chester (1869-1924). The original story, titled after its hero, was followed by *Blackie Daw* and *Wallingford in His Prime.*

the Get-Rich-Quick-Wallingford of the brokerage office

GETTYSBURG

Gettysburg, a borough in southern Pennsylvania, was the scene of the crucial battle that marked the turning point in the victorious sweep of the Confederate Army into Pennsylvania during the Civil War. The battle, in which Meade defeated Lee, lasted from July 1st to 3rd, 1863. A national cemetery and a military park now commemorate the heroic event and the great oration that President Lincoln delivered on this hallowed ground.

another Gettysburg to stem the tide of the enemy's sweep

GIBBET

Gibbet, in Farquhar's *Beaux' Stratagem,* is a footpad who "piqued himself on being the best-behaved man on the road." He also boasted of conducting himself with all appropriate civility in the exercise of his profession.

polite in his thievery as Gibbet

GIBBON, EDWARD

Gibbon is the great English historian (1737-1794) who wrote *The Decline and Fall of the Roman Empire,* hailed by friend and enemy alike as the high-water mark of historical writing, even while it is assailed for a bias and prejudice which often leads the author to enlarge on one element while he reduces others, equally important, to notes.

a Gibbonian prejudice apparent throughout

GIBEONITE

The Gibeonites were made to be "hewers of wood and drawers of water" for the Israelites (*Josh.,* ix, 27). The name has ever since connoted a slave's slave, a workman's laborer, a Jack-of-all-work, and a drudge.

a Gibeonite, serving them all by turn

GIBIL

Gibil, also known as Girru, was the Assyro-Babylonian fire-god often appealed to in invocations against magic and sorcery.

exorcised by Gibil

GIBRALTAR

Gibraltar, the impregnable rock fortress, symbolizes solidity and strategic position for purposes of guarding and control. In ancient times it was named Mount Calpe and was supposed to be the European support of one of the Pillars of Hercules straddling the strait. Its modern name is derived from the Arabic *Gibel al Tari,* "mountain of Tari," the Arab general who in 710 landed there and defeated the army of Roderick, the Gothic king of Spain. The precipitous mountain is now the emblem of strength, eternal endurance, stability, and safety.

Cape Diamond, Quebec, the Gibraltar of the New World

GIBSONESQUE

Gibsonesque recalls the pictures and style of Charles Dana Gibson (1867-1944), the famous American illustrative artist and portraitist who created the typically American "Gibson Girl" of the late nineteenth and early twentieth centuries. Wearing a pomadour hair-style and a velvet ribbon with a cameo at her neck, and with a tiny waist-line and swirling skirts, she was represented in all the feminine occupations of her time, chaperoned in ballrooms or playing tennis and indulging in other out-of-door pastimes. Directness, simplicity, and economy of line mark the style of this popular artist of the Gay Nineties and the Horse-and-Buggy epoch.

demure and sweet as a Gibson Girl with Gibsonesque modishness and charm

---

GIDE, ANDRE

André Gide (1869-1951), French novelist, essayist and critic, is best known for his internationally acclaimed novels *The Counterfeiters* and *The Immoralist,* though it is as an essayist and critic that his unusual gifts won for him the Nobel prize for literature in 1947. His *Journals,* recently published in this country, and his philosophical discourses and aesthetic *causeries* are all written in the introspective method with such distinction that he is considered the finest of contemporary French stylists. His great delicacy of expression and individual grace have influenced writers of all countries.

with Gide-like contemplation

GIDEON

Gideon was the great religious leader who became the liberator of the Hebrew people. When the vast and well-organized army of the Midianites was about to overwhelm them, "Gideon's army," a hastily recruited and unwieldy mob that he reduced and trained to a small but trusty handful of 300 energetic and determined men, defeated and routed the enemy in a patriotic struggle. Thereafter he was held in great esteem and revered as a judge in Israel for a period of forty years (*Judges,* vi, 11).

an impassioned Gideon's army-like resistance

GIGANTES

The Gigantes, mythological children of Uranus (Heaven) and Ge (Earth), were creatures of monstrous size with fearful faces and dragon tails. Attacking heaven with huge rocks and tree-trunks in an endeavor to unseat the gods, they were worsted by their betters with the assistance of Hercules, and buried in punishment under Mount Aetna and other famous volcanoes. The origin of the Gigantomachy, their fabled contest with the Olympian gods, is probably to be explained mythopoeically as a description of the violence of volcanic upheavals.

monsters with Gigantean impiety

GILBERT and SULLIVAN

Gilbert and Sullivan is from the team of Sir William Gilbert, who wrote the lyrics, and Sir Arthur Sullivan, who furnished the music for a series of operas, musical comedies on light, entertaining subjects, with topsy-turvy plots, crazy dialogue, and catchy tunes, among them *The Mikado* and *Pinafore.* The operas are so popular and so highly individual in type that any story of that general sort is characterized as a Gilbert-and-Sullivan story, light, amusing, entertaining, melodious, rollicking, and irresponsible.

with the mad joy of a Gilbert and Sullivan opera

GIL BLAS

Gil Blas is a picaresque romance by LeSage, borrowed from old Spanish romance. The hero, Gil Blas, tells the tale and makes his own commentaries which disclose him to have been timid, but audacious; shrewd in fooling others, but gullible himself; good-natured, easy, and full of good intentions which he never quite fulfilled. The name is apt to be applied to a person having those same qualities.

an incurable Gil Blas

GILDEROY

Gilderoy, of the "higher than Gilderoy's kite" fame, was hanged in England from the highest gallows ever erected, where his body swung like a kite. The expression became common thereafter.

with all the grim horror of a Gilderoy

GILEAD

Gilead was an ancient mountainous district of Palestine. East of the Jordan, it was famous for its soothing balm that was esteemed in the ancient world for its fragrance and medicinal qualities (*Jeremiah,* viii, 22).

a modern-day balm from Gilead to soothe all pain

GILES, SAINT

Saint Giles, a seventh century hermit saint said to have been wounded in the knee accidentally by the King of France while hunting, was thereafter called the patron saint of cripples.

the village St. Giles

GILGAMESH

Gilgamesh is the hero of a Babylonian epic that recounts his adventures with his friend Engidu. He frees the town of Uruk, spurns the goddess Ishtar, is smitten with disease, finds the Source of Life and is healed, and opens the paradise of heroes. In his search for eternal life after his friend's death, he meets an ancestor who tells him the story of the great flood of Biblical times. The work abounds in philosophical advice of this sort:

Fill, O Gilgamesh, thy belly,
Day and night be joyful!
Daily be glad!
Day and night make merry!
Let thy garments be white,
Anoint thy head, and purify thyself.
With the children at thy side,
Enjoy the wife of thy bosom.

a comfortable sort of Gilgameshean hedonism

GILL, HARRY

Harry Gill, in Wordsworth's ballad of *Goody Blake and Harry Gill,* is a hard-hearted farmer who detects Goody Blake, a poor old dame, in the act of pilfering a few sticks of wood from her neighbor's ground in the bitter winter cold. When he forces her to relinquish her loot, in requital she invokes upon him the curse that he may "never more be warm." Ever after, "his teeth they chatter, chatter still."

as stingy as Harry Gill

GILLS, SOL

Sol Gills, in Dickens' *Dombey and Son,* is a warm-hearted and simple-minded ships'-instruments maker, "who smelt like a weedy sea-beach when the tide is out." His "newly awakened manner" he might have acquired by having stared for three or four days successively through every optical instrument in his shop. Old prints of ships, outlandish shells, seaweeds, and mosses decorated the chimney piece of his home, and ships' biscuit was always plentiful on his table.

nautically minded as Sol Gills

GILPIN, JOHN

John Gilpin, a London linen-draper and captain of a train-band, finds himself on a runaway steed which leads him into all sorts of ridiculous adventures. This story was told to Cowper by Lady Austin, to "divert him from his melancholy," and Cowper turned it into an amusing poem, entitled *The Diverting History of John Gilpin.*

swift as John Gilpin's ride

GINEVRA

Ginevra, the beautiful young bride of Lord Lovel, on her wedding night, in the gay games that were part of the marriage festivities at the castle, hid in a trunk that snapped shut as the lid closed. She was never found until years after when her bones were discovered in the old chest. Haynes Bailey makes use of the story in a ballad of the sad sort popular in that day, called *The Mistletoe Bough,* songful and sentimental.

Ginevra-like, shut herself up in a trunk

GIOTTESQUE

Giottesque refers to the style or work of Giotto di Bondone (1266-1337), great Florentine painter and architect, who took Nature for his teacher and whose paintings are characterized by their imaginative, pictorial invention and dramatic expression. An Italian proverb, *round as Giotto's O,* refers to a dull and stupid person. The Pope, wishing to commission some art decorations, sent a messenger to secure specimens from the chief artists of Italy. When Giotto drew a circle with red paint, the astonished messenger asked if that were all. Giotto answered, "Send it, and we shall see if His Holiness understands the hint," thus reproving the Pope by showing him that a mere specimen of a work of genius is about equal to a brick as a sample of a finished building.

moralizes with Giottesque terseness

GISELLE

Giselle, the heroine of the ballet libretto by Gautier based on a story by Heinrich Heine and set to music by Adam, is a Rhineland peasant girl who loves Albrecht, a neighboring noble disguised as a villager. Hilarion, a gamekeeper suitor whom she spurned, swears revenge. Excessively fond of dancing, Giselle has been warned by her mother to abstain, lest she die before her wedding-day and become one of the Willis, ghostly dancing maidens who lure travelers to their death by night. When the jealous Hilarion reveals to Giselle that Albrecht is betrothed to a princess, the grief-stricken maiden dances wildly in a transport of despair, stabs herself, and becomes one of the Willis, from whose enticements, however, she manages to save her beloved Albrecht by counseling him to cling to the cross on her grave.

like Giselle, powerless to resist the rhythm of the dance

GISHZIDA

Gishzida was the Babylonian sun-god, stationed as guardian of the door of heaven.

Gishzida's torrid rays

GJALLARHORN

Gjallarhorn, in Norse mythology, is the horn sounded by Heimdall, the guardian of Asgard (Heaven), to summon the gods to battle at Ragnarok. Its clarion tones were heard throughout the universe.

like the trumpet blast of Gjallarhorn

GLADSTONIAN

Gladstonian is from William Ewart Gladstone, illustrious nineteenth century statesman responsible for introducing the Bill of Rights for the common people into English politics, and a strong advocate of Home Rule for Ireland. Fair, sane, liberty-loving, his spirit in politics has been preserved in the word Gladstonian.

eventually there comes to every country a liberating Gladstone

---

GLASSE, MRS.

Mrs. Glasse is the name of the real or fictitious author of a cookery-book, first edited in 1747 and very famous in that day. She is popularly thought to have begun a recipe for cooking hare with this humorous but dispensable bit of advice, "First catch your hare."

directions as superfluous as those of Mrs. Glasse

GLAUCUS

Glaucus (1) was a god of the sea, a prophet, and patron of fishermen and sailors. Originally a Boeotian fisherman, he became immortal through eating a marvelous herb.

Glaucus (2) was a Greek legendary figure also from Boeotia. The owner of large herds of horses, he was torn to pieces by his mares for having despised the power of Aphrodite in refusing to allow them to breed.

Glaucus (3), the grandson of Bellerophon, was a gallant soldier and the leader of the Trojans' Lycian allies at Troy. When he encountered Diomedes in combat, he abstained from battle because the two were bound by ties of ancient hospitality. Simple and credulous, he exchanged his own golden armor (worth 100 oxen) for Diomedes' inferior bronze panoply (worth a mere 9 oxen). This kind of one-sided bargain has ever since been known by the phrase *Glaucus's swop.*

Glaucus (4) was a son of Minos of Crete. While a mere lad, he was suffocated and drowned by falling into a vat of honey. When the seer Polyidus was at first unable to restore him to life, he was buried alive with the boy. In the tomb a wise serpent, one of the symbols of immortality, showed the seer a magic herb with which he could restore Glaucus to life again. Whereupon the two of them were released from their tomb.

a barter as ill-considered as Glaucus's

GLORIANA

Gloriana, in Spenser's *Faerie Queene,* is the excellent and glorious queen of fairy land. Representing the sovereign Queen Elizabeth, she kept an annual feast for twelve days, during which adventurers appeared before her to undertake whatever task she chose to impose upon them. On one occasion, twelve valiant knights presented themselves before her, and their exploits form the plan of Spenser's allegory.

a resplendent Gloriana

GLOVER, CATHERINE

Catherine Glover, the heroine of Scott's *Fair Maid of Perth,* was "universally acknowledged to be the most beautiful young woman of the city or its vicinity." The daughter of Simon the glover, she becomes the bride of Henry Smith, an armorer.

lovely as Katie Glover

GNATHO

Gnatho ("puff-cheek") is the name of the vain and boastful parasite in Terence's comedy *The Eunuch.* The name was used proverbially in the Roman and the later Greek comedy to designate a toadying parasite and a sycophant, ready with words of flattery and praise for anyone offering a free dinner.

a Gnatho searching for a meal-ticket

GOBBO

Gobbo was the impudent, sharp, mischievous young servant to Shylock in Shakespeare's *Merchant of Venice.* Hence, he is the impertinent, clownish, saucy young hanger-on in any employ, always ready to leave one master without notice for a better stipend and more freedom.

a rascally Gobbo

GOBSECK

Gobseck is the avaricious moneylender and usurer in Balzac's novel of the same name. He is a type of miser.

a penny-pinching Gobseck

GODEY

Godey will recall *Godey's Magazine,* the first magazine of feminine fashions and of etiquette in America, edited by Antoine Godey, and noted for its artistic and finely executed colored prints of beautifully dressed women. The prints are now collector's items.

with the genuine Godey look so much affected today

GODIVA

Godiva was a beautiful, virtuous, and compassionate lady, wife of Leofric, who assured her, when she besought him to relieve Coventry of a burdensome tax, that he was as willing to lift the tax as she would be to ride naked through the streets of the town. She held him to his promise, and rode through the streets, clothed only in her long hair, but only after the people had been directed to stay indoors and not to look out. Only one person, thereafter called Peeping Tom, looked out. The tax was lifted, Godiva won the undying love and respect of her people, and the story has appeared and reappeared in song and story. Tennyson has a poem *The Lady Godiva.*

the purity of a Godiva

GODWINIAN

Godwinian is from William Godwin (1756-1836), a charming, enthusiatic person, daring in his theory of utter freedom from law, written and unwritten, personal or natural; of living every man to himself; of abandonment of all social convention; hence, radical, independent, liberal. He had a tremendous influence on many of the young Romantic poets, among them Wordsworth and Shelley in their extreme youth.

dangerous Godwinian theories

GOETHE

Johann Wolfgang von Goethe (1749-1832), versatile German genius, poet, prose-writer, dramatist, and art-critic, is best known for his lyrics that mark one of the high-water crests of German poetry and for major works like *Faust.* The inaugurator of the literary movement known as *Sturm und Drang,* the "storm and stress" impetuosity of thought and style, he had a universal mind that was able to embrace all domains of human activity. His many-sided and versatile talents scattered profound maxims of practical wisdom throughout all of his writings, and his ardent classicism represents for all time the epitomized spirit of his age.

with Goethean versatility of thought

GOG AND MAGOG

Gog and Magog are first mentioned in *Ezekiel* (38) as having been cursed repeatedly as evil rulers of an evil land. The two names were later combined in the name of a giant, Gogmagog, in Geoffrey of Monmouth's tales, and they are commemorated, probably whimsically, by two wooden statues fourteen feet high, in Guildhall in London. Burned in the Great Fire, they were so dear to the London people that they were rebuilt in 1708, on the same site.

evil as Gog and Magog

GOGH, VINCENT VAN

Vincent van Gogh (1853-1890) was the famous Dutch painter associated with the post-impressionist school. Settling at Arles in France's Provence, he painted numerous pictures of peasants at labor and recreation, warmly colored landscapes, vibrant cypresses, and richly tinted still-lifes. His name is widely associated with his urgent yellows, and he considered that shade to be the color of madness. He committed suicide while insane, and is the subject of Irving Stone's fine novel, *Lust for Life.*

has Van Gogh's fondness for yellow

GOLCONDA

Golconda, a city in India where diamonds were found and cut, a center of the diamond trade, has now come to mean either any mine of wealth, or simply great wealth.

a princess out of Golconda

GOLDSMITHIAN

Goldsmithian is from Oliver Goldsmith (1728-1774), facile humorist, novelist, and dramatist. Gay, irresponsible, witty, generous, and tenderhearted, he stumbled upon good fortune when he began writing of his native village and the people he knew best, incidentally poking fun at the manners, society, and ambitions of his time. Although he lived literally from hand to mouth most of the time, he was known to and beloved by the greatest men of London, and was a member of the famous Literary Club.

the gentle nature of a Goldsmith

as bad as Goldsmith, giving away his last shilling

Oh for another Goldsmith, natural, vivid, versatile

GOLGOTHA

Golgotha is the Aramaic name for Calvary, the place of the crucifixion and the passion of Jesus Christ. Hence, it suggests blood, intense agony, and anguish of spirit.

except they meant to memorize another Golgotha

it will lead to a new Golgotha

GOLIATH

Goliath was the violent champion of the Philistines, of huge size. For many days he came forth, more boastfully each time, to challenge the Children of Israel to send out a champion to meet him. He met no response until David, a shepherd boy, son of Jesse, advanced, armed only with his shepherd's sling, but declaring himself armed "with the strength of the Lord God," and approaching "in the name of the Lord God of Hosts," killed Goliath with the first stone out of his sling.

he is a very Goliath in threats, but there will come a David

GOMORRAH

Gomorrah was a city on the north side of the Dead Sea. Along with Sodom, the other of the infamous "cities of the plain," it was destroyed by God with fire for its carnal wickedness. The name is now used generically for any extremely sinful and sensual place.

Gomorrahean sensuality and corruption

GONERIL

Goneril is the eldest of Lear's three daughters (v. *Regan, Cordelia*) in Shakespeare's *King Lear.* Masculine and unnatural, she is a type of filial ingratitude.

harsh as Goneril to her father

GONZALO

Gonzalo, in Shakespeare's *Tempest,* is an honest old counselor, the friend and adviser of Prospero.

advice as sound as Gonzalo's

GOODFELLOW, ROBIN

Robin Goodfellow is another name for Puck, a spirit full of mischief and tricks, playing pranks especially in a household and on household servants. He is airy and whimsical, but primarily mischievous.

the Robin Goodfellow of the house, laughing and beloved

GOODY TWO-SHOES

Goody Two-Shoes is the name of a well-known character in nursery literature. Her *History* was published by Newberry in 1765, and it is thought to have been written by Goldsmith, who had a turn for this type of mock-history, sly and playful. It recounts how Goody, owning only one shoe, became extravagantly ecstatic on the acquisition of two and told her blessings to every one she met. The means by which she gained learning and wisdom of a smugly pious sort and, as a result of that, her fortune, are related with delicate satire.

counting her blessings like Goody Two-Shoes

GOOSE GIBBIE

Goose Gibbie, in Scott's *Old Mortality*, is a half-witted lad in the service of Lady Bellenden. He first "kept the turkeys, and was afterwards advanced to the more important office of minding the cows."

a simple-minded Goose Gibbie

GORBODUC

Gordobuc was a mythical king of Britain who divided his realm between his sons Ferrex and Porrex. The latter slew the former, his elder brother, and was in turn killed by his mother. Both parents were then slain in an uprising of the people, whom the nobles then massacred. This bloody saga of greed and sordid discontent was made the subject of an early English tragedy in blank verse by Norton and Sackville (1561).

an envy that could reannihilate the family of Gorboduc

GORDIUS

The Gordian knot is from Gordius, King of Phrygia, who tied a knot he said could be untied only by one who would rule Asia. Alexander the Great settled that by cutting the knot with his sword, and, incidently, ruled Asia. The phrase is often used of a situation so complicated as to seem impossible to resolve, one that can be settled only by drastic action.

boldly cuts the Gordian knots in any situation

GORGIAS

Gorgias (c.s. 485-375 B.C.) was the Sicilian sophist and teacher of rhetoric who was as remarkable for his longevity as for his oratory, which stressed beauty of sound and expression rather than content. His poetic prose rhythms and ornamentation made him tremendously popular with the Athenians, and he lectured extensively throughout Greece. Plato's dialogue on the subject of eloquence is named after him.

prose as ornamental as that of Gorgias

GORGIBUS

Gorgibus is the honest, simple-minded burgess in Molière's comedy *Les Précieuses Ridicules*. He is distressed, perplexed, and resentful of the perverse affectation of elegance of his daughter and his niece, whose fastidious preciosity centers on an excessive love of finery and of gingerbread gentility.

perplexed as Gorgibus by ostentation

GORGONS

The Gorgons were the legendary three sisters, with snakes instead of hair, all so terrible in aspect that any beholder was turned into stone. Medusa is the sister most often mentioned by name. The name signifies "queen" of anything that is so ugly that no human can survive looking at it. Her sisters were named Euryale ("wide wanderer") and Sthenno ("mighty").

Medusa with Gorgonian terrors guards the ford
stared like the Gorgon's head
Gorgonian effect

GORIOT PERE

Père Goriot is the title character of a novel (1834) by Honoré de Balzac. A modern Lear, he laboriously amasses great riches, making personal sacrifices for his two daughters and eventually signing over his entire fortune to them, only to be heartlessly deserted by them in his old age.

a parent as neglected as Père Goriot

GOSHEN

Goshen was the part of Egypt reserved by Joseph for the Israelites. Near the eastern side of the Delta, it was a land of plenty and abundance and contained the treasure cities of Rameses and Pittim. The name has come to be synonymous with any place of wealth and comfort.

seeking a spiritual Land of Goshen

GOTHA

Gotha is the name of a town in the German province of Thuringia. Since 1764 it has been famous in the title of an annual social register, the *Almanach de Gotha.* Published in French and German, it contains the genealogy of the principal royal and aristocratic families of Europe, and inclusion in it is a mark of social prestige and success.

as aristocratic as a page from Gotha

GOTHAMITE

Gothamite is from Gotham, the name given to the city of New York in Washington Irving's half-satirical and wholly amusing *Salamagundi Papers,* in which the inhabitants of the town were noted for their foolishness.

the million Gothamites shot in and out of subways endlessly

GOTHIC

Gothic suggests the architectural style that prevailed in Europe from the twelfth to the sixteenth centuries and was characterized by great height, pointed arches, rib vaulting, and the flying buttress. The name is used disparagingly in referring to the barbarous and rude qualities of the Middle Ages. In literature it describes the grotesque and horrible elements of the type of novel designated by its name. A detailed mixture of the sublime and the bizarre, it is the antithesis of classicism.

Gothic in its macabre gruesomeness

GOULD, JAY

Jay Gould (1836-1892), was an American financier and capitalist, a socialite, and one of America's Four Hundred. His name has become the synonym for wealth obtained through Yankee resourcefulness, smart deals, clever exploitation and manipulation furthered by eventual high social prominence. Willingness to work at the outset was a prime factor in his beginnings. A keen brain to see, and courage to seize opportunity explain his rapid rise to wealth.

the Gould or Midas touch

GOWK-THRAPPLE, MAISTER

Maister Gowk-thrapple is a covenanting preacher referred to as the "chosen vessel," in Scott's *Waverly.*

with the vehemence of some pulpit-drumming Gowk-thrapple

GRACCHI

Tiberius and Caius Sempronius Gracchus, the sons of Cornelia, daughter of Scipio Africanus, though of aristocratic birth, were tribunes of the Roman People and political reformers who tried to solve the economic crisis caused in their time by the failure of the conservative and aristocratic Roman Senate to administer its growing lands on a fair and sound principle. They both met with violent deaths, Tiberius by murder (133 B.C.), Caius by suicide after defeat (121 B.C.), because their liberalism was opposed by the reactionary Senate, which felt — as in recent times critics accused Franklin D. Roosevelt on the same grounds — that they had "betrayed their own class."

liberals and reformers like the Gracchi

a Gracchan determination for reform

GRACES

The Graces, three sisters, bosom friends of the Muses, are usually shown with their arms around each other to indicate that where one Grace is found, the others are sure to be. The sister-goddesses, daughters of Jupiter and Eurynome, were represented as beautiful and modest virgin-attendants of Venus. They were the source of all favor, loveliness, and grace, and their names were Aglaia, Euphrosyne, and Thalia.

assiduously courting the Graces

GRACIOSA

Graciosa is the lovely princess in an old and popular fairy-tale. She is the object of the implacable ill-will and malice of a step-mother named Grognon, whose evil designs are always thwarted by Percinet, a fairy prince, who is in love with Graciosa.

rescued like Graciosa

GRADASSO

Gradasso, in the epics of Boiardo and Ariosto, is the king of Sericana who is renowned for his deeds of martial prowess. Instigated by a desire to win the sword and courser of Rinaldo, he invades France, followed by all his vassals, "crowned kings," who must always salaam before him when they address him. The name was popularly employed by Italians to designate a bully.

like Gradasso, requires obeisance to be done before him

GRADGRIND

Gradgrind, a dried-up and utterly matter-of-fact and practical person in Dickens' *Hard Times,* is so material in all his evaluations that he ruthlessly disregards all intangible and spiritual values, smothers all natural and spontaneous emotion, and represses all imagination in his children. He is led to recognize the existence of feeling, and to attain a more nearly human state of mind, only when his favorite son falls into disgrace.

shows a surprising spontaneity; both parents are veritable Gradgrinds
ought to be rescued from the Gradgrind atmosphere

GRAIAE

The Graiae were goddesses of Greek mythology who were represented as gray-haired women, personifications of old age. Their names were Pemphredo ("Horrifier"), Enyo ("Shaker"), and Deino ("Terrifier"), and they had only one tooth between them and one eye which they passed back and forth. They protected their sisters, the Gorgons, and guarded their home. Perseus stole their eye and refused to return it to them until they conducted him to the Nymphs. The latter gave him the winged sandals and the helmet that made him invisible, thus enabling him to surprise the Gorgons and slay Medusa without interference from the Graiae.

old ladies as toothless as the Graiae

GRAM

Gram, in Teutonic mythology, is the name of the sword of Siegfried, noted for its trenchant sharpness.

a blade as keen as Gram

GRANDET, PERE

Père Grandet, a type of avarice and miserliness, is the father of the Eugénie of Balzac's *Eugénie Grandet,* whom he cold-bloodedly sacrifices to his greed.

a heartless Père Grandet

GRANDISONIANISM

Grandisonianism refers to qualities resembling those of Sir Charles Grandison, title-character of Richardson's novel and the ideal representative of masculine character and sentiment, as

Clarissa Harlowe (*q. v.*) is that author's embodiment of the ideal female. A felicitous union of the good Christian and the perfect English gentleman, he was dubbed by Sir Walter Scott as "the faultless monster that the world ne'er saw." The prototype of the character is said to have been Robert Nelson, reputed author of *The Whole Duty of Man.*

a paragon of Grandisonianism

GRANGOUSIER

Grangousier, the father of Rabelais' *Gargantua,* is the name for one with so enormous a gullet that it will swallow anything regardless of the size. The King of Utopia, he married, in "the vigor of his old age," Gargamelle, daughter of the king of the Parpaillons, who bore him the giant. He is described as a man in his dotage, whose favorite pastime was to draw scratches on the hearth with a burnt stick while watching the broiling of his chestnuts.

omnivorous as Grangousier

GRANI

Grani, in Teutonic mythology, was the marvelous horse of Siegfried, and its swiftness was said to exceed that of the winds. In Wagner's *Goetterdaemmerung,* it is the steed of Brunhilde (*q. v.*).

faster than Grani

GRANT, ULYSSES

Ulysses Grant (1822-1885) was appointed U. S. General of the Union Armies and led the Union to victory. When an official objected to the appointment on the ground that Grant drank, Lincoln replied, "Tell me the name of the brand he uses. I'll order some for the rest." Grant was direct, forceful, effective, successful.

with the blunt decisions of a Grant

GRATIANO

Gratiano, in Shakespeare's *Merchant of Venice,* is the loquacious friend of Antonio and Bassanio, and he "talks an infinite deal of nothing, more than any man in all Venice." When Bassanio marries Portia, Gratiano marries Nerissa, her maid.

Another Gratiano is a stock character in Italian *commedia dell' arte.* Represented as a Bolognese doctor, he wore a mask with a black nose and forehead and red cheeks. His character is that of a pedantic bore and a tedious proser.

outdoing Gratiano in garrulity

GRAUSTARK

Graustark is the name of a mythical principality in central Europe that was popularized in George Barr McCutcheon's novel of the same name. Set in an imbroglio of political and amorous intrigues, plottings and counterplottings, the story told of the love of Yetive, the Princess Royal of Graustark, for an American, Grenfall Lorry, and of her willingness to renounce her throne for that love. However, with high sentimentality it concluded with a special dispensation of happiness when her ministry legalized the union and enabled her issue to succeed to the throne. So popular was this whimsical bit of escapism to Americans of the early decades of the century that it resulted in a sequel, *The Prince of Graustark.*

with Graustarkian intrigue and scheming

GRAY, AULD ROBIN

Auld Robin Gray is the elderly husband in an old Scotch ballad by Lady Ann Barnard, in which the girl sings of the kindness of Robin Gray and his generosity that provides for her old father and mother, but reveals and declares her unwavering love for her sweetheart Jamie who has gone to sea and will have come back too late. Jeanie's appreciation of her husband's kindness is apparent throughout the ballad, as is her own spirit of unselfishness, sacrifice, renunciation, and longing.

admittedly an Auld Robin Gray situation

GRAY, DORIAN

Dorian Gray, the title-character of Oscar Wilde's celebrated novel, is a brilliantly perverse product of late Victorianism. Sinister and handsome, he indulges rampantly in monstrous excesses of depravity, vice, and sin, and becomes the more radiantly beautiful as his actions befoul his character the more shamefully. Age and the growing marks of degeneracy appear not on his physical mien but on a painting of him, executed by an artist friend when the subject was a pure young man, until he is compelled to relegate the likeness to a bolted attic, where, in a transport of remorse for having finally slain the artist, he lunges at the remindful portrait, stained with all the horrors of his actual life, rends it with a knife, and dies with the picture's blemishes transferred to his own person at last.

as unmarked by his immorality as Dorian Gray

GRAY, THOMAS

Thomas Gray (1716-1771), English elegiac poet best known for his "Elegy in a Country Churchyard," also wrote odes that marked an epoch in the history of British poetry. An admirer of ballads, he revived the poetic diction of the past and was that rare combination of a Romanticist and a satirical humorist as well. With a protean variety he wrote as a speculative philosopher, a critic of art and music, a meteorologist, and a nature-lover, though he is remembered chiefly for the few poems in his rather tenuous output that reveal his characteristic sadness.

with the Thomas Gray flair for gloom

GREATHEART

Greatheart is the kindly man marked by the qualities suggested in his name, who guided Christiana and her children to the Celestial City in Bunyan's *Pilgrim's Progress.*

the Greatheart of the community

GREAVES, SIR LAUNCELOT

Sir Launcelot Greaves is the hero of Smollett's novel bearing his name. A sort of travesty of Don Quixote, a wellborn, handsome and virtuous English squire, though crack-brained, he wandered over England in the reign of George II, redressing wrongs, discouraging moral evils not recognizable by law, degrading immodesty, punishing ingratitude, and reforming society. An old sea captain was the Sancho Panza of his adventures.

a busybody like Sir Launcelot Greaves

GRECO, EL

El Greco (1548-1614), born Dominico Theotocopuli on the island of Crete, was given his more popular name because of his long residence in Spain, though he continued to sign his more important pictures with his Greek initials. His paintings are characterized by increasing eccentricity and mounting individuality with the passage of the years, as seen in his perverse love of strange chilly coloring and the startlingly livid effects of his ashen tones. Even the gauntness of his figures has a spectral and visionary quality. The initiator of truth and realism in art and the immortalizer of the spirit of the Spanish people in such paintings as "The Burial of the Count Orgaz," he is also associated with great religious subjects, such as "The Disrobing of Christ."

gaunt and grisly as an El Greco

GREEKS BEARING GIFTS

Greeks bearing gifts is a phrase originating from the warning "Beware the Greeks bearing gifts," born of the occasion when the Greeks, apparently departing from Troy, presented to their evident conquerors, the Trojans, a great wooden statue of a horse, so large that a portion of the city wall had to be leveled to get the statue in. At night, when all the city was asleep, hundreds of Greek warriors came out of the statue to open the gates of the city to the Greeks who sacked and burned Troy. In modern terms, the phrase means beware of an enemy or a self-seeking person suddenly turned friendly or generous.

may be genuine, but smacks of the Greeks bearing gifts
too suddenly flattering; beware the Greek bearing gifts

GREELY, HORACE

Horace Greely (1811-1872) was the daring, intrepid, and invincible founder and editor of the *New York Tribune*. Also a famous anti-slavery agitator, and advocate of the "emancipation of labor," he was a close friend of Abraham Lincoln. His name is synonymous with courage, fearlessness, and boldness amounting to defiance in any stand one takes. He also represents the best traditions of newspaper editing, genial companionship, and brilliant repartee. In urging opportunism he said, "Go West, young man."

true Greely invective and art
the Greely flavor

GREEN, GEORGE A'

George a' Green is the hero of the old English prose romance dating from the time of Queen Elizabeth, *The History of George a' Green*. By occupation a pinner or penner (i.e., keeper of the public pen or pound for the housing of strays), he resisted Robin Hood, Will Scarlett, and Little John single-handed when they attempted to commit a trespass in his town of Wakefield. The name is used for anyone who is resolute-minded, or one who will do his duty come what may.

the determined resistance of George a' Green

GRETNA GREEN

A Gretna Green couple indicates a pair married at Gretna Green, Scotland, without benefit of clergy, i.e., simply by announcing before witnesses their intention to marry without license, or fee, or ceremony. It was tantamount to an elopement to have married at Gretna Green, and many of the marriages so announced were so short-lived that a law was finally passed forbidding such marriages.

evidently a Gretna Green romance

GRIDE, ARTHUR

Arthur Gride, an old usurer in Dickens' *Nicholas Nickleby,* has an air and attitude of "stealthy, cat-like obsequiousness" and an expression that is "concentrated in a wrinkled leer, compounded of cunning, lecherousness, slyness, and avarice." Expressive of his covetous and griping penury is the fact that there is not one spare fold or plait in his costume, the trousers of which are so scantily cut as to display his shrunken spindle-shanks in their full ugliness.

as penny-pinching as Arthur Gride

GRIEG, EDVARD

Edvard Grieg (1843-1907), a Norwegian composer, wrote music that grew out of the folk songs of Norway and reflected the rugged spirit of the forests, streams, and mountains of Norway. There is a certain vitality and originality in Grieg's music that is unmistakable once it has been perceived. It is vigorous and hauntingly personalized.

nationalistic as Grieg's music

GRIMM BROTHERS

The Grimms were authors of fairy tales known to all the world from their translation from German into every other language. The name Grimm has come to be synonymous with any altogether absorbing, fabulous, and fanciful tale.

fantastic and absorbing as Grimm

GRIMWIG

Grimwig is the name of a choleric old gentleman in Dickens' *Oliver Twist*. He is fond of contradictions and generally ends each one with the words "or I'll eat my head." Kindly but opinionated, he is the friend of Brownlow, the benevolent elderly gentleman who befriends the hero of the novel.

a cantankerous and opinionated Grimwig

GRISELDA

Griselda, the emblem of the patient wife, is tried by her husband in cruel ways. Two of her children are taken away, where she does not know, but she supposes them killed. In reality they are carefully reared elsewhere. Finally her husband sends her away, and brings her back only when her children have grown, she to welcome them, he to praise her for the patience she has shown through all her adversity. Her story is told by Boccaccio, Petrarch, and Chaucer.

the fortitude of a Griselda

GROLIERESQUE

Grolieresque refers to the ornamental book-binding designed by Jean Grolier de Servières (1479-1565), treasurer-general of France and bibliophile famous for his love of books that were distinctive in subject, paper, printing, and binding. Many of his decorations were devised by himself, as the Grolier scroll, which is characterized by arabesque figures and leaf-scrolls executed in gold lines.

a rare edition with a Grolieresque binaing

GROTIUS, HUGO

Hugo Grotius (1583-1645), famous Dutch theologian, historian, and jurist, laid the corner-stone for the developed study of international law with his celebrated *De Iure Belli et Pacis,* "the rights of war and peace." In it he presented the theory of natural rights, emphasizing the distinction between inviolable essential justice and ever-changing civil law.

a Grotian flair for distinction

GRUB-STREETER

A Grub-Streeter is any poor poet, poor in pocket and poor in output, compelled by his poverty to live in cramped quarters, named for Grub Street in London where most of the struggling writers lived.

memories of Grub Street dogged his mind

GRUNDY, MRS.

Mrs. Grundy is known from the question, "What will Mrs. Grundy say?" It was constantly asked in Morton's *Speed the Plough*. Hence, Mrs. Grundy means society at large, a kind of personified social arbiter, narrow regularity, and supercritical judgment.

fear of Mrs. Grundy alone keeps social conventions alive

Mrs. Grundy—the fetish of society

GRYPS

Gryps was the mythological pictorialization of the fabulous griffin, a composite creature with the body of a lion and the head and wings of an eagle. An emblem of vigilance, it lived between the Hyperboreans of the far north and the one-eyed Arimaspians, from the latter of whom it guarded a treasure of gold. Because these Arimaspians, mounted on horseback, attempted to steal the precious hoard, Gryps became the unrelenting enemy of horses.

fanciful as Gryps

GUDRUN

Gudrun, the heroine of a famous North-Saxon poem dating from the thirteenth century, is the daughter of Attila and is betrothed to Herwig, king of Heligoland. But a rejected suitor, Hartmuth, king of Norway, carries her off and subjects her to all sorts of menial work because she refuses to marry him. One day her brother and her lover appear on the scene, and she is rescued to marry Herwig and to pardon Hartmuth. She is a perfect model of angelic mercy, heroic fortitude, and pious resignation.

like Gudrun, she pardons those who injure her

GUINEVERE

Guinevere was King Arthur's queen, whose guilty love for Lancelot, chief of the Knights of the Round Table, introduced disloyalty into the ideal kingdom King Arthur sought to establish. Finally it brought her own downfall, along with that of Arthur, Lancelot, and the whole Round Table. Her beauty and grace, her love, and her tragic remorse, have been made the subject of many stories, chief among them Tennyson's *Guinevere,* in *The Idylls of the King.*

the tragic remorse of a Guinevere
with the fatal loveliness of young Guinevere

GULA

Gula was the Assyro-Babylonian deity presiding over life and death as the goddess of healing. She was the consort of Ninurta, a solar deity and the god of war, the chase, and agriculture.

cured by Gula

GULLIVER

Gulliver is a character invented by Swift, in his *Gulliver's Travels,* to go on a journey to four imaginary lands, each to satirize some one aspect of life as Swift saw it, and to represent with bitterness and cynicism the follies and wrongs of the existing political and social system. Oddly enough, Swift managed to write the satire in such a way that it is the perfect fairy-story book for children, who see nothing of the bitter diatribe he meant it to be. The name has come to mean fantastic, romantic, absurd, incredible, and satirical.

as huge a liar as Gulliver
magnificent Gulliver fabrication

GUMMIDGE, MRS.

Mrs. Gummidge is the forlorn housekeeper for Mr. Peggoty in Dickens' *David Copperfield.* Her reply to any one who tried to comfort her plaints by assuring her that the rain, the cold, sickness, death, and other universal troubles were common to every one, was always, "I know, I know, but I feel it worse." Hence, the name means doleful, lugubrious, mournful, and also suggests pleasure in discomfort.

a Mrs. Gummidge-enjoyment of ill-health
lost as Mrs. Gummidge in favorable situations

GUNGNIR

Gungnir, in Scandinavian mythology, is the unerring spear of Odin (*q.v.*). Never failing to hit its target, it also represents the stinging and mordant nature of the god's satire. Oaths were sworn by this symbol of his strength.

marksmanship as accurate as Gungnir's

GUNTHER

Gunther, in the *Nibelungenlied,* is the King of Burgundy and the brother of Kriemhilde (*q.v.*). Determined to wed Brunhilde, the martial queen of Issland, he had to surpass her in three trials of strength and skill. The first was hurling a spear that could hardly be lifted by three men, the second was throwing a stone that took twelve brawny champions to carry, and the third was jumping. Worsted by Gunther who was assisted by his friend Siegfried wearing his invisible cloak, she behaved so obstreperously after the marriage that Gunther had to avail himself of his friend's help again. Siegfried entered the chamber in his cloud-cloak and wrestled with the bride till all her strength was gone, drawing a ring from her finger and depriving her of her girdle, after which she became a submissive wife. But Gunther, with unpardonable ungratefulness, was privy to the murder of Siegfried, and was himself slain by Kriemhilde.

thankless as Gunther

GUPPY

Guppy is a vulgar young law clerk in Dickens' *Bleak House.* He is so importunate and self-important that the name now means any smart young employee who makes a nuisance of himself.

a new young Guppy started work today

GURTH

Gurth, in Scott's *Ivanhoe,* is the surly and uncouth Saxon swineherd, the thrall and bondsman of Cedric, and the brave and clever squire of Ivanhoe.

a rude and harsh Gurth

GURTON, GAMMER

Gammer Gurton is the heroine of an old English comedy concerning the loss of a needle—a serious event in a remote village of that time. The straying implement is eventually found sticking in the breeches of Hodge, the owner's husband!

as sharp as Gammer Gurton's needle

GUY OF WARWICK

Guy of Warwick is the hero of a famous English legend which celebrates his surpassing prowess and feats of strength that were accomplished in order to give him the fair Felice as his bride, since she had refused to listen to his suit until he would first distinguish himself by knightly deeds. After slaying Saracens, giants, boars, and dragons, he became a hermit in Warwick, living in a cave he hewed himself. Daily he went to his own castle unrecognized and lived on his wife's alms by begging her bread. On his deathbed he sent her a ring, by which she recognized her lord and went to close his dying eyes. The romance is mentioned by Chaucer in the *Canterbury Tales.*

mighty as Guy of Warwick

GUYON, SIR

Sir Guyon is a knight in Spenser's *Faerie Queene.* He destroys the witch, Acrasia, and her residence, the Bower of Bliss, and represents the quality of temperance and self-control. He holds in check not only all inferior sensual appetites but also the impulses of passion and the impulse for revenge. His very name is derived from the Spanish *guiar,* meaning to "guide," and Prudence is his companion.

as temperate as Sir Guyon

GWYN, NELL

Nell Gwyn (1650-1687), the "child of the London streets," started life as an orange-seller in the neighborhood of the Drury Lane Theater, to the stage of which she progressed as the most celebrated comedy actress of her day. Pepys adored the playing of "pretty, witty Nell," and Dryden wrote many plays especially to suit her airy, wanton personality and her flair for the delivery of risqué lines. Piquante and with beautiful reddish-brown hair as her best beauty feature, she was reckless, generous, indiscreet, witty, and high-spirited, though she was so illiterate that it was all she could do to scrawl her initials at the end of letters that others had written for her. The faithful and adored mistress of Charles II until his death, she bore him two sons.

vivacious and indiscreet as Nell Gwyn

GYAS

Gyas, in Vergil's *Aeneid,* is a companion of Aeneas, noted for his bravery. At the naval games exhibited by Aeneas in honor of his father Anchises on the first anniversary of the latter's death, Gyas commanded the ship "Chimaera," of which Menoetes (*q.v.*) was the timid pilot.

a trusted companion like Gyas

GYES

Gyes, or Gyas, was one of the hundred-handed giants, represented generally as friendly to the gods and not at variance with them as most of the other giants of Greek mythology. He and his brothers Briareus and Cottus were sons of Uranus (Heaven) and Ge (Earth), and they were slain by Hercules.

as supple as hundred-handed Gyes

GYGES

Gyges was a Lydian shepherd who became king of his country by killing Candaules (*q. v.*), his predecessor (c. 685 B.C.). According to Plato, he had found a hollow bronze horse in a cave in the earth. Opened, it was found to contain a corpse with a golden ring on one finger. Gyges took the ring and found that it had the magical ability of making its wearer invisible. When Candaules' wife was forced by the king to expose her naked beauty before Gyges, she became so enraged that she gave the latter the choice of murdering the king or of being put to death himself. With the aid of his magic ring he followed her instructions, succeeded to the throne and married her. He sent such sumptuous presents to Delphi that the phrase "the riches of Gyges" became a proverb.

as wealthy as Gyges

GYMNOPAEDIA

The Gymnopaedia was a Spartan festival held in July to honor the tutelary deity of Laconia, Artemis Orthia. Young men danced naked, sang hymns, and exhibited their gymnastic prowess. The principal feature of the holiday was, however, the dread *diamastigosis,* or "public flogging," at which the nude youths were lashed sadistically, much to the delight of the spectators who came from far and wide to witness the famed Spartan ability to endure pain without an outcry.

athletes as hardy as those at the Gymnopaedia

GYMNOSOPHIST

The Gymnosophists, or "naked philosophers," were Hindu ascetics and mystics so-called by the Greeks because of their belief that food and clothing interfered with the purity of their thought. Consequently, they often lived as hermits in forests, whence the Greeks called them specifically *Hylobioe,* or "wood-dwellers."

a nudist colony full of Gymnosophists

H

HABAKKUK

Habakkuk, one of the minor Hebrew prophets and poets, wrote about the menace which Chaldean power presented to the existence of Israel. After describing the greed and violence of these people, he denounced them for their evil gains, their iniquity, and "for giving their neighbor drink." Condemning them for the vanity of their idolatry, he concluded with a hymn to Jehovah for the deliverance of his people.

like Habakkuk, aware of the might of his neighbor

HADES

Hades, one name for the god of the lower world, is more often used for the lower world itself. In the Bible, it names the abode of the dead, also, generally, the abode of condemned spirits.

incarcerated in hopeless Hades

HADRIAN

Hadrian succeeded to the throne of Rome (117-138 A. D.) through his friendship with Plotina, the wife of his predecessor, Trajan. An extremely cultured man, he lived for some time in Athens as benefactor of that classic city. He spent much time traveling throughout the Empire's provinces, which enjoyed great prosperity and peace during his lifetime. A patron of the arts, he erected many magnificent monuments throughout the Empire and crammed his beautiful villa at Tivoli with masterpieces of Greek sculpture and art.

buildings of Hadrianic majesty
a Hadrianic devotion to art

HAEMON

Haemon was the son of Creon, the tyrant of Thebes, and the fiancé of Antigone. Passionately devoted to his betrothed, he killed himself by her side when she was condemned by his father to be entombed alive for having violated his edict in burying her brother Polynices.

a devoted Haemon, a suicide by his love's side

HAGAR

Hagar was the concubine-wife of Abraham, who with her son Ishmael was, at the behest of Sarah, Abraham's wife, sent forth into the desert, where a well of water was made, by divine Providence, to spring up for their refreshment.

a pitiable Hagar, with no protecting Providence

HAGEN

Hagen, the murderer of the hero Siegfried in the *Nibelungen Lied*, was a pale-faced, one-eyed dwarf who knew everything. Always bent on malice and mischief, he was finally killed by Kriemhilde Siegfried's wife, who cut off his head with the hero's sword.

an ugly and baleful Hagen

HAGGAI

Haggai was one of the minor Hebrew prophets, contemporary with the rule of Darius I (c. 520 B.C.). He addressed his four prophecies to Zerubbabel, the governor, and the people, rebuking them for their failure to complete the temple and attributing the severe drought of the time to their failure to do so. His exhortations goaded them to the task of finishing it.

a persuasive Haggai

HAGGARD, RIDER

Sir Henry Rider Haggard (1856-1925) was the popular British writer of fantastic and incredible novels of discovery. Most of his themes were drawn from the South African scene with which he was familiar from his years of government service in the Transvaal. *King Solomon's Mines* was suggested by the Zimbabwe ruins, and his archaeological bent was also reflected in the novel which he wrote in collaboration with Andrew Lang, *The World's Desire,* a romance of Helen of Troy. Equally romantic, imaginative, and exotic was his account of a mysterious, ageless and beautiful African queen whose power was absolute, *She* (*Who Must Be Obeyed*). Its sequel *Ayesha, or The Return of She; Allan Quartermaine,* and *The People of the Mist* were other bizarre novels that added to his fame.

an incredibly fanciful Haggard-like theme

HAIDEE

Haidee, the heroine of Byron's *Don Juan,* is a beautiful Greek maiden, the daughter of Lambro, a rich pirate. After rescuing Don Juan from shipwreck and resuscitating him, she fell in love with him. When Lambro had him arrested and deported from the island on which they lived, Haidee went insane and died after a lingering illness brought on by her broken heart.

heartbreak as fatal as Haidee's

HAKLUYT, RICHARD

Richard Hakluyt (1553-1616), geographer and navigator, and man of note in several countries, published an account of all the English explorations and discoveries in all parts of the globe, covering a period of 1500 years, an account widely read in the sixteenth century and the inspiration of many an adventurous romance. Coleridge's *Ancient Mariner* got its inception from the mention of an albatross in Hakluyt's book.

the albatross of Hakluyt fame
many a Hakluyt-inspired story lights the world

HALGAVER

Halgaver is an English moor in Cornwall that was famous for an annual carnival held there in the middle of July. The name is familiar, however, principally from the phrase "Summoned before the mayor of Halgaver." This mayor is actually an imaginary person before whom it is threatened to arraign those who have committed no offense against the laws, but who are simply guilty of being untidy and slovenly.

slatternly enough to bring before His Honor of Halgaver

HALIBURTON, RICHARD

Richard Haliburton, an adventurous young Princeton man, went gaily forth hither and yon all over Europe and in many countries in a series of journeys he recorded in the *Royal Roaa to Romance* and other fascinating and exciting stories. Suddenly there was no word of or from Richard Haliburton; he disappeared as completely as if the world had swallowed him, which is perhaps exactly what happened.

the Haliburton spirit

HAMADRYADS

(see *Dryads*)

HAMELIN

Hamelin is the North German town made familiar by Robert Browning's famous poem of *The Pied Piper.* In 1284 this legendary magician freed the town of a plague of rats by playing on his pipe. When the authorities defaulted on their promise and refused to pay him the covenanted recompense, he led away the children of the town, who followed the weird enchantment of his music over the fields and beyond the hills. They were never seen again.

like Hamelin, a town shorn of its youth

HAMILCAR

Hamilcar Barca ("lightning") was the famous Carthaginian general and statesman defeated by Rome in the first Punic War (264-241 B. C.). An overseas expansionist and imperialist, he established an economic sphere of influence in Spain for his country's commercial interests in compensation for the loss to Rome of the Carthaginian control and exploitation of Sicily and Sardinia. It was said that he pledged his son Hannibal to undying hatred of Rome and eternal vengeance, an oath that the son tried to accomplish in the second Punic War.

like Hamilcar, he placed his country's foreign policy in the hands of its commercial interests

---

HAMILTONIAN

Hamiltonian is from Alexander Hamilton (1757-1804), famous for exceptional sagacity and logic, and revered in America for his invaluable contribution to the Constitution. He was intimately associated with Washington as aide-de-camp, as personal secretary, as Secretary of the Treasury, and in many other relations. His policy of a strong central government, of establishing public credit through a national bank, and of foreign trade, all contributed to a philosophy he disseminated through a series of papers called the *Federalist.* Personal grace, eloquence, and affability added force to his political influence.

with Hamiltonian grace
the Hamiltonian policies

HAMLET

Hamlet, the chief character in Shakespeare's *Hamlet,* was the son of the king of Denmark, who had been secretly killed by Hamlet's uncle, who then married the queen. Hamlet, to whom the truth is revealed, resolves upon revenge, but while he is clever in his mental processes, more than ordinarily intelligent in his analysis, and courageous and subtle in his plotting, he finds himself incapable of carrying out his planned revenge. Melancholy over his disillusionments and his own futility, and painfully aware of his actual inability to put his purposes into effect, he becomes brooding and pathetically ineffective.

a brooding Hamlet, sure he is born to set things right
too much humility makes Hamlets of us all

HANCOCK, JOHN

John Hancock (1737-1793) was the famous American Revolutionary statesman who became the first signer of the Declaration of Independence. Hence, his name has become synonymous with an original and sensational signature of a distinguished or epochal character. A member of the Continental Congress and a president of that group, he also became the first governor of the State of Massachusetts.

a signature as breath-taking as John Hancock's

HANDEL AND HAYDN

The numerous Handel and Haydn Societies that have sprung up since the time of George Friedrich Handel (1685-1759) and Franz Joseph Haydn (1732-1809) have glorified the pure and nobly classical melodic lines of their music. Of all of Handel's more than 40 operas, 23 oratorios, and works for small chamber orchestras, none is perhaps better known than his magnificent setting of the sacred story in *The*

Messiah. "Papa" Haydn, the first great master of the symphony and the string quartet, is equally beloved for his "Surprise" and "Clock" symphonies, and his oratorios, *The Creation* and *The Seasons.* The charming graciousness of the music of both these masters recreates, when heard today, the mannerly era of minuets, powdered wigs, and courtly gentlemen in velvet knee breeches and black silk stockings.

as smoothly gracious as Handel and Haydn

HANDY ANDY

Handy Andy, the good-natured but blundering hero of Samuel Lover's novel of that name, furnishes a convenient nickname for any jack-of-all-trades, regardless of what the original story made of him; hence, versatile, useful, helpful, handy.

established a profitable Handy Andy service

HANNIBAL

Hannibal was the son of Hamilcar Barca of Carthage and was the implacable enemy of Rome. Just as his father had unleashed the First Punic War (264-241 B.C.), so Hannibal, in revenge for that defeat, planned and executed his intrepid crossing of the Alps in order to attack Rome in the Second Punic War (218-202 B.C.). After Scipio defeated him at Zama, the site of the last battle of the war, the Romans pursued him vindictively from refuge to refuge until to escape them he was forced to take poison in 182 B.C. He was hated by Romans everywhere for his craftiness, cruelty and perfidiousness.

Hannibalic craftiness

HANSWURST

Hanswurst is a pantomimic character introduced into old German comedies and marionette plays. A buffoon, clown, and fool, he is noted for his clumsiness, his gourmandizing appetite, and his Falstaffian dimensions.

fat as Hanswurst

HARDCASTLE, KATE

Kate Hardcastle is the daughter of Squire Hardcastle, a country gentleman of the old school, and is the lively heroine of Goldsmith's *She Stoops to Conquer.* In love with young Marlowe, the bashful and diffident hero, she finally prevails over his timidity in proposing to her by posing as a barmaid in her own home, which Marlowe mistakes for an inn.

a determined Kate Hardcastle

HARDOUIN, JEAN

Jean Hardouin (1646-1729) was the learned French Jesuit and librarian to Louis le Grand. His name occurs in the phrase "Even Hardouin would not object," spoken in endorsment of only the most self-evident and indisputable of truths. He was so intellectually fastidious that he questioned the accuracy of all recorded history and even denied the authenticity of Vergil's *Aeneid* and of Horace's *Odes.* A numismatist himself, he placed no trust in the genuineness of most coins or medals, and he regarded with suspicion all councils before that of Trent as chimerical inventions. The name now connotes an authoritarian whom it is impossible to convince of the truth or existence of anything, if he does not himself champion its claim.

as alerted for error as Hardouin

HARDY, THOMAS

Thomas Hardy (1840-1928) was the great English novelist and poet who, in a manner all his own and in a setting that characterizes all of his finest work, described the futilities and sardonic ironies of life as seen on the melancholy moors and somber heaths of "Wessex," scene of the action of novels like *The Return of the Native, Tess of the D'Urbevilles, The Mayor of Casterbridge,* and *Jude the Obscure.* A fatalist by philosophy, he studied the inexorable workings of destiny in what he saw as the chief disturbing power in life, women.

a setting as ominous and portentous as that of a Hardy novel

HARI, MATA

Mata Hari was the assumed name of a glamorous and alluring dancer on the French stage, who was arrested and executed in 1917 by the French on charges of espionage. Her sobriquet may be derived from the Malayan word for "sun," as her art was exotic and seductively eastern. In any case, her name still connotes scheming and dangerous subversive activites as a spy and the fatal and irresistible charm of a *femme voilée,* impenetrably mysterious.

plotting with all the aplomb of Mata Hari

HARLEQUIN

Harlequin is a fantastic buffoon in early Italian comedy, carrying a wooden sword and indulging in all sorts of extravagant clowning. He typifies drollery, fantasy, and buffoonery.

jumping about like a harlequin

HARLEY

Harley is *The Man of Feeling* in Mackenzie's novel of that name. He is characterized by fine sensibility, benevolence, and bashfulness that results from excessive delicacy. This work (1771) by a Scottish author is a rather disconnected series of sketches about a weak and sentimental hero.

another overly sensitive Harley

HARLOWE, CLARISSA

Clarissa Harlowe is the unhappy heroine of Richardson's novel of that name. In order to avoid a loveless marriage proposed by her parents, she succumbs to the blandishments of an unscrupulous roué named Captain Lovelace, who abuses her trust by seducing her in order to satisfy his dominant sensuality. Overwhelmed with proud grief and shame, she refuses his subsequent offer of marriage and retires from the world to die of a broken heart.

for each scheming villain there is a Clarissa Harlowe somewhere

---

HARMODIUS AND ARISTOGITON

Harmodius and Aristogiton were Athenian youths who were revered as tyrannicides and champions of liberty for their attempt at freeing the city from the misrule of Hippias and Hipparchus (514 B.C.). Hipparchus, frustrated in his attempts at entering upon a love affair with Harmodius, publicly insulted the latter's sister. In collusion with his friend Aristogiton, the young Harmodius plotted to slay the tyrants, but the plot failed partly, only Hipparchus being despatched. Harmodius was instantly slain by the despots' bodyguard, and Aristogiton was tortured and put to death. When the city was ultimately freed, statues of the heroes were erected, which were so admired by Xerxes that he carried them off to Persia. Copies still exist today.

champions of liberty like Harmodius and Aristogiton

HARMONIA'S NECKLACE

Harmonia's necklace was an unlucky possession that brought evil to all into whose hands it passed. When Harmonia, the daughter of Mars and Venus, was married to King Cadmus of Thebes, she received from her husband as a wedding gift this ancient equivalent of the Hope Diamond. The work of Hephaestus (Vulcan), the necklace later proved fatal to Eriphyle (see *Amphiaraus*), to Arsinoë, the first wife of the former's son, Alcmaeon, and to Callirrhoë, his second wife. It was then dedicated to Apollo at Delphi.

accursed as Harmonia's necklace

HAROLD, CHILDE

Childe Harold (*Childe* was originally a title of honor) is the hero of Byron's metrical romance of that name, a youth disillusioned with life, wandering over the world. Expressing his personal and usually embittered reaction to all that he sees, he is especially responsive to whatever is restless, tempestuous, and uncontrollable in nature. Byron's poem is made a vehicle for his own feelings, enthusiasms, bitterness, despair, and anger. The poem, nevertheless, is marked by outbursts of brilliant description of oceans, mountains, and places of unsurpassed beauty.

always striking a tragic Childe-Harold attitude

HAROUN AL RASCHID

Haroun al Raschid was a caliph of Bagdad concerning whom so many fabulous and fantastic tales have been woven that any person going too far in incredible and romantic imaginings is said to be Haroun-al-Raschiding.

no more Haroun-al-Raschiding for him

HARPAGON

Harpagon, the hero of Molière's comedy *L' Avare,* is represented as a wretched miser whose greed has reached that point where it is without pride and whose dread of losing his wealth has subdued his desire of being thought to possess it. The name is a synonym for covert, apprehensive miserliness.

gloating, like Harpagon, over his bank account

HARPIES

The Harpies were horrible creatures of mythology, having a woman's head and body, but bird-claws, -feet and -wings. They were rapacious, destructive, seizing upon the souls of the dead, and executing filthy vengeance. Malign creatures, they were predatory, grasping, ravenous people, clawing either another's possessions or reputation to pieces with joy.

the Harpies, gloatingly destructive

HARPOCRATES

Harpocrates was the Greek name of the Egyptian deity Horus, the god of the sun. Represented as an infant with his finger laid over his mouth, he was mistakenly assumed to be the god of silence as well.

as silent as Harpocrates

HARRIS, MRS.

Mrs. Harris is an imaginary character in Dickens' *Martin Chuzzlewit.* Though she never appears in person in the pages of the novel, Mrs. Sarah Gamp (*q. v.*) constantly refers to her as the authority behind her own fabrications and fancies and the originator of any bits of self-praise in which she chooses to indulge.

more quoted and more mythical than Mrs. Harris

HARTE, BRET

Bret Harte (1839-1902) was the early American master of the short story, familiar for such popular works as *The Luck of Roaring Camp* and *The Outcasts of Poker Flat.* Combining humor, pathos, and powerful character portrayal, he set his locales in a terrain of mining gulches and Western gambling houses. In his pioneer pictures he is a sort of latter-day James Fenimore Cooper.

picturesque as a Bret Harte mining town

HARUM, DAVID

David Harum, the shrewd and tender-hearted banker, the good neighbor and standby, and on occasion the smart horse-trader in Westcott's novel *David Harum,* sees all, knows all, and says little. But when he does speak it is with the wise common sense and humorous philosophy of the traditional shrewd thinker of New England.

with a David-Harum penetration and shrewdness

HATCHWAY, LIEUTENANT

Lieutenant Jack Hatchway, in Smollett's *Adventures of Peregrine Pickle,* is a retired naval officer living on pension of half-pay. He is the boon companion and attendant of Commodore Trunnion (*q. v.*).

nautical as Lieutenant Hatchway

HATHOR

Hathor was the Egyptian goddess of love and its pleasures and joys. In art she was often represented as having the head, horns, or ears of a cow. An Hathoric capital is the crown of an architectural column, which is carved so as to represent the head and face of this deity.

wallowing in Hathoric delights

HATTERAICK, DIRK

Dirk Hatteraick, in Scott's *Guy Mannering,* is a Dutch smuggler and a thorough and desperate villain whose character is redeemed from utter depravity only by his one virtue of integrity to his employers. "I was always faithful to my ship-owners, always accounted for cargo to the last stiver," he says. He is imprisoned with the lawyer Glossin for shooting Meg Merrilies and kidnaping Henry Bertrand, and during the night when Glossin contrives to enter the smuggler's cell, a quarrel ensues during which Hatteraick strangles Glossin and then hangs himself.

a Dirk Hatteraick at villainy

HAWTHORNE NATHANIEL

Nathaniel Hawthorne (1804-1854), novelist and diplomat, loved solitude, but he was nevertheless a public figure and an ambassador to foreign countries, where he was valuable, affable, and successful. He was the supreme novelist of the somber backgrounds of New England, of the shadowy region of religion and superstitious belief. His *Scarlet Letter* registers the constant New England awareness of sin, sin shown as a spiritual force in individual lives—sometimes one's own sin, sometimes shadows of the sin of earlier generations working out their retribution "to the third and the fourth generations." Hawthorne's work in general suggests somber, gloomy superstition and penance; his personality showed reserve, reticence, and pleasant and affable solitariness.

an elfish and alien Hawthorne

HEADSTONE, BRADLEY

Bradley Headstone, an ungainly schoolmaster in Dickens' *Our Mutual Friend,* had mechanically acquired a great store of knowledge, but always seemed to be taking stock of it lest anything should be missing. "He could do mental arithmetic mechanically, sing at sight mechanically, blow various wind instruments mechanically, even play the great church organ mechanically." From constant questioning of his pupils he had acquired a suspicious manner, or rather a manner "that would be better described as lying in wait." Falling in love with Lizzie Hexam, he tried to murder his rival, Wrayburn.

a mind as automatic as Bradley Headstone's

HEBE

Hebe was the eternally youthful, rosy, healthy, dimpled cupbearer to the gods on Mount Olympus, referred to always as blooming, young, delightful. Her name is used to refer to any such person, and particularly to attractive waitresses.

served by a dimpled Hebe

HECATE

Hecate, the Greek goddess of the earth, moon, and infernal regions, is sometimes represented as a beneficent dispenser of blessings, but more often as a terrible creature of infernal power. She was queen of all the witches, dispenser of curses, and dealer in sorcery.

tremble at the dreaded name of Hecate

HECTOR

Hector, "one of the most admirable conceptions of Homer's genius," is the most illustrious of the Trojan soldiers in Homer's *Iliad.* He was slain by Achilles in vengeance for Hector's slaying of Achilles' friend Patroclus. Achilles then dragged his body in insulting triumph three times around the walls of Troy before ransoming it to Hector's father, Priam, king of Troy.

valorous as a Hector
a Hector, raging like the force of fire

HECTOREAN

Hectorean refers to the cheap sort of soldier who in later times wished to resemble Hector. They were swaggering, domineering fellows, imitators of the real Hector. Hence they were called *Hectorean,* and their bullying was called *hectoring;* both words suggest swashbuckling, domineering, blustering fellows.

blustering about the stage in hectorean style

HECUBA

Hecuba was the wife of Priam, king of Troy, mother of his fifty sons and fifty daughters, and the subject of a very moving tragedy by Euripides. After the fall of Troy she was carried into slavery by the Greeks, but on the coast of Thrace she succeeded in avenging the murder of her son Polydorus by slaying Polymester to whom he had been sent with a hoard of gold for safety during the siege of Troy. Later transformed into a dog, she leaped into the sea.

Hecuban pathos
Hecuban vengeance

HEEP, URIAH

Uriah Heep, a clerk in Dickens' *David Copperfield,* constantly refers to himself as "so very 'umble, sir" but is in reality a crafty, hypocritical, scheming, disloyal rascal whose name has become the synonym for the meanest sort of hypocrisy, sham, pretense, and double-dealing.

a pleasant manner, but Uriah Heep eyes

HEGELIAN

Hegelian refers to the philosophical system of George William Hegel (1770-1831), German logician and dialectician, who established the doctrine of Absolute Idealism known as Hegelianism. The leading metaphysical movement of the early part of the nineteenth century, its law of the identity of thought and being made for a complete and final philosophy. Hegel then proceeded to apply his principles to art, comparative religions, history, and politics.

a system of thought as complete as Hegel's

HEGIRA

Hegira is the name given to Mahomet's flight from Mecca to Medina (A.D. 622), with which event the Mohammedan era began. The word is now used generally of any mass flight, departure, or exodus.

the pitiable hegira began

HEIDRUM

Heidrum, in Scandinavian mythology, is the she-goat in Valhalla who furnishes the heroes there with abundant quantities of mead. Feeding on the tree Laedrad, she supplies enough of the liquid from her teats to give every one a full bowl daily. Her name means "the bright-flowing stream."

copious as the streams of Heidrum

HEIMDALL

Heimdall was the Scandinavian sentinel god who guarded Bifröst, the bridge of the gods to heaven, against assault by the giants. He was said to need sleep less than a bird and to be able to see to a distance of 100 leagues by night as well as day. He could hear grass grow, and the wool on sheep's backs as well.

vigilant and alert as Heimdall

HEINE, HEINRICH

Heinrich Heine (1797-1856) was the great nineteenth century poet who wrote some of the most familiar and most beloved lyrics of all time. Of Jewish descent, but a convert to Christianity, he suffered in later life from an incurable disease of the spine that necessitated his confinement to bed. Masterpieces of credulous folklore like *Die Lorelei,* and simple, emotional outpourings such as *Du Bist wie eine Blume,* are characteristic of his many *Leider* which challenged contemporary musical composers like Schumann and Schubert to set them to songs.

the limpid lyrical simplicity of a Heine

HELA

Hela was the Scandinavian queen of the dead. Frightful and ferocious in appearance, she was described as having a body that was black and livid from congealed blood. Her castle was set in the midst of eternal damp, snow, ice, and darkness. Inexorable, she would release no one who had once entered her domain. Only those who died of old age or sickness entered her realm, the souls of heroes passing to Valhalla instead.

frightful and bloody as Hela

HELENA

Helena, the heroine of Shakespeare's *All's Well That Ends Well,* is famous for her romantic passion for Bertram and her patient submission to the most adverse vicissitudes. She is the type of lovely woman, patient and hopeful, of strong character, and sustained through trials by her enduring and heroic faith.

a patient Helena, unbowed by circumstance

HELEN OF TROY

Helen was the beautiful Grecian princess who was sought in marriage by all the greatest of the princes, all of whom, on her marriage to Menelaus, agreed to unite in her defense in case she were ever to be carried away. Her abduction by Paris was the cause of the great Trojan war, celebrated in Homer's *Iliad.*

like another Helen, fired another Troy

fair as Helen, Sparta's pride

HELENUS

Helenus, a son of Priam and Hecuba, was famous for his soothsaying powers. He deserted his countrymen during the siege of Troy either voluntarily or because he was ensnared by Ulysses, who wanted to get his prediction on when the fall of the beleaguered city would occur. According to another version, he was not a traitor, but was taken prisoner by the Greeks. After the capture of Troy he fell to the share of

Pyrrhus, whose kingdom and captive wife, Andromache, he inherited on his master's death.

a prophetic Helenus, able to predict the fall of his own country

---

HELIADES

The Heliades were the daughters of Helios. (*q. v.*). Phaëthusa, Lampetie, and Phoebe by name, they bewailed the death of their brother Phaëthon (*q.v.*) so bitterly that the gods in pity transformed them into popular-trees and their tears into amber.

as full of tears as the Heliades

HELICONIAN

Heliconian refers to Helicon, the celebrated mountain in Boeotia, Greece, that was said to be sacred to Apollo and the Muses. On its slopes were found Aganippe and Hippocrene (*q.v.*), the sacred fountains that were reputed to be the source of poetic inspiration to all who drank of them. The slopes of the beautiful mountain were covered with snow the greater part of the year.

an inspirational Heliconian drink

HELIOS

Helios was the son of Hyperion (*q.v.*), and the god of the sun. Homer describes him as rising from Oceanus, the earth-encircling stream, in the East traversing the heavens in his four-horse chariot, and descending in the evening into the darkness of the West and Oceanus. Later poets tell of his resplendent palace in the East and also assign him an alternate one in the West. His horses were supposed to feed on herbs grown in the *Fortunatae Insulae* (*q.v.*). The god who sees and hears everything, he was identified in later times with Apollo. On his sacred island of Sicily he kept his wonderful flocks of sheep and oxen. The famous Colossus of Rhodes was a representation of him.

all-seeing and all-knowing as Helios

HELLE

Helle was the daughter of Athamas and Nephele. With her brother Phrixus she fled from her step-mother Ino, entrusting herself to the back of the ram with the golden fleece. Borne through the air on this living vehicle, she became dizzy and fell into the sea near the straits of Sigeum. The section of the eastern Mediterranean into which she plunged was thereafter named the Hellespont, or "sea of Helle," in her honor.

a dizzying fall like Helle's

HELMER, NORA

Nora Helmer, the principal character in Ibsen's *A Doll's House*, is a young wife and mother treated like a child by her husband and kept in the narrow domestic seclusion of home and family interests. Frivolous and immature, she blunders into forgery and other errors because of her limited and confined knowledge of life. When she awakens to a realization of the seriousness and earnestness of it, she leaves her pampering home to seek emancipation and education away from it.

coddled like Nora Helmer

HELOISE

(see *Abelard* and *Héloise*)

HENGIST AND HORSA

Hengist and Horsa were the brother-leaders of the Jutes who were the first post-Roman invaders of England (449 A.D.). Called in by the British king Vortigern to assist in defending him from the Picts, they founded the kingdom of Kent. Horsa was subsequently killed in a battle with that monarch.

a Hengist and Horsa team of invaders

HENRIETTE

Henriette, in Molière's *Femmes Savantes,* is the young, simple, and natural daughter of Chrysale. She has become proverbial in French as the type of a perfect woman and domestic ideal.

ingenuous as Henriette

HENRY VIII

Henry VIII (1369-1415), the Tudor king of England sometimes known as "Bluff King Hal," became notorious for the number of his marriages and his establishment of the Church of England in defiance of papal refusal to grant or acknowledge divorce. He dismissed Cardinal Wolsey for failing to get Catholic sanction for separation from Catherine of Aragon, his first wife. By Anne Boleyn he became the father of Queen Elizabeth, after which he beheaded Anne on a charge of adultery. Jane Seymour, his third wife, died. Anne of Cleves he subsequently divorced, though Catherine Howard met the same fate as Anne Boleyn. His last wife, Catherine Parr, survived him. "A despot under the forms of law," he was an industrious and subtle monarch as well as the gross, corpulent epicure and sensualist that his name has since suggested.

as much married as Henry VIII

HEPHAESTUS

(see *Vulcan, Mulciber*)

HEPHZIBAH

Hephzibah ("my delight is in her") is the wife of Hezekiah and the mother of Manasseh (*2 Kings,* xxi, 1). In *Isaiah,* lxxi, 4, it is also an ideal name for the restored New Jerusalem of prophecy.

perfect as Hephzibah

HERA

Hera, in Greek mythology, is the daughter of Cronus and the sister-wife of Jupiter, who listens to her counsels and shares his secrets with her. In the Homeric poems her character is not very amiable; she is jealous, obstinate, quarrelsome, and shrewish. Once she so annoyed her royal spouse that he hung her up in the clouds, chaining her hands and suspending two anvils from her feet. Corresponding to the Roman Juno, she is the goddess of marriage and presides over childbirth, though she jealously persecutes all the children her husband had by mortal mothers. In art she is represented as a majestic and matronly woman, with a beautiful forehead and large, expressive eyes. She wears a crown or diadem, and a sceptre and peacock are her usual attributes.

a marriage favored by Hera

HERACLITUS

Heraclitus, the Weeping Philosopher of Ephesus (flourished c. 500 B.C.), forsook the noble and privileged social position into which he had been born for a life of study in seclusion. Because of his aristocratic opinions and melancholy philosophy, he was frequently contrasted with Democritus (*q.v.*), the Laughing Philosopher. Considering all things to be in a constant state of flux and change, he maintained that fire was the original form of all matter. The difficult and abstract nature of his subject matter and his condensed style of writing caused him to be dubbed as "the Obscure" by ancient critics.

it is better to be a weeping Heraclitus than a laughing Democritus

HERCULES

Hercules was the strongest and most famous of all the heroes of Greek mythology. It is related that in his cradle he strangled the two serpents Hera had sent to destroy him. The oracle of Delphi promised him that on the completion of twelve labors, since known as the Labors of Hercules, he should become immortal. All were supposedly impossible except to a Hercules; they included cleansing the Augean stables, carrying Cerberus out of Hell (Hercules brought the monster up to show him and returned him), fights with a lion, tiger, and a stag, the capture of wild horses, procuring the girdle of the Queen of the Amazons, and other amazing tasks. Finally Hercules, immortal, joined the gods on Mount Olympus.

with Herculean strength
a herculean task

HEREWARD THE WAKE

Hereward the Wake, or Watchful, was the Saxon patriot and outlaw who fought against the Normans. In 1070 he was besieged for three months on the island of Ely by William the Conqueror, but managed to escape with some of his followers after his allies deserted him. The subject of an historical novel by Charles Kingsley, he was named to signify "sword-keeper."

vigilant as Hereward

HERMAPHRODITUS

Hermaphroditus, the son of Hermes and Aphrodite, was a handsome lad who inherited the beauty of both his parents. Salmacis, the nymph of the fountain in which he bathed, was excited by love for him and entreated him vainly for conjuncture. In desperation she embraced him forcibly, begging the gods to unite her physically with him forever. Her request granted, their bodies were fused together, the composite retaining the characteristics of both their original sexes. The resultant creature has ever since been regarded as the symbol of indissoluble marriage.

Hermaphroditus with Salmacis engraved on his body

HERMES

Hermes was the herald of the gods, trader, artful dodger, and patron of thieves. At a few hours of age it is said that he escaped his cradle, stole Apollo's oxen, and strung strings across a turtle shell to make the first lyre. Apollo made him return the oxen, but was so charmed by the music of the lyre that he spared the baby-thief, and was his friend for life. The Romans called him Mercury.

ravishment more keen than Hermes' pipe
winged as Hermes' heels

HERMIONE

Hermione is the wife of Leontes, king of Sicilia, in Shakespeare's *Winter's Tale.* Suspected of infidelity, she is cast into prison, deprived of her child Perdita, and supposed to have died. In actuality, however, she is merely kept concealed until her daughter Perdita is of marriageable age, when Leontes discovers his mistake and is reconciled to her. The character of Hermione shows dignity without pride, love without passion, and tenderness without weakness.

like Hermione, the victim of unjust suspicions

HERMOD

Hermod, in Scandinavian mythology, is a son of Odin, and the messenger of the gods. On the horse Sleipnir (*q.v.*) he journeyed to Hel, the lower world, clearing its gate by a tremendous leap without touching it, in the futile attempt to bring Baldur back to earth.

HEZEKIAH

Hezekiah, king of Judah from c. 719 to 691 B. C., restored the service of Jehovah and was victorious over the Philistines in the early part of his reign (*2 Kings,* xviii). High-spirited and patriotic, he later resisted the cruel and hard subservience to Assyrian power that had been imposed on his people by his father Ahaz. Organizing a revolt in spite of the warnings of Isaiah, he became humble and penitent after Sennacherib had stripped and plundered his land, sparing only the city of Jerusalem.

ill-timed as the revolt of Hezekiah

HIAWATHA

Hiawatha, a Mohawk chieftain who "came to bring peace," was made memorable in Longfellow's poem *Hiawatha.* To him, legend attributes the power to talk with birds and beasts, so that all the forces of nature were friendly to him, and he was friendly to all men. Hence, his name indicates friendliness, beneficence, and magic.

the happy freedom of the Hiawatha days is not known to the reservation

---

HICKATHRIFT, TOM

Tom Hickathrift is a famous character in a legendary tale named after him. A poor laborer of the time of William the Conqueror, he possessed such superhuman strength that, armed with an axletree and cartwheel only, he killed a marsh-dwelling giant near Norfolk, England, and accomplished many other feats of such public importance that he was knighted and made governor of East Anglia.

strength like that of Tom Hickathrift

HILKIAH

Hilkiah, high priest in the time of Josiah, discovered the Book of Law in the temple, which revealed to the king the great need for reformation (*2 Kings,* xxii, 8).

a discovery as important as that of Hilkiah

HILL, SAM

Sam Hill is a polite name for the devil, origin unknown. The term has become an opportunity for the polite world to be angrily profane without being accused of profanity. "What the Sam Hill do I care?" It may be a corruption of the Biblical name Samaël (Samuel), in the old Jewish demonology the prince of the devils, who in the guise of a serpent tempted Eve. Many Rabbis, however, say that he is the angel of death, armed with a sword or bow and arrows.

ambiguous as Sam Hill

HIPPARCHUS

Hipparchus (c. 150 B.C.) was the Greek mathematician who invented trigonometry. He also calculated the length of the solar year and the lunar month, and discovered the precession of the equinoxes from watching the morning risings of stars. Determining their positions according to latitude and longitude, he catalogued some 800 fixed stars.

as mathematically minded as Hipparchus

HIPPOCAMPUS

Hippocampus was a fabulous hybrid with the head and fore quarters of a horse and a fish-like caudal appendage, resembling a dolphin's tail. In classical art the god of the sea is pictured as riding on this creature.

as sure of his surf board as though it were trusty Hippocampus

HIPPOCLIDES

Hippoclides is the classical prototype of indecorous conduct and carefree indifference. After his talents had been approved above those of all the other suitors for the hand of Agariste, daughter of Cleisthenes, the tyrant of Sicyon, he insouciantly whistled away his reward by ordering the flute-player to pipe a dance at the wedding feast. Whereupon, he danced, "probably so as to please himself," standing on his head and maneuvering his legs in the air, much to the horror of the staid and decorous guests. When Cleisthenes solemnly said, "Hippoclides, you have danced away your marriage," the flippant youth replied with a shrug of the shoulders and a nonchalant "Hippoclides doesn't care."

breezy and inappropriate as Hippoclides

HIPPOCRATIC

Hippocratic refers to Hippocrates (460-377 B.C.), the "Father of Medicine" and the most celebrated physician of antiquity. The perfect type of doctor, learned, humane and calm, he wrote over 72 works of medicine, including the *Epidemics,* the *Prognostics* and *Air, Earth and Locality,* a treatise dealing with the effects of environment on health. Honoring his true scientific spirit, the Hippocratic oath still enjoins faithfulness to the best traditions of the profession.

works with Hippocratic perfection

HIPPOCRENE

Hippocrene was the spring sacred to the Muses on the slopes of Mount Helicon (*q. v.*). Its waters were said to be the source of poetic inspiration to all who imbibed them, and it was said to have been produced by a stroke of the hoof of Pegasus (*q. v.*).

drink of Hippocrene's fount

HIPPODAMIA

Hippodamia, in Greek mythology, was the wife of Pirithous (*q. v.*). At her nuptial feast the celebrated battle of the Centaurs and Lapiths arose from the attempt of the former, inflamed with wine and lust, to abduct the bride.

Another Hippodamia, daughter of Oenomaus, became the wife of Pelops when he fraudulently outwitted her father in a chariot race, victory in which was imposed as the condition of winning her. To avoid being speared by Oenomaus if he should lose the race, Pelops had bribed the former's charioteer to loosen a pin in one of his chariot's wheels. When Pelops later refused the reward he had promised to Myrtilus, the charioteer who had betrayed Oenomaus, a curse was placed on his house.

drunken as a guest at Hippodamia's wedding

HIPPOLYTE

Hippolyte, the daughter of Ares (Mars), and the queen of the Amazons, was slain by Hercules in that hero's attempt to procure her girdle. According to another story, she marched into Attica at the head of her army in order to take vengeance on Theseus for having abducted her sister Antiope. Defeated, she died of grief. In another account, she, and not Antiope, became the wife of Theseus and the mother of Hippolytus.

like Hippolyte on the hunt and ready for the kill

HIPPOLYTUS

Hippolytus was the son of Theseus by Hippolyte, the queen of the Amazons. Phaedra, Theseus' later wife, fell passionately in love with the chaste youth but accused him falsely of attempting to seduce her when he rejected her amorous advances. Cursed by his father, he was riding in a chariot along the shore, when his horses, frightened by a bull, overturned the chariot and dragged him to his death. When Theseus later learned of his son's innocence, Phaedra killed herself. Another myth had it that the virgin-goddess, Diana, to whom he was devoted, attempted to restore him to life. He is the subject of a tragedy by Euripides.

a chaste Hippolytus of a youth

HIPPOMENES

Hippomenes, the son of Megareus and the great-grandson of Poseidon (Neptune), was the suitor of Atalanta (*q. v.*), the huntress and sports-woman, who succeeded in beating her in the foot-race that was the test for success in winning her in marriage. On Aphrodite's advice he carried in the race three of the golden apples of the Hesperides, dropping them at strategic intervals and racing on to the finish as she stopped to pick them up. Because he forgot to thank Aphrodite for his success, the goddess in punishment transformed him into a lion.

clever as Hippomenes in gaining the woman he wants

HIPPONAX

Hipponax of Ephesus (c. 540 B.C.) was a Greek satirical poet of great coarseness. In retaliation for having been ridiculed in a statue portraying his ugliness, he lampooned the artists, Bupalus and Athenis, so savagely that both were driven to hang themselves in despair.

a satirical and merciless Hipponax

HITLER, ADOLF

Adolf Hitler (1889-1945), master manipulator of Germany, dictator, from his apparently innocent beginning after World War I became a dangerous figure in the 1920's, culminating in his insidious request for the Sudeten in 1939, "the single thing that Germany wanted." This request was granted by Chamberlain and Daladier representing England and France at the Munich Conference. From that springboard Hitler plunged into World War II. When Germany faced defeat, Hitler was reported a suicide in a gruesomely mysterious story and a grotesque situation. Only his henchmen saw and reported his death; none of the opposing forces ever found the body.

a demagogic Hitler

HOBSON, TOBIAS

Tobias Hobson was a liveryman of 17th century England who rented to all comers the horse nearest the door and no other. The customer's choice must be that horse; otherwise he got none. The name is now applied to any situation when a person imposes his own choice, regardless of another's desires. "Hobson's choice" really means "this or nothing."

Hobson's choice is a convenience —to Hobson

HODUR

Hodur was the blind god of war in Norse mythology. At the instigation of Loki, he destroyed his brother Baldur without meaning to. He is the type of night and darkness, and his name connotes unwitting destruction and gullibility.

a gullible Hodur, malicious without meaning

HOENIR

Hoenir, in Scandinavian mythology, was one of the three gods who created Ask and Embla, the first man and woman. After Odin had granted them human spirit and Loder had given them blood, Hoenir bestowed mind and sense on them. Though he was physically strong and beautiful, he was himself stupid and dull mentally.

richly endowea by Hoenir

HOGARTH, WILLIAM

Hogarthian is from William Hogarth (1697-1764), a celebrated painter and caricaturist, whose satirical pictures of the period have never been surpassed. He made society, politics, and eighteenth century manners in general the butt of his comic satire. Keen, satirical, comic drawing today is characterized as Hogarthian.

a second Hogarth, making tangible the thoughts and movements of the mind

other pictures we see; Hogarth's we read

HOLMES, OLIVER WENDELL

Oliver Wendell Holmes (1809-1894), genial Bostonian, was a born humorist, a doctor of medicine, master of ceremonies, writer of occasional verses, and one of the most loved figures of his time. His play of fancy and fun is apparent in *The Boys* and in his delightful *Breakfast Table* series, which set him high among the literary men of Boston in its brightest days.

with genial Holmesian grace

HOLMES, SHERLOCK

Sherlock Holmes is the chief character in a series of detective stories by Sir Arthur Conan Doyle (1859-1930), whose remarkable skill in solving mysteries by reasoning has never been surpassed in mystery fiction. The name is loosely applied to any one with unusual penetration, keenness, and skill in solving mysteries.

he is your Sherlock-Holmes type of hero, marvelously retracing invisible steps

HOLOPHERNES

Holophernes is a pedantic schoolmaster in Rabelais' *Gargantua.* In the period of five years and three months he was able to teach the title character a dubious and futile accomplishment—the recital of the *A B C's* in reverse.

In Shakespeare's *Love's Labour's Lost,* Holofernes is likewise a pedant who is fantastically vain of his empty knowledge. Under this name Shakespeare ridiculed John Florio, the philologist and lexicographer, and satirized the literary affectations of the Lyly school.

a match for Holophernes in useless erudition

HOMERIC

Homeric is from Homer, greatest of all epic poets, who recorded tremendous world events on an epic scale never surpassed, involving gods and men in the events of the great Trojan war. The characters mentioned in the *Iliad* and *Odyssey* have become a part of the vocabulary of the world, and the style and the events are of "inextinguishable greatness." Homeric has therefore come to mean on a grand scale, as in the expressions *Homeric scorn, Homeric laughter, Homeric wrath,* all meaning epic, inextinguishable, irrepressible, unappeasable.

a Homeric grandeur unsurpassed

Homer's unappeasable wrath

HONEGGER, ARTHUR

Arthur Honegger (1892-) is the leader of the ultramodern school of French music and the head of the famous group of composers known as "The Six" (Auric, Durey, Milhaud, Poulenc, Taillefere, and himself). Creator of the oratorio *King David* and of the biblical drama *Judith,* he is best known for his powerful musical description of an American transcontinental locomotive, *Pacific 231,* which amid strident cacophonies illustrative of hissing steam and grinding wheels depicts with noisy realism the power and glory of motion and masterfully harnessed kinetic energy.

rhythmic and fast as Honegger's locomotive

HONEYCOMB, WILL

Will Honeycomb is a middle-aged beau, a friend of Sir Roger in Addison's *Spectator,* genial, graceful, somewhat affected and pretentious, but courtly and gallant, much given to recalling his success among the ladies.

he is a pleasant old Will Honeycomb—the town would miss him

HONEYMAN, CHARLES

Charles Honeyman, in Thackeray's novel of *The Newcomes,* is a fashionable and free-and-easy clergyman and preacher, the brother-in-law of Colonel Newcome.

an easy-going Charles Honeyman

HONEYWOOD

Honeywood is a character in Goldsmith's *The Goodnatured Man,* distinguished for his exaggerated generosity and humble self-abnegation.

an amiable Honeywood

HOOD, ROBIN

Robin Hood, a merry English outlaw whom rumor said to be the outlawed Earl of Huntingdon, was courteous, just, gallant, but reckless, daring, saucy, an infallible archer and uncatchable. He lived in Sherwood Forest with other outlawed gentlemen, merry knaves all, a care-free life. His sense of social justice led him to rob the rich to give to the poor; his daring led him into many an escapade out of which his saucy ingenuity led him, to the delight of the whole countryside and the despair of the law. Gay, merry, reckless. loyal, just, he, with his merry men, is the most loved character of early England, and probably the first man to build up among Englishmen a government by the consent of the governed, and that on English soil among outlaws. The *Robin Hood Ballads* and Scott's *Ivanhoe* give pictures of Robin Hood and his men.

a mocking Robin Hood among the politicians

HOOVERIZE

Hooverize is from Herbert Hoover, President (1929-33) of the United States, who was during and after World War I administrator of aid to Europe. A statesman of high order, idealistic but practical, accomplishing great good and making no fanfare about it, he is still the sane and sensible voice concerning the conservation and distribution of food supplies. Hooverize has come to mean to regulate the consumption of vital materials when there is need for a larger supply, to save in one's own use, to economize in that particular.

the old Hooverizing comes out periodically under a new name

HOP O' MY THUMB

Hop o' My Thumb is a legendary character originally appearing in fairy tales—a tiny person who steals an ogre's seven-league boots and rescues his larger brothers. Later a popular figure in puppet plays and childrens' stories, he is always dwarfed or tiny, always saving the day at the last minute by doing something the normal persons in the story did not think to do. The name consequently suggests the accomplishment of a tiny or less gifted person in helping a more able person.

an invaluable little Hop o' My Thumb person

HORAE

The Horae, daughters of Zeus and Themis, were goddesses presiding over the changes of seasons, the social order, and the works of man. Keeping watch at the gates of heaven, they were represented in art as blooming maidens carrying flowers, fruits, etc. Eunomia (Wise Legislation), Dice (Justice), and Irene (Peace) by name, they promoted the earth's fertility by the various kinds of weather which they sent to mortals.

to judge from the weather, the Horae must be confused at their job

---

HORATIAN (HORACE)

Horatian refers to the *bon vivant* philosophy of Quintus Horatius Flaccus (65-8 B.C.), one of the greatest of the Roman poets. Maecenas, the richest man in Rome of the day, was his patron and the great Augustus his friend. His four books of *Odes* teem with the good humor of an Epicurean in affairs of love and wine (he refers to himself as "a pig from the sty of Epicurus"), but they also reflect the lofty moral sense of the Stoic philosophy. Vivid pictures of the Roman society of his day, as found in both palace and tavern, illuminate his pages, and his felicitous phrases have enriched literature with a plethora of oft-quoted expressions. His *Satires* have had a profound influence on men like Pope and other later exponents of that form of literary expression. To be Horatian means, therefore, to be gallant and gay in wine-bibbing conviviality, to be a humorist in the ways of the world, and to have a flair for coining quotable, terse and long-remembered phrases.

his philosophy of life is eagerly Horatian
has a Horatian love for wine
a neat and Horatian epigram

HORATII AND CURIATII

The Horatii and the Curiatii were the champions of Rome and Alba respectively in a war between those two cities. The three brothers on each side decided the issue of the conflict between the rival powers, when it was agreed that on the outcome of this miniature battle would hinge the status of the larger groups. Though only one Horatius survived the early stages of the combat, by superior prowess he killed the three Curiatii in single-handed combat. On his triumphant return to his victorious city, Horatius killed his own sister because she bewailed the death of her lover, one of the Curiatii. Condemned to the death penalty, he was later spared on appeal to the people.

a miniature battle, like that of the Horatii and the Curiatii

---

HORATIO

Horatio is the loyal, devoted, and sensible friend of Hamlet in Shakespeare's tragedy of the melancholy prince. Of this paragon of friends Shakespeare has Hamlet say:
"Give me that man that is not passion's slave, and I will wear him in my heart's core, ay, in my heart of hearts, as I do thee."

a sensible Horatio to counsel him

HORATIUS AT THE BRIDGE

(see *Cocles, Horatius*)

HORNER, JACK

Jack Horner was the celebrated personage in the literature of the nursery whose "witty tricks and pleasant pranks" are fully described in Halliwell's *Nursery Rhymes of England.* According to one account, he was the steward of the Abbot of Glastonbury whom the latter sent to present Henry VIII with a dish, beneath the crust of which were found the deeds to twelve manors. Before making the presentation, however, Jack Horner removed the "plum," the deed to the manor of Wells, and kept it for himself and his descendants, telling his master that the sovereign had given it to him.

tricky as Jack Horner

HORN GATE

The Horn Gate is one of the two gates of sleep in the lower world, the other being of Ivory. Through that of Horn, true visions or dreams are sent to man in the upper world, according to Vergil's *Aeneid.* Through the Ivory Gate, resplendent with shining white, false dreams issue.

a dream that could come only from the Horn Gate, for it came true

---

HORUS

(see *Harpocrates*)

HOSEA

Hosea, who flourished in the eighth century B.C., was the first of the minor Hebrew prophets. His reproof to apostate Israel is stated symbolically as marriage to a faithless wife, a comparison drawn from the outward facts of his own life. For he himself was unhappily married to an unfaithful woman, Gomer, who left him to become the concubine of a wealthy man in order to satisfy her craving for luxury. Hosea then purchased her back as his slave, pardoning her for her recreancy.

wronged as Hosea

HOTSPUR

Hotspur is a name given to Sir Henry Percy for his energetic temper in warfare, and he appears as a character in Shakespeare's *Henry IV,* where Hotspur is presented as brave, high-spirited, honest, impatient of pretenses, as well as insatiably energetic, hotheaded, and reckless.

valuable enough, but a Hotspur on occasion

HOTTENTOTISM

Hottentotism refers to the peculiarly clicking and clacking nature of the language spoken by the Hottentots, a South African people of short stature and ungainly build who were first encountered by whites in Cape Colony. These Dutch immigrants named them after their own words *hateren tateren,* meaning to "stammer" and "stutter." Hence, the term Hottentotism refers to any speech that seems inarticulate and agglutinative to an outsider.

hemming and hawing like a Hottentot

HOUDINI

Houdini was an American magician whose feats of magic were so unusual and so nearly incredible that his name is now used of any person whose achievements partake of the magical, or defy explanation on any ordinary grounds. To be a Houdini means to do the apparently impossible (1874-1926).

outwitting Houdini

HOUYHNM

Houyhnm, in *Gulliver's Travels* by Swift, is the name of one of the horses gifted with reason and noble qualities, who rule over the Yahoos (*q. v.*), a race of brutish and degraded people. Hence, the name refers to any superior horse regarded as having human characteristics. Its coining is obviously purposeful and onomatopoetic, being designed to imitate equine whinnying and neighing.

unpronounceable as Houyhnm

HOWARD, JOHN

John Howard (1726-1790) was the famous British philanthropist honored for his efforts to improve the condition of prisons and prisoners. According to Burke, "He visited all Europe

... to dive into the depths of dungeons; to plunge into the infection of hospitals; to survey the mansions of sorrow and pain; to take the dimensions of misery, depression, and contempt; to remember the forgotten; to attend to the neglected.... It was a voyage of discovery, a circumnavigation of charity."

a new John Howard to clean up our prisons

HOYLE

Edmond Hoyle (1672-1769) was the English compiler of rules and instructions for the playing of card games, especially of whist, who supported himself in part by giving lessons in such games. Systematizing the regulations, he drew up a treatise for the use of his pupils, but after it was published it gained such wide currency that it was regarded as definitive and authoritative. Though his laws were superseded by new compilations in 1864, the phrase *according to Hoyle* has become proverbial in the English language to indicate a supreme arbiter.

need Hoyle to get out of this impasse

HRAESVELGER

Hraesvelger is a Scandinavian giant arrayed in the plumage of an eagle. Inhabiting the northern fringe of the heavens, he creates winds and storms by spreading and beating his wings. His name means "the swallower of corpses."

a wing-spread like Hraesvelger's

HRIMFAXE

Hrimfaxe, in Scandinavian mythology, is the horse of Nott, or Night. Every morning foam that congeals into dew falls from his bit. His name means "rime mane."

Hrimfaxe passing over the fields

HRIMTHURSAR

Hrimthursar is a Scandinavian frost giant who lives under one of the roots of Yggdrasil, the world-tree that nourishes all nature.

windows congealed by Hrimthursar

HRINGHAM

Hringham, in Scandinavian mythology, is the ship that became the blazing funeral-pyre of Baldur. The largest of all vessels, it made the whole earth quake when it was launched.

a mighty trans-oceanic Hringham

HUBBARD, ELBERT

Elbert Howard (1859-1915), individualist and philanthropist in his own way, independent and fascinating writer and social prophet, was one of the most interesting figures of his time. He established the Roycroft shops in East Aurora on the principle that every homeless wanderer has some skill, some craft, and needs only the opportunity to work at it. His shops were built one after another to use that skill, in silver designing, woodcraft, carpentry, printing. His *Little Journeys* was a series of biographies, short, delightful, arresting; his magazine, *The Philistine,* made a stimulating difference in magazines, attractively printed in the Roycroft Shops. He was lost on the "Lusitania."

the blatant assertion of a Hubbard

HUDIBRASTIC

Hudibrastic is from *Hudibras,* Samuel Butler's highly satirical mock-heroic poem, characteristic of eighteenth century satire and burlesquing the efforts of the Commonwealth to suppress the amusements of the people.

writes Hudibrastic editorials against all reforms

UDSON, HENDRICK

endrick Hudson was the English avigator and explorer who on his ird voyage (in the *Half Moon*) dis- overed the river named after him nd sailed up it as far as Albany 1609). On his fourth voyage (in the *iscovery*) he reached Hudson Bay, here mutineers set him adrift in a nall boat with eight other men. The nall craft disappeared, and there is o further record of the fate of the en (1611).

an intrepid sailor like Hendrick Hudson

UGGINS AND MUGGINS

uggins and Muggins, humorous cari- atures of boastfulness and preten- on, were the Mr. and Mrs. Vulgarity f Pretension Hall. Possibly an ety- ological corruption of the Dutch hrase for "high and mighty," the ames are now used as the embodi- ent of the self-assured arrogance of e pompous, though ignorant.

as pretentious and ignorant as Huggins and Muggins

UGH OF LINCOLN

ugh of Lincoln, the subject of the *rioress's Tale* in Chaucer, was the nglish boy martyr and saint said to ave been stolen by Jews in 1255, en tortured for ten days and cruci- ed. Nineteen of the richest Jews of incoln were hanged for taking part the affair, and the boy was buried state. The earth miraculously re- ised to hide his body, which was ubsequently credited with working any wonders.

thaumaturgical as the body of Hugh of Lincoln

IUGIN

Iugin, in Scandinavian mythology, is ne of Odin's two pet ravens who erch upon the god's shoulders when e is seated on his throne. Every day at dawn he flies out over the earth to report to his master all that he has seen and heard. His name denotes "mind," "thought," and "intellect," and his fellow raven is named Munin, or "memory."

the Hugin of the newscasters

HUGO VICTOR

Victor Hugo (1802-1885), French dramatist and novelist, wrote romances and adventures that are excitingly dramatic. *Toilers of the Sea* and *Les Misérables* are packed with material enough for a hundred stories, splendid with action, emotion, tense situations and narrow escapes. His Jean Valjean is known to the world. With Dumas, fellow giant among storytellers, he has held the world spellbound and breathless with his vigorous and profound tales.

crowds his canvas as Hugo crowds his pages

with the revelations of a Hugo

HUITZILOPOCHTLI

Huitzilopochtli, the war-god and principal deity of the Aztecs, was born of a virgin. In the great pyramid temple at Tenochtitlan he was worshiped with a ritualistic feast at the December solstice, at which his image, baked in a loaf of bread, was broken and eaten by his votaries. War dances and a wholesale sacrificial massacre of captives were also held in his honor. On their southern migration he conducted the Nahuas, whose conquest of the Mayas promoted the highest civilization of the time in North America, and whose religion included ritualistic cannibalism and human sacrifice.

like Huitzilopochtli, reveling in carnage

HULDAH

Huldah was the Hebrew prophetess to whom king Josiah sent Hilkiah (*q. v.*), the high priest who discovered the Book of Law, to inquire why the wrath of the Lord was kindled against Israel. She predicted that devastation and evil would be brought against the land because of the idolatrous burning of incense before other gods, but that Josiah himself would be spared the sight and gathered unto his fathers as the reward for his humility and tender heart.

clairvoyant as Huldah

HUMPHREY, DUKE

Duke Humphrey is a name used in an old English expression, *to dine with Duke Humphrey,* that is, to have no dinner at all. The phrase is said to derive from the fact that a part of the public walks in old St Paul's, London, was called Duke Humphrey's Walk, and that those who did not have the money to buy a meal were accustomed to promenade and idle here in the hope of securing an invitation.

so hungry he must have dined with Duke Humphrey for the last month

---

HUNCAMUNCA

Huncamunca, in Fielding's *Tom Thumb the Great,* is the gentle and amorous daughter of King Arthur.

a sweet and clinging Huncamunca

HUNKER

A Hunker, in United States political history, was a member of the conservative wing of the Democratic party and opposed to the Barnburners in the years from 1845 to 1848. Hence, Hunkerism denotes hostility to progress and opposition to innovation, and a Hunker may be defined as a conservative old fogy.

reactionary as a Hunker

HUNS

The Huns were fierce nomadic Asiatic horsemen who had roved the Wall of China in the pre-Christian era, later migrated westward and conquered the Gauls. Under Attila, called "The Scourge of God," a leader so terrible that "no grass ever grew where his horse's hoofs had trod," they forced even Rome to pay tribute. Later they defeated the armies of the Eastern Empire, and were themselves crushed only when the Italians, Franks, and Burgundians united against them. This was a significant event in that it determined Christian rather than barbarian dominion over Europe. The devastating raids of the Huns have led the civilized world to use that name of any people reckless of civilization.

sweeping along like the Huns

HUNTER, MR. AND MRS. LEO

Mr. and Mrs. Leo Hunter, characters in Dickens' *Pickwick Papers,* are distinguished for their desire to cultivate all the social "lions" of their day and to make the acquaintance of all the celebrities of London in order to lend lustre to their parties. Celebrity-hunters *par excellence,* they are the nineteenth century prototype of the autograph-collectors and social climbers of our times. Mrs. Hunter, a poetess, is the author of the immortal "Ode to an Expiring Frog."

like Mr. and Mrs. Hunter, they invite only celebrities to their parties

---

HUR, BEN

Ben Hur, hero of General Lew Wallace's book *Ben Hur,* was a young Jew of fine family, converted to Christianity in the time of Christ. Drawn with unerring accuracy, the exciting and dramatic events of the book are set against the background of Rome in the first century, the time of spectacles and games in the arena, chariot races, great celebrations, and involving Roman politics, Roman domestic life in noble families, Christ and his miracles, in short, all the grandeur that was Rome. Through it all Ben Hur moves, the center of storm and stress, but never failing in loyalty to his friends, his family, his faith.

a derring-do Ben Hur

HUSS, JOHN

John Huss (1369-1415) was the great Bohemian religious reformer and popular preacher who was excommunicated from the church for his advocacy of the doctrines of Wycliffe. Tried for heresy, he was condemned and burned at the stake. His followers then launched the conflict known as the Hussite War in revenge for the martyr.

with the religious ardor of John Huss

HYACINTHUS

Hyacinthus was a beautiful Spartan youth whom Apollo loved and unintentionally killed in a game of quoits. Another version of the myth says that Zephyrus (or Boreas) also loved the lad and from jealousy of his preference for Apollo caused that god's quoit to drive against the boy's forehead. His spilt blood was transformed by Apollo into the flower that bears his name, and on its leaves appeared the letters AI, AI, the Greek word for alas, alas!

struck, like Hyacinthus, by a quoit

HYADES

The Hyades were a Greek class of nymphs. Seven in number, their names were said to be Ambrosia, Eudora, Pedile, Coronis, Polyxo, Phyto, and Dione (or Thyene). Placed among the stars to form the constellation Taurus, they were thought to threaten rain when they rose with the sun.

a day influenced by the Hyades

HYBLAEAN

Hyblaean refers to the smoothly flowing honey produced at Hybla, a famous town on the East coast of Sicily, some 12 miles north of Syracuse. Hence, the epithet has come to mean honeyed, suave, and mellifluous.

bland as Hyblaean honey

HYDRA

The Hydra was a monster with seven or nine heads. When certain Greek heroes were sent to conquer the monster they found that the moment they struck off one head two sprung out in its place. Hence, hydra-headed means any difficulty or situation that grows worse on attack. Hercules finally killed it by preventing with a firebrand any regrowth of the heads.

rapidly becoming a hydra-headed situation

HYGEIA

Hygeia was the Greek goddess of health, a daughter of Asclepius (*q.v.*). In art, she is usually pictured as a lovely virgin holding a cup in her hand and giving a drink from it to a serpent. The serpent or snake was regarded as the symbol of rejuvenescence, because in sloughing his skin he was thought to renew his youth and health. These sacred snakes were thus believed to heal the sick by licking them.

a blooming Hygeia, lustrous with health

HYLAS

Hylas was a beautiful youth passionately loved by Hercules, whom he accompanied on the Argonautic expedition. As he went ashore on the coast of Mysia to draw water from a fountain, he was abducted by the amorous local water nymphs, the

Naiads. Though Hercules in jealous grief launched a protracted search for his companion, he never found him.

as handsome as Hylas

HYMENEAL

Hymeneal is from Hymen, the god of marriage, who is pictured carrying the nuptial torch. In general the name represents the rites, ceremonies, and festivities having to do with marriage occasions.

there let Hymen oft appear in pomp and feast and revelry

HYMETTAN

Hymettan refers to the marble, and heath-honey for which Hymettus, a lovely mountain fringing Athens, was famous in antiquity. From the color of the shrubs and vegetation growing on this tree-denuded mountain came Pindar's celebrated description of the Greek capital as "the city of the violet crown." Hymettan honey was, and still is today, delightfully smooth and clear.

amber-colored and smooth as Hymettan honey

HYMIR

Hymir, in Scandinavian mythology, was a water-demon and giant personifying the inhospitable and stormy sea. He owned the kettle that was taken by Thor to brew the ale for Aegir's feast to the gods. For cutting the line with which Thor hauled up the Midgard serpent, he was flung by the ears into the sea.

as savage as Hymir

HYPATIA

Hypatia, celebrated female philosopher of Alexandria, was the daughter of Theon the mathematician. Combining great eloquence with rare beauty, modesty, and intellectual gifts, she taught astronomy and commented with the Neoplatonists on Plato and Aristotle. Because of her intimacy with Orestes, the pagan prefect of the city, she became the object of attack for Christian monks and Cyril, archbishop of Alexandria. Incited by them, a fanatical mob tore her from her chariot in 415 A.D., dragged her to a Christian church where they stripped her naked, cut her to pieces with oyster shells, and burned her piecemeal. She is the heroine of an historical novel by Charles Kingsley (1853).

a modern Hypatia, the friend of intellectual men

HYPERBOREANS

The Hyperboreans, or "dwellers beyond Boreas," the North wind, were a fabulous people of the remote, northernmost end of the earth. Supposed by the Greeks to be favorites of Apollo, they were therefore reputed to live in a land of perpetual sunshine, where the sun rose and set only once a year, and to enjoy everlasting youth and health, perfect happiness, and eternal peace and springtime. Many geographical positions were assigned to this ideal land, including the island of Britain.

delightfully idyllic as the land of the Hyperboreans

HYPERION

Hyperion, one of the Titans of Greek mythology, was a son of Uranus (Heaven) and Ge (Earth), and the father of Helios (the sun), Selene (the moon), and Eos (Aurora, the dawn). In later usage he was identified with Helios himself and regarded as the incarnation of light and beauty. His name is used as the title of one of Keats' poetical fragments and of Longfellow's prose romance.

a romantic and handsome young Hyperion

HYPNOS

Hypnos was the son of Night and the Greek god of sleep, the equivalent of the Latin *Somnus*. The brother of Thanatos (Death) and Oneiros (Dreams), he was usually represented in art as a beautiful youth sleeping or holding an inverted torch in his hand. English words like *hypnotic* and *hypnosis* are derived from his name.

under the spell-binding power of Hypnos

HYPSIPYLE

Hypsipyle was the daughter of Thoas, king of Lemnos. When the Lemnian women, jealous of their husbands, conspired to slay them all, Hypsipyle aided her father to escape. When the Argonauts spent a year on the island and married the women, Hypsipyle bore Jason two sons. The truth that she had helped her father to avoid destruction having been divulged, she was banished, captured by pirates, and sold to Lycurgus, king of Nemea. As nurse to his son, she inadvertently caused the child's death at the claws of a dragon, by laying him on the ground in order to escort the Seven Against Thebes (*q. v.*) to a spring. Saved from the anger of the king, she was finally rescued by her sons.

a life as eventful as Hypsipyle's

I

IACHIMO

Iachimo is the Italian libertine who plays the villain in Shakespeare's *Cymbeline.* In spite of his cunning art and audacity, he meets with failure when he attempts to seduce Imogen, the wife of Posthumus, though he manages to conceal the defeat of his project with a daring imposture.

another Iachimo, disappointed in his salacious intentions

IAGO

Iago is a character in Shakespeare's *Othello,* who, moved by envy and hatred of Othello, conceives the subtle and diabolical revenge of falsely persuading Othello that his adored wife, Desdemona, was unfaithful to him. Presenting what seems to be incontrovertible proof, he thereby brings about the frenzied grief and jealousy that ends with Othello's tragic killing of Desdemona and his own tragic remorse. Iago has ever since been the synonym for diabolical and cruel malice.

contrived with Iago-like duplicity to breathe a taint of suspicion on a purity he dare not assail

IAPETUS

Iapetus, a Titan, was the father of Prometheus, the creator of mankind, and so himself regarded as the original ancestor of all humanity. He was recognized by the Semites under the name of Japhet, as god and ancestor of the people found to the north and west of Syria.

prehistoric as Iapetus

IASION

Iasion was the mortal son of Zeus and Electra, who united with the goddess Demeter in "the thrice ploughed field," and was punished for his presumption. By him Demeter became the mother of Plutus (*q.v.*), originally an agricultural deity of abundant crops. The myth probably derives from a ritualistic worship, signifying the fertilization and fecundation of the fields.

entreat Iasion to increase the yield of your fields

IBANEZ, VICENTE BLASCO-

Vicente Blasco-Ibañez (1867-1928), distinguished Spanish republican, social reformer, and novelist, lived as an exile in Paris and Italy for his activities as a political agitator and anti-monarchist. Unpopular with Spanish women for his strong antifeminist opinions, he developed a flair for writing stories with an appeal for men and women alike, and many of them lent themselves with effortless naturalness to casting in the form of cinema scripts. The most famous of these novels were *The Shadow of the Cathedral, Blood and Sand, The Four Horsemen of the Apocalypse,* and *Our Sea.*

a Blasco-Ibañez sort of plot

IBSEN, HENRIK

Henrik Ibsen (1828-1906) was a great Norwegian dramatist who leveled shafts of satire against the false standards of society in problem plays that are at once pessimistic, bitterly satirical, and tragic. Among the most famous are *Hedda Gabler, Ghosts, Peer Gynt,* and *A Doll's House.*

a ruthless Ibsen, laying human nature bare with merciless realism

IBYCUS

Ibycus was a Greek lyric poet of the latter part of the sixth century B.C. Legend says that he was assaulted and killed by a gang of robbers and that just before he expired he pointed to a flock of herons flying overhead and prophesied to the thieves, "Those birds will avenge me." In a town later, one of the brigands spotted a flock of similar birds and said to his companion, "There go the avengers of Ibycus." Because his scoffing remark was overheard and reported to the authorities, he and his villainous colleagues were apprehended and brought to justice. Schiller has used the story as the subject of one of his poems.

avengers as sure as those of Ibycus

ICARIAN

Icarian is from Icarus, the son of Daedalus, who dreaming he could fly with wings, affixed them to his body with wax. They melted and dropped him into the sea when he flew too near the sun; hence, Icarian means foolhardy, daring, impractical.

explore the unknown with inept Icarian wings

ICARIUS

Icarius was a legendary resident of Attica, who entertained and gave kind hospitality to Dionysus (Bacchus). The gift of wine which he received as token of the god's gratitude he shared with the neighboring peasants, who killed him for his generosity in their frenzied intoxication. When his daughter Erigone found his body, she hanged herself from grief. His faithful dog Maera became one of the dogs associated with the constellation known as the Dog-star.

generous to a fault, as was Icarius

ICHABOD

Ichabod, son of Phinehas, was named the Hebrew equivalent of "inglorious" (*i.e.*, the glory has departed) because he was born immediately after the death of his father and grandfather (*1 Samuel*, iv, 21). The name has since been used with the same allusion to discredit and abasement. Whittier's *Ichabod* criticized Daniel Webster for his attitude on slavery, and the notions of disgrace, ignominy, and shame still accompany the orginal name of this posthumous son of sorrow.

dishonored as innocent Ichabod

ICTINUS

Ictinus was the celebrated Greek architect of the fifth century B.C. With Callicrates as his colleague he designed the magnificent temple of the Parthenon on the Athenian Acropolis, compensating for the optical illusion of concavity and monotony created by the unusually brilliant atmosphere of Athens by introducing numerous "architectural refinements" into the structure, such as slight curves in the vertical lines of the columns and in the horizontal lines of the flooring. These careful adjustments gave to this most exquisite of ancient temples full and harmoniously flowing lines.

architectural plans as subtle as those of Ictinus

IDES OF MARCH

The Ides of March refers to the 15th of that month, the day of which the Roman soothsayer warned Caesar, and the day on which the great Roman Dictator was assassinated in 44 B.C. Hence, it has been used of any approaching crucial day.

dreading his Ides of March—the deadline that haunted his dreams

---

IDOMENEUS

Idomeneus was the Cretan king celebrated in Homer for his beauty and his bravery at Troy. Having vowed to sacrifice to Poseidon (Neptune) the first thing that he would encounter on his safe return from Ilium, he was accordingly compelled to kill his own son. When Crete was visited by a plague in punishment, he was banished from his own country and went, an exile, to Italy.

as handsome as Idomeneus

IDUNA

Iduna was the daughter of the dwarf Svald in Scandinavian mythology. The wife of Bragi, she was abducted by a giant and rescued by Loki, who changed her into a nut and himself into a falcon. She was keeper of the golden apples, the eating of which bestowed everlasting youth on the gods. Personifying the season of the year from March to September, she suggests the annual disappearance of fertility during the remaining months of the year. Thus, her apples are symbolic of the fruits of the earth in general, and she herself is goddess of both youth and springtime.

IFURIN

Ifurin, in Celtic mythology, was the Hades of the ancient Gauls. A dark region infested by serpents and savage beasts, it was the scene of dreadful torments. In it the wicked were chained in horrendous caverns, plunged into the lairs of dragons, or subjected to a ceaseless distillation of poison.

dreadful and dark as Ifurin

IGNATIUS, ST.

St. Ignatius (c. 29-115 A.D.), bishop of Antioch and one of the fathers of the early Christian church, is pictured in art as accompanied by lions or chained and exposed to them, in allusion to his martyrdom under the emperor Trajan, who condemned him to be made the food of lions and other wild beasts for the delectation of the spectators. According to tradition, Ignatius was the little child whom Jesus set in the midst of His disciples for their example.

a death as gory as that of St. Ignatius

IKHNATON

Ikhnaton, or Akhenaten (known also as Amenhotep IV), was an Egyptian king of the XVIII dynasty (1375-1358 B.C.). A religious revolutionary, he established a new cult, that of Aten, the sun god or solar disc, and gave himself the name that means "Aten is satisfied." Establishing a new capital at Tell el-Amarna, he married Nefertiti, a great beauty who is still admired from the well-known bust extant from ancient times, and who exerted a strong influence on her young husband's religious ideas. His pacific reign, though short-lived, and his neglect of foreign affairs cost his country its Syro-Palestinian empire.

a faddist in religion, like Ikhnaton

ILIAD

The word *Iliad* has come to be used of any long recital of an interminable succession of sorrows and afflictions, an analogy with the woes suffered by both the Greeks and the Trojans at the siege of Troy. The full catalogue of disasters there, as recounted by Homer in his epic, followed in a train upon the "wrath of Achilles," the expressed cause of the subject matter of the long poem. Its twenty-four books abound in all the negative emotions and constitute one of the earliest literary inventories of the horrors of war and bloodshed. Formerly ascribed to Homer alone, it has in recent times been an experimental station for literary critics who claim to find internal evidence (inconsistencies, differences in tone and style, etc.) sufficient in quantity to discredit any one-man authorship.

recounted an Iliad of misfortunes

IMHOTEP

Imhotep, originally a human being who built the Step Pyramid, was later deified as the Egyptian god of knowledge and science, especially of medicine, corresponding, thus, with the Greek Asclepius. The first born of Ptah and Sekhmet, he became the protector of craftsmen, builders and scribes.

skilled as Imhotep in medicine

IMOGEN

Imogen, the daughter of *Cymbeline* in Shakespeare's play of the same name, is distinguished for her unswerving fidelity and magnanimity to her mistaken husband, by whom she is unjustly suspected and persecuted. By some critics she is supposed to be the most tender and most artless of all Shakespearean women.

faithfulness to crown even Imogen's

INCAN

Incan refers to the high civilization and culture of the South American Indians of the Quechuan tribes living originally on the Peruvian highlands. After their consolidation by Manco Capac in the eleventh century, they extended their empire from northern Ecuador to central Chile. Their political system was an extreme form of communism under a despotic head, who was known as the Inca and who governed through privileged castes of officials and priests. He traced his descent from the sun, which was the highest god of their religion. Developing one of the most advanced civilizations of native America, the people attracted the attention of the Spanish *conquistadores* because of their fabulous wealth in gold and their great architectural and engineering achievements.

dazzled by desire for Incan gold

INDRA

Indra, in Hindu mythology, is the god presiding over the firmament and the middle realm (the air). The lord of lightning, thunder, and storms, he is the dispenser of rain. In the later Puranas, he fell from primary to secondary rank and is represented as being both amorous and deceitful. Clothed in a royal robe with 1000 eyes, he is pictured in art as armed with an axe and a thunderbolt and as riding on an elephant. In Anglo-Indian phraseology, alto-cumulus clouds are known as *Indra's sheep*.

Indra riding the storm clouds

INGE, WILLIAM RAPLH

William Ralph Inge (1860-), Anglican prelate, scholar, and writer, was known as "the gloomy Dean" of St. Paul's London because his sermons attracted great attention for their pessimism and their caustic and critical attitude toward the ways of modern life. Among his writings reflective of this characteristic are *Christian Ethics and Modern Problems, Faith and Knowledge,* and *Our Present Difficulties.*

more pessimistic than Dean Inge

INGERSOLL, ROBERT GREEN

Robert Green Ingersoll (1833-1899) was an eminent lawyer and speaker, much criticized in the nineteenth century for what seemed anti-Christian doctrine; hence, unchristian, heretic, agnostic.

many an Ingersoll, many a Paine is misinterpreted by his own generation

---

INGERSOLL, ROBERT HAWLEY

Robert Hawley Ingersoll (1859-1928) was an American industrialist who rose to fame as an example of the national "success story" of the nineteenth century. Developing the mail-order business and the chain-store system with success, he introduced in 1892 the famous one-dollar watch that was heralded with the slogan "the watch that made the dollar famous." Though this venture endeared him in the hearts of every American schoolboy, he was insolvent by 1921 and was forced to sell his assets to the Waterbury Clock Company.

disdainfully proud of his Ingersoll

INGRES, JEAN AUGUSTE

Jean Auguste Ingres (1780-1867) was the leading French painter of the classical school. His works are familiar from the numerous illustrative engravings made from them for reproduction in classical textbooks and the like. The most popular of these subjects include "Ambassadors of Agamemnon in the Tent of Achilles," "Oedipus and the Sphinx," "Venus Anadyomene," "Jupiter and Thetis," "Vergil reading the Aeneid," and "Romulus and Acron." He also painted many romantic and historical subjects such as "Francesca da Rimini" and "Jeanne d'Arc."

as illustrative of ancient times as an Ingres

INNOCENTS ABROAD

Innocents Abroad, originated from Mark Twain's *Innocents Abroad,* recounting the travels and the ridiculous adventures of unsophisticated American tourists thrown into a European world of old romance. The phrase suggests unsophistication and a breach of conventionality by unaccustomed travelers.

waved goodbye to another group of Innocents going abroad

INO

Ino, the daughter of Cadmus and Harmonia, and the wife of Athamas, was transformed into a sea-goddess by Dionysus after her husband went berserk, killed her one son, and drove her to leap into the sea with the other. It was she who saved Ulysses (Odysseus) when his raft was wrecked, and the hero would have drowned had she not given him her scarf to buoy him up in the storm-tossed waters.

a lady life-guard, as comely as Ino

IO

Io, in Greek mythology, beloved of Zeus, was changed into a heifer by Juno, then guarded by Argus. Another story relates that Io was so tormented by a gadfly sent by the jealous Juno that she swam across the Ionian Sea (hence, the name "Ionian") to escape it, and wandered thereafter through all of Europe.

tormented like Io

IOLAUS

Iolaus was the son of Iphicles and half-brother of Hercules, to whom he was both charioteer and faithful companion. He also assisted the hero in some of his famous labors, helping to slay the Lernaean Hydra. After Hercules' death, he was the first to offer sacrifices to him and to worship him as a demigod. His name still stands for loyalty and devotion in friendship.

has his devoted Iolaus
a friend as loyal as Iolaus

ION

Ion, the eponymous ancestor of the Ionian branch of the Greek people, was the son of Apollo and Creüsa, whom the unwed mother abandoned in a cave for fear of the anger of her father, Erechtheus of Athens. According to Euripides, the infant was taken by Hermes to Delphi, where he was raised as a servant of the temple. Creüsa and her husband, Xuthus, later came to the shrine to ask for offspring, and Apollo ordered Xuthus to adopt as his son the first person he should meet on leaving the temple. Creüsa, indignant over her husband's supposed recognition of a bastard son, would have killed Ion, had not the priestess of Apollo effected a reconciliation between mother and son by producing the original swaddling clothes in which the infant had been exposed.

a recognition as miraculous as Ion's

IPHICRATES

Iphicrates was the son of an Athenian shoemaker who became famous for the innovations he introduced into the armor and discipline of his city-state's army. He renamed the troops *Peltasts,* because they carried a small, light, leather shield (*pelte*). Clothing them in a linen corslet instead of the old heavy coat of mail and equipping them with light weapons, he made them more mobile and flexible in maneuver than the other armies of the time. As general, he defeated the Spartans near Corinth (390 B.C.) and in Thrace (387 B.C.), and was able to lift the Spartan siege of Corcyra (373 B.C.).

Iphicratean innovations in army equipment

IPHIGENIA

Iphigenia was the daughter of Agamemnon and Clytemnestra, and the sister of Orestes and Electra. When the Greek armies mustered at Aulis on their way to Troy, they were unable to secure a favorable wind because Agamemnon had killed a favorite deer belonging to Diana (Artemis). Calchas, the soothsayer, consequently declared that Iphigenia must be sacrificed in order to appease the wrath of the goddess. Under pretext of marrying her to Achilles, Agamemnon sent for his daughter to have her sacrificed. But when she was on the point of being slain, Diana carried her in a cloud to her temple in the land of the Taurians. Later, after Orestes and Electra had slain their mother and her paramour, Aegisthus, for having murdered Agamemnon on his return from Troy, Orestes was sent to Tauris to atone for his matricide. With his faithful friend, Pylades, he succeeded in rescuing Iphigenia and bringing her back to their native land. This latter phase of the story is told in Euripides' play, *Iphigenia among the Taurians.*

Iphigenia is a symbol of purity and innocence as the intended victim of a human sacrifice. The scene at Aulis is depicted in a wonderful mosaic at Pompeii and in Gluck's charming opera.

with Iphigenian innocence

IRENE

Irene, the daughter of Zeus and Themis (*q. v.*), was worshiped in Athens as the goddess of peace and plenty. The Roman *Pax,* she was represented in art as a lovely maiden holding a cornucopia in her left arm and an olive branch or the staff of Mercury in her right.

supplicate Irene for calm and repose

IRIS

Irisdescent is from Iris, the goddess of the rainbow and messenger of the gods, for whom a many-colored flower, the iris, is named; hence, colorful, glowing, prismatic.

all the radiance of Iris
bright as the bow of Iris

IRONSIDES, OLD

Old Ironsides, a sobriquet coming from the name *Ironsides* and applied to the U. S. frigate, "Constitution," is now applied to a person who has had many perilous experiences and is consequently hardened and determined. *Ironsides* took part in the bombardment of Tripoli in 1804 and played a gallant role in the War of 1812.

the Old Ironsides of the Board of Trustees

IRUS

Irus was the gigantic, indigent, and gluttonous beggar of Ithaca, who became a sycophantic parasite to the suitors for Penelope during the absence of her husband Odysseus (Ulysses). His real name was Arnaeus, but it was changed in derision to Irus, in allusion to the rainbow (Iris) hues of his flesh after he was given a severe drubbing and felled with one blow by the hero, whom he had challenged in disguise after his return from Troy.

a tramp as gluttonous as Irus

IRVING, SIR HENRY

Sir Henry Irving (1838-1905) was the stage name of John Henry Brodribb, great English Shakespearean actor and the first of his profession to be knighted. The well-known portrayer of *Hamlet, Macbeth,* and *Othello,* he was professionally associated with the equally well-known and beloved Ellen Terry for a period of 22 years, and with her won great acclaim for their performances of *The Merchant of Venice, Romeo and Juliet, Much Ado About Nothing, Twelfth Night,* and *King Lear.* He achieved endearing fame in his eight American tours, and was buried with honor in Westminster Abbey.

declaiming Shakespeare like another Irving

IRVING, WASHINGTON

Washington Irving (1783-1859) was a New Yorker of the Hudson River locale. Ambassador to England and to Spain, essayist and story-writer, he was pleasant, affable, and gracious in personality and in literary style. A keen sense of humor, a flair for the ridiculous and for caricature, and an ardent interest in his immediate surroundings marked his talk and his writings. Along with these he was gifted with a talent for description, apparent in his *Knickerbocker's History of New York.* His life in England and in Spain is reflected in *The Sketch Book* of England, and in *The Alhambra* stories of Spain, while his own Hudson River scene appears in *Rip Van Winkle, Sleepy Hollow,* and others. In short, the name Irving suggests complete enjoyment of one's surroundings and a sharing of that pleasure.

with Irving's pleasant expansiveness
a genial raconteur of Irving-like observations

ISAAC

Isaac, the Hebrew word for "he laughs," was the only child of aged parents, Abraham and Sarah. In early childhood angelic intervention released him from the altar at which he was about to be sacrificed by his father in obedience to a divine command. For this last-minute salvation he became an early prototype of martyr, though the rest of his life was marked by a patriarchal, restful, pious, and contemplative character. He lived a nomadic pastoral life, married Rebekah, and became the father of Esau and Jacob.

last-minute rescue like Isaac's

ISABELLA I

Isabella I, called *la Católica* (1451-1504), the queen of Castile and wife of Ferdinand V, is best known as the patron and benefactress of Columbus. When all others had listened to his plans for a voyage of discovery with incredulity and derision, she said, "I will assume the undertaking for my own crown of Castile, and am ready to pawn my jewels to defray the expenses of it, if the funds in the treasury should be found inadequate." Though she was a remarkable example of staid sobriety, clear intellect, religious fervor, and patriotism, an innate bigotry influenced her to attempt the introduction of the dread Inquisition and to proscribe the Jews.

as generous to aid as Isabella

ISAGORAS

Isagoras was an Athenian political despot and archon (508 B. C.) who in order to enforce his aristocratic government banished 700 families, replaced the democratic council of Five Hundred by a selected group of Three Hundred, and was forced to get Sparta to occupy his city with troops to support his policies. His fellow citizens staged a successful revolt and drove the hated oligarch into exile.

wholesale banishments like those enforced by Isagoras

ISAIAN

Isaian refers to the Hebrew prophet Isaiah and to the book of the Old Testament that bears his name. The first of the great prophets, he ministered to the kingdom of Judah from about 740 to 701 B.C., and exerted an even greater literary and religious influence than Jeremiah. The great Assyrian invasion of Sennacherib called forth his oratorical faculties, and his object was to warn, stimulate, and console his people. The vanity of idol-gods, the omnipotence of Israel's helper, the sinfulness and infirmity of the Israelite people, and their high spiritual destiny were his important themes.

fulminating an Isaian warning

ISENBRAS

Sir Isenbras was the proud and presumptuous hero of medieval romance, who was visited by all sorts of punishments. When he had become penitent and humble, his afflictions were turned into blessings.

reduced from glory like Sir Isenbras

ISHMAEL

Ishmael was the son of Abraham and Hagar, of whom it had been prophesied that his hand would be against all men, and every man's hand against him. In his childhood his mother, with Ishmael, had been cast out into the desert at the insistence of Abraham's wife Sara, and there had been protected by the direct help of God, and so saved from death.

a bitter Ishmael

ISHTAR

Ishtar (known also as Astarte and Astoreth) was the Babylonian and Assyrian "Great Mother," the goddess of sexual reproduction and fertility. Mistress and queen of heaven, she was regarded by the Greeks and Romans as the moon goddess, though Venus was her planet. To symbolize the vicissitudes of the earth in its destruction and revival of fruits with the passing of the seasons, she murdered her own husband, Tammuz, and then restored him to life after a mourning period of barrenness and grief. Among the Assyrians she was also the goddess of war, and was armed with a bow and arrows, fire, and a sword.

as fruitful as Ishtar wills

ISIS

Isis was the Egyptian goddess of the moon and the queen of heaven. The wife of Osiris, with whom she ruled the lower world, she became by him the mother of Horus (*q. v.*). Representative of the female productive force of Nature, she was often symbolized by the cow. Since she was also regarded as a token of mystery, her head was frequently veiled. Her rites were popular in imperial Rome, where her priests and servants were distinguished by the wearing of linen garments. She was thought of as teaching agriculture and the arts to mankind.

as productive as Isis

ISLAM

Islam, the Arabic word signifying *submission to God,* refers to the Mohammedan religion and to the whole body of its believers. Its five cardinal duties include daily prayers, almsgiving, monthly fasting, bearing witness to the existence of only one god, and a pilgrimage to Mecca before death. Its exponents are characterized by a burningly ardent, almost fanatical zeal, and a rather vicious persecution of the "infidels."

as zealous as an Islamite

ISLAND OF ST. BRANDAN

The Island of St. Brandan was named after the sixth century Irish abbot who went in search of the Islands of Paradise. A marvelous flying island, it mysteriously eluded all the expeditions that were sent in quest of it, including the last sent from Spain in 1721. Sometimes seen only by accident, the illusory goal always succeeded in disappointing the most hopeful search.

elusive as St. Brandan's isle

ISMENIAS

Ismenias was the cacophonous Theban musician of whom Atheas, King of the Scythians, said, "I liked the music of Ismenias better than the braying of an ass."

unmusical as the efforts of Ismenias

ISOCRATES

Isocrates (468-338 B.C.) was one of the canon of ten great Athenian orators. In spite of a weak voice and "stage nerves," he taught rhetoric, wrote speeches for litigants at law, and composed political discourses on the subject of a Pan-Hellenic political unification of Greece. So ardently did he espouse this cause that he committed suicide after Chareronea, "the battle fatal to liberty," in which Philip of Macedon defeated Thebes and Athens. His rhetorical style was flowingly luxurious and ornamented with elaborate figures and rhythmic clauses. Through Cicero it had profound influence on English political oratory of the nineteenth century.

Isocratean prose, rhythmic and balanced

ISOLDE

Isolde was the beautiful Irish princess who married King Mark of Cornwall, but had come to love Tristan. The story of their tragic love is told in Wagner's opera, *Tristan and Isolde.* The original story says that Isolde fell in love with Tristan after having drunk a love philter by mistake.

There is another Isolde, of Breton, *Isolde of the White Hands,* whom Tristan later married, after he had made his search for the Holy Grail.

the passion of Isolde

ISRAEL

Israel was the name bestowed on Jacob, the patriarch and ancestor of the Jewish people, after he had wrestled with the angel at Peniel (*Genesis,* xxxii, 24). Subsequently it became the ethnic name for his descendants, the 12 Israelite tribes, until the division of the kingdom; thereafter it was affixed to the northern part. Figuratively it connotes a chosen people, elect and authentic.

as privileged by protocol as an Israelite

ISRAFEL

Israfel, the angel of music, according to the legend, will sound the trumpet at the resurrection. Israfel is first mentioned in the Koran as "the angel Israfel, whose heartstrings are a lute, and who has the sweetest voice of all God's creatures."

None sang so wildly and so well
As the angel Israfel

ITHURIEL

Ithuriel was the angel commissioned by Gabriel, in Milton's *Paradise Lost,* to search through Heaven for Satan, who had eluded the vigilance of the angelic guard and effected an entrance into the garden. Inasmuch as the slightest touch of his spear exposed deceit, his quest was successful.

the detecting spear of Ithuriel

ITINERARIA

The Itineraria were road-maps of Roman antiquity, complete with route directions, distances, and a travelers' guide. One of them gave the course for a pilgrimage from Bordeaux to Jerusalem, via Arles, Milan, Constantinople, and Antioch. These Itineraria were, thus, the prototype of the motorists' *Blue Books* of a generation ago and of the *Esso* road maps of today.

bewildered without his Itinerarium

ITYS

(see *Philomela*)

IVANHOE

Ivanhoe is the hero of Sir Walter Scott's novel of twelfth century England. The son of Cedric of Rotherwood, he is disinherited for associating with the Normans, and as the favorite of King Richard I he goes on the Third Crusade. Disguised as a palmer, he returns to England and his father's house. A model of courage and chivalry, he defeats all comers at a tournament, is reconciled with his father and marries Rowena, his father's ward.

an Ivanhoe to champion his Rowena

IVANOVITCH, IVAN

Ivan Ivanovitch was the imaginary person who symbolized the Czarist Russian people before the hammer and the sickle of the Soviet supplanted him. He embodied their peculiarities in the same way in which John Bull represents the British, Uncle Sam the Americans, and Jean Crapaud the French. He was described as a lazy and good-natured person.

no Ivan Ivanovitch in Russia today

IVAN THE TERRIBLE

Ivan IV, surnamed "the terrible" because of the demoniac cruelty latent in his neurotic character, ruled Russia from 1533-1584, at first under the regency of his mother and of the powerful Russian aristocracy known as the boyars, and later as absolute autocrat. The first to assume the title of Czar, he conquered Kazan and Astrakhan, engaged in a long war with Poland and Sweden over Livonia, and ravaged the city of Novgorod, massacring great numbers of its population. His despotic acts reached a climax in the death of his own beloved son, caused by a blow Ivan struck at him in a fit of anger.

outdoing Ivan in fury

IVORY GATE

Ivory Gate is the gate of sleep through which false and illusive dreams enter, while the Horn Gate is the gate through which true dreams enter. These gates are mentioned by Vergil (*Aeneia* VI) as being at the entrance to the lower world.

IXION

Ixion, the king of the Lapithae and father of the Centaurs, dared to express his love for Hera. Punished by Zeus for this, he is pictured as being bound by the hands and feet to a wheel that rolls perpetually in the air. *Ixion's wheel,* therefore, means unending torture.

bound to an Ixion wheel of duty

IZDUBAR

Izdubar was a semi-mythical Babylonian king and the hero of twelve ancient legends of that country. Remarkable for his prowess as a hunter, he was a prototype of huntsmen.

an Izdubar on the hunt

J

JABBERWOCK

The Jabberwock, from Lewis Carroll's *Through the Looking-Glass,* is a mythical monster, used now of any imaginary fear that could not credibly exist.

always looking for a non-existent Jabberwock

JABEZ

Jabez, in *1 Chronicles,* iv, 9, was so named because his mother bore him with "sorrow." A man "more honorable than his brethren," he called on the Lord to "bless me indeed and enlarge my coast" and subsequently became the possessor of extensive riches and the head of a family of Judah.

more honorable even than Jabez

JACK-A-LENT

Jack-a-Lent was a small stuffed puppet, probably an effigy of Judas Iscariot, carried in Mardi Gras processions and set up to be pelted as a game in Lent. Hence, by extension the name has come to mean any simple-minded or insignificant fellow.

an absurd Jack-a-Lent nonentity

JACK-AMEND-ALL

Jack-Amend-All was one of the nicknames given to Jack Cade, the Irish rebel leader of a peasant insurrection in 1450 (see *Cadean*). He promised to remedy all abuses, personally led some 20,000 armed men to secure "redress of grievances," and was killed while resisting arrest.

as glib with his promises as Jack-Amend-All

JACK AND JILL

Jack and Jill (or Gill) are the familiar characters in the old English nursery tale about a lad and a lassie who carried a pail up a hill for water and came stumble-tumbling down with it. By extension Jack has come to be a generic name for a gallant, a husband, or a master, and Jill similarly connotes a sweetheart, wife, or female servant, as in the proverbial expression *every Jack shall have his Jill,* based on Shakespeare's

Jack shall have his Jill,
Nought shall go ill;
The man shall have his mare again,
and all shall be well.

a good Jack makes a good Jill

JACK AND THE BEAN STALK

Jack, the hero of this popular Teutonic nursery tale, sold a cow, exchanged it for a bag of beans, and was scolded by his angry mother, who threw out ali the beans. One of them, however, sprouted and grew so magically that it reached the sky. Jack climbed it, found and robbed a giant, descended the stalk, and cut it to foil and kill the pursuing giant. Allegorically interpreted, the giant is the All-Father and the three treasures that Jack finds in his possession are a harp (the wind), money bags (the rain), and the red hen that laid golden eggs (the genial sun).

returned with his prize quicker than Jack came down the bean stalk

JACK, COLONEL

Colonel Jack is the hero of Defoe's novel, *The History of the Most Remarkable Life and Extraordinary Adventures of the truly Hon. Colonel Jacque, vulgarly called Colonel Jack.* A thief, he goes to Virginia and passes through all the gradations of colonial life, from the state of a servant to that of an owner of vast plantations and a retinue of slaves.

a success story like that of Colonel Jack

JACK-IN-THE-GREEN

Jack-in-the-Green was a popular puppet character in the May-day games of England. Participating in a pageant representing Melva, or Melvas, king of the country now known as Somersetshire, he was disguised in green boughs as he lay in ambush to abduct King Arthur's wife on her way to the hunt.

secluded as Jack-in-the-Green, hiding behind a bush and ready to steal a kiss

JACK OF NEWBURY

Jack of Newbury was a title given to John Winchcomb, the greatest clothier in England in the time of Henry VIII. He kept one hundred looms in his house at Newbury, and armed and clothed at his own expense one hundred of his men, to aid the king against the Scotch at Flodden Field.

a modern Jack of Newbury, master of the garment industry

JACK SIXTEEN-STRING

Jack Sixteen-String was the popular sobriquet of John Rann, a notorious English highwayman. After having been several times tried and acquitted, he was at last hanged at Tyburn on the 30th of November, 1774. He was remarkable for foppery in his dress, and received his nickname from his fancy habit of wearing fine silk stockings and breeches with eight strings at each knee.

as spruced up as Jack Sixteen-String

JACK THE GIANT-KILLER

Jack the Giant-Killer is the hero of a Teutonic legend that became localized in England. A valiant Cornishman, he killed a huge giant named Cormoran by contriving to make him fall into a pit and then tapping him on the head with a pickax. He subsequently destroyed a great number of Welsh monsters, being aided in his task by a coat of invisibility, a cap of knowledge, an irresistible sword, and shoes of incredible swiftness — treasures which he tricked a foolish giant into giving him. For his invaluable services in ridding the country of these undesirables, he was knighted by King Arthur, married to a duke's daughter, and presented with a large estate.

a public benefactor like Jack the Giant-Killer

JACK THE RIPPER

Jack the Ripper was the sobriquet of an undetected criminal who committed a series of ten gruesome murders in the East End of London in 1888 and 1889. He was thought to have been a sadist and a pervert with an aversion for women, since his victims were common prostitutes whom he took a fiendish delight in mutilating.

saaistic as Jack the Ripper

JACKSON, STONEWALL

Stonewall Jackson is the sobriquet given to Thomas Jonathan Jackson (1824-1863), brilliant Confederate general in the Civil War. The nickname had its origin in an expression used by General Bee, on trying to rally his men at the battle of Bull Run, July 21, 1861 — "There is Jackson, standing like a stone wall." He was the successful strategist in charge of the brilliant Shenandoah Valley campaign in the following year. The name connotes sturdy endurance and powerful resistance against assault.

another Stonewall Jackson, a tower of strength

JACKSONIAN

Jacksonian is from Andrew Jackson, (1767-1845), whose public fame records vigorous personal and social independence, sporting blood, and military prowess. His record shows that he "dared" the British, in twenty-five minutes defeated them in the battle of Orleans and was therefore idolized by the people. He was a lawyer, later a senator, but resigned because he "felt out of place in so slow and dignified a body." Later judge of the State Supreme Court, he finally became seventh President of the United States. There he was famous for the Nullification Act, and for his clairvoyant announcement in 1830 that "our Federal Union must be preserved." His veto of the renewal of the charter of the U.S. national bank, and the first proscription of public servants for political opinion were equally audacious.

need some Jacksonian courage today
Jacksonian directness

JACOB'S LADDER

Jacob's Ladder is the ladder of which Jacob dreamed when he slept at Bethel, with a stone for a pillow, and saw the angels of the Lord ascending and descending the ladder. The Lord was standing above, promising Abraham the land on which he lay and bestowing His blessing and the promise of His presence to him and his children always, wherever they might be.

sees a Jacob's ladder from any field

JACQUARD, JOSEPH MARIE

Joseph Marie Jacquard (1752-1834) was the French inventor of the apparatus named after him for the loom-weaving of elaborately figured patterns. Although it was fiercely opposed by the silk-weavers of the day, who feared that its adoption would throw large numbers of them out of work because of its great labor-saving possibilities, it was accepted widely and by 1812 there were 11,000 looms of this type in use in France. The name today suggests the richly variegated figures and designs that are used to embellish sweaters and men's hosiery. Jacquard also invented a machine for weaving nets, and reticulated patterns came into decorative use in woven fabrics as a result of this.

with a complicated Jacquard pattern

JACQUERIE

Jacquerie is from Jacques, a common name for a French peasant. Historically, the Jacquerie was the French peasant insurrection (1358) that occurred when King John was a prisoner in England. The peasants were dubbed "Jacques Bonhomme" ("Jack Goodman") by the contemptuous nobles. Even in the French Revolution (1789-1802) it was a natural and safe name to give to the revolutionists against the aristocratic government. Hence, Jacquerie signifies any revolt of peasants.

imitating the insidious openness of the Jacquerie

JAEL

Jael was the wife of Heber the Kenite, who, loyal to her people, allowed Sisera, leader of their enemy, to come into her tent for rest and refuge from his pursuers, and there, while he was at rest, drove a nail into his temple as her contribution to the deliverance of her people.

the Jaels and the Judiths of history had a courage of their own

---

JAFFIER

Jaffier is a prominent character in Otway's *Venice Preserved.* Joining with Pierre and others in a conspiracy against the Venetian senate, he communicates the secret to his wife Belvidera. She is concerned about the safety of her father, himself a senator, and prevails on Jaffier to disclose the plot. With pledges and assurance of pardon for himself and his friends, he does so. But on discovering the insincerity of the senate, who forthwith condemn the conspirators to death, he stabs his friend Pierre to prevent his being tortured on the wheel, and then proceeds to kill himself.

as trusting as Jaffier

JAMES, JESSE

Jesse James was a noted American outlaw, respected and feared throughout the West, and so daring in his exploits, robbing banks and trains, that stories of his doings, real and fictitious, made the most exciting of dare-devil reading in his day, and the basis of books for boys ever since. He was treacherously slain by one of his own band on April 3, 1882.

playing innocently at their desperate Jesse James games

JAMES, HENRY

Henry James (1843-1916) was the son of a Swedenborgian theologist and the brother of William James, distinguished psychologist. A famous novelist himself, author of *Daisy Miller, The Bostonians, The Portrait of a Lady,* and *The Turn of The Screw,* he also wrote essays of literary criticism, such as *French Poets and Novelists* and *The Life of Hawthorne.* His writings are characterized by great psychological subtlety and are couched in idiomatic, picturesque English. All his people have an elaborately complex preoccupation with themselves. A sensitive impressionist, a cosmopolite who after years of London residence became a naturalized British citizen, he shows an abstract interest in the workings of the human psyche and successfully catches the most elusive gestures and meanings.

with Jamesian disinterest and subtlety

JAMES, ST.

St. James, son of Zebedee, brother of John, and one of the twelve apostles, became the patron saint of Spain, because after he had returned to Judea following a missionary tour of the Iberian peninsula and had been beheaded at Herod's order, the body of the martyr was miraculously translated back to the scene of his earlier conversions. His shrine at Compostela became an object of pilgrimage. July 25th was the date of his martyrdom.

under the protection of St. James

JAMES, WILLIAM

William James (1842-1910) was the brother of novelist Henry James (*q.v.*) and equally celebrated in the fields of anatomy, physiology, psychology, and philosophy. A keen analyst and the brilliant and vivid expounder of "pragmatism" and "radical empiricism," he established himself as leader of the physical school of American thinkers with his authoritative two-volume *Principles of Psychology.* With brilliant analogies he turned his interests to include religious and moral problems. He showed an amazing aptitude for translating the cumbersome terminology of his highly technical field into terms readily appreciable to the layman. Other writings include *The Will to Believe, Pragmatism, Varieties of Religious Experience,* and *A Pluralistic Universe.*

a Jamesian talent for expressing the abstruse in simple terms

---

JANNES AND JAMBRES

Jannes and Jambres were the two magicians of Pharaoh who imitated some of the miracles of Moses (*2 Timothy,* iii, 8, 9). The paraphrast Jonathan says they were the sons of Balaam.

imitative as Jannes and Jambres

JANOTISM

Janotism, the word for a trifling or dawdling ineptitude, is from the French proper name *Janot* or *Jeannot,* the diminutive of *Jean* (John). *Janot* itself is used proverbially to designate a simpleton, a dawdler, or one who exercises a silly ingenuity.

without being a Janot, who has not sometimes in conversation committed a Janotism?

JANSENISTS

The Jansenists were the followers of Cornelis Jansen (1585-1638), Catholic theologian and bishop of Ypres in Flanders, who advanced the doctrine of irresistible grace and complete natural depravity, including the belief in loss of free will, predestination, and limited atonement. Rigorous in morals, they were opposed to frequent communion and were bitterly hostile to the Jesuits. One of the centers of their creed was in the nunnery of Port Royal, near Paris, and in 1653 they were condemned by Pope Innocent X. In the 18th century they dressed themselves with notable austerity and plainness of style, whence the word *Jansenist* refers also to any peculiarity of dress in that epoch.

ascetic as the Jansenists

JANUARIUS, ST.

St. Januarius (about 272-305 A.D.) was the Christian prelate and bishop of Beneventum sentenced to martyrdom in the persecution ordered by Diocletian and Maximian. Judged by Timotheus, he was successful in escaping death by several tortures. He passed through a fiery furnace unscathed, was thrown to licns who fawned on him, miraculously healed the wicked Timotheus of sudden blindness, and was finally executed by the sword of his persecutor after the latter had had his sight restored by the saint. The patron saint of Naples, he is worshiped in a miraculous ceremony in May and September of each year. Two phials supposed to contain his blood are enshrined in that city, and when they are exhibited on these occasions the coagulated substance turns to fluid and deliquesces.

liquefies like St. Januarius's blood

JANUS

Janus, a Roman deity, two-faced god of gates and doors presiding over all beginnings and endings, was reputedly the porter of heaven, the "opener and shutter." He is always represented as looking two ways, hence, rather loosely typifying double-dealing or two-faced and deceitful. In the original meaning, the name is given to January. The temple dedicated to Janus in Rome had its doors opened in time of war and closed in time of peace, to indicate that in war the god had gone out to help the warriors, and that in peace he was inside as a safeguard to the city.

the Janus of the busy intersection

JAPHETH

Japheth was the son to whom Noah gave the stone which had the power of bringing rain from heaven at the will of whoever possessed it. It was for a long time preserved by the Turkish Moguls.

a rain-maker like Japheth

JAQUES

Jaques is the morose and cynical moralizer who attends on the exiled duke in Shakespeare's *As You Like It.* Purely contemplative, he thinks constantly and yet never does anything. His whole absorption is in occupying his mind, while he is completely oblivious of his body and his fortunes. After a youth spent in wanton dalliance, he has become a querulous old man.

absorbed in moodiness as Jaques

JARGAL, BUG

Bug Jargal is the title character of Victor Hugo's novel of the same name, the subject of which concerns itself with a revolt of the negroes in Santo Domingo. Bug Jargal is a negro of innate nobility who falls in love with a white woman.

crossing the color line, like Bug Jargal

JARLEY, MRS.

Mrs. Jarley is the good-natured, kind-hearted proprietress of a wax-work show, who befriends Little Nell in Dickens' *Old Curiosity Shop.* She lent her name to a kind of parlor entertainment of the time, called *Mrs. Jarley's Wax-Work.* In it living persons represented wax figures in a variety of tableaux depicting well-known people. They were put through stiff, mechanical motions, and resembled wire-drawn puppets.

with the automaton's grace of one of Mrs. Jarley's figures

JARNDYCE, JOHN

John Jarndyce is the guardian of Esther Summerson and the owner of *Bleak House* in Dickens' novel of that name. He is a shrewd and genial philanthropist, and always explains his fits of temper or moodiness by saying, "The wind is in the east." He is a litigant before the court in the interminable case over the trusts under a will, the famous suit of *Jarndyce vs. Jarndyce,* a satire on the dilatory methods of English jurisprudence.

involved in a law-suit as involved as that of Jarndyce vs. Jarndyce

---

JARVIE, BAILLIE NICOL

Baillie Nicol Jarvie is a prominent and well delineated character in Scott's novel *Rob Roy.* A magistrate of Glasgow, he is petulant, conceited, purse-proud, tactless, and intensely prejudiced, uniting with these vexatious characteristics qualities of sincerity and kind-heartedness. Though he does nothing in the story but give bail, take a journey, and marry his maid, his generous courage and Highland blood make him both original and interesting.

as Scotch as Baillie Nicol Jarvie

JASON

Jason was the Grecian youth who organized the Argonauts to go on an expedition to find the Golden Fleece, which he secured with the help of Medea, whom he married, to discard her later for a Corinthian princess. Jason now means a seeker for gold, or sometimes a fortune-hunter.

rich, and many Jasons come in quest of her

JAVERT

Javert is the crafty, inexorable, and ubiquitous captain of police in Hugo's *Les Misérables,* who, no matter through how many years it extends, never gives up the search for a wanted person. In Hugo's story, at the most crucial moment of what seems to be a final escape for Jean Valjean, Javert stands waiting. He knows only one emotion, devotion to duty; one wish, to be known to have done what has been committed to him to do.

the Javert of the system

JAY, JOHN

John Jay (1745-1829) was a distinguished American jurist and statesman active in pre-Revolutionary agitation. While Minister to Spain he was called to Paris by Franklin in order to negotiate for peace with Great Britain in 1782. Later he collaborated with Hamilton and Madison in the writing of the *Federalist* to explain the new Constitution. Chief Justice of the Supreme Court from 1789 to 1795, he drafted Jay's Treaty, settling outstanding difficulties with the government of Great Britain. Also governor of New York State from 1795 to 1801, this illustrious patriot led a long life of public service.

a peace-maker of the John Jay type

JEAMES

Jeames was an old English form of James, so pronounced and often so spelled until the end of the eighteenth century. A character by this name is the hero of Thackeray's *Jeames's Diary*. The appellation has acquired currency as a designation of a footman or a flunkey, and was applied in nineteenth century London to that capital's *Morning Post*, as the organ of the "haristocracy."

as British as the name Jeames

JEANNOT

Jeannot is the French term, generally derogatory, for a trifler, one who is minutely great. In the familiar Horatian phrase, a Jeannot is the sort of person who, after great preparation to produce some mighty effect, brings forth only a ridiculous mouse.

a painstaking Jeannot

JEFFERSON, JOSEPH

Joseph Jefferson was an eminent and beloved American actor of the nineteenth century, famous for his inimitable interpretations of many dramatic roles. He was probably responsible for the general knowledge and the permanence of the popular interest in many of them, including *Rip Van Winkle* and the role of Bob Acres (*q.v.*) in *The Rivals*.

with a Joseph-Jefferson sympathy with his role

JEFFERSONIAN

Jeffersonian, from Thomas Jefferson (1734-1826), relates to his political views which favored a strong state government and democratic doctrines rather than centralized federal doctrines. He drafted the Declaration of Independence, destroyed titles, made an aristocracy impossible, and believed in extreme simplicity. Accessible to people of all degrees, he was one of the strongest influences in the establishment of the principles that built the United States.

Jeffersonian simplicity
Jeffersonian doctrines

JEHOIACHIN

Jehoiachin became king of Judah in 598 B.C. at the age of eighteen. After a reign of only three months, he was carried in captivity to Babylon by Nebuchadnezzar (*2 Chronicles*, xxxvi) and imprisoned there for the entire reign of that monarch, though his mother, wives, and the 10,000 other leading personages and artisans taken along in the deportation were allowed to live in comparative freedom. In 561 B.C. he was finally released by Evil-merodach and supported in royal state at the expense of that king.

uprooted like Jehoiachin and his people

JEHU

Jehu, young king of Israel, anointed by one of Elijah's prophets, was noted for his aggressive and extensive battles in which his men were mounted on chariots. Hence, the expression "drives like Jehu" means to rush along recklessly and dangerously.

Fast as Jehu drove for a crown
For the driving is like the driving of Jehu . . . for he driveth furiously
II Kings, ix, 20

JEKYLL-HYDE

Dr. Jekyll and Mr. Hyde, from *Dr. Jekyll* in Stevenson's story by that name, was a man who by the use of a powerful drug could transform himself from the respected and admirable professional man that he was into a vicious person who committed atrocious deeds. The name is now used for any person who does things apparently inconsistent with his supposed nature.

leads a Jekyll-and-Hyde existence
to follow the Jekyll-and-Hyding from the outset

JELLYBY, MRS.

Mrs. Jellyby is an untidy character in Dickens' *Bleak House.* A sham philanthropist, she spends all her time and a limited amount of capital on foreign missions, such as helping the poor fanmakers and flower girls of Borrioboolah Gha, but would bundle into the street a poor beggar dying of starvation on her doorstep.

as hypocritical as Mrs. Jellyby

JENKINS

Jenkins was a cant name for any snobbish penny-a-liner journalist in nineteenth century England. First given in *Punch* to a writer for the London *Morning Post,* it poked fun at the author of articles describing persons and events in fashionable and aristocratic society. All these chronicles betrayed the innate servility, priggishness, and vulgarity of the writer's character.

a fawning social climber like Jenkins

JENKINS, WINIFRED

Winifred Jenkins is Miss Tabitha Bramble's maid and the sweetheart of the title character in Smollett's *Expedition of Humphry Clinker.* The archetype of Mrs. Malaprop (*q.v.*), she makes a meaningless mess of the English language and commits ridiculous errors in speaking and writing.

absurd as Winifred Jenkins in her gossip

JENKINSON, EPHRAIM

Ephraim Jenkinson is a swindling knave in Goldsmith's *Vicar of Wakefield.* He dupes and wins the confidence of Dr. Primrose by his venerable appearance, his apparent piety, his learned talk about "cosmogony," and his loudly declaimed admiration of the good Doctor's views on the subject of monogamy.

a hypocritical Ephraim Jenkinson

JENKINSON, MRS. MOUNTSTUART

Mrs. Mountstuart Jenkinson is an epigrammatic lady in Meredith's *Egoist* (1879). An avid quoter of platitudes, she has a flair for achieving the improper by always saying "the remembered if not the right thing."

out-of-place as a remark by Mrs. Mountstuart Jenkinson

JEPHTHAH

Jephthah's daughter is the maiden whose story is told in *Judges,* xi. When her father fought the Ammonites, he vowed that if he were granted the victory he would offer up as a burnt sacrifice whatever came first to greet him out of his own gates on his return home. His own daughter, his only child, was the first to come to greet him and acquiesced in the need to keep his vow, asking only that she might have two months with her maidens before the sacrifice.

pale as Jephthah's daughter

JEREMIAD

Jeremiah, one of the four great prophets, wrote both the book bearing his name and *Lamentations,* predicting the evil that would befall and constantly bewailing and lamenting. Hence, the name is used of a person making doleful predictions, and a jeremiad is a long recital of lamentable happenings.

reciting the endless jeremiad of his life

JERICHO

Jericho was the ancient Palestinian city miraculously destroyed by Joshua and his army. When they had marched around the walls seven times, they blew trumpets and raised so loud a shout that the stones crumbled and fell in ruin. Proverbially, in allusion to the place where David's servants were sent to stay till their beards were grown (2 *Samuel,* x), it has come to signify any place of retirement in obscurity or any distant and out-of-the-way spot.

a shout loud enough to bring down the walls of Jericho

JEROBOAM

Jeroboam, a man of energy and ability, was the king of Israel who led the ten northern tribes to secession and revolt from the southern tribes under Rehoboam (1 *Kings,* xi-xiv). Because he set up golden calves as images of Jehovah, he was denounced for the capital sin of idolatry.

Jeroboam who made Israel to sin

JEROME, ST.

St. Jerome, or Hieronymus (A.D. 340-420), was one of the four great Latin Fathers. After a period of dissipation as a student in Rome, he embraced asceticism, living as a hermit in the desert of Chalcis on the Syrian frontier. Subsequently as spiritual counselor of several noble Roman ladies, ardent Christians, he attacked hypocrisy and censured the frivolous unsparingly. His life-long admiration of pagan literature is apparent in many of his writings, in spite of his outward attempts to quell it, and it was said that he would fast first in order to read Cicero afterwards. He even dreamed that when he was summoned before the Judgment Seat and professed himself a follower of Christ, he was rebuked with the words, "You lie, you are a Ciceronian, not a Christian." Among his numerous works the best known is his Vulgate edition of the Bible, with the Old Testament translated from the Hebrew into Latin and the New Testament translated from the Greek.

as ascetic and pious as St. Jerome

JERONIMO

Jeronimo, or Hieronymo, is the principal character in Thomas Kyd's play *The Spanish Tragedy.* On finding his application to the king ill-timed, he says, "Go by, Jeronimo," an expression that became proverbial and popular slang to signify a putting or thrusting aside without notice. Overcome by grief, he employs exaggerated language and rant that was ridiculed by other writers of the day for its lackadaisical inflation.

as maudlinly sentimental as Jeronimo

JESSICA

Jessica, the beautiful daughter of Shylock in Shakespeare's *Merchant of Venice,* is "a most beautiful pagan, a most sweet Jew." Taking her father's jewels and money, she elopes with her Christian lover, Lorenzo.

forced like Jessica to elope

JESUIT

The Jesuits, a religious order founded by Ignatius Loyola in 1534 and originally resisting the authority of the sovereign in religious matters, were later missionaries and explorers in the early nineteenth century in America. Finally, because so many of the society became shrewd, crafty, and evasive, these qualities became inseparably attached to the name, and are most often implied in the word "jesuitical."

crafty as any Jesuit

JEW, THE WANDERING

(see *Khartaphilos*)

JEZEBEL

Jezebel, the wicked wife of Ahab, a king of Israel, "painted her face and (at)tired her head, and looked out at a window" to see young Jehu. At his command her eunuchs threw her down from her window, and Jehu trod her under foot because "the whoredoms of (Jezebel) and her witchcrafts are so many" (2 *Kings,* ix). The name is now proverbially used to designate a showily dressed woman with painted face and frail morals. It has been so used from the time of the Puritans.

and the dogs shall eat Jezebel, and there shall be none to bury her

JINGLE, ALFRED

Mr. Alfred Jingle is an impudent, chattering swindler and actor rescued from prison and reformed by Mr. Pickwick in Dickens' *Pickwick Papers.* He is represented as never speaking a coherent or connected sentence, but stringing together disjointed phrases, generally without verbs.

as ungrammatical as Alfred Jingle

JOAN OF ARC

Joan of Arc (1412-1431), a young French peasant girl aflame with fervid patriotism, claimed a vision bade her to deliver France. When Charles in the desperation of the French situation gave her the rank of military commander and the disposal of troops, in one week she compelled the English to raise the siege of Orleans and Charles was crowned king. The Maid of Orleans, as she was afterward known, fell to the English, however, and was burned as a witch. Her name now implies personal leadership, at any risk or sacrifice, in a cause to which one feels himself to be consecrated. Excellent accounts of her religious enthusiasm and inspired leadership are to be found in Mark Twain's *Joan of Arc* and Bernard Shaw's *Saint Joan.*

a modern Joan of Arc
a Joan of Arc vision

JOAN, POPE

Pope Joan is the name of a scandalous figure in the list of Supreme Pontiffs of the Roman Church. Supposedly an English woman educated at Cologne, Athens, and Rome, she assumed the name Joannes Anglicus and was so celebrated for her learning that she was elected to the papacy in either 855 or 1100, the double date being due to the attempt to fill in lacunae in the lists of Popes at those times. As she was proceeding to the Lateran Basilica, she was seized with the pains of childbirth on the road between the Colosseum and the church of St. Clement. She died and was buried without any honors, after a pontificate of about two years. At least a hundred and fifty authors between the 13th and 17th centuries repeated this doubtful story, probably with the intention of shaking the popular reverence for the Papal See.

as doubtful as the papacy of Joan

JOB

Job, one of the richest and greatest men of the East in his time, is identified in the Septuagint appendix with King Jobab of Edom. Satan persuaded God to allow him to test his loyalty by depriving him of his fortune, tormenting him by physical ills and suffering. Eventually Job curses the day of his birth, rebukes his friends for their desertion, and wishes for death. After learning to submit without complaint, this paragon of piety (whose very name means "one afflicted, hated, or persecuted") is restored to his former estate to teach the lesson that seeming adversity is only a means to spiritual prosperity.

The enormity of his trials has permeated colloquial speech with such expressions as "as poor as Job's turkey," "Job's news," and "Job's post," the last used of one who brings bad news. A *Jobation* is a long and tedious reproof.

patient as Job
Job-like, vindicating himself

JOB'S FRIENDS

Job's "friends" were Eliphaz, Bildad, and Zophar. Suspecting him of having incurred the punishment of heaven for his sins, they have become bywords for false or blundering friendship. Like the expression "Job's Comforter," they connote people who profess to comfort but achieve the opposite.

as hypocritical as Job's friends

JOCASTA

Jocasta was the wife of Laius, king of Thebes, and mother of Oedipus (*q. v.*), whom she married unwittingly. To Oedipus she bore Eteocles and Polynices (see *Seven against Thebes*) and their sisters, Antigone and Ismene. On discovering that she was married to her own son, the murderer of her husband, she hanged herself. Her name connotes the ultimate in discovery of horrible and unspeakable truth. A pitiful victim of an inevitable Fate, she suffered not as the result of wilful erring but because of the pitilessness of blind destiny.

a destiny as blind as that of Jocasta

JOE

Joe, the fat boy in Dickens' *Pickwick Papers,* is a somnolent lad who dedicates his energies to eating and sleeping, from the latter of which he can be prodded only by "sundry taps on the head with a stick." He even falls asleep while masticating a huge piece of pie. Lazy and unctuous, he wallows in a constant lethargy.

like Joe, he lives to eat

JOHN-A-DREAMS

John-a-dreams is a name apparently coined to suit a dreaming, stupid character, so lost in his own thoughts that he is scarcely conscious of his surroundings.

Yet I, a dull and muddy-mettled rascal, peak like John-a-dreams, unpregnant of my cause, and can say nothing
Shakespeare

an incurable John-a-dreams

JOHN THE BAPTIST

John the Baptist was the son of aged parents, Zachariah and Elizabeth, upon whose death he retired into the desert, subsisting on wild locusts and honey during his long meditation there. Later he baptized Jesus, his cousin, though he seemed to feel unworthy to perform this office for the Christ whose forerunner he declared himself to be. During his denunciatory teachings he publicly rebuked Herod Antipas for his marriage with Herodias, the mother of Salome, whom she instigated to demand the prophet's head as a reward for her dancing.

a forerunner like John the Baptist

JOHN, LITTLE

(see *Little John*)

JOHN, PRESTER

Prester John, Priest John (*le prêtre Jean*), was probably an imaginary personage, but with so much semblance of actuality that Louis IX of France commissioned a friar to explore Central Tartary in search of him. It proved to be a search that revealed only the story that a Tartar Khan had been converted by Prester John. Meantime, marvelous tales of his kingdom in Asia, his wealth, his adventures, and the expansion of his power were told, and these are still the foundation of many stories. His name therefore suggests the same fantastic setting up of a kingdom in far places that the name Marco Polo connotes.

beyond the realms of Prester John

JOHN, ST.

St. John, the evangelist, apostle, and "disciple whom Jesus loved," is represented in art as writing his gospel, or bearing a chalice from which a serpent issues, in allusion to his driving the poison from a cup presented to him to drink. He is sometimes also pictured in a cauldron of boiling oil, referring to the tradition of his being plunged into such a cauldron before his banishment to the isle of Patmos.

persecuted like St. John

JOHNSONIAN

Johnsonian is from Dr. Samuel Johnson (1709-1784), who rose from abject poverty and through constant struggle against handicaps to be the greatest literary figure in London. A brilliant conversationalist in a time of noted wits, he was an intimate of Burke, Reynolds, and Garrick. He was a doctor of the Universities of Dublin and Oxford, and was conceded to have had "the most penetrating mind and the most clear and forceful although ponderous style of his time." His personal peculiarities included a huge body, a head that "rolled on its neck," a lurching gait, a refusal to be contradicted or to admit himself worsted in an argument, and whip-lash repartee that was as famous as his more positive accomplishments. His kindness to the poor and disabled; his graciousness on occasion; his contempt for social conventions and his rugged pride and independence are all well known through Boswell's affectionate *Life of Johnson.*

the Johnsonian method—if his pistol missed fire, he knocked you down with the butt

JOLIET, LOUIS

Louis Joliet (1645-1700) was the Canadian-born explorer and hydrographer who was sent on an expedition to take supplies to a mining party searching for copper in the region of Lake Superior and met Marquette at Saulte Ste. Marie. In 1672 he was put in charge of an expedition to discover the great river described by the Indians, found the Mississippi, and sailed down it as far as Arkansas. An adventurous and energetic woodsman and an indefatigable traveler, he conducted further missions of exploration in the Gulf of St. Lawrence and the Hudson Bay area.

facing the unknown as venturesome as Joliet

JOLLY ROGER

The Jolly Roger is the black flag of piracy, with a white skull and crossbones on a black field. Symbol of bold adventure, fearless spirit, and extreme daring, the name is sometimes loosely used of a dare-devil type of sailor.

likes to sail under a Jolly Roger

JONAH

Jonah, a Hebrew prophet fleeing from God's command, took refuge aboard a ship which was pursued by tempests so frequent and so terrible that the sailors finally determined by lot whose sin was causing their persecution and flung Jonah into the sea. Hence, Jonah is used of any person who brings ill luck to an undertaking. The name also sometimes implies the end of the story, when God caused Jonah to be swallowed by a whale, but touched by Jonah's repentance, caused the whale to throw him out on dry land three days later; hence, repentance, and miraculous deliverance from apparent doom.

incredible as the story of Jonah and his whale

JONATHAN

Jonathan was the son of Saul, king of Israel, and his friendship for David, whom Saul hated and persecuted, has become proverbial for a tender and loyal devotion of one man for another. He "stripped himself of his robe and gave it to David, with his sword, bow, and girdle." Again in 1 *Samuel* we read that "the soul of Jonathan was knit with the soul of David, and Jonathan loved him as his own soul." Equally typical of the gentleness of Jonathan is the phrase "Jonathan's arrows," meaning to shoot to give warning and not to hurt.

a gentle and unharming Jonathan

JONATHAN, BROTHER

Brother Jonathan, a name humorously used to refer to the United States, is commonly supposed to have originated in Washington's constant and witty references to Jonathan Trumbull, governor of Connecticut (1740-1789). He wondered "What will Jonathan think?" in every important situation.

little dreamed that all Europe would be marveling at Brother Jonathan

---

JONES, DAVY

Davy Jones is a familiar name among sailors for death by drowning, formerly for the evil spirit supposed to preside over the demons of the sea. He was pictured as being of the height of a gigantic wave, and having three rows of sharklike teeth in his cavernous mouth. He also had frightful eyes and nostrils emitting blue flames, and was constantly on the lookout for a new sailor lad to add to his crew. "Davy Jones's Locker" is the final resting place of those who perish at sea.

fearful of sailing into Davy Jones

JONES, EMPEROR

Emperor Jones is the central figure in Eugene O'Neill's play of that name, picturing the fear that possessed a negro who, on an island inhabited by native blacks, had, by virtue of his self-assurance, his air of magnificence and competence and his consequent glory in their eyes, made himself "Emperor." The play features his abject terror and his panic-stricken flight when his "subjects" turned against him. Emperor Jones suggests not only an assumed and spurious command, power, and magnificence, but abject and pitiable fear and panic.

a pitiable, abject, Emperor-Jones fear

JONES, TOM

Tom Jones, the friendly, frank, attractive and generous youth who nevertheless gets himself into some unsavory situations and has many a lapse from virtue, is the hero of Fielding's novel, *Tom Jones*. He is brought up by a kindly gentleman who turns out to be his own uncle. Tom inherits all his uncle's money and marries a rich wife, an ending that satisfied the current demand for a happy ending in stories. The name, however, is used for a pleasant and attractive young scapegrace.

world is full of Whiteheaded Boys and Tom Joneses who come into good fortune without conscious effort

---

JONSON, BEN

Ben Jonson (1573-1637), poet and dramatist of Shakespeare's time, author of "Drink to me only with thine eyes," titled *To Celia,* was a master of song and a dramatist of considerable ability, author of *Every Man in His Humor*. A loyal friend, a boon companion, and inspired writer, he is characterized in Shakespeare's epitaph, "O rare Ben Jonson!"

with Jonsonian song

JORDAN

The river Jordan was the Styx of Christian religious belief, for it was the river which separated the wilderness of this world from the promised land to come. Hence, to *cross the Jordan* meant to die and enter paradise, and *Jordan passed* signified that death was already over and the reward achieved.

crossing a metaphoric Jordan, he found a happier life

JORMUNGANDAR

Jormungandar, in Scandinavian mythology, is the fearful serpent that encompasses the whole earth. The offspring of Loki, it was hurled down by the gods into the ocean surrounding Midgard, where it will remain until Ragnarok (*q. v.*). It is so huge that it holds its tail in its mouth.

dreadful as Jormungandar

JOSE, DON

Don José, in Byron's *Don Juan,* is the father of the hero and the henpecked husband of Donna Inez, a bluestocking.

In Bizet's *Carmen,* Don José is a soldier and the jealous lover of the gypsy girl. Disgraced and jailed for abetting her in her activities with a ring of smugglers, he stabs her when she jilts him for Escamillo, a popular toreador.

goaded by jealousy like Don José

JOSEPH

Joseph, son of Jacob and Rachel, his father's favorite, to whom Jacob gave a coat of many colors, was so envied by his brothers that they sold him to Midian who in turn sold him into Egypt. There, in service to Potiphar, he angered Potiphar's wife by refusing her advances, was accused by her and imprisoned, but interpreted the dreams of the prisoners, and was finally summoned to interpret Pharaoh's dream. He was freed, elevated to a position to serve and to save his brothers and his father, and to "live in the favor of the Lord in the land of Egypt."

wearing a Joseph's coat

JOSEPH OF ARIMATHEA

Joseph of Arimathea was a rich Israelite who lived about 30 A.D. and secretly believed in Jesus Christ. He benevolently took the body of the crucified Christ and laid it reverently in his own tomb. He is supposed by some to have introduced Christianity into Britain, establishing a monastery at Glastonbury. According to late medieval legend, it was he who brought the Holy Grail to Montsalvat (see *Parsifal*).

as charitable as Joseph of Arimathea

JOSEPH, ST.

St. Joseph, the husband of Mary, is the patron of carpenters because he was of the same craft himself. In art he is represented as an aged man with a budding staff in his hand.

the guild of St. Joseph

JOSEPHUS

Flavius Josephus (A.D. 37-100) was a celebrated Jewish statesman and soldier who received Roman citizenship as a reward for his abilities by the grant of Vespasian and Titus. He wrote two sound historical works in Greek, the *Early History of the Jews* and a *History of the Jewish Wars* from the capture of Jerusalem by Antiochus Epiphanes in 170 B.C. to its capture in A.D. 70 by Titus.

another Josephus to record the sufferings of the Jewish people

---

JOSHUA

Joshua, successor to Moses as leader of the Children of Israel, led them at God's command across the Jordan, the waters of which parted for their passage, into the land of Canaan, where in one of the many conflicts with the Canaanites Joshua commanded the sun and the moon to stand still. "The sun stood still and the moon stayed until the people had avenged themselves upon their enemies." The name Joshua has become a synonym for the exertion or the assumption of superhuman power, and is sometimes used of one who can, or thinks he can, stop the unstoppable. The same Joshua took the city of Jericho by compassing it seven times with the sounding of trumpets and shouting, and the city walls fell flat.

need a Joshua to stop the wheels of time

JOSSE, MONSIEUR

Monsieur Josse is a silversmith and jeweler in Molière's comedy *L'Amour Médecin.* When asked by a friend consulting him as to the best way of curing a lady pining from love, he recommends a handsome present of jewelry, seeking to advance his own self-interests by disposing of some of his merchandise. The friend replies, "You are a jeweler, Monsieur Josse," intimating that his advice is not disinterested.

a Monsieur Josse at furthering his own interests

JOTUNHEIM

Jotunheim, in Scandinavian mythology, is the home of the giants, or Jotun, who personify the hostile powers of nature. One of the nine worlds, it is found in the northwest, where the ocean reaches the fringes of the universe. One of the roots of the ash tree Yggdrasil extends into it.

born and bred in Jotunheim

JOURDAIN, MONSIEUR

Monseiur Jourdain is the hero of Molière's comedy, *Le Bourgeois Gentilhomme.* He is represented as an elderly tradesman who suddenly acquires tremendous wealth and desires to emulate those brought up in the front ranks of society. Discovering that he has been speaking prose all his life, he wishes to give it the air of poetry and foolishly apes graces and accomplishments which cannot be easily acquired after the early part of life is past.

nouveau riche as M. Jourdain

JOVE

Jove, also called Jupiter and Zeus in classical mythology, is the father of the gods, king of gods and men, and ruler of the skies and the universe. He had supreme power over the heavens, controlled the rains (*Pluvius*) and all the phenomena of the sky. As *Tonans* he spoke in thunder, and as *Fulminator* he announced his decrees by lightning bolts. All the gods appealed to him for favor, which he dispensed with "joviality" or refused for disobedience. Juno, called by the Greeks Hera, was his sister-wife, and was extremely jealous of his extra-marital philanderings.

the all-ruling Jove

JOYCE, JAMES

James Joyce (1882-1941) was the brilliant Irish author whose prose works (*Portrait of the Artist as a Young Man, Ulysses,* etc.) have done more to influence the technique of twentieth-century literary style than those of any other writer. The possessor of a vast and labyrinthine vocabulary to which he added many new words culled from numerous languages or coined by himself, he also originated the "stream of consciousness" method of recording thoughts and impressions with the random, meandering course of a dream-monologue.

with Joycean invention
the vocabulary of a Joyce
has the analytical powers of a Joyce

JUAN, DON

Don Juan was a legendary courtier whose life was given over to the gay pursuit of pleasure; hence, the term Don Juanism indicates a refined libertinism. His adventures have been made the theme of operas, poems, and stories. Among the most fantastic of the stories is one recounting his visit to the tomb of a man he had killed, and his inviting the statue on the tomb to dinner. The statue, according to the story, came and carried Don Juan to hell. The name stands for loose living, libertinism, and recklessness.

faithless as Don Juan in love

JUBAL

Jubal, a descendant of Cain and the son of Lamech and Adah, is the reputed inventor of musical instruments, either the harp and the organ, or the lyre and the flute. His name is the Hebrew word for "blast of trumpets," and he is the patron of all musicians who play either of the instruments which he invented.

as tinkling as Jubal's harp

JUDAS

Judas was the disciple of Christ who went to the priests and offered, for thirty pieces of gold, to betray Christ to them. That night he came "with a multitude" and addressed Jesus and kissed Him, the sign that was to identify Him as the man to be taken before Caiaphas the High Priest. The "Judas kiss" has ever since meant the show of affection that is actually cover for dastardly betrayal. According to the Bible, "Judas with his money purchased a field, but therein fell and perished."

a Judas at the table

JUDITH

Judith is the heroine of a well-known book with her name in the Old Testament Apocrypha. A beautiful woman of Bethulia, she put both her life and her chastity in jeopardy by venturing alone into the tent of Holofernes, a general of Nebuchadnezzar's, with whom her native town was at war. She accomplished her purpose, assassination, and escaped with the head of Holofernes. Whereupon her fellow-townsmen, inspired by her courage, rushed upon the foe and routed them.

the cold courage of a Judith

JUDY

Judy is one of the inimitable and perennial pair, Punch and Judy, in the famous old puppet show wheeled about on a miniature portable stage. It was as much a part of London street life as the hurdy-gurdy was of the New York pavements. Judy is the wife, ridiculously and comically beaten by her grotesque and ugly husband Punch, to the never-ending delight of London street crowds of all ages.

had played Judy to his Punch long enough

JUGGERNAUT

Juggernaut, an uncouth image of the Hindu deity Krishna, a form of Vishnu, is dragged on festival occasions through the streets on a massive car with wide and terrible wheels, under which in a frenzy of fanaticism devotees throw themselves to be crushed. The name has come to be used in connection with persons who sacrifice themselves, or are ruthlessly sacrificed, to a cause that destroys them. It is often used of a custom or belief that demands victims.

sacrificed to the Juggernaut of filial duty

JUGURTHA

Jugurtha was the bastard grandson of Masinissa, king of Numidia. Ambitious, unscrupulous, and cunning, he had learned of the venality of many Roman generals and senators and aspired to be sole monarch of his country. This necesssitated his putting to death his two cousins, co-rulers, but he did not hesitate over the deed, feeling sure that he could buy off Rome. In the war that followed this violation of Roman honor he was successful at first, by bribing the consul for an easy peace. Finally he was, however, captured, brought to Rome to adorn the triumphs of Marius, the victor, and starved to death in a dungeon in 104 B.C.

Jurgurthan liberality in bribing

JUKES FAMILY

Jukes is the fictitious name of an actual family of Dutch extraction, whose history was written up in 1874 by R. L. Dugdale, a sociologist, in order to show the effects of defective heredity. Their members for several generations exhibited a high incidence of disease, abnormality, delinquency, poverty, and crime, and one of the original progenitors of this inferior breed, Ada Jukes, became known as "the mother of criminals." Their total cost to society over a span of 75 years was estimated at $1,308,000.

a clan approximating the fabulous Jukes in notoriety

JULIA

Julia was the daughter of Augustus and Scribonia, and the Roman Emperor's only child. Beautiful, sophisticated, and immoral, she was banished for her adulterous profligacies by her own father's stern legislation for marriage and against adultery. In 2 B.C. she was exiled to the tiny island of Pandataria off the Campanian coast and kept in disgraceful segregation until her death in A. D. 14. She had been married three times before her downfall, to Marcellus, Agrippa, and Tiberius.

a sinful Julia, trifling with the marriage vows

JULIAN

Julian, from Julius Caesar, is applied to the month of July, named in his honor. It also refers to the calendar he directed to be evolved, still used by the Eastern Church, and to the "Julian year."

outdated as the Julian calendar

JULIAN THE APOSTATE

Julian the Apostate, emperor of Rome from 361 to 363 A.D., was brought up with distaste for the Christian faith because of his consuming passion for the Greek classics. As monarch he endeavored to revive the pagan religion, thereby making himself extremely unpopular with Christians everywhere in the ancient world. He even wrote a satire *Against the Christians.* Bitter and aggressive, though a man of high moral character, he was killed during an expedition against the Persians. It was said that he was murdered by a Christian and that his last words were *Vicisti, Galilaee,* "Thou hast conquered, Galilean," but it is unfounded and seems like a vindictive fiction circulated by his spiritual antagonists.

as much a pagan and an anti-Christ as Julian

JULIET

Juliet is the central figure in Shakespeare's *Romeo and Juliet,* a story of the two single-minded, very young, very much in love members of two prominent feuding families in Italy. Their love is the subject of one of the most tender and romantic tales in literature; their tragic end is brought about in their attempt to elude the marriage Juliet's family had planned for her.

Juliet is conceded to be the perfect picture of youth, purity, passion, and girlish love.

fond and sad as Juliet

JUMALA

Jumala, in Finnish mythology, is the supreme god, invisible and all-governing. The deity of the air and heavens and the protector of flocks, he is often vaguely described without attributes or qualities to distinguish him as a person or individual. The name also means godhead in general, and as such can be used as a generic title for any deity.

as desolate and abandoned as Jumala's shrine

JUNG, CARL G.

Carl G. Jung (1875-) was the brilliant Swiss psychologist and psychiatrist who founded the analytic school and believed in studying the patient's present problem rather than in unearthing his childhood fixations. Dividing all people into two classes, introverts and extroverts, he was at variance with Freud in believing the libido (energy or driving force) to be not a manifestation of the sex instinct, but rather of the will to live. Among his distinguished books are *Psychology of the Subconscious, Studies in Word Association,* and *Modern Man in Search of a Soul.*

like Jung, he divides all humanity into two classes

JUNKER

The Junkers constituted a caste of Prussian aristocracy that was narrow-minded and reactionary. Selfishly devoted to maintaining their own social and political privileges, they comprised the military clique that supplied the German army with its highest commanders and officers. The young men were especially characterized by ostentatious arrogance, overbearing hauteur, and supercilious conceit, and any person exhibiting these traits may be called a Junker.

from his youth up a Junker of Junkers

JUNNER

Junner, one of the Scandinavian giants, is said by the poets to represent the "eternal principle." His skull forms the heavens; his eyes, the sun and moon; his shoulders, mountains; and his bones, rocks. Hence, heaven is known as "Junner's skull," and rivers as the "ichor of old Junner."

with the shoulders of Junner

JUNO

Juno, queen of heaven and jealous wife and sister of Jove, beautiful and courted, is the guardian of women, of national wealth, of war. Described by Homer as "she of the beautiful ox-eyes," and admitted to be all-powerful on Mount Olympus, she dealt out good and evil to the gods and goddesses according to whether they pleased or displeased her. To the Greeks she was known as Hera (*q.v.*).

regal Juno

Juno's unrelenting hate

JUPITER

(see *Jove* and *Zeus*)

JUSTINIAN

Justinian is from Justinianus (483-565), Emperor of the East, the man who compiled the best of the Roman laws, collecting all that had been good before and all that were new in his own day. These constitute Roman law, as it was received in all Europe.

new judge is a true Justinian

JUTURNA

Juturna was the nymph of a healing fountain in Latium, the waters of which were used in most Roman sacrifices. She was loved by Jupiter, who rewarded her with immortality and dominion over the waters, naming her the goddess of fountains. The *Lacus Juturnae,* or pool of Juturna, was located in the Roman forum between the temples of Castor and Vesta. Vergil, in the *Aeneid,* says that she was the sister of Turnus (*q.v.*).

loves the rippling waters like Juturna

JUVENALIAN

Juvenalian refers to burning invective and coarse satire such as that found in the sixteen satirical poems of Decimus Junius Juvenal, who lived in the 1st century A.D. He denounced the vices, abuses, and follies of Roman life with bitter indignation. A master of irony and of grim epigrammatic statement, and a pessimist who saw only the gray skies of life, he condemned the whole female sex and scorned the rich in tones of gross exaggeration. A social satirist writing with a serious purpose, he was admired and translated by Dryden, and Johnson's "London" is an imitation of Juvenal's critical lampooning of Rome.

scornfully ranting Juvenalian vehemence

JUVENTAS

Juventas was the Roman personification of youth and charm. The counterpart of the Greek Hebe (*q.v.*), she represented the radiant springtime of life as a graceful and lovely maiden.

with the youthful loveliness of Juventas

K

KA

KA is the unknown god, the inexplicable, in Hindu theology. Sometimes given as an epithet to Prajapati and Brahma, the name is also that of any independent deity or abstraction thereof. Any chief object of worship is thus one's Ka.

an inscrutable Ka to worship

KAABA

Kaaba, the Arabic word for a "square house," is the name of a shrine of Mecca, in the direction of which all Mohammedans turn to pray. It is said to have been built by Abraham on the spot where Adam first worshiped after his expulsion from Eden. In the north-east corner is a stone seven inches long, said to be a ruby sent down from heaven. From being kissed so often by devout but sinful man it is now black in color.

sacred as Kaaba

KABIBONOKKA

Kabibonokka, a North American Indian and the son of Mudjekeewis, was the Indian Boreas, who dwelt in Wabasso (the North). He paints the autumn leaves scarlet and yellow, sends the snow, binds the rivers in ice, and drives away the sea-gull, cormorant, and heron.

such a season as Kabibonokka sends for hunters

KALANOS

Kalanos was a Brahman gymnosophist (*q.v.*) who burned himself alive in the presence of Macedonians three months before the death of Alexander the Great (323 B. C.), whose approaching end he had predicted.

the foresight of a Kalanos

KALI

Kali is the goddess of destruction and the bloody consort of Siva, in Hindu mythology. Worshiped with obscene rites and human sacrifice, she was known as Kali the Black, and was represented as dripping with blood, festooned with snakes, and adorned with skulls. The fierce creature was also known as Durga the ten-armed.

like Kali, exulting in carnage

KALPA-TAROU

Kalpa-Tarou, in Hindu mythology, is "the tree of the imagination" from which may be gathered whatever a person desires.

all his wishes granted by Kalpa-Tarou

KAMA

Kama is the Hindu god of love. Corresponding to Cupid, he is usually pictured as a youth riding a parrot or a sparrow and carrying a bow of sugarcane, a bowstring of bees, and five arrows each tipped with a flower supposed to conquer one of the senses. Even the god Brahma acknowledges and succumbs to his power.

sweet as Kama's shafts
stung by one of Kama's bees

KAMADHENU

Kamadhenu, in Hindu mythology, is the fabulous cow that gratifies and grants all wishes.

enriched by Kamadhenu

KANTIAN

Kantian is from Immanuel Kant (1724-1804), a philosopher who believed in the supremacy of reason as the basis of morals and judgment, and in the transcendental nature of human understanding. He believed in God, freedom, and immortality, and held that activity of the mind is the basis of all civilization.

a Kantian disciple

KARENINA, ANNA

Anna Karenina, the tragic heroine of Tolstoi's novel by that name, embittered by a disappointing marriage to a much older man, seeks true romance with a young lover, but finds that too unsatisfying, and eventually takes her own life. The whole is a famous and dramatic story of a futile search for personal happiness; hence, unsatisfied, futile, frustrated, tragic.

disenchanted as Anna Karenina

KAROON

Karoon, or Korah, according to the commentators of the Koran, was the wealthiest and most beautiful of all the Israelites. It was said that he built a large palace, which he overlaid with gold. The Croesus of the Mohammedans, he guarded his wealth in a labyrinth.

as rich in gold as Karoon

KATERFELTO

Katerfelto was a celebrated quack or influenza doctor. A tall man dressed in a long black academic gown and square cap, in 1782 he exhibited in London his solar microscope, creating great and gullible excitement with it by merely showing the infusoria of muddy water in its lens. Katerfelto is now a generic name for any charlatan or impostor.

microscopic tricks as misunderstood as that of Katerfelto

KATHARINE

Katharine is the daughter of Baptista, the rich gentleman of Padua, in Shakespeare's *Taming of the Shrew.* Beautiful, rich, and young, she has so ill a temper that nobody will marry her. Petruchio of Verona, however, does so, and so subdues her imperious temper by his indomitable will and fantastic conduct that she becomes the model of a submissive wife. She even gives Bianca, her sister, most excellent advice concerning the duties of marital respect and obedience.

a brawling termagant to outdo Katharine

KAY, SIR

Sir Kay, a foster-brother of King Arthur, is a rude, boastful, envious knight of the kitchen in King Arthur's court, as recorded in Tennyson's *Idylls of the King.* His discourteous treatment of Sir Gareth, his insolence to Sir Lancelot, his treacherous trickery, all make him an unworthy knight.

every group is sure to have an occasional Sir Kay to stir up trouble

---

KEATS, JOHN

John Keats (1795-1821), the great English lyrist, wrote verse that ranked with Shelley's in exquisite melody, sheer beauty of fancy, and a certain joy of youth, enthusiasm for beauty, and delight in the sense of being. His theory that a thing of beauty is a joy forever, that beauty alone is assured of survival, colors all his own poetry, marked as it is by a beautiful imagery, romantic situation, and lyric perfection.

with the true Keats love of beauty
lost in a Keatsian world of color and beauty

KEDAR

Kedar, a son of Ishmael (*Genesis,* xxv, 13), is the eponymous ancestor of a tribe of Arabian nomads famous for their flocks and their tents, which became proverbial adornments of poetic and figurative speech. Thus, as in the following, *Kedar's tents* refers to houses in the wilderness of this world or to the world itself:

Ah me! ah me! that I
In Kedar's tents here stay.
No place like that on high:
Lord, thither guide my way.
Crossman.

In *Isaiah,* xxi, 16, these people are said to furnish mighty archers, and in xlii, 11, to inhabit villages, which were probably merely military encampments.

transient as Kedar's tents

KEDERLI

Kederli is an Arabian prototype of the dragon-slayer, the St. George of Mohammedan mythology. After slaying a ferocious monster to save a damsel exposed to its fury, he drank the water of life and rode about the world to bring assistance to all warriors who invoked him.

the superhuman aid of a Kederli

KELLER, HELEN

Helen Keller (1880-), after an illness in childhood, became deaf, dumb, and blind, but by means of the wisdom of her parents and the amazing understanding and skill of her teacher, Anne Sullivan Macy, she learned to understand, hear, and speak, and grew to become a force in the world, speaking, writing, and talking with a broader experience and knowledge than is accorded to the ordinary person. She has served on many philanthropic and charitable committees, has written articles and books, and has achieved in short an amazing demonstration of what intelligence and will can do toward overcoming what may seem a hopeless handicap.

the perseverance of a Helen Keller

KEMBLE, FANNY

Fanny Kemble (1809-1893) was a famous English actress in both comedy and tragedy, the highest representative of drama on the stage in her day, and immensely popular in the United States, where she was acclaimed and beloved almost beyond belief. Even to this day she is named by the critics as the acme of superb acting.

can never hope to reach the Fanny Kemble level

KEMPIS, THOMAS A

Thomas á Kempis (1380-1471) was a celebrated monk and mystic noted for the beautiful spirit of his personal life, and for the marvelous copies he made of religious books, including the Bible. His reputation now rests largely on his *Imitation of Christ,* a classic for people of all faiths, perhaps written but perhaps only transcribed by Thomas á Kempis. His name is synonymous with devout, mystic religious, spiritual, and self-sacrificing living.

a sort of Thomas á Kempis tract

KEPLER, JOHANNES

Johannes Kepler (1571-1630) was a somewhat mystical German astronomer, influenced by the Copernican principles. Though he also wrote on optics and approximated the law of refraction as well as doing some pioneer work in the invention of calculus, his most famous achievement was the formulation of the three laws of planetary motion, named *Kepler's laws* after him. Realistic enough to discover that the planets move in ellipses with the sun in one of the foci, he romantically supposed that they must also move according to musical intervals and geometric constructions, insisting that the arrangement of the universe must be congruent with some beautiful harmony.

hears the Keplerian music of the spheres

KETCH, JACK

Jack Ketch (died 1686) was a celebrated hangman and executioner, notorious for his barbarity, who lived in the time of James II and made himself universally odious by his butchery of Monmouth (1685) and of many other brave and noble victims of the "Bloody Assizes," in which about 300 persons were executed after short trials and about 1,000 more were sent as slaves to American plantations. Though some think the name to be a sobriquet derived from Richard Jacquett, the master of the manor of Tyburn near London, the place of execution, the name is probably original. According to Macaulay, it was given thereafter to all who succeeded him.

reveling in the carnage of Jack Ketch

KEVIN, ST.

St. Kevin, in Irish folklore and one of Thomas Moore's *Melodies,* was a chaste paragon of virtue who retired to an island where he vowed no woman should ever land to touch him. Kathleen, who loved him, tracked him to his place of retirement, whereupon St. Kevin hurled her from a rock to her death. Her ghost rose smiling from the tide and never left the place where the saint lived. A bed in the rock at Glendalough is known as the bed of St. Kevin.

woman-shy as St. Kevin

KEY, FRANCIS SCOTT

Francis Scott Key (1779-1843) was the American lawyer and patriot best known for his composition of *The Star-Spangled Banner,* the national anthem inspired by an experience during the War of 1812. Sent on a mission to exchange prisoners, he was detained by the British during their bombardment of Fort McHenry, the key to the defenses of Baltimore. At sight of the flag still flying over the fort on the morning following the attack, he scribbled the poem on the back of an envelope, just as the words came to him. The next day it was handbilled and distributed throughout the Chesapeake city. After the war he returned to his practice of law, and wrote no further noteworthy verse.

a unique inspiration like that of Francis Scott Key

KEYNE, ST.

St. Keyne's is the name of a well or spring at St. Michael's Mouth, Cornwall. It memorializes Keyna the Virgin, who by prayer created a body of water which has this tradition associated with it: "If the bridegroom drinks therefrom before the bride, he will be master of the house; but if the bride gets the first draught, the grey mare will be the better horse." A ballad of Southey's records how a groom, destined to be a henpecked husband, was tricked by his bride who had taken a bottle of the water to the church with her, so that all his post-ceremonial haste to get to the well before her was in vain.

drank of St. Keyne's before her spouse

KHAN, GENGHIS

Genghis Khan (spelled also Jenghis Khan) was a Mongol conqueror in Asia (1164-1227), known for his amazingly far-reaching schemes and intrigues involving the destinies of whole peoples in their scope. His operations included the invasion and subjugation of Persia. His most infamous devastation is recorded in DeQuincey's *The Flight of the Tartar Tribe,* and he appears again in modern tales, among them Harold Lamb's *Genghis Khan* and *Tamerlaine.*

emulating the expeditions of a Genghis Khan

KHAN, KUBLA

Kubla Khan (1216-1294), the grandson of Genghis, was the founder of the Mongol dynasty in China. He was both more humane than the Khans preceding him and less effeminate than those to follow. An ardent Buddhist, he made his religion that of the state, though he was interested in and tolerant of other religions as well. He chose as his capital the site of the city known today as Peiping. As patron of the arts and literature he made his love of splendor manifest in his sumptuous court, his costly entertainments, his magnificent winter and summer palaces, great hunting expeditions, etc. Marco Polo visited him with his father and uncle from 1275 to 1292. Coleridge's poem, named in his honor, still evokes the brilliance and romantic lure which history associates with him.

an imagination as splendid as that of Kubla Khan

KHARTAPHILOS

Khartaphilos, Pilate's porter, is said to have been the original Wandering Jew. When the officers were dragging Jesus out of the hall, he is said to have struck Him with his fist in the back and to have said, "Go quicker, man; go quicker." Whereupon Jesus replied, "I indeed go quickly, but thou shalt tarry till I come again." Khartaphilos later became a Christian and took the name of Joseph. At the end of every hundred years he falls into a trance or an ecstacy, upon which, when he recovers, he returns to the same state of youth he was in when he abused Jesus, being about thirty years of age. Thus living a perpetual life, he remembers periodically every circumstance of the death and resurrection of Christ, as he wanders over the earth.

as everlasting as Khartaphilos

KHAYYAM, OMAR

Omar Khayyam (died about 1123), the "tent-maker," was the well-known Persian poet, astronomer, and freethinker who was one of a group of eight appointed to reform the Moslem calendar. He published a series of astronomical charts and an algebraic system, but is best loved for his *Rubaiyat,* a collection of quatrains in which the 1st, 2nd, and 4th lines rhyme. Totaling 500 epigrams, some of them are traditionally mystic and pantheistic, while the majority, however, protest against the bigotry and austerity of the Sufis. Called "the Voltaire of the East" because of his delicate wit and his fine satire against the ignorant clergy of his religion, he praises wine, love, and all ephemeral earthly joys, but denounces inexorable fate. The whole poem is familiar to English readers through the fine translation by Edward FitzGerald, first published in 1859.

a Khayyamesque love for the delicate things that pass

KHEM

Khem is the Egyptian god of generation and reproduction, identified by the Greeks with Pan. As a procreative deity he naturally functioned also in the role of garden-god, as which he was represented under the form of an asp.

productive as Khem

KHUFU

Khufu, or Cheops, was the first king of the IVth (Memphite) dynasty of Egypt, and the traditional dates of his reign run from 2900 to 2877 B. C. According to Herodotus, he closed all temples, abolished sacrifices, and subjected his people to all kinds of misery in order to build the largest of the pyramids at Gizeh. Working the Egyptians in relays of 100,000 men every three months, he even put to sale the beauty of his daughter in order to finance the stupenduous project. The princess was said to have had enough money left over from the official contributions of her lovers to build herself a small pyramid.

as monumentally useless as Khufu's memorial

KIAK-KIAK

Kiak-Kiak, or god of gods, is the name of a Burmese idol worshiped in Pegu. He is destined to sleep for 6,000 years, after which he will awake and the end of the world will come.

drowsy as Kiak-Kiak

KIDD, CAPTAIN

Captain Kidd was a notorious pirate, commisioned by the British to sail out of New York to suppress piracy on the high seas. He went to the East Indies, and there became himself a pirate. Returning to New York with great plunder, he was reputedly bought and resold by some of the most famous of American financiers, and was himself executed for piracy in 1701. His deeds have been told and enlarged until he has become a superman, according to modern standards.

boys are at the Captain Kidd stage

KIEPERT, HEINRICH

Heinrich Kiepert (1818-1899) was the distinguished German cartographer, geographer, and philologist whose maps of the ancient world are familiar to every student of ancient times, of collegiate or of secondary school level. An authority on the Mediterranean "ancient circle of lands," he was also the author of *Travels in Asia Minor*, *A Textbook of Ancient Geography*, and many other scientific books. His most important collections of maps are found in the *Atlas of Hellas*, the *Atlas of the Ancient World*, and the *Atlas Antiquus*, the latter having been issued in the English, French, Russian, Dutch, and Italian languages, as well as in their native German.

with a fancy for map-making such as Kiepert's

KIERKEGAARD, SOREN

Soren Kierkegaard (1813-1855) was the melancholic Danish philosopher and theological writer who influenced such contemporary schools of social pessimism as that championed by Jean Paul Sartre in France and known as Existentialism. Of delicate and morbid temperament, the frustrated Kierkegaard maintained that all religion is a matter for the individual, and that the relation of that individual to God must involve suffering. He believed eternity to be more important than time, and sin worse than suffering. Man is an egoist bound to despair and unable to comprehend God with mere reason, since all thought ends in paradox. His most famous work, *Either-Or*, contains a discussion of the ethical and aesthetic sides of life. Ibsen modeled his character of Brand (in the play by that name) on him.

with morbid Kierkegaardian pessimism

KILKENNY CATS

The Kilkenny Cats come from the old story of two cats that, like the gingham dog and the calico cat, fought until they ate each other up except for their tails. The name is probably a remnant of an old satire based on a feud that destroyed the towns of Kilkenny and Irishtown.

like the remnants of the Kilkenny cats

fight like the Kilkenny cats

KILMANSEGG

Miss Kilmansegg is the heroine of *A Golden Legend*, by Thomas Hood. An heiress with great expectations and an artificial leg of solid gold, she represents something both alluring and repellent at the same time, something which only the most covetous would desire.

as dubiously promising as Miss Kilmansegg

KINDHART

Kindhart was a dentist by that name in the reign of Queen Elizabeth. He is mentioned by Rowland in his *Letting of Humours-Blood in the Head-vaine* and in Rowley's *New Wonder.* The name has since been used with jocular irony for any tooth-drawer.

the most painless Kindhart of his profession

KING LOG

King Log is a king who rules in peace and quiet, but who never makes his power felt. The allusion is to the fable of "The Frogs Desiring a King," in which the denizens of marsh and pool ask Jupiter for a king. He first throws them down a log of wood, but when they grumble at so inert and spiritless a monarch, he substitutes a stork or serpent, which immediately begins to devour them with unappeasable voracity. Finding that neither their liberty, property, or persons are secure under such a tyrant, they beseech Jupiter to send them another king. Instead of indulging their new desire, however, the king of the gods sent them this sententious message: "They that will not be contented when they are well, must be patient when things go amiss."

a reign as quiescent as that of King Log

KING OF YVETOT

King of Yvetot was the title assumed by the lord of a small municipality in France in the eleventh century. Béranger has made him a model potentate, a good monarch not known in history, but happier than any other. The title has since been metaphorically applied to any ruler of large pretentions but insignificant authority, a kind of historical nonentity.

authoritative as the King of Yvetot

KING PETAUD'S COURT

The Court of King Petaud is a kind of sanctuary where all are talkers with no hearers, all are kings with no subjects, all are masters and none servants. It derives its origin from an assemblage of beggars, who formerly held meetings under the presidency of the most adroit or the poorest among their number. This superior being took the title of King Petaud (from the Latin *petere,* to beg). The phrase also denotes a place of confusion, where everything is out of order and everybody is master, though nobody is able to make order.

as confused as the Court of King Petaud

KIPLINGESE

Kiplingese (Kiplingesque) is a name used of Rudyard Kipling's (1865-1936) dialect style in his stories of the British soldiers in India, *Soldiers Three, Barrack-Room Ballads,* and others. The English of Tommy Atkins in India, some critics thought it a low-brow style and ridiculed it mercilessly.

> "How Kipling would have
> changed Keats: 'St. Hagnes
> Heve! 'Ow bloomin' chill it
> was, The 'are with all, etc.
>
> From Aldrich's letter
> to Mark Twain.

KISTNERAPPAN

Kistnerappan is a water-deity of India, to whom persons at the point of death are carried for purification from all defilement. He pours a little water from the Ganges into the palms of their hands.

baptized by Kistnerappan

KIT-CAT CLUB

The Kit-Cat Club was formed in 1688 by the leading English Whigs of the day, and held its meetings in the Shire Lane house of Christopher Cat, a pastry-cook who supplied the mutton pies and after whom the club was named. Sir Godfrey Kneller painted forty-two portraits of the club's members, but in order to accommodate them to the rather diminutive dimensions of the club room, he had to make them only three-quarter length. Hence, a three-quarter length portrait is still called a kit-cat.

as reduced in size as the Kit-Cat Club

KITELY

Kitely is a rich city merchant in Ben Jonson's *Every Man in His Humour.* Uxorious in his affection for his wife and lavish in his generosity and esteem, he is at the same time extremely jealous of her.

a jealous old Kitely of a husband to dog her every step

KLAUS, PETER

Peter Klaus is the hero of an old popular traditional German tale. The prototype of Rip Van Winkle, he is represented as a goat-herd from Sittendorf, who leading his herd to pasture one day was silently beckoned to by a young man. Led into a deep dell enclosed by craggy precipices, he found twelve knightly personages playing at skittles in utter silence. Drinking from a can of wine which exhaled a delicious fragrance, Peter felt inspired with new life, but then sank into a deep and lethargic slumber. When he awoke, he found himself again on the plain where his goats were accustomed to graze, but none of them were in sight. Descending the mountain and entering the village, he found everything altered and new faces about him everywhere. At last by mutual inquiries he recognized a few of his former friends, much older now, who informed him that he had been asleep for twenty years.

couldn't have looked more different to Peter Klaus

KLINGSOR

Klingsor is the evil magician in Wagner's *Parsifal.* Barred from admission to the knighthood that guarded the Holy Grail, he gained possession of the sacred spear that had wounded Christ by having Kundry seduce Amfortas, chief of the knights. When Parsifal came to retrieve the spear, he foiled Klingsor's attempts at his undoing, and Klingsor and his enchanted castle were destroyed.

a kind of Klingsorian malice
spiteful as Klingsor

KNEIPPISM

Kneippism refers to the therapeutic methods for the treatment of diseases, mental and physical, preached and practiced by Sebastian Kneipp (1821-1897), Bavarian priest, hydropathist, and writer, known as Father Kneipp. A special feature of his hydrotherapy was based on walking barefoot over dewy grass. Known also as "Kneipp's cure," it stimulated the scientific investigation of more advanced curative effects of special baths and mineral waters.

like a Kneippist, loves to go barefoot

KNEPH

Kneph was the ram-headed deity of ancient Egypt, the local god of Thebes. Later identified with Amon, the god of reproduction, he was still further merged with the sun-god, Amen-Ra, "the father of gods, the fashioner of men, the creator of cattle, and the lord of all being." In this latter capacity he was represented as a man wearing the solar disk and two waving plumes on his head, and the ruins of Karnak represent the remains of his great temple. Identified by the Greeks with Zeus Ammon (of whom Alexander the Great claimed to be a descendant), he gave forth oracles at his shrine in the Libyan desert.

horns like Kneph's

KNICKERBOCKER

Knickerbocker is the name now given to New York and to New Yorkers, as well as to the population as a whole. Irving's famous *Knickerbocker's His-*

tory of New York purports to have been written by Diedrich Knickerbocker, an old Dutch Burgher. The name is still used of the old Dutch settlers, and the city itself was called "Father Knickerbocker."

the Knickerbocker aristocracy is all but gone today

KNOX, JOHN

John Knox (1505-1572) was the Scottish reformer, theologian, and writer who was opposed to clerical abuses in religion and preached for greater simplicity in worship. A royal chaplain in England until Mary Tudor's accession, he fled to Geneva where he met John Calvin. Returning to Scotland, he published several religious tracts, one of which, *Blast of the Trumpet against the Monstrous Regiment of Women,* offended Queen Elizabeth. Other works include a *Treatise on Predestination* and a *Book of Common Order,* the latter a prayer book. He inveighed against image-worship and called Mary Queen of Scots a Jezebel. He organized the Presbyterian Church in Scotland and wrote the *History of the Reformation.*

earnest as John Knox in his religious simplicity

KOHINOOR

Kohinoor, Persian for "mountain of light," is the name of the famous diamond fabled to bring ill-luck to its possessor. Its history involved many romantic stories since it was wrested from the Rajah of Punjab in 1849. Presented to Queen Victoria on the annexation of the Punjab in 1849, it is regarded figuratively as the most splendid and superb specimen of anything.

lustrous as the gem from Kohinoor

KORAH

Korah was the leader of the rebellion against Moses and Aaron in the desert (*Numbers,* xvi). His descendants constituted the guild of temple musicians, and eleven of the Psalms are attributed to his sons.

fomenting rebellion like Korah

KORAN

The Koran is the sacred book of the Mohammedans and the basis for their civil, religious, commercial, social, legal, and military regulations. In 114 *suras* or chapters, it professes to contain the personal revelations of the deity to Mohammed, each one of which may properly be called a Koran. Its contents consist chiefly of warnings, arguments in favor of specific doctrines, and narratives for enforcing morals. Its ideal is the day of judgment, and it includes realistic descriptions of the torments of hell and of the delights of paradise.

as full of warnings as the Koran

KOSCIUSKO, THADDEUS

Thaddeus Kosciusko (1746-1817) was the distinguished Polish patriot who offered his services to the Continental army in the American Revolution. He fought so valiantly at Yorktown and during the siege of New York that Washington appointed him colonel of engineers in charge of the fortification of West Point. Made brigadier general in 1783, he was awarded the order of Cincinnati, which carried the privilege of citizenship and an annual pension with landed estates. His charming manner made him one of the most popular of American officers. Returning to Poland, he was named dictator in charge of an unsuccessful rebellion against Muscovite tyranny. After imprisonment in Russia, he made another trip to America, then spent the rest of his life in France and Switzerland, plotting for the freedom of his native land. Shortly before his death he emancipated his serfs in order to demonstrate his belief in liberty, equality, and fraternity.

with the freedom-loving ardor of Kosciusko

KRAFFT-EBING, RICHARD VON

Baron Richard von Krafft-Ebing (1840-1902), German psychiatrist and physician, was the forerunner of Sigmund Freud and Havelock Ellis in the study of sexual aberrations and their causes. His *Psychopathia Sexualis* contains a series of case-histories of his clinical patients who suffered an interesting variety of erotic frustrations, fetishisms, and sadistic and masochistic perversions. Though now outmoded in its scientific approach and in the validity of its conclusions, it has made such absorbing reading for the layman interested in risqué and titillating subject matter that the very "forbidden" nature of the work itself was sufficient to send it into its 17th edition in 1924. It will probably always be found on the library shelves of those interested in *erotica curiosa.*

hastily shoving Krafft-Ebing under the pillow

KREISLER, FRITZ

Fritz Kreisler (1875-   ), Austrian-born virtuoso violinist and composer, has captured the love and admiration of the world by his wistful and nostalgic interpretations, freshness of charm, and gracious execution. A popular concert performer everywhere, always generous with his response to encores, he is already, though still living, a legend of indefinable distinction. His style is uniquely mannered and a blend of classical simplicity with the arch and flirtatious echoes from an atmosphere of Viennese cafés.

haunting as the music of Kreisler

KRIEMHILDE

Kriemhilde, a beautiful Burgundian lady, was the sister of King Gunther and the wife of Siegfried, King of the Netherlanders, on whom she brings ruin by a gossiping tongue. She tells Brunnhilde, Gunther's beloved, that it is Siegfried who has taken her ring and magic girdle, thus forcing her to come into Gunther's possession. This so enrages Brunnhilde that she prevails on Hagen the Dane to murder Siegfried. Next, Kriemhilde tattles to Hagen that Siegfried is vulnerable only in a spot between his shoulders, a hint which enables the Dane to slay her husband as he stoops to drink from a brook.

In Part II of the great epic Kriemhilde is bent on revenge, since in addition to slaying her husband, Hagen has also seized her treasure, the Nibelungen hoard, and buried it secretly beneath the Rhine. Marrying Etzel, King of the Huns, she invites Hagen and her brother Burgundians to visit her in Hungary. This is a mere snare, as a mêlée is provoked in the dining hall. It ends in the slaughter of all the guests except Hagen and Gunther, whose heads Kriemhilde promptly cuts off.

a vindictive Kriemhilde, quick to avenge her wrongs

KRISHNA

Krishna (the Dark One) was the eighth avatar, or incarnation, of Vishnu, the form in which that deity is the most popular object of worship in northern India. The son of a king, he was brought up amid lowly cowherds and milkmaids to save him from a massacre of the innocents. The many miraculous feats which he performed in his childhood form a large part of his legend. His flute music was thought to be the "call of the Infinite" to "leave all and follow me." The fact that he was killed by the wound of an arrow in his heel is akin to the single point of vulnerability found in semi-divine heroes of other countries and peoples (*e.g.*, Achilles' heel in Hellenic lore, and Siegfried's shoulder in Teutonic mythology).

flute-music as alluring as that of Krishna

KRISS KRINGLE

Kriss Kringle is a sort of St. Nicholas. On Christmas Eve, arrayed in a fur cap and strange apparel, he goes to the bedrooms of all good children, where he finds a stocking hung up in expectation of his visit. In it he leaves a present. The German *Pelznichel,* he is also the terror of the young, who propitiate him as a kind of Teutonic Mumbo-Jumbo.

gifts from Kriss Kringle or a whipping from the Pelznichel?

KROOK, MR.

Mr. Krook is the toper and dipsomaniac in Dickens' *Bleak House.* During a lifetime of Bacchic revels he has taken so much alcohol into his system that it ignites and he dies by spontaneous combustion.

a thirst second only to Mr. Krook's

KRUPP FAMILY

Friedrich Krupp (1787-1826), German ironmaster and founder of the Krupp Works at Essen, was the progenitor of the family that was to control the destinies, whether for war or for peace, of nearly all the countries of Europe up to our own time. His son Alfred (1812-1887) developed the process of casting steel and entered upon the manufacture of army ordnance, the Prussian military adopting his breech-loading rifle in 1861. Alfred's son, Friedrich Albert, continued the munitions monopoly, and at his death the German government allowed the husband of his only child, Bertha, to prefix the name *Krupp* to his own, so that this both proud and fearful name might not become extinct. The "Big Berthas" of World War I were named after this last direct descendant of the original founder.

a name as pregnant with history as Krupp

KU KLUX

The Ku Klux Klan is a secret organization originally founded to "control and affright" any one who violated civil, political, or personal rights of any people, but the organization, with too flexible a basis, itself became lawless and committed so many outrages that it was suppressed in 1872. It has sprung up again in one connection or another at various times since, and seems never to die out entirely. Attacking minorities, it fosters vicious prejudices and racial hatreds.

how the Vigilantes, the Ku Kluxes, the Molly Maguires do change color as time goes on

---

KUMARA

Kumara, the "ever youthful," is the celebrated Hindu war-god. One of the most famous Sanskrit poems concerns the legendary history of this god. Seven cantos of it have been translated into English verse by R. T. H. Griffith.

a belligerent young Kumara

KUNDRY

Kundry is the woman in Wagner's *Parsifal* who was doomed to eternal laughter because she had scoffed at Christ on the cross. Become a seductress under the spell of Klingsor, the magician, she corrupted Amfortas, the chief of the knights of the Holy Grail, causing the sacred spear which had pierced the side of Christ to pass into Klingsor's hands. When it was retrieved by Parsifal, who resisted her wiles, she was redeemed from her curse and sank lifeless, but absolved of her guilt.

cunning and seductive as Kundry

KUNIGUNDE

Kunigunde (died about 1039) was the wife of Henry II of Germany. A tradition says that she and her husband had both taken vows of chastity, and that she submitted to the ordeal of fire when her own reputation had been unjustly impugned. She is said to have vindicated herself by walking barefoot over hot irons without scathing herself. After her husband's death she withdrew from public life into a convent which she had founded, and devoted the rest of her life to pious works. For this and for her perfect chastity and virtue she was canonized in 1200.

as blameless and pure as Kunigunde

KUVERA

Kuvera, or Kubera, is the chief of the Yakshas, the ogres, demons, and gnomes of Hindu mythology. Dwelling in darkness, he is represented as being frightfully deformed and as riding in a car drawn by hobgoblins. Later, analogous to the Greek Pluto, he became the god of riches, subterraneous or otherwise.

as rich and as ugly as Kuvera

L

LABADISTS

The Labadists were a sect of 17th and 18th century Christian communists, followers of Jean de Labadie (1610-1674), a French Jesuit and pietist who became a Protestant and founded an ascetic community which did not long survive him. Gaining many adherents in the Netherlands, he was zealous in preaching a return to primitive Christianity.

as fervent as the Labadists in his piety

LABAN

Laban was the avaricious and covetous Syrian father-in-law of Jacob (*Genesis,* xxiv, 29-60). Laughing in his sleeve while bargaining with the simple Jacob, he attempted to deceive him by giving Leah instead of Rachel to be his wife, though he was punished for his duplicity by a dwindling flock and by Rachel's theft of his teraphim. Extremely obsequious in his courtesy, he typifies craft and double-dealing.

fraudulent as Laban

LABERIUS

Decimus Laberius (105-43 B.C.), outspoken Roman capitalist and writer of mimes, was a forthright political critic of Julius Caesar. His rebukes of the Dictator brought on him the disgrace of being ordered to appear on the stage as an actor in his own mimes. *Necesse est multos timeat quem multi timent* ("It is necessary that he whom many fear also be made to fear many") was one of his barbs at the despot, and when he spoke the line the eyes of every one in the audience stole toward Caesar.

with fearless Laberian candor

LA CHAISE, PERE

Père La Chaise, the most famous of Parisian cemeteries, was named after Francois d'Aix de la Chaise (1624-1709), Jesuit priest and confessor of Louis XIV, whose secret marriage to Mme. de Maintenon (*q.v.*) he promoted. The burial ground, opened in 1806, is situated on Mont Louis to the northeast of Paris, the site of a religious retreat to which he often retired. It is adorned with numerous sculptural works, commemorating the famous persons interred in it.

as full of marble statuary as Père La Chaise.

LACHESIS

Lachesis is the one of the Greek Fates who spins the thread of life, hence, controls and selects the experiences of a lifetime. See *Clotho* and *Atropos.*

while Lachesis sits, inscrutable, and spins

LACONIAN

Laconian is from Laconia, an ancient country in the south of Greece with Sparta as its capital. Like Spartan, it refers to the qualities of the Dorian inhabitants of the country who were famous for their plain living and their military machine. They were rigorous disciplinarians, frugal and austere in their habits. To them it was honorable to steal, but dishonorable to be caught at it. At their religious festival of the Gymnopaedia they sadistically flogged their young men to harden their bodies, and homosexuality was encouraged among them. On going into battle they were told to come back with their shields or on them (*i.e.*, dead). Like *laconic,* the word *Laconian* also refers to a terse manner of speaking.

the boorish manners of a Laconian

LADAS

Ladas was a runner famous for his fleet feet and was employed by Alexander the Great. He is mentioned in the works of Catullus, Martial, and others. The name has always connoted prize-winning speed and swiftness, and was given to Lord Rosenbery's English Derby winner in 1894.

a Ladas as swift as lightning

LADISLAW, WILL

Will Ladislaw is a clever but mediocre artist in George Eliot's *Middlemarch.* As the second husband of Dorothea Brooke, he succeeds in making her happy by gratifying her desire for joint intellectual achievement, a desire in which she had been frustrated by her first husband, a pedantic and self-centered cleric.

a Will Ladislaw, artistic enough to satisfy an ambitious intellectual

---

LAELAPS

Laelaps, in Greek mythology, was the storm-wind, personified as the swift dog which Procris received from Artemis (Diana) and gave to her husband Cephalus (*q.v.*). Zeus later turned it into stone, when it had overtaken the Teumessian fox which he sent to punish the people of Thebes.

ominous rumblings of Laelaps filling the skies

LAELIUS, CAIUS

Caius Laelius (born 186 B.C.), Roman consul and bosom friend of Scipio Africanus the Younger (*q.v.*), was surnamed *Sapiens,* "the Wise," because of his broad learning and philosophical depth. An eminent orator and litterateur as well, he is said to have ghost-written some of the comedies of his friend Terence. He is the principal speaker in Cicero's dialogue *On Friendship,* and according to that writer he and Scipio used to become "incredibly childish and . . . collect shells and pebbles on the beach" during their vacations at the seashore.

a Laelius to discourse wisely on friendship

LAENAS

Laenas was the name of a Roman family of the Popilian gens, noted for its sternness, arrogance of character, and cruelty. Caius Popilius Laenas, a consul in 172 B.C., was later special ambassador to King Antiochus of Syria, whom the Roman senate wished to dissuade from hostilities against neighboring Egypt. Just as Antiochus was ready to march on Alexandria, Popilius Laenas delivered the senate's instructions for the monarch to read and consider. With his cane he described a circle in the sand around the king, ordering him not to stir beyond it until he had given a satisfactory reply. Such self-assured temerity frightened Antiochus, who yielded at once to Rome's wishes.

with the bold haughtiness of a Laenas

LAERTES

Laertes is the fiery and impetuous son of Polonius and the brother of Ophelia in Shakespeare's *Hamlet.* In the combination of vengeance and death at the close of the play, he wounds Hamlet with a poisoned rapier. In the scuffle that follows they exchange foils inadvertently, and Laertes too is wounded. After an exchange of forgiveness Laertes dies repentant, and Hamlet follows.

Another Laertes, in Greek mythology, was the father of Ulysses (*q.v.*).

as rash as Laertes in the execution of vengeance

LAESTRYGONIAN

Laestrygonian refers to the savage race of cannibal giants encountered by Ulysses in the *Odyssey*. Having destroyed eleven of the hero's twelve ships, they proceed to kill and devour many of his comrades before the remnant succeeds in escaping. Antiphates and Lamus are mentioned as being kings of the Laestrygonians, and the ancient Greeks located them on the east coast of Sicily. The Romans, however, placed them in the south of Latium, in the neighborhood of Formiae, which they supposed to have been founded by Lamus, one of their kings.

with Laestrygonian bloodthirstiness

LAFAYETTE

The Marquis de Lafayette (1757-1834) was the French patriot and officer who withdrew from military service in his own country to aid the Americans in their Revolutionary War and was commissioned a major general in the Continental Army (1777). The intimate friend of George Washington, he promoted American interests in France and was influential in causing his own country to adopt the tricolor flag. A conservative liberal in favor of a constitutional monarchy, he abstained from politics in his post-American years because he was opposed to Napoleonic policies, though he was in command of the National Guard in the Revolution of 1830.

an international patriot like Lafayette

LAFITTE, JEAN

Jean Lafitte, celebrated French buccaneer and pirate, flourished from 1809 to 1821. The head of a band of privateers, he also found smuggling a lucrative trade. During the War of 1812 he divulged to the Americans the British plans for the attack on New Orleans, which many of his men aided the United States to meet and repel. After the war he established his freebooters' headquarters at Galveston, Texas, but they were attacked and destroyed by an American warship in retaliation for his capture and scuttling of a United States merchantman. He then transferred the scene of his activities to the Spanish main and disappeared mysteriously from history around the year 1825.

dreams of sailing the bounding main with Lafitte and his men

LAFONTAINE, JEAN

Jean de la Lafontaine (1621-1695), famous French writer of animal fables, *contes*, and poetry, was the intimate friend of Racine, Boileau, and Molière. Tales of his absent-mindedness abound in his biographers. When he was introduced to his own son by an unsuspecting third party, he said, "Ah, yes, I thought I had seen him somewhere!" He fought a duel with an admirer of his wife, and then proceeded to ask the rival to be sure to visit him at his home. It is said that he habitually went promenading with his silk stockings worn wrong side out. In the easy and sparkling narration of his fables, he says outrageous things in most polite and courtly fashion. A master of satire, he was much admired for the boldness of his political expressions and for his ingenious moralizing.

as clever as Lafontaine at disguising his criticisms under allegory

---

LAGADO

Lagado is the capital city of Balnibarbi in Swift's *Gulliver's Travels*. It is celebrated for its grand academy of researchers who try to extract sunbeams from cucumbers and to calcine ice into gunpowder. In his description of this fantastic scientific laboratory, Swift ridicules the speculative philosophers and the false and chimerical pretenders to science who were so common in his time.

nonsensical as Lagadonian research-problems

LAIS

Lais was a beautiful courtesan who was brought to Corinth from Sicily as a slave when only seven years old. As she matured, she was renowned for possessing the most beautiful figure of her age (c. 420 B.C.).

Another courtesan of the same name (c. 340 B.C.) was a rival of Phryne (*q.v.*) in beauty and was stoned to death by the women of Thessaly, who were jealous of her comeliness.

has the figure of Lais

LAIUS

Laius was the king of Thebes, husband of Jocasta, and father of Oedipus (*q.v.*), by whom he was unwittingly killed in spite of his efforts to avert destiny. Having learned from an oracle that he was fated to perish at the hands of his own son, he exposed Oedipus immediately after birth, with his feet pierced and tied together. The infant with "swollen feet" was found by a Corinthian shepherd, however, and raised as the son of that city's ruler. When Oedipus was grown and had learned of his fate, he rushed away from Corinth, thinking that his destiny for patricide and incest applied to the Corinthian king and queen. On the road from Delphi he found his real fate, killing Laius in a scuffle arising from an argument as to who was to turn out of the other's way on the narrow road, and proceeding on to blind marriage with his own mother.

no plan of a mere Laius can forestall fate

LAKSHMI

Lakshmi, the wife of Vishnu in Hindu mythology, is the goddess of fortune, prosperity, and abundance. She is also the luck or fortune, personified, of a king or kingdom. Elsewhere described as the goddess of beauty she is represented in art as being of a bright goiden color and as seated on a lotus. It is said that she was born from the sea of milk that was churned from ambrosia.

Lakshmi smiled on the attempt

LALAGE

Lalage, or "Chatterbox," was a common Greek name for a courtesan, and was used as a term of endearment for one who lisped coaxingly or prattled of love. The famous Horatian ode beginning *Integer vitae scelerisque purus* is dedicated to just such a Lalage, *dulce loquentem.*

adores his prattling Lalage

LALLA ROOKH

Lalla Rookh, in Thomas Moore's poem of the same name, is the daughter of the emperor of Delhi, who on her splendid wedding-journey to Kashmir to meet her husband-to-be, Aliris, the Sultan of Bucharia, is escorted and entertained by a young Persian poet named Feramorz. To amuse and divert her royal progress he relates to her the four poetical tales that make up the bulk of the work. She falls intensely in love with him, and by the time she reaches the glittering towers and palaces of the lovely vale of Kashmir, she would prefer to fly to the desert with the romantic bard. He, however, has disappeared, as heart-broken she is ushered into the presence of her betrothed. Agreeably surprised, she discovers him to be her young lover, who had assumed the gallant disguise of escort in order to win her love without any aid of royal rank.

as perfect an ending as the love of Lalla Rookh

LAMARCKIAN

Lamarckian refers to the evolutionary theories of the Chevalier de Lamarck, Jean Baptiste (1744-1829), a forerunner of Charles Darwin. This distinguished French naturalist, botanist, and student of medicine discovered that changes in environment cause corresponding structural changes in animals and plants by inducing new or increased use of certain organs and parts and by adaptive modification of others leading to disuse and eventual atrophy. Detecting the principles of inheritance, he also maintained that all such acquired characters can be transmitted to offspring. He, too, was responsible for the classification of animals into vertebrates and invertebrates.

with a Lamarckian flair for detecting the effects of environment

---

LAMB, CHARLES

Charles Lamb (1775-1834), a clerk in the South Sea offices, close friend of Wordsworth and Coleridge, was a "child of London" who loved it so much, its theatres and its shops and its crowds, that he could not be persuaded to leave it even for a day. At his desk he jotted down the pleasant wanderings of his mind on any subject that at the moment occurred to him, in a style ruminative, chuckling, pleasant, easy, and inimitable, the whimsies of a mind amusing itself between tasks, essays so charming that they have become a pattern for pleasant familiar writing ever since. He frequently collaborated with his sister, Mary (*Tales from Shakespeare*).

every man ought to number one Charles Lamb among his friends, for the good of his soul.

LAMIA

Lamia was a mythological female phantom whose name was used as a bugbear to frighten children. A Libyan queen of great beauty, and beloved by Jupiter, she was robbed of her children by the jealous Juno, whereupon she embarked upon a career of murdering other people's children. Become a fearful fiend, she had the ability to take out her eyes and put them in again at will. She is the subject of a poem by Keats. In a later age, a belief arose in a plurality of Lamiae, handsome specters with the head and breasts of a woman and the body of a serpent. By voluptuous enticements they lured young men to them in order to feed upon their flesh and suck their blood.

with the fatal allure of Lamia
a Lamian vampire

LAMMLE, ALFRED

Alfred Lammle is the fortune-hunting sharper and swindler in Dickens' *Our Mutual Friend.* He and Sophronia Akershem marry, each having been tricked into believing the other wealthy, and each being disappointed in his expectations.

an Alfred Lammle to smell out her money

LAMOTTE, COMTE and COMTESSE

Comte Marc de LaMotte (1754-1831) and his wife Jeanne (1756-1791) were French adventurers involved in the affair of the Diamond Necklace. As mistress of Cardinal de Rohan, the Comtesse de LaMotte, posing as an intimate of Marie Antoinette, induced her lover to purchase a necklace consisting of 155 large diamonds, knotted together by 747 small ones, in order to secure the Queen's favor. Delivered to the Comtesse on Feb. 1, 1785, it thereupon vanished from sight, its stones turning up subsequently in small packages in England and throughout France.

When the jewelers who had made the necklace complained to Queen Marie Antoinette for payment, the Cardinal was arrested and brought to trial, but was acquitted. The Comtesse, though condemned to be flogged, branded, and imprisoned, managed to escape from confinement. Her husband, who had disappeared, was believed to have taken the jewel cache to England. And, at the bottom of the mystery, Cagliostro (*q.v.*), an Italian impostor who was somehow connected with the plot, was confined in the Bastille for one year in punishment for complicity.

a jewel theft as mysterious as the LaMotte affair

LANCELOT

Lancelot, chief among King Arthur's Knights of the Round Table, the "flower of chivalry," the most trusted, the bravest and most invincible of all the knights, was sent by King Arthur to meet and escort his royal bride Guinevere on her journey from her father's kingdom to Arthur's court. He fell in love with Guinevere, and she, having on his approach to her retinue believed him to be Arthur, had "let her heart go forth to meet him." At first faithful to Arthur, their love for each other was nevertheless conscious and finally declared, and the Round Table, with all its principles founded in honor, dissolved therefore. The story is told in Malory's *Morte d'Arthur*, and in more recent form in Tennyson's *Idylls of the King*, and is referred to in innumerable tales. The tournaments, journeys, and the court scenes all emphasize the courtliness of Lancelot, as well as the agony of his conflict between devotion to the king and love for the queen, and his anguish of guilt.

a chivalrous Lancelot

LAND OF NOD

The Land of Nod is the state or condition of drowsy slumber, represented as a place which people visit in their dreams. The reference may be drawn from the description of the conduct of the first murderer in *Genesis*, iv, 16: "And Cain went out from the presence of the Lord, and dwelt in the land of Nod." In this passage Nod seems to mean a vagrant or vagabond, as when Cain was driven out he lived a nomadic life, with no fixed abode, until he built his city.

aimlessly wandering in the Land of Nod

LAND O' THE LEAL

Land o' the Leal is the Scottish Dixey land, a hypothetical country of happiness, loyalty, and virtue. Caroline Oliphant so designated heaven in her song of that name, and this is now its accepted meaning, inasmuch as it is a place to which only the *leal,* that is, the "loyal," may aspire.

elected by merit to the Land o' the Leal

LANGUISH, LYDIA

Lydia Languish, the romantic and fashionably languishing young girl in Sheridan's comedy *The Rivals,* is determined to marry only a penniless unknown youth who will elope with her. It is her protest against the conventional "fortunate" marriage her family has arranged for her with a person she has never seen. Following the eighteenth century pattern of a double identity, Sheridan makes her penniless and devoted lover, Ensign Beverly, in reality the Captain Jack Absolute she is supposed to marry. Lydia's rage at the deception, her petulance, her general sixteen-year-old behavior leads young Absolute a merry chase.

she's a romantic young Lydia Languish

LANTERN LAND

Lantern-Land is the land of literary charlatans, the inhabitants of which are graduates in the arts, doctors, professors, prelates, etc., in Rabelais' *Pantagruel.* The author designates as inmates of this country the divines attending the Council of Trent who wasted their time in great displays of learning to little profit. Hence, to "lanternize" means to spend one's time in learned trifles.

a bit of vaporous research of the kind conducted in Lantern-Land.

LAOCOON

Laocoön was a son of Priam and Hecuba, and a Trojan priest. He opposed the reception of the Wooden Horse into Troy, believing it some ruse on the part of the Greeks, whom Vergil has him describe in the famous words *timeo Danaos et dona ferentes* ("I fear the Greeks even when they bear gifts"). For flinging his spear at the Horse he and his two sons were killed by two sea-serpents, which first entwined the boys and then involved and crushed their father as he was endeavoring to rescue them. His death was regarded as due to his impiety to the Horse, sacred to Athena who favored the Greeks. One of the most famous sculptural groups of antiquity depicts his cruel death.

as involved as Laocoön
Laocoöntian agonies

LAODAMIA

Laodamia was the daughter of Acastus and the wife of Protesilaus, the first Greek to spring ashore at Troy despite the fact that he knew it meant instant death. According to one version of this perfect love story, Laodamia begged the gods to allow her a three-hour interview with her dead husband, at the end of which she accompanied him to the lower world. Another version says that after his death she had an image made of him, which she always kept in her sight. A slave detected her embracing it, and supposing it to be a lover informed her father, who had it burned to divert her from her grief. Whereupon, she is said to have cast herself into the flames, inconsolable in her bereavement.

as devoted to her husband as Laodamia

LAODICEAN

The Laodiceans were originally members of the Christian church who were scorned because they were "neither hot nor cold, but lukewarm." Persons who are indifferent to things spiritual, casual about their blessings and their good fortune, and completely absorbed with their own possessions, with no need for anything else, are still called Laodicean.

a fatal Laodicean attitude

LAOMEDON

Laomedon was the father of Priam and the founder and king of Troy. He bargained with Apollo and Neptune to build his city walls, but when the task was completed he failed to pay the promised reward. In punishment, Neptune sent a sea-serpent to ravage his land, and a maiden chosen by lot had to be sacrificed to it periodically. When it came the turn of Hesione, Laomedon's own daughter, he bargained with Hercules to save her, but again defaulted on his agreement. Consequently, Hercules killed him.

perfidious trickery worthy of Laomedon

LAO-TSE

Lao-tse (604-531 B.C.), the founder of Taoism, was the great Chinese philosopher and moralist who formulated the liberal religion that in later times degenerated into a system of magic. His practices stressed good conduct and righteousness, and belittled the significance of empty ceremonies and rituals. Especially popular among the common people, his religion resembled Quietism in the simplicity of its social and political organization.

with the piety and simplicity of Lao-tse

LAPHAM, SILAS

Silas Lapham is the hero of W. D. Howell's novel (1885), *The Rise of*

Silas Lapham, depicting the rise and decline of a typical self-made American business-man.

a self-made Silas Lapham

LAPITHAE

The Lapithae, or Lapiths, were monstrous giants inhabiting the mountains of Thessaly. They defeated the Centaurs, a hybrid race of creatures, half-man and half-horse, at the wedding feast of Pirithous, their king, and were said to have invented bits and bridles for horses.

gigantic as a Lapith

LAPUTA

Laputa is a flying island inhabited by scientific quacks and speculative philosophers, and is described by Swift in *Gulliver's Travels.* These dreamy and wool-gathering savants are so absent-minded and engrossed in their imponderable thoughts that they employed attendants called "flappers" to flap them on the mouth and ears with an inflated bladder when their attention was to be called from "high things" to vulgar, mundane affairs.

a Laputan endeavoring to extract sunbeams from cucumbers

LARA

Lara, in Lord Byron's poem of the same name, is the assumed name of Conrad, the Corsair. Represented as a chief long absent from his own domains, he returns at length, squired by a single page. Dark hints and surmises are made against him by Sir Ezzelin, a noble whom he encounters at Lord Otho's banquet, and who seems to have some knowledge of how Lara spent the time of his prolonged absence. Most opportunely for the reputation of Lara, Ezzelin disappears at the very time when he should have substantiated his innuendoes. A peasant, however, is witness to the concealment of a corpse on the night of Ezzelin's disappearance, and the reader is left to draw his own conclusions. Proud and ascetic, Lara then heads a rebellion, and is eventually shot by Lord Otho.

insinuations as dark as those against Lara

LARES

The Lares are the spirits of ancestors, the protectors of state and of families, and the gods of the Roman household, guarding its fortunes if propitiated by a proper shrine and proper respect and ceremony, otherwise visiting evil upon the state or the family. The Penates were the household gods, their images set in the entrance of dwellings. Lares and Penates have now come to mean the possessions dear to a family. One may lose his home, move away, but he takes his Lares and Penates with him.

our Lares and Penates established in a new setting

LAROUSSE, PIERRE

Pierre Larousse (1817-1875) was a distinguished French lexicographer and encyclopedist. With a grammarian's zeal he edited improved textbooks for school instruction and a journal for teachers. He is best known today, however, for his comprehensive and monumental *Grand Dictionnaire* of the French language, and his name suggests the precise and informational definitions found in dictionaries.

with a knowledge as encyclopedic as Larousse's

LARUNDA

Larunda, daughter of Almon, was the nymph who informed Juno of the love affair between Jupiter and Juturna (*q.v.*). In punishment, Jupiter silenced her by depriving her of her tongue. He then ordered Mercury to conduct her to the lower world, but on the descent the messenger-god fell in love with her and made her the mother of the two Lares (*q.v.*). Though the silent goddess of the underworld, she became, as supposed mother of the Lares, the benefactress of the Romans.

more silent even than Larunda

LARVAE

(see *Lemures*)

LA SALLE, ROBERT

Robert Cavelier de La Salle (1643-1687) was the famous French explorer, settler, trader, and adventurer in America. Having made an expedition to Lake Ontario and claimed to have discovered the Ohio River, he sailed down the Mississippi as far as the Gulf of Mexico, conferring the entire valley on his monarch, Louis XIV, and naming it Louisiana in his honor. He returned to France to organize a colonizing expedition to the New World, landed by mistake at Matagorda Bay, Texas, and was murdered by his own men on his way to the mouth of the Mississippi.

intrepid as La Salle in journeying into the unknown

LATINUS

Latinus, the eponymous ancestor of the Latin race, was the son of Faunus and king of the Laurentians, a people of Latium, in ancient Italy. The father of Lavinia, he had betrothed his daughter to Turnus, aboriginal king of the Rutulians, but when Aeneas arrived in Italy he favored him as son-in-law because he had been warned by a divine oracle to give Lavinia in marriage to a stranger who would come. Latinus, consequently, offered an alliance to the Trojan hero but was overridden by his queen, Amata, and other Latin chieftians. Aeneas, therefore, had to win the Italian princess by the protracted warfare that is the subject of the last six books of Vergil's *Aeneid.*

as obedient to a warning as Latinus

LATONA

Latona, or Leto, was the daughter of the Titans Coeus and Phoebe. Loved by Jupiter, she conceived Apollo and Artemis (Diana), but, as the time for her delivery approached, no land would receive her from fear of Hera's jealousy of her divine husband's dalliance with Latona. Consequently, Ortygia (later named Delos), then a floating island, was secured to the bottom of the Mediterranean by anchor to provide a safe place for the birth of her divine twins. When some Lycian rustics later insulted her as she knelt with the infant deities in her arms to quench her thirst at a small lake, she changed them into frogs. Proud and imperious, she resented Niobe's boast of superiority in number of children (the latter had seven sons and seven daughters), and had them all slain by the arrows of her twins.

a Latona-like avenger of insult

LATUDE, JEAN HENRY

Jean Henry Latude (1725-1805) was a dissipated French army officer who played a hoax on Mme. de Pompadour in order to make himself a hero in her eyes. Sending her an infernal machine or a box of poison, he then apprised her of a supposed plot against her life. When his ruse was detected, he was sent to the Bastille without trial for thirty-five years of imprisonment, marked by several escapes and returns to incarceration (1749-1784). At the outbreak of the French Revolution he was finally liberated and voted a pension to requite him for this great injustice. The heirs of Mme. de Pompadour were also compelled to pay him an indemnity of 60,000 francs.

unjust as the punishment of Latude

LAUNCE

Launce is the foolish servant of Proteus and a punning clown in Shakespeare's *Two Gentlemen of Verona.* He addresses amusing reproaches to Crab, his ill-natured dog.

an amusing Launce-like punster

LAUNFAL, SIR

Sir Launfal was the steward of King Arthur who retired in poverty to Carlyoun because of his intense dislike for Queen Gwennere (Guinevere). In a forest there he met the fair Tryamour, who gave him an inexhaustible purse and promised to come to him whenever he needed her help. Returning to court with his great wealth, he was again tempted by Gwennere, who on being repulsed told Arthur that he had insulted her person by comparing her unfavorably with Tryamour. When Arthur told him he would be burned alive unless he produced this paragon of women, Tryamour came to his rescue. Set at liberty, Launfal accompanied his mistress to the isle of Oleron, and no man ever saw him more. He is the subject of a metrical romance by Chestre (1430) and his name is used for the hero of Lowell's *Vision of Sir Launfal.*

riches as unfailing as Sir Launfal's

LAURA

Laura was the lovely lady from Avignon celebrated by Petrarch in his sonnets and in some of his other poems. He saw her first in 1327, and from that time adopted her beauty as the theme of his songs. Tradition says she was Mme. Hugues de Sale, and that she died of the plague in 1348. The name is used of any beautiful woman who is the subject of praise in poetry.

celebrates a new Laura with every change of scene

LAURENCIN, MARIE

Marie Laurencin (1885-) is the distinguished French modernist painter. Her art is the quintessence of femininity and has earned her the title of the Sappho of painting because of the ethereal daintiness of her subjects. Women are almost her exclusive interests, and she paints them with large black dots for eyes and noseless faces. Somewhat narcissistic, she has used herself frequently as model. She has designed decorations and costumes for the *Comédie Française* and for Diaghilev's *Ballets Russes.* Her ladies, alluring in pastel pinks and blues, are reproduced on the powder boxes and perfumes of expensive lines of cosmetics.

as dainty and fragile as a Marie Laurencin

LAURIE, ANNIE

Annie Laurie, the famous and beautiful daughter of Sir Robert Laurie, was made the subject of a love-lyric by William Douglas, a song so beautiful in its melody, so haunting in its beauty, and so deeply lovely in its feeling that it has become one of the most famous and beloved of universal love songs. *Annie Laurie* is now used of any rarely lovely maiden who can inspire so deep and tender an emotion.

a maid to inspire an Annie-Laurie devotion

LAVERNA

Laverna was an ancient Roman spirit of the underworld who later became the protectress of thieves and impostors because she was friendly to all operations that occur in the darkness. At her altar on the Aventine hill and in her grove on the Via Salaria, robbers invoked her aid to enable them to carry out their plans successfully without losing their reputation for piety and honesty. The gate known as the Porta Lavernalis was named after her, and her own name may be derived from the Latin *levare,* in the sense of "shoplift."

blessed by Laverna in all his clandestine goings-on

LAVINIA

Lavinia was the daughter of Latinus and Amata, the rulers of ancient Latium, and the second wife of Aeneas. Previously betrothed to Turnus, king of the aboriginal Rutulians, she was the innocent cause of the dissension that led to the long war between the Trojan immigrants and the indigenous Italian people. The story is told in the last six books of Vergil's *Aeneid.*

as fought over as Lavinia

LAVOISIER, ANTOINE

Antoine Lavoisier (1743-1794), the French founder of the science of modern chemistry, was in turn director of the gunpowder works of his country, farmer-general, and member of the commission to establish a uniform system of weights and measures. He also composed the system of nomenclature at the basis of modern chemical terminology, explained the process of combustion, and conducted many quantitative experiments. Arrested by the Revolutionary Convention, he was guillotined.

an embryonic Lavoisier among his test tubes and beakers

LAWRENCE, D. H.

David Herbert Lawrence (1885-1930) was the distinguished British novelist and poet whose outlook and style were deeply influenced by his study of psychoanalytical doctrines. *Sons and Lovers,* one of his most famous novels, is a melancholy study of the effects of a mother-complex on an impressionable young man. Another work, *Lady Chatterley's Lover,* though a searching study of erotic frustrations and fixations, has been widely banned for pornography. The author's psychological researches are contained in his *Fantasia of the Unconscious* and *Psychoanalysis of the Unconscious.*

the neurotic sexuality of a character by D. H. Lawrence

LAWRENCE OF ARABIA

Thomas E. Lawrence (1888-1935), known as Lawrence of Arabia, was the British explorer, soldier, and writer who learned colloquial Arabic during a walking trip through Syria. Because of the great confidence which he inspired in the Arabs, he led their revolt against the Turks in 1917 and was such a master of guerrilla tactics that he won the sobriquet of "El-Orens, destroyer of engines." Later disgusted with Allied failure to make good on their moral obligations to the Arabs, he changed his name to Shaw and withdrew into a secluded private life to write *The Seven Pillars of Wisdom* and *Revolt in the Desert.* Shortly before his death in a motorcycle accident he published his fine prose translation of the *Odyssey.*

another Lawrence of Arabia, betrayed in his commitments

LAWRENCE, ST.

St. Lawrence was the Christian martyr killed in the persecution by Valerian in A.D. 258. When called upon to exhibit the ecclesiastical treasures entrusted to his keeping, he produced the church's poor people. Sentenced to be burned alive on the gridiron, he addressed the judge ironically in the midst of his agonies and said, "I am roasted enough on this side; turn me around and eat me." His festival falls on August 10 at approximately the time at which the meteorites known as "the tears of St. Lawrence" appear in the sky, and in England alone some 228 churches have been dedicated to him.

a St. Lawrence to befriend the poor

LAZARILLO DE TORMES

Lazarillo de Tormes is the roguish hero of the earliest Spanish picaresque novel, formerly attributed to Diego Hurtado de Mendoza (1553) and somewhat in the *Gil Blas* style. Its object is to satirize all classes of society. Lazarillo is a light, jovial, audacious man-servant who sees his masters in their undress and exposes their foibles.

a Lazarillo of the bed-chambers

LAZARUS

Lazarus is the name most commonly used for the beggar in the parable of the rich man and the beggar at the gate. The parable relates that the rich man, having died and being in torment, beseeches that Lazarus, having died and being in bliss, might bring him water to cool his tongue, and might appear to the rich man's family to tell them of the need for generosity and virtue. He is told only that "if his family had not listened to Moses and the prophets, neither will they be persuaded, though one rise from the dead." Lazarus is also the brother of Mary and Martha, the one who sickened and died, and whom Jesus, late a guest in their house, returned to restore to life. References to both stories are frequent.

poorer than Lazarus

LEAH

Leah was the daughter of Laban (*q.v.*) and became Jacob's first wife through a ruse (*Genesis*, xxix, 32). The mother of six sons and one daughter, she is styled as one of the builders of Israel (*Ruth*, iv, 11) because of her fruitfulness.

a substitute wife like Leah

LEANDER

(see *Hero and Leander*)

LEAR

Lear, from *King Lear*, in Shakespeare's play of that name, was the great king who hit upon the unwise idea of giving away his kingdom to his three daughters while he still lived. Depending upon their affection to maintain him in regal honor, he determined the degree of that affection and the consequent importance of their shares by their own statement of affection. Disappointed and angered when his favorite daughter Cordelia answered only that she "loved him as a daughter should love a father," he bestowed the kingdom on the effusive and calculating Goneril and Regan, with the resulting tragedy of their neglect, abuse, and repudiation and his own desolation and death.

unhappy as Lear
mistaken as Lear
with the tragic faith of a Lear
a disillusioned Lear

LEATHERSTOCKING

Leatherstocking, also called Natty Bumppo, is the chief character in Cooper's five novels known as the *Leatherstocking Tales.* In the *Deerslayer* he is the young rifleman, and in *The Prairie* the old trapper, but always the romantic hero of frontier America, stepping from one hair-raising adventure to another in a series of events that are still exciting to read. Many a *Superman* story could be made from the tales of *Leatherstocking.*

yearning to be a Leatherstocking hero
no Leatherstocking ever tread more silently

LEDA

Leda was the daughter of Thestius and the wife of Tyndareus. Jupiter fell in love with her and visited her amorously in the guise of a swan, so that it was assumed that her children (Castor and Pollux, Helen of Troy, and Clytemnestra) issued from the two eggs she brought forth after her amour with the god. The subject of *Leda and the Swan* was very popular to Renaissance painters and has been favored ever since by artists who employ classical subjects.

as seductive as Leda
as fond as Leda was of birds

LEE, ROBERT E.

Robert E. Lee (1807-1870) was the commander-in-chief of the Confederate armies in the American Civil War and served as military adviser to Jefferson Davis. Defeated at Gettysburg in the great battle of July 1st to the 4th, 1863, he continued to plan brilliant defensive strategies for his inferior forces until he was compelled to surrender to Grant at Appomattox Court House in 1865. Washington College, of which he was president from the close of the war till his death, renamed itself Washington and Lee University in his honor. His name still connotes the courteous and gallant aristocracy of the old South.

with the gracious hospitality of Robert E. Lee

LEGREE, SIMON

Simon Legree is the heartless slave-driver and overseer of a plantation in Harriet Beecher Stowe's *Uncle Tom's Cabin,* a story of slavery. The name has come to be used of any cruel, unfeeling taskmaster driving his employees or others under his control beyond reasonable or possible exertion.

the Simon Legrees of industry have long since fled to cover

LEIBNITZIAN

Leibnitzian refers to the philosophy and works of Baron Gottfried von Leibnitz (1664-1716), the famous German discoverer of differential calculus and student of theology, natural science, law, politics, history, and philosophy. His *Systema Theologicum* is an attempt to find common ground between Catholicism and Protestantism, while his *Theodice* contains a discussion of the problem of evil and a defense of the facile type of optimism that was ridiculed by Voltaire in *Candide.* A friendly rival of Newton, he is perhaps better known for his philosophical axiom *nihil nisi intellectus ipse,* "nothing except the intellect itself" (*i.e.* the nature of the faculty of thought determines the nature of thought).

Leibnitzian defense of this as the best possible world

LEIGH, AURORA

Aurora Leigh, the heroine of Elizabeth Barrett Browning's poem of the same name, is "the representative of the spiritual and aesthetic spirit of the age, through whom are exemplified the noble ends and the high office of true art."

as artistically representative as Aurora Leigh

LEILAH

Leilah and Mejnoun are a pair of model lovers in Persian romance. Leilah is the type of feminine beauty, chastity, and ardent affection, whose love for Mejnoun compares with that of the bride for the groom in the *Song of Solomon.*

In Byron's *The Giaour,* Leilah is a beautiful slave girl, the concubine of Hassan, the Caliph of the Ottoman Empire. She flees from the seraglio with her paramour, the infidel Giaour, is overtaken by an emir, and cast into the sea in punishment.

like Leilah yearning for her Mejnoun

LELEGES

The Leleges, descended from an Egyptian ancestor, Lelex, were an ancient marauding race of raiders who, along with the Pelasgians, were reputed to have been the most ancient inhabitants of the islands of the Aegean Sea and

Caria and of continental Greece. A warlike and migratory people, they made their living by piracy.

as prehistoric as the Leleges

LEMNIAN

Lemnian refers to the island of Lemnos in the north Aegean Sea. The proverbial phrase *Lemnian deeds* alludes to actions of unusual barbarity and cruelty, and arose from two horrible massacres perpetrated by the residents of the island. The first was the murder of all the men and male children by the Lemnian women, because they had discovered that their husbands liked the Thracian women better than themselves. The second was the slaughter of all children born of Athenian mothers and Lemnian fathers, and was prompted by the men's suspicion of the children's habit of speaking the Attic dialect. Lemnos was also the center of the cult of Hephaestus (Vulcan), because it was on that island that the god fell when Zeus hurled him out of heaven.

atrocious Lemnian inhumanity

LEMURES

The Lemures were the spirits of the dead and were believed to wander about like ghosts at night and to torment and frighten the living. Some writers divided them into two classes: the Lares, or the souls of good men, and the Larvae, or the souls of evil men. The latter gives us our word *larva* for the young of certain types of insects. To propitiate these spirits the Romans celebrated the festival of the Lemuria.

hounded by the Lemures

LENAEA

The Lenaea, or "feast of the vats," was an ancient Greek festival in honor of Dionysus, wh may, hence, also be called Lenaeus, "god of the vat." It was celebrated in January with a sacrifice, procession, and dramatic exhibits.

merry-making at the Lenaean vintage

LENIN

Nikolay Lenin (1870-1924) developed Russian communism out of Bolshevism, especially the dictatorship of the proletariat. His embalmed body has been placed on permanent exhibition in Moscow, and he is venerated for his far-reaching social reforms for the betterment of the Russian people.

the Lenin philosophy

LENORE

Lenore, a name probably chosen for its euphony, is used in Poe's lyric lament for a lost love. *Lenore* is also the subject of a ballad by Buerger, in which Lenore's lover, who had died months before, reappears riding a charger, catches up Lenore and rides with her forty miles in two hours, and then is seen no more until the day of her burial, when he appears at her grave.

as lovely as a lost Lenore

LENTULUS SURA

Publius Cornelius Lentulus Sura, Roman consul in 71 B.C., was the man of chief note in the crew of Catiline (*q.v.*). Though ejected from the senate in consequence of his infamous life and morals, he believed that his distinguished birth and former high rank would enable him to become the chief of the conspiracy of 63 B.C. He also put foolish credence in a flattering Sibylline prophecy to the effect that he would be the third Cornelius to rule Rome (Sulla and Cinna, dictators before him, had belonged to this family). His typical irresolution and procrastination, however, along with

Cicero's vigilance saved Rome. Overcautious and slow, he was executed by strangulation in the Capitoline prison.

a hesitant Lentulus to spoil things by delay

LEON, PONCE DE

Ponce de Leon (1460-1521), the Spaniard who discovered Florida, heard from the Indians of a fountain in the Bahamas, the waters of which rejuvenated those who drank of it, and spent much time in a futile search for it. Because of that search his name is used jocularly of elderly people who are constantly seeking means to make them seem younger than they are. Hawthorne used the idea in his story, *Dr. Heidegger's Experiment.*

pursuing his furtive Ponce de Leon experiments

LEONIDAS

Leonidas was the king of Sparta who was sent with a small army to hold the pass of Thermopylae (480 B.C.) when Greece was invaded by the Persians. His forces totaled about 5000 men, of whom only 300 were Spartans. Leonidas and his gallant band drove back the enemy hordes with immense slaughter as they attempted to force the pass. But a Malian traitor, Ephialtes, led the Persians around the Greek rear by another mountain pass. Leonidas thereupon dismissed all the Greeks except his Spartans, insisting that they alone had been sent with the express duty of holding the strategic position. Then he charged the enemy with his gallant band, hopeless now of preserving their lives and anxious only to sell them dearly. In the desperate battle that ensued, Leonidas and his men fell in heroic action.

resolute and fearless as Leonidas

LEONTES

Leontes is the king of Sicily and the jealous husband of Hermione in Shakespeare's *Winter's Tale.* Unduly suspicious of his friend Polixenes, he would have had him murdered had not the latter fled. Hermione is confined to prison and her daughter Perdita is abandoned in Bohemia. But when Polixenes' son Florizel and Perdita grow up to be lovers, Leontes and Hermione are at length reunited. The picture of the jealous king is masterful in its psychology. Excited by the most trivial causes and eager to snatch at proofs, he is saturnine and moody, often ashamed of his own feelings. Selfish and vindictive, he also fears ridicule because of his tendency to degrade the object of his passion by sensual fancies.

unreasonably jealous and vindictive as Leontes

LEPORELLO

Leporello is the Don's amusing and cowardly valet in Mozart's opera *Don Giovanni.*

a craven Leporello

LERNA

A Lerna of ills, derived from the Latin phrase *malorum Lerna,* refers to a very great evil by reference to Lake Lerna, where Hercules destroyed the Hydra (*q.v.*) which had brought incalculable harm to Argos.

hopeless, Lernaean calamity

LESBIA

Lesbia is the name given Clodia, the favorite of Catullus (87-54 B.C.). It is also a name for a female inhabitant of the island of Lesbos. The word *Lesbian* has more recently been used of homosexual relations among women, with reference to the character of the great Greek poetess, Sappho, who came from Lesbos.

beautiful as Catullus's Lesbia

LESCAUT, MANON

(see *Manon*)

LETHEAN

Lethear is from Lethe, the river of oblivion in Hades, whence the terms "the waters of oblivion" and "Lethean," both meaning obliteration of all memory of the past.

exerts a Lethean influence
silent as the gentle Lethe's tide

LEUCOTHEA

Leucothea (white goddess") is the name given to Ino (*q.v.*) after she was received among the marine deities. It is also the name of one of the three Sirens, sister sea-nymphs who usually resided on a small island near Cape Pelorus in Sicily. By their melodious singing they enticed sailors ashore and killed them. Later writers represented them as presiding over the music of the spheres. The names of Leucothea's sisters were Parthenope and Ligeia.

Another Leucothea, or Leucothoë, was the daughter of the Babylonian king Orchamus and Eurynone. Loved and dishonored by Apollo, she was buried alive by her father. Apollo in atonement transformed her into a sweet-smelling incense shrub.

singing as irresistible as Leucothea's

LEVANA

Levana was the Roman goddess of childbirth and the protectress of children. She either lifted children from the ground or induced their fathers to acknowledge the legitimacy of their birth by raising them from the ground.

even Levana couldn't force him to admit his parenthood

LEVIATHANIC

Leviathanic refers to anything resembling the massive and strange sea-monster described in the Old Testament as a kind of crocodile, serpent, or whale. The name also alludes to a dragon invoked by enchanters in order to cause solar and lunar eclipses. In other Scriptural passages it designates an Egyptian Pharaoh. Thomas Hobbes' treatise on absolutism and the state was named after it, with the allusion that political society is an illusory animal larger than man. Dr. Samuel Johnson was dubbed the "Leviathan of literature" because of his formidable critical powers.

leviathanic in scope and magnitude

LIBER

Liber was an ancient Italian deity presiding over the cultivation of the vine and the fertility of the fields. His festival, the Liberalia, celebrating the first fruits of the vintage, was held in Rome on the 17th of March. A general spirit of creativeness and fecundity, he was identified in later times with Bacchus (Dionysus), though the fact that he was in origin quite distinct is attested to by the existence of a female counterpart of him. Called Libera, she was subsequently identified with Proserpina.

brimming over with the spirit of Liber

LIBERTAS

Libertas was the Roman goddess of liberty to whom several temples were consecrated in Rome. In the one on the Aventine hill the census records were preserved. In art she is pictured as a matron wearing the pileus, or liberty cap, a Phrygian felt hat worn by manumitted slaves. She also appears with a wreath of laurel, thus signifying both freedom and glory.

with the spirit of Libertas firing him

LIBITINA

Libitina was an ancient Italian divinity, identified by later Romans with Proserpina because of her connection with the lower-world, death, and burial. Funeral equipment was stored in her temple in Rome, where persons could hire or buy everything necessary for the disposal of their dead. An undertaker was called a *libitinarius,* and his business *libitina.* The name was also used by the poets in the sense of death as the consummation of life. In this connection Libitina seems to have been confused with Venus Lubentia, or Lubentina, goddess of gardens, vineyards, and voluptuous pleasures, though Plutarch explains the inconsistency by saying that one and the same goddess presides over both birth and death.

Libitina consummated his life

LIBRO D' ORO

The Libro d' Oro, or "golden book," was a roll or register of noble families of an Italian state or province in the Middle Ages, with a list of their landed estates included. Hence, the name connotes any list of titles of honor or a social register.

a social-climber headed for the Libro d' Oro

LIBURNIANS

The Liburnians were a people inhabiting the Adriatic coast of Dalmatia in ancient times. Bold and skillful sailors, they supported themselves by commerce and navigation. Because their ships were remarkable for their swift sailing, the Romans employed craft modeled after them and known as Liburnians. Light vessels and rapid pursuit ships of this type enabled Augustus to win the naval victory over Antony and Cleopatra at Actium in 31 B.C.

guiding his canoe as swiftly as a Liburnian

LICINIUS

Licinius, tribune of the Roman plebs from 376 to 367 B.C., was surnamed Stolo because of the care with which he dug up the shoots springing from the roots of his vines. It was he who laid the cornerstone of Rome's greatness by adjudicating and terminating the bitter quarrel between that city's patricians and plebeians. By legislation he limited the amount of land and cattle which any individual might own and regulated affairs between debtors and creditors. Later brought to trial, he was condemned and fined for transgressing his own land law.

a modern Licinius to protect the interests of the underprivileged

---

LIGEIA

Ligeia was the sister of Leucothea (*q.v.*) and Parthenope, and one of the three Sirens, sea-nymphs whose melodious singing enticed sailors to their death near Cape Pelorus in Sicily. The name is also applied to any fair and alluring nymph. Edgar Allen Poe used the name as the title of one of his famous stories.

By . . . fair Ligeia's golden comb,
Wherewith she sits on diamond rocks, Sleeking her soft alluring locks.

Milton

LILITH

Lilith, according to the Talmud, was Adam's first wife, and in popular tradition she is mentioned as an evil spirit roaming at night, attacking children. Literary references are made to both of these stories. Goethe mentions her in the Walpurgis night scene of *Faust.* Bliss Carmen writes:

Well now I know
Where the lost Lilith went long ago
The rosy Lilith and the pure white Eve.
Of Adam's first wife Lilith it was told,
The witch he loved before the gift of Eve.

Lilith is consequently used of the alluring, seductive, rosy love as opposed to chaste conjugal affection.

For Eve like ocean foam was white,
And Lilith—roses dipped in red

LILLIPUTIAN

Lilliputian is from Lilliput, a fictitious region in Swift's *Gulliver's Travels,* in which the people were pygmies and all other things were dwarfed. The whole is a biting satire on the England in which Swift lived, and in which he was so bitterly disappointed because it had yielded him so little recognition. He wrote, he said, "in protest against that despicable little animal, Man."

uncomfortable as the Lilliputians made Gulliver with their arrows

---

LIMBO

Limbo was a region supposed by ancient theologians to lie off the border of hell. The souls of those not admitted to heaven or Purgatory awaited the general resurrection here. Pious patriarchs deceased before the birth of Christ inhabited the *Limbus Patrum.* Infants dying unbaptized went to the *Limbus Infantum.* To these popular opinion added the *Limbus Fatuorum,* or "Fools' Paradise," in which all vanity and nonsense were contained. Dante's limbo, in which the distinguished spirits of antiquity were confined, is located in the outermost of the circles of Hell. In modern speech, *to be in limbo* means to be relegated to obscurity, to be cast aside, forgotten and out-of-date.

lying in a limbo of neglect

LINCOLN, ABRAHAM

Abraham Lincoln (1809-1865) came up through poverty to be President of the United States during the period of the Civil War. He was a President marked by integrity, foresight, intelligence, and a wisdom acclaimed through all the decades since. Persistence in educating himself, a passion to right wrong, a courage to translate that feeling into action, a resolution that carried him through any opposition, a belief and trust in God—these combined to command the respect of the world. A tragic intensity strangely coupled with a saving sense of humor marked all his days. In the sternest situation he never lost either his courage or his human compassion, nor, on occasion, his ability to laugh. These qualities, even more than his political achievements, cling to his name today, a name universally revered. Drinkwater's play, *Abraham Lincoln,* interprets his character marvelously.

towered above other men like a Lincoln

LIND, JENNY

Jenny Lind (1820-1887), noted Swedish-American singer, was famed both in Swedish and in German opera. Sponsored in America by P. T. Barnum in a barnstorming tour, she became so popular both for her unsurpassed operatic soprano voice and for her beautiful character and generosity that her name is still synonymous with song, womanliness, and grace. She is still known by the name then given her, "the Swedish nightingale."

suggests the graciousness of sweet-voiced Jenny Lind

LINDABRIDES

Lindabrides is the heroine of a celebrated romance, *The Mirror of Knighthood.* Her name has become a synonym for a kept woman, a mistress, in which sense it was used by Scott in *Kenilworth* and *Woodstock.*

a courtesan expensive as Lindabrides

LINDOR

Lindor is a poetical name formerly in use for a rustic gallant or swain, a lover *en bergère* (in a pastoral background).

Spare us those most tedious and insipid persons of all Arcadia . . . Do not bring down upon us Corydon and Lindor

Sir W. Scott

LINNE, HEIR OF

The Heir of Linne, in Percy's *Reliques,* was a profligate and spendthrift "who wasted his substance in riotous living." When all was spent, he sold his estate to John o' the Scales, his steward, reserving to himself only a "poor and lonesome lodge in a lonely glen." After he had gone through the proceeds of the sale, he attempted to hang himself but the rope broke and disclosed to him three money chests and a note from his father: "Once more, my son, I set thee clear; amend thy life, or a rope at last must end it." His steward, having refused to grant his former master a test loan, was forced by a stranger to return to the Heir his estate at the price for which he had secured it.

prodigal as the Heir of Linne

LINUS

Linus was a Greek mythological hero whose untimely death was commemorated in the *Song of Linus,* a dirge sung at the annual harvest and expressing sorrow over the passing of summer and the brevity of the changing seasons. One version of the myth makes him the son of Apollo and an Argive princess and says that he was torn to pieces by dogs. Another states that he was the son of Apollo and Terpsichore, and the musical instructor of Orpheus and Hercules, the latter of whom killed Linus with his own lyre when rebuked by his teacher.

sorrowful music worthy of Linus

LIR

King Lir, the father of Fionmala in Irish legend, was so bereaved on the death of Fingula, the girl's mother, that he sought consolation in marriage to Aoife, a wicked witch. In spite she transformed the children of Lir into swans, doomed to float on the water till they heard the first mass-bell ring. Thomas Moore, in his *Irish Melodies,* has versified the tale.

murmuring mournfully, Lir's lovely daughter

LISA, MONA

Mona Lisa, the famous painting of La Gioconda, wife of Francesco del Giocondo, was painted about 1500 by Da Vinci. The face is beautiful in its regularity of feature, but famous particularly for its inscrutable smile, interpreted in numberless ways, never twice the same. DaVinci worked four years on the portrait, and then declared it unfinished. The painting came into new prominence in this century when it mysteriously disappeared from the Louvre, where it had been kept for years under careful guard. It was traced to Florence, Italy, and returned to the Louvre in 1914.

a Mona Lisa smile
the inscrutability of a Mona Lisa

LISMAHAGO, CAPTAIN

Captain Lismahago is the superannuated officer on half-pay in Smollett's *Humphry Clinker.* A hard-featured and forbidding Scotchman of extraordinary dress and manners, he is pompous, conceited, rude, disputatious, and full of national pride. His unusual adventures among the Indians are quite worthy of Cervantes. This poor but proud captain succumbs to the wintry smiles and snug fortune of Miss Tabitha Bramble.

as argumentative as Captain Lismahago

LISZT, FRANZ

Franz Liszt (1811-1886) was the musician who at nine years of age gave his first concert, and was a notable figure of Paris at twelve. He had not only a mastery of the piano that made him a world figure, but a generosity to other musicians that has made him a beloved memory to many a great artist. He developed what is known as the symphonic poem. Essentially a virtuoso, he was instinctive in his knowledge of the elements of brilliant and effective performance.

the brilliant performance of a Liszt

LITTLE EVA

Little Eva is the angelic daughter of St. Clair, wealthy Louisiana planter in Mrs. Stowe's *Uncle Tom's Cabin.* The pet of Uncle Tom, who rescues her from drowning, the frail child dies prematurely, her death forming one of the most pathetic episodes in the story.

delicate as Little Eva

LITTLE JOHN

Little John, really John Little, a huge and brawny fellow, on first encountering Robin Hood gave him a sound thrashing, which so delighted Robin Hood that he promptly dubbed him Little John. He also added John to his band of outlaws by having him so baptized, standing godfather to him—a scene well pictured in Scott's novel, *The Talisman.* Little John became one of the most colorful, faithful, and devoted of the Merry Men.

a devoted and invaluable Little John

LITTLE LORD FAUNTLEROY

Little Lord Fauntleroy is the name of a book by Frances Hodgson Burnett, picturing a beautiful boy perfectly dressed, with curls, a velvet suit, and lace collar. Always ready for inspection, always adored, always the darling of the Victorian feminine heart, he is today absurdly unready for the natural activities of the average boy's life. Appealing as the story was in its day, the name has now become a term of opprobrium, of scorn and torment, a name for a sissy, the antithesis of Tom Sawyer or Penrod.

any little Lord Fauntleroy fares badly today

LITTLE NELL

Little Nell, a child of great loveliness, was the constant companion of her grandfather, and the center of sentimental interest in Dickens' *Old Curiosity Shop.* She was a "child of great purity in a world of worldliness, selfishness, and crime," according to Dickens' description.

she is one of the rare Little Nells of this generation

LITTLE PEDLINGTON

Little Pedlington is an imaginary locality in which humbug, quackery, cant, affectation, selfishness, and other social vices abound. It is described in a work of the same name by John Poole, and is a good-natured and amusing satire on the contemporary condition of literature, art, criticism and society of 19th century England.

pretentious enough to lead the debates of Little Pedlington

LITTLE RED RIDING-HOOD

Little Red Riding-Hood is the central figure in a nursery tale about a little girl clad in a red cloak who was sent to carry a basket of food to her sick grandmother, only to find, instead, a wolf in her grandmother's bed. The child's conversation with the supposed grandmother and the element of danger introduced are suspenseful enough to make the story a favorite with small children, who love to be frightened by a story told them in the safety of their own nursery. In French *Riding-Hood* is known as *Chaperon Rouge,* in German as *Rothkaeppchen.*

many a Little Red Riding-Hood finds grim reality

LITYERSES

Lityerses was a son of Midas, the king of Phrygia. He was said to have required all visitors to help him in the harvest and, if they did not exceed him in industry, to have killed or severely beaten them. A mightier hero (Hercules ?) arrived and put an end to his tyranny by slaying him. In origin he was probably some kind of harvest divinity. In fact, a harvest song was associated with his name.

For thee the Lityerses-song again
Young Daphnis with his silver voice doth sing.

Matthew Arnold

LIVIA

Livia (born 58 B.C.) was the famous wife of the emperor Augustus. A woman of ability, lofty character, and austerity, she was imbued with the stern spirit of the aristocracy of the Roman Republic. In an age of luxury, when more frivolous ladies were learning to wear silk, she still had homespun and linen made in her own household to be used for clothing. Her strict morality was set as a pattern to be followed by other Roman matrons, and she disapproved heartily of the lax conduct of Julia, her husband's daughter by a previous marriage and ultimately disgraced by a life-long exile. On the accession of Tiberius, her son by a previous marriage, to the throne, she ambitiously attempted to obtain an equal share in the government but was foiled in her design by her moody son.

the strait-laced morality of a Livia

LIVIAN

Livian refers to the work and style of Titus Livius (59 B.C.-17 A.D.), a friend of Augustus in spite of his personal preference for the old republican constitution of Rome. He wrote the perennially popular history of Rome *Ab Urbe Condita* ("from the founding of the city") in 142 books. His purpose was ethically slanted to commemorate the deeds of the Roman people from the landing of Aeneas in Italy to 9 B.C. and to describe the city's greatness and decline in morals so that his readers might draw helpful lessons. Though his intense patriotism sometimes blinded him to Roman faults, his graphic powers of description and his sense of the dramatic in recounting the exploits of the popular heroes of monarchical and republican Rome make his work uniquely interesting reading.

with a Livian love of Rome and her heroes

LIVINGSTONE, DAVID

David Livingstone (1813-1873) was the famous Scottish missionary and explorer of the "Dark Continent" who did more than any other man to ascertain the geography of Africa, covering more than one-third of its huge size. At first repulsed by the Boers, he went on numerous expeditions into the interior, discovering the Zambesi River and its celebrated Victoria Falls and exploring the watershed of Central Africa and the sources of the Nile. The story of his rescue, when ill and immobilized in cannibal country, by Henry M. Stanley is famous for its classically restrained interchange of courteous formalities: "Dr. Livingstone, I presume?" and "Mr. Stanley, I presume?" The great and beloved "Doctor" was subsequently buried with honor in Westminster Abbey.

the Christian zeal and fearlessness of Dr. Livingstone

LLOYD'S

Lloyd's is the great insurance house of London, so named from Edward Lloyd's old coffee-house (1688) that was its first headquarters. It is now the greatest underwriters' association in the world, and although originally a commercial and maritime company, headquarters for information about shipping, it now insures the widest range of risks in the world.

no Lloyd's can insure happiness

LOATHLY LADY

Loathly Lady was the hideous hag whom Sir Gawain married because no one else would have her. At the moment of their marriage, however, she was transformed into a beautiful woman, having previously been under the power of a malignant enchanter. The story symbolizes the power of love to beautify.

transformed like Loathly Lady

LOCHINVAR

Lochinvar is the young gallant of the old Scotch ballads, also of Scott's *Marmion,* who dashes in at the moment of the marriage procession and carries his ladylove away from her waiting bridegroom, a "laggard in love and a dastard in war." Typical of many similar ballad themes, the name Lochinvar has become the synonym for any gay and dashing young lover who appears suddenly to abduct his fair one in the face of law and authority.

always a Lochinvar to come to her rescue

LOCOFOCOS

Locofocos, from the Latin *loco foci,* "in place of a fire," was the name of Lucifer-matches that was given to an ultra-radical American political group in the nineteenth century. It was so called because at a meeting in Tammany Hall in 1835 the lights were suddenly extinguished with the hope of breaking up the turbulent assembly. But those who were in favor of extreme measures instantly drew from their pockets their locofocos and relighted the gas.

as radical as a Locofoco

LOCUSTA

Locusta has become a by-word for a professional poisoner. A woman talented in the ways in which to slip powerful poisons unnoticed into foods and beverages, she was employed by Agrippina to destroy Claudius and by Nero to kill Britannicus. She was put to death during the reign of the emperor Galba, who acceded to the throne for about six months in the year following Nero's suicide (68 A.D.).

a Locusta concocting her lethal brew

LOGISTILLA

Logistilla, or "Reason," is the good fairy in Ariosto's *Orlando Furioso,* and the sister of Alcina the sorceress and Morgana. She teaches Ruggiero how to master the hippogriff, a beast with the head and claws of a griffin and the hoofs and tail of a horse. To Astolpho she gives a magic book and a horn of wonderful power.

found his Logistilla to administer to his needs

LOHENGRIN

Lohengrin was the son of Parsifal and the hero of the German version of the swan-knight legend. Sent from the castle of the Holy Grail to help Elsa, the young Duchess of Brabant, he came to her on a boat drawn by a swan and married her on condition that she not ask his origin. The promise broken because of Elsa's curiosity, Lohengrin left her with his magic swan, and Elsa sank into a lifeless swoon. The story is exquisitely told in Wagner's music-drama *Lohengrin.*

as mysterious as Lohengrin
Lohengrin's secretiveness

LOKI

Loki, the god of destruction in the old Norse folk tales, is sometimes a helper, sometimes a hindrance to the other gods, but in general he is used in old

legends as the god of mischief and discord, the one who will "lead forth the hosts of Hell on the last day." Though an evil principle, he is pictured as seductive and alluringly beautiful. For treacherously contriving the death of Baldur he was bound to a rock with the intestines of his sons, while two serpents continually dropped torturing venom on his limbs.

a malignant Loki

LOLLIUS

Lollius was a mysterious author, real or mythical, referred to by the writers of the Middle Ages and cited by Chaucer apropos of the story of Troy. So vain, however, have been all attempts to discover and identify him, that he has come to be regarded as the *ignis fatuus* of antiquaries. "Of Lollius," says one of these baffled investigators, "it will become every one to speak with deference." According to Coleridge, "Lollius, if a writer of that name existed at all, was a *somewhat somewhere*." The name may, therefore, be used to describe anything elusive and improbable.

as hard to find as Lollius

LOMBARD

Lombard was the English word for a banker or money-lender, so-called because the first bankers were Italians from the province of Lombardy, who set up business in Lombard Street, London, in the Middle Ages. They exercised a monopoly in pawnbroking until the reign of Queen Elizabeth.

needs the genius of a Lombard to rescue him

LONDON, JACK

Jack London (1876-1916) was the popular American author, sailor, beachcomber, hobo, and soap-box Socialist, whose adventurously thrilling life started at the age of seventeen when he went to sea to serve before the mast. In 1897 he joined the rush to the Klondike, and later served as war correspondent to Japan in 1904 and to Mexico in 1914. The voyage around the world which he undertook with Martin Johnson in a fifty-foot yacht is recorded in *The Cruise of the Snark*. Others of his nomadic journeys ended in numerous jailings for vagrancy. Some of the most spirited of his fine novels are *The Call of the Wild, The Sea Wolf, John Barleycorn, Martin Eden,* and *The Strength of the Strong.*

a restless and roaming Jack London

LONGCHAMPS

Longchamps, near the Bois de Boulogne in Paris, is the destination sought by the fashionably dressed Parisians on Wednesday, Thursday, and Friday of Passion Week, as they display their sartorial perfection in a procession of private carriages and hired cabs. Originally there was a famous nunnery there to which all who could, went to hear the religious women sing the *Ténèbres*, a performance for which they had achieved fame. The custom grew into a fashion, and though the convent no longer exists, the route is still followed by all the smartly dressed men and women who wish to display their spring fashions.

modish as the procession to Longchamps

LONGFELLOW, HENRY WADSWORTH

Henry Wadsworth Longfellow (1807-1882), known as the poet of the hearth and home, was nevertheless one of the most widely travelled men of his time, with a broad European background. He was a language professor at Bowdoin even before he became popularly recognized as a poet. But it is as a lover of America, a painter of the American scene, of home and family that he made his appeal to the American people. Hence, his name connotes home-loving, peaceful, contented and natural happiness.

with all the tranquillity and graciousness of a Longfellow home scene

LONGINUS

Longinus (220-273 A.D.) was a celebrated Greek rhetorician and Neo-Platonic philosopher. The counselor of Queen Zenobia of Palmyra, he was put to death by Aurelian for his association with that monarch. Attributed to him is the profoundly analytical work on literary criticism, known as *On the Sublime*. In it the author analyses the qualities in writing that make for grandeur and nobility of effect, finding them to be exalted ideas, strong emotion, artistic construction, and felicitous phrasing. Avoidance of bombast and turgidity of expression is as necessary as the presence of the positive values. He illustrates his points with a wealth of quotation, and finds Homer, Plato, and Demosthenes to be the authors who are most worthy of his praise.

Thee, bold Longinus! all the Nine inspire, And bless their critic with a poet's fire

Alexander Pope

LONG TOM COFFIN

Long Tom Coffin is a sailor of noble daring and a man of action, the heroic Leatherstocking of the seas, in Cooper's *The Pilot*. Probably the most widely known sailor character in fiction, he is a simple-hearted hero who loses none of his reality or individuality in his nobleness of soul.

yearning for a voyage on the seas with someone like Long Tom Coffin for a companion

LORD BURLEIGH

Lord Burleigh is a minister of state in Mr. Puff's tragedy of the "Spanish Armada" introduced into Sheridan's farce of *The Critic*. With his head too full of state affairs and politics to give him time to utter a word, he merely shakes his head expressively while Mr. Puff explains what the eloquently comprehensive nod means. Hence comes the expression *as significant as the shake of Lord Burleigh's head.*

a sagacious shake of the head that would have done honor to Lord Burleigh

LORELEI

The Lorelei was originally the name of a rock in the Rhine river, which gave a remarkable echo that probably accounted for the well-known legend found in Heinrich Heine's famous poem. Personified as a maiden who threw herself into the river in despair over her faithless lover, she was supposed to have been transformed into an alluring siren whose voice lured fishermen and sailors to destruction. As she sits combing her golden hair, whoever sees her loses his sight or reason, and he who listens to her strange song is condemned to wander with her forever.

an irresistible Lorelei of song

LORENZO

Lorenzo is the name of a character in Edward Young's *Night Thoughts*. A person of a thoroughly debauched and reprobate life, he is supposedly the embodiment of imaginary atheism and unavailing remorse and despair.

a wanton and worthless Lorenzo, with nothing left to believe in

LORENZO THE MAGNIFICENT

Lorenzo the Magnificent (1449-1492) was the grandson of Cosimo de' Medici, and succeeded to the great wealth and power of that Florentine family. Statesman, ruler, and patron of the arts and letters, he was an immoral and tyrannical prince, though he contrib-

uted greatly to the prosperity and intellectual achievements of his city-state. A versatile and elegant prose-writer and poet, he promoted the Tuscan dialect till it became the standard speech of Italy, and gathered about him men of genius in all fields, giving momentum to the cultural forces of the Renaissance.

with the touch of a Lorenzo for detecting and promoting genius

---

LORETTO

Loretto, a town in Ancona province, Italy, is the site of the *Santa Casa,* a house surrounded by a church. The reputed house of the Virgin Mary at Nazareth, the sanctuary was miraculously transported by angels to Fiume in 1291, thence to Recanati in 1294, and finally to a plot of land belonging to the Lady Loretto in its present location. Another Loretto is the Mariazel in Austria, famous for its ancient and ugly, ebony miracle-working image, to which two pilgrimages were made every year.

traveling through the air like the house of Loretto

LOTHARIO

Lothario, a flirtatious and prominent character in Rowe's *The Fair Penitent,* was a libertine so infamous that his name is applied to any careless, licentious, and gay deceiver.

lured by Lothario's honeyed words

LOTI, PIERRE

Pierre Loti was the pen-name of Louis Viaud (1850-1923), the finest French descriptive writer of his day. The pseudonym is said to have been due to the great shyness of his early life, because of which his playmates dubbed him *le Loti,* an Indian flower which blushes unseen. A French naval officer, he saw service in many exotic waters and ports of call, the scenes of which are reflected in such works as *Mme. Chrysanthème,* a fantastic novel of Japanese life. His other novels, such as *Pêcheur d'Islande,* the most popular, abound in the impressionistic details of remembered colors, sounds, and perfumes which make his style at once both sensual and ethereal. Dreamy originality and idyllic romanticism pervade his sensitive art.

the slumbrous memory-stirrings of Loti

LOTOPHAGI

The Lotophagi, or Lotus-eaters, dwelled in the fabulous land visited by Odysseus on his return from Troy. They fed on the fruit of the lotus, the taste of which was so savory that any one who ever ate of it forgot his home and sank into a languorous lethargy. A Lotus-eater, therefore, refers to a person whose life is one of dreamy, carefree ease. Indifferent to the work-a-day activities of the outer world, he is a voluptuary whose only concern is for indolent pleasures.

sunk in Lotophagean inertia
wrapped in lotophagous oblivion

LOT'S WIFE

Lot's wife was turned into a pillar of salt for looking back on the city of Sodom as, escorted by two angels, she was escaping from its destruction with her husband and two unmarried daughters (*Genesis,* xix). Mention of her thus suggests a fatal curiosity and unwise inquisitiveness.

as unwise in her curiosity as Lot's wife

LOUIS XIV

Louis XIV, the "Sun King" (1638-1715), was monarch of the Golden Age of French letters and art. His name in the form Louis Quatorze is used to designate the architecture, design, and furnishings of the time as marked by a formal classicism of exterior and by the beginning of the florid and rococo in interior. Rich and elaborate carving, gilding, and inlay characterize the furniture of the period. The king himself deprived the Huguenots of their rights, causing thousands of them to flee France, and contributed to the lowering of the social morality. His inordinately ambitious and despotic absolutism is reflected in his words *L' état c'est moi*, "I am the state." The condition of France's poor classes started its plunge to the intolerable despair that precipitated the Revolution in the time of Louis XVI.

flashy and authoritarian as Louis XIV

LOUIS XV

Louis XV (1710-1774) was known as *le Bien-Aimé*, "the Well Beloved." The extravagant influence of his mistress Mme. de Pompadour led to disordered finances and mass discontent and hatred of the king in spite of his sobriquet, however, and caused him to utter with ominously prophetic nonchalance *Après moi le déluge*, "After me the storm." His next mistress, Mme. du Barry, was in ascendancy over him from 1768 to 1774, and his whole private life seems to have been one long record of vulgarity and vice. The art and decoration of this period, known as Louis Quinze, shows a fantastic and extravagant rococo style marked by excessive use of broken curves, shells, scrolls, mirrors, and white and gold color.

foppish and fancy as Louis XV

LOUIS XVI

Louis XVI (1754-1793) brought France to the brink of misery and discontent through the extravagance of his wife Marie Antoinette and her court, in spite of his efforts to relieve the tax-burdened condition of his people. His irresolute character cost him the confidence of both Royalists and Revolutionists, so that he and his family were forcibly brought by the Parisian mob from Versailles to the Tuileries palace, which was twice invaded by organized rabble and its Swiss Guard massacred. When the Republic was declared, he was deposed by the National Convention and he and his wife were guillotined. The art and decoration of this period, known as Louis Seize, is marked by a reaction from the rococo of Louis XIV and XV, and pastoral motives and the influence of Pompeian frescoes appear in the rather plain ornamentation.

a potentate as wavering and irresolute as Louis XVI

LOUYS, PIERRE

Pierre Louys (1870-1925) was the French novelist and poet who won notoriety by his *Aphrodite*, a story of Alexandrian morals in the early Christian era that was considered too vivid and sensual when it first appeared. Both his style and his subject matter were felt to be delicately decadent and too carnally alluring in the afterglow of Victorianism in which they were born. Just as voluptuous and impure as his prose are the *Chansons de Bilitis*, poems purporting to be translations from the Greek and centering on glorification of Lesbian love.

decadence of the sort meditated by Pierre Louys

LOVELACE

Lovelace is both the hero and the villain of Richardson's *The History of Clarissa Harlowe*. This suave personage, whom Crabbe calls "rich, proud, and crafty, handsome, brave, and gay," is represented as an unscrupulous fop and voluptuary who devotes his life and talents to the undermining of female virtue. Inflamed with passion for Clarissa, he resorts to drugging her in order to overcome her resistance to his advances. The most finished picture of a self-possessed and insinuating libertine of the time ever drawn, his character is an expansion of that of Lothario in Rowe's *Fair Penitent.* Though he makes a belated offer of marriage to Clarissa, the wronged maiden dies of mortification and shame.

a twentieth-century Lovelace, handy with a Mickey Finn

LOWELL, AMY

Amy Lowell, a twentieth century New England poet, early advocated and practiced complete emancipation from the old romantic subjects and the established verse forms of her time. She flaunted and preached abandonment of regularity, but embodied in her work beauty and rhythm, and seems less and less startling as more and more poets have followed her lead.

amused at the steady calmness of Amy Lowell's revolt

LOWELL, JAMES RUSSEL

James Russel Lowell (1819-1891), American editor, essayist, and poet, spoke with earnestness and force, even in his verse, on subjects that came close to his heart and to the heart of the American people. While personal affections and love of home and the home scene mark much of his work, his *Present Crisis,* written at the time the struggle in Texas was imminent, *Biglow Papers* at the time of the Mexican War, and *The Commemoration Ode* in memory of those who had died in the war, rank higher than the rest. Essentially, as poet and as editor, he is the zealous patriot.

with a Lowell zeal

LOYOLA, IGNATIUS

Ignatius Loyola (1491-1556) was the Spanish soldier who during a convalescence from wounds received in battle resolved to devote himself to the Church. Living thereafter as an ascetic, he made a pilgrimage barefoot to Jerusalem. Later he planned and was the founder of the Society of Jesus, known as the Jesuit Order and intended for the conversion of infidels and a counteraction to Protestantism. The Society is famous for both its learning and its zeal, aggressive and propagandistic in type, whence the very name *Jesuit* (*q.v.*) has come to mean crafty and double-dealing.

a conversion as miraculous as that of Loyola

LREUX

Lreux was King Arthur's seneschal or steward, introduced in romances of the Round Table as a detractor, coward, and boaster.

boastful as Lreux

LUA

Lua, or Lua Mater, an earth goddess, was one of the early Italian deities to whom were dedicated all arms and spoils taken in battle.

donated their weapons willingly to Lua

LUBBERLAND

Lubberland is the Land of Cockaigne (*q.v.*), an imaginary place of idleness and plenty, or of laziness.

dreaming of Lubberland

LUCIA DI LAMMERMOOR

Lucia di Lammermoor, known also as Lucy Ashton, is the heroine of Donizetti's opera of that name and of Scott's *Bride of Lammermoor.* Lord Henry Ashton, her brother, arranged a marriage between his sister and Lord Arthur Bucklaw in order to recoup the family's fortunes, though Lucia is in love with Edgar Ravenswood, whose family has long been in a state of hostility with the Lammermoors. While Edgar is absent in France on an embassy, Lucia is made to believe, by feigned letters, that he is unfaithful to her, and in a frenzy of indignation consents to marry Bucklaw. On her wedding night, however, her reason breaks, she stabs her husband, goes mad, and dies.

ill-omened as Lucia di Lammermoor's wedding

LUCIA, ST.

St. Lucia was a virgin martyr of the primitive church in Syracuse, who perished during the persecution of Diocletian in A.D. 304. She had persuaded her mother, who had been miraculously cured of an illness, to distribute her wealth to the poor and needy, and for this she was denounced by her own lover. In torture no force could budge her from the spot whereon she stood, and even boiling oil and burning pitch could not hurt her. Finally she was slain with a sword. Her festival is held on the 13th of December, and she is revered as a patroness of those who suffer with eye afflictions. In art she is represented as bearing her eyes in her hand or on a salver.

as impervious to pain as St. Lucia

LUCIAN

Lucian (A.D. 115-200) was the great Greek writer of satirical dialogues and fantastic tales, and a rhetorician and philosopher besides. His questioning spirit and hatred of sham influenced later writers like Rabelais and Swift. In the *Dialogue of the Gods* he pokes fun at many of the Greek myths, while in the *Dialogue of the Dead,* with its grim irony and melancholy, he exposes the vanities and pretenses of living men. The tale of *The Cock* shows the advantages of poverty over wealth. With gentle humor or biting ridicule he denounces the foolish foibles of mankind.

analytical as Lucian's mordant humor

LUCIFER

Lucifer is one of the names of the Devil, being applied to him from an allegorical interpretation by the Church fathers of a passage in *Isaiah* (xii, 12), in which the king of Babylon is likened to the morning star. Wierus makes him the highest officer of justice in the infernal court or empire. The name is, in fact, not properly a profane or Satanic title. It is the Latin word for *light-bringer,* the morning star, and was a Christian name in early times, borne even by one of the early Popes. It acquired its present connotation from the apostrophe of the ruined king of Babylon: "How art thou fallen from Heaven, O Lucifer, son of the morning!" Thence, Milton took the name as the title of his demon of pride, making this name of the pure herald of daylight hateful ever after to Christian ears.

with Lucifer's pride in evil-doing

LUCINA

Lucina was the goddess of childbirth who presided over the bringing to light of new-born babes. The patron of women at the time of delivery, she was identified with the Greek goddess, Ilithyia, and her name was used as an epithet for Juno and Diana in their duties of protecting pregnant women.

a midwife adept as Lucina

LUCIO

Lucio is a fantastic character in Shakespeare's *Measure for Measure.* Without being absolutely depraved or intentionally bad, he has become, through lack of thoughtful consideration, both vicious and dissolute. Talkative and dissipated, he is totally ungoverned by temperament.

a Lucio of easy-going and unrestrained manners.

LUCRETIA

Lucretia, the wife of Collatinus, was the noble Roman matron who was raped during her husband's absence by the sensual Sextus Tarquinius, a young prince of the royal house of early Rome and a guest in Lucretia's home. She revealed the outrage to her husband and father who vowed to avenge her, but in spite of their consolations she refused to continue her dishonored life, lest it might become a bad example for less virtuous ladies. After her suicide the scandalous incident led to the expulsion of the Tarquin kings of Rome and to the foundation of the Republic in 509 B.C. Chaucer and Shakespeare tell the story in English, the latter in his famous *Rape of Lucrece.*

with the undeviating virtue of a Lucretia

LUCRETIAN

Lucretian refers to the work and style of Titus Lucretius Carus (c. 99-55 B.C.), the great Roman philosophical poet who wrote *De Rerum Natura* ("Concerning the Nature of the Universe"). He explains in this didactic poem in six books the atomic structure of the universe and everything in it, whereby everything acts according to the laws of Nature and not of the gods. He taught that popular religion and its superstitions kept man from a full enjoyment of life and made him afraid of death and torment in the after life. Condemning luxury and praising simple tastes and the beauties of Nature, he described in wonderful detail the entire birth and progress of civilization.

with Lucretian realism
Lucretian emphasis on the atom

LUCULLAN

Lucullan Feast is derived from Lucullus (c. 110-57 B.C.), a Roman consul and general who amassed a great fortune. He expended great amounts of money on sumptuous entertainments, particularly on banquets, so that a Lucullan feast is really the acme of abundance and extravagance in food and in the appurtenances of a banquet.

in every respect a Lucullan occasion

LUDDITES

The Luddites were riotous workmen, in the manufacturing districts of England, who in 1811 attempted to prevent the introduction of power-looms under the notion that machinery would throw men out of work. In 1816 they reappeared with intention to sabotage the looms, but were put down, after a short and sharp riot in London, by the police and military. The real leaders went about in women's clothes, and, hence, were called "Lud's wives." The name is said to derive from a Ned Lud of Leicester, an imbecile who was continually hounded by bands of boys. One day he chased a set of tormentors into a house and broke two stocking-frames. From him General Lud, the leader of the rioters, took his name.

with a hatred of the mills as bitter as that of a Luddite

LUGGNAGG

Luggnagg is an imaginary island mentioned by Swift in *Gulliver's Travels* as being located to the southeast of Japan. The fact that its inhabitants live forever affords the satirist an opportunity to point out the evil of such a destiny, if it is not accompanied by corresponding health, strength, and intellect.

as everlasting as an inhabitant of Luggnagg

LUKE, ST.

Luke, evangelist, physician, and author of the third of the New Testament gospels, was the faithful companion of St. Paul on several of his missionary journeys. In Rome his fidelity prompted him to stay by Paul's side during his first imprisonment and at the end of his second. Because tradition says that he painted a portrait of the Virgin Mary, he is regarded as the patron saint of painters, and in art is usually

LYNCH, JUDGE

Judge Lynch, whose name has come to connote extralegal methods of trial and punishment, was a planter and justice of the peace in Virginia. Since he lived several miles from any law court, his neighbors selected him to pass sentence on Tory offenders during the disorganized conditions attending the Revolutionary War. His name has ever since stood for violent and illegal measures, mob-law, or law administered by private persons, usually with severity.

arbitrary in his judgment, the Judge Lynch of his community

LYSANDER

Lysander was the distinguished Spartan diplomat and general who, subsidized by Cyrus of Persia to pay his sailors, brought the Peloponnesian War to an end in 405 B.C. He was later unsuccessful in his attempt to abolish hereditary royalty in his own city-state.

a Lysander to challenge dynastic right to power

LYSIAS

Lysias (458-380 B.C.) was the wealthy Athenian orator who fled from Athens when the tyranny of the Thirty stripped him of his property and his brother of his life in 404 B.C. In financial need thereafter, he became a professional ghost-writer of forensic speeches, of which he composed more than two hundred. His unusual skill lay in his ability to put himself in his client's place and character, so that the client could speak words not his own as though they were natural and original with him. He is said to have written a defense for Socrates, which the great philosopher refused to use. The language of his speeches, though it varies with some flexibility to conform to the personalities and circumstances of the litigants who commissioned them, is always agreeably simple and natural, clear, vivid, and orderly, as devised by this master chameleon.

as flexible as Lysias at stepping into another's personality

LYSIPPUS

Lysippus, the great Sicyonian sculptor who was the favorite artist of Alexander the Great, established his own "canon," or standard, for the proportions of the perfect human figure. It made the head one-eighth of the total height, shortened the torso, made the body thinner and leaner and thus increased its apparent height. His most celebrated statue was the *Apoxyomenus*, a long-legged athlete scraping the cleansing oil from his skin with a strigil. Because he alone portrayed Alexander's courage in visible form, he was the portraitist of that military genius from boyhood up. 316 B.C. was the last fixed point in his career.

the long-legged gracefulness of a figure by Lysippus

LYSISTRATA

Lysistrata, "Dismisser of Armies," is the heroine of Aristophanes' comedy of the same name (411 B.C.). She artfully suggests to the women of Athens that, since their husbands had failed to bring the protracted Peloponnesian War to an end, they themselves force peace by withholding all marital favors from them and obliging them to chastity and sexual abstinence as long as the war would continue. The women follow her leadership and amid scenes of gross indecency humiliate their unhappy spouses until peace is finally declared.

a demobilization as prompt and effective as that brought about by Lysistrata

M

MAAT

Maat, the daughter of the Sun, was the Egyptian goddess of truth, justice, and law. Wearing an ostrich plume on her head, she lead the souls of the dead to Osiris (*q.v.*). In art she is represented as standing by in scenes of judgment, as the weighing of the soul takes place.

a vengeful Maat to lead him to justice

MAB

Mab was a mischievous fairy in English folklore, credited with control of the farm maids by pinching and pulling them and interfering with their sleep if they were untidy and shiftless about their work. She did the work for them while they slept, if they were neat and orderly or if they set a creambowl and junket out for her at night. Akin to Puck in harmless mischief or in petty revenge for misdeeds, Mab was universally popular.

an uneasy overture to Mab
with Mab's favor blest

MACADAM, SIR JOHN

Sir John L. MacAdam (1756-1836) was the British engineer and surveyor general of roads who introduced the method of using broken stones for road-building material, making the surface of the highway convex instead of concave as before. He is the eponymous namer of the modern macadamized road.

ingenious at highway-design as Sir John MacAdam

MACAIRE, ROBERT

Robert Macaire is the name of a heavy villain, a bold and shameless brigand in *Chien de Montargis, Chien d'Aubry,* and a large number of derivative French plays. It may be applied to any audacious criminal, and is also used as a sportive designation of a picaresque rogue and even of the adroit French people in general. Actually, Richard (not Robert) Macaire was a French knight of the era of Charles V, and he is said to have assassinated Aubry de Montdidier, one of his companions, in the forest of Bondy in 1371. As the dog of the murdered man exhibited unappeasable hostility toward the killer, Macaire was arrested on suspicion and required to fight a combat with the animal, which forced him to confess his guilt before it finally killed him. The character of Macaire has since been a favorite one on the French stage.

as guilty as Robert Macaire

MACARONI

Macaroni was the name given to the silk-stockinged society dandy, the fashionably dressed exquisites and coxcombs of eighteenth century London. It was derived from the Macaroni Club, founded about 1760 by a group of flamboyant young men who had traveled on the Continent and affected foreign manners, especially those of Italy. They introduced Italian maccheroni at Almack's (*q.v.*), and were roisteringly fond of gambling, drinking, and swashbuckling. Though now almost out of use as a name with which to designate a fop, it is preserved in the American song *Yankee Doodle*:

"Stuck a feather in his cap
And called it Macaroni."

as fancily clad and mincing as a Macaroni

MACAULAY, LORD

Thomas Babington Macaulay (1800-1859), brilliant English biographer, essayist, and historian, was also a statesman of note. Highly educated, amazingly well informed, he had a flair for words, a passion for history and a keen sense of effective detail. His writing is brilliant, convincing and crystal clear. His *History of England,* designed to have covered a long range, was so detailed that in execution it covered only a short period, but it is as entrancing as a novel. His biographies are a complete revelation not only of the man concerned but of the times in which he lived.

conversational as a Macaulay history
Macaulayan in clarity

MACBETH

Macbeth, in history was a Scotch king said to have procured the throne by killing Duncan on the field of battle and to have reigned for ten fairly good years. In Shakespeare's play *Macbeth,* the story accepted for literary reference, he is a Scotch thane and general who murdered Duncan as he slept, a guest in Macbeth's own castle. From the very moment of the deed which made him king, Macbeth lived in a torment of remorse and increasing desperation, constantly in danger of betraying, and finally actually betraying his deed. Hence, the name means ambitious, treacherous, desperate, remorseful, tragic.

the frightful desperation of a Macbeth

MACBETH, LADY

Lady Macbeth was the wife of the Scottish nobleman Macbeth, and queen of Scotland after she had connived with her husband to kill their guest, King Duncan, while he slept, that they might reign in his stead. The sovereignty was an empty honor, for from that moment Lady Macbeth's life became an intensity of agonized watchfulness lest her remorseful and distraught husband betray himself to the nobles, a thing he eventually did.

uneasy as Lady Macbeth
insistent as Lady Macbeth

MACCABEES

The Maccabees were a family of Jewish patriots of the second and first centuries B.C. Correctly called Hasmonaeans, they are associated with the four books of the Apocrypha, known as *Maccabees.* The priest Mattathias and his five sons rose in revolt against Antiochus Epiphanes of Syria, who had endeavored to abolish the Jewish religion and to substitute the Greek cults. The names of Mattathias's five sons were John, Simon, Judas, Eleazar, and Jonathan. The most heroic in accomplishment was Judas, whose exploits are the subject of Handel's great oratorrio, *Judas Maccabaeus.*

with the intense national spirit of the Maccabees

MACDUFF

Macduff is a Scottish thane in Shakespeare's tragedy of *Macbeth.* He was a Scotch nobleman whose castle of Kennoway was surprised by Macbeth, and his wife and babies savagely butchered. Macduff vowed vengeance and joined the army of Siward to dethrone the tyrant. On reaching the royal castle of Dunsinane, he engaged Macbeth in combat and slew him.

a vengeance as satisfied as Macduff's

McFINGAL

McFingal is the hero of Trumbull's Hudibrastic political poem of the same name, composed about 1775. He is represented as a typical burly New England squire, whose sympathies are on the side of the Tory, or royalist, party of the American Revolution, though he can not keep himself from prophesying the success and prosperity of the rebels. He is constantly engaged in controversy with Honorius, the champion of the Whigs, or rebels.

conservative as McFingal

MacFLECKNOE

MacFlecknoe, in Dryden's famous satire, is Thomas Shadwell, a worthless contemporary poet laureate and dramatist who repeatedly intimated his superiority to Dryden as a writer of plays. He was actually a wretched poet, so distinguished for his bad verses that his name has become proverbial for a poetaster. There was an historical Flecknoe, an Irish priest, doggerel writer, sonneteer, and playwright, though Dryden's MacFlecknoe is an aged prince who for many years has reigned: "without dispute, Through all the realms of Nonsense, absolute." Shadwell is MacFlecknoe, son of the venerable monarch and his successor to the throne of dullness. Therefore, as scion of an obscure nonentity, he is of even lesser parts.

like MacFlecknoe, he "never deviates into sense"

McFLIMSEY, MISS FLORA

Miss Flora McFlimsey is a modish young woman in W. A. Butler's satirical poem "Nothing to Wear." Though she shops continually, she always complains of the limitations and gaps in her wardrobe.

ransacking her closets like Miss Flora McFlimsey

McGUFFEY, WILLIAM

William McGuffey (1800-1873) was the author of a series of readers used in the little red schoolhouses of America. To "know your McGuffey" meant not only the ability to read, but to know the many bits of information carefully included in the selections used, to have learned most of the important American documents there reprinted "by heart", and to have been exposed to bits of the world's finest literature. The name has come into new prominence by reason of Henry Ford's advertising for copies in his effort to restore the little red schoolhouse with its full complement of the books studied.

knew his McGuffey

MACHAON

Machaon was the son of Asclepius (*q.v.*). He and his brother Podalirius were the surgeons of the Greek host at Troy, having brought with them to the siege troops from Tricca, Ithome, and Oechalis. He was killed by either Paris or Eurypylus, and after death received divine honors.

the Machaon of the invading army

MACHEATH, CAPTAIN

Captain Macheath is the handsome, light-hearted, and profligate highwayman and hero in Gay's *Beggar's Opera*. A bold-faced ruffian, he is game to the very last.

he hears the sound of coaches and six, takes the road like Macheath, and makes society stand and deliver

Thackeray

MACHIAVELLIAN

Machivellian is from the Italian diplomat Machiavelli (1469-1527), infamous for his crafty, wily, astute political doctrines. His policy was openly declared: no means was too dishonest, low, or cunning to be used if it worked to build up a strong central government; no ruthlessness or brutality wrong if it served the end for which it was destined. Hence, his name stands for any policy, wily, crafty or unscrupulous, if only it will further an intended purpose.

the world still has its Machiavellis, and his policies will always have their adherents

MAC IVOR, FLORA

Flora MacIvor, the heroine of Scott's *Waverley,* is the sister of the Highland chief Fergus MacIvor. Famous for her beauty and her allegiance to the cause of the Jacobites, she refuses to marry Waverley but enters a convent to take the veil after the execution of her brother by decapitation.

like Flora MacIvor, chooses a cloistered life

MACSTINGER, WIDOW

The Widow MacStinber, in Dickens' *Dombey and Son*, is a determined and dauntless husband-hunter. With rigid chin and brandishing fists, she brings her victims within "the range of a brisk battery of slaps," as she demonstrates the fact that her nature corresponds to her name. A woman of "fell inflexibility," she and her daughter Juliana represent to Captain Cuttle "a series of ages of oppression and coercion," though she succeeds in inveigling Captain Jack Bunsby into becoming her reluctant bridegroom.

a termagant like the Widow MacStinger

MAC TAB, MISS LUCRETIA

The Honorable Miss Lucretia MacTab is the stiff old maiden aunt in Colman's comedy *The Poor Gentleman.* Sister of one of the oldest barons in Scotland, she lived on the bounty of the husband of a deceased niece, named Worthington, always snubbing her host for not appreciating the honor of such a noble hanger-on, and always committing the most ludicrous mistakes from her extravagant vanity and family pride.

lives in the past like Miss Lucretia MacTab

MADAMA BUTTERFLY

Madama Butterfly, or Cio-Cio San, is the heroine of Puccini's opera based on a drama by David Belasco and John Luther Long. She marries an American naval lieutenant, Pinkerton, according to her native Japanese rites, bears him a son, and is discarded by him for a wife of his own nationality. Since she can no longer live with honor, she chooses to die according to the proud dictates of her people by committing hara-kiri. A noble and ardent woman, she is a moving and tragic figure in her insistence on honor and dignity.

betrayed like Madama Butterfly

MADELON

Madelon, the daughter of Gorgibus, is one of the characters satirized by Molière in *Les Précieuses Ridicules.* She affectedly changes her name to Polixène, thinking it to be more genteel.

a pretentious Madelon

MADISON, DOLLY

Dolly, or Dorothea, Madison (1768-1849) was one of the most famous "first ladies" of the White House and the most charming hostess in Washington while her husband James was secretary of state (1801-1809) and president of the United States of America (1809-1817). A woman of unusual social grace and plump beauty, she made of her home a center for diplomats and cultured people of all types. Her published *Memoirs ana Letters* are a source of considerable information on national and international affairs of the time.

the entertaining hospitality of a Dolly Madison.

MADOC

Madoc was a legendary Welsh prince reputed to have discovered America, where he established a colony on the southern branches of the Missouri about the year 1170. He is the hero of a poem by Robert Southey, who harmonizes this event with the Aztec founding of the empire of Mexico.

the exploring zeal of a Madoc

MADONNA

Madonna was an old Italian form of address, like the modern *signora* or *madama*. Since the first council of Ephesus (431) declared Mary to be the Mother of God, the name has been in universal use for the Virgin Mary as Mother, and for paintings and statues of her. Raffael's *Madonna of the Chair* in the Pitti Gallery, Florence, is a splendid example. The name, therefore, connotes adoration, worship, purity, and the essence of motherhood.

the Assumption is a noble picture, because Titian believed in the Madonna

Ruskin.

MADOR, SIR

Sir Mador, in Arthurian romance, was the Scottish knight whom Lancelot du Lac engaged in single combat in order to prove the innocence of Queen Guinevere, falsely accused and defamed by Sir Mador of having poisoned his brother. The contest lasted from noon till evening, when Lancelot finally achieved a complete victory over his antagonist. The two men thereafter became close friends, when Sir Mador was finally convinced of the Queen's innocence.

a reconciliation worthy of Sir Mador

MAECENAS

Caius Cilnius Maecenas was a wealthy Roman of the Augustan age. He was a liberal patron of the poets Vergil, Propertius, and Horace, to the last named of whom he gave the oft-mentioned Sabine farm of Horatian odes. The name Maecenas has come to be used proverbially to denote any munificent friend of literature.

a young author in search of a Maecenas

MAELSTROM

The Maelstrom, a famous whirlpool off Norway, was believed capable of sucking in vessels at great distances. Hence, the name indicates any vortex of power, influence, or opinion that draws people into its orbit. It suggests power, destruction, far-reaching, irresistible and inescapable.

the maelstrom of their ideologies

MAENAD

The name Maenad means literally a "mad woman." Devotees of Dionysus (Bacchus), the Maenads were known also as Bacchantes. They roamed the woods with the thyrsus, or wand wreathed with ivy and vine leaves and tipped with a pine cone. Orgiastic secret rites and much wine-tippling characterized their behavior. Today the name may be used of any woman beside herself with sexual or inebriated frenzy.

a frenzied Maenad with her bottle

MAEVIUS

(see *Bavius and Maevius*)

MAFFIA

Maffia is the name of a Sicilian secret society that operated over the law, demanding protection money by blackmail and avenging any injury done to its members. Politically influential, the Maffiosi controlled elections and labor conditions through their activities. The Camorra in Naples was a similar group of vigilantes. Figuratively, the designation Maffia may be applied to any society that operates at hostility with the law and perpetrates criminal outrages to gain its ends.

vindictive as the Maffia

MAGDALENE

Magdalene is the woman in the Bible, a sinner, who came into the house of Simon where Christ sat at supper and washed his feet with her tears, wiped them with her hair, anointed them with the ointment from an alabaster box, and was by Christ forgiven of her sins. The word is now used of a penitent woman, though more commonly of a reformed prostitute.

the gentleness of a Magdalene

MAGELLAN, FERDINAND

Ferdinand Magellan (1480-1521) was the famous Portuguese navigator and explorer who, in the service of Emanuel of Portugal, discovered the Spice Islands. Dropped from the employ of his own monarch, he offered his services to Charles V of Spain and set out with five vessels on a second voyage to the Spice Islands via the western route. Sighting South America near Pernambuco, he explored the estuary of the La Plata river. He crushed a mutiny among his men, and from October 21 to November 28 of 1520 he sailed through the strait now known by his name. He discovered the Philippines, where he made an alliance with the treacherous native ruler on whose behalf he undertook the expedition to the island of Mactan on which he was killed. The survivors of his party escaped, and one of his vessels succeeded in completing the circumnavigation of the earth.

intrepid as Magellan in facing the unknown

MAGI

Magi is the Latin for "wise men," in the Vulgate translation of the Bible. They are the traditional three Kings of the East who came to pay homage to the infant Jesus. Melchior is represented as an old man with a long beard, offering gold in acknowledgement of the sovereignty of Christ. Jaspar is a beardless youth, who offers frankincense in recognition of His divinity. Balthazar is a Moor, who tenders myrrh in token of His sorrow. They were also regarded as the patron saints of travelers. Originally the Magi were a priestly caste of the Medes and Persians, and later of the Zoroastrians. Losing their high repute, they became known as fortune-tellers and "magicians."

omniscient as the Magi

MAGLIABECCHI, ANTONIO

Antonio Magliabecchi (1633-1714) was the greatest bookworm that ever lived. A Florentine bibliophile and scholar, he never forgot what he had once read, and could even turn at once without reflection to the exact page of any reference. The librarian of Duke Cosimo III, he amassed a personal library numbering 30,000 volumes. Granted to Cosimo, it is now part of Florence's *Biblioteca Nazionale.*

a memory like Magliabecchi's

MAGUIRE, MOLLY

Molly Maguire was a name given in 1843 to a radical group of men in Ireland, a secret association who disguised themselves in women's dress and disturbed the agents of the absentee landlords. The name was later adopted by the Irishmen in the Pennsylvania coal regions, where they were active terrorists from about 1850 until 1870, when the organization was suppressed. The name is now sometimes loosely used as a general name for any group who, disguised in appearance, activate group disapproval of what they consider a general abuse.

the Molly Maguires are a' watchin'

MAGWITCH, ABEL

Abel Magwitch, the escaped convict in Dickens' *Great Expectations,* sums up his life as an unbroken series of "in jails and out of jails," and says that he was "locked up as much as a silver teakettle . . . put out of this town and put out of that town, and stuck in the stocks, and whipped, and worried, and drove." His first memories of infancy, indeed, were of himself thieving turnips for a living, since "summun had run away from me . . . and he'd took the fire with him and left me very cold."

a waif and a foundling like Abel Magwitch

MAHARAJAH

Maharajah is the name applied to the ruling chiefs of the native Hindu tribes or to a prominent religious teacher among them. In Sanskirt the name means *great prince* or *king.*

with a maharajah dignity

MAHLER, GUSTAVE

Gustave Mahler (1860-1911) was the much discussed Bohemian conductor and composer of impressive, romantic, and melancholically philosophical symphonies, choral works, and songs. He made music vaster in dimension by scoring for unprecedentedly large orchestras and by adding more movements to the symphonic form. His compositions are of a soul-searching and lugubrious nature, frequently preoccupied funereally with death and futility. To many critics they are too lush and overblown, their extreme length leading to inordinate and tedious repetitions and stress. His works include nine symphonies with more or less programmed content, two of them, the Second and Eighth, including choral groups, on the analogy of Beethoven's Ninth; *Das Lied von der Erde* ("The Song of the Earth"), a series of Chinese poems scored to music for a contralto, a tenor, and full orchestra; and many songs.

emotionally ardent as a Mahlerite

MAHOMET

Mahomet or Mohammed (570-632), the Arabian prophet who founded Islam, called Mohammedanism, after facing many dangers and much persecution was finally exiled and fled from Mecca to Medina, a flight called the Hegira. By word and by sword, and with a religious fervor that has not been surpassed, Mahomet propagated the principles which are recorded in the Koran. He wrote, partly inspired by visions, according to his own statement, and partly recording his own beliefs and the principals by which his millions of followers today are guided.

short as Mahomet's dream

MAHU

Mahu is the fiend and prince who urges and instigates to theft. This venerable patron of those who make their living by stealing is mentioned by Shakespeare in *King Lear* (Act IV, Scene I) along with Obidicut, the fiend of lust; Hobbididance, the prince of dumbness; Modo, of murder; and Flibbertigibbet, of moping and mowing.

lured by Mahu's mania

MAIA

Maia was a daughter of Atlas, and the eldest and most beautiful of the seven sisters known as the Pleiades, sometimes called mountain goddesses. In a grotto of Mount Cyllene, in Arcadia, she was seduced by Zeus and made the mother of the god Mercury (Hermes). In Italian mythology she is known as Maia Majesta and is thought to be the Bona Dea, an earth goddess or divinity of the springtime, similar to Fauna and Ops. Sacrifice was made to her by the priest of Vulcan on the first day of her eponymous month, May.

Maia treading the vernal flowers

MAID MARIAN

Maid Marian was a personage in the morris-dance, and dressed sometimes like a woman, sometimes like a strumpet. The name is therefore used to describe women of an impudent, masculine, unchaste, or virago-like character. Though the morris-dances were, as their name implies, of Moorish origin, yet they were commonly adapted in

England to the popular story of Robin Hood, whose fair mistress Matilda, or Marian, was the very person here originally represented. As Queen of May, she has a golden crown upon her head and in her left hand carries a red pink as an emblem of summer. She was "sovereign of the woods, chief lady of the game, her clothes tucked to the knee, and dainty-braided hair, with bow and quiver armed," according to Drayton.

no Maid Marian to be the outlaw's mistress

MAINTENON, MME. DE

Madame de Maintenon (1635-1719) was the second wife of Louis XIV of France, a woman of rare beauty and great talents, governess of a son of Louis, secretly married to the king in 1685—a woman Macaulay records as "of rare understanding, rational and sprightly conversation, serene, tactful, and truly delightful." Madame de Sévigné pictures her extreme grace. She advised the king on matters of state, discussed important questions with foreign ministers, determined policies, and was universally respected. She never lost her delightful manner to the king, even in his extreme and difficult age. Her letters, now published in English, show her grace, intelligence, and high breeding.

with a Madame de Maintenon intelligence and charm

MALACHI

Malachi, the last of the Hebrew minor prophets, is the reputed author of the Old Testament book named after him and dating to the Persian period (c. 464-424 B.C.). He reproves the priests for their laxity in the ritual on which he lays great stress, and denounces the people for foreign intermarriage, foretelling the coming of Elijah.

condemnatory as Malachi

MALAGIGI

Malagigi, in medieval romance, is brought up by the fairy Orlando to become a great enchanter and magician. He is also one of Charlemagne's paladins.

the wizardry of a Malagigi

MALAGROWTHER, SIR MUNGO

Sir Mungo Malagrowther is an embittered old courtier in Scott's novel *The Fortunes of Nigel.* A talented man of distinguished birth, he is unamiable by nature and mutilated by accident. Grown old, deaf, and peevish, he endeavors by malicious and caustic wit to retaliate on an unfriendly world. Soured by misfortune, he tries to make everyone as discontented as himself.

as crabbed and morose as Sir Malagrowther

MALAPROP, MRS.

Mrs. Malaprop is an amusing character in Sheridan's play *The Rivals.* A coquettish old dowager, she made a great pretense to learning, according to the fashion of her time. Her name, which Sheridan coined from the French expression *mal apropos* (meaning "inappropriate," "out of place"), indicates her facility for choosing words close to the sound but laughably far from the meaning of the ones she really wanted, as when she speaks of the terrible "allegories on the banks of the Nile," but means "alligators." Hence, the name suggests someone who is bombastically absurd, pretentious, ridiculous, and ignorant, though wishing to seem learned.

ridiculously Malapropish as usual

MALBECCO

Malbecco is a character in Spenser's *Faerie Queene.* A morose and cankered old man, very wealthy but miserly and mean, he is married to a beautiful young wife of whom he is inordinately jealous. Malbecco seems to be the impersonation of self-inflicted torments, though Helenore, his wife, set fire to his house and eloped with Sir Paridel. Malbecco thereupon cast himself over a high rock, and all his flesh vanished into thin air, leaving behind nothing but his ghost, which was metamorphosed into Jealousy.

like Malbecco, he "dotes, yet doubts; suspects, yet fondly loves."

MALORY, SIR THOMAS

Sir Thomas Malory, who flourished around the year 1470, was the English compiler and translator of that celebrated prose epic of the age of chivalry and knighthood, *Le Morte d'Arthur.* Printed by Caxton in 1485, it is an abridged version of the entire corpus of French Arthurian romance. It has been the source of information and inspiration to all writers in the period, and its author has been identified with Sir Thomas Malory, an English knight who, as the result of differences with a neighboring priory, was imprisoned from the year 1451 on. If so, Malory must have finished his work in jail.

dreams of Malory's knights errant and fair ladies

MALTHUSIAN

Malthusian is from T. R. Malthus (1766-1834), an economist who held that the existing economic evils were due to a too rapidly rising population, and that they could and should be corrected by some natural but compulsory restraint. He asserted that social welfare, general economy, and high standards of living would be the result of "prudential restraint" of population. His many followers were called Malthusians.

impracticable as the Malthusian doctrine

MALVOLIO

Malvolio, in Shakespeare's *Twelfth Night,* is the incredibly conceited steward to Olivia, whom he imagines to be in love with him. Though proud and grave by character, he is gulled into believing that he cuts an attractive figure before his mistress, and his naturally cold and austere dignity are made all the more ludicrous as he makes unsolicited advances to her.

as foolish in his conceit as Malvolio

MAMBRINO

Mambrino was the Moorish prince, in the romantic poems of Boiardo and Ariosto, who owned an enchanted golden helmet that rendered the wearer invisible. It was the object of eager quest by Charlemagne's paladins, and was borne away by the knight Rinaldo. Its celebrity is due to its mention in Cervantes' *Don Quixote,* where the Don is represented as fully believing that he had found it, whereas what he had really come upon was a highly polished copper basin worn by a barber to protect his new hat during a shower.

as proud of his discovery as if he had found Mambrino's golden helmet

---

MAMMON

Mammon, the god of wealth, is mentioned both in the Bible and in mythology as the embodiment of riches. The Bible says, "ye cannot serve God and Mammon." Milton says, "Mammon, the least erected spirit that fell from heaven, admiring more the gold of heaven's pavement than its glory." In any case, Mammon means this world's goods, and Mammonism the worship of them.

a worshiper of Mammon

MAN IN THE MOON

Man in the Moon is the name popularly given to the illusion caused by the dark lines and spots on the earth's satellite, as they are visible to the naked eye. One of the most popular and ancient superstitions in the world, the figure is supposed to be that of a man leaning on a pitchfork on which he carries a bundle of thorns or brushwood, in punishment for the theft of which he was confined to the moon. The belief is mentioned in Shakespeare's *Midsummer-Night's Dream* (Act III, Scene I) and *Tempest* (Act II, Scene II). The origin of the fable may be the story in *Numbers* (xv, 32-36) of the man who was stoned to death for gathering sticks on the Sabbath, though another tradition states that the man is Cain with his dog and thornbush, the bush being emblematic of the fall from grace, and the dog being the "foul fiend." Classical poets made the man out to be Endymion (*q.v.*), taken to the moon by Diana.

an exile as remote as that of the Man in the Moon

MAN WITH THE IRON MASK

The Man with the Iron Mask is a name used to designate an unknown French prisoner whose identity has never been satisfactorily established. Wearing a black velvet mask secured behind the head with steel springs, he was brought with great secrecy to the castle of Pignerol about the year 1679. Subsequently he was imprisoned on the isle of Ste. Marguerite and in the Bastille, always with orders that he be killed if he revealed himself. Until his death on November 19, 1703, he was never permitted to undo the mask even in the presence of his physician, though he was always treated with the utmost respect. In 1703 he was interred in the cemetery of St. Paul under the name of Marchiali. Many conjectures have been hazarded as to the identity of this mysterious prisoner. Though Voltaire supposed him to have been a twin brother of Louis XIV, whose birth was concealed to prevent the civil dissensions which it might one day have caused in France, there have been numerous other equally feasible suggestions.

as baffling as the Man with the Iron Mask

MANDEVILLE, SIR JOHN

Sir John Mandeville (1300-1372), the assumed name of a French physician, probably a native of England, wrote of ostensibly his own travels in Egypt, India, China, as well as of lands to the north. He related such incredible things as having seen sheep growing on trees, men without heads, their eyes in their shoulders, or with ears so long they hang to their knees. True or not, the book made its valuable contribution to a knowledge of geography, even while it placed Mandeville among the world's most fantastic and entertaining liars.

with his most entertaining Mandevillian stories

MANES

The Manes, or Di Manes, were the deified souls of the departed, worshiped by the Romans with divine honors. Collectively they were thought to be hostile, and so were called by euphemism "the kindly ones." Having supernatural powers, they were also identified with the Di Inferi, or gods of the lower world, Dis, Proserpina, and Hecate. On their festivals, which were held three times a year, these deities were supposed to come forth from their abode and offerings were made to them to placate them. If properly propitiated, they were regarded as protecting divinities. Sometimes their name is used of the lower world itself, as the home of these departed spirits, and also of the punishments meted out there.

worships his ancestors as devoutly as if they were potent Manes

MANET, EDOUARD

Edouard Manet (1832-1883) was the founder of the French school of impressionism in painting. His *Olympia* is a portrait of a nude woman reclining on a couch which is spread with a white sheet, contrasting with a black cat at the nude's feet and the head of a negress carrying a bouquet of flowers in the background. Works like *The Garden* gave rise to the open-air group of painters, who stressed the value of outdoor lighting to pictorial effects.

a nude as striking as Manet's Olympia

MANFRED

Manfred, the hero of Byron's drama of the same name, is a being estranged from all human creatures and indifferent to all human sympathies. Dwelling in the magnificent solitude of the central Alps, he communes only with the seven spirits which he acquired by selling himself to the Prince of Darkness. They are earth, ocean, air, night, mountains, winds, and the star of his own destiny, and he invokes them by his sorceries. He is haunted by the fearful memory of the Lady Astarte, whom he had loved and destroyed. When he goes to the hall of Arimanes to see and speak to her, he is told that he will die on the following day. When the Spirit of his Destiny comes to him then, he proudly dismisses it and dies.

a romantic recluse of the Manfred type

MANICHAEUS

Manichaeus, or Manes, or Mani (216-277 A.D.), was the Persian sage and founder of Manichaeism, a dualistic religious philosophy which taught that light and goodness, personified as God, are in perpetual conflict with chaos and evil. The servant of a rich widow who left him her great wealth, Manichaeus traveled to Turkestan, India, and China, announcing himself to be an apostle of Christ, claiming that he received divine revelations and that he was the final prophet of God to come to this world. Bitterly denounced by the Magians, he was finally crucified by Shapur I, king of Persia.

Manichaean conflict with the powers of evil

MANLIUS

Manlius Torquatus, a popular hero in the early annals of the Roman Republic, gained his surname by defeating in single-handed combat a gigantic Gaul and stripping from him his twisted ornamental necklace (*torquis*) in 361 B.C. As consul during the Latin War of 340 B.C., he forbade any single skirmishes between his scouts and those of the enemy. So strict and harsh were his orders, known ever since as *Manliana imperia,* that he demanded the execution of his own son for violating them. Hence, the name *Manlian* connotes severe penalties and impartial sentencing.

as impersonal toward his own son as Manlius

MANLY

Manly is one of the characters in Wycherley's *Plain Dealer,* described by the author as "of an honest, surly, nice humor, supposed first in the time of the Dutch War to have procured the command of a ship, out of honor, not interest, and choosing a sea-life only to avoid the world." This violent and uncouth character has been better characterized by Leigh Hunt as "a ferocious sensualist, who believed himself as great a rascal as he thought everybody else." He does, however, present an excellent contrast to the hypocritical Olivia.

a misanthropic escapist like Manly

MANOA

Manoa is a fabulous city of unbounded wealth, great size, and formidable population, the capital of El Dorado (*q.v.*), the Indian chief whose body was powdered daily with gold dust. Supposed by the Spaniards of the 15th century to be situated between the Orinoco and Amazon rivers, and by Sir Walter Raleigh (1595) to lie in Guiana, it was the object of many a quest, great outlay of money, and severe privation and suffering.

the Manoa of his dreams

MANON (LESCAUT)

Manon Lescaut, the heroine of Abbé Prévost's novel replete with pathos, *L'Histoire du Chevalier des Grieux et de Manon Lescaut*, is a girl of strong desires who, en route to become a nun, meets the handsome young Des Grieux at a coach stop in an inn. Lovers at first sight, they flee together to Paris, where Manon is driven to physical unfaithfulness to her lover and high-class prostitution by her overwhelming desire for the luxuries with which wealthier paramours can provide her. Apprehended by the gendarmes, she is sent with a cargo of common streetwalkers to a French penal colony near New Orleans, whither Des Grieux follows her. They escape together to the desert, where the unfaithful and wretched Manon dies of exposure. The story inspired operas by Auber, Balfe, Massenet, and Puccini.

with Manon's fatal love for finery

MANTALINI

Mantalini is a fop of extravagant habits in Dickens' *Nicholas Nickleby*. An exquisite man-milliner, he is noted for his white teeth, minced oaths, and gorgeous morning gown. He lives on the earnings of his wife, Mme. Mantalini, a fashionable milliner near Cavendish Square, whose industry he bankrupts with his luxurious and sybaritic cravings and with whom he is continually quarreling and threatening suicide.

like Mantalini, parasitically content to be supported by his wife

MANU

Manu is a mythical Hindu sage, or one of the fourteen ancestors of the human race. Present mankind is derived from the seventh Manu, who, like Noah, survived the great deluge in an ark. He is also the reputed author of the Code of Laws, supposed to have had its origin sometime between 400 B.C. and 200 A.D., discussing the creation of the universe, the condition of the soul after death, the duties of caste, and so forth.

a descent as illustrious as that from some ancient Manu

MARAH

Marah is the name of the halting place where the wandering Israelites found only bitter water after they had crossed the Red Sea (*Exodus*, xv, 23-25). Taken as a name by Naomi, the mother-in-law of Ruth, in her sorrow, the word has come to connote grief and barren disappointment.

lamenting by the waters of Marah

MARAT, JEAN PAUL

Jean Paul Marat (1744-1793), one of the three leaders of the French Revolution, was generally believed to be the most cruel of all, and the one to whom the extreme terrors were attributed. He was finally stabbed by Charlotte Corday, who gained admission to his apartment under the pretext of having for him a desired list of persons to be guillotined. His associates were Danton and Robespierre.

the fate of a Marat

MARATHON

Marathon is the plain in Attica, some 22 miles northwest of Athens, on which the Athenians defeated the Persians against overwhelming odds when they invaded Greece in 490 B.C. From the dispatch of a fast runner, Phidippides, to Sparta to summon reinforcements comes our use of the word to signify a long-distance race, though it is often erroneously ascribed to a reputed rapid carrying to Athens of news of the victory. Both because of the battle and the race, the name today connotes extreme heroism and endurance in the face of insuperable difficulties.

Marathonian heroism

MARCELLUS

Marcus Claudius Marcellus (268-208 B.C.) was the famous Roman general who slew Britomartus, king of the Insubrian Gauls, insingle-handed combat, thus winning the *spolia opima,* or "richest spoils," awarded only to champions in such contests. He was the third and last in the history of the Roman republic to earn this unique distinction, granted only when leaders of hostile armies spared their troops battle and settled the issue between themselves. In spite of the elaborate defense works of Archimedes, he also succeeded in wresting Syracuse by siege from Hannibal. Known as the "sword of Rome," he was killed in ambush by Carthaginian forces, when consul for the fifth time in 208 B.C.

Another and later Marcellus was the son of Octavia, sister of Augustus, and the latter's heir designate. The untimely death of this youth of great promise inspired Vergil to write the touching tribute to his memory at the end of the sixth book of the *Aeneid.* During the poet's public reading of this passage, Octavia swooned from the grief which its pathos caused her to feel, and is said to have paid Vergil handsomely in appreciation, so much per line.

like Marcellus, a leader willing to expose himself to the enemy's chief

---

MARCHIONESS

The Marchioness is a poor, abused, half-starved girl in Dickens' *Old Curiosity Shop.* As the "small servant" to Sampson and Sally Brass, she is constantly ill-fed and mistreated by her employers. Eventually she aids in bringing them to justice and marries Dick Swiveller, the devil-may-care fellow who conferred on her the wistfully ironic sobriquet.

the pathetic little Marchioness of a hard-hearted employer

MARGARET

Margaret is the heroine of Goethe's *Faust* and, as Marguérite, of Gounod's opera of the same name. She falls in love with the title-character, who had made a compact with Mephistopheles, is seduced by him, and bears him a child. Overwhelmed with shame, she destroys the infant and is condemned to death. Gaining admission to the dungeon in which she is imprisoned in an effort to save her, Faust finds her huddled on a bed of straw, singing wild snatches of ancient ballads. Her reason gone, she opposes all his efforts to rescue her. At last morning dawns, and Mephistopheles hurries Faust off as Margaret dies and is taken to heaven, exalted by love above her lowly station, her shame, and her guilt.

like Margaret, both guiltless and guilty

MARIAMNE

Mariamne (60-29 B.C.) was the first wife of Herod the Great, who put her to death in a fit of jealous rage. She is the subject of works by Voltaire and Hebbel.

the doom of a suspected Mariamne

MARIANA

Mariana, in Shakespeare's *Measure for Measure,* is the lovely lady who lived in a grange surrounded by a moat. Though betrothed to Angelo, the deputy of Duke Vincentio, she is wronged by him in his wicked passion for Isabella. Pleading successfully with the Duke for his pardon, she is ultimately permitted to marry him. Her forsaken state suggested to Tennyson the subject of two poems titled after her.

jilted like Mariana

MARITORNES

Maritornes (Spanish for *bad woman*) is a stunted, vulgar, and lewd Asturian wench who figures as a servant at an inn in Cervantes' *Don Quixote*. The hyperbolic imagination of the Don takes the inn for a castle, and Maritornes for the daughter of the lord who owns it. Fancying her to be in love with his gallant figure, he supposes her hair, "rough as a horse's tail," to be "silken threads of finest gold."

the Maritornes of the tavern, a lascivious trollop

MARIUS

Caius Marius (157-86 B.C.) was the brilliant Roman military strategist who ended the prolonged war against Jugurtha, overthrew the Teutons and Cimbri, Germanic tribes that had invaded Italy and Gaul, and reorganized the Roman army, recruiting professional soldiers and volunteers from all classes of society. He made his troops dependent directly on him for bonuses and rewards. A liberal, he married the aunt of Julius Caesar and was the implacable enemy of the reactionary and conservative senatorial man Sulla, on whose supporters he inflicted cruel massacres through proscription during the latter's absence from Italy for the war against Mithradates (which Marius had hoped to conduct himself). He died insane, leaving dictatorial powers in the hands of Sulla.

a strategist and army-man of Marius's caliber

MARIVAUDAGE

Marivaudage is a word coined by French literary critics to describe the peculiarly humorous style of Pierre Carlet de Chamblain de Marivaux (1688-1763), novelist and playwright who began his literary career with the composition of travesties of Homer and Fénelon, later writing a novel, *Marianne,* and finding his chief support in writing comedies for the Comédie Italienne. *Jeu de l'Amour et du Hasard* ("Game of Love and Chance") and *Arlequin Poli par l'Amour* ("Harlequin Refined by Love") are among his most famous plays. The topical matter of much of his writing concerns the metaphysics of making love.

His style derives its peculiar effects from his diction, which employs common words where dignified ones are expected and *vice versa,* thus producing comical reactions through surprise and shock. Crébillon described it as "an introduction to each other of words which have never made acquaintance, and which think that they will not get on together." Marivaudage refers to any such fantastic embroidery of language. The author also developed for the theater the idiosyncratic trick of having his characters tell each other and the audience in frank language exactly what they are thinking or what they suppose themselves to be thinking.

diction replete with Marivaudages

MARK, KING

King Mark was a treacherous ruler of Cornwall, according to Arthurian romance. Uncle of Tristan (*q.v.*), he lived in the castle of Tintagel and was married to Isolde, who betrayed him because of her love for Tristan. Cuckolded, he unwittingly caused the mortal wounding of Tristan and the *Liebestod,* or "love death," of Isolde. The illicit love of his nephew and his wife was proverbial in the Middle Ages and is the subject of Wagner's great music-drama.

unsuspecting as Mark of his unfaithful wife

MARK, ST.

St. Mark, the evangelist and author of the second gospel, is represented in art as a man in the prime of life, sometimes habited as a bishop or holding a pen and a book and accompanied by a winged lion (as the historian of the resurrection).

the lion of St. Mark

MARLEY, JACOB

Jacob Marley, in Dickens *Christmas Carol,* is the former business partner of Scrooge, and his ghost appears to reprove the miserly misanthrope on Christmas eve.

the warning apparition of a Jacob Marley

MARLOVIAN

Marlovian refers to the life and works of Christopher Marlowe (1564-1593), English poet-dramatist and personal friend of Sir Walter Raleigh. In *Tamburlaine the Great* he was the first writer to discover the stately dignity of blank verse as a vehicle for dramatic expression. The verse of *Dr. Faustus, The Jew of Malta,* and *Edward II* is equally distinguished for its freedom and power and for its variety. The author of shorter poems as well, he was denounced as an atheist and an immoral and licentious person. He was killed in a tavern brawl, supposed to have originated in some lewd love affair.

Marlovian in its rolling sonority

MARLOW, YOUNG

Young Marlow, the hero of Goldsmith's *She Stoops to Conquer,* is a swaggerer who is shy and diffident before ladies of his own class but has a penchant for domestics and low women. Kate Hardcastle finally tricks him into marriage by posing as a barmaid.

as much at home with working girls as Young Marlow

MARMION

Marmion is the hero of Sir Walter Scott's poem of the same name. An English knight, he is valiant and sagacious, but profligate and unscrupulous as well. Engaged to Constance de Beverly, he prefers the fortune of Lady Clare, whose lover, Ralph de Wilton, he has overcome and left for dead on a field of battle. After various adventures in Scotland he finally falls in battle on the field of Flodden, and De Wilton regains Lady Clare.

as brave in the sight of gold as Marmion

MARNER, SILAS

Silas Marner is the hero of George Eliot's novel of the same name. A poor hand-weaver, he has had his life wrecked by a false accusation of theft. He is consoled by the great mutual affection existing between himself and a small foundling girl he finds by chance.

like Silas Marner, the victim of an injustice

MARPLOT

Marplot is one of the characters in Mrs. Centlivre's comedy *The Busybody.* A silly and cowardly fellow, he is very inquisitive to know everybody's business. A calling name, the word *marplot* designates one who by meddling interference frustrates or spoils a plan.

curiously instrusive as Marplot

MARQUETTE, JACQUES

Jacques, or *Père,* Marquette (1637-1675) was the famous French Jesuit missionary and explorer in Canada and the Great Lakes region. On an expedition among the Ottawa Indians he founded the mission of St. Ignace on the Straits of Mackinac. This intrepid and zealous monk also accompanied Joliet on the famous voyage down the Mississippi to the mouth of the Arkansas River, returning to Lake Michigan via the Illinois River. In 1681 he published his diary and notes of the voyage, thereby stimulating further discovery and the establishment of settlements by brave pioneers.

pioneering with the religious fervor of Père Marquette

MARS

Mars was the Roman god of war, whose priests, the Salii, danced in full armor. The Campus Martius in Rome was named after him. Martial and martialist, meaning warlike and warrior, come from his name. Terrible and majestic, his march shakes the world. His counterpart in the Greek pantheon was Ares.

heroic Ajax, marching like Mars

MARSI

The Marsi were a brave and warlike people living in the central Italian Apennines. Proverbial for their valor, they instigated the revolt of Rome's allies against her in the "Social" or Marsian war, with the franchise in Rome as their demand. They were also acquainted with the medicinal properties of herbs as a cure for snakebite. Hence, they were regarded as magicians and said to be descended from Circe.

as belligerent and hardy as the Marsi

MARSYAS

Marsyas was the Phrygian satyr who found the flute that Athena had thrown away, disgusted at the manner in which it distorted her features to play it. Discovering that it emitted beautiful tones of its own accord, he rashly challenged Apollo, the god of music, to a contest in which the Muses were to be the judges. Playing the cithara, Apollo easily won the verdict over the flute playing of Marsyas. In punishment for the satyr's arrant presumption, he was tied to a tree and flayed alive by the god. Statues of the foolish Marsyas were commonly found in ancient cities, doubtless intended to serve as a warning against boastful effrontery and arrogant audacity. The statuary group of Athena, Marsyas and the Flute, exists in a Roman copy of Myron's celebrated marble sculptures.

as foolhardy and conceited as Marsyas

MARTHA

Martha was the sister of Mary and Lazarus, whose house in Bethany Jesus frequently visited (*John* xi, 1 ff.; *Luke*, x, 38-42). In medieval and later Christian allegory she symbolizes the active and energetic physical life, as contrasted with the contemplative and meditative spiritual life of Mary. Thus, one speaks of the *way of Martha*, as opposed to the *way of Mary*, Martha being the tidy and bustling housewife concerned only with domestic chores and business.

prosaic-minded as Martha

MARTIAL

Marcus Valerius Martial (c. 40-104 A.D.) was the Roman epigrammatic poet born in Spain. He came to the Italian metropolis and lived there for thirty-five years, first dwelling in poverty in a tenement and later the owner of a small house in the capital and a villa at Nomentum, the means for which were largely accumulated from servile flattery to the emperors Titus and Domitian, his patrons. His fourteen books of *Epigrammata* exhibit wit, satire, a fertile imagination, and felicitous phrasing. One book celebrated the opening in 80 A.D. of the great Flavian amphitheater known as the Colosseum. Many of his poems are mottoes suitable for accompanying gifts sent to friends (*Xenia*), others express gratitude for presents received at banquets (*Apophoreta*). In concise and pointed language, though he does not give the real names of the persons he satirizes, he writes with coarse and gross obscenity about debauchees, gluttons, drunkards, legacy-hunters, perverts, and hypocrites of all types.

a gallery of characters as varied as those that roam the pages of Martial

---

MARTIN OF TOURS

Saint Martin of Tours (315-399) was the French prelate, bishop, and patron saint of France, whose festival falls on the 11th of November. Born of heathen parents, he divided his cloak with a beggar, had a vision of Christ announcing his charity with approbation, and was converted to Christianity, influencing his mother to do likewise. Because Martinmas, his feast, occurred on the same day as a pagan festival which it supplanted, some of the latter's qualities were confused with him, thus causing him to be considered the patron of taverns and innkeepers, drinking, reformed drunkards, and jovial meetings.

Martin of Tours presiding over the hilarity

MARTINET, JEAN

General Jean Martinet was the French army officer of Louis XIV who devised a new and uniform system of military drill still known by his name. Accidentally shot and killed by his own artillery at the siege of Duisburg in 1672, he made the army manageable and efficient. The name is usually used in the derogatory sense of a strict disciplinarian, a drillmaster, and a stickler for decorum and etiquette. Martinetism refers to a rigid adherence to principle.

another Martinet, watchful against any breach of propriety

MARX, KARL

Karl Marx (1818-1883) was the editor of a German radical newspaper who later founded the Communist economic philosophy known as dialectical materialism. The friend and associate of Friedrich Engels, he wrote the "Manifesto of the Communist Party" in 1840. Devoting much of his time to the labor movement and to the organization of workers into unions, he also wrote *Class Struggles in France* and the monumental *Das Kapital,* which was finished after his death by his friend Engels. The latter years of his life were lived as a political refugee and exile in Paris, Brussels, and London.

Marxian devotion to the interests of the laborer and common man

---

MARY OF BETHANY

(see *Martha*)

MASCARILLE

Mascarille, in three comedies by Molière, is the name of the skilfully intriguing valet whose character is marked by the lying ingenuity and effrontery for which any reference to him has become synonymous.

a Mascarille at duplicity

MASKWELL

Maskwell is the name of a sinister hypocrite in Congreve's *Double Dealer.*

a Maskwell at equivocation

MASOCHISM

Masochism is from Leopold von Sacher Masoch (1836-1895), the Austrian novelist whose name has become a byword in the repertoire of psychiatry. In his works he depicted the degenerate state in which "masochists" can obtain sexual satisfaction only through physical pain and torture or degrading humiliation. Masochism is thus the complement of Sadism.

exhibits strong traits of masochism

MASON AND DIXON

Mason and Dixon refers to the boundary line separating the free state of Pennsylvania from the former slave states of Maryland and Virginia. Drawn by Charles Mason and Jeremiah Dixon, two English mathematicians and surveyors, between 1763 and 1767, it gained proverbial celebrity since the time of the excited congressional debate on the question of excluding slavery from Missouri in 1820, when the eccentric John Randolph of Roanoke made great use of the phrase. Mason and Dixon now connotes segregation, prejudice, and suppression of minority groups.

a sharper line of discrimination than that drawn by Mason and Dixon

---

MASTER LEONARD

Master Leonard, in the fantastic system of Middle Age demonology, was a powerful devil in the infernal court. Grand master of the "sabbats," or nocturnal assemblages of demons and sorcerers, he presided over their orgies in the representation of a three-horned goat with a black human countenance. Stolen children were thought to be brought to him to be marked by one of his horns with a sign which they bore during their novitiate, and they there had to renounce God, the Holy Virgin, and the Saints.

a regular Master Leonard, adept at black magic

MATHER, COTTON

Cotton Mather (1663-1728), the son of Increase, was the famous American Congregational clergyman who preached of fire, brimstone, and the torments of Hell. Though his father's *Cases of Conscience Concerning Evil Spirits* was credited with disapproving of executions for witchcraft, Cotton at first countenanced them, later withdrawing his support on the ground they were unfair. *Wonders of the Invisible World* and *Essays to Do Good* were among the works of this pious decrier of worldliness.

warning with the grim earnestness of Cotton Mather

MATISSE, HENRI

Henri Matisse (1869-) is the renowned French post-impressionist painter and the leader of the Fauvists. A painter of light, he achieves the effect of modelling and illusion of space by using pure tones on a large scale, rather than as the impressionists did by juxtaposition of minute touches of color. Successful in an expressive distortion of his subjects, he is an artist of revolutionary tendencies, producing bulk in his figures by the use of shadow rather than of contour. His favorite subjects are small feminine figures, brilliantly illuminated interiors, and still life.

as distorted in outline as a Matisse

MATSYA

Matsya, in Hindu mythology, is the name of the first avatar or incarnation of Vishnu. In the form of a fish he saved Manu (primeval mankind) from the deluge by pulling his ark to a high crag.

saved by a miraculous Matsya

MATSYS' FLY

Quintin Matsys (1466-1530), the Flemish artist, painted a fly on the silk-stockinged leg of one of his male models so realistically that Mandyn, a rival artist, tried to brush it off with his handkerchief.

illusory as Matsys' fly

MATTHEW, ST.

St. Matthew was a tax-collector at Copernaum who, at the summons of Jesus, became one of the twelve apostles. Traditionally regarded as the author of the first gospel, he is pictured in art as a winged man bearing a lance.

evangelizing like St. Matthew

MATUTA

Matuta, or Mater Matuta, was the Roman spirit of the dawn and morning, hence, of creation and birth. The female counterpart of Janus (*q.v.*), she became later a protectress of childbirth. She was venerated by the Greeks as Leucothea.

Matuta paling in the skies

MAUPASSANT, GUY DE

Guy de Maupassant (1850-1893), realist and inimitable master of "naturalistic" short-story writing, was the godson and protégé of Flaubert. *Boule de Suif,* the first work with which he attracted wide attention, was immediately proclaimed a masterpiece of the objective viewpoint with which the name of Maupassant is associated. Until his death from insanity he wrote countless tales, novels, verse, and some theater pieces.

the ironic cruelty of a story by Maupassant

MAUSOLUS

Mausolus was the king of Caria in Asia Minor from 377 to 353 B.C. His wife, Artemisia, honored him by erecting a splendid and costly tomb that was accounted one of the Seven Wonders of the World. His statue and some of the sculptures from the tomb are now in the British Museum, and his name has given us the word *mausoleum.*

entombed with the majesty of Mausolus

MAVERICK, SAMUEL

Samuel Maverick (1803-1870) was a Texan pioneer, rancher, and member of the convention that established the Republic of Texas. Later, mayor of San Antonio and a member of the first legislature of the State of Texas, he owned a 385,000 acre cattle ranch. The term *maverick* for an unbranded yearling derives from his practice of not branding his calves. Hence, the word has come to mean something acquired dishonestly, by expropriating another's unmarked cattle or unoccupied land.

enough land to satisfy Samuel Maverick

MAXIMILIAN OF MEXICO

Maximilian, brother of Francis Joseph, Emperor of Austria, became the unwilling puppet and pawn of international intrigue when the French convinced him to accept the throne of Mexico (April 10, 1864) after their partial conquest of that country. With his wife Carlota he established himself in Mexico City, and, still aided by the French, he drove the rebel Juarez over the nothern frontier. But when the United States government refused to recognize his imperial rights, the French withdrew their support and their army, and betrayed of aid in an enterprise not of his own choosing, this unhappy tool of diplomacy was captured, court-martialed, and shot by Juarez in 1867.

victimized like Maximilian

MAYEUX

Mayeux is the name of the hunchback who figures prominently in countless French caricatures and tales. The popularity of the character has made it the recognized type of a man dreadfully deformed, vain and licentious, but brave and intelligent withal.

unsightly and lecherous as Mayeux

MAYO

William and Charles Mayo, brothers and physicians, built up in Rochester, Minnesota, a clinic where ailing people had so true a diagnosis and were treated with such skill, intelligence, and fairness that the clinic became known to all the world. Their standard of training for the doctors who worked with them was so high, and is still so carefully maintained, that the name goes on, even though the Mayos themselves have died.

the Mayo tradition

MAZDAKITE

A Mazadakite was a follower of Mazdak, a Persian religious reformer of the late fifth century A.D. Originally a Magian priest, he founded a sect which practiced community of property and of wives, simplicity of life, and vegetarian abstention from meat. He was put to death by consent of King Kobad.

a meatless table fit for a Mazdakite

MAZEPPA, IVAN

Ivan Mazeppa (1644-1709), once a chief of the Cossacks, became a page in the Polish royal court, where he had an affair with a countess. The count, on discovering it, punished Mazeppa by having him lashed naked to the back of a wild horse which was then loosed. The horse dashed madly about until it died of exhaustion, and Mazeppa was nursed back to health by some native tribesmen. Byron has Mazeppa tell the story to Charles XII in his highly dramatic poem, *Mazeppa's Ride.*

a Mazeppa nightmare

MAZZINI, GIUSEPPE

Giuseppe Mazzini (1805-1872) was a great Italian patriot, democrat, and agitator. A member of the *Carbonari,* a secret society formed for expelling Murat and the French and establishing a republic in Italy, he was imprisoned and exiled to Marseilles. He then organized *Young Italy,* a revolutionary society to work for the unification of that country under republician institutions. On the outbreak of the 1848 revolution, he returned to his country and established the Republic of Rome in 1849, but when Papal control of the city was re-established he was again exiled. Inciting rebellious demonstrations in Mantua, Milan, and Genoa, he aided to organize Garibaldi's expeditions. An uncompromising republican until his death, he refused to accept a seat in Parliament under a monarchical government.

intransigent as Mazzini to monarchy

MEANDER

The Meander, a river in Asia Minor, flows into the Aegean Sea so slowly and by so many windings and turnings that its name has been applied to persons who habitually wander slowly, circuitously, in a leisurely fashion. It is also the name of an artistic design, the fret—or key pattern.

came meandering along in his usual aimless fashion

MECCA

Mecca, the birthplace of Mohammed, is therefore so sacred to all Mohammedans that every Moslem is required to make a journey to Mecca once a year. The name is now also applied to any supremely desirable goal or to any end sought by great numbers of people.

the Mecca toward which they strive

MECK, NADEJDA VON

Nadejda von Meck, the widow of a wealthy Russian railway engineer, was the patroness of Peter Ilitch Tschaikovsky from 1877 to 1890, making him financially independent and able to concentrate exclusively on the composition of his great musical scores. Rich and autocratic, she conducted a platonic friendship with him, stipulating that there must be no personal relationship except through the medium of correspondence. Though it was inevitable that they meet physically at concerts, it is said that they never conversed with each other, Tschaikovsky simply acknowledging her with a bow. His Fourth Symphony was dedicated to her. For some reason or another their friendship was abruptly severed three years before his death, Mme. von Meck apparently feeling that she was neglecting her family through her passionate devotion to his music.

seeking a benefactress like Mme. von Meck

MEDEA

Medea, a Colchian princess celebrated for her skill in magic, fell in love with Jason after she had helped him to obtain the Golden Fleece. Later, deserted by Jason, she turned murderess, killed their two sons and Jason's new wife, Creusa of Corinth, and fled in a chariot drawn by dragons to Athens, where she married King Aegeus. She is the symbol of magic, vengeance, and cruelty.

fled like Medea in her dragon car

MEDES AND PERSIANS

The Medes and Persians were peoples noted even today for the fact that their laws, once made, were not subject to change. The phrase, "a law of the Medes and Persians," means there is no possibility of any change, modification, or even relaxation of the law exactly at it stands; hence, unchangeable, impregnable, permanent.

fear not; this is not the land of the Medes and Persians

MEDICI

The Medici, one of the most noble and wealthy of Renaissance Italian families, with distinguished members in many arts and dignities, were later concerned in so many infamous tyrannies and intrigues, most of them under Catherine de Medici (1519-1589) who had made France miserable under successive reigns of her sons, that the house of Medici came to a shameful end. In the days of their glory they were made the subjects of innumerable portraits, so that the style of dress then prevalent became familiar to the world, and to this day the collar high at the back and rolling outward at the side is called the Medici collar.

a match for the Medici in intrigue

MEDUSA

Medusa was the most famous of the Gorgons. In lieu of hair, writhing serpents fringed her head, and she had wings, brazen claws and enormous teeth. At first Medusa was beautiful, but for becoming the mother of Pegasus (Poseidon was the father) in one of Athena's temples, the virgin goddess made her head so fearful that anyone who looked at it was turned to stone. When Perseus killed her he presented her head to Athena, who placed it on her aegis, a short cloak covered with scales and an impenetrable shield.

fearful Medusan hair

MEGAERA

Megaera, a daughter of Nox (Night) and Acheron, the river of woe in the lower world, was one of the three Furies who visited punishment on the wicked in Tartarus. Like her sisters, Tisiphone and Alecto, she brandished a flaming torch as, with snakes writhing in her hair, she meted out retribution with her whip.

cruel Megaeran vengeance
vindictive as Megaera

MEISTERSINGER

A Meistersinger was a member of one of the workingmen's guilds that were founded in Germany (1300-1500) for the purpose of cultivating the musical and poetic arts. The successors of the Minnesingers (*q.v.*), they often chose subjects of Biblical origin, which they presented in a lyrical setting to the accompaniment of a harp. The four novitiate degrees that had to be passed in contest before a candidate rose to the eminence of a *Meister* ("Master") were satirized for their pedantry by Wagner in his great comic opera, *Die Meistersinger von Nuernberg.*

the soloist of the male chorus, as jealous of his preeminence as a Meistersinger

---

MEJNOUN AND LEILAH

Mejnoun and Leilah are ideal lovers in Persian literature, patterned after Pyramus and Thisbe of Greek culture and Romeo and Juliet of later times. Esteemed among the Arabians as the most beautiful, chaste, and impassioned of lovers, they are regarded by the Mohammedans in the same light in which the Song of Songs is regarded among the Jewish people. Their amours are celebrated in the verse of many Oriental languages.

as perfectly mated as Mejnoun and Leilah

MELAMPUS

Melampus, "Black Foot," was the son of Amythaon and the brother of Bias. A famous Greek soothsayer and physician, he became the ancestor of a family of seers and prophets. Because his ears were licked, while he slept, by two young serpents which he had saved from death, he could understand the voices of birds and of beasts. Instructed by Apollo in the art of divination, he was the first to introduce the worship of Dionysus (Bacchus) into Greece. By his discovery of the herb malampodium, named after him and a kind of hellebore (a cure for insanity), he relieved the women of Argos of the madness that had seized them because of their opposition to the cult of Dionysus. He and his brother Bias were regarded as symbols of cunning and force.

listening like Melampus to the bird voices

MELANTIUS

Melantius is a brave and honest soldier in Beaumont and Fletcher's play *The Maid's Tragedy*. Incapable of suspecting evil till it becomes impossible to be ignorant of it, he believes everyone to be true and honest until actually convicted of criminal conduct. Then, however, he becomes a relentless and unshrinking punisher of guilt.

as fair-mindedly naive as Melantius

MELBA, NELLIE

Nellie Melba (1859-1931) was born with the family name Armstrong, but took her stage name from her birthplace near Melbourne, Australia. Though this sensational operatic coloratura soprano was a cold and unemotional actress, the liquid tones of her voice and its virtuosity made her the greatest successor to Adelina Patti (*q.v.*). Famous for her interpretation of the role of the mad *Lucia di Lammermoor* in Donizetti's opera, she was created a dame of the British empire in 1918. Various gastronomic delicacies, including Melba toast and Peach Melba, were named after her.

a diva of the quality of Nellie Melba

MELCHIZEDEK

Melchizedek ("king of righteousness") was the priest-king of Salem to whom Abraham paid tithes (*Genesis,* xiv, 18 ff.). In the *Epistle to the Hebrews* (v, 6-10) he is mentioned as the spiritual prototype of Christ, because he combined ideally the priestly and royal offices.

righteous as Melchizedek

MELEAGER

Meleager was the son of the Calydonian king, Oeneus, and of Althaea (*q.v.*) He distinguished himself as one of the Argonauts, and by his skill in throwing the javelin. Diana (Artemis) sent a wild boar to ravage Calydon, because

Oeneus had neglected to pay her homage. All the princes of the age assembled to hunt it down, but Meleager alone could kill it. He then gave it to Atalanta, his beloved, but when his mother's brothers took it from her, Meleager in a rage slew them. Whereupon his mother caused his own destruction by burning the extinguished firebrand, on the preservation of which his life depended. Repenting, she put an end to her own life, and Meleager's sisters wept so inconsolably over him that Diana changed them into guinea-hens and transported them to the island of Leros.

stalking his prey like Meleager

MELESIGENES

Melesigenes is an appellation sometimes given to Homer, on the supposition that he was born on the banks of the Meles, a river of Ionia where the great epic poet was born. Another story relates that the river-god himself was his father.

blind as Melesigenes

MELIBOEUS

Meliboeus is a shepherd and one of the interlocutors in Vergil's *1st Eclogue*. His name has given us the word Melibean, referring in rhetoric and poetry to prose passages or lines of verse spoken or sung with alternating and antiphonal responses.

a pastoral Meliboeus, wandering over the hills with the sheep

---

MELICERTES

Melicertes was the son of Athamas, king of Thebes, and Ino. When his father was seized with madness for having incurred the anger of Hera by being unfaithful to his wife, Nephele, Ino cast herself with Melicertes into the sea. Both were transformed into marine deities, Ino becoming Leucothea, and Melicertes changing into Palaemon. The Romans identified him with Portunus, the protecting genius of harbors.

made the port with the aid of Melicertes

MELISANDE

(see *Pelléas and Mélisande*)

MELISSA

Melissa, in Greek mythology, was the nymph reputed to have discovered the use of honey. Bees were consequently named after her. In legend, another Melissa was the wife of Periander, tyrant of Corinth, who accused her unjustly of infidelity and murdered her in a raptus of jealousy.

Melissan sweetness

MELPOMENE

(see *Muse*)

Melpomene was the Muse of tragedy. In ancient works of art she was pictured as having vine leaves in her hair and wearing the cothurnus, a shoe with elevated soles worn by tragic actors in order to add to their height and dignity. Though she properly inspired the writing of tragic drama, by transference the name may be applied to a fine tragic actress.

the brooding air of Melpomene
Melpomenean talent for tragedies

MELUSINA

Melusina was the daughter of the fairy Pressina and Elenas, king of Albania. Herself a fay, she was condemned to become every Saturday a serpent from the waist downward, because she had imprisoned her father in a high mountain in order to avenge an insult her mother had received from him. Having married Raymond, Count of Poitiers, she was seen by him during her loathsome transformation, an indiscretion on his part caused by his violation of a solemn promise never to visit her on a Saturday. He then immured her in a subterranean dungeon of the castle of Lusignan, named after her. A *Melusinan cry* is a proverbial expression for a sudden scream, recalling that with which the unfortunate fairy discovered her lord's intrusion.

with Melusina's hatred of Saturdays

MELVILLE, HERMAN

Herman Melville (1819-1891), author of the classic of seafaring, *Moby Dick,* ran away from home in his youth to become a mariner on a whaler and later deserted ship to live among cannibal natives on the Marquesas Islands. An enlisted seaman on the frigate *United States,* he devoted his last years to the writing of many fine novels reflecting his passionate love of adventure at sea, including *Typee, Omoo, Mardi, White Jacket, Redburn,* and *Pierre: or the Ambiguities.*

down to the sea (in imagination) with Herman Melville

MEMNON

Memnon was the Ethiopian son of Eos (Aurora), the goddess of the dawn, and Tithonus, and came to the Trojan War to help his uncle, King Priam. After he was killed by Achilles, the ancients declared the dew to be the tears of his mother who wept every morning over his death. The more eastern of the granite statues of Amenophis II at Thebes, Egypt, was supposed by the Greeks to be that of Memnon. As the rays of the rising sun touched it, it was said to give forth the music of a lyre.

soft as Memnon's harp at morning
mournful as Memnon's harp
silent as the lips of Memnon

MENAECHMUS

Menaechmus is the name of the twin brothers who are the heroes of a comedy by Plautus that is based on their confused identities and that furnished the main source for Shakespeare's *Comedy of Errors.* The wife, father-in-law, and mistress of the one Menaechmus, who had been kidnapped and transported to Epidamnus when still a child, mistake his brother from Syracuse for him and conclude that he is insane, since he fails to recognize them. Only when the twins confront each other is the puzzle solved.

alike as Menaechmus to Menaechmus

MENALCAS

Menalcas is the name of a shepherd in the pastoral poetry of Theocritus and Vergil. The name is given to the inveterate enemy and treacherous rival of Colin Clout in Spenser's *Shepherd's Calendar.* Since the time of the bucolic poets it has been used for any rustic swain or herdsman.

Spend some months yet among the sheepwalks of Cumberland; learn all you can, from all the shepherds you can find,—from Thyrsis to Menalcas.

Sir E. Bulwer-Lytton

MENANDER

Menander (342-292 B.C.) was an Attic poet and the most famous of the playwrights of New Comedy, a kind of comedy of manners entirely fictitious and lacking the satire of actual individuals found in Aristophanes (*q.v.*). He presented the life of contemporary Athens in its serious, pathetic, and amusing phases. Love entanglements are a central feature of all his plots—seduction of a girl, abandonment of her child and its later recognition by means of a trinket, followed by the reconciliation and marriage of the parents. Courtesans, scheming slaves, amorous young men, and stingy fathers are among the stock *dramatis personae.* St.

Paul quotes his "Evil communications corrupt good manners" (1 *Cor.*, xv, 33). "Whom the gods love die young" is also one of his proverbs.

a complicated love problem for Menander to solve

MENDELIAN

Mendelian is from Gregor Mendel (1822-1884), Austrian scientist who worked out a chart of probabilities in the matter of transmission of certain tendencies and characteristics among plants and animals. The conclusions he reached by his process constitute a system called Mendelian.

immutable Mendelian law

MENDELSSOHN-BARTHOLDY

Felix Mendelssohn (1809-1847) "inherited music." He, like Liszt, gave his first concert at nine, was giving improvisations at the age of twelve, and was soon a composer of ability and influence. His music was not so spectacular and dramatic as that of many other composers, but smooth and fluent, even while it has the charm and sparkle and gayety that had marked his youth. His violin concerto, considered the most perfect of its type, symphonies, and incidental music to the *Midsummer-Night's Dream* are typical of his grace and charm.

a pleasant Mendelssohn air

MENELAUS

Menelaus was a son of Atreus (whence called Atrides), and the brother of Agamemnon. The king of Sparta and husband of Helen, who eloped with Paris and thus brought on the Trojan War, he is represented in classical literature as being unfortunate in both love and war. In the *Iliad* he is overshadowed in importance by his brother, but in the *Odyssey* he is pictured as reconciled to Helen after the fall of Troy and living with her again at Sparta.

as unlucky as Menelaus

MENOETES

Menoetes is the pilot of the ship "Chimaera" in Vergil's *Aeneid*. His vessel took part in the naval contest at Drepanum in Sicily, where Aeneas celebrated the first anniversary of the death of his father Anchises by various games and feats of skill. For Menoetes' timidity in standing out from the shore, in order to avoid certain hidden rocks, and consequent defeat by another craft, Gyas, the commander of the "Chimaera," hurled him headlong into the sea, much to the amusement of the spectators.

an overcautious Menoetes, fearful of imaginary dangers

MENTOR

Mentor is the faithful friend and companion of Ulysses (Odysseus) in Homer's *Odyssey*. When the hero left to take part in the siege of Troy, he gave Mentor charge of his home on the island of Ithaca and appointed him to be guardian and adviser of his son Telemachus.

Another Mentor, who flourished around 356 B.C., was the most celebrated silver-chaser and master of the toreutic art of working and adorning metal among the ancient Greeks. His vases and cups were highly prized as art-works by the Romans.

no Mentor to counsel him

MEPHISTOPHELIAN

Mephistophelian is from Mephistopheles. A name for the fiend next in importance to Satan, it refers to the devil, the Prince of Evil, and was adopted by Goethe in *Faust* for the fiend. The guide of Faust, he is represented as a cold, scoffing, sardonic personage; hence, anything devilish, crafty, relentless, sardonic.

Mephistophelian scheme
the grace and seductiveness of a Mephistopheles
Mephistophelian mockery and glee

MERCURY

Mercury was the messenger of the gods, the god of commerce and of eloquence, consequently dexterous, swift, nimble, clever, and the bearer of news and tidings. Combined with his cleverness and nimbleness was his skillful thievery. The inventor of letters and the conductor of souls to the lowerworld, he was known to the Greeks as Hermes. Winged sandals and a staff (the caduceus, symbol of the medical profession) are his familiar attributes.

swift as Mercury

MERCUTIO

Mercutio is Romeo's friend in Shakespeare's *Romeo and Juliet.* He is a kind-hearted, sprightly, and witty nobleman, the finished portrait of a fine gentleman of his time. Displaying alert intelligence, imagination, and courage, this gay and reckless madcap is mortally wounded in a quarrel with Tybalt. When asked if he is hurt, he replies, "A scratch, a scratch; marry, 'tis enough."

a carefree, gallant young Mercutio

MERIMEE, PROSPER

Prosper Mérimée (1803-1870) was the distinguished French writer and inspector-general of historical remains who is best known for his novels *Colomba, Carmen, Arsène Guillot,* and *L'Abbé Aubain*, though his short stories such as *Mateo Falcone* exhibit a rare and classic perfection of form. Of them it was said that they are "tales that one reads in an hour, rereads in a day, tales which fill the memory and occupy the thoughts forever." This famous archaeologist and talented linguist, who translated extensively from Russian literature and introduced it to western Europe, had a reputation for cold-blooded cynicism, scepticism, and apathy (rather than sympathy) in observing suffering humanity, because of the extreme objectivity with which he recorded his characters' thoughts and emotions.

a detachment worthy of Mérimée

MERLIN

Merlin, magician, sage, and seer of early Norman and English romances, was made one of the principal characters in Geoffrey of Monmouth's romances and in Tennyson's *Idylls of the King.* With all his wisdom, he fell victim to the wiles of the lovely and wicked fairy Vivian, a sorceress, and was betrayed into revealing his magic, whereupon, according to one version, he was imprisoned forever in a hawthorn bush by his own arts.

with the all-knowing air of a Merlin

MEROPE

Merope was the daughter of king Oenopion of Chios and the beloved of Orion, who cleared her father's island of wild beasts in order to win her. Impatient over her father's delay in granting her to him in marriage, he attempted to gain her by violence, but was made drunk and blinded by Oenopion in revenge.

Merope is also the name of the one of the Pleiades who became the least visible star in the constellation because she was ashamed of having had intercourse with Sisyphus, a mortal man.

abashed as Merope

MERRILIES, MEG

Meg Merrilies is a weird, half-crazed gypsy woman in Scott's *Guy Mannering.* Akin to the ancient sibyls, she has some of the traits of the witches in *Macbeth*. A nurse in the Bertram family, she is forced to assist in the kidnapping of her charge, Harry, and loses her life in an effort to restore him.

demented as Meg Merrilies

MERRY-ANDREW

Merry-Andrew was an assistant to a mountebank, whose business it was to divert the attention of the crowd from the quality of the goods to the merriment of the occasion. The name now signifies any running accompaniment to a less-than-creditable or mysterious performance, to divert attention from anything that will not bear scrutiny.

hard to tell whether he is an enthusiastic bystander or a hired Merry-Andrew.

MESMER, FRANZ

Franz Mesmer (1733-1815) is the name of a physician who studied medicine and evolved the idea of the curative power of the magnet and of animal magnetism. He began to use that in his own practice and was allowed to present his findings to a committee of physicians and scientists, but they made an adverse report. Mesmer introduced the science into Paris in the late eighteenth century, and that form of hypnotism is called Mesmerism, after him.

a strange mesmeric influence
an unexpected Mesmer

MESSALINA

Valeria Messalina was the great granddaughter of Octavia (sister of Augustus) and wife of the emperor Claudius (41-54 A.D.). During her life she acquired a reputation for licentiousness and profligacy that has become proverbial. In 48 A.D., though still married to Claudius, she undertook a second marriage to a handsome young Roman Senator, Silius, in a plot to supplant the doting Claudius on the throne. For this *lèse-majesté* she and Silius were put to death by the tribune Narcissus.

adulterous as Messalina
as profligate as Messalina

MESSIANIC

Messianic is from the Messiah, the name for the expected deliverer of the Jewish people, by the Christians applied to Christ. The word is sometimes used of any deliverer.

fired with Messianic ambition

METHUSELAH

Methuselah was the oldest patriarch of the Bible who lived nine-hundred-sixty-nine years. Hence, the phrase expressing the so-far greatest known age is "old as Methuselah."

the Methuselah of the village

METIS

Metis was the daughter of Oceanus and Tethys in Greek mythology. Zeus married her and devoured her in her first month of pregnancy because he feared that her offspring would be stronger than himself. The child, however, turned out to be Athena, who sprang fully armed from the head of the king of the gods. The name *Metis* means "prudence" or "wisdom."

a pregnancy as distasteful to her husband as that of Metis

MEZENTIUS

Mezentius was the Etruscan tyrant of the city of Caere. Expelled by his subjects because of his cruelties, he fled to Turnus, king of the Rutulians, and offered him his services in the war against Aeneas, the rival of Turnus for the hand of Lavinia, daughter of Latinus, king of Latium. Killed by Aeneas, he was called by Vergil in the *Aeneid* "a despiser of the gods." The expression *Mezentian cruelty* stems from such atrocities as the tyrant's binding of living persons face to face with dead ones, leaving them there to perish of starvation.

another act of Mezentian horror

MICAH

Micah is the name of the Ephraimite who stole 1,100 shekels of silver from his mother, then repented and made restitution (*Judges,* xvii).

Another Micah (8th century B.C.) was the sixth of the Hebrew minor prophets. He predicted imminent judgment on Israel, extending also a Messianic hope.

a thief repentant as Micah

MICAWBER

Micawber, the cheerful ne'er-do-weli in Dickens' *David Copperfield,* was always optimistic, always affectionately assuring his constantly increasing family and his trusting wife, with irritating insouciance, that "something would turn up." He was noted for his long speeches and ambitious style.

endless Micawber optimism
the pleasant air of a Micawber
an incurable Micawber attitude

MICHAEL

Michael, the archangel in Milton's *Paradise Lost,* is commander-in-chief of the heavenly armies that drove the rebellious angels out of heaven. He is mentioned five times in the Bible, always as fighting, and in *Daniel* (x) is mentioned as the archangel having special charge of the Israelites as a nation; hence, protector, guardian, commander, militant. September 29 is celebrated as Michaelmas Day.

a victorious Michael

MICHEL, COUSIN

Cousin Michel is a humorous personification of the German people. The name signifies a stupid dolt and indicates the weaknesses and follies of that nation's character, especially their proverbial slowness, heaviness, and credulity. It is also a contemptuous designation of any simple and coarse rustic.

dull-witted as Cousin Michel

MICHELANGELO

Michelangelo (1475-1564), Italian sculptor, painter, and poet, worked with supreme intelligence and powerful imagination. He produced what are still the grandest artistic conceptions in existence in their dignity, grandeur, and power. Vasari credits his Sistine Chapel frescoes with a perfection of anatomy and a grandeur of style that have never been equalled.

the dignity of a Michelangelo
with Michelangelo's majestic art

MIDAS

Midas, mythical Phrygian king to whom Dionysus promised to grant one wish, wished that everything he touched might turn to gold, but when even his food and drink turned to precious metal he begged to have the power taken from him. He is pictured with an ass's ears, reputedly the punishment Apollo visited upon him when Midas had decided for Pan and against Apollo in a contest. Hence, Midas means great wealth, but not necessarily great intelligence or happiness.

the Midas touch

MIDGARD

Midgard ("mid-yard") in Scandinavian mythology is the name of the earth. The abode of humanity, it was thus distinguished from Asgard, the home of the gods, and Utgard, the home of the giants. Fashioned by Odin, Vili, and Ve out of the brow of the giant Ymir, whom they had slain, it was joined to heaven by the rainbow bridge of the gods.

a resident of Midgard

MIDSHIPMAN EASY, MR.

Mr. Midshipman Easy, the title-character of Frederick Marryat's novel (1836), is the spoiled son of a philosopher who enlists in the British navy and leads a dashing and adventurous life.

the Mr. Midshipman Easy of the ship

MIGGS

Miss Miggs, the impersonation of an old shrew, is Mrs. Varden's maid in Dickens' *Barnaby Rudge.* She is a tall, gaunt spinster who has various ways of wreaking her hatred on the opposite sex, the most cruel of which lies in often "honoring" them with her company and discourse. This paragon of piety and ill temper is proud of her virtue and religion, though full of weakness and malignity. Slander is the staple of her conversation. She pursues Tappertit with her attentions, but ultimately becomes a turnkey.

a warped and Miggs-like old maid

MIGNON

Mignon is the name of the young Italian girl in Goethe's *Wilhelm Meister.* Represented as beautiful and mysterious, she secretly fell in love with Wilhelm, her protector. Since he exhibits only kindness and compassion for her, she dies the victim of her own hopeless attachment. Carlyle said of her, "When she glides before us through the mazes of her fairy dance, or whirls her tambourine and hurries round us like an antique Maenad, we could almost fancy her . . . . disengaged from the clay of this world."

an ethereal Mignon

MILANION

Milanion was the husband of Atalanta of Calydon, whom he defeated in a foot race by dropping at strategic intervals three golden apples that had been given to him by Aphrodite to prevent his death as loser of the contest. The beauty of the apples so impressed Atalanta that while she stooped to gather them up, Milanion sped on to the goal. Subsequently both he and his wife were transformed into lions for having profaned the grove of Zeus by their embraces. Another Atalanta of Boeotia, of whom the same stories are told, married Hippomenes, also a swift-footed runner.

a ruse as clever as that of Milanion

MILL, JOHN STUART

John Stuart Mill (1806-1873) was the English philosopher and economist whose father inculcated in him the desire to be the chief exponent of the utilitarian philosophy. A precocious child and student, he is said to have read Plato and Demosthenes with complete understanding at the age of ten. Interested in French literature and social conditions, he founded the Utilitarian Society to read and discuss essays on the subject. The author of a *System of Logic, Principles of Political Economy,* and *Thoughts on Parliamentary Reform,* he sympathized with the advanced Radical party, was an advocate of women's suffrage, and popularized universal ethical hedonism, or the belief that only pleasure and pleasant consciousness possess ultimate value.

examines his pleasures as carefully as Mill

MILLAIS, SIR JOHN

Sir John E. Millais (1829-1896), along with Holman Hunt and D. G. Rossetti, was the distinguished British artist who originated the Pre-Raphaelite movement in 19th century painting. Their idea was "to present on canvas what they saw in Nature," and to achieve this Millais' pictures are characterized by detailed and minute imitations of Nature. He studied all persons and objects directly from original models, and painted them in a simple and realistic manner. "The Eve of St. Agnes," remarkable for its painting of moonlight, belongs to his mature period. His "Christ in the House of His Parents" was his contribution to the great trilogy of Pre-Raphaelite art, and was complemented by Hunt's "Light of the World" and Rossetti's "Girlhood of Mary Virgin."

the naturalness and simplicity of a Millais

MILLER, DAISY

Daisy Miller, the heroine and title-character of a novel (1878) by Henry James, is an innocent and naive American girl who while traveling abroad becomes the victim of a scandal.

unsophisticated as Daisy Miller

MILLER, JOE

Joe Miller (1684-1738) was the reputed author of the first joke-book, popular in its day, but as time went on and all the world became familiar with the jokes, a "Joe Miller" became a term of derision, indicating a joke too old, feeble, and stale to move in current circles. As a matter of fact, Joe Miller, an actor, was so dull and slow and sober-minded that he did not even smile at any joke, and it became funny among his fellow actors to attribute any witty quip to Joe Miller: "Who said that?" "Probably Joe Miller!" Upon his death his family was in dire want, and an actor-friend assembled all the jokes current under Joe Miller's name, for their benefit.

another Joe Miller joke

MILLET, JEAN

Jean Millet (1814-1875) was the famous French genre and landscape painter of the Barbizon school, named from a village on the outskirts of Fontainebleau forest. The son of a peasant, he passed his boyhood working in his father's fields and acquiring a deep love for the peasant types and rural occupations depicted in so many of his finest art works. The intimate friend of Rousseau, he is best known for such paintings as *The Sower, The Gleaners, The Angelus, Harvesters Resting, Potato Diggers, Man with the Hoe, Woman Feeding Chickens, The Milkwoman,* and *Woman Shearing Sheep.* In his sturdy figures, painted without models, one feels the strength and movement of their bodies even through their clothes.

a peaceful rural atmosphere such as one finds in Millet's pictures

---

MILO

Milo of Croton in southern Italy was a celebrated athlete who was for six times victor in the wrestling contests at Olympia and as many times at Delphi. A follower of Pythagoras, he commanded the army that defeated the Sybarites in 511 B.C. Many stories were told of his inimitable strength. He was said to have carried a four-year old heifer through the stadium at Olympia and thereafter to have eaten all of it in a single day. In his old age he attempted to rend the trunk of an oak tree which had been partially split open. But the wood closed upon his hands, holding him fast to be the prey of ravening wolves.

the superhuman strength of a Milo

MILTIADES

Miltiades (540-489 B.C.) was the tyrant of the Chersonese at the time of the Persian invasion of Thrace, and the hero of the battle of Marathon. Beloved by the Athenians for his victory in that heroic struggle, he succeeded in getting them to entrust him with seventy ships to conduct an attack on the island of Paros. His purpose, of which the people of Athens knew nothing, was the satisfaction of a private enmity, and when the expedition failed he was impeached and fined for his deception. Unable to pay the fine, he was cast into prison where he died of a wound received in the Parian adventure. His name suggests the tragic spectacle of a man who was once a hero in the eyes of his countrymen and then fell from favor into disgrace.

forgotten as the heroic achievements of Miltiades

MILTONIC

Miltonic refers to John Milton (1608-1674), one of the six greatest English poets, known particularly for the majestic epic poem of his later years, *Paradise Lost,* ranging as it does in a field "unattempted yet in prose or rhyme," comprising Heaven, Earth, and Hell, characterizing angels, devils, and Man, written in sonorous, majestic organ tones to justify the ways of God to Man. Milton was also a statesman, for twenty years secretary to Oliver Cromwell and the English Commonwealth, a service overshadowed by his fame as a poet, although his *Areopagitica*, on the freedom of the press, has never been surpassed. In 1652 he became totally blind.

with Miltonic majesty
the organ voice of Milton

MIME

Mime, in the story of the *Nibelungenlied,* is a dwarfed smith who reveals to Siegfried the secret of the magic ring and helps him to win it by forging the sword with which the hero slays the dragon, Fafner, which is guarding the golden hoard. The brother of the dwarf Alberich, he is finally slain for his treachery.

a dwarfish Mime, hopping about the forge

MIMI

Mimi, the heroine of Puccini's melodious opera *La Bohème,* is a fragile and lovely Parisian seamstress adored by the poet Rodolfo. Their tender romance, typifying that of the working girl and the starving artist, is of the love-in-a-garret variety and fluctuates between idyllic happiness and equally passionate desperation. Their friends are bohemian and mercurial in temperament, their story one of universal and haunting pathos. Delicate in health, Mimi quarrels with her lover, droops in sadness, and during a reconciliation dies of tuberculosis, to the despair of Rodolfo and all lovers of Puccini's exquisite music.

beauty as fragile and delicate as Mimi's

MIMIR

Mimir, in Scandinavian mythology, was the god of eloquence and wisdom. He was the guardian of a well in which wit and wisdom lay hidden, and from which he drank every morning out of the horn Gjallar. Odin once drank from this fountain, and by so doing became the wisest of gods and men. But he had to purchase the privilege and distinction with the cost of one eye, which Mimir exacted from him.

wise and omniscient as Mimir

MINERVA

Minerva, the goddess of wisdom, is said to have sprung full-grown from the brow of Jove, representing thinking power personified. It was her special mission to guide warriors to prudence, courage, and perseverance, which explains her being pictured with helmet, shield, and a coat of mail. Her name is commonly used to indicate wisdom in general, and she was known to the Greeks as Athena. In Athens, of which she was tutelary patroness, stands the majestic temple honoring her virginity, and so named the *Parthenon.*

an omniscient Minerva

MINNA

Minna is sister to Brenda, and is one of the heroines in Scott's novel *The Pirate.* Characterized by credulity, simplicity, and sober vanity, she is distinguished with talents, strong feelings, and spirited enthusiasm.

a credulously enthusiastic Minna

MINNEHAHA

Minnehaha is the heroine of Longfellow's poem *The Song of Hiawatha.* Her name is derived from the Indian root words *mini* for "water" and *haha* for "cascade," as its origin is shown in the poet's words:

"From the waterfall he named her,
Minnehaha, Laughing Water."

An Indian maiden of the Dakota tribe, she became the bride of the Sioux brave. During a famine she succumbed to hunger.

sporting like Minnehaha in the pool at the bottom of the falls

---

MINNESINGER

A Minnesinger, or "Singer of Love," was one of a class of lyric poets and musicians of medieval Germany who flourished from the 12th to the 14th centuries. Singing in the Swabian Middle High German, they chose their themes from love, women, springtime, and the beauties of nature. Usually of noble birth and knightly rank, they presented their verses of varied meters in poetical contests. Walther von der Vogelweide ("Bird Meadow") was one of the best known of these German troubadours.

a modern Minnesinger, crooning of love

MINOS

Minos was a son of Jupiter and Europa, and brother of Rhadamanthus. Marrying Pasiphaë, the daughter of the Sun, he had by her two daughters, Ariadne and Phaedra, and two sons. Because he refused to sacrifice to Poseidon a beautiful bull that the god had given him, Poseidon caused Pasiphaë to conceive an impure lust for the animal, the issue of which was the hybrid monster known as the Minotaur, for the housing of which Minos commissioned Daedalus to construct the labyrinth. Athenian legend pictured him as a cruel despot who exacted annual tribute in the form of seven youths and seven maidens, destined to be food for the Minotaur ("bull of Minos").

Archaeological researches have untangled the history behind the legend from the mythopoeic and imaginative additions of Greek writers, and the labyrinth, or "place of the double axe," is now taken to be the extremely intricate and rambling palace itself, situated at Cnossus. The annual tribute is identified by means of frescoes depicting a popular sport of bull-vaulting, or somersaulting in mid air over the back of a plunging bull, grasped by the horns as it charges to effect the leap. For this sport Athenians, doubtless, were forcibly trained.

According to other traditions, Minos was a king and lawgiver in Crete, who was so distinguished for his incorruptible justice that after death he was made supreme judge in the lower world (Aeacus and Rhadamanthus were his colleagues). The name Minos is now believed to have been the family name of a dynasty or a title signifying ruler, such as that of Pharaoh in Egypt, rather than a personal name.

the unswervingly equitable justice of a Minos.

MINOTAUR

The Minotaur, a monster with the head of a bull and the body of a man, was shut up at Cnossus, Crete, in the labyrinth built by Daedalus, where Athens had to feed him with young men and maidens until he was killed by Theseus. Hence, monstrous, infamous, menacing, a force destructive of youth.

the minotaur of war, to whom we sacrifice our youth.

MIRABEL

Mirabel is the name of a much traveled Monsieur in Beaumont and Fletcher's *Wildgoose Chase.* A sophisticated fellow and proof against all the wiles of the fair sex, he is represented as a great defier of all ladies in the way of marriage, and a very dissipated and licentious character to boot.

Mirabel is also the name of two of the *dramatis personae* in Farquhar's comedy *The Inconstant,* an old gentleman and his son. The former is an odd compound between the peevishness incident to his years and his fatherly fondness for his son. The latter is an incorrigible libertine and rake.

sophisticated in his bachelorhood as Mirabel

MIRAMONT

Miramont is an ignorant, testy, and honest old man in Fletcher's comedy *The Elder Brother.* A great admirer of learning, he is himself without more of it than enables him to sign his name.

illiterate as Miramont

MIRANDA

Miranda is the lovely daughter of Prospero in Shakespeare's *The Tempest.* Brought up on a desert island with the companionship of her father and the few serving folk, she is peculiarly unsophisticated and brings to every experience and situation the childlike innocence, but the carefully tutored mind, of an unspoiled and pure maiden. Hence, girlish, innocent, pure.

an eager-eyed Miranda

MIRIAM

Miriam, the sister of Moses and Aaron, was a Hebrew prophetess who was noted for her intense zeal for her God and her people (*Exodus*, xv, 20). Because she later claimed equal honor with Moses, she was smitten with leprosy, but was restored by his intercession.

like Miriam's sin of presumption

MISENUS

Misenus was the trumpeter of Aeneas in Vergil's *Aeneid.* Presumptive and bold, he challenged Triton to a contest in musical skill, and was dragged into the sea and drowned for his audacity. The promontory of Misenum, to the north of the spaciously beautiful bay of Naples, was named after him.

as conceited and cocksure as Misenus

MITE, SIR MATTHEW

Sir Matthew Mite is a returned East India merchant in Foote's satirical play *The Nabob.* Purse-proud, he decks his servants with the most costly exotic flowers, and squanders his wealth on sycophants and flatterers, overpowering everyone with the profusion of his wealth. Astounding the ignorant with jargon about rupees, lacs, and jaghires, he is represented as dissolute, vainglorious, ungenerous, and tyrannical. Ashamed of the humble friends of his youth, he both hates the aristocracy and yet is childishly eager to be numbered among them.

Sir Andrew Mite, with all the pomp of Asia behind him

"a letter worthy of Sir Andrew Mite, in which Clive orders 'two hundred shirts, the best and finest that can be got for love or money'."

Macaulay

MITHRADATES

Mithradates Eupator, or "the Great," was king of Pontus in northern Asia Minor and one of Rome's most formidable enemies. A series of three wars had to be undertaken against him to curb and destroy his overweening ambitions. In the first (88-84 B.C.) he was defeated by Sulla and forced to pay a heavy indemnity; in the second (83-81 B.C.) he succeeded in defeating the Roman army that had invaded Pontus. Pompey worsted him in the third war

(74-64 B.C.), forcing him to flee into the Crimea, where he attempted to take his life by poison. Ancient authorities speak with awe of his courage and superhuman military ability, of his great physical strength and size, his skill at hunting, riding, and fighting, his insatiable desire for food and drink, and his mastery of twenty-two languages. According to Cicero, Mithradates precipitated the final war against his kingdom by an act of outrageous cruelty, ordering all Roman citizens in Asia Minor (some 80,000) to be massacred on a single day.

the subtle cunning and ambition of a Mithradates, challenging Rome to come to grips

---

MITHRAS

Mithras, one of the principal deities of the ancient Persians, was god of light and the personification of the Sun. An all-seeing and omniscient deity, he waged persistent war against the powers of darkness and was regarded as the mediator between Ormuzd, the principle of good, and Ahriman, the principle of evil. In art he was represented as a handsome youth kneeling on a bull, into the neck of which he has sunk a knife. He is also pictured as a lion. Worshiped in subterraneous crypts, he included in his rites baptism, anointing with honey, and a feast of bread and consecrated wine.

beneficent as the sunlight of Mithras

MJOLLNIR

Mjöllnir, in Scandinavian mythology, is the name of the terrible hammer which Thor uses against the giants. A type of the thunderbolt, it is never lost, however far it is cast, for it always boomerangs back into the user's hand. Whenever desired, it becomes so small that it can be put into a pocket. After Ragnarok it will pass into the hands of Thor's sons, Modi and Magni.

the pounding of a Mjöllnir

MNEMOSYNE

Mnemosyne was the daughter of Uranus (Heaven) and Ge (Earth). A Titaness, she was the goddess of Memory and became by Zeus the mother of the nine Muses. Her name has given us the word *mnemonic,* "pertaining to the memory," and a mnemonic device is consequently something which enables a person to remember and to recall a fact whenever he wishes.

Mnemosyne sharpening the edges of recollection

MNEVIS

Mnevis, in Egyptian mythology, is the sacred black bull of Heliopolis, worshiped as the incarnation of the god Ra.

jet-black as Mnevis

MOBY-DICK

Moby-Dick, the animating force in a story by Herman Melville, is a great white whale being pursued through the seas by a sailor who seeks vengeance for the loss of his leg in an encounter with the whale. The pursuit involves many a picture of life aboard ship with a motley crew.

gigantic as Moby-Dick

MODO

Modo is the fiend who instigates and incites to murder. He is mentioned by Shakespeare in *King Lear* (Act IV, Scene I) as one of the five that possessed "Poor Tom." See *Mahu* for the others.

Modo prompting him to bloodshed

MODRED

Modred, in the romance of *The Round Table,* is distinguished as the treacherous knight. He hated Sir Lancelot, and sowed discord among the knights. Revolting from his uncle, King Arthur he seduced his wife and was mortally wounded in the battle of Camlan in Cornwall. He was buried on the island of Avalon.

a master of treachery, outdoing even Modred

MOERAE

Moerae is the Greek name of the Parcae or Fates, and is derived from the word *meros*, meaning "lot." They are represented as the three daughters of Nox (Night) and Erebus (Hell, or the lower world) in order to symbolize the uncertainty and obscurity of fortune. All-powerful goddesses who presided over the destiny of man, Clotho held the distaff or spindle to spin the thread of doom, while Lachesis drew it out to determine its length, and Atropos severed it when its duration was reached.

futile to protest the will of the Moerae

MOGUL, GRAND

The Grand Mogul, emperor of the Mongol Empire of Hindustan with his capital at Delhi, was leader of the eastern world, with all its opulence and magnificence. The last emperor was dethroned for rebellion in 1857. Grand Mogul is now applied to a person either truly great or assuming to be great and self-important.

undoubtedly thought himself the Grand Mogul of the occasion

MOHOCK

The Mohocks were gay young blades that infested the streets of London in the eighteenth century for no other purpose than their own entertainment. Nevertheless, they were one of the minor perils and the major fears of the unlighted London streets, since they were perfectly willing to rob the well-lined citizen or lord of any considerable amount, or to commit annoying minor outrages. They were apparently kin to the rollicking companions of Prince Hal and Falstaff of Shakespearean fame.

armed against the Mohocks
the Mohocks' insistent pleasantries

MOKANNA

Mokanna, or Al-Mokanna, was the name of the eighth century impostor from Khorassan, Persia, who is the subject of Moore's *Veiled Prophet of Khorassan*. Terribly deformed in appearance, he wore a veil under pretense of shading the dazzling light of his countenance.

disillusioned by the removal of Mokanna's veil.

MOLIERE

Molière is the pseudonym of Jean Baptiste Poquelin (1622-1673), one of the greatest comic dramatists in all literature, who ridicules humanity by drawing outrageous caricatures of its foolish and typical figures. With swift massive strokes he presents the misanthrope, the hypocrite, the miser, the fool, the materialist, so that the vice he represents is laughed out of court. A man of infinite wit, full of life, laughter and whim, he excelled in farce. He has made the world laugh, as Dickens and as Thackeray, each in his own way, made the world laugh its own follies out of countenance. Molière has besides treated many a risqué subject with delicacy and without offense.

the Molière wit

MOLMUTIUS

Dunwallo Molmutius was a legendary king of Britain, said to have promulgated the Molmutine code of laws by which the privilege of sanctity was bestowed upon temples, cities, the roads leading to them, and even plows.

Shakespeare, in *Cymbeline* (Act III, Scene I), says of him:

"Molmutius made our laws;
Who was the first Britain which did put his brows within a golden crown, and called himself a king."

sacrosanct by Molmutian decree

MOLOCH

Moloch was the Phoenician fire-god to whom human sacrifices were offered. Especially were first-born children given to Moloch. The name has loosely become the symbol of any devotion that requires frightful sacrifice, and is used as a designation of any dread influence at whose shrine human sacrifice is offered.

the Moloch of public opinion

MOMUS

Momus, the god of censure and of mockery, is said to have censured even Prometheus, because in the little man he created he had not left a door in his breast so that one might look in and see his secret thoughts. He jeered bitterly at all gods and all men, but finally he saw Aphrodite, so beautiful and so perfect that he could see no fault in her, and consequently grieved himself to death.

one has an uncomfortable sense that Momus lurks in a corner of their house

---

MONET, CLAUDE

Claude Monet (1840-1920), famous French landscape painter and one of the greatest of the impressionists, became notorious as a student for the "doodlings," drawings, and caricatures with which he embellished his school books. *A plein-air* artist in maturity, he executed beautiful paintings of nature with wonderful effects of light and shadow, such as the series of views along the Seine river and those of Rouen cathedral under different lights. *Un Déjeuner sur l'Herbe* ("Picnic on the Grass") is one of the best known of his oils.

the play of light caught impressionistically by a Monet

MONETA

Moneta is a surname of Juno as the goddess who gives warnings and counsel. The temple of Juno Moneta stood on the northern summit of the Capitoline hill, and in it was established the Roman public mint. Hence, she was also regarded as the protectress of money, the very name of which is derived from this epithet of hers.

needs the advice of Moneta to protect his finances

MONIPLIES, RICHARD

Richard, or Richie, Moniplies is the servant of Nigel Olifaunt, in Scott's *Fortunes of Nigel.* He is an honest, self-willed, conceited, and pedantic Scotchman.

opinionated as Richie Moniplies

MONROE, JAMES

James Monroe (1758-1831), one of the most distinguished Americans in the Hall of Fame, served in the American Revolution, was a member of the Continental Congress, and United States minister to France and England. Twice governor of Virginia, he also was one of the negotiators of the Louisiana Purchase, and was President of the United States during the so-called "era of good feeling," named from the absence of party and factional quarrels during his term. He is most renowned, however, for his promulgation of the Monroe Doctrine on December 2, 1823, outlawing European intervention in American affairs and forbidding further territorial expansion of European powers on the American continent.

time for the party harmony of the Monroe era

MONTAGUES AND CAPULETS

The Montagues and Capulets have become symbols of deadly enmity and fatal feuding, since Shakespeare wrote his tragedy of *Romeo and Juliet.* Their Italian names were Capelletti and Montecchi, and they were members of two rival houses of Verona in the latter part of the 13th and the early 14th centuries. Montague is the proud father of Romeo, and Lady Capulet, mother of Juliet, is a haughty Italian matron who offers to poison Romeo to revenge the death of Tybalt and yet exhibits great tenderness in her lamentation over the death of her daughter and the grim irony perpetrated by the intransigence of the two noble families.

factionalism as intense as that of the Montagues and the Capulets

---

MONTAIGNE

Michel Montaigne (1533-1592), great French essayist, was the first man to dare to put on paper his own thoughts exactly as he thought them, to say what he as an individual thought on a great variety of subjects. With no aim to instruct or to record, he simply indulged in glorious and untrammelled talk on paper. In his essays one finds the richness, truth, and force of the sincere expression of an original mind, concerning almost everything that was occupying the minds of men in his century. His name suggests the words natural, unrestrained, delightful, original, varied.

poured it out Montaigne-fashion, as he thought it

MONTESINOS

Montesinos is a legendary hero whose history and adventures are described in the ballads and romances of chivalry. Having received some offense at the French court, he is said to have retired into Spain, where he acquired his name from his fondness for wild and mountainous scenery. His cavern is supposed to be in the heart of La Mancha, and it was immortalized by Cervantes in his account of the visit of Don Quixote to the Cave of Montesinos. It is about sixty-five feet in depth. Entrance is more easily effected now than in Cervantes' time, and it is frequently resorted to by shepherds as a refuge and a shelter from the cold and from storms.

a recluse in the Cave of Montesinos

MONTESPAN, MME. DE

Mme. Françoise de Montespan (1641-1707) was the brilliant and haughty beauty who became the favorite and mistress of Louis XIV of France. Her husband disapproved of the "honor" and wore mourning for a while. To Louis she bore seven children, the oldest of whom were legitimatized in 1673. A cultivated and amusing conversationalist, she was the friend and patroness of Corneille, Racine, and La-Fontaine. From her great estates she spent vast sums of money on hospitals and charities. She believed in witchcraft, love potions, and had the "black mass" said over her. As discarded mistress, replaced in the sensual monarch's favor by Mme. de Maintenon (*q.v.*), she withdrew from court and spent her last years in penance at the Convent of St. Joseph.

scintillatingly beautiful as Mme. de Montespan.

MONTESQUIEU, CHARLES

Charles Montesquieu (1689-1755) was a distinguished French lawyer, litterateur, and political philosopher, who is best known for his *Lettres Persanes,* or "Persian Letters," a satire on contemporary French society purporting to be represented as seen through the eyes of two Persian tourists. He also wrote a history of the grandeur and decline of the Roman empire and *L'Esprit des Lois,* "The Spirit of the Laws," which profoundly influenced political thought in Europe and America of the time.

The enemy of Voltaire, he had a moderate and mild desire for human improvement and a sure instinct in political science. Tolerant in his views on politics and religion, he had a great admiration for English character and system of government.

as mild in his desire for reform as Montesquieu.

MONTEZ, LOLA

Lola Montez (1818-1861) was the British adventuress and dancer whose real name was Marie Gilbert.

During the course of her much-traveled lifetime she collected three husbands, and was mistress of the aged Louis I of Bavaria who created her Baroness of Rosenthal and Countess of Lansfield. On him she exerted such great influence that she actually controlled the Bavarian government, until her liberal and anti-Jesuit policies goaded the Austrian people and the Jesuits alike to oust her.

She appeared on the stage in New York, Philadelphia, and Australia, eventually settling in New York where she wrote *The Art of Beauty* and devoted her last years to the cause of helping fallen women.

another cosmopolitan and sophisticated Lola Montez

MOPSUS

Mopsus was the son of Apollo and Manto (the daughter of Tiresias), and a celebrated prophet. At Colophon he had a prophetic contest with Calchas and was so superior that the latter died of grief. When he disputed with Amphilochus for possession of the town of Mallos in Cilicia, both were killed by each other's hand. There was also another seer of the same name who accompanied the Argonauts and died in Libya of a snakebite.

a prediction worthy of Mopsus

MORDECAI

Mordecai, in the Old Testament book of *Esther,* is a Jew of the tribe of Benjamin who becomes a prime minister of Ahasuerus (Xerxes) in the Persian court. His deliverance of his cousin Esther and his people from Haman is commemorated by the feast of Purim.

a liberator like Mordecai

MORGAN, J. P.

Morgan, from J. P. Morgan (1837-1913), great American financier and capitalist, influential in the financial structure of the world, was the symbol of American capitalism and power in his day. Hence, his name stands for wealth, but particularly for financial power and control. Morgan is also noted for philanthropy and for his world-famous art collection.

wished for the Midas-touch of the Morgans

MORGAN, SIR HENRY

Sir Henry Morgan (1635-1688) was the famous sea-roving Welsh leader of American buccaneers. Said to have been kidnapped and sold as a slave in his youth, he was appointed admiral of a powerful group of freebooters and pirates wth whom he sacked Porto Bello, Panama, Cuba, Maracaibo, and Gibraltar. After a treaty had been signed between England and Spain, he was called to the former country to account for his actions. He is said to have so gained the favor of the king in explaining his conduct that he was appointed lieutenant governor and commander-in-chief of Jamaica.

dreams of joining Henry Morgan's sea-wolves

MORGANA, FATA

Fata Morgana, the sister of King Arthur and pupil of Merlin, lived at the bottom of a lake, and from there dispensed her treasures to whom she would. Her name is now given to the mirage that occasionally appears over the surface of a lake.

searches every lake for a Fata Morgana treasure

MORGANTE

Morgante is the hero of Pulci's romantic poem *Morgante Maggiore.* A ferocious pagan knight, he is conquered and converted to Christianity by Orlando, whose fast friend he becomes. He acquires great renown for his gentleness, generosity, kindness of heart, and chivalrous defense of ladies in distress. He dies of the bite of a crab, as if to show on what trivial chances depends the life of the strongest.

a brute as gentle as Morgante

MORGIANA

Morgiana is the clever, faithful, female slave of Ali Baba in the *Arabian Nights' Entertainments.* She pries into the forty jars, and discovers that all but one contain a man. Taking oil from the only one containing it, she makes it boiling hot, and pours enough into each jar to kill the thief concealed therein. At last she kills the captain of of the gang, and marries her master's son.

like Morgiana, looking into everything around her

MORGLAY

Morglay was the name of the sword of Sir Bevis of Hampton. Derived from the Welsh roots for "great" and "sword," it became so famous that it has been ever since a generic name for any sword. *Claymore* is an inversion of the word.

wielding his trusty Morglay

MORPHEUS

Morpheus is the son of Somnus (Sleep), and is the god of dreams. The name means "fashioner" or "molder," because he shapes and fashions the dreams that come to mortals. Morphine, the drug inducing sleep, is named after him.

court Morpheus in vain

MORRIS, DINAH

Dinah Morris, the heroine of George Eliot's *Adam Bede,* is a beautiful young woman whose devotion to religion and duty leads her to become a Methodist field preacher.

the Dinah Morris of the pulpit

MORS

Mors is the Roman personification of death and a deity of the lower world, represented as the daughter of Nox (Night) and Erebus (Hell, or the lower world). The Greeks knew this concept as Thanatos, and considered him to be the brother of Sleep (Hypnos).

Mors sweeping near with her dark robes

MORSE, SAMUEL

Samuel F. Morse (1791-1872) was the American artist and portrait painter who became the founder and first president of the National Academy of Design. He is better known, however, for his invention of the magnetic telegraph and the Morse alphabet, or code, for the transmission of messages without wires. Voted $30,000 by Congress for experimentation, he established a line between Washington and Baltimore with the help of Ezra Cornell. May 24, 1844, the first wireless message crackled over the air ways: "What hath God wrought!"

Morse-coded the message across the room

as revolutionary as Morse once seemed

MOSES

Moses, chosen leader of the people of Israel with Aaron, and obedient to the commands of God, delivered the Children of Israel out of the land of Egypt by means of many visitations of divine wrath upon Pharaoh, and led them to the Promised Land. He was guided by the pillar of cloud by day and the pillar of fire by night, and by miraculous provision for their needs during the period of their journeying. Moses, hence, represents a guide, a leader, a counselor, deliverer, and savior, as well as a law-giver, for it was he who brought to the Israelites the direct commandments of God and the laws by which they were to be governed. He is the only man revered as the direct agent of God to His people.

meek as Moses
need a Moses to guide

MOTH

Moth is a page to Don Adriano de Armado, in Shakespeare's *Love's Labor's Lost.* Light as his name, his jesting, playful, versatile, and cunning personality is an excellent foil to the stiff, weak, and melancholy Armado. Moth is also the name of a fairy in the same playwright's *Midsummer-Night's Dream.*

a nimble-witted and jocose Moth

MOTHER BUNCH

Mother Bunch is the subject and supposed writer of a popular 18th century book, entitled "Mother Bunch's Closet newly broke open, containing Rare Secrets of Art and Nature . . . . recommended to all Ingenious Young Men and Maids, teaching them, in a Natural Way, how to get Good Wives and Husbands. By a Lover of Mirth and Hater of Treason." The cabinet of this lovelorn-advising prototype of Dorothy Dix and Beatrice Fairfax, when broken open reveals numerous potent love-spells, ones teaching the blooming damsel to recall the fickle lover or to fix the wandering gaze of the cautious swain, attracted by her charms. A typical "recipe" involves the placing of a pared St. Thomas's onion on a clean handkerchief under one's pillow, in order to conjure by dream the likeness of "him who is to be your husband."

tried all the advice of Mother Bunch to escape her spinsterhood

---

MOTHER CAREY

Mother Carey, of "Mother Carey's Chickens" fame, is an expression applied by sailors to the stormy petrel, a small oceanic bird popularly supposed to be a harbinger of storms. Some regard the words to be a corruption of *Mater Cara,* an affectionate appellation of the Virgin Mary used by Italian sailors in invoking her kindness as the special patroness of mariners in forewarning them of impending tempests. When it was snowing, Mother Carey was said to be plucking her goose.

no Mother Carey to warn them of danger

MOTHER DOUGLAS

Mother Douglas was a famous procuress of the 18th century. Foote represented her in *The Minor* as the character known as Mrs. Cole, and she also figures in Hogarth's *March to Finchley.* This celebrated Madame conducted a superbly furnished menage, decorated with expensive pictures by old masters, "at the north-east corner of Covent Garden," where she died June 10, 1761. She had grown very fat, and with pious, upturned eyes used to pray for the safe return of her "babes" from battle.

the ingratiating, managerial Mother Douglas of the bordello

MOTHER GOOSE

Mother Goose is said to have been a Boston woman whose daughter, Elizabeth Goose, married an industrious printer, who, when his son was small, was annoyed by the jingles his mother-in-law, Mother Goose, was constantly singing to her grandson. Finally he saw in the situation, he thought, a chance to make fun of her and perhaps turn a pretty penny for himself by assembling the ditties and printing them (1719) under the title, *Mother Goose's Melodies for Children.* Many of the songs, of course, had their origin elsewhere, but knowing them, Mrs. Goose had repeated them. They are short, utterly realistic, crazily fantastic sometimes, highly objective, all made to amuse children.

She had Mother-goosed them to sleep

MOTHER SHIPTON

Mother Shipton is the pseudonym of T. Evans Peerce, a Welsh prophetess of the reign of Henry VIII. She foretold many modern inventions, including the steam engine and the telegraph, and the deaths of Wolsey, Lord Percy, and others. She also predicted that the end of the world would occur in the year 1881.

a prophetic Mother Shipton

MOWGLI

Mowgli, in Rudyard Kipling's *Jungle Books,* is the native Indian boy who is suckled by wolves and reared among the animals of the jungle, whose leader he eventually becomes.

the instincts of a Mowgli.

MOZARTEAN

Mozartean refers to music of the charm, delicacy, and rococo perfection of form written by Wolfgang Amadeus Mozart (1751-1791), the chief exponent of the Viennese school of classical music. A child prodigy at the age of six, he concertized throughout European courts on the harpsichord, violin, and organ, later becoming royal chamber composer to Emperor Joseph II of Austria. Living in poverty and ill health in spite of commissions from royalty, he is said to have been poisoned in Berlin by a rival named Salieri, and was buried in an unknown grave in potter's field. An unusually prolific composer of fragile and haunting appeal, he wrote over 600 works, including 48 symphonies, sonatas, concerti, chamber music, and operas like the *Marriage of Figaro, The Magic Flute,* and *Don Giovanni.*

an ethereally elfin Mozartean air

MUCKLEWRATH, HABAKKUK

Habakkuk Mucklewrath, in Scott's *Old Mortality,* is a fanatical preacher in the Covenanters' army.

fiery as Habakkuk Mucklewrath

MULCIBER

Mulciber is a surname of Vulcan, the fire-god and smithy. Since Mulciber means "the smelter" of metals, it seems to have been given to Vulcan as a euphemism, so that he would not consume by fire the dwellings of men but rather aid them in their pursuits by being kindly.

(see *Vulcan*)

flaming as the furnace of Mulciber
Mulciberian fires

MULLER, MAUD

Maud Muller, the simple but beautiful maiden of Whittier's poem *Maud Muller,* raking the hay one day as the judge rides by, looks out with envy of his wealth and good fortune, while the judge through all his years looks back with wistful memory to the thought of the simple country maiden he might have won.

a wholesome Maud Muller

MULVANEY

Mulvaney, one of the three soldiers in Kipling's *Soldiers Three,* is noted for his sharp observations of the behavior of all the persons of the British Army in India who fall under his eye, including the wives and the children of officers in the compound. Mulvaney, gigantic, philosophical, is witty and correct in his curt, pointed, and always funny straight-from-the-shoulder shots at human foibles, a formidable Argus in any social circle.

luckily no Mulvaney in the compound

MUMBO-JUMBO

Mumbo-Jumbo is an African bogie feared by the natives as an evil power, a malignant and hideous personification uttering meaningless but terrifying jargon. Today, among certain African tribes, the tradition is maintained by having a native in masquerade, wearing a headdress of pom-poms, engaged to ward off evil powers and "to keep the women in subjection." Vachel Lindsay uses this old fetish in his poem, *The Song of the Congo*. It is also used for any meaningless jargon.

the Mumbo-Jumbo of secret societies

never had the proper reverence for ceremonial mumbo-jumbo

MUMMIUS, LUCIUS

Lucius Mummius was the Roman general and politician who, as consul in 146 B.C., captured, sacked, and razed the cultured Greek city of Corinth, because his emissaries to the Achaean League there had been rather arrogantly addressed and haughtily handled by the Corinthians. As he proceeded to massacre the entire population of the city, his soldiers threw dice over possession of priceless works of art. All of the great Greek city's movable wealth was sent back to Rome. This was one of the most thorough and systematic instances of loot, pillage, and plunder recorded in ancient history.

the arrant devastation of a Mummius

MUNCHAUSEN, BARON

Baron Munchausen is one of the most audacious and successful liars in literature. He is the pretended author of a book of most fantastic, incredible, but entertaining tales, actually written by a German named Rudolph Raspe (1785) under the name of Munchausen. Titled *Baron Munchausen's Narrative of his Marvellous Travels and Campaigns in Russia*, the volume recounts the most extravagant fictions, and the name suggests mendacious exaggeration.

he's a regular Munchausen; no one believes him, but every one likes to hear him talk

---

MUNIN

Munin, or "Memory," was the name of one of Odin's two ravens. Perched on his shoulders as he sat on his throne, they flew forth into the world daily in order to report to their master everything that they had seen or heard. Munin's mate was named Hugin.

an informer, like Munin, to keep one posted on the news

MUSE

The Muses were inspiring goddesses of song and divinities presiding over the different kinds of poetry and over the arts and sciences. The daughters of Zeus and Mnemosyne (Memory), they were born near the famous Pierian spring at the foot of Mount Olympus. Nine in number, their names were Thalia, Clio, Euterpe, Melpomene, Terpsichore, Erato, Polyhymnia, Urania and Calliope (*qq.v.*). They favored Mount Helicon in Boeotia where were their favorite fountains, Aganippe and Hippocrene, and also haunted Mount Parnassus and its Castalian spring. Apollo, the god of the lyre, was their leader.

Muse-like in her love for song

MUSPEL

Muspel, or Muspellsheim, one of the nine worlds in Scandinavian mythology, was a region of fire and heat, lying to the south of Ginnunga-gap. From it, at Ragnarok, Surtur will collect flames to set fire to the universe and devastate Bifrost, the rainbow bridge leading to heaven.

a fiery heat more intense than that at Muspel

MUSSOLINI

Benito Mussolini (1883-1945) was the Fascist dictator of Italy after World War I, who in World War II threw his fortunes in with Hitlerite Germany. Eventually his own countrymen turned against him, and he died a horrible death at the hands of his own people.

the Caligulas and Hitlers and Mussolinis of the world pronounce their own doom

---

MUT

Mut, in Egyptian mythology, is "the mother," the consort of Amon-Ra, the solar deity, and the mother of Chunsu, the moon. She is the personification of the female principle.

fruitful as Mut

MYRMIDONS

The Myrmidons were an Achaean race living in Thessaly, whom Achilles ruled and led to the siege of Troy. Noted for their brutal savagery and lust for plunder, they were supposed to have been originally ants living on the island of Aegina, which Zeus metamorphosed into human beings so that Aeacus (*q.v.*) might have somebody over whom to rule.

more ferocious and barbaric than the Myrmidons

MYRON'S COW

Myron, the celebrated Greek sculptor who flourished about 450 B.C., cast a bronze "cow in the market-place of Athens" that was so true to life and realistic that even as it seemed to low a bull mistook it for a living animal. His next most famous statue, the *Discobolus,* or "discus (quoit) thrower," is extant in a marble copy from Roman times depicting a handsome athlete in the act of tossing a discus. It succeeds in catching the fleeting, dramatic moment so characteristic of his work. Since he expressed only the body in movement, his statues are quite emotionless in their realism.

life-like as Myron's cow

MYRRHA

Myrrha, in classical mythology, was the daughter of Cinyras, the king of Cyprus. Aphrodite smote her with an unnatural passion for her father, because she had refused to honor the goddess, and as the fruit of an incestuous union she bore Adonis. When Cinyras detected her crime and sought to kill her, Myrrha was transformed into a myrtle.

a Myrrha with a father-complex

MYRTILUS

Myrtilus, in Greek mythology, was the charioteer who cursed Pelops when the latter treacherously threw him into the sea after his victory in the race with Oenomaus (see *Hippodamia*). His curses brought innumerable woes on the descendants of Pelops.

Myrtilan maledictions

N

NAAMAN

Naaman was the Syrian captain who as a young man drew his bow at a venture and mortally wounded King Ahab. When he later acquired leprosy and heard of the healing powers of the prophet Elisha from an Israelite slave girl in his household, he went to Elisha and was cured by bathing in the Jordan, thereafter becoming a worshiper of Jehovah (*2 Kings*, v).

miraculous as the healing of Naaman

NABOTH

Naboth is the defenseless man in *1 Kings* (xxi) from whom Ahab took a possession, his vineyard. Since Naboth refused to sell or exchange his coveted family inheritance, Jezebel, Ahab's wife, had him treacherosuly arrested on a charge of treason. With the connivance of false witnesses she succeeded in getting him condemned to death by stoning. This tragic murder, an act of royal encroachment, stirred up popular resentment and that of the prophet Elijah against Ahab and his wicked spouse. *Naboth's vineyard* is now proverbial for a piece of property which a superior desires and wrests from one not in a position to defend himself or prevent the wrong.

as coveted as Naboth's vineyard

NAGLFAR

Naglfar, in Scandinavian mythology, is the ship of the giants on which they will embark on the "last day" to do battle with the gods at Ragnarok (*q.v.*). It is made of the nails of corpses.

ill-omened as the vessel Naglfar

NAHUM

Nahum was the seventh of the Old Testament minor prophets. Flourishing before the fall of Ninevah (606 B.C.), he predicted that event as coming along with a general wrathful vengeance on the enemies of Judah.

a Nahum at crying woe

NAIADS

The Naiads were nymphs inhabiting springs, rivers and lakes. Like the other nymphs, they were represented as young and beautiful, and in consequence of the very meaning of the word *Nymph* ("young marriageable women," and "brides") they consorted amorously with satyrs, gods and even mortals. In art they were depicted as lightly clad, garlanded with flowers and carrying water in an urn.

a Naiad drawing water from the spring

NAMA

Nama, a daughter of the race of man and beloved by the angel Zaraph, wished only to love purely, intensely, and holily. But she fixed her love on a seraph more than on her Creator, and was therefore condemned to abide on earth, "unchanged in heart and frame," as long as the earth would endure. When time is no more, however, she and her angel lover will be admitted into those courts "where love never dies." Her story is told in Moore's *Love of the Angels.*

with Nama's intensity of love

NANA

Nana, the heroine of Emile Zola's novel of the same name, is a beautiful creature of the slums who is betrayed and forced into the life of a cheap prostitute. Following a successful venture on the stage in which her sensual body becomes the toast and the desire of all

Paris, she amasses and squanders a vast fortune as a courtesan and the mistress of a series of wealthy lovers, whom she drags to ruin and involves in her own vengeful fate. She finally succumbs to poverty and smallpox.

like Nana, a femme fatale to every man she met

NANCY

Nancy, in Dickens' *Oliver Twist,* is the protector of Oliver and the mistress of sadistic Bill Sikes, who brutally murders her. Though of depraved and dissolute life, she has naturally good instincts.

a fiend looking for his Nancy

NANNA

Nanna is the wife of Baldur, famed for her piety and loyalty in Scandinavian mythology. When the blind Hodur slew her husband, she cast herself on his funeral pyre and was destroyed and buried with him. She is also the flower-goddess who strews the earth with blossoms in the springtime.

Nanna's fragrant carpet on the earth

NAOMI

Naomi, mother-in-law of Ruth in the Old Testament, is characterized by courage, motherly affection, and wisdom. When a famine fell among her own people of Judah, she bravely accompanied her husband and two sons to the land of Moab in search of better living. After her sons had married Orphah and Ruth, she was cruelly widowed and bereft of her two sons as well. With fortitude she returned again to her own people, accompanied by her loyal daughter-in-law, Ruth, whose "Whither thou goest, I will go" is indicative of the nobility of soul which the older woman inspired in her. Saying "Call me not Naomi (pleasant), but call me Mara (bitter), for all hath gone bitterly with me," she sent Ruth out to glean in the poor people's corner of the field of Boaz, a kinsman. When it was discovered that this land had once belonged to Naomi's husband, Boaz undertook the obligation due a widowed relative by redeeming the field for Naomi and marrying Ruth. Thus, from adversity these two brave women came to find happiness again.

Naomi's courage in facing the future

NAPAEAE

The Napaeae were the nymphs of glens, vales and sylvan dells. See *Nymphs.*

a glen for dancing Napaeae

NARAKA

Naraka, the hell of the Hindus, has twenty-eight divisions, in some of which the victims are mangled by ravens and owls; in others they are doomed to swallow boiling-hot cakes and walk over burning sands. Each division has its name: Rurava (fearful) is for liars and false witnesses; Rodha (obstruction) for those who plunder a town, kill a cow, or strangle a man; Sukara (swine) for drunkards and those who steal gold.

doomed by his deeds to Naraka

NARASINHA

Narasinha, in Hindu mythology, is the "man-lion" or fourth incarnation of Vishnu, in form half mortal, half leonine.

terrifying as Narasinha

NARCISSUS

Narcissus was the youth so beautiful that when he saw his own image mirrored in the surface of a pool he fell in love with it and pined away because he could not substantiate the image. He was finally transformed into the flower we call the narcissus, and his name is preserved in *narcissistic,* meaning inordinate admiration of oneself or of one's own qualities.

a little narcissistic perhaps

NASH, BEAU

Richard "Beau" Nash (1674-1761) was the master of ceremonies in Bath, a fashionable society resort in England in the eighteenth century, where all the famous and the pseudo-famous went to "drink the waters," to see and to be seen. It was a place where rank and fashion were of prime importance, and admission to certain public Assembly Rooms was so carefully exclusive that an arbiter was essential. "Beau" Nash was that arbiter. Booth Tarkington's *Monsieur Beaucaire* introduces "Beau" Nash in his authentic character, "the depth of his bow registering with perfect accuracy the height of the recipient's standing."

must pass muster with the "Beau" Nash of the occasion.

NASTROND

Nastrond is a noisome and horrible marsh in the underworld, where the impenitent and the wicked will be punished in the future life. According to Scandinavian mythology, serpents pour forth venom incessantly from its high walls.

deserving of eternal incarceration in Nastrond

NATHAN

Nathan was the Old Testament prophet, the adviser and counselor of David (*2 Samuel,* vii), whom he rebuked for his sin against Uriah (*q.v.*). He later promoted Solomon's succession to the throne. A similarly idealized Jewish sage is the title-character of Lessing's *Nathan der Weise* (the Wise).

advice as sagacious as Nathan's

NATHANAEL

Nathanael, who *John* (i, 45-51) says was without guile, was one of the disciples of Jesus. He is possibly to be identified with either Bartholomew or with "the disciple whom Jesus loved."

a guileless Nathanael

NAUSICAA

Nausicaa is one of the loveliest characters in the *Odyssey*. The daughter of Alcinous, king of Phaeacia, she was surprised by Odysseus, a stranger shipwrecked on her shores, as she was playing with a golden ball after washing the household linen with her maidens. With maidenly courtesy and sweetness, she escorted Odysseus to her father's palace for hospitality. The virginal charm of her character suggests both courage and dignity, grace and kindness.

the charming hospitableness of a Nausicaa
kind as Nausicaa

NAVIUS

Navius was a famous seer in the time of Tarquinius Priscus, king of Rome, whom he offended by opposing in a census proposal. Then Tarquin ordered him to divine whether what he was thinking of in his mind could be done or not. When Navius declared that it could, the king proffered him a whetstone and a razor and ordered him to cut the stone in two with the instrument. Navius proceeded to do so without any trouble, thus becoming proverbial for achieving the impossible.

a Navian facility for doing the impossible
as sharp as Navius's razor

NAZARITE

A Nazarite was a Hebrew devotee consecrated to abidance by the vows enjoined in *Numbers,* vi. These included abstinence from wine and other intoxicants, wearing the hair long and uncut, and refusal to touch a dead body.

as teetotaling as a Nazarite

NEAERA

Neaera is the name of a lovely maiden mentioned by the Latin poets Horace, Vergil, and Tibullus. In classical poetry she is a beautiful nymph. The name has been introduced into modern pastoral verse as that of a mistress, sweetheart, or true-love.

playing with the ringlets in his Neaera's hair

NEBO

Nebo was the Assyro-Babylonian god of science and literature, said to have invented cuneiform writing. His temple was at Borsippa, but his worship was carried wherever Babylonian letters penetrated. God of wisdom and agriculture as well, he was regarded as the patron of scribes, learned men, and the priesthood, and was also the protector of schools.

a manner of writing as curious as Nebo's

NEBUCHADNEZZAR

Nebuchadnezzar, King of Babylon, destroyed the Temple and levelled the walls of Jerusalem (586 B.C.). He became the most powerful monarch of the age, and was so proud that he was punished by the loss of his reason and of his throne. Restored, he recognized God's power as higher than his own.

with Nebuchadnezzar's new humility

NEFERTEM

Nefertem was an Egyptian god worshiped at Memphis. In art he is depicted as wearing the lotus-flame on his head, and symbolizing procreation and generation.

blessed by Nefertem with a large brood

NEFERTITI

Nefertiti, a great Asiatic beauty who lived in the first half of the 14th century B.C., was the wife of Egyptian king Ikhnaton. Her thrilling and unusual pulchritude is appreciable even today in a magnificent portrait bust, extant from antiquity, depicting her tapering oval face, slanting eyes, and high cylindrical, Cossack-like headgear. She profoundly influenced the ideas of her husband, "the Religious Revolutionary," in establishing a new cult, that of the sun-god or "solar disk."

a beauty as delicate as that of Nefertiti

ovoid as the face of Nefertiti

NELL, LITTLE

(see *Little Nell*)

NELSON, LORD

Lord Nelson (1758-1805) was the hero of the great British naval exploits against France and Spain, and the subject of the notorious love-scandal with Emma, Lady Hamilton, a vain and amorous woman of little or no moral principles, whom he met while her husband was British ambassador at the court of Naples. In an assault on Calvi, on the island of Corsica, he lost the sight of his right eye, and in an attack on Santa Cruz was shot through the right elbow, suffering subsequent amputation of that arm. Victor over the combined fleets of Napoleon and Spain at the battle of Trafalgar (1805), the signal for which was given in the memorable words "England expects that every man will do his duty," he was shot and killed by an enemy sharpshooter in that engagement. Charming in manner, he won the affection of everybody he met and became the love-slave of Lady Hamilton, who plunged him into diplomatic intrigue as well as gambling debts and bore him an illegitimate daughter. With an insatiable vanity and appetite for praise, his career was marked by his passionate attachments to women.

like Lord Nelson, victorious in the lists of battle and love

NEMEAN LION

The killing of the Nemean lion was the first of the labors of Hercules. The beast inhabited Nemea in Argolis, southern Greece, and kept the people there in a constant state of alarm. Its skin was so tough that the hero's club made no impression on the animal, so Hercules caught it in his arms and squeezed it to death. Ever after he wore its skin as a mantle.

an embrace to strangle the Nemean lion

NEMESIS

Nemesis was the goddess of retributive punishment, particularly of murders and atrocious crimes, the "queller of the proud and arrogant" whom she punished by reducing them to the level of an ordinary situation. Nemesis is the eye-for-an-eye, tooth-for-a-tooth justice, dealt out by Fate. In one modern view, it is suggested that Nemesis is really remorse and the suffering brought about by remorse, but the old view that crime brings its own punishment is the true spirit of the old belief.

consciousness of impending discovery is the worst weapon of Nemesis

---

NENIAE

Neniae were funeral poems sung in primitive times at Rome by female relatives of the deceased, or by hired performers. These obituaries of ancient times gave place later to elegiac funeral orations and eulogies.

mumbling an incoherent Neniae of grief

NEOPTOLEMUS

Neoptolemus, the son of Achilles, was so named because he came late to the siege of Troy, after his famous father had already fallen. One of the heroes concealed in the wooden horse, he showed himself cruel and vindictive at the fall of the city, killing aged and defenseless king Priam without mercy. He secured Andromache, Hector's widow, as his war-prize and concubine. Because he had golden hair he was also known as Pyrrhus.

as cruel and merciless as Neoptolemus at the fall of Troy

NEPHELOCOCCYGIA

Nephelococcygia, "cloud-cuckoo-town," is an imaginary place built in the clouds in Aristophanes' *Birds,* a satire on Athenian frivolity and credulity, castles-in-the-air, and the inert luxury and ease in which the masses of Athens of that day indulged. Occupying the whole horizon, it cut off the gods from all connection with mankind, and even from the power of receiving sacrifices, so as to force them to surrender at discretion to the birds. In modern usage, the name represents an imaginary and non-existent place of perfect happiness and content.

wool-gathering in Nephelococcygia

NEPOS, CORNELIUS

Cornelius Nepos, Roman historian of the first century B.C., was a contemporary and friend of Cicero, Atticus, and Catullus. Associated with his name are the biographies *Vitae Excellentium Imperatorum* (Lives of Outstanding Generals) and *De Viris Illustribus,* a series of twenty-four biographies of eminent Greeks and Romans, designed to bring out the character of their heroes rather than to stress the historical events of their lives.

a biography with Nepos's stress on character-delineation

In his long and peaceful reign he gave his time to the codification and establishment of religious practices among his rude subjects. Instructed by the nymph Egeria (*q.v.*), who visited him in a grove near Rome and who honored him with her love, it was he who first appointed the priestly colleges of pontiffs and the Vestals. He also founded the temple of Janus, which remained always shut during his reign in token of abiding peace.

as versed as Numa in religious lore

NURIEL

Nuriel, another form of Uriel in Rabbinical mythology, is the name of an angel who presided over hailstorms.

sleet and ice storms that must have come from Nuriel

NUTBROWN MAID

The Nutbrown Maid is the heroine of a ballad of uncertain date and origin, preserved in Percy's *Reliques*. A perfect female character, exposed, like Boccaccio's Griselda, to the severest trials, she submits without a murmur to unmerited hardships. Henry, Lord Clifford, and Lady Margaret Percy, who becomes his wife, are the originals of the ballad. Lord Clifford, having a miserly father and ill-natured stepmother, leaves home to become the head of a band of robbers. He woos and wins the Nutbrown Maid by telling her of the hardships she will face as the wife of a banished and penniless man. When she declares her love in spite of his handicaps, he reveals himself as the owner of large estates.

a love as pure as that of the Nutbrown Maid

NYCTYMENE

Nyctymene was the daughter of Epopeus, king of Sicyon. Having been dishonored in incestuous relation by her father, she concealed herself in shame in the shade of forests, where she was metamorphosed by Athena into an owl.

blinking myopically like Nyctymene

NYDIA

Nydia is the blind flower girl in Bulwer-Lytton's *Last Days of Pompeii.* A sensitive creature, she leads Glaucus, an aristocrat whom she loves with futile pathos, and Ione, her successful rival in his favor, from the doomed city, drowning herself in sorrow after effecting their escape.

a blind Nydia, hands out and groping sensitively

NYM

Nym is the name of an arrant rogue and thieving, cowardly knave in Shakespeare's *Merry Wives of Windsor.* A corporal in Falstaff's "army," he has his name apparently derived from *nim,* an old word meaning to pilfer or steal that is still common among British thieves.

as thieving and untrustworthy as Corporal Nym

NYMPHS

The Nymphs were female deities of lesser rank whom the Greeks believed to inhabit all phases of nature—rivers, springs, fountains, the sea, mountains, trees, grottoes, etc. The very name means "a young, marriageable woman" or "a bride," and in token of this significance they were represented as being young, beautiful, fond of music and the dance, and as spending their time in somewhat promiscuous amorous dalliance with satyrs, gods, and even mortals. This latter channeling of their energies and enthusiasm has led to the meaning behind the word *nymphomania,* an inordinate sexual desire on the part of women. Because many of the Nymphs were believed to inspire those who came into contact with them, prophetic powers were assigned to these goddesses. Hence, all persons who had espied a Nymph in a stream or a spring passed into a state of frenzied rapture and ecstasy and were called *nympholepts*, that is," ones taken by a Nymph."

They were classified under the following categories indicative of their locale, and are listed individually under: (1) the Oceanids; (2) the Nereids; (3) the Naiads; (4) the Oreads; (5) the Napaeae; and (6) the Dryads or Hamadryads.

OEDIPUS

Oedipus was a legendary king of Thebes, whose father, Laius, having been warned that his infant son would kill him, had the child exposed to perish. But a shepherd found him, and years later, never having known his own identity, Oedipus killed Laius in a quarrel. Long after, accepting the challenge that he who solved the riddle of the Sphinx should have the throne of Thebes and the hand of Jocasta, widow of Laius, Oedipus solved the riddle, possessed the throne, and married Jocasta, by whom he had several children. On discovering that Jocasta was his mother, Oedipus lived in an agony of remorse and suffered many misfortunes. Jocasta hanged herself and Oedipus put out his eyes. His experiences are the subject of Sophocles' tragedies *Oedipus at Colonus* and *Oedipus Tyrannus*. The name has been used by psychologists as the Oedipus complex, to indicate unnatural affection for one parent and hatred of the other.

an Oedipus complex
an unimaginable Oedipus situation

OENEUS

Oeneus was king of Grecian Calydon, and the father of Meleager, Tydeus, and Deianira. He incurred the wrath of Artemis by neglecting to sacrifice to her, whereupon the goddess sent a great boar to ravage his land until Meleager succeeded in killing it during the great Calydonian boar-hunt. Oeneus was said by tradition to have been the first to plant the vine.

forgetful as Oeneus in religious matters

OENOMAUS

Oenomaüs, the son of Ares, was the father of Hippodamia (*q.v.*), whose suitors he challenged either to win her hand by defeating him in a chariot race, or else to suffer death for losing. Pelops bribed Oenomaüs's charioteer Myrtilus to loosen a pin in one of the wheels, thus overcoming Oenomaüs by strategy.

a competition devised by an Oenomaüs

OENONE

Oenone was a Phrygian nymph and resident of Mt. Ida. Married to Paris, she was abandoned by him in favor of Helen of Troy, even though she possessed the gift of divination and warned him of the trouble that would result from his journey to Greece. Just before Troy fell to the Greek siege, Paris had been wounded by one of the arrows of Heracles and sought the assistance of Oenone, who had told him that only she could help him if he should be wounded. Indignant at his desertion of her, Oenone refused to help him. Later repenting, she hastened after him, and on finding him already expired, she killed herself from grief. She is the subject of a beautiful poem by Tennyson.

an injured wife, as slow to forgive as Oenone

OENOPION

Oenopion was a king of Chios and the father of Merope. The giant Orion was a suitor for the hand of Merope, but, as Oenopion constantly deferred their marriage, Orion once, when intoxicated, raped her with violence. For this Oenopion blinded him while asleep, and expelled him from the island. When Orion later returned to seek revenge, Oenopion was not to be found, his friends having concealed him.

procrastinating like Oenopion

OG

Og, king of Bashan, according to Rabbinical mythology, was an antediluvian giant who saved himself from the flood by climbing on the roof of the ark. After the passage of the Red Sea,

Moses first conquered Sihon, and then advanced against the giant Og, whose bedstead, made of iron, was more than 15 feet long and nearly 7 feet wide. Og plucked up a mountain to hurl at the Israelites, but he got so entangled with his cumbersome burden that Moses was able to kill him without a great deal of difficulty.

as huge as Og

OGIER THE DANE

Ogier the Dane, one of Charlemagne's paladins, was the son of Geoffrey, king of Denmark. One of the popular heroes of medieval romance, he lived an enchanted life on the isle of Avalon and defended France from the heathen paynims. He is still the national hero of Denmark.

a heroic Scandinavian like Ogier the Dane

OGLEBY, LORD

Lord Ogleby is a character in the comedy *Clandestine Marriage* by Garrick and Colman. A superannuated peer who affects gayety and the graces of youth, he is at heart kind and benevolent.

a senile and ludicrous lover like Ogleby

OGYGES

Ogyges was the mythical first ruler of Thebes, in whose reign a great flood was said to have occurred. His name is also connected with Attic legend, for in Athens an Ogygian flood is likewise mentioned. His name connotes prehistoric and primeval.

of Ogygian ancientness

OGYGIA

Ogygia was an island in the Mediterranean or the great Western Ocean. The abode of Calypso, the nymph who detained Ulysses in hospitality there, promising him immortality if he would remain with her, it presented such a scene of sylvan beauty that it charmed even Mercury, who was sent from Olympus to order the nymph to release Ulysses.

lovely as Calypso's isle, Ogygia

O. HENRY

O. Henry (1862-1910) is the pen name of Sidney Porter, the author of short stories concerning the ordinary man, the four million instead of the Four Hundred. In fact, he named one of his collections *Stories of the Four Million.* He uses the most possible and usual of situations, and shows the humor, the pathos, the tragedy, but above all the naturalness of happenings, as few other writers have done. The surprise ending is a surprise simply because it is so natural. From the moment of the appearance of his stories they were hailed as a breath of fresh air in the atmosphere.

O. Henry realism

OKIE

Okie, originally the name for a resident of Oklahoma, has now come to suggest the social problems of a small group of poor people, dispossessed of their land through no fault of their own. John Steinbeck, in his powerful novel *The Grapes of Wrath,* first focused attention on a family of this class, who were forced to leave their home land because of poor soil, erosion, and drought, and driven to live the nomadic life of migratory workers in the rich gardens of southern California. There they were unwanted, except in time of seasonal crop-harvesting, and subjected to a livelihood of want, need, and gypsy-like squalor.

uprooted like an Okie and driven to migrate.

OLDBUCK, JONATHAN

Jonathan Oldbuck is the whimsical antiquary who gives name to Scott's novel *The Antiquary*. He is devoted to the study and amassing of old coins and medals and all kinds of Roman archaeological relics. A sarcastic and irritable misogynist (from early disappointment in love), he is withal humorous, kind-hearted, and faithful to his friends.

as passionate a numismatist as Oldbuck

OLD MAN OF THE SEA

The Old Man of the Sea is a monster encountered by Sindbad in the *Arabian Nights' Entertainments*. He managed to fasten himself upon the sailor's shoulders so firmly that he could not be dislodged by the utmost efforts of his unfortunate victim. After carrying him about for a long time, Sindbad at last succeeded in intoxicating him and effecting his escape.

an inescapable critic and bore, like the Old Man of the Sea

OLD MORTALITY

Old Mortality is the itinerant antiquary in Scott's novel of that name. It is said to be a picture of Robert Patterson, a religious fanatic who frequented country churchyards in the south of Scotland, and whose occupation consisted in clearing the moss from the tombstones, renewing with his chisel the half-effaced inscriptions, and repairing the emblems of death with which the monuments were adorned.

puttering about in the graveyard like Old Mortality

OLD NICK

Old Nick is a humorous and colloquial name for the devil, used in familiar talk and in common folk tales rather than in the more sonorous and majestic references. The term is used in the same sense and in the same contexts as the Old Boy, Old Scratch, and the like, and means malicious, mean, devilish and tormenting. It is derived from *Neck* or *Nikr,* a dangerous Scandinavian water-demon, popularized into disrepute by British sailors. Macaulay, however, in his essay on Niccolo Machiavelli, the unscrupulous Florentine statesman, says, "Out of his surname they have coined an epithet for a knave—and out of his Christian name a synonym for the Devil."

he has the old Nick in him

OLIBRIUS

Olibrius is the name used to dub a wrong man in a wrong place, a misfit in his job. The name is said to take its origin from a Roman knight, named Olibrius, who was proclaimed emperor by surprise in 472 A.D., but who turned out to be wholly unsuited for the office.

as inappropriate as Olibrius

OLIFAUNT, NIGEL

Nigel Olifaunt, the hero of Scott's *Fortunes of Nigel*, is an impoverished but proud young Scottish lord of Glenvarloch. After various adventures at the court of King James I, whom he induces to repay a debt to his father's estate, he succeeds in freeing it from a mortgage and in marrying Margaret Ramsay.

the vicissitudes of a Nigel Olifaunt

OLIVER (1)

Oliver, the son and heir of Sir Rowland de Boys, in Shakespeare's *As You Like It,* so hated his youngest brother, Orlando, that he persuaded him to wrestle with a professional champion, hoping thus to kill his brother. When Orlando won, Oliver tried to set fire to his chamber, then pursued him to the forest of Arden. When Oliver was rescued from a preying lioness and a snake by his forgiving brother, he repented of his ill-conduct, though his name still connotes a faithless guardian.

an Oliver of a brother to maltreat him

OLIVER (2)

Oliver was a favorite paladin of Charlemagne and accompanied Roland in riding by his side. The exploits of these two young heroes were so similar that it is difficult to keep them distinct. What Roland did Oliver also did, and what Oliver did Roland did, giving rise to the proverb *a Roland for an Oliver,* meaning tit for tat or retaliatory action. At length the two met in single combat and fought for five consecutive days on an island in the Rhine, but neither gained the least advantage.

plays the Oliver to his opponent's Roland

OLIVIA

Olivia is the name of a treacherous woman and female Tartuffe in Wycherley's *Plain Dealer.* A creature of the most unblushing effrontery, she is a master of hypocrisy.

Another Olivia, in Shakespeare's *Twelfth Night,* is the rich countess courted by Orsino through the medium of his supposed page, Viola. The niece of Sir Toby Belch, she employs Malvolio (*q.v.*) as her steward. After rejecting Orsino she marries Sebastian, Viola's twin brother.

deceitful as Olivia
jilted by an Olivia

OLYMPIAD

An Olympiad was an interval of time, reckoned in units of four years, among the ancient Greeks. It was based on the periods between the celebration of the great Olympic games, the first of which was held in 776 B.C. and the last in 393 A.D.

computes her age in Olympiads

OLYMPIAN

Olympian is from Mount Olympus, the home of the gods who seem endowed with a power, a happiness and delight, and even a rage beyond the lot of mortals to know, and their home is bathed in a brightness above the brightness of earth. It is a mountain 6000 feet high between Macedonia and Thessaly.

flew into an Olympian rage

OLYMPIAN GAMES

The Olympian Games were established in 776 B.C. to be held every fourth year in honor of Zeus. The contestants had to be Hellenic, untarnished by any crime against the state or against the gods. Spectators came from all parts of the world; the victor was crowned with a garland of wild olive; heralds proclaimed his name; his own city received him as a conqueror, and artists and poets perpetuated his fame. Later, contests in oratory, poetry, and music were added to the contests of physical skill. During the games war was outlawed, and the whole period was marked by great trade, much traffic, and a stimulation of friendly world-intercourse and travel. The Olympian games persist to this day, but with universal participation permitted; and much the same fame and acclaim attach to the victors.

as permanent as the Olympian games

OMPHALE

Omphale was a queen of Lydia to whom Hercules was sold as a maid for three years in expiation of his murder of Iphitus. The hero fell in love with her, living an effeminate life in her society, spinning wool and wearing her womanly garments, while she donned his lion skin. Her name, in abnormal psychology, connotes transvestitism or cross-dressing, a neurotic fetishism for wearing clothing of the opposite sex. She herself is a type of sadistic virago or masculine woman.

under Omphale's persuasion, a maid-servant for his wife

ONAN

Onan was the brother of Er, and the second son of Judah and Shuah (*Genesis,* xxxviii, 4, ff.). When Er died childless, Judah commanded Onan, "Go in unto thy brother's wife (Tamar, *q.v.*), and marry her, and raise up seed to thy brother." Onan, however, rebelled against complying fully with his father's order, "spilling it on the ground, lest that he should give seed to his brother." His violation of the custom of *levirate marriage* (*i.e.,* union with the widow of a deceased brother and the subsequent granting of a posthumous descendant and heir to his memory and estate) so displeased Jehovah that Onan was slain for his wickedness. The derivative medical term *onanism* refers to self-pollution or to an unconsummated union.

unbrotherly as Onan

ONCA

Onca, in Phoenician mythology, was the goddess of wisdom.

take a lesson from Onca

ONESIMUS

Onesimus ("profitable") was a slave belonging to the household of Philemon, a Christian living in Colossae. After stealing some of his master's property, he fled to Caesarea or Rome, where he was converted by Paul and became one of his disciples (*Col.,* iv, 9). When he returned to his master, he brought with him Paul's *Epistle to Philemon.*

a regenerate Onesimus

ONIAS MENELAUS

Onias Menelaus was the corrupt high priest of the Jews (172-162 B.C.), whose abuses led to the Maccabean revolt.

corrupt as Onias Menelaus

OPHELIA

Ophelia, daughter of Polonius and beloved of Hamlet, in Shakespeare's *Hamlet*, is finally driven to madness and suicide by Hamlet's inexplicable neglect and later his apparent forgetfulness of their love, in his either feigned or actual obsession to avenge his father's murder.

the tragic bewilderment of a neglected Ophelia

OPIMIUS, LUCIUS

Lucius Opimius was the Roman politician who, as consul in 121 B.C., opposed the reforms of Caius Gracchus and led the mob that killed the great liberal and 3000 of his followers. Because the autumn of that same year was one of extraordinary heat, its vintage was so unusually fine that it was named *Opimian wine* in his honor. Later convicted of accepting a bribe from Jugurtha, he was exiled to Dyrrachium where it is said he died in great poverty.

wine of Opimian smoothness

OPPENHEIM, E. PHILLIPS

E. Phillips Oppenheim (1866-1946) was the British novelist who became famous as the popular author of more than 100 stories of adventure, intrigue, espionage, international jewel thefts and secret diplomacy. His first such, *Expiation*, was written when this highly imaginative author was only twenty-one years of age.

mysterious as an Oppenheim thriller

OPPIAN

Oppian was an author who wrote two Greek hexameter poems on hunting and fishing, the *Cynegetica* and *Halieutica* respectively. A third poem, the *Ixeutica,* on bird-catching, is no longer extant, though it too was attributed to this contemporary of the emperor Caracalla (A.D. 211-217).

a modern field and stream enthusiast, inspired by Oppian

OPS

Ops, the wife of Saturn, was the goddess of agriculture, the harvest, plenty, fertility, and power. Especially the protectress and patroness of husbandmen, she was identified with the Greek Rhea.

invokes Ops to prosper his crops

ORBILIAN

Orbilian is from Orbilius, the teacher of the Roman poet Horace, whom the latter called *plagosus,* "the flogger," because of his disciplinary strictness. An Orbilian stick is a cane or birch-rod used in the instruction of refractory pupils.

descends to Orbilian tactics to gain his ends

ORC

Orc is an imaginary mailed beast, dragon, ogre, named after a sea-monster killed by Orlando, in Ariosto's *Orlando Furioso.* He was also a man-eating giant who spared women.

fabulous as Orc

ORCUS

Orcus, in Roman mythology, is the name of the lower world, the abode of the dead. It is also used as a personified reference to the god of the infernal regions, Pluto. In poetry it often appears as a word for Death.

sent his opponent's spirit in flight to Orcus

OREADS

The Oreads were the nymphs of mountains and grottoes. In the Homeric *Hymn to Aphrodite* they are described as belonging "neither to mortals nor to immortals; long do they live and they eat immortal food . . . but when the doom of death stands near them, first the fair trees wither upon the earth . . . and the soul of he nymphs therewith leaves the light of the sun."

scouring the mountains for sight of an Oread

ORESTES

Orestes was the son of Agamemnon and brother of Electra. When he grew to manhood, he avenged his father's death by murdering his mother. He was driven to madness by the Furies that unrelentingly pursued and tormented him; hence, tormented, pursued by furies, crazed. (See *Agamemnon, Electra, Clytemnestra, Pylades, Iphigenia.*)

pursued by unrelenting Furies

ORGOGLIO

Orgoglio, or "Arrogant Pride," is the giant, tall as three men, and the son of Earth and Wind, in Spenser's *Faerie Queene.* Finding the Red Cross Knight at the fountain of Idleness, he beats him with his club, imprisons him, and makes him his slave. Una, hearing of these misfortunes, tells King Arthur who liberates the knight and slays the giant.

proud as Orgoglio

ORGON

Orgon is the silly bourgeois duped by his brother-in-law Tartuffe in Molière's comedy named after the latter. His credulity is proverbial, gulling him to disbelieve his own senses and to see everyone and everything through the rose-colored glasses of his own honest heart.

as gullible as Orgon

ORIANA

Oriana, in the romance of *Amadis de Gaul,* is a daughter of Lisuarte, an imaginary king of England. She is beloved by Amadis, and is represented as the fairest, gentlest, and most affable, courteous, and faithful woman in the world. The name was also given to Queen Elizabeth, extolling her purity and loveliness.

a beauty as matchless as Oriana's

ORILLO

Orillo, in *Orlando Furioso,* is a magician and robber who lived at the mouth of the Nile. As the son of an imp and fairy, he had the ability of restoring any part of his body that might be injured by an opponent. When his head was cut off, he could even put it back on his neck. When Astolpho fled with his severed head, Orillo pursued him on horseback, but Astolpho, knowing that the secret of the magician's power lay in one particular hair, cut all of it from the head. Orillo thereupon expired.

as indestructible as Orillo

ORION

Orion was a mighty giant and hunter, famous for his masculine beauty. Blinded by Oenopion for ravishing Merope, he was expelled from Chios. Following the sound of a Cyclops' hammer, he found Vulcan, who gave him Cedalion as a guide to the abode of the sun. Commanded to proceed to the east by an oracle, he exposed his eyeballs to the rays of the rising sun and recovered his sight. Later slain by Diana, he was placed among the stars, where he forms the most splendid of all the constellations, appearing as a giant wearing a lion's skin and a girdle, and wielding a club.

a hunter as mighty as Orion

ORLANDO

Orlando (see *Roland*), the nephew of Charlemagne, is the hero of many romantic tales of Charlemagne and his paladins. Irving calls him a "mirror of knightly virtue, more willing to do great things than to talk of them." He is generous compassionate, valiant, and courageous beyond belief.

as romantic as an Orlando

ORMUZD

Ormuzd, or Oromasdes, is the name of the supreme deity of the ancient Persians and of their descendants, the Parsees and Guebers. Embodiment of the principle of good, he was created by the will of the great eternal spirit Zervan-Akharana, simultaneously with Ahriman, the principle of evil, with whom he is in everlasting conflict. Ormuzd is the creator of the earth, sun, moon, and stars, to each of which he originally assigned its proper place, and whose various movements he continues to govern.

like Ormuzd and Ahriman, intransigent opponents

ORPHEUS

Orpheus was the legendary Thracian god who played the lyre so sweetly that he could enchant wild beasts, reverse the currents of streams, and cause trees to draw up their roots and walk after him. When his wife, Eurydice, died, he followed her to the underworld and prevailed on Pluto to allow her to return to earth with him—on condition that he not look back at her as she followed him until they had reached the upper world. So ardent was he to see her again that he violated the condition, and she was lost to him forever. Later, when he ignored the invitation of the Thracian women to join them in their orgiastic worship of Dionysus, they tore him to pieces and cast his body to a stream that carried him to the shores of Lesbos, where to this day there is a shrine to him. He was supposed to be the founder of the Orphic mysteries concerning the immortality of the soul.

lulled by music sweet as Orphean strains
like the strains of Orpheus' lyre

ORSINO

Orsino, the Duke of Illyria, in Shakespeare's *Twelfth Night,* is at first in love with Olivia, whom he courts through the emissary Viola, his supposed male page. When the latter's disguise is revealed, Orsino marries her and Olivia marries Sebastian, Viola's brother.

an Orsino, confusing his amours

OSBORNE, JOHN

John Osborne, in Thackeray's *Vanity Fair,* is the avaricious and arrogant merchant who disinherits his son George for marrying Amelia Sedley, the daughter of a bankrupt.

stubborn in pride like John Osborne

OSIRIS

Osiris is the name of the great Egyptian deity, the phases of whose life represent the vicissitudes of human life. His envious brother (or son), Set, called Typhon by the Greeks, tricked him into a chest which he promised he would give to whomever it fit. The chest was thrown into the sea and floated away, but Isis, wife of Osiris, finally found it and brought the god's body back to Egypt. Set then cut it up into fourteen pieces which he scattered about. Isis was able to find only thirteen, since fishes of the sea had already eaten the remaining one. A wooden substitute had to be supplied for the missing part in the reassembling of Osiris's body. Horus, son of Osiris and Isis, finally vanquished and killed his father's murderer.

Osiris was god of light, health, verdure, agricultural fertility, and the source of fruitfulness in general. In the lower world he was regarded as ruler and judge of the dead. His symbol was an open eye.

a puzzle like that of joining the parts of Osiris's body

OSRIC

Osric is the affected and euphuistic young courtier and king's herald who summons Hamlet to sword-play with Laertes in Shakespeare's tragedy of the melancholy Dane. A hair-splitter in thought, he is absurdly dainty and extravagant in expression.

as pretentious of speech as Osric

OSSA ON PELION

Ossa and Pelion are two mountains in Thessaly, piled on top of each other, according to legend, by giants who had planned to scale Mount Olympus. The phrase is now used to refer to obstacles impossible to overcome, burdens or troubles heaped one upon another until the whole is insupportable.

it's the Ossa-on-Pelion aspect of the task that makes it so impossible

OSSIAN

Ossian was the fabulous Celtic warrior and typical pagan bard of the third century, who narrated the adventures of Finn and his band of heroes. James Macpherson's purported translation of the cycle was published in 1760, and it shows great romantic beauty in its descriptions of wild scenery. Its rhythmic prose is couched in short, balanced clauses, and has a tone of lofty sadness in spite of its general grandiloquence.

dreams of Ossian and his warriors of ancient times

OTHELLO

Othello was a Moor of Venice so valorous, gallant, and noble that, in spite of his color, he won the love of Desdemona, the daughter of a noble senator. But he was driven to insane jealousy by the envious and malicious Iago, and only after he had killed Desdemona did he learn that she was innocent and wholly faithful to him. In tragic remorse he killed himself. His name is used not only to indicate valor, but a too-ready yielding to jealousy, and an unbearable remorse, the remorse that makes the tragedy of Shakespeare's *Othello.*

a frenzied Othello

O'TRIGGER, SIR LUCIUS

Sir Lucius O'Trigger, the ostentatiously militant, fortune-hunting Irishman in Sheridan's *The Rivals*, counts that day lost that does not involve him in a gentleman's quarrel of some sort, duels preferred. Part of the comedy in the play rises from Sir Lucius persuading Bob Acres that his honor demands a duel.

a joyous Lucius O'Trigger

OTUS

(see *Ephialtes*)

OUIDA

Ouida was the *nom de plume* of Marie Louise de la Ramée (1839-1908), English romantic novelist of great popularity in the latter part of the last century. Her most widely read novel, *Under Two Flags,* like her many others, brims with love affairs and episodes of fashionable life that have made her pseudonym into the adjective *Ouidaesque,* connoting romantic happy endings. A resident of Florence, in later life, the author wrote charming novels of Italian peasant life and animal and children's stories as well.

spun a Ouidaesque tale of romantic adventure

OUTIS

Outis, meaning "nobody" in Greek, is the assumed name which Ulysses in the *Odyssey* palms off as his real name upon Polyphemus, a Cyclops, whose single eye he destroys while the monster is stretched out on the ground in drunken sleep.

a punning name like Outis

OVERDO, JUSTICE

Justice Overdo, a prominent and celebrated character in Ben Jonson's *Bartholomew Fair*, is the overzealous official who, in his enthusiasm for detecting illegal actions at the Fair, is himself ridiculously apprehended as a malefactor.

as exaggerated as Justice Overdo

OVERREACH, SIR GILES

Sir Giles Overreach is a character in Massinger's comedy *A New Way to Pay Old Debts.* The counterpart of Sir Giles Mompesson, a noted usurer who was outlawed for his misdeeds, he is a bold and unscrupulous oppressor, greedy of wealth, intensely proud and inordinately ambitious. He is finally outwitted by his victims.

shady practices like those of Overreach

OVIDIAN

Ovidian suggests the character and work of Publius Ovidius Naso (43 B.C. -18 A.D.), whose poetry was fashionable in sophisticated Roman circles. In A.D. 8 he was banished by imperial decree of Augustus to the Black Sea region, probably because of his immoral *Ars Amatoria* ("Art of Love") and his friendship with the licentious Julia, the emperor's daughter, who likewise was exiled for life. Principally elegiac in form, his work is neat, facile, and vivid, and he was one of the smoothest of the Roman versifiers. The purpose of his work was to amuse, though he fulfilled a larger role as well in influencing Chaucer, Spenser, Marlow and Shakespeare. As a guide to Greek mythology and Roman legend, his *Metamorphoses* and *Fasti* have become indispensable to the cultured man.

with Ovidian elegance and smoothness

Ovidian urbanity and licentiousness

OWAIN

Owain is the name of the Irish knight of King Stephen's court who is fabled to have entered and passed through St. Patrick's Purgatory by way of performing penance for having lived a life of violence and rapine. The legend of the descent, composed by Henry, an English Benedictine monk of the abbey of Saltrey, in 1153, was the first to make known to the world the story of the Purgatory of St. Patrick, entrance to which was effected through a cave through which living sinners passed who were desirous of expiating their evil deeds while still in the flesh.

a penitential Owain, punishing himself for his sins

P

PACHOMIUS

Pachomius, who established the first community of monks and nuns on an island in the Nile at Tabenna, Egypt, was born of heathen parents about the year 292. A conscript in one of the campaigns of Constantine, he was converted to Christianity on his return in 314. According to legend, an angel called him to establish a monastery for cenobites, and at his death he had founded nine of them (with some 3000 monks) and a nunnery.

a religious hermit like Pachomius

PACOLET

Pacolet, a dwarf in the old romance of *Valentine and Orson,* is the owner of an enchanted steed made of wood and capable of incredible swiftness of motion. With it he rescues the twin brothers from the dungeon of Ferragus. The *horse of Pacolet* is a popular French allusion to speed and capacity for going anywhere, and by transference the very name Pacolet has come to mean a fast horse.

with the speed of Pacolet

PACTOLUS

Pactolus, the ancient name of a river of Lydia in Asia Minor (the modern Bagouly), connotes wealth in gold, for its waters were said to flow over golden sands from the time that Midas (*q.v.*) bathed in the stream to rid himself of the curse brought on him by his unwise request that everything he touch turn to that precious metal. Flowing past Sardis, this tributary of the Hermus was one of the principal sources of the wealth and riches of Lydia.

all his wealth flowed into the Pactolus

PADALON

Padalon is the name of the underworld in Hindu mythology. The abode of departed spirits, it was thought to be of octagonal shape and to have its eight gateways guarded by the same number of deities.

down to the fiery floor of Padalon
left for Padalon many years ago

PADEREWSKI, IGNACE JAN

Ignace Jan Paderewski (1860-1941), distinguished Polish concert pianist and patriot, made his professional debut in Vienna in 1887, in Paris two years later, in London in 1890, and swept on to fame in the United States in 1891. Beloved as an interpreter of Chopin, Rubinstein, Liszt and Schumann, he was the composer of an opera (*Manru*), a symphony, several concertos, and the celebrated *Minuet* as well. During World War I he was a leader of the Polish cause, organizing a "general committee of assistance for the victims of the war in Poland," and touring America to raise funds for the relief of his countrymen. For ten months after the war he served his country as Prime Minister and Minister of Foreign Affairs. To the very end of his life, when his musical powers were feeble and his impressive leonine mane of hair thinning, he still toiled unceasingly and with passionate devotion for the liberty and well-being of his country.

a new Paderewski of the keyboard

PAEAN

Paean ("the healing") was the name of the physician of the gods and was sometimes used as the surname of Asclepius (*q.v.*), the god of medicine. The name was later used to invoke in more general sense any deliverer from evil or calamity, and was thus transferred to Apollo and to the hymn dedicated to him at Sparta. Sometimes accompanied by a dance, the name was also used for the warlike song sung before or during a battle.

a propitious Paean guard your health

PAGANINI

Paganini (1784-1840) was an Italian violinist, a genius and a prodigy at nine, who became a most brilliant performer. In fact, his performances are said to have occasioned extraordinary excitement among the audience, and later a contemporary critic wrote that his audiences went wild with enthusiasm, that Paganini created a "furor wholly unequalled in the history of music." He was the first to accomplish really distinguished and marvelous virtuoso performances on a single string, a feat that excited great astonishment and admiration. His name suggests genius, brilliant execution, and effective showmanship. He was also a brilliant composer of difficult violin literature such as the *Devil's Trill* sonata.

with a Paganini showmanship
with a Paganinian brilliance of execution

PAGES, THE

The Pages are a family in Shakespeare's *Merry Wives of Windsor.* Mr. Page is distinguished for his uxoriousness, and Mrs. Page, one of the ladies to whom Falstaff proposes amorous dalliance, joins with Mrs. Ford in a plot to dupe and disgrace him. William Page, the son, is a schoolboy and brother to Anne. She rejects both Slender, her mother's choice for her hand, and Dr. Caius for her own preference, Fenton. Slender, a shy and awkward booby, is too faint-hearted to urge his suit further than to sigh in audible whispers, "Sweet Anne Page!"

at variance as the Pages in choosing a son-in-law

PAINE, THOMAS

Thomas Paine (1737-1809) rendered signal service to America in its early days, both through his magazine, *The Pennsylvanian,* and his *Common Sense,* advocating rebellion and separation from England. In 1776 he published *The Crisis,* the famous "these are the days that try men's souls" pamphlet meant to counteract a general spirit of gloom that followed the war. Sent to France to negotiate a loan, and again at the time of the French Revolution, he was there imprisoned, but released at the instance of James Monroe. He returned home, resumed his seat in the Convention, and was given $3000 and three hundred acres of land in New York for "signal service to his country." In 1795, however he so offended his friends by his *Age of Reason* that he was generally calumniated, and only now is beginning to be remembered again for his service to his country.

the delayed recognition of a Thomas Paine

PAKHT

Pakht, also known as Sekhet, was an Egyptian goddess with the head of a lioness or cat. Crowned with the solar disk and the uraeus serpent, she was associated with Ptah, her husband, in the triad of supreme gods worshiped at Memphis. Called "the eye of Ra," she represented the destructive heat of the sun and annihilated the souls of the wicked in the lower world.

the intense gaze of Pakht

PALAEMON

Palaemon, a surname of Melicertes, son of Ino, was a sea-god friendly to the shipwrecked. By the Romans he was identified with Portunus, the protecting god of harbors.

Palaemon is also the name of a shepherd in Vergil's third *Eclogue.* Chosen to serve as umpire in a musical contest between Damoetas and Menalcas, he declares his inability to reach a decision in such an important controversy, after hearing the competitors.

an umpire as irresolute as Palaemon
with Palaemon's aid he brought his craft out of danger

PALAMEDES

Palamedes, the son of Nauplius, king of Euboea, was celebrated in Greek mythology for his inventive genius and was said to have been the first to make measures, scales, dice, lighthouses, and the discus (quoit). He also furnished four letters to the Greek alphabet of Cadmus. Hence, the name is sometimes used as an appellation of any ingenious man. When Ulysses feigned madness in order to avoid going to the Trojan war, plowing up the seashore and sowing it with salt, Palamedes placed the hero's infant son Telemachus in his path to expose his deception. Hated and persecuted by Ulysses for this, he was, according to some accounts, treacherously accused of treason by the hero and condemned to death on false evidence.

has the inventive genius of a Palamedes

PALAMON AND ARCITE

Palamon and Arcite were two noble Theban youths whose friendly rivalry for the love of Emilia is told in Boccaccio's *Teseide* and Chaucer's *Knight's Tale*. Imprisoned by Duke Theseus in a dungeon in Athens, they both fell in love with Emilia, the Duke's sister-in-law, and when they obtained their liberty the Duke appointed a tournament, promising Emilia to the victor. Arcite prayed to Mars to grant him victory, Palamon besought Venus to grant him Emilia, and both obtained their petition. Arcite won the victory but, being thrown from his horse, died. Palamon, though not the winner, won the prize for which he had fought.

a Palamon and Arcite competition

PALES

Pales, in Roman mythology, was the tutelary deity of shepherds, flocks, and cattle. Worshiped with great solemnity at the festival of the Palilia on April 21 (the date on which Rome was founded in the year 753 B.C.), the god is represented in some writers as male, in others as female, though sylvan in character by all. The rites consisted of a purification of shepherds and their flocks, which were driven through the flames of burning straw, and similar ceremonies still adhere to the customs of several eastern European nations.

Pales must be prospering your herds

PALESTRINA, GIOVANNI

Giovanni Palestrina (1526-1594) was a great Italian composer of ecclesiastical music and the protégé of Pope Julius III. Developing medieval church modes for use in masses, hymns, litanies, magnificats, motets, and madrigals, he reformed religious music by relying on simple masses of harmony without polyphonic embellishment. Simplicity, solemnity, and sacramental and penitential devotion characterize the impressive music of Palestrina.

as sacred as a Palestrina mass

PALINURUS

Palinurus is the name of the unvigilant pilot of Aeneas in Vergil's *Aeneid*. Falling asleep at the helm, he tumbled into the sea and swam to the coast of Lucania in Italy, where he was murdered by bandits. Proceeding to the lower world, he was unable to cross the Styx because his body had not been given burial. Eventually Aeneas satisfied this need. His name has been given to the promontory near which he went overboard, and he has been still further immortalized in modern times by ichthyologists, who have given the name *Palinurus vulgaris* to the sea-crayfish or langouste.

as unwary in a boat as Palinurus

PALLADIUM

The Palladium was the venerable statue of Pallas (Athena, Minerva) said to have fallen from heaven on the plain of Troy. It represented the goddess in full panoply of war, and the safety of the city depended on its presence on the citadel at Troy. Stolen through the craft of Diomedes and Ulysses, it could no longer guard the city, which subsequently fell. Aeneas was also said to have taken it to Italy, where it later stood in Rome's temple of Vesta. It has come to mean any safeguard or protection.

has lost his Palladium

PALLAS

Pallas is a surname of Athena, won from that goddess's victory over a giant or a maiden of that name, or perhaps the name of some other deity whom she absorbed. Harmoniously blending both power and wisdom, she was the preserver of the state, the protectress of agriculture (she created the olive-tree and invented the plow and the rake), and the patroness of all useful arts, such as weaving. The embodiment of all knowledge, she was a virgin divinity to whom the owl, serpent, and cock were sacred. Her beauty was severe and masculine, and she was the granter of victory in war.

Pallas-like perfections

PAMELA

Pamela is the heroine of the novel of the same name, subtitled *Virtue Rewarded,* by Richardson. A simple and innocent country girl who becomes servant to a dissolute master, Mr. B., she inspires him with a lecherous passion, which, however, she resists so pertinaciously that her rectitude awakens in him a deep admiration. In the end, this pure, modest, and meek creature is rewarded by becoming his wife.

Pamelan power to resist temptation

PAN

Pan, the son of Mercury and Penelope in Greek mythology, was the god of woods, shepherds, and huntsmen. Represented as a grim, shaggy being with horns, pointed ears, a tail, and goat's feet, he was fond of music, playing on pipes of straw, and also possessed prophetic powers. With his terrific voice he sometimes startled travelers, appearing before them suddenly and startling them with the awe and terror now known as *panic.* The early Christians believed that at the moment of Christ's crucifixion a deep groan was heard throughout the Grecian isles, telling that the great god Pan was dead and all the gods of Olympus dethroned. His name still connotes carefree life in sylvan retreat, freedom from responsibility or obligation.

a piping Pan, young and gay

PAN, PETER

Peter Pan is a fanciful, whimsical, altogether charming creation of Sir James Barrie. An elfish boy who never grew up, he lives through a series of situations that smack of fairyland and dream, born of whimsicality, imagination, and fantasy. Peter Pan has caught and held the spirit of youth and childhood, and has captivated the universal heart of youth in people of all ages.

Barrie himself is the Peter Pan of literature

PANAETIUS

Panaetius was a celebrated Stoic philosopher who lived in Rome for some years as an intimate friend of Scipio Africanus and Laelius, dying in Athens around B.C. 111. His principal work was a treatise on moral obligation, from which Cicero took the greater part of his work *De Officiis.*

more stoical than Panaetius

PANCRAS

Pancras (Latin Pancratus), the patron saint of children, was a Christian boy martyr who suffered death at the age of fourteen, in 304 A.D., by order of Diocletian. In art he is represented as treading on a Saracen and bearing either a stone and a sword, or a book and a palm-branch, the former emblems alluding to his hatred of infidelity and to the implements of his martyrdom. A church in London is dedicated to him, and a borough in the northern part of the metropolis is named after it and him.

a child surely protected by St. Pancras

PANDAREOS

Pandareos, in Greek legend, was the Milesian who stole the golden dog made by Hephaestus and gave it to Tantalus. In punishment, his daughters were carried off by the Harpies.

a thieving Pandareos

PANDARUS

Pandarus is the uncle of Cressida in Shakespeare's play *Troilus and Cressida.* Represented as procuring for the young Trojan the love and affections of his niece, he is a stock type of the pimp or go-between. His name has passed into the English word *pander,* formerly spelled *pandar.*

he has found the services of a Pandarus

PANDEMONIUM

Pandemonium is the name given by Milton to "the high capital of Satan and his peers." Hence, as the abode of all the demons, it is a place of lawlessness and connotes wild uproar, uncontrolled noise and utter tumult.

the place was a pandemonium
pandemonium broke loose

PANDEMOS

Pandemos ("of all the people") was a surname of Aphrodite as the goddess of marriage and family life. Later separated from the realm of Aphrodite Urania (that of spiritual love), Pandemos personified worldly passion and sensual lust.

aroused by Pandemos

PANDORA

Pandora is the girl mentioned in the phrase, *Pandora's box.* She is sometimes said to have been the first woman, on whom all the gods and goddesses bestowed gifts on her wedding to Epimetheus. One story goes that she opened her box, and all the ills of the world flew out to trouble the children of men; another that all the blessings of the world, except Hope, flew away, never to be recovered.

a stunned Pandora

PANGLOSSIAN

Panglossian is from the proper name Pangloss, meaning "all tongue." In Voltaire's *Candide* there is an optimist philosopher by this name. Dr. Pangloss is a learned pedant in Colman's "The Heir at Law." Very poor but very conceited, he is proud of being an LL.D and an A.S.S. (the latter mythical academic degree being *Artium Societatis Socius,* or "Associate of the Society of Arts"). He is a satirical portrait of the mercenary tutor of the period.

pedantic and pompous as Dr. Pangloss

PANTAGRUEL

Pantagruelian is from Pantagruel in Rabelais' satire, *Gargantua and Pantagruel,* a drunkard whose broad, cynical, coarse good humor nevertheless strikes out with deep satire. Like Gargantua, he was fantastically huge — "whole armies could find shelter under his tongue, and cities in his mouth and throat." *Pantagruelian* in its general sense suggests buffoonery, jovial but serious mockery, coarse good humor, and tremendous size.

Pantagruelian dimensions

PANTALEON, ST.

Pantaleon, the patron saint of physicians, was himself a doctor and born probably at Nicomedia in Bithynia, Asia Minor. Attendant and personal physician of the emperor Galerius, he was put to death as a martyr, in 305 A.D., for his Christian persuasion.

St. Pantaleon to aid him in the diagnosis

PANTALOON

Pantaloon is a witless old man in Italian comedy, the stooge and the shadow accent to the clown. He is dressed in a suit reaching to his heels, spectacles and slippers, and is an old buffoon. The patron saint of Venice, Pantaloon may be derived from the Italian words *pianta leone,* the "planter" of the "lion" of St. Mark.

contented to play Pantaloon to any good clown

PANTIBIBLIA

Pantibiblia is a legendary city of Babylonia in antediluvian days. It was used as a storehouse for books. The name is a compound of two Greek roots, meaning "all" and "books."

a library large enough to fill Pantibiblia

PANURGE

Panurge is a rogue, the companion of Pantagruel, a rake, a borrower, a spendthrift, tippler, and libertine, but a boon companion, ready for any kind of work, any kind of knavery or roguishness. In fact, he is so ready that *panurgic* and *panurgy* have come to mean aptness and readiness in all kinds of work. With Rabelaisian wit he is made mirthful, full of ingenious mockery, an endless questioner, an objector to all advice, utterly non-moral, but "he had a good heart."

the questions of a Panurge

PANZA, SANCHO

Sancho Panza, the squire of Cervantes' *Don Quixote*, is really a foil for his master, round, pot-bellied, short, selfish and self-important. Not until he is made mayor of a town does he appear as an amusing person in his own right, ignorant, credulous, and grotesque to be sure, but shrewd, full of common sense and especially full of proverbs.

addicted to Sancho-Panzian proverbs

PAPHIAN

Paphian is from Paphos, a town on the west coast of the island of Cyprus and the chief seat of the worship of Aphrodite (Venus), who is said to have landed there after her birth among the waves. There too she had a celebrated temple, the high-priest of which exercised religious superintendence over the entire island. Aphrodite is often spoken of as Cypria or Paphia, and the name connotes the meretricious love of an erotic votary of Venus, a prostitute, or a lewd and wanton woman.

seeking Paphian adventures on the street

PAPHNUTIUS

Paphnutius, the sainted Bishop of Thebes, was famed for the purity, chastity, and perfect sanctity of his life. A participant in the first ecumenical council, he also attended the Synod at Tyre in 335 A.D. He is portrayed in Anatole France's *Thais* as the holy man tempted by the pagan and glamorous courtesan.

less open to temptation than Paphnutius

PAPINIAN

Aemilius Papinian, celebrated Roman jurist and praetorian prefect for the emperor Septimius Severus, wrote 37 books of legal *Quaestiones* and 19 books of *Responsa* (verdicts), excerpts from which are now extant in the Digest of Law made by Justinian. When Caracalla, Severus's son, murdered his brother Geta and asked Papinian to defend him before the Senate, the jurist replied, "Parricide is not so easy to defend as to commit," refusing to undertake the assignment. For his failure to yield to his scruples, Caracalla had him put to death.

as legally learned as Papinian

PARACELSUS

Paracelsus, made popular in Browning's poem *Paracelsus,* was actually a Swiss alchemist (1493-1541) proficient in the superficial knowledge and the jargon of alchemy, magic, and quackery. He performed some famous cures, and finally proclaiming an "elixir of life," he professed means to prolong life indefinitely. Although later a vagabond and a loose liver, Paracelsus nevertheless gave importance to pharmaceutical chemistry.

sad as a lost Paracelsus

PARAN

Paran was the name of the wilderness between Midian and Egypt, the refuge of Ishmael when he was expelled from the camp of Abraham (*Genesis*, xxi, 21). It was one of the stations of the wilderness journey of the Israelites before they entered Canaan, and from it spies were sent forth to reconnoitre and make their reports.

arid as Paran

PARCAE

The Parcae is the collective name for the Fates, Clotho, Lachesis and Atropos, said to control human destinies. The thread of life Clotho unwinds, Lachesis spins, and Atropos cuts. Other words are Fortune, Life, Destiny, Fate.

the watching eyes of the Parcae

PARIAH

A Pariah is an outcast, a low person not received by a community, and is derived from the original non-Brahmanic low-caste among some of the tribes of Burmah. It was adopted in general use to mean unacceptable, outcast, taboo, of persons seriously detrimental to a community or to a large group.

an unhappy Pariah

PARIAN

Parian is from Paros, one of the larger of the Aegean islands known as the Cyclades and inhabited by prosperous Ionians. Its most celebrated product was its beautiful white statuary marble, which was used extensively by ancient sculptors. *Parian verse* means verse marked by stinging satire, as found in the work of Archilochus (*q.v.*), a native son. The *Parian Chronicle* is a famous inscription, now preserved at Oxford, which in its perfect state contained a chronological account of the principal events in Greek history from the time of Cecrops, 1582 B.C., to the archonship of Diognetus, 264 B.C.

poetry of Parian character

PARIBANOU

Paribanou is a fairy in the story of "Prince Ahmed" in the *Arabian Nights' Entertainments.* The tent which she gave to her husband was capable of contracting to the size of a toy for the hand of a lady, or of expanding great enough to house the armies of powerful sultans for them to repose in its shade.

as adaptable as Paribanou's tent

PARIDEL

Sir Paridel is a fickle and inconstant libertine in Spenser's *Faerie Queene*. The model for this male coquette, whose passionate delight was to enslave women and then desert them, is said to have been the Earl of Westmoreland.

Paridel is also used as an appellation for a young gentleman who travels widely to seek adventure merely because he is rich, young, idle, and fanciful.

Thee too, my Paridel, she marked thee there,
Stretched on the rack of a too-easy chair,
And heard thy everlasting yawn confess
The pains and penalties of idleness.
Pope, *Dunciad, iv*

indolent as Paridel

PARIS

Paris was the Trojan prince who persuaded the beautiful Helen, wife of his host Menelaus, King of Sparta, to flee with him to Troy. To the obloquy of seducing the wife of his host he added the danger involved in abducting Helen, whose suitors had been so noble and so many that when Helen had chosen Menelaus as her husband they had bound themselves to avenge any possible abduction by any means necessary. Paris, graceful, accomplished, seductive, and treacherous, brought on the Trojan war when he took Helen to Troy.

an irresponsible Paris

PARJANYA

Parjanya, in Vedic mythology, is the god of the rain. He is sometimes identified with Indra, the great national god of the Indo-Aryans, a deity who wields the thunderbolt, brings down the rain, subjugates his enemies, and rewards his devotees with booty. The elephant Airavata which he rides is the personification of a rain cloud.

Parjanya riding through the skies on his elephantine cloud

PARMENIDES

Parmenides, celebrated Greek philosopher born about 510 B.C., is the interlocutor in Plato's dialogue of that name. Founder of the Eleatic school, he taught the differences between reality and illusion. The only possible object of knowledge, he believed, is the actual universe, which is a single, eternal, indivisible, and unchangeable whole. Of things that are changeable and perishable, and phenomena such as motion, we can have only conjectures.

unchanging as Parmenides' "truth"

PARNASSUS

Parnassus was the hill of poetry, a mountain of delights, of trees and fountains, the haunt of the Muses and Apollo and sacred to them. The Delphic oracle was near and the Castalian spring, whose waters gave poetic power. Parnassus is therefore used to indicate attempts at and success in poetry.

Lowell, who strove Parnassus to climb

hard to climb as Parnassus

PAROLLES

Parolles ("Words") is the name of the boastful and cowardly follower of Bertram in Shakespeare's *All's Well That Ends Well.* Steeped in baseness, he is a man of vain words who pretends to knowledge which he does not have and to hypocritical sentiments which he does not feel. In one scene he is taken blindfold among his old acquaintances and led to vilify their characters under the impression that he is speaking to and gratifying their enemies. A slandering pretender and a faithless villain, "he hath outvillained villainy so far, that the rarity redeems him."

as insincere in speech as Parolles

PARRHASIUS' CURTAIN

In a contest between the celebrated 4th century painters, Parrhasius and Zeuxis, the latter exhibited a picture of some grapes that were so realistic that birds flew down to peck them. Triumphantly he then ordered Parrhasius to draw the curtain from his easel that he might see the painting behind it. But Parrhasius had painted the curtain itself so that Zeuxis had to concede him the victory, since he had deceived only birds but Parrhasius had deceived him.

as life-like as Parrhasius' painted curtain

PARROT, POLL

Poll Parrot, a mindless repeater of words other people use, means a silly babbler, insignificant and unworthy of attention. The name also indicates the empty-headed people who borrow other people's ideas and by repeating them, acquire a reputation for good thinking.

a sort of Poll-Parrot patriotism

PARSIFAL

Parsifal was the pure knight in Wagner's poem (1877) and opera (1879) of the same name. Reared in a forest in complete ignorance of chivalry, he arrived at the castle of the Holy Grail where Amfortas, the chief of the knights guarding it, had lost the sacred spear that pierced the side of Christ through yielding to the seductions of Kundry, the female accomplice of Klingsor, the magician. When Parsifal went to Klingsor's enchanted castle to retrieve the spear, he resisted the attempts of Kundry on his chastity. Klingsor cast the sacred spear at Parsifal but the latter seized it suspended in mid-air. Klingsor and his castle were then destroyed, and Parsifal redeemed Kundry, healed Amfortas of his wound by touching it with the spear, exposed the Holy Grail, and became king of the knights.

as chaste as Parsifal
Parsifalian ignorance of evil

PARTHENIA

Parthenia ("virginal purity"), in Sidney's *Arcadia,* is the wife of Argalus, who assumes the armor of a knight in order to avenge her husband's death at the hands of Amphialus.

an Amazonian Parthenia

PARTHENON

The Parthenon is the "temple of the virgin" Athena, built of Pentelic marble on the Athenian Acropolis and erected under the administration of Pericles (447-438 B.C.) by the architects Ictinus and Callicrates and the sculptor Phidias. Subtle architectural refinements make it the greatest of all Doric temples and one of the most superb masterpieces of building of all time. The *cella* or main shrine contained the gold-and-ivory statue of Athena by Phidias. Its gracious curves and chaste majesty conspire to awe all who see it. It remained intact until 1687, when the Venetians blew out the roof by firing gunpowder stored in the temple by the besieged Turks.

sublime and majestic as the Parthenon

PARTHENOPE

Parthenope was one of the three Sirens, whose alluring singing drew sailors to shipwreck and ruin. She became enamored of Ulysses, and in her grief at not winning him threw herself into the sea and was cast up on the shore where

Naples later stood, for which reason that city was originally called by her name.

like Parthenope, a suicide from heartbreak

PARTHIAN

The Parthians were a Persian people who by reason of their skill with the bow and arrow were formidable to Rome. If defeated, they were apt to turn in flight to shoot a final and usually fatal arrow. The army of Crassus was destroyed by the Parthians (53 B.C.) who captured and killed Crassus by pouring molten gold down his throat, "to satisfy his thirst for gold." The expression "a Parthian arrow" means a parting shot, an arrow shot while the warrior is fleeing, a last word.

fled like a Parthian
a Parthian's flying arrow

PARTINGTON, MRS.

Mrs. Partington is an anecdotal character by Sydney Smith, who, according to her creator, tried with a mop to stem a high tide of the Atlantic Ocean during a storm at Sidmouth, England, in 1824, in order to keep it out of her home. She is an emblem of the futility of enterprise and the vainness of opposition to the inevitable.

Another Mrs. Partington was likewise an imaginary old lady, whose laughable sayings were recorded by the American humorist B. P. Shillaber (1814-1890). She is a Mrs. Malaprop or Tabitha Bramble, distinguished for her amusing affectations and her misuse of learned words.

as senseless as Mrs. Partington

PARTRIDGE

Partridge, the attendant of *Tom Jones* in Fielding's novel of that name, is the quondam schoolmaster turned barber. Noted for his fidelity, shrewdness, and childlike simplicity, he exhibits strong and naive excitement when he goes to the theater to see David Garrick in *Hamlet.*

as flustered as Partridge at the theater

PARTULA

Partula, according to Tertullian (quoted in *Aulus Gellius,* iii, 16), was the Roman goddess of pregnancy who determined the length of time of a woman's gestation.

should ask Partula how soon she will have her child

PASIPHAE

Pasiphaë was the daughter of Helios (the sun), the sister of Circe, and the wife of Minos, king of Crete, to whom she bore Phaedra, Ariadne, and Androgeos. When Minos defaulted on his promise to sacrifice a beautiful snow-white bull to Poseidon (Neptune), the sea-god inspired Pasiphaë with a zoophilic passion for the bull, and the fruit of her perverse love was the Minotaur (*q.v.*), the monstrous creature, half-bull and half-man, housed in the Labyrinth. The legend probably derived from a cult of the bull in Minoan Crete.

as devoted to her pets as Pasiphaë to the bull

PASQUINADE

Pasquinade is from Pasquin, a 15th century Roman cobbler noted for his caustic wit. After his death a wooden statue dug up during some street repairs was set up opposite his old shop and jocularly used as a bulletin board for any sort of caustic comment such as Pasquin had habitually made. It eventually came to be the bulletin on which to make public any jibe or lampoon against anyone, a sort of attack eventually called a pasquinade. The victims finally set up a rival statue, called Marforio, in the Capitol, where replies to the pasquinades were posted. In jest or in earnest, all such writings were anonymous, consequently safe and correspondingly free in expression.

public as a pasquinade

PASTEUR, LOUIS

Louis Pasteur (1822-1895) was the eminent French chemist who discovered the successful treatment for rabies, and what is even more widely useful, the method of checking fermentation —now called pasteurizing—by means of sterilizing fluid by high temperature followed by rapid cooling, which destroys undesirable bacteria but leaves original qualities intact. Pasteur's story is marvelously told in one chapter of De Kruif's *Microbe Hunters.*

the persistence of a Pasteur

PATAGONIAN

Patagonian is from the inhabitants of Patagonia, the tallest known race, remarkable for their large feet and huge figure. They were marked persons wherever they went, and Patagonian is applied humorously to extraordinarily tall and large persons. The country is at the southern extremity of South America.

escorted by a Patagonian bell-boy

PATELIN

Patelin, an artful dodger and cheat in a French farce of the fifteenth century, is a name still in currency to designate a subtle and crafty man who by flattery and insinuation entices others to grant him his desires. When he wanted Josseaume to sell him cloth on credit, he gained his end obliquely by saying of his father, "He did sell on credit, or even lend to those who wished to borrow." The French phrase *savoir son Patelin* means, therefore, the talent to bamboozle, and Patelinage connotes foolery and buffoonery.

as scheming and knavish as Patelin

PATRICK, SAINT

Saint Patrick (372-460?) is the patron saint of Ireland to whom is commonly ascribed clearing the snakes out of the island, although there is no authentic basis for the story. March 17 is Saint Patrick's Day, celebrated the world over by Irishmen "wearing the green." History credits Saint Patrick with having established a purgatory on earth, off Ireland and in a place of punishment, to give reality to the idea of eternal punishment for sins.

routed them as with a St. Patrick charm

PATROCLUS

Patroclus, the son of Menoetius, was the intimate friend of Achilles, whom he accompanied to the siege of Troy. When Achilles sulked in his tent because of an affront from Agamemnon, the Greeks lost heavily to their foe until Patroclus donned Achilles' armor and turned the tide of the fighting. He was, however, slain by Hector on whom Achilles subsequently vowed and exacted vengeance. Patroclus' name stands for loyalty and devotion in friendship.

has his devoted Patroclus
avenged his Patroclus

PATTERNE, SIR WILLOUGHBY

Sir Willoughby Patterne, in Meredith's *Egoist* (1879), is the embodiment of masculine self-appreciation, conceited and ostentatiously exemplary.

a model as perfect as Sir Willoughby Patterne

PATTI, ADELINA

Adelina Patti (1843-1919), Spanish-born Italian coloratura soprano of operatic fame, began her artistic career at the age of seven in a New York concert hall. Making her debut as *Lucia di Lammermoor* (*q.v.*) in 1859, she soon became the leading prima donna at Covent Garden, London, in Paris and other continental capitals. After marrying Baron Cederström, her third husband and a Swedish-born naturalized Englishman, she retired in the late 80's, making only occasional appearances on the private stage of her castle in Wales and to sing "Home, Sweet Home" at Albert Hall in London. Avoiding Wagnerian roles, she associated herself exclusively with the Italian repertoire. After Jenny Lind, she was generally considered to be the greatest soprano of the nineteenth century.

warbling like Adelina Patti

PAUL AND VIRGINIE

Paul and Virginie are the juvenile playmates and faithful lovers of Bernardin de St. Pierre's idyllic romance, *Paul et Virginie,* "a tropical Arcadian romance which for a time reigned supreme over French, English, and German imaginations of a certain caliber, and rendered the name *Virginie* triumphant in France." The story achieved the same sensational popularity in its day (1787) that *Uncle Tom's Cabin* did in a later one, and its title characters have become archetypes of constant devotion, pastoral charm, and simple content. When returning from France to their island home, Mauritius, Virginie is shipwrecked and drowned, and Paul, conforming to the destiny imposed upon him by this type of sentimental effusion, shortly thereafter dies of heart-break.

as dependent on one another as Paul and Virginie

PAUL, SAINT

Saint Paul, a Jew (?-67 A.D.), was a Roman citizen by birthright, a rigid Pharisee by education, a student of law under Gamaliel, and an eminent rabbi in Jerusalem. After he had been for years a persecutor of Christians and was said to have had to do with the martyrdom of Stephen, he was converted by Samuel and ordained to preach to the Gentiles. He is said to have had speech with St. Peter, and to have established many Christian churches, to which he later wrote epistles, now a part of the New Testament. He was consistently noted for energy of thought and action and for zeal in all his undertakings.

bold as a Paul before Agrippa

PAULINA

Paulina is the turbulent, hot-tempered, and voluble wife of Antigonus, a Sicilian nobleman in Shakespeare's *Winter's Tale.* The friend of Queen Hermione, she takes care of her when the latter is unjustly sent to prison by her jealous husband, King Leontes, and after a time presents her again to Leontes as a statue "by that rare Italian master, Julio Romano." A character strongly drawn from real life, Paulina is a warm-hearted woman, fearless in asserting the truth and firm in her sense of right. But heedless, impatient, and bold, she injures, from excess of zeal, those whom she most wishes to serve.

a fiery-tempered and garrulous Paulina

PAUSANIAS

Pausanias was a traveler and geographer who lived in the second half of the second century A.D. and recorded in ten books a detailed description of all the sites most worth seeing in Greece. This *Periegesis* or *Itinerary of Hellas* had the value of an ancient Baedeker or a guide-book for tourists, detailing with great minuteness all cities, sanctuaries, and tombs throughout the Hellenic peninsula, and supplying a full inventory of the artistic treasures, such as statues and paintings, contained in them. As well as cataloguing these artefacts according to their locations in ancient times, he also discusses the villages, rivers, and roads to be followed en route to each site and gives the history, economic condition, and landscape of the places which he personally visited.

the Pausanias of the museum

PAVLOVA, ANNA

Anna Pavlova (1886-1931) was the greatest star of the Russian ballet when it was first presented to the western world. A supporter of Fokine's reforms in the traditional ballet, she danced to much of his choreography, including the famous "Swan," "Les Sylphides." and others. Unsympathetic to Diaghilev, she went on tour with a company of her own. She had wonderful dramatic ability and consummate grace of movement, and her name is still synonymous with supreme grace in the dance.

with Pavlovan grace of movement

PAVOR

Pavor was the Roman god of fear, and the attendant of Mars in war. This ancient personification of panic and rout in battle has now come into the realms of psychology and psychiatry, as in the phrases *pavor diurnus* and *pavor nocturnus* for groundless fear by day and the unreasoning fear of children by night, respectively.

Pavor passing through the entire army

PAX

Pax was the Roman goddess personifying peace. Called Irene by the Greeks, she was represented as a daughter of Zeus and Themis, and one of the Horae. In Rome a magnificent temple was dedicated to her by the emperor Vespasian. On coins she is portrayed as a beautiful maiden, holding in her left arm a cornucopia, and in her right hand either an olive branch or the staff of Mercury.

may Pax bless the land

PEACHUMS, THE

The Peachums are a family in Gay's *Beggar's Opera.* Peachum himself is a pimp and a receiver of stolen goods who makes of his house a resort for thieves, pickpockets, and base villains. Mrs. Peachum advises her beautiful daughter Polly to be "somewhat nice" in her deviations from virtue, though Polly preserves unspotted the purity of her character in spite of the corrupt milieu. The bride of Macheath, the leader of a band of highwaymen, she remains loyal and constant in her affection, even though she knows of his numerous illicit affairs with other women, and is ultimately deserted by him.

a Polly Peachum, unspoiled by the raffish character of her home

---

PECKSNIFF

Pecksniff is an unctuous, pretentious hypocrite in Dickens' *Martin Chuzzlewit,* always canting high moral principles, even while he was carrying out the most nefarious and despicable of schemes and violating every high principle. Always blatantly pronouncing for high standards, he was a disloyal, drunken deceiver and humbug.

sleek as a Pecksniff

PEEBLES, PETER

Peter Peebles is the litigious pauper in Scott's *Redgauntlet.* He is represented as vain, hardhearted, and credulous, and a liar and ne'er-do-well to boot.

as quarrelsome as Peter Peebles

PEEL, JOHN

John Peel (1776-1854) of *D'ye ken John Peel* musical fame (a composition written extempore by J. W. Graves) was a celebrated English hunter and sportsman who collected a fine pack of hunting hounds at Caldbeck, Cumberland, and maintained them for some fifty-five years.

hears the hunting horn of John Peel every time he sees a deer

---

PEELER

Peeler, the name for the Irish police, is from Sir Robert Peele, an English Minister who established the Irish constabulary (1814). The British chose his given name with which to dub their policemen "Bobbies."

on the lookout for a Peeler

PEEPING TOM

Peeping Tom was the one person in Coventry who disobeyed the edict and looked out the window when Lady Godiva rode through the street naked (1057) to fulfil the condition that would free the town from a burdensome tax. Tom was thereafter called Peeping Tom, and the name is now given to any person surreptitiously looking in on anyone's privacy.

the Peeping Tom of the village

PEGASUS

Pegasus, the winged horse that sprang from the blood of Medusa when Perseus struck off her head, was caught by Bellerophon with a golden bridle. Bellerophon rode Pegasus when he conquered the Chimaera, but fell to earth when he attempted to soar to heaven. Pegasus is called the horse of the Muses, which they rode as they sang; hence, it suggests flights of poetry.

soars on Pegasian wing
rides his Pegasus merrily

PEGGOTY, CLARA

Clara Peggoty, in Dickens' *David Copperfield*, is the faithful servant of David's mother and his own devoted nurse. Poor but upright, she is characterized by a rugged, abiding honesty. The cheerful creature is so plump that she bursts the buttons of her clothes when she laughs. The sister of Dan Peggoty, the retired boatman who migrates to Australia with Little Em'ly, and the aunt of Ham, who is drowned while trying to rescue James Steerforth, Clara marries Barkis the carrier (*q.v.*).

like Clara Peggoty, as honest as she is plump

PEITHO

Peitho was the Greek goddess of persuasion, called Suada or Suadela by the Romans. Wielding her influence particularly in affairs of love, she was often represented as an attendant of Aphrodite and sometimes identified with that deity.

invokes Peitho to prosper his suit

PELASGIANS

The Pelasgians were a prehistoric people and the first to inhabit Greece. Claiming descent from a mythical hero Pelasgus, they spread widely throughout the Hellenic peninsula and the isles of the Grecian archipelago, establishing the worship of Dodonaean Zeus, Hephaestus, the Cabiri, and other divinities as they came. Herodotus says that they spoke a barbarous (*i.e.* non-Greek) language and that they were an agricultural people, possessing a considerable knowledge of the useful arts. Their most ancient architectural remains in Greece are characterized by masonry of massive, uneven, and unhewn stones laid without clay cement. Such structure is known after them as Pelasgic, or Cyclopean, and is well seen at Mycenae and Tiryns.

as ancient as the Pelasgians

PELEUS

Peleus, the son of Aeacus of Aegina, was the king of the Myrmidons at Phthia in Thessaly. Twice involved in murder (once that of his half-brother, then that of his father-in-law, Eurytion), he fled to Iolcos where Acastus purified him, though the latter's wife treacherously accused Peleus of attempting to ravish her, whereas he had really refused her own overtures. The Nereid Thetis, destined to marry a mortal but having the power, like Proteus, of assuming any form she pleased, attracted him and he held her fast, as instructed, until she consented to marry him. The gods took part in the bridal rites, and Eris (Strife) was the only one not invited. By Thetis Peleus became the father of the hero Achilles, known as Pelides or "son of Peleus." Though too old to accompany his son to the siege of Troy, he survived his death.

an embrace as tight as Peleus's

PELIAS

Pelias was the son of Poseidon and Tyro, and was exposed with his twin-brother, Neleus, by his mother at birth. Later he became ruler of Iolcos, having expelled Cretheus, the king, who had married his mother. When Jason, Cretheus's grandson, came to claim the throne, Pelias set him the task of fetching the golden fleece in order to get rid of him. After Jason's successful return, Pelias was cut to pieces and boiled by his own daughters, who had been told by Medea that in this manner they might restore their father to vgor and youth. His son, Acastus, held funeral games in his honor, expelling Jason and Medea for the latter's crime. Among the daughters of Pelias was Alcestis (*q.v.*), the wife of Admetus.

as drawn and quartered as Pelias

PELLEAS AND MELISANDE

Pelléas and Mélisande are the title characters of a play by Maurice Maeterlinck and an opera by Claude Debussy. Mélisande is married to Golaud, but falls in love with his brother, Pelléas. Though their love is chaste and innocent, Golaud kills Pelléas. Mélisande dies after disclaiming any guilt or infidelity.

he loves with the futility of a Pelléas the innocent love of a Mélisande

---

PELOPS

Pelops was the son of Tantalus and the grandson of Jupiter. He was slain and served up before the gods by his own father, who wished to test the omniscience of the Olympians. They were not deceived, however, and would not touch the cannibal feast. But Demeter (Ceres), absorbed in grief for the loss of her daughter, Proserpina, tasted of the shoulder before she discovered what it was. Jupiter restored Pelops to life, and replaced his shoulder with one of ivory, whence the *ivory shoulder of the sons of Pelops* became a proverbial phrase for the distinguishing or distinctive mark of anyone, since all the descendants of Pelops bore this trait. The southern part of Greece was named Peloponnesus after him, meaning "island of Pelops."

as branded by heredity as Pelops and his sons

PENATES

The Penates were the guardian deities of the individual Roman household and of the collective state regarded as a large household comprising all family ones. They were similar to and often identified with the Lares. Originally gods of the storehouse or pantry (Latin *penus*), they had their shrine in every home and a perpetual fire was kept on the hearth for them. When one, therefore, invokes his Penates, he invokes the spirit of his house and abundance for protection.

prayed to his Penates to protect his home

PENDENNIS, ARTHUR

Arthur Pendennis, the hero of Thackeray's novel *The History of Pendennis,* is a hack who becomes a successful young writer. A vain and impulsive young man, imprudent in his love affairs, he has a lively intellect in spite of his conceit and selfishness, but otherwise possessing no attractive points of character except for his capacity for love.

as vain and selfish as Pendennis

PENELOPE

Penelope was the wife of Ulysses, a great hero in the Trojan War and wanderer always in search of new adventure. When for years, on his way back from Troy, her husband had not returned and her court was filled with importunate suitors, Penelope still refused to consider any proposal, but finally agreed to decide "when her tapestry was finished." Each night, however, she ravelled what she had woven during that day. Hence, the name Penelope means a trusty, constant, and faithful wife, and a resourceful person.

it is the Penelopes who keep the world steady
with a Penelopean faith

PENROD

Penrod, the irrepressible, mischievous, average American boy in Booth Tarkington's novel *Penrod and Sam,* is representative of twentieth century boyhood and life as Tom Sawyer is of the nineteenth century, in being energetic, enthusiastic, boyish, irrepressible, and troublesome.

the young Penrods of the neighborhood

PENTECOST

Pentecost is the Jewish harvest festival and also the day that marks the giving of the law on the fiftieth day after the departure of the Children of Israel from Egypt. Pentecost is also the Christian festival celebrating the descent of the Holy Spirit upon the apostles on the day of the Jewish festival.

the light of speech descends like a tongue of the Pentecost

PENTHESILEA

Penthesilea was the daughter of Ares (Mars), and was queen of the Amazons. When Hector was slain by Achilles, she came to the aid of the Trojans, but was herself worsted and killed by the great Greek hero who subsequently mourned over the dying Amazon and admired her beauty, youth, and courage. When Thersites ridiculed his tears, Achilles slew him too, whereupon Diomedes, a relative of the scoffer, threw Penthesilea's body into the Scamander river. According to other versions, however, Achilles himself gave the queen honorable burial on the banks of the Xanthus.

a brave and courageous Penthesilea

PENTHEUS

Pentheus, the son of Echion and grandson of Cadmus, was the king of Thebes who opposed the introduction of the rites of Bacchus (Dionysus) into Thebes. For treating the god with contempt, he was driven mad and his palace hurled to the ground. Curious about the nature of the new religion, he mounted a tree to spy on the doings of the frenzied and inspired female celebrants, among them being his own mother and her sisters, Ino and Autonoë. Believing him to be a wild beast, they seized him and tore him to pieces in their haunts on Mt. Cithaeron.

haunted by devils like Pentheus by the Maenads

PEPYS, SAMUEL

Samuel Pepys (1633-1703) wrote the most remarkable bit of "unconscious literature" in existence in the most remarkable period of English history. His diary was written in code and meant only for his own perusal. Consequently he wrote with unrestrained freedom concerning all the events of his days, from his own quarrels with his wife, his yearning for a carriage of his own, his trifling deviations from virtue, what they had for dinner, through the Great Plague in London, the Great Fire, the restoration of the king, and the coronation of the returned king. The whole is a juicy, free, original, highly amusing, and most valuable account of the seventeenth century in England.

with the naive revelations of a Pepys

PERDICARIS, ION

Ion Perdicaris was the naturalized American citizen who, in company with two British subjects, was kidnapped by Ahmed Raisuli, Riff brigand, and offered to the Sultan of Morocco, his superior, for ransom. Lest this incident become a *casus belli,* the Moroccan leader had to accede to Raisuli's terms, for the U. S. Secretary of State John Hay forced his hand by sending him this famous, succinct message, "Perdicaris alive or Raisuli dead."

terse as the demand for Perdicaris

PERDITA

Perdita, the daughter of King Leontes and Queen Hermione of Sicily, in Shakespeare's *Winter's Tale,* is a type of noble simplicity and pastoral sweetness. As a child, disowned by her father who was jealous of his wife, she was set adrift and exposed on the coast of Bohemia, where a shepherd raised her as his own daughter. Florizel, son of King Polixenes, fell in love with her, but, as marriage was forbidden by his father, the young lovers fled to Sicily, where ultimately Leontes and Hermione were reconciled, Perdita recognized, and Florizel united to her in wedlock.

Under this name the beautiful Mary Darby Robinson was known to her paramour, George IV, who fell in love with her while she was playing the role of Perdita in a stage presentation of the play. The licentious monarch took the name of Florizel.

a Perdita waiting for a happy ending

PERDIX

Perdix was the nephew of Daedalus, and the inventor of the saw, chisel, compass, and potter's wheel. So skillful was he that he excited the jealousy of Daedalus, who threw him headlong from the Athenian Acropolis into the sea. But Athena caught him in his fall, and changed him into the bird which was named after him, the *perdix,* or partridge.

as inventive as Perdix

PEREGRINUS PROTEUS

Peregrinus Proteus was a celebrity-seeking Cynic philosopher of the second century A. D. Expelled from his native town of Parium in Mysia because of suspicions of patricide, he became the head of a Christian community in Palestine, where his fanaticism led to his imprisonment, and his martyr-like posturing to his liberation. Later excommunicated from the church because he was detected profaning its rites, he joined the sect of Cynics in Egypt. There followed a short-lived search for fame in Rome, from which he was banished for insulting Antoninus Pius. Teaching in Athens (Aulus Gellius was one of his pupils), he offended Herodes Atticus and was forced to realize that his popularity was diminishing. Determined to stage one last sensation, he declared publicly that he would immolate himself on a funeral pyre at the Olympic games in 165. Lucian witnessed this last ambitious attempt to scale the walls of fame and immortality, helping the publicity-mad Peregrinus in part to achieve his desire by describing the event in the still extant *De Morte Peregrini.* This curious character is the subject of a novel by Wieland. This German attempt to rehabilitate Peregrinus's character was translated into English in 1796.

as thirsty for fame as Peregrinus Proteus

PERIANDER

Periander, the son of Cypselus, was tyrant of Corinth from B.C. 625 to 585. His rule was mild and beneficent at first, patronizing literature, philosophy, and the arts. But later he consulted Thrasybulus, the tyrant of Miletus, on means for ruling securely. The latter is said to have taken Periander into a field of corn and cut off the ears that were taller than the rest, thereby advising him to be stern and oppressive of individual superiorities. He acquired a reputation for justice and experience that promoted him to inclusion in the list of Seven Sages of Greece.

wise and sagacious as Periander

PERICLEAN

Periclean refers to the statesmanship and culture of Pericles (490-429 B.C.), the distinguished Athenian after whom the greatest period of his city is known and in whose lifetime Greece produced more men of genius than all the rest of the world ever produced in so short a time. He established ideal Athenian democracy, rule by popular assembly, and a pattern for civilization. Encouraging naval power, he established sea supremacy for his native city-state, but eventually made the mistake of enslaving allies. He also instituted pay for soldiers, jurymen, and public officials, acts which, according to the historians, "destroyed patriotism, discredited labor, destroyed frugality, fostered idleness, and eventually sapped democracy."

More realistically, he adorned Athens with the beautiful art works and public buildings, such as the Parthenon (*q.v.*) and the monumental marble Propylaea, or gateway to the Acropolis, that made that city the wonder and admiration of all the contemporary world. His enemies, unable to encompass his own ruin, attacked him through his talented friends, Aspasia his consort, Phidias the sculptor, and Anaxagoras the philosopher (*qq.v.*), and even falsely ascribed to his ambitious schemes the ruinous Peloponnesian War which broke out between Athens and Sparta two years before his death in 429 B.C. So great, however, was his genius that the name of Pericles will for all time allude to one of the golden ages of intellectual enlightenment, democracy, and culture.

glorious as when Pericles ruled Athens

Periclean intellectuality

PERIGNON, PIERRE

Pierre Pérignon (1638-1715) was the French Benedictine monk who, as supervisor of the vineyards in his cloister, discovered the process of making effervescent wines such as sparkling burgundy and champagne.

a toast in Pérignon's vintage

PERIPATETIC

Peripatetic, literally "one who walks about," was the name originally given to Aristotle, from his habit of strolling about the Lyceum gymnasium of Athens to converse among and instruct the youths who had come there for education. Later the word passed current for his philosophy or any adherent thereto. In more recent times, following its original etymological meaning, it is used of rambling or discursive speech or of a wanderer and itinerant

the Peripatetic of the park

PERNELLE, MME.

Mme. Pernelle, in Molière's *Tartuffe*, is a scolding old woman, the mother of Orgon.

anile as Mme. Pernelle

PERONELLA

Peronella, derived from a character in ancient mysteries, is the subject of a fairy tale. She is represented as a pretty country lass who, at the offer of a fairy, changes place with an old and decrepit queen and receives the homage paid to rank and wealth. But tiring of the exchange, she afterward gladly resumes her original beauty and rags.

many a money-mad Peronella
as bored as Peronella by her power

PERRAULT, CHARLES

Charles Perrault (1628-1703) was educated at Orleans and pursued an official career in Paris, writing occasional historical and biographical essays, though he is known today only as the author of many familiar and charming fairy tales. In 1676 Mme. de Sévigné mentions that there was a taste at court for allegorical stories and Oriental tales, and Perrault was doubtless influenced by this fashion to publish (in 1697) *Sleeping Beauty, Little Red Riding Hood, Bluebeard, Puss-in-Boots, Cinderella* and others in a volume the frontispiece of which read "Tales of Mother Goose" (*Contes de ma mère l'oie*). The quaint mixture of naiveté and satire found in his tales has made them part of the world's legacy of ever-popular literature.

Perraultian imagination

PERSEPHONE

(see *Proserpina*)

PERSEUS

Perseus, son of Zeus, was sent to fetch the head of Medusa, one of the Gorgons. By trickery he possessed himself of winged sandals, a magic wallet, a helmet that made him invisible, a sickle from Hermes, and a mirror. He looked at Medusa in the mirror lest a straight glance might turn him to stone, cut off her head, put it in the wallet, and was invisible, therefore escaping the pursuing Gorgons. He used Medusa's head to turn Atlas into a mountain, and disposed of all people at enmity with his friends by showing them Medusa's head. Mythology is full of the great deeds of Perseus, all showing him ingenious, resourceful, unscrupulous, and amazing.

rival the mighty accomplishments of a Perseus

PERSIUS

Aulus Persius Flaccus (A.D. 34-62) was a virtuous, gentle, and pleasing Roman youth and satirical poet. The pupil of Cornutus the philosopher, to whom in his will he bequeathed his books and his money (typical of his profession, the legatee accepted the former but spurned the latter), he was deeply admired and beloved by the Stoic Paetus Thrasea, of whose noble wife, Arria (*q.v.*), Persius was a relative. His six short *Satires* are often obscure and hard to understand. The third is directed against sloth and urges self-control. The fourth calls for virtue and self-knowledge in men who hold public office, and the fifth concerns the nature of true freedom.

a self-absorbed Persius, intent on philosophical inquiry

PETER

Peter, originally called Simon, was a fisherman of Capernaum who became a disciple of John the Baptist, and later one of the twelve apostles of Jesus. After the crucifixion he preached and proselytized in Palestine. Imprisoned by Herod Agrippa, he escaped and established the church at Antioch. Regarded by Catholics as the vicar of Christ on earth, he was martyred in Rome during the Neronian persecution in 67 A.D.

Simon called Peter, the fisher of men

PETER THE HERMIT

Peter the Hermit (1050-1115), a French monk commissioned by the Pope to preach a crusade, went through all France preaching to crowds in streets and in the fields. He roused them to indignation by his stories of the treatment of pilgrims by the infidels and of the profanation of holy places, until his followers, too impatient to wait for the organized Crusades, set forth, ill-equipped and unprotected. Thousands of women and children died of exposure, thousands were killed by infidels, and the rest were slaughtered. This expedition was known as the First Crusade.

blind followers of any Peter the Hermit

PETIPA, MARIUS

Marius Petipa (1819-1910) was the great choreographer and dancing-master who dictated the destiny of Czarist Russian ballet from 1863 to the early years of the twentieth century, formalizing it along the strict lines of Franco-Italian tradition. Collaborating with composer Tschaikovsky in the production of ballets of five- and six-act length such as *Le Lac des Cygnes* ("Swan Lake"), *La Belle au Bois Dormant* ("The Sleeping Beauty"), and *Casse-Noisette* ("Nutcracker"), he maintained tremendously high technical standards, exacting of his dancers almost superhuman virtuosity.

the perfect grace of a Petipa pose

PETIT ANDRÉ

Petit André was the name of a celebrated executioner in the time of Louis XI. He is introduced as a character in Scott's *Quentin Durward.*

the deft touch of a Petit André

PETRARCHAN

Petrarchan is from Petrarch (1304-1374), famous Italian poet noted especially for his love sonnets so perfect that they became the pattern for many of the great poets. The most important were addressed to Laura, and followed the pattern *abba, abba,* with *c, d,* and *e* variously arranged for the sestet, all in the ten-syllable iambic verse, the first eight lines proposing and the last six embellishing the single idea. Petrarchan means, therefore, poetry stately in theme, single in idea, undeviating in form from the sonnet pattern, regular, complete, rhythmic and dignified in expression.

the high Petrarchan strain

PETRONIUS

Petronius, the *arbiter elegantiae,* director of court manners and elegance in Nero's time (54-68 A.D.), was a refinde voluptuary. He is the author of a book, the *Satyricon,* a record of the vices of the time, and extremely licentious, as were the "elegancies" over which he presided in Nero's libidinous court.

the licentiousness of a Petronius

PETRUCHIO

Petruchio, the clever lover in Shakespeare's *Taming of the Shrew,* tamed the shrewish but beautiful Katherine by out-heroding Herod, flouting her, humiliating her, berating her publicly, and all but beating her. He neglected her in every conceivable and fantastic fashion, going to any length to outdo her own bad manners, until finally he subdued her to a beautiful wifely adoration. Hence, Petruchio implies adroit, successful, outwitting, clever.

finds she has married a Petruchio

PHAEACIAN

Phaeacian refers to the gay, luxurious Phaeacians, a sea-faring people who inhabited the island of Scheria at the western extremity of the earth and whose king Alcinous entertained

Odysseus, when he was shipwrecked on their isle in the *Odyssey*. They are described as easy-going, self-indulgent epicures, whence a glutton was called *Phaeax* by Horace. Though the ancients identified Scheria with Corcyra (Corfu), it is better to regard the Phaeacians' paradise as altogether fabulous.

as indolent and effortless as a Phaeacian

PHAEDO

Phaedo, a native of Elis who was taken prisoner and sold as a slave at Athens, afterwards obtained his freedom and became a devoted follower of Socrates, at whose death he was present. Plato's dialogue bearing his name as title concerns a discussion of death and immortality, marshalling as arguments in favor thereof the theory of reminiscence and the existence of eternal ideas in which the soul is a partaker. The fate of the soul after the dissolution of the body and the judgment and retribution awaiting it in the next world are then considered. Cato of Utica is said to have sought fortitude and solace through the reading of this work on the night before his patriotic suicide, caused by the triumph of the Caesarean cause in Rome's civil war.

manumitted, like Phaedo, of fear of death

PHAEDRA

Phaedra was the daughter of Minos and the wife of Theseus. Enamored of Hippolytus, his son by a previous wife, she attempted to seduce the chaste young man. Rebuffed, she accused him of trying her virtue. When Theseus learned of Hippolytus's innocence after the accidental death of his son, Phaedra killed herself. A classical prototype of a passion-ridden, adulterous woman, she is the subject of tragedies by Euripides and Racine. The French play was one of the favorite vehicles of Sarah Bernhardt.

she has Phaedran designs on his virtue

PHAEDRUS

Caius Julius Phaedrus, Thracian slave and freedman in the household of Augustus, composed in the Latin language some 97 animal fables borrowed from Aesop and having advice and entertainment as their object. Serious and satirical, they concern themselves with life's injustices and social and political evils of the day. To people oppressed under the tyranny of Tiberius and Caligula, they suggested the lesson of humble resignation. Because insinuations concerning leading members of the imperial staff could easily be read under these allegories, he got into trouble and was imprisoned by Sejanus, notorious praetorian prefect under Tiberius. Phaedrus is the source of the expression "adding insult to injury."

innuendoes as concealed as those of Phaedrus

PHAETON

Phaëton, or Phaëthon ("the shining"), was the son of Helios (the sun) and Clymene, who entreated his father for permission to drive the chariot of the sun across the heavens one day, as a proof of his divine descent. Losing control of the unruly steeds, he set the world on fire and was punished by Jupiter for his presumption by being struck with a thunderbolt and thrown into the river Eridanus, or Po. His sisters, the Heliadae, who had yoked the steeds to the chariot, were metamorphosed into poplars, and their tears into amber.

ambitious as Phaëton, playing with fire

PHALARIS

Phalaris was the tyrant of Agrigentum in Sicily who reigned from B.C. 570 to 564 and was proverbial for his inhuman cruelty. He commissioned Perillus of Athens to design and execute for him a brazen bull suitable for the execution of criminals. They were shut up in the effigy, and, fires being lighted below the belly, the metal was made red hot. The cries of the victims sounded like the bellowing of a bull, as they reverberated against the bronze. Phalaris admired the ingenious device, but tested its efficacy on the inventor himself. Later he perished during a sudden outbreak of popular fury.

as sadistic as the bull of Phalaris

PHAON

Phaon, an old and ugly boatman at Mitylene on the island of Lesbos, was transformed into a young and beautiful lad by Aphrodite, as a reward for ferrying her across the sea without accepting payment. After his rejuvenation, Sappho is said to have fallen passionately in love with him and to have leaped from the Leucadian cliff when he slighted her and refused her affections.

dreams of being Phaon, for whom the clock turned back

PHARAOH

Pharaoh, a title given to the kings of Egypt, is best known as the magnificent, tyrannical, and obstinate king of Egypt during the time of the captivity of the Children of Israel, when Moses and Aaron time after time carried out certain instructions, only to be told the Israelites could not yet go out of the land. The words, "but Pharaoh hardened his heart," appear again and again in the story of the latest years of their captivity; hence, obstinate, tyrannical, cruel. Out of this story grew the spiritual, "Let My People Go."

with the magnificence of the Pharaohs

PHARISEE

A Pharisee, in ancient Hebrew religion, was a "separatist," one of a class of self-righteous and hypocritical people strictly observant of the external forms of Jewish ritual but without regard for the spirit behind it.

The Talmud mentions these classes of Pharisees: the "Dashers," who dashed their feet against the stones so that people might think them absorbed in holy thought; the "Mortars," who wore a cap which would not allow them to see passers-by; the "Bleeders," who mortified themselves by inserting thorns in their garments; the "Cryers," who insisted "Let me know my duty, and I will do it"; the "Almsgivers," who sounded a trumpet to summon the poor; the "Stumblers," who shut their eyes before women; the "Immovables," who stood at their prayers; the "Pestles," who bent themselves double; the "Strong-shouldered," who walked with their backs bent as if carrying on their shoulders the whole burden of the law; and the "Dyed Ones," called by Jesus "Whited Sepulchres," whose externals of devotion cloaked moral uncleanness.

as smug in his superiority as a Pharisee

PHARNACES

Pharnaces, the son of Mithradates the Great, was ruler of Pontus from 63 to 47 B.C. A partisan of Pompey in the civil war between Caesar and that leader, he was defeated by the greater Roman at Zela, in 47, and is the subject and object of the terse announcement of victory sent by Caesar to the Senate, *veni, vidi, vici.*

immortalized in defeat like Pharnaces

PHAROS

Pharos, a small island off the coast of Alexandria, Egypt, was united to the mainland by Alexander the Great by means of a mole nearly a mile in length, thus forming the two harbors of the city. On this island Ptolemy Philadelphus erected a white marble lighthouse, said to have been the first of its kind and accounted one of the Seven Wonders of the ancient world, in order to guide mariners to the larger of the two sea-harbors, the one on the eastern side of the mole. The name *Pharos* has since been applied to any similar structure, as a beacon or watch-tower, or to a conspicuous light, as of a torch or lantern. In ecclesiastical usage the word connotes a chandelier for holding candles.

an indispensable Pharos, directing him to safety

PHEBE

Phebe is a light-hearted shepherdess in Shakespeare's *As You Like It*. When she meets and falls in love with Rosalind disguised as a man in the forest of Arden, she deserts her erstwhile swain Silvius. Ultimately Rosalind persuades her to return her affections to him and marry him.

falls in love as easily as Phebe

PHEMIUS

Phemius was the celebrated bard and minstrel who sang to the suitors in the palace of Odysseus (Ulysses) during the hero's absence. Derived from the Greek word *pheme* for "speech," the name has since Homer's time been used for any sweet singer and poet of mellifluous strain.

a dulcet-voiced Phemius to entertain them

PHIDIAN

Phidian refers to the majestic sculptural style of Phidias (500-432 B.C.), leading Athenian sculptor of the Periclean Age and supervisor of all the art works erected in "the city of the violet crown" in that period. He created three statues of Athena for erection on the Acropolis, one of them being the magnificent chryselephantine (gold and ivory) cult statue for her temple, the Parthenon. Another colossal work of his was the cult statue of Zeus at Olympia, it too being wrought in the same technique, with the flesh represented in ivory and the robes in gold. After disproving a charge brought by enemies of Pericles to the effect that he had misappropriated some of the gold for Athena's statue, he was convicted of impiety for having introduced his own likeness and that of Pericles on the goddess's shield, and died in prison.

majestic Phidian art

PHIDIPPIDES

Phidippides was the celebrated courier who was sent by the Athenians to Sparta in B.C. 490 to ask for aid against the Persians at the battle of Marathon. Herodotus says that he covered the distance of 150 miles separating the cities in a matter of two days, so fleet of foot was he. While he was racing across Mount Parthenius on the frontiers of Argolis and Arcadia, the god Pan appeared to him, promising the Athenians his aid in the great conflict. After the great victory the Athenians introduced the worship of that god in their city.

sprinting along like Phidippides

PHILAENI

The Philaeni were two patriotic Carthaginian brothers who acted as emissaries and arbiters for their country in a boundary dispute with the neighboring land of Cyrene. It had been agreed that deputies should start at a fixed time from each of the cities and that the place of their meeting should form the limit of the two territories. But as the Philaeni advanced much farther than the Cyrenaean party, they were accused of having started before the others. At length the rival delegation agreed to accept the new boundaries if the Philaeni would submit to being buried alive there in the sand. Courageously devoting themselves to their country's interests, they were thereafter venerated by the people who paid high honors to their memory and erected altars to them where they had died. From these the place was called "The Altars of the Philaeni."

magnanimous and brave as the Philaeni

PHILANDER

Philander, in *Orlando Furioso,* is a Dutch knight who played *Joseph* to the *Potiphar's wife* of his host Argeo, a Servian baron and husband of Gabrina. After he had unwittingly murdered Argeo and accepted forced marriage with the adulteress, she grew tired of him and poisoned him.

In Fletcher's *The Laws of Candy,* Philander is a prince of Cyprus ardently in love with the princess Erota. The name, a usual one for any lover in old romances, now connotes a sort of male coquette, intent on furtive satisfaction of amorous impulses without serious purpose of involvement.

debonair and flirtatious as Philander

PHILEMON

(see *Baucis and Philemon*)

PHILETAS

Philetas of Cos, Greek poet, critic, and grammarian of the late fourth century B.C., and tutor of Ptolemy II and Theocritus (*q.v.*), wrote erotic and elegiac verse that was imitated by Ovid. Athenaeus says that he was so extraordinarily thin and light-weight that he had to ballast himself against the wind — to prevent it from sweeping him off his feet — by fastening heavy lead balls on his shoes!

as skinny as Philetas

PHILIP

Philip was one of the twelve apostles. He is sometimes identified with Philip the Evangelist, who was appointed to take charge of the distribution of alms to widows. According to *Acts,* xxi, 9, he had four daughters who were virgin prophetesses.

clairvoyant as the daughters of Philip

PHILIP OF MACEDON

Philip II of Macedon (382-336 B.C.), celebrated father of Alexander the Great, was the original exponent of methods of national aggrandizement by means of "fifth columnistic" boring-from-within, and by exerting bribery, trickery, and "false peace" hopes against his intended victims. A cunning diplomatist and military genius, he was successful in waging aggression against all Greece with his newly organized weapon, the "phalanx" army, crushing the combined efforts of Athens and Thebes to stop his career of conquest. After being chosen commander of the entire Hellenic peninsula in a new war he was about to launch against Persia, Philip was murdered by Pausanias, probably in complicity with his own wife Olympias, angered because she had been supplanted by a new consort. Many pithy and proverbial sayings are accredited to him, as in his reply to some Olynthiac traitors who had manoeuvered their city into his hands and now were deprecating the scurrilous names they were being called at his court: "The Macedonians are a rude and boorish people, and call a spade a spade."

strategy-minded as Philip of Macedon

PHILIPPIC

Philippic comes from Demosthenes' orations against Philip of Macedonia, so famous for their powerful invective that any vituperative oratory directed against a powerful person is now called a philippic.

having delivered his philippic, he strode out

PHILISTINES

Philistines are worshipers of material and mechanical prosperity, scornful of culture and beauty and all intangible values. The name is now loosely applied to persons who are willing to throw arts and culture overboard.

you will have the Philistines upon you!
lost in their own Philistinism

PHILOCTETES

Philoctetes, being present at the death of Hercules, received from him certain arrows which had been dipped in the gall of the Lernaean hydra. On his journey to Troy he was wounded in the foot by one of these arrows (or by a water-snake), and as the wound ulcerated it emitted such an intolerable stench that his companions treacherously abandoned him on the solitary island of Lemnos. In the tenth year of the war, however, an oracle declared that Troy could not be taken without the arrows of Hercules. Philoctetes, yielding to the supplications of Ulysses and Diomedes, repaired to Troy. His wound was healed by Asclepius or his sons, and with the aid of the arrows Philoctetes killed Paris and helped to bring about the capitulation of Troy. Sophocles' *Philoctetes* is one of the most famous of Greek tragedies.

as noisome as Philoctetes' wound
longer in healing than Philoctetes' wound

PHILOMELA

Philomela was the daughter of Pandion, a legendary king of Attica. Tereus, the king of Thrace, had married Procne, Philomela's sister, but he seduced Philomela, after which he deprived her of her tongue and hid her in a remote place to prevent her from telling Procne of his infidelity. Philomela, however, found Procne, and by means of symbols woven in a tapestry conveyed to her the situation. They avenged themselves on Tereus by killing Itys, his son by Procne, and serving him to Tereus for dinner. Whereupon Tereus pursued them until the gods changed Philomela into a nightingale, Procne into a swallow, and Tereus into a hoopoe.

sad as the song of Philomela

PHILOXENUS

Philoxenus of Cythera (435-380 B.C.) was one of the most distinguished Greek writers of dithyrambs, choral lyrics in honor of Dionysus. An innovator, in his *Cyclops* he introduced a solo passage set to lyre accompaniment. So painfully frank and truthful was he that the baldness of his opinions caused him to spend part of his life in prison at Syracuse, Sicily. For he offended Dionysius, the tyrant of that city, who had asked him to criticize and correct one of his poems, by telling him that the best way of revising it would be to draw a thick black line through the entire paper on which the effort was written.

as brutally frank as Philoxenus

PHILYRA

Philyra, a beautiful nymph and the daughter of Oceanus, attracted the amorous attentions of Cronus, who, in order to escape the detection of his jealous wife Rhea, transformed himself into a horse in order to woo her. The result of their union was the centaur Chiron, half-man and half-horse. Afterwards Philyra herself was metamorphosed into a linden-tree.

the leafy arms of Philyra

PHINEHAS

Phinehas was a high priest of Israel who was distinguished for his religious zeal. He stopped a plague at a critical time by punishing an offender who had undertaken a mixed marriage and whose wife had insisted on retaining her own religion.

a Phinehas at averting evil

PHINEUS

Phineus was a king of Thrace who possessed the power of prophecy. He was harassed by the Harpies for his cruelty toward his sons, whom he had deprived of sight because of a false accusation made against them by their step-mother Idaea, who charged them with having behaved improperly to her. Whenever Phineus wanted to eat, the Harpies came and took away, devoured, or defiled his food. The gods also afflicted him with blindness.

Phineus was also the name of Andromeda's betrothed, whom Perseus turned into stone with the help of the Gorgon's head.

with the prophetic air of a Phineus

PHLEGETHON

Phlegethon was one of the rivers of the lower world in Greek mythology. Its very name signifying "burning" or "flaming," in its channel rolled waves of fire instead of water. Nothing could grow on its scorched and desolate shores.

Fierce Phlegethon, Whose waves of torrent fire inflame with rage
Milton

PHLEGYAS

Phlegyas, a son of Ares (Mars), was king of Orchomenos in Boeotia. He was the father of Ixion and Coronis, the latter of whom was ravished by Apollo and became the mother of Asclepius. Enraged at this, Phlegyas plundered and set fire to the god's temple at Delphi. For his impiety he was killed by Apollo's arrows and condemned to severe punishment in hell, where a huge stone was suspended over his head to keep him in a state of continual alarm.

an anxiety as imminent as that of Phlegyas

PHOEBE AND PHOEBUS

Phoebe and Phoebus are surnames of Artemis (Diana) and Apollo, respectively. Meaning "radiant" or "bright," they refer to the twin deities as illuminating the heavens with the celestial orbs of the moon and the sun, the moon being regarded as the female counterpart of Phoebus, the sun.

Phoebe reflecting the pure light of Phoebus

PHOENIX

The Phoenix, an emblem of immortality in Egyptian mythology, was a rare bird with red and gold plumage. Coming out of Arabia to Heliopolis every 500 years, it burned itself on the altar there and rose from its ashes, young and beautiful again. By transference the name has come to signify a person of unusual or superlative excellence, a paragon, or a prodigy. In Christian belief it is also an emblem of the resurrection of the dead.

as self-renewing as the Phoenix

PHOOKA

Phooka, or Pooka, is a mischievous, malignant, and diabolical spirit or apparition, usually inhabiting a bog or a marsh. This specter, according to Irish mythology, sometimes appears as an eagle or a black horse, but, always an evil goblin, it rushes to destruction whoever sees it.

a malevolent Phooka to haunt him

PHORBAS

Phorbas was the son of Lapithes in Greek mythology. After freeing the island of Rhodes from a plague of serpents, he challenged Apollo to a boxing match and was slain for his presumption against the immortals.

another aspiring Phorbas of the ring

PHORCUS

Phorcus, or Phorcys, was Homer's "old man of the sea" and the father of many monsters, including Scylla, the Gorgons, the Hesperian dragon, and the Graiae, who were gray from birth and had but one eye and tooth common to the three of them. One of the harbors of Ithaca was dedicated to this ancient spirit of the sea, so prolific of dreadful creatures.

explore the depths of Phorcus's domain

PHORMIO

Phormio is a parasite in Terence's comedy of the same name. He is an accommodating gentleman who adjusts himself to the humor of everyone and reconciles all differences between the opposing characters of the comedy, thus making himself indispensable to the solution of their difficulties. Parasites, in general, in ancient Greek and Latin comedies were men who sought free dinners and subsistence from the well-to-do, repaying them for their largesse with flattery and buffoonery and proffering them the services of a factotum.

obliging and obsequious as Phormio

PHOSPHOR

Phosphor ("light-bearer"), in Greek mythology, was the morning star. The son of Eos (dawn), he was the harbinger of day. The Latin Lucifer, he was identified with the planet Venus, when it shines in the east before daybreak.

pale as the rays of Phosphor

PHRIXUS

Phrixus, the brother of Helle (*q.v.*), rode through the air and crossed the Hellespont on the ram with the golden fleece that was given by Hermes to aid him in escaping the intrigues of his stepmother who had designated him for sacrifices to Zeus. In safety, Phrixus gave the ram to Aeetes, king of Colchis and father of Medea (*q.v.*). After Phrixus and Aeetes had sacrificed it to Zeus, its golden fleece was fastened to an oak-tree in the grove of Ares, and Jason and the Argonauts later carried it away.

an escape as miraculous as that of Phrixus

PHRYGIAN

Phrygian refers to the culture of this Asia Minor people, at one time a part of the empire of Croesus (*q.v.*) and of the Persians. Celebrated for high intellectuality and splendor in their early period, they contributed the wild and plaintive *Phrygian mode* and highly developed flute music to the Greeks. Associated with their name are also the frenzied orgiastic rites of Dionysus and of Cybele, the Mother of the Gods. Their characteristic head-dress, the *Phrygian cap,* a close-fitting, conically shaped head-protection worn by Orientals, is identified in more recent times with the so-called "Liberty cap" of the French Revolution, and is seen also on the head of that goddess (though wingless) on United States ten-cent pieces. *Phrygianize* meant specifically to frizzle or curl the hair, and *Phrygian stone* was a kind of pumice used extensively in dyeing. *Opus Phrygicum* was embroidery of great richness, heavy and ornate with gold.

After the Persian conquest, however, this talented people lost their intellectual éclat and became equally proverbial for submissiveness and stupidity.

as sumptuously luxurious as a Phrygian

PHRYNE

Phryne was a famous Greek *hetaera,* or courtesan, of the fourth century B.C. and mistress of Praxiteles, the great sculptor, who made two statues of her, one of gilded bronze which she dedicated at Delphi, the other of marble. When he offered to present her with any statue in his possession, she cleverly decided to ascertain his professional preference by having one of her slaves tell him that his studio was on fire. When he exclaimed that he was ruined if his Eros had perished, she wisely chose it. When accused of impiety, she was defended by the great orator Hyperides, who appealed to the emotions of the jury by throwing open her dress and exposing the beauty of her bosom. She became so wealthy from practicing her trade that when Alexander the Great destroyed Thebes she offered to rebuild it at her own expense.

an irresistibly charming Phryne

PHUT

Phut, or Put, was one of the four sons of Ham (*Genesis*, x, 6). He furnished mercenary soldiers to the armies of Tyre, Egypt, and Gog, and became the ancestor of the Libyans, whose favorite weapon was the bow.

archers from the land of Phut

PHYLLIS

Phyllis, daughter of King Sithon of Thrace, was betrothed to Demophon, son of Theseus and Phaedra of Athens. Before the nuptials her fiance went to his native city to settle his affairs, and, as he tarried there longer than Phyllis had expected, she thought that he had forgotten and deserted her. She hung herself in grief and despair, but was metamorphosed by the gods into an almond-tree.

Another Phyllis is a country lass in Vergil's third and fifth *Eclogues.* The name appears frequently thereafter in pastoral poetry for a rustic maiden in general.

at their savory dinner set
Of herbs, and other country messes,
Which the neat-handed Phyllis dresses.
Milton, *L'Allegro*

PHYSIGNATHUS

Physignathus ("puffcheeks") is the King of the Frogs in the mock-heroic epic and parody, the pseudo-Homeric *Batrachomyomachia* (*q.v.*), or "Battle of the Frogs and Mice." The son of Pelus ("mud"), he is slain by Troxartas ("bread-nibbler") for having inadvertently caused the drowning of Psicharpax, another mouse whom he had taken for a ride on his back, when he dived at sight of a water-snake.

with cheeks as distended as Physignathus

PICKETT, GEORGE EDWARD

George Edward Pickett (1825-1875) was the brilliant Confederate major general in charge of the Gray position at Fredericksburg, Maryland. On July 3, 1863, he led 4500 men in the famous charge over half a mile of rough terrain to dislodge the Union forces from their location on Cemetery Ridge at Gettysburg. The attempt was impossibly arduous, and Pickett's forces were routed with the loss of three fourths of the division.

a charge as suicidal as Pickett's

PICKLE, PEREGRINE

Peregrine Pickle, the hero of Smollett's novel of the same name, is a handsome but savage young reprobate bent on sowing his wild oats. An ungrateful spendthrift and profligate, he is fond of practical jokes that end in annoyance for other people, but himself suffers with brutal temper the misfortunes brought on him by his own wilfulness.

as passionate as Peregrine Pickle

PICKWICKIAN

Pickwickian is from Mr. Pickwick, in Dickens' *Pickwick Papers,* a lovable delightful, genteel and benevolent person, pictured as wearing spectacles, breeches, short black gaiters, and having a bald head and "good round belly." He is dressed in the colorful height of fashion, says the most brazen things in the most polite and innocent manner. Asked in a courtroom whether he had used a certain expression in an insulting sense, he answered, "No, your honor, merely in a Pickwickian sense." He gathers a few friends into a group, the Pickwick Club, and travels about with them, advising, admonishing, sponsoring, and in general having a good time with them, to the great delight of the world.

starving in a Pickwickian sense
the Pickwickian advice to shout with the largest mob

PICO DELLA MIRANDOLA

Pico della Mirandola (1463-1494), tall, handsome, yellow-haired Renaissance humanist, philosopher, and scholar, was the protégé of Lorenzo de' Medici and a student of Arabic, Hebrew, Chaldee, and the cabala, as well as of Greek and Latin. In 1486 he posted in Rome a list of 900 questions in philosophy and theology, declaring that he could publicly defend any or all against a disputant. The debates never occurred, but he was accused of heresy by Innocent III for some of the these. Later absolved by Alexander VI, he was reconverted to orthodoxy by Savonarola. The collector of a precious library, he died at the age of 31 under somewhat mysterious circumstances, leading to the suspicion that he had been poisoned by his secretary.

a linguist and polyglot like Pico della Mirandola

PICTI

The Picti were Iberian or Caledonian aborigines who inhabited eastern Scotland from about A.D. 296 to 844, at which time they amalgamated with the Scots to form one nation. At continual warfare with the Romans during their administration of the island, they were thus named from their habit of painting their entire bodies with woad, an herb of the mustard family with yellowish flowers that was used rather extensively by ancients for staining or tattooing purposes. Before the practice of applying cosmetics to the face was common among Anglo-Saxons, a woman who painted her face was known figuratively as a Pict.

covered with pigment like a Pict

PICUMNUS AND PILUMNUS

Picumnus and Pilumnus, in Roman religion, were rustic deities of agriculture, matrimony, and childbirth. Picumnus, husband of Pomona, concerned himself with manuring of the soil, and, hence, was also called Stercutus or Sterquilinus (from *stercus* for dung). His brother and double, Pilumnus, was named from the *pilum,* or pestle used by bakers, since it was he who first invented the pounding of grain. Vergil, in the *Aeneid,* makes him the ancestor of Turnus (*q.v.*). Both brothers were also guardians of pregnant women and of new-born children, protecting them from assault and evil.

Picumnus and Pilumnus attend your crops!

PICUS

Picus was a prophetic divinity and king of Latium in Italy. The son of Saturn, he was himself the father of Faunus. His legend is based on the belief that the woodpecker is a soothsaying bird, sacred to Mars. Enamored of Pomona, he is said to have rejected the erotic overtures of Circe, whereupon the enchantress changed him into a woodpecker who retained the prophetic powers which he had formerly possessed as a man.

Picus tapping his code message on my tree

PIED PIPER

The Pied Piper of Hamelin is a legendary character who contracted to free the town of Hamelin of a plague of rats by playing on his flute. When he had fulfilled his contract, the city fathers refused the full promised payment, whereupon he charmed all the children of the town to follow his magical music and led them into the side of a mountain, which opened and closed after them forever. Only one lame child, who could not keep up with them, was left. The story is best known through Robert Browning's poem, *The Pied Piper of Hamelin Town.*

a Pied Piper effect on children

PIERIAN

Pierian is from Pieria, the birthplace of Orpheus and the nine Muses. It is near Mount Olympus and in antiquity there was a sacred fountain in the vicinity that was considered dear to the Muses (Pierides). The waters of this spring were commonly supposed to inspire all who drank of them. Hence, the name suggests poetic inspiration coming from any source.

writes with Pierian inspiration
he has Pierian learning

PIERIDES

Pierides is a surname given to the Muses because of their residence at Pieria, a fountain near Mount Olympus. It is also the name of the nine daughters of Pierus, king of Emachia, Macedonia, to whom he gave the names of the nine Muses. Pleased by the brilliance of their appellations, they became overly ambitious and challenged the divine Muses to a song-contest. Conquered in the concert, they were transformed into magpies for their presumption.

no match to challenge the Pierides

PIERRETTE

Pierrette is the lovable little French pantomime figure, dressed usually in a ballet skirt and bright peasant waist and smart little cocked hat, popular in street and carnival shows. She is a tender-hearted and wise little foil for the Pierrot who plays opposite her in fanciful and delightful whimsical stories. Her name suggests a spirit loving, tender, comforting, but saucy, gay, and smart.

a charming little Pierrette of a daughter

PIERROT

Pierrot, originally the small but droll valet in French pantomine, is usually dressed in a white jacket with wide reveres and huge buttons, wide white pantaloons. The whole role is borrowed from old Italian comedy. In France he usually plays opposite a Pierrette, and is gay, jesting, comical, saucy at his work, but at heart fearful, pessimistic, and sad. He needs the sympathetic understanding of Pierrette and her optimistic and wise gayety. He has his counterpart in the gay, impudent, harmless circus clown in America.

a Pierrot-like courage in the face of his discouragement

PILATE

Pontius Pilate was the Roman procurator in Judea (A.D. 26) at the time Christ was delivered up to be crucified. It was the time of the Feast of the Passover, when it was customary to release a prisoner, and Pilate, apparently unwilling to give the order to have Christ crucified, questioned whether he should not be released. But the people, directed by the high priests, demanded that Barabbas be released and Christ crucified. Against his own convictions, Pilate yielded to the populace. In 38 A.D. Pilate was banished and killed himself.

like Pilate's unhappy consent

PINCH, TOM

Tom Pinch is Pecksniff's ungainly employee in Dickens' *Martin Chuzzlewit*. Guileless, eccentric, and excessively modest, he is remembered for his inexhaustible kindheartedness.

as good at heart as Tom Pinch

PINCHBECK

Christopher Pinchbeck (died 1732), a maker of musical clocks in Brummingham, invented an alloy resembling gold, and made jewelry in imitation of good jewelry. All sham and imitation articles have since been characterized as pinchbeck.

bought a quantity of pinchbeck trash

PINCHWIFE

Pinchwife is the foolish city husband in Wycherley's comedy *The Country Wife* (1673). Believing that a woman's innocence depends on her worldly ignorance, he vainly watches over his wife, whom he tries to keep in a state of benighted rusticity.

as vigilant over his spouse as Pinchwife

PINCIAN

Pincian refers to the Pincian Hill in northern Rome and standing near the Quirinal within the Aurelian wall of the eternal city. Designated as the Collis Hortorum, or "hill of gardens," it is famous for its elaborately landscaped gardens and floral vegetation.

gardens as lushly exuberant as the Pincian

PINDARIC

Pindaric is from the Greek Pindar (522-443 B.C.), who wrote songs for festivals, verses to celebrate the Olympic games, chariot races and the like —the forerunner of what is now known as occasional verse. His verse was so graceful and so completely appropriate to every occasion that all such poems, particularly the majestic and lyric odes, are called Pindaric odes, and the spirit the Pindaric spirit. Chief among our own are Tennyson's *Ode to the Duke of Wellington,* and Lowell's *Commemoration Ode*.

with Pindaric majesty

PINKERTON

Pinkertons is a famous detective agency founded in Chicago by Allan Pinkerton (1819-1884). The work of its trained detectives was so effective that the name came to be applied to any one successful in the legal ferreting out of mysterious situations. Jocosely, it refers to persons given to persistent and unrestrained inquiry into other people's affairs.

there goes the neighborhood Pinkerton

PIP

Pip is a childish corruption of the name Philip Pirrip, the hero of Dickens' *Great Expectations*. An orphan brought up by the Gargerys, he is suddenly transported into the world of high fashion, where he lives as a fine gentleman because of the largesse of an unknown benefactor who turns out to be a convict he had befriended as a poor boy.

from rags to riches like Pip

PIPPA

Pippa is an Italian peasant girl who works in a silk factory, in Browning's dramatic idyll *Pippa Passes* (1841). On her single holiday, New Year's, as she trips along singing cheerfully, she unwittingly influences for good at crucial moments in their lives several persons who would seem least susceptible to her influence.

a situation needing the magical touch of a Pippa

PIRITHOUS

Pirithous, son of Ixion, was king of the Lapithae, a wild Thessalian people. His intimacy with the hero Thesus has become one of the standard and proverbial examples of friendship, constancy and loyalty. When Pirithous married Hippodamia, the wedding feast was disturbed by the Centaurs in a fight that was the subject of sculptures on the temple of Zeus at Olympia and on the Athenian Parthenon. Later the two friends resolved to wed daughters of Zeus, Theseus abducting Helen from Sparta, Pirithous aspiring to carry off Pluto's queen, Proserpina. They were foiled in this latter attempt, however, and chained to a rock in the lower world. Hercules freed Theseus who had dared the outrage only to please his friend, but Pirithous remained forever in torment in Hades, bound to his father's celebrated wheel (see *Ixion*).

fired by Pirithouan ambition

PISISTRATUS

Pisistratus was the tyrant of Athens who seized the government of the city in 560 B.C. by espousing the cause of the working classes and getting himself voted a bodyguard, ostensibly for the purpose of protecting himself from his political enemies but actually designed to enforce his authority. Twice expelled (in 560 and 556-554 B.C.), he entrenched himself so firmly after his second return that he governed until his death in 527 B.C. Ambitious and resourceful, he exercised a benevolent and moderate despotism. He and his sons, Hippias and Hipparchus (the Pisistratids), beautified Athens with new temples and fine roads, and patronized art and letters.

rode to power like Pisistratus

PISO

Piso was the name of a distinguished Roman family whose appelative is connected with agriculture, the most honorable pursuit of the ancient Romans, being derived from *pisere,* to grind corn. Lucius Calpurnius Piso, consul in 112 B.C., received the surname Frugi for his "integrity" and "deservingness." The later annals of the family show a deviation from its pristine virtue. Cnaeus Calpurnius Piso was a profligate young noble who dissipated his wealth and joined the conspiracy of Catiline (*q.v.*) to recoup it. Lucius Calpurnius Piso, consul in 58 B.C. and father of Julius Caesar's last wife Calpurnia, was an unprincipled debauchee and a cruel and corrupt magistrate with a record for extortion in his administration of Macedonia.

a family as pedigreed as the Pisones

PISTOL

Pistol is Falstaff's lieutenant and blustering crony in Shakespeare's *Merry Wives of Windsor, Henry IV,* part two, and *Henry V*. A bully, rogue, and coward, he mouths bombastic blank verse as he swaggers about. Always poor and despicable in every sense, he is in part redeemed by his love for his wife.

bombastic as Pistol, whenever he opens his mouth

PISTOR

Pistor, "the baker," was a surname of Jupiter at Rome, because when the Gauls were besieging that city in 390 B.C. he suggested to the defenders, who had taken their stand in the citadel on the Capitoline hill, that they throw loaves of bread down among their enemies. This act of waste, he pointed out, would make the Gauls believe that the besieged had a superfluity of food and would outlast any attempt to starve them out.

outdoes Pistor in kitchen waste

PITCHER, MOLLY

Molly Pitcher, traditional heroine of the Revolutionary war, is said to have gone out with her husband and manned the guns, and that in a day when women stayed at home and sewed a fine seam. Her name means courageous, heroic, fearless.

Molly Pitcher would have found hundreds of her kind today

PITTACUS

Pittacus, one of the "Seven Sages" of Greece, was a native of Lesbos renowned as a warrior, statesman, philosopher, and poet. In 611 B.C. he overthrew the regime of Melanchrus, tyrant of his native land, and in 606 he killed in single combat Phrynon, the commander of the Athenians with whom his people disputed the possession of Sigeum. Appointed absolute ruler of Lesbos for ten years in 589 B.C., he voluntarily resigned his power at the end of that period, when he felt that order had been finally established.

as wise as Pittacus

PITYS

Pitys was one of the many sylvan nymphs pursued by Pan with amorous intent. When she fled from the embraces of the ardent deity, she prayed for deliverance and was metamorphosed into a pine-tree.

under the cool shade of Pitys' spreading arms

PLAGIARY, SIR FRETFUL

Sir Fretful Plagiary, in Sheridan's *Critic,* is a dramatist who plagiarizes from obscure and little-known works. Though he affects a sincere desire to have his plays criticized, he is bitterly offended by any adverse comments. He is a satirical caricature of the playwright Richard Cumberland, who was noted for his vanity and his irritability.

an insincere Sir Fretful Plagiary

PLANCUS

Plancus was the surname of a distinguished Roman family of the Munatia gens. It signified a person having flat splay feet with low arches and broad soles. Lucius Munatius Plancus, to whom Horace addressed one of his odes (I, 7), sided with Octavius in his civil war with Antony and sponsored the motion in the Senate to confer upon the former the title of Augustus.

feet like those of a Plancus

PLATAEA

Plataea was the name of a city in Boeotia, Greece. In 480 B.C. it was destroyed in the Persian invasion of Hellas by Xerxes, and in the following year, still in ruins, it was the scene of the great victory over Mardonius at which the independence of Greece was secured. In consequence of this triumph, it was declared inviolable and sacred.

a victory as memorable as that at Plataea

PLATO

Plato (427-347 B.C.), great Greek philosopher and pupil of Socrates, was the author of dialogues of inquiry into the nature of courage (*Laches*), friendship (*Lysis*), love (*Symposium*), beauty (*Hippias Major*), temperance (*Charmides*), and numerous others named, like the above, after the principal interlocutor. While living in the court of the tyrant Dionysius of Syracuse, he offended him by his plain speaking, was sold into slavery, but was later ransomed and returned to Athens. He set up his school of philosophy known as the Academy, in which he taught according to the Socratic method of question and answer. He wrote on knowledge as a qualification of the statesman (*Alcibiades*) and evolved the notion of the ideal state, which he discusses in his *Republic*. Arguing the immortality of the soul and the idea of a pre-existence, he taught, "Become like God . . . become holy, wise, and just."

with Platonic wisdom

PLATONIC

Platonic, from Plato (427-347 B.C.), is most often used to refer to a love that seeks and delights in community of interests, spirit, thought, and finds complete satisfaction therein, quite apart from sexual attraction. The term platonic is frequently used of a completely friendly and interesting, stimulating attraction, rather impersonal, but securely and openly established.

a calm, platonic friendship

PLAUSIBLE, LORD

Lord Plausible, in Wycherley's *Plain Dealer,* is an insinuating fop whose words have the ring of truth though they are as affected and specious as his appearance.

specious as Lord Plausible

PLAUTUS

Titus Maccius Plautus (c. 254-184 B.C.) was the earliest of the great Roman comic playwrights. Twenty of his comedies still survive, and they all reproduce Greek plots with Greek characters and settings. The stock plot of nearly all of them centers around a knavish slave who abets his young master, against the wishes of his stingy father, to rescue a young courtesan from the clutches of a pimp. She subsequently turns out to be a free-born Athenian lady and the lovers happily marry. The plays are characterized by broad, racy humor, intrigue, and burlesque. The *Menaechmi* influenced Shakespeare's *Comedy of Errors,* and the *Aulularia* was adapted by Molière for *L'Avare* (The Miser).

a comedy with Plautine bawdiness

PLEIADES

The Pleiades were the seven daughters of Atlas and Pleione. Virgin companions of Artemis, they went hunting with her in Boeotia, where they were pursued by Orion. Praying to the gods to be rescued from him, they were metamorphosed into doves and placed among the stars, where they formed a constellation. According to another account, they killed themselves from grief over the death of their sisters, the Hyades. Only six of the group are described as visible in the heavens, the seventh, named Sterope, having become invisible from shame, because she alone had loved a mortal man, Sisyphus. Their rising in Italy is about the beginning of November. Their names are Electra, Maia, Taygete, Alcyone, Celaeno, Merope, and Sterope, the "lost" or invisible Pleiad.

as close as the Pleiades

PLIABLE

Pliable, in Bunyan's *Pilgrim's Progress,* is an untrustworthy neighbor of Christian. He accompanies him as far as the first difficulty, the Slough of Despond, then backslides and deserts him.

a friend as reliable as Pliable

PLIANT, SIR AND LADY

Sir Paul Pliant, in Congreve's *Double Dealer,* is an uxorious old husband married to Lady Pliant, a wanton and licentious woman.

a marital relationship like that of the Pliants

PLINY THE ELDER

Pliny the Elder (A.D. 23-79), noble Roman author with an insatiable thirst for knowledge and encyclopedic output, read constantly, slept little, and took an immense profusion of notes. His greatest achievement, the *Historia Naturalis,* deals in 37 books with universal physics; the geography and ethnology of Europe, Asia, and Africa; the physiology of man; zoology; medical properties of plants; minerals and metallurgy; and a digression on the history of art. His curiosity in the natural phenomena of the great eruption of Vesuvius that occurred in the last year of his life led to a fatal close-range investigation. Though he took the precaution of tying a pillow over his head as a protection against the hail of pumice stones, he was asphyxiated by sulphurous fumes.

memoranda worthy of Pliny the Elder in bulk

PLINY THE YOUNGER

Pliny the Younger (A.D. 61-113), nephew of the foregoing, was a Roman consul in A.D. 100 and governor of the province of Bithynia from 111 to 113. A professional epistolographer, he wrote nine books of letters to his friends and had published in a tenth his official correspondence with the emperor Trajan. All self-consciously stylized and intended for publication, they range in subject from descriptions of his villas and accounts of public affairs to interpretations of dreams, ghost stories, murder cases, and how to treat Christians.

letters as marked for posterity as those of Pliny the Younger

PLOWMAN, PIERS

Piers Plowman, a peasant, is the chief character in William Langland's 14th century metrical tale, *The Vision of Piers Plowman.* He goes to sleep and dreams he sees "a faire field filled with folk" of all sorts, all the social wrongs of the time, the corruption of the church, the injustices of the laws and the courts. Langland makes a scathing attack on social conditions, purporting it to be the dream of the simple English laborer. *Piers Plowman* is revived periodically in England as a part of social reform campaigns.

the dreams of a Piers Plowman

PLUTARCH

Plutarch (A.D. 46-120), "prince of biographers," was the Greek who wrote *Parallel Lives,* translated under the title *Plutarch's Lives,* the greatest biography yet produced concerning Roman and Greek statesmen and soldiers. With a great store of anecdotes Plutarch compares their lives, painting, says a great French critic, "man as he is . . . the greatest characters and the most admirable actions of the human species . . . in a record that kindles the enthusiasm of youth and commends itself to the sober wisdom of age."

with the perspicacity of a Plutarch

PLUTO

Pluto, ruler of the lower world, is often referred to as a beneficent power below the earth's surface dispensing wealth out of the ground, but he is more often considered wholly as the deity exerting absolute power in his realm. His wife is Proserpina, daughter of Ceres (Demeter).

seeking mercies of Pluto, god of the world below
dark as Pluto's palace
Pluto's glooming reign

PLUTUS

Plutus was the personification of riches; hence, plutocratic is applied to persons deriving their power from their wealth. Plutus is sometimes represented as blind, giving to the evil and the good alike; as lame, coming slowly; and with wings, forsaking quickly.

crude and plutocratic magnificence

PLUVIUS

Pluvius, the "sender of rain," was a surname of Jupiter among the Romans. To him they offered sacrifices during long-protracted droughts, in order to elicit his merciful and beneficent manifestation in the form of showers. The name became prevalent in journalese of a few decades ago, and many a baseball game was dispelled and broken up by an "ill-disposed Jupiter Pluvius."

Pluvius bless the produce

POCAHONTAS

Pocahontas (1595-1617), daughter of Powhatan, an Indian chief of the Mohawks, rescued Captain John Smith when her father was about to have him killed. She was married to one of Powhatan's captains. Meantime, an Englishman had secured her, demanded and got a ransom for her, but did not give her up. History records that she later married John Rolfe, with whom she went to England.

with Pocahontas's ready plea

PODALIRIUS

Podalirius, son of Asclepius, was the brother of Machaon, along with whom he led the Thessalians of Tricca, Greece, against Troy. He and his brother were skilled in the medical art, serving as surgeons of the Greek host. On his return from Troy, Podalirius was cast by a storm on the coast of Syros, in Caria, where he is said to have settled.

the Podalirius of the battalion

PODSNAP, MR.

Mr. Podsnap, in Dickens' *Our Mutual Friend,* is a pompous, self-satisfied, and smug member of British middle-class society. A representative of strait-laced and stiff-starched Philistinism, he is continually protesting against things likely to "bring a blush into the cheek of the young person" (the last-named being his own daughter, in the presence of whom he is very careful of the proprieties). This pretentious and respectable creature is further distinguished by his intimate knowledge of the exact designs of Providence, which generally happen to coincide with his own. The word *Podsnappery* designates this lumbering etiquette of the fossil gentry.

prudish, decorous as Mr. Podsnap

POE, EDGER ALLAN

Edgar Allan Poe (1809-1849), American editor, critic, poet, and writer of short stories, won immediate acclaim in Europe on the publication of his first poems, when the critics hailed him as "the first American writer." Highly imaginative, sensitive, temperamental and moody, his first poetry touched the purely mystical, purely beautiful, in complete accord with his declared theory that poetry is not meant to convey ideas, but to be in itself music and to create beauty. His stories stand supreme among short stories of mystery, horror, and analytical reasoning. *Murders in the Rue Morgue, The Pit and the Pendulum, The Gold Bug,* for example, all have the magic of details so managed that they carry complete belief.

as temperamental as a Poe

POICTESME

Poictesme is a fantastic and imaginary land where nothing is impossible and the fabulous transpires with the ease of reality. This miraculous place, located somewhere in Europe and having about it the air of medieval Provence, southern France, is in one of the stories in James Branch Cabell's *Two Heroes of Poictesme* and in the series known as the "Biography of Manuel."

as ideal and legendary as Poictesme

POLEMON, ANTONIUS

Antonius Polemon, renowned sophist and rhetorician of the early part of the second century A.D., had Aristides as his most famous disciple. So harassed by gout was he for the greater part of his life that he determined to put an end to his miserable existence. He had himself immured in the tomb of his ancestors at Laodicea, where he died of hunger at the age of sixty-five.

like Antonius Polemon, he thought death more merciful than suffering

---

POLEMON OF ATHENS

Polemon of Athens, a celebrated Platonic philosopher, was riotously profligate in his youth. One day, as he was nearing his thirtieth year, he led a band of revelers tumultuously into the school of Xenocrates, intending to disrupt its proceedings. But he was so much interested in the discourse, which chanced to be on the subect of temperance, that he tore off his Dionysian garland and became a rapt listener. From that day on he practiced abstinence and continued to attend the school, of which he became the head on the death of Xenocrates in 315 B.C.

a conversion as sudden as that of Polemon

POLLIO, ASINIUS

Caius Asinius Pollio (75 B.C. - 5 A.D.) was a distinguished Roman soldier, orator, historian, and politician. Consul in 40 B.C., he was the first to recognize the literary genius of Vergil and secured for him the restitution of his confiscated estate. Patron of the arts and literature, he brought aid to many writers, including Horace. He himself wrote a *History of the Civil Wars,* tragedies, and erotic poems. He also introduced the practice of public declamation of new literary works by reciting to an audience from his own, and constructed the first public library in Rome.

a Pollio to befriend his talents

POLLIO, VEDIUS

Vedius Pollio, a friend of the emperor Augustus, used to feed the lampreys in the fish tanks on his estates with human victims. Whenever a slave exasperated him, the poor wretch was forthwith tossed into the ponds as food for the blood-sucking eel-like fishes. Pollio died in 15 B.C., leaving a large part of his property to the emperor. It was this Pollio who erected the beautiful villa of Pausilypum ("rest from care"), which has given its name to the celebrated grotto of Posilipo between modern Naples and Pozzuoli, at the entrance of which the tomb of Vergil is still shown.

fiendishly inhumane as Vedius Pollio

POLLUX

(see *Dioscuri*)

POLLYANNA

Pollyanna, a young girl in Mrs. Porter's book of that name, is so constantly cheerful and optimistic that her name has become the synonym for rather purblind optimism and credulousness.

the Pollyannas of the world

POLO, MARCO

Marco Polo, thirteenth century Venetian traveler in Asia, first sold jewels to a Tartar chief, then was sent with a Persian envoy to the court of Kubla Khan, the Great Mogul of China and Tartary. Later he went to the Pope to ask him for a hundred scholars to teach the Mongols, and afterward to China on many an important mission. In Venice again, leading an attack against the Genoese, Marco was imprisoned, and in prison wrote his adventures, so remarkable that for hundreds of years they were considered fictitious, until recent research and travel have established both their veracity and Marco Polo's great service to the progress of navigation and commerce. A French historian declares that Marco Polo stands with Alexander the Great and Christopher Columbus in having contributed most to our knowledge of the globe.

a fabulous Marco Polo story
the range of a Marco Polo

POLONIUS

Polonius is the sententious, pedantic, preachy father of Ophelia in Shakespeare's *Hamlet*. He is the lord chamberlain of the king, and lets no occasion go by without adding his usually trite but sometimes astute preachment. He was a double-dealer who owes his literary immortality to his quotability.

the sententiousness of a Polonius

POLYBIUS

Polybius (202-120 B.C.) was the great Greek historian of the Roman Republic. Brought to Rome as a hostage after Rome had defeated Greece at the battle of Pydna (168 B.C.), he became the tutor of Scipio Africanus the Younger, with whom he formed an enduring friendship. His *History* is full of admiration of the Roman constitution and traces Rome's dramatic rise to supremacy from the First Punic War to the end of the Third Macedonian War (264-146 B.C.). Earnestly devoted to accuracy, he had a high sense of historical truth and realized that "war is a fearful thing but not so fearful that we should submit to anything in order to avoid it."

Polybian admiration for republicanism

POLYCLEITUS

Polycleitus was the great Argive sculptor who flourished from 450 to 420 B.C. Seeking to delineate the perfect proportions of the human body in his statues, he evolved a "canon," or standard, that made the head one-seventh of the total height of the figure. Plotted as mathematical exercises, his most famous statues were the *Doryphorus,* a stocky young man bearing a spear and advancing toward the spectator, and the *Diadumenos,* a youth binding the fillet of victory around his head. His figures, though squarely built and "all of one pattern," have a calm and reposed attitude, and his canon was approved by Galen, the Roman physician of much later times.

square-shouldered as a statue by Polycleitus

POLYCRATES

Polycrates was the wealthy and powerful tyrant of the Greek island of Samos in the sixth century B.C. Amasis, king of Egypt and his friend, advised him to part with something he prized highly in order to lessen the possibility of the gods' envy of his fabulous fortune. Accordingly, Polycrates cast a seal ring of great value into the sea. A few days later a humble fisherman presented him with a fish which, when it was opened in his kitchens, was found to have swallowed the ring. Amasis, thereupon, renounced his friendship with the tyrant on the ground that he was doomed by heaven. Not long after, Polycrates was crucified by the Persian satrap Oroetes (522 B.C.).

a Polycrates doomed by his own riches

POLYDAMAS

Polydamas was a Grecian athlete, famous for his stature and strength, and victor in the Olympic games in 408 B.C. Many marvelous tales were related of him, as that, when unarmed, he killed a huge and fierce lion. He was also said to have opposed and stopped a racing chariot in full career, to have lifted a mad bull from the ground, and the like. He met his death in attempting to stop or to sustain a falling boulder.

a mighty Polydamas with bulging biceps

POLYDORUS

Polydorus, one of the sons of Priam and Hecuba of Troy, was sent with a large hoard of gold to king Polymnestor of Thrace for safekeeping, when Troy was about to fall. After the destruction of the city, Polymnestor's greed for the gold induced him to kill the youth and throw his body into the sea. When it was washed upon the coast and recognized by Hecuba, she took vengeance upon the murderer by killing his own two children and putting out his eyes.

money lust such as that which killed Polydorus

POLYGNOTUS

Polygnotus was the famous Greek painter of the first half of the fifth century B.C. Born on the island of Thasos, he was later granted Athenian citizenship as the reward for his paintings in the Theseum and Painted Porch of the Attic city. He executed the *Capture of Troy* and *Descent of Odysseus to Hades* in the Lesche, or clubhouse, at Delphi. Each of these large murals contained at least seventy figures, and was described in detail by Pausanias (*q.v.*) the Periegete. His subjects were chiefly mythological and contained only meager attention to landscape. He lived on intimate terms with Cimon and his sister Elpinice.

a Polygnotus of the modern world

POLYHYMNIA

(see *Muse*)

Polyhymnia was the Muse of sublime song and was pictured in a pensive and meditating attitude. Hymns, sacred songs and ecclesiastical music in general fall within the province in which she exerted her inspirational powers.

a song of Polyhymnian solemnity

POLYNICES

(see *Seven against Thebes*)

POLYPHEMUS

Polyphemus, a cruel giant with one eye in the middle of his forehead, was chief among the Cyclopes. He cared nothing for the gods, and devoured human flesh. Polyphemus at one time captured Ulysses, confined him with his twelve companions in a cave, but Ulysses blinded Polyphemus in his sleep, and with his companions got out of the cave by clinging to the bellies of the sheep in the cave when they were let out to graze.

void of discretion as Polyphemus, strong and blind

POLYXENA

Polyxena was the virgin daughter of Priam and Hecuba of Troy and is the tragic heroine of Euripides' play, *Hecuba.* Fallen into Greek hands at the destruction of her city, she was taken by her captors to the coast of Thrace, where the ghost of Achilles appeared to them and demanded that Polyxena be sacrificed to him as his war-prize. The hero's son, Neoptolemus (Pyrrhus, *q.v.*), promptly despatched her on the tomb of his father, her own pride preferring death to slavery.

a not-unwilling Polyxena, contemplating death with stoical mind

---

POMONA

Pomona was the Roman goddess of fruit and fruit-trees, and her name is derived from the Latin word *pomum,* meaning fruit. In art she was depicted as holding fruits in the folds of her gown and a pruning-knife as well. She was loved by several rustic deities, including Silvanus, Picus and Vertumnus (*q.v.*).

looking like Pomona in her orchard

POMPADOUR, MME.

Madame Pompadour (1721-1764), the brilliant and beautiful French woman who had the favor of Louis XV, was by him titled the Marquise de Pompadour, and for twenty years not only influenced his policies, but herself maintained many of the powers of the royal throne. Receiving and corresponding with foreign states, she appointed ministers and was active in diplomacy. This brilliant, powerful, influential woman is now chiefly remembered for the style of head-dress affected by her and named in her honor.

the Madame Pompadour in the case

POMPEIA

Pompeia, daughter of Quintus Pompeius Rufus and Cornelia, and granddaughter of the dictator Sulla, was married to Julius Caesar in 67 B.C. and divorced by him in 61 because she was suspected of amorous rendezvous and dalliance with Clodius (*q.v.*), who had stealthily introduced himself dressed as a woman into her husband's house while she was celebrating the mysteries of the Bona Dea, exclusively for women. She is, therefore, the target of the expression, "Caesar's wife must be above suspicion."

another Pompeia at making a cuckold of her husband

POMPEII

Pompeii was an ancient city destroyed by an eruption of Vesuvius (A.D. 79). All traces were lost until some laborers digging a well in 1713 uncovered utensils and vases which led to exploration and excavations that uncovered the entire ruins. The excavations afforded the most perfect picture that inanimate objects can give of Roman life eighteen hundred years before. Pompeian usually refers to the colors, art, decorations, and furnishings found still intact in the houses of the city. The whole story of the city and its destruction is used as a background of Bulwer-Lytton's fascinating novel, *The Last Days of Pompeii.*

still as the halls of Pompeii

POMPEY

Pompey (106-48 B.C.), a member of the First Triumvirate comprising himself, Crassus and Caesar, boasted that he had "taken the city gates" of eight hundred cities and put friends of Rome in power in all of them. He was accorded a triumph so great that it aroused the envy of Julius Caesar. Princes and kings were his spoil; twelve million people in Africa, Asia and Europe had been subjugated by him. Finally he was sole consul until the powerful Caesar crossed the Rubicon (49 B.C.) to oppose him and defeated him. Pompey escaped being led in chains through the Rome that had so recently acclaimed him only by flight to Egypt where he was murdered.

a Pompey in chains

POOH-BAH

Pooh-Bah, prominent character in Gilbert and Sullivan's *Mikado,* is the pompous, officious holder of nearly every office called into play in the opera. Ludicrously referring a person to one official after another, all personified in Pooh-Bah himself, he practically makes the comedy of the play. The name, consequently, means a person holding many offices, proud of his high position, or blatantly advertising his own importance.

happy in his Pooh-Bah capacities

POOR RICHARD

Poor Richard was the assumed name of Benjamin Franklin in a series of Almanacs written from 1732 to 1757. They are distinguished for their inculcation of such virtues as temperance, frugality, order, justice, cleanliness, chastity, and honesty, and are a mine of maxims and proverbial wisdom.

as edifying as Poor Richard

POPE, ALEXANDER

Alexander Pope (1688-1744), English poet famed for the acerbity of his satire and friend of Addison and Swift, is celebrated as the author of such classics as *The Rape of the Lock,* a parody of epic style in mock-heroic vein; the *Essay on Criticism;* and the *Essay on Man,* many lines and couplets of which have become household expressions. His translations of the *Iliad* and *Odyssey,* though still popular, are somewhat marred by the brilliance of his own individualism and the over-adorning of the classic simplicity of the originals by the "fill" necessary to round out the rhymed couplet he chose to be the vehicle of his versions. His forte really lay in parody, lampoon, and retort that could be both abusive and scurrilous.

a pen like Pope's dagger

POPPAEA

Poppaea Sabina was the beautiful but morally licentious wife of Nero's best friend, Otho, and subsequently of Nero himself. An ambitious and cruel woman, she persuaded Nero to murder his mother Agrippina (59 A.D.), because she was opposed to their union and to divorce, and slay his innocent and virtuous first wife, Octavia. Luxurious of habits, she was said to bathe in milk and lived riotously with the emperor in his *Golden House.* She died in pregnancy from a kick administered by her choleric husband, who later, grief-stricken, had her embalmed and deified like an oriental queen.

Poppaean luxuriousness
as licentious as Poppaea
Poppaean allure

PORCIA

Porcia, the daughter of Cato of Utica, who committed suicide when the republican opposition to Caesar's dictatorship collapsed, was married to Marcus Brutus, the assassin of her father's despotic enemy. On the night before the fateful Ides of March in 44 B.C., she persuaded her husband to divulge to her the conspiracy against Caesar's life, wounding herself in the thigh to demonstrate her courage and trustworthiness. After the death of Brutus in 42 B.C., she put an end to her own life, devoted to her husband to the end.

secrets revealable only to a Porcia

PORSENA, LARS

Lars Porsena was king of the Etruscan town of Clusium at the end of the 6th century B.C. In order to restore Tarquinius Superbus to the throne he marched against Rome at the head of a vast army, occupied the Janiculum hill, and would have entered the city by the bridge connecting it with the hill, had it not been for the superhuman prowess of Horatius Cocles (*q.v.*). He then laid siege to the city, which soon began to feel the pinch of famine. A young Roman named Caius Mucius thereupon resolved to deliver his people by murdering the invader, but killed the royal secretary by mistake. Seized and threatened with torture, he put his right hand in the altar fire to show how indifferent a Roman could be to pain. Porsena admired his courage and let him go free, but not before Mucius Scaevola (as he was thereafter called) warned him to make peace with Rome, inasmuch as 300 noble youths had sworn to take his life and he was only the first to whom the lot had fallen. After receiving twenty hostages, Porsena consequently was content to lift his siege and to withdraw from Rome. Such was the explanation by which Roman vanity accounted for one of the earliest and greatest disasters to befall the city. In actual fact, Rome seems to have been completely conquered by Porsena and compelled to pay him tribute. The story is told in Livy's history and reworked in Macaulay's *Lays of Ancient Rome.*

has no Lars Porsena to champion his claims

PORTHOS

Porthos, one of the *Three Musketeers,* immortalized in Dumas' novel, shares in the adventure of Aramis and Athos, along with D'Artagnan, in one gay or hazardous escapade after another over the face of Europe. (see *Athos, Aramis, D'Artagnan.*)

always has his Porthos ready

PORTIA

Portia, the literary character best known through Shakespeare's romantic *Merchant of Venice,* is a beautiful, rich heiress, whose suitors are, by the terms of her father's will, to win her only by choosing the right one of three caskets. Bassanio, the Venetian her heart favors, is the fortunate person, and she endears herself to him by going at once to Venice to help save his friend Antonio from death for debt at the hands of Shylock, a creditor. This she accomplishes by means of her brilliant mind. Her name suggests wealth, beauty, bright and happy love, along with generosity and unusual intelligence.

surprised at his Dolly Varden — turned Portia

PORTUNUS

Portunus was the Roman protecting genius of harbors (*portus*) or of gates (*portae*), or of both, since the ancients themselves were somewhat doubtful and uncertain of his functions. Identified with the Greek Palaemon (*q.v.*), he was represented with a key in his hand, and his festival, the *Portunalia,* was observed on the 17th of August. In the boat-race that formed part of the funeral-games held in honor of Anchises, the father of Aeneas, in Vergil's *Aeneid* (v, 241-3), Portunus gives one of the galleys a shove "into port."

Portunus brought his craft to safety

POSEIDON

Poseidon, brother of Jupiter, husband of Amphitrite, and god of the sea identified with Neptune, is usually pictured riding a dolphin or seahorse, carrying a trident, and attended by a train of sea maidens. In his palace in the depths of the sea he kept his horses with brazen hoofs and golden manes. He is credited with great power, and literature uses the words *majestic, loud-sounding, earth-shaking,* and *ruler of the sea,* in reference to him.

steering his great ship like a Poseidon commanding the waves

POSTHUMUS, LEONATUS

Leonatus Posthumus is husband to Imogen, in Shakespeare's *Cymbeline.* Persuaded of his wife's infidelity, he jealously and rashly plots her death as punishment, but his unjust scheme miscarries.

as suspicious of his wife as Leonatus Posthumus

POSTVERTA AND PRORSA

Postverta ("turned backward") and Prorsa ("turned forward") were epithets for a Roman goddess of prophecy and childbirth, sometimes regarded as one deity, Carmenta, sometimes as two, designated as Carmentes or by the above names. The deity was invoked either according to the position of the child during latter pregnancy or depending on whether recourse to divine knowledge of the past or future was desired. Her festival fell on January 11 and 15, and the cult still survives in modern Italy, where women in labor supplicate Carmenta.

the assistance of Postverta or Prorsa?

POTIPHAR'S WIFE

Potiphar's wife, the spouse of the Egyptian official to whom Joseph was sold as a slave, attempted to lure the

Biblical hero into passionate relations with her, and, stung by his frequent rebuffs to her desire, accused him falsely of attempting to violate her, using as evidence the very garment which she herself had torn from him in her sensual frenzy. She was believed, and her wounded vanity and frustrated concupiscence were in part satisfied by his consequent imprisonment. In *Genesis,* xxxix, she is not given a proper name, though according to the Koran her name was Zuleika, other Arabian writers calling her Rail.

as lecherous as Potiphar's wife

POUNDTEXT, PETER

Peter Poundtext, in Scott's *Old Mortality,* is a thumpingly evangelistic preacher and "indulged pastor" with the Covenanters' army.

a revivalistic Peter Poundtext

POYSER, MRS.

Mrs. Poyser, in George Eliot's *Adam Bede,* is a keen-witted farmer's wife. Clever, vigorous, and ready of tongue, she is also amusingly shrewish.

a voluble Mrs. Poyser

PRAJAPATI

Prajapati, in Vedic lore, is a special genius presiding over procreation. The name signifies literally "lord of creatures," and refers to the supreme deity and cosmic principle as progenitor and creator of everything. It is applied to Soma, Indra, Savitri, Brahma, and the Rishis, as fathers of the human race.

like Prajapati, worried over his offspring

PRAXITELES

Praxiteles was born at Athens c. 390 B.C. and became one of the most famous of the Greek sculptors. One original marble statue of his still exists, the famous group of Hermes and the infant Dionysus, whom the beautiful older god is holding in his arms. His Aphrodite of Cnidus and statues of Eros (see *Phryne*) and Apollo exist in Roman copies. These works all show the dreamy, sensuous and graceful qualities of his style, as distinguished from the majestic grandeur of Phidias.

a figure for Praxiteles to sculpt

PRE-RAPHAELITE

Pre-Raphaelite refers to the group of artists who in England (1847) made an effort to imitate the naturalness and the artistry of color and figure of early Italian painting before Raphael. The group included Millais and the Rossettis in art; Morris and Swinburne in poetry. The name is now loosely used of any painters who consciously work for the Italian attention to detail and depth of color.

the Pre-Raphaelite atmosphere extended even to the habitués of the museum

---

PRIAM

Priam was a son of Laomedon and the last king of Troy. By Hecuba, his wife, he sired fifty sons and fifty daughters, including Hector, Paris, Troilus and Cassandra. In the *Iliad* and *Aeneid* he is pictured as grieving inconsolably over the death of so many of his sons and the sorrows of his people, but well-disposed to Helen, the cause of the siege of Troy. He bravely entered the Greek camp alone to ransom the body of his favorite son, Hector, who had been slain by Achilles. The night on which Troy fell to the Greeks he was murdered by Pyrrhus (Neoptolemus), the son of Achilles.

prolific as Priam
with the pathos of Priam

PRIAPUS

Priapus, the son of Dionysus (Bacchus) and Aphrodite (Venus), was the god of procreation and the personification of the fructifying principle in Nature. Worshiped particularly as the god of gardens and vineyards, the protector of flocks, bees and all garden produce, he was represented in art mostly in the form of *hermae* (square pillars, broad at the base, with a sculptured head on the top and a phallus below) carrying fruit in his garment and a sickle or cornucopia in his hand. In Roman times he was little more than a grotesque scarecrow frightening off birds from gardens.

a garden with Priapean plenty
Priapean abundance

PRIG, BETSEY

Betsey Prig, in Dickens' *Martin Chuzzlewit,* is an ignorant day-nurse who becomes a friend of Mrs. Gamp (*q.v.*). Acid and sharp of disposition, and contemptuously derisive and offensive in manner, she finally quarrels with her over the existence of Mrs. Harris (*q.v.*).

a narrow-minded Betsey Prig

PRIMROSE, DOCTOR CHARLES

The Reverend Doctor Charles Primrose, the title-character of Goldsmith's *Vicar of Wakefield,* is celebrated for the simplicity of his character and for his support of the Whistonian theory that it is unlawful for a priest of the Church of England to take a second wife. Unskilled in the world, genuinely pious, and beloved by all who know him, he is devout and charitable, and he submits with bravery and fortitude to the misfortunes that assail his virtuous household. The moral picture that he presents is affecting and even sublime.

a pious Charles Primrose in matters of marriage

PRIMROSE, GEORGE

George Primrose, in Goldsmith's *Vicar of Wakefield,* is proverbial for misdirected and short-sighted good intentions. He went to Amsterdam to teach English to the Dutchmen, without reflecting until he landed that he should first know something about Dutch himself.

as lacking in foresight as George Primrose

PRIMROSE, MOSES

Moses Primrose, impractical, unsophisticated younger son of Dr. Primrose, in Goldsmith's *Vicar of Wakefield,* was sent by his father to the fair to sell or trade a horse, to recoup the family fortunes. He returned with a dozen pair of "gold"-rimmed, brass spectacles a sharper had given him in exchange for the horse. His name has ever since been used of the gullible, easily duped young greenhorn, prey of sharpers and swindlers.

a Moses Primrose among the wolves
a bewildered Moses Primrose

PRIMROSE, MRS. DEBORAH

Mrs. Deborah Primrose, the wife of the vicar, in Goldsmith's *Vicar of Wakefield,* is noted for her boasted skill in housewifery, her vanity and pride in her children and husband, and her desire to appear genteel. Her wedding gown is a standing simile for things that wear well.

as serviceable as Mrs. Primrose's wedding gown

PRISCIAN

Priscian, who flourished about 450 A.D., was a famous Latin grammarian working at Constantinople under Anastasius, the emperor of the East. His most renowned work was the *Institutio Grammatica,* an eighteen-book exposition of the rules of Latin syntax. So much authority did it gain that the phrase "to break Priscian's head" came to mean to violate rules of grammar.

Priscian's head is often bruised without remorse
in every sentence a blow to Priscian's head

PRISCILLA, THE PURITAN MAID

Priscilla Mullens, in Longfellow's *Courtship of Miles Standish,* was patterned after a real personage. In the poem she is represented as the Puritan maid who, when courted by John Alden serving as proxy and intercessor for the military Miles Standish, demurely suggested to the younger man that he speak for himself.

as bold in her modesty as Priscilla Mullens

PROCNE

Procne was the daughter of King Pandion of Athens and the wife of Tereus, king of Thrace. In revenge for her husband's infidelity and rape of her sister Philomela (*q.v.*), she killed her son, Itys, and served him to his father in a cannibal feast. When Tereus pursued her and Philomela, Procne was metamorphosed into a swallow and her sister into a nightingale.

a Procne with the air of an injured wife

PROCRIS

(see *Cephalus*)

PROCRUSTEAN

Procrustean is from Procrustes, a notorious robber who fitted his captives to a bed by stretching them to the required length or by cutting their legs down to that length, as the case required. The word Procrustean, therefore, suggests persons who are so opinionated that they insist that others' views be either cut down or extended to meet their own. Sometimes it connotes persons whose abilities must be stretched to perform the duties of a situation or curtailed not to overstep the province of their authority.

the Procrustean bed of British proprieties

PROETIDES

The Proetides were the three daughters of Proetus, co-king of Argos, Lysippe, Iphinoë, and Iphianassa by name. When they arrived at the age of maturity they were seized with madness, either because they despised the worship of Dionysus or from presumption in comparing their beauty with that of Hera (Juno). The frenzy spread to the other women of Argos, until at length Proetus had to agree to divide his kingdom with Melampus and Bias, his brother, when the former promised him that he could cure the women of their insanity. After the cure was effected, Malampus and Bias married two of the daughters.

as mad as the Proetides

PROMETHEAN

Promethean is from Prometheus, a Titan, who, according to Greek mythology, stole fire from heaven for the use of man. Hence, he is known as a benefactor to man. Jupiter, in punishment, chained him to a rock, where his liver was eaten every day by an eagle and every night restored, until Hercules rescued him. Another story relates that he fashioned a man of clay and breathed into him the fire of life. Hence, he is life-bringing and creative. His name means "Fore-thought," and his punishment is the subject of Aeschylus' magnificent play, *Prometheus Bound.*

hopeful as Prometheus
warm as the spark Prometheus stole
like the vulture that is every day quarrying on Prometheus' liver

---

PRONUBA

Pronuba, a surname of Juno among the Romans, described that deity as one presiding over the rites of marriage, in which capacity she was represented as holding a pomegranate, the emblem of fertility. As a married woman herself, the spouse of Jupiter, she was thought of as attending the bride and assisting in the ceremonies in the role of bridesmaid and matron of honor. Her festival, the Matronalia, was celebrated on March 1.

a stately Pronuba to escort the bride

PROPERTIAN

Propertian refers to the style of Sextus Propertius (c. 50-15 B.C.), Roman elegiac poet who wrote four books of elegies in which he claimed to be the first to treat Italian subjects in Greek strains. His principal theme is his love for Cynthia (Hostia), though his work is rich in mythological references and adornments that are often obscure. Sonority of language and richness of sounds characterize his highly stylized poetry, though his personality, his passions and melancholy, his self-absorption in reflections on death overlay all the ornate decoration of his art.

shows Propertian self-pity
has Propertian obscurity

PROSERPINA

Proserpina, known also as Persephone and Core (daughter), was the child of Zeus and Demeter (Ceres). Pluto, god of the lower world, saw her as she was gathering lilies in a field and kidnaped her to become his wife and the formidable queen of the Shades. Demeter thereupon grieved for her daughter so much that she refused to allow the earth to produce any crops unless she would be restored to her, but as Proserpina had eaten part of a pomegranate while in the lower world, she was obliged to spend one-third of the year there and allowed to stay with her mother only for the rest of the year. During this latter period the earth produces, but is sterile and barren when the lovely maiden is ruling over the dead.

Allegorically interpreted, Proserpina is the seed-corn which is entrusted to the ground and concealed there for part of the year; when she returns to her mother, she becomes the corn which rises from the ground to feed mankind. Mystic philosophers interpreted her disappearance and return as alluding to the burial of the body of man and the immortality of his soul.

the golden lilies of a Proserpina

PROSPERO

Prospero, the central figure in Shakespeare's *The Tempest,* is the rightful Duke of Milan, dispossessed by his brother and set adrift with his daughter, Miranda. Reaching a desert island he calls into play the magic he had learned and like a guiding providence commands the services of Ariel, a spirit of speed and light, and Caliban, a malignant and menial dwarf. Never once even in that deserted region does Prospero lay aside his high wisdom or his nobility of mind. When finally, by means of his magic, he raises the tempests and wrecks his brother's ship, he punishes him by discomforts and fears, but finally forgives him and on the reconciliation he renounces his magic as no longer needed.

the Prospero of the dreary term of captivity

PROSS, SOLOMON

Solomon Pross, alias John Barsad, in Dickens' *A Tale of Two Cities,* is a rogue and thorough-going villain. He does spy service for the British, robs his own sister, Miss Pross, and ends up as a turnkey in a Paris prison.

as rascally an informer as Solomon Pross

PROTAGORAS

Protagoras (480-411 B.C.), celebrated Greek philosopher and an intimate friend of Pericles, was the first of the Sophists and also the first of the famous Hellenic sages to teach for pay. His instructions were so highly valued and priced that Plato says that he made more money than Phidias and ten other sculptors. In 411 B.C. he was impeached by Pythodorus, one of the Four Hundred, on a charge of impiety for having questioned the reality of the immortal gods ("I am unable to know whether they exist or not"). The impeachment was followed by conviction and banishment, or, as others affirm, only by the burning of the book *On the Gods* in which he made the statement. The coiner of the proverb "Man is the measure of all things," he is also said to have been the first to make a systematic study of grammar, distinguishing parts of speech and syntax.

another Protagoras, suspected of atheism

PROTESILAUS

Protesilaus, the husband of Laodamia (*q.v.*), was one of the Greeks who went to the siege of Troy. The first casualty, he fell by the hand of Hector as he was the first hero to leap from the prow of his ship. His dead body being sent home to Laodamia, she prayed to be allowed to converse with him for three hours only. Her prayer granted, Mercury conducted Protesilaus to the upper world, and when the hero died for the second time his wife expired with him.

like Protesilaus, the first Commando to fall

PROTEUS

Protean is from Proteus, son of Neptune. Called "the old man of the sea," he was capable of assuming different forms at will, a power he used to escape the task of prophesying. At midday, the story goes, Proteus rose from the sea to sleep among the flock of seals he tended for Neptune, and if caught at that time he was bound to prophesy, though to escape capture he assumed every possible shape. Caught, he predicted the future truthfully, and went back into the sea.

change, like Proteus

forms and variety of beauty are Protean

PROTOGENES

Protogenes was a distinguished Greek painter of the latter part of the fourth century B.C., and was noted for the extreme care he lavished on every detail in his work. A resident of Rhodes, he lived in poverty and obscurity until his fiftieth year, when a fellow-artist of note, Apelles, offered him fifty talents a piece for each of his finished paintings, thus leading the Rhodians to infer what a great artist they had living among them. Some of his finest works were: *Ialysus in Rhodes;* a *Resting Satyr,* painted during the siege of the island by Demetrius Poliorcetes in 305 B.C.; and portraits of king Antigonus and of Aristotle's mother.

as meticulous draftsmanship as that of Protogenes

PROUDHON, PIERRE J.

Pierre Joseph Proudhon (1809-1865), French writer, social philosopher, and economist, is regarded as the father of anarchism. Active in the Socialist movement in Paris, he was a vigorous critic of all contemporary forms of political government. Some of his famous works are: *What is Property?; Principles of Political Organization; Economic Contradictions; Capacity of the Working Classes; Revolutionary Ideas;* and *The Philosophy of Misery.*

a radical new Proudhon

PROUSTIAN

Proustian refers to the manner of Marcel Proust (1871-1922), valetudinarian author of the sixteen-volume novel, *Remembrance of Things Past,* and discoverer of the "involuntary memory," according to which the past does not die but clings to evocative sense-impressions that can summon forth long trains of memory within us. For example, a particular cake dipped in tea enables the narrator to relive his entire childhood. Proust believed that we do not correctly appreciate or evaluate direct experiences but that only in recollection can we really understand their import. His continuous novel is characterized by perspicacious analysis of persons belonging to the bourgeois world and exclusive society of Paris, and delves into the motives behind their every thought and action so intensely that digest of the work requires great amounts of concentration and time. Novelistic attention to homosexuality was first sponsored by him on a large scale in the section of the novel entitled "Cities of the Plain."

with penetrating Proustian analysis
long waves of Proustian memories

PRUSIAS

Prusias II, king of Bithynia from 192 to 148 B.C., was Hannibal's perfidious host during the latter years of the great Carthaginian's life. Though Hannibal was an invited and honored guest at his court, Prusias treacherously connived with a Roman embassy sent to persuade him to surrender the onetime invader of Italy for punishment. Hannibal, however, thwarted both the double-dealing Prusias and implacable Rome by taking poison when he detected the plot. For all his sycophantic service to Rome, Prusias met the gratitude usually in store for deceitful men of no honor — in 154 B.C. he was forced to make restitution to Rome for all his Pergamene conquests.

untrustworthy with guests as Prusias

PRY, PAUL

Paul Pry, from a short play by John Poole, is a meddlesome, idle, trifling fellow, a general nuisance, always looking into other people's affairs; hence, meddlesome, interfering, snooping.

the inevitable Paul Pry of the campus

PRYNNE, HESTER

Hester Prynne, in Hawthorne's *Scarlet Letter,* is the heroine who is led astray into adultery, by Puritan clergyman Arthur Dimmesdale, and forced to wear a scarlet *A* on her breast as penance and punishment for not revealing the name of her partner. Tortured by his conscience, the clergyman confesses his guilt years later.

as scorned as Hester Prynne

PSYCHE

Psyche ("soul") was so beautiful that Venus, in jealousy, ordered her son, Cupid, to cause her to fall in love with some monster. Smitten himself, however, the love-god wooed her in a palace in which he installed her, visiting her only at night. Forbidden to look on his countenance, Psyche yielded to her curiosity and the urgings of her jealous sisters. Holding a lamp before his radiant beauty as he slept, she wakened him by accidentally spilling a drop of oil on him. Angry, the god left her. Seeking her lover in many a country, Psyche performed various superhuman tasks enjoined on her by Venus. After all were accomplished, Jupiter consented to her union with Cupid in heaven.

This beautiful allegorical fable is told in *The Golden Ass* by Apuleius and in Walter Pater's *Marius the Epicurean.* The name Psyche, meaning *mind, soul, spirit,* is a part of many words relating to the immaterial and the sentient — psychic, psychological, psychiatry, psychoneurosis, etc.

like the awakened eyes of winged Psyche
pure as Psyche

PTAH

Ptah was the principal deity of Memphis in ancient Egypt. The shaper of the world and father of gods and men, he was worshiped there as early as the first dynasty of kings. Sometimes called the Egyptian Hephaestus (*q.v.*), he was considered as the creative force of the universe. He is represented in human form, generally swathed as a mummy and holding the scepter of life, power, and force.

aboriginal as Ptah

PTOLEMY

Ptolemy was the masculine personal name of the Macedonian, or XXIst, dynasty of Egyptian kings, fourteen or sixteen in number. Ptolemy I, "Soter" (Savior), who lived from 367 to 283 B.C. and who established the succession, was one of the generals and "Diadochi" (followers) of Alexander the Great. He founded the museum and great library of Alexandria, making his capital the cultural center of the world at that time. His son(Ptolemy II, or "Philadelphus," built the great Pharos (*q.v.*), one of the seven wonders of the ancient world.

Surnames of the Ptolemies to follow were "Euergetes" (benefactor); "Philopator" (father-loving); "Epiphanes" (illustrious); "Philometor" (mother-loving); and "Auletes" (flute-player), the father of the famous Cleopatra. With all are associated splendor, munificence, and culture.

the wealth and power of a Ptolemy

PUBLICOLA

Publicola, or Poplicola, was a Roman cognomen signifying "one who courts the people" or "friend of the people." Publius Valerius Publicola aided in expelling the Tarquin kings from Rome in 509 B.C. and was honored for his patriotism by being elected co-consul with Brutus. He liberated the people by proposing several laws, and ordered the lictors, consular attendants, to lower the fasces (emblems of the power to punish) before the populace, as an acknowledgment that the people's power was superior to that of the consuls. So popular was this champion of the citizenry that he was elected consul three times after his initial honor, in 508, 507, and 504 B.C.

as demagogic as Publicola

PUBLILIUS PHILO

Quintus Publilius Philo, Roman politician and consul in 339 B.C., was a distinguished general in the Samnite wars and sponsored the three bills known as the *Publilian Laws.* These laws were aimed at depriving the conservative and privileged patricians of the monopoly of the government by elevating the down-trodden plebeians to an equality with their superiors. All classes of citizens, rich and poor alike, were now to be eligible for all public offices of a secular nature.

another Publilius to champion the lower classes

PUCCINI, GIACOMO

Giacomo Puccini (1858-1924), born of a family already renowned in Italian musical annals of the time, himself achieved even greater celebrity as the composer of many beloved and immortal operas. Among them are *Manon Lescaut; La Bohème* (see *Mimi*), the production of which at Turin in 1896 made him world-famous; *Tosca; Madama Butterfly* (*q.v.*); and *La Fanciulla del West* ("The Girl of the Golden West"). Exquisite lyrism of melodic line, tender pathos, and wistful or somber tragedy mark and individualize his ever-popular music.

a Pucciniesque phrase of haunting beauty

PUCK

Puck, an elf, is a mischievous sprite, a hobgoblin, a fantastic whimsical spirit. Capable of transforming situations, he mischievously misleads travelers by dancing before them as a lantern on dark roads. He squeezes juice into sleeping eyes so that a person on waking will fall in love with the first person he sees. He does this in Shakespeare's *Midsummer Night's Dream,* and in general has a good time with mortals. He climaxes all with the wise observation, "Lord, what fools these mortals be!" Puck is, in short, the embodiment of the whimsical, tricksy, carefree spirit.

the spirit of Puck was loose in the carnival crowd

PUDDING, JACK

Jack Pudding is a name for a zany, buffoon, or clown. Every nation seems to call such characters by the name of the dish or viand preferred there. Thus, in French a simpleton is known as a Jean Potage; in Dutch, as Pickel-Herringe; in German, Hans Wurst; and in Italian, Macaroni.

as pudding-headed as Jack

PUDICITIA

Pudicitia was the personification of modesty, purity, chastity, propriety, and decency among the Greeks and Romans, and she was worshiped at an altar dedicated to her in Athens. In Rome two sanctuaries were consecrated to this deity, one to her as *Pudicitia patricia* or patrician honor, the other to her as *Pudicitia plebeia* or plebeian honor.

a votary of Pudicitia

PUFF

Puff is a bold and impudent literary quack and the author of the play rehearsed in Sheridan's *Critic.* In his own words, "I open with a clock striking, to beget an awful attention in the audience; it also marks the time, which is four o'clock in the morning, and saves a description of the rising sun, and a great deal about gilding the eastern hemisphere."

a Puff-like charlatan

PULITZER, JOSEPH

Joseph Pulitzer (1847-1911), the publisher of the *New York World* in 1883, combined aggressiveness, sensationalism, and wit with a crusader's zeal, exposing abuses and sponsoring worthy causes, using any means to that end. Cartoons, pictures, colored supplements, startling headlines, sensationalism, all were means of increasing circulation so that he might reach more and more people with the ideas on the editorial page. Finally Pulitzer provided money for a School of Journalism at Columbia University and established prizes for the best work by a reporter during any one year, as well as prizes for the best drama, novel, biography, history, verse, editorial, and cartoon of the year. His name stands for newspaper work that is aggressive, fearless, public-spirited, ingenious, and philanthropic, and for zealous crusading for any sound forward movement for the public good.

with Pulitzer's own zeal

PUMBLECHOOK, UNCLE

Uncle Pumblechook, in Dickens' *Great Expectations,* is a pompous old man who bullies Pip, the hero, when he is a poor boy, and fawns on him obsequiously when he has a prospect of becoming rich. He is noted for saying, "Might I, Mr. Pip, — may I, —" (*scilicet,* shake hands).

a boot-licker like Pumblechook

PUNCH

Punch, the hook-nosed, grotesque, hump-backed figure in the famous Punch and Judy puppet show displayed in a little portable stage on any London street, is as much a feature of street amusement as the hurdy-gurdy of early New York pavements. Punch strangles his child and beats his wife, to the intense delight of all spectators, bearing out the statement that "the drollery and wit of a piece of wood is doubly droll and farcical."

a cruel Punch in his own household

PUNIC

Punic refers to Carthage, Rome's great rival in the domination of the ancient Mediterranean region. It suggests the three Punic Wars between the rivals, fought in the years 264-241, 218-202, and 149-146 B.C. Phoenician, Carthaginian and Punic alike connote craftiness, faithlessness and perfidy.

Punic honor is no honor

PURE, SIMON

Simon Pure is the name of a Pennsylvania Quaker in Mrs. Centlivre's comedy, *A Bold Stroke for a Wife.* Visiting London for a quarterly meeting of his sect, he lost a letter of introduction from an American friend, Mr. Holdfast, to Obadiah Prim, a stern Englishman who is guardian of Anne Lovely, an heiress. Colonel Feignwell found the letter and undertook the imposture of Simon Pure. Thus the real Simon Pure was treated as a fraud until Feignwell had secured Prim's unconditional consent that he marry Miss Lovely.

the true, and not the fictitious, Simon Pure

PURGON

Purgon is a comic physician in Molière's *Malade Imaginaire.* His name suggests that his favorite remedy for illness, feigned or real, is a liberal recourse to purgatives.

the Purgon of the sickroom

PURITANIC

Puritanic, originally used of the Puritans (1559) and their religious and political views and rules, is now used of any rather strict and narrow views concerning group or personal behavior, or of rather intolerant and narrow social restrictions. Hence, it means narrow, intolerant, severe, prudish.

a puckish mind with Puritanic training

PUSHAN

Pushan, in the Vedic hymns, represents Surya the sun, and is a god who protects and multiplies cattle and the other possessions of mankind. This celestial shepherd deity is also the guardian of roads and journeys, and conducts the souls of the dead.

Pushan brings increase to the flocks

PUSS-IN-BOOTS

Puss-in-Boots is the hero of a nursery tale by Perrault, in which he secures a rich wife and a fortune for his young master by passing him off as a titled nobleman. Therefore, it connotes useful, clever, indispensable.

a useful Puss-in-Boots introduced him

PYGMALION

Pygmalion is the Greek sculptor who carved an ivory statue of Galatea so beautiful that he fell in love with it and prayed Aphrodite that she would bring it to life. His prayer granted, he married the beautiful maiden. A modern play, Shaw's *Pygmalion,* has revived the knowledge of and interest in the story, and the word is now applied to any creation brought about by a person's own effort and admiration, and come to be part of his daily life.

mute as Pygmalion

PYGMY

A Pygmy, in ancient history, is the name of a member of a race of dwarfs, a Nile-dwelling tribe of small stature. It is now used of any unnaturally small or dwarfish person, any unimportant and futile person, or one of small power or of entirely insignificant efforts.

a pygmy in the hall of giants

PYLADES

Pylades was the son of Strophius, king of Phocis, and Anaxibia, a sister of Agamemnon. After Agamemnon had been treacherously murdered by his wife, Clytemnestra, their son, Orestes was brought to Phocis for safety until he should be old enough to undertake, with his sister, Electra, as accomplice, the revenge-murder of their adulterous mother. Whiles Orestes was at Phocis he contracted his proverbial friendship with Pylades, and the two of them form a team of friends characterized by ever-faithful devotion, as well-known as Damon and Pythias. Pylades later married Electra, the sister of his friend. (See *Orestes, Electra,* etc.)

helped by his Pylades

PYRAMUS

Pyramus was a Babylonian lad who loved Thisbe, his neighbor. Forbidden by their parents to marry, they exchanged vows through the partition wall separating their homes and arranged a tryst outside the city. Thisbe came first to the agreed upon white mulberry tree, but was frightened by a lion and ran to a cave for shelter. In her trepidation she dropped her veil which the lion mangled and covered with blood. Finding it later, Pyramus thought she had been killed and stabbed himself. Distraught at the sight of her dying lover, when she emerged from her shelter, Thisbe likewise stabbed herself. The mulberry tree ever after bore blood-red berries. Originally an Asiatic tale, the story was later told by Ovid in his *Metamorphoses* and is found in the burlesque by Nick Bottom and his rustics in Shakespeare's *Midsummer Night's Dream.*

with Pyramus's hasty belief

PYRGOTELES

Pyrgoteles, one of the most renowned gem-engravers of ancient Greece, was a contemporary of Alexander the Great and carved cameos and intaglios of rare and exquisite beauty and perfection. Alexander considered his genius as unique as that of Apelles, the portrait painter, and Lysippus, the sculptor, and designated him as the only artist who was permitted to engrave seal-rings for the king.

a carnelian fine enough to have been wrought by Pyrgoteles

PYRRHA

Pyrrha was the wife of Deucalion (*q.v.*), who entered an ark with him to escape the deluge sent by Zeus in revenge on mankind for its sins. When the flood had subsided they repopulated the earth by casting stones ("the bones of their mother") over their shoulders. Those tossed by Pyrrha turned into women, Deucalion's into men.

the fertility of a Pyrrha

PYRRHIC VICTORY

A Pyrrhic victory is from Pyrrhus, the king of Epirus, who battled Rome victoriously in 279 B.C., but exclaimed as he looked on his battered army, "One more such victory over the Romans and we are lost!" The term implies a victory so costly that the victor as well as the vanquished suffers.

a tempered rejoicing over the Pyrrhic victory

PYRRHONIAN

Pyrrhonian is from the Greek skeptic philosopher Pyrrho (360-270 B.C.) who espoused absolute skepticism. He believed nothing not proved and was therefore excited at nothing, all of which contributed to his composure and tranquillity. His general attitude was: It might not be true. Pyrrhonian is, therefore, used of persons who wrap themselves in the calm of disbelief.

his Pyrrhonian slant counteracts any value his opinion might have

---

PYRRHUS

Pyrrhus, the son of Achilles, was so-named because of his hair. He was also called Neoptolemus because he came to Troy late in the course of the war. One of the heroes concealed in the Wooden Horse, he is pictured as exerting great cruelty on the fall of the city, killing aged king Priam at a holy altar, sacrificing Polyxena, Priam's daughter, at the tomb of Achilles, and taking Andromache, Hector's wife, as his slave-concubine.

shows the cruelty of a Pyrrhus
Pyrrhic viciousness

PYTHAGOREAN

Pythagorean is from Pythagoras (6th century B.C.), a Greek philosopher and the first to define a philosopher as a man who loved wisdom alone. He adopted the theory of the transmigration of souls, and by means of his unusual and carefully developed methods of influencing the minds of men, attracted many followers to his brotherhood. But like many too-exclusive groups, they became so haughty and arrogant that they were finally divested of their political power and destroyed, although their ideas persist even to this day.

with a Pythagorean air of mystery
Pythagorean doctrines

PYTHEAS

Pytheas of Massilia (ancient Marseilles) was a celebrated Greek navigator and explorer who lived in the time of Alexander the Great, or shortly thereafter. In one of his voyages he reached Britain and Thule, the latter variously identified as one of the Shetlands, Iceland, Norway, or an Orkney, and supposed to be the most northerly region of the world. In a second trip he coasted along the whole of Europe from Gadira (Cadiz) to the Tanais (Don), afterwards describing the voyage in his *Periplus* ("sailing around"). He stated that *ultima Thule* was a six days' sail from Britain and said that the day and night were each six months long there.

an intrepid Pytheas of the high seas

PYTHIAN

Pythian refers to Pythius, an epithet of Apollo as the slayer of the Python, the huge serpent that was engendered near Delphi from the mud of the deluge. In memory of that event, Pythian Apollo, or Pythius, instituted the Pythian games, held every four years from about 586 B.C. on and involving musical contests as a prominent feature. Pythia was the name of the priestess of the god at his Delphic shrine. Since she was inspired by him to utter his oracles, the name may now be used of anyone going into ecstasies or frenzies like her.

a Pythian seizure of prophecy

PYTHIAS

Pythias, or Phintias, was the noble Pythagorean of Syracuse, memorable for his loyal and constant devotion to his friend, Damon. When Dionysius I. tyrant of the city, had condemned him to death, he begged leave to go to his home first to arrange his affairs, offering Damon as hostage to guarantee his return. When Pythias came back just in season to save the life of Damon, Dionysius was struck by so rare and noble an example of mutual friendship that he pardoned him, entreating to be admitted as a third into their sacred fellowship.

like Pythias, unfailing to his friend in time of peril

Q

QUADRIFRONS

Quadrifrons ("four-faced") was used as a surname of Janus (*q.v.*) from the time when the Romans of ancient Italy found an image of the god with four foreheads after their conquest of the Faliscans. Afterwards they built a temple of Janus Quadrifrons which had four gates. The multiplicity of the god's faces was ascribed to the fact that he was the divinity presiding over the year with its four seasons.

a region with the seasons clearly demarcated by Quadrifrons

QUASHEE

Quashee is a cant generic name for a negro, especially a West Indian one. Often used as a proper name, it is derived by modern etymologians from the Ashanti word for a boy born on a Sunday, *kwasi,* though Linnaeus, famous eighteenth century botanist, applied the name quassia to a tree in Surinam, Dutch Guiana, in honor of a negro called Quassi or Quasha, who employed its bark as a remedy for fever and who enjoyed such a reputation among the other natives as to be almost worshiped by some.

as black as Quashee

QUASIMODO

Quasimodo is the foundling hunchback adopted by Archdeacon Frollo in Victor Hugo's *Notre Dame de Paris.* A man of great strength, but a complete monster of misshapen deformity, he has nonetheless a tender and courteous nature, and serves as the bell-ringer of the cathedral. The name is used popularly to designate any hideously ugly man.

repellent to look at as Quasimodo

QUEEN DICK

Richard Cromwell, the ineffectual Lord Protector of England (1658-59), was sometimes called Queen Dick. The phrase *to happen in the reign of Queen Dick* means never, since Cromwell was never Queen.

last heard of in the reign of Queen Dick

QUEEN LABE

Queen Labe is a sorceress ruling over the City of Enchantments, in the story of Beder from the *Arabian Nights' Entertainments.* Like the Greek Circe, she practices a diabolic art that transforms men into horses, mules, and other animals. Beder marries her, defeats her plots against him, and turns her into a mare. When she is restored to her own shape by her mother, she turns the tables against the young prince and metamorphoses him into an owl, until he finally escapes her vengeance after numerous adventures.

powerful as Queen Labe in her control over men

QUEEN OF HEARTS

The original Queen of Hearts was Elizabeth, the daughter of James I of England, and the queen of Bohemia (1596-1662). This unfortunate woman was so called in the Low Countries because of her amiable character and engaging manners. When her fortunes were at their lowest ebb, she never departed from her dignity. Neither poverty nor distress seemed to have any effect on her other than to render her more an object of admiration than before. A Queen of Hearts today is everybody's sweetheart or darling, a woman beloved simultaneously by many people.

as much a charmer as the Queen of Hearts

QUEEN OF TEARS

Queen of Tears was a name given to Mary of Modena, the second wife of James II of England. "Her eyes," says Noble, "became eternal fountains of sorrow for that crown her own ill policy contributed to lose." Any contrite or lachrymose woman, inconsolable and lavish with weeping, may be called a Queen of Tears.

weeping as copiously as the Queen of Tears

QUEENSBURY, MARQUIS OF

Sir John Sholto Douglas, the eighth Marquis of Queensbury (1844-1900), was a peer of Scotland and a patron of pugilism. With John G. Chambers he drew up and established the rules for prizefighting that were adopted in 1866 by the Amateur Athletic Club of England.

a blow not according to the Marquis of Queensbury

QUEER CARD

A Queer Card is an eccentric person who does not act in accordance with social rules. The name stems from the game of whist, in which, when a wrong card is played, the partner says, "That is a queer card." Transferred to the player, it means that he is a queer card to play in such a manner.

the Queer Card of the bridge table

QUEER STREET

Queer Street is an imaginary abode for people in any kind of difficulty. *To live in Queer Street* means to be of doubtful solvency, and to be marked in a tradesman's ledger with a *quaere* (inquire) reminds the merchant to make inquiries about this customer. In other phrases Queer Street means perplexity or puzzledom.

that has put me in Queer Street

QUELCH, JOHN

John Quelch (1665-1704) was a British pirate and sea-roving freebooter who plundered Portuguese vessels off the coast of Brazil and returned to Marblehead, Massachusetts, with his loot. He was apprehended, brought to trial, and convicted by the testimony of his accomplices. His subsequent execution by hanging was officially defended as a case of judicial murder.

a buccaneer in the tradition of John Quelch

QUERNO

Camillo Querno of Apulia, Italy, heard that pope Leo X was a great patron of poets and went to Rome with a harp in his hand to sing his *Alexias*, an endless and dull poem containing 20,000 verses. Introduced to His Holiness as a buffoon, he was promoted to the laurel. The character is mentioned in Alexander Pope's *Dunciad*:

"Rome in her Capitol saw Querno sit,
Throned on seven hills, the Antichrist of wit."

an ambitious dullard like Querno

QUETZALCOATL

Quetzalcoatl was a traditional Aztec king and hero-god who introduced culture among his people and was worshiped as the inventor of arts and crafts and the founder of Mexican civilization. A god of peace, he was averse to human sacrifice and was pictured as white and bearded. At the insistence of his wicked brother, Tezcatlipoca, he drank some magic pulque, wandered to the ocean, and sailed away eastward to Tlapallan, the land of the rising sun, promising, however, to return. The myth seems to represent the conflict between night and day and the rival powers of light and darkness. The patiently waiting Aztecs at first mistook Cortez for their returning god, thereby aiding the progress of the invader.

the civilizing influence of a Quetzalcoatl

QUICKLY, MISTRESS

Mistress Quickly, hostess of a tavern in Eastcheap, broadly indulgent to all her rather miscellaneous transients and habitués, was herself good-humored, non-moral, of easy virtue, but withal womanly when there was need of womanly wisdom. She appears in Shakespeare's *The Merry Wives of Windsor* and in the *Henry* plays, and her name is common in many of the earlier popular tales.

a rough Mistress-Quickly womanliness

QUIDNUNC

A Quidnunc is a political Paul Pry (*q.v.*), a pragmatical village politician or jobber. Quidnunc is the chief character in Murphy's farce, *The Upholsterer, or What News?* The words are Latin, and mean "What now?" or "What's new?" The original of this inquiring political busybody was the father of Dr. Arne and his sister, Mrs. Cibber, who lived on King Street, Covent Garden, London, and is mentioned in *The Tatler*.

the Quidnunc of the party

QUILP

Quilp, a hideous and ferocious scheming dwarf in Dickens' *Old Curiosity Shop*, enjoys tormenting others. He is malignant, hideous, and sadistic.

a Quilp-like malice
his Quilpish tendencies

QUIMBY, PHINEAS P.

Phineas Parkhurst Quimby (1802-1866) was an American mental healer and hypnotist with offices in Portland, Maine. His religious philosophy of health through faith and mental happiness gave Mary Baker Eddy, one of his consultants, some of the basic ideas of her system of Christian Science.

a faith-healer like Phineas P. Quimby

QUINCE, PETER

Peter Quince is the carpenter peasant among the rustics who, in *Midsummer Night's Dream*, presented a crude play in honor of the Duke's wedding. The staging of the play by the unsophisticated Quince and his companions furnishes the hilariously comic element in the play.

the "very tragical mirth" of a Peter Quince

QUINTILIAN

Marcus Fabius Quintilian (35-95 A.D.), distinguished Roman rhetorician who was born in Spain, found renown in Italy's capital as a teacher of eloquence, numbering Pliny the Younger among his pupils and achieving a fame preeminent to the point of being proverbial. He was the first public instructor to receive a regular salary from the imperial exchequer of Vespasian. The twelve books of his great work, the *Institutio Oratoria*, deal with the complete education of a Roman and with educational methods of the day, with a list of authors to be studied by aspiring orators and containing the writer's appraisal of their style and value. His conception of the purpose of education — to create a man of character and culture, not a pedant — is admirably akin to that of the Humanists of a later day. Keen judgment, careful discrimination, and pure taste pervade the work.

a literary taste as impeccable as Quintilian's

QUIRINUS

Quirinus was the name of the Italic deity of the Sabine community that settled on the eponymically known Quirinal, one of the seven hills of ancient Rome. The name seems to be derived from *quiris*, the Sabine word for lance or spear. When this community was embodied into the city of Rome, Quirinus was included in its state gods, along with Jupiter and Mars, with the latter of whom the older deity was then identified. A god of war and agriculture, he had his festival, the Quirinalia, celebrated on February 17. The name was given to Romulus as a surname after his deification, and was also applied to Janus and Augustus.

may Quirinus prosper the battle

QUIRITES

Quirites, a word of uncertain origin, was applied to the citizens of the body politic of Rome from earliest times, though it was restricted in use for reference to them in their civil capacities as distinct from any military ones. Suetonius says that Caesar once checked an insurrection among his troops by addressing them as Quirites. If the appellative is derived from *quiris,* the Sabine word for lance, then the name must have referred to people as citizens because they had the census privilege of bearing arms, though not actually doing so. Others claim its derivation to come from the name of the capital of the Sabine people, who left their own town of Cures to form an amalgam with the Romans.

at election time the Quirites all turn out

QUISLING

Vidkun Quisling (1887-1945), a Norwegian, in World War II played into the hands of the invading Germans for personal gain so infamously that not only in Norway but throughout the world his name from that moment became the synonym for treachery to one's country. He was sentenced to be executed for his infamy.

has the makings of a quisling

QUIXOTIC

Quixotic is from Don Quixote, chief character in Cervantes' (1547-1616) romance of that name. He is crazily tenacious of certain chivalrous and romantic ideas and pursues them through a series of ridiculous and fantastic events, all so shot through with an innate love of honor, nobility and sacrifice that the word quixotic has come to mean unselfish. Sometimes it suggests unwarranted helpfulness, generosity, and service, as well as a noble but crazy attempt to realize the impossible. "The most truly comic book of all time," in the consensus of the world, started as a burlesque of the old code of chivalry.

rejects such a quixotic proposal

R

RA

Ra was the god of the midday sun and the supreme deity worshiped at Memphis, in Egypt. Represented in the morning by Mentu, the rising sun, and in the evening by Atmu, the setting sun, he was often pictured as a hawk-headed man crowned with the solar disc and the uraeus, Egyptian serpent-symbol of divinity and the sovereignty of royalty. The son of Nut, the sky, he battled each night with the serpent Apepi, and was thought to be the progenitor of the Pharaohs.

Ra reigning with all his splendor in the heavens

RAB

Rab is the dog hero of Dr. John Brown's novel (1859) about the faithful mastiff of a Scotch carrier and his wife, who grieved so excessively over the death of his master and mistress that he had to be shot.

canine devotion like Rab's

RABELAISIAN

François Rabelais (1483-1553), celebrated French novelist, was as stupendous a figure in the world of gigantic mirth as Dante was in the world of infernal horrors or Homer in a world of heroic action. Rabelais created the most tremendous piece of foolery in the world. He drew on his apparently endless stores of absurdity and mirth, with a mind that knew no limits to its creation of such persons and situations, gross, robust, extravagant, and fantastic beyond belief, as appear in *Pantagruel* and *Gargantua*. With broad satire that is without gravity and without spleen, he races from one grotesque jest to another, a "privileged lunatic with the license of a jester."

earth-shaking Rabelaisian mirth

RACHEL

Rachel was the sister of Leah, the younger daughter of Laban, and the cousin-wife of Jacob, who served her father for seven years in order to gain her as his wife. When Leah was substituted by craft, he served another seven years to secure her (*Genesis*, xxix). Childless for a while after her marriage, she gave Jacob her maid Bilhah to be his concubine, even adopting the two offspring of the union, Dan and Naphtali. Later she bore Joseph and died in giving birth to Benjamin.

a marital prize like Rachel

RACHMANINOFF, SERGE

Serge Rachmaninoff (1873-1943), when young an admirer of Tschaikovsky, wrote his first considerable music at nineteen, and it was acclaimed throughout the world. His music suggests the spirit of Russia, the minor key of deep pathos and dark struggle with all its muffled repetitions. Gloom, intensity, depth, and a forward march, these are persistent motifs, no matter what the intervals and the interruptions. His artistry as a piano virtuoso was equally as compelling as his musical compositions.

persistent as a Rachmaninoff theme

RACINE, JEAN

Jean Racine (1639-1699) was a great French tragic dramatist with a careful, delicate and disciplined style. With unsurpassed unity of construction and elegance of diction, he says of his plays, according to one of his prefaces, that they are always "trying for a simple situation . . . which never departs from the natural into the extraordinary . . . (but) goes step by step to the end, sustained by the interest, feelings and passions of the characters." His plots are borrowed from Greek, Roman and Biblical sources, but he gives to them a naturalness that is deep and universal.

the brilliant Racine etching of character

RADEGUND

Radegund, in Spenser's *Faerie Queene,* is the Queen of the Amazons. Worsting Sir Artegal in single combat, she made him dress in woman's clothing and forced him to spin flax in token of his feminine subservience. Britomart rescued Artegal from his shame and beheaded Radegund.

a bellicose Radegund

RAFFLES

A. J. Raffles is an amateur gentleman burglar of silk-stockinged society in *The Amateur Cracksman* (1899), *Mr. Justice Raffles* (1909), and other stories by E. W. Hornung, British journalist and novelist.

thieves with the sleek aplomb of Raffles

RAGNAROK

Ragnarok is the twilight of the gods, the doomsday of the world to precede its regeneration in a golden age, in Norse mythology. Though the gods strive in vain to avert it, it is heralded by the triumph of evil and followed by a horrendous winter lasting three years, a universal deluge, and the devouring of the sun and moon by the wolves Fenrir and Managarme. Its final phase is an internecine lethal combat between the gods led by Odin and the giants and monsters led by Loki. The whole creation, mankind, giants, and gods, perish alike in a shower of fire and blood. Only Vidar and Vali, Odin's sons, survive to reconstruct the universe on an imperishable basis for Lif and Lifthraser, a human couple who repeople the world with progeny.

as cataclysmic as Ragnarok

RAHAB

Rahab is the harlot whose house is built on the walls of Jericho, in *Joshua,* ii and vi. When two spies sent out by Joshua to reconnoitre and view her land come to her, she hides them from a searching party by concealing them under stalks of flax laid out on her roof. Convinced that they and their people are on the Lord's side, she bargains with them for protection for herself, her father, and his entire family on the return of their conquering army, and lets them down by a cord through her window. They caution her to bind a line of scarlet thread in that same window as a safeguard for all under her roof at the destruction of the city, and when it finally falls, Joshua has her and all her household brought in safety to Israel.

a bargain with Rahab

RAHU

Rahu, in Hindu mythology, is the demon who causes eclipses of the sun and the moon. Stealing into heaven one day to quaff some of the nectar of immortality, he was discovered and informed against by those enemies of his, and Vishnu cut off his head. As he had already taken some of the nectar into his mouth, the head was immortal, and he ever after hunted the sun and moon, which he caught occasionally and swallowed, thereby causing eclipses. He typifies the ascending astronomical node, the tail or descending node being called Ketu. The name Rahu is derived from a verbal root meaning to "abandon" or "void," hence, also black, or darkness.

Rahu shadowing the sun

RAJPUT

Rajput designates a member of a Hindu warrior-caste claiming descent from the ancient Shatriya. Noted for their military spirit, they now number nearly 600 tribes in various parts of northern India, and give its name to Rajputana. Fine, brave men, they retain a strongly developed feudal instinct, and proud of their blood and lineage, they are extremely punctilious on all points of etiquette. The name also indicates a substantial landholder, who claims proprietary rights to the territory on which he is settled.

as arrogant and martial as a Rajput

RALEIGH

Sir Walter Raleigh (1552-1618) was an English courtier, soldier, and statesman in London, with a passion for the sea and seafaring. He was an explorer, an adventurer, a colonizer in North America, where he named Virginia for the virgin queen. Stirring, romantic, daring, able, Raleigh was the most striking figure of a striking time. And like many another famous Englishmen, despite his devotion to the Queen he was sent to the tower and beheaded. He appears in Kingsley's *Westward Ho.*

a very Raleigh for courtliness
with the amazing energy of a Raleigh

RAMESES

Rameses was the name of twelve kings of the XIXth and XXth Egyptian dynasties. The one celebrated as being the pharaoh of the oppression in *Genesis* and *Exodus* and who impressed the Israelites into forced labor gangs to build the treasure cities of Pithom and Ramses, Rameses II (1292-1225 B.C.), warred successfully against the Hittites, the daughter of whose king he triumphantly married. Elaborating the temples at Karnak and Luxor, he also built the great mortuary temple of the Rameseum with the colossal statues of himself that are familiar through innumerable reproductions. The name Rameses suggests tyrannical power and splendor.

as despotic as Rameses

RAMMAN

Ramman was the Assyro-Babylonian god of wind and storms, and was designated as "the thunderer" or "the roarer." Symbolical of retributive justice, he is called Rimmon in *2 Kings,* v, 18, in the passage concerning Elisha's permission to Naaman to bow down with his master in the deity's presence. Hence, the phrase *to bow down in the House of Rimmon* means to submit and conform to some reprehensible or immoral requirement or custom.

prostrated himself before Ramman

RAMONA

Ramona, a half-breed Indian girl, is the heroine of Helen Hunt Jackson's novel dealing with the wrongs inflicted on American Indians by the early settlers in southern California.

the Ramona of the pueblos

RAMSBOTTOM, MRS.

Mrs. Ramsbottom was the pseudonym of Theodore Edward Hook (1788-1841), British humorist, novelist, and editor of *John Bull,* a London newspaper. Under this imaginary name appeared a series of letters which, following the example of Smollett's *Winifred Jenkins,* relied for merriment on atrociously bad spelling. Their author was the original of Mr. Wagg in Thackeray's *Vanity Fair.*

as preposterous as Mrs. Ramsbottom's spelling

RAN

Ran, in old Norse mythology, is the death-deity of the sea who catches drowning men in her net and draws them into the depths. The wife of the sea-god Aegir, she bears him nine daughters who represent the boisterous surf and turbulent waves.

snatched to a watery grave by Ran

RANDOM, RODERICK

Roderick Random, the hero of Smollett's novel of the same name, is an unprincipled and adventurous Scotsman in quest of a fortune, at one time reveling in prosperity and at another plunged into destitution. Inherently mean and conspicuous for his reckless libertinism, selfishness, and revengeful mischievousness, he is on occasion lavish and humorous. Rescued from starving by his kind-hearted adherent, Strap, whose money he borrows and whose clothes he wears, he repays him by treating him as a menial servant and by beating him when the dice run against him.

an opportunist like Roderick Random

RAPHAEL

Raphael (1483-1520), one of the giants among artists, is noted especially for the complete unity of his composition, every detail of background, subject, and atmosphere being in harmonious accord, even while attention is being centered on the mysterious beauty of feature that marks his pictures. He blended the Hellenic and Christian at a time when the Hellenic was still the classic standard and the Christian was in the forefront of attention. The *Sistine Madonna* is one of his most famous paintings.

the complete Raphael-like harmony

RAPHAEL OF CATS

"Raphael of Cats" was the sobriquet given to Gottfried Mind (1768-1814), Swiss cretin painter, sketcher, and lithographer, whose interest in subjects centered on animals, especially cats, and children.

a feline proud as a model for the "Raphael of Cats"

RASIEL

Rasiel is an angel who is spoken of in the Talmud as the tutor of Adam. In Milton's *Paradise Lost* and in the Apocryphal book of Tobit he is named Raphael, however. He travels with Tobias into Media and back again, overcoming Asmodeus (*q.v.*). Milton calls him "the sociable spirit" and "the affable archangel." In the book of Enoch he is "the angel of the spirits of men."

an instructive Rasiel in teaching one how to overcome evil

RASKOLNIKOV

Raskolnikov is the protagonist of Dostoevsky's *Crime and Punishment*. He is a student who murders a pawnbroker and her daughter in order to relieve the sordid poverty of his social milieu. Though his guilt is suspected, it is never proved. He scorns his conscience as the voice of "herd morality," but in the end yields to it and achieves salvation through meekness and the spiritual purification of confession.

the gnawing conscience of a Raskolnikov

RASPUTIN, GRIGORI E.

Grigori E. Rasputin (1871-1916), Russian monk and court intriguer, had little if any formal education and to the end of his life was unable to write correctly. The son of a peasant who acquired the name of Rasputin (Russian for "debauchee"), he had the same passionate nature, magnetic power, and great physical endurance of his sire. After acquiring a wife and three children, he left them in order to consecrate himself to religion, gaining the reputation of a holy man among the peasantry and rising to a position of unhealthy influence over the czarina. The rule of his orgiastic religious philosophy was "Sin in order that you may obtain forgiveness; be united with me in soul and body, for I am elected the dispeller of darkness and evil." His baneful power and meddlesome effect on church and state politics led to his assassination by a group of Russian noblemen.

an unctuous and lecherous Rasputin

RASSELAS

Rasselas is the title-character of Samuel Johnson's philosophical romance (1759) on the theme of the vanity of human happiness. An Abyssinian prince, he is confined in Happy Valley, an earthly paradise walled in by high mountains, with his sister, Nekayah, and the poet Imlac. Resolved to escape and find the most desirable lot of humankind, he does so only to discover that all ways of life have their disadvantages and that Happy Valley is the most felicitous home for him after all. The mad astronomer, who imagines that he possesses the regulation of the weather and the distribution of the seasons, is one of the story's most original characters.

a restlessly roaming Rasselas, seeking a new type of happiness

---

RATSEY, GAMALIEL

Gamaliel Ratsey was a notorious English highwayman who masked his face on his forays and indulged in broad and rough humor. Hanged at Bedford in 1605, he is celebrated for his exploits in *Ratsey's Ghost,* a rare tract of the time.

a black silk-stocking masking his visage à la Gamaliel Ratsey

---

RATTLIN, JACK

Jack Rattlin is a celebrated naval character and a typical seaman, in Smollett's *Roderick Random.*

a swashbuckling Jack Rattlin

RAVEL, MAURICE

Maurice Ravel (1875-1937) was the French composer of distinctive, impressionistic musical pieces such as *Rhapsodie Espagnole, Daphnis and Chloe,* and *Ma Mère l'Oye* ("Mother Goose"). His music is sensuous, richly though often strangely harmonic, and melodically elusive, and his name is coupled with that of Debussy (*q.v.*) as typical of an epoch in French music. *La Valse* is a satirical musical exposition of an elegant waltz danced beneath the blaring, dazzling splendor of a great crystal chandelier. Best known of his works is perhaps his *Bolero,* written to be danced by Ida Rubenstein, a work which, unhandicapped by a purposeful monotony of thematic material, moves by insidiously pulsating Spanish rhythms through a series of repetitions of the theme and mounts gradually to a great crescendo played by full orchestra. Its great composer died of insanity shortly after its composition.

repetitious as Ravel's Bolero

RAVENSWOOD, EDGAR

Edgar Ravenswood, the hero of Scott's *Bride of Lammermoor,* is a Scotch royalist, intrepid, melancholic, haughty, and revengeful. He falls in love with Lucy Ashton (*q.v.*), daughter of Sir William Ashton, Lord-Keeper of Scotland. The lovers plight their troth at the Mermaid's Fountain, but Lucy is compelled by her mother to marry Frank Hayston, laird of Bucklaw. In a fit of insanity she attempts to murder the bridegroom and dies in convulsions. Her brother sees Edgar at the funeral of Lucy and appoints a meeting for a duel, but on his way to the site Edgar is lost in the quicksands of Kelpiesflow.

In Donizetti's opera *Lucia di Lammermoor,* Edgar is so heartbroken at Lucy's death that he immediately kills himself, that "his marriage with Lucy, forbidden on earth, may be consummated in heaven."

like Edgar Ravenswood, denied the right to love

RAZOR

Razor is an intriguing valet in Vanbrugh's *Provoked Wife.*

a sharp and scheming Razor

REASON, GODDESS OF

The Goddess of Reason was a personification of the intellectual powers which distinguish man from the rest of the animal creation, and the deification was perpetrated in 1793 by the revolutionists in France. The goddess was substituted as an object of divine worship for the saints of the Christian faith. It was decreed that the metropolitan church of Notre-Dame be converted into a Temple of Reason, and that a festival be instituted for the first day of each decade, to supersede the Catholic ceremonies of Sunday. The first festival of this sort was held with great pomp on the 10th of November. Mlle. Candeille, of the Paris Opera, was the first Goddess, but Mme. Momoro, wife of a printer, was the most celebrated. The "deity" wore a red Phrygian, or Liberty, cap, a white draped gown, an azure mantle, and tricolor ribbons. Her head was filleted with oak-leaves, and in her hand she carried the pike of Jupiter-Peuple. She sat upon an antique seat, entwined with ivy, and borne by four citizens. Young girls, dressed in white and crowned with roses, preceded and followed her. The services of the occasion consisted of speeches, processions, and patriotic hymns.

an intellectual Goddess of Reason

REBECCA THE JEWESS

Rebecca the Jewess is the actual heroine of Scott's *Ivanhoe*. She is the beautiful, modest, brave, and high-souled daughter of Isaac, a wealthy money-lender of York, and falls secretly and hopelessly in love with Ivanhoe, whom she nurses when he is wounded. At his marriage to Rowena, she departs from England to seek consolation and peace with her kindred in Grenada.

a love-affair as hopeless as Rebecca's

REBECCAITE

A Rebeccaite was a member of the band of Welsh rioters who, exasperated by the heavy and vexatious tolls to which they were subjected, undertook in 1843 to demolish the gates and toll-houses on the turnpikes in the rural districts of Pembrokeshire and Caermarthenshire. In that and the following year they committed various other excesses throughout the mining and manufacturing districts of the principality. Their name was derived from an odd and preposterous interpretation of the following passage in *Genesis* xxiv, 60: "And they blessed Rebekah, and said unto her, . . . let thy seed possess the gate of those which hate them."

The captain called himself Rebecca and dressed in female apparel, as did his bodyguard, who were addressed as his daughters. Their marches and attacks were always made by night. The insurrection was ultimately suppressed by the police and the military.

a secret society like the Rebeccaites

REBEKAH

Rebekah, the sister of Laban, is pictured idyllically in *Genesis* (xxii, xxiv) for her beauty, hospitableness, and generosity. When the servant of Abraham is seeking a bride for his master's son, Isaac, he finds her drawing water from a well and, in accord with a vow he had to choose as bride-to-be the one who would grant him a drink for himself and his camels, he requests that she permit him and his beasts to refresh themselves from her well. When she courteously complies, he makes suit in Isaac's name and gains Rebekah.

Later her character is portrayed less attractively, when she exhibits partiality toward Jacob, one of the two sons she bore Isaac, preferring him to Esau, his brother, teaching him to deceive his blind father and assisting him in his subsequent flight to her brother Laban for refuge.

gracious as Rebekah at the well

RECAMIER, MME.

Mme. Jeanne Françoise Recamier (1777-1849) was a glamorous French society beauty and wit whose salon attracted notables of literary and political celebrity during the Consulate and the Empire. Exiled from Paris by Napoleon because of suspicion of disaffection with the government, she was a close friend of Chateaubriand throughout her mature life. Her *Souvenirs et Correspondance* afford an intimate view of the famous people of her day.

with the esprit of Mme. Recamier

RED CROSS KNIGHT

The Red Cross Knight, in Spenser's *Faerie Queene,* is St. George, the patron saint of England, and typifies, in teh obvious interpretation, Holiness, of the perfection of the spiritual man in religion. In a narrower political sense, his adventures are intended to shadow forth the history of the Church of England. The fairy queen sends him out to be the champion of Una (Truth) by slaying the dragon which has been ravaging her father's kingdom. Having achieved this feat, he marries Una and departs to engage in other adventures assigned him by the fairy queen.

like the Red Cross Knight, urging his way to escort Truth to her home

---

REDGAUNTLET, SIR EDWARD HUGH

Sir Edward Redgauntlet, in Scott's novel titled after the family name, is a Jacobite conspirator who favors the young Pretender to the throne, Charles Edward, and scruples at no means of upholding his cause. He is represented as possessing the power of contorting his brow into a terrific frown, which makes distinctly visible the figure of a horseshoe, the fatal mark of his race. This political enthusiast and fanatic accompanies the Pretender into exile and retires to a monastery in France.

a frown as ominous as Redgauntlet's

REDLAW, MR.

Mr. Redlaw is the title character in Dickens' *The Haunted Man.* A professor of chemistry in an ancient college, he bargains with the spectre that haunts him to leave him, with the stipulation that, wherever he go, he should give again "the gift of forgetfulness" bestowed on him by the spectre. From that moment on the chemist carries in his touch the infection of sullenness, selfishness, discontent, and ingratitude. On Christmas day, however, the infection ceases, and all those who have suffered by it are restored to love and gratitude.

a gift, like Mr. Redlaw's, for forgetting

RED MAN

Red Man, or *Homme Rouge,* in the popular superstition of Brittany, France, is the demon of tempests. He commands the elements and precipitates into the waves the voyager who seeks to molest him in the solitude which he loves. There was a prevalent belief in France that a mysterious Red Man appeared to Napoleon, and foretold his reverses.

The name is also given to the American Indian beacuse of the copper color of his skin.

a tempest that must have been raised by the Homme Rouge

RED RIDINGHOOD

(see *Little Red Ridinghood*)

REED, WALTER

Walter Reed (1851-1902), American army surgeon and curator of the Army Medical Museum, in 1900 was appointed head of the commission to investi-

…iend or foe. Though Isengrin often …es him to the direst straits, Rey… generally outwits him in the end.

…unning as Reynard

…DAMANTHINE

…amanthine is from Rhadaman… a Greek judge in mythology so …d for his severe and immovable …ice that it is said that after his …th he was made one of the judges … the lower world.

inexorable Rhadamanthine justice
Rhadamanthine voice of the past

RHAMPSINITUS

Rhampsinitus was the Egyptian Pharaoh (Rameses III, as he has been identified) who built a treasury into which he stored and sealed an immense cache of riches. The architect had artfully left a movable stone in the structure, however, and through this aperture his sons proceeded to pilfer from the treasure in regular visits. When the king inspected his wealth and noticed its diminution, he set a trap in which one of the architect's sons was caught. To preserve their secret and their father's honor, the sons agreed that the free one should cut off the other's head and carry it away before Rhampsinitus should come to see what his trap had caught. The story is told in Herodotus.

as frustrated in his plan to catch the thief as Rhampsinitus

RHEA

Rhea, an ancient Greek earth-goddess, was known under a variety of names throughout Asia Minor, the most common being Cybele and "Mother of the Gods." Her worship had a wild and orgiastic character, and the Corybantes were her enthusiastic priests, who, with drums, cymbals, horns, and in full armor, performed their frenzied dances in the forests of Phrygia. In Rome the Galli (*q.v*) were her priests, and the lion was regarded as sacred to her. Symbolizing the creative annual revival of nature in the springtime, she was reputed to be the protector of agriculture and the arts of life.

revered with frenzy fit for Rhea

RHEA SILVIA

Rhea Silvia, or Ilia as she is sometimes called, was the daughter of Numitor, in Roman mythology. Forced to become a Vestal Virgin by her usurping uncle Amulius, who wished to retain his right to power by making her officially incapable of bearing issue, she was violated by Mars and became the mother of Romulus and Remus. In a fury over her defection from the chastity he had enjoined on her, Amulius had her cast into the Tiber river, the god of which took her to be his immortal wife.

unwilling chastity like that of Rhea Silvia

RHEINGOLD

The Rheingold, in Richard Wagner's version of the Germanic myth, is a treasure snatched from the river Rhine by the dwarf Alberich, who renounces love in order that he may create from the gold a ring that will make him all-powerful. Robbed of it by Wotan, he puts a curse on it, making it the instrument of death and disaster for all who possess it. To ransom Freia, Wotan subsequently gives it to the giants, and Fafner the dragon guards it in the forest. Siegfried slays him and gives the ring to Brunnehilde. When she immolates herself on the hero's funeral pyre, love removes the curse from this object of dissension and greed, and the ring is returned to the custody of the Rhine-maidens.

as coveted as the Rheingold

RHESUS

Rhesus, son of the Muse Terpsichore, was a warlike king of Thrace who marched to the assistance of Priam when the Greeks began their assault on Troy. There was a prophecy that the city would never be taken if the snow-white horses of Rhesus should once drink of the water of the river Xanthus and graze on the Trojan plains. To avert its fulfillment, Diomedes and Ulysses kill the Trojan guard, Dolon, having first learned from him the password to his camp. Then they slay Rhesus on his first night in the Trojan camp and lead away his horses.

inadequate protection, like that given to Troy by Rhesus's steeds

---

RHIPAEI MONTES

The Rhipaei Montes, or Rhipaean Mountains, constituted a range of forests supposed by the ancient Greeks to be located at and mark the northernmost extremity of the earth, though there are various statements as to the exact position of the lofty chain. The name seems to have been given quite indefinitely to all the mountains in the northern parts of Europe and Asia. Thus, they are sometimes identified with the Hyperborean hills. Late geographical writers place the Rhipaeans on the frontiers of Asiatic Sarmatia, and state that the river Tanais (Don) rises in them. According to this, they may be regarded as a western branch of the Ural Mountains.

as remote as the Rhipaeans

RHODES, CECIL

A Rhodes Scholar is a man of such superior attainments that he is selected from his region to receive one of the scholarships for Oxford set up by Cecil Rhodes (1853-1902), an Englishman who went to Africa for his health, amassed a fortune in diamonds, and became a South African statesman. The scholarships are open to 100 candidates annually from the British dominions; 96 from the United States, four annually to each of the eight regions of six states each; six, two annual[l] students of Germany. To be a R[hodes] scholar, therefore, indicates super[ior at]tainments and superior charact[er.]

a born Rhodes scholar — h[is] parents' dream

RHODOPE

Rhodope, a celebrated Greek cou[rtesan] famous for her beauty, was at one [time] enslaved, but rescued from her sla[very] by the poet Sappho's brother who [fell] in love with her. In rage, Sappho a[t]tacked Rhodope in her poetry, succeeding only in making her name and fame immortal.

the infamous fame of a Rhodope

RHOECUS

Rhoecus, in Greek mythology, was the name of a handsome youth whom the Dryad of an oaktree rewarded with her love when he had saved the tree from falling by ordering his servants to prop it up, thereafter asking for her charms as payment for his forethought. She adjured him to be faithful and constant in love, and sent a bee as emissary to remind him of the occasions for meeting her in their frequent rendezvous. One day he impatiently drove the bee away, because he was more interested in the game of dice that he was engaged in playing. The Dryad then avenged her wounded pride by making him blind.

Rhoecus was also the name of the Samian architect and sculptor, who, around 640 B.C., invented the art of casting statues in bronze and iron.

tasting like Rhoecus the vengeance of a woman scorned

RIALTO

Rialto (from the Italian *rivo alto*, "deep stream") is the name of the ancient commercial quarter of the city of Venice, containing warehouses and places of business. The name was also given to the marble bridge spanning the Grand Canal and connecting this quarter with the island of San Marco. Since this bridge was lined with shops and traders' booths, the term denotes any mart, bazaar, or place of exchange. In theatrical parlance, Rialto refers to the section of Broadway habituated by actors and containing the offices of theatrical managers and agents.

teeming as the Rialto at noon

RICHARD THE LION-HEARTED

Richard the Lion-Hearted (1157-1199) was the central figure among the Christian monarchs of the Crusades, for which he raised money by robbing the Jews, selling offices and royal lands — "I would sell London could I find a purchaser." His adventures were romantic beyond pen to describe, and have been made the theme of many a story, Scott's *The Talisman* chief among them. His enemies fought him and admired him; Saladin sent him choice foods when he lay sick; Mohammed sent a wonderful Arabian steed when his horse had been killed. He was daring, energetic, enthusiastic, ruthless.

stern as Richard in Bosworth Field
an admired but formidable Richard

RICHELIEU

Richelieu (1585-1642), Cardinal and Prime Minister under Louis XIII, one of the most remarkable figures of the seventeenth century, was virtually sovereign of France and swayed the destiny of all Europe. Master of diplomacy and intrigue, he trampled out the independence of the old feudal aristocracy to make the king supreme in France, and crushed the power of Austria and Spain to make France supreme in Europe, relentlessly pursuing these two purposes through diplomacy, intrigue and war. Sir Henry Irving got much of his fame on the stage by playing the part of Richelieu in the famous play of that name.

with brilliant Richelieu strategy

RIDD, JOHN

John Ridd, the hero of Blackmore's novel *Lorna Doone*, is a brave and sturdy farmer who rescues the title character from the band of outlaws who had kidnaped her in infancy. Later knighted, he marries her.

a rescuer as gallant as John Ridd

RIENZI

Rienzi (1313-1354), talented Roman orator and tribune, rose from the ranks, led a revolt against the barons who were robbing and outraging citizens, and was made tribune. His success went to his head and he was driven from Rome by the people, only to be returned seven years later by papal decree. He ruled well, but was killed in a tumult fostered by the barons. His two short periods of power were spectacular, and have been made glamorous by Byron in *Childe Harold,* by Bulwer-Lytton in a novel, *Rienzi,* and by Wagner in his opera of that name.

a tragic Rienzi, the last of the tribunes

RIFFIAN

Riffian refers to the belligerent and fanatical nature of the Riffs, the Berber inhabitants of the north Moroccan coastal hills.

with Riffian fanaticism

RIGOLETTO

Rigoletto is the hunchback jester and favorite of the Duke of Mantua, in Verdi's opera named after him and based on Victor Hugo's *Le Roi S' Amuse*. The father of the beautiful Gilda, he is forced to submit to her rape by the sleek and lecherous Duke, and then prevented from carrying out his vengeance by his daughter, who substitutes her own life for that of his intended victim.

a doubly betrayed Rigoletto

RIMA

Rima is the "bird girl" heroine of W. H. Hudson's *Green Mansions*. A primitive and shy creature, she lives in the woods and understands the language of its feathered inhabitants.

a timid Rima, the friend of birds

RIMSKI-KORSAKOV

Nikolai Rimski-Korsakov (1844-1908) was one of Russia's greatest nationalistic composers and one of the famous "Five" of musical history in that country, his colleagues being Cui, Borodin, Balakirev, and Moussorgsky. Despising Tschaikovsky for being too "Western" in his art, Korsakov concentrated seductive Slavic and Asiatic barbarity of tonal effect, broken rhythms, and subtle sensuality in his glittering orchestrations which mark him as one of the greatest technicians with the symphony orchestra. *Scheherezade* and *Le Coq d'Or* are among his most popular works.

the perfect tonal clarity of a Rimski-Korsakov orchestration

RINALDO

Rinaldo, a famous warrior and one of the most renowned of Charlemagne's paladins, in Tasso's *Jerusalem Delivered*, is violent and headstrong, but gallant, ingenuous, and generous as well. In a raptus of rage he kills Charlemagne's nephew, Bertholet, with a chess-board, and is banished and outlawed in punishment. After various adventures he departs for exploits in the Holy Land and makes peace with the emperor on his return. Angelica, the lovely infidel princess for whom kings and nations are warring, is madly in love with Rinaldo, who, however, spurns her and leaves her to deplore her unrequited love.

We stare at a dragoon who has killed three French cuirassiers as a prodigy; yet we read, without the least disgust, how Rinaldo slew his ten thousands

Macaulay

RINDE

Rinde, or Rind, is one of Odin's wives and the mother of Vale in Scandinavian mythology. She represents the frozen surface of the earth when it is crusted and covered by snowflakes.

a perilous footing on Rinde

RIQUET

Riquet with the Tuft, in French fable, was a prince of surpassing ugliness but of great wit and good sense. A fairy bestowed on him the power of communicating these gifts to the person he should love best. Enamored of a very beautiful but excessively stupid and vapid princess, he made her clever and intelligent by the exercise of his power. She, in return and by virtue of a similar power invested in her by the same fairy, made him become the handsomest man in the world.

a transformation as complete as Riquet's

RISHI

A Rishi, in sacred Hindu literature, is a poet or singer of sacred songs. There were seven Rishis, all born of Brahma's brain. Holy men, inspired seers, and hearers of eternal voices, they were regarded as sages of especial wisdom and influence among all peoples, and at their death they were transported to the heavens to become the constellation known as Ursa Major.

pours forth his inspired oracles like a Rishi

ROBBIA, DELLA

Luca della Robbia (1400-1482) was the Florentine goldsmith and sculptor who established an atelier unique for its artistic craftsmanship with terra cotta medallions of bambini. His nephew and pupil, Andrea (1437-1528), and the latter's two sons perpetuated the technique of Robbia ware with their enameled and brightly colored relief sculptures, adorned with characteristic wreaths of brilliantly hued fruit and flowers. Decorative tiles for pavements and bathrooms also were produced in their workrooms.

an imitation plaque of a Della Robbia

ROBERT THE DEVIL

Robert the Devil, hero of a thirteenth century French romance, was given over to the Devil before birth and ran an unparalleled career of cruelties and crime till he was miraculously reclaimed and did seven years' penance in Rome in the guise of a fool and a dumb person, living among the dogs and wearing mean clothes. Commanded by an angel to fight the Saracens, he defeated them but refused the hand of the king's daughter, retiring to the forests to die a holy death. In Normandy it is thought that his wandering ghost is doomed to expiate his crimes until the day of judgment. A paraphrased account of the story furnished the libretto for Meyerbeer's opera of the same name. The name was popularly given to Robert Damiens (1714-1775) for his attempt to assassinate Louis XV.

unending penance, like Robert the Devil's

ROBESPIERRE

Maximilien Robespierre (1758-1794). one of the terrible triumvirate, Danton, Marat, and Robespierre, of the French Reign of Terror, was cruel, ruthless, and personally responsible for some of the worst of the decrees of the period. After the most incredible atrocities, he was himself denounced and guillotined.

a fated Robespierre

ROBIGUS

Robigus was the Roman god who averted blight, red mildew, and excessive heat from the newly planted fields. At his festival, the Robigalia, celebrated on April 25, a procession was held in his honor and a red dog was sacrificed to the god. The English word *rubiginous,* meaning rust-colored or affected with rust, is derived from his name.

implored Robigus to protect his crops

ROBIN AND MAKYNE

Robin and Makyne are the hero and heroine of an old Scottish pastoral. Robin is a shepherd for whom Makyne languishes in love, but when she goes to him to declare her passion he turns a deaf ear to the damsel who goes home to weep. Later the tables are turned, and Robin goes to Makyne to plead for her heart and hand. She, disillusioned and angry, replies, "The man that will not when he may shall have not when he would."

a love as unrequited as that of Robin and Makyne

ROBINSON, JACK

Jack Robinson was a folklore person appearing in old tales. Always called to the rescue in an emergency, he is now known only in the phrase, "before you can say Jack Robinson," meaning before one could call for help; hence, quick, swift, instantaneous.

no convenient Jack Robinson appeared

ROBOTIAN

Robotian refers to the nature of a Robot (derived from the Polish word *robota*, "work"), one of a class of grotesque creatures in Karel Capek's fantastic melodrama *Rossom's Universal Robots* (R.U.R., 1921). Artificially manufactured automatons that perform all hard work, these brutal and insensitive beings are as totally devoid of sensibility as machine-made bulldozers run off the assembly lines in groups of thousands. Hence, the word Robotian may be used to describe any mechanical and uninspired creation that is without spirit or soul, or anything that is done in a perfunctory way.

with demoniac Robotian energy

ROB ROY

Rob Roy was the pseudonym popularly given to a celebrated Highland freebooter, the Robin Hood of Scotland, Robert Macgregor (1671-1734). Because of the outlawry of his clan by the Scottish parliament in 1662, he assumed the name of Campbell. He engaged in cattle-rustling and demanded tribute for protection against thieves in the hills east of Loch Lomond, terrain that is still spoken of as the Rob Roy country. Arrested and sentenced to exile, he was pardoned in 1727. He is the hero of Sir Walter Scott's novel named after him, and in its introduction the author gives details of the outlaw's life.

the protection-money racket à la Rob Roy

ROBSART, AMY

Amy Robsart, in Scott's *Kenilworth,* a trusting girl secretly married to the Earl of Leicester, was kept prisoner at Cumnor Hall, Oxfordshire, lest the marriage should hinder her husband's advancement at court. She escaped and went to Kenilworth, his ancestral hall, to get herself acknowledged, but was despatched back to Cumnor and murdered. In real life, Amy Robsart (1532-1560) married Robert Dudley, courtier and favorite of Queen Elizabeth. She was found dead at the foot of a staircase, probably a suicide.

a beautiful Amy Robsart to be his secret wife

ROCH, SAINT

Saint Roch was an early fourteenth century patron invoked in times of pestilence. He devoted his life to those afflicted with the plague. Depicted in a pilgrim's habit, lifting his robe to display a plague-spot on his thigh, he is accompanied by an angel who is applying his healing touch to the sore. Sometimes he is escorted by a dog, bringing bread in his mouth, in allusion to the legend that a hound brought him food daily while he was perishing in a forest of pestilence. From this, the expression *St. Roch and his dog* has come to mean a pair of inseparable friends. The good Saint's festival day, August 16th, was formerly celebrated in England as a general harvest-home.

the St. Roch of the epidemic

ROCHESTER, MR.

Edward Fairfax Rochester is the passionate and self-willed employer of the governess-heroine of Charlotte Brontë's novel *Jane Eyre.* Prevented from openly loving Jane by an insane wife closeted in his home, he is blinded and crippled in an attempt to rescue the madwoman from the burning house which she herself had fired. Freed at last to live a happy life, he marries Jane.

cursed like Mr. Rochester by a skeleton-in-the-closet

ROCINANTE

Rocinante, Don Quixote's charger in Cervantes' novel *Don Quixote,* was a nag chiefly skin and bone, lean, scraggy, and full of blemishes. But it was dear to the heart of the hero and good enough to carry him head-on into his romantic and crazy adventures.

charges his Rocinante-Ford into any obstacle

ROCKEFELLER

John D. Rockefeller, one of the world's extremely wealthy men and a philanthropist, established in 1913 the Rockefeller Foundation, "to promote the well-being of mankind throughout the world." He specified that the money should be used through charitable, educational, and religious agencies. Later he established The Rockefeller Institute for Medical Research and a general Rockefeller Foundation.

as liberal with his dimes as John D.

RODERIGO

Roderigo is a Venetian gentleman in Shakespeare's *Othello*. He had been in love with Desdemona, and when she eloped with his rival conceived a violent hatred of the noble Moor. Taking advantage of this temper for his own ends, Iago told his dupe that Othello would change and advised him to "put money in thy purse." And the burden of his counsel always ends on these words.

as easily deceived as Roderigo

RODILARDUS

Rodilardus is the name of the huge cat that attacked and scared Panurge in Rabelais' *Pantagruel*. From a Latin multiple base, it means "gnaw-bacon."

a Rodilardus of a tomcat

RODINESQUE

Rodinesque refers to the strength and massiveness of physique found in the sculptured figures of François Rodin (1840-1917), leading French exponent of the modern naturalistic school of sculpture. The vigorous and heavy, though graceful, masculinity of his *Penseur* (The Thinker) is characteristic of his art ideal. *The Bronze Age* was so unusual a departure in the field of art that it raised a storm of criticism. *St. John the Baptist* and *The Kiss*, depicting the illicit embrace of Paolo and Francesca da Rimini (*q.v.*), are among his finest Romantic conceptions, though in genre subjects such as the *Man with a Broken Nose* and the *Aged Courtesan* he exhibits the realism of the Hellenistic school. His most ambitious work, *The Portal of Hell*, a composition six meters in height, required twenty years in completion.

a Rodinesque bulk and grace

RODOMONTADE

Rodomontade is from Rodomont, a brave, fierce, but boasting and swaggering Saracen lover in Ariosto's *Orlando Furioso*. He was vain and bragging. A rodomontade is any speech or statement extolling one's own achievements unduly.

his dinner-table rodomontade finished

ROE, RICHARD

Richard Roe is a fictitious name used as routine for that of a party, usually the defendant, in any legal transaction when the actual name is either not known or is for some reason being withheld. It is commonly used instead of a name in form papers to indicate the space in which an actual defendant's name is to be written. The plaintiff is, of course, John Doe.

here, sirs, without doubt, is the Richard Roe of the case

seems to me a potential Richard Roe

ROENTGEN, WILHELM

Wilhelm Roentgen (1845-1923) was the famous German physicist who discovered X-rays and was awarded the Nobel prize for his researches in 1901. In his honor, the study and use of X-ray in diagnosis and treatment of disease is known as Roentgenology.

eyes as penetrating as Roentgen's rays

ROGERS, WILL

Will Rogers (1879-1935) was a humorous, far-seeing, sensible American, whose broad wisdom saw the American picture as a whole, with its virtues and its vices, its needs and its best courses. He expressed what he felt about it all in a wise, drawling, keen commentary in the vernacular of the people. "My ancestors did not come over in the Mayflower. They went down to meet it," illustrates his pungent way of stating a fact. His practical sense concerning political situations, usually expressed in a single sentence and boxed in the press, was syndicated and reached practically the whole of the reading public, so that his death was a serious loss to America.

the genuine Will-Rogers-wit

ROGET, PETER MARK

Peter Mark Roget (1779-1869), English physician, inventor, scholar, and author who aided in establishing the University of London, is best known for his *Thesaurus of English Words and Phrases,* which passed its twenty-eighth edition during his lifetime. This indispensable manual for writers, enabling them to find effective synonyms, is one of the standard works on English vocabulary and has made of its own author's name a synonym for careful vocabulary and choice diction.

word-conscious as Roget

ROIS FAINEANTS, LES

Les Rois Fainéants, or "the do-nothing kings" of France, were Clovis II and the Merovingian successors of Dagobert I, who were little more than figure-heads. Hence, the name *fainéant* denotes a person of ineptitude and weakness of character, an inefficient, lazy, and useless idler and dawdler.

more incompetent than all the Rois Fainéants

ROISTER DOISTER, RALPH

Ralph Roister Doister is the title-character of the earliest known English comedy, written by Nicholas Udall and printed in 1566. A blustering, swaggering soldier (resembling Plautus's *Miles Gloriosus*), he has a sycophantic parasite to flatter him into imagining that every woman he sees is in love with him. A note he sends to one of his ladies fair was intended to read:

"Sweet mistress, whereas I love you (nothing at all regarding your substance and richness) chief of all
For your personage, beauty, demeanor and wit."

But the emissary entrusted with reading it to the lady in question changed the punctuation and inflection of its oral delivery to create this gem of double sense:

"Sweet mistress, whereas I love you nothing at all,
Regarding your substance and richness chief of all."

In the final scene Roister Doister is made to reveal himself the arrant coward he really is, when the male slaves whom he thinks to be routing him are really maidservants with mops and pails.

conceited and posturing like Ralph Roister Doister

ROLAND

Roland was a renowned paladin whose romantic adventures were the basis of many of the songs and tales of the troubadours of Northern France. His final adventure records his being hemmed into a mountain pass in A.D. 778 and set upon by wild mountaineers who destroyed him and his men before Charlemagne could reach him with aid. There were no written accounts; therefore popular imagination seized upon the story, as the English did the story of Robin Hood, and built up many legends of heroism and chivalry, especially the *Song of Roland,* of universal fame.

a Roland's pride and courage

ROLANDE, CHILDE

Childe Rolande appears in Browning's poem, *Childe Rolande to the Dark Tower Came,* inspired by a line from *King Lear.* According to the fragment of story available, the Childe had been sent to Elfland to "bring back his faire sister Helen," and from this slender suggestion imagination has had to build whatever story has been since told; hence, mysterious, romantic, appealing, fanciful.

a far-fetched Childe Rolande conception

ROLFE, JOHN

John Rolfe (1585-1622) was the English émigré and colonist at Jamestown, Virginia, who discovered a method of curing tobacco, made it an article of export, and laid the foundation of Virginia's trade and prosperity. He is better known for his romantic marriage to Pocahontas in 1614, thus stabilizing relations between the Indians and white settlers, though he was probably killed by the aborigines in 1622.

the insidious effects of Rolfe's weed

ROMANY

Romany is the name for a gypsy, a rover, hence, anything suggestiong the gypsies. The name originally meant a roving person of low caste, usually a lover of music. Konrad Bercowitz revived an interest by his magazine stories, and the name Romany appears in song and story more and more frequently, with an air of happy, free, untrammeled, gypsy life, with all the free and passionate currents of life running deep.

the Romany road of love and freedom

ROMEO

Romeo, the lover in Shakespeare's *Romeo and Juliet,* is a Montagu while Juliet is a Capulet, and the two families were at enmity with each other. When Romeo and Juliet fell in love, the family situation imposed secrecy and finally brought about a situation that ended in the tragic death of both. Meantime Romeo's love was so deep, so passionate, so tender and graceful in expression, so utterly young, that Romeo has become the name for such lovers the world over.

a yearning Romeo

ROMOLA

Romola, the title-character of George Eliot's novel, is the beautiful and high-minded daughter of an aged Florentine scholar of the fifteenth century. After an unhappy marriage to the hedonistic Tito Melema, a Greek distinguished for his handsome appearance and his great learning, she finds peace and relief from her morally weak husband by coming under the influence of Savonarola and by living a life of faith and service in nursing the plague-stricken.

an altruistic Romola to the sick

ROMULUS AND REMUS

Romulus and Remus were twin grandsons of Numitor, and the sons of Mars and Rhea Silvia, Numitor's daughter. Numitor had been king of Alba but was deposed by his wicked brother, Amulius, and the twins were exposed for death. They were, however, rescued by Faustulus, a royal herdsman, and raised by him and his wife, Acca Larentia. Livy assumes the origin of the wolf-suckling tale (Latin, *lupus*) to arise from the fact that Acca Larentia was called *Lupa* (Latin for "prostitute") because of her easy-going ways with other men. In any case, in B.C. 753 Romulus founded Rome and killed Remus for deriding and jumping over his walls. As sole king he invited slaves, exiles, and fugitives from justice elsewhere in Italy to populate his city, and furnished them with wives by abducting the neighboring Sabine maidens while they were attending a public festival in Rome. This historic Rape of the Sabine Women occasioned a war with the Sabines that was terminated only by the intervention of the abducted maidens themselves. Legend says that Romulus was carried to heaven in a thunderstorm as he was reviewing his troops in the Campus Martius, but there was another (more probable) rumor that he was torn to pieces by his councillors for his despotic ways.

brotherly as Romulus and Remus

RON

Ron was the name of King Arthur's invincible and unerring spear. Fashioned of ebony, it was "long and broad and well contrived for slaughter."

the ranks fell as though massacred by Ron

ROSALIA, SANTA

Saint Rosalia, or Rosalie, was a native of Palermo, Sicily, who died around 1160. The niece of King William II of the island, she was carried by angels to an inaccessible mountain, where she lived for many years as a hermit on Monte Pelegrino (Pilgrim Mountain). She is said to have worn away a part of the rock with her knees in her constant devotions. If anyone doubts the credibility of the statement, he is shown an extant depression in the stone, and a chapel with a marble statue to commemorate the event has been built there. In Christian art, Saint Rosalie is depicted in her cave with a cross and a skull, or in the act of receiving a rosary and a chaplet of roses from the Virgin.

knees as indefatigable as Saint Rosalie's

ROSALIND

Rosalind is the vivacious and witty daughter of the banished duke in Shakespeare's *As You Like It*. When she is forbidden by her uncle Frederick, the usurper, to marry her lover, Orlando, she and her cousin Celia flee to the forest of Arden, Rosalind assuming male attire for safety and calling herself Ganymede, thereby posing as the brother of Celia. The latter has donned the guise of a peasant girl and renamed herself Aliena. Yet even through her cross-dressing Rosalind appears with charming womanly tenderness and delicacy that is essentially feminine. She marries Orlando, and Celia falls in love with his brother Oliver.

an alluring Rosalind in slacks

ROSCIUS

Quintus Roscius was the Roman comic actor whose histrionic ability was so highly esteemed by his countrymen that it became the fashion to call anyone distinguished for Thespian talent by the name of Roscius. His art procured him the favor of many of Rome's aristocracy, including the dictator Sulla who presented him with a gold ring, the symbol of equestrian rank. He also enjoyed the friendship of the orator Cicero, who spoke of him in terms of affection and admiration. Having realized an immense fortune, he died in 62 B.C.

the Roscius of the American stage

ROSEMARY

Rosemary, the evergreen shrub of the mint family, with pungent leaves and refreshing perfume, is derived from the Latin *ros marinum* for "sea dew." Both Venus, the love-goddess, and Rosemary were offspring of the sea, and so both were thought to be useful in love-making. The name, as well as the shrub, connotes remembrance, as when Ophelia in *Hamlet* says, "There's rosemary, that's for remembrance." According to tradition, the herb was believed to strengthen the memory. In the language of flowers, the name means "fidelity in love."

as constant in love as Rosemary

ROSENCRANTZ AND GUILDENSTERN

Rosencrantz and Guildenstern are time-serving courtiers in Shakespeare's *Hamlet*. Sycophants and spies, they offer their services for all jobs, and are willing to be hired to betray anyone and to do any "genteel" hard or dirty work to please the king. The latter sets them to lure Hamlet to his death.

a team as nefarious as that of Rosencrantz and Guildenstern

49, "The die is cast!" and in the following Civil War he became the master of Italy. "Crossing the Rubicon" means any significant step openly taken that marks an irrevocable and vital change.

as ominous as Caesar's step across the Rubicon
peace lies this side the Rubicon

RUDGE, BARNABY

Barnaby Rudge, hero of Dickens' novel of the same name, is a half-witted young man who keeps a talking, evil-looking raven as a companion. Accidentally involved in the Gordon No-Popery riots, he is apprehended, condemned to death, but pardoned.

There comes Poe with his raven, like Barnaby Rudge,
Three fifths of him genius and two fifths sheer fudge.
Lowell

RUDOLPH OF MAYERLING

Rudolph of Hapsburg (1858-1889) was the Austrian Archduke and only son of Emperor Franz Joseph. Patron of the arts and husband of Princess Stephanie of Belgium, he is now remembered chiefly for his amour with the Baroness Marie Vetsera, a romantic interlude with a mysterious and tragic dénouement, for in January of 1889 the bodies of Rudolph and the Baroness were found in the royal hunting lodge of Mayerling, outside of Vienna. Though official murder to hush up the scandal was suspected, the terse imperial announcement of the tragedy termed it a suicide compact, and all investigation was forthwith suppressed.

a rendezvous as illicit as Rudolph's in Mayerling

RUDRA

Rudra, in the Rig-Vedic sacred literature of the ancient Hindus, is the lord of the Maruts, or storm-gods. Himself the chief god of storms and fire, he could also cause or cure disease. In later literature he was merged with Siva.

Rudra riding the storm-clouds

RUGGIERO

Ruggiero is a young Saracen knight in Ariosto's *Orlando Furioso*. Nursed by a lioness on the death of his mother, he is brought up by Atlantes, a magician, who gives him a hippogriff, or winged horse, and a veiled shield, the dazzling splendor of which causes everybody who sees it to quail and go blind. After winning too cheap a victory by its accidental exposure, he throws it into a well. He deserts the Saracen army for Charlemagne's, is Christianized, and after numerous adventures and narrow escapes marries Charlemagne's niece, Bradamante.

as radiant as Ruggiero's shield

RUMINA

Rumina was the Roman goddess-protector of nursing mothers who safeguarded them as they suckled their young. Her sanctuary stood at the foot of the Palatine hill in a spot called the *ficus ruminalis*, the "fig tree" beneath which legend said that Romulus and Remus had been suckled by the wolf.

invoked Rumina to keep her supplied with milk

RUMPLESTILZCHEN

Rumplestilzchen, an evil dwarf in a German nursery tale, spins straw into gold for a beautiful miller's daughter who had the impossible task enjoined on her by the king she subsequently marries. The dwarf had, however, put her under promise to give him her first child as reward for his services, and when as queen she delivers her first-born, Rumplestilzchen appears to claim his due. Her grief and despair are so great that he tells her that she may keep her child if she can find out his name in three days. Convinced that she will never think up a name as outlandish as his own, he is overheard by one of her messengers as he is exulting in the remote place in which he lives. When the queen identifies him correctly, his chagrin and rage are so intense that he destroys himself on the spot.

raging like Rumplestilzchen in his frustration.

RUPRECHT, PRINZ

Prinz Ruprecht was formerly, in some villages of northern Germany, a personage clad in high boots, white robe, mask, and enormous flaxen wig who at Christmas time received from parents the presents designed for their children. He then went about from house to house to deliver them. Everyone received him with great welcome and hospitality, and like St. Nicholas he was supposed to exercise a secret supervision over children, keeping watch especially over naughty ones and chastising them.

another Ruprecht of a hobgoblin

RUSKIN, JOHN

John Ruskin (1819-1900) was first a writer concerning beauty and art, using a prose that had the beauty and color of poetry in *The Stones of Venice, The Seven Lamps of Architecture,* and *Of Queen's Gardens.* Later he became a reformer, believing that only a happy, healthy people can either appreciate or produce true art. Thus, he turned his attention to the social and economic principles that would make England happy and healthy, and wrote in a starkly simple prose *Fors Clavigera,* letters to workingmen. Hence, his name suggests both young, enthusiastic love of beauty, and stern economic thinking.

poetic as Ruskin's prose

RUSTAM

Rustam, the Persian Hercules and subject of the national epic *Shah-Nameh,* was revered for his victory over the white dragon named Asdeev. The miraculous exploits attributed to him even in his childhood must have been the aggregate of feats performed by several people of the same name. Matthew Arnold's poem *Sohrab and Rustam* tells of the tragic mistake of his old age, when in single-handed combat he slew Sohrab, his own son, whose birth had been concealed from him by the boy's mother.

a Rustam at conflict with his own son

RUTH

Ruth is the Moabitess and widowed daughter-in-law of Naomi (*q.v.*), in the Old Testament book bearing her name. An emblem of faithful devotion and filial love, she clung to Naomi in time of famine and left her own people to follow her to Bethlehem, where she eventually married her marital kinsman, Boaz, becoming by him the father of Obed and a revered ancestress of the house of David. She is remembered for her unselfish words of comfort to Naomi, when the latter entreated her to go her own way and leave her: "Whither thou goest, I will go; and where thou lodgest, I will lodge; thy people shall be my people, and thy Lord my Lord; where thou diest, will I die; and there will I be buried."

a daughter-in-law as devoted as Ruth

RUY BLAS

Ruy Blas, in Victor Hugo's drama of the same name, is a Spanish valet and the lover of the queen. After having killed his master for threatening to expose the queen's illicit infatuation, he poisons himself to save her honor.

another Ruy Blas at protecting womanly honor

RYANCE, KING

King Ryance, or Ryence, is a king of Ireland and Wales and possessor of the sword Marandaise, in Arthurian lore.

He sent to King Arthur for his beard, to enable him, with those of eleven other kings whom he had already discomfited, to border his mantle. Meeting with an angry refusal, he entered Britain with a large army to enforce his demand, but was captured and sent as a prisoner to Arthur. According to some accounts, he later gave his daughter Guinevere, in apology, to be Arthur's wife.

a request as absurd as that of King Ryance

RYPAROGRAPHER

Ryparographer (Greek for "filthy writing") is the name Pliny the Elder called Pyricus the painter, because he confined himself to the drawing of gross and foul pictures, in which genre he showed considerable talent. Thus, any type of pornographic or caricatured art or writing may be called ryparography, and Rabelais has been dubbed "the ryparographer of wits."

as salaciously pictorial as a work by the original Ryparographer

S

SABAEAN

Sabaean refers to Saba, an ancient kingdom in southern Arabia whose people were descendants of one of several persons named Sheba (*q.v.*), or Seba. The inhabitants were renowned for their wealth and for their costly export products of spices, perfumes, and gems.

> *Sabaean odors from the spicy shore of Araby the bless'd*
> Milton, *Paradise Lost*

SABAZIUS

Sabazius was a Phrygian or Thracian nature-god, partially identified with the Greek Zeus and Dionysus. An orgiastic festival, the Sabazia, was held in his honor at Athens. His symbol was a snake, the token of the yearly revival of nature and one of the objects of his worship. A golden serpent was passed across the bosoms of the initiated underneath their clothes and was withdrawn from below, in significance of an old rite of adoption mentioned by Demosthenes (*On the Crown*). Some etymologists explain his name from an Illyrian word for the "beer god," others as related to the Jewish "Sabbath."

> *snake cultists as frenzied as Sabazius's devotees*

SABINE

The Sabines were an ancient Italic people subjugated by the Romans under Romulus in a war made by the Sabines after the Romans had abducted their maidens to be wives to the conglomerate population of the new city of Rome. The Sabines were finally reconciled to their captors on the plea of those same women, and became one with the early Roman people. Their land is still beautiful wooded and rolling country to the north and east of Rome, and they were a sturdy, vigorous folk.

> *Sabine sturdiness*

SABRA

Sabra, in old ballads of *St. George and the Dragon,* was the daughter of Ptolemy, king of Egypt, and was rescued by St. George from the fangs of the monster. Ultimately marrying her deliverer, she is represented as pure in mind, saintly in character, and a perfect citizen, daughter, and wife. She bore triplets named Guy, Alexander, and David, and died from the "pricks of a thorny brake."

> *a deliverance as miraculous as Sabra's*

SABRINA

Sabrina, the Latin and poetical name of the Severn river in England, is represented in Milton's *Comus* as the virginal daughter of Locrine and his concubine Estrildis. Locrine's wife and queen, Guendolen, vowed vengeance against Estrildis and her daughter, collected an army, and defeated Locrine. Thrown into the river which bears her name, Sabrina was metamorphosed into the nymph who aids distressed maidens.

> *invokes Sabrina to hear her woes*

SACCO-VANZETTI

Nicola Sacco (1891-1927) and Bartolomeo Vanzetti (1888-1927) were Italian-born political radicals who were tried and convicted on a charge of murdering a shoe-factory paymaster and guard at South Braintree, Massachusetts, and for theft of a $16,000 payroll. When their case was appealed, doubt of their guilt became prevalent and their cause was espoused by many notable people, including Edna St. Vincent Millay. World-wide protests were launched, but in spite of them they were electrocuted on August 23, 1927, after the case was reviewed and the trial and verdict affirmed to be fair and just.

a cause célèbre of the eminence of the Sacco-Vanzetti dispute

---

SACHS, HANS

Hans Sachs (1494-1576) was an itinerant shoemaker and journeyman who wandered through Germany, studying the art of the Meistersingers (*q.v.*). He composed some 6000 songs and was celebrated by Goethe. He is depicted as the principal character in Wagner's opera *Die Meistersinger von Nürnberg*.

a musical cobbler like Hans Sachs

SACRIPANT

Sacripant is the king of Circassia and lover of Angelica, in Ariosto's *Orlando Furioso*. Represented as false, brave, noisy, and hectoring, he has his steed stolen from beneath his very legs without his knowledge by Brunello, a thief, at the siege of Albracca. The name is a synonym for boastful vanity, braggart courage, and cowardice.

as unaware of his loss as Sacripant

SADDUCEES

The Sadducees were a religious and political group in Judea opposed to the Pharisees, and were wealthy, aristocratic, and conservative officers of the army and the state. They rejected the notion of retribution in a future life, personal immortality, and fate, but respected the law of the Pentateuch and freedom of the will. They were vigorous in the administration of justice, but eventually sided with Rome and vanished from history.

Sadducean opposition

SADE, MARQUIS DE

The Marquis de Sade (1740-1814), French soldier and author of two obscene novels, *Justine* (1791) and *Juliette* (1798), in addition to another work on immorality, *Les Crimes de l' Amour* (1800), was himself imprisoned for a large part of his life beacuse of an unnatural offense and a poisoning perpetrated at Aix in 1772. Sadism, a sexual perversion in which ecstasy is brought about by the infliction of pain on the person loved, was described by him in his writings and received its name from him because of his own vicious acts of sexual atrocity. He died in an insane asylum, maddened by his incontinent licentiousness.

degenerate as the Marquis de Sade

SAEHRIMNIR

Saehrimnir, in Scandinavian mythology, is the boar whose flesh replenishes itself magically. Served daily at the banquets of Valhalla, it is cooked whole every morning and renews itself every night.

as inexhaustible as Saehrimnir's flesh

SAGITTARY

Sagittary, or Sagittarius ("the archer"), was an imaginary monster introduced into the armies of the Trojans by the fable-writer Guido da Colonna. A terrible archer, half-man and half-beast, he was identified with the centaur Chiron, who was placed in the heavens to form the constellation of that name after his death. He was described as neighing like a horse and as having eyes that sparkled like fire and struck dead like lightning.

as unerring as the aim of Sagittary

SAHARA

The Sahara, a vast desert in North Africa, comprising millions of acres of sand and oases, ranging from below sea level to 8800 feet altitude, is useless and arid and in great parts not traversable, consequently synonymous with vast, arid, empty, terrifying, impassable.

no one has yet attempted the Sahara-like passage.

SAKHRAT

Sakhrat, in Mohammedan mythology, is a sacred emerald, a single grain of which grants miraculous powers to the possessor, and the reflection from which colors the sky blue. Upon it rests Mount Caf, the fabulous mountain that encircles the earth and is the home for giants and fairies.

as luminous as Sakhrat tinging the heavens

SALACIA

Salacia, the wife and female counterpart of Neptune among the Romans, was the regnant goddess of the sea. Her name is obviously connected with the Latin *sal* for "brine," accordingly denoting the salty sea.

a draught seasoned with Salacia's bitter brine

SALAMIS

Salamis, an island off the coast of Attica, Greece, was the scene of a great naval battle on October 20, 480 B.C., in which the Greeks under Themistocles defeated the overwhelmingly superior Persian fleet of Xerxes in the waters of the narrow channel.

a sea victory comparable to Salamis

SALIC LAW

Salic Law is from the 5th century Salian Franks who had a code of law forbidding women to inherit land, and in France, later, from succeeding to the crown. The name has been generally applied to any law excluding women from the rights that might, without that law, be common to men and women alike. Strictly, it refers only to women's exclusion from succession to royal power, in countries where it is in force.

a kind of domestic Salic law was imposed by the boys of the family

SALII

The Salii, or "leaping priests" of Mars, in March of every year danced all around Rome, wearing high conical hats and carrying the *ancilia,* or sacred shields that had fallen from heaven as a portent of Rome's dominion. Beating on these shields with staves, they chanted ancient rituals, and a luxurious banquet ensued for these whirling dervishes of antiquity. The proceedings were probably intended to avert demons and to make the crops abundant.

hopping and jumping like the Salii

SALLUSTIAN

Sallustian refers to the luxurious splendor in which Caius Sallustius Crispus (86-35 B.C.) passed the latter part of his life. This Roman democrat and Caesarian had once been horsewhipped by Milo for an amorous intrigue with his wife and was expelled from the Senate on charges against his character that were founded on his reputation for libertinism. After his governorship of Numidia, to which Caesar had appointed him, he retired from public affairs to enjoy the great wealth he had amassed by extortion as governor of that province. His lavish pleasure-gardens, the *horti Sallustiani* on the Quirinal hill in Rome, were worthy of a monarch and, indeed, later did become imperial property. He is also known to classical scholars as the author of two extant historical monographs, on *Catiline* (*q.v.*) and *Jugurtha* (*q.v.*), written in a terse and moralistic vein.

gardens of Sallustian magnificence

SALMACIS

Salmacis was the nymph of a fountain near Halicarnassus in Caria, in whose waters the youth Hermaphroditus bathed. Enamored of the beautiful son of Hermes and Aphrodite, she made advances to him. When they were rejected, she embraced him closely and prayed the gods to blend them into one, which they obligingly did. Hence, the word *hermaphrodite* is used to refer to a person combining the characteristics of both sexes in one body.

an embrace as close as Salmacis's

SALMONEUS

Salmoneus, king of Elis, son of Aeolus, and brother of Sisyphus, in Greek mythology, was celebrated for his arrogance, presumptuousness, and impiety. He ordered sacrifices to be offered to himself, as if he were a god, and even imitated the attributes of Jupiter, making a noise like thunder by driving a chariot of bronze and throwing firebrands in token of thunderbolts. For his impudence Jupiter struck him with a genuine bolt and hurled him into the infernal regions for punishment.

Salmoneus-like, requiring homage of all who saw him

SALOME

Salome (c. 14-60 A.D.), artful, cruel daughter of Herodias, more than once induced Herod to put to death persons she wanted out of the way, among them her own husband and Herod's wife. She is the same Salome, actually the niece of Herod and his stepdaughter upon his marrying her mother Herodias, who had danced before the king so pleasingly that he had promised her any favor. Whereupon, instigated by her mother, whose marriage to Herod had been denounced by John the Baptist, she asked for the head of John the Baptist and her request was granted. Oscar Wilde in luscious poetic drama and Richard Strauss in opera have portrayed her wanton charms.

the heartless easy cruelty of a Salome

SALT RIVER

Salt River is an imaginary stream up which defeated political parties are supposed to be sent to oblivion, and those who attempt to uphold the party have the task of rowing up this ungracious watercourse. J. Inman says that the phrase *to row up Salt River* had its origin in the fact that there was a small stream of that name in Kentucky, the passage of which was made difficult and laborious by its tortuous meandering and by an abundance of shallows and bars. The real application of the phrase was, thus, to the unhappy wight who had the task of propelling a boat up the stream.

relegated in defeat to Salt River

SALUS

Salus was the Roman goddess of health, prosperity, and the public welfare. In the first capacity she was partially identified with the Greek deity Hygeia. In her temple on the Quirinal Hill in Rome she was officially worshiped on the 30th of April, in conjunction with Pax, Concordia, and Janus. In art she is represented with a rudder and a globe at her feet; or sometimes she is in a sitting position, pouring from a patera a libation on an altar, around which a serpent is winding.

invokes Salus for her family's weal

SAM, UNCLE

Uncle Sam is the name applied to the United States, a personification pictured as a lanky figure in a high hat and a suit featuring the stripes and the starred blue ground of the national flag. The name perhaps originated in the War of 1812 when Samuel Wilson, locally known as Uncle Sam, stamped the goods to be shipped by the government "U.S.," and, hence, was called Uncle Sam because they had gone through his hands.

calling to Uncle Sam for rescue

SAMAEL

Samael, in old Jewish demonology, is the prince of demons who in the guise of a serpent tempted Eve. According to some Rabbins, however, he is the angel of death who is armed with a sword or with a bow and arrows. Elsewhere, he is identified with Asmodeus (*q.v.*).

seductive as Samael

SAMARITAN

Samaritan, from Samaria, a province city "out of which what good may come?" was a city originally captured, its tribes deported *en masse,* and the whole area filled with other captives or slaves of the Assyrian king. These made the population of Samaria, at the time of Christ, a people of whom no good was expected; hence, the strength of the parable of the good Samaritan who befriended the stricken stranger after the better people, the priest and the Levite, had passed him by.

with Samaritan anonymity

SAMBO,

Sambo, the cant designation of a member of the negro race, is a name properly applied to the male offspring of a negro and a mulatto, the female issue being called Zamba. It is derived from the Spanish *zambo,* "bow-legged."

legs as crooked as poor black Sambo's

SAMPSON, DOMINIE

Dominie Sampson is a homely and awkward schoolmaster, in Scott's *Guy Mannering.* "No uncommon personage in a country where a certain portion of learning is easily attained by those who are willing to suffer hunger and thirst in exchange for acquiring Greek and Latin," he always expresses his astonishment by saying "Pro-di-gi-ous!" A poor, humble, and pedantic scholar, he is both irascible and old-fashioned in his ways.

the Dominie Sampson of the village

SAMSON

Samson is the strong man of the Bible who in his youth "killed a lion between his hands." Later, to punish the Philistines, he loosed three hundred foxes, tied tail to tail with a fire-brand between the tails, among their ripened grain and their olive orchards. Caught and bound by the Philistines, he broke the bonds and with the jaw-bone of an ass "slew thousands of them." He lost his strength to his enemies' ruse when they had Delilah, of whom he was enamored, tease him into revealing that his strength lay in his hair, whereupon, while he slept hidden, men cut it. Shorn of his strength, imprisoned, and blinded, he was occasionally brought forth as a spectacle to amuse the thousands of people at celebrations. When his hair had meantime grown, on an occasion he stood between two supporting pillars and suddenly pulled them together, destroying himself and three thousand of the pleasure-seekers.

Samsonian strength
a Samsonian revenge

SAMUEL

Samuel, the son of Elkanah and Hannah, was made a prophet when at eight years of age he heard the Lord call to him in the night and answered, "Speak, Lord, Thy servant heareth." It was Samuel who later converted Saul and anointed him King of Israel, although much later he prophesied against Saul and anointed David as his successor.

a Samuel, responsive to the Lord's call

SANBALLAT

Sanballat was the Samaritan who plotted unsuccessfully to defeat Nehemiah's plans for rebuilding the walls of Jerusalem (*Neh.*, iv). He then invited the Jewish prophet and governor to a conference at Ono, intending to slay him by treachery, but neither his persuasions nor his threats moved the shrewd Nehemiah.

a treacherous Sanballat

SAND, GEORGE

George Sand was the pseudonym of Mme. Amantine Lucile Aurore Dudevant (1804-1876), the most prolific authoress in the history of the French novel. Mistress of Chopin, Liszt, de Musset and others, she consorted freely in male society. Affecting many of the ways of men so that she might mix openly in their company, she carried her enthusiasm for them to the point of wearing male attire and smoking. She was, however, by no means masculine herself, but accomplished her purpose — that of giving other women and herself, in particular, free access to the company of men — without detracting from her own feminine appeal. *Jeanne* and *Consuelo* are two of her famous novels.

a free-living George Sand

SANDALPHON

Sandalphon, in Jewish angelology, is a tall angel of intense fire, one of the three who preside over mankind, receiving the prayers of the Israelites and weaving crowns from them to bring them before God. Longfellow made the superstition the subject of a beautiful poem.

flaming as Sandalphon in all his glory

SANGRADO, DOCTOR

Doctor Sangrado, in LeSage's *Gil Blas*, is a physician who prescribes copious bloodletting and the drinking of hot water as the panacea for all sorts of ailments. By the author's contemporaries the character was generally thought to be intended for the celebrated Helvetius, a French philosopher and propounder of the doctrine of sensationalism, or sensualism, whose great work *De l'Esprit* was condemned by the Sorbonne and publicly burned.

as useful as Doctor Sangrado's panacea

SANGREAL

Sangreal was the drinking vessel said to have been carved from a single emerald and to have been used by Christ at the Last Supper. At the Crucifixion it was filled with the blood which flowed from the wounds with which he was pierced, and then carried to England by Joseph of Arimathea, where it remained for many years as an object of pilgrimage and devotion. But at length it disappeared, one of its keepers having violated the condition of strict virtue in thought, word, and deed, which was enjoined on those who had charge of it. Thenceforth many knights-errant, especially those of the Round Table, spent their lives in searching for it, and Sir Galahad was at last successful in finding it.

Various miraculous properties were attributed to the cup, such as the power of prolonging life, preserving chastity, and the like. In some legends it was said to have been brought down from heaven by a group of angels and entrusted to the charge of an order of knights, who guarded it in a temple-like castle atop the inaccessible mountain Montsalvat, whence it would be borne away and vanish from their sight if approached by any but a perfectly pure and holy person. At the death of Parsifal (*q.v.*), Sangreal, the sacred lance, and the silver trencher were carried up to heaven and have never since been seen on earth.

as venerable as Sangreal, intolerant of contact with evil

SANHEDRIN

The Sanhedrin, or Sanhedrim, was the supreme ecclesiastical council and judicial tribunal of the ancient Jewish nation, and probably took its form from the seventy elders appointed to assist Moses in the government. The president was called "Ha-Nasi" (the prince), and the vice-president "Abba" (father). The seventy members sat in a semi-circle, thirty-five on each side of the president. All questions of the "Law" were dogmatically settled by this body, and those who refused obedience were excommunicated. The name Sanhedrin may be used figuratively for any assembly or council.

arraigned before the Sanhedrin

SANSCULOTTE

Sansculotte ("without breeches") was the name given to republicans and members of the lower classes in the days of the French Revolution, because they had adopted the fashion of wearing long pantaloons instead of the knee-breeches and silk stockings worn by men of the court and the nobility. Originally contemptuously applied by the rich as a term of reproach for the poor, it was adopted by the republican revolutionists as a designation of honor and synonymous with "patriot." It now connotes either anarchist and communist or a shabbily dressed man.

a violent and radical Sansculotte

SANS-GENE, MME.

Mme. Sans-Gêne ("without constraint") was the name given to Catherine, the wife of Marshal LeFebvre, because she retained in the exalted position she occupied in her maturity the naive, outspoken, and unconventional ways of her earlier life, having been a laundress of lowly birth at the time of her marriage (1783). The name denotes any woman so frank and unsophisticated as to be almost unmannerly.

unrestrained as Mme. Sans-Gêne

SANTA CLAUS

Santa Claus, or St. Nicholas (died A.D. 326), patron saint of children, is usually represented as an old man dressed in red, with white whiskers, red cheeks, and twinkling eyes, who comes from the North, where he sits all the year contriving presents he will bring to the children of the world on Christmas Eve. He is immortalized by Clement Moore in *The Night Before Christmas* and made real by an editorial in the *New York Times* by Frank Church on *Is there a Santa Claus?* The term is now used of any person who goes about distributing goods or bounties indiscriminately with or without reason, and is sometimes used opprobriously with political implications.

a Santa-Claus politician
the Santa Claus among the nations
a Santa-Claus figure

SAPPHIRA

Sapphira was the wife of Ananias, with whom she shared the same fate. Both were miraculously struck dead for their hypocrisy and falsehood in lying to the apostle Peter (*Acts,* v) and withholding part of the sum of money they had received from the sale of a possession, thus defaulting on a communal sharing of all property among the disciples.

another Sapphira in money matters

SAPPHO

Sappho, a Greek writer of the 7th century B.C., was one of the two great leaders of the Aeolian school of lyric poetry (Alcaeus was the other) and is considered by many to have been the greatest poetess of all time, even though — except for her complete Ode to Aphrodite — the nine ancient volumes of her verse exist today only in fragments. These fragments, however, are of highly evocative delicacy, and their subject matter is principally love, both tender and passionate. She was the center of a female literary and musical society, and the recipients of her love were all girls within her group. Hence, a native of the island of Lesbos, she has had her name used to designate homosexual love among women, which is known as Sapphism or Lesbianism. The rather common story that she threw herself from the Leucadian cliff because of unreciprocated love for Phaon, a youth, is clearly a later invention, contrived to cover up the abnormality of her libido and at variance with the known facts of her life as gleaned from her own poems. Because of the exquisite perfection of her poetry she was known in antiquity as the Tenth Muse.

Sapphic emotional intensity

SARACEN

A Saracen was originally a nomad of the deserts, but in history and in literature appeared as first an Arab, then as any Moslem hostile to the Crusaders. The suggestion of enmity to the Crusaders is emphasized particularly in Scott's incomparable novel, *The Talisman.*

Saracen cruelty

SARAH

Sarah ("princess"), the sister-wife of Abraham (*Genesis,* xvii), accompanied him from Ur of the Chaldees to Canaan and thence to Egypt, whither they were driven by a famine. Pharaoh entertained them in his palace until he learned of the incestuous relationship and sent them on their way with a rebuke. Being childless, she gave Abraham her handmaid, Hagar (*q.v.*), as concubine, but when in old age she herself bore Isaac, she was moved by jealousy to force Hagar and her son Ishmael to leave. She died at the age of 127.

the longevity of a Sarah.

SARASWATI

Saraswati, in Hindu mythology the consort and wife of Brahma, is the patron goddess of poetry, painting, sculpture, eloquence, and music. The personification of speech by whom knowledge is conveyed to mankind, she was known as Vach in earlier times and regarded as the overseer of sacrifice.

as great a civilizing influence as Saraswati

SARDANAPALUS

Sardanapalus, the Greek form of the Assyrian name Ashurbanipal, was the king of Nineveh and Assyria who flourished from 668 to 624 B.C. Noted for his luxury and voluptuousness, he was so effeminate that Arbaces, the Mede, conspired against him. Myrra, an Ionian slave and his favorite concubine, roused Sardanapalus from his wanton lethargy and induced him to appear at the head of his armies. Though he won three successful battles, he was finally defeated and persuaded by Myrra to immolate himself as the Medes were besieging his palace. She herself set fire to the pyre and jumped into the flames to perish with her beloved master. The name Sardanapalus now connotes any luxurious, extravagant, and self-willed person.

a modern-day Sardanapalus, sleekly effeminate

SARPEDON

Sarpedon, in Greek mythology, was the son of Zeus and Europa, and the brother of Minos and Rhadamanthus, two of the judges in the lower world. He became king of the Lycians in Asia Minor, and Zeus granted him the privilege of living for three generations.

His grandson, also named Sarpedon, was the Lycian prince who became an ally of Priam in the Trojan war, where he distinguished himself by his bravery and valor. Slain by the spear of Patroclus, friend of Achilles, he was anointed by Apollo and his body borne by Hypnos (Sleep) and Thanatos (Death) to his native Lycia for burial.

the longevity of a Sarpedon

SARTO, ANDREA DEL

Andrea del Sarto, a celebrated Florentine painter (1487-1531), was noted for correct design, harmonious coloring, and skill in chiaroscuro. For a time, for political and perhaps financial reasons, he painted portraits at the direction of Francis I, a work that went against his grain, according to Browning's interpretation in his *Andrea del Sarto.* Left to himself he painted masterpieces. His name is now used sometimes to indicate the marvelous character-painting in his pictures, and sometimes to indicate making one's art a means to an end.

with an Andrea-del-Sartean character delineation

SATANIC

Satanic is from Satan, Prince of Evil and father of iniquity, a name universally used for the personification of evil, as well as for the abstract principle of evil. According to the Talmud, Satan had been an archangel cast out from heaven for disobedience and revolt. Milton apparently follows this version for his Satan in *Paradise Lost,* in heaven called Lucifer, after his fall called Satan.

Satanic ingenuity

SATURN

Saturn (Latin for "sower" or "planter") was the ancient Italic god of seed-time and harvest who became the first king of Latium. Worshiped as the god of agriculture, civilization, and social order, he was at an early time identified with the Cronos of the Greeks, and, hence, was said to be the son of Coelus (Heaven) and Terra (Earth), and the husband of Ops (Plenty). Dethroned by his brother Titan and imprisoned, he was set at liberty by his son, Jupiter, who, however, divided his kingdom with Neptune and Pluto. Saturn fled to Italy, where his reign was so mild and beneficent that men called it "the golden age."

The word *saturnine,* derived from Saturn the planet, refers to the astrological qualities usually attributed to the influence of that body, and means gloomy, heavy, sullen, and cynical.

an age as prosperous as that of Saturn

SATURNALIAN

Saturnalian is from Saturnalia, a mid-December Roman festival celebrating Saturn with great mirth and license. Slaves were served at table by their masters, jesting without let or hindrance; a king was chosen from among them; gifts were exchanged — it was a period of gayety and good feeling.

the convention was a Saturnalian occasion

SATYR

A Satyr is one of a group associated with Dionysus (Bacchus), representing the luxuriant vitality of nature. Ears pointed at the top and two small horns growing out of the top of the forehead mark most of the pictures of satyrs. The Italians associated them with Fauns. They are fond of wine, of sensual pleasure, sleep and music, and are shown in voluptuous dances with nymphs.

Satyr-leer

SATYRANE

Satyrane, the son of a satyr in Spenser's *Faerie Queene,* is born and bred in the forests and shows the strength and bravery of man in his natural state. The faithful squire of Una (*q.v.*), he delivers her from the lust of the fauns and satyrs. He represents Martin Luther of the Reformation, a time in which it was very difficult to separate Truth (Una) from Error (Archimago), with whom Una subsequently falls in.

the natural goodness of a Sir Satyrane

SAUL

Saul, the son of Kish, was the first king of Israel. Brave, patriotic, and energetic, he was summoned by Samuel, the seer, to the throne and the deliverance of his people from the Philistine yoke. Rash and fickle, he sought to charm away his innate melancholy and despondency by the music of David, of whose popularity he forthwith became suspicious and jealous. Killed by the Philistines, Saul was succeeded by David.

a melancholic Saul

SAVONAROLA

Girolamo Savonarola (1452-1498), a Florentine monk and reformer, denounced the corruptions of the Church and advocated political liberty, engaging many of the most influential families and persons in his doctrines. He finally established a new constitution on Christian principles and became immensely popular, but when he refused to submit to papal authority there was a reaction. The people turned against him, his enemies gained the ascendancy, and he was tortured, condemned, and put to death. His story is told in Eliot's *Romola.*

another Savanarola sacrificed

SAWYER, BOB

Bob Sawyer, in Dickens' *Pickwick Papers,* is a jovial, though impecunious, young medical student and practitioner who endeavors to prosper his business by a variety of ingenious devices.

an interne as inventive as Bob Sawyer

SAXNOT

Saxnot, in Germanic mythology, is one of the names of the god of war appearing in Anglo-Saxon as a son of Odin (Woden). He is probably the same as Tiu, the sky-god and war-god of the ancient Teutonic peoples.

their martial tumult whipped up by Saxnot

SCAEVOLA

Caius Mucius Scaevola ("left-handed") was a young Roman patrician who entered the camp of King Porsena with the intention of killing the Etruscan, as he was blockading Rome. Having stabbed Porsena's secretary by mistake, he was ordered to be burned alive. Scaevola thereupon thrust his right hand into a sacrificial fire and held it there without flinching. Amazed at his firmness, Porsena granted him his life, and when told by Scaevola that 300 other young Romans were pledged to make the same attempt on his life, he made proposals of peace to the Romans and evacuated their territory.

as impervious to pain as Scaevola

SCALAE GEMONIAE

The Scalae Gemoniae, or "Stair of Sighs," was a flight of steps leading from the Roman forum to the top of the Capitoline hill. The bodies of criminals who had been executed in the Mamertine prison nearby were thrown out on these stairs and dragged down them to the Tiber river, into which they were then flung.

disgraced on the Scalae Gemoniae

SCAPINO

Scapino, from the Italian word for a sock or short stocking, was a mask on the Italian stage, represented as a cunning and knavish servant of Gratiano, the loquacious and pedantic Bolognese doctor. Derived from his name, the word *scapinade* means an act of deception and cheating, any piece of trickery.

In Molière's comedy, *Les Fourberies de Scapin,* the hero, Scapin, is a wily and intriguing valet who dupes his master.

outdoes Scapin in his scapinades

SCARAMOUCH

Scaramouch was a military personage in an old Italian comedy, dressed in a Spanish or Hispano-Neapolitan costume of grotesquely decorated black. His character was that of a cowardly boaster and fool, very valiant with words. In the end he always received a beating from Harlequin. The name is used to mean a clowning buffoon, a braggadocio, and a ne'er-do-well.

the ridiculous boasting of a Scaramouch

SCHAMIR

Schamir, in the Persian and other traditions incorporated by the Jews into the Solomon legends, is the worm which was able to cut the hardest stone and aided Solomon to hew the stones for the Temple. The myth is generally understood as referring to a natural crystal or diamond.

needs Schamir to cut through the impervious

SCHEHEREZADE

Scheherezade, daughter of the Grand Vizier of the Indies, marries the Sultan, knowing that it is his habit to kill each bride at daybreak the day after the marriage because of the infidelity of women. Scheherezade, however, has made ready a store of tales to tell the Sultan for a thousand and one nights, leaving each story unfinished until the next night, when she also starts a new one. They are so fascinating that the Sultan cannot forego hearing the end of each one. They are the stories of *The Arabian Nights.*

fascinating Scheherezadian stories

SCHLEMIHL, PETER

Peter Schlemihl is the hero of a story of the same name by Chamisso (1781-1838). Meeting an old man in a gray suit (the Devil), just after he has been disappointed in an application for assistance to a nobleman, he sells him his shadow for the purse of Fortunatus. The name is a synonym for any person who makes a desperate and silly bargain, or for any poor, foolish, and unfortunate fellow.

a bargain as ridiculous as Peter Schlemihl's

SCHOPENHAUERIAN

Schopenhauerian refers to Arthur Schopenhauer (1788-1860), the brilliant but pessimistic German philosopher. His *The World as Will and Representation* presents the theory that man will always have unsatisfied cravings and that he should deny the "will to live." Only in the contemplation of works of art can one find temporary relief from ennui and dissatisfaction.

has Schopenhauerian pessimism
Schopenhauerian unhappiness

SCHUBERT, FRANZ

Franz Schubert (1797-1828), Austrian composer distinguished for his inexhaustible melodiousness, is most famous for his *Lieder,* musical settings in song of romantic German ballads and lyrics. From the *Erlking*, which he composed when he was only 18, to the end of his tragically short life he wrote about 600 amazingly artistic songs,

Die Schöne Müllerin, a set of 20, and the *Winterreise* being among the most popular. His amazingly rich store of tuneful airs poured itself forth in seven complete symphonies (that in C major being dubbed *Himmlische lang,* "of heavenly length"), two incomplete ones (the B minor of which is the popular "Unfinished"), and a great quantity of sonatas, chamber music, and operas. The epitaph of this short-lived genius, dead of typhus at the age of 31, reads:
"Music has here entombed a rich treasure, but still fairer hopes."

Schubertian melody

SCHUMANN, ROBERT

Robert Schumann (1810-1856), German musical composer of the Romantic School, was one of the greatest exponents of the art of writing *Lieder,* musical settings in song for German lyric poems. His famous piano concerto and the "Spring" and "Rhenish" symphonies also continue his popularity today, as do piano pieces like the *Traumerei* ("Dreaming"), *Papillons* ("Butterflies") and *Kinderszenen* ("Childhood Scenes"). A nature prone to passionate intensity and morbid introspection led to his insanity and death in early life, after which his beloved wife Clara (*née* Wieck) dedicated herself to the interpreting and the popularization of his music for piano.

haunting as a Schumann air

SCHUMANN-HEINCK

Mme. Ernestine Schumann-Heinck (1861-1936) was the great contralto of German birth but United States citizenship. Distinguished for her magnificent singing of Wagnerian roles at the Metropolitan Opera, she is perhaps even better, certainly more affectionately, remembered for her warm qualities of motherhood. Deeply sentimental by nature, she was grievously distressed by the emotional turmoil caused her by World War I, in which her sons fought on opposite sides of the trenches. Yet she carried on heroically, singing for American troops everywhere. She called all doughboys, with motherly bursts of affection, her "sons."

the motherly warmth of Schumann-Heinck

SCIPIO AFRICANUS

Publius Cornelius Scipio Africanus Major, "the elder," (235-183 B.C.) was the Roman consul who saved his father's life in one of the earliest battles of the Second Punic War and later put a successful end to the savage conflict by defeating Carthaginian Hannibal in Africa in 202 B.C. Known as the "thunderbolt of war," he was honored by the Senate with the cognomen *Africanus.*

Publius Cornelius Scipio Africanus Minor, "the younger," (185-129 B.C.) was the adoptive grandson of Africanus Major. He besieged and destroyed Carthage at the end of the Third Punic War (149-146 B.C.) and is said to have wept as he ordered the plow to be run over the site of the once great city and salt to be sown in the furrows to ensure the sterility of its soil. His grief was caused by his foreseeing the ultimate and inevitable destruction of Rome itself. A patron of arts and letters, he established a literary coterie that included men like Terence and Polybius. He also had a great admiration for Greek culture and was called a Philhellene for this reason.

Scipionic generalship
Scipionic patronage of culture

SCIRON

Sciron was the notorious brigand and robber who frequented the frontier between Attica and Megara in ancient Greek legend. On a precipitous rock, named Scironian after him and overlooking the sea, he compelled wayfarers to wash his feet. While they were thus employed, he kicked them into the sea, where a giant tortoise devoured his victims. He was later slain by Theseus.

a highwayman of Scironian exploits

SCONE

The Stone of Scone, indicating royalty generally, is the stone upon which Scottish kings from time immemorial had sat when they were crowned. Tradition says it is the stone that served as Jacob's pillow when he dreamed of the ladder reaching into heaven. Edward I carried it, with other royal regalia, to London when he took Scotland back as a fief forfeited to England by treason, and today it is used as the seat of the throne chair at the coronation of all English kings. The stone is said to have borne the carved legend:

"Where'er this stone is found,
The Scot shall monarch of that realm be crowned."

And James VI of Scotland did become James I of England.

sits on an imaginary Stone of Scone

SCOPAS

Scopas of Paros was the eminent fourth century B.C. Greek sculptor who was famous for his power of expressing pathos, suffering, and passion on the faces of his marble figures. The group of Niobe and her children was attributed to him, and he was also the architect of the temple of Athena Alea, at Tegea, and responsible for the bas-relief sculptures of the Mausoleum at Halicarnassus.

the anguish of a figure by Scopas

SCOTLAND YARD

Scotland Yard is the name of a short street in London, near Trafalgar Square. It was formerly the site of the London police headquarters, now removed to New Scotland Yard on the Thames Embankment. Specifically, it is a name for the London police and detective bureau. It was immortalized in fiction through the exploits of Conan Doyle's *Sherlock Holmes.*

needs Scotland Yard to solve the mystery

SCOTT, WALTER

Sir Walter Scott (1771-1832) was among the greatest of the world's story-tellers in the nineteenth century, first in verse, then in prose. The "troop of horse," as he declared, had always surged through his brain, and his work features the daredevils of history, pageants, tournaments, crusades, battles, stirring action, and brave knights rescuing fair ladies. He used a headlong, vigorous narrative, cared more for action than for accuracy, and races a reader through a story with breathless interest.

colorful as a Scott tournament

SCRIBLERUS, MARTINUS

Martinus Scriblerus is the character ridiculed for his universal but superficial learning, his lack of judgment, and his perverted taste, in the *Memoirs of the Extraordinary Life, Works, and Discoveries of Martinus Scriblerus,* usually published in Pope's works, but generally attributed to Arbuthnot. Martin's father, Cornelius Scriblerus, is equally noted for his pedantry and absurdities about the education of his son. The *Scriblerus Club,* organized by Swift in 1714, numbered among its members Pope, Bolingbroke, Arbuthnot, and Gay, and set as its object the ridiculing of inferior literary work.

a Martin Scriblerus, versed inadequately in everything he teaches

---

SCROOGE

Ebenezer Scrooge is the grasping, selfish, wealthy old employer in Dickens' *Christmas Carol.* Hard-fisted, miserly, unloved, he is changed into a kindly old man, happy for the first time, when he has a visitation from spirits on Christmas Eve and is led to visit Bob Cratchit's humble home, where the real spirit of Christmas prevails.

the Scrooge selfishness
a Scrooge transformation

SCUDAMOUR

Sir Scudamour, in Spenser's *Faerie Queene,* is the knightly lover of Amoret, whom he finally marries.

chivalrous as Sir Scudamour

SCYLLA

Scylla, of Scylla and Charybdis fame, was actually a dangerous rock on the Italian side of the Strait of Messina, in avoiding which seamen had to steer into Charybdis, an equally dangerous whirlpool on the Sicilian side. The ancients personified her as a monstrosity, daughter of Crataeis, and believed that she barked like a dog and had 12 feet and 6 long necks and heads, each of which contained 3 rows of sharp teeth. Vergil, differing from this Homeric account, speaks of several Scyllae and places them in the lower world. Following the prevailingly accepted description as given in the *Odyssey,* however, when we speak of being between Scylla and Charybdis we mean to be beset by terrific difficulty however we move.

appeasment or war? Scylla or Charybdis?

SCYTHIAN

The Scythians were an ancient nomadic people, mentioned by Hesiod, Herodotus and other writers as inhabiting the steppes north of the Black Sea in southern Russia. Living in horse-drawn covered wagons, they were expert in cavalry exercises and archery. The proverbial phrase *Scythian defiance* arose from their contumelious rejection of the attempts of Darius of Persia to absorb their land. They sent an ambassador to his tent with a bird, a frog, a mouse, and five arrows, but with no verbal mesage. The import was explained to Darius as follows: either fly away like a bird, or hide your head in a hole like a mouse, or swim across the river like a frog, or in five days you will be laid prostrate by Scythian arrows.

Famed for their savagery, these people were drunken barbarians, noted for their intemperance in all things.

as arrogant and defiant as a Scythian

SEB

Seb was the Egyptian god of the primeval earth, and the father of Osiris. Identified by the Greeks with Kronos, he is represented in art as bearing a scepter and the ankh, or emblem of life, and balancing a goose on his head.

an ancient and chthonian Seb

SEBASTIAN, ST.

St. Sebastian, a third century martyr, was a soldier by profession and captain of the first cohort under Maximian and Diocletian. After making many converts to Christianity, he was ordered by the latter emperor to cease his proselytizing. Bound to a stake, he was shot with arrows, but when Irene, a devout woman, came by night to take his body for burial, she found him still alive and carried him to her house, where she dressed his wounds.

When he had recovered, he went to Diocletian and reproached him for his impiety, whereupon the emperor ordered him to be beaten to death with rods. Finally executed, he was thrown into the *cloaca maxima,* the principal sewer of Rome, but in a vision he appeared to another Christian lady, Lucina, and directed her to bury him "by the Catacombs, near to the footprints of the Apostles." On this spot the Basilica of St. Sebastian was erected, which became a place of pilgrimage in the middle ages.

A young and beautiful man, he became a popular subject for the Renaissance painters, his undraped body being represented in many fine pictures, such as that by Sodoma in the Pitti Palace, Florence. His festival is celebrated on the 20th of January, and he is especially invoked against the plague.

invulnerable as St. Sebastian

SEBEK

Sebek, in Egyptian mythology, is a deity of evil, a malignant influence, and the protector of reptiles. He is depicted with a crocodile head, representing the destructive power of the sun, and is seemingly a double of Set.

malevolent and long-faced as Sebek

SEDLEY, AMELIA

Amelia Sedley, the lovely and gentle girl in Thackeray's *Vanity Fair,* moves through the fashionable, calculating, and insincere world she belongs to as the personification of kindness, amiability, and guilelessness, in contrast to the scheming and guileful Becky Sharp. Amelia serves to accentuate Thackeray's theory that simple goodness is the ultimate good.

contented to be an amiable Amelia Sedley

SEDLEY, JOSEPH

Joseph Sedley, brother to Amelia in Thackeray's *Vanity Fair,* is a fat, sensual, and epicurean dandy and India official. Vain, lazy, and easy-going, he becomes one of Becky Sharp's victims.

a sensual and voluptuous Joseph Sedley

SEJANUS, AELIUS

Aelius Sejanus (died 31 A.D.), Roman courtier, intriguer, and prince of machination, was Prefect of the Praetorian Guard under the emperor Tiberius, whose confidence he gained by feeding his suspicions of others. His overweening ambition made him envious of Drusus, Tiberius's son, whom he contrived to poison. When the morose emperor withdrew to his villa on Capri, Sejanus became all-powerful and tyrannically cruel in Rome, until Tiberius became apprehensive of his power, denounced him, and had him sentenced to death. So hated was he that after his fall the populace tore his body to pieces and cast it into the Tiber. His name is synonymous with a corrupt use of power.

a hateful, Sejanus-like informer

SEJUS

Sejus was a Roman clerk who owned a horse of the same breed as those of Diomedes, excelling all other horses in all points of comparison. But this horse also brought bad luck to all who owned it, and Sejus was put to death by Mark Antony, as were later owners of the steed, Dolabella, Cassius, and Antony himself. Whence, the expression *the horse of Sejus* connotes ominous misfortune and disaster.

cursed by the horse of Sejus

SELENE

Selene is the Greek goddess of the moon, the daughter of Hyperion and Thea, and the sister of the Sun. Sometimes identified with Artemis, she was also considered the equivalent of the Latin Luna. She fell in love with Endymion (*q.v.*), most beautiful of men, whom she contrived to cast into a perpetual sleep, visiting him amorously every night. By him she had fifty daughters, one of them called Erse ("the dew"). In art she is represented as riding in a chariot drawn by two white horses.

an argent Selene riding the skies

facts or of a situation so involved that there is no way out — an inescapable dilemma.

Congress wallowing in a Serbonian bog

SERGESTUS

Sergestus, one of the companions of Aeneas and reputed progenitor of the Sergian family at Rome (see *Catiline*), took part in the naval games at Drepanum in Sicily on the occasion of Anchises' death (*Aeneid,* vi). In command of a craft named the "Centaur," Sergestus ran the vessel on the rocks, with difficulty preserving the members of his crew.

as clumsy a pilot as Sergestus

SERGIUS

St. Sergius was a soldier martyr (c. 300 A.D.) whose cult is celebrated chiefly by the Eastern Church and is especially popular in Syria and Russia. Sergiopolis, a town named after him, is a place of pilgrimage for the devout, and his festival is held on the 7th of October. In art he is represented as wearing a military costume.

saved by the intercession of St. Sergius

SERIC

Seric refers to the Seres, a people vaguely identified as Chinese by the Greeks and Romans, and mentioned as producers of silk and of silken garments. Hence, in Roman writers of the Augustan age and later, the word connotes extravagance and wealth, since silk robes were worn only by rich and somewhat dissolute persons. Our words *serge* and *silk* are derived etymologically from the name of this people, the Seres.

a diaphanous Seric vestment

SERVIUS TULLIUS

Servius Tullius, sixth king of early Rome, was born of a slave woman, Ocrisia. On his head appeared a miraculous flame that burned without harming him, thus betokening his father to be Vulcan the fire-god. Marrying the daughter of Tarquinius Priscus, he succeeded him to the throne, framing a new constitution that granted the plebeians political independence and assigned to property-wealth the influence that had previously belonged to patrician birth alone. He also built the Servian wall around the city. His own daughter, Tullia, conspired with Lucius Tarquinius, her husband, to perpetrate his murder, and she even guided her chariot exultantly over his prostrate body. The scene of this incident was thereafter known as *Vicus Sceleratus,* or "Wicked Street."

impervious to flame as Servius Tullius

SESAME

Sesame, the magic password "Open, Sesame!" used by Ali Babi to open the robber's cave in the *Arabian Nights' Entertainments,* is now used to indi cate free passage into any place from which the ordinary person is excluded. It also admits one to any exclusive council or assemblage, or even to knowledge generally assumed to be secret and confided to only a few specified persons.

gracious considerateness is the "Open, Sesame" to the best society

a little child lisps an "Open, Sesame" to the hardest heart

SESHAT

Seshat was the Egyptian goddess of writing and learning, worshiped at Memphis and at Heliopolis. Her name is from the Egyptian root meaning "to instruct" or "ordain."

chirography as taught by Seshat

SESOSTRIS

Sesostris, in Greek legend, was an Egyptian pharaoh said to have conquered the world, especially Ethiopia, the greater part of Asia, and the Thracians in Europe. Returning to Egypt after an absence of nine years, he brought with him hordes of captives, whom he employed in the erection of numerous public works. Historically he is identified with Ramses, the second king of the 19th dynasty, and memorials of Ramses-Sesostris abound throughout the whole of Egypt.

the conquering career of a Sesostris

SET

Set, called Typhon by the Greeks, was the Egyptian god of evil, and brother and implacable opponent of Osiris. Originally a war-god and granter of victories, he was the oldest of all the Egyptian gods and the ruler of Upper Egypt. Appreciation of his character changing, he began to personify the powers of darkness and was regarded as the deadly enemy of all good. He is represented in art as having the head of a fabulous animal with high square ears and a pointed snout.

like Set, a destroyer of all virtue

SETEBOS

Setebos is a Patagonian deity mentioned in Shakespeare's *Tempest* and Browning's *Caliban on Setebos*. He is worshiped by Sycorax, the foul witch who is the dam of Prospero's slave Caliban. That Shakespeare did not invent this false god but rather had read about him in the books of American discovery of his time is clear from a passage in Eden's *History of Travayles*: "The giants, when they found themselves fettered, roared like bulls and cried upon Setebos to help them."

His art is of such power,
It would control my dam's god, Setebos,
And make a vassal of him.

Tempest, i, 2.

dark as the powers of Setebos

SETH

Seth, the third son of Adam (*Genesis*, iv, 25), was so named by Eve, "for God hath appointed me another seed instead of Abel, whom Cain slew." After living for 105 years, he begat Enos, then lived for another 807 years, making a total lifetime of 912 years.

the longevity of a Seth

SEVEN AGAINST THEBES

The Seven against Thebes were the champions of Polynices in his claim for the throne of Thebes. When Polynices and his brother, Eteocles, succeeded to rule at the death of Oedipus, their father, they had agreed to share sovereignty in alternate years, but Eteocles refused to vacate at the end of his year. Adrastus, father-in-law of Polynices and king of Argos, enlisted the support of Tydeus, Capaneus, Hippomedon, Parthenopaeus and Amphiaraus. With himself and Polynices numbering "seven," Adrastus then laid siege, each champion attacking one of the seven gates of Thebes. The brothers slew each other in combat and the Argive army was routed. Though Creon, the new king, forbade burial for the body of Polynices, the latter's heroic sister, Antigone, violated the edict and was herself destroyed.

attacked with the violence of the "Seven"

SEVEN SLEEPERS OF EPHESUS

The Seven Sleepers of Ephesus, according to early Christian tradition, were seven noble youths who at the time of the Decian persecution in the 3rd century took refuge in a cave, were discovered and walled in for a cruel death. They were, however, cast into a divine sleep which lasted for 230 years, during which a faithful dog that accompanied them remained standing and on guard. Soon after they awoke they died, and their bodies were taken in a large stone coffin to St. Victor's church in Marseilles. Their names were Constantine, Dionysius, John, Maximian, Malchus, Martinian and Serapion. This legend of divine sleep, care, and protection is matched in the Koran.

slept as soundly as the Seven of Ephesus

SEVIGNE, MME. DE

The Marquise de Sévigné (1626-1696), a brilliant woman whose life and social position admitted her to the French court and to acquaintance with some of the best people of her time, was separated from a beloved daughter by the latter's marriage. In a series of letters to that daughter, Mme. de Sévigné wrote most delightfully and charmingly of everything that concerned her personal and social life, reflecting with wonderful clarity the whole picture of French life in her day.

a Madame de Sévigné quality in the keen, illuminating and charming letters

SEXTUS TARQUINIUS

Sextus Tarquinius was the son of Tarquinius Superbus, early king of Rome. He and some other young princes, inflamed with wine in camp during military service, discussed the comparative virtues of their wives and decided to visit them unannounced in order to test their virtue. At sight of Lucretia, Sextus conceived a lustful desire for her, returning to her house later in the night and threatening to charge her with misconduct with a slave if she did not yield to his insistent advances. Having shamefully raped her, though she was the wife of his father's cousin, Collatinus, he departed. On her subsequent exposure of him, she committed suicide. Such a frenzy of popular indignation swept Rome that he and his father were banished from the city and a republic proclaimed, in 509 B.C. Shortly thereafter, Sextus was murdered at Gabii, his own principality.

the dishonorable intentions of a Sextus Tarquinius

SFORZA, GIACOMUZZO

Giacomuzzo Attendolo (1369-1424) was the founder of the illustrious ducal house of Milan. The son of a peasant day-laborer, he changed his name to Sforza ("Force") from the following incident: consulting his hatchet as to whether he should go to the wars as constable under Joanna II of Naples, he flung it against a tree, saying, "If it sticks fast, I will go." Because he threw it with amazing force, it did stick fast and he enlisted, later serving as soldier, mercenary, and condottiere in the armies of Pope Martin V. His notural son, Francisco (1401-1466), established the dukedom of Milan by force and strategy.

makes his decisions as fortuitously as Giacomuzzo Sforza

SGANARELLE

Sganarelle is a stock character, often a dupe, in several of Molière's comedies. In *Le Mariage Forcé* he is a humorist of fifty-four who has a mind to marry a fashionable young woman but vacillates with instinctive doubts and scruples, at last being cudgeled into compliance by the brother of his intended. The plot of the play is founded on an adventure of the Count de Grammont, who on leaving England was followed by the brothers of *la belle* Hamilton. With their hands on the pommels of their swords they asked him if he had not left something behind. He instantly repaired his lapse of memory by making their sister the Countess de Grammont.

Another Sganarelle is a simple-minded valet in Molière's *Festin de Pierre.* He is ever halting between fear of being drubbed by his master, Don

Juan, and the deeper horror of abetting or witnessing the latter's crimes. In the other plays the name is usually assigned to a bluff, wilful, and domineering character. In *L'Ecole des Maris* he is married to a woman who quarrels with a stranger for interfering with her husband when he is beating her.

a domineering Sganarelle of the home

SHADRACH

Shadrach, a companion of Daniel, was one of three youths (the names of the others were Meshach and Abednego) who were cast into the fiery furnace of Nebuchadnezzar and came forth unscathed and unharmed because of their great religious faith. Their song for deliverance is found in the Old Testament apocryphal book, *The Song of the Three Children.*

as miraculous as the saving of Shadrach

SHAFTON, SIR PIERCIE

Sir Piercie Shafton, in Scott's *Monastery,* is a fantastic character drawn in imitation of the pedantic courtiers of Queen Elizabeth's reign. Made to talk in the bombastic and high-flown style which Lyly rendered fashionable by his *Euphues,* Sir Piercie turns out to be the grandson of one Overstich, a tailor.

the verbal elegance of Sir Piercie Shafton

Shaftonian ornateness of language

SHAKESPEAREAN

Shakespearean means having to do with Shakespeare's work, or is reminiscent of the qualities of William Shakespeare (1564-1616). Apropos of his works, the word means universal, broadly human, comprehensive, vivid, running the whole gamut of human emotions, vices, and virtues, in completely unified and highly developed dramatic form. Of his personal qualities, it signifies all-embracing observation, perfect mimicry, deep understanding, utter tolerance, penetrating insight into the springs of human action, and a nature capable of every mood, from the deepest compassion to the most hilarious and unrestrained mirth.

Shakespearian perception of motives

SHALOTT, LADY OF

The Lady of Shalott, the central figure in Tennyson's poem by that name, sits and weaves in a tower, forbidden to look out of the window, but permitted to see the world passing by in a mirror that hangs before her. She obeys until one day in the mirror she sees a knight come riding by to Camelot. Despite the curse that will come upon her if she looks out, she turns to the window, the mirror breaks, the curse comes upon her, and she dies. She had also entertained an unrequited love for Lancelot du Lac.

finally rebelled against her sheltered Lady of Shalott existence

---

SHALLOW

Shallow is a foolish, dull country justice in Shakespeare's *Henry IV* and in *The Merry Wives of Windsor.* A fellow with no understanding, but with an endless babble of nothings and repetitions, he is idiotically restless, endlessly asking questions without even sensing the significance of replies. His name suggests the utterly useless, witless and irresponsible petty official.

all the Shallows of all the city halls

SHAMASH

Shamash is the Assyro-Babylonian sun-god, worshiped at Larsa and Sippar as the deity presiding over plantlife and the weather. He beneficently routs the storms of winter and spreads the earth with verdure. He also dispels the evil spirits and demons of disease, and personifies righteousness, order, and justice.

fields glowing with the blessings of Shamash

SHANDY, MRS. ELIZABETH

Mrs. Elizabeth Shandy is the mother of *Tristram Shandy* in Sterne's novel. A submissive nonentity, she is a character profoundly individual from her very lack of individuality.

meek and submissive as Mrs. Shandy

SHANDY, TRISTRAM

Tristram Shandy is the nominal hero of Lawrence Sterne's novel, *The Life and Opinions of Tristram Shandy, Gent.* His father, Walter Shandy, is an absurd theorist and pedant who believes in the virtue of a generous nose, though poor Tristram's is crushed at birth, and who thinks Trismegistus the noblest of all names and Tristram the worst, yet through an accident, Tristram is the name given to his son. Mrs. Shandy, Tristram's mother, is a good lady of the pococurante school and a meek nonentity. Uncle Toby, the principal character, is a retired captain, kind, gallant, and courageous.

has the misfortunes of a Tristram Shandy

SHARP, BECKY

Becky Sharp, a keen and shrewd young minx, penniless and calculating, in Thackeray's *Vanity Fair,* is even in her school days astute enough to attach herself to Amelia Sedley, a "profitable" pleasant girl, wealthy and well connected. Through Amelia's family and friends, and by means of her amiability, Becky climbs to a stratum of high society, where, by a career of pretense, craft, and intrigue, she has herself a profitable time, quite careless of the happiness, rights, or reputation of other people. Her methods of sharp, calculating, and brittle social climbing have ever since been characterized by her name.

more than the usual number of Becky Sharps

SHATRIYA

A Shatriya is a member of the Hindu warrior caste, fabled to have sprung from the right arm of Brahma. From the Shatriya class, also called Rajputs, a sovereign was chosen for the country.

belligerent as a Shatriya

SHAVIAN

George Bernard Shaw (1856-1951), dramatist and critic, with the sword of his wit cut through the wrongs of the world, exposed its ills, and proposed his own remedies toward its health in education, in religion, in politics, in domestic life, and toward peace. He poked fun at the average man, his sentimentalism, his romanticism, his muddling, with an incisive satire that is so insidious and so subtle that it sometimes misses fire. He loved to be startling, was one of the world's best laughers, and feared no one. His work has been, if not an instrument of reform, at least a stimulus to it. He attributed his longevity to his vegetarianism.

joined a Shaw scolding-society
the Shavian wits

SHEBA, QUEEN OF

The Queen of Sheba was the rich queen of the Sabeans in Southern Arabia whose fame rests upon her visit to Solomon's kingdom to test his wisdom and grant her tribute to his wealth and glory. She said, "The half was not told me," when she actually saw Solomon in all his glory. Hence, the name implies wealth, tribute, wonder.

sighs like David's son for Sheba's queen
proud as Sheba's queen

SHELLEY, PERCY BYSSHE

Percy Bysshe Shelley (1792-1822), the most lyric voice of the nineteenth century, dreamed and sang of a freedom, a liberty, a joy untrammeled by the material needs of the world. His youthful and ardent spirit led him into revolt and left him yearning to make the world young and free and joyous. But the world was satisfied with the lyric beauty and melody and music of his phrases, regardless of his theme. He is the poet of inexhaustible song; he is the Skylark, the West Wind, young, mad, and joyous.

the glad joy of a Shelley

SHEM

Shem, one of the three sons of Noah, was the ancestor of the Semitic races and lived a total of 602 years (*Genesis,* x, 21).

imitating Shem's longevity

SHEOL

Sheol is the place of departed spirits and the abode of the dead mentioned in *Proverbs,* xxvii, 20. In the *Psalms* it is a land of forgetfulness in which nothing is known of the upper world. The Hades of the New Testament, it came to mean the same thing as Gehenna, inasmuch as Old Testament descriptions of it pictured it as being the place of punishment.

the fires of Sheol

SHEPPARD, JACK

Jack Sheppard (1702-1724) was the notorious English robber who became the subject of a narrative by Defoe, a novel by Ainsworth, and a painting by Sir James Thornhill. Reared in crime by "Edgeworth Bess" Lyon, he committed almost daily robberies in the environs of London until he was captured by Jonathan Wild, his enemy. Condemned to death, he escaped prison through the assistance of "Edgeworth Bess," but was later recaptured and hanged at Tyburn.

burglary as audacious as that of Jack Sheppard

SHERATON, THOMAS

Thomas Sheraton, a noted 18th century designer and maker of furniture, made pieces marked by straight lines, graceful proportions, delicate and sometimes ingenious construction, with little carving except in the reeding of the tapered legs. The design is so harmonious in almost any setting that it continues to be sought today.

a genuine Sheraton
Sheratonian grace

SHERIDAN

Philip Henry Sheridan (1831-1888), who succeeded Sherman, was a Union officer remembered principally for his famous twenty-mile ride from Winchester to Cedar Creek battlefield, where he turned defeat into victory. The ride is recorded dramatically in Read's poem, *Sheridan's Ride.*

a dashing Sheridan

SHERMAN, GENERAL

William Tecumseh Sherman (1820-1891), Grant's successor, is the celebrated American Civil War general famous for his march through Georgia to the sea, leaving lamentable devastation in his wake.

a victorious ruthless Sherman march

SHESHA

Shesha, in Hindu mythology, is a thousand-headed serpent, regarded as the symbol of eternity. His coils, floating on the primeval waters, form the couch of Vishnu. One of his heads supports the earth and destroys it periodically by belching forth fire. The other heads form the canopy of Vishnu's couch. He is also worshiped as Ananta, the infinite or endless.

a problem as multi-headed as Shesha

SHIMEI

Shimei is the name of the malcontent of the tribe of Benjamin who cursed David during the rebellion of Absalom (*2 Samuel,* xvi, 5 ff.).

splenetic as the curses of Shimei

SHRI

Shri is the Hindu goddess of beauty, love, and good fortune. The wife of Vishnu, she has many other names, including Loka Mata ("the mother of the world"), Jaladhija ("ocean-born"), Padma ("the lotus"), and Lakshmi ("good sign"). Bright gold in color, she is pictured seated on a lotus, and is said to have been born from the sea of milk that was churned from ambrosia.

a beauty more golden than Shri's

SHYLOCK

Shylock, the wealthy money-lender in Shakespeare's *Merchant of Venice,* was so badly treated by Antonio, an arrogant Venetian merchant, and his friends that he gladly welcomed the opportunity for revenge that opened when, after he had lent Antonio money, Antonio could not pay. Having made a "merry bond" that in case he were not paid he might demand a pound of flesh, he claimed the forfeit. The court granted his claim but stayed him in the execution of it by accusing Shylock, by an old law, of an attempt on the life of a Venetian citizen. It then demanded the forfeit of his wealth and the renunciation of his religion. Loosely speaking, Shylock stands for cruelty, revenge, greed, but also for injury, desolation and bereavement.

bereft as a Shylock

SIAMESE

Siamese, from Eng and Chang of Siam, congenitally united twins, means literally twins physically joined at birth, and figuratively, more generally, any persons who are constantly associated, who are always together, inseparable companions.

unavoidable as a Siamese twin

SIBYLLA

Sibylla is the personification of the sibyls, Apollo-inspired prophetesses who are said to have written books of predictions concerning the Greek and Roman world. The Cumean sibyl was the best known and most universally revered of them. The books, most carefully preserved and guarded always, were destroyed when the Capitol was burned in 82 B.C. The reproductions were naturally inaccurate, perhaps in many cases spurious. The name sibyl still suggests these prophetic utterances.

prognosticating like Sibylla

SIDDONS, MRS.

Sarah Siddons (1755-1831), famous English actress and daughter of Roger Kemble of the great Kemble dramatic line, was distinguished by a perfect figure, great beauty, and was rather majestic in type. She was the most popular and gifted tragic actress of her day. The critics and the historians of the stage all record the completeness of her power to identify herself with the part she played, and to transport her audience into the situation she presented.

today's Mrs. Siddons

SIEGFRIED

Siegfried, the hero of the *Nibelungen Lied* legends and of Wagner's *Nibelungen Ring* operas, grows up in the forest with Mime, the smith, and becomes a young warrior of unusual strength. He wins the gold from the Nibelungs and, with the Tarnhelm cape to make him invisible, does great deeds. To make himself invulnerable, he kills a dragon and bathes in its blood. except where a leaf lights between his shoulder blades while he bathes. He weds Kriemhilde, sister of Gunther, who learns from Kriemhilde of Siegfried's one vulnerable spot, and kills him. The story of the youth and strength and deeds of Siegfried is a part of the literary heritage of the world.

a Siegfried vulnerability

SIF

Sif, in Scandinavian mythology, was the wife of Thor, and the patron of the family and of wedlock. She was famous for the beauty of her hair, which Loki cut off while she was asleep. Thor compelled him to get her a new head of hair made of gold, that should grow like natural hair. This he obtained from the dwarfs. The myth of Sif's tresses reflects her personification of Mother Earth, who annually is stripped of her foliage in autumn, regaining an even more glorious crown of leaves (*i.e.*, hair) in the springtime.

as proud of her tresses as Sif

SIGISMUNDA

Sigismunda, the heroine of one of the tales in Boccaccio's *Decamerone*, is the daughter of Tancred, prince of Salerno, and falls in love with Guiscardo, one of her father's pages. Tancred, discovering her guilt, upbraids her for her conduct but finds her insensible to shame and reproof. He sends her Guiscardo's heart in a golden cup, whereupon the bereft maiden drains a poisonous draught, after having poured some of it on her lover's heart. In English the tale of the tragic pair is best known through Dryden's *Sigismonda and Guiscardo*.

a widow as pale and poetic as Sigismunda

SIGUNA

Siguna is the wife of Loki, in Scandinavian mythology, and is celebrated for the constancy of her devotion to him. She sits by him in the subterranean cavern in which he is chained, and holds out a vase to catch the venom dropped by the serpents which hang over him. When she goes out to empty the receptacle, some poison falls on the god's limbs, and his consequent writhings cause earthquakes.

as devoted in her nursing as Siguna

SIGURD

Sigurd is the hero of an old Scandinavian saga which is the foundation of the German epic, the *Nibelungen Lied.* He discovered Brynhild, a beautiful Valkyrie, encased in complete armor and lying in a death-like sleep, to which she had been condemned by Odin for some offense. Sigurd awoke her and fell in love with her, engaged on oath to marry her, and took his departure. Subsequently meeting Gudrun, he was given a charmed love potion by her mother, causing him to forget Brynhild. This ill-starred union was the cause of a volume of woes. Sigurd is the Icelandic or Old Norse form of Siegfried (*q.v.*).

a Sigurd to deliver her from confinement

SIKES, BILL

Bill Sikes, in Dickens' *Oliver Twist*, a thief, murderer, and burglar, abused Oliver, killed Nancy Sikes, the one person who befriended Oliver, and in general represented the brutality and cruelty and criminality of his class at that time in London. He has been immortalized as a type by Henry Irving's impersonation of him in a play by that name.

a Bill Sikes household

SIKH

A Sikh is a member of a religious sect of northern India that professes monotheism and the principle of human brotherhood, rejects caste, and enjoins purity of life. Distinguished as fighters, the Sikhs furnished a famous contingent in the British Indian army.

the valor of a Sikh

SILENCE

Silence is a foolish country justice in Shakespeare's *King Henry IV*, Part II. A man of untamable mirth when he is tipsy, he is of asinine dullness when abstinent and sober.

like Master Silence, he had been merry twice and once in his time

---

SILENUS

Silenus, an elderly satyr, the constant companion of Dionysus (Bacchus), is represented as a jovial old baldheaded man with a pug nose, fat, and too intoxicated to walk. Therefore he was always riding or being supported by other satyrs. He was a lover of sleep, wine, and music, the inventor of the flute, and a prophet who would prophesy only when he was drunk, asleep, and surrounded by chains of flowers, at which time he was in the power of mortals. He was lazy, debauched, wanton, and a winebibber.

an intemperate Silenus

SILHOUETTE, ETIENNE DE

Etienne de Silhouette (1709-1767) was the French controller general of finances whose reforms brought on him the contempt and ridicule of the nobles because of his attempts to reduce the pensions of privileged people. Deriding him for his cheapness and economies, the nobility gave his name to low-priced articles, including the outline profiles now called after him.

operating on the low budget of an Etienne de Silhouette

SILK-STOCKING

Members of the conservative Federalist or Whig Party in United States politics of the early nineteenth century were called "Silk-Stockings," because their wealth enabled them to wear the then costly silken hosiery. In New York and other Amercan cities, the ward in which the rich residents are predominantly influential politically is still known as the "Silk-Stocking District."

The name, apart from this usage, denotes an aristocratic or an elegant person of sybaritic character, since silk hosiery was formerly regarded as extravagant and even reprehensible morally. As applied chiefly to men, "Silk-Stocking" betokens an effeminate fop of luxurious habits or an indolent wastrel and profligate who spends his energies in libertinism.

Hopkins was elected by the Silk-Stockings on the one hand and the Short-Hairs on the other

the class of men who rejoice in slippered ease: the people call them "Silk-Stockings"

SILVANUS

Silvanus was the deity presiding over woods, forests and fields. Also the protector of the boundaries of fields, he delighted especially in plantations. His tutelary functions included their fertility and driving away wolves. By the Latin poets he was depicted as a genial old man in love with Pomona.

a skilled Silvanus at caring for trees

SILVER, JOHN

John Silver is the one-legged pirate and treacherous buccaneer in Stevenson's *Treasure Island*. Called "Long John" because of his height, he wore a patch over one eye. For young readers he epitomizes the typical portrait of the rum-swilling, skull-and-cross-bones-flying villain of the seas who makes trembling victims walk the plank, much to the fascinated horror of his audience.

a malicious peg-leg of the John Silver school

SIMEON

Simeon was the devout Jew of Jerusalem to whom the Holy Ghost revealed that "he should not see death before he had seen the Lord's Christ." When he beheld the child Jesus in the temple, he uttered the song now known as the *Nunc Dimittis*: "Lord, now lettest thou thy servant depart in peace, according to thy word: For mine eyes have seen thy salvation, which thou hast prepared before the face of all people; A light to lighten the Gentiles, and the glory of thy people Israel."

the pious belief of Simeon

SIMEON STYLITES

Simeon Stylites (390-459 A.D.) was the most famous of the Syrian ascetics and "pillar saints." He spent the last thirty-seven years of his life living on different pillars, each loftier and narrower than the preceding, the last being sixty-six feet high. He preached from his perilous perch, making many converts and acquiring great influence. Daniel the Stylite, of Constantinople, lived thirty-three years on a similar pillar, and was frequently blown from it by the storms from Thrace. Tennyson's poem on Simeon Stylites says:

"I, Simeon of the Pillar by surname,
Stylites among men — I, Simeon,
The watcher on the column till the end."

as vigilant as Simeon Stylites

SIMON

Simon, surnamed Magus (magician), was a Samarian who "used sorcery and bewitched the people of Samaria, giving out that himself was some great one." Called "the great power of God" by the credulous townfolk, he was later converted and baptized by Philip the apostle. When he had received the Holy Ghost through the laying on of the hands of Peter and John, he offered them money to grant him too the power to make a similar use of his hands. He was sharply rebuked by Peter for being so mercenary as to think "that the gift of God may be purchased with money" (*Acts,* viii).

Simon was also the name of the man of Cyrene who was compelled to bear Jesus' cross (*Mark,* xv, 21), and of the tanner of Joppa in whose seaside house Peter lodged (*Acts,* ix, 43).

Simonian thaumaturgy

SIMON, SIMPLE

Simple Simon, a character in Mother Goose, a wandering foolish one, asks for samples of pie and other goodies without any intention of buying. The name is now used of any aimless, inane, rambling person, willing to get something for nothing, blithely asking for anything that seems desirable to him.

had a Simple-Simon follower

SIN

Sin is the Assyro-Babylonian moon-god. The lord of wisdom, he dispels darkness and evil and sends dreams and oracles. The chief seats of his worship were at Ur and Haran.

a dream winging from Sin's moon

SINAI

Sinai is the name of the mountain from which the commandments and the Law were given to Moses (*Exodus*, xix). Described as a wilderness and a desert, it was from very early times regarded as a sacred place, as dedicated perhaps to the Babylonian moon-god Sin (*q.v.*). It was also known as Mount Horeb.

as revered as Sinai

SINDBAD THE SAILOR

Sindbad the Sailor, a wealthy man of Bagdad, related his seven incredible and fabulous adventures, fascinating and bold. Among them is the story of the time he compassionately took on his back, to carry him across a small brook, an apparently helpless, little old man who turned out to be the Old Man of the Sea and refused to get off. To get rid of him, Sindbad finally gave him so much strong drink that he loosed his hold and Sindbad shook him off. The stories have fascinated readers to this day.

the glorious mendaciousness of a Sindbad tale

SINDRE

Sindre, in Old Norse mythology, is a dwarf who makes a wager with Loki that he can make three treasures that will surpass those possessed by the god. He then creates a boar with golden bristles, a golden ring (Draupner), and Thor's hammer. The name is also used generally for any member of a race of dwarfs.

a dwarfed and stunted Sindre

SINIS

Sinis, or Sinnis, was a robber and brigand who haunted the isthmus of Corinth, killing the travelers whom he captured by tying them to the top of a fir-tree, which he bent like a sling-shot and then let spring up again. He himself was punished by being treated to the same kind of death by Theseus.

catapulted by Sinis

SINN FEIN

Sinn Fein ("we ourselves") was the name of an Irish society founded by Arthur Griffith in 1905 to promote national home manufacturing for that country and to further its economic independence of Britain. It later became active politically, advocating extreme republicanism and fomenting the revolt of 1916. The revival of nationalistic Irish literature and culture was also among its goals.

as Celtic as the Sinn Fein

SINON

Sinon, the prototype of all treacherous and perfidious people who deceive in order to betray, was the crafty Greek who accompanied his relative, Ulysses, to the siege of Troy. Allowing himself to be taken prisoner, he persuaded the Trojans to take into their city the wooden horse, filled with armed men, which the Greeks had constructed as a pretended atonement for the Palladium (*q.v.*). The Trojans fell victims to his persuasions and dragged the horse into their city; whereupon Sinon, in the dead of night, let the Greeks out of the horse to take Troy.

a smoothly persuasive Sinon

SIR COURTLY NICE

Sir Courtly Nice is the principal character in a comedy of the same name (1685) by John Crowne. He is an insignificant but self-important fop and "Silk-Stocking," a simpering dandy like the contemporary Sir Fopling Flutter in Etherege's *The Man of Mode.*

more of a coxcomb and exquisite than Sir Courtly Nice

SIR MARTIN MAR-ALL

Sir Martin Mar-all is an inept and blundering knight, the principal character of *The Feigned Innocence,* a comedy (1668) by Dryden.

spoiled as though by Sir Martin Mar-all

SIREN

The Sirens were three sister nymphs who lived on an island near Sicily and enticed sailors ashore by their singing, then killed them. Their song was so irresistible that one great hero, Ulysses (Odysseus), longing to hear it, had the ears of the crew stuffed with wax and himself lashed to the mast, so that he might hear them and yet be unable to guide or to order others to guide the ship to their shores. Hence, their name signifies alluring, irresistible, dangerous. Their names are usually given as Parthenope, Ligeia, and Leucothea.

the siren-voices lured him through the doors

SISERA

Sisera was the Canaanite commander-in-chief of the army of the tyrant Jabin, who had oppressed the children of Israel for twenty years. During the war against Barak and the prophetess Deborah, his army "with its 900 chariots of iron" was totally annihilated, and Sisera himself fled for sanctuary to the tent of Jael, the wife of Heber, an ally. After this treacherous woman had given him refreshment and covered him over with a mantle (presumably for purposes of concealment), she took a hammer and drove a nail through his temples, pinning his head to the ground. His body was subsequently delivered into the hands of Barak (*Judges*, iv).

a Sisera, betrayed in hiding

SISTER ANNE

Sister Anne was the instrument of salvation for Fatima, the seventh and last of the wives of Blue-beard. This unfortunate lady, having been condemned to death by her husband, obtained the favor of a brief delay. Sister Anne ascended the highest tower of the castle to watch for her brothers, who were expected to make them a visit at about that time. When the distraught Fatima called up to her for news of hope on the horizon, for a long time Sister Anne could only disappoint her with announcement of clouds of dust raised by flocks of sheep. Finally, and in the nick of time, however, she proclaimed the happy arrival of the brothers, who forthwith despatched the arch-villainous Blue-beard.

Sister Anne at the lookout to descry aid

SISYPHEAN

Sisyphean is from the fabulous Sisyphus, avaricious and deceitful King of Corinth, so crafty that when Death came for him he outwitted Death and bound him in fetters. For this and because of his other crimes, he was doomed eternally to roll a great stone uphill, but at the top of the hill the stone always rolled back again. Sisyphean toil has always therefore meant unending, laborious toil, always needing to be done over again when it is apparently finished.

the Sisyphean labors of the household

SITA

Sita, in Hindu mythology, is the bride of the god Rama, or Vishnu, and was carried off by the giant Ravana. She is said not to have been born in normal fashion, but to have sprung from a furrow while her father, Janaka, king of Mithila, was plowing.

searching the furrows for Sita

SIVA

Siva, who with Brahma and Vishnu forms the sacred Hindu trinity of Creator, Preserver, and Destroyer, is named by euphemistic use of the Hindu word for "kind" or "gracious." Himself the transformer of forces and the destroyer of life, he exercises this function, however, only in order to enable subsequent regeneration and reproduction. The lingam, or phallus, and the sacred bull are two of his many emblems. One of his aspects is that of a stern asceticism that works miracles by means of penance and meditation. Also god of the arts and especially of dancing, he is called Nataraja in his sphere as cosmic dancer. Durga is his spouse.

founa death ana transfiguration at the hands of Siva

SKADHI

Skadhi, in Old Norse mythology, is a giantess, the wife of Njord. She suspends a poisonous serpent over the face of the captured Loki, and is represented by a wild mountain stream, plunging down from high rocks. Her name, meaning "to harm," is related to the English word *scathe.*

a woman as gigantic and baleful as Skadhi

SKANDA

Skanda, in Hindu mythology, is the younger brother of Ganesha, and the son of Siva. The god of war, he is represented as having six arms and as riding on a peacock. He is also called Kartikkeya.

war incited by Skanda

SKEGGS, MISS CAROLINA

Miss Carolina Wilhelmina Amelia Skeggs is one of the town ladies who impose upon the innocent family of the Vicar, in Goldsmith's *Vicar of Wakefield.* A false pretender to gentility, she boasts of her aristocratic connections and acquaintance, and prides herself on her taste for Shakespeare and love of musical glasses. In the end, however, she turns out to be no better than she should be.

as full or false pretensions as Miss Skeggs

SKIDBLADNIR

Skidbladnir, old Norse for "a thin plank" and "a leaf," is the name of the ship made by the dwarfs and given to Frey, in Scandinavian mythology. It was so capacious that it could hold all the gods with full panoply of weapons and armor, and, when the sails were set, it always had a fair wind. When not required for navigation, it could be folded up like a piece of cloth and tucked in Frey's pocket.

as adjustable as Skidbladnir

SKIMMINGTON

Skimmington is a word of unknown origin, but supposed to be the name of some notorious scold of old English times. Used only in the phrase *to ride Skimmington,* in the sense of creating a row or a disturbance, it was employed to describe a species of mock triumphal procession in honor of a man who had been beaten by his wife. In the cavalcade the henpecked husband (or his next neighbor) rode behind a woman, with his face to the horse's tail, holding a distaff in his hand and seeming to work on it, while the woman beat him with a ladle and the retinue made hideous noises with frying-pans, meat-cleavers, and the like. Those who attended this mournful procession were wont to sweep the threshold of the houses in which fame affirmed the mistresses to exercise paramount authority, which was given and received as a hint that their inmates in turn might be made the subject of a similar ovation.

as shrewish as Skimmington's spouse

SKIMPOLE, HAROLD

Harold Skimpole, in Dickens' *Bleak House,* is a mild-mannered, selfish, and unprincipled sentimentalist and sponger upon his friends. A shiftless and aesthetic amateur artist, he is said to represent a caricature of some of the more prominent character-traits of Leigh Hunt.

dilettantish as Harold Skimpole

SKIRNIR

Skirnir is the Old Norse messenger of the gods, especially of Frey. He won that god's magic sword, which would of its own accord spread a field with carnage, by getting him Gerda for his wife.

as swift as if brought by Skirnir

SKULD

Skuld, in Scandinavian mythology, is the name of one of the three Norns or Fates. She represents the future, and her very name is related to the word *shall.*

resigned to the will of Skuld

SLAWKENBERGIUS, HAFEN

Hafen Slawkenbergius is the name of an imaginary author who is quoted in Sterne's *Life and Opinions of Tristram Shandy, Gent.* as a great authority on all learning connected with the subject of noses. Distinguished by the inordinate length of his own nose, Slawkenbergius relates a quaint and singular tale about another man with an enormous nasal appendage.

no nose can be justly amputated by the public, not even the nose of Slawkenbergius himself

Carlyle

SLEEPING BEAUTY

Sleeping Beauty is the heroine of a celebrated nursery tale, *La Belle au Bois Dormant,* by Charles Perrault (*q.v.*), relating how a princess was shut up by fairy enchantment, to sleep a hundred years in a castle, around which sprang up a dense, impenetrable wood. At the expiration of the appointed time she was delivered from her imprisonment by a handsome young prince, before whom the forest opened itself to afford him passage. The story's prototype may be found in the sleeping Brynhild and her awakening and deliverance by Sigurd (q.v.), though its origins may be traced as far back as the story of Epimenides, a Cretan poet, who sheltered himself from a torrid sun while in search of a lost sheep, and fell asleep in a cave for fifty-seven years (see also the *Seven Sleepers of Ephesus*).

Perrault's version of a beautiful woman awakening to love is romantically rendered in Tschaikovsky's ballet score for this subject, and is also familiar in Tennyson's metrical rendition.

like the prince in the nursery tale, he sought and found his Sleeping Beauty within the recesses which so long concealed her from mankind

Macaulay

these precincts . . . are silent, vacant, yet comfortably furnished, like Sleeping Beauty's castle

Carlyle

SLEIPNIR

Sleipnir, in Scandinavian mythology, is the horse of Odin. The noblest of his race, he carries his master over land and sea alike. He is of a gray color, has eight legs, and typifies the wind, which blows from eight principal points. Like Pegasus, he is the courser of the poet's soul and is emblematic of lofty inspiration.

no Sleipnir to whisk him to his goal

SLENDER, ABRAHAM

Abraham Slender is a country lout and a booby in Shakespeare's *Merry Wives of Windsor.* Cousin to Shallow (*q.v.*), he is a silly provincial youth in love with Mistress Anne Page, but he is too faint-hearted to win so fair a prize. His portrait is that of an awkward, obstinate, and confused suitor who is ill-at-ease among civil people, but at home in rude sports and proud of exploits at which the town would laugh.

fell as short of his fair goal as Slender

during the second Punic war (218-202 B.C.). When Syphax was captured by Masinissa, a Numidian prince allied to Rome, she too fell into his hands, as he fell prey to her beauty. Masinissa was, however, restrained from marrying her by Scipio, who feared her influence on his loyalty to Rome and wished to claim her as a captive to grace his Roman triumph. To save her from this disgrace, Masinissa sent her poison, which she courageously drank. Nathaniel Lee and Corneille wrote tragic plays centering on her as heroine.

with the undaunted courage of a Sophonisba

SORBONIST

Sorbonist, a designation for a learned person in France, is from the Sorbonne, an educational institution of theology, science, and literature that is now a part of the University of Paris. Founded by Robert de Sorbon, chaplain and confessor of Louis IX, in 1257, it was then designed as a place of learning for theological students of impoverished means. Its amphitheater is now the scene of the annual congress of the learned societies of France.

with the higher degrees of a Sorbonist

SORDELLO

Sordello was a renowned 13th century Provencal poet whom Dante and Vergil met in Purgatory, sitting alone, with a haughty aspect, and eying them like a lion on the watch. On finding that Vergil was his countryman, he sprang forward to embrace him with joy, accompanying him partway on his journey. Browning wrote a philosophical and narrative poem of his progress in experience and education till he reached the stature, name, and fame of poet. He chose him as in some sort an ideal man, identified with the cause of liberty and human progress, and exemplifying the highest and best results of culture.

the lion-like repose of a Sordello

SORREL, HETTY

Hetty Sorrel is the first love of Adam Bede, the bookish carpenter-hero of George Eliot's novel of that name. After she is seduced by Arthur Donnithorne, a weak but good-natured youth, Adam marries Dinah Morris.

unfaithful as Hetty Sorrel

SOSIA

Sosia is a servant of Amphitryon, or Amphitruo, in Plautus's play of that name. Mercury, availing himself of his power to assume disguises at pleasure, figures in the play as the double of Sosia, who is consequently led to doubt his own identity. Hence, by an extension of the term, the name is given to any person who bears a close or striking resemblance to another and thus seems to be a duplicate of the other or even to eclipse that other. Dryden and Molière have both adapted the *Amphitruo* to the stage of their time.

a Sosia more faithful than the original

SOTENVILLE, MONSIEUR

M. Sotenville ("fool in the city") is the name of a pompous, stolid, provincial French noble of the seventeenth century who figures in Molière's comedy of *George Dandin*. He aggravates his intrinsic insignificance and vacuity by aping the manners of the court *noblesse*.

as pretentiously pedigreed as M. de Sotenville

SOTER

Soter is a Greek surname meaning savior, deliverer, or preserver. It was applied as an epithet to many gods and men, including Zeus, Poseidon, and Ptolemy I of Egypt.

thinks of himself as the Soter of his age

SOUTHCOTT, JOANNA

Joanna Southcott (1750-1814) was the English religious fanatic and visionary who claimed to be the "bride of the Lamb." At the age of 64 she announced that she was about to become the mother of Shiloh, the "true Messiah," but died ten days after her prophecy had proven false. Her followers, known as Southcottians, numbered some 100,-000. She was the author of several books of prophecy.

a Southcottian parthenogenesis

SPARTACUS

Spartacus, successively a Thracian shepherd, soldier, and chief of banditti, was taken prisoner on one of his predatory expeditions and sold to a trainer of gladiators. While detained in the school of Lentulus at Capua, of whose company he was a member, he boldly led seventy of his fellows in an outbreak in 73 B.C., hiding in the crater of Vesuvius and collecting an army of slaves and desperadoes which for two years resisted the Roman armies and ravaged Italy from the foot of the Alps to the southernmost corner of the peninsula. He was finally defeated and slain in 71 B.C. by Marcus Licinius Crassus, though his courage and daring were so great that he had actually stabbed his horse before the battle, determined that he would not submit to the ignominy of flight.

the daring lawlessness of a Spartacus

SPARTAN

Spartan is from Sparta, a city not walled in but depending for its protection on the valor of its inhabitants, consequently developing fighters rather than talkers. The Spartans were bound by laws drawn up by Lycurgus and approved by the Delphic oracle. Their money was iron, consequently undesirable to own. They ate at a common table, kings and people together, and all were silent at meals. Children were property of the state, trained to despise danger, the pains of toil, and to endure suffering without flinching. All were inured to prefer death to dishonor and to subdue all personal feeling to the state. Youths were forced to forage for food, and punished for failure to find it, or for being caught while finding it. Strangely enough, the system contributed not a single great man to the world. Spartan means endurance, stoicism, unflinching calmness.

Spartan endurance
Spartan silence

SPEED

Speed is the name of the clownish manservant of Valentine, one of Shakespeare's *Two Gentlemen of Verona*. He is a quick-witted rogue and an inveterate punster.

as full of word-plays as Speed

SPENCERIAN

Spencerian is from P. R. Spencer (1800-1864), founder of American business colleges. He was the person who established as standard the very fine-line, slightly shaded, slanting style of handwriting used in those colleges and "by genteel persons everywhere." It is now a mark of the nineteenth century as surely as are Godey styles and haircloth sofas.

(To be distinguished from Spenserian)

the Spencerian hand of Victorian America

SPENLOW AND JORKINS

Spenlow and Jorkins is a law firm in Dickens' *David Copperfleld.* Each member escaped criticism by shunting the responsibility to the other partner. It is now an expression used to indicate any settled policy of shifting blame for hard dealings.

never both in; a conventional Spenlow-Jorkins arrangement

SPENLOW, DORA

Dora Spenlow, in Dickens' *David Copperfield,* is the pretty but frail and impractical child-wife of the hero and title-character. She worshiped her husband with an idolatrous love.

as unfit for marriage as Dora Spenlow

SPENS, SIR PATRICK

Sir Patrick Spens is the hero of the famous old Scottish balad in which he is represented as having been sent by the king of Scotland on a mission to Norway in the wintertime, and as having been lost with his whole crew in mid-ocean on the homeward voyage. In one of the islands of the Orcadian group, a large tumulus, or grave mound, has been known to the inhabitants as his last resting-place from time immemorial, though there is nothing factual to attest to the manner of his death or the cause of his mysterious disappearance.

as inexplicable a disappearance as that of Sir Patrick Spens

SPENSERIAN

Spenserian is from Edmund Spenser, sixteenth century poet unequalled either for the untrammeled and purely imaginative beauty of his poetic conceptions, the fanciful and romantic tales he created, or for the perfect fluency and melody of his word combinations. "They would have music even were there no meaning attached," is the opinion of the ages. The most lyric and melodious of the later poets, among them Shelley and Keats, admittedly imitated Spenser, and consciously studied him to imbue themselves with those poetic qualities.

flowing Spenserian measures

SPES

Spes was the deified Roman personification of Hope, equivalent to the Greek goddess Elpis. Several temples were dedicated to her in ancient Rome. In art she is represented as a youthful figure, walking lightly in full attire, and holding a flower in her right hand while her left raises the hem of her garment, as if to avoid any obstacle in her path.

bases his fortune on Spes

SPHINX

The Sphinx, originally a monster with a human head and the body of a lion, proposed to all travelers the riddle: "What walks on four legs in the morning, two legs at noon, and three legs at night?" He destroyed all who could not answer. Finally the Thebans offered their land and the hand of their queen, Jocasta, to any man who could answer the riddle. Oedipus answered: "Man, who walks on four legs in infancy, two legs at maturity, and three legs, one a staff, in age." The Sphinx slew herself in rage, and Oedipus claimed the land of Thebes. Statues were erected to the Sphinx, the most famous at the foot of the pyramids, where she sits looking westward, attentive and inscrutable, with an expression of depth, majesty, serenity, and mystery.

inscrutable as the Sphinx
sphinx-like silence

SPINOZA

Benedict Spinoza (1632-1677) was born in Holland of Spanish and Portuguese Jewish parents. He was finally excommunicated by the Jews for his heretical doctrines. While often characterized as an atheist and a blasphemer, he was conceded to be a calm, reflective, diligent scholar and a peaceable domestic man. He is elsewhere recorded as having an all-composing calmness, mathematical method, precise thinking, and to have led a most devout life, a life "one unbroken hymn, but not pious."

methodical as Spinoza

SPOLIA OPIMA

The Spolia Opima, in Roman history, were the "rich spoils" or the "spoils of honor" taken by a Roman general from the leader of an enemy force after defeating that leader in single-handed combat, the outcome of which granted victory to the side of the winner. These distinguished spoils of armor were then dedicated to Jupiter Feretrius, "the striker." Only three times in the annals of early Rome were they taken: once, by Romulus from Acron, following the Rape of the Sabines; then, by Aulus Cornelius Cossus from the Etruscan Tolumnius; and last, by Marcus Claudius Marcellus from the Gaul Viridomarus. So rarely did this honor befall that *Spolia Opima* now designates the supreme rewards or achievements of men in competition.

feats worthy of the honor of Spolia Opima

SPOONERISM

A Spoonerism is a *lapsus linguae*, or slip of the tongue, caused by the inadvertent transposition of the sounds in two or more words. Attributed to nervous tension, these unintentional errors in speech were named after William Archibald Spooner (1844-1930), Anglican clergyman and educator who perpetrated such garblings as the "shoving leopard of his flock" for "loving shepherd of his flock," and "sew the ladies into their sheets" for "show the ladies into their seats."

Spooner's fallibility of speech

SPURINNA VESTRITIUS

Spurinna Vestritius was the name of the haruspex, or diviner, who warned Julius Caesar to beware of the Ides of March. Like that of Cassandra, his name is therefore indicative of ominous foresight.

no Spurinna to warn him

SQUARE AND THWACKUM

Mr. Square is a "philosopher" in Fielding's novel *The History of Tom Jones, a Foundling*. He is always disputing with Thwackum, a fellow tutor, and in their characters Fielding satirizes the theological pedantry of education. Square insists on the natural virtue of man, while Thwackum deduces everything from original sin.

as disputatious as Square and Thwackum

SQUEERS

Squeers is the brutal, self-seeking, obsequious, stingy, dishonest schoolmaster in Dickens' *Oliver Twist*. He was master of Dotheboys Hall, where he had his own despicable methods of "doing the boys" to his own great profit and their great misery. He is representative of the dishonest, tricky, altogether cruel and self-seeking heads of institutions by which the rights and the happiness of the inmates are completely ignored.

the Squeers are all stirring uneasily

SQUIRE OF DAMES

The Squire of Dames is a personage introduced by Spenser in the *Faerie Queene*, Book III, canto vii. His gallant adventures have caused his name to be used to express a person devoted to the fair sex, or even a pimp, though in the poem he chivalrously performs the tasks enjoined on him by Columbell, his sweetheart.

a wandering Squire of Dames

STANDISH, MILES

Miles Standish (1584-1656) was the English soldier who emigrated to America in the "Mayflower" and became a military leader of the Pilgrims. The subject of Longfellow's famous poem, he was the shy, bashful suitor of Priscilla and deputed John Alden to propose for him. Priscilla, however, with more of an eye for John, uttered the immortal "Speak for yourself, John, " and Miles Standish became a rejected candidate.

bashful in love as Miles Standish

STANLEY, HENRY M.

Sir Henry Morton Stanley (1841-1904) was a British-born youth who ran to sea and was adopted by the New Orleans merchant after whom he is named. After serving as a newspaper correspondent in Asia Minor, Crete, and Spain, he was commissioned by the New York *Herald* to lead the expedition in search of David Livingstone (*q.v.*), whom he rescued November 10, 1871, greeting him with the absurdly formal remark "Dr. Livingstone, I presume?" Later becoming an African explorer of note, he wrote *Through the Dark Continent* and *In Darkest Africa.* A repatriated British citizen in later life, he had the honor of having the Stanley Falls in the upper Congo named after him.

pompous and ceremonious as Henry Stanley

STATIRA

Statira, Persian queen of the fourth century B.C., and sister and wife of Darius III, was celebrated as being the most beautiful woman of her time. She was taken captive by Alexander the Great and died in 331 B.C. Statira was also the name of Darius's daughter, whom Alexander married in order to fuse the European and Asiatic portions of his far-flung empire. Roxana (*q.v.*) was her rival for the affections of the conqueror.

a beautiful and queenly Statira

STATOR

Stator is the epithet of Roman Jupiter as the courage-inspiring "stayer-of-flight" of armies in battle, and as "giver of victory." As establisher, he preserves the existing order, or status quo of things.

saved from rout and defeat by Stator

STEERFORTH, JAMES

James Steerforth, in Dickens' *David Copperfield,* is the schoolmate who befriends David, but later turns into the gay and attractive libertine who seduces and abandons Little Emily.

a persuasively blandishing Steerforth

STEIN, GERTRUDE

Gertrude Stein (1874-1946) was the brilliant, though mostly unintelligible, American author (*Tender Buttons, Four Saints in Three Acts, Wars I Have Seen,* etc.) who elected to make France her spiritual home. Critic and patron of the arts, she established a salon that included Picasso, Matisse, Cézanne and other eminent Gallic painters. She also exerted a significant influence on such American writers as Dos Passos and Hemingway. Her style is characterized by alternatingly naive and abstruse principles, and she works for rhythmic effects in her prose.

a Steinese jargon

STELLA

Stella was the name given by Sir Philip Sidney, in a series of exquisitely beautiful amatory poems entitled *Astrophel and Stella,* to Penelope Devereux (afterward Lady Rich), at one time the loadstar of his affections, and generally admitted to have been the finest woman of her age. Stella means "star," and Astrophel, a sort of metagrammatic translation of an element in the author's first name and his beloved's pet name into Greek, means "star-lover."

Swift also gave the name Stella to his one-time pupil, Miss Esther (Greek *aster* for "star") Johnson, whom he privately married in 1716.

a paragon of womankind to outshine Stella

STELLENBOSCHE

Stellenbosche, originally a verb, refers to the town of Cape province, South Africa, known as Stellenbosch. In the early days of the Boer War (1899-1902) it was used as a British military base, and officers who had not distinguished themselves at the front were "sent back to Stellenbosch," whence the term *Stellenbosched* became so widely used that men were said to have been treated so even if sent to some other place. The name is now applied to any person who is failing in the position to which he has been assigned, but is saved from the embarrassment of dismissal by mild demotion to another position, usually a sinecure. American slang calls the process being "kicked upstairs."

a Stellenbosche promotion

STENTORIAN

Stentorian is from Stentor, the Greek herald in the Trojan war whom Homer describes as "great-hearted, brazen-voiced Stentor, accustomed to shout as loud as fifty other men." The derivative adjective is now applied to any prodigiously loud, resonant, or bellowing voice or announcement.

roared for help with the lungs of a Stentor

STEPHEN, SAINT

Saint Stephen (*Acts,* vi and vii) was the deacon of the early church at Jerusalem. Falsely accused of blasphemy, he was stoned to death, thus becoming the first Christian martyr. Though the legal forms of stoning were observed by his executioners, the death of the "proto-martyr" was tumultuary in character.

as pelted with stones as Stephen

STEROPES

Steropes is the name of one of the Cyclopes, a gigantic one-eyed race of men inhabiting the seacoasts of Sicily. Sons of Coelus (heaven) and Terra (earth), they were said by Hesiod to have been three only in number, the names of Sterope's brothers being Arges and Brontës. Homer described them as wild, insolent, and lawless shepherds who devoured human beings. A later tradition represented them as Vulcan's assistants in fabricating thunderbolts for Jupiter.

as cannibalistic as Steropes
Steropean lawlessness

STEVENSONIAN

Robert Louis Stevenson (1850-1894), the inimitable story-teller the world knows through *Treasure Island* and *Kidnapped,* and through his *Child's Garden of Verses,* is one of the best beloved of English writers. Stevenson kept his spirit of youth, gayety, charm, his exuberant enthusiasm in a good yarn, and his scrupulously careful artistry in the face of a losing fight against ill health. Breadth of mind, wealth of anecdote and charm of style animate his essays and letters with his inexhaustible spirit of *camaraderie.*

Stevensonian courage
Stevensonian charm

STEYNE, MARQUIS OF

The Marquis of Steyne, in Thackeray's *Vanity Fair,* is a cynical and profligate old nobleman who is soundly thrashed by Colonel Rawdon Crawley for his lecherous attentions to Becky Sharp, Crawley's wife. This unprincipled roué causes a separation between the couple.

another Marquis of Steyne at making a cuckold out of any husband

---

STHENEBOEA

Stheneboea was one of the many "Potiphars' wives" of classical antiquity. The Lycian wife of Proetus, the king of Argos, she conceived an erotic passion for young Bellerophon, who was a guest in her husband's home. When her efforts to seduce the chaste youth were spurned, in a rage of shame she accused him before her husband of attempting to violate her. Unwilling to ignore the sacred bonds of hospitality by which he was bound to him, Proetus, however, despatched Bellerophon with a sealed letter for Iobates, the father of Stheneboea, requesting him to put the accused to death. The mission against the Chimaera was one of the futile attempts by which Iobates endeavored to encompass the hero's punishment.

an illicit passion like Stheneboea's

STHENO

Stheno, in Greek mythology, was one of the Gorgons, the three daughters of Phorous and Ceto. Like her sisters, Euryale and Medusa (*q.v.*), Stheno's hair was entwined with hissing serpents and her body covered with impenetrable scales. All had wings, brazen claws, and enormous teeth, and whoever looked upon them was turned to stone. The name *Stheno* may thus be used to describe any hideously ugly or repulsive woman.

a hag of Sthenonian horror

STIGGINS, REVEREND MR.

The Reverend Mr. Stiggins, in Dickens' *Pickwick Papers,* is a Methodist parson who is spiritual adviser to Mrs. Weller. A hypocritical puritan and killjoy, he is a temperance lecturer with a secret passion for pineapple rum.

like the Rev. Mr. Stiggins, a teetotaler only in public

STOCKWELL GHOST

The Stockwell Ghost was a name given to a supposed supernatural agent who produced a train of extraordinary disturbances and strange noises in Stockwell, near London, in the year 1772, by which the superstitious inhabitants were thrown into abject fear and consternation. When the author of the imposture, a servant by the name of Anne Robinson, was at length detected, her "magic" was found to lie merely in an unusual dexterity aided by the credulity of the spectators.

as fraudulent as the Stockwell Ghost

STOIC

(see *Zeno*)

A Stoic is a follower of the school of philosophy founded by Zeno (342-270 B.C.). Marked by austerity and unbending morality, it included bearing with composure any lot Destiny might bring, or any physical pain, in short, priding oneself on showing neither suffering nor emotion. Diogenes introduced a note of cynicism when he went about in daylight, carrying a lantern and looking for an honest man. The emperor and philosopher, Marcus Aurelius, was a Stoic whose principles were published as *The Sayings of Marcus Aurelius.*

the stoicism of a true philosopher

STOKE POGES

Stoke Poges is the name of the village in Buckinghamshire, England, in which the remains of Thomas Gray (*q.v.*) are buried. In its quiet cemetery he is said to have composed his famous *Elegy in a Country Churchyard.*

a resting-place as still as Stoke Poges

STONEHENGE

Stonehenge ("hanging stones") is the prehistoric, monumental pile of huge stones on Salisbury Plain, Wiltshire, England. It consists of two concentric megalithic circles of horseshoe shape, within which originally stood five trilithons (groups of two upright stones having a third resting horizontally on them). Possibly an ancient temple of the sun, it is thought to date back as far as the seventeenth century B.C., and to be a cultural record of the late Neolithic or early Bronze age.

a rock-pile as impressive as Stonehenge

STRABO

Strabo (64 B.C. - A.D. 19) was the Greek Stoic and traveler whose *Geographica* describes in seventeen books the physical geography of all the countries in the Roman world, detailing the history and customs of their inhabitants and the flora and fauna of the lands. He tells how the Indians capture elephants and apes, how the Arabians make fresh water out of brine, and how the Egyptians feed the sacred crocodiles of their country. He also describes the Hanging Gardens of Babylon, the whales in the Persian Gulf, and the perfumes and spices of the Sabaeans.

as well-traveled as Strabo

STRAP, HUGH

Hugh Strap is the name of the simple, generous, and faithful friend and adherent of Roderick Random (*q.v.*), in Smollett's account of the adventures of that notorious personage. About the shabby treatment Strap receives from his friend, Sir Walter Scott said, "We believe there are few readers who are not disgusted with the miserable reward assigned to Strap in the closing chapter of the novel. Five hundred pounds (scarce the value of the goods he had presented to his master) and the hand of a reclaimed street-walker, even when added to a Highland farm, seem but a poor recompense for his faithful and disinterested attachment."

received the compensation of Hugh Strap

STRAUSS

The name of Strauss, epitomizing the spirit of gay Vienna in the reign of Franz Josef, recalls the gracious, charming. and captivating waltzes of Johann Strauss senior (1804-1849), composer of some 150 waltzes and numerous polkas and galops, and of his son Johann junior (1825-1899). The latter succeeded his father to the leadership of the famous Strauss orchestra, and is beloved for his lilting and melodious operettas (*Die Fledermaus*) and unforgettable dance-music (*The Blue Danube, Southern Roses,* etc.).

light-hearted as a Strauss waltz

STREPHON

Strephon is the name of the shepherd in Sidney's *Arcadia* who pays court to a beautiful lady. His is, therefore, a stock name for a lover of the pastoral poetry type in general.

the young Strephons came to dance with Phyllis and Amaryllis

STRULDBRUGS

The Struldbrugs are wretched inhabitants of Luggnagg in Swift's imaginary *Travels* of Lemuel Gulliver. Born with a mark on their forehead, they are supported at public expense after achieving the age of fourscore years, when they are declared dead in law. They are immortal, however, and since they can never die, they eke out a miserable existence, lacking intellect, vigor, and strength.

Struldbrugsian leeches on society

and with impunity for their assassins. From their confiscated estates the murderers were rewarded. Sulla then established a stringent constitutional reform in favor of the privileged classes, though his measures to curb the power of the people were abolished after his death.

another Sullan "reform," favoring the few

SULPICIUS RUFUS, SERVIUS

Servius Sulpicius Rufus (105-43 B.C.) was a great Roman orator and jurist who helped make Roman Law a permanent force in the world, codifying its principles and interpreting and defining them. He is the author of a famous letter of consolation to Cicero on the death of the latter's daughter, an epistle that was admired by St. Ambrose as worthy of a Christian.

the sound legal principles of a Sulpicius Rufus

SUMMANUS

Summanus was an ancient Roman or Etruscan divinity, equal to or even higher than Jupiter with whom he shared dominion of the heavens. As Jupiter was god of the heaven in full day, Summanus was the ruler of nocturnal skies, hurling his thunderbolts during the night. His name is probably derived from the Latin *sub mane*, indicating that he was the god of the time before morning, or "early morning."

Summanus brooding over the darkened skies

SUMMERSON, ESTHER

Esther Summerson is the lovable heroine of Dickens' *Bleak House.* The ward of John Jarndyce, and an illegitimate child, she finally discovers that Lady Dedlock (*q.v.*) was her mother.

a love-child as charming as Esther Summerson

SURFACE, CHARLES

Charles Surface, the younger brother of Joseph, in Sheridan's comedy *The School for Scandal,* is a gay and amiable prodigal and libertine. Warm-hearted, fascinating, and generous, his character is, as his name would indicate, completely but ingratiatingly superficial. He is the accepted lover of Maria Teazle.

an extravagant rake like Charles Surface

SURFACE, JOSEPH

Joseph Surface, in Sheridan's *The School for Scandal,* is the elder brother of Charles (*q.v.*). An artful and mean hypocrite, he affects great seriousness, gravity, and sentimentality, and earns his sobriquet, "the Tartuffe of sentiment." Contrary to Charles, whose character on the surface exhibits all the qualities opprobrious to moralists, Joseph makes a pious and fraudulent show of those deemed praiseworthy.

as sanctimonious as Joseph Surface

SURTUR

Surtur, in Scandinavian mythology, is the formidable fire-giant who, with flames collected from Muspelheim, the abode of intense fire and heat peopled by a host of fiends, is to be the implacable foe of the gods. At Ragnarok (*q.v.*) he will lead the giants to destroy the immortals and set fire to the universe.

a holocaust worthy of Surtur

SURYA

Surya is the Hindu sun-god, sometimes known as Savitar. This deity of light and warmth is represented in art as driving in a vehicle drawn by four or seven horses.

the beneficent rays of Surya

SUSANNA

Susanna, according to her *History* in the Old Testament Apocrypha, was the beautiful and virtuous wife of Joachim, and was accused of adultery during the Babylonian captivity by some elders whose advances she had resisted when surprised in her bath. Daniel proved her innocence and imposed on the lecherous elders the death penalty which they had demanded for her. The scene of the elders peeping salaciously at her nude body as she bathes is depicted in a painting by Rembrandt (1637).

surprised in her privacy like Susanna

SVENGALI

Svengali is the sinister and villainous musician in Du Maurier's novel *Trilby*. Possessing powers of hypnotism, he gets Trilby, an art model, under his spell and makes her the toast of Paris as an incomparable concert singer when mesmerized. Ultimately his power over her is broken. His name suggests villain and hypnotist, one who forces people to do things they would ordinarily not do.

a sleek and sinister Svengali

SWARGA

Swarga, in Hindu mythology, is a terrestrial paradise and heaven situated on the summit of Mount Meru, a sacred spot in the center of the world. It is inhabited by beautiful nymphs and the souls of faithful warriors, and is the delightful abode of Indra and a place of frequent resort for the other gods.

a garden-spot as lovely as Swarga

SWEDENBORGIAN

Swedenborgian is from Emanuel Swedenborg (1688-1772), who claimed intimate communion with the spirit world and power to converse with spirits and with angels. From his youth he was engrossed in reflection upon God, salvation, and the spiritual affections of man, until he came to believe that he had attained a perception of things not visible to the senses. Emanuel Kant records that Swedenborg, his guest at the time, suddenly announced a fire at Stockholm, three hundred miles away, and reported in detail its progress exactly as it was later reported by courier. Swedenborg is now entirely associated with his religious convictions, and his followers are an organized body.

with Swedenborgian clairvoyance

SWIFTIAN

Jonathan Swift (1667-1745), the greatest satirist of his age, was an embittered, gloomy man, lashing out at humanity and particularly at the political institutions of his time in *Gulliver's Travels*. A book that sells over the counter as a child's fairy tale, it is in reality the bitterest known satire of that "detestable little animal, man," according to Swift. Brilliant, incisive, disappointed, a misanthrope, Swift writes prose that is terse, trenchant, clear, with here and there a flash of whimsy.

Swiftian bitterness

SWINBURNE, ALGERNON

Algernon Swinburne (1837-1909), among the greatest of English lyric poets, incurred great criticism in his day because of the paganism and unconventionality of his verse. Many of his poems and plays follow Greek models and have Greek subjects (*Erechtheus, Atalanta in Calydon, The Garden of Proserpine*). Revolutionizing the system of metrics in English poetry, he released verse from the control of the iambic foot and introduced it to the freer use of the choriamb, the dactyl, and the anapest. Reveling in the beauty of sensuous language and rhythm, he was a peerless master of the felicitous phrase.

intricate Swinburnian rhythms

SWITHIN, SAINT

Saint Swithin, a ninth century bishop of Winchester, England, worked fabulous cures even after his death. July 15 is called St. Swithin's day, and there is a popular belief that rain on that day portends rain for forty days thereafter, a belief that persists even though so often proved untrue. It is based on the legend that it rained for forty days immediately after Swithin's death, signifying his displeasure at an attempt of the monks to bury him in the chancel of the church instead of in the open churchyard, as he had directed.

an untrustworthy Swithin

SWIVELLER, DICK

Dick Swiveller, in Dickens' *Old Curiosity Shop,* is a careless and lighthearted young man, whose flowery orations and absurd quotations provoke laughter. Vain, dissipated, and bombastic as he is, his genuine kindness of heart enlists sympathy in spite of his other qualities.

as high-flown as Dick Swiveller

SYBARITE

Sybarite is from Sybaris, a wealthy Greek city of Southern Italy where the people lived in fabulous extravagance and careless luxury, seeking only personal and sensuous pleasure. Hence, the name means luxurious, abandoned, voluptuous.

Sybaritic extravagance

SYCORAX

Sycorax is the foul witch mentioned in Shakespeare's *Tempest* as the mother of Prospero's slave, Caliban. She imprisoned Ariel for declining to obey her commands.

obscured by those foul and impure mists which the raven wings of Sycorax brushed from fern and bog

Sir W. Scott

SYLVIA

Sylvia is a "holy, fair and virtuous" lady in Shakespeare's *Two Gentlemen of Verona.* She is the epitome of desirable girlish beauty, purity and bewitching loveliness.

"Who is Sylvia?
What is she?
That all the swains adore her?"

The name suggests adorable, pleasing, fascinating, and unattainable.

a Sylvia, immortalized in verse

SYMPLEGADES

The Symplegades, in the legend of the Argonauts, were two huge floating rocks at the northern end of the Bosporus, gateway to the Euxine (Black) Sea. At times they were driven together by the winds and crushed all that came between them. The crew of the *Argo,* warned of their clashing by an oracle, sent a pigeon flying through the strait ahead of them. After the rocks had closed on it, the *Argo* slid through on their rebound. The islands thenceforth became fixed and remained open ever after.

jaws that gnash like the Symplegades

SYNTAX, DOCTOR

Doctor Syntax is the simple, pious, amiable, and henpecked clergyman in Combe's *Tour of Dr. Syntax in Search of the Picturesque.* Moralizing in eight-syllabled verse, the author, William Combe (1741-1823), sent his character "in search of consolation" and "in search of a wife" in subsequent books.

a questing Dr. Syntax

SYRINX

Syrinx was the Arcadian nymph whom the enamored god Pan pursued in an effort to overcome her chastity. When she fled into the river Ladon, of which her father was eponymous god, she prayed for metamorphosis in order to escape from her pursuer. At her own request she was changed into a reed, of which Pan then made his flute.

as slender and willowy as Syrinx

SYRTES

The Syrtes were two gulfs off the north coast of Africa, the Greater Syrtis near what is today Tripoli, the Lesser near Tunis. Both were proverbially dangerous to mariners, the one from its sandbanks and its quicksands, the other from its shelving rocky shores.

avoid the Syrtes on your route

T

TABARD

Tabard is the name of the ancient inn at Southwark, London, at which the pilgrims assembled to start their journey to Canterbury Cathedral, in Chaucer's *Canterbury Tales.* The sign of the inn, which represented a short outer jacket worn in bad weather by commoners and monks, gave it its name. Though the hostelry itself was condemned and demolished in 1866, its name is perpetuated in that of numerous contemporary collegiate literary fraternities, known as Tabard Societies and Tabard Clubs.

drinking inspiration at the sign of the Tabard

TABITHA-DORCAS

Tabitha, or Dorcas, was a Christian woman and disciple of Joppa, who was known for her "good works," including the making of coats and garments for the poor. Hence, numerous church sewing circles are known as "Dorcas societies." She was miraculously raised from the dead and restored to life by the apostle Peter (*Acts* ix, 36-41).

a Tabitha with needle and thread

TACITEAN

Tacitean refers to the works and style of Cornelius Tacitus (c. 55-117 A.D.), one of the greatest of the world's historians. Having suffered under the tyrannous rule of Domitian, he was biased in judgment and threw emphasis on the evil aspects of Rome's emperors rather than on their good qualities. His *Annals* recount the events of the reigns of Tiberius, Caligula, Claudius and Nero, the *Histories* those of the emperors from Galba to Domitian. Likewise the author of the *Agricola,* a biography of his father-in-law, an excellent governor of Britain, and the *Germania,* an account of the folkways and tribes of ancient Germany, he wielded an incisive pen. His style is marked by great compression, and he says almost more by insinuation and innuendo than by overt statement.

Tacitean insinuations

TAFFY

Taffy is a corruption of the Welsh pronunciation of the name David, or Davy, and has come to be a generic designation of a Welshman. It also connotes thievery, from the famous Mother Goose rhyme:

Taffy was a Welshman,
  Taffy was a thief,
Taffy came to my house
  And stole a piece of beef.
I went to Taffy's house,
  Taffy wasn't home,
Taffy came to my house
  And stole a marly bone.

a Taffy by birth

TAGES

Tages was a mysterious Etruscan and the grandson of Jupiter. A boy with the precocious wisdom of an old man, he sprang suddenly out of the ploughed earth and instructed Tarchon and the Etruscans in the augural art of interpreting the meaning of lightning flashes. All his sayings were recorded in the twelve books of the haruspices, divining from the entrails of animals killed in sacrifice, and other types of auspices, such as studying the feeding and flying habits of birds.

as precocious as Tages

TAGLIONI

Taglioni was the name of a renowned Italian family of ballet dancers that included: Filippo (1777-1871), ballet master at Stockholm, Vienna, and Warsaw, and creator of the ballet *La Sylphide;* Maria, his daughter (1804-1884), of whom Thackeray said in *The Newcomes* that the young men of that era "will never see anything so graceful as Taglioni in *La Sylphide,*" and whom Balzac also mentions frequently in his novels; Paul (1808-1884), Filippo's son, maître de ballet at the Royal Theater in Berlin; and Paul's daughter, Maria (1833-1891), prima ballerina in London, Berlin, and Naples.

So celebrated was Maria, the elder, for her artistry that a style of multiple skirt in vogue around 1835 was named a *taglioni* after her, as was a kind of overcoat fashionable at the same time.

dancing as airily as Taglioni

TAJ MAHAL

Taj Mahal ("crown of buildings") is the name of the exquisite white marble mausoleum at Agra, India, erected by the Mogul emperor Shah Jehan (1631-1645) in honor of his favorite wife, Mumtazi Mahal. This ethereal and graceful structure contains the remains of both husband and wife. Its beautiful design and rich decorations make it one of the finest specimens of Saracenic architecture.

a resting place as sumptuous as the Taj Mahal

TALASSIUS

Talassius, in Roman legend, was a senator of the time of Romulus. During the rape of the Sabine women, designed to afford female companionship for the young bachelor town of Rome, a maiden of uncommon beauty was carried off for Talassius, and the persons conducting her shouted *Talassio, Talassio* ("She is for Talassius"), in order to protect her from the designs of any other man. Hence, Livy says, arose the wedding cry with which a bride of historical times was conducted to the home of her groom. This explanation was offered since the Romans of later days did not have the faintest idea of the etymological descent or meaning of this part of the marriage ceremony.

reserved for Talassius

TALIESIN

Taliesin is the name of the legendary or mythical Cymric-Celtic bard of the sixth century. The poems known as the *Book of Taliesin* and collected in the fourteenth century are attributed to him by Welsh authorities.

a poet of the antiquity of Taliesin

TALLEYRAND

Charles Talleyrand (1754-1838) was a famous diplomat known for his love of liberty and justice and prominent in the Third Estate in France. In disfavor as French ambassador in England, he was ordered from England by Pitt and proscribed by Robespierre. Therefore he came to the United States where he was warmly received, both because of his love of liberty and because of his exquisite social grace, tact, and wit. He was genuinely respected for his finesse and diplomacy, his wisdom and penetration, which had "the certainty of an instinct."

with Talleyrand's own grace

TALTHYBIUS

Talthybius was the faithful herald of Agamemnon at the siege of Troy. On their return to Mycenae at the close of the war, he is supposed to have saved Orestes, his master's son, from the murderous fury of Clytemnestra, the boy's mother, when she and her paramour slew Agamemnon. Talthybius

thirsty lips reached to drink, and under a fruit-laden tree whose branches lifted out of his reach when his hand grasped for the fruit to appease his hunger. Hence, tantalizing means something in plain view but unattainable.

a Tantalus punishment

TAPLEY, MARK

Mark Tapley, the bodyservant of Martin Chuzzlewit in Dickens' *Martin Chuzzlewit,* was irrepressibly and resolutely jolly. In fact, the more difficult the situation, the more determinedly jolly was Mark.

a Mark-Tapley optimism

TAPPERTITIAN

Tappertitian refers to the youthful bumptiousness and cocksure conceit of Simon Tappertit, the ambitious apprentice to Gabriel Varden in Dickens' *Barnaby Rudge*. The embodiment of self-confidence and aplomb, he aspires to the hand of Dolly Varden, Gabriel's daughter.

with Tappertitian resolve to marry the boss's daughter

TARHEEL

A Tarheel is any native of the North Carolina pine-barrens, where, barefoot or shod, backwoodsmen are apt to have the pitch of the turpentine pine on their heels.

a horde of young Tarheels

TARPEIAN ROCK

The Tarpeian Rock was a cliff at the southwest corner of the Capitoline hill in Rome, from which condemned criminals were hurled. It was named in allusion to Tarpeia, the daughter of the officer in command of the citadel on that hill when it was besieged by Titus Tatius and the Sabines during the reign of Romulus. She bargained with the enemy to betray the city if they would give her what they wore on their left arms. She was referring to the golden bracelets worn on the arms of the Sabine men, but when she admitted them within the walls they rewarded her perfidy by crushing her under their shields, which they also carried on their left arms.

a traitress worthy of Tarpeia's end

TARQUINIUS PRISCUS

Tarquinius was the name of a family in the annals of early Rome. The fifth and seventh kings of that city were of this stock. The former, Lucumo Tarquinius, emigrated from Tarquinii, the family seat in Etruria, to Rome with his wife Tanaquil, a woman of high rank and skilled in the Etruscan science of augury. When they reached the Janiculum hill, an eagle seized Tarquin's cap, carried it away to a great height, and put it back on his head again, an act which Tanaquil interpreted as betokening the highest honor. Settling in Rome, he took the name of Lucius Tarquinius Priscus, and his wealth, courage, and wisdom endeared him to Ancus Marcius, the fourth king then reigning, who appointed him guardian of his children. When Ancus died, the senate and the people unanimously elected Tarquin to the vacant throne.

His reign was distinguished by great exploits in war and by the erection of many public buildings in peace, including the mighty sewers which can still be seen draining into the Tiber. After a reign of 38 years he was murdered at the instigation of the sons of Ancus Marcius, who did not, however, secure the reward they desired, the throne. For Tanaquil succeeded in placing on it Servius Tullius (*q.v.*), whom she had raised in her palace from boyhood, and in whom she had seen a portent of high position, when a divine fire cropped his hair without harming him.

the Tarquinius and Tanaquil of their community, outstanding and capable newcomers

TARQUINIUS SUPERBUS

Lucius Tarquinius Superbus, son-in-law of Servius Tullius (*q.v.*), sixth king of early Rome, murdered the latter in order to become seventh and last king of the city. Reigning tyrannically, he exiled or killed all the patricians whose wealth he coveted, and protected himself with a bodyguard. He made Rome the head of the Latin Confederacy, and with the spoils of his wars erected the Capitoline temple, in the vaults of which he deposited the three Sibylline books he had purchased from a Sibyl, or prophetess, for 300 pieces of gold.

In his unsuccessful attempt to take the city of Gabii, he resorted to a cunning ruse by sending his son Sextus (*q.v.*) into it, covered with bloody welts and pretending to be ill-treated by his father. The gullible inhabitants entrusted the command of their armies to him, and on a hint from his father, who struck off the heads of the tallest poppies in his garden before the eyes of Sextus's messenger, he put to death all the leading men of the place, and then had no difficulty in compelling it to submit to his father.

In the midst of his prosperity, Tarquinius fell from power because of his son's shameful rape of Lucretia (*q.v.*), a married Roman lady. He was deposed and banished from the city with all his family, and, after numerous attempts to reinstate himself on the throne, he died at Cumae, a wretched and lonely old man. The surname *Superbus* had been given him because of his arrogance, cruelty, and despotism.

as overweening and dictatorial as Tarquinius Superbus

TARTARIN

Tartarin of Tarascon is the hero of Alphonse Daudet's quixotic novel of the same name. It concerns the fabulous doings of Tartarin, who, having invested himself with considerable (but fanciful) prestige as a hunter, is compelled to live up to his reputation in a series of absurd undertakings. The name now connotes any ridiculous or braggart person who is forced into impossible situations by his boasting.

a ridiculous Tartarinesque figure
as boastful as Tartarin

TARTARUS

Tartarus is the name of the infernal regions of classical mythology, or specifically that part of them where the impious and guilty were punished for their crimes. Among its famous denizens were Ixion, Tantalus, Sisyphus and the Danaids. In the *Iliad* it is placed beneath the earth, as far below Hades as Heaven is above the earth, and closed by iron gates. Later poets used the name as synonymous with Hades. Vergil describes it and its inhabitants in the sixth book of the *Aeneid*.

suffered Tartarean agonies

TARTUFFIAN

Tartuffian is from Tartuffe, the principal character in Molière's *Tartuffe*. He is a hypocritical, malicious and pretentious person, posing as a priest and religious devotee, pretending to great piety even while he swindles his benefactor. So grotesque and so enormous is his hypocrisy that he is the arch-pretender and hypocrite of French literature. It was said that the character of Tartuffe depicted the confessor of Louis XIV, whom Molière once saw eating truffles (French, *tartufes*).

Tartuffian hypocrisy

TARZAN

Tarzan, childhood favorite of adventurous American youth, is the hero of a comic strip and movies based on a series of novels by Edgar Rice Burroughs, including *Tarzan of the Apes* (1914) and *Tarzan Returns* (1915). A white child abandoned in African jungles through the disaster of his parents, he was reared by an ape and became a tree-swinging, wild phenomenon of the forests, the uncivilized though strong and handsome object of search for a party of British explorers. Taken back to England to learn culture and love, he still yearned for the primitive simplicity of his former haunts and eventually returned to his back-to-nature ways.

with Tarzanian grace and power

TATAR

A Tatar, known erroneously also by the designation Tartar, is a member of a branch of the Ural-Altaic race that includes Cossacks, Turks, Mongols, and Kirghis Tatars. Their habitat is Siberia and Chinese Tartary, and from 1644 to 1912 China was ruled by a Tatar dynasty, the Manchu. When hordes of this savage race pillaged eastern Europe in the reign of St. Louis of France (1226-1270), that monarch exclaimed, with mistaken etymology, over their barbarous deeds, "Well may they be called Tartars, for their deeds are those of fiends from Tartarus!"

The name Tatar, or Tartar, is therefore used to denote a person of violent, irritable, savage, and rebellious temper. And the expression *to scratch a Russian and find a Tatar* means to find that what one thought to be harmless is quite unexpectedly the opposite.

living with that Tatar has all the charms of moving about in a hornets' nest

---

TATTERSALL'S

Tattersall's is the name of the London sporting establishment at which horses were auctioned and traded in market. Opened in 1766 by Richard Tattersall, it became the center of credit-betting for English horse races. Hence, the name is applicable to any large horse market anywhere.

a horse fair as famous as Tattersall's

TATTLE

Tattle, in Congreve's comedy *Love for Love,* is represented as a dull-witted beau and dandy, conceited about his conquests and amours, yet valuing himself for the secrecy with which he guards and protects them.

a lover as indiscreet as Tattle

TAURI

The Tauri were a wild and savage cave-dwelling people who lived in the Tauric Chersonese (the modern Caucausus) of ancient Sarmatia (southern Russia). Inhospitable to travelers and strangers, they sacrificed all who fell into their hands to Diana. Euripides' *Iphigenia among the Taurians* recounts how the heroine and title-character saved her brother, Orestes, from death by human sacrifice among these people.

with Taurian inhospitality

TEAGUE

Teague is a nickname and contemptuous term for an Irishman, about equal to Pat or Paddy. Derived from the Irish word for *clown,* the name appears in Scott's edition of the works of Jonathan Swift (vol. xviii, 203), in Shadwell's play *The Lancashire Witches,* in Howard's *The Committee,* and in Farquhar's *Twin Rivals,* where the name is that of a servant boy who is characterized by wit, blundering, whisky-toping, and laziness. When used with the same connotations, Teagueland means Ireland.

an indolent Teague, content with his bottle of Irish "spirits"

TEARSHEET, DOLL

Doll Tearsheet is a coarse, sharp-tongued strumpet with a brawling temper in the Second Part of Shakespeare's *King Henry IV*. A wench who tipples with Falstaff, she drinks too much "canaries — and that's a marvelous searching wine."

as vulgar and sottish as Doll Tearsheet

TEAZLE, LADY

Lady Teazle, the imprudent young wife of exacting but kindly old Sir Peter Teazle in Sheridan's *School for Scandal,* is a lively and innocent country girl, a little intoxicated by her new wealth and social position, but wholesome enough not to be wholly spoiled by it.

many a Lady Teazle, charming and indiscreet

TEIRTU

Teirtu, in Celtic mythology, was the possessor of a magic harp that played and ceased to play according to the desire of the owner. He would not give it away of his own free will, nor could anyone take it from him by force.

as automatic as Teirtu's harp

TELAMON

Telamon was the son of Aeacus, king of Aegina, and the brother of Peleus. Having assisted the latter in slaying their half-brother Phocus, he was driven from home and came to the island of Salamis, where he married the king's daughter and succeeded to the throne. Telamon numbered among the heroic exploits in which he participated the Calydonian boar-hunt and the Argonautic expedition. A friend of Hercules, he assisted him in his attack on Laomedon of Troy, and was himself the first to scale that city's walls. His name meaning "bearer," a *telamon* in architecture is a male figure used as a supporting column or pilaster in holding up an architrave.

led the attack with Telamonian audacity

TELCHINES

The Telchines, in Greek mythology, were a primitive people associated with the islands of Crete, Cyprus and Rhodes, and were regarded in one aspect as skilled artisans and workers in metal, as tillers of the soil and ministers of the gods. Though reputed to be the inventors of the useful arts, they were said to have been destroyed by Apollo, who had assumed the guise of a wolf, or by an inundation sent upon them by Zeus.

In another aspect, they were considered to be sorcerers and envious demons, whose very eyes brought on destruction. They could bring on hail, rain, and snow, and had the power to assume any shape they desired. Mixing Stygian water with sulphur, they thereby destroyed animals and plants. As metallurgists in bronze and iron, they made the sickle of Cronos and the trident of Poseidon.

a Telchinic metamorphosis

TELEGONUS

Telegonus was the son of Odysseus and Circe, conceived during the hero's enforced detainment on the enchantress's isle of Aeaea. After Odysseus had returned to Ithaca, Circe sent Telegonus forth in search of his father. Shipwrecked on the Ithacan coast and assailed by hunger, he began to plunder the fields. Informed of the depredations caused by the stranger, Odysseus and his son Telemachus (born of Penelope) went out to fight him, but Telegonus succeeded in killing his father, unknowingly, with a spear given him by Circe. At the order of Athena, Telegonus, accompanied by Penelope and Telemachus, went to Circe with the body of Odysseus to bury it on her island. Telegonus then married the widowed Penelope, who bore him a son, Italus.

unintentional patricide like that committed by Telegonus

TELEMACHUS

Telemachus, the son of Odysseus and Penelope, took care of his father's estate during the latter's twenty long years of absence, and finally went in search of news concerning him to Nestor at Pylos and to Helen and Menelaus at Sparta. Though he is a bit diffident and indecisive when compared with the heroic stature of his father, he assisted him in slaying the extravagant suitors after his return.

Telemachean concern for his father
Telemachean worries

TELEPHUS

Telephus, in Greek legend, was the son of Hercules and Auge. Uncertain of his parentage, he was told by the Delphic oracle to go to Mysia in Asia Minor, where he would find his mother and become king of the country. After achieving this, he attempted to prevent the Greeks from landing on his coast on their way to Troy, because he was allied by marriage to Priam. Dionysus, however, caused him to trip over a vine, and he was wounded by Achilles. Since the wound would not heal and could not be cured by anyone except the one who had inflicted it, he went to the Trojan camp, where Achilles, instructed by an oracle that Troy could not be taken without the aid of Telephus, cured him by means of the rust of the spear with which the wound had been inflicted. In return, Telephus showed them the route which they had to take.

wounded as hopelessly as Telephus

TELL, WILLIAM

William, or Wilhelm, Tell was the boldest of the Swiss mountaineers and the liberator of his country from the tyrannical rule of Albrecht Gessler, Austrian governor of three forest cantons of Switzerland. Tell carried Leuthold, a herdsman whose daughter had been insulted by an emissary of Gessler, to safety across the lake, greatly incensing the latter, who placed the ducal cap of Austria on a pole and commanded the people to do reverence before it. When Tell refused, Gessler ordered him to shoot an apple from his little boy's head. The excellent marksman succeeded in his perilous task, but in so doing let fall a concealed arrow and was asked with what object he had hidden it. "To kill thee, tyrant, if I had failed in the task you imposed on me," answered Tell, who, though Gessler ordered him chained to be devoured alive by reptiles, was rescued by the peasantry, shot Gessler, and liberated his country.

an unflinching patriot of the William Tell type

TELLUS

Tellus, in Roman mythology, was personified as the terrestrial globe and worshiped as a divinity of the earth associated with agricultural ceremonies such as the Fordicidia (*q.v.*). Resembling Ceres in fecundity and productivity, she was revered as the goddess of the cultivated fields, whose sown seed she received and nourished.

blessed by Tellus with abundant crops

TEMPE

Tempe was a romantic vale between Mount Olympus and Mount Ossa in Thessaly, northern Greece. Abounding in breathtakingly poetic scenery, it was famous for its mild climate and was one of the favorite haunts of Apollo and the Muses. Hence, the name connotes *poetry, inspiration, romance, scenery* and the like, and any beautiful valley may be called a Tempe.

scenery of Tempean beauty and allure

TENES

Tenes, or Tennes, was the son of Proclea and Cycnus, king of Colonae in the Troad, and the brother of Hemithea. Cycnus's second wife, Philonome, fell in love with her step-son and endeavored to seduce him, but when she could make no inroads on his chastity, she accused him of attempting her rape. Cycnus, believing her charges, put both his son and his daughter into a chest and cast them adrift at sea. But the chest floated to the coast of the island of Leucophrys, the inhabitants of which made Tenes their king, renaming their isle Tenedos in his honor.

spurning her attentions like Tenes

TENNYSONIAN

Alfred Tennyson (1809-1892), Victorian poet, rejoices in the progress of the time, recognizes with satisfaction and wonder the political, social, and scientific advance, and predicts, in *Locksley Hall,* wonders yet to be. He was at heart a romanticist, sentimental, emotional, and colorful. His attention to detail, the love of color evident in his constant use of words expressing color, his love of chivalry and courtliness in *The Idylls of the King,* along with his deep understanding of people of all sorts, would set him apart, even without the perfect melody of his songs.

Tennysonian chivalry
Tennysonian pageantry

TERAH

Terah is the name of the father of Abraham, in *Genesis,* xi, 26. Migrating with his family from Ur of the Chaldees to Haran, he achieved the ripe old age of 205 years. *Joshua* (xxiv, 2) suggests that he practiced idolatry, worshiping gods rather than Jehovah.

the longevity of a Terah

TERENCE

Terence (185-159 B.C.), a manumitted African slave, was second only to Plautus as a writer of Latin comedies. His six plays were adapted from Greek sources and, like those of Platus, concerned the love entanglements of rich and amorous young men. He is more elegant and refined than Plautus, and suave urbanity replaces the latter's saucy impudence. Sentimental portraiture in his characterizations and smooth, limpid diction are hallmarks of his style. The *Andria* influenced Thornton Wilder's *Woman of Andros.*

a comedy of Terentian elegance

TEREUS

Tereus, the son of Ares (Mars), and a king of Thrace, married Procne, daughter of the king of Athens, and became by her the father of Itys. Having lecherously seduced her sister Philomela, he cut out the latter's tongue and hid her in the country, so she could not tell Procne of his infidelity and of her rape. But Philomela depicted her misfortunes in some embroidery, which she sent to Procne, who, to revenge her, killed Itys and served him up at a cannibal feast to his father. When Tereus in a rage was about to kill the sisters, they were all transformed into birds, Philomela into a nightingale, Procne into a swallow, and Tereus into a hoopoe or hawk.

with Tereus's interest in his wife's sister

TERMAGANT

Termagant is a name given to the god of the Saracens in medieval romances, where he is co-partner of Mahound. Originally a man, as is obvious in *The Picture* by Massinger, "A hundred thousand Turks assailed him, every one a Termagant (Pagan)," he was subsequently transformed into a female from the custom of representing him on the stage in Eastern robes, like those worn in Europe by women. The expression *outdoing Termagant* (*Hamlet,* iii, 2) is due to the fact that the degree of boisterous, brawling rant was the measure of villainy. Termagant being considered the paragon of all that is bad, he was represented as settling everything with club law, and bawling so as to split the ears of the audience.

even more violent than Termagant

TERMINUS

Terminus was the Roman deity who presided over boundaries and frontiers. His worship was instituted by Numa, who ordered everybody to mark the limits of his property by stones consecrated to Jupiter. At these stones annual offerings of cakes and first-fruits were presented at the festival of the Terminalia on the 23rd of February. A public "great god Terminus" stood in the Capitoline temple of Jupiter in Rome, and other sculptural images of the deity generally represented him as without arms and terminating from the waist-down in a pedestal.

sharply demarcated by Terminus

TERPANDER

Terpander was the father of Greek music and lyric poetry. A native of Lesbos in the first half of the seventh century B.C., he came to Sparta and established the first music school in Greece there. Adding three additional strings to the lyre of his day, he introduced the seven-stringed instrument for greater sonority. He also invented the Aeolian and Boeotian musical modes, and composed many songs, of which only the titles have come down to us.

like the sweet strains of Terpander's lyre

TERPSICHORE

(see *Muse*)

Terpsichore was the Muse of dancing and choral song. Derived from her name is the word terpsichorean, meaning "pertaining to dancing." Colloquially, a dancer my be called a terpsichorean. In ancient works of art she was represented with the lyre and plectrum, a small pick for twanging the strings.

incomparable terpsichorean grace
the talent of Terpsichore

TERRA

Terra, in Roman religion, is, like Tellus (*q.v.*), a personification of the earth as a bounteous goddess. Fructifying the seeds entrusted to her bosom, she rewards agriculturists with opulent harvests.

rewarded for his toil in the fields by an appreciative and generous Terra

TERTULLIAN

Tertullian (A.D. 160-230), Latin ecclesiastical writer and father of the church, was a pagan converted to Christianity. Versed in philosophy, science, and law, he had an imperious and intransigent character. In his *Apologeticus* he pleads for protection for Christians from the attacks of pagan mobs and from illegal trials. Elsewhere he attempts to regulate minutely the conduct of his brethren in the midst of pagan society, and shows a strong personal asceticism. A rigorous moralist, he refused pardon to persons convicted of sin, even if they were penitent.

the condemnatory moral purity of a Tertullian

TESS OF THE D'URBERVILLES

Tess of the D'Urbervilles, the heroine of Thomas Hardy's novel of the same name, is a village girl who confesses to her husband on their wedding day that she has been corrupted by the erotic attentions of another man. When her horrified husband repudiates her, she kills her former paramour and betrayer and is condemned to execution.

like Tess, the victim of another's lust

TETHYS

Tethys, in Greek mythology, was a Titaness and the daughter of Uranus (Heaven) and Ge (Earth). She became the bride of Oceanus, to whom she bore the Oceanids, or ocean nymphs, and numerous river gods.

disporting in the waves like Tethys

TEUCER

Teucer, the son of Telamon of Salamis, and the brother of Ajax, was the best archer among the Greeks at the siege of Troy. When his father refused to receive him on his return from the war, because he had not avenged the death of Ajax, he went on to found a new home on the island of Cyprus, where he established a second town called Salamis and became its first king.

unerring as Teucer with bow and arrow

TEUFELSDROECKH, HERR

Herr Teufelsdroeckh (Mr. Devil's-dung) is the eccentric German philosopher and Professor of Things in General at the University of Weissnichtwo (I-know-not-where). The hero of Carlyle's *Sartor Resartus* (the tailor retailored), he expounds on the philosophy of clothes because "to look through the Show of things into Things themselves he is led and compelled." The satire's purpose is to expose the illusions and shams which govern so extensively man's intellect and his social life.

as opinionated about clothes as Herr Teufelsdroeckh

TEZCATLIPOCA

Tezcatlipoca was one of the Aztec gods of the polytheistic ancient Mexican race. To him was sacrificed annually the handsomest and noblest captive of the year, as a moral lesson to the people of the transience of riches and pleasures, and of the ever-present possibility of poverty and sorrow. In his last month of life, the victim was married to four beautiful women and feasted and adorned richly, like a king, to be paraded through the streets in all his beauty and pride. On the fatal day, he was led up the steps of the temple, at the top of which stood the priests to tear out his heart. His body was then butchered and his flesh consumed with cannibalistic fury.

barbarous and cruel as Tezcatlipoca

THACKERAYAN

Thackerayan is from William Makepeace Thackeray (1811-1863), one of the three great novelists of the nineteenth century (Dickens, Eliot, and Thackeray). Thackeray was a humorist, a caricaturist, and an inimitable word-painter of the follies and foibles, the goodness and gentleness, the mistakes and virtues of eighteenth century English drawing-room society. "To cure the evils of society by laughing at them" was his serious aim. Delightful, genial, for many years caricaturist for the London comic paper *Punch,* illustrator of his own stories, Thackeray was one of the most beloved persons in England, and immensely popular as a lecturer in the United States.

the famous, sly Thackerayan asides

THAIS

Thaïs was a celebrated Greek *hetaera,* or courtesan, who accompanied Alexander the Great on his conquering tour of Asia. After his death she became the mistress of Ptolemy I, by whom she had two sons, Leontiscus and Lagus, and a daughter, Irene.

Another courtesan of the same name is the heroine of Anatole France's *Thaïs* and of Massenet's opera. After she has successfully tempted a holy man, Paphnutius, to forswear his religious vows, she repents and embraces an ascetic life herself.

a Thaïs to tempt one from his virtue

THALES

Thales (640-546 B.C.), Ionian natural philosopher and accounted one of the Seven Sages of Greece, accomplished many wonderful things for his time, including the prediction of the solar eclipse that occurred in the reign of the Lydian king Alyattes, and the diverting of the course of the Halys river in that country. Philosophically he maintained that water or moisture was the one element of which the earth was formed and that everything eventually resolves itself into water. The founder of the geometry of lines, he was accredited as being the father of abstract geometry.

has Thales's passion for water

THALESTRIS

Thalestris, according to Greek mythological history, was the queen of the Amazons who went with three hundred women to meet Alexander the Great, with the hope of raising a race of little Alexanders.

a perfect Thalestris, whom it is unwise to offend

THALIA

(see *Muse*)

Thalia was the Muse of comedy and also one of the three Charites, or Graces. As Muse she was represented as carrying a comic mask, a shepherd's staff or a wreath of ivy.

a gracious Thalia of the comic stage

THALLO

Thallo was the Greek goddess of the blooming springtime, and one of the Horae, deities of the order of Nature and of the seasons. They guarded the doors of Olympus, and promoted the fertility of the earth by the changing types of weather they brought. Thallo's sister, Carpo, was the Hora of autumn.

Thallo arraying the earth with verdure

THAMYRIS

Thamyris, in Greek mythology, was a Thracian poet and minstrel of such surpassingly presumptuous conceit that he boasted he could conquer the Muses themselves in a contest of song. In consequence of his arrogance, he was deprived of his sight and the power of music. He was represented in art with a broken lyre in his hand.

another Thamyris, vain about his voice

THANATOS

Thanatos was the Greek god of death, a deity of the lower world. The son of Nyx (Night), he was the brother of Hypnos (Somnus, Sleep). His name among the Romans was Mors.

the grim approach of Thanatos

THAUKT

Thaukt, in Scandinavian mythology, was the pitiless hag who alone of all mortals refused to weep for Baldur, the god of light, when he was detained in Hel, the lower world, by its mistress, Hela. Though Hela consented to release him if he were so beloved on earth that all would sorrow in his absence, and though all gods and men, even stones and trees, complied with her terms, Thaukt remained sitting in her cavern obdurately, and answered the messengers who entreated her to weep:

"Thaukt will wail
With dry tears
Baldur's bale-fire.
Let Hela keep her own."

a dry-eyed and stony-hearted Thaukt

THAUMASTE

Thaumaste is the name of a great English scholar in Rabelais' celebrated satirical romance. He went to France to argue in sign-language and dumb-show with Pantagruel. Overcome by Panurge, he expressed himself as fully delighted, for "Panurge had told him even more than he had asked."

gesticulating like Thaumaste

THAUMATURGUS

Thaumaturgus, or "wonder-worker," was a surname given to Gregory, bishop of Neo-Caesarea, in Cappadocia, in the third century, because of the numerous miracles ascribed to him.

Thaumaturgus of the West was the appellation conferred on St. Bernard (1091-1153) for his ascetic life, studious solitude, and stirring eloquence. The disastrous crusade of 1146 was urged on by his fervid zeal. His burning words fired innumerable legions, which hurried to the East, almost depopulating many castles and cities.

as eloquent as Thaumaturgus of the West

THECLA

Thecla, a first century Christian famous for her virtues and her miracles, is one of the most popular saints in the Greek church, her festival falling on the 24th of September. Coming under the personal instruction of St. Paul, she was accused by her relatives of being a Christian, because she broke her engagement to Thamyris, her pagan fiancé. Protected by the sign of the cross, she cast herself on the funeral pyre that had been built for her, but a sudden rain extinguished the flames. Exposed to wild beasts and tied to bulls at Antioch in order that she might be torn asunder, and thrown into a pit full of venomous serpents, she was delivered from all these attempts to destroy her. Converting many heathens, she retired to a life of prayer in a mountain solitude.

heaven-sent, Theclan deliverance

THELEME

Thélème is the name under which Voltaire has personified the will, in his composition entitled *Thélème and Macare*. Macare connotes austerity.

never discovered his own personal Thélème

THELEMITE

A Thelemite is a do-as-you-please libertine, and the name is acquired from Rabelais' Abbey of Thélème, an elegant and gay imaginary establishment stored with everything which can contribute to earthly happiness. It was given to Friar John, by Grangousier, as a recompense for his services in subjecting the people of Lerne. Its motto was *Fais ce que voudras* ("Do what thou wilt"), and the whole regulations of the convent were such as to assure a succession of diverting recreations.

a hedonistic Thélèmite

THEMIS

Themis was the goddess of justice, a daughter of Uranus (Heaven) and Ge (Earth). She was also a prophetic divinity. The mother of the Fates (Moerae), she was represented as having scales in one hand and a cornucopia in the other. Homer makes her the personification of the order of things established by law, custom and equity. She was, therefore, supposed to reign in the assemblies of men.

enough to exasperate Themis

THEMISTOCLEAN

Themistoclean is from Themistocles (514-449 B.C.), a sagacious, versatile, but ambitious and unscrupulous Athenian statesman who succeeded Aristides the Just. He believed in mastery of the sea, and to that end built up a great sea power; he even persuaded the whole Athenian population to abandon their city and embark in ships, from which they won the battle of Salamis.